EXAM✓CRAM

D1036258

CompTIA A+
(Exams 220-602, 220-603, 220-604)

Charles J. Brooks

CompTIA A+ Exam Cram (Exams 220-602, 220-603, 220-604)

Copyright © 2008 by Pearson Education, Inc.

All rights reserved. No part of this book shall be reproduced, stored in a retrieval system, or transmitted by any means, electronic, mechanical, photocopying, recording, or otherwise, without written permission from the publisher. No patent liability is assumed with respect to the use of the information contained herein. Although every precaution has been taken in the preparation of this book, the publisher and author assume no responsibility for errors or omissions. Nor is any liability assumed for damages resulting from the use of the information contained herein.

ISBN-10: 0-7897-3564-4

ISBN-13: 978-0-7897-3564-5

Printed in the United States of America

First Printing: May 2007

10 09   6 5

Trademarks

All terms mentioned in this book that are known to be trademarks or service marks have been appropriately capitalized. Que Publishing cannot attest to the accuracy of this information. Use of a term in this book should not be regarded as affecting the validity of any trademark or service mark.

Warning and Disclaimer

Every effort has been made to make this book as complete and as accurate as possible, but no warranty or fitness is implied. The information provided is on an "as is" basis. The author and the publisher shall have neither liability nor responsibility to any person or entity with respect to any loss or damages arising from the information contained in this book.

Bulk Sales

Que Publishing offers excellent discounts on this book when ordered in quantity for bulk purchases or special sales. For more information, please contact

U.S. Corporate and Government Sales
1-800-382-3419
corpsales@pearsontechgroup.com

For sales outside the U.S., please contact

International Sales
international@pearsoned.com

Library of Congress Cataloging-in-Publication Data

Brooks, Charles J.

  CompTIA A+ exam cram (exams 220-602, 220-603, 220-604) / Charles J. Brooks.

    p. cm.

  ISBN 0-7897-3564-4

  1. Electronic data processing personnel--Certification. 2. Computer technicians--Certification--Study guides. I. Title.

  QA76.3.B776 2007

  004--dc22

                              2007019513

Publisher
Paul Boger

Associate Publisher
David Dusthimer

Acquisitions Editors
Rick Kughen
Jeff Riley

Development Editor
Rick Kughen

Managing Editor
Patrick Kanouse

Project Editor
Mandie Frank

Copy Editor
Barbara Hacha

Indexer
Ken Johnson

Proofreader
Mike Henry

Technical Editor
Mark Reddin

Publishing Coordinator
Cindy Teeters

Contents at a Glance

		Introduction	1
CHAPTER 1	Basic PC Terms and Concepts	5
CHAPTER 2	PC System Boards	59
CHAPTER 3	Microprocessors	121
CHAPTER 4	Random Access Memory	159
CHAPTER 5	Data Storage Systems	179
CHAPTER 6	Ports and Peripherals	225
CHAPTER 7	Installing, Upgrading, Configuring and Optimizing PC Components	281
CHAPTER 8	Basic Troubleshooting and Preventative Maintenance Techniques	327
CHAPTER 9	Advanced PC Troubleshooting	373
CHAPTER 10	Portable Computer Fundamentals	435
CHAPTER 11	Maintaining and Repairing Portable Computers	489
CHAPTER 12	Windows Operating Systems	511
CHAPTER 13	Major Windows Structures	575
CHAPTER 14	Installing and Upgrading Operating Systems	621
CHAPTER 15	Optimizing Operating Systems	665
CHAPTER 16	Operating System Utilities	691
CHAPTER 17	Basic Operating System Troubleshooting and Maintenance	739
CHAPTER 18	Printers and Scanners	797
CHAPTER 19	Printer and Scanner Servicing	851
CHAPTER 20	Basic Networking Concepts	889
CHAPTER 21	Installing Local Area Networks	933
CHAPTER 22	Wide Area Networking	969
CHAPTER 23	Network Troubleshooting	1031
CHAPTER 24	Security	1071

CHAPTER 25 Safety and Environmental Issues   1129

CHAPTER 26 Professionalism and Communication   1159

CHAPTER 27 Advanced PC Component Installations and Upgrades   1189

Index   1225

On the CD

APPENDIX A Practice Essentials Exam

APPENDIX B IT Tech Practice Exam

APPENDIX C Depot Practice Exam

APPENDIX D Remote Support Practice Exam

Table of Contents

Introduction 1

How This Book Is Organized 1

Conventions Used in This Book 2

Special Elements 2

Test Taking Tips 3

Chapter 1:
Basic PC Terms and Concepts 5

Introduction 6

The PC System 6

System Unit Cases 7

Form Factors 9

Power Supplies 11

System Boards (Motherboards) 16

Microprocessor 17

Chipsets 21

Memory Units (RAM and ROM) 21

Basic Input/Output Systems 24

System Configuration Settings 27

Expansion Slots 28

Adapter Cards 31

Data Storage Devices 34

Removable Storage 39

Peripherals and Ports 41

Video Displays 46

Printers 47

Exam Prep Questions 48

Answers and Explanations 54

Challenge Solution 57

Chapter 2:
PC System Boards **59**

Introduction. 60

System Board Form Factors 60

    ATX System Boards 60

    BTX System Boards 62

    Low-Profile Form Factors. 66

    Pentium Chipsets 66

    System Bus Speeds 72

Expansion Slots. 73

    PCI Local Bus 73

    PCI-X. 76

    PCI Express 77

    AGP Slots. 80

    Audio Modem Risers and Communication Networking Risers. . 82

I/O Ports 84

    Onboard Disk Drive Connections 85

    SCSI Connections. 90

Processor Socket Specifications 91

    AMD Slots and Sockets 93

DRAM Sockets 95

CMOS RAM 96

    CMOS Setup Utilities 96

Exam Prep Questions. 109

Answers and Explanations 116

Challenge Solutions 118

Chapter 3:
Microprocessors **121**

Introduction. 122

Intel Microprocessors. 122

    The Pentium Processor 122

    Advanced Pentium Architectures 124

    Intel Dual-Core Processors. 130

    Advanced Intel Microprocessor Technologies 133

AMD Processors 135

    Athlon 64 Processors 136

    Duron Processors 137

    Athlon Dual-Core Processors 137

    Opteron Processors 141

Microprocessor Clock Speeds 144

Processor Power Supply Levels 145

Configuring Microprocessors and Buses 146

Fans, Heat Sinks, and Cooling Systems 147

    BTX Thermal Module 149

    Advanced Cooling Systems 149

Cache Memory 152

Exam Prep Questions 153

Answers and Explanations 156

Challenge Solution 157

Chapter 4:
Random Access Memory **159**

SRAM and DRAM 160

    SRAM 163

Memory Overhead 164

    Error Checking and Correcting 164

    Cache Memory Operations 166

RAM Packaging 168

    RIMM 169

    RAM Speed Ratings 170

Exam Prep Questions 174

Answers and Explanations 176

Challenge Solution 178

Chapter 5:
Data Storage Systems **179**

Introduction 180

    Personal Video Recorders 182

    RAID Systems 184

    Floppy Disk Drives 190

    Magnetic Tape Drives 191

Optical Storage 193

    CD-ROM Drives 193

    DVDs 197

Disk Drive Interfaces 199

    Internal Disk Drive Interfaces 199

    IDE/ATA Interface 200

    Serial ATA Interface 202

    Floppy Drive Interface 203

    Small Computer System Interface 204

Removable Storage 213

    Flash Memory 214

Exam Prep Questions 218

Answers and Explanations 222

Chapter 6:
Ports and Peripherals **225**

Input/Output Interfaces 226

    Initiating I/O Transfers 226

    System Resource Allocations 227

Ports, Cables, and Connectors 228

    PS/2 Connectors 229

    Universal Serial Bus 230

    IEEE-1394 FireWire Bus 236

    Multimedia Connections 239

    Legacy Ports 244

    Parallel Printer Ports 245

    RS-232 Serial Ports 248

    Game Ports 249

Typical Peripheral Systems 251

    Keyboards 251

    Pointing Devices 252

Exam Prep Questions 274

Answers and Explanations 278

Challenge Solutions 280

Chapter 7:
Installing, Upgrading, Configuring, and Optimizing PC Components **281**

    Installing Storage Devices 282

        Installing Internal Storage Devices 282

        HDD Installation 283

        Installing SCSI Adapter Cards 292

        Installing CD-ROM/DVD Drives 300

        Installing CD-RW and DVD-RW Drives 301

        Installing a Floppy Disk Drive 302

        Installing External Storage Devices 303

    Upgrading and Optimizing Disk Drives 305

        HDD Upgrading 305

        Disk Drive Subsystem Enhancements 306

    Installing Video/Monitor Systems 308

    Installing Standard PC Input Devices 310

        Installing Scanners 311

        Installing Bar Code Scanners 312

        Installing Sound Cards 312

        Installing Digital Cameras 313

        Installing Adapter Card–Based Peripherals 314

        Installing Devices Using USB, IEEE-1394, PCMCIA,
        and IrDA 316

        Upgrading Peripheral Devices 320

    Exam Prep Questions 321

    Answers and Explanations 324

    Challenge Solutions 325

Chapter 8:
Basic Troubleshooting and Preventive Maintenance Techniques **327**

    Basic PC Troubleshooting 329

        Diagnostic and Repair Tools 330

        Gathering Information 331

        Initial Troubleshooting Steps 333

        Symptoms/Error Codes 336

        Determining Hardware/Software/Configuration Problems 339

    Using a Multimeter 343

        Field-Replaceable Unit Troubleshooting 349

Basic Preventive Maintenance 350
   Cleaning 350
   Preventive Maintenance Procedures 352
   Protecting Display Systems 355
   Protecting Hard Disk Drives 357
   Protecting Removable Media Drives 358
   Protecting Input Devices 360
   Preventive Maintenance Scheduling 361
Exam Prep Questions 365
Answers and Explanations 368
Challenge Solutions 370

Chapter 9:
Advanced PC Troubleshooting 373
Advanced Diagnostics 375
Isolating Power Supply Problems 375
   Checking a Dead System 376
Troubleshooting the System Board 379
   System Board Symptoms 379
   Configuration Checks 381
   Hardware Checks 382
   Troubleshooting Keyboard Problems 386
   Troubleshooting Mouse Problems 390
   Troubleshooting Video Systems 393
   Troubleshooting HDDs 400
   Troubleshooting CD-ROM and DVD Drives 406
   Troubleshooting FDDs 410
   Troubleshooting Tape Drives 413
   Troubleshooting Other Removable Storage Systems 414
   Troubleshooting Port Problems 415
IEEE-1394 Adapters and Ports 419
   Troubleshooting Sound Cards 421
   Troubleshooting Front Panel Connections 423
Exam Prep Questions 425
Answers and Explanations 430
Challenge Solutions 432

Chapter 10:
Portable Computer Fundamentals **435**

   Inside Portables 437
   Portable System Boards 438
      Microprocessors in Portables 440
      Pentium IIIM and 4M Processors 441
      Pentium M Processors 442
      Centrino 443
      Pentium M Celerons 443
      Core Duo Processors 444
      AMD Mobile Processors 445
   Portable Memory 446
      Upgrading Portable Memory 448
   Portable Drives 450
      Upgrading/Replacing Portable Drives 451
   Portable Display Types 452
      Liquid Crystal Displays 452
   Portable Keyboards 455
   Trackballs 457
   Touch Pads 457
   Pointing Sticks 458
   External Portable I/O 459
      Peripheral Storage Devices 460
      External FDDs 460
      External CD-ROM Drives 460
      External CD-RW and DVD-RW Drives 461
      Removable Storage 462
      Installing External Storage Devices 463
   PC Cards 464
      Cardbus 464
      Adding PC Card Memory 465
      Installing PC Cards 466
      Installing PC Card Support 467
      Mini PCI Express Cards . . . . · 468

Networking Portables 469

    Wireless Networking with Portables 470

Portable Power Sources 473

    Power Consumption 475

    Power Management 475

Docking Stations 477

    Port Replicators 478

Portable System Upgrading 478

    Upgrading Batteries 479

    Upgrading PC Cards 480

Exam Prep Questions 482

Answers and Explanations 485

Challenge Solutions 487

Chapter 11:
Maintaining and Repairing Portable Computers **489**

Troubleshooting Portable Systems 490

Common LCD Display Problems 492

    Replacing the LCD Panel 494

Troubleshooting Portable Keyboards 496

Troubleshooting Touch Pads 496

Troubleshooting Portable Unique Storage 497

Troubleshooting Infrared Ports 499

Troubleshooting PCMCIA 500

Troubleshooting Portable Power Issues 501

Troubleshooting Docking Stations/Port Replicators 503

Portable Preventative Maintenance 505

    Rough Handling 505

    Thermal Issues 507

    Cleaning 507

Exam Prep Questions 508

Answers and Explanations 509

Challenge Solutions 510

Chapter 12:
Windows Operating Systems **511**

  Operating Systems 512
    Graphical User Interfaces 513
  The Windows NT Product Line 515
    Windows 2000 518
    Windows XP 519
    Windows 2003 Server 521
    Windows Vista Operating Systems 521
  Navigating Windows 2000/XP 521
    Windows 2000/XP Desktops 523
    Drop-Down Menus 528
    The Taskbar 530
    Start Menu 531
    Windows 2000 Control Panel 535
    Windows Explorer 543
    Windows XP Interface Variations 547
    Windows XP Media Center Interfaces 552
  Command Prompt Procedures 557
    Working from the Command Line 558
  Exam Prep Questions 565
  Answers and Explanations 570
  Challenge Solutions 572

Chapter 13:
Major Windows Structures **575**

  Introduction 576
  The PC Hardware Startup Process 576
  Windows 2000/XP Structures 581
    System Memory Management 583
    Windows 2000/XP Registries 586
  Windows 2000/XP File Systems 590
    Managing Partitions 590
    High-Level Formatting 593
    FAT Disk Organization 593
    NTFS Disk Organization 597

Files and Filenames 608
    File Types. 608
    Windows 2000/XP Files 609
    File Encryption and Compression 610
Exam Prep Questions. 614
Answers and Explanations 617
Challenge Solutions 620

Chapter 14:
Installing and Upgrading Operating Systems **621**

Introduction. 623
Installing Windows 2000/XP 623
    Installation Methods. 624
    Hard Disk Drive Preparation 629
    Managing Patches and Service Packs. 630
    Troubleshooting General Setup Problems 632
Installing Windows 2000 Professional. 633
    Windows 2000/XP Setup Problems. 636
Installing Windows XP Professional 638
    Windows XP MCE Hardware Requirements. 640
    Windows XP Setup Problems. 641
Operating System Upgrading 643
    Upgrading to Windows 2000 643
    Upgrading to Windows XP. 646
    Performing Local Upgrades 648
Upgrade Problems 650
    Dual Booting. 651
Loading and Adding Device Drivers 654
    2000/XP Device Drivers 654
    SATA Drivers 655
    Finding Drivers. 656
    Driver Signing. 656
Exam Prep Questions. 658
Answers and Explanations 661
Challenge Solutions 663

Chapter 15:
Optimizing Operating Systems **665**

Introduction 666
Optimizing Windows 2000/XP Performance 666
Optimizing Virtual Memory 667
Optimizing the Disk Drive System 668
Managing Temporary Files 670
Optimizing System Services 673
Modifying the Startup Process 674
Monitoring System Performance 676
Monitoring Application Performance with System Monitor . . . 678
Software Maintenance 684
Exam Prep Questions 687
Answers and Explanations 688
Challenge Solutions 689

Chapter 16:
Operating System Utilities **691**

Windows Disk Management Tools 692
Disk Cleanup 693
CHKDSK 694
HDD Defragmentation 695
Backups 698
Removable Storage Utility 708
Windows 2000/XP System Management Tools 709
Event Viewer 709
Windows 2000/XP System Information 712
Windows XP System Restore 714
Task Manager 714
Device Manager 716
MSCONFIG.EXE 720
Remote Desktop and Remote Assistance Features 721
File Management Tools 722
System Editors 722
Dr. Watson 724
Command-Line Utilities 725

Windows Troubleshooting Help Files 727
    Internet Help 729
Exam Prep Questions 730
Answers and Explanations 735
Challenge Solutions 737

Chapter 17:
Basic Operating System Troubleshooting and Maintenance **739**

Introduction 742
General OS Troubleshooting Process 743
Troubleshooting Startup Problems 744
    General Bootup/Startup Problems 745
    Windows 2000/XP Startup Tools 746
    Using Windows XP System Restore 759
    Windows 2000/XP Startup Problems 763
Common OS Operational Problems 767
    Optional Devices Do Not Operate 767
    Troubleshooting Stop Errors 768
    Windows 2000/XP Application Problems 770
    Windows-Related Printing Problems 776
Using Remote Desktop/Assistance 779
    Configuring the Remote Desktop Function 779
    Conducting Remote Desktop Sessions 780
    Using Remote Assistance 783
Exam Prep Questions 787
Answers and Explanations 791
Challenge Solutions 794

Chapter 18:
Printers and Scanners **797**

Introduction 799
Printer Types 799
    Fonts 800
    Basic Printer Components 801
    Dot-Matrix Printers 804
    Dot-Matrix Printer Mechanics 804
    Thermal Printers 807

Inkjet Printers 809

Laser Printers 811

Dye Sublimation Printers 815

Printer Installation 816

USB Printers 818

Networked Printers 818

Wireless Printer Interfaces 819

Infrared Printer Ports 820

Legacy Printer Interfaces 821

Printer Drivers 824

Printer Control Panel Configuration 826

Printer Calibration 827

Printer Options and Upgrades 828

Printing in Windows 831

Establishing Printers in Windows 834

Printer Properties 836

Network Printing with Windows 837

Scanners 838

Exam Prep Questions 842

Answers and Explanations 847

Challenge Solutions 850

Chapter 19:
Printer and Scanner Servicing **851**

Introduction 853

Servicing Printers 853

General Printer Troubleshooting 854

Troubleshooting Dot-Matrix Printers 858

Dot-Matrix Printer Power Supply Problems 859

Dot-Matrix Consumables 859

Printhead Not Printing 861

Printhead Not Moving 862

Paper Not Advancing 862

Troubleshooting Inkjet Printers 863

Inkjet Printer Configuration Checks 863

Inkjet Consumables 863

Printhead Not Printing 865

Printhead Not Moving. 865

Paper Not Advancing. 866

Troubleshooting Laser Printers 866

Laser Printer Consumables. 867

Printer Is Dead or Partially Disabled. 868

Print on Page Is Missing or Bad. 869

Paper Does Not Feed or Is Jammed 871

Troubleshooting Scanners. 873

Image Quality Problems 874

Checking the Host System 875

Interface Cables. 876

Preventive Maintenance and Safety Issues 876

Dot-Matrix/Inkjet Printers 877

Laser Printers 877

Laser Safety Issues 878

Exam Prep Questions. 879

Answers and Explanations 884

Challenge Solutions 887

Chapter 20:
Basic Networking Concepts **889**

Local Area Networks 890

LAN Topologies 891

Network Control Strategies 894

Network Connectivity Devices. 897

Network Transmission Media. 900

Copper Cabling. 901

Fiber-Optic Cable. 906

Plenum Cable 909

Wireless Infrared Links 910

Wireless RF Links 911

Network Architectures. 913

Ethernet 914

Networking Protocols 920

Exam Prep Questions. 922

Answers and Explanations 928

Challenge Solutions 931

Chapter 21:
Installing Local Area Networks **933**

Installing and Configuring LAN Components 934

LAN Adapter Cards 934

Installing LAN Cards 936

Optimizing Network Adapters 937

Installing Wireless LANs 938

Installing Network Components in Windows 2000/XP
Control Panels 946

Configuring Clients in Windows 2000/XP 950

Configuring Protocols in Windows 2000/XP 950

Networking with Novell NetWare 953

Sharing Network Resources 955

Network Shares 956

Mapping a Drive 961

Exam Prep Questions 963

Answers and Explanations 965

Challenge Solutions 967

Chapter 22:
Wide Area Networking **969**

Introduction 971

Internet Connectivity 971

Internet Service Providers 972

IP Addresses 974

Internet Domains 978

Internet Access Methods 979

LAN Access to the Internet 980

Dial-Up Access 983

ISDN Connections 988

Digital Subscriber Lines 990

Cable Modems 996

Installing Digital Modems 998

Satellite Internet Access 1000

Wireless Internet Access 1002

Voice Over IP 1003

TCP/IP 1005

The TCP/IP Suite 1006

Internet Resources 1010

The World Wide Web 1011

File Transfer Protocol 1012

Email 1013

Secure Sockets Layer Protocol 1014

Telnet 1015

Web Browsers 1016

Establishing Internet Browser Security Options 1017

Exam Prep Questions 1021

Answers and Explanations 1027

Challenge Solutions 1030

Chapter 23:
Network Troubleshooting **1031**

Basic Network Troubleshooting 1032

Network Troubleshooting Tools 1034

Troubleshooting LAN Problems 1038

Service Access Problems 1038

Checking the NIC 1039

Checking Cabling 1041

Checking Connectivity Devices 1041

Windows-Related LAN Problems 1042

Troubleshooting Wireless Networks 1046

Troubleshooting Network Printing Problems 1049

Troubleshooting WAN Problems 1052

Troubleshooting Broadband Problems 1053

Troubleshooting Dial-Up Problems 1056

Windows Modem Checks 1061

Troubleshooting Browser Problems 1063

Exam Prep Questions 1065

Answers and Explanations 1067

Challenge Solutions 1069

Chapter 24:
Security **1071**

  Introduction 1074
  Computer Security 1074
    Access Control 1075
    PC Hardware Security 1078
    Environmental Security Issues 1084
    Software Security 1084
  Windows Network Security 1087
    Administering Windows Networks 1088
    Establishing Wireless Security 1101
  Malicious Program Security 1108
    Viruses 1108
    Establishing and Implementing Malicious Software
      Protection 1112
    Social Engineering 1118
    Phishing 1119
    Pharming 1119
    Session Hijacking 1120
    Identity Theft 1120
  Exam Prep Questions 1122
  Answers and Explanations 1125
  Challenge Solution 1128

Chapter 25:
Safety and Environmental Issues **1129**

  Work Area and Safety Issues 1130
    The Work Area 1131
    Personal Safety 1132
    Avoiding Laser and Burn Hazards 1136
  System Protection 1138
    Power Line Protection 1138
    Electrostatic Discharge 1143
  Hardware Disposal Procedures 1148
  Exam Prep Questions 1150
  Answers and Explanations 1155
  Challenge Solutions 1158

Chapter 26:

Professionalism and Communication **1159**

Customer Service Skills 1160

Prepare 1162

Establish Rapport 1163

Establish Your Presence 1163

Be Proactive 1164

Listen and Communicate 1164

Follow Up 1169

Be Responsive 1170

Be Accountable 1171

Be Flexible 1172

Be Professional 1172

Establish Integrity 1173

Handle Conflicts Appropriately 1176

Telephone Techniques 1177

Handle Paperwork and Finish Up 1179

Maintain an Orderly Work Area 1179

Exam Prep Questions 1181

Answers and Explanations 1184

Challenge Solutions 1187

Chapter 27:

Advanced PC Component Installations and Upgrades **1189**

Introduction 1191

System Board Compatibility Issues 1191

Replacing System Boards 1193

Removing the External I/O Systems 1193

Removing the System Unit's Cover 1194

Removing the Adapter Cards 1195

Removing the Cables from the System Board 1195

Removing the System Board 1196

Replacing System Board Field Replaceable Unit Devices 1196

Installing Microprocessors 1197

Installing Slot Processors 1199

Configuring Processor Speeds 1199

Fans, Heat Sinks, and Cooling Systems 1199

Installing Memory Modules 1202

Replacing Power Supplies 1203

Installing Power Supplies 1204

Power Supply Upgrade Considerations 1205

System Upgrading and Optimizing 1206

System Board Upgrading 1206

Exam Prep Questions 1218

Answers and Explanations 1221

Challenge Solutions 1222

Index 1225

On the CD

Appendix A
Practice Essentials Exam

Appendix B
IT Tech Practice Exam

Appendix C
Depot Practice Exam

Appendix D
Remote Support Practice Exam

About the Author

Charles J. Brooks is currently co-owner and vice president of Educational Technologies Group Inc., as well as co-owner of eITPrep LLP, an online training company. He is in charge of research and product development at both organizations. A former electronics instructor and technical writer with the National Education Corporation, Charles taught and wrote on post-secondary EET curriculum, including introductory electronics, transistor theory, linear integrated circuits, basic digital theory, industrial electronics, microprocessors, and computer peripherals. Charles has authored several books, including the first five editions of *A+ Certification Training Guide*, *The Complete Introductory Computer Course*, and *IBM PC Peripheral Troubleshooting and Repair*. He also writes about networking, residential technology integration, and convergence.

Dedication

Thanks to my wife, Robbie—you're the best. I couldn't do this without her support. I thank my dad, Ralph, who has taken up personal computing a little later in life than some and knows exactly what he wants out of it. Finally, Robert, Jamaica, Michael, and Joshua—you guys light up my life.

Acknowledgments

I want to thank Jeff Riley, Rick Kughen, and all the folks at Que Publishing for their excellent support on this and our other Que publication efforts. It's a real privilege to work with high-quality people and a high-quality organization.

I also want to thank all the people who have purchased our products in the past and were willing to give us feedback to make them better. As always, good luck with your certification efforts—although I hope you don't need any luck after using our materials to prepare.

We Want to Hear from You!

As the reader of this book, *you* are our most important critic and commentator. We value your opinion and want to know what we're doing right, what we could do better, what areas you'd like to see us publish in, and any other words of wisdom you're willing to pass our way.

As an executive editor for Que Publishing, I welcome your comments. You can email or write me directly to let me know what you did or didn't like about this book—as well as what we can do to make our books better.

Please note that I cannot help you with technical problems related to the topic of this book. We do have a User Services group, however, where I will forward specific technical questions related to the book.

When you write, please be sure to include this book's title and author as well as your name, email address, and phone number. I will carefully review your comments and share them with the author and editors who worked on the book.

Email: scorehigher@pearsoned.com

Mail: David Dusthimer
           Associate Publisher
           Que Publishing
           800 East 96th Street
           Indianapolis, IN 46240 USA

Reader Services

Visit our website and register this book at www.examcram.com/register for convenient access to any updates, downloads, or errata that might be available for this book.

Introduction

CompTIA has rolled out the most dramatic structural change in the history of the A+ certification program. Since its inception, the A+ certification has been divided into two sections: core hardware components and troubleshooting and operating system structures and troubleshooting. Originally you had two choices for the operating system exam: DOS/Windows or Apple OS.

The new exam structure introduces an Essentials exam that covers basic hardware and operating system technologies. To complete the A+ certification, you also must pass one of three advanced exams: Depot Technician, Technical Support Technician, or IT Technician exams. These exams are designed to align with commonly used PC repair and service job titles.

All four exams are fixed length and linear. However, they are also dynamic in nature, as they have been for the last two exam revolutions. There were no beta exams used to validate the current question pools. Instead, new questions will be added to the pool over time. CompTIA will routinely inject new questions into the exams as unscored items until their psychometric validity can be established. After validation, the questions will be returned to the question pools as scored items, thus creating a dynamic test pool that is continually being renewed.

How This Book Is Organized

This book has been designed to prepare its users to challenge the October 2006 version of the A+ Certification exams from the Computer Technology Industry Association. A+ Certification is a two-step process: You must pass the Essentials exam and one of the other advanced exams. For more information on CompTIA and the A+ exams, visit http://www.comptia.org.

This book will provide you with the knowledge and skills required to pass the A+ exam and become a certified computer service technician. A+ certification is recognized nationwide and is a hiring criterion used by companies such as AT&T, IBM, Microsoft, and Hewlett-Packard. Therefore, becoming A+ certified will enhance your job opportunities and career advancement potential.

There was much discussion beforehand about how to produce this book. Should it be four books (one per test), two books (one for Essentials and one to cover the three advanced exams), or should it all be in one book. As it turns out, the four exams are so intertwined and the questions have so much overlap among the exams that it made sense to produce one bigger book that covered everything.

The first eight chapters are exclusively tied to the 220-601 Essentials exam. On the other hand, Chapter 27 is the only chapter that doesn't have any reference to the Essentials exam. All the chapters in between have elements from Essentials and from one or more of the advanced exams. The objectives being covered in each chapter are spelled out at the beginning of the chapter.

Each chapter concludes with a collection of multiple-choice questions that can be used for test-prep purposes.

The appendices are fixed-length representations of each A+ exam: Essentials, IT Technician, DepotTechnician, and Remote Support Technician.

Conventions Used in This Book

Each chapter begins with a list of CompTIA objectives that establishes a foundation and systematic approach to the material in the chapter.

Each page is populated with Exam Alerts that point out the presence of known exam-related materials.

Each chapter concludes with multiple-choice exam-prep questions to prepare you for the real exams.

Special Elements

In this edition, we have added a new feature called Challenges to each chapter to challenge students to apply what they are learning to scenario-based situations that require more than a single word or sentence to evaluate.

NOTE

This is a note that presents some key information that may not necessarily be essential information for taking the exam.

EXAM ALERT

This is a tip that will prove useful in preparing for one or more of the exams.

CAUTION

This is a caution that something you might accidentally do could have undesirable results—so take care!

Test Taking Tips

The A+ exam is an objective-based, fixed length, timed test delivered in a multiple-choice format. There are two general methods of preparing for the test. If you are an experienced technician using this material to obtain certification, use the testing features at the end of each chapter and the final four chapters to test each area of knowledge. Track your weak areas and spend the most time concentrating on them.

If you are a newcomer to the subject of serious computer repair, plan a systematic study of the materials, reserving the testing functions until each chapter has been completed.

In either case, after you complete the study materials, use the various testing functions available on the CD to practice taking the test. Use the Study and Exam modes to test yourself by chapter or on a mixture of questions from all areas of the text. Practice until you are very certain that you are ready. The CD will provide you with explanations of questions and answers for your review.

► Answer the questions you know first. You can always go back later and work on questions you don't know.

► Don't leave any questions unanswered. They will be counted as incorrect.

► There are no trick questions. The correct answer is in there somewhere.

► Get plenty of hands-on practice before the test, using the time limit set for the test.

► Make certain to prepare for each test category listed previously. The key is not to memorize, but to understand the topics.

► Take your watch. The A+ exam is a timed test. You will need to keep an eye on the time to make sure that you are getting to the items that you are most sure of.

► Get plenty of rest before taking the test.

CHAPTER 1

Basic PC Terms and Concepts

Terms you'll need to understand:

- ✓ System board
- ✓ Form factor
- ✓ System unit
- ✓ Microprocessor
- ✓ RAM
- ✓ ROM BIOS
- ✓ Adapter card
- ✓ Disk drive
- ✓ Chipset

- ✓ Power supply
- ✓ Video display
- ✓ Expansion slots
- ✓ Keyboard
- ✓ Mouse
- ✓ Printer
- ✓ Pointing devices
- ✓ Signal cables

Techniques to master:

Essentials 1.1—Identify the fundamental principles of using personal computers.

- ✓ Identify the names, purposes, and characteristics of storage devices.

- ✓ Identify the names, purposes, and characteristics of motherboards.

- ✓ Identify the names, purposes, and characteristics of power supplies.

- ✓ Identify the names, purposes, and characteristics of display devices.

- ✓ Identify the names, purposes, and characteristics of input devices.

- ✓ Identify the names, purposes, and characteristics of adapter cards.

- ✓ Identify the names, purposes, and characteristics of ports and cables.

Introduction

This chapter covers a portion of the names, purposes, and characteristics of the personal computer areas of the CompTIA A+ Certification—Essentials examination under Objective 1.1. All the objectives under Domain 1.0 of the CompTIA A+ Essentials Exam expect the potential candidate to show basic knowledge of fundamental personal computer (PC) principles.

This objective asks you to identify typical PC components, know what they are called, know what they look like, and know a little bit about what they do. There is almost nothing in the exam that asks you to know how these components work.

The PC System

As a technician, you should know and be able to identify the components found in a typical personal computer system. The PC is modular by design. It is called a system because it includes all the components required to make a functional computer.

- ▶ System unit—The main computer cabinet, usually referred to as a case, housing the primary components of the system. This includes the main logic board (system board or motherboard), processor, memory, disk drive(s), switching power supply, and the interconnecting wires and cables. The system unit also includes expansion cards to provide audio, video, networking, and other functionality. Expansion cards vary from system to system.

- ▶ Keyboard—The most familiar computer input device, the keyboard is used to introduce characters and commands into the system.

- ▶ Mouse—An input device used with graphical user interfaces to point to, select, or activate images on the video monitor. By moving the mouse along a surface, the user can cause a cursor on the display to move in a corresponding manner.

- ▶ Video display—A visual output device that displays characters and graphics on a screen.

- ▶ Printer—A hard copy output device that applies data to paper. Normally, methods of placing information on a page include dot-matrix printer, inkjet printer, or laser printer.

- ▶ Speakers—Audio output devices used to deliver voice, music, and coded messages.

System Unit Cases

The system unit case is typically a metal chassis and removable cover that includes a plastic front panel for aesthetic purposes. This box typically contains the basic parts of the computer system. PCs have been packaged in various case designs. Each design offers characteristics that adapt the system for different environments. Primary characteristics for case design include the following:

▶ Ventilation characteristics

▶ Total drive capacity

▶ Portability

▶ Mounting methods for the printed circuit boards

▶ Footprint (the amount of desk space the case takes up)

Within this list of characteristics, PC case designs fall into four basic styles:

▶ Desktops—PC units that are designed to sit horizontally on a standard desktop behind a keyboard and mouse, usually with the display monitor sitting on top of the case (hence the name). These cases are typically wider than they are tall.

▶ Low-profile desktops—A special variety of desktop case, referred to as low-profile desktops, that reduces the vertical height of the unit by using a short bus-extender card, called a backplane, that mounts in an expansion slot and permits option adapter cards to be mounted in the unit horizontally.

▶ Towers—Tower cases are designed to sit vertically on the floor beneath a desk to provide more usable workspace on the desktop. Mini towers and mid towers are short towers designed to take up less vertical space. Tower cases also can be placed on a desktop. Internally, their design resembles a vertical desktop unit. They are considerably less expensive than the larger towers because of the smaller amount of materials needed to produce them. Unlike their taller relatives, mini towers do not provide abundant space for internal add-ons or disk drives.

▶ Portables (laptops)—To free users from the desk, an array of portable PCs have been developed. These units package the system unit, input units, and output unit into a single, lightweight package that can be carried along with the user. The capabilities of modern portable computers make them the equivalent of desktop or tower units in most respects.

Different PC case styles are depicted in Figure 1.1.

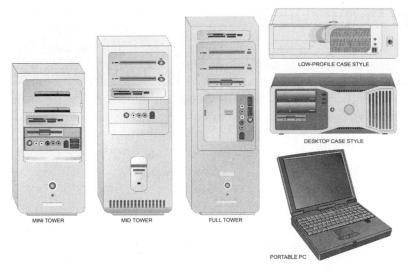

LOW-PROFILE CASE STYLE

DESKTOP CASE STYLE

MINI TOWER

MID TOWER

FULL TOWER

PORTABLE PC

FIGURE 1.1 PC case designs.

Inside the System Unit

The system unit is the main portion of the microcomputer system and is the basis of any PC system arrangement. The components inside the system unit can be divided into four distinct subunits: a switching power supply, the disk drives, the system board, and the options adapter cards, as illustrated in Figure 1.2.

The major components of interest in a PC system are the following:

▶ Power supply—The component in the system that converts the AC voltage from the commercial power outlet to the DC voltage required by the computer circuitry.

▶ System board—The main component of a personal computer. It contains the major structures that make up a computer system.

▶ Disk drives—The system's mass storage devices that hold data for an extended time, even when power is removed from the system. Disk drives include hard disk drives, CD-ROM/DVD drives, floppy disk drives, and tape drives.

▶ Adapter cards—Interface cards used to enhance the basic system with additional functions. Examples of common adapter cards include video display adapters, modems, and Local Area Network (LAN) cards.

▶ Signal cables—Connecting cables, typically configured in a flat ribbon format, that pass control signals and data between system components such as the disk drives and the system board.

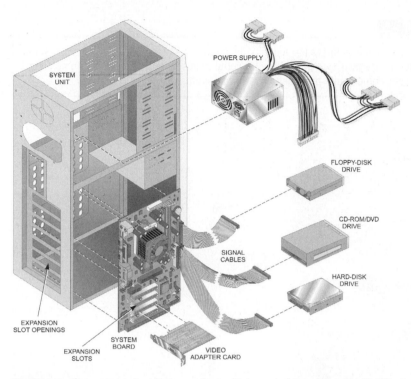

FIGURE 1.2 Components inside the system unit. Layout of components will differ based on the case style. A typical tower unit is shown here.

EXAM ALERT

Know the names of all the components of a typical PC system and be able to identify them by sight.

Form Factors

Form factor is a term used to describe specifications for physical dimensions and electrical compatibility that enables components from different manufacturers to work together. In a PC, form factor is used to describe system board and adapter card sizes, mounting hole patterns for system boards and power supplies, microprocessor placement, and airflow. These factors determine whether component A (such as a system board) will fit properly with component B (such as a system unit case) and connect to component C (such as a power supply). This concept is illustrated in Figure 1.3.

> **NOTE**
>
> Although most manufacturers use industry-defined form factors to create their PCs, some manufacturers use their own proprietary PC components so that they are not compatible with the same components produced by their competitors.

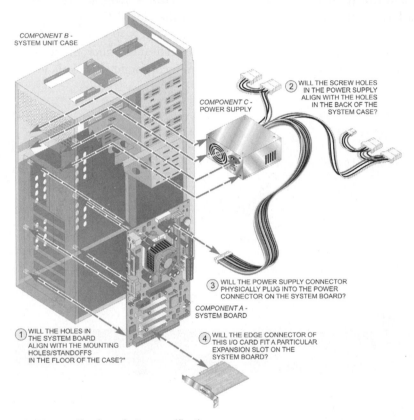

FIGURE 1.3 Key form factor specifications.

You should be aware of three major active form factors: ATX, BTX, and NLX.

▶ The Advanced Technology Extended (ATX) form factor was introduced in the mid 1990s as an upgrade to the IBM PC-AT standard that had become the pseudo standard form factor for PCs. It continues to be the most widely used form factor currently in use with PC components.

▶ The Balanced Technology Extended (BTX) form factor is a newer scalable form factor specification that provides for a wide range of system sizes and profiles. Its main goal is to establish component positions that optimize cooling inside the case to support higher component operating speeds. The BTX form factor design is incompatible with the ATX standard, except that you are able to use ATX power supplies with BTX boards and systems.

▶ The new low-profile extended (NLX) form factor, which is the replacement form factor specification from Intel for the older LPX low-profile specification. The NLX specification is designed to support newer PC technologies, such as larger memory modules, advanced microprocessors, and their cooling systems. The NLX system incorporates a backplane that mounts in a slot on the main board and enables adapter cards to be plugged in horizontally. This is one of the major keys to its low profile.

Power Supplies

The desktop and tower PC's system's *power supply* unit is a shiny metal box that provides electrical power for every component inside the system unit. It converts commercial electrical power received from a 120Vac, 60Hz (or 220Vac, 50Hz outside the U.S.) outlet into other levels required by the components of the system. The power supply delivers power to the system board and its expansion slots through the system board power connectors.

Several bundles of cable emerge from the power supply to provide power to the components of the system unit and to its peripherals. Typical desktop/tower power supplies produce four (or five) levels of efficiently regulated DC voltage. These are +3.3, +5V, –5V, +12V, and –12V. The power supply unit also provides the system's ground. The +3.3V and +5V levels are used by the microprocessor. Other integrated circuit (IC) devices on the system board and adapter cards use the +5V level. Figure 1.4 illustrates the typical power-supply connections found in a desktop or tower PC.

While voltage levels associated with PC power supplies are consistent from model to model, their ability to deliver power to the PC system is not. When selecting power supplies for a given PC application, such as a simple email/web browsing machine versus a high end game machine, it is important to select a power supply that can deliver enough energy to drive all the components in the system. This capability is expressed in the power supply's wattage rating. PC power supplies come in fairly standard wattage increments such as 400 watts, 500 watts, and up.

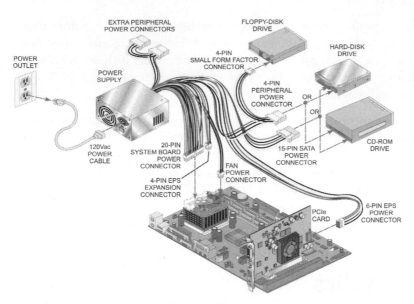

FIGURE 1.4 System power-supply connections.

EXAM ALERT

Be aware of how the power delivery capabilities of a PC power supply are expressed.

The other factor to take into account when dealing with power supplies is their form factor. The power supply's form factor is typically tied to the form factor of the system unit chassis (that is, an ATX power supply should be used in an ATX case). However, some power supplies are designed to work with multiple case form factors.

System Board Power Connectors

The power supply delivers power to the system board and its expansion slots through the system board power connector, as depicted in Figure 1.5. The standard ATX system board connector is a 20-pin connector that is keyed so that it cannot be installed incorrectly. It provides the system board components and the individual expansion slots with up to 1 ampere of current each. All the voltage levels provided by the power supply are available to adapter cards through the system board's expansion slot connectors.

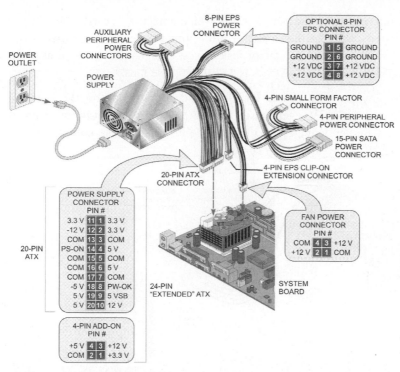

FIGURE 1.5 The system board power connector.

In addition to the lines that deliver different voltages to the system board, this connection contains a signal line that the system board can use to turn off the power supply. This is a power-saving feature referred to as a *soft switch* and enables the system to shut itself off under control of the system software. This enables power-management components of the operating system software to manage the hardware's power usage.

Newer power supplies offer a 4-pin clip-on extension to the standard 20-pin ATX power connector to adapt it to meet the minimum requirements of the *Entry-Level Power Supply (EPS)* specification. This enhanced specification calls for additional conductors to provide additional 12-volt supply sources to the system board so it can deliver higher current capabilities required by high-end peripherals.

Other Power Supply Connectors

The other power supply bundles are used to supply power to optional devices, such as the disk drives, CD-ROM/DVD drives, and tape drives. These bundles provide a +5 and a +12Vdc supply, as described in Figure 1.6. The larger 4-pin connector, referred to as the peripheral power connector, is carried over from older PC designs, whereas the smaller 4-pin floppy connector has gained widespread usage with smaller form factor disk drives. The 4-pin connector also can be used to power other devices such as additional case fans.

The +5V supply provides power for electronic components on the optional devices, whereas the +12V level is used for disk drive motors and other devices that require a higher voltage. As the figure illustrates, these connectors are keyed, so they must be plugged in correctly.

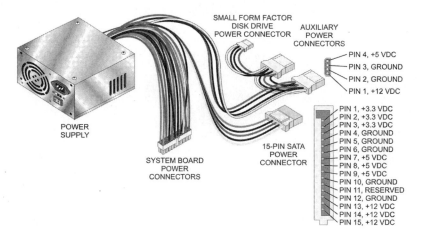

FIGURE 1.6 Auxiliary power connectors.

More advanced power supplies offer additional power connection options, as illustrated in Figure 1.7. The wide-flat 15-pin Serial ATA (SATA) connectors are used to supply power to the newer SATA style disk drive units.

The 6-pin PCI Express (PCIe) power connectors are used to supply additional power to adapter cards mounted in the system board's PCIe expansion slots. Some of these cards may require more current from the power supply than the system board can deliver through its expansion slots.

The 8-pin EPS connector provides the full implementation of the EPS specification for those system boards that require, or accommodate, this connector. The full EPS implementation delivers even more 12Vdc power sources to the system board than standard ATX 20, 20+4, and 24-pin connections. These advanced connectors are keyed, so they cannot be plugged in incorrectly.

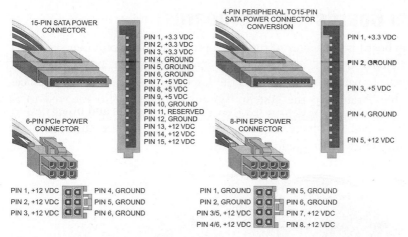

FIGURE 1.7 Advanced auxiliary power connectors.

AC Adapters

Most of the PC's basic components receive their power to operate either directly from the system's power supply unit or indirectly through the system board's expansion slots. However, many peripheral devices must have an additional source of electrical power to operate. Larger peripherals such as monitors, printers, and scanners usually obtain this additional power through their own connection to a commercial AC outlet. These devices are typically large enough and require enough additional power to include their own built-in power supply.

However, several other external peripheral devices, such as modems, disk drives, and USB devices, do not require significant amounts of additional power. These devices rely on small, inexpensive AC power adapters for their additional power needs. These units are self-contained power supplies that plug into the outlet and deliver a designated level of DC voltage at their output plugs.

One of the problems associated with these adapters is that they are not standardized. They come in many sizes and power/voltage/current ratings. For this reason, most peripheral systems that rely on AC adapters include them as part of the package.

Replacement adapters must meet the specification for the original. The best choice is to contact the device manufacturer to find a replacement that you can be sure will work. The alternative is to find a third-party or universal replacement for the defective adapter. However, you must find a unit that has the correct voltage/current ratings and a tip that will plug into the device.

Portable computers employ removable AC adapters to recharge their batteries and to operate the computer when they are being used in a desktop fashion.

System Boards (Motherboards)

The system board is the center of the PC-compatible microcomputer system. It contains the circuitry that determines the computing power and speed of the entire system. In particular, it contains the microprocessor and control devices that form the "brains" of the system. System boards are also referred to as *motherboards* and *planar boards*. A typical system board layout is depicted in Figure 1.8.

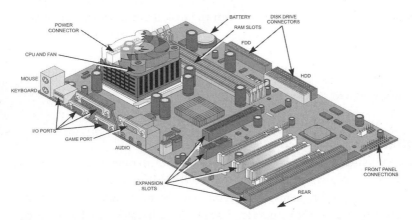

FIGURE 1.8 Parts of a typical system board.

The major components of interest on a PC system board are the following:

▶ Microprocessor/CPU—The "brains" of the system. This component performs mathematical and logical computations at incredible speeds.

▶ Primary memory—Most of the system's primary memory is located on the system board and typically exists in three forms:

   ▶ Random access memory (RAM), which is quick enough to operate directly with the microprocessor and can be read from and written to as often as desired. RAM is a volatile type of memory; its contents disappear when power is removed from the memory.

   ▶ Read-only memory (ROM), which contains the computer's permanent startup programs. ROM is nonvolatile; its contents remain with or without power being applied.

   ▶ Cache memory, which is an area of special high-speed RAM reserved for improving system performance by holding information that the microprocessor is likely to use. Blocks of often-used data are copied into the cache area to permit faster access times.

▶ Expansion slot connectors—Also referred to as *expansion bus connectors*, these are structures mounted on the system board that enable the edge connectors of adapter cards to be plugged in to expand the capabilities of the system. The connectors interface the adapter to the system's I/O channel and system buses.

▶ Chipset—Microprocessor-support devices that coordinate the operation of the system.

▶ Disk drive interface connections—These are standard connectors that provide the physical interface between the disk drive units and the disk drive controller circuitry on the system board. This circuitry is part of the system board's chipset.

▶ Standard I/O connections—Many input/output (I/O) connection types have become standards in the PC environment and have been integrated directly into the system board structure (serial ports, parallel ports, universal serial bus [USB] ports). These have developed into standard blocks of I/O connections that are placed along the back edge of the system board.

EXAM ALERT

Know the parts of a typical system board and make sure that you can identify these components (and variations of them) from a pictorial or photographic representation. You must be familiar with their relative sizes and typical placements on different types of system boards.

NOTE

For orientation purposes, the end of the board where the keyboard connector, expansion slots, and power connectors are located is generally referred to as the rear of the board.

Although the figure shows typical appearances and locations of system board devices on an ATX form factor board, the BTX and NLX specifications move these components around within the system unit to provide better system performance and optimized space considerations, respectively.

Microprocessor

The *microprocessor* is the major component of any system board. It can be thought of as the "brains" of the computer system because it reads, interprets, and executes software instructions, and also carries out arithmetic and logical operations for the system.

The original PC and PC-XT computers were based on the 8/16-bit 8088 microprocessor from the Intel Corporation. The IBM PC-AT system employed a 16-bit 80286 microprocessor. The popularity of the 80286-based IBM PC-AT introduced many standards that are still being addressed by PCs today.

Intel continues to produce ever more powerful microprocessors for the PC market. These include devices such as the 80386DX and SX, the 80486DX and SX, the Pentium (80586), the Pentium Pro (80686), and Pentium II/III/4 processors. All are backward compatible with the 8088—that is, programs written specifically for the 8088 can be executed by any of the other processors.

Intel used the SX notation to define reduced function versions of existing microprocessors (the 80486SX, for example, was a version of the 80486DX that had some functionality removed). SX devices were normally created to produce price variations that kept the Intel product competitive with those of other manufacturers.

Other microprocessor manufacturers, including American Micro Devices (AMD) produce work-alike versions of the Intel processors that became known as *clone processors*. In response to clone microprocessor manufacturers using the 80×86 nomenclature, Intel dropped the use of the 80×86 numbering system following the 80486 processor and adopted the Pentium name so that it could copyrighted.

The Pentium architecture has appeared in many implementations and improvements. It has also appeared in a number of package styles and connection configurations. For A+ certification purposes, the only microprocessors specified are the Pentium class Intel and AMD processors.

Pentium Processor Package Types

Pentium microprocessors have employed a variety of package styles. In desktop and tower systems, the system boards employ socket-mounted or slot-mounted processors so that they can be replaced or upgraded easily. This permits a failed microprocessor to be exchanged for a working unit. It also enables the system board to be upgraded with improved processors when they become available (provided that the new processor uses the same socket).

Beginning with the 80386DX processor, microprocessor manufacturers began using a type of IC package called a *pin grid array (PGA)* package for microprocessors. This arrangement, depicted in Figure 1.9, placed the actual integrated circuitry chip in a thin, square, or rectangular package with connecting pins sticking straight down from the bottom of the package. Variations of this package type are still used with different microprocessors. The size of the package, the number of pins attached to it, and the scale of the IC chip circuitry inside the package change as processing power increases.

In older systems, the microprocessors were forcibly inserted and removed from their sockets using an IC extractor tool. As the typical microprocessor's pin count increased, so did the amount of force required to install or remove it. To overcome this, special zero insertion force (ZIF) sockets were implemented that allowed the microprocessor to be set in the socket without force and then clamped in place. An arm-activated clamping mechanism in the socket shifts to the side, locking the pins in place.

EXAM ALERT

Know which system board structure makes it easy to install upgrade processors in a PC system.

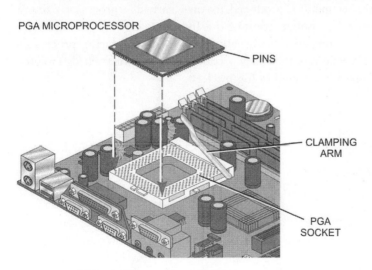

FIGURE 1.9   PGA microprocessors and sockets.

In Figure 1.9 the microprocessor is at the bottom of the cubic structure to the left (looking from the back of the board) of the system board. The cubelike structure actually includes the socket that the microprocessor is mounted in, a large block of metal called a *heat sink*, and finally, a fan unit that moves air across the heat sink unit to remove heat from the microprocessor.

The notches and dots on the various microprocessor packages are important keys when installing or replacing them. They specify the location of the IC device's number 1 pin. This pin must be lined up with the pin-1 notch of the socket for proper insertion. The writing on the microprocessor package is also significant. It contains the number that identifies the type of device in the package and normally includes a speed rating for the device.

In a move to decrease the impact of clone processors, Intel changed the Pentium packaging to a proprietary cartridge and plug-in slot and microprocessor cartridge arrangement with the Pentium II processor. Cartridge processor packages place the microprocessor in a plastic package that snaps into a special slot connector on the system board. The cartridge is tall and thin in comparison to the socket-mounted processor assembly and is held in place by a plastic support mechanism that includes a fan/heat sink module. These units are easy to locate because they look very different from any of the other components attached to the system board.

The original argument for the change to cartridges centered on claims that the socket and pin arrangement had reached its speed limit and the slot technology was supposed to provide the development pathway to higher speed processors. AMD, Intel's main competitor, produced its own cartridge processor using a mirror image connection configuration of the Intel cartridge and slot arrangement. However, both companies eventually returned to producing processors with pin and socket versions of their new processors. A slot and cartridge microprocessor arrangement is depicted in Figure 1.10.

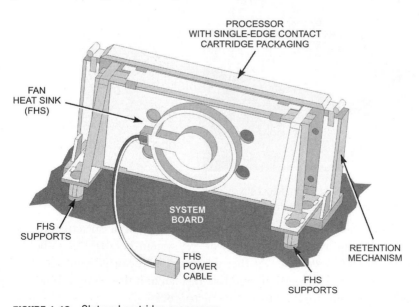

FIGURE 1.10 Slot and cartridge processors.

Chipsets

Microprocessor manufacturers and third-party integrated circuit manufacturers produce microprocessor-support *chipsets* that provide auxiliary services for each type of microprocessor. IC technology can place millions of transistor circuits on a single small piece of silicon.

Such very large scale integration (VLSI) devices are commonly referred to as *application-specific integrated circuits* (*ASIC*s). In some highly integrated Pentium system boards, the only ICs that remain are the microprocessor, a ROM BIOS (basic input/output system) chip, a three-IC chipset, and the system's memory modules.

All Pentium-based system boards rely on some variation of the Pentium/PCI chipset. Figure 1.11 illustrates the relatively compact structure provided by a typical Pentium/PCI chipset. As the figure illustrates, the *chip count* on a typical Pentium-class system board involves only seven major ICs, including the microprocessor, a memory controller called the North Bridge that coordinates all of the system's processor and memory operations with the activities in the rest of the system, and an I/O controller called the South Bridge that coordinates slower system devices and buses with the primary buses used by the North Bridge.

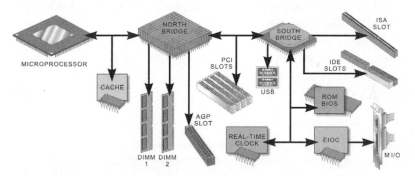

FIGURE 1.11   A basic Pentium chipset architecture.

Memory Units (RAM and ROM)

All computers need a place to temporarily store information while other pieces of information are being processed. In computers, information storage is usually conducted at two levels: primary memory (made up of semiconductor RAM and ROM chips) and mass storage (usually involving different types of magnetic and optical drives).

ROM devices store information permanently and are used to hold programs and data that do not change. RAM devices retain the information stored in them only as long as electrical power is applied to the IC. Any interruption of power will cause the contents of the memory to vanish. This is referred to as *volatile memory*. ROM, on the other hand, is nonvolatile. It retains the information even of power is removed from the device.

EXAM ALERT

Be aware of which memory types are volatile and what this means.

Semiconductor RAM and ROM devices can hold different amounts of data depending on how their internal architectures are designed. When discussing memory capacities of semiconductor memory devices it is common to refer to them in terms of bytes. A byte is made up of eight bits (binary-digits) of information—the bit being the smallest unit of information that can be represented in a digital system.

In most of the PC architecture, information is handled in some increment of bytes referred to as *word size*. For example, microprocessors are designed to handle information in multiple numbers of bytes—a 64-bit processor ideally handles information in 8-byte chunks. This value is referred to as the processor's word size. The word sizes of different devices in the PC may not always match, such as a 64-bit processor and a 32-bit memory device or an 8-bit bus (communication pathway) within the system. When this occurs, the words must be broken up into word sizes the bus or component can handle and exchanged in multiple communications.

EXAM ALERT

Know that RAM and ROM memory capacities are specified in terms of bytes.

RAM

RAM modules on Pentium-class system boards are supplied in the form of snap-in dual inline memory modules (DIMMs). These modules are mounted vertically in special snap-in slots on the system board. DIMMs slide into the slots and are secured in place by locking tabs at each end of the slot. They are keyed so they cannot be plugged in backward. A typical DIMM module is depicted in Figure 1.12.

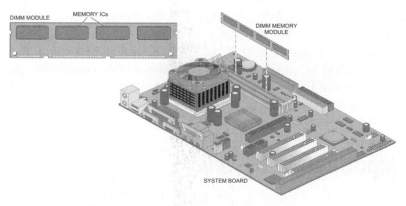

FIGURE 1.12 A DIMM memory module.

RAM module capacities are typically specified in terms of mega (millions) bytes (MB) or giga (billion) bytes (GB). Typical memory module capacities currently range from 256MB to 1GB. However, these values continue to increase as newer memory technologies are devised.

While the capacity of the module is specified in bytes, the geometry of the device involves an x-by-y format that corresponds to word size. A 512MB memory module designed to work directly with a 64-bit microprocessor would be designed to deliver data in 8-byte words (64 bits×8 million words).

PCs are typically sold with less than their full RAM capacity. This enables users to purchase a less-expensive computer to fit their individual needs and yet retain the option to install additional RAM capacity if future applications call for it.

ROM

Every system board contains a ROM IC that hold the system's basic input/output system program. The BIOS program contains the basic instructions for communications between the microprocessor and the various input and output devices in the system. Until recently, this information was stored permanently inside the ROM chips and could be changed only by replacing the chips.

EXAM ALERT

Remember which type of memory device in a PC is used to store information on a permanent basis if necessary.

Advancements in Electrically-Erasable Programmable Read Only Memory (EEPROM) technology have produced flash ROM devices that enable new

BIOS information to be written (downloaded) into the ROM device to update it. This can be done from an update disk, or it can be downloaded from another computer. New information can be flashed as into these devices as often as necessary. Unlike RAM ICs, the contents of the flash ROM remain after the power has been removed from the chip. In either case, the upgraded BIOS must be compatible with the system board it is being used with and should be the latest version available.

Basic Input/Output Systems

When a PC is turned on, the entire system is reset to a predetermined starting condition. From this state, it begins carrying out software instructions from its BIOS program. This small program is stored in an EEPROM memory IC located on the system board.

The information stored in this device represents all the inherent intelligence that the system has until it can load more information from another source, such as a disk drive or remote server computer. Taken together, the BIOS software (programming) and hardware (the ROM chip) are referred to as *firmware*. Some I/O devices, such as video and network adapter cards, have additional firmware that act as extensions to the system's BIOS.

During the execution of the BIOS firmware routines, three major sets of operations are performed. First, the BIOS performs a series of diagnostic tests (called *POST* or *power-on self tests*) on the system to verify that it is operating correctly. The main functions provided by the POST are illustrated in Figure 1.13.

Next, the BIOS places starting values in the system's various programmable devices. These intelligent devices regulate the operation of different portions of the computer's hardware. This process is called *initialization*. The end of the POST/initialization process is typically marked by an audible signal such as a single beep. The system initialization process is shown in Figure 1.14.

Finally, the BIOS performs the bootstrap loader sequence in which it searches the system for a special program that it can use to load other programs into RAM. This program is called the *Master Boot Record (MBR)*. The boot record contains information that enables the system to load a much more powerful control program, called the disk operating system, into RAM memory. After the operating system has been loaded into the computer's memory, the BIOS gives it control over the system. From this point, the operating system oversees the operation of the system. This operation is referred to as *bootup* and is depicted in Figure 1.15.

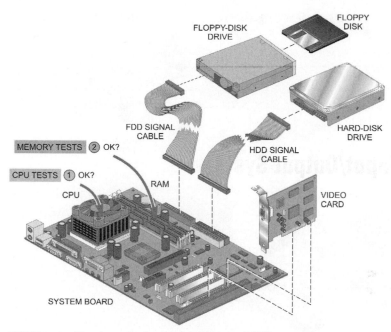

FIGURE 1.13 The steps of a bootup: phase one—POST.

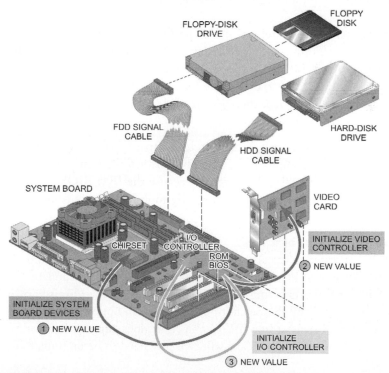

FIGURE 1.14 The steps of a bootup: phase two—initialization.

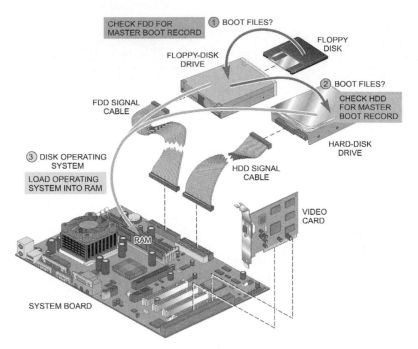

FIGURE 1.15   The steps of a bootup: phase three—bootup.

The boot process may take several seconds to perform, depending on the configuration of the system. If the computer is started from the OFF condition, the process is referred to as a *cold boot*. If the system is restarted from the ON condition, the process is called a *reset*, or a *warm boot*. If a warm boot is performed, or if the POST has been disabled, the amount of time required for the system to get into operation is decreased.

A system's BIOS program is one of the keys to its compatibility. For example, to be IBM PC-compatible, a computer's BIOS must perform the same basic functions that the IBM PC's BIOS does; however, because the IBM BIOS software is copyrighted, the compatible's software must accomplish the same results that the original did, in some different way.

When a major PC component is upgraded, the system's BIOS (along with any associated BIOS extension devices) should be updated with the latest compatibility firmware. All newer PCs have the capability to electrically update the BIOS information without removing the device from the system. This is known as *flashing the BIOS*. If the BIOS does not possess the flash option and does not support the new component, a new BIOS chip that does support it must be obtained. If not, the entire system board will typically need to be upgraded.

EXAM ALERT

Be aware of how information stored in the system's BIOS is updated in most newer PCs.

Challenge #1

A friend is having trouble starting up her computer and she has asked you for help. When you turn the system on, the video display comes on and you can hear the disk drive spinning. Several screens display and then you hear a single beep from the computer. From your knowledge of system bootups, what can you tell your friend about her system? See the solution to this challenge at the end of this chapter.

System Configuration Settings

Each time the system is turned on or reset, the BIOS startup routine checks the system's configuration settings to determine what types of optional hardware devices have been included in the system. PCs feature a battery-powered RAM area that holds some of the system's advanced configuration information. This configuration storage area is known as *CMOS RAM*.

Most system-board designs include a removable, rechargeable battery on their system boards to maintain the CMOS information when the system is turned off. These batteries are typically disk-shaped coin cell batteries that are easy to identify on the system board. However, some systems have no separate rechargeable batteries for the CMOS storage. Instead, the CMOS storage area and real-time clock (RTC) functions have been integrated with a 10-year non-replaceable battery in an independent RTC chip. The RTC function keeps track of time and date information for the system.

Because these configuration settings are the system's primary method of getting information about what options are installed, they must be set to accurately reflect the actual options being used with the system. If not, an error will occur. You should always suspect configuration problems when a machine fails to operate immediately after a new component has been installed.

PCs possess the capability to automatically reconfigure themselves for new options that are installed. This feature is referred to as *Plug-and-Play (PnP)* capability. PnP is a set of system design specifications that enables options added to the system to automatically be configured for operation. Under PnP, the user is not involved in setting hardware jumpers or CMOS entries. To accomplish this, the system's BIOS, expansion slots, and adapter cards are designed in a manner so that the system software can reconfigure them automatically.

During the startup process, the PnP BIOS examines the system for installed devices. Devices designed for plug-and-play compatibility can tell the BIOS what types of devices they are and how to communicate with them. This information is stored in an area of the CMOS memory so that the system can work with the device. Plug-and-play information will be scattered throughout the remainder of the text as it applies to the topic being covered.

CMOS Setup Utility

During the startup process, the BIOS places a prompt on the display to tell the user that the CMOS Setup utility can be accessed by pressing a prescribed key or key combination (these keys vary from PC to PC, but common keys are Esc, F2, and Delete). If the designated keys are not pressed within a predetermined amount of time, the BIOS program will continue with the bootup process.

If the keys are pressed during this time, the bootup routine will be held up, and the CMOS Setup utility will open so that changes can be made to the basic configuration of the system. The values input through the Setup utility are stored in the system's CMOS configuration registers, where they are examined each time the system is booted up.

User must navigate through the CMOS Setup utility using the keyboard's arrow keys and page-up and page-down keys. CMOS utilities typically place directions for navigation and exiting along the bottom of the display.

Every system board model has a specific BIOS designed around the chipset it employs. Therefore, each CMOS utility must address the chipset-specific functions for that system board design. This leads to different options that users can access and configure for each chipset type.

Expansion Slots

In PC systems, the system board can communicate with various optional I/O and memory systems through adapter cards that plug into its expansion slots to expand the capabilities of the basic system for different uses. Most PCs use standardized expansion slot connectors that enable various types of peripheral devices to be attached to the system. Optional input/output devices, or their interface adapter boards, are plugged into these slots to connect the devices to the system's address, data, and control buses.

Several types of expansion slots are in use today. A particular system board may contain only one type of slot, or it may have a few of each type of expansion slot. Be aware that adapter cards are compatible with particular types of slots, so it is important to know which type of slot is being used. These expansion slots are depicted in Figure 1.16.

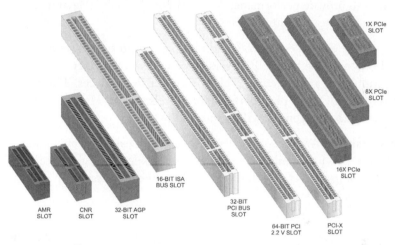

FIGURE 1.16 Expansion slot connectors.

The following expansion slot types are commonly found on Pentium-class system boards:

▶ Peripheral Component Interconnect (PCI) slots—These 32/64-bit slots have been the most widely used expansion slots in the Pentium PC environment. They replaced the earlier 16-bit Industry Standard Architecture (ISA) slot as the main expansion slot in the PC. These slots can conduct data transfers at rates between 132 and 528MBps.

▶ Accelerated Graphics Port (AGP) slots—The AGP slot is a 32-bit derivative of the PCI bus that was developed to provide a specialized interface for advanced video graphics adapters. Data passes back and forth between the system board and the AGP adapter card at rates of up to 2.1GBps.

▶ Audio Modem Riser (AMR) slot—A special expansion slot specification developed to handle specialized modems and sound cards that interact directly with the system.

▶ Communications and Networking Riser (CNR) slot—The CNR slot is a revised expansion slot specification that replaces the AMR slot. Like the AMR specification, the CNR slot is designed to handle special communication and audio cards.

▶ PCI Extended (PCI-X) slots—A high-performance version of the original PCI bus specification. These buses maintain the same connectors and form factor as the original PCI bus. They employ advanced signaling techniques to provide performance levels of 266 and 533MHz and data transfer rates up to 2.1 and 4.3GBps.

▶ PCI Express (PCIe) slots—A collection of high-speed serial versions of the PCI bus standard. These PCI versions employ proprietary slot specifications that are not compatible with other PCI devices. The serial versions of the PCI slot push performance levels to 2.5GHz and data transfer rates to between 250MBps and 4GBps.

▶ Industry Standard Architecture slots—You can still expect to encounter these 16-bit, non plug-and-play, legacy slots on older Pentium system boards. ISA slots, however, will soon pass into history because no new system boards include ISA.

The ISA bus, also known as the Advanced Technology (AT) bus, served as the standard expansion slot specification for many years and through several generations of processors. The reason this slot has continued well into PnP systems is that so many ISA compatible adapter cards and devices were manufactured. Users have steadfastly hung on to these adapters and devices until the industry stopped including the slot in new designs. The ISA slot ran at 8.33MHz and could transfer data at a whopping 8MBps.

EXAM ALERT

You should be able to recognize different expansion slot types from graphics of system board layouts. The most efficient way to do this is to memorize the size relationships between the different types and be aware of how they are most commonly arranged on the system board.

In ATX systems, expansion slots are normally located along the left-rear portion of the system board in positions that permit connections from the back plates of the adapter cards to protrude through the back panel of the system unit case. In other case types, the location of the slots may be in other places.

Adapter Cards

The openness of the original IBM PC-XT and PC-AT architectures, coupled with their overwhelming popularity, led manufacturers to develop a wide assortment of expansion devices for them. Most of these devices communicate with the basic system through adapter cards that plug into the expansion slots of the system board. They typically contain the interfacing and controller circuitry for the peripheral. In some cases, however, the entire peripheral may be included on the adapter card. Typical adapter cards used with PCs are the following:

▶ Video adapter cards

▶ Modems

▶ Local area network cards

▶ Sound cards

Video Adapter Cards

The video adapter card provides the interface between the system board and the display monitor. The most common type of video adapter card currently in use is the Video Graphics Array (VGA) card like the one depicted in Figure 1.17. The system uses it to control video output operations.

Unlike most other computer components, the VGA video standard uses analog signals and circuitry rather than digital signals. The main component of most video adapter cards is an ASIC device called the *Integrated Video Controller*. It is a microprocessor-like chip that oversees the operation of the entire adapter. It is capable of accessing RAM and ROM memory units on the card. The video RAM holds the information that is to be displayed on the screen. Its size determines the card's maximum video resolution and color capacities.

Most current video adapter cards are designed to use the system's AGP slot. High-end video adapter cards such as those used by artists and serious game players are designed to plug into more advanced PCI-X or PCIe slots. However, in some cases, the VGA adapter circuitry is built directly into the system board circuitry. With these onboard video system boards, the display monitor plugs directly into the VGA or other video connector on the back of the board. Video adapter cards with more advanced capabilities can still be added to systems with onboard video. However, it may be necessary to disable the onboard video before doing so. As Figure 1.17 illustrates, the video output connector is a three-row, DB-15 female connector used with analog VGA displays. Higher-end video cards are likely to include more than one VGA connector, as well as other high performance video connectors, such as DVI/HDMi, S-Video, and Component/RGB.

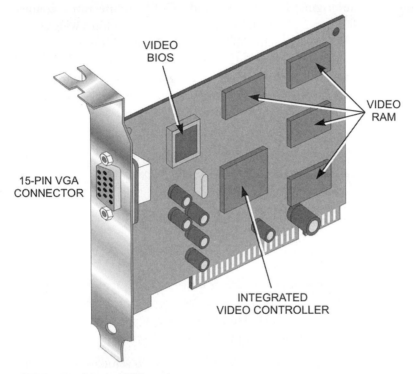

VIDEO BIOS

VIDEO RAM

15-PIN VGA CONNECTOR

INTEGRATED VIDEO CONTROLLER

FIGURE 1.17   A typical VGA card.

Other Adapter Cards

The video display adapter card is typically the only adapter card required in the Pentium system; however, many other input/output functions can be added to the system through adapter cards. Some of the most popular I/O cards in modern Pentium systems are the following:

▶ Internal modem cards—Devices used to carry out data communications through telephone lines.

▶ Local area network cards—Also called *network interface cards (NICs)*, these are used to connect the local system to a group of other computers so they can share data and resources

- ▸ Sound cards—Used to provide high-quality audio output to the computer system.

- ▸ TV tuner cards—Used to input cable television signals to the computer for viewing and recording.

Figure 1.18 shows samples of these cards and their connections. Although they represent the most common options added to computer systems, many other I/O devices can be plugged into expansion slots to enhance the operation of the system.

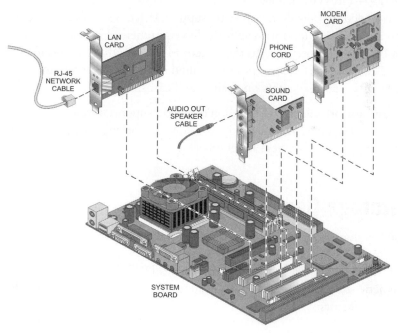

FIGURE 1.18 Typical I/O cards.

Still other adapter cards can be added to the system to provide additional connectivity and functionality. Other adapter cards routinely used in PC systems are the following:

- ▸ SCSI adapters—Most PCs include a built-in Integrated Drive Electronics (IDE) interface for peripherals. Many disk drive arrangements and peripherals are designed to use a small computer system interface (SCSI). For these devices to be used with the PC, a SCSI host adapter must be installed in one of the expansion slots to facilitate communications between the system and the device.

▶ SATA disk drive adapters—While most new PCs include Serial ATA disk drive interfaces as an integral part of the system board, there are several suppliers of plug-in SATA adapters that can be used to add these newer storage systems to older EIDE system boards, or to increase the number of disk drive interfaces in the system.

▶ USB adapters—Most new PCs include high-speed Universal Serial Bus connections. However, you can install additional USB connection points in the system by installing a USB adapter card in one of the expansion slots.

▶ IEEE-1394 FireWire adapters—Although most newer PCs include a USB connection, they do not directly support IEEE-1394 FireWire connections commonly used with audio/video equipment. However, you can add a FireWire adapter card to the system to support this bus specification. Also, it has become common for sound card manufacturers to include IEEE-1394 adapters on their sound cards.

▶ Wireless network adapters—PCs don't directly support wireless networks or printers. However, you can add a wireless networking adapter card so the system can support these functions.

Data Storage Devices

Most secondary memory systems for computers have involved storing binary information in the form of magnetic charges on moving magnetic surfaces; however, optical storage methods such as CD-ROM and DVD have recently moved to rival magnetic storage for popularity. Magnetic storage has remained popular because of three factors:

▶ Low cost-per-bit storage

▶ Intrinsically nonvolatile nature

▶ Successful upward evolution in capacity

The major magnetic storage media are hard disks, magnetic tape, and floppy disks.

Hard Drives

The system's data storage potential is extended considerably through high-speed, high-capacity hard-disk drive units such as the one shown in Figure 1.19. Hard-disk drives are the mainstays of mass data storage in PC-compatible systems. These units store much more information than floppy disks do. Modern hard drives typically have storage capacities ranging up to several hundred gigabytes. Hard drives also differ from floppy-disk units in that they use rigid disks that are permanently sealed in a nonremovable, air-tight portion of the drive unit.

FIGURE 1.19 Inside a hard-disk drive.

Two or more platters are usually mounted on a common spindle, with spacers between them, to enable data to be recorded on both sides of each disk. The drive's read/write mechanism is sealed inside a dust-free compartment along with the disks. The organizational structure of a typical hard disk is illustrated in Figure 1.20.

Typical hard disks may have between 315 and 2,048 tracks on each side of each platter. The term *cylinder* refers to the collection of all the tracks possessing the same number on different sides of the disks (that is, track0/side0, track0/side1, track0/side2, and so on). Each track on the hard drive is divided into 17 to 65 equal-size *sectors*, depending on the diameter of the disk. Sectors generally contain 512 bytes. The high speed at which the hard disk spins provides very rapid data transfer rates.

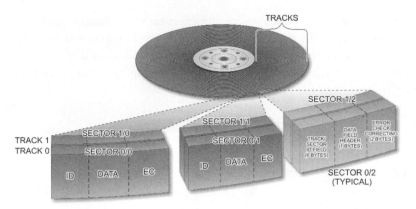

FIGURE 1.20 The organizational structure of a magnetic disk.

EXAM ALERT

Be able to describe the organization of PC-compatible disks (that is, sectors, tracks) and recognize examples of them associated with different disk types.

CD-ROM Drives

Soon after the compact disc (CD) became popular for storing audio signals on optical media, the benefits of storing computer information in this manner became apparent. The term *disc* is used instead of disk to differentiate between magnetic disks and optical discs. With a CD, data is written digitally on a light-sensitive material by a powerful, highly focused laser beam.

Data is encoded by the length and spacing of the blisters (pits) and the lands between them. The recorded data is read from the disc by scanning it with a lower-power, continuous laser beam. The scanning laser beam comes up through the disc, strikes the aluminized data surface, and is reflected back. There is no physical contact between the reading mechanism and the disc.

The information on a compact disc is stored in one continuous spiral track, unlike magnetic disks where the data is stored in multiple concentric tracks. The CD storage format still divides the data into separate sectors; however, the sectors of a CD-ROM disc are physically the same size. The disc spins counter-clockwise and slows down as the laser diode emitter/detector unit approaches the outside of the disc.

CDs are created and marketed in two standard storage capacity ratings—as a 74-minute, 650MB CD-R version and as an 80-minute, 702MB CD-R/RW. These differences are a function of the burning process used to store data on the discs. Most CD-Rs on the market employ the 80-minute/702MB format. You may also encounter some 90-minute/790MB and 99-minute/870MB discs in the market. This additional storage capacity requires that an overburn feature in the CD writer's software be used.

DVD Drives

Newer compact disc technologies have produced a high-capacity disc, called a *digital versatile disc*, *digital video disc*, or *DVD* for short. Like CDs, DVDs are available in DVD-ROM (write-once) and DVD-RAM (rewritable) formats. These discs have capacities that range between 4.7GB and 17GB of data. Transfer rates associated with DVD drives range between 600kbps and 1.3Mbps.

DVDs are available in 120mm and 80 mm diameter versions. They are also available in single-sided or double-sided discs, and may incorporate single-layer or special double-layer recording capabilities. A single-sided, single layer 120mm DVD can hold up to 4.7GB of data, while a single-sided, dual layer DVD is boosted to a capacity of 8.5GB. Double-sided, single-layer DVDs hold up to 9.4GB, while double-sided, double-layer discs can hold 17.1GB.

The single-sided, single-layer 80mm DVD holds 1.4GB, while single-sided, double-layer 80mm DVDs hold 2.6GB. Likewise, double-sided, single-layer DVDs hold 2.8GB, while double-sided, double-layer 80mm discs hold 5.2GB.

The drives used for DVDs are backward compatible with old CD-ROM discs, and newer DVD drives can be used to read CD-R and CD-RW discs. Currently, there are two standards in the rewritable DVD field: the DVD-RAM standard being presented by the DVD consortium and the DVD-RW standard developed by a group of manufacturers that includes Philips, Sony, and Hewlett-Packard. The DVD-RAM format supports 2.6GB of storage per disc; the DVD-RW standard supports 3.0GB per disc.

Physically, the DVD drive looks like and operates in the same manner as the traditional CD-ROM drive. Newer manufacturing methods for the discs permit the minimum length of the pits and lands to be smaller. Therefore, they can be squeezed closer together on the disc. DVD drives also employ higher-resolution lasers to decrease the track pitch (distance between adjacent tracks). Together, these two factors create the high data densities offered by DVD.

Tape Drives

Tape drives are another popular type of information storage system. These systems can store large amounts of data on small tape cartridges. Tape drives are generally used for applications that store large amounts of information that will not need to be accessed often, or quickly. Such applications include making backup copies of programs and data. This type of data security is a necessity with records such as business transactions, payroll, artwork, and so on.

Floppy Drives

The PC uses floppy disk drives (FDD) to store data on small, removable, flexible magnetic disks. The typical floppy disk is a flexible 3.5-inch diameter mylar disk that has been coated with a ferromagnetic material. It is encased in a protective hard plastic envelope that contains a low-friction liner to remove dust and contaminants from the disk as it turns within the envelope. Floppy disks are relatively inexpensive and are easy to transport and store. In addition, they can easily be removed and replaced if they become full.

Like the hard disk, a floppy is divided into tracks and sectors. A typical IBM floppy disk has 40 or 80 tracks per surface. The tracks are divided into 8, 9, or 18 sectors each. In a PC-compatible system, each sector holds 512 bytes of data.

In most cases, the floppy-disk drive connects to the system board using a 34-pin ribbon cable. The cable has a color stripe along one edge to indicate the presence of pin #1. This pin must be oriented correctly at both ends of the cable. Typically, the cable can provide for one or two floppy drives that will automatically be recognized as logical drives A: and B: by the system. The drive connected to the end of the cable will be designated as drive A:.

It is also useful to note that many newer systems do not include floppy drives and in the near future, floppies will probably disappear altogether.

> **NOTE**
>
> Over long periods of time (such as 10 years), data will disappear from a magnetic disk, making magnetic storage only a semipermanent storage solution.

Removable Storage

Removable storage includes all the removable technologies we have already described (floppies, CD/CD-RWs and DVD/DVD-RWs, and tapes). Other types of emerging and/or lesser-known removable storage systems include cartridge-mounted high-capacity floppy disks (Zip drives), solid-state USB drives (IC memory devices configured to operate like a mechanical disk drive), and PC Card drives. PC Card versions of removable storage can hold miniature (1.8-inch) mechanical or solid-state disk drives.

Many current PC designs include special front-panel memory card reader/writer units that handle different types of memory modules used with other digital electronic devices, such as Personal Digital Assistants (PDAs) and digital cameras. This enables digital information, such as audio and video data stored on those memory modules, to be shared between the computer and the device for processing. Figure 1.21 depicts a 9-in-1 front-panel memory card unit that accepts eight types of memory modules and supplies a single front-mounted USB connection port. As the figure illustrates, these units provide multiple openings that are compatible with different standard memory module types.

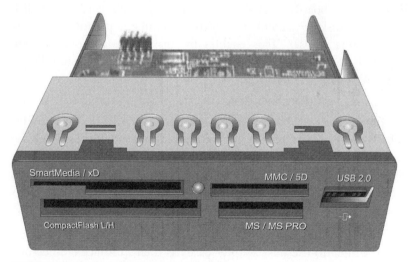

FIGURE 1.21 Front panel memory card reader.

Most external removable storage systems connect to and operate from standard I/O ports (USB, FireWire, SCSI, ECP Parallel). This enables the operating system's PnP operation to detect the new hardware attached to the system. However, most of the devices are nonstandard in nature and require that an OEM applications package be installed to control them. However, USB memory drives automatically load USB drivers and function as another drive in the system (for example, drive E:). In the case of PC Card mounted removable storage systems, the entire peripheral is PnP and hot swappable (meaning that you can connect and disconnect them without powering down your system).

Connecting Storage Devices to the System

Five interface architectures are commonly used to connect HDD, CD-ROM, DVD, and tape drives to PC systems:

- ▶ SCSI

- ▶ Parallel ATA (PATA also known as IDE/EIDE)

- ▶ Serial ATA-SATA

- ▶ IEEE-1394

- ▶ USB

In pre-Pentium systems, the SCSI and PATA drives employed host adapter cards that plugged into the system board's expansion slots. For many generations, Pentium-based system boards have directly supported a standard set of disk drive interfaces. The disk drive control circuitry is an integral part of the microprocessor's supporting chipset. This enables the disk drives to communicate directly with the system through signal cables that plug into the system board without using a host adapter card.

On older Pentium boards this involved three berg strip connectors: one 34-pin strip for the floppy disk drive and two 40-pin strips for PATA hard disk and CD-ROM/DVD drives, as illustrated in Figure 1.22. These connectors can be mounted anywhere on the system board, but they tend to be placed toward the front-right side so that they are close to the disk drive cage of an ATX system. Newer system boards provide two 7-pin connectors to accommodate SATA drives. These drives can operate at much higher speeds than the older PATA drives.

SCSI systems continue to use host adapter cards as their interface connectors. An internal SCSI drive must be capable of connecting to the type of SCSI cable being used. In a PC this is usually a 50-pin ribbon cable. The SCSI interface is also used to connect external drives to PC systems. In external situations, a Centronics connector is normally employed with the SCSI cable.

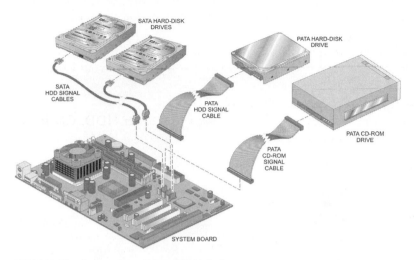

FIGURE 1.22 System board/disk drive interfaces.

Most external I/O devices, including external data storage devices, use the USB interface. This interface has gained prominence because of its high-speed transfer capabilities and flexibility. Many audio/video devices include an IEEE-1394 interface. Like the SCSI interface, a host adapter card may be required to implement the IEEE-1394 interface in a PC system.

Peripherals and Ports

Peripherals are devices and systems that are added to the basic system to extend or improve its capabilities. These devices and systems can be divided into three general categories: input systems, output systems, and memory systems. Peripheral devices are attached to the system through I/O port connections. Ports offer standard hardware connection and logical interface schemes that enable I/O device manufacturers to develop their products to predefined standards. PCs offer a wide variety of different port types to accommodate as many diverse device types as possible.

The standard peripherals used with PCs are keyboards, video display monitors, and mice. The next most common peripheral is the printer, which is used to produce hard-copy output on paper. Figure 1.23 depicts a sample system with these devices. Many other types of peripheral equipment are routinely added to the basic system.

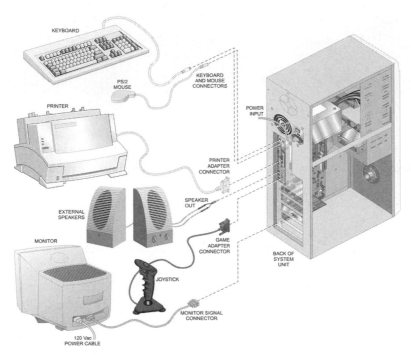

FIGURE 1.23 Typical PC peripherals.

External Devices and Connections

Many of the system board-related functions have been grouped into a standard-ized block of connections. Figure 1.24 illustrates typical connectors found on the back panel of ATX systems. The back panels of specific PCs may have all the connections depicted in the figure, or they may have a subset of these connec-tions.

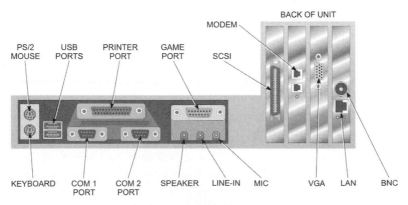

FIGURE 1.24 Typical back panel connections.

EXAM ALERT

Memorize the appearance, type, and pin configuration of the standard PC port connectors (for example, parallel ports use 25-pin female D-shell connectors and VGA/SVGA displays employ 15-pin, 3-row female D-shell [DB-15F] connectors).

The panel features two 6-pin PS/2 mini-DIN connectors. The (0.25 inch), 6-pin mini-DIN connector was adopted from the IBM PS/2 line of computers. This connector type is specified in the ATX form factor for both the mouse and the keyboard. The lower connector is designated for keyboards equipped with PS/2 connectors, whereas the upper connector is intended for use with a PS/2 mouse.

Because these connectors are physically identical, it is relatively easy to confuse them. To compensate for this possibility, manufacturers have color coded these connectors—purple indicates the connection is for the keyboard, and green is used for the mouse. To the right of the keyboard and mouse ports are two USB connectors for attaching devices to the system using this high-speed serial interface.

Most PCs use detachable keyboards that are connected to the system by a signal cable. This cable may plug into the PS/2 keyboard connector or one of the USB connectors. These connectors are keyed so they cannot be misaligned. The most widely used display device for current PCs is the color VGA/SVGA display. The display monitor's signal cable normally connects to a 15-pin, 3-row female D-shell (DB-15F) connector at the back of the system unit. The mouse can be connected to the PC through the 6-pin mini-DIN or one of the USB connectors.

The complete master I/O block contains a DB-9M COM port connector for use with serial devices and a DB-25F parallel-port connector for SPP, EPP, and ECP parallel devices. This board also features a game port and built-in audio connections. The two-row DB-15F connector is the standard for the PC game port and is used to attach joysticks and other game-playing devices. The audio block features standard 1/8-inch RCA minijacks for the microphone, audio-in, and speaker connections.

Some peripheral devices interact with the basic system architecture through adapter cards that plug into the system board's expansion slots. The peripheral devices connect to the adapter cards through expansion slot openings in the back of the system unit. The physical port connector on the back of the computer may be located directly on the adapter card where the port circuitry is, or it may be connected to the port circuitry through an internal signal cable.

In the expansion slots to the right of the I/O block are a DB-15F VGA video connector, a 50-pin Centronics SCSI bus connector, two RJ-11 jacks for an internal modem (one is for the phone line and the other is used to attach a traditional telephone handset), and an RJ-45 combination for making LAN connections with the system's network interface card (NIC). The DB-15F connector used with VGA video devices uses a three-row pin arrangement to differentiate it from the two-row DB-15F game port connector. This prevents them from being confused with each other. The RJ-45 jack on the NIC card is used with Unshielded Twisted Pair (UTP) LAN cabling.

Many front-panel designs provide standardized connection points (hardware ports) for input and output devices (usually USB, IEEE-1394, headphones, and Mic). Historically, I/O connections were all made at the rear of the system unit, out of sight of the user and the public. This also served to keep connecting cables out of the way. However, as PC technology has advanced so that peripheral devices can be connected and disconnected while the system is in operation, many manufacturers have provided additional connections on the front panel. With this move, users do not have to gain access to the back of the unit to connect such devices to the system.

Keyboards

The keyboard type most widely used with desktop and tower units is a detachable, low profile 101/102-key model. To produce data from a key press, the keyboard detects and identifies the pressed key and then encodes the closure into a digital character that the computer can use. These units are designed to provide the user with a high degree of mobility and functionality. The key tops are slightly concave to provide a comfortable feel to the typist. In addition, the key makes a noticeable tap when it bottoms out during a keystroke.

Pointing Devices

Mice, joysticks, trackballs, and touch pads belong to a category of input devices called *pointing devices*. They are all small, handheld input devices that enable the user to interact with the system by moving a cursor or some other screen image around the display screen, and to choose options from an onscreen menu instead of typing commands from a keyboard. Because pointing devices make it easier to interact with the computer than other types of input devices, they are friendlier to the user.

The most widely used pointing device is the *mouse*. Mice are handheld devices that produce input data by being moved across a surface, such as a desktop. The mouse has become a standard input device for most systems because of the popularity of graphics-based software.

The *trackball mouse* detects positional changes through the movement of a rolling trackball that it rides on. As the mouse moves across a surface, the mouse circuitry detects the movement of the trackball and creates pulses that the system converts into positional information.

Typical mice may have one, two, or three buttons that can be pressed in different combinations to interact with software running in the system. When the cursor has been positioned onscreen, one or more of the mouse buttons can be "clicked" to execute an operation or select a variable from the screen. Specialized graphics software enables the user to operate the mouse as a drawing instrument. Some of the more exotic mice possess more than three buttons—many of which are user programmable—making them popular choices with gamers.

A newer mouse design, called a *wheel mouse*, includes a small wheel built in to the top of the mouse between the buttons. This wheel enables the user to scroll up and down the video screen without using scrollbars or arrows. Some scrolling functions, such as click-and-drag text highlighting in a word processor, can be awkward when the text extends off the bottom of the screen. In faster computers, the automatic scroll functions in some software packages will take off at the bottom of the screen and scroll several pages before stopping. The wheel in the mouse is designed to control this type of action. Some mice manufacturers have turned the wheel into an additional button, so that if you press down on the wheel, the system interprets it as a mouse click. This button is generally user customizable.

Joysticks are popular input devices primarily used with computer video games. They can also provide a convenient computer/human interface for a number of other applications. These peripherals are X-Y positioning devices with a *gimbal* (handle) that can be moved forward, backward, left, right, or at any angular combination of these basic directions to move a cursor or other screen element across a video display. Buttons on the joystick can be used in the same manner as buttons on a mouse.

Touch pads (or *touch panels*) are pointing devices that supply X-Y positioning for cursors and other screen elements. The touch pad typically replaces the mouse in the system. The user controls the screen element by moving a finger across the pad surface. Clicking and double-clicking functions associated with mice can be accomplished by tapping a finger on the pad. Touch pads come as an integral part of many portable computers. However, they can be obtained as add-on devices that plug into standard USB or PS/2 mouse ports. Figure 1.25 depicts typical input devices used with PC systems.

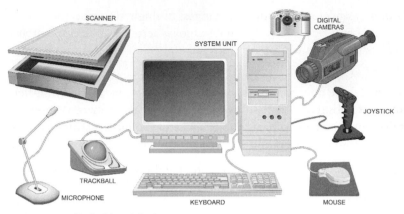

FIGURE 1.25 Typical input devices.

Video Displays

There are two technologies commonly used to display video output from a personal computer: the color cathode ray tube (CRT) display monitor and liquid crystal display (LCD) flat-panel displays. In the past, the video display function was dominated by the CRT display, similar to the one shown in Figure 1.28, as standard video output equipment. The color CRT monitor is sometimes referred to as an *RGB monitor* because the three primary colors that make a color CRT are red, green, and blue.

However, LCD displays are rapidly replacing the CRT in this role. These monitors are not as bulky as CRT-based monitors so they take up less space than the same size CRT monitor. They are also lighter and use less energy than CRT monitors. Figure 1.26 depicts different monitor types commonly used with PS systems.

FIGURE 1.26 CRT and flat-panel video displays.

The video display's normal external controls include

- ▶ Brightness and contrast—*Brightness* refers to the total light output produced by the display. If the brightness setting is too low, image detail is lost. If the brightness setting is too high, the image will appear washed out or faded. *Contrast* is the ratio between the brightest white and the darkest black that can be produced. This setting is a major contributor to perceived picture quality. A high contrast ratio produces a sharper picture than a lower setting.

- ▶ Horizontal and vertical sizing—Horizontal and vertical sizing refers to the fit between the image being displayed and the physical screen dimensions. The image size may be adjusted so that all the viewable area of the image does not fit within the dimensions of the physical screen, either lengthwise (horizontally) or from side to side (vertically).

- ▶ Horizontal and vertical position—Horizontal and vertical positioning refers to the placement of the screen image within the confines of the screen. The image size may match the physical dimensions of the screen but not be centered correctly, causing some part of the image to be outside the viewing area.

- ▶ Skew—The sides and top/bottom of picture are drawn in so that the image is not a rectangle.

The controls for these functions are located in different positions on the monitor, depending on its manufacturer. In addition, each function may be directly addressable or may be accessed through a menu system. There is also a power on/off switch on the monitor. Its location varies from model to model as well. If the monitor receives power through the system unit's power supply, the monitor's power switch can be set to On and the monitor will turn on and off along with the system.

Printers

Printers are widely used peripheral devices that provide hard copy output. The most common method of connecting newer printers to PCs is through high-speed USB, FireWire, or direct network connections. However, there is still a large installed base of printers that communicate with the host system through a standard parallel interface.

Older parallel printers are connected to the 25-pin female D-shell connector at the rear of the system. There are also many older printers that use serial interfacing so that they can be located further from the computer. Serial printers normally plug into a 9-pin or 25-pin male D-shell connector on the computer.

Exam Prep Questions

1. Which type of storage is volatile?

○   **A.** RAM

○   **B.** CD-ROM

○   **C.** Disk

○   **D.** ROM

2. Nonvolatile data can be stored in _____.

○   **A.** Registers

○   **B.** Cache

○   **C.** ROM

○   **D.** RAM

3. Which IC pin is used to align a microprocessor for insertion in a socket?

○   **A.** Pin 0

○   **B.** Pin 1

○   **C.** Pin 10

○   **D.** Pin 8

4. Hard-disk and floppy-disk drive tracks are composed of _____.

○   **A.** Sectors

○   **B.** Clusters

○   **C.** FRUs

○   **D.** Magnetic spots

5. An optical CD-ROM disc typically contains _____ of information.

    ○ **A.** 420MB

    ○ **B.** 500MB

    ○ **C.** 680MB

    ○ **D.** 1.2GB

6. Which of the following interfaces employs a 50-pin cable?

    ○ **A.** An internal SCSI interface

    ○ **B.** An EIDE interface

    ○ **C.** A VESA bus

    ○ **D.** An LPT port

7. Which type of interface would you normally expect to encounter when installing an external CD-ROM drive in a newer PC?

    ○ **A.** ISA

    ○ **B.** IDE

    ○ **C.** SCSI

    ○ **D.** USB

8. For computer bootup purposes, the first set of instructions is stored in the _____.

    ○ **A.** CMOS

    ○ **B.** ROM BIOS

    ○ **C.** CPU

    ○ **D.** RAM

9. From the figure depicting PC components, what type of component is labeled as C?

   ◯ **A.** Hard drive

   ◯ **B.** System board

   ◯ **C.** Power supply

   ◯ **D.** Signal cable

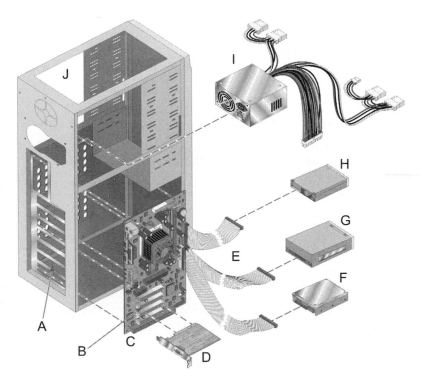

10. From the figure depicting PC components shown in question 9, which component is used to enhance the basic functions of the system, such as video display capabilities and networking?

   ◯ **A.** A

   ◯ **B.** B

   ◯ **C.** C

   ◯ **D.** D

11. From the figure depicting basic system board components, identify the microprocessor.

- ○ **A.** A
- ○ **B.** B
- ○ **C.** C
- ○ **D.** D

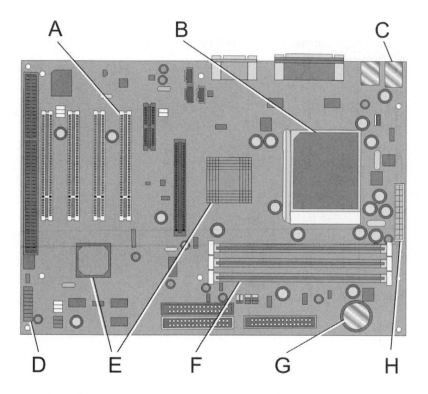

12. From the figure depicting basic system board components shown in question 11, the expansion slots are identified as ____.

- ○ **A.** A
- ○ **B.** C
- ○ **C.** D
- ○ **D.** E

13. From the figure depicting basic system board components shown in question 11, which component is considered to be the "brains" of the PC system?

  ○ **A.** C

  ○ **B.** B

  ○ **C.** E

  ○ **D.** F

14. Which system component executes software instructions and carries out arithmetic operations for the system?

  ○ **A.** The microprocessor

  ○ **B.** The CMOS RAM

  ○ **C.** The BIOS

  ○ **D.** The U and V pipes

15. PC systems use a _____ connector for the VGA video function.

  ○ **A.** 9-pin, female D-shell

  ○ **B.** 15-pin, male D-shell

  ○ **C.** 15-pin, female D-shell

  ○ **D.** 25-pin, male D-shell

16. During startup, the memory of a computer is tested by _____.

  ○ **A.** The CPU

  ○ **B.** The CMOS setup program

  ○ **C.** The POST

  ○ **D.** The interrupt controller

17. A good example of firmware is _____.

  ○ **A.** RAM memory

  ○ **B.** CD-ROM

  ○ **C.** Operating system

  ○ **D.** ROM BIOS

18. Which of the following constitutes a valid computer startup sequence?

    ○ **A.** POST, initialization, bootup

    ○ **B.** Initialization, bootup, POST

    ○ **C.** Bootup, POST, initialization

    ○ **D.** Initialization, POST, bootup

19. When you are discussing the memory capacity of a memory module, the capacity is specified in _____.

    ○ **A.** Gigabits

    ○ **B.** Megabits

    ○ **C.** Bytes

    ○ **D.** Dibits

20. Which one of the following types of memory can be used to permanently store data and instructions in a PC?

    ○ **A.** RAM devices

    ○ **B.** ROM devices

    ○ **C.** Cache devices

    ○ **D.** I/O memory devices

21. How is information stored in the system's BIOS updated in most newer PCs?

    ○ **A.** By physically removing and replacing the BIOS device on the system board

    ○ **B.** By replacing the RTC module so the variable information stored in CMOS will update the BIOS on startup

    ○ **C.** By electronically flashing the BIOS with new information

    ○ **D.** By electronically removing the information from the BIOS, using new downloaded BIOS software to rewrite the BIOS and then restoring it to the BIOS chip

22. What system board structure makes it easy to install upgrade processors in a PC system?

    ○ **A.** An SEC cartridge

    ○ **B.** A ZIF socket

    ○ **C.** A PGA socket

    ○ **D.** A flashable BIOS

23. Which system board structures enable users to install multiple adapter cards in a system to expand its features for different types of uses?

   ○ **A.** Expansion bus slots

   ○ **B.** Chipsets

   ○ **C.** DIMM slots

   ○ **D.** Backplanes

24. You are helping a nontechnical user over the telephone and you need to have him plug in his SVGA monitor. How would you describe the connector and number of pins in the SVGA connector?

   ○ **A.** 15-pin, 3-row D-shell

   ○ **B.** 9-pin, 3-row D-shell

   ○ **C.** 50-pin 2-row D-shell

   ○ **D.** 6-pin, round mini-DIN

25. You have upgraded a user's PC significantly and need to install an upgrade power supply to handle all the new equipment you've installed. You use the Internet to check pricing and features and find thousands of power supply listings. What power supply specification is key in choosing a new power supply for the system?

   ○ **A.** Amperage

   ○ **B.** Amp Hours

   ○ **C.** Voltage

   ○ **D.** Wattage

Answers and Explanations

1. A. RAM is a volatile type of memory; its contents disappear when power is removed from the memory.

2. C. Read-Only Memory (ROM), which contains the computer's permanent startup programs. ROM is nonvolatile and its contents remain with or without power being applied.

3. B. There are notches and dots on the various ICs that provide important keys when a microprocessor is replaced. These notches and dots specify the location of pin 1. This pin must be lined up with the pin-1 notch of the socket.

4. A. Typical hard disks can have as many as 10,000 tracks on each side of each platter. Each track on the hard drive is divided into between 17 and 65 equal-size sectors, depending on the diameter of the disk. Sectors generally contain 512 bytes.

5. C. The average storage capacity of a CD-ROM disc is about 680MB.

6. A. An internal SCSI device must be capable of connecting to the type of SCSI cable being used. In a PC this is usually a 50-pin ribbon cable.

7. D. Most newer external CD-ROM drives employ USB interface connectors.

8. B. When a PC is turned on, it begins carrying out software instructions from its BIOS program. This small program is permanently stored in the ROM BIOS memory IC located on the system board. The information stored in this chip represents all the inherent intelligence that the system has until it can load more information from another source, such as a disk drive or remote server computer.

9. B. Refer to Figure 1.2   Components inside the system unit.

10. D. Refer to Figure 1.2   Components inside the system unit. Adapter cards provide for significant upgrading and enhancement of the basic PC system. These cards are used to add advanced video display adapters, dial-up modems for communicating over telephone lines, and network adapters for connecting local computers together.

11. B. Refer to Figure 1.8   Parts of a typical system board.

12. A. Refer to Figure 1.8   Parts of a typical system board.

13. B. Refer to Figure 1.8   Parts of a typical system board.

14. A. The microprocessor is the major component of any system board. It can be thought of as the "brains" of the computer system because it reads, interprets, and executes software instructions, and also carries out arithmetic and logical operations for the system.

15. C. The VGA/SVGA adapter on the back of the computer has a 15-pin, 3-row female D-shell connector.

16. C. The BIOS performs a series of diagnostic tests (called *POST* or *power-on self-tests*) on the system to verify that it is operating correctly. While performing its normal tests and bootup functions, the BIOS displays an active RAM memory count as it is being tested.

17. D. The BIOS software (programming) and hardware (the ROM chip) are referred to as *firmware*. Some I/O devices, such as video and network adapter cards, have additional firmware that act as extensions to the system's BIOS.

18. A. When a PC is turned on the entire system is reset to a predetermined starting condition. From this state, it begins carrying out software instructions from its BIOS program. This small program is permanently stored in the ROM memory IC located on the system board. First, the BIOS performs a series of diagnostic tests (called POST or

power-on self-tests) on the system to verify that it is operating correctly. Next, the BIOS places starting values in the system's various programmable devices. These intelligent devices regulate the operation of different portions of the computer's hardware. This process is called *initialization*. Finally, the BIOS performs the bootstrap sequence where it searches the system for a special program that it can use to load other programs into RAM and start the operating system.

19. C. Memory capacities are typically specified in an a-by-b format. Under this format, the capacity of the device (in bytes) is derived by multiplying the two numbers and then dividing by eight (or nine for parity chips).

20. B. ROM devices store information permanently and are used to hold programs and data that do not change. RAM devices retain the information stored in them only as long as electrical power is applied to the IC. This is referred to as *volatile memory*. ROM, on the other hand, is nonvolatile. It retains the information even if power is removed from the device.

21. C. When a major PC component is upgraded, the system's BIOS should be updated with the latest compatibility firmware. All newer PCs have the capability to electrically update the BIOS information without removing the device from the system. This is known as *flashing the BIOS*. If the BIOS does not possess the flash option and does not support the new component, a new BIOS chip that does support it must be obtained. If not, the entire system board will typically need to be upgraded.

22. B. Special Zero Insertion Force (ZIF) sockets were designed that allowed the microprocessor to be set in the socket without force and then be clamped in place. An arm-activated clamping mechanism in the socket shifts to the side, locking the pins in place.

23. A. Bus slots (also called *expansion slots*) are standard structures in most PC system boards and enable various types of peripheral devices to be added to the system. The system board communicates with the various optional I/O and memory systems through adapter cards that plug into its expansion slots.

24. A. Video display monitors are attached to the video adapter card in the system unit (or to built-in adapters on the system board in some cases) via a signal cable or cables. The signal cable permits the monitor to be positioned away from the system unit if desired. With CRT VGA/SVGA monitors, the signal cable is permanently attached to the monitor and plugs into the video adapter card using a 3-row, 15-pin D-shell connector.

25. D. When upgrading power supplies, power consumption (expressed as wattage rating) is an important consideration so that enough power will be delivered to drive all components installed.

Challenge Solution

1. Because the system reaches the single beep, you can tell that the basic hardware in her system is working okay. Between the time the system is turned on and the single beep is presented, the system is performing POST tests and initializing basic system hardware components. After the beep, the system searches for a boot record and tries to load an operating system. The problem must be related to one of these activities.

CHAPTER TWO

PC System Boards

Terms you'll need to understand:

- ✓ Slot 1
- ✓ Slot 2
- ✓ Slot A
- ✓ Socket A
- ✓ Socket 7
- ✓ Socket 8
- ✓ Socket 423
- ✓ Socket 478
- ✓ Socket 370
- ✓ Socket LGA775
- ✓ Socket 939
- ✓ PCI slots
- ✓ PCI-X slots

- ✓ PCIe sLots
- ✓ AGP slots
- ✓ Chipsets
- ✓ USB (Universal Serial Bus) interface
- ✓ FireWire interface
- ✓ AMR (audio modem riser) slots
- ✓ CNR (communication network riser) slots
- ✓ PATA interfaces
- ✓ SATA interfaces
- ✓ SCSI interfaces
- ✓ CMOS setup

Techniques to master:

- ✓ Essentials 1.1—Identify the fundamental principles of using personal computers.
- ✓ Identify the names, purposes, and characteristics of motherboards.
- ✓ Form factor (for example, ATX / BTX, micro ATX / NLX)
- ✓ Components
    - ✓ Integrated I/Os (for example, sound, video, USB, serial, IEEE 1394 / FireWire, parallel, NIC, modem)
    - ✓ Memory slots (for example, RIMM, DIMM)

- ✓ Processor sockets
- ✓ External cache memory
- ✓ Bus architecture
- ✓ Bus slots (for example, PCI, AGP, PCIE, AMR, CNR)
- ✓ EIDE/PATA
- ✓ SATA
- ✓ SCSI technology
- ✓ Chipsets
- ✓ BIOS/CMOS/Firmware
- ✓ Riser card/daughter board

Introduction

This chapter covers the motherboard areas of the CompTIA A+ Certification—Essentials examination under Objective 1.1. The system board is the main component in a PC-compatible microcomputer system. The system board contains the components that form the basis of the computer system. Even though the system board's physical structure has changed over time, its logical structure has remained relatively constant. Since the original PC, the system board has contained the microprocessor, its support devices, the system's primary memory units, and the expansion-slot connectors.

Technicians must be aware of the characteristics of different types of system boards in the marketplace. This will enable them to make intelligent choices about repairing, upgrading, or exchanging system boards.

System Board Form Factors

Although the term *form factor* generally refers to the physical size and shape of a device, with system boards it also refers to their case style and power supply compatibility, as well as to their I/O connection placement schemes. These factors must be considered when assembling a new system from components, and in repair and upgrade situations where the system board must be replaced.

One of the first considerations when installing or replacing a system board is whether it will physically fit (form factor) and work with the other system components (compatibility). In both of these situations, the following basic issues must be dealt with: the system board's form factor, its case style, and its power-supply connection type.

> **NOTE**
>
> CompTIA's 2006 A+ exam deals only with ATX, BTX, and NLX form factors.

ATX System Boards

Intel developed the ATX form factor for Pentium-based systems as an evolution of the older Baby AT form factor that first integrated the standard I/O functions onto the system board. It has been the predominant PC form factor for some time. The ATX specification basically rotates the Baby AT form factor by 90 degrees, relocates the power-supply connection, and moves the microprocessor and memory modules away from the expansion slots.

Figure 2.1 depicts a Pentium-based ATX system board that directly supports the floppy disk drive (FDD), hard disk drive (HDD), serial, and parallel ports. The board is 12 inches (305mm) wide and 9.6 inches (244mm) long. A revised mini-ATX specification allows for 11.2 inch-by-8.2 inch system boards. The mounting-hole patterns for the ATX and mini-ATX system boards require a case that can accommodate ATX boards.

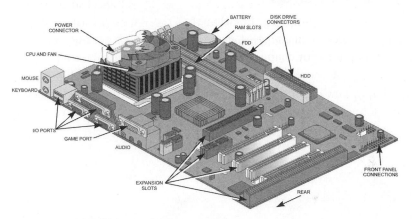

FIGURE 2.1   An ATX Pentium system board.

EXAM ALERT

Be able to identify the major components of an ATX system board from a graphical representation.

The power-supply orientation enables a single fan to be used to cool the system. This feature results in reduced cost, reduced system noise, and improved reliability. The relocated microprocessor and memory modules enable full-length adapter cards to be used in the expansion slots while providing easy upgrading of the microprocessor, RAM, and I/O devices.

The fully implemented ATX format also has specifications for the power-supply and I/O connector placements. In particular, the ATX specification for the power-supply connection calls for a single 20-pin power cord between the system board and the power-supply unit. This cable provides a +3.3V (DC) supply along with the traditional +/– 12V (DC) and +/– 5V (DC) supplies. A software-activated power switch can also be implemented through the ATX power-connector specification. The PS-ON and 5VSB (5V Standby) signals can be controlled by the operating system to perform automatic system shutdowns.

As mentioned in Chapter 1, "Basic PC Terms and Concepts," newer ATX power supplies include a 4-pin, 12V EPS clip-on extension to the standard 20-pin ATX power connector. The additional conductors provide additional current-carrying capabilities to support newer microprocessors and high-end peripherals.

BTX System Boards

The BTX form factor specification is designed to provide better thermal handling capabilities, better acoustic characteristics, and provisions for newer PC technologies. The BTX form factor is not compatible with the older ATX specification. It moves key components, such as the microprocessor, chipset, and video controller, to new general locations on the system board to achieve better airflow (and cooling) characteristics inside the system unit. Figure 2.2 depicts the recommended full-size version of a BTX system board.

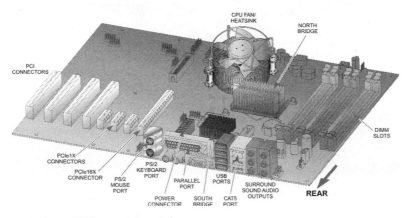

FIGURE 2.2 BTX system board.

The microprocessor has been moved toward the front center section of the board, as have the chipset devices. The major source of cooling in the BTX system is the *thermal module* depicted in Figure 2.3. The thermal module mounts to the front of the system unit and sits directly over the microprocessor and chipset components to provide inline airflow across the components. This reduces the need for additional cooling fans and heat sinks, which in turn lowers the cost of the unit. BTX thermal modules come in two varieties: a standard height Type I version, which is designed for full-height cases, and a low-profile Type II version designed for small form factor cases.

This configuration also improves the *acoustics* of the unit, which is becoming an area of greater concern as PCs are increasingly being used as media servers. *Media servers* are specialized PCs designed specifically for delivering audio and video services in the home setting. In these applications, the sound levels generated by cooling and case fans can reach unacceptable levels.

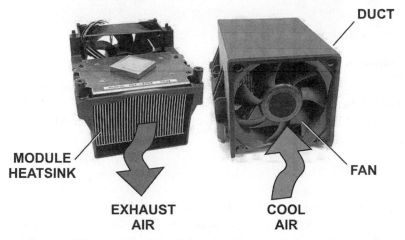

FIGURE 2.3 BTX thermal modules draw cool air in from the top, pulling it over the top of the processor and venting the heated air from the vents on the sides of the module.

BTX Options

The BTX specification offers four board widths that share common core design characteristics. The length of all the board types is 266.7mm. One of the core design characteristics is that in each version the expansion slots have been moved to the right side of the BTX boards, making BTX designs incompatible with other PC form factors. The standard BTX board versions are described in Figure 2.4 and include the following:

▶ PicoBTX—This is the smallest BTX variation at a width of 203.2mm. It includes only a single expansion slot.

▶ NanoBTX—This BTX version increases the board width to 223.53mm and provides for two expansion slots.

▶ Micro BTX—This medium-size BTX version includes four expansion slots on a board that is increased to a width of 264.16mm.

▶ BTX—The full-size BTX specification extends the number of expansion slots from the four in the smaller variations to a total of seven. The board width for the full version is 325.12mm.

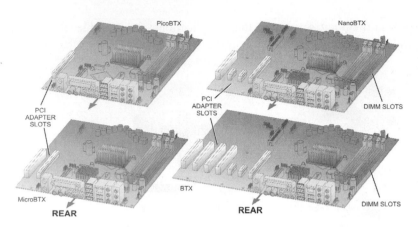

FIGURE 2.4 Standard BTX size variations.

BTX system boards routinely include SATA interface connections, USB 2.0 ports, and PCI Express (PCIe) expansion slots. The larger the board, the more adapter slots and slot types are included. Typical expansion slots used in BTX systems include PCI-5V, PCI-3.3V, AGP-3.3V, AGP-1.5V, and PCI Express slots. The dual inline memory module (DIMM) slots are located near the micro-processor and its chipset components.

The various BTX system board sizes are intended to allow the same technologies to be used in tower, desktop, and low-profile configurations. Figure 2.5 illustrates how these variations are implemented in the different case styles.

The BTX specification makes provisions for using ATX power supplies as well as low-profile form factor (LFX) and compact form factor (CFX) small form factor power supplies.

The BTX back panel moves the rear panel I/O connectors, depicted in Figure 2.6, to the center of the back panel. This layout is the result of better placement of the I/O controller on the system board. Most BTX back panels include PS/2 mouse and keyboard connectors, VGA (Video Graphics Array) video connections, and legacy parallel printer/serial ports. In addition, the BTX back panel may offer a variety of consumer audio and video connection combinations.

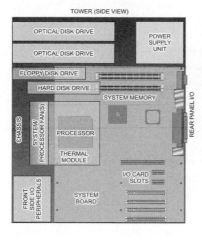

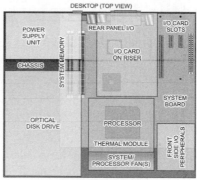

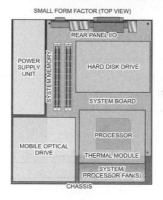

FIGURE 2.5 BTX implementations.

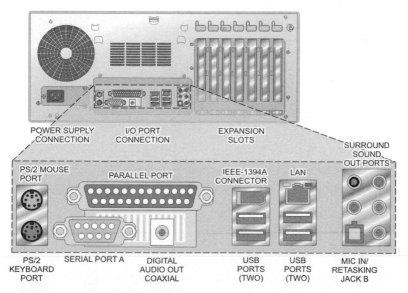

FIGURE 2.6 Typical BTX back panel layout.

Low-Profile Form Factors

Low-profile cases employ short backplanes to provide a lower profile than traditional desktop units. In low-profile cases, the adapter cards are mounted horizontally on the backplane card that extends from an expansion slot on the motherboard. The expansion slot openings in the back panel of the case are horizontal as well. To accommodate the lower profiles, special lowered power supply versions have also been developed.

The low-profile extended (LPX) form factor, also referred to as the slim-line form factor, was designed to reduce the height of the system unit. As such, the specification applied to system unit cases, power supply units, and expansion cards. LPX never became an official standard but it gained enough industry support that millions of cases and power supply units were produced. LPX system boards typically incorporated built-in video so that no adapter card was needed for this function. Finally, LPX units typically had poor ventilation characteristics—the low case height and horizontally mounted adapter cards tended to trap heat near the system board surface.

The new low-profile extended (NLX) form factor, depicted in Figure 2.7, did become a legitimate standard for cases, power supplies, and system boards. However, manufacturers have chosen to produce low-profile units based on microATX and miniATX designs. These form factors followed the ATX design specification but reduced the size of the unit (and its associated costs) by limiting the number of expansion slots.

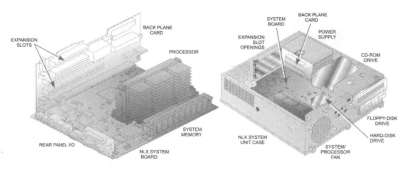

FIGURE 2.7 NLX components.

Pentium Chipsets

Integrated circuit manufacturers develop different chipsets to support different processor types. The typical Pentium chipset consists of a memory controller (called the *North Bridge*), a PCI host bridge (referred to as the *South Bridge*), and in some older versions, a Super (or enhanced) I/O controller. The memory controller provides the interface between the system's microprocessor, its various memory sections, and the PCI bus.

In turn, the host bridge monitors the microprocessor's address bus to determine whether addresses are intended for devices on the system board, in a Peripheral Component Internconnect (PCI) slot, or in one of the system board's other expansion slots. It also provides the interface between the PCI bus, the IDE (Integrated Drive Electronics) bus, and the ISA bus (if present). The Super I/O controller chip interfaces the standard PC peripherals (LPT, COM, and FDD interfaces) to the ISA bus.

This typical chipset arrangement may vary for a couple of reasons. The first is to include a specialized function, such as an advanced graphics port (AGP) or USB interface. The second reason is to accommodate changes in bus specifications such as PCI-X or PCIe slots. Figure 2.8 shows an advanced Pentium/PCI chipset design that includes an AGP slot. Notice that the AGP slot is local to the North Bridge—meaning that it has very fast access to the microprocessor.

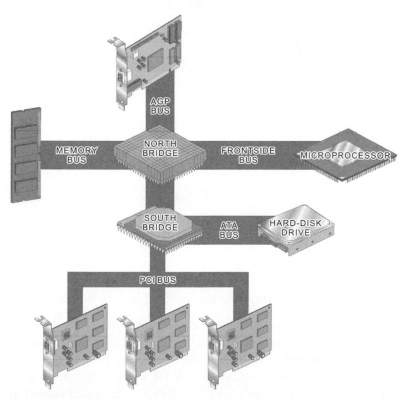

FIGURE 2.8 Pentium chipset with an AGP slot.

Figure 2.9 depicts an advanced Pentium/PCI chipset that provides advanced PCIe expansion buses for multiple "links." Notice that each PCIe link is attached directly to the South Bridge (with the exception of a special PCIe link for the high-end video display adapter).

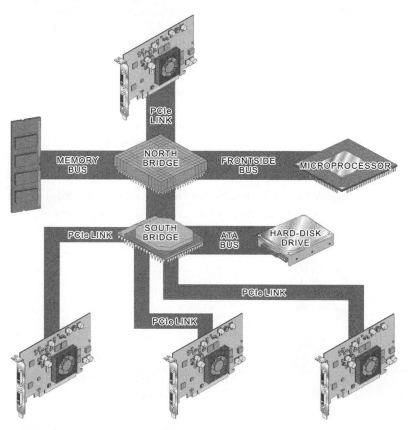

FIGURE 2.9 Advanced Pentium/PCIe chipset.

It is normal to consider the ROM BIOS as an integral part of any chipset model because it is designed to support the register structure of a particular chipset. One of the major functions provided by the BIOS is the Chipset Features configuration screen in the CMOS setup routine described later in this chapter.

Technicians can use this tool to optimize the system settings to provide maximum internal performance. However, these settings tend to be very technical and require an extensive understanding of the specific system's component structure to configure. Therefore, replacing a ROM BIOS chip on a system board is not as simple as placing another ROM BIOS IC (integrated circuit) in the socket. The replacement BIOS must have correct information for the specific chipset it is being used with.

Dual-Core Intel Chipsets

Intel has also introduced a new series of system board chipsets to support the Pentium D line of processors. These include the Intel 975X, 955X, 945G, 945GZ, 945P, and 945PL Express chipsets. Figure 2.10 depicts the block diagram of a typical Pentium D processor chipset. The chipset described in the figure is the 955X chipset. This chipset is primarily intended to support Pentium D and Pentium Extreme Edition processors. However, Intel also lists it as supporting all other Intel microprocessors using the LGA775 socket.

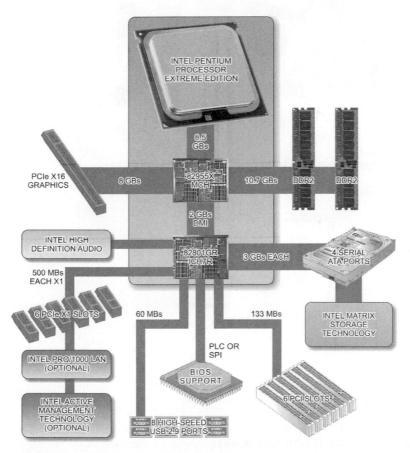

FIGURE 2.10 An Intel dual-core processor chipset.

Chipsets designed to support the Pentium Extreme Edition processors with hyperthreading technology include the Intel 975X, 955X, 945G, 925XE, 925X, and 915G Express chipsets. Figure 2.11 depicts the block diagram of a typical Pentium Extreme Edition processor chipset. This particular chipset is the 975X chipset designed for high-performance gaming, multimedia, and business applications. Notice the extremely fast front side bus capabilities, the number of PCIe options available, and the number of different I/O options supported.

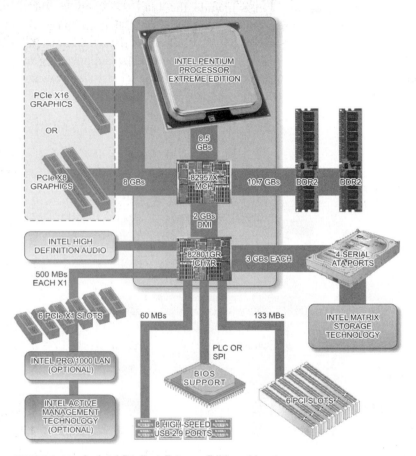

FIGURE 2.11 An Intel Pentium Extreme Edition chipset.

The 910GL Express chipset is used with the Intel Celeron D processor. Likewise, a low-power chipset has been developed to support the Core Duo processors in mobile computing environments. This chipset is the Intel 945GTExpress chipset. Figure 2.12 depicts the block diagram of the Pentium Celeron D processor chipset. Notice the reduced set of features compared to the previous chipset architectures. Also notice the reduced speeds associated with the major buses and I/O connections.

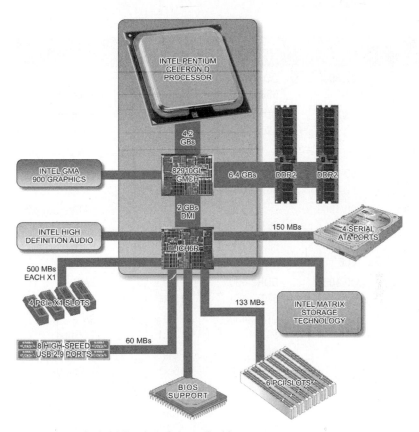

FIGURE 2.12 An Intel Pentium Celeron D chipset.

Table 2.1 compares the attributes of the different dual-core Pentium chipsets.

TABLE 2.1 Dual-Core Pentium Chipset Specifications

PRODUCT	FSB SPEEDS	MEMORY TYPES	EXPANSION BUSES	DISK DRIVE SUPPORT
Pentium D				
975X Express	800/1066	DDR2.533 /667 (8GB)	PCIe × 16/×1	SATA – 3Gbps
945G Express	533/800/ 1066	DDR2.400/ 533/667	PCIe × 16/×1 (4/6)	SATA – 3Gbps/4
945GZ Express	533/800	DDR2.400/ 533	PCIe × 1 (4/6)	SATA – 3Gbps/4

TABLE 2.1 *Continued*

PRODUCT	FSB SPEEDS	MEMORY TYPES	EXPANSION BUSES	DISK DRIVE SUPPORT
945P Express	533/800/ 1066	DDR2.400/ 533/667	PCIe × 16/×1 (4/6)	SATA – 3Gbps/4
945PL Express	533/800	DDR2.400/ 533	PCIe × 16/×1 (4/6)	SATA – 3Gbps/4
Pentium EE				
975X Express	800/1066	DDR2.533/ 667 (8GB)	PCIe × 16/×1	SATA – 3Gbps
955X Express	800/1066	DDR2.533/ 667 (8GB)	PCIe × 16/×1	SATA – 3Gbps
945G Express	533/800/ 1066	533/800/ 1066	PCIe × 16/×1 (4/6)	SATA – 3Gbps
925XE Express	800/1066	DDR2.400/ 533	PCIe × 16/×1	SATA – 1.5Gbps
925X Express	800	DDR2.400/ 533	PCIe × 16/×1	SATA – 1.5Gbps
915G Express	533/800	DDR/ DDR2.533	PCIe × 16/×1	SATA – 150Mbps
Celeron D				
910GL Express	533	DDR-333/ 400	PCIe × 1 (4/6)	SATA – 150Mbps

System Bus Speeds

Microprocessor and chipset manufacturers are continually developing products to speed up the operation of the system. The first method used to speed up the system is to separate the speed at which the internal core of the processor runs from that of all the buses and devices external to it. In the Pentium processor, two speed settings can be established for the microprocessor—one is the *core speed* at which the internal microprocessor operations take place, and the second is a derivative bus speed for its external bus transfers. These two operational speeds are tied together through an internal clock multiplier system.

The second method is to speed up the movement of data across its data buses. As the previous chipset figures in this chapter have shown, the buses operating directly with the microprocessor and North Bridge, referred to as the *Front Side Bus (FSB)*, are running at one speed, whereas the PCI bus is running at a different speed, and the peripheral devices are running at still another speed. In Pentium processors, a parallel bus called the *Back Side Bus (BSB)* connects the microprocessor with its internal L2 cache.

The chipset devices are responsible for coordinating data and control signal flow between the different buses (much like highways and streets where traffic travels at different speeds). The devices in the chipset act as on/off ramps and stoplights to effectively coordinate information movement across the buses. For example, with a current Pentium system board, the processor may run at 3.0GHz internally, while the front side bus runs at 800MHz (200 MHz × 4), the PCI bus runs at 33MHz, and the IDE bus runs at 100MHz.

Expansion Slots

The system's expansion slots provide the connecting point for most of its I/O devices. Interface cards communicate with the system through the extended microprocessor buses made available through these slots. The PCI expansion bus specification has become the dominant expansion bus and slot configuration for PCs. Continued advancement of the PCI architecture has prevented it from being replaced by another type of bus/slot architecture.

The original ATX Pentium class system boards contained a mixture of ISA and PCI slots. Subsequent generations added AMR or CDR slots for specialized audio/modem functions. Most of these designs also added an AGP slot to support high-speed video display functions. Current ATX and BTX designs have completely discarded the ISA, AGP, AMR/CDR slots, and provide different versions of the PCI slot (that is, PCI and PCI-X or PCI and different PCIe slot types).

With the exception of the ISA slot, all the other expansion bus specifications mentioned include slot-addressing capabilities and reserve memory space to allow for plug-and-play reconfiguration of each device installed in the system. However, because no identification or reconfiguration capabilities were designed into the ISA bus specification, the presence of ISA-compatible slots on the system board can seriously disrupt plug-and-play operations.

PCI Local Bus

The Peripheral Component Interconnect local bus design incorporates three elements: a low-cost, high-performance local bus; the automatic configuration of installed expansion cards (PnP); and the capability to expand with the introduction of new microprocessors and peripherals. The data-transfer performance of the PCI local bus is 132MBps using a 32-bit bus and 264MBps using a 64-bit bus. This is accomplished even though the bus has a maximum clock frequency of 33MHz.

The PCI peripheral device has 256 bytes of onboard memory to hold information as to what type of device it is. The peripheral device can be classified as a controller for a mass-storage device, a network interface, a display, or other hardware. The configuration space also contains control, status, and latency timer values. The latency timer register on the device determines the length of time that the device can control the bus for bus-mastering operations.

The PCI bus specification uses multiplexed address and data lines to conserve the pins of the basic 124-pin PCI connector. Within this connector are signals for control, interrupt, cache support, error reporting, and arbitration.

The original PCI bus employed 32-bit address and data buses. Its specification also defined a 64-bit multiplexed address and data bus variation for use with 64-bit processors, such as the Pentium. Its clock line was originally defined for a maximum frequency of 33MHz and a 132MBps transfer rate; however, it can be used with microprocessors operating at higher clock frequencies (66MHz under the PCI 2.1 specification).

The PCI 2.2 and PCI 2.3 versions of the bus implemented two new slot structures to provide a true 64-bit data bus, as illustrated in Figure 2.13. The new PCI specification runs at 66MHz to provide a 264MBps data throughput. The slot also features a reduced 3.3Vdc power supply voltage to decrease signal interference levels generated by the 33MHz operations. Adapters placed in the 32-bit section of the PCI 2.2 slot can operate with the 5Vdc or 3.3V supply levels. The back portion of the slot remains pin- and signal-compatible with the older 32-bit PCI slots. It retained its +5Vdc operating voltage to remain compatible with older PCI 1.1 and 2.0 adapters.

An additional PCI bus improvement has been developed using a new slot layout for PCI 2.3. This slot is similar to the PCI 66-32/64 intermediate slot in size and appearance. However, it is keyed in such a manner that only adapter cards designed for this slot (or universal PCI cards) can be inserted. The slot also features a reduced 3.3Vdc power supply voltage to decrease signal interference levels generated by the 66MHz operations.

PCI Configuration

The PCI standard is part of the PnP hardware standard. As such, the system's BIOS and system software must support the PCI standard. Although the PCI function is self-configuring, many of its settings can be viewed and altered through the CMOS setup utility.

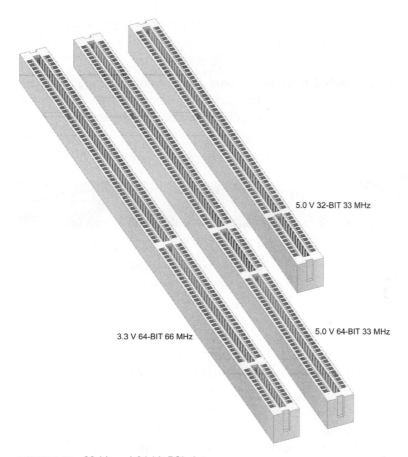

5.0 V 32-BIT 33 MHz

3.3 V 64-BIT 66 MHz

5.0 V 64-BIT 33 MHz

FIGURE 2.13 32-bit and 64-bit PCI slots.

During a portion of the bootup known as the *detection phase*, the PnP-compatible BIOS checks the system for devices installed in the expansion slots to see what types they are, how they are configured, and which slots they are in. For PnP-compatible I/O cards, this information is held in a ROM device on the adapter card.

The BIOS reads the information from all the cards and then assigns each adapter a *handle* (logical name) in the PnP Registry. It then stores the configuration information for the various adapters in the Registry as well.

Next, the BIOS compares the adapter information to the system's basic configuration in search of resource conflicts. After evaluating the requirements of the cards and the system's available resources, the PnP routine assigns system resources to the cards as required.

Because the PnP process has no method for reconfiguring legacy devices during the resource assignment phase, it begins by assigning resources, such as IRQ assignments, to these devices before servicing the system's PnP devices.

Likewise, when the BIOS detects the presence of a new device during the detection phase, it disables the resource settings of its existing cards, checks to determine what resources are required and available, and then reallocates the system's resources as necessary.

EXAM ALERT

Know the process the PnP system employs to allocate resources to a new device in an existing system.

Depending on the CMOS settings available with a particular PCI chipset, the startup procedure may be set up to configure and activate all the PnP devices at startup. With other chipsets, it may also be possible to check all cards, but enable only those actually needed for startup. Some CMOS routines contain several user-definable PCI configuration settings. Typically, these settings should be left in default positions. The rare occasion for changing a PCI setting occurs when directed to do so by a product's installation guide.

Systems may, in theory, contain an unlimited number of PCI slots. Only four slots are included on most system boards because of signal loading considerations. The PCI bus includes four internal interrupt lines (INTa through INTd, or INT1 through INT4) that enable each PCI slot to activate up to four different interrupts. PCI interrupts should not be confused with the system's IRQ channels, although they can be associated with them if required by a particular device. In these cases, IRQ9 and IRQ10 are typically used.

PCI-X

PCI bus versions after PCI 2.3 were given a designation of PCI-X (along with a description of their operating speeds, such as PCI-X 66). These PCI-X specifications are enhanced versions of the 64-bit 66MHz PCI 2.3 bus specification.

▶ PCI-X 1.0 was based on the previous PCI 2.3 architecture and offers support for 3.3V and universal PCI cards. Therefore, conventional 33/66MHz PCI cards can be used in PCI-X 1.0 slots. Conversely, PCI-X 1.0 cards could be used in standard PCI slots. PCI-X 1.0 provides 66 and 133MHz bus speed options.

▶ PCI-X 2.0 was derived from PCI-X 1.0 and introduced an Error Correction Code (ECC) feature to improve data transfer reliability. It also introduced two new speed options: PCI-X 266MHz (which provides 2.13GB/sec transfer rates) and PCI-X 533MHz (with 4.26 GB/sec transfer rates).

All the PCI-X versions are backward compatible with the original PCI specifications (that is, they employ the same form factors, pin-outs, connector, 32/64-bit bus widths, and protocols as the original PCI specification). However, the slowest board installed in one of the PCI-X slots determines the operating speed for all the PCI devices. Although these versions offered some improvements over previous PCI versions, they have never been widely used in desktop PCs or network workstations. Instead, boards with these slots have typically been used in more powerful network server computers.

PCI Express

Originally, there was a PCI-X 1066 expansion slot version envisioned. However, as signal speed increases in parallel bus connections, it becomes much more difficult to reliably transmit and receive data. The electrical quantities associated with insulated, parallel conductors eventually outweigh the advantages of sending multiple bits of data at the same time. When this point is reached in any type of communications setting, the answer is always to implement some type of serial (one bit at a time using one communication path) method of moving the information from point A to point B.

The PCI specification shifted to a serial PCI expansion scheme called PCI Express (PCIe). The Pentium/PCIe chipset employs the same software driver support as traditional PCI interfaces. However, under PCIe, the data moving back and forth across the bus is formed into serialized packets before being sent and is then converted back to parallel format after it has been received.

The basic PCIe architecture employs two low-voltage differential signal (LVDS) pairs of data lines that carry data back and forth at rates up to 5.5GBps in each direction. Each two-pair communication path is referred to as a *lane* and is capable of transmitting one byte at a time in both directions at once. This full-duplex communication is possible because each lane is made up of one send and one receive path.

Under the PCIe specification, PCIe switching devices can combine multiple PCIe lanes together to provide additional bandwidth between the PCIe host and the PCIe device. Each complete connection between a host and a device (or slot) is referred to as a *link*. Figure 2.14 illustrates the relationship between PCIe lanes and links. In this example, two PCIe lanes are routed to a particular PCIe slot configuration to provide a two-lane (×2) link capable of carrying twice as much information as a single-lane link (×1).

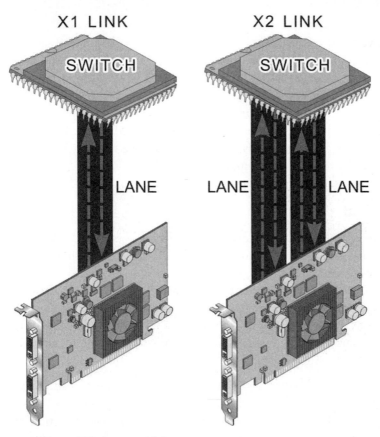

FIGURE 2.14 PCIe lanes and links.

The PCIe specification supports ×1, ×2, ×4, ×8, ×12, ×16, and ×32 lane links. However, available PCIe chipsets provide for only 20 lanes, and 16 are typically used for the ×16 PCIe graphics slot. The PCIe switches depicted in the figure are built into the South Bridge of the chipset and provide links to most of the PCIe expansion slots. In some chipset versions the ×16 slots are connected directly to a PCIe switch in the North Bridge. To date, this slot is the most successful implementation of the PCIe standard. The other four lanes can be distributed between any combination of ×1, ×2, or ×4 slots.

PCIe Slots

PCIe employs four slot connector sizes. The ×1 slot contains 36 contact positions. The ×4 slot is physically larger and has 64 pins, the ×8 version uses 98 pins, and the ×16 has 164 pins. Figure 2.15 shows the different PCIe expansion slots and their pin assignments.

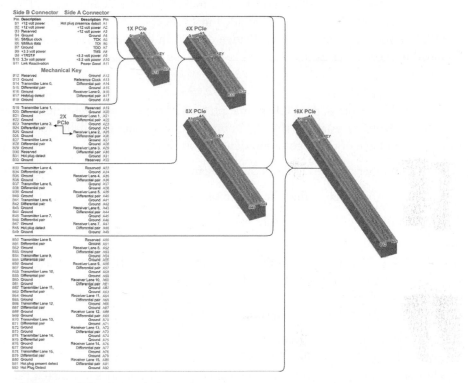

FIGURE 2.15 PCIe slots and pinouts for each.

The number and arrangement of PCIe slots on system boards is largely up to the discretion of the system board manufacturer. The BTX form factor specification calls for one ×16 slot and two ×1 slots for its system boards. The ×16 slot replaces the traditional AGP slot (covered in the next section of this chapter) for the graphic display adapter. Some system boards include two ×16 slots, whereas others offer a mixture of ×8, ×4, and ×1 slots. These system boards may also include some number of traditional PCI slots.

It is permissible to plug PCIe adapter cards with fewer lanes into a larger slot (for instance, a ×8 card into a ×16 slot). The card's edge connector will not fill the slot, but the electrical contact connections should line up properly and the card should function correctly. The PCIe host adapter (known as a *PCIe switch*) portion of the chipset will automatically assess the card in the slot during start-up and assign the required number of lanes to the slot. The unused lanes are then available for use in other PCIe slots.

System boards designs may include both traditional PCI and PCIe slots. A *PCI-to-PCIe bridge* translates PCIe information into standard PCI signals. This bridging enables standard PCI devices to be included in the PCIe system. The bridging circuitry is starting to be included in PCIe chipsets. On these boards, the PCI bridge is part of the South Bridge device. In other cases, the bridge is included in the adapter card.

PCIe Configuration

During the PnP process, the PCIe switch portion of the chipset negotiates with any PCIe devices to establish the maximum number of lanes available for the link. The outcome of the negotiation depends on three factors:

▸ The number of physical lanes the link can support

▸ The number of lanes that the device requires

▸ The number of lanes the PCIe switch can support

If the device, such as an advanced PCIe video card, contains 16 lanes, it will need to be inserted into an ×16 slot. However, if the device has only 8 lanes, the PCIe switch will detect this and allocate only the 8 lanes required. If the link supports more than 16 lanes, the extra lanes will be ignored.

If the device has more lanes than the link can furnish, the device and the switch throttle back to the number of lanes available. The one situation where this would not be the case is where the physical edge connector does not match the physical connector.

AGP Slots

Many ATX system board designs include an advanced Accelerated Graphics Port (AGP) interface for video graphics. The AGP interface is a variation of the PCI bus design that has been modified to handle the intense data throughput associated with 3D graphics.

EXAM ALERT

Know what type of device is plugged into an AGP slot.

The AGP specification was introduced by Intel to provide a 32-bit video channel that runs at 66MHz in basic 1× video mode. The standard also supports three high-speed modes: 2× (5.33MBps), 4× (1.07GBps), and 8× (2.1GBps).

The AGP standard provides for a direct channel between the AGP graphic controller and the system's main memory, instead of using the expansion buses for video data. This removes the video data traffic from the PCI buses. The speed provided by this direct link permits video data to be stored in system RAM instead of in special video memory. System boards designed for portable systems and single-board systems may incorporate the AGP function directly into the board without using a slot connector.

As illustrated in Figure 2.16, three types of slot connectors have been used to deliver the AGP function for system boards used in desktop and tower units. The system board typically features a single slot that is supported by a Pentium/AGP-compliant chipset. The original slot configuration had a key located toward the rear of the board. These slots were used with 3.3V (2×) adapters.

The second AGP slot version moved the key toward the front of the board, so it was not physically compatible with the older AGP adapters. These slots were used with 1.5 V (4×) adapters. The final revision of the AGP slot is the universal AGP slot that removes all keys so that it can accept any type of AGP card (including universal adapters). These slots can be used with 3.3V, 1.5V, and 0.8V (2×/4×/8×) adapters.

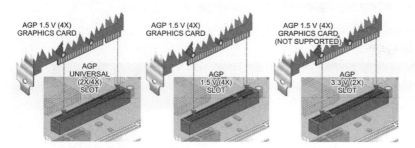

FIGURE 2.16 AGP slots.

The newer 8× specification employs a lower supply voltage (0.8) than the 2× and 4× specifications. When upgrading an AGP card or a system board containing an AGP slot, you should always consult the system board and AGP adapter card's documentation to verify their compatibility with each other. Usually the Chipset Features page of the CMOS setup utility provides user-configurable AGP slot parameters that can be used to manually configure the adapter's parameters. The default setting for this option is Autodetect. In this mode, the PnP process will detect the card and assign the correct voltages and maximum speed settings for that type of card.

Table 2.2 compares the capabilities of the various bus types commonly found in personal computers. It is quite apparent that the data-transfer rates possible with each new version increase dramatically. The reason this is significant is that the expansion bus is a speed-limiting factor for many of the system's operations. Every peripheral access made through the expansion slots requires the entire computer to slow down to the operating speed of the bus.

TABLE 2.2   Expansion Bus Specifications

BUS TYPE	TRANSFER RATE	DATA BITS	ADDRESS BITS	DMA CHANNELS	INT CHANNELS
ISA	8MBps	16	24	8	11
PCI 2	132/264MBps	32/64	32	None	3
PCI 2.1	264/528MBps	32/64	32	None	3
PCI-X 1.0	1.06GBps	64	64	None	3
PCI-X 2.0	2.13/4.26GBps	64	64	None	3
PCIe	250MBps per lane	Serial	None	None	None
AGP	266/533/1,070MBps	32	32	None	3

EXAM ALERT

You must be able to identify standard expansion slot types from different ATX system board outline drawings.

Audio Modem Risers and Communication Networking Risers

Intel developed an audio/modem standard for system board designs that separates the analog and digital functions of audio (sound card) and modem devices.

This standard includes an expansion slot connection, called the Audio Modem Riser (AMR), and a companion expansion card format, known as the Mobile Daughter Card (MDC). The analog portion of the function is placed on the MDC riser card and the digital functions are maintained on the system board. These components are depicted in Figure 2.17.

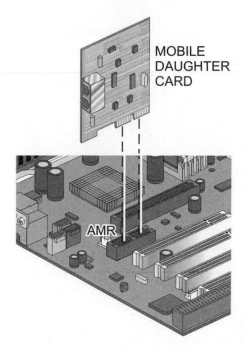

FIGURE 2.17 Audio Modem Riser components.

AMR slots are already being replaced in Pentium systems by a new design called the Communications and Networking Riser (CNR) card, depicted in Figure 2.18. This specification improves on the AMR specification by including support for advanced V.90 analog modems, multichannel audio, telephone-based dial-up networking, and USB devices, as well as 10/100 ethernet-based LAN adapters.

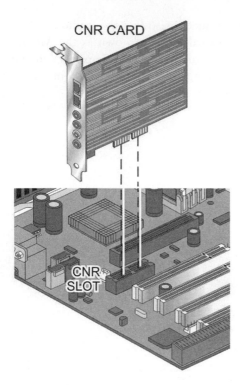

FIGURE 12.18 Communications and Networking Riser card components.

I/O Ports

Many of the PCs standard I/O port circuits have been integrated directly into the system board's chipset and BIOS/CMOS structures. The corresponding hardware ports were grouped into a standardized block of connections in the ATX specification, as illustrated in Figure 2.19. These connectors are placed along the back edge of the system board and extend through the back panel of the system unit. The back panels of specific PCs may have all the connections depicted in the figure, or they may have some subset of these connections.

The panel features two (0.25 inch) 6-pin PS/2 mini-DIN connectors specified for both the mouse and the keyboard. The lower connector is designated for keyboards equipped with PS/2 connectors, and the upper connector is intended for use with a PS/2 mouse. Because these connectors are physically identical, it is relatively easy to confuse them. To compensate for this possibility, manufacturers have color coded these connectors—purple indicates that the connection is for the keyboard, and green is used for the mouse.

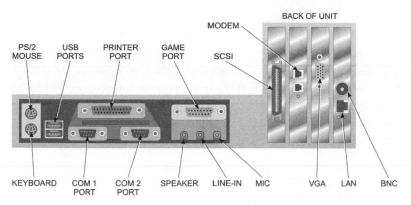

FIGURE 2.19 Standard ATX back panel connections.

To the right of the keyboard and mouse ports is a DB-9M D-shell COM port connector for use with serial devices, a DB-25F D-shell parallel-port connector for SPP, EPP, and ECP parallel devices, and a digital coaxial audio output connector.

Next are two stacks of two USB connectors. An IEEE-1394 FireWire port tops the first stack. These are high-speed serial interface ports that allow various peripheral devices to be attached to the system. The second stack is topped with an RJ-45 connector to accommodate CAT5 local area networking. These connectors are keyed so they cannot be misaligned.

Other integrated I/O ports commonly found on the back of PC systems include additional serial ports, integrated DB-15F D-shell VGA display connectors, and 1/8 inch RCA jacks for speakers, microphones, and line-in sources.

> **EXAM ALERT**
>
> You must be able to identify standard I/O connection types from different ATX/BTX system board drawings by their relative sizes and locations.

Onboard Disk Drive Connections

Pentium system boards provide the system's hard-disk/CD-ROM/DVD drive and floppy-disk drive controller functions and interface connections. There are currently three common disk drive connection interfaces provided on system boards: Parallel Advanced Technology Attachment (PATA) and Serial AT Attachment (SATA) connectors for IDE drives, and (possibly) a FDC interface connection.

PATA and SATA interfaces are designed to serve a particular type of drive that places the bulk of the drive controller circuitry on the disk unit instead of on an adapter card. These drives are referred to as *IDE drives*. The IDE designation was originally used to refer to all ATA devices until the advent of the serial ATA interface. At this point, discussions of IDE drives and their interfaces had to be segmented into terms of parallel and serial ATA drives. Figure 2.20 provides an example of a system board that supplies the system's PATA and SATA host adapter connections, along with the FDC interface connection.

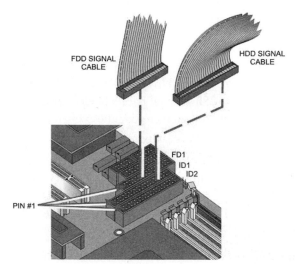

FIGURE 2.20 System board disk drive connections.

The FDC portion of the chipset can control two floppy-disk drives whose signal cable connects to the system board at the 34-pin BERG connector, labeled FD1. As with any disk-drive connections, caution must be taken when connecting the floppy-disk drive signal cable to the system board; pin 1 of the connector must line up with the signal cable's indicator stripe.

PATA Connections

The parallel IDE host adapter portion of the chipset furnishes two complete IDE channels—IDE1 and IDE2—that can handle one master and one slave device each. The IDE hard drives and CD-ROM drives are attached to the system board via signal cables that connect to two 40-pin BERG connectors labeled ID1 and ID2. Traditionally, cables used with internal disk drives have been flat, ribbon cables. However, newer rounded cables are available for connecting disk drives to the system board. The connectors at the ends of the cables are the same, but the rounded cables are supposed to take up less space, provide better air flow through the case, and be more flexible so they are easier to work with. There are several versions of the PATA/IDE interface. Fortunately, most of these versions are concerned only with the software and drivers that control the flow of information through the interface.

System boards that used the original PATA/IDE specification provided one 40-pin connector on the board and offered a single IDE channel that could control two IDE devices (one master and one slave). Eventually, system boards that support the Enhanced IDE (EIDE) standards for communications and feature two physical IDE connectors were introduced to the market.

Each EIDE channel is capable of handling its own master and slave devices. Over time, the EIDE interface has been redefined to provide faster transfer rates, as well as to handle larger storage capacities. EIDE interfaces can also be used to control drive units such as a tape or CD-ROM. The EIDE interface is often described as an ATAPI (AT Attachment Packet Interface) or a Fast ATA (Fast AT Attachment) interface.

The original PATA/IDE interface employed 40-wire cables between the system board interfaces and the drive units. Of these 40 wires, only 7 were ground wires. As transfer speeds across the PATA cabling increased, the large separation between each signal line and its respective return ground line resulted in decreased reliability over this cable.

For transfer rates greater than 33MHz, the original 40-wire cable was replaced by an 80-wire version that alternates ground and signal lines. This arrangement reduces interference between signal lines, which greatly increased the reliability of each line at higher frequencies. These cables have a maximum length specification of 18 inches.

The 80-wire cables still use the 40-pin IDE connector at each end to remain compatible with standard PATA connections. These cables are typically color coded to prevent them from being confused with older 40-wire cables, which are typically gray. However, when newer EIDE devices are connected to the system using an older 40-conductor cable, they will default to operating speeds compatible with the older IDE standards.

Many PATA cable manufacturers also color code the connectors on their cables to suggest where each connector should be attached in the system. The blue connector is intended to be connected to the system board's PATA interface. The black connector should be connected to the master device and the gray connector is used for a slave device, if one is used on the same IDE channel, as illustrated in Figure 2.21.

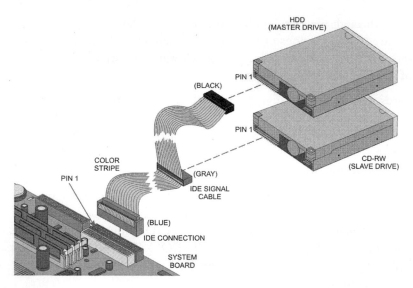

FIGURE 2.21 PATA drive connections.

This color code is just a suggestion—physical configuration jumpers on the devices control the actual designation of master and slave devices. If PATA devices are not connected according to the color code they will still function properly. Procedures for configuring PATA devices are covered in detail in Chapter 7, "Installing, Upgrading, Configuring, and Optimizing PC Components."

Serial ATA Connections

As with all other parallel I/O schemes, the PATA specification eventually ran into performance limitations (speed and distance) associated with parallel transmissions. The SATA interface specification was designed to replace the PATA interface and overcome its electrical constraints. Although it replaces the physical interface connection and cabling structures, the SATA specification remains compatible with the supporting ATA software embedded in existing operating systems.

Figure 2.22 depicts the flat 7-pin SATA signal cable connector and its configuration. Four of the wires are used to form two differential signal pairs (A+/A– and B+/B–), whereas the other three wires are used for shielded grounds. The cable is only 0.5 inches wide. This feature makes cable routing inside the system unit simpler and provides less resistance to airflow through the case. The maximum length for an internal SATA cable is specified as 36 inches (1 meter).

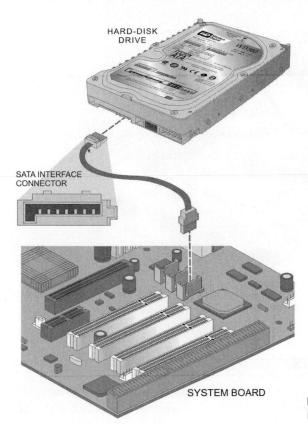

HARD-DISK
DRIVE

SATA INTERFACE
CONNECTOR

SYSTEM BOARD

FIGURE 2.22 The Serial ATA
interface connector.

Unlike its PATA counterpart, the SATA interface has made provisions for connections outside the system unit case. This type of connection is referred to as
the external SATA or eSATA interface. Figure 2.23 illustrates the implementation
of a single-lane external SATA interface. An eSATA interface consists of a SATA
cable that links the SATA interface on the system board to an eSATA connector
on one an expansion slot cover mounted in the rear of the system unit. A shielded eSATA cable is used to connect the drive unit to the slot-mounted interface.
The maximum cable length for the external eSATA cable is 6 feet (2 meters).

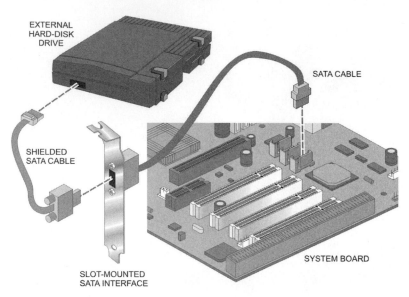

EXTERNAL
HARD-DISK
DRIVE

SATA CABLE

SHIELDED
SATA CABLE

SLOT-MOUNTED
SATA INTERFACE

SYSTEM BOARD

FIGURE 2.23   eSATA interface connections.

SCSI Connections

No industry-accepted equivalents exist for onboard SCSI adapters. Although a few such system board designs are available, they are not standard boards and have probably been created to fill the specific needs of a particular application. Therefore, SCSI devices require that a SCSI host adapter card be installed in most systems.

The built-in SCSI connector on the system board will normally be made through a 50-pin BERG header. Like the IDE drives, support for the onboard SCSI controller must be established through the CMOS setup utility. The system BIOS provides support for the built-in SCSI controller through its CMOS setup utility, whereas add-on adapter cards feature a BIOS extension on the card. Figure 2.24 shows typical SCSI connections.

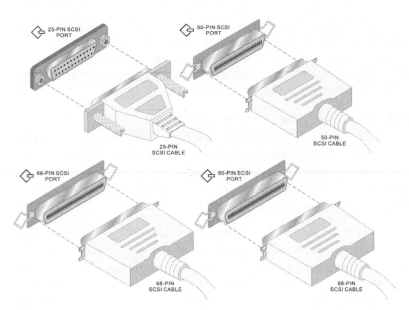

FIGURE 2.24   SCSI connections.

Processor Socket Specifications

Intel has always developed lines of upgrade microprocessors for its original offerings. These are referred to as *OverDrive processors*. An OverDrive unit may be the same type of microprocessor running at a higher clock speed, or it may be an advanced architecture microprocessor designed to operate from the same socket/pin configuration as the original. To accommodate this option, Intel created specifications for eight socket designs, designated Socket 1 through Socket 8.

The specifications for Socket 1 through Socket 3 were developed for 80486SX, 80486DX, and 80486 OverDrive versions that use different pin numbers and power supply requirements. Likewise, the Socket 4 through Socket 6 specifications deal with various Pentium and OverDrive units that have different speeds and power supply requirements.

The Socket 7 specification enabled system boards to be configured for different types and versions of microprocessors using different internal core and FSB operating speeds. Its design includes provision for a Voltage Regulator Module (VRM) to allow various power settings to be implemented through the socket.

The Socket 7 specification corresponds to the second generation of Pentium devices that employ SPGA packaging. It is compatible with the Socket 5, straight-row PGA specification that the first-generation Pentium processors employed. Finally, the Socket 8 specification is specific to the Pentium Pro processor.

An upgraded Socket 7 specification, referred to as Super Socket 7, was developed to extend the use of the Socket 7 physical connector. This upgrade added support signals required for implementing AGP slots and the 100MHz front-side bus (FSB) specification. Microprocessors designed to use the Super Socket 7 specification include AMD's K6-2, K6-2+, and K6-III, along with Intel's Pentium MMX and Pentium Pro.

Although the Intel Slot 1 design was originally developed for the Pentium II, it also serves the Celeron and Pentium III processor designs. Like Socket 7, the Slot 1 specification provides for variable processor core voltages (2.8 to 3.3) that permit faster operation and reduced power consumption. In addition, some suppliers have created daughter boards containing the Pentium Pro processor that can be plugged into the Slot 1 connector. This combination Socket 8/Slot 1 device is referred to as a *slotket processor*.

The Slot 2 specification from Intel expands the Slot 1 SECC technology to a 330-contact (SECC-2) cartridge used with the Intel Xeon processor.

In a departure from its proprietary slot connector development, Intel reversed direction and introduced a new ZIF socket standard, called Socket 370, for use with its Celeron processor. There are two versions of the Socket 370 specification. The first is the PPGA 370 variation intended for use with the Plastic Pin Grid Array (PPGA) version of the Celeron CPUs. The other is the Flip Chip Pin Grid Array (FC-PGA) version.

NOTE

When Intel retreated from the slot processor designs and returned to sockets for its processors, it abandoned the linear socket numbering system and began referring to the socket by its pin count (for example, Socket 370 is a socket that has 370 pins—the company originating the use of the socket gets to specify what each pin represents).

The term *flip chip* is used to describe a group of microprocessors that have provisions for attaching a heat sink directly to the microprocessor die. The processors in this category include the Cyrix III, Celeron, and Pentium III. Although the PPGA and FC-PGA processors will both plug into the 370 socket, that does not mean they will work in system board designs for the other specifications.

The original P4 was delivered in a Socket 423 configuration. Subsequent versions have been produced using Socket 478 or flip chip LGA775 sockets. Intel has continued to employ the LGA775 socket arrangement for a number of its newer processor designs, including

- Pentium 4 (2.66—3.800GHz)

- Celeron D (2.527—3.333GHz)

- Pentium 4 Extreme Edition (3.2GHz, 3.400—3.73GHz)

- Pentium D (2.80—3.40GHz)

Intel has also offered a variety of front-side bus speed options through this socket type, including 133MHz /533FSB, 200MHz /800FSB, 266MHz /1066FSB; and 333MHz/1333FSB speeds. The LGA775 package features 250 power and 273 ground pins to accommodate the processor's 130 watts of power dissipation.

AMD Slots and Sockets

AMD produced a reversed version of the Slot 1 specification for its Athlon processor by turning the contacts of the Slot 1 design around. They titled the new design Slot A. While serving the same ends as the Slot 1 design, the Slot A and Slot 1 microprocessor cartridges are not compatible.

In addition, a 462-pin ZIF socket specification was adopted for the PGA versions of its Athlon and Duron processors. This has been followed by a line of advanced sockets to keep pace with the updated features of the AMD processors:

- Socket 563—Athon XP-M (low power mobile)

- Socket 754—Athlon 64

- Socket 939—Athlon 64/Athlon 64 FX

- Socket 940—Opteron/Athlon 64 FX

- Socket 462/Socket A—Athlon, Duron, Athlon XP, Athlon XP-M, Athlon MP, and Sepron

- Socket AM2 —A 940-pin socket also known as Socket M2, replaces the current Socket 754 and 939 offerings—Athlon 64, Athlon 64 FX, and Athlon 64 X2

> ▶ Socket S1—A 638-pin mobile processor socket that replaces the Socket 754 for Athlon 64 mobile processors and future dual core AMD processors.

> ▶ Socket F—A 1207-pin socket that replaces the Socket 940 for dual-processor applications

Table 2.3 summarizes the attributes of the various industry socket and slot specifications.

TABLE 2.3   Industry Socket Specifications

NUMBER	PINS	VOLTAGES	MICROPROCESSORS
Socket 1	169 PGA	5V	80486 SX/DXx, DX4 OverDrive
Socket 2	238 PGA	5V	80486 SX/DXx, Pentium OverDrive
Socket 3	237 PGA	5/3.3V	80486 SX/DXx, Pentium OverDrive
Socket 4	237 PGA	5V	Pentium 60/66, 60/66 OverDrive
Socket 5	320 SPGA	3.3V	Pentium 75-133, Pentium OverDrive
Socket 6	235 PGA	3.3V	Never implemented
Socket 7	321 SPGA	VRM (2.5V–3.6V)	Pentium 75-200, Pentium OverDrive
Socket 8	387 SPGA	VRM (2.2V–3.5V)	Pentium Pro
Slot 1	242 SECC/SEPP	VRM (1.5V–2.5V)	Celeron, Pentium II, Pentium III
Slot 2	330 SECC-2	VRM (1.5V–2.5V)	Xeon
Super Socket 7	321 SPGA	VRM (2.0V–3.5V)	AMD K6-2, K6-2+, K6-III, K6-III+, Pentium MMX
Socket 370	370 SPGA	VRM (1.1V–2.5V)	Cyrix III, Celeron, Pentium III
Slot A	242 Slot A	VRM (1.2V–2.2V)	AMD Athlon
Socket A	462 SPGA	VRM (1.2V–2.2V)	AMD Athlon, Duron
Socket 423	423 FC-PGA	VRM (1.7V)	Pentium IV (1.3GHz–2.0GHz)
Socket 478	478 FC-PGA	VRM (1.5V–1.7V)	Pentium IV Xeon (1.4GHz–2.2GHz)
Socket 603	603 INT-PGA	VRM (1.5V–1.7V)	Pentium IV (1.4GHz–2.2GHz)

TABLE 2.3 *Continued*

NUMBER	PINS	VOLTAGES	MICROPROCESSORS
Socket 418	418 INT-PGA	VRM (1.7V)	Itanium/Intel (733MHz–800MHz)
FC-LGA775 (Socket T)	775 LGA	1.2V–1.4V	Pentium 4/Extreme Edition/D; Celeron D
Socket 563	563 microPGA	1.5–1.75V	Athlon XP-M
Socket 754	754 PGA	0.8–1.55V	Athon 64
Socket 939	939 PGA	0.8–1.55V	Athon 64, Athlon 64 FX
Socket 940	940 PGA	0.8–1.55V	Opteron, Athlon 64 FX

Challenge #1

Your company does not want to replace all of its computers at this time. In fact, what it really wants to do is spend a little money to upgrade all its computers as much as it can now and wait as long as possible to replace them. Because you are the Technical Service Manager, the company has asked you for a plan to upgrade the systems. You know that nearly all the systems in the company are Pentium II 350MHz machines. What is the most current, fastest upgrade you can recommend to your board of directors?

DRAM Sockets

Pentium system boards supply special 168-pin, 184-pin, or 240-pin snap-in sockets to hold the system's SDRAM, DDR-DRAM or DDR2-DRAM DIMMs. The sockets and DIMMs are keyed so that they cannot be plugged in backward. DIMM sockets are quite distinctive in that they are typically arranged side-by-side and may involve between three and four slots. However, they can be located anywhere on the system board.

Some system boards feature a three-DIMM slot arrangement, referred to as a *split-bank arrangement*. When you are working with these boards, you must refer to their user's manual to determine what types of memory can be used because split-bank arrangements use a different specification for DIMM slot 1 than for DIMM slots 2 and 3. The odd slot is usually organized into one bank, whereas the other two slots combine to form the second bank. If you are not careful when populating these slots, you may create a situation in which the system's memory controller cannot access all the installed RAM.

EXAM ALERT

Be aware of situations that will cause the system to "see" less than the actual amount of installed RAM.

Challenge #2

You have been assigned to upgrade the memory in a number of your office's computers. When you open them, you discover that they have a three-slot DIMM arrangement. Also, you cannot locate a system board user's manual for these computers. You install a 128MB DIMM in each slot. When you start the computer, you see from the POST that the system recognizes only 256MB of RAM. What happened to the other 128MB of RAM, and how can you get the system to recognize it?

CMOS RAM

The configuration of every PC-compatible system is controlled by settings established in its CMOS setup utility. Therefore, every technician should be aware of the contents of typical CMOS utilities and be able to properly manipulate the parameters they contain to achieve a fully functional unit and optimize its performance.

CMOS Setup Utilities

The CMOS setup utility can be accessed during the POST process by pressing a designated key. The CMOS setup utility's Main Menu screen, similar to the one depicted in Figure 2.25, appears whenever the CMOS setup utility is engaged. This menu enables the user to select different configuration functions and exit choices. The most used entries include the Standard CMOS Setup, BIOS Features Setup, and Chipset Features Setup options. Selecting these, or any of the other Main Menu options, will lead you into the corresponding submenus.

Other menu items typically include Power Management Setup, PnP/PCI Configuration, Integrated Peripherals, and Password Maintenance Services. The CMOS setup utility of a particular BIOS may contain these same options, or options that perform the same functions under a different name, or it may not contain some of these options at all.

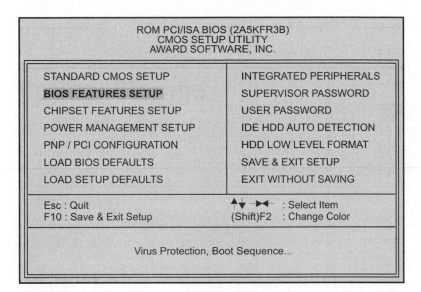

FIGURE 2.25 The CMOS Main Menu screen.

BIOS designers have built two options (Auto Configuration and Default Settings) into newer versions to help users deal with the complexity of the advanced CMOS configuration. Newer system boards use an auto-configuration mode that takes over most of the setup decisions. Working well in most cases, this option produces settings for an efficient, basic level of operation for standard devices in the system. However, it doesn't optimize the performance of the system. To do that, it's necessary to turn off the autoconfiguration feature and insert the desired parameters into the configuration table. Two options typically exist for the autoconfiguration function: Auto Configure with Power-On Defaults and Auto Configure with BIOS Defaults.

The autoconfiguration power-on defaults provide the most conservative system options from the BIOS and the most effective method of detecting BIOS-related system problems. These settings replace any user-entered configuration information in the CMOS setup registers, disabling the turbo speed mode, turning off all memory caching, and setting all wait states to maximum, thus enabling the most basic part of the system for starting.

If these default values fail to boot the system, it indicates possible hardware problems such as incorrect jumper settings or bad components.

If you have entered an improper configuration setting and cannot determine which setting is causing the problem, using the autoconfiguration with the BIOS defaults provides more flexibility than the power-on option. This selection also replaces the entered configuration settings with a new set of parameters from the BIOS and likely gets you back into the CMOS setup screen so that you can track down the problem. This is also the recommended starting point for optimizing the system's operation.

> **CAUTION**
>
> **Set Values with Caution**   The settings in these menus enable the system to be configured and optimized for specific functions and devices. The default values are generally recommended for normal operation. Because incorrect setup values can cause the system to fail, you should change only setup values that really need to be changed. If changes are made that disable the system, pressing the Insert key on reset will override the settings and start the system with default values.

The standard CMOS setup screens from various BIOS manufacturers all provide the same basic information. They can be used to set the system clock/calendar, establish disk-drive parameters and video display type, and specify which types of errors will halt the system during the POST.

Time and Date

PC chipsets include a Real-Time Clock (RTC) function that keeps track of time and date information for the system. During the startup process, the operating system acquires the time and date information from the CMOS RTC module. This information is updated in the system once every second.

The CMOS uses military time settings (for example, 13:00:00 = 1 p.m.). The PgUp and PgDn keys are used to change the setting after it has been selected using the arrow keys. Most BIOS versions support daylight saving time by adding an hour when daylight saving time begins and subtracting it when standard time returns.

All system boards employ a rechargeable battery to maintain the system's configuration information when it is turned off. In newer systems, the most common battery type is a replaceable 2032 coin cell battery. These are plentiful and easy to change if they become defective. However, in other systems there are no rechargeable batteries for the CMOS storage. Instead, the CMOS storage area and RTC functions have been integrated with a 10-year nonreplaceable lithium cell in an independent RTC IC module.

If the power source or the backup battery becomes defective, the system's capability to keep proper time and date information will be impaired. On older system boards, the backup battery was completely responsible for maintaining the information in the RTC. With newer systems, there is a 5Vdc level present on the system board even when the system is turned off. On these boards, the power supply and the battery in the RTC module work together to keep the time and date information correct.

If the time is incorrect on a PC system, the easiest way to reset it is through the operating system; however, if the system continually fails to keep good time, you should replace the battery. If that doesn't work, check for corrosion on the battery contacts. Clean the contacts with a pencil eraser and retry the battery. Next, you should try replacing the RTC module. If this does not correct the timekeeping problem, the electronic circuitry that recharges the battery may be defective, and in this case you need a new motherboard.

> **EXAM ALERT**
>
> Be aware of where to go to reset the system clock and what to check if the clock fails to keep proper time.

Disk Drive Support

Most BIOSs possess autodetect options that automatically detect the type of hard drives installed in the system and load their parameters into the CMOS. However, they also provide an entry for user-definable drive settings. Systems with PATA drive capabilities support up to four IDE drives. In older BIOS versions, the CMOS typically did not display information about CD-ROM drives or SCSI devices; however, newer versions show both types of devices when running in autodetect mode.

When the Auto Detect selection is chosen, the BIOS attempts to detect IDE devices in the system during the POST process and to determine the specifications and optimum operating modes for those devices. The drive specifications can also be selected from a built-in list of drive parameters, or they can be entered directly using the User option at the end of the list.

Four translation modes can be selected for each drive type: Auto, Normal, Large, and LBA. In Auto mode, the BIOS attempts to determine the best operating mode for the drive. In Normal mode, the BIOS will support a maximum Cyl/Hds/Sec (CHS) setting of 1024/16/63.

For larger drives (greater than 1,024 cylinders or 504MB), the Large and LBA modes are used. The Large option can be used with large drives that do not support logical block addressing (LBA) techniques. For drives that do support logical block addressing, the LBA mode should be selected. In this mode, the IDE controller converts the sector/head/cylinder address into a physical block address that improves data throughput. Care must be taken when changing the translation mode setting in CMOS because all data on the drive can be lost in the process.

In the case of errors detected during the POST process, some BIOSs can be set up to halt on different types of errors or to ignore them and continue the boot-up process. These settings include

▶ No Errors—The POST does not stop for any errors.

▶ All Errors—The POST stops for all detected errors and prompts the user for corrective action.

▶ A series of "All But" options—The POST stops for all errors except those selected (that is, all but disk or keyboard errors).

Finally, the screen displays the system's memory usage. The values displayed are derived from the POST process and cannot be changed through the menu. The BIOS displays the system's total detected RAM, base memory, extended memory, and other memory (between the 640kB and 1MB marks). In most CMOS displays, the total memory does not equal the summation of the base and extended memory. This is because the BIOS reserves 384kB for shadowing purposes. Newer BIOS versions may show only the total installed system memory.

Advanced BIOS Features Setup Screen

The Advanced BIOS Features Setup screen provides access to options that extend the standard BIOS functions. Many BIOSs include a built-in virus warning utility that produces a warning message whenever a program tries to write to the boot sector of an HDD partition table. If a warning message is displayed under normal circumstances, a full-featured antivirus utility should be run on the system.

CAUTION

The virus warning utility should be enabled for normal operations; however, it should be turned off when you conduct an upgrade to the operating system. The built-in virus warning utility checks the drive's boot sector for changes. The changes that the new operating system will attempt to make to the boot sector will be interpreted as a virus, and the utility will act to prevent the upgrade from occurring.

EXAM ALERT

You should know that BIOS virus-detection functions should be disabled when performing an operating system upgrade.

This screen is used to configure different bootup options. These options include establishing the system's bootup sequence. Most BIOS versions typically provide user-definable boot sequences for up to four devices. The most commonly used sequence checks the first hard drive as the first boot source. Newer BIOS versions can be configured so the system checks the CD-ROM drive for a boot sector first. You should enable the CD-ROM as the primary boot option when you are installing an operating system or when the system will not boot from the HDD. In these cases, the operating system CD can be used to start the system for installation or troubleshooting purposes.

EXAM ALERT

Know the possible disk seek configuration possibilities and be aware of how they might affect the system in different circumstances.

Challenge #3

Your system will not boot up to the hard drive, so you place a bootable CD-ROM in the drive and try to restart the system. You watch the startup sequence closely and discover that the system does not appear to check the CD-ROM drive for a disc. What should you do to get the system to look for a disc in the CD-ROM drive as part of the bootup activities?

Advanced Chipset Features Setup Functions

The Advanced Chipset Features screen contains advanced setting information that system designers and service personnel use to optimize the chipset. The options and submenus associated with this page can vary greatly from chipset to chipset. The options that you can configure here depend on the functions the chipset provides (for example, FSB options, processor speed/voltage options, AGP configurations, thermal throttling, memory timing options, and so on).

The Auto Configuration option selects predetermined optimal values for the chipset to start with. When this feature is enabled, many of the screen's fields are not available to the user. When this setting is disabled, the chipset's setup parameters are obtained from the system's CMOS RAM. Many of the system's memory configuration parameters are established in this screen.

PnP/PCI Configuration Functions

In most newer PCs, the BIOS, the peripheral devices, and the operating system employ Plug and Play technology that enables the system to automatically determine what hardware devices are installed in the system and allocate system resources to those devices as required to configure and manage them. This removes some of the responsibility for system configuration from the user or the technician. All three of the system components listed previously must be PnP-compliant before automatic configuration can be carried out.

The BIOS holds information about the system's resource allocations and supplies it to the operating system as required. This information can be displayed through the CMOS PnP/PCI Configuration screen. The operating system must be PnP-compatible to achieve the full benefits of the PnP BIOS. In most PCs, the standard operating system is Windows 2000 or Windows XP, which are both PnP-compliant.

Basically, the PnP device communicates with the BIOS during the initialization phase of the startup to tell the system what type of device it is, where it is located in the system, and what its resource needs are. This information is stored on the device in the form of firmware. The BIOS stores the PnP information it collects from the devices in a special section of the CMOS RAM known as the Extended System Configuration Data (ESCD) area. This information is stored in the same manner as standard BIOS settings are stored.

The BIOS and operating system both access the ESCD area each time the system is restarted to see if any information has changed. This enables the BIOS and the operating system to work together in sorting out the needs of the installed devices and assigning them needed system resources.

EXAM ALERT

Know which portion of the BIOS is responsible for implementing the PnP process.

If no changes have occurred in the contents of the ESCD since the last startup occurred, the BIOS will detect this and skip that portion of the boot process. When a PnP operating system checks the ESCD to see if any hardware changes have occurred, it will react accordingly and record any changes it finds in the hardware portion of its Registry. On some occasions, the system's PnP logic may not be able to resolve all of its resource needs, and a configuration error will occur. In these cases, the technician or the user will have to manually resolve the configuration problem. The BIOS and the operating system typically provide interfaces to the hardware configuration information so that users can manually override the system's PnP resource assignments.

Challenge #4

Your local area network connection to the Internet crashes often and tends to be down for some time. For these occasions you want to establish a dial-up connection to the Internet from your office computer. Your boss does not want to buy a new PnP modem for your use. However, you have an old internal ISA modem in your desk drawer and want to install it in your system to perform this function through your office phone connection. What do you have to do to make this modem work in your plug-and-play system?

Integrated Peripherals Setup Functions

In most Pentium-based systems, the standard I/O functions are configured through the BIOS Integrated Peripherals screen, depicted in Figure 2.26. This screen provides configuration and enabling settings for the system board's IDE drive connections, floppy-disk drive controller, onboard UARTs, and onboard parallel port.

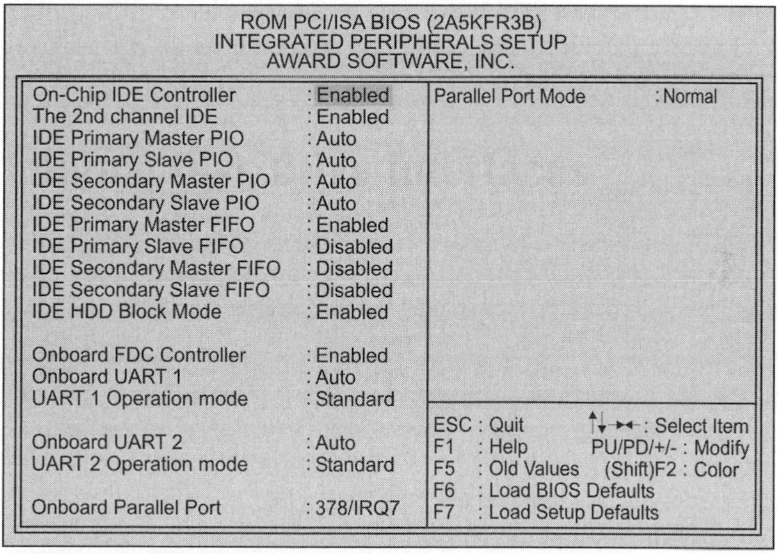

```
                    ROM PCI/ISA BIOS (2A5KFR3B)
                    INTEGRATED PERIPHERALS SETUP
                         AWARD SOFTWARE, INC.

  On-Chip IDE Controller      : Enabled   Parallel Port Mode      : Normal
  The 2nd channel IDE         : Enabled
  IDE Primary Master PIO      : Auto
  IDE Primary Slave PIO       : Auto
  IDE Secondary Master PIO    : Auto
  IDE Secondary Slave PIO     : Auto
  IDE Primary Master FIFO     : Enabled
  IDE Primary Slave FIFO      : Disabled
  IDE Secondary Master FIFO   : Disabled
  IDE Secondary Slave FIFO    : Disabled
  IDE HDD Block Mode          : Enabled

  Onboard FDC Controller      : Enabled
  Onboard UART 1              : Auto
  UART 1 Operation mode       : Standard
                                            ESC : Quit        ↑↓→← : Select Item
  Onboard UART 2              : Auto        F1  : Help       PU/PD/+/- : Modify
  UART 2 Operation mode       : Standard    F5  : Old Values   (Shift)F2 : Color
                                            F6  : Load BIOS Defaults
  Onboard Parallel Port       : 378/IRQ7    F7  : Load Setup Defaults
```

FIGURE 2.26   The Integrated Peripherals screen.

IDE Functions

The Integrated Peripherals screen is used to enable the onboard IDE controller. As mentioned earlier, the second IDE channel can be enabled or disabled independently of the first channel, provided that the controller has been enabled.

Any of the four possible devices attached to the interface can be configured for master or slave operation.

The system's SATA drives and their operating modes are also enabled and configured through the CMOS setup utility. You can typically select among enabling the PATA interface controller, the SATA interface controller, or both. Because the SATA controller is an integral part of the IDE subsystem, you may see options for enabling up to six IDE devices in the CMOS Setup utility. The IDE rules still apply to the four PATA devices in the system.

The IDE HDD Block Mode selection should be set to Enabled for most new hard drives. This setting (also referred to as *Large Block Transfer*, *Multiple Command*, and *Multiple-Sector Read/Write* mode), supports LBA disk-drive operations. If the Auto mode option is selected, the system will determine which mode is best suited for each device.

Implementing Ports

The other onboard I/O functions supported through the CMOS utility can include enabling/disabling the FDD controller, enabling and configuring the system's onboard USB and IEEE-1394 FireWire ports, selecting the logical COM port addressing and operating modes for the system's two built-in UARTs, and selecting logical addressing and operating modes for the parallel port. Other onboard functions configured through this screen include onboard audio and local area networking interfaces, as well as built-in support for game ports and MIDI music ports, on those system boards that offer them.

All newer PCs rely on high speed USB and/or IEEE-1394 ports as their major I/O connections. The controller functions for these ports are typically integrated into the system board's chipset circuitry. They are also enabled/disabled through its CMOS setup utility.

If the system supports a legacy serial communications port, the chipset includes a UART device that can be configured to support half-duplex or full-duplex transmission modes for dialup networking, or to support an infrared communications port, provided the system board is equipped with one. This port enables wireless communications with serial peripheral devices over short distances.

The parallel printer port can be configured for Standard Parallel Port (SPP) operation, for extended bidirectional operation (Enhanced Parallel Port, or EPP), for fast, buffered bidirectional operation (Extended Capabilities Port, or ECP), or for combined ECP+EPP operation. The normal CMOS setting should be selected unless both the port hardware and driver software support EPP and/or ECP operation.

EXAM ALERT

Remember that ECP and EPP modes for the parallel port must be enabled through the CMOS setup utility.

Enhanced Parallel Port Operations

When EPP mode is selected in the port's configuration register, the standard and bidirectional modes are enabled. The functions of the port's pins are redefined under the EPP specification. When the EPP mode is enabled, the port can operate either as a standard, bidirectional SPP parallel port, or as a bidirectional EPP port. The software controlling the port will specify which type of operation is required.

The ECP mode provides a number of advantages over the SPP and EPP modes. In particular, it offers higher performance than either of the other modes. As with the EPP mode, the pins of the interface are redefined when ECP mode is selected in the system's CMOS. The ECP port is compatible with the standard LPT port and is used in the same manner when no ECP operations are called for. However, it also supports high-throughput DMA operations for both forward- and reverse-direction transfers.

Because both of the advanced parallel port modes operate in a bidirectional, half-duplex manner, they require an IEEE-1284-compliant cable. Standard parallel cables designed for older SPP operations may not support these qualities.

EXAM ALERT

Be aware that a non-IEEE-1284 rated parallel printer cable should not be used with bidirectional EPP or ECP devices.

Infrared Port Operation

Infrared Data Association (IrDA) ports provide short-distance wireless connections for different IrDA-compliant devices, such as printers and personal digital assistants. Because the IrDA port communicates by sending and receiving a serial stream of light pulses, it is normally configured to work with the UART of the system's second serial port. This arrangement is established through the Integrated Peripherals page of the CMOS setup utility. In this manner, the infrared port is assigned the system resources that are usually reserved for the COM2/COM4 serial ports.

To enable the IrDA port, the mode for the COM2 UART must be set to automatic and one of the infrared protocol settings (HPSIR or ASKIR) must be selected. In addition, the transmission duplex mode must be selected (usually half duplex). The operations of the infrared port and the second serial port are mutually exclusive. When the Infrared option is enabled in CMOS, the second serial port will be disabled.

Challenge #5

A customer brings in a computer that has a laser printer and a scanner connected to the parallel port. The scanner is connected directly to the computer's parallel port and the printer is connected to the scanner. The customer cannot get the scanner to work, but the printer operates correctly. What two actions should you perform to determine why the scanner does not work correctly?

Power Management Functions

The Power Management fields enable the user to select from different power saving modes: Doze, Standby, Suspend, or Hibernate. These are green PC-compatible power-saving modes that step the system incrementally down from maximum power usage. The Doze setting causes the microprocessor clock to slow down after a defined period of inactivity. The Standby mode shuts down the hard drive and video after a period of inactivity. Everything in the system except the microprocessor shuts down in Suspend mode. Certain system events, such as IRQ and DRQ activities, cause the system to wake up from these modes and resume normal operation. In Hibernate mode, the system saves the current information in memory to the hard disk drive and shuts down. When the system is restored form Hibernate mode, the environment is returned to the state it was in when Hibernate mode was initiated.

PC Health Status

The PC Health menu, shown in Figure 2.27, displays status information for the critical elements of the system board, including the microprocessor temperature, fan speeds, and actual voltage levels. The page also enables you to establish set points for issuing notifications and alarms when these variables are outside of the desired ranges of operation.

Temperature monitoring can be as simple as tracking the microprocessor's package temperature, or it can include monitoring the case temperature in multiple locations. Key voltage levels tracked by the BIOS include the microprocessor core voltage, the expansion slot voltages, and the various voltage levels being provided to the system board by the power supply.

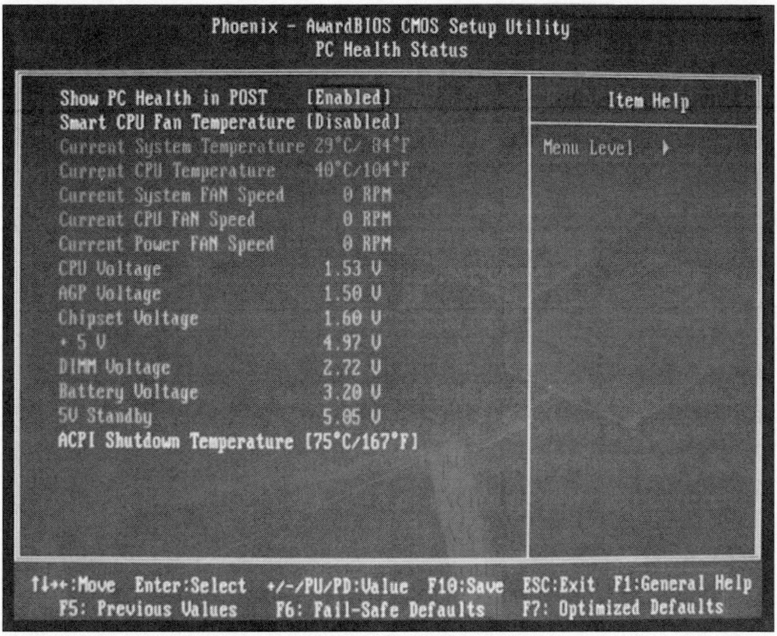

```
                    Phoenix - AwardBIOS CMOS Setup Utility
                              PC Health Status

    Show PC Health in POST      [Enabled]                    Item Help
    Smart CPU Fan Temperature   [Disabled]
    Current System Temperature  29°C/ 84°F       Menu Level   ▶
    Current CPU Temperature     40°C/104°F
    Current System FAN Speed         0 RPM
    Current CPU FAN Speed            0 RPM
    Current Power FAN Speed          0 RPM
    CPU Voltage                   1.53 V
    AGP Voltage                   1.50 V
    Chipset Voltage               1.60 V
    + 5 V                         4.97 V
    DIMM Voltage                  2.72 V
    Battery Voltage               3.20 V
    5V Standby                    5.05 V
    ACPI Shutdown Temperature  [75°C/167°F]




    ↑↓←→:Move  Enter:Select  +/-/PU/PD:Value  F10:Save  ESC:Exit  F1:General Help
        F5: Previous Values     F6: Fail-Safe Defaults   F7: Optimized Defaults
```

FIGURE 2.27 The PC Health Menu screen.

Finally, this screen enables you to establish warning and system shut down levels that will either warn the user that something is going wrong, or will go ahead and shut the system down to protect the microprocessor from harm.

Security Subsystem

Most BIOSs offer a variety of security options that can be set through the CMOS setup utility. Figure 2.28 displays a typical Security Configuration screen. Typically, these options include setting User passwords to control access to the system and Supervisory passwords to control access to the CMOS setup utility. The User password option enables administrators to establish passwords that users must enter during the startup process to complete the boot process and gain access to the operating system. However, this password does not provide access to the CMOS setup utility. The Supervisory password option establishes a password that must be used to access the CMOS setup utility (where the User and Supervisory password options are configured).

EXAM ALERT

Be aware of the types of passwords that can be established through the CMOS Setup utility.

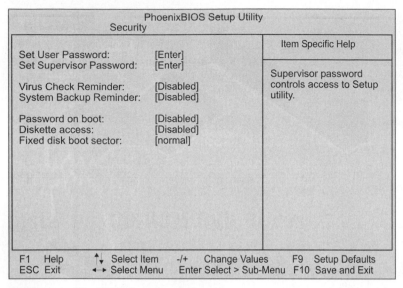

FIGURE 2.28 The CMOS Security configuration.

The Security Configuration screen may also include options for setting virus check and backup reminders that pop up periodically when the system is booted. In addition to enabling these settings, administrators can also specify the time interval between notices.

One of the main sets of security options in the CMOS setup utility consists of those that can be used to control access to the system. For the most part, these options cover such things as access permitted through the floppy drive and access to the boot sector of the drive.

Because the CMOS password controls access to all parts of the system, even before the bootup process occurs, there is some inconvenience in the event that the user forgets a password. When this occurs, it will be impossible to gain access to the system without completely resetting the content of the CMOS RAM. On some system boards, this can be accomplished by shorting a special pair of jumpers on the board.

With other systems, you will need to remove or short across the backup battery to reset the CMOS information. It will also be necessary to unplug the power from the commercial outlet to reduce the voltage to the CMOS registers. When the content of the CMOS is reset, you must manually restore any nondefault CMOS settings being used by the system.

EXAM ALERT

Be aware of the effects of forgetting a CMOS password and know what steps must be taken to restore the system in this event.

Exam Prep Questions

1. What type of expansion bus is based on a 124-pin slot?

   ○ **A.** ISA

   ○ **B.** PCI

   ○ **C.** AGP

   ○ **D.** PC-bus

2. Which IRQ resources are assigned in the PnP configuration process?

   ○ **A.** Motherboard devices

   ○ **B.** ISA devices

   ○ **C.** PCI devices

   ○ **D.** Legacy devices

3. What type of expansion card is plugged into an AGP slot?

   ○ **A.** Graphics

   ○ **B.** Modem

   ○ **C.** Network

   ○ **D.** Sound

4. What is the maximum data throughput when connecting an Ultra ATA 66 hard-disk drive with a 40-pin IDE cable?

   ○ **A.** 10Mbps

   ○ **B.** 33Mbps

   ○ **C.** 66Mbps

   ○ **D.** They will not work together.

5. From the figure depicting an ATX motherboard, identify the ISA expansion slot.

○ **A.** A

○ **B.** B

○ **C.** C

○ **D.** D

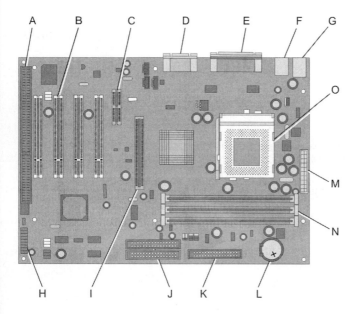

6. From the figure depicting an ATX motherboard shown in question 5, identify the AGP expansion slot.

○ **A.** A

○ **B.** B

○ **C.** I

○ **D.** N

7. From the figure depicting an ATX motherboard shown in question 5, identify the IDE connectors.

○ **A.** C

○ **B.** J

○ **C.** K

○ **D.** M

8. From the figure depicting an ATX motherboard shown in question 5, identify the battery.

○ **A.** G

○ **B.** H

○ **C.** L

○ **D.** O

9. From the figure depicting an ATX motherboard shown in question 5, identify the DIMM slots.

○ **A.** B

○ **B.** I

○ **C.** H

○ **D.** N

10. Locate the serial port connector in the diagram of an ATX back panel.

○ **A.** A

○ **B.** B

○ **C.** C

○ **D.** D

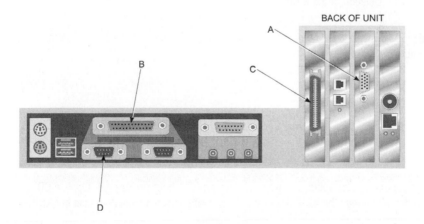

11. From the figure depicting an ATX back panel shown in question 10, locate the printer port.

   ○ **A.** A

   ○ **B.** B

   ○ **C.** C

   ○ **D.** D

12. What should you do first if the system clock fails to keep proper time after being reset by the operating system?

   ○ **A.** Reload the operating system

   ○ **B.** Replace the battery

   ○ **C.** Clean the battery contacts

   ○ **D.** Replace the motherboard

13. What may happen when you change the translation mode setting for an existing IDE drive?

   ○ **A.** Loss of all data on the drive

   ○ **B.** Access limited to the first 504MB of the drive

   ○ **C.** Slower drive access times

   ○ **D.** Deletion of the MBR

14. Which CMOS functions should be disabled when performing an operating system upgrade?

   ○ **A.** EPP and ECP

   ○ **B.** PnP resource allocation

   ○ **C.** BIOS virus-detection functions

   ○ **D.** RAM memory checks

15. When your computer boots, you want it to search for a boot sector on a floppy, a CD-ROM drive, and then the hard disk drive. What boot sequence should you set in CMOS?

   ○ **A.** A, C, SCSI

   ○ **B.** A, C, CD-ROM

   ○ **C.** CD-ROM, A, C

   ○ **D.** A, CD-ROM, C

16. During which portion of the startup process does the BIOS communicate with the system's PnP devices?

    ◯ **A.** During the POST

    ◯ **B.** During the initialization phase

    ◯ **C.** During the OS bootstrap operation

    ◯ **D.** During the CMOS configuration process

17. Which utility must be used to enable the ECP and EPP modes for the parallel port?

    ◯ **A.** DMA setup

    ◯ **B.** CMOS setup

    ◯ **C.** Printer driver

    ◯ **D.** BIOS initialization

18. What types of devices can be used with a half-duplex/bidirectional parallel printer cable? (Select all that apply.)

    ◯ **A.** USB devices

    ◯ **B.** SPP devices

    ◯ **C.** EPP devices

    ◯ **D.** ECP devices

19. What are the effects of forgetting a CMOS password?

    ◯ **A.** You cannot start the computer.

    ◯ **B.** You cannot boot to the operating system.

    ◯ **C.** You cannot log in to the computer.

    ◯ **D.** You cannot shut down the computer.

20. What action must be taken to restore the system if the CMOS password is forgotten in an ATX system?

    ◯ **A.** Change the Password Enable setting in CMOS

    ◯ **B.** Remove the battery

    ◯ **C.** Short the CMOS-enabling jumper and remove the battery

    ◯ **D.** Unplug the computer from the wall and remove the battery

21. Where is the PnP information stored in the BIOS?

◯   **A.** The RTC module

◯   **B.** The ESCD area

◯   **C.** The PnP Registry

◯   **D.** The Device Manager

22. The system's time and date configuration can be performed in the _____.

◯   **A.** Memory cache

◯   **B.** North Bridge

◯   **C.** CMOS setup

◯   **D.** South Bridge

23. What is the major difference between EPP and ECP operation of the parallel port?

◯   **A.** DMA mode

◯   **B.** Bidirectional

◯   **C.** 16-bit transfers

◯   **D.** Serial transfers

24. Which parallel port type has the highest throughput?

◯   **A.** ECP

◯   **B.** EPP

◯   **C.** XPP

◯   **D.** SPP

25. What type of communication is possible with an IEEE-1284 parallel cable?

◯   **A.** Bidirectional, half-duplex

◯   **B.** Bidirectional, full-duplex

◯   **C.** Simplex

◯   **D.** Selectable half- or full-duplex

26. If you place a bootable floppy in drive A: and the system boots to drive C:, what action should you take to correct this?

- ○ **A.** Reconfigure the drive seek sequence in the operating system Control Panel
- ○ **B.** Reconfigure the drive seek sequence in the CMOS setup utility
- ○ **C.** Disconnect the IDE cable to the drive to force the system to boot from the floppy drive
- ○ **D.** Reconfigure the floppy jumpers to make it a bootable drive

27. What type of BIOS password should be set on machines that are open to public use?

- ○ **A.** User access
- ○ **B.** Remote Access
- ○ **C.** Admin
- ○ **D.** Supervisory

28. You are responsible for computers in your area of the building. You need to secure them so that only your employees can access the systems but they cannot change CMOS settings. What type of CMOS password should you set for these machines?

- ○ **A.** User access
- ○ **B.** Remote Access
- ○ **C.** Admin
- ○ **D.** Supervisory

29. Where should you establish an Administrators password on a computer that will be installed in an Internet cafe?

- ○ **A.** In the CMOS setup utility.
- ○ **B.** In the BIOS.
- ○ **C.** In Windows.
- ○ **D.** If you set a password in this environment, users will not be able to access the system.

Answers and Explanations

1. B. The PCI bus specification uses multiplexed address and data lines to conserve the pins of the basic 124-pin PCI connector.

2. D. Because the PnP process has no method for reconfiguring legacy devices during the resource assignment phase, it begins by assigning resources, such as IRQ assignments, to these devices before servicing the system's PnP devices.

3. A. The AGP interface is a variation of the PCI bus design that has been modified to handle the intense data throughput associated with three-dimensional graphics.

4. B. All Ultra ATA versions support 33.3MBps data rates when used with a standard 40-pin/40-conductor IDE signal cable.

5. A. Refer to Figures 2.1. For more information, see the section "ATX System Boards."

6. C. Refer to Figure 2.1. For more information, see the section "ATX System Boards."

7. B. Refer to Figure 2.1   An ATX Pentium system board. Along with the I/O port connections, Pentium system boards moved the hard- and floppy-disk drive controller functions and interface connections to the system board. For more information, see section "ATX System Boards

8. C. Refer to Figure 2.1   An ATX Pentium system board. For more information, see the section "ATX System Boards."

9. D. Refer to Figure 2.1   An ATX Pentium system board. For more information, see the section "ATX System Boards."

10. D. Refer to Figure 2.18   Standard ATX back panel connections. For more information, see the section "I/O Conenctions."

11. B. Refer to Figure 2.18   Standard ATX back panel connections. For more information, see the section "I/O Ports."

12. C. If the time is incorrect on a PC system, the easiest way to reset it is through the operating system; however, if the system continually fails to keep good time, you should start by checking for corrosion on the battery contacts. Clean the contacts with a pencil eraser and retry the battery. If that doesn't work, try replacing the battery. Next, you can try replacing the RTC module. If this does not correct the timekeeping problem, the electronic circuitry that recharges the battery may be defective, and in this case you will need a new motherboard.

13. A. Care must be taken when changing the disk drive translation mode setting in CMOS because all data on the drive can be lost in the process.

14. C. BIOS antivirus functions should be turned off when conducting an upgrade to the operating system. The built-in virus warning utility checks the drive's boot sector for changes. The changes that the new operating system will attempt to make to the boot sector will be interpreted as a virus, and the utility will act to prevent the upgrade from occurring.

15. D. The BIOS Features Setup screen is used to configure different bootup options. These options include establishing the system's bootup sequence. The sequence can be set so that the system checks the floppy drive (A:) for a boot sector first, or so that it checks the hard drive (C:) without checking the floppy drive. Other boot options include CD-ROM drives or a SCSI drive.

16. B. The PnP device communicates with the BIOS during the initialization phase of the startup to tell the system what type of device it is, where it is located in the system, and what its resource needs are.

17. B. One of the onboard I/O functions supported through the CMOS Setup utility includes selecting the operating modes for the parallel port. The parallel printer port can be configured for normal PC-AT-compatible standard parallel port (SPP) operation, for extended bidirectional operation (extended parallel port, or EPP), for fast, buffered bidirectional operation (extended capabilities port, or ECP), or for combined ECP+EPP operation. The normal setting should be selected unless both the port hardware and the driver software support EPP and/or ECP operation.

18. C, D. Because both of the advanced parallel port modes (EPP and ECP) operate in a bidirectional, half-duplex manner, they require an IEEE-1284-compliant cable. Standard parallel cables designed for older SPP operations may not support these qualities.

19. B. Because the CMOS password controls access to all parts of the system, even before the bootup process occurs, there is some inconvenience in the event that the user forgets his or her password. When this occurs, it will be impossible to gain access to the system without completely resetting the content of the CMOS RAM.

20. D. On some system boards, resetting the content of the CMOS can be accomplished by shorting a special pair of jumpers on the board. With other systems, you will need to remove or short across the backup battery to reset the CMOS information. In ATX systems, it will also be necessary to unplug the power from the commercial outlet to reduce the voltage to the CMOS registers. When the content of the CMOS is reset, you must manually restore any nondefault CMOS settings being used by the system.

21. B. The BIOS stores the PnP information it collects from the devices in a special section of the CMOS RAM known as the *Extended System Configuration Data (ESCD)* area. This information is stored in the same manner as standard BIOS settings are stored. The BIOS and the operating system both access the ESCD area each time the system is restarted to see if any information has changed. This enables the BIOS and the operating system to work together in sorting out the needs of the installed devices and assigning them needed system resources.

22. C. The Standard CMOS setup screens from various BIOS manufacturers all provide the same basic information. For example, they can be used to set the date and time via the system clock/calendar. During the startup process, the operating system acquires the time and date information from the CMOS RTC module. This information is updated in the system once every second.

23. A. The ECP mode supports high-throughput DMA operations for both forward- and reverse-direction transfers.

24. A. The ECP mode offers higher performance than either the SPP or the EPP mode.

25. A. Because both of the advanced parallel port modes operate in a bidirectional, half-duplex manner, they require an IEEE-1284-compliant cable. Standard parallel cables designed for older SPP operations may not support these qualities.

26. B. The Drive A: option in the Drive Seek Sequence setting should be enabled if the system cannot boot to the hard-disk drive and you have a clean boot disk or emergency repair floppy. If you disable the A: seek function in the CMOS setup utility (by not selecting it as part of the boot seek sequence), you will not be able to use the A: drive to troubleshoot hard-drive problems. The system then would never access the floppy drive to see if it had a bootable disk in it; however, you can always enter the CMOS setup utility and include it as part of the troubleshooting process.

27. D. The Supervisory password is used to control access to the system's CMOS setup utility. Because this system is opened for public use, setting a User password would prevent users from accessing the system. The Supervisory password will prevent intentional malicious access to the CMOS where users could disable the system.

28. A. The User password option enables you to establish password access to the systems that you can share with your employees. This will prevent other employees from accessing the systems without giving your employees access to the CMOS setup utility.

29. A. The first line of system protection in this situation is setting a Supervisory password in the CMOS Setup utility to prevent users from accessing and manipulating the system's configuration settings.

Challenge Solutions

1. You can potentially upgrade your Pentium II/Slot 1 machines to Pentium III class microprocessors that will run at up to 1GHz.

2. The three-bank split bank slot arrangement has separated the memory into a 128MB section for the first slot and only 128MB for the second bank of two slots. These devices are not compatible with the organization of the board's slot configuration. You need to obtain the system board's user's manual to determine what types and sizes of memory devices can be used. (If this occurs when you are using the specified types of memory devices, you may have a bad DIMM device in one of the slots.)

3. You must go into the CMOS Setup utility and make sure that the CD-ROM drive is one of the options selected in the Drive Seek Sequence.

4. There are several things that you should do to make this modem work in your system. The item we are most interested in, at this point, is the configuration information required by the CMOS. Older BIOS versions required that you manually disable the COM2 setting and reserve an IRQ setting for the modem in the PnP/PCI Configuration window. Windows 2000 and Windows XP operating systems will detect the presence of an ISA device and reserve a set of resources for it; however, you are still required to supply an acceptable device driver program for the device.

5. If you consider the nature of the two devices, you will realize that the scanner is basically an input device (actually a bidirectional device), so its data must move back to the parallel port, whereas the printer is an output device, so information normally travels from the port to the printer. Check the parallel cables to make sure that they are IEEE-1284 compliant. The port must be configured for bidirectional support in the CMOS. Check the CMOS settings to make sure that EPP or ECP modes are selected.

CHAPTER THREE

Microprocessors

Terms you'll need to understand:

✓ Hyperthreading

✓ Throttling

✓ Overclocking

✓ L1 cache

✓ L2 cache

✓ L3 cache

✓ Voltage Regulator Module

✓ PGA socket

✓ SPGA socket

✓ Flip Chip Pin Grid Array (FC-PGA) sockets

✓ Single-Edge Contact cartridge

✓ Pentium processors

✓ Duron processors

✓ Opteron processors

✓ Athlon processors

✓ Dual-core processors

Techniques to master:

✓ Essentials 1.1—Identify the fundamental principles of using personal computers.

✓ Identify the names, purposes, and characteristics of processor/CPUs.

✓ CPU chips (for example, AMD, Intel)

✓ CPU technologies

  ✓ Hyperthreading

  ✓ Dual core

  ✓ Throttling

✓ Micro code (MMX)

✓ Overclocking

✓ Cache

✓ VRM

✓ Speed (real versus actual)

✓ 32 versus 64 bit

✓ Identify the names, purposes, and characteristics of cooling systems—for example, heat sinks, CPU and case fans, liquid cooling systems, and thermal compound.

Introduction

This chapter covers the microprocessor areas of the CompTIA A+ Certification—Essentials examination under Objective 1.1. It also covers the cooling systems area of the objective. Computer technicians are often asked to upgrade existing systems with new devices, such as a new microprocessor. Therefore, every technician should be aware of the characteristics of possible CPU upgrades and be able to determine whether a particular upgrade is physically possible and worthwhile.

The successful technician must be aware of the capabilities of the different microprocessors that are available for use in a system. Technicians must know what impact placing a particular microprocessor in an existing system may have on its operation. They must also be able to identify the type of processor being used and the system setting necessary to maximize its operation.

Intel Microprocessors

There were originally several competitors in the PC-compatible microprocessor market. However, over time the market has narrowed to two major players competing for market domination: Intel and American Micro Devices (AMD). Intel has set the standard for processor performance throughout most of the personal computer era. However, AMD has shown itself a worthy opponent, frequently taking the market lead with speed increases and new innovations.

For the most part, the previous generations of microprocessors have disappeared from the marketplace, leaving the Pentium and its clones as the only processor types that need to be discussed in detail. The following sections first look at the advancements Intel has produced and then focus on the AMD processors that compete with them.

The Pentium Processor

When IBM was designing the first PC, it chose the Intel 8088 microprocessor and its supporting chipset as the standard CPU for its design. This was a natural decision because one of IBM's major competitors (Apple) was using Motorola microprocessors for its designs. The choice to use the Intel microprocessor still affects the design of PC-compatible systems. In fact, the microprocessors used in the vast majority of all PC-compatible microcomputers include the Intel 8088/86, 80286, 80386, 80486, and Pentium (80586 and 80686) devices.

The original Pentium processor was a 32/64-bit design housed in a ceramic pin grid array package. Its registers and floating-point sections were identical to those of its predecessor, the 80486. It had a 64-bit data bus that enabled it to handle quad word data transfers. It also contained two separate 8kB caches, compared to only one in the 80486. One cache was used for instructions or code, and the other was used for data.

This original Pentium architecture has appeared in three generations. The first generation, codenamed the P5, came in a 273-pin PGA package and operated at 60 or 66MHz speeds. It used a single +5V (DC) operating voltage, which caused it to consume a large amount of power and generate a large amount of heat. It generated so much heat during normal operation that an additional CPU cooling fan was required.

The second generation of Pentiums, referred to as P54Cs, came in a 296-pin Staggered Pin Grid Array (SPGA) package and operated at 75, 90, 100, 120, 133, 150, and 166MHz in different versions. For these devices, Intel reduced the power-supply voltage level to +3.3V (DC) to consume less power and provide faster operating speeds. Reducing the power-supply level in effect moved the processor's high- and low-logic levels closer together, which means that less time is required to switch back and forth between them. The SPGA packaging made the second generation of Pentium devices incompatible with the first-generation system boards.

The second-generation devices also employed internal clock multipliers to increase performance. In this scenario, the system's buses run at the same speed as the clock signal introduced to the microprocessor; however, the internal clock multiplier causes the microprocessor to operate internally at some multiple of the external clock speed (for example, a Pentium operating from a 50MHz external clock and using a 2× internal multiplier is actually running internally at 100MHz).

The third generation of Pentium designs, designated as P55C, employed a 296-pin SPGA arrangement. This package adhered to the 321-pin Socket-7 specification designed by Intel. The P55C was produced in versions that operate at 166, 180, 200, and 233MHz. This generation of Pentium devices operated at voltages below the +3.3V level established in the second generation of devices. The P55C was known as the Pentium MMX (Multimedia Extension) processor. Figure 3.1 shows the pin arrangements for PGA and SPGA devices. Notice the uniformity of the PGA rows and columns versus the staggered rows and columns of the SPGA device.

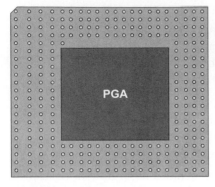 

FIGURE 3.1 PGA and SPGA arrangements.

Advanced Pentium Architectures

Intel has continued to improve its Pentium line of microprocessors by introducing additional specifications including the Pentium MMX, Pentium Pro, Pentium II, Pentium III, and Pentium 4 processors. At the same time, Intel's competitors have developed clone designs that equal or surpass the capabilities of the Intel versions.

Pentium MMX Processors

The Pentium MMX processor extended the multimedia and communications processing capabilities of the original Pentium device by the addition of 57 multimedia-specific instructions to the instruction set. Intel also increased the onboard L1 cache size to 32KB. The cache was divided into two separate 16KB caches: the instruction cache and the data cache. The typical L2 cache used with the MMX is 256KB or 512KB, and employs a 66MHz system bus.

The Pentium MMX processor was produced in 166, 200, and 233MHz versions and used a 321-pin SPGA Socket-7 format. It required two separate operating voltages. One source was used to drive the Pentium processor core; the other was used to power the processor's I/O pins.

Pentium Pro Processors

Intel departed from simply increasing the speed of its Pentium processor line by introducing the Pentium Pro processor. Although compatible with all the software previously written for the Intel processor line, the Pentium Pro was optimized to run 32-bit software. However, the Pentium Pro did not remain pin-compatible with the previous Pentium processors. Instead, Intel adopted a 2.46 inch×2.66 inch, 387-pin PGA configuration to house the Pentium Pro processor core, and an onboard 256KB (or 512KB) L2 cache with a 60 or 66MHz system bus. The L2 cache complements the 16KB L1 cache in the Pentium core. Figure 3.2 illustrates this arrangement. Notice that although the L2 cache and the CPU are on the same PGA device, they are not integrated into the same IC. The unit is covered with a gold-plated copper/tungsten heat spreader.

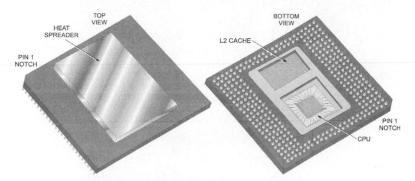

FIGURE 3.2   The Pentium Pro microprocessor.

The L2 onboard cache stores the most frequently used data not found in the processor's internal L1 cache as close to the processor core as it can be without being integrated directly into the IC. A high-bandwidth cache bus (referred to as the *back-side bus*) connects the processor and cache unit. The bus (0.5 inch in length) allows the processor and external cache to communicate at a rate of 1.2GBps.

The Pentium Pro was designed to be used in single-microprocessor applications as well as in multiprocessor environments such as high-speed, high-volume file servers and workstations. Several dual-processor system boards have been designed for twin Pentium Pro processors. These boards are created with two Pentium Pro sockets so that they can operate with either a single processor or with dual processors. When dual processors are installed, logic circuitry in the Pentium Pro's core manages the requests for access to the system's memory and 64-bit buses.

Pentium II Processors

Intel radically changed the form factor of the Pentium processors by housing the Pentium II processor in a new Single-Edge Contact (SEC) cartridge, depicted in Figure 3.3. This cartridge uses a special retention mechanism built in to the system board to hold the device in place.

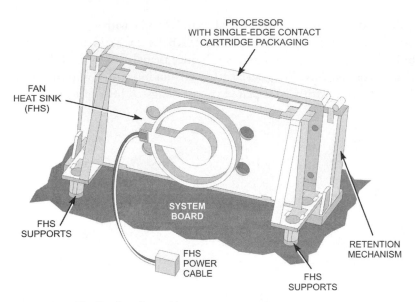

FIGURE 3.3 The Pentium II cartridge.

The proprietary 242-contact socket design is referred to as the *Slot 1 specification* and was designed to enable the microprocessor to operate at bus speeds in excess of 300MHz.

The cartridge also requires a special Fan Heat Sink (FHS) module and fan. Like the SEC cartridge, the FHS module requires special support mechanisms to hold it in place. The fan draws power from a special power connector on the system board or from one of the system's options power connectors.

Inside the cartridge is a substrate material on which the processor and related components are mounted. The components consist of the Pentium II processor core, a TAG RAM, and an L2 burst SRAM. TAG RAM is used to track the attributes (read, modified, and so on) of data stored in the cache memory.

The Pentium II includes all the multimedia enhancements from the MMX processor, as well as retaining the power of the Pentium Pro's dynamic execution, and features up to 512KB of L2 cache and employs a 66 or 100MHz system bus. The L1 cache is increased to 32KB, and the L2 cache operates with a half-speed bus. Figure 3.4 depicts the content of the Pentium II cartridge.

EXAM ALERT

Know which microprocessor employs half-speed cache.

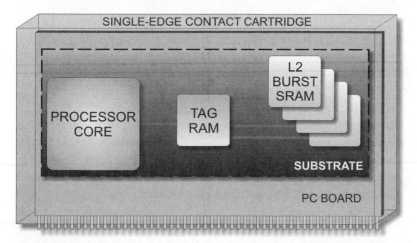

FIGURE 3.4 Inside the Pentium II cartridge.

A second cartridge type, called the *Single-Edged Processor Package (SEPP)*, was developed for use with the Slot 1 design. In this design, the boxed processor is not completely covered by the plastic housing as it is in the SEC design. Instead, the SEPP circuit board is accessible from the backside.

EXAM ALERT

Remember which components Intel included in the SEC cartridge.

Intel followed the Pentium II processor with an improved low-cost design it called the Pentium Celeron. The first version of this line of processors was code named the Covington. This processor was built around a Pentium II core without a built-in cache. Later, the Celeron Mendocino version featured a 66MHz bus speed and only 128KB of L2 cache. Initially, this version was packaged in the SECC cartridge.

Pentium III

Intel quickly followed the Celeron release with a new Slot 1-compatible design it called the Pentium III. The original Pentium III processor (code named Katmai) was designed around the Pentium II core, but increased the L2 cache size to 512KB. It also increased the speed of the processor to 600MHz, including a 100MHz front-side bus (FSB) speed.

Later versions of the Pentium III and Celeron processors were developed for the Intel Socket 370 specification. This design returned to a 370-pin, ZIF socket/SPGA package arrangement.

The first pin grid array versions of the Pentium III and Celeron processors conformed to a standard called the Plastic Pin Grid Array (PPGA) 370 specification. Intel repackaged its processors into a PGA package to fit this specification. The PPGA design was introduced to produce inexpensive, moderate-performance Pentium systems. The design topped out at 533MHz with a 66MHz bus speed.

Intel upgraded the Socket 370 specification by introducing a variation called the *Flip Chip Pin Grid Array (FC-PGA)* 370 design. Intel made small modifications to the wiring of the socket to accommodate the Pentium III processor design. In addition, it employed a new 0.18 micron IC manufacturing technology to produce faster processor speeds (up to 1.12GHz) and front-side bus speeds (100MHz and 133MHz). However, the new design provides only 256KB of L2 cache.

Pentium III and Celeron processors designed with the 0.18 micron technology are referred to as Coppermine and Coppermine 128 processors, respectively (the L2 cache in the Coppermine 128 is only 128KB). Further developments of the Coppermine versions, referred to as Tualatin, employed 0.13 micron IC technology to achieve 1.4GHz operating speeds with increased cache sizes (256KB or 512KB).

Xeon Processors

Intel has produced three special versions of the Pentium III that they have collectively named the Pentium Xeon, as shown in Figure 3.5. These processors are designed to work with an edge connector-based Slot 2 specification that Intel has produced to extend its Slot 1/boxed-processor scheme to a 330-contact design. Each version features a different level of L2 cache (512KB, 1MB, 2MB).

The Xeon designs were produced to fill different high-end server needs. The Xeon processor functions at speeds up to 866MHz and is built on the 0.18-micron process technology. The processor allows for highly scalable server solutions that support up to 32 processors.

Pentium 4 Processors

Intel then released the Pentium 4 (Williamette 423) microprocessor. The Pentium 4 was a new processor design based on 0.18-micron IC construction technology. It employed a modified Socket 370 PGA design that uses 423 pins and boasts operating speeds up to 2.0GHz.

The system's FSB bus was increased from 64 to 128 bits and operates at up to 400MHz. The bus is actually clocked at 100MHz but data was transferred four times in a single clock cycle (referred to as a *quad-pumped bus*). Therefore, the bandwidth of the bus is considered to be 400MHz.

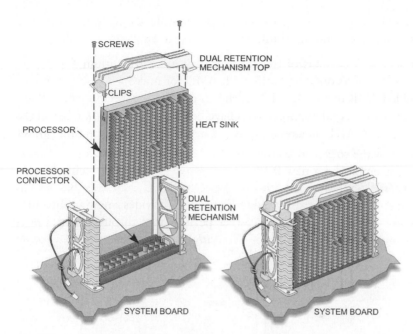

FIGURE 3.5   The Xeon processor.

In addition to the new front-side bus size, the Pentium 4 features new WPNI (Williamette Processor New Instructions) instructions in its instruction set. The L1 cache size has been reduced from 16kB in the Pentium III to 8kB for the Pentium 4. The L2 cache is 256kB and can handle transfers on every clock cycle.

The operating voltage level for the Pentium 4 core is 1.7Vdc. To dissipate the 55 watts of power (heat) that the microprocessor generates at 1.5GHz, the case incorporates a metal cap that acts as a built-in heat sink. Firm contact must be maintained between the microprocessor's case and its built-in heat sink feature.

Newer .13-micron versions codenamed Northwood operate at speeds up to 3.06GHz. This newer Pentium 4 design employs an improved 478-pin version of the chip that increased the L2 cache size to 512KB. This type of P4 processor has been produced in versions that run at 2.0, 2.2, 2.4, 2.8, and 3.06GHz. The 2.4GHz version increased the speed of the quad-pumped bus to 533MHz (133×4). Some variations of the 2.4 to 3.06 processors were produced with support for 800MHz FSB operations.

The evolution of the Pentium 4 processor topped out with the delivery of a 3.2 and 3.4GHz version in 2004. The 3.06MHz version of the P4 brought Hyperthreading Technology (HTT) to the Intel line of processors. *Hyperthreading* is an architecture that enables multiple program threads to be run in different sections of the processor simultaneously. Basically, the structure fools the operating system into thinking that two processors are available.

The most advanced versions of the P4 processor are the Pentium 4 Extreme Editions (P4EE). In its ongoing battle with AMD for microprocessor supremacy, Intel added 2MB of Level 3 (L3) cache to the Xeon core and called them P4EE. Later versions of these processors have been clocked at 3.73GHz and are equipped with 1066MHz front-side buses. They are available in either Socket 603 or LGA 775 versions.

Itanium Processors

The Intel Itanium processor, depicted in Figure 3.6, provides a new architecture specifically for servers. It maximizes server performance through special processing techniques Intel refers to as *Explicitly Parallel Instruction Computing (EPIC)*.

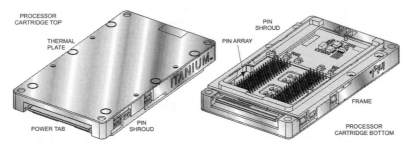

FIGURE 3.6 The Itanium processor.

The Itanium processor design features a new three-level, onboard cache system. The L1 cache size is 32KB operating fully pipelined, the L2 cache size is 96KB, and the new L3 cache is available in two sizes: 2MB or 4MB. The cartridge's edge connector specification provides separate voltage levels for the processor and cache devices to improve signal integrity.

Because Itanium processors are designed to be available 100% of the time, they tend to be very expensive—often more expensive than the complete network operating system that they are running. However, the cost of the processor is nothing compared to the cost of most online businesses going down for just one hour.

Intel Dual-Core Processors

Dual-core processors provide two execution cores in one physical processor package. The two cores are actually produced on the same piece of silicon (on the same die). This enables the system to divide processing tasks between the two cores. Therefore, it can do twice as many things, such as editing video while downloading audio streams, in a given amount of time and appear to be running much faster. Fitting two processors into a single package theoretically doubles the computing power of the device without having to clock it twice as fast. Figure 3.7 depicts a dual-core processor arrangement.

FIGURE 3.7   Dual-core processors.

Intel has launched the Pentium D and Pentium Extreme Edition (EE) lines of dual-core processors. The Extreme Edition versions employ Intel's hyper-threading technology that enables a single processor core to simulate dual-logical processors that can be used to work on different program segments simultane-ously. Including the hyperthreading technology in a dual-core processor pack-age enables it to process four different threads simultaneously (it functions like four different single-core processors). Table 3.1 lists the key characteristics of the Intel dual-core processors.

TABLE 3.1   Intel Dual-Core Processors

PROCESSOR	CLOCK FREQUENCY	L2 CACHE	FRONT-SIDE BUS SPEED	CLOCK MULTIPLE	CORE VOLTAGE	POWER DISSI-PATION
Pentium D 805	2.667GHz	2 ×1MB	533MT/s	20×	1.25/1.4V	95W
Pentium D 820	2.800GHz	2 ×1MB	800MT/s	14×	1.2/1.4V	95W
Pentium D 830	3GHz	2 ×1MB	800MT/s	15×	1.2/1.4V	130W
Pentium D 840	3.2GHz	2 ×1MB	800MT/s	16×	1.2/1.4V	130W
Pentium D 920	2.8GHz	2 ×2MB	800MT/s	14×	1.2/1.337V	130W
Pentium D 930	3GHz	2 ×2MB	800MT/s	15×	1.2/1.337V	130W
Pentium D 940	3.2GHz	2 ×2MB	800MT/s	16×	1.2/1.337V	130W
Pentium D 950	3.4GHz	2 ×2MB	800MT/s	17×	1.2/1.337V	130W

(continues)

TABLE 3.1 *Continued*

PROCESSOR	CLOCK FREQUENCY	L2 CACHE	FRONT-SIDE BUS SPEED	CLOCK MULTIPLE	CORE VOLTAGE	POWER DISSI-PATION
Pentium D 960	3.6GHz	2 ×2MB	800MT/s	18×	1.2/1.337V	130W
Pentium Extreme Edition 840	3.2GHz	2 ×1MB	800MT/s	16×	1.2/1.4V	130W
Pentium Extreme Edition 955	3.466GHz	2 ×2MB	1066MT/s	13×	1.2/1.337V	130W
Pentium Extreme Edition 965	3.733GHz	2 ×2MB	1066MT/s	14×	1.2/1.337V	130W

As Table 3.1 shows, most of the dual-core Intel designs employ an 800MHz FSB to communicate with the rest of the system. So far, the exceptions to this are the Pentium EE 955 and EE 965 processors that use a 1066MHz FSB. The table specifies the front-side bus speed in terms of Mega Transfers per second (MT/s). This is a realistic measurement of the bus's channel speed instead of its clock speed. For instance, if the bus transfers data on both the rising and falling edges of its clock signal, a 400MHz clock would effectively yield a 800MT/s throughput rate.

In both designs, the two cores communicate with each other through a special bus interface block, or through the FSB. They can also access each other's L2 caches through this interface. However, each core can use only half of the FSB bandwidth frequency when working under heavy load. The 8XX models include 1MB of L2 cache for each core, whereas the 9XX models have enlarged the L2 cache to 2MB for each core.

The Smithfield core used in the first Pentium D models is made up of two Prescott Pentium 4 processor cores and includes 1MB of Level 2 cache for each processor. This is all placed on a 206mm chip, which makes the Pentium D core roughly twice the physical size of the Prescott processor. Newer Pentium D 920, 930, 940, and 950 processors are based on the Presler core, which is a derivation of pairing two Cedar Mill cores. This core is produced using 65nm technology and can work with the same chipsets as the Smithfield core.

All the current and planned dual-core processors from Intel are designed to use a new type of socket called the Land Grid Array (LGA) 775. Unlike previous socket types, the LGA775, also referred to as *Socket-T*, places contact pins on the system board and contact pads on the bottom of the microprocessor.

A hinged metal rim folds down over the microprocessor package and holds its contact pads securely against the signal pins on the system board. A locking arm is used to clamp the processor package in place. The heat sink and fan unit are connected directly and securely to the system board on four points. Figure 3.8 shows the LGA775 socket arrangement.

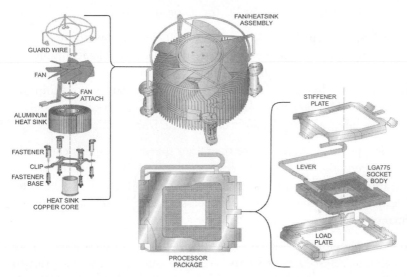

FIGURE 3.8   The LGA775 socket.

Advanced Intel Microprocessor Technologies

Both dual-core processor types incorporate advanced technologies into their feature sets. All Smithfield-based processors support the Intel Execute Disable Bit (XD bit) virus protection, EM64T 64-bit extension, and enhanced SpeedStep technologies. The Presler designs also include Virtualization Technology (VT), which enables a single machine to run multiple operating systems at once.

XD-bit technology is used to separate areas of memory into regions for distinct uses. For example, a section of memory can be set aside exclusively for storing processor instructions (code), and another section can be marked only for storage of data.

In the case of Intel processors, any section of memory marked with the XD attribute means it's only for storing data. Therefore, processor instructions cannot be stored there. This is a popular technique for preventing malicious software from taking over computers by inserting their code into another program's data storage area and then running that code from within this section. This is known as a *buffer overflow attack*.

EM64T is a 64-bit microprocessor architecture and corresponding instruction set that is an extension of the x86 instruction set used with all Intel processors. Intel has included this technology and instruction set in its Pentium 4, Pentium D, Pentium Extreme Edition, Celeron D, and Xeon processors.

Enhanced Intel SpeedStep Technology (EIST) enables the operating system software to dynamically control the clock speed of a processor. Running the processor at higher clock speeds provides better performance. However, running the processor at a lower speed provides for reduced power consumption and heat dissipation. This *throttling* technique is used to conserve battery power in notebooks, extend processor life, and reduce noise from cooling devices.

Each processor type has a range of core operating speeds at which it can work. For example, a Pentium M processor designated as a 1.5GHz processor can actually operate safely at any speed between 600MHz and 1.5GHz. The Intel dual-core designs leave some margin for processor overclocking to satisfy the PC performance enthusiast.

The SpeedStep technology enables the user or the operating system to change the speed setting in 200MHz increments. Windows operating systems prior to Windows XP require a special driver and a dashboard application to provide speed control for the processor. However, Windows XP has SpeedStep support built in to its Control Panel's Power Management Console.

Hyperthreading Software Support

The presence of two microprocessors does not automatically double system performance. The controlling operating system software must distribute tasks to all available processor resources. This requires the OS to handle multiple program execution threads that can run independently. The problem is that software has not traditionally been written with multiple threading capabilities. Most existing software applications are single threaded—they are written so only one task is worked on at a time. In these cases, the dual-core processor performs just like its single-core version.

On the other hand, modern operating systems can deliver multitasking operation—operations where the system works on more than one application at a time. The operating system switches from one task to another in a predetermined order. This is done so quickly that the system appears to be working on multiple tasks at the same time. Operating systems can use processors with hyperthreading technology to provide smooth and responsive operations during intensive multitasking operations.

AMD Processors

Advanced Micro Devices (AMD) offers several clone microprocessors: the 5 ×86 (X5), 5×86 (K5), K6, K6PLUS-3D, and K7 microprocessors. The X5 offers operational and pin compatibility with the DX4. Its performance is equal to that of the Pentium and MMX processors. The K5 processor is compatible with the Pentium, and the K6 is compatible with the MMX. Both the K5 and K6 models are Socket 7–compatible, enabling them to be used in conventional Pentium and Pentium MMX system board designs (with some small modifications). The K6 employs an extended 64KB L1 cache that doubles the internal cache size of the Pentium II.

The K6PLUS-3D is operationally and performance compatible with the Pentium Pro, and the K7 is operationally and performance-compatible with the Pentium II. However, neither of these units has a pin-out compatibility with another processor.

AMD continued to produce clone versions of Pentium processors. In some cases, the functions and performance of the AMD devices went beyond those of the Intel design they are cloning. Two notable AMD Pentium clone processors are the Athlon and the Duron.

The Athlon is a Pentium III clone processor. It is available in a Slot 1 cartridge clone, called the *Slot A specification*. Figure 3.9 depicts the cartridge version of the Athlon processor along with a Slot A connector.

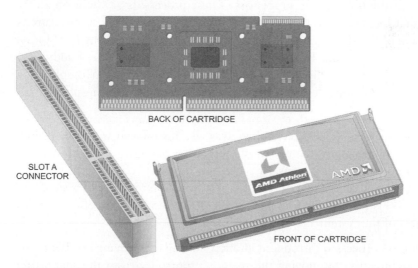

BACK OF CARTRIDGE

SLOT A
CONNECTOR

FRONT OF CARTRIDGE

FIGURE 3.9 The Slot A Athlon processor.

The Athlon is also available in a proprietary SPGA Socket A design that mimics the Intel Socket 370 specification. The Socket A specification employs a 462-pin ZIF socket and is supported by only two available chipsets.

The first Athlon version was the K7 version that ran between 500MHz and 700MHz, provided a 128KB L1 cache and a 512KB L2 cache, and employed a 100MHz system bus. Subsequent Athlon versions have included the K75, Thunderbird, Thoroughbred, and Barton versions. These versions are constructed using the 0.18-micron manufacturing technology.

The K75 processor ran between 750 MHz and 1 GHz. Like the K7 version, it provided a 128KB L1 cache and a 512KB L2 cache, and employed a 100MHz system bus. The Thunderbird version ran between 750MHz and 1.2 GHz, provided a 128KB L1 cache and a 256KB L2 cache, and employed a 133MHz system bus. The Thoroughbred featured 256KB of L2 cache and the standard 64+64KB L1 cache. It operated at speeds up to 2.8GHz.

A later evolution of the Athlon processor was given the title of Athlon XP. These versions were based on the Thoroughbred and the newer Barton core versions. The Barton versions feature a 512KB L2 cache, a slower clock speed, and a maximum processor speed of 3.0GHz.

Athlon 64 Processors

AMD made several technology changes to the Athlon processor when it unveiled its Athlon 64 line of processors. These processors are built on a new K8 core that includes AMD's AMD64 64-bit architecture. This architecture is an extension of the x86 instruction set that was originally created by Intel for its 80x86 line of processors. In addition, the Athlon 64 implemented additional internal registers to handle SSE (Streaming Single-Instruction/Multiple Data Extensions) instructions designed to support independent floating-point math operations.

A new No-Execute (NE) bit technology was also introduced with the Athlon. NE technology marks different areas of memory as being for use with data, or as being reserved for instructions. Any attempt to execute code from a memory page that has been tagged as a no-execute page will result in a *memory access violation error*. This feature makes it more difficult for certain types of malware to take control of the system and execute its payload.

The Athlon 64 processor introduced another considerable change to Pentium-class PC architecture by moving the memory controller from the supporting system board chipset into the microprocessor package. This effectively removes the front-side bus from the system architecture and improves memory access operations by avoiding external bus access overhead.

Instead of continuing the traditional FSB structure, AMD adopted a special bidirectional, serial/parallel I/O bus and controller technology from the HyperTransport Technology Consortium for its Athlon 64 processors. The HyperTransport (HT) technology handles the I/O functions previously performed across the FSB at speeds much higher that existing FSB clocking. AMD also employs this bus to interconnect multiple processor cores to provide efficient cooperation between the cores.

The Athlon 64 FX is a special designation given to some Athlon 64 versions. These processors are typically clocked faster than the traditional Athlon versions to make them more interesting to gamers and other enthusiasts.

There are two common socket sizes used with Athlon 64 processors: a 754-pin socket for a value/budget version of the Athlon 64 that provides only a 64-bit, single-channel memory interface, and a 939-pin version that is the standard for all other Athlon 64 versions.

Duron Processors

The Duron processor is a Celeron clone processor that conforms to the AMD Socket A specification. The Duron features processor speeds between 600MHz and 800MHz. It includes a 128KB L1 cache and a 64KB L2 cache and employs a 100MHz system bus. Like the newer Celerons, the Duron is constructed using 0.18-micron IC manufacturing technology.

Athlon Dual-Core Processors

AMD took the lead in the processor development races by pushing dual-core processors to the forefront. Unlike the Intel dual-core processors discussed earlier in the chapter, AMD designed its dual-core devices to fit in the same 939-pin socket interface it was already using for its single-core Athlon 64 processor. In addition, the existing Athlon 64 chipset had been designed with this possibility in mind. These features make upgrading to dual-core processors relatively easy and attractive. All that is required is to physically exchange the microprocessor packages and perform a logical upgrade by flashing the system's ROM BIOS with programming to support the new processor.

Figure 3.10 provides a block diagram of the AMD Athlon 64 X2 Dual-Core processor design. Like the Intel processors, the dual processor cores in the 64 X2 can communicate with each other through the System Request Interface.

This interface enables the communications to take place at the core clock speed of the processors. The AMD multicore technology also changed the front-side bus arrangement found in existing Pentium/PCI systems. This portion of the system has been redesigned in a Direct Connect Architecture that directly connects the processor, the memory controller, and the I/O controller to the CPU. Therefore, there is no loss due to I/O manipulation and bottlenecks associated with the operation of the front-side bus.

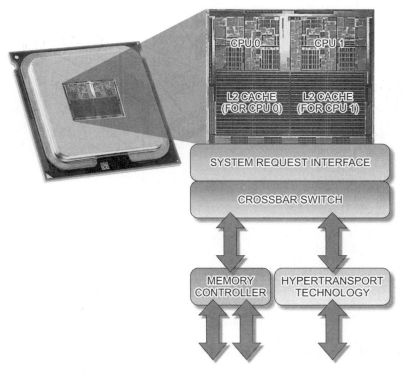

FIGURE 3.10   The AMD dual-core processors design.

Notice in Figure 3.10 that in the AMD 64 processors, a 128-bit ECC memory controller has been integrated into the microprocessor die. This gives the processors direct access to the memory controller (in contrast to having to access an external bus to get to the North Bridge).

The complete line of AMD64 devices (single and dual core) offers AMD's advanced HyperTransport bus interface technology for high speed I/O communication. In the AMD processors, this interface consists of an integrated HyperTransport controller and a 16-bit, 1GHz bus that interconnects the cores of the multicore AMD processor through its Direct Connect Architecture and provides 8GBps transfer rates. The HyperTransport interface also connects the processor package to the system board's chipset. This connection scheme is illustrated in Figure 3.11.

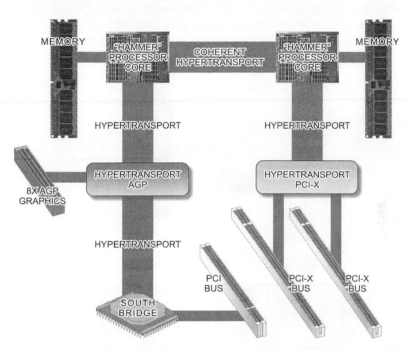

FIGURE 3.11 HyperTransport links.

The AMD 64 X2 has been built on two different microprocessor core types: the Toledo core and the Manchester core. Both versions include dual AMD64 microprocessor cores. These cores are rated to operate at core voltages between 1.35V and 1.4V. Likewise, they both contain dual 64+64 (Data/Instructions) L1 cache memory units. They also run identical microprocessor instruction sets and extensions. Finally, they both work with Socket 939 structure and provide 1GHz HyperTransport high-speed I/O interfaces.

In the Toledo core, each processor core is supported by a 1MB full speed L2 cache. On the Manchester core, the L2 cache is limited to 512KB for each core. Power consumption for the Toledo core is 89 or 110 watts, depending on the version, whereas the power consumption in the Manchester core is 110W max.

Models built on the Toledo core include the 4400+ and 4800+ processors, and Manchester models include the 3800+, 4200+, and 4600+ processors. The 4400+ runs on a 2.2GHz clock and the 4800+ uses a 2.4GHz clock. On the Manchester side, the 3800+is designed for a 2.0GHz clock, the 4200+ uses a 2.2GHz clock, and the 4600+ model employs a 2.4GHz clock.

The Athlon 64 X2 is supported by a number of chipsets from many manufacturers. In at least one case, the chipset designed to support the AMD dual-core processor is a single chip, as illustrated in Figure 3.12. The AMD processors provide direct connection to the system's DDR memory through its Direct Connect Architecture, and the nFORCE chipset handles the PCIe graphics, ethernet networking, and SATA disk drive interfaces.

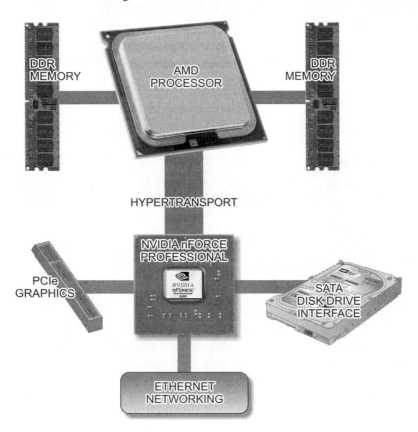

FIGURE 3.12 A single-chip AMD chipset.

Like the dual-core Intel processors, the Athlon 64 X2 supports a 64-bit extension to the x86 instruction set, enhanced virus protection with supported operating systems, and speed throttling features. In the AMD environment, these features are known as AMD64, NX (no execute bit), and CoolnQuiet. The functions associated with these features are roughly the same as those of the Intel EM64T, XD bit, and SpeedStep features described earlier in this chapter.

Opteron Processors

AMD has also produced a line of dual-core, high-end Opteron processors for network server and workstation units. These units are built on AMD's K8 core and are intended to compete with Intel's Xeon line of processors. The original 1XX Opteron versions were built for a 939-pin socket. However, newer 2XX and 8XX 940-pin versions have been introduced for the newer Socket M2 (AM2) specification. As mentioned in Chapter 2, "PC System Boards," several Athlon 64, Athlon 64 FX Athlon64 X2, and Sempron processors versions have been developed to use the Socket M2 specification. Table 3.2 lists the prominent features of the dual-core Opteron processors from AMD.

Socket AM2—A 940-pin socket also known as Socket M2, replaces the current Socket 754 and 939 offerings: Athlon 64, Athlon 64 FX, and Athlon 64 X2.

TABLE 3.2 AMD Dual-Core Opteron Processors

MODEL	CLOCK FREQUENCY	L2 CACHE	MEMORY	MULTI-PLIER	VOLTAGE	TDP	SOCKET
165	1.8GHz	2 ×1MB	up to PC-3200	9×	1.35/1.3V	110W	Socket 939
170	2.0GHz	2 ×1MB	up to PC-3200	10×	1.35/1.3V	110W	Socket 939
175	2.2GHz	2 × 1MB	up to PC-3200	11×	1.35/1.3V	110W	Socket 939
180	2.4GHz	2 ×1MB	up to PC-3200	12×	1.35/1.3V	110W	Socket 939
185	2.6GHz	2 ×1MB	up to PC-3200	13×	1.35/1.3V	110W	Socket 939
265/865	1.8GHz	2 ×1MB	up to PC-3200R	9×	1.35/1.3V	95W	Socket 940
270/870	2.0GHz	2 ×1MB	up to PC-3200R	10×	1.35/1.3V	95W	Socket 940
275/875	2.2GHz	2 ×1MB	up to PC-3200R	11×	1.35/1.3V	95W	Socket 940
280/880	2.4GHz	2 ×1MB	up to PC-3200R	12×	1.35/1.3V	95W	Socket 940
285/885	2.6GHz	2 ×1MB	up to PC-3200R	13x	1.35/1.3V	95W	Socket 940

Table 3.3 summarizes the characteristics of common Intel and AMD micro-processors. Both companies add new or upgraded processors to their product lines on a regular basis. Therefore, this list is not intended to be a complete list of all existing processors, just the main ones in existence up to the time when the text was created.

TABLE 3.3   Microprocessor Characteristics

MICRO-PROCESSOR	DIAMETER SIZE (mm)	VRM (VOLTS)	SPEED (MHz)	CACHE ON DIE (KB)	CACHE ON CART-RIDGE	CACHE ON BOARD (KB)	SOCKETS OR SLOT TYPES
Pentium	23.1 ×23.1	2.5–3.6	75—166	L1—8+8	-	L2—256/512	Socket 7
Pentium MMX	25.4 ×25.4	2.0–3.5	166—233	L1—16+16	-	L2—256/512	Socket 7
AMD - K6-2:K6-3	33.5×33.5	2.2–3.3	300—550	L1—32+32	-	L2—256/512	Super Socket 7
Pentium Pro	24.2 ×19.6	3.1–3.3	150, 166, 180, 200	L1—8+8	L2—256/512/1000	-	Socket 8
Pentium II/III Celeron (.25 micron)	25.4×25.4 18×62× 140 Box	1.5–2.6	233.1000	L1—16+16	L2—256/512 128 kB	- -	Slot 1
Xeon II/III (330) (.25 micron)	27.4 ×27.4 18 × 87 × 125 Box	1.5–2.6	500/550 700/90	L1—16+16	L2—512 kB/ 1 MB/2 M	- -	Slot 2
Pentium III Celeron (.25 micron)	25.4 ×25.4 Slug 27.4 × 27.4 Opening	1.1–2.5	300—566	L1—16+16 L2—128/256	- -	- -	Socket 370 PPGA
Pentium III (Coppermine) Celeron (.18 micron)	9.3 ×11.3	1.1–2.5	667–1000	L1–16+16 L2–128/256	- -	- -	Socket 370 FC-PGA
Pentium III (Tualatin) Celeron (.13 micron)	31 ×31	1.1–2.5	800–1500	L1—16+16 L2—128/256/512	- -	- -	FC-PGA2
Pentium 4 (.18 micron)	31 × 31	1.75	1300–2000	L1—12+8 L2—256	- -	- -	Socket 423 FC-PGA

TABLE 3.3 *Continued*

MICRO-PROCESSOR	DIAMETER SIZE (mm)	VRM (VOLTS)	SPEED (MHz)	CACHE ON DIE (KB)	CACHE ON CART-RIDGE	CACHE ON BOARD (KB)	SOCKETS OR SLOT TYPES
Pentium 4 (.18 micron) (.13 micron)	31 ×31 33 × 33	1.75– 1.50	1400– 2000 1800– 3400	L1— 12+8 L2— 512	- -	- -	FC-PGA2
Pentium Xeon (.18 micron)	31 × 31	1.4–1.8 1.7	1400– 2000	L1— 12+8 L2—256	- -	- -	Socket 603 FC-BGA
Pentium Xeon (.13 micron)	35 × 35	1.4–1.8 1.475	1800– 3400	L1— 12+8 L2—512	- -	- -	Socket 603 FC-BGA2
Itanium (.18 micron) (266 MHz)	71.6 × 127.7	1.7	733/800	1— 16+16 L2— 512	L3— 2 MB 4 MB	- -	PAC-418
Celeron D	125.0 × 90nm × 81mm	1.25– 1.4	2133.3333	L1— 12+16KB /L2— 256KiB	-	-	Socket 478/ LGA775
Pentium 4 Extreme Edition	169.0 × 130nm × 237mm	1.2/1.25 –1.337 /1.4	3200– 3733	L1— 12+8/ L2— 2x1024KiB or 2x2048KiB	L3.2MB	-	FC-LGA775
Pentium D	230.0/376.0 × 90/65nm × 206/ 280mm	1.2/1.25 –1.337 /1.4	2667– 3600	L1— 24+32KB /L2— 2x1024KiB or 2x2048KiB	-	-	FC-LGA775
Athlon/Duron	9.1 ×13.1	1.75	800– 1400	L1— 64+64	L2— 256kB	-	Slot A 242 CPGA
Athlon/Duron Socket A ORGA	11.1 × 11.6	1.75	733.1800 3200	1400– 64+64	L1— 256kB	L2— - 462	-
Athlon XP-M	68.5 × 130nm × 144mm	1.5–1.75	1333. 2333	L1— 64+64	L2— 128KiB/ 256KiB/ 512KiB	-	Socket A/462

(continues)

TABLE 3.3 *Continued*

MICRO-PROCESSOR	DIAMETER SIZE (mm)	VRM (VOLTS)	SPEED (MHz)	CACHE ON DIE (KB)	CACHE ON CART-RIDGE	CACHE ON BOARD (KB)	SOCKETS OR SLOT TYPES
Athon 64	105.9/68. 5/76 × 130/130/ 90nm×193/ 144/84mm	1.25– 1.40, 1.35,1.4, 1.5	2133. 3333	L1— 64+64	L2— 1024KiB/ 512KiB	-	Socket 754/939
Athon 64 FX	233.0 × 90nm × 199mm	1.50– 1.55, 1.50, 1.35/1.4	1.3.1.35V, 2200– 2800	L1— 64+64	L2— 1024KiB	-	Socket 754/939/ 940/AM2
Opteron	114.0/105.9 ×90/ 130nm × 115/193mm	1.50– 1.55/1.35 –1.4	1400– 2400/1600 –3000	L1— 64+64	L2— 1024KiB	-	Socket 939/940

NOTE

The PC industry has added a new measurement to contend with. This is the kiB (kibibyte or kilo binary byte) as presented in the table above. The kiB is related to the kilobyte (KB) but is intended to remove the inaccuracy that exists between the 1000 units generally attributed to the term *kilo* and the 1024 units it represents in digital systems. Therefore, when you see a PC quantity specified in kiB it represents 1024 bytes.

Microprocessor Clock Speeds

In the Pentium processor, two speed settings are established for the microprocessor: one speed for its internal core operations and a second speed for its external bus transfers. These two operational speeds are tied together through an internal clock multiplier system. The Socket 7 specification enabled system boards to be configured for different types of microprocessors using different operating speeds. In older systems, the operating speed of the microprocessor was configured through external settings.

Prior to Pentium II, all Pentium processors used 50, 60, or 66MHz external clock frequencies to generate their internal operating frequencies. The value of the internal multiplier was controlled by external hardware jumper settings on the system board.

Pentium II processors moved to a 100MHz external clock and front-side bus. The Pentium III and all slot processors up to 1GHz continued to use the

100MHz clock and FSB. However, beginning with the Pentium III Coppermine, the external clock speed was increased to 133MHz. At the same time, the Celeron processors retained the 66MHz clock and bus speeds up to 800MHz.

The Pentium 4 processors use external clocks of 100MHz and 133MHz. From these clock inputs, the Pentium 4's internal clock multipliers generate a core frequency of up to 3.06GHz and front-side bus frequencies of 400MHz, 533MHz, and 800MHz. They have also used four different special memory buses with different memory types. In Pentium 4 systems, it is possible to set independent clock speeds for the memory and front-side buses. The different memory bus configurations are designed to work with different types of advanced RAM and run at speeds of 400, 600, and 800MHz.

Newer processors, such as Intel's 3.46GHz Pentium 4 Extreme Edition, Pentium D dual core and the Core 2 Duo, possess a 1066MHz FSB capability that works with 266MHz quad-pumped (that is, multiplied by 4) DDR2 RAM.

Processor Power Supply Levels

Beginning with the Pentium MMX, Intel adopted dual-voltage supply levels for the overall IC and for its core. Common Intel voltage supplies are +5/+5 for older units and +3.3/+3.3, +3.3/+2.8, +3.3/+1.8, and +3.3/1.45 for newer units.

Clone processors may use compatible voltages (especially if they are pin compatible), or may use completely different voltage levels. Common voltages for clone microprocessors include +5, +3.3, +2.5, and +2.2. The additional voltage levels are typically generated through special regulator circuits on the system board. In each case, the system board's user's guide should be consulted anytime the microprocessor is replaced or upgraded.

From the second generation Pentiums forward, system boards have employed Voltage Regulator Modules (VRMs) to supply special voltage levels associated with different types of microprocessors that might be installed. The VRM module may be designed as a plug-in module so that it can be replaced easily in case of component failure. This is a somewhat common occurrence with voltage regulator devices. It also enables the system board to be upgraded when a new Pentium device is developed that requires a different voltage level or a different voltage pairing.

Some multiprocessor system boards have spaces for two or more VRM modules to be installed. The additional modules must be installed in VRM sockets to support additional processors. VRMs can also be a source of server board failures. You should always check the processor voltages on a malfunctioning system board to verify that they are being supplied correctly.

Configuring Microprocessors and Buses

Most system boards feature autodetection functions as part of the PnP process that automatically detect different FRU components on the board (processors, fans, RAM modules, and adapter cards) and synchronizes the different bus speed configurations. For example, the autodetect feature examines the installed microprocessor and the installed RAM modules to configure the front-side bus for maximum microprocessor-memory operations.

Similarly, the chipset may detect an advanced video adapter card in one of the expansion slots and adjust the expansion bus speed to maximize the performance of the video display. Likewise, the system autodetects the installed hard drives and CD-ROM drives and adjusts the IDE bus speed to provide the best drive system performance based on what it finds.

Finally, the system evaluates the information it has acquired about its components and buses and configures the North and South Bridges to provide synchronization between their other buses and the PCI bus that connects them. The PCI bus speed (and by default its AGP video slot derivative) does not change to accommodate different installed components. Its speed is established as a derivative of the microprocessor clock (not to be confused with the advertised speed rating of the microprocessor).

The BIOS version must support the parameters of the microprocessor so that the PnP process can correctly configure the device and the chipset. If a microprocessor upgrade is performed and the BIOS code does not fully support the new processor, all the problems described earlier can occur.

The processor configuration settings must be correct for the type of microprocessor installed in the system. If the core voltage level is set too high, the microprocessor will probably overheat slowly, or burn out, depending on the amount of voltage applied. Conversely, if the voltage level is configured too low for the installed processor, the system will most likely refuse to start. Likewise, setting the speed selection incorrectly can cause the system to think that a different processor is installed in the system.

For example, if an 850MHz Pentium III processor is installed in a system whose BIOS supported processor speeds only up to 600MHz, the BIOS will report a processor speed of only 600MHz during the POST portion of the startup. The system will be limited to running at 600MHz. For this reason, the capabilities of the system BIOS should always be examined when performing microprocessor upgrades.

However, as described earlier in this chapter, newer processors possess speed step capabilities that enable them to reduce their operating speeds in steps depending on their usage levels. This is a power-saving feature and must be considered before assuming that a newer system is incorrectly configured.

EXAM ALERT

Know why a processor would show an incorrect speed rating.

Similarly, different groups of PC enthusiasts, such as gamers, make a practice of manually configuring the microprocessor clock to run at a higher speed than the IC manufacturer suggests. This is referred to as *overclocking* the processor and is done to squeeze additional performance out of the system.

Because the basic microprocessor is running faster than designed, both the front-side bus and the PCI bus run faster than their stated values by a factor directly proportional to the amount that the microprocessor is overclocked. The additional speed also generates additional heat from both the processor and its supporting devices. This requires the installation of addition fans and cooling systems to prevent damage from the additional heat generated.

Challenge #1

Your company's board of directors approves your recommendation for upgrading existing systems as outlined in the previous chapter. When you upgrade the first system, you find that it is running at only 450MHz. What should you do to get the system up to the speed you recommended to the board?

Fans, Heat Sinks, and Cooling Systems

All Pentium processor requires the presence of a heat-sinking device and a microprocessor fan unit for cooling purposes. As Figure 3.13 illustrates, these devices come in many forms, including simple passive heat sinks and fan-cooled, active heat sinks.

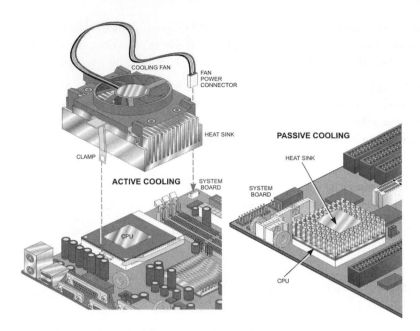

FIGURE 3.13 Typical microprocessor cooling systems.

Passive heat sinks are finned metal slabs that can be clipped or glued with a heat-transmitting adhesive (referred to as *thermal compound* or *paste*) onto the top of the microprocessor. The fins increase the surface area of the heat sink, enabling it to dissipate heat more rapidly. *Active heat sinks* add a fan unit to move air across the heat sink. The fan moves the heat away from the heat sink and the microprocessor more rapidly.

ATX-style systems employ power supplies that use a reverse-flow fan that brings in cool air from the back of the unit and blows it directly onto the microprocessor. For this to work properly, the system board must adhere to the ATX form factor guidelines and place the microprocessor in the correct position on the system board.

Slot-based cartridge processors (Pentium II, III, and 4 processors) also require special heat sink and fan support structures that work with the cartridge package. These units mount vertically on the system board beside the processor cartridge and provide support for the heat sink as well as the fan unit.

The support mechanism is designed so that it plugs into standard predrilled holes in the system board. For repair or upgrading purposes, the fan unit can be removed from the support mechanism and replaced.

Because slot processors are typically used in ATX-style systems, the processor cartridge assembly is typically mounted directly beneath the power supply vent to achieve additional cooling benefits.

In newer Pentium systems, the BIOS interrogates the processor during startup and configures it appropriately. This prevents the user from subjecting the processor to potentially destructive conditions, such as overclocking. In addition, these systems can monitor the health of the processor while it is in operation and take steps to compensate for problems such as overheating. This normally involves speeding up or slowing down the processor fan to maintain a given operating temperature.

The fan module must be one supported by the installed BIOS. If a fan unit is installed that does not have proper stepping in the BIOS routines, the system will not be able to correctly control the fan speed. Therefore, it may not be able to keep the processor cool enough for proper operation. Also, some fans are built better than others. For instance, fans that use ball bearings instead of slip ring bearings tend to run smoother and make less noise. However, they are usually more expensive than the slip ring versions.

BTX Thermal Module

The BTX form factor design is based on creating specific airflow zones within the case. The component responsible for generating the airflow is the BTX Thermal Module. The thermal module combines a heat sink and fan into a special duct that channels the air across the system board's main components. The duct fits tightly against large air vents in the front center portion of the case. The fan draws air in from the front and pushes it directly over the microprocessor mounted under the assembly in a linear flow pattern. The air continues toward the back of the case, passing over the graphics card and major chipset components. A fan in the power supply unit draws some of the air across the memory devices before exhausting it out through the rear of the unit. Figure 3.14 depicts the flow of air through the BTX case.

Advanced Cooling Systems

As system designers continue to push microprocessors for more speed, they also increase the amount of power that they dissipate. The latest microprocessor design techniques have created processors that generate more than 80 watts of power that must be dissipated as heat. This is comparable to the heat generated by a heat lamp. It is beyond the capabilities of most processor fans and heat sinks to effectively dissipate this much heat.

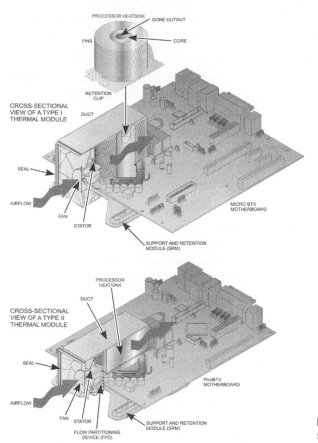

FIGURE 3.14 Airflow in a BTX system.

Simple air-cooling systems cannot create a large enough temperature differential to cool the processor. Therefore, system designers have begun to equip very high-speed systems with refrigerated cooling systems. Originally, the designers adopted water-based cooling systems that cooled and circulated water to carry heat away from the processor. Figure 3.15 depicts the components of a water-based cooling system typically used to cool processors that have been configured to run in overclocking conditions.

The water cooler system consists of the following:

► A water reservoir tank

► A water pump that circulates water throughout the cooling system

▶ A condenser coil radiator with fans that cool the water and exhaust heat into the outside atmosphere

▶ A CPU cooling block that connects directly to the microprocessor and extracts heat from it

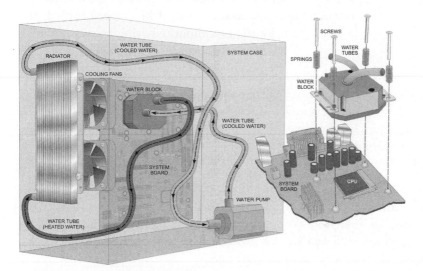

FIGURE 3.15 Water-based microprocessor coolers.

The water pump operates from inside the reservoir tank and forces cooling water through the system. Most of the pumps for these systems are adaptations of home aquarium pumps and are designed for 120Vac operation; therefore, they must have an external power cord.

The CPU cooling block consists of a copper-finned heat sink that mounts to a bracket installed around the microprocessor. Pentium 4 system boards have standard hole patterns already supplied to permit such devices to be attached to them. The heat sink is enclosed in a water jacket that circulates cooling water around the fins. This water jacket removes more heat from the processor faster than an air-cooled heat sink.

Heated water from the CPU cooler is pumped through the radiator. The radiator is composed of several coils of tubing to maximize the surface area that is used to dissipate heat. The additional fans push air across the coils and speed up the radiation process in the same manner as conventional CPU fans do for air-cooled heat sinks. The cooled water returns to the reservoir for recirculation.

Cache Memory

One method of increasing the memory-access speed of a computer is called *caching*. This memory management method assumes that most memory accesses are made within a limited block of addresses. Therefore, if the contents of these addresses are relocated into a special section of high-speed SRAM, the microprocessor could access these locations without requiring any wait states.

The original Intel Pentium had a built-in first-level cache that could be used for both instructions and data. The internal cache was divided into four 2KB blocks containing 128 sets of 16-byte lines each. Control of this cache is handled directly by the microprocessor. The microprocessor's internal first-level cache is also known as an *L1 cache*. Many of the older Pentium system boards extended the caching capability of the microprocessor by adding an external, second-level 256KB/512KB memory cache. The second-level cache became known as an *L2 cache*.

With the Pentium Pro, Intel moved the 256KB or 512KB L2 cache from the system board to the processor package. This design technique continued through the Pentium II and III slot processors so that the 256KB/512KB L2 cache resided in the microprocessor cartridge.

In its Celeron and Coppermine devices, Intel moved the L2 cache (128KB/256 KB and 256 KB/512 KB, respectively) onto the actual microprocessor die. Moving the L2 cache onto the die made the microprocessor directly responsible for managing the cache and enabled it to run at full speed with the microprocessor. In all these systems, no cache existed on the system board.

When Intel designed the Itanium processor, it built in capabilities for managing an additional external level of cache in the microprocessor cartridge. This additional cache level was dubbed *L3 cache*. The Xeon processor has continued this design concept and improved it by moving a 1MB or 2MB L3 cache onto the microprocessor die. Again, the external cache is able to run at full speed with the microprocessor.

The computer industry has taken a more liberal definition of L3 cache—it sometimes refers to L3 cache as cache memory mounted on system boards with processors that possess onboard L1 and L2 cache. Practical sizes for cache memories run between 16KB and 512KB. However, the newest microprocessors (Xeon and Itanium) used for server computers have created a third level: L3 cache. These microprocessors can support up to 4MB of cache in the cartridge.

EXAM ALERT

Know where the L1 cache memory is located in different Pentium class processors.

Exam Prep Questions

1. Which microprocessor has cache memory that operates at half the core bus speed of the other microprocessor sections?

   ○ **A.** Pentium Pro

   ○ **B.** Pentium II

   ○ **C.** Pentium III

   ○ **D.** Celeron

2. Which of the following is not a component of a Pentium II SEC cartridge?

   ○ **A.** Processor core

   ○ **B.** TAG RAM

   ○ **C.** 262-contact socket interface

   ○ **D.** L2 burst SRAM

3. What is the major difference between Pentium II and Pentium III microprocessors?

   ○ **A.** The L2 cache is enlarged to 512KB.

   ○ **B.** Improved microprocessor die.

   ○ **C.** Improved 128-bit system bus.

   ○ **D.** Lower voltage requirements.

4. Which types of system board sockets can accept a Pentium III microprocessor? (Select all that apply.)

   ○ **A.** Slot 1

   ○ **B.** Super Socket 7

   ○ **C.** Socket 370

   ○ **D.** Socket A

5. Which processors can be used in a Socket 370 system?

   ○ **A.** Pentium MMX, Celeron

   ○ **B.** Celeron, Pentium III

   ○ **C.** Pentium III, Pentium 4

   ○ **D.** Celeron, Duron

6. Which microprocessor can use a Slot 1 connection?

   ○ **A.** Athlon K7/550

   ○ **B.** Duron/600

   ○ **C.** Celeron/266

   ○ **D.** Pentium Pro

7. What is the appropriate socket for the original Celeron microprocessor?

   ○ **A.** Slot 1

   ○ **B.** Super Socket 7

   ○ **C.** Socket 370

   ○ **D.** Slot A

8. What is the appropriate socket for the Pentium II microprocessor?

   ○ **A.** Slot 1

   ○ **B.** Super Socket 7

   ○ **C.** Socket 370

   ○ **D.** Slot A

9. If you upgrade a 600MHz processor to a 1.00GHz version and the system still shows a 600MHz processor during the POST, what type of problem is indicated?

   ○ **A.** Insufficient RAM

   ○ **B.** Incompatible operating system

   ○ **C.** Incompatible motherboard BIOS

   ○ **D.** Defective microprocessor

10. What is the appropriate socket for the Pentium 4 microprocessor?

   ○ **A.** Socket A

   ○ **B.** Super Socket 7

   ○ **C.** Socket 370

   ○ **D.** Socket 423

11. What is the appropriate socket for the Duron microprocessor?

○ **A.** Socket A

○ **B.** Super Socket 7

○ **C.** Socket 370

○ **D.** Socket 423

12. What is the appropriate socket for the Pentium Pro microprocessor?

○ **A.** Socket 7

○ **B.** Super Socket 7

○ **C.** Socket 8

○ **D.** Socket 370

13. What is the appropriate socket for the Pentium MMX microprocessor?

○ **A.** Socket 7

○ **B.** Super Socket 7

○ **C.** Socket 8

○ **D.** Socket 370

14. Which processors can be used in a Slot A system board? (Select all that apply.)

○ **A.** Athlon K7/550

○ **B.** Duron/600

○ **C.** Celeron/266

○ **D.** Pentium II/233

15. Which microprocessor works with a 66MHz front-side bus?

○ **A.** P75

○ **B.** Pentium MMX

○ **C.** PIII/450

○ **D.** Duron/600

16. Explain how an older Socket 7 system knows what type of processor is installed in the system.

- ○ **A.** CMOS Setup utility
- ○ **B.** Interrogation of the microprocessor
- ○ **C.** Orientation of the microprocessor
- ○ **D.** Jumpers on the motherboard

Answers and Explanations

1. B. The Pentium II L1 cache is increased to 32KB, whereas the L2 cache operates with a half-speed bus.

2. C. The Pentium II's proprietary 242-contact socket design is referred to as the *Slot 1 specification*.

3. A. The original Pentium III processor (codenamed Katmai) was designed around the Pentium II core, but increased the L2 cache size to 512KB.

4. A, C. Intel followed the Pentium II processor with a new Slot 1–compatible design it called the *Pentium III*. Later versions of the Pentium III and Celeron processors were developed for the Intel Socket 370 specification.

5. B. Later versions of the Pentium III and Celeron processors were developed for the Intel Socket 370 specification.

6. C. Initially, the Celeron was packaged in the Slot 1 (SECC) cartridge.

7. A. The original Celeron used Slot 1.

8. A. The Pentium II used Slot 1. Refer to Table 3.3, "Microprodessor Characteristics."

9. C. If an 850MHz Pentium III processor were installed in a system whose BIOS supported processor speeds only up to 600MHz, the BIOS would report a processor speed of only 600MHz during the POST portion of the startup. The system will actually be limited to running at 600MHz.

10. D. The Pentium 4 uses Socket 423 or Socket 478. Refer to Table 3.3, "Microprocessor Characteristics."

11. A. The Duron uses Socket A. Refer to Table 3.3, "Microprocessor Characteristics."

12. C. The Pentium Pro used Socket 8. Refer to Table 3.3, "Microprocessor Characteristics."

13. B. The Pentium MMX uses Super Socket 7. Refer to Table 3.3, "Microprocessor Characteristics."

14. A, B. The Athlon K7 version runs between 500MHz and 700MHz, provides a 128KB L1 cache and a 512KB L2 cache, employs a 100MHz system bus, and uses Slot A. The Duron processor is a Celeron clone processor that conforms to the AMD Socket A specification.

15. B. In the Pentium MMX processor, the multimedia and communications processing capabilities of the original Pentium device were extended by the addition of 57 multimedia-specific instructions to the instruction set. Intel also increased the onboard L1 cache size to 32KB. The cache has been divided into two separate 16KB caches: the instruction cache and the data cache. The typical L2 cache used with the MMX is 256KB or 512KB, and employs a 66MHz system bus.

16. D. The Socket 7 specification enabled system boards to be configured for different types of microprocessors using different operating speeds. In older systems, the operating speed of the microprocessor was configured through external settings (jumpers on the motherboard).

Challenge Solution

1. The old BIOS supported processor speeds up to only 450MHz. You now have processors capable of running 1GHz. You must upgrade the system BIOS to support higher operating speeds for the processor. With many Slot 1 system boards, you will not have any problems upgrading to 1GHz, provided that you get the newest BIOS version; however, this is not true for every system board. You should have checked the chipset and BIOS information before purchasing the new microprocessors. There is a chance that you will be able to upgrade to only 600MHz.

CHAPTER FOUR

Random Access Memory

Terms you'll need to understand:

✓ DRAM

✓ SRAM

✓ SDRAM

✓ DDR / DDR2 RAM

✓ Rambus

✓ Parity checking

✓ Error Correction Code

✓ DIMM

✓ Refresh

✓ Cache memory

✓ RIMM

Techniques to master:

✓ Essentials 1.1—Identify the fundamental principles of using personal computers

✓ Identify the names, purposes and characteristics of memory

✓ Types of memory (for instance, DRAM, SRAM, SDRAM, DDR / DDR2, RAMBUS)

✓ Operational characteristics

    ✓ Memory chips (8, 16, 32)

    ✓ Parity versus nonparity

    ✓ ECC versus non-ECC

    ✓ Single-sided versus double-sided

SRAM and DRAM

This chapter covers the memory section of the CompTIA A+ Certification—Essentials examination under Objective 1.1. The system's microprocessor relies on the system board's memory units to correctly store and reproduce the data and programs that it needs for its operations. The operation of the system's memory units is so critical that if a single bit gets lost or becomes corrupt, a major interrupt error is created that in most cases results in a shutdown of the system.

Because the operation of the system's RAM structures is so critical, every technician should be aware of the characteristics of different RAM devices and should be able to determine whether a particular device is suited to a given application and whether it physically fits the system in question.

All the memory types designated under this objective are based on two types of semiconductor RAM technologies: static RAM (SRAM) and dynamic RAM (DRAM). Although they both perform the same basic storage functions, their methods of doing so are completely different. SRAM stores bits in a manner so that they will remain valid as long as power to the chip is not interrupted. DRAM requires periodic refreshing to maintain data, even if electrical power is applied to the chip.

Dynamic RAM stores data bits on rows and columns of integrated circuit (IC) capacitors. Capacitors lose their charge over time. This is the reason that dynamic RAM devices require data-refreshing operations. Static RAM uses IC transistors to store data and maintain it as long as power is supplied to the chip. Its transistor structure makes SRAM memory much faster than ordinary DRAM. However, it can store only about 25% as much data in a given size as a DRAM device. Therefore, it tends to be more expensive to create large memories with SRAM.

Whether the RAM is made up of static or dynamic RAM devices, all RAM systems have the disadvantage of being volatile. This means that any data stored in RAM will be lost if power to the computer is disrupted for any reason. On the other hand, both types of RAM have the advantage of being fast, and are capable of being written to and read from with equal ease. ROM, on the other hand, is classified as nonvolatile memory, meaning that data stored in ROM is not lost when the power is shut down.

SRAM is used in smaller memory systems, such as cache and video memories, where the added cost of refresh circuitry would increase the cost-per-bit of storage. Cache memory is a special memory structure that works directly with the microprocessor. Video memory is a specialized area that holds information to be displayed on the screen. DRAM is used in larger memory systems, such as the system's main memory, where the extra cost of refresh circuitry is distributed over a greater number of bits and is offset by the reduced operating cost associated with DRAM chips.

> **EXAM ALERT**
>
> You should be aware that all forms of RAM are volatile, and you should know what that means in terms of storing data.

Advanced DRAM

Both types of RAM are brought together to create an improved DRAM, referred to as *Enhanced DRAM (EDRAM)*. By integrating an SRAM component into a DRAM device, a performance improvement of 40% can be gained. An independent write path allows the system to input new data without affecting the operation of the rest of the chip. These devices are used primarily in L2 cache memories.

Another modified DRAM type, referred to as *Synchronous DRAM (SDRAM)*, employs special internal registers and clock signals to organize data requests from memory. Unlike asynchronous memory modules, SDRAM devices operate synchronously with the system clock. After an initial Read or Write access has been performed on the memory device, additional accesses can be conducted in a high-speed burst mode that operates at one access per clock cycle.

Special internal configurations also speed up the operation of the SDRAM memory. The SDRAM device employs internal interleaving techniques that permit one side of the memory to be accessed while the other half is completing an operation. Because there are two versions of SDRAM (two-clock and four-clock), you must make certain that the SDRAM type you are using is supported by the system board's chipset.

Advanced SDRAM

Advanced versions of SDRAM include the following:

> ▶ EDO-DRAM—Extended Data Out (EDO) memory increased the speed at which RAM operations were conducted by cutting out the 10-nanosecond wait time normally required between issuing memory addresses. This was accomplished by not disabling the data bus pin between bus cycles. EDO is an advanced type of fast page-mode DRAM, also referred to as hyper page-mode DRAM. The advantage of EDO-DRAM was encountered when multiple sequential memory accesses

were performed. By not turning off the data pin, each successive access after the first access was accomplished in two clock cycles rather than three.

▶ SDR-SDRAM—Single Data Rate SDRAM. This version of SDRAM transfers data on one edge of the system clock signal.

▶ SGRAM—Synchronous Graphics RAM. This type of SDRAM is designed to handle high-performance graphics operations. It features dual-bank operations that permit two memory pages to be open at the same time.

▶ ESDRAM—Enhanced SDRAM. This advanced form of SDRAM employs small cache buffers to provide high data access rates. This type of SDRAM is used in L2 cache applications.

▶ VCM-SDRAM—Virtual Channel Memory SDRAM. This memory design has onboard cache buffers to improve multiple access times and to provide I/O transfers on each clock cycle. VCM-SDRAM requires a special chipset to support it.

▶ DDR-SDRAM—Double Data Rate SDRAM. This is a form of SDR-SDRAM that can transfer data on both the leading and falling edges of each clock cycle. This capability doubles the data transfer rate of traditional SDR-DRAM. It is available in a number of standard formats including SODIMMs for portables.

▶ EDDR-SDRAM—Enhanced DDR-SDRAM. An advanced form of DDR-SRAM that employs onboard cache registers to deliver improved performance.

▶ DDR2—Double Data Rate SDRAM 2. DDR2 is an improved version of the DDR memory devices that effectively conducts data transfers four times on each bus cycle. These devices employ advanced electrical interface technologies to improve the effective clock frequency of the memory module over older DDR devices. These interface technologies include bigger prefetch buffers, off-chip driver devices, and on-chip termination. Improved manufacturing processes enable the DDR2 operating voltage to be dropped to 1.8V. DDR2 devices are not compatible with DDR slots. The notch in the edge connector of the DDR2 device is in a different location than that of a DDR module.

▶ RDRAM—Rambus DRAM. A proprietary type of synchronous dynamic RAM designed by the Rambus Corporation. At one point, RDRAM was being considered as the main memory choice for all Intel processors, but licensing discussions did not work out and usage of RDRAM has diminished significantly. The technology has been given a variety of names, including Rambus DRAM (RDRAM), Direct Rambus DRAM (DRDRAM), and RIMM. However, the term RIMM actually refers to the plug-in memory module form factor used with the RDRAM devices.

SRAM

Like Dynamic RAM, SRAM is available in different types. Many of the memory organization techniques described for DRAM are also implemented in SRAM:

- ▶ Asynchronous SRAM—Standard SRAM that delivers data from the memory to the microprocessor and returns it to the cache in one clock cycle.

- ▶ Synchronous SRAM—Uses special clock signals and buffer storage to deliver data to the CPU in one clock cycle after the first cycle. The first address is stored and used to retrieve the data while the next address is on its way to the cache.

- ▶ Pipeline SRAM—Uses three clock cycles to fetch the first data and then accesses addresses within the selected page on each clock cycle.

- ▶ Burst-mode SRAM—Loads a number of consecutive data locations from the cache, over several clock cycles, based on a single address from the microprocessor.

In digital electronics terms, a *buffer* is a holding area for data shared by devices that operate at different speeds or have different priorities. These devices permit a memory module to operate without the delays that other devices impose. Some types of SDRAM memory modules contain buffer registers directly on the module. The *buffer registers* hold and retransmit the data signals through the memory chips.

The data-holding aspect permits the module to coordinate transfers with the outside system. The retransmission factor lowers the signal drain on the host system and enables the memory module to hold more memory chips. Registered memory and unbuffered memory modules cannot be mixed. The design of the chipset's memory controller dictates which types of memory the computer can use.

Memory Overhead

DRAM devices, commonly used for the system's RAM, require periodic refreshing of their data to prevent it from disappearing. Some refreshing is performed by the system's normal memory reading and writing cycles. However, additional circuitry must be used to ensure that every bit in all the memory registers is refreshed within the allotted time frame.

The extra circuitry and inconvenience associated with refreshing may initially make DRAM memory seem like a distant second choice behind static RAM. However, because of the simplicity of DRAM's internal structure, the bit-storage capacity of a DRAM chip is much greater than that of a similar static RAM device, and it offers a much lower rate of power consumption. Both of these factors contributed to making DRAM memory the economical choice in certain RAM memory systems.

EXAM ALERT

Be aware of what DRAM refreshing is and why it is performed.

Error Checking and Correcting

Another design factor associated with RAM is data error detection. A single incorrect bit can shut down the entire system instantly. With bits constantly moving in and out of RAM, it is crucial that all the bits be transferred correctly. The most popular form of error detection in PC compatibles is *parity checking*. In this method, an extra bit is added to each word as it's stored in RAM and checked each time the word is accessed. Like refreshing, parity checking requires additional circuitry and memory overhead to operate.

EXAM ALERT

Know that parity is a method of checking stored data for errors by adding an additional bit to each word when it is stored in memory.

Parity checking is a simple self-test used to detect RAM read-back errors. When a data byte is stored in memory, the occurrences of logic "1s" in the byte are added together by the parity generator/checker chip. This chip produces a parity bit that is added to, and stored along with, the data byte. Therefore, the data byte becomes a 9-bit word. Whenever the data word is read back from the memory, the parity bit is reapplied to the parity generator and recalculated.

The recalculated parity value is then compared to the original parity value stored in memory. If the values do not match, a parity-error condition occurs and an error message is generated. Traditionally, there are two approaches to generating parity bits; the parity bit may be generated so that the total number of 1-bits equals an even number (*even parity*), or an odd number (*odd parity*).

To enable parity checking, an additional ninth bit is added to each byte stored in DRAM. On older systems, an extra memory chip was included with each bank of DRAM. In newer units, the extra storage is built in to the DIMM modules. Whether a particular system employs parity check depends on its chipset. Many newer chipsets have moved away from using parity checking. In these cases, DIMMs with parity capability can be used, but the parity function will not function. In Pentium systems, the system board's user's guide or the BIOS Extended CMOS Setup screen should be consulted to determine whether parity is supported. If so, the parity function can be enabled through this screen.

When a parity error occurs, a Non-Maskable Interrupt (NMI) signal is generated in the system, causing the BIOS to execute its NMI handler routine. This routine will normally place a parity error message onscreen, along with an option to shut down the system or to continue. In other cases, the system will show a short memory count during the POST and lock up without an error message.

> **NOTE**
>
> Another possible outcome when a parity error occurs is that the system will count the memory, lock up, and reboot itself. If the memory error occurs higher in the physical memory device, this situation can occur after the operating system and applications have been loaded and started running.

> **EXAM ALERT**
>
> Be aware of the types of problems that can create an NMI error and what the consequences of these problems are.

Error Correction Code (ECC) SDRAM is a type of SDRAM that includes a fault detection/correction circuit that can detect and fix memory errors without shutting down the system. Occasionally, the information in a single memory bit can change states, which, in turn, causes a memory error to occur when the data is read from memory.

Using a parity memory scheme, the system can detect that a bit has flipped when the memory is read, but it can only display a "Parity Error" message and freeze up. Although this prevents the bad data from being used or written away in the system, it also erases all current data from RAM. An ECC memory module has the capability to detect and correct a single-bit error or to detect errors in two bits. The latter condition causes a parity error shutdown to occur as described earlier.

EXAM ALERT

Know the difference between parity and ECC error-detection systems.

In some applications, stability is of the utmost concern for system design. In these systems, advanced RAM types that include ECC capabilities are used. ECC provides additional data integrity by detecting and often correcting errors in the information they process. However, the additional data manipulation that goes on inside the memory devices causes ECC RAM to provide lower performance than its non-ECC counterparts.

Challenge #1

You are called on to check out a failing computer in the production department. When you arrive, you find that the system is continually locking up and rebooting during the POST process. What type of problem does the system probably have and what should you do about it?

Cache Memory Operations

One method of increasing the memory-access speed of a computer is called *caching*. This memory-management method assumes that most memory accesses are made within a limited block of addresses. Therefore, if the contents of these addresses are relocated into a special section of high-speed SRAM, the microprocessor can access these locations without requiring any wait states. Cache memory structures are normally small to keep the cost of the system as low as possible. However, it is also very fast, even in comparison to fast DRAM devices.

Cache memory operations require a great deal of intelligent circuitry to operate and monitor the cache effectively. The cache controller circuitry must monitor the microprocessor's memory-access instructions to determine whether the specified data is stored in the cache. If the information is in the cache, the control circuitry can present it to the microprocessor without incurring any wait states. This is referred to as a *hit*. If the information is not located in the cache, the access is passed on to the system's RAM and it is declared a *miss*.

The primary objective of the cache memory's control system is to maximize the ratio of hits to total accesses (hit rate) so that the majority of memory accesses are performed without wait states. One way to do this is to make the cache memory area as large as possible (thus raising the possibility of the desired information being in the cache). However, the relative cost, energy consumption, and physical size of SRAM devices work against this technique. Practical sizes for cache memories working directly with the microprocessor run between 16KB and 512KB. Additional levels of onboard and remote cache can be much larger. However, these caches require more management circuitry.

The Intel 80486 and the original Pentium microprocessors (Pentium I and Pentium MMX) had a built-in first-level cache, referred to as *L1 cache*, that was used for both instructions and data. The internal cache in these units was divided into four 2KB blocks containing 128 sets of 16-byte lines each. Control of the internal cache was handled directly by the microprocessor. However, many system boards that supported these processors extended their caching capabilities by adding an external, second-level 256KB/512KB memory cache, referred to as an *L2 cache*.

With the Pentium Pro processor, Intel moved the 256KB or 512KB L2 cache from the system board to the processor package. This design technique continued through the Pentium II and III slot processors, so that the 256KB /512KB L2 cache resided in the microprocessor cartridge. In its Celeron and Coppermine devices, Intel moved the L2 cache (128KB/256KB and 256KB/512KB, respectively) onto the actual microprocessor die. Moving the L2 cache onto the die made the microprocessor directly responsible for managing the cache and enabled it to run at full speed with the microprocessor. In all these systems, no cache existed on the system board.

When Intel designed the Itanium processor, it built in capabilities for managing an additional external level of cache in the microprocessor cartridge. This additional cache level was dubbed *L3 cache*. The Xeon processor has continued this design concept and improved it by moving a 1MB or 2MB L3 cache onto the microprocessor die. Again, the external cache is able to run at full speed with the microprocessor. The Pentium 4 Extreme Edition processor from Intel and upcoming AMD quad-core Opteron processors include an L3 cache as standards.

The computer industry has taken a more liberal definition of L3 cache, sometimes referring to L3 cache as cache memory mounted on system boards where the processors already possess onboard L1 and L2 cache.

RAM Packaging

Pentium system boards employ dual inline memory modules (DIMMs) to fill the system's onboard RAM functions. DIMMs are made up of a number of IC memory devices mounted on a printed circuit board. The printed circuit board has a number of contacts along its lower edge that slips into a DIMM socket mounted on the system board.

Standard DIMM packages come in 168-pin modules for older EDO, FPM, PC66, PC100, and PC133 SDRAM memory, 184-pin boards for DDR memory, and 240-pin boards for DDR2 memory. These modules are designed to work efficiently with different Pentium-class microprocessors and memory bus schemes. The number of ICs on the module may vary and may be electrically arranged to provide various storage capacity/word size options. Figure 4.1 illustrates the different types of DIMMs. To use any of these modules, the system board must have DIMM slots that match the module and a chipset that can support that type of memory.

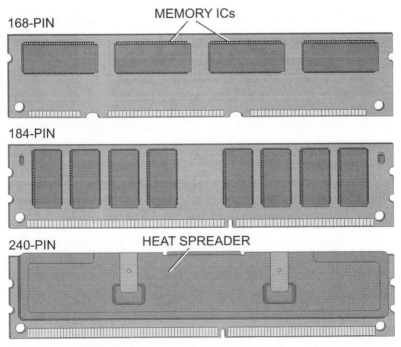

FIGURE 4.1 DIMM types.

DIMM storage capacities are typically specified in an a-by-b format. Under this format, you can derive the total capacity of the device (in bytes) by multiplying the two numbers and then dividing by eight (or nine for DIMMs with parity chips).

Non-parity DIMMs typically come in 32-bit and 64-bit bus widths to service more powerful microprocessors. However, DIMMs that include a parity-checking bit for each byte of storage come in 36-bit and 72-bit versions.

When examining DRAM memory, you will encounter some DRAM package configurations designated as SS and some as DS. This refers to *single-sided* modules and *double-sided* modules. Single-sided modules place all the DRAM chips on one side of the module, whereas double-sided modules place half of the total memory on each side of the module.

There are many theories about how this affects memory performance; for example, the two sides are two separate banks of memory and take time to switch between them, or separating the chips on each side of the module lets them run cooler and perform more efficiently.

In reality, the performance of a DRAM module is contolled by the types of IC devices it employs and how the module designer lays out the physical connections on the printed circuit board. However, you should not mix these two types of memory even if they have the same capacity. You should consult the system board's user's/installation guide to determine what types of memory it will support.

RIMM

RIMMs are special 168-, 184-, and 242-pin memory modules designed to hold the RDRAM devices developed by the Rambus Corporation. Although these devices are often referred to as Rambus Inline Memory Modules, according to the Rambus company this is not actually the source for the acronym RIMM.

Figure 4.2 shows that RIMMs look similar to DIMMs. However, they have a different pin and notch arrangement. The RDRAM high-speed transfer modes generate considerably more heat than normal DIMMs. Therefore, RIMM modules include an aluminum heat shield, called a *heat spreader*, to protect the chips from overheating. Newer SDRAM technologies have adopted this heat sink feature with their DDR and DDR2 memory modules.

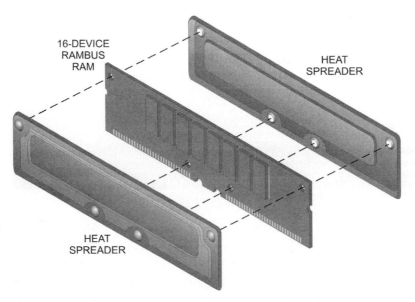

16-DEVICE RAMBUS RAM

HEAT SPREADER

HEAT SPREADER

FIGURE 4.2 RIMM modules.

The Rambus design requires that its memory modules be installed in sets of two. Any unfilled memory slots must have terminators (referred to as *CRIMMs*).

RAM Speed Ratings

Another important factor to consider when dealing with RAM is its speed, which is generally marked on the RAM module. DRAM modules are marked with a numbering system that indicates the number of clock cycles required for the initial read operation, followed by information about the number of reads and cycles required to move a burst of data. For example, a fast page-mode DRAM marked as 6-3-3-3 requires 6 cycles for the initial read and 3 cycles for each of three successive reads. This will move an entire 4-byte block of data. EDO and FPM operated with bus speeds up to 66MHz.

SDRAM devices are marked differently. Because they are designed to run synchronously with the system clock and use no wait states (they work at the same speed as the front-side bus [FSB]), a marking of 3:3:3 at 100MHz on an SDRAM module specifies that the following:

▶ The CAS signal setup time is three bus cycles.

▶ The RAS to CAS changeover time is three cycles.

▶ The RAS signal setup time is three clock cycles.

The bus speed is specified in MHz. These memory modules have been produced in the following versions:

▶ PC66 (66MHz or 15 nanoseconds)

▶ PC83 (83MHz or 12 nanoseconds)

▶ PC100 (100MHz or 10 nanoseconds)

▶ PC133 (133MHz or 8 nanoseconds)

▶ PC150 (150MHz or 4.5 nanoseconds)

▶ PC166 (166MHz or 4 nanoseconds)

The PC66 and PC83 specifications were the first versions produced using this system. However, they never gained widespread acceptance. On the other hand, the PC100, PC133, PC150, and PC166 versions did gain acceptance.

Continued advancements in memory module design have made the MHz and CAS setup time ratings obsolete. Onboard buffering, along with advanced clocking and access strategies, have made these measurements inconsequential. Instead, memory performance is now measured by total data *throughput* (also referred to as *bandwidth*) and in terms of gigabytes per second (GBps). For example, some of the new standard specifications include the following DDR modules designed for use with double-pumped front-side buses:

▶ PC1600 (1.6GBps/200MHz/2:2:2)

▶ PC2100 (2.1GBps/266MHz/2:3:3)

▶ PC2600 (2.6GBps/333MHz/3:3:3)

▶ PC3200 (3.2GBps/400MHz/3:3:3)

To understand this relationship, multiply the actual clock speed (100MHz) by the data rate (x2). This gives the effective clock speed of the memory module (200MHz). Then multiply the data rate and the bus size (8 bytes) together to produce an effective data transfer rate of 1600 MBps (1.6GBps).

Likewise, a number of specifications exist for Double Data Rate 2 (DDR2) modules designed for use with quad-pumped front-side buses. These include the following:

▶ PC2-3200 (3.2GBps/200MHz/3:3:3)

▶ PC2-4200 (4.267GBps/266MHz/3:3:3)

▶ PC2-5300 (5.333GBps/333MHz/3:3:3)

▶ PC2-6400 (6.4GBps/400MHz/3:3:3)

The PC2-3200 DDR2 memory module running at 200MHz using DDR2-400 memory devices yields a bandwidth of 3.2GBps. The PC2-XXXX designation denotes that the module is built on DDR2 technology.

Like SDRAM, DDR, and DDR2 memory, RDRAM memory has been used to create standardized memory modules that include the following:

▶ PC-600 RDRAM (1.2GBps/300MHz)

▶ PC-700 RDRAM (1.42GBps/355MHz)

▶ PC-800 RDRAM (1.6GBps/400MHz)

▶ PC-133 RDRAM (1.066 GBps/133MHz)

▶ PC-1066 RDRAM (2.133GBps/533MHz)

▶ PC1200 RDRAM (2.4GBps/600MHz)

▶ PC-3200 dual-channel RDRAM (3.2GBps/400MHz)

▶ PC-4200 dual-channel RDRAM (4.2GBps/533MHz)

▶ PC-4800 dual-channel RDRAM (4.8GBps/600MHz)

▶ PC-6400 dual-channel RDRAM (6.4GBps/800MHz)

EXAM ALERT

Be able to recognize memory module types and correlate them to the bus speed specifications.

The system board's documentation will provide information about the types of devices it can use and their speed ratings. This information can also be obtained from the system board manufacturer's website. If not available there, some memory manufacturers provide this information on their websites. It is important to install RAM that is compatible with the bus speed the system is running.

Normally, installing RAM that is rated faster than the bus speed will not cause problems. However, installing slower RAM, or mixing RAM speed ratings in a system can cause the system to not start or to periodically lock up.

EXAM ALERT

Be aware of the consequences of mixing RAM with different speed ratings within a system.

Dual Channel Memory

All of the major memory technologies (DDR, DDR2, and RDRAM) have adopted dual channel memory architectures to effectively double data throughput between the RAM modules and the North Bridge. Dual channel systems employ two 64-bit data channels with two independent memory controllers to create a total bandwidth of 128-bits per transfer between the memory modules and the microprocessor. For example, the bandwidth of a PC-1600 DDR module using dual channel architecture would be boosted from 1.6GBps to 3.2GBps.

Dual channel memory is typically installed in matching pairs. It is possible to use different memory module sizes and speeds in some system boards, but other boards will have compatibility issues. Therefore, manufacturers sell dual channel memory modules in matched pairs.

Exam Prep Questions

1. Which of the following qualifies memory as volatile?

   ◯ **A.** The data disappears if the power goes off.

   ◯ **B.** The data will not disappear if the power goes off.

   ◯ **C.** The data is rewritable.

   ◯ **D.** The component is a potential fire hazard.

2. Which type of memory is considered volatile?

   ◯ **A.** RAM

   ◯ **B.** Magnetic memory

   ◯ **C.** ROM BIOS

   ◯ **D.** CD-ROM disks

3. Which type of RAM is faster, EDO-DRAM or fast page-mode DRAM?

   ◯ **A.** EDO-DRAM is faster.

   ◯ **B.** Fast page-mode DRAM is faster.

   ◯ **C.** They are both the same.

   ◯ **D.** There is no such thing as fast page-mode DRAM.

4. What is the process of recharging a DRAM's memory bits called?

   ◯ **A.** Strobe

   ◯ **B.** Latency

   ◯ **C.** Refresh

   ◯ **D.** Survey

5. What is the term used to describe the method of checking memory for errors by adding a status bit to each byte?

   ◯ **A.** ECC

   ◯ **B.** CAS

   ◯ **C.** Parity

   ◯ **D.** Refreshing

6. What type of system error will a memory parity error create?

    ◯ **A.** A fatal exception error

    ◯ **B.** An NMI error

    ◯ **C.** A corrupt Windows operating system file

    ◯ **D.** A GPF error

7. What method is used to correct single-bit errors in RAM?

    ◯ **A.** Refreshing

    ◯ **B.** Parity

    ◯ **C.** ECC

    ◯ **D.** Latency

8. Where is the L1 cache located in a PC system?

    ◯ **A.** On the RAM

    ◯ **B.** On the motherboard

    ◯ **C.** On the microprocessor PCB

    ◯ **D.** On the microprocessor die

9. How many total bits need to be stored in RAM to provide parity for a 64-bit data bus?

    ◯ **A.** None

    ◯ **B.** 64

    ◯ **C.** 72

    ◯ **D.** 128

10. What are the effects of mixing RAM modules with different speed ratings?

    ◯ **A.** The system will run at the speed of the slowest RAM stick.

    ◯ **B.** The system will run normally.

    ◯ **C.** The system will run at the speed of the memory bus.

    ◯ **D.** The system may not run, or will crash periodically.

11. If the RAM count presented during the POST does not equal the amount of RAM actually installed in the system, what type(s) of problem is the system having? (Select all that apply.)

   ○ **A.** Wrong RAM speed

   ○ **B.** Mixed RAM types

   ○ **C.** Split-bank RAM arrangement

   ○ **D.** Voltage regulation from the power supply

12. Cache memory is used to _____.

   ○ **A.** Increase the speed of data access

   ○ **B.** Increase the size of memory available to programs

   ○ **C.** Store data in nonvolatile memory

   ○ **D.** Augment the memory used for the operating system kernel

13. Which of the following are types of RAM? (Select all that apply.)

   ○ **A.** RDRAM

   ○ **B.** ECC SDRAM

   ○ **C.** CAS DRAM

   ○ **D.** ASYNC RAM

14. What is the clock speed for a DDR 1600 DIMM?

   ○ **A.** 133MHz

   ○ **B.** 200MHz

   ○ **C.** 233MHz

   ○ **D.** 300MHz

Answers and Explanations

1. A. Whether the RAM is made up of static or dynamic RAM devices, all RAM systems have the disadvantage of being volatile. This means that any data stored in RAM will be lost if power to the computer is disrupted for any reason. ROM, on the other hand, is classified as nonvolatile memory.

2. A. Whether the RAM is made up of static or dynamic RAM devices, all RAM systems have the disadvantage of being volatile. This means that any data stored in RAM will be lost if power to the computer is disrupted for any reason. On the other hand, both types of RAM have the advantage of being fast, and are capable of being written to and read from with equal ease. ROM, on the other hand, is classified as non-volatile memory.

3. A. Extended Data Out (EDO) memory increases the speed at which RAM operations are conducted by cutting out the 10-nanosecond wait time normally required between issuing memory addresses. This is accomplished by not disabling the data bus pins between bus cycles. EDO is an advanced type of fast page-mode DRAM also referred to as *hyper page-mode* DRAM. The advantage of EDO-DRAM is encountered when multiple sequential memory accesses are performed. By not turning off the data pin, each successive access after the first access is accomplished in two clock cycles rather than three.

4. C. DRAM requires periodic refreshing to maintain data, even if electrical power is applied to the chip.

5. C. The most popular form of error detection in PC compatibles is parity checking. In this method, an extra bit is added to each word in RAM and checked each time it is used. Parity checking is a simple self-test used to detect RAM read-back errors. Like refreshing, parity checking requires additional circuitry and memory overhead to operate.

6. B. When a parity error occurs, an NMI signal is co-generated in the system, causing the BIOS to execute its NMI handler routine. This routine will normally place a parity error message onscreen, along with an option to shut down the system or to continue. In other cases, the system will show a short memory count during the POST and lock up without an error message. Another possibility is that the system will count the memory, lock up, and reboot itself. If the memory error occurs higher in the physical memory device, this situation can occur after the operating system and applications have been loaded and started running.

7. C. Using a parity memory scheme, the system can detect that a bit has flipped when the memory is read, but it can only display a "Parity Error" message and freeze up. Although this prevents the bad data from being used or written away in the system, it also erases all current data from RAM. An ECC memory module has the capability to detect and correct a single-bit error, or to detect errors in two bits.

8. D. The microprocessor's internal first-level cache is also known as an *L1 cache*.

9. C. DIMMs come in 36- and 72-bit versions that include a parity checking bit for each byte of storage (for example, a 36-bit DIMM provides 32 data bits and 4 parity bits—one for each byte of data).

10. D. Installing slower RAM or mixing RAM speed ratings within a system may cause it not to start or to periodically lock up.

11. C. The system may have an incorrect RAM module installed in a split-bank system board arrangement. Using wrong RAM speed or mixed RAM types can cause the system to lock up, but should not produce a short RAM count. The system could also have a bad RAM module installed.

12. A. One method of increasing the memory-access speed of a computer is called *caching*.

13. A, B. RDRAM and ECC SDRAM are both types of actual RAM modules. There are no such devices as CAS DRAMs or ASYNC RAMs.

14. B. The effective clock speed of the memory module (200MHz) is the effective data transfer rate of 1600MBps divided by the bus size (8 bytes).

Challenge Solution

1. Even though there is no mention on the screen of a parity error or memory failure, the fact that the failure occurs during the POST indicates a hardware failure of some type. From the information presented in this chapter, you should be able to determine that the symptoms presented seem to indicate that you may have a bad memory location in a RAM device. You must isolate the bad device and replace it with one that will work properly.

CHAPTER FIVE

Data Storage Systems

Terms you'll need to understand:

✓ Thumb drive

✓ SCSI interface

✓ PATA interface

✓ SATA interface

✓ Flash drive

✓ Tape drives

✓ SD card

✓ Hard disk drives

✓ Flash memory

✓ CD-ROM drives

✓ DVD drives

✓ RAID systems

✓ Memory Stick

✓ CompactFlash cards

Techniques to master:

Essentials 1.1—Identify the fundamental principles of using personal computers.

✓ Identify the names, purposes, and characteristics of storage devices.

✓ FDD

✓ HDD

✓ CD/DVD/RW (for example, drive speeds, media types)

✓ Removable storage (tape drive, solid state such as thumb drive, flash and SD cards, USB, external CD-RW and hard drives)

Introduction

This chapter covers the storage devices areas of the CompTIA A+ Certification—Essentials examination under Objective 1.1.

All personal computers include one or more mass storage subsystems. The most widely used mass storage devices have typically involved covering some medium (such as disks or tape) with a magnetic coating. However, optical storage technologies such as compact discs (CDs) and digital versatile discs (DVDs) have made great inroads into the digital data storage market. In addition, many small form factor flash storage technologies have been introduced to the PC market.

Modern PC systems feature hard drives with storage capacities that typically range well into the hundreds of gigabytes (GB) of storage as standard equipment. The physical makeup of a hard disk subsystem is depicted in Figure 5.1. It involves a controller (either on an I/O card or built in to the system board), a a signal cable, a power cable, and a disk drive unit. In some cases, floppy and hard disk drive signal cables may look similar. However, some slight differences in their construction prevent them from being compatible.

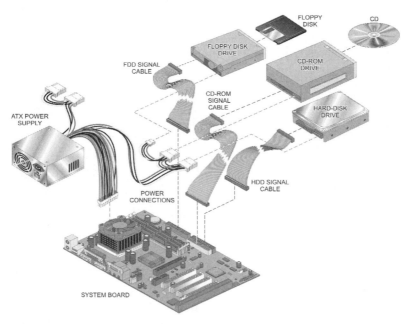

FIGURE 5.1 Components of the HDD subsystem.

The basic organization of both hard and floppy disk drives is similar in many respects. Both have precision synchronous motors with drive spindles that turn the disk(s), and a set of movable R/W (read/write) heads that are positioned by a digital stepper motor, or voice coil. In addition, both systems have intelligent control circuitry to position the R/W head and to facilitate the transfer of information between the disk and the host PC's memory. Figure 5.2 depicts the major components of a typical magnetic disk drive system.

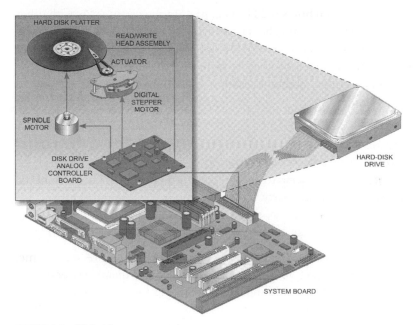

FIGURE 5.2 Disk drive components.

The heart of the disk drive's circuitry is the disk-drive controller. The controller is responsible for providing the necessary interfacing between the disk drive and the computer's I/O channel. It does this by decoding the computer's instructions to the disk drive, and generating the control signals that the disk drive must have to carry out the instruction. The controller must also convert back and forth between the parallel data format of the computer's bus and the serial format of the disk drive.

In addition, the controller must accurately position the R/W heads, direct the read and write operations, check and correct data received from the processor, generate error-correction codes for outbound data, and mark the location of defective sectors on the disk, closing them to use. After all of these responsibilities, the disk controller must also provide addressing for the tracks and sectors on the disk, and control the transfer of information to and from the internal memory.

EXAM ALERT

Memorize the major components that make up a magnetic disk drive and their functions.

The system's CMOS setup holds the HDD configuration settings. As with other configuration settings, these must be set correctly for the installed drive. Typical HDD information required for the CMOS setup includes its capacity, the number of cylinders, the number of read/write heads, the number of sectors per track, the amount of signal precompensation applied, and the track number to be used as the landing zone for the read/write heads when the drive is shut down.

In Pentium-class systems, the PnP BIOS and operating system work with system-level drives to autodetect the drive and supply its configuration information to the CMOS Setup utility. Otherwise, this information must be obtained from the drive manufacturer or a third-party technical support center and then entered manually. Most BIOS tables also provide a user-definable HDD entry, where the drive's geometry values can be entered manually into the CMOS settings.

The other important hard-disk drive specifications to consider are access time, seek time, data transfer rate, and storage capacity. These quantities designate how much data the drive can hold, how fast it can get to a specific part of the data, and how fast it can move it to the system.

Personal Video Recorders

Personal video recorders (PVRs), also known as *digital video recorders (DVRs)*, are hard disk drive based devices designed to record digitized audio and video for storage and replay. These devices have become very popular with television viewers because they are able to perform recording and replay functions more simply than existing video cassette recorders do. However, they have also been an important component in the development of media center PCs that allow users to integrate their PC functions with audio/video entertainment systems in their homes and offices.

There are two types of PVRs: PC-based PVRs and standalone PVRs. PC-based PVR systems employ a video capture card to capture and digitize video images in MPEG-1 or MPEG-2 formats for storage on the hard drive. Standalone PVRs are designed specifically to be digital video recorders. These units contain a firmware-based operating system and application software. There are two popular standalone PVR systems in the marketplace: TiVo and ReplayTV. These systems involve subscription services to deliver television programming information and scheduling controls.

The PC-based PVR is a specialized multimedia version of the PC, which includes a video capture card, a fast hard disk drive, lots of RAM, a TV tuner, and a high-end video card. A typical PC-based PVR is depicted in Figure 5.3. Mainstream PC manufacturers have attempted to create these PCs in case styles similar to those encountered in consumer A/V electronics products (stereo receivers, tape decks, and amplifiers). This has been done in an effort to make media center PCs blend in with the "family room" environment.

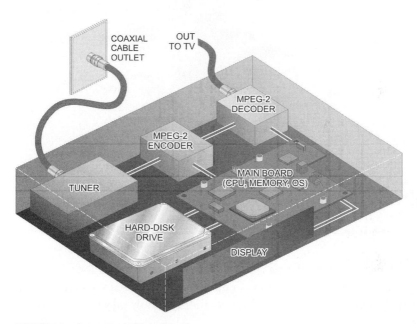

FIGURE 5.3 A personal video recorder.

The PC-based PVR also requires software to help the user select and control the recoding, organization, and playback of audio and video media. The key to the popularity of PVRs is the capability to record multimedia materials at the same time you are watching or listening to another piece of material.

Several applications software packages are available for this function; some are even available as freeware. Microsoft has entered the PC-based PVR market by including PVR control software in its Windows XP operating system. This version is known as Windows XP Media Center Edition. Media Center Edition is a special superset of the Windows XP Professional operating system. PVR control is also an intergal feature of Microsoft's Vista operating system versions.

RAID Systems

As software applications pushed storage capacity requirements past available drive sizes, it became logical to combine several drives to hold all the data produced. In a desktop unit, this can be as simple as adding an additional physical drive to the system. Wide area and local area networks connect computers so that their resources (including disk drives) can be shared. If you extend this idea of sharing disk drives to include several drive units operating under a single controller, you have a *drive array*. A drive array is depicted in Figure 5.4.

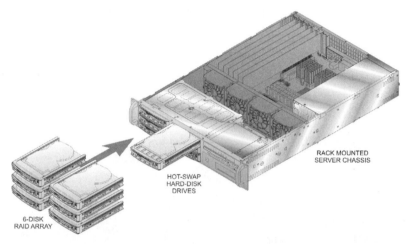

FIGURE 5.4 A drive array.

Drive arrays have evolved in response to storage requirements for local area networks. They are particularly useful in client/server networks, in which the data for the network tends to be centrally located and shared by all the users around the network.

In the cases of multiple drives within a unit, and drives scattered around a network, each drive assumes a different letter designation. In a drive array, the stack of drives can be made to appear as a single large hard drive. The drives are operated in parallel so that they can deliver data to the controller in a parallel format. If the controller is simultaneously handling eight bits of data from eight drives, the system will see the speed of the transfer as being eight times faster. This technique of using the drives in a parallel array is referred to as a *striped drive array*.

It is also possible to use a small drive array as a data backup system. This is referred to as a *mirrored drive array*, in which each drive is supplied with the same data. In the event that the data from one drive is corrupted, or one of the drives fails, the data is still safe. Both types of arrays are created through a blend of connection hardware and control software.

The most common drive arrays are RAID systems. RAID is an acronym for *redundant array of inexpensive disks*. Later use of the term RAID exchanges the word *independent* for *inexpensive*. Five levels of RAID technology specifications are given by the RAID Advisory Board.

▶ RAID 0—The RAID Advisory Board designated the classic striped array described earlier as RAID level-0 (RAID 0—Striped Disk Array Without Fault Tolerance). Likewise, the mirrored drive array previously described is labeled RAID 1. The operation of a striped disk array is shown in Figure 5.5.

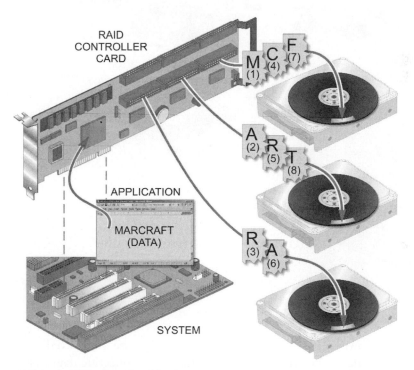

FIGURE 5.5 Operation of a striped array.

EXAM ALERT

Remember which RAID solution is based on mirroring.

▶ RAID 1 (Mirroring and Duplexing) is a redundancy scheme that uses two equal-sized drives, where both drives hold the same information. Each drive serves as a backup for the other. Figure 5.6 illustrates the operation of a mirrored array used in a RAID 1 application. Duplicate information is stored on both drives. When a file is retrieved from the array, the controller reads alternate sectors from each drive. This effectively reduces the data read time by half.

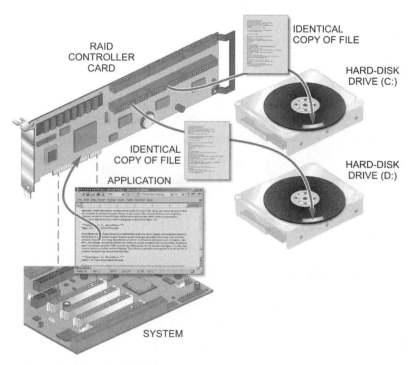

FIGURE 5.6 Operation of a mirrored array.

▶ RAID 2 (Data Striping with Error Recovery) interleaves data on parallel drives, as shown in Figure 5.7. Bits or blocks of data are interleaved across the disks in the array. The speed afforded by collecting data from the disks in a parallel format is the biggest feature of the system. In large arrays, complete bytes, words, or double words can be written to and read from the array simultaneously.

The RAID 2 specification uses multiple disks for error-detection and correction functions. Depending on the error-detection and correction algorithms used, large portions of the array are used for nondata storage overhead. Of course, the reliability of the data being delivered to the system is excellent, and there is no need for time-consuming corrective read

operations when an error is detected. Arrays dealing with large systems
may use between three and seven drives for error-correction purposes.
Because of the high hardware overhead, RAID 2 systems are not normally used with microcomputer systems.

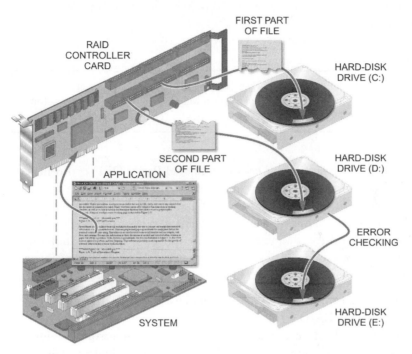

FIGURE 5.7 Interleaved data on parallel drives.

When the array is used in this manner, a complex error-detection and
correction algorithm is normally employed. The controller contains circuitry based on the algorithm that detects, locates, and corrects the error
without retransmitting any data. This is a very quick and efficient
method of error detection and correction.

In Figure 5.6, the data block being sent to the array is broken apart and
distributed to the drives in the array. The data word already has a parity
bit added to it. The controller generates parity for the block and stores it
on the error-detection drive. When the controller reads the data back
from the array, it regenerates the error-check character and compares it
to the one written on the error-check drive. By comparing the error-
check character to the rewritten one, the controller can detect the error
in the data field and determine which bit within the field is incorrect.
With this information in hand, the controller can correct that bit as it is
being processed.

▶ RAID 3 (Parallel Transfer with Parity Striping) allows the drives of the array to operate in parallel like a RAID 2 system. However, only parity checking is used for error detection and correction, requiring only one additional drive. If an error occurs, the controller reads the array again to verify the error. This is a time-consuming, low-efficiency method of error correction.

> **NOTE**
>
> A variation of RAID 3 referred to as RAID 53 (High I/O Rates and Data Transfer Performance RAID) combines RAID 0 striped arrays with RAID 3 parallel segments. The result is a high-performance RAID 3 system.

▶ RAID 4 (Independent Data Disks with Shared Parity Disk) controllers interleave sectors across the drives in the array. This creates the appearance of one very large drive. The RAID 4 format is generally used for smaller drive arrays, but can be used for larger arrays as well. Only one parity-checking drive is allotted for error control. The information on the parity drive is updated after reading the data drives. This creates an extra write activity for each data read operation performed.

▶ RAID 5 specifications (Independent Data Disks with Distributed Parity Blocks) alter the RAID 4 specifications by allowing the parity function to rotate through the different drives. Under this system, error checking and correction is the function of all the drives. If a single drive fails, the system is capable of regenerating its data from the parity information on the other drives. RAID 5 is usually the most popular RAID system because it can be used on small arrays, and it has a high level of error recovery built in. The operation of a RAID 5 array is shown in Figure 5.8.

As the figure illustrates, the data block being sent to the array is broken apart and distributed to the drives in the array. The data word already has a parity bit added to it. The controller generates parity for the block and stores it on the error-detection drive. When the controller reads the data back from the array, it regenerates the error-check character and compares it to the one written on the error-check drive. By comparing the error-check character to the rewritten one, the controller can detect the error in the data field and determine which bit within the field is incorrect. With this information in hand, the controller can correct that bit as it is being processed.

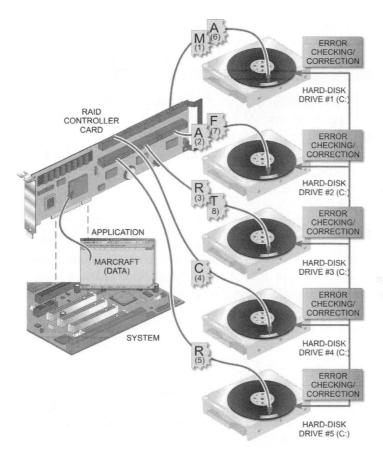

FIGURE 5.8 Operation of a RAID 5 array.

EXAM ALERT

Know how many drives are required to implement a RAID 5 array.

This creates the appearance of one very large drive to the system. Under this specification, the parity function rotates through the different drives. Error checking and correction is the function of all the drives. If a single drive fails, the system is capable of regenerating its data from the parity information on the other drives. RAID 5 is the most popular RAID system because it can be used on small arrays (as small as three drives), and it has a high level of error recovery built in.

A variation of RAID 5 that implements two independent error-correcting schemes (Independent Data Disks with Two Independent Distributed

Parity Schemes) has been devised and labeled RAID 6. This format is relatively expensive, but it provides an extremely high fault-tolerance level for critical applications. This RAID level requires at least two additional drives to operate.

▶ RAID 10 (Very High Reliability/High Performance RAID) combines mirroring and striping to produce a high-performance, high-reliability backup system. This arrangement combines RAID 1 striped array segments with mirroring to provide increased performance to a RAID 1 installation.

Floppy Disk Drives

Few new desktop and tower PCs include a floppy disk drive as a standard component. Rewritable CDs and flash drives have replaced the floppy disk in many cases. However, floppies are still widely used to boot failing PC systems to a command prompt for troubleshooting purposes. Emergency start disks are covered in Chapter 17, "Basic Operating System Troubleshooting and Maintenance."

EXAM ALERT

Be aware of common floppy disk uses.

The discussion of general disk-drive operations earlier in the chapter applies to both hard and floppy drives alike. However, the physical construction and operation of the drives are quite different. The FDD is an exposed unit, with an opening in the front to allow the floppy disk to be inserted and removed. In addition, the R/W heads are open to the atmosphere and ride directly on the surface of the disk. Modern 3 1/2-inch floppy disk drives have an ejection button that kicks the disk out of the drive when the button is pushed.

Data moves back and forth between the system's RAM and the floppy disk surface. Along the way, it passes from the system RAM, to the Floppy Disk Controller (FDC), through the floppy drive signal cable, and into the floppy drive's analog control board. The analog control board converts the data into signals that can be applied to the drive's read/write heads, which in turn produce the magnetic spots on the disk surface.

Under direction of the operating system, the FDC divides the 3 1/2-inch floppy disk into 80 tracks per side, with 9 or 18 512-byte sectors per track. When the disk is formatted to use nine sectors per track it is referred to as a *double-sided, single-density (DSSD)* disk. However, when the formatting is increased to use 18 sectors per track it is referred to as a *double-sided, high-density disk (DSHD)*. These options provide the system with 737,280 (720KB) or 1,474,560 (1.44MB) total bytes of storage on each disk. Table 5.1 lists the operating specifications for a typical 3 1/2-inch floppy disk drive.

TABLE 5.1   Typical Floppy Disk Specifications

DRIVE UNIT PART	DSSD	DSHD
Tracks	80	80
Heads	2	2
Sectors per Track	9	18
Bytes per Sector	512	512
Formatted Capacity	720KB	1.44MB
Unformatted Capacity	1MB	2MB
Rotational Speed (RPM)	300	300
Recording Density (bits/inch)	8,717	17,432
Tracks per Inch	135	135
Transfer Rate Unformatted (kbps)	250	500

The FDC also supplies interface signals that permit it to be connected to microprocessor systems with or without DMA capabilities. In most systems, however, the FDC operates in conjunction with the system's DMA controller and is assigned to the DRQ2 and DACK2 lines. In operation, the FDC presents a DRQ2 request for every byte of data to be transferred. In addition, the disk-drive controller is assigned to the IRQ6 line. The FDC generates an interrupt signal each time it receives a Read, Write, or Format command from the system unit. An interrupt will also be generated when the controller receives a Ready signal from one of the disk drive units.

Magnetic Tape Drives

Tape drives are available in a variety of types and configurations. Tape drives intended for desktop computers are available in both 5 1/4-inch and 3 1/2-inch drive form factors. These units are designed for mounting inside the system unit as part of the system's permanent drive capabilities.

Removable tape cartridges like the one depicted in Figure 5.9 are inserted into the front of the drive and locked into place by an internal mechanism. The drive's read/write heads access the tape through an opening in the front of the cartridge. Likewise, a capstan in the drive is used to turn a drive wheel inside the cartridge, which in turn moves both tape spools simultaneously.

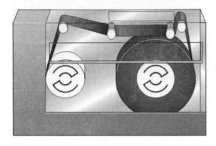

FIGURE 5.9 Data storage cartridge.

The drive also has a sensor, that detects the position of the tape's write-protect switch. This switch disables the drive's write circuitry so that important data on the tape cannot be written over by mistake.

With the exception of their front panels, internally mounted tape drives share a great deal of their form with internal floppy and hard drive units. They feature a signal interface connection to connect them to their controller and to standard options power supply connectors that deliver power to the drive.

Internal tape drives are available for most of the standard drive interface types (that is, floppy drive connections, as well as EIDE and internal SCSI buses). In many cases, tape drives are supplied with proprietary controller cards that plug into one of the system's expansion slots. Other older models are even capable of using the system's B: drive floppy connection as their interface connection.

For portable systems, tape drives are designed as external units that connect to one of the portable's external port or bus connections. These units typically employ one of the PC's standard I/O port or extension bus connections to communicate with the system (that is, external SCSI, USB, or IEEE-1394 buses). These units usually include an external housing for aesthetic purposes. They also normally derive power independently from the host computer through their own detachable power pack unit.

Because tape drives are not considered standard PC peripherals, they are not directly supported by the available operating systems. These operating systems support the bus or port operation, but not the drive. However, the backup utility in newer versions of Windows will treat tape drives as another storage device after their drivers have been installed.

Tape drive manufacturers normally supply device drivers for their own tape drives. In most cases, the manufacturer provides the entire application software package for the tape drive. These packages are installed under the operating system in the same manner as other application packages.

Optical Storage

Although magnetic disk drives have dominated the secondary memory function in PCs for decades, newer optical storage technologies have taken a large share of that category over the last 20 years. The main optical storage contenders in the PC market are the CD-ROM disc and the DVD, or Digital Versatile Disc, and their variants. Continued development and success of these two storage media has led to lower costs and greater demand. Practically every new PC sold comes with at least one CD/DVD drive installed. In many cases they include more than one drive.

CD-ROM Drives

The mechanics of a CD-ROM drive are similar in many respects to those of magnetic disk drive. These drives employ variable speed motors to turn the CD in the drive. Discs are loaded in the drive by a tray that extends from the front of the drive when its access button is pressed. When the button is pressed again, the tray retracts into the drive and properly aligns the disc with the drive spindle. Like magnetic drives, CD-ROM drives have an actuator motor that moves the laser/detector module in and out under the disc. Figure 5.10 shows the physical construction of a typical CD-ROM drive.

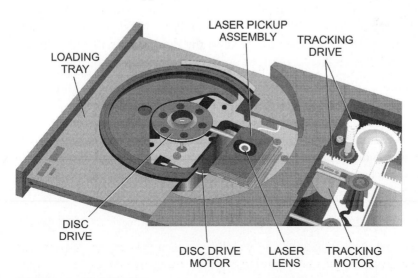

FIGURE 5.10 CD-ROM drive.

EXAM ALERT

Memorize the major components that make up an optical disc drive, along with their functions.

A powerful, highly focused laser beam is used to write digital data on light-sensitive material inside the CD. The writing laser is pulsed with the modulated data to be stored on the disc. When the laser is pulsed, a microscopic blister is burned into the optical material, causing it to reflect light differently from the material around it. The blistered areas are referred to as *pits*, and the areas between them are called *lands*. Figure 5.11 illustrates the writing of data on the optical disc.

NOTE

Mass produced commercial CDs and DVDs use a negative image of a master copy of the optical material (that was burned by a laser) to physically stamp impressions of the recorded lands and pits into each piece of optical material, which is then encased in the transparent CD material.

The recorded data is read from the disc by scanning it with a lower-power, continuous laser beam. The laser diode emits the highly focused, narrow beam that is reflected back from the disc. The reflected beam passes through a prism and is bent 90 degrees, where it is picked up by the diode detector and converted into an electrical signal. Only light reflected from land areas on the disc is picked up by the detector. Light that strikes a pit is scattered and is not detected. The lower power level used for reading the disc ensures that the optical material is not affected during the read operation.

With an audio CD, the digital data retrieved from the disc is passed through a digital-to-analog converter (DAC) to reproduce the audio sound wave. However, this is not required for digital computer systems because the information is already in a form acceptable to the computer. Therefore, CD players designed for use in computer systems are referred to as *CD-ROM drives*, to differentiate them from audio CD players. Otherwise, the mechanics of operation are very similar between the two devices.

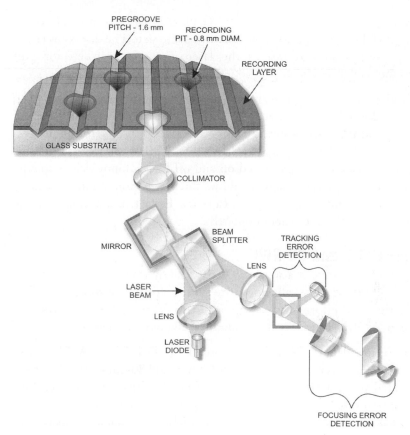

FIGURE 5.11 Writing on a CD-ROM disc.

CD-ROM Discs

A typical CD-ROM disc is 4.7 inches in diameter, and consists of an acrylic substrate, an aluminized, mirror-finished data surface, and a lacquer coating. The scanning laser beam comes up through the disc, strikes the aluminized data surface, and is reflected back. Because there is no physical contact between the reading mechanism and the disc, the disc never wears out. This is one of the main advantages of the CD system. The blisters on the data surface are typically just under 1 micrometer in length, and the tracks are 1.6 micrometers apart. The data is encoded by the length and spacing of the blisters, and the lands between them.

The information on a compact disc is stored in one continuous spiral track, unlike hard disks, where the data is stored in multiple, concentric tracks. The compact disc storage format still divides the data into separate sectors. However, the sectors of a CD-ROM disc are physically the same size. The disc spins counterclockwise, and it slows down as the laser diode emitter/detector unit approaches the outside of the disc.

The disc begins spinning at approximately 500RPM at its inner edge and slows down to about 200RPM at its outer edge. The spindle motor controls the speed of the disc so that the track is always passing the laser at between 3.95 and 4.6 feet per second. Therefore, CD-ROM drives must have a variable-speed spindle motor, which cannot just be turned on and off like a floppy drive's spindle motor. The variable speed of the drive allows the disc to contain more sectors, thereby giving it a much larger storage capacity. In fact, the average storage capacity of a CD-ROM disc is about 680MB.

CD Writers (CD-R and CD-RW)

Another type of CD drive is a write once, read many (WORM) drive. As the acronym implies, these drives allow users to write information to the disc once and then retrieve this information as with a CD-ROM drive. After information is stored on a WORM drive, the data cannot be changed or deleted.

CD writers record data on blank CD-recordable (CD-R) discs. A CD-R is a WORM media that is generally available in 120mm and 80mm sizes. The drives are constructed using a typical 5.25-inch half-height drive form factor. This form factor is convenient in that it fits into a typical PC drive bay. The CD-R technology has continued to evolve into a recordable, rewritable compact disc, called a *CD-RW disc*. These discs can be recorded, erased, and rewritten.

The physical construction of the CD-R disc is considerably different from that of the CD-ROM disc. The writable disc is constructed as described in Figure 5.12. The CD-R disc is created by coating a transparent polycarbonate substrate with an opaque polymer dye. The dye is covered with a thin layer of gold and topped with a protective lacquer layer and a label. The CD-R writing mechanism is not as strong as that of a commercial CD-ROM duplicator. Instead of burning pits into the substrate of the disc, the CD writer uses a lower-power laser to discolor the dye material.

The CD-R disc format is identical to that of a CD-ROM, and information written on it can be read by a typical CD-ROM drive. The spiral track formation and sectoring are the same as those used with CD-ROM discs. In addition, the CD writer can produce recordings in the standard CD book formats (that is, red, yellow, orange, and green).

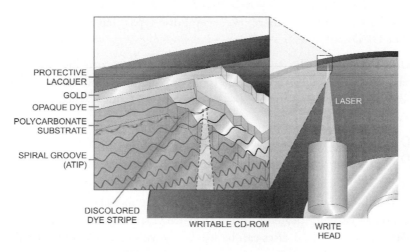

PROTECTIVE LACQUER
GOLD
OPAQUE DYE
POLYCARBONATE SUBSTRATE
SPIRAL GROOVE (ATIP)
DISCOLORED DYE STRIPE
WRITABLE CD-ROM
LASER
WRITE HEAD

FIGURE 5.12 Writable CD-R disc.

During the write operation, the CD writer uses a medium-intensity laser to write the data on the thermally sensitive media. The laser light is applied to the bottom side of the disc. It passes through the substrate to the reflective layer and is reflected back through the substrate. The light continues through the drive's optics system until it reaches the laser detector.

When the polymer is exposed to the light of the writing laser, it heats up and becomes transparent. This exposes the reflective gold layer beneath the polymer. During readback, the reflective layer reflects more light than the polymer material does. The transitions between lighter and darker areas of the disc are used to encode the data.

CD writers are typically able to write to the CD-R at up to 52× CD speeds and to CD-RWs at speeds up to 32×. These settings have nothing to do with playback speeds. CD-RW drives are specified in a record (write CD-R) × rewrite (write CD-RW) × read speed format (for example, a 52 × 32 × 52 CD-RW can read at 52×, write at 52×, and rewrite at 32× speeds) .

DVDs

DVD drives and discs are identical in form factor and appearance to CD-ROM drives and discs. In fact, DVD drives are backward compatible with old CD-ROM discs, and newer DVD drives can be used to read CD-R and CD-RW discs. The discs are inserted into the front of the unit just like CD-ROM discs. The drive's circuitry senses the type of disc being used and automatically adjusts for it.

Within the DVD specification, there are several disc types that are associated with different DVD standards:

▶ DVD Recordable (DVD-R) and (DVD+R)—Separate recordable DVD formats where the media can be used to record data only once and then the data becomes permanent on the disc. The disc cannot be recorded onto a second time.

▶ DVD Rewritable (DVD-RW) and (DVD+RW)—Separate rerecordable DVD formats where data on the disc can be erased and recorded over numerous times.

▶ DVD-RAM—A specialized DVD format where the media can be recorded and erased repeatedly. The DVD-RAM specification is non-standard, so DVD-RAM discs can be used only with drives manufactured by the companies that support the format.

There are two variations of the DVD-R disc: DVD-RG and DVD-RA. The DVD-RG designation is associated with general-use media, and the DVD-RA standard is provided for authoring and mastering DVD video and data. DVD-RA media is generally not available for general use. The DVD-RAM format supports 2.6GB of storage per disc, and the DVD-RW standards supports 4.7GB per disc.

The DVD industry has produced standards for DVD drives that make these disc type distinctions less important than they used to be. The standards have led to DVD multidrives that provide transparent compatibility between DVD-R, DVD-RW, and DVD-RAM discs. These drives can read, or read and write to DVDs in any of these formats.

As mentioned in Chapter 1, "Basic PC Terms and Concepts," DVDs are available in single-sided or double-sided discs, as well as single-layer or dual-layer recording capabilities. Dual-level DVDs place two organic dye recording levels inside the disc, separated by a transparent spacer layer. The top layer (L1) has a metal reflector above the recording material while the lower level (L0) is backed up by a semitransparent metal reflector.

The drive's optics controller focus the reading (or writing) laser at the desired recording level. A table of contents is written on the L0 level and represents the contents of the entire disc.

Disk Drive Interfaces

PC storage devices fall into one of two general categories: internal or external. Internal devices are typically mounted in the system unit's drive bays and connect to the system board or one of its adapter cards. External devices normally connect to one of the system's standard I/O port connectors. Whereas internal devices typically derive their power from the system unit's power supply, external storage devices tend to employ separate, external power supply units.

Modern PCs employ one of two standard system-level interface types to communicate with their internal disk drive systems: Integrated Drive Electronics (IDE), also known as the *AT Attachment (ATA) interface*, or small computer system interface (SCSI) interfaces. Both interface types place most of the controller electronics directly on the drive unit. Therefore, data travels in parallel between the computer and the drive unit. The controller circuitry on the drive handles all the parallel-to-serial and serial-to-parallel conversions. This permits the interface to be independent of the host computer design. The system sees the entire HDD system as an attachment to its bus systems.

Most newer external HDD and CD-ROM/DVD drives employ USB or IEEE-1394 FireWire interfaces. However, there are external disk drive systems that employ SCSI interfaces or local area networks to communicate with the system.

Internal Disk Drive Interfaces

Most internal hard drives and CD-ROM/DVD drives typically connect to one of the system board's parallel IDE/EIDE-ATA (PATA) interface connections, or one of its Serial ATA (SATA) interface connections. On some system boards you will find only PATA connectors, on others you will find only SATA connectors, and on some you will find a mixture of both. A mixed version system board layout is depicted in Figure 5.13.

The other internal drive option is the SCSI interface. Most PC system boards do not physically or logically (in the BIOS) support SCSI interface devices. Therefore, an adapter card–based controller is usually required to accommodate these drives. The host adapter card plugs into one of the system board's expansion slots and provides a BERG pin connector for the system's internal SCSI ribbon cable.

However, there are many versions of the SCSI standard and several types of SCSI connecting cables. An internal SCSI CD-ROM drive must be capable of connecting to the type of SCSI cable being used. The SCSI interface that employs a Centronics-type connector is the most widely used method for connecting external CD-ROM drives to systems.

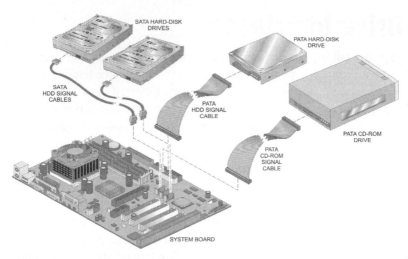

FIGURE 5.13 Mixed disk drive interface connections.

IDE/ATA Interface

The original IDE interface standard was also referred to as the ATA interface (IDE and ATA were involved in the same standard). This interface was introduced on adapter cards and supported two drive units that shared a single communications channel (one cable). When two drives were attached to the cable, one was designated as the *master* drive and the other as the *slave* drive. With the introduction of the ATX form factor specification, the IDE host adapter function and physical interface was integrated into the system board.

IDE systems store their low-level formatting information directly on the drive. This information is placed on the drive by its manufacturer and is used by the controller for alignment and sector sizing of the drive. The IDE controller extracts the raw data (format and actual data information) coming from the read/write heads and converts it into signals that can be applied to the computer's buses. Therefore, the system basically sees the drive as an extension of its buses. The IDE interface used a single 40-pin ribbon cable to connect the hard drive to the host adapter card or system board and supported a maximum throughout of 8.3MBps.

Advanced EIDE Specifications

A variety of IDE-related specifications exist. Updated IDE specifications have been developed to enable more than two drives to exist on the interface. This was accomplished by creating two separate IDE channels, with two controllers and two 40-pin interface connections. The first channel is referred to as the *primary* channel and the other is the *secondary* channel. Each channel is capable of handling its own master and slave drive independent of the other channel.

This new IDE specification is called *Enhanced IDE (EIDE)*, or the *ATA-2* interface, and actually includes the ATA-2/EIDE/ATAPI specifications (the ATAPI standard is a derivative of the ATA-2 standard). The AT Attachment Packet Interface (ATAPI) specification provides improved IDE drivers for use with CD-ROM drives and new data transfer methods. This specification provides maximum throughput of 16.7MBps through the 40-pin IDE signal cable.

The ATA standards provide for different programmed I/O (PIO) modes that offer higher performance capabilities, as illustrated in Table 5.2. Most IDE devices are now capable of operating in modes 3 or 4. However, the IDE port must be attached to the PCI bus to use these modes. Some system boards place only the IDE1 connection on this bus, whereas the IDE2 connection is a function of the ISA bus. In these cases, devices installed on the IDE2 connector will be capable only of mode-2 operation.

TABLE 5.2   ATA PIO Modes

PIO MODE	TRANSFER	ATA VERSION
0	3.3MB/sec	ATA-1
1	5.2MB/sec	ATA-1
2	8.3MB/sec	ATA-1
3	11.1MB/sec	ATA-2
4	16.6MB/sec	ATA-2
4	33.3MB/sec	ATA-3/Ultra DMA 33
4	66.6MB/sec	ATA-4/Ultra DMA 66
4	100MB/sec	ATA 100

An additional development of the ATA standard has provided the ATA-3/Ultra ATA 33 specification that boosts throughput between the IDE device and the system to 33.3MBps. This standard still employs the 40-pin IDE signal cable. It relies on the system to support the 33.3MBps burst mode transfer operation through the Ultra DMA (UDMA) protocol.

IDE enhancements called ATA-4/Ultra ATA 66 and Ultra ATA 100 provide even higher data throughput by doubling the number of conductors in the IDE signal cable. The IDE connector has remained compatible with the 40-pin IDE connection, but each pin has been provided with its own ground conductor in the cable. The Ultra ATA 66 specification provides 66MBps, and the Ultra ATA 100 connection provides 100MBps.

Both Ultra ATA versions support 33.3MBps data rates when used with a standard 40-pin/40-conductor IDE signal cable. Therefore, Ultra ATA 66 and 100 devices can still be used with systems that don't support the new IDE standards. These operating modes must be configured correctly through the system's CMOS Setup utility.

EXAM ALERT

Remember how the Ultra ATA 66 interface cable can be identified.

Serial ATA Interface

The newest ATA implementations from the IDE development community are the SATA standards. These interface standards have been developed to compete with other interface types that employ serial data transmission types. Serial ATA interfaces employ two data channels: one for sending and one for receiving. The original SATA 1.5Gbps specification supported data transfer rates at up to 150MBps (also expressed as 1.2Gbps because the SATA encoding scheme is only 80% efficient) using 250mV differential signaling techniques.

An improved 3Gbps version of the SATA standard has been introduced that boosts the maximum data transfer rate for the interface to 2.4 Gbps (or 300 MBps). At this time, SATA drives are not fast enough to keep up with this interface, so the actual operating speed is determined by the capabilities of the drive. 3Gbps SATA devices are designed to be backward compatible with older 1.5Gbps controllers. However, some devices must be manually configured to work with some older SATA interfaces. This standard is sometimes mistakenly referred to as the SATA II interface.

The seven-wire data cable used with the SATA connection is considerably different from the traditional ribbon cables used with parallel interfaces. They are thin and flexible and their connectors are just 8mm wide. These cables can range up to a meter in length, meaning that there is no problem connecting a disk drive that is mounted in the top bay of a large tower case.

With SATA drives there is no master/slave relationship or configuration to perform. Each SATA drive has its own host connector and cable. Host connectors can be located on a host adapter card that plugs into one of the system board's PCI expansion slots, or it can be mounted directly on the system board. Figure 5.14 depicts a typical SATA adapter card. These cards may contain between one and four SATA connectors. There is no particular connection order that needs to be followed because there is no master/slave—primary/secondary PATA interface to configure.

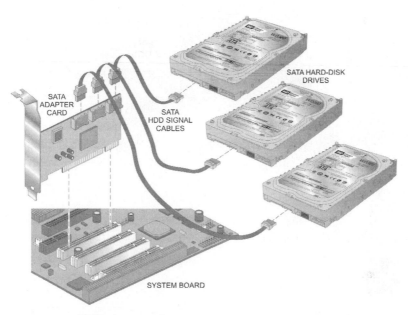

FIGURE 5.14 SATA adapter card.

It's permissible to mix PATA and SATA drives in a system as long as the system board or host adapter card supports both types of interfaces. This enables SATA drives to be added to older PATA systems by installing a host adapter card, without removing the existing PATA drives.

Depending on the system board and drive types installed, you may need to load device drivers for the SATA controller after a Windows operating system detects the new drive in the system. These drivers should be located on the installation disc that comes with the drive or adapter card. You should also check the manufacturer's Internet web page for the latest drivers available.

Floppy Drive Interface

A single ribbon cable is used to connect the floppy drive to the system board's FDD adapter connector when present. The signal cable has two 34-pin, two-row BERG headers along its length. The other end of the cable terminates in a 34-pin, two-row BERG header. A small colored stripe normally runs along one edge of the cable, as illustrated in Figure 5.15. This is the Pin #1 indicator stripe that marks the side of the cable, which should be aligned with the #1 pin of the FDD connector and the disk drive's signal connector. The location of this pin is usually marked on the drive's printed-circuit board.

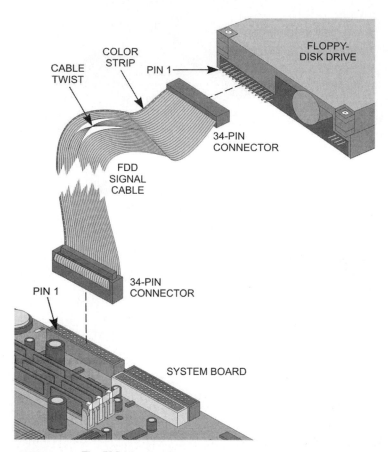

FIGURE 5.15 The FDD signal cable.

The interface connection enables the FDC to manage two floppy disk drive units. The floppy disk drive connected to the 34-pin header at the end of the cable will be designated as drive A by the system. A floppy drive attached to the connector in the middle of the cable will be designated as the B drive. A small twist of wires between the A and B connectors reroutes key lines that determine which drive is which.

Small Computer System Interface

The small computer system interface, often referred to as the "scuzzy" standard, like the IDE concept, provides a true system-level interface for the drive. Nearly all the drive's controller electronics are located on the peripheral device. As with the IDE host adapter, the duties of the SCSI host adapter are reduced to mostly physical connection functions, along with some signal compatibility handling.

With this arrangement, data arrives at the system interface in a form that is already usable by the host computer.

The SCSI interface can be used to connect diverse types of peripherals to the system. As an example, a SCSI chain could connect a controller to a hard drive, a CD-ROM drive, a high-speed tape drive, a scanner, and a printer. Additional SCSI devices are added to the system by daisy-chaining them together: The input of the second device is attached to the SCSI output of the first device, and so forth.

SCSI Specifications

The original SCSI-1 specification established a data bus width of 8 bits and permitted up to eight devices to be connected to the bus (including the controller). The maximum speed of the SCSI-1 bus is 5MBps (1 byte × 5MHz = 5MBps). The maximum recommended length for a complete standard SCSI chain is 20 feet (6m). However, unless the cables are heavily shielded, they become susceptible to data corruption caused by induced noise.

Therefore, a maximum single SCSI segment of less than 3 feet (1m) is recommended. Don't forget the length of the internal cabling when dealing with SCSI cable distances. You can realistically count on about 3 feet of internal cable, so reduce the maximum total length of the chain to about 15 feet (4.5m). This specification became known as *Narrow SCSI*.

> **EXAM ALERT**
>
> Memorize the permissible lengths stated for SCSI cables and chains.

An updated SCSI specification was developed by the ANSI committee to double the number of data lines in the standard interface to 16 bits (2 bytes). It also adds balanced dual-line drivers that allow much faster data transfer speeds to be used. This implementation is referred to as *Wide SCSI-2*. The specification expands the SCSI specification into a 16/32-bit bus standard and increases the cable and connector specification to 68 pins. This enhancement enabled the SCSI bus to transfer data twice as fast (2 bytes × 5MHz = 10MBps).

A different improvement to the original specification increased the synchronous data transfer option for the 8-bit interface from 5Mbps to 10Mbps. This implementation became known as *Fast SCSI-2*. Under this system, the system and the I/O device conduct nondata message, command, and status operations in 8-bit asynchronous mode. After agreeing on a larger, or faster file-transfer format, they conduct transfers using an agreed-on word size and transmission mode. As the speed of the bus was increased, it caused cross talk to occur earlier, which cut the maximum usable cable length in half (from 6 meters to 3 meters, or about 10 feet). Fast SCSI-2 connections use 50-pin connectors.

A third version brought together both improvements and became known as *Wide Fast SCSI-2*. This version of the standard doubles the bus size to 16 bits and employs the faster transfer methods to provide a maximum bus speed of 20MBps (2 bytes × 10MHz = 20MBps) supporting a chain of up to 15 additional devices. The maximum cable length is still specified at 3 meters because the bus can run at 10MHz.

The next step in the evolution of the specification was to speed up the bus again. The newer version, referred to as *Ultra SCSI* (*ultra* meaning *ultrafast*), pushed the bus speed from 10MHz to 20MHz, using the original SCSI-1 interface. This move increased the maximum transfer rate from 5MBps to 20MBps (1 byte × 20MHz), but it also reduced the maximum useful cable length of 1.5 meters. This distance tends to physically limit the number of devices that you can attach to the cable; however, it is still suitable for most installations. The Ultra SCSI specification also makes provisions for a special high-speed serial transfer mode and special communications media, such as fiber-optic cabling. This update has been combined with both wide and fast revisions to produce the following:

- ▸ Ultra SCSI
- ▸ Ultra2 SCSI
- ▸ Wide Ultra SCSI
- ▸ Wide Ultra2 SCSI
- ▸ Wide Ultra3 SCSI

Of course, the next logical SCSI standard advancement was to again increase the data bus width. This revision is called *Wide Ultra SCSI*. The addition of the wide specification doubles the number of devices that can be serviced by the interface. Likewise, the ultra designation indicates a speed increase due to improved technology. Combining the two technologies yielded a 4× increase in data throughput (Wide Ultra SCSI= 40MBps compared to Ultra SCSI = 20MBps and Wide and Fast SCSI = 10MBps), while still keeping the cable length at 1.5 meters.

At this point, the SCSI development community could not increase the speed of the bus using the existing hardware interface. Increasing the speed again would limit the maximum cable length to the point where it would be unusable in the real world. To increase the bus speed to 40MHz, the specification switched to Low-Voltage Differential (LVD) signaling techniques described later in this section.

By employing LVD technology, the Ultra2 SCSI specification doubled the data throughput of the 8-bit SCSI bus (1 byte × 40MHz = 40MBps). However, the presence of the LVD technology enabled the maximum cable length for this specification to be increased to 12 meters. Single LVD devices connected solely to a single controller may use up to 25 meters of cable.

Then the SCSI community mixed the LVD technology with the increased bus width of the Wide SCSI specification to produce Wide Ultra2 SCSI. This specification increased the maximum data throughput to 80MBps (2 bytes × 40MHz = 80MBps), while the cable length remained at 12 meters.

The next improvement to the SCSI technology was the introduction of Double Transition (DT) clocking techniques. DT clocking enabled an Ultra 160 SCSI controller to send data on both the rising and falling edges of its clock cycles. Although the bus width remained at 16 bits and the bus clock frequency stayed at 40MHz, the new technique increased the maximum throughput to 160MBps (2 bytes × 40MHz × 2 =160MBps). The maximum cable length also remained at 12 meters with the new specification, although the specifications for the cable type had to be made more stringent.

A later SCSI specification, referred to as *Ultra 320 SCSI*, increased the clock speed from 40MHz to 80MHz, while still employing the DT clocking scheme. Together, these steps boosted the maximum bus speed to 320MBps (2 bytes × 80MHz × 2 = 320Mbps), using a 16-bit bus and supporting up to 15 external devices. The Ultra 320 SCSI connection employs a special 80-pin Single Connector Attachment (SCA) connector.

A newer Ultra 640 SCSI specification increases the throughput of the interface to 640MBps.

Serial SCSI

As with other PC interface technologies, the SCSI interface has moved to serial transfer techniques to increase its data throughput. This has created a number of serial SCSI implementations including Serial Attached SCSI (SAS), Internet SCSI (iSCSI), and IEEE-1394 (FireWire) interfaces.

The SAS specification allows for much higher speed data transfers than previously available, and is backward-compatible with the SATA interface. Although SAS uses serial communication instead of the parallel method found in traditional SCSI devices, it still employs SCSI commands to interace with SAS target devices (also referred to as *end devices*)—such as disk drives, CD-ROM/DVD drives, RAID arrays, scanners, and printers. The SAS standard also provides support for SATA devices and device hot swapping.

The simplest SAS conenction would be to connect a SAS device to a SAS Initiator port. SAS *Initiators* are the controllers that service the SAS interface for the host system. They may be incorporated into system board chipsets, or located on an adpater card. However, the SAS architecture is designed to use SAS Expanders that enable multiple SAS devices to communicate with the SAS Initiator. the SAS system resembles the tiered-star network structure. *Expanders* are circuits built into devices that handle communications between different SAS devices and the Initiator.

Unlike parallel SCSI solutions, SAS requires no terminator packs and can support up to 16,3,84 interconnected devices. Transfer speeds for serial attached SCSI connections include 1.5Gbps, 3.0Gbps, and 6.0Gbps for each initiator-to-target pathway. The structure of the SAS architecture permits these transfer speeds to be realized on each conenction instead of being shared between devices and the host. SAS interfaces are typically found in high performance chipsets designed for network server applications. However, some of these boards and devices find their way into high-end desktop PC system boards.

Internet SCSI is a network protocol standard that permits use of the SCSI protocol over TCP/IP networks. This protocol is employed in local area networks—covered in Chapter 20, "Basic Networking Concepts"—to implement Storage Area Networks (SANs). These networks are used to backup and retreive large amounts of data for users in business networks.

The IEEE-1394 interface is widely used as a high-speed serial interface beteeen audio/video devices, such as digital cameras, camcorders, and older Apple iPod designs, and PC systems. As mentioned in Chapter 1, this interface is a direct competitor of the USB ports commonly used in newer PCs and is discussed in detail in Chapter 6, "Ports and Peripherals."

SCSI Cables and Connectors

The SCSI standard has been implemented using a number of cable types. In PC-compatible systems, the SCSI interface uses a 50-pin signal cable arrangement. Internally, the cable is a 50-pin flat ribbon cable. However, 50-pin shielded cables, with Centronic connectors, are used for external SCSI connections. The 50-pin SCSI connections are referred to as *A-cables*.

Advanced SCSI specifications have created additional cabling specifications. A 50-conductor alternative cable using 50-pin D-shell connectors has been added to the A-cable specification for SCSI-2 devices. A second cable type, referred to as *B-cable*, was added to the SCSI-2 specification to provide 16- and 32-bit parallel data transfers. However, this arrangement employed multiple connectors at each end of the cable and never received widespread acceptance in the market.

A revised 68-pin P-cable format, using D-shell connectors, was introduced to support 16-bit transfers in the SCSI-3 specification. A 68-pin Q-cable version was also adopted in SCSI for 32-bit transfers. The P and Q cables must be used in parallel to conduct 32-bit transfers.

For some PS/2 models, IBM used a special 60-pin Centronics-like connector for its SCSI connections. The version of the SCSI interface used in the Apple Macintosh employs a variation of the standard that features a proprietary miniature 25-pin D-shell connector.

In addition, SCSI devices may be classified as internal or as external devices. An internal SCSI device has no power supply of its own and therefore must be connected to one of the system's options power connectors. On the other hand, external SCSI devices come with built-in or plug-in power supplies that need to be connected to a commercial AC outlet. Therefore, when choosing a SCSI device, always inquire about compatibility between it and any other SCSI devices installed in the system.

These cabling variations create a hardware incompatibility between different SCSI devices. Likewise, there are SCSI devices that will not work with each other because of software incompatibilities.

Figure 5.16 depicts a 25-pin D-shell, a 50-pin Centronics, and a 68-pin Centronics-type and an 80-pin SCA SCSI connector used for external connections. Inside the computer, the SCSI specification employs 50-pin and 68-pin ribbon cables with BERG pin connectors, or the 80-pin SCA connector for Ultra 320 devices.

There are a variety of different connector types used with Serial Attached SCSI interfaces. A simple SAS connection employs the SATA connector described earlier in this chapter to provide the physical interface. This connector selection enables SATA drives to be connected to the SAS port. However, connectors on SAS devices have a key that prevents them from being connected to a SATA interface—these devices cannot operate from a SATA interface.

SAS host ports employ a 7-pin signal connector that provides two differential pairs of signal wires: one transmit pair and one receive pair. SAS devices may use the same 7-pin keyed connector as the one used on the host, or it may have a 14-pin version that provides for two complete SAS physical links: a primary channel (referred to as a *phy* or *lane*) and a secondary lane. This secondary physical link is optional and is not connected on single-phy SAS devices and SATA drives. The wiring in the SAS cable cross-connects the transmit pair at the host to the receive pair on the device.

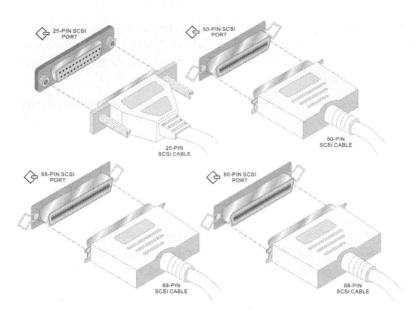

FIGURE 5.16 SCSI connectors.

Some internal SAS connections employ a 35-pin wide-SAS connector (five SATA connectors configured side-by-side) may be employed to create a four-lane connection that supports ribbon cable or round cable interconnections. External four-lane connections employ a 25-pin connector. The power connection is identical to the 15-pin SATA power connection. It provides 3.3V, 5V, and 12V supplies to the SAS device.

SCSI Signaling

You should also be aware that two types of signaling are used with SCSI interfaces: single-ended (SE) and differential. Single-ended signaling transmits signals in a straightforward manner where the information is applied to a signal line and referenced to ground. Differential signaling applies reciprocal versions of the same signal to two wires in the cable and compares them at the other end of the cable. This differential signal technique provides exceptional noise rejection properties and enables the signal to be transmitted much further (from 3/6 meters using SE up to 25 meters using differential) before it significantly deteriorates. For this reason, a single-ended interface uses half as many active conductors in the cable as differential cables do. The other conductors in the SE cable are used to provide grounds for the individual signal cables. In a differential cable, the ground conductors are used to carry the differential portion of the signal.

Single-ended and differential SCSI cables are available for A, P, and Q applications. Because they are electrically different, confusing them with each other would be problematic (using a differential cable to connect single-ended devices could damage the devices because of the missing ground capabilities). For this reason, the industry has adopted different symbols, as illustrated in Figure 5.17, to identify SE and differential cables and devices. These symbols are placed on the connectors of the cables and ports so that they are not confused with each other. Fortunately, most PC applications use single-ended connections. And therefore you are unlikely to run into differential cables or devices.

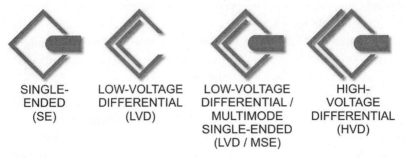

| SINGLE-
ENDED
(SE) | LOW-VOLTAGE
DIFFERENTIAL
(LVD) | LOW-VOLTAGE
DIFFERENTIAL /
MULTIMODE
SINGLE-ENDED
(LVD / MSE) | HIGH-
VOLTAGE
DIFFERENTIAL
(HVD) |

FIGURE 5.17 SCSI symbols.

The following two differential signal specifications are used in the SCSI environment:

▶ High-Voltage Differential (HVD)—The high differential refers to the +5Vdc and 0Vdc signal levels used to represent data bits. These voltage levels were implemented with the original SCSI-1 bus and have been included with all the specifications up to the Wide Ultra SCSI version.

▶ Low-Voltage Differential (LVD)—This is similar to the move in microprocessors to reduce the core voltage to 3.3V to make them run faster and consume less power. LVD interfaces operate on 3-volt logic levels instead of the older TTL-compatible 5-volt levels.

Unlike the earlier HVD interfaces that were incompatible with SE devices, LVD SCSI devices operate in what is known as *multimode* (that is, they can shift back and forth between traditional SE mode and LVD mode). The LVD is backward-compatible with single-ended SCSI. However, connecting one single-ended peripheral to a multimode LVD bus will cause the entire bus to switch to the single-ended mode for protection.

With the switch, the single-ended limitations on data throughput and cable length come into play. LVD mode was not defined in the original SCSI standards. If all devices on the bus support LVD, operations at up to 12 meters are possible at full speed. However, if any device on the bus is singled-ended only, the entire bus switches to single-ended mode and the distance is reduced to the 3/6 meters.

To add a single-ended peripheral to an LVD bus and preserve the data throughput and cable length of the LVD, you can add a SCSI expander called an *LVD-to-SE* or *LVD/MSE-to-LVD/MSE converter*. This converter divides the SCSI domain into two bus segments. One segment can operate at the LVD data throughput rate and cable length, and the other segment uses the single-ended data throughput and cable length ratings. Most LVD controllers employ a single-ended connector for connecting to slower tape drives so that they can preserve the speed and cable length of the LVD segment.

The speed capabilities of the SCSI interfaces make them attractive for intensive applications such as large file servers for networks, and multimedia video stations. However, the PATA and SATA interfaces are generally more widely used because of their lower cost and nearly equal performance. Table 5.3 contrasts the specifications of the PATA, SATA, and SCSI interfaces.

> **EXAM ALERT**
>
> Know the number of devices that can be attached to IDE, EIDE, SATA, and standard SCSI interfaces.

TABLE 5.3   PATA, SATA, and SCSI Specifications

INTERFACE	BUS SIZE	# DEVICES	ASYNC. SPEED	SYNC. SPEED
IDE (ATA-1)	16 bits	2	4MBps	3.3/5.2/ 8.3MBps
EIDE (ATA-2)	16 bits	2	4MBps	11/16MBps
SATA 1.5/3.0	Serial	4	150/300MBps	-
SCSI (SCSI-1)	8 bits	7	2MBps	5MBps
Wide SCSI (SCSI-2)	8/16 bits	15	2MBps	5MBps
Fast SCSI (SCSI-2)	8/16 bits	7	2MBps	5/10MBps
Wide Fast SCSI (SCSI-2)	8/16 bits	15	2MBps	10/20MBps
Ultra SCSI	8 bits	7	2MBps	10/20MBps

TABLE 5.3 *Continued*

INTERFACE	BUS SIZE	# DEVICES	ASYNC. SPEED	SYNC. SPEED
Wide Ultra SCSI (SCSI-3)	16 bits	15	2MBps	10/20/ 40MBps
Ultra2 SCSI	8 bits	7	2MBps	10/20/ 40MBps
Wide Ultra2 SCSI	16 bits	15	2MBps	10/20/40 /80MBps
Wide Ultra3 SCSI	16 bits	15	2MBps	10/20/40 /160MBps
Ultra320 SCSI	16 bits	15	2MBps	10/20/40/ 320MBps
Ultra640 SCSI	Serial	15	2MBps	640MBps
Serial SCSI	Serial	16,384	1.5/3.0/ 6.0 Gbps	NA

Removable Storage

In a PC, *removable storage* includes all the removable technologies we have already described (floppies, CD/CD-RWs, DVD/DVD-RWs, and tapes). However, there are still several other types of emerging and lesser-known removable storage systems. These systems include cartridge-mounted high-capacity floppy disks (Zip drives), solid-state USB drives (IC memory devices configured to operate like a mechanical disk drive), and PC Card drives. PC Cards drives are removable storage devices that can hold miniature (1.8 inch) mechanical or solid-state disk drives.

Most external storage systems employ the PC's standard I/O ports (ECP Parallel, SCSI, USB, or FireWire). This permits the system's PnP operation to detect the new hardware attached to the system. However, most of the devices are nonstandard in nature and require that original equipment manufacturers application packages be installed to control them. On the other hand, newer flash memory drives automatically load USB drivers and function as another drive in the system (drive E:). These removable storage systems have the advantage of being *hot swappable*—they can be added to or removed from the system while it is in operation.

Flash Memory

Flash memory is an all-electronic storage technology that can be written to, erased, and rewritten in the same manner as a magnetic disk drive. When power is removed from the memory module, the data stored inside remains and does not dissipate. This technology has been used to create a number of digital memory devices for use in PDAs, digital cameras, video game units, and notebook computers.

There are many types and form factors of flash memory devices currently in use. The original flash memory systems associated with personal computers involved making ROM-BIOS devices so that they could be updated electronically, and PCMCIA cards developed as memory adapter cards for portable computer systems.

Subsequently, many new form factor flash memory systems have been introduced into both the personal computer and consumer electronics markets. The most notable formats include USB flash memory drives, CompactFlash cards, Memory Sticks, and Secure Digital cards. They all provide small form factor, power-free storage capacity. Figure 5.18 shows the various flash memory card types commonly available.

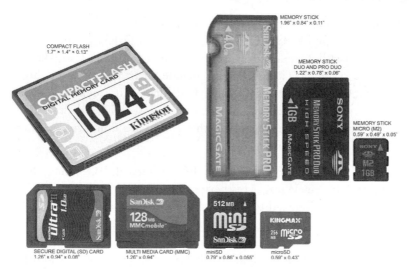

FIGURE 5.18 Flash memory cards.

The memory card reader has become a common feature on new desktop PCs. These units are installed in one of the system's disk drive bays and provide a physical and logical interface for various flash memory device types. In addition to providing an interface to connect additional disk-drive-like storage to the PC, it also allows digital information from other non-PC digital devices, such as digital pictures and video clips from cameras and different types of files from PDAs, to be moved back and forth between the device and the PC.

USB Flash Drives

A *USB flash drive* is a flash memory unit equipped with a USB interface and connector and mounted in a high impact plastic or metal case. This enables USB drives to plug into a standard USB port and function as an additional disk drive. They are removable and rewritable and can hold up to 64GB of data. However, the most popular sizes for these devices range between 512MB and 2GB. Figure 5.19 depicts a USB drive being plugged into a computer's standard USB port.

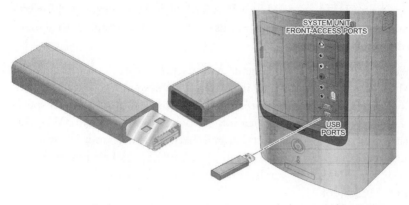

FIGURE 5.19   Connecting a USB drive.

Because the USB drive is based on flash memory technology, it does not require any power when it is not connected to the USB port. When it is installed, it draws power directly from the USB port. Most USB drive manufacturers supply a protective cap that snaps over the USB connector when the drive is not in use. The caps typically include an opening for attaching a chain or cord to the drive, which allows it to be attached to a key ring or other personal device for convenient carrying.

The appearance of Boot from USB options in the CMOS setup utilities of newer system boards has made it possible to install operating systems and diagnostic utilities on USB drives so that they can be used for emergency startup purposes.

USB drives are also referred to as *pen drives*, *thumb drives*, *flash drives*, or *USB keys*. Although they are sometimes referred to as Memory Sticks, this is an improper reference because that name is a trademark of the Sony Corporation and describes a different memory card specification. USB drives are supported directly by modern versions of Linux, Apple, and Windows operating systems.

CompactFlash Cards

The CompactFlash (CF) card is another flash memory form factor specification. CF cards are very thin flash memory-based devices that provide battery-free, removable data storage. These units are widely used in the professional camera market.

There are multiple form factors within the CF specification. The Type I CF card is 1.7 inches × 1.4 inches × 0.13 inches (43mm × 36mm × 3.3mm). Type II CF cards measure 1.7 inches × 1.4 inches × 0.19 inches (43mm × 36mm × 5.0mm) in size. Otherwise, the Type I and Type II cards are the same. CF cards are available in storage capacities up 137GB and can offer data transfer rates up to 16MBps for Type II CF cards and 66MBps for newer CF 3.0 devices. These cards employ Ultra DMA 33 and Ultra DMA 66 techniques developed for traditional parallel disk drive interfaces (discussed later in this chapter) to achieve these transfer rates.

The connector and socket arrangement used with CF cards is similar to the older PCMCIA Card connector used in portable PC systems. However, the CF card and socket has only 50 pins (instead of the 68 pins in the PCMCIA specification). The CF connection specification supports both 3.3V and 5V operation, allowing CF cards to be interchanged between 3.3V and 5V systems. Therefore, any CF card can operate at either voltage. Special 68-pin PCMCIA Type II to CF Type II adapters can be used to enable CF cards to be installed in a standard PCMCIA slot.

CF cards provide complete PCMCIA compatibility. In addition to flash memory applications, CF cards have been developed to fill a wide range of I/O functions for PCs. Common I/O devices available in a CF form factor include dial-up modems, ethernet network adapters, 802.11b WiFi wireless network adapters, serial ports, and Bluetooth wireless ports, to mention a few. Type I CF cards can be used in both Type I and Type II CF slots. On the other hand, Type II CF cards will fit only in CF Type II slots.

There is a special 1-inch hard drive designed to fit in a Type II CF card slot. These drives, called *microdrive cards*, can store up to 8GB of data. Like other electromechanical HDDs, microdrives must be formatted and have an operating system installed to be useful. Microdrive cards consume more power than other CF cards and devices, so they may not work properly in all systems with CompactFlash support.

Memory Sticks

Memory Stick is a proprietary 1.96 inches × 0.84 inches × 0.11 inches (50.0 × 21.5 × 2.8mm) removable flash memory card format introduced by the Sony

Corporation. These devices are available in transfer rates of 2.5MBps and storage capacities ranging up to 128MB. A newer version of the Memory Stick, known as *Memory Stick Pro*, offers greater storage capacities (theoretically ranging up to 32GB) along with higher data transfer rates (20MBps).

Small-form-factor versions of the Memory Stick, called the *Memory Stick Duo* and *Memory Stick Pro Duo* 1.22 inches × 0.78 inches × 0.06 inches (31.0mm × 20.0 × 1.6mm) have been developed to compete with the very successful *SD flash device* format. These devices feature 4GB storage capacities and transfer rates up to 20MBps.

Finally, an even smaller *Memory Stick Micro (M2)* device, 0.59 inch × 0.49 inch × 0.05 inch (15 × 12.5 × 1.2mm) is available and also provides data transfer rates up to 20MBps and capacities that theoretically range up to 2GB.

Secure Digital Cards

Secure Digital (SD) is a flash memory card format used in a variety of different portable devices, including digital cameras, notebook computers, and PDAs. SD cards generally measure 1.26 inches × 0.94 inch × 0.08 inch (32mm × 24mm × 2.1mm), but can be as thin as 0.055 inch (1.4mm). These cards are based on an older Multi Media Card (MMC) form factor, but tend to be slightly thicker than MMC cards. New miniSD 0.79 inch × 0.86 inch × 0.055 inch (20 × 21.5 × 1.4mm) and *microSD* 0.59 inch × 0.43 inch × 0.039 (15mm × 11mm × 1mm) formats have also been introduced to provide even smaller form factor memory devices to the market.

SD cards are sold according to their storage capacities as well as their data transfer rates. SD cards are available in 2GB, 4GB, and 8GB versions. Transfer rates for SD cards are specified in terms of 150KBps multiples (for example, a 1x version runs at 150KBps and a 2x device transfers data at 300KBps rates). Basic SD cards transfer data at 6x speeds—the speed of a standard CD-ROM drive. Higher speed 1.01 SD cards operate at transfer rates up to 66x and SD 1.1 cards operate at 133x speeds.

Mini and Micro SD cards can be used in standard SD slots by first inserting them in special adapters. Likewise, the standard SD devices can be used in CompactFlash or PC Card slots with an adapter. Some SD cards come with built-in USB connectors to provide dual purpose usage of the device. Most SD cards also offer security feature such as a locking write-protect switch on the side of the device to prevent accidental overwriting of the contents and onboard digital rights management (DRM) software to prevent unauthorized copying of the contents (this feature is intended for use by the software, music, and movie industries to protect their materials from copying).

Exam Prep Questions

1. Which of these configurations can be set on an IDE drive? (Select all that apply.)

   ○ **A.** Master

   ○ **B.** Primary

   ○ **C.** Single

   ○ **D.** Slave

2. How is IDE support provided for system boards that have integrated IDE controllers?

   ○ **A.** Through the BIOS firmware

   ○ **B.** Through an installed driver

   ○ **C.** By the operating system

   ○ **D.** Through an installed application

3. What is the maximum permissible length for a standard SCSI daisy chain, including the internal cable?

   ○ **A.** 10 feet

   ○ **B.** 15 feet

   ○ **C.** 20 feet

   ○ **D.** 25 feet

4. How many devices can be daisy-chained on a single standard SCSI controller?

   ○ **A.** 2

   ○ **B.** 7

   ○ **C.** 8

   ○ **D.** 15

5. What is the maximum permissible length for a standard SCSI cable segment?

   ○ **A.** 3 feet

   ○ **B.** 6 feet

   ○ **C.** 9 feet

   ○ **D.** 12 feet

6. If you are working on an older Pentium system board that supports four PATA drives, how could you install two large HDDs, a CD-ROM/DVD drive, a CD writer drive, and an IDE tape drive?

   ○ **A.** Install a SATA adapter card and use SATA devices for some of or all the drives

   ○ **B.** Install an IDE adapter card

   ○ **C.** This type of motherboard can support only four PATA devices

   ○ **D.** This type of motherboard can use only two PATA devices

7. How many SCSI devices can be attached to a Wide SCSI host adapter?

   ○ **A.** 7

   ○ **B.** 8

   ○ **C.** 15

   ○ **D.** 16

8. What is the maximum length for an external standard SCSI daisy chain?

   ○ **A.** 3 feet

   ○ **B.** 10 feet

   ○ **C.** 15 feet

   ○ **D.** 20 feet

9. What is the maximum permissible length for a Fast SCSI daisy chain?

   ○ **A.** 10 feet

   ○ **B.** 15 feet

   ○ **C.** 20 feet

   ○ **D.** 25 feet

10. An internal SCSI ribbon cable is outfitted with a _____ connector.

   ○ **A.** 25-pin

   ○ **B.** 40-pin

   ○ **C.** 50-pin

   ○ **D.** 68-pin

11. Which of the following is not a valid SCSI connector?

   ○ **A.** 25-pin DB

   ○ **B.** 34-pin Centronics

   ○ **C.** 50-pin Centronics

   ○ **D.** 68-pin Centronics

12. Which part of the system is responsible for assigning drive letters to IDE drives?

   ○ **A.** BIOS

   ○ **B.** User

   ○ **C.** IDE controller

   ○ **D.** Operating system

13. On an ATX system board that integrates the PATA interface connections into the board, how many devices can be attached to each interface connection?

   ○ **A.** 1

   ○ **B.** 2

   ○ **C.** 3

   ○ **D.** 4

14. How many SCSI devices can be attached to a Wide SCSI host adapter?

   ○ **A.** 7

   ○ **B.** 8

   ○ **C.** 15

   ○ **D.** 16

15. How many wires are there in a standard IDE signal cable?

   ○ **A.** 50

   ○ **B.** 40

   ○ **C.** 25

   ○ **D.** 8

16. Which of the following devices is based on flash memory technology?

- ○ **A.** SD cards
- ○ **B.** Floppy disks
- ○ **C.** CD-ROM discs
- ○ **D.** DVD discs

17. The mechanism in a CD-ROM/DVD drive is responsible for positioning the drive's read mechanism in the correct position is the _____.

- ○ **A.** Collimator
- ○ **B.** Spindle
- ○ **C.** Stepper motor
- ○ **D.** Head actuator

18. What part of a hard disk reads the information stored on a disk?

- ○ **A.** Spindle
- ○ **B.** R/W head mechanism
- ○ **C.** Platter
- ○ **D.** Drive controller

19. What are floppy disk generally used for in newer PCs?

- ○ **A.** Install OEM printer drivers
- ○ **B.** Booting a failing system into Safe Mode
- ○ **C.** Loading third-party device drivers into a Windows system
- ○ **D.** Booting a failing system to a command prompt environment

20. Which of the following types of cables can be used to connect hard drives to a typical BTX system board? (Select all that apply.)

- ○ **A.** EIDE
- ○ **B.** SATA
- ○ **C.** SCSI
- ○ **D.** IEEE-1394

Answers and Explanations

1. **A, C, D.** Most IDE drives come from the manufacturer configured for operation as a single drive or as the master drive in a multidrive system. To install the drive as a second (or slave) drive it is usually necessary to install, remove, or move a jumper block.

2. **A.** The IDE controller structure is an integrated portion of most PC system boards. This structure includes BIOS and chipset support for the IDE version that the board will support, as well as the IDE host connector.

3. **C.** Maximum recommended length for a complete standard SCSI chain is 20 feet (6 meters).

4. **B.** A system's first SCSI controller can handle up to 7 devices; an additional SCSI controller can boost the system to support up to 14 SCSI devices.

5. **A.** A maximum single SCSI segment of less than 3 feet (1 meter) is recommended.

6. **A.** The older system described in the question employs a two-channel IDE system-level interface that supports up to four PATA devices. The only reasonable option for adding the number and types of devices described in the question to the system is to install a SATA adapter card.

7. **C.** A Wide SCSI (SCSI-2) controller can control up to 15 additional devices.

8. **C.** Maximum recommended length for a complete standard SCSI chain is 20 feet (6 meters). You can realistically count on about 3–5 feet of internal cable, so reduce the maximum total length of the chain to about 15 feet (4.5 meters).

9. **A.** The Fast SCSI (Fast SCSI-2) specification allows transfers of up to 10MBps and reduces the maximum length of the SCSI chain to about 10 feet. Fast SCSI allows up to seven devices to be connected using a 50-pin connector.

10. **C.** The SCSI interface uses a 50-pin signal cable arrangement. Internally, the cable is a 50-pin flat ribbon cable.

11. **B.** The version of the SCSI interface used in the Apple Macintosh employs a variation of the standard that features a proprietary miniature 25-pin D-shell connector. A 50-pin shielded cable with Centronics-like

connectors is used for external SCSI connections. A revised 68-pin P-cable format, using Centronics connectors, was introduced to support 16-bit transfers in the SCSI-3 specification.

12. D. Under Microsoft operating systems, the primary partitions of multiple IDE hard drives are assigned the first logical drive identifiers. If an IDE drive is partitioned into two logical drives, the system will identify them as the C: drive and the D: drive. If a second IDE drive is added as a slave drive with two additional logical drives, the system will reassign the partitions on the first drive to be logical drives C: and E:, and the partitions on the slave drive will be D: and F:.

13. B. The EIDE controller supplies two IDE interfaces that can each handle a master and a slave device in a daisy-chained configuration.

14. C. A Wide SCSI (SCSI-2) controller can control up to 15 additional devices.

15. B. The IDE interface used a single 40-pin ribbon cable to connect the hard drive to the host adapter card or system board and supported a maximum throughput of 8.3 MBps.

16. A. Secure Digital (SD) is a flash memory card format used in a variety of different portable devices, including digital cameras, notebook computers and PDAs. SD cards generally measure 1.26" × 0.94" × 0.08" (32mm × 24mm × 2.1 mm), but can be as thin as 0.055" (1.4mm).

17. D. Like magnetic drives, CD-ROM drives have an actuator motor that moves the laser/detector read or read/write module in and out under the disc to position it in the correct place for reading (or writing).

18. B. In order to perform a read or write operation, the address of the particular track and sector to be accessed is applied to a stepper motor, which moves a read/write (R/W) head over the desired track. As the desired sector passes beneath the R/W head, the data transfer occurs.

19. D. While many new PC systems do not include a floppy disk drive as a standard component, many operating systems have provisions for creating an Emergency Start or Emergency Repair disk based on a floppy disk. These disks are designed to be used for booting the failing system to a command prompt when the operating system or hard disk drive is not functioning properly.

20. A, B. Most newer system boards offer built-in EIDE and SATA drive connections as standards for connecting disk drives to the system.

CHAPTER SIX

Ports and Peripherals

Terms you'll need to understand:

- ✓ USB port
- ✓ FireWire/IEEE-1394 port
- ✓ HDMI
- ✓ DVI
- ✓ Composite video
- ✓ Component (RGB) video
- ✓ Aspect ratio
- ✓ Joystick

- ✓ Mouse
- ✓ Trackball
- ✓ CRT monitor
- ✓ HDTV
- ✓ Touch screens/pads
- ✓ LCD display
- ✓ S-video

Techniques to master:

Essentials 1.1—Identify the fundamental principles of using personal computers.

- ✓ Identify the names, purposes, and characteristics of display devices; for example, projectors, CRT and LCD.
- ✓ Connector types (for example, VGA, DVI/HDMI, S-video, Component / RGB).
- ✓ Settings (such as V-hold, refresh rate, resolution).
- ✓ Identify the names, purposes, and characteristics of input devices; for example, mouse, keyboard, bar code reader, multimedia (web and digital cameras, MIDI, microphones), biometric devices, touch screen.

- ✓ Identify the names, purposes, and characteristics of adapter cards.
  - ✓ Video including PCI/PCI-E and AGP
  - ✓ Multimedia
  - ✓ I/O (SCSI, serial, USB, parallel)
  - ✓ Communications, including network and modem
- ✓ Identify the names, purposes, and characteristics of ports and cables; for example, USB 1.1 and 2.0, parallel, serial, IEEE 1394 / FireWire, RJ45 and RJ11, PS2/mini-DIN, Centronics (for instance, mini, 36) multimedia (such as 1/8 connector, MIDSI COAX, SPDIF).

Input/Output Interfaces

This chapter covers the I/O Ports and Peripherals areas of the CompTIA A+ Certification—Essentials examination under Objective 1.1. The PC-compatible architecture has always permitted a variety of peripheral devices to be added to the system. Most of these devices are designed to employ some type of PC-compatible I/O connection method. The computer technician must be able to

▸ Recognize the type of port the device requires

▸ Locate standard I/O port connections on a PC

▸ Determine what type of cabling is needed to add peripheral devices to a PC

The PC's input and output units enable it to communicate with the outside world. An *I/O unit* typically consists of interface circuitry, a peripheral device and some type of standard connection point or port connector. The interface circuitry may be located on a plug-in adapter card or in one of the system board's chipset components.

The I/O port connector may be mounted on the back of an adapter card, on the back of the system board so that it is accessible from the rear of the system, on the front panel of the system unit case, or somewhere on the system board. The peripheral device can plug directly into one of the port connectors, or it can be attached to the system through some type of standard signal cable.

Initiating I/O Transfers

While executing a program, the microprocessor constantly reads information from or writes information to memory locations. The program is also likely to call on the microprocessor to read from or write to the system's I/O devices. Regardless of how the peripheral is connected to the system (serial or parallel), one of the following four methods is used to initiate data transfer between the system and the peripheral device:

▸ Polling—The microprocessor examines the status of the peripheral under program control.

▸ Programmed I/O—The microprocessor alerts the designated peripheral by applying its address to the system's address bus.

▸ Interrupt-driven I/O—The peripheral uses the system's Interrupt Controller to alert the microprocessor that it's ready to transfer data.

▶ DMA—The intelligent peripheral uses the system's DMA controller to assume control of the system's buses to conduct direct transfers with primary memory.

System Resource Allocations

Each I/O controller or interface in the system requires certain system resources to support its operation and interaction with the system. Most intelligent devices in the PC system will require at least two of the following system resources:

▶ IRQ interrupt channels

▶ DMA channels

▶ I/O port address allocations

▶ Buffer memory address allocation (in system RAM)

Table 6.1 lists the standard system resources allocated to I/O devices, controllers, and ports.

TABLE 6.1   Standard I/O Resources

DEVICE	I/O PORT ADDRESS	IRQ/DMA CHANNEL
DMA Controller (South Bridge)	000–01F	-
Interrupt Controller (South Bridge)	020–03F	-
Timer/Counter (South Bridge)	040–05F	IRQ0
Keyboard Controller	060–06F	IRQ1
Real-Time Clock, NMI Mask (South Bridge)	070–07F	IRQ8
DMA Page Register (South Bridge)	080–09F	-
Interrupt Controller (South Bridge)	0A0–0BF	-
Clear Math Coprocessor Busy	0F0	-
Reset Math Coprocessor	0F1	-
Math Coprocessor	0F8–0FF	IRQ13
Second IDE Controller	170–177	IRQ15
First IDE Controller	1F0–1F7	IRQ14
Game Port	200–207	

(continues)

TABLE 6.1 *Continued*

DEVICE	I/O PORT ADDRESS	IRQ/DMA CHANNEL
Parallel Printer Port #2	278–27F	IRQ5
Serial COM Port #2	2F8–2FF	IRQ3
Parallel Printer Port #1	378–37F	IRQ7
MGA/First Printer Port	3B0–3BF	
CGA	3D0–3DF	
FDD Controller	3F0–3F7	IRQ6/DRQ2
Serial COM Port #1	3F8–3FF	IRQ4
USB Controller	FF80–FF9F	IRQ10
PS/2 Mouse Port	-	IRQ12
Serial COM Port #3	3E8–3EF	IRQ4
Serial COM Port #4	2E8–2EF	IRQ3

Resources for Legacy Ports and Devices

In Pentium-based systems the PnP BIOS normally detects all the ports and devices in the system and allocates the appropriate resources to each. The exception to this is the presence of non-PnP devices, also referred to as *legacy devices*.

Older ISA adapter cards typically had no PnP function and had to be configured manually. In these situations, the system had no way to reconfigure the card, so you had to tell it which resources were required for it. This function is performed through the PnP and PCI Setup screens in the CMOS setup routine and reserves certain resources so that they are available for the legacy device.

When you manually configure such a device, you must be aware of which system resources it needs and what settings it can work with. This information can typically be found in the device's installation guide. If the guide is not available, you should check the Internet for the manufacturer's website to determine whether any configuration information is available there. In addition, there may be third-party sites on the Internet that can supply the configuration information that you need for the device.

Ports, Cables, and Connectors

A variety of peripheral devices can be added to a PC-compatible system. Most of these devices are designed to employ some type of standard PC-compatible I/O connection method. The computer technician must be able to recognize what type of port the device requires, locate standard I/O port connections, and determine what type of cabling is required to successfully connect the port and the device to successfully add peripheral devices to a PC system.

The Universal Serial Bus (USB) port has emerged as the go-to port for nearly everything in the PC. This has led to the steady disappearance of the older ports from newer PC models. In addition, new devices are not being designed with older port types as an option. However, these legacy ports are still found and used in millions of existing computers and peripherals in the world. Therefore, they are covered later in the chapter.

The standard I/O port types commonly found on new computers include the following:

▶ PS/2 keyboard and mouse ports

▶ USB ports

▶ IEEE-1394 (FireWire) ports

▶ Infrared ports

▶ Audio connections

PS/2 Connectors

PC-compatible systems still offer a pair of round (quarter-inch) 6-pin mini-DIN connectors (also referred to as *PS/2 connectors*) for connecting the keyboard and mouse to the system. These connectors are built in to the system board, and their controllers are an integral part of the chipset.

When the ATX form factor specification adopted identical connectors for both the keyboard and mouse, it introduced an opportunity to plug these devices into the wrong connector. Although they are physically the same, the pin assignments and signal levels are completely different, as Figure 6.1 illustrates. Later PC system boards and peripherals have adopted an informal color-coding system to avoid this confusion—the keyboard connector and port are color coded purple, whereas the mouse connection is green.

> **EXAM ALERT**
>
> Be aware that it is quite possible to confuse the PS/2 mouse and keyboard connections on most PC systems.

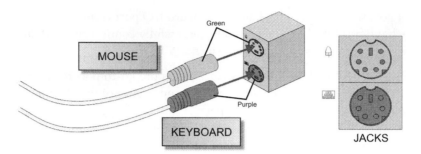

FIGURE 6.1   Mouse and keyboard connectors.

Although many newer peripheral devices can safely be unplugged and reattached to the system while power is applied, this is not so with the standard keyboard or mouse. Plugging these devices in to the system while power is applied
can cause the system board or the device to fail because of the power surge and
electrostatic discharge (ESD) that might occur between the keyboard and the
system board.

EXAM ALERT

Be aware that plugging non-hot-swappable devices such as the keyboard into the system while it is turned on can damage parts of the system.

Universal Serial Bus

The most widely used I/O interface scheme in current PCs is the Universal
Serial Bus. This high-speed serial interface has been developed to provide a fast,
flexible method of attaching up to 127 peripheral devices to the computer. USB
peripherals can be daisy-chained, or networked together, using connection hubs
that enable the bus to branch out through additional port connections. This
connection format has been designed to replace the system's traditional serial-
and parallel-port connections. A practical USB desktop connection scheme is
presented in Figure 6.2.

EXAM ALERT

Memorize the number of devices that can be attached to a USB port.

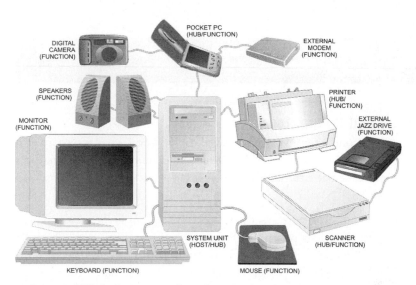

FIGURE 6.2 USB desktop connection scheme.

In this example, some of the peripheral devices are simply devices that perform a certain function (such as a keyboard), whereas others serve as both devices (functions) and as connection hubs. These latter devices are referred to as *compound devices*. The system provides a USB host connection that serves as the main USB connection. USB devices can be added to or removed from the system while it is powered up and fully operational. This is referred to as *hot swapping* or *hot plugging* the device. The plug-and-play capabilities of the system will detect the presence (or absence) of the device and configure it for operation.

The USB management software dynamically tracks what devices are attached to the bus and where they are. This process of identifying and numbering bus devices is known as *bus enumerating*. The USB specification promotes *hot-swap* peripheral connections that do not require the system to be shut down. The system automatically detects peripherals and configures the proper driver. Instead of simply detecting and charting devices at startup in a PnP style, the USB controller continuously monitors the bus and updates the list whenever a device is added to or removed from it.

While hot swapping USB devices typically does no harm to the system hardware or the device, the Windows operating system requires that you stop the device's operation using the Safely Remove Hardware tool. An icon for this tool appears in the notification area of the Windows taskbar while the USB device is active. Failure to stop the device's operation before physically removing it from the USB port will cause Windows to generate an "Unsafe Removal of Device" error. It may also cause the system to crash and lose any unsaved data.

EXAM ALERT

Be aware of the need to use the Safely Remove Hardware tool prior to removing USB devices from a Windows system.

USB Cabling and Connectors

USB transfers are conducted over a four-wire cable. The signal travels over a pair of twisted wires (D+ and D–) in a 90-ohm cable. The differential signal and twisted-pair wiring provide minimum signal deterioration over distances and high noise immunity.

A Vbus and Ground (GND) wire are also present. The Vbus is the +5Vdc power cord. The interface provides power to the peripheral attached to it. The root hub provides power directly from the host system to those devices directly connected to it. Hubs also supply power to the devices connected to them. Even though the interface supplies power to the USB devices, they are permitted to have their own power sources if necessary. In these instances, the device must be designed specifically to avoid interference with the bus power-distribution scheme. The USB host's power-management software can apply power to devices when needed and suspend power to them when not required.

The USB specification defines two types of plugs: series-A and series-B. Series-A connectors are used for devices where the USB cable connection is permanently attached to devices at one end. Examples of these devices are keyboards, mice, and hubs. Conversely, the series-B plugs and jacks are designed for devices that require detachable cabling (printers, scanners, and modems, for example). Both are four-contact plugs and sockets embedded in plastic connectors. The sockets can be implemented in vertical, right-angle, and panel-mount variations. Smaller 5-pin USB plugs and jacks (referred to as *Mini-A* and *Mini-B*) have been developed for the USB 2.0 specification, and an even smaller Micro-USB connector version has been proposed for the future. These connectors are intended for use with smaller devices such as digital cameras, cell phones, and Personal Digital Assistants (PDAs). These connector selections are designed to provide rugged connections that are not prone to damage from repeated or incorrect usage.

The connectors for both series are keyed so that they cannot be plugged in backward. All hubs and functions possess a single, permanently attached cable with a series-B connector at its end. The connectors are designed so that the A- and B-series connections cannot be interchanged. Figure 6.3 depicts the USB cable and connector versions. The icon used to represent a USB connector is depicted in the centers of the A and B plug connectors.

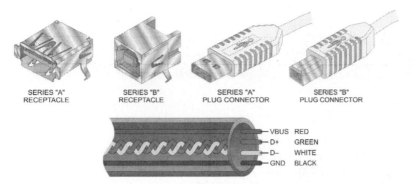

FIGURE 6.3 The USB cable and connectors.

EXAM ALERT

Be able of describe the construction of a USB cable.

USB Architecture

When USB devices are daisy-chained together, the resulting connection architecture forms a tree-like, tiered-star configuration, like the one depicted in Figure 6.4. In this type of configuration, information passes back and forth between devices (nodes) attached at different tier levels and the host PC located at the Root Hub level. In the process, the information may pass through hubs at several different tier levels. The system knows where all the devices are located in the architecture through the enumeration process that is performed when the system is first powered up, or when a device is added to or removed from the structure.

The USB system is composed of a USB host and USB devices. The devices category consists of hubs and nodes. In any system, there is one USB host. This unit contains the interface that provides the USB host controller. The controller is actually a combination of USB hardware, firmware, and software.

Hubs are devices that provide additional connection points for other USB devices. A special hub, called the *root hub*, is an integral part of the host system and provides one or more attachment points for USB devices.

ATX and BTX system boards routinely feature built-in USB host ports. ATX boards feature a pair of USB port connectors as part of their master I/O connection block. BTX boards may provide five or more USB connections. You can also install PCI card-mounted USB ports to attach even more USB devices to the system. These host ports function as the system's root hub.

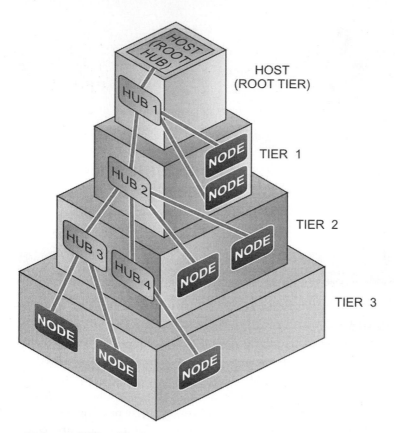

FIGURE 6.4 USB architecture.

In the case of built-in USB ports, the operation of the port connections is controlled by settings in the system board's CMOS setup utility. In most cases, it will be necessary to access the CMOS setup utility's PCI configuration screen, enable the USB function, and assign the ports IRQ channels to use. If no USB device is being used with the system, the IRQ allocation should be set to NA to free up the IRQ line for use by other devices.

Although the tiered architecture described in Figure 6.4 approaches the complexity and capabilities of local area network architectures, the overhead for managing the port is much easier to implement. USB devices can be added to or removed from the system while it is fully operational. In reality, this means that the USB organizational structure is modified anytime a device is added to or removed from the system.

USB Data Transfers

Unlike traditional serial interfaces that transmit framed characters one at a time, data moves across the USB in the form of *data packets*. Packet sizes vary with the type of transmission being carried out. However, they are typically 8, 16, 32, or 64 bytes in length.

The USB specification provides for the following four types of transfers to be conducted:

▶ Control transfers—Used by the system to configure devices at startup or time of connection. Other software can use control transfers to perform other device-specific operations.

▶ Bulk data transfers—Used to service devices that can handle large batches of data (scanners and printers, for example). Bulk transfers are typically made up of large bursts of sequential data. The system arranges for bulk transfers to be conducted when the bus has plenty of capacity to carry out the transfer.

▶ Interrupt transfers—Small, spontaneous transfers from a device that are used to announce events, provide input coordinate information, or transfer characters.

▶ Isochronous transfers—These involve large streams of data. This format is used to move continuous, real-time data streams such as voice or video. Data delivery rates are predetermined and correspond to the sampling rate of the device.

> **EXAM ALERT**
>
> Be aware of the USB high-speed data streaming mode.

USB devices are rated as full-speed and low-speed devices based on their communication specification. Under the USB 1.1 specification, USB devices run at 1.5 Mbps (low speed) and 12Mbps (full speed) speeds. The length limit for cables serving low-speed devices is 9 feet 10 inches (3 meters). On the other hand, high-speed USB devices operate under the USB 2.0 specification (also referred to as *high-speed USB*) and support data rates up to 480Mbps. The maximum cable length for full-speed USB communication is 16 feet 5 inches (5 meters).

EXAM ALERT

Know the length limits for full- and low-speed USB devices. It should help you to remember that the low-speed distance is actually shorter than the high-speed length.

The low-speed USB data rate is sufficient for many PC peripherals, such as telephones, keyboards, mice, digital joysticks, floppy drives, digital speakers, and low-end printers. The higher bandwidth of high-speed USB enables peripherals such as higher-resolution, full-motion video cameras, high-resolution scanners and printers, fast data storage devices, and broadband Internet connections to operate smoothly.

High-speed USB ports are available on PCI adapter cards for upgrading older PC systems. Likewise, USB drivers for Windows 2000 and Windows XP can be downloaded from the Microsoft Windows update website.

IEEE-1394 FireWire Bus

While the USB specification was being refined for the computer industry, a similar serial interface bus was being developed for the consumer products market. Apple Computers and Texas Instruments worked together with the Institute of Electrical and Electronic Engineers (IEEE) to produce the FireWire (or IEEE-1394) specification. The bus offers a very fast option for connecting consumer electronics devices, such as camcorders, digital music players, and the original iPods from Apple, to the computer system.

The FireWire bus is similar to USB in that devices can be daisy-chained to the computer using a single connector and host adapter. The entire interface requires a single IRQ channel, an I/O address range, and a single DMA channel to operate. FireWire is also capable of using the high-speed isochronous transfer mode described for USB. The original IEEE-1394a FireWire specification (now referred to as *FireWire 400*) provides data transfer rates up to 400Mbps. However, an improved IEEE-1394b standard provides an additional electrical signaling method that permits data transmission speeds of 800Mbps (FireWire 800) and greater. Its high-speed capabilities make FireWire well suited for handling components, such as video and audio devices, which require real-time, high-speed data transfer rates.

A single IEEE-1394 connection can be used to connect up to 63 devices to a single port. However, up to 1,023 FireWire buses can be interconnected. PCs most commonly employ a PCI expansion card to provide the FireWire interface. Whereas AV equipment typically employs 4-pin 1394 connectors, computers normally use a 6-pin connector, with a 4-pin to 6-pin converter. The maximum segment length for an IEEE-1394 connection is 4.5 meters (14 feet). Figure 6.5 depicts the FireWire connector and plug most commonly used with PCs.

> **EXAM ALERT**
>
> Remember how many devices can be attached to a single IEEE-1394 port.

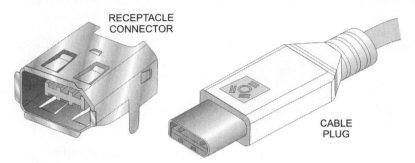

RECEPTACLE
CONNECTOR

CABLE
PLUG

FIGURE 6.5 FireWire plug and connector.

The IEEE-1394 cable is composed of two twisted-pair conductors similar to those used in the local area networks. The IEEE-1394b version of the standard also supports new transport media, including glass and plastic optical fiber, as well as Category 5 copper cable. With the new media comes extended distances; for example, 100 meters over CAT5 cabling. Like USB, FireWire supports both PnP and hot swapping of components. It also provides power to the peripheral devices through one pair of the twisted conductors in its interface cable.

Infrared Ports

The Infrared Data Association (IrDA) has produced a wireless peripheral connection standard based on infrared light technology, similar to that used in consumer remote control devices. Many system board designs include an IrDA-compliant port standard to provide wireless communications with devices such as keyboards, mice, character printers, personal digital assistants, and notebook computers. Figure 6.6 illustrates an IrDA-connected printer. The same technology has been employed to carry out transfers between computer communications devices such as modems and local area network cards.

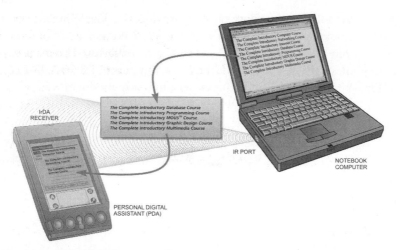

FIGURE 6.6 An IrDA device connection.

The IrDA standard specifies four protocols that are used with different types of devices:

- ▶ IrLPT—Used with character printers to provide a wireless interface between the computer and the printer.

- ▶ IrDA-SIR—The standard infrared protocol used to provide a standard serial port interface with transfer rates ranging up to 115kbps.

- ▶ IrDA-FIR—The fast infrared protocol used to provide a high-speed serial port interface with transfer rates ranging up to 4Mbps.

- ▶ IrTran-P—Used to provide a digital image transfer standard for communications with digital image capture devices.

These protocols specify communication ranges up to 2 meters (6 feet), but most specifications usually state 1 meter as the maximum range. All IrDA transfers are carried out in half-duplex mode and must have a clear line of sight between the transmitter and receiver. The receiver must be situated within 15 degrees of center with the line of transmission.

EXAM ALERT

Remember that the IrLPT port is a new, high-speed printer interface that can be used to print from a wide array of computing devices.

The Windows operating system supports the use of infrared devices. The properties of installed IrDA devices can be viewed through its Device Manager. Likewise, connections to another IrDA computer can be established through the Windows Network Dial-up Connections applet. By installing a Point-to-Point Protocol (PPP) or an IrDA LAN protocol through this applet, you can conduct wireless communications with other computers without a modem or network card.

Challenge #1

Your assistant is setting up an IrDA printer in a remote location. He has called you because he cannot get the system to see the infrared printer connection. To check the printer, the assistant connected it to the host computer using a normal parallel interface and it ran successfully. Which items should you suggest that your assistant check to verify the operation of the infrared port?

Multimedia Connections

Another noticeable change in PC systems is the rapid integration of the PC with consumer audio and video (A/V) systems. Special hardware and operating system versions have been produced under the banner of media centers in an effort to integrate mainstream PC systems for home entertainment applications. Figure 6.7 depicts a typical PC media center and its I/O components.

This integration has led to the inclusion of many connector types commonly found in consumer A/V systems. These connections range from the standard RCA minijacks and plugs associated with traditional PC sound cards to advanced video cables and connectors used with high-definition television (HDTV) systems. They enable A/V source components such as AM/FM stereo receivers, MPEG players, and DVD and CD players to be connected to the PC system. They also enable the PC system to operate with advanced A/V output devices, such as large screen, HD televisions and high-end stereo amplifiers and speaker systems.

Figure 6.8 depicts common audio connector schemes. To the left of the figure are the typical microphone, speaker, and line-in connectors found on PC sound cards. On the right side of the figure are plugs and connectors used for stereo audio connections. Audio connections are typically made with 1/4-inch RCA minijacks and plugs (you may also encounter 1/8 inch or 3/32 inch submini RCA jacks). Audio connectors typically use a red connector and jack for the right stereo channel and a white connector for the left channel.

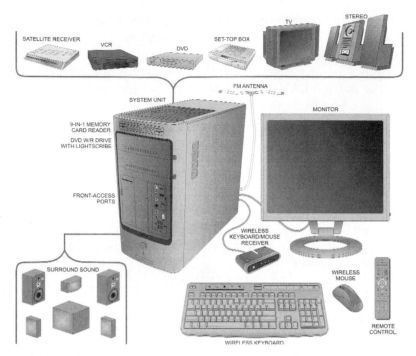

FIGURE 6.7 Media center components.

Most sound card manufacturers now color-code the standard A/V connections on their products. The microphone connection is generally pink while the headphone (lineout) connection is green. If the card features a Line In connection, it is generally a light blue color. MPC-3 CD-In connectors are generally black, MPC-3 Aux-In connectors are white, and subwoofer connections are orange. These colors are not an official industry standard, so you should consult the card's documentation when installing and configuring it.

For many years, the standard video connection for PCs has been the three-row, 15-pin VGA D-shell connector used to connect video adapter cards to video monitors. This connector has remained in used through the VGA standard upgrade—SVGA, XGA, UXGA video displays. However, as the PC is increasingly integrated into home entertainment systems, standard consumer electronics connectors have been adopted to accommodate these applications. Just as the PC industry has developed standardized connections for most components, consumer electronics connections are standardized by function. Figure 6.9 shows different video connection options adopted from the consumer A/V market.

> ▶ Composite Video—A video connection scheme where all video color and synchronization information is transmitted as one combined signal. These cables and connectors are typically color-coded yellow. This is

typically the cheapest and lowest quality method of transporting audio signals.

▶ Component Video—An analog video connection method where three color video signals (RGB) are transmitted on separate lines and combined inside the video equipment. Luminance and synchronization signals are added to one or more of the color signal lines. This method delivers signal quality levels between the composite video and the S-Video method described next. Component video connections are typically color coded as red, blue, and green.

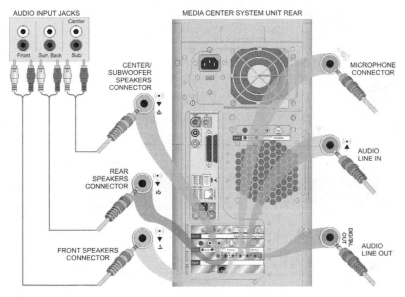

FIGURE 6.8   Audio connection methods.

Digital component video is also referred to as *4:2:2*. These numbers represent an encoded luminance factor followed by a Blue Difference (Pb) and a Red Difference (Pr) value that make up the color signal. Digital component video can be used with 480p, 720p, 1080i, and 1080p video display systems.

▶ S-Video—A high-performance multipin video cable and connector specification that splits the video signal into separate color components, chrominance, and luminance channels to provide high quality video output.

▶ Digital Video Interface (DVI)—A relatively new video signal connection scheme adopted from high definition (HD) television systems. DVI is a video-only connection scheme. DVI can deliver quality video in video systems running resolutions up to 1080p.

▶ High Definition Media Interface (HDMI)—An advanced version of the DVI interface that offers high-definition video and multichannel (up to eight) audio transfers in a single cable. Like the DVI interface, HDMI is capable of handling signals for video systems running resolutions up to 1080p.

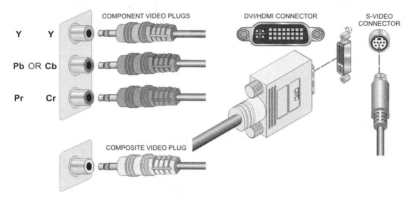

FIGURE 6.9 Advanced video connection options.

EXAM ALERT

Know which types of connectors are associated with different video standards.

MIDI Connections

Most sound cards possess only the capability to capture audio signals, digitize them, and play them back as they were recorded. Some sound cards have the capability to generate synthetic sounds that are not a function of a digitizing process. Musical instrument makers created the Musical Instrument Digital Interface (MIDI) standard to enable music synthesizers and other electronic music devices to communicate with computers and with each other.

The MIDI specification began as a hardware connectivity format that included a protocol for exchanging data and a cabling scheme for hooking devices together. The agreement was so widely accepted by the music industry that virtually every electronic instrument manufactured today conforms to the MIDI standard.

A typical MIDI system contains a MIDI-equipped computer, a keyboard controller/synthesizer, and an audio mixer/recorder, along with related sound modules. The computer contains a MIDI interface card. Advances in MIDI software have led to systems where the mixer has been eliminated in favor of software mixing. Sophisticated MIDI systems with a large number of instruments still opt for hardware mixing consoles. MIDI software contains programming called *MIDI Machine Control* (MMC) that actually controls intelligent MIDI devices, such as mixers, stage lights, and so on. A *sound module* is a hardware component containing ROM devices that hold the sampled sounds of the real instruments.

MIDI devices communicate serially through round, 5-pin DIN connectors, as described in Figure 6.10. Three types of connections are possible in a MIDI system. These are the MIDI-In, MIDI-Out, and MIDI-Thru connections. A single connection cable can be used for all three connection types. The synthesizer/controller requires two connections to the MIDI interface in the computer. The first deals with the controller portion of the keyboard. A MIDI cable runs from MIDI-Out of the controller to MIDI-In of the interface. On the synthesizer side of the keyboard, a MIDI-In from the keyboard must be connected to MIDI-Out of the interface card.

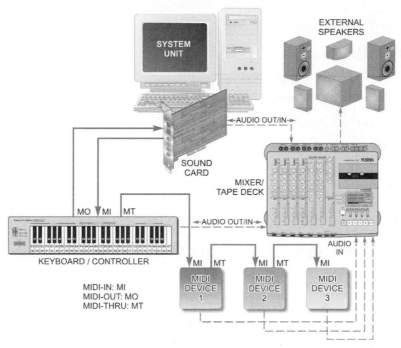

FIGURE 6.10   MIDI cable connections.

To continue the MIDI connection scheme, the interface would require an additional MIDI-Out connection. Alternatively, MIDI-Thru connections can be used to serially connect all the other MIDI devices to the system. The various devices are connected to the mixer/recorder through audio out/in patch cords.

MIDI data transfers are conducted serially. Each MIDI device contains a MIDI controller, as does the MIDI adapter card in the computer system. In the MIDI device, the data produced by the equipment is applied to the MIDI controller, which converts the data into the MIDI data format. The signal passes serially to the MIDI adapter card in the computer. After processing, the computer sends it back to the MIDI device.

Challenge #2

Your company is moving strongly into multimedia systems that include professional electronic music and video devices. Your boss is aware that some kind of FireWire devices are used with audio/video equipment and that there is MIDI equipment used by professional musicians. The boss has asked you which type of interface the company should standardize on. What should you tell the boss about this?

Legacy Ports

As indicated earlier in this chapter, three port types have been I/O standards since the original IBM PCs were introduced:

▶ Centronic parallel ports

▶ RS-232C serial ports

▶ Game ports

To their credit, these older ports are still included on many PCs. However, with the advent of several newer, faster, and more flexible connectivity schemes, these ports are becoming legacy ports and will probably disappear from PCs in the near future.

Table 6.2 summarizes the types of ports typically found on the back panel of system units, along with their connector and pin count information. These ports and connector types are described in Figure 6.11.

TABLE 6.2   Typical I/O Ports and Connectors

PORT	CONNECTOR
Keyboard	PS/2 6-pin mini-DIN
Mouse	PS/2 6-pin mini-DIN
COM1	DB-9M
COM2	DB-9M

TABLE 6.2 *Continued*

PORT	CONNECTOR
LPT	DB-25F
VGA	DB-15F (three row)
Game	DB-15F (two row)
Modem	RJ-11
LAN	BNC/RJ-45
Sound	RCA 1/8-inch mini or 3/32-inch sub minijacks
SCSI	Centronics 50-pin
USB	4-pin USB socket

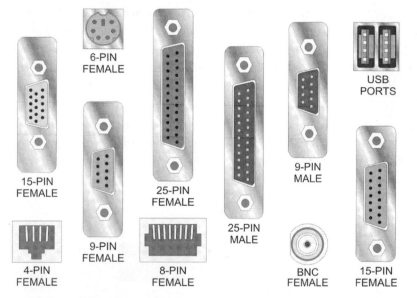

FIGURE 6.11 Typical I/O port connectors.

EXAM ALERT

Memorize the appearance, type, and pin configuration of the standard PC port connectors (parallel ports use 25-pin female D-shell connectors).

Parallel Printer Ports

Parallel printer ports have been a staple of the PC system since the original PCs were introduced. In their day, the parallel port's capability to quickly transfer bytes of data in parallel mode caused it to be adopted to interface a number of peripheral devices to the PC. These devices include CNC mills and lathes; X-Y plotters; fast computer-to-computer transfer systems; high-speed, high-volume, removable disk backup systems; and optical scanners.

The Centronics Standard

The original Centronics interface that existed prior to the original IBM PC employed a 36-pin D-shell connector on the printer adapter and a 36-pin Centronics connector on the printer end. The Centronics connector on the printer features a female slotted connector with contacts embedded on the top and bottom of the slot.

The IBM version of the interface, which became known as the Standard Parallel Port (SPP) specification for printers, reduced the pin count to 25 using a 25-pin, female D-shell connector at the computer's back panel. However, at the printer end of the cable, IBM continued with the standard 36-pin Centronics connector. Some printer connections employ a 36-pin mini-Centronics connector at the printer end of the cable.

Figure 6.12 shows a typical parallel printer connection using the IBM version of the Centronics standard. This interface enables the computer to pass information to the printer, 8 bits at a time, across the eight data lines. The other lines in the connection carry control signals (handshaking signals) back and forth between the computer and the printer.

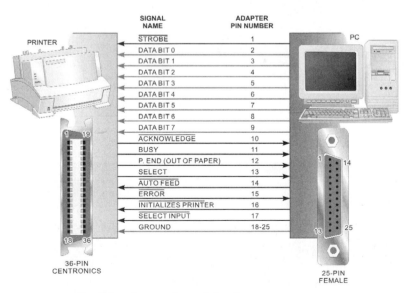

FIGURE 6.12 Parallel-port connector and signals.

Because parallel signals can deteriorate quickly with long lengths of cable, the length of a parallel printer cable should be less than 10 fcct. If longer lengths are needed, the cable should have a low-capacitance value. The cable should also be shielded to minimize Electromagnetic Field Interference (EFI) peripherals.

EXAM ALERT

Know the recommended length of a standard parallel printer cable.

EPP and ECP Parallel Port Operations

Enhanced Parallel Port (EPP) and Extended Capabilities Port (ECP) ports can be converted between unidirectional and bidirectional operation through the CMOS setup screen. If a parallel port is being used to support a bidirectional I/O device, such as a local area network adapter or a high-capacity storage device, this feature would need to be checked. The parallel cable should also be checked to see that it complies with the IEEE-1284 standard for use with bidirectional parallel ports. Using a traditional SPP cable could cause the device to operate erratically or fail completely.

EXAM ALERT

As you study the I/O ports in this chapter, be aware of which ports provide bidirectional, half-duplex, and full-duplex operation.

When EPP mode is selected in the port's configuration register, the standard and bidirectional modes are enabled. The functions of the port's pins are redefined under the EPP specification. When the EPP mode is enabled, the port can operate either as a standard bidirectional parallel port, or as a bidirectional EPP port.

The ECP mode provides a number of advantages over the SPP and EPP modes. The ECP mode employs DMA operations to offer higher performance than either of the other two modes.

EXAM ALERT

Remember that the ECP specification employs DMA operations to provide the highest data throughput for a parallel port.

RS-232 Serial Ports

Before the widespread acceptance of newer USB and FireWire serial ports, serial communications were conducted using one of the PC's standard RS-232 asynchronous communication (COM) ports.

When data is transferred *asynchronously*, the receiving system is not synchronized with the sending system. The standard serial ports in a PC employ this transmission method. The transmitted material is sent character by character (usually ASCII), with the beginning and end of each character framed by character start and stop bits. Between these bits, the bits of the character are sent at a constant rate, but the time interval between characters may be irregular.

Over a given period of time, synchronous communications are much faster than asynchronous methods. This is because of the extra number of bits required to send each character asynchronously. PC serial ports and analog modems use asynchronous communications methods, whereas digital modems and local area network adapters use synchronous methods.

RS-232 Interfaces and Cables

Historically, the most popular serial interface standard for PCs has been the Electronic Industry Association (EIA) RS-232C interface standard. The IBM version of the RS-232C standard calls for a 25-pin, male D-type connector. It also designates certain pins for data transmission and receiving, along with a number of control lines. The standard was developed to cover a wide variety of peripheral devices, and therefore not all the lines are used in any given application. Normally, only nine of the pins are active for a given application. The other lines are used for secondary, or backup, lines and grounds. Different device manufacturers may use various combinations of the RS-232C lines, even for peripherals of the same type.

In addition to defining the type of connector to be used and the use of its individual pins, the RS-232 standard also establishes acceptable voltage levels for the signals on its pins. These levels are generally converted to and from standard digital logic levels. These levels can produce a maximum baud rate of 20,000 baud over distances less than 50 feet.

> **EXAM ALERT**
>
> Know the maximum recommended length of an RS-232 cable.

The system's first serial port has typically been implemented in a 9-pin D-shell male connector on the computer. Figure 6.13 depicts a typical 9-pin to 25-pin connection scheme. Notice the crossover wiring technique employed for the TXD/RXD lines displayed in this example.

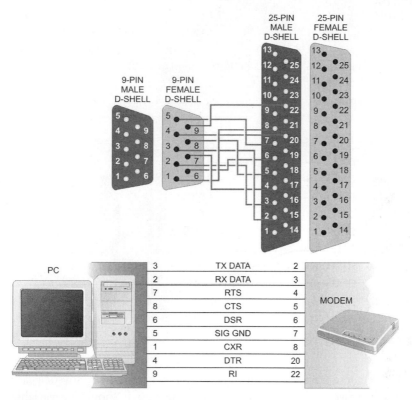

FIGURE 6.13   A 9-pin to 25-pin RS-232 cable.

In cases where systems with serial ports are located close enough to each other, a null modem connection can be implemented. A *null modem connection* allows the two serial ports to communicate directly without using modems. A typical null modem connection scheme is illustrated in Figure 6.14.

Game Ports

The IBM version of the game control port enables two joysticks to be used with the system. The adapter converts resistive input values into relative joystick positions in much the same manner as described in the previous section. This adapter can also function as a general-purpose I/O converter, featuring four analog and four digital input points. As with the parallel printer and RS-232 serial ports, the game port has mostly been replaced on newer PC models by USB ports and devices.

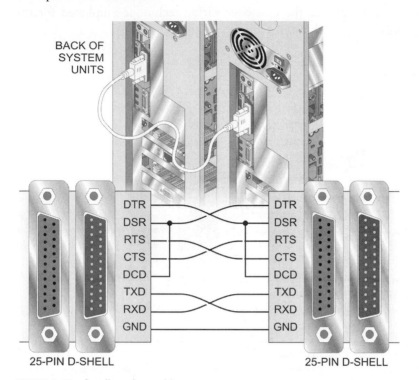

FIGURE 6.14 A null modem cable.

The input to the game port is generally a pair of resistive joysticks. Joysticks are defined as having two variable resistances, each of which should be variable between 0 and 100 kilohms. Joysticks may have one or two normally open fire buttons. The order of fire buttons should correspond with that of the resistive elements (A and B or A, B, C, and D). The wiring structure for the two-row, 15-pin D-shell female connector is shown in Figure 6.15.

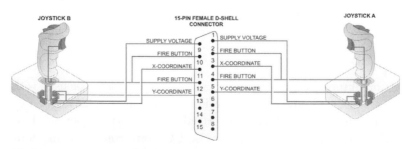

FIGURE 6.15 Game-port connections.

Typical Peripheral Systems

Peripherals are devices and subsystems that are added to the basic PC system to extend its capabilities. These devices and systems can be divided into three general categories: input systems, output systems, and memory systems. The standard peripherals associated with personal computers typically include two input devices and two output devices. The typical input devices are the keyboard and the mouse. Likewise, most systems employ two output devices: the VGA display monitor and the character printer.

Keyboards

The alphanumeric keyboard is the most widely used input device for microcomputers. Inside, a keyboard is basically an X,Y matrix arrangement of switch elements, as shown in Figure 6.16. To produce meaningful data from a key press, the keyboard must be capable of detecting and identifying the pressed key and then encoding the key closure into a data form the computer can use.

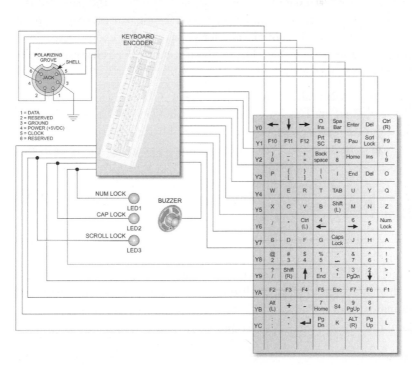

FIGURE 6.16   A 101-key keyboard.

The keyboard's *keyboard encoder* scans the lines of the matrix sequentially at a rate much faster than it is humanly possible to close one of the key switches and release it. Pressing a key shorts a particular strobe line to a sense line, which the encoder interprets as the key corresponding to that location in the matrix. When it detects a key closure, the encoder pauses for a few milliseconds to enable the switch closure to settle out and sends an interrupt request signal to the system. Afterward, the keyboard encoder stores the closure in its buffer and continues scanning until all the rows have been scanned. A typical encoder scans the entire keyboard within 3 to 5 milliseconds.

Each time the keyboard encoder receives a valid key closure from the matrix, it generates two serially coded characters: a scan code that corresponds to the key closure and a break code that is generated when the key closure is broken. The encoder notifies the system unit that it is ready to transmit a scan code by sending it a start bit, followed by a serial string of coded bits.

On the PC system board, an intelligent keyboard controller portion of the system's chipset handles the keyboard-interfacing function. When the keyboard controller receives the serial data from the keyboard, it checks the parity of the data, converts it into a scan code, and generates a keyboard interrupt request (IRQ1) to the system. The keyboard encoder transmits the codes to the keyboard controller through the cable. The keyboard controller releases the code to the system's keyboard interrupt handler routine.

Finally, the keyboard-handling routine sends the ASCII character code to the program that called for it. The program, in turn, delivers the code to the activated output device (monitor, modem, or printer). This is referred to as an *echo* operation and may be suppressed by programming so that the character is not displayed.

Pointing Devices

Mice, joysticks, trackballs, and touch pads belong to a category of input devices called *pointing devices*. They are all small, handheld input devices that allow the user to interact with the system by moving a cursor, or some other screen image, around the display screen to choose options from an onscreen menu, instead of typing commands from a keyboard. Pointing devices make it easier to interact with the computer than other types of input devices.

Mice

The most widely used pointing device is the mouse. A *mouse* is a handheld device that produces input data by being moved across a surface, such as a desktop. The mouse has become a standard input device for most systems because of the popularity of GUI-based software. The most common mouse type is the *track-ball mouse*, depicted in Figure 6.17. The trackball mouse detects positional changes through the movement of a rolling trackball that it rides on. As the mouse is moved across a surface, its circuitry detects the movement of the track-ball and creates pulses that the system converts into positional information.

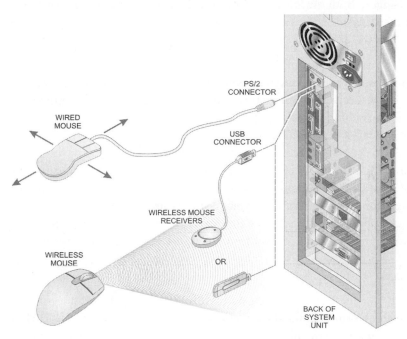

FIGURE 6.17 A typical trackball mouse.

The movement of the mouse causes the trackball to roll. Inside the mouse, the trackball drives two small wheels that are attached to the shafts of two poten-tiometers (one X and one Y). As the trackball rolls, the wheels turn and the resistance of the potentiometers varies proportionally. The varying resistance is converted to an analog signal that undergoes an analog-to-digital conversion process, by which it is changed into a digital input that represents the movement of the mouse.

The trackball mice use opto-coupling techniques to generate a string of digital pulses when the ball is moved. These devices are referred to as *opto-mechanical mice*. The trackball turns two perforated wheels by friction. Light from light-emitting diodes shines through holes in the wheels (which are not attached to potentiometers) as the mouse moves. The light pulses are detected by a photo-conductive device that converts them into digital voltage pulses. The pulses are applied to counters that tabulate the distance (both X and Y) that the mouse moves.

Another popular type of mouse is the *optical mouse*. In these mice, a light-emitting diode and light sensor arrangement has replaced the trackball. The mouse detects motion by emitting an infrared light stream, which is reflected off the surface when the mouse moves. The sensor detects the movement and direction by subtle changes in the angle of the received light and converts it into X,Y position changes. Both trackball and optical mice have similar appearances, except for the trackball underneath the mouse.

As the figure indicates, there are currently two methods used to connect mice to the system: through the 6-pin PS/2 mouse connector or through one of the system's USB ports. Some wireless mice employ an infrared (IR) link between the mouse and an IR receiver, which then communicates with the computer through a USB port.

Joysticks

Two major types of joysticks can be used with PC-compatible systems: analog and digital joysticks. The analog version employs two resistive potentiometer elements, one for the X-direction and one for the Y-direction. Both potentiometers are mechanically connected to the movable gimbal that causes the resistance elements to produce variable levels of output signal when the gimbal is moved along the X-axis, Y-axis, or at some angle between them (this varies both the X and Y voltages).

The computer's game port interface uses these analog signals to produce digital X,Y coordinate information for the system. When this type of joystick is used to position a screen image, the position of the image on the screen corresponds to the X,Y position of the gimbal.

A somewhat simpler design is used in the construction of digital joysticks. The gimbal is used to mechanically open and close different combinations of an internal, four-switch arrangement, as depicted in Figure 6.18. The joystick produces a single-byte output, which encodes the gimbal's movement in any of eight possible directions. Unlike analog joysticks, the position of the controlled image on the screen does not correspond to the X,Y position of the gimbal. Instead, the gimbal position produces only the direction of movement for the screen image. When the gimbal is returned to its neutral position, the screen image simply stops where it is.

Touch-Sensitive Screens

Touch-sensitive screens, or simply *touch screens*, employ different sensing mechanisms to divide the display screen into rows and columns that correspond to X,Y coordinates and to detect the location of any contact made with the screen. When a user touches an area of the screen, the screen coordinate for the point is captured and passed to the system as input information. The supporting software application matches that coordinate with items displayed on the screen and determines what type of action is appropriate for the definition of the corresponding screen item.

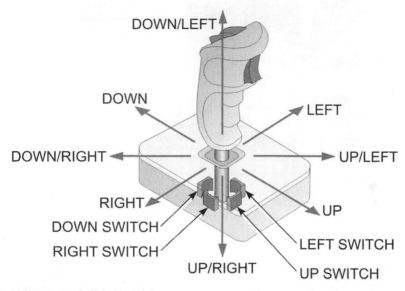

FIGURE 6.18 A digital joystick.

These input devices are widely used in business settings for *Point of Sale* (*POS*) operations, such as computerized cashier stations. They are also popular as input devices for customer information and service kiosks (self-service computer stations). The lack of easily detachable items and mechanical mechanisms makes the touch screen very attractive for these applications.

Two techniques are commonly used to construct touch screens. The first technique employs see-through membranes arranged in rows and columns over the screen, as illustrated in Figure 6.19.

When the user presses the touch-sensitive panel, the transparent strips are pressed together. When strips from a row and a column make contact with each other, their electrical qualities change. The signal generated between the two strips is decoded to an approximate X,Y position on the screen by the panel's decoding circuitry.

The second type of touch-sensitive screen technology employs infrared techniques to section the screen. Banks of LEDs and sensors arranged around the face of the monitor divide the screen into a grid pattern. When an object interrupts the signal paths between a pair of horizontal and vertical LEDs and sensors, a decodable signal is produced that can be related to an X,Y coordinate on the screen.

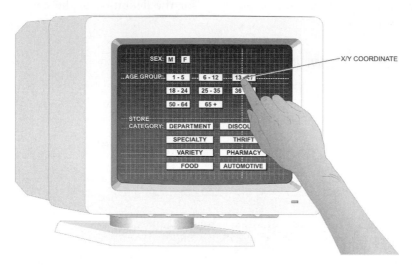

FIGURE 6.19 A membrane strip touch screen.

The main drawback associated with touch screens involves the excessive arm movements required to operate the system. It is also true that the human fingertip is not a fine enough pointing device to select small points on the screen. Therefore, the location of a small item pointed to onscreen may not be exact because of the relative size of the fingertip. The software designer must create screen displays that take this possibility into account and compensate for it where touch screens are used.

Touch-sensitive panels are built-in units on some monitors, whereas other units are designed as add-ons to existing monitors. These units clip, or strap, onto the body of the monitor and hang down in front of the screen. In add-on units, the coordinate mismatch problem can be compounded by the addition of parallax errors. The distance between the screen and the sensors and the angle at which the user views the display are responsible for these types of errors. *Parallax error* causes the image to appear at a different location than it actually is.

Biometric Input Devices

Biometric authentication involves using uniquely personal physiological characteristics to verify that people are who they say they are. Every person possesses unique physical characteristics that differentiate him or her from everyone else. Even identical twins have separate and distinctive DNA, voice patterns, fingerprints, eye features, and other characteristics. The qualities most often involved in biometric authentication include voice patterns, fingerprints, palm prints, signatures, facial features, and retinal and iris scans.

In each case, a *biometric scanning device* is required to convert the physiological quantity into a digital representation. The results are stored in a database where they can be used in an authentication process. The underlying application will use the truly unique qualities of the data as a basis to compare future access requests to. If the data from a future authentication request matches the key points of the stored version, access will be granted. The biometric authentication device most widely used with PCs is the fingerprint scanner, depicted in Figure 6.20.

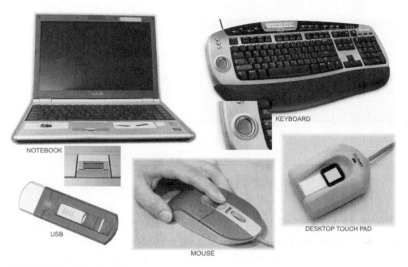

FIGURE 6.20   Fingerprint scanners.

Barcode Scanners

A special type of optical scanner called *barcode scanners* or *barcode readers* is designed to optically read information that has been encoded in a standard striping arrangement. Figure 6.21 shows a handheld barcode scanner. The stripes in the code are created in different widths of dark and light stripes to represent numbers and letters. Some scanners have trigger mechanisms that must be engaged to read barcodes, whereas other models are triggerless and automatically recognize barcode patterns when they are exposed to them.

A light source in the barcode reader is scanned across the coded stripes and the light/dark image is reflected to the photo sensor in the reader. Decoder circuitry in the reader converts the light level changes into digital code. The decoded information can be transmitted directly to a host computer, or it may be stored in the reader and downloaded into a host computer in a batch transfer operation. Some scanner models must be pressed directly on the code to get a reading, whereas other models have a "depth of field" range that describes how far away from the code they can be and still get a reading.

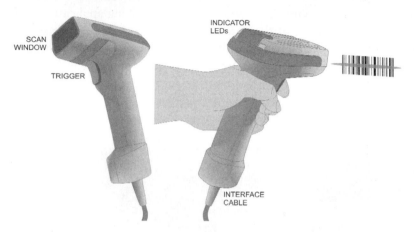

FIGURE 6.21   A handheld barcode scanner.

Video Capture Cards

Video capture cards are responsible for converting video signals from different sources into digital signals that can be manipulated by the computer. The video capture card samples the incoming video signal by feeding it through an analog-to-digital converter. The digitized output from the analog-to-digital converter is applied to a video compressionapplication-specific integrated circuit (ASIC).

The compression chip reduces the size of the file by removing redundant information from consecutive frames. This reduction is necessary because of the extreme size of typical digitized video files. Video-compression schemes can reduce the size of a video file by a ratio of up to 200:1. The audio signal is not compressed, but it is synchronized to the video signal so that it will play in the right places when the video is rerun.

Sources for video capture normally include CD and DVD players, VCRs, and camcorders. Some capture cards include an radio frequency (RF) demodulator and a TV tuner so that video can be captured from a television broadcast signal or a cable TV input. The signals received from analog video-producing devices can be composite TV or analog S-video signals. However, newer digital video capture cards feature DVI or HDMI connections to support digital HDTV signals.

The connection points for a typical video capture card are displayed in Figure 6.22. Low-end analog video capture cards supply an input connector for the video source. Other analog capture cards may supply both an input and output connection scheme. More advanced digital capture cards provide connection types that can act as both inputs and outputs.

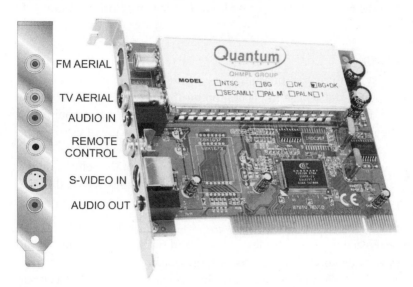

FIGURE 6.22 Video capture connections.

A video decoder circuit is used to convert analog video signals into a stream of digital signals. However, these are not the RGB digital signals useful to the video adapter card. The characteristics of the decoded TV signal are defined in television industry terms as *YUV*. The *Y* portion of the term refers to the luminance of the signal color, and the *UV* portion describes the color component of the signal.

One of the jobs of the video capture card is to convert the YUV format into an RGB VGA-compatible signal. An encoding circuit samples the incoming analog signal and then performs an operation known as *color space conversion* on it. Color space conversion is the process of converting the YUV signal into the RGB format acceptable to the video adapter's screen memory.

When the digitized video is recalled for output purposes, the file is reapplied to the compression chip, which restores the redundant information to the frames. The output from the compression chip is applied to the digital-to-analog portion of the video-processing circuitry. In the case of analog capture cards, the video signals are converted back into the proper video format and are applied to the video-out connector at the back plate of the card.

More expensive video capture cards, referred to as *video editing cards*, contain special hardware to provide video editing and processing functions, such as rendering figures and performing MPEG encoding. They may also feature dual-monitor capabilities that enable you to attach two monitors to the card and spread the display across the two screens. This enables you to work in one screen and view the results in the other without opening and closing windows to do so.

Video Displays

The video display monitor has long been one of the most popular methods of displaying computer data. For many years the most widely used version of this output device in PCs was the cathode-ray tube (CRT) video display monitor. At the heart of the monitor is the cathode-ray tube familiar to many of us from the television receivers we have in our homes. In fact, the early personal computers used televisions as video units. The basic difference between the television and a monitor is that no radio-frequency demodulation electronics are used in the video monitor.

However, newer, lightweight, reduced power consumption display technologies have begun to replace the CRT display in home and office PCs. Originally, the popularity of portable computers created a large market for lightweight, low-power display devices. The main devices used in this market are the liquid crystal display (LCD) monitors. These devices do not use a CRT tube or its supporting circuitry, so the weight associated with the CRT and its high-voltage components is not present. The flat-panel nature of these devices also works well in the portable computer because of its reduced size.

In addition to their use in portable PCs, LCD displays have gained widespread acceptance in the large screen, high-definition television market. Coupled with the explosion of digital A/V systems, this has helped the PC become a pivotal component in home entertainment systems, using the LCD television as a video display and a television/video viewing system.

Video projectors can also be used with portable PCs to display presentations on a large screen. Most video projectors connect to the PC's VGA output connector. However, many projector models include component video, S-video, DVI, or HDMI inputs that allow it to be used with home entertainment equipment.

Basic CRT Display Operations

A CRT is an evacuated glass tube with an electron gun in its neck and a fluorescent coated surface opposite the electron gun. A typical CRT is depicted in Figure 6.23. When activated, the electron gun emits a stream of electrons that strike the fluorescent coating on the inside of the screen, causing an illuminated dot to be produced.

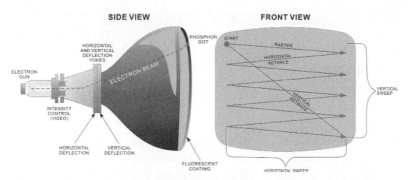

FIGURE 6.23 Cathode-ray tube operation.

The sweeping electron beam begins at the upper-left corner of the screen and moves across its face to the upper-right corner, leaving a line across the screen. This is called a *raster line*. On reaching the right side of the screen, the trace is blanked out, and the electron beam is repositioned to the left side of the screen, one line below the first trace in an operation called the *horizontal retrace*. At this point, the horizontal sweep begins producing the second display line on the screen. The scanning continues until the horizontal sweep reaches the bottom of the screen. At that point, the electron beam is blanked again and returned to the upper-left corner of the screen in a move referred to as the *vertical retrace*, completing one field.

As the beam moves across the screen, it leaves an illuminated trace, which requires a given amount of time to dissipate. The amount of time depends on the characteristics of the fluorescent coating and is referred to as *persistence*. Video information is introduced to the picture by varying the voltage applied to the electron gun as it scans the screen. The human eye perceives only the picture because of the blanking of the retrace lines and the frequency at which the entire process is performed.

Typically, a horizontal sweep across the screen requires about 63 microseconds to complete, and a complete field requires approximately 1/60 of a second, or 1/30 of a second per frame. The National Television Standards Committee (NTSC) specifies 525 lines per frame, composed of two fields of 262.5 lines, for television pictures. The two fields, one containing the even-numbered lines and the other containing the odd-numbered lines are interlaced to produce smooth, flickerless images. This method of creating display images is referred to as *interlaced scanning*, which is primarily used with television. Most computer monitors use noninterlaced scanning methods.

Standard VGA monitors employ a 31.5KHz horizontal scanning rate, whereas Super VGA monitors use frequencies between 35 and 48KHz for their horizontal sync, depending on the vertical refresh rate of the adapter card. Standard VGA monitors repaint the screen (vertical refresh) at a frequency of 60 or 70Hz, whereas Super VGA vertical scanning occurs at frequencies of 56, 60, and 72Hz.

Color CRT Monitors

The monitor we have been discussing so far is referred to as a *monochrome* monitor because it is capable of displaying only shades of a single phosphor color. A color monitor, on the other hand, employs a combination of three color phosphors, red, blue, and green, arranged in adjacent trios of dots or bars, called *pixels* or *PELs*. By using a different electron gun for each element of the trio, the individual elements can be made to glow at different levels to produce almost any color desired. The electron guns scan the front of a screen in unison, in the same fashion as described earlier for a monochrome CRT. Color CRTs add a metal grid in front of the phosphor coating called a *shadow mask*. It ensures that an electron gun assigned to one color doesn't strike a dot of another color. The basic construction of a color CRT is shown in Figure 6.24.

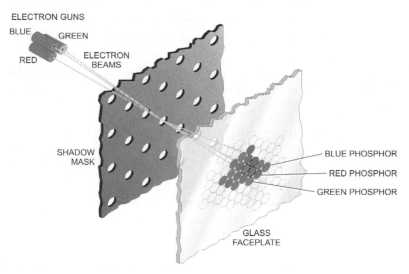

FIGURE 6.24 A color CRT construction.

Video Adapters

At the heart of any video adapter is the video controller. This device is a specialized microprocessor-like device that develops the video signals for the display. It employs a video DAC (Digital-to-Analog Converter) to convert digital data from the PC into the analog signal used to drive the video display. The video controller also generates horizontal (HSYNC) and vertical (VSYNC) synchronization signals to control the placement of dots on the display screen. As described earlier, these signals are used to sweep the electron beam across and down the screen to paint the image on the display screen.

After a line or a page of text has been displayed onscreen, it must be rewritten periodically to prevent it from fading away. For the rewrite to be performed fast enough to avoid display flicker, the contents of the display are stored in a special memory, called the *screen memory*. This memory is typically located on the video adapter card in the form of discrete memory devices or as an integral part of the video controller IC. On the other hand, some newer systems use sections of the system's onboard memory for the video screen memory function. In our example of 25 lines of text at 80 characters per line, the memory must be able to hold at least 2,000 bytes of screen data for a single display.

The adapter card's extended BIOS and device drivers set the rates for these signals, which are required to support the vertical refresh rate of the monitor (that is, if the video adapter card has lower vertical resolution capabilities than the monitor, the screen image will be created at the vertical resolution of the adapter card). If this is a problem, there are three options: update the video BIOS, update the adapter card's device drivers, or get a better video adapter card.

The *vertical hold* control setting located on the monitor is used to fine-tune the response of the monitor to the vertical refresh signal received from the video adapter and the operation of the monitor's VSYNC generating circuitry. These variations can cause the display to roll, jump, or flash.

Video adapters also have a video BIOS ROM that is similar to the ROM BIOS on the system board. The video BIOS acts as an extension of the system BIOS and is used to store firmware routines that are specific only to video functions.

You should also be aware that the video adapter circuitry can be integrated directly into the system board. In these cases there is no video adapter card present in the system—only a three-row, 15-pin D-shell VGA connector on the back panel of the system unit. Although the system board may come with integrated video capabilities, you are not necessarily stuck with them. You can typically deactivate the onboard video interface circuitry and install a higher performance video card in the system at any time.

Specialized Video Cards

High-end computers, such as media center computers or specialized gaming computers typically employ a high-end video adapter card to display streaming video and other multimedia presentations. This type of video adapter card, depicted in Figure 6.25, normally includes at least a heat sink and possibly a snap-on fan unit to cool its video controller IC. The operating speeds and complexity of these devices has increased to the point where *active cooling* methods are required. Cooling units that include fans require a power source to drive the fan. This connection can be made to a special connector on the video adapter card, to a jumper on the system board, or to a special power supply connector.

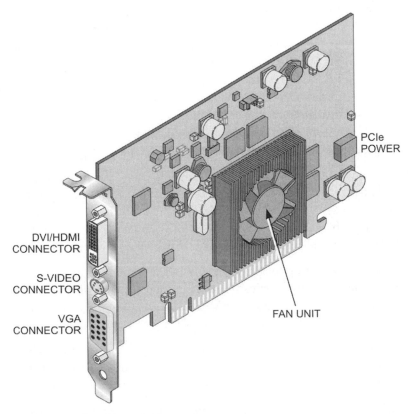

DVI/HDMI
CONNECTOR

S-VIDEO
CONNECTOR

VGA
CONNECTOR

PCIe
POWER

FAN UNIT

FIGURE 6.25   An advanced video card.

DVI- and HDMI-capable cards are specialized video adapters that provide both analog and digital video signals to accommodate both analog and digital monitors. The DVI standard specifies a single plug and connector arrangement that can accommodate traditional legacy VGA connections as well as newer digital interfaces. The DVI interface operates with signal bandwidths that support Ultra Extended VGA (UXGA) video display specifications, as well as HDTV signals.

High-end video adapter cards normally include a heat sink and possibly a snap-on fan unit to cool the video controller IC, as illustrated in Figure 6.25. The operating speeds and complexity of these devices has increased to the point where active cooling methods are required. Cooling units that include fans require an additional power connection to drive the unit. This connection can be made on a special connector on the video card or to the system board.

Some very high-end video adapters provide internal VGA-to-TV converters that enable them to deliver output directly to a typical television display. This output signal is provided through standard RCA minijacks mounted on the back of the card. In addition to standard VGA and SVGA compatible outputs, these cards generate NTSC-compatible (or European PAL-compatible) raster scan video signals compatible with television sets. These signals can be delivered in the form of composite TV or analog S-video formats.

One of the major forces driving high-end video adapters and sound cards is the PC games market. PC gamers want the highest quality video they can obtain to enhance their gaming experiences. PC games are typically very demanding on the PC's hardware components including video adapters, processors, memory systems, disk drive subsystems, and sound cards. With some online multiplayer games, a disadvantage in hardware capabilities can make the difference between winning and losing.

Therefore, a good game system would provide the fastest video adapter card and its supporting expansion slot. This involves PCIe adapter slots and video cards with as much video memory onboard as possible. Some newer chipsets designed to support gaming applications include support for dual 16X PCIe slot video cards. This specification is called the Scalable Link Interface (SLI) specification and enables both cards to operate simultaneously. Additional advances have yielded twin, dual-slot (quad) PCIe system boards to host four video adapters.

EXAM ALERT

Be aware of multislot video adapter card systems.

Screen Resolution

The quality of the image produced on the screen is a function of two factors: the speed at which the image is retraced on the screen and the number of pixels on the screen. The more pixels on a given screen size, the higher the image quality. This quantity is called *resolution* and is often expressed in an X by Y format. Using this format, the quality of the image is still determined by how big the viewing area is (for instance, an 800 × 600 resolution on a 14-inch wide display will produce much better quality than the same number of pixels spread across a 27-inch display).

Standard VGA resolution is defined as 720 × 400 pixels using 16 colors in text mode and 640 × 480 pixels using 16 onscreen colors in graphics mode. However, improved-resolution VGA systems, referred to as *Super VGA (SVGA)*, are now commonly available in formats of 1024 × 768 with 256 colors, 1024 × 768 with 16 colors, and 800 × 600 with 256 colors. The SVGA definition continues to expand, with video controller capabilities ranging up to 1280 × 1024 (with reduced color capabilities).

IBM produced its own Extended Graphics Array standard, called the XGA. This standard was capable of both 800 × 600 and 1024 × 768 resolutions, but added a 132-column, 400-scan line resolution. Unfortunately, IBM based the original XGA on interlaced monitors and therefore never received a large following. However, several newer XGA standards have made it to the market, such as the following:

> ► Super XGA (SXGA) specification capable of displaying 1280 × 1024 resolution

> ► Ultra XGA (UXGA) specification capable of displaying 1600 × 1200 resolution

> ► Wide UXGA (WUXGA) specification that is capable of displaying 1920 × 1200 resolution

The maximum resolution/color capabilities of a particular VGA adapter are ultimately dependent on the amount of onboard memory the adapter possesses. The standard 640 × 480 display format, using 16 colors, requires nearly 256KB of video memory to operate (640 × 480 × 4/8=153,600 bytes). With 512KB of video memory installed, the resolution can be improved to 1024 × 768, but only 16 colors are possible (1024 × 768 × 4/8=393,216 bytes). To achieve full 1024 × 768 resolution with 256 colors, the video memory has to be expanded to a full 1MB (1024 × 768 × 8/8=786,432 bytes). A summary of the different video standards is presented in Table 6.3.

TABLE 6.3   Video Standards Summary

VIDEO STANDARD	RESOLUTION IN PIXELS	REFRESH RATE	HORIZONTAL SWEEP RATE	BUFFER ADDRESS
VGA (Video Graphics Array Adapter)	720 × 400 640 × 480	60 or 70Hz	31.5KHz	0A0000– 0BFFFF
Super VGA (SVGA)	1280 × 1024 1024 × 768 800 × 600	50, 60, or 72	35– 48KHz	0A0000– 0BFFFF

TABLE 6.3 *Continued*

VIDEO STANDARD	RESOLUTION IN PIXELS	REFRESH RATE	HORIZONTAL SWEEP RATE	BUFFER ADDRESS
XGA	1024 × 768 800 × 600	44/70	35.5KHz	0A0000– 0BFFFF
Super XGA (SXGA)	1280 × 1024	60/70/72 /75/80 /100Hz	24.8– 82 Hz (analog) 65KHz (digital)	0A0000– 0BFFFF
Ultra XGA (UXGA)	1600 × 1200	60/70/72 /75/80 /100Hz	21-100KHz (analog) 31-100KHz (digital)	0A0000– 0BFFFF
Wide UXGA (WUXGA)	1920 × 1200	60/70/72 /75/80 /100Hz	24–100KHz (analog) 31–100KHz (digital)	0A0000– 0BFFFF

Dot Pitch

While x by y resolution specifications are largely a function of the video controller card, from the monitor's point of view, resolution can be expressed as a function of how close pixels can be grouped together on the screen. This form of resolution is expressed in terms of *dot pitch*. A monitor with a .28 dot pitch has pixels that are located .28mm apart. In monochrome monitors, dot pitch is measured from center to center of each pixel. In a color monitor, the pitch is measured from the center of one dot trio to the center of the next trio.

EXAM ALERT

Be able to explain the definition of dot pitch.

Digital Television Resolutions

The convergence of computer video and digital television has introduced a whole new set of video resolution definitions and terms to the computer industry. The television industry has established a new Advanced Television Systems Committee (ASTC) and has produced new high-definition digital television specifications that offer much better viewing than the old NTSC standard.

Digital televisions can produce displays in two general formats: *interlaced displays*, like those used in NTSC television that use two different frames to create a complete picture, and *progressive displays* (or noninterlaced displays) that paint the entire picture in one sequential set of horizontal lines. Under the new specifications, interlaced display resolutions are denoted by a lowercase "i" following the *vertical resolution* description, and progressive resolutions are designated by a lowercase "p". The vertical resolution value is fixed by the specification, whereas the horizontal resolution is allowed to vary to permit different standard video sources to be displayed on a digital display device.

Different content sources employ different width-to-height ratios when displaying mages (for example, standard television, high definition television, DVDs, camera phones, and so on). The mathematical relationship between the width and height of images is called the *aspect ratio*. For example, displaying NTSC programming on a digital television set produces a display screen of 640 pixels by 480 pixels. The ratio of these two values is expressed as a 4:3 aspect ration. On the other hand, theater quality video is presented in an aspect ration of 16:9. The goal of the HDTV specification is to bring home entertainment displays up to the level of these displays.

Where aspect ratio most often becomes apparent is when viewing a movie from a DVD. You are often given two viewing options: full screen and wide screen. These options refer to the aspect ratio you want to display the film in. If you select full screen and you are watching on a traditional NTSC display, the version of the film altered to provide a 4:3 aspect ration will fill up the screen. To accomplish this, the film has been edited and picture elements that do not fit in the 4:3 box have been cut off, which is referred to as *letter boxing*. Figure 6.26 illustrates the difference between displaying images in 4:3 vs. 16:9 resolutions.

On the other hand, if you select the wide screen option and you are watching an NTSC display, you will see the complete width of the movie, including all the screen elements, but you will have black bars at the top and bottom of the display. If you were watching the movie on a digital display with a 16:9 aspect ratio, the movie would fill the screen without losing any picture. As you might expect, if you watch an NTSC program on a wide-screen digital display, you will see black bars at both sides of the display.

16:9 Ratio

4:3 Ratio

FIGURE 6.26 Aspect ratio effects.

Digital Display Definitions

The new digital television display standards have also caused a reevaluation of display-related terms.

► Low Definition TV (LDTV)—Display systems that produce lower resolutions than the NTSC standard. These systems are digital and provide video for Internet distribution, where higher bandwidth video streams associated with higher resolution video streams would slow down or crash the system. Typical resolutions associated with LDTV are 240p and 288p. Screen refresh rates used with LDTV include 24, 30, and 25Hz. LDTV is used with Apple iPods, the original Sony Playstations, and video CDs.

▶ Standard Definition TV (SDTV)—Digital display systems that have lower resolutions than the high definition TV specification calls for. These include the standard digital television displaying NTSC broadcasts. SDTV resolutions include 480i for displaying NTSC programming and 480p for European PAL-M programming. SDTV screen refresh rates are 60, 24, and 30Hz. For PAL and SECAM formats, the resolutions are 576i and 576p using 50 and 25Hz refresh rates.

▶ Enhanced Definition TV (EDTV)—A gray area of picture quality that falls between traditional NTSC/PAL picture quality and the definitions set for HDTV images. DVD players with progressive scan output are a good example of EDTV. The EDTV image has a horizontal resolution of 704 pixels regardless of the aspect ratio—the picture is stretched to fit 4:3 or 16:9 aspect ratios.

▶ High Definition TV (HDTV)—Under the ATSC standard, HDTV is any image being displayed at a resolution of 720 or more using a 16:9 aspect ratio. Cinematic video is produced in 720p or 1080p formats using a 24-frame per second refresh rate. Noncinematic HDTV images are produced in 720p or 1080i formats with refresh rates of 24, 25, 30, 50, or 60Hz, depending on the producer of the content. In computer terms, these are screen resolutions of 1280×1024 and 1920×1080, respectively.

Sound Cards

The sound-producing capabilities of early PCs were practically nonexistent. They included a single small speaker that was used to produce beep-coded error messages. Even though programs could be written to produce a wide array of sounds from this speaker, the quality of the sound was never any better than the limitations imposed by its small size. This led various companies to design audio digitizer cards for the PC that could both convert sound into digital quantities that the computer could manipulate and play back digitized sound produced by the computer. These cards are referred to as *sound cards*.

A typical audio digitizer system is depicted in Figure 6.27. A microphone converts sound waves from the air into an encoded analog electrical signal. The analog signal is applied to the audio input of the sound card. On the card, the signal is applied to an analog-to-digital (AD)converter circuit, which changes the signal into corresponding digital values.

The sound card takes samples of the analog waveform at predetermined intervals and converts them into corresponding digital values. Therefore, the digital values approximate the instantaneous values of the sound wave.

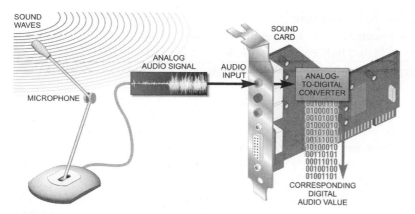

FIGURE 6.27 A typical audio digitizer system.

The *fidelity* (the measure of how closely the original sound can be reproduced) of the digital samples is dependent on two factors: the accuracy of the samples taken and the rate at which the samples are taken. The accuracy of the sample is determined by the resolution capabilities of the A/D converter. *Resolution* is the capability to differentiate between values. If the value of the analog waveform is 15.55 microvolts at a given point, how closely can that value be approximated with a digital value?

The number of digital output bits an A/D converter can produce determines its resolution capabilities. For example, an 8-bit A/D converter can represent up to 256 (2^8) different values. On the other hand, a 16-bit A/D converter can represent up to 65,536 (2^{16}) different amplitudes. The more often the samples are taken, the more accurately the original waveform can be reproduced.

Playback of the digitized audio signal is accomplished by applying the digital signals to a digital-to-analog (D/A) converter at the same rate the samples were taken. When the audio files are called for, the sound card's software driver sends commands to the audio output controller on the sound card. The digitized samples are applied to the audio output IC and converted back into the analog signal.

The analog signal is applied to an audio preamplifier that boosts the power of the signal and sends it to an RCA or mini RCA jack. This signal is still too weak to drive conventional speakers. However, it can be applied to an additional amplifier, or to a set of speakers that have an additional amplifier built in to them.

A CD-quality audio signal requires a minimum of 16-bit samples, taken at approximately 44kHz. If you calculate the disk space required to store all the

16-bit samples collected in one minute of audio at this rate, the major consideration factor associated with using digitized audio becomes clear ($16 \times 44,000 \times 60 \times 8 = 5.28MB$). High-end sound cards are designed to handle from five to seven independent surround sound channels, in addition to an additional low frequency effect subwoofer channel. With stereo sound, this doubles to 10.56MB.

To handle the level of sound processing required to provide this amount of sound data, most sound cards are based on specialized microprocessors called *Digital Signal Processors (DSPs)* that process audio signals. These integrated circuit devices employ complex mathematical algorithms to manipulate sound data to create the musical notes, at the correct pitch and with the correct effects (reverb, chorus, and delays). These sound cards may also employ multiple DMA channels to move digital audio data between the system and the sound card.

Sound Card Connections

Most sound cards support microphones through a stereo RCA jack. Microphone jacks typically are color coded pink. A very similar green speaker jack is also usually present on the back of the card. Depending on the card, the jack might be designed for mono or stereo output. When stereo connections are provided, the jack is wired so that it can deliver separate sound channels through the same connection. The RCA miniplug used with this connection must also have a stereo configuration.

A separate Line In connector is provided for making connections with audio equipment that has audio industry standard Line Out connections. These are nonamplified signals meant to be transported between devices. Because the signal has not been amplified, it is considered to be cleaner from a sound quality point of view.

Advanced sound cards may include a number of multimedia connectors. Figure 6.28 shows an advanced sound card that offers connectors for full 7.1 Surround Sound outputs. It also features Sony/Philips Digital Interface Format (S/PDIF) digital/optical Toslink connectors to transfer multichannel DVD sound to external A/V equipment associated with home theater systems. The RCA minijacks for the Front Out and Rear Out functions are stereo connectors that provide for separate Left and Right sound channels. The Center/LFE jack provides the Center sound speaker and the Low Frequency Effect (LFE) subwoofer channels. This sound card example also provides two onboard connectors along the top of the card that allow it to directly interface with CD players and other auxiliary audio sources.

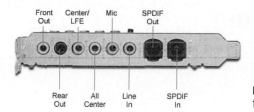

FIGURE 6.28 Advanced sound card connections.

Other sound cards feature IEEE-1394 FireWire ports and two-row, 15-pin D-shell MIDI/joystick connectors, as well as telephone answering ports.

Exam Prep Questions

1. Which of the following should be avoided when the computer is in operation?

   ○ **A.** Removing CD-ROM disks

   ○ **B.** Exchanging mice trackballs

   ○ **C.** Pushing the On/Off switch

   ○ **D.** Swapping keyboards

2. Which standard ATX ports are often confused with each other?

   ○ **A.** The serial port and the VGA/SVGA port

   ○ **B.** The docking port and the parallel ports

   ○ **C.** The NIC card and modem connector ports

   ○ **D.** The mouse and keyboard connections

3. Describe the first step to installing a USB device.

   ○ **A.** Install the USB driver in the Add New Hardware Wizard

   ○ **B.** Enable the USB driver in Device Manager

   ○ **C.** Enable USB resources in CMOS

   ○ **D.** Right-click the USB device icon in the taskbar and select Enable

4. How many devices can be attached to a single Universal Serial Bus (USB) host?

   ○ **A.** 63

   ○ **B.** 127

   ○ **C.** 255

   ○ **D.** 511

5. Which new serial interface is the fastest?

   ○ **A.** IrDA

   ○ **B.** ECP

   ○ **C.** IEEE-1394

   ○ **D.** USB

6. When can you safely disconnect a PS/2 keyboard from a computer?

  ○   **A.** When the computer is turned off

  ○   **B.** Anytime the computer is running

  ○   **C.** While the computer is booting

  ○   **D.** While the operating system is in Safe Mode

7. The type of connectors usually associated with Audio-in and Audio-out ports are

_____.

  ○   **A.** 25-pin D-shells

  ○   **B.** RCA mini jacks

  ○   **C.** RJ-11 jacks and plugs

  ○   **D.** 15-pin D-shells

8. Which terms are used to describe the dot information produced by a color monitor? (Select all that apply)

  ○   **A.** Picture pod

  ○   **B.** Pixel

  ○   **C.** Trilogy

  ○   **D.** Picture element

9. What is used to prevent the spreading of the electron beam on a color monitor?

  ○   **A.** Shadow mask

  ○   **B.** Color shield

  ○   **C.** Glass faceplate

  ○   **D.** Phosphor shield

10. Suppose that you are purchasing a new VGA monitor. Which of following is the best dot pitch?

  ○   **A.** .30

  ○   **B.** .28

  ○   **C.** .32

  ○   **D.** .29

11. Which device or port uses IRQ8 in a PC-compatible system?

- ○ **A.** Keyboard buffer
- ○ **B.** Math coprocessor
- ○ **C.** RAM refresh controller
- ○ **D.** Real-time clock module

12. At what I/O port addresses does the system communicate with the primary hard disk (IDE) controller?

- ○ **A.** 0F8–0FF
- ○ **B.** 1F0–1f8
- ○ **C.** 200–207
- ○ **D.** 278–27F

13. What type of connectors are normally found on PC-compatible keyboards? (Select all that apply.)

- ○ **A.** A 6-pin mini-DIN connector
- ○ **B.** A 15-pin D-shell connector
- ○ **C.** A USB connector
- ○ **D.** An RJ-45 connector

14. Which type of I/O port employs a two-row, 15-pin, D-shell female connector?

- ○ **A.** VGA port
- ○ **B.** ATX mouse port
- ○ **C.** LAN port
- ○ **D.** Game port

15. Which video display standard is capable of providing a maximum output resolution of 1600×1220 pixels?

- ○ **A.** WVXGA
- ○ **B.** SXGA
- ○ **C.** UXGA
- ○ **D.** SVGA

16. Select the option that is not found on the back plate of a typical audio sound card.

   ○ **A.** Line-In

   ○ **B.** Line-Out

   ○ **C.** Speaker

   ○ **D.** Microphone

17. If you want to establish a component video connection between a media server PC and a television/video display unit, what connection standard offers the best performance?

   ○ **A.** SVGA

   ○ **B.** S-video

   ○ **C.** DVI

   ○ **D.** HDMI

18. Which DMA channel has a dedicated function in a standard PC?

   ○ **A.** Channel 6 for the FDD controller

   ○ **B.** Channel 2 for the FDD controller

   ○ **C.** Channel 3 for the EPP port controller

   ○ **D.** Channel 1 for the keyboard controller

19. How many pins are there in a USB connector?

   ○ **A.** 2

   ○ **B.** 4

   ○ **C.** 8

   ○ **D.** 16

20. What is the proper way to remove a USB mass storage device?

   ○ **A.** Click on the Safe Hardware Removal icon in the taskbar

   ○ **B.** USB devices are hot swappable and can be installed or removed at any time

   ○ **C.** Use the New Hardware Wizard to remove the device from the system and then disconnect it

   ○ **D.** Disable the device in the Device Manager and then physically remove it from the system

21. How many pins are there in a XVGA connector?

   ○ **A.** 9

   ○ **B.** 15

   ○ **C.** 25

   ○ **D.** 50

Answers and Explanations

1. D. Plugging hot-swappable devices such as the keyboard into the system while it is turned on may cause a system crash or even damage parts of the system.

2. D. When the ATX specification adopted the same connector for both the keyboard and mouse, it introduced the possibility of plugging these devices into the wrong connector. Later ATX models and peripherals adopted an informal color-coding system (purple for keyboards and green for mice).

3. C. Installing a USB device normally involves enabling the USB resources in the CMOS Setup screen.

4. B. The specification allows 127 devices (128 – 1) to be attached to the USB host. The host accounts for one of the 128 possible USB addresses.

5. C. FireWire (IEEE-1394) is capable of using the high-speed isochronous transfer mode described for USB to support data-transfer rates up to 400Mbps. This actually makes the FireWire bus superior to the USB bus.

6. A. Many newer peripheral devices can safely be unplugged and reattached to the system while power is applied, but this is not so with the standard keyboard. Plugging the keyboard into the system while power is applied may cause the operating system or even the system board to fail due to the power surge and electrostatic discharge (ESD).

7. B. The microphone and speakers are plugged into the appropriate RCA minijacks on the back of the sound card.

8. B, D. A color monitor employs a combination of three color phosphors, red, blue, and green, arranged in adjacent groups of dots or bars, called pixels or PELs. A picture element, also referred to as a *pixel*, is created in

a liquid crystal display's screen at each spot where a row and a column of electrodes intersect.

9. A. Color CRTs add a metal grid called a shadow mask in front of the phosphor coating. It ensures that an electron gun assigned to one color doesn't strike a dot of another color.

10. B. Resolution can be expressed as a function of how close pixels are grouped together on the screen. The closer the pixels are to one another, the sharper the image. This form of resolution is expressed in terms of dot pitch. A monitor with a .28 dot pitch has pixels that are located .28mm apart.

11. D. Real time clock module. In an ATX PC system, IRQ8 is used by the system for the Real-Time Clock Interrupt.

12. B. 1F0-1F7. The I/O Port addresses used by the system to communicate with the primary hard disk controller is 1F0–1F7.

13. A, C. A 6-pin mini-DIN connector or a USB connector. The ATX and BTX systems use either the PS/2 6-pin mini-DIN connector or a USB connector for keyboards.

14. D. Game port. The game port connector is a 15-pin D-shell female type connector.

15. C. UXGA. The Ultra XGA (UXGA) video display standard is capable of providing a maximum output resolution of 1600×1200 pixels.

16. A. Line-In. Most sound cards support microphones through a mono RCA mini jack. A similar green speaker jack is also normally present on the back of the card. A separate Line-In connector is provided for making connections with audio equipment that have audio industry standard Line-Out connections.

17. D. High definition multimedia interface (HDMI) is an advanced version of the DVI interface that offers high definition video and multichannel (up to eight) audio transfers in a single cable. Like the DVI interface, HDMI is capable of handling signals for video systems running resolutions up to 1080p.

18. B. Channel 2 for the FDD controller. DMA channel 2 is used for the FDD in a standard PC.

19. B. USB transfers are conducted over a four-wire cable. The signal travels over a pair of twisted wires (D+ and D–) in a 90-ohm cable. The four wires are connected to four pins within the connector end.

20. A. While hot swapping USB devices typically does no harm to the system hardware or the device, the Windows operating system requires that you stop the device's operation using the Safely Remove Hardware tool before doing so. An icon for this tool appears in the notification area of the Windows taskbar while the USB device is active. Failure to stop the device's operation before physically removing it from the USB port will cause Windows to generate an "Unsafe Removal of Device" error. It may also cause the system to crash and lose any unsaved data.

21. B. IBM produced the extended graphics array standard, called the XGA. This standard was capable of both 800×600 and 1024×768 resolutions using a XVGA (Extended Video Graphics Array) 15-pin, three-row D-shell connector.

Challenge Solutions

1. The properties of installed IrDA devices can be viewed through the Device Manager. Likewise, connections to another IrDA computer can be established through the Windows Network Dial-up Connections applet. By installing a Point-to-Point Protocol (PPP) or an IrDA LAN protocol through this applet, you can conduct wireless communications with other computers without a modem or network card.

2. You should tell your boss that the industry standard interface for professional music and multimedia work is MIDI. The IEEE-1394 (or FireWire) specification is widely used with consumer electronics A/V equipment.

CHAPTER SEVEN

Installing, Upgrading, Configuring, and Optimizing PC Components

---

Terms you'll need to understand:

✓ Partition

✓ Volume

✓ MFT

✓ FAT

✓ Active partition

✓ Primary partition

✓ Logical drives

✓ Device drivers

✓ Field-Replaceable Units

✓ IDE

✓ SCSI

✓ ATA

✓ Pin #1 indicator stripe

✓ Adapter cards

Techniques to master:

Essentials 1.2—Install, configure, optimize, and upgrade personal computer components.

✓ Add, remove, and configure internal and external storage devices.

✓ Drive preparation of internal storage devices including format/file systems and imaging technology.

✓ Install display devices.

✓ Add, remove, and configure basic input and multimedia devices.

Tech Support 1.1—Install, configure, optimize, and upgrade personal computer components.

✓ Add, remove, and configure display devices, input devices, and adapter cards, including basic input and multimedia devices.

Installing Storage Devices

This chapter covers the Install, Upgrade, Configure, and Optimize PC Components areas of the CompTIA A+ Certification—Essentials examination under Objective 1.2. It also covers the Install, Upgrade, Configure, and Optimize PC Components areas of the Tech Support examination under Objective 1.1.

Every technician should be aware of typical personal computer components that can be exchanged in the field. Technicians should be able to install, connect, and configure these components to upgrade or repair an existing system. The following sections of this chapter present standard procedures for installing and removing typical Field-Replaceable Units (FRUs).

For installation purposes, storage devices fall into one of two categories: internal and external. Internal devices are typically mounted in the system unit's drive bays. External devices normally connect to options adapter cards installed in the system board's expansion slots. Whereas internal devices typically derive their power from the system unit's power supply, external storage devices tend to employ separate, external power supply units.

Installing Internal Storage Devices

Most internal storage devices conform to traditional disk drive form factors. Therefore, the hardware installation procedures for most storage devices are the same. To install a storage device in a disk drive bay, disconnect the system's power cord from the back of the unit. Slide the device into one of the system unit's open drive bays, and install two screws on each side to secure the unit to the disk drive cage. If the unit is a 3 1/2-inch drive, and it is being installed into a 5 1/4-inch drive bay, you will need to fit the drive with a *universal mounting kit*. These kits attach to the drive and extend its form factor so that it fits correctly in the 5 1/4-inch half-height space.

Connect the device's signal cable to the proper interface header on the system board (or on an I/O card). Then connect the signal cable to the storage device. Use caution when connecting the disk drives to the adapter. Make certain that the Pin #1 indicator stripe on the cable aligns with the Pin #1 position of the connectors on both the storage device and its controller. In most cases, the connector is keyed so that it cannot be plugged in backward. Proper connection of a signal cable is depicted in Figure 7.1. Finally, connect one of the power supply's optional power connectors to the storage device.

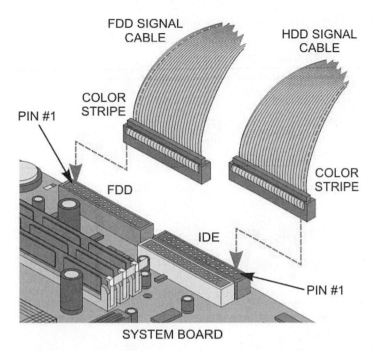

FIGURE 7.1 Connecting a drive's signal cable.

HDD Installation

The hard disk drive (HDD) hardware installation process is similar to that of other storage devices, as illustrated in Figure 7.2. Slide the hard drive unit into one of the system unit's open drive bays, install two screws on each side to secure the drive to the system unit, and connect the signal and power cables to it. For parallel ATA (PATA) drives, attach the black connector on the cable to the master drive and the gray connector to the slave drive.

It is a good idea to confirm the PATA drive's master/slave/single setting, or the SCSI drive's ID configuration setting, before installing the unit in the drive bay. Likewise, in a SCSI system, make sure that the drive is correctly configured and terminated for its position in the system before performing the physical installation. These settings are harder to configure after the drive has been placed in the drive bay.

Finally, the signal cables must be attached to the interface connectors. For PATA drives this connector is found on the system board. Plug the blue connector from the signal cable into the interface connector on the system board. Figure 7.3 provides an example of the proper alignment of the PATA and floppy disk drive (FDD) cables with their system board interface connectors. Check the markings on the system board and the drive to ensure that the Pin #1 alignment stripe is aligned with Pin #1 at each end.

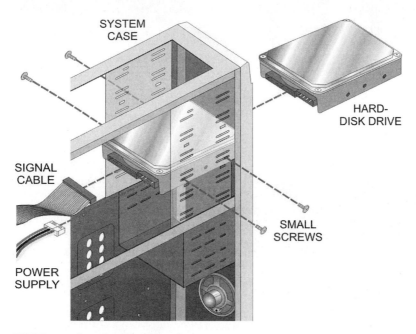

FIGURE 7.2 Securing the drive unit.

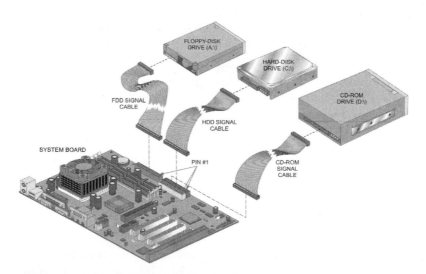

FIGURE 7.3 HDD and FDD system board connections.

EXAM ALERT

You must be able to identify IDE system board connections from different system board drawings by their relative sizes and locations.

When you are installing the HDD signal cable in an IDE-based system, you should recall that there are two similar types cables used with PATA devices. The newer ATA-4/Ultra ATA 66, Ultra ATA 100, and Ultra ATA 133 IDE enhancements provide higher data throughput by doubling the number of conductors in the signal cable to 80.

The PATA connector has remained compatible with the original 40-pin IDE connection, but each pin has been provided with its own ground conductor in the cable. All three Ultra ATA versions support 33.3Mbps data rates when used with a standard 40-pin/40-conductor IDE signal cable. Therefore, Ultra ATA 66, 100, and 133 devices can still be used with systems that don't support the newer PATA standards, but they will operate well below their potential.

EXAM ALERT

Remember how the Ultra ATA 66 interface cable can be identified, and know the effects of using the older signal cable on these faster interfaces.

When dealing with SCSI systems, verify that the SCSI host adapter and all the SCSI devices installed in the system are supported and will work together. For example, a standard SCSI-I host adapter will not support a Fast-Wide SCSI device. The physical cable and the communication speed differences between the two specifications will not match.

When handling hard drives, make sure to practice proper Electrostatic Discharge (ESD) precautions to prevent damage to the drive's electronic control circuitry. For instance, the hard drive should be kept inside its antistatic bag until installation. Also, make sure that during installation, you are wearing an antistatic device, such as a grounded wrist or ankle strap. If a replacement hard drive is being installed for repair or upgrading purposes, the data on the original drive should be backed up to some other media before replacing it (if possible).

After completing the hardware installation process, the drive must be configured and formatted. Hard disk drives are created in a variety of storage capacities and geometries. When the disk is created, its surface is electronically blank.

With system-level drive types, the manufacturer performs the low-level formatting process. To prepare the disk for use by the system, three levels of preparation must take place. The order of these steps is as follows:

1. Verify the CMOS configuration for the drive.

2. Partition the drive.

3. High-level format the drive.

The system's CMOS setup holds the hard drive's configuration settings. As with other I/O devices, these settings must be established correctly for the type of drive being installed. Newer BIOS versions possess autodetection capabilities that enable them to find and identify the drives in the system. The physical geometry of the drive might be different from the logical arrangement that the controller displays to the CMOS. The Integrated Drive Electronics (IDE) controller handles the translation between the drive parameters the system believes to exist and the actual layout of the drive.

However, if the BIOS does not support autodetection, you must move into the CMOS Setup utility and identify the drive type being installed. The Hard Disk C: Type entry is typically located in the CMOS Setup utility's main screen. Move to the entry and scroll through the HDD selections until an entry is found that matches the type you are installing. In some cases, such as with SCSI drives, the CMOS configuration entry must be set to None Installed before the drive will operate correctly. Store this parameter in the CMOS configuration file by following the directions given on the menu screen. This utility can also be used to manually configure various IDE channel selections. Both IDE channels can be Enabled, Disabled, or placed in Autodetect mode through the CMOS.

With the rapid increase that occurs in hard disk drive capacities, it is not uncommon for a new drive to show up as something less when the system is started. The most common reason for this is that the system's BIOS version does not support the size of the new drive and reverts to its maximum support capabilities. It is always a good idea to check the drive support capabilities of the system BIOS before installing a hard disk drive. You may need to flash the BIOS with the latest upgrade version to support the new drive.

You may also gain additional support by updating the operating system with the latest patches and service packs. In the case of Windows XP Professional, the move to Service Pack 1 (SP1) increased Windows capability to handle larger drives beyond 137GB.

EXAM ALERT

Be aware of the possible need to upgrade BIOS and operating systems to support larger hard disk drive installations.

Configuring PATA Drives

The PATA interface has been the standard PC disk drive interface for some time. The IDE controller structure is an integrated portion of most PC system boards. This structure includes BIOS and chipset support for the IDE versions the board will support, as well as the physical PATA host connector.

EXAM ALERT

Remember that IDE bus driver support is built in to the BIOS of system boards that have integrated IDE host adapters.

These include providing the select signals to differentiate between the master and slave drive of the channel. Most PATA drives come from the manufacturer configured for operation as a master drive. To install the drive as a second, or slave, drive, it is usually necessary to install, remove, or move a jumper block to the Slave setting, as illustrated in Figure 7.4.

Choosing the Cable Select (CS) setting shifts responsibility for the master and slave roles of the drives to their positions along the signal cable. If both drives are set to CS, the drive attached to the middle (gray) connector becomes the slave drive. The drive attached to the connector at the end of the cable (black) becomes the master drive. Older 40-conductor IDE cables did not support the Cable Select function by default. Special CS versions of the IDE cable were required to implement the chip select option. Eighty conductor cables support the cable select option. These versions placed the master drive connector in the center of the cable and the slave drive at the end of the cable.

If the Cable Select option is being used and drive connections are switched, there is a possibility that the BIOS and operating system may incorrectly identify the drives and attempt to boot to the wrong drive.

NOTE

Most drives have graphical directions for configuring the drive as master, slave, or cable Select options.

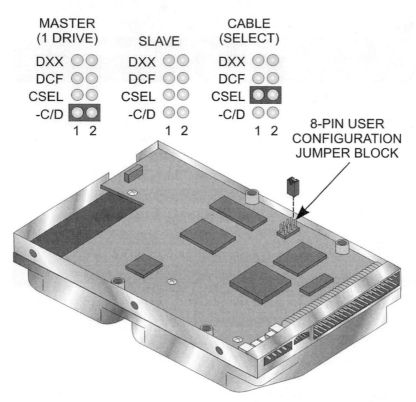

FIGURE 7.4 PATA master/slave settings.

EXAM ALERT

Memorize the three configuration options that can be set on a PATA drive.

After the PATA hardware has been installed, its operating mode must be configured correctly through the system's CMOS Setup utility. Newer system boards
possess an autodetect feature in the BIOS that communicates with the hard
drives and automatically configures them for optimum use with the system. The
CMOS Setup utility can be used to manually configure IDE channel parameters. Both IDE channels can be Enabled, Disabled, or placed in Autodetect
mode through CMOS settings.

In the FAT-based system, the primary partition of the drive attached to the ID1
connector will always be designated as a logical C: drive. On an IDE drive that
is partitioned into two logical drives, the system will identify them as drives C:
and D:. The hierarchy of assigning logical drive designations in the IDE

interface calls for the primary partitions to be assigned sequentially from ID1 master, ID1 slave, ID2 master, to ID2 slave.

The next step is to assign letters to the extended partitions on each drive in the same order (*drive partitions* are logical divisions of hard-disk drives and are covered in detail in the following section). For example, if a second drive is attached to ID1 as a slave, its primary partition will be designated as a logical D: drive. The system will reassign the partitions on the first drive to be logical drives C: and E:, and the partitions on the slave drive will assume the letters D: and F:.

Challenge #1

You are installing PATA drives in a new system. The buyers want to include a large HDD, a standard CD-ROM drive, and a rewritable CD-ROM drive. Your supervisor wants to place the Windows XP operating system files on the primary partition of the drive and keep the application programs and data files on the extended partition. To accomplish this, you connect the hard drive to the system board's IDE1 connector and the two CD-ROM drives to the cable connected to its IDE2 connector. Then you partition the drive into two equal size logical drives. Where will users have to go to find the data files on the drive?

Installing SATA Drives

The physical installation of Serial ATA (SATA) drives is performed in the same manner as PATA drives, with the exception that there is no master/slave configuration that needs to be made. Before installing the drive in the drive bay, connect the signal cable to the drive. Figure 7.5 shows the connectors on a typical SATA drive unit. The larger connector is the power connector, and the smaller one is the signal cable connector. Both connectors are keyed at the drive so they will connect in only one way. Therefore, they cannot be connected backward. The jumpers beside the signal connector are not for user configurations and should not be moved.

Next, install and secure the drive unit in an open disk drive bay. Then attach the power supply cable to the drive and the signal cable to the host adapter (either on a SATA adapter card or on the system board). You are now ready to start the system.

When you start the system, it should automatically detect the presence of the new drive. If not, you should restart the system and enter the CMOS Setup utility during the startup process. Entering the CMOS Setup utility is accomplished by pressing a specific key (such as Alt or Esc) while a prompt is displayed on the screen. Check with your BIOS manufacturer if you are not sure which key(s) need to be pressed during bootup to reach the CMOS Setup utility. Enable the

SATA interface controller under the Integrated Peripherals' Onboard Devices submenu, as illustrated in Figure 7.6.

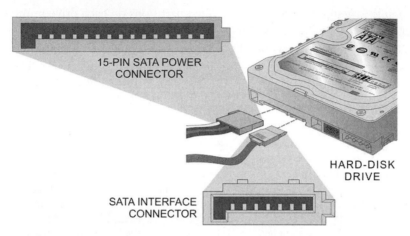

FIGURE 7.5 SATA connections.

```
CPU Type          Intel(R) Pentium(R) D
CPU Speed                3.20GHz/800MHz
CPU L2 Cache Size        2048KB x2
Plug and Play OS              [Yes]
Primary Video Adapter        [PCI]
PS/2 Mouse                   [Auto Detect]
Onboard PATA/SATA Adapters   [Both]
SATA Mode                    [RAID]
USB Legacy Mode Support      [Auto]
Onboard LAN                  [Enabled]
Onboard LAN Boot ROM         [Disabled]
Onboard 1394                 [Enabled]
Onboard Audio                [Auto]
Supervisor Password          Disabled
```

FIGURE 7.6 Enabling the SATA interface.

You may need to enable the SATA DMA options and disable the IDE channel that is being used for the SATA drive. These options are typically established through the IDE Function Setup page of the Integrated Peripherals menu, as shown in Figure 7.7. Then reboot the system and allow the Plug-and-Play (PnP) process to detect the additional drive. The presence of the drive should now show up in the Standard CMOS Setup page.

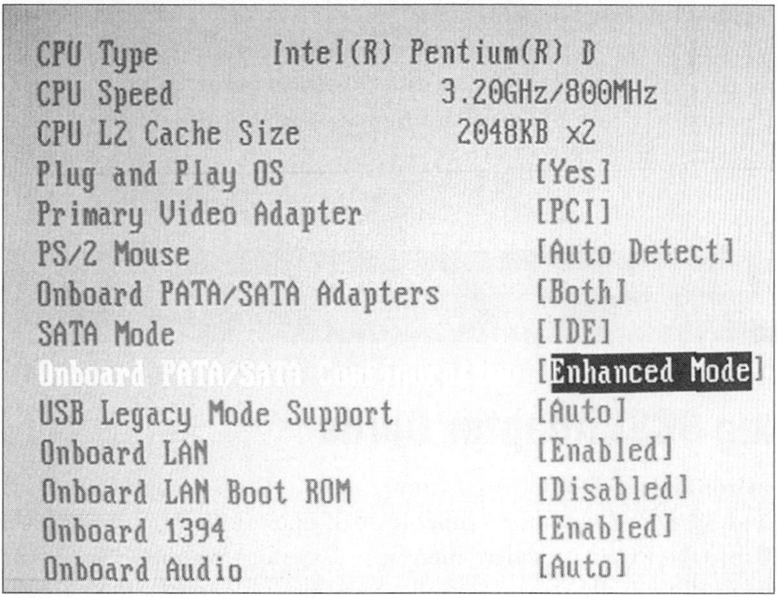

```
CPU Type          Intel(R) Pentium(R) D
CPU Speed                   3.20GHz/800MHz
CPU L2 Cache Size           2048KB x2
Plug and Play OS            [Yes]
Primary Video Adapter       [PCI]
PS/2 Mouse                  [Auto Detect]
Onboard PATA/SATA Adapters  [Both]
SATA Mode                   [IDE]
Onboard PATA/SATA           [Enhanced Mode]
USB Legacy Mode Support     [Auto]
Onboard LAN                 [Enabled]
Onboard LAN Boot ROM        [Disabled]
Onboard 1394                [Enabled]
Onboard Audio               [Auto]
```

FIGURE 7.7 Configuring the SATA interface in CMOS.

If the SATA drive you are installing is the system's boot drive, you may have to change the boot order sequence in the CMOS setup to boot from a SATA drive. Because SATA is a new interface type, older systems may recognize the presence of a SATA host adapter card and mistakenly classify it as a SCSI device. It may also represent the drive simply as a model number in the listing. You should be aware of these possibilities and treat them as normal events, even though the drive is not SCSI.

You may also need to load device drivers to enable the operating system to work with the SATA drive. Because SATA drives are not native to Windows operating systems, you will need to install the manufacturer's drivers for Windows so that it can recognize the SATA device. Download the SATA drivers from the website of the company that manufactured the SATA adapter card (or system board) you are installing.

If you are installing the SATA drive in a system with existing disk drives, you can load the drivers at any time. However, if you are performing a new Windows operating system installation on the drive, the drivers must be added during the installation process when requested by the Setup routine.

If the SATA drive being installed is the boot drive in a Windows system, the SATA drivers will need to be loaded during the text mode phase of the Windows installation process. When the Windows 2000 or XP setup program produces a "Setup did not find any hard disk drives installed in your system" during an installation, or an "Inaccessible boot device" message during a Windows operating system upgrade, you must install third-party device drivers to support the drive and continue the installation process. Windows Setup provides an F6 function key option to pause the installation process so that these mass storage device drivers can be installed.

EXAM ALERT

Know how to add third-party mass storage device drivers to the system during the Windows installation process.

Installing SCSI Adapter Cards

In the PC environment, SCSI devices are not standard. Even though newer system boards and operating systems do support SCSI operation, it has never been incorporated into the PC as a standard interface. Therefore, to use SCSI devices with a PC, you will typically need to install a SCSI host adapter card.

Before you install the SCSI host adapter card in the system unit, check its documentation for any manual configuration information and set up the card as required. PCI SCSI host adapter cards possess PnP capabilities that enable the system to automatically configure them with the system resources they need to operate. PnP SCSI adapters are normally configured by default for ID=7. However, you can change this setting by using the card's OEM software to update the BIOS extension on the card. This will cause the PnP process to configure the card with resources for the new ID setting when it is started again.

NOTE

You should always remove power from the system before adding or removing devices from inside the system unit. You should also use an antistatic wrist strap or other ESD prevention devices to protect the system from damage due to the discharge of potentially harmful electrostatic buildup from your clothes or body. The system should be disconnected from the AC power source before touching the system with a wrist strap on. It is not enough to just turn the system off, because some portions of Advanced Technology Extended (ATX) and Balanced Technology Extended (BTX) systems remain energized even when the system is turned off.

To install the SCSI host adapter card, remove the system unit's cover and select an appropriate expansion slot for the card (that is, PCI, PCI-X, or PCIe). Make certain that there is enough clearance for the card at the selected slot and remove the corresponding expansion slot cover from the back panel of the system unit. Then, insert the card into the empty expansion slot and secure it to the system unit back panel with a retaining screw.

After the SCSI host adapter card has been installed in the system and secured, the cables must be attached to the card and the devices it supports. This could involve internal ribbon cables, internal serial cables, external cables with D-shell connectors, or a combination of internal and external cables. One of the major tasks in getting parallel SCSI systems installed and operating has always been properly terminating the cables that run to the different SCSI devices in the system. Many newer SCSI adapters have autotermination capabilities built in to them to reduce the effort required to achieve satisfactory termination. As with any type of device you are installing in a PC system, you should refer to the adapter's documentation to determine its termination and configuration needs. Connect any external power supply connections to the SCSI peripherals and start the system.

The Windows 2000 and Windows XP operating systems offer support for most SCSI adapters. These operating systems should detect the new SCSI adapter if it is PnP-compatible and install the correct drivers for it. If Windows does not detect the device, or it does not install the drivers, you will need to manually load drivers for the adapter. In some cases this involves loading the drivers through the Windows Add Hardware applet in the Control Panel. In other cases, the system may ask for an OEM installation/driver disk or CD so that it can upload the drivers required to support the card.

Configuring SCSI Addresses

The original SCSI specification allows up to eight SCSI devices to be connected together. The standard SCSI1 port can be daisy-chained to permit up to six external peripherals to be connected to the system. To connect multiple SCSI devices to a SCSI host, all the devices, except the last one, must have two SCSI connectors: one for SCSI-In, and one for SCSI-Out. Which connector is used for which function does not matter. However, if the device has only one SCSI connector, it must be connected to the end of the chain.

It is possible to use multiple SCSI host adapters within a single system to increase the number of devices that can be used. The system's first SCSI controller can handle up to 7 devices, whereas the additional SCSI controller can boost the system to support up to 14 SCSI devices.

EXAM ALERT

Remember how many devices can be daisy-chained on a standard SCSI interface, and which ID numbers are assumed automatically.

Each SCSI device in a chain must have a unique ID number assigned to it. Even though there are a total of eight possible SCSI ID numbers for each controller, only six are available for use with external devices. The SCSI specification refers to the SCSI controller as SCSI-7 (by default), and then classifies the first internal hard drive as SCSI-0. If two devices are set to the same ID number, one or both of them will appear invisible to the system. This type of identification is also used for wide SCSI. The difference is that the bus can now support up to 16 devices with the bus being 16 bits wide. The addressing scheme changes from SCSI-0 to SCSI-15.

With older SCSI devices, address settings were established through jumpers on the host adapter card. Each device had a SCSI number selection switch or a set of configuration jumpers for establishing its ID number. Figure 7.8 illustrates a three-jumper configuration block that can be used to establish the SCSI ID number. In the figure, an open jumper pair is counted as a binary 0 and a shorted pair represents a binary 1. With a three-pair jumper block, it is possible to represent the numbers 0 through 7. In PnP systems, the BIOS will configure the device addresses using information obtained directly from the SCSI host adapter during the bootup process.

EXAM ALERT

Be aware of how SCSI ID priorities are set.

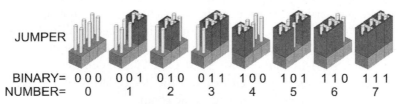

JUMPER								
BINARY=	0 0 0	0 0 1	0 1 0	0 1 1	1 0 0	1 0 1	1 1 0	1 1 1
NUMBER=	0	1	2	3	4	5	6	7

FIGURE 7.8 Configuring a SCSI ID number.

All newer BIOS versions are able to detect SCSI drives during the PnP process and can even be set to boot to a SCSI device. In addition, all current Windows versions offer native SCSI support. Because SCSI drives use a system-level interface, they require no low-level formatting. Therefore, the second step involved in installing a SCSI drive is to partition it.

SCSI Termination

The SCSI daisy chain must be terminated with a resistor network pack at both ends. Single-connector SCSI devices are normally terminated internally. If not, a SCSI terminator cable (containing a built-in resistor pack) must be installed at the end of the chain. SCSI termination is a major cause of SCSI-related problems. Poor terminations cause a variety of system problems, including the following:

▶ Failed system startups

▶ Hard drive crashes

▶ Random system failures

Several types of termination are commonly used with SCSI buses. They differ in the circuitry that is used to terminate the bus. The better the termination method, the better the quality of signal moving along the bus, making it more reliable. In general, the slower bus specifications are less particular in the termination method required, whereas the faster buses require better termination techniques. The different types of termination commonly used with SCSI systems include the following:

▶ Passive termination—This is the simplest and least-reliable method of termination. It employs nonactive resisters to terminate the bus. Passive termination is fine for short, low-speed SCSI-1 buses; however, it is not suitable for faster SCSI buses.

▶ Active termination—Adding active elements such as voltage regulators to the resistors used in passive termination provides for more reliable and consistent termination of the bus. Active termination is the minimum requirement for any of the faster single-ended SCSI buses.

▶ Forced perfect termination (FPT)—FPT is a more advanced form of active termination, in which diode clamps are added to the circuitry to force the termination to the correct voltage. FPT virtually eliminates any signal reflections or other problems and is the best form of termination of a single-ended SCSI bus.

Newer SCSI buses that employ low-voltage differential signaling require special types of terminators. In addition, there are special LVD/SE terminators designed for use with multimode LVD devices that can function in either LVD or SE modes. When the bus is in single-ended mode, they behave like active terminators. LVDs are currently more popular than HVDs because LVDs can support the Wide Ultra 2 SCSI, so the bandwidth is effectively doubled from 80 to 160MB/sec.

Newer SCSI technologies often provide for automatic cable termination. Many of the latest internal SCSI cables provide the termination function on the cable itself. The terminator is permanently applied at the end of the cable. For this reason, you should always verify the type of SCSI cables and components you are using before installation. This will help to ensure that your SCSI installation process moves along as effortlessly as possible.

In these systems, after a SCSI component has been installed, the system queries the device to detect modifications to the SCSI configuration. It then provides termination as required to enable the system to operate properly. In addition, these intelligent systems can also assign SCSI IDs as required. Even in these systems, you can still manually select ID numbers for the devices. In many cases, this is the best option because it enables you to document each SCSI component's ID for future reference.

Challenge #2

You are installing SCSI devices in a new system. Inside the case is a SCSI host adapter card, a hard disk drive, and a CD-ROM drive. The SCSI cabling runs from the host adapter to the hard drive and ends at the CD-ROM drive. External to the case, you must make connections for a SCSI flat bed scanner and a SCSI printer. The external cabling runs from the host adapter to the scanner and ends at the printer. Where should the terminator packs be installed?

Logical and Physical Drives

Before a disk drive can have a high-level format applied to it so that it can be used to perform useful functions for the system, the drive must be partitioned. *Partitioning* is the practice of dividing a physical drive into multiple logical storage areas and then treating each area as if it were a separate disk drive. This is normally done for purposes of organization and increased access speeds. However, drives may also be partitioned to enable multiple operating systems to exist on the same physical drive. Figure 7.9 illustrates the concept of creating multiple logical drives on a single physical hard drive.

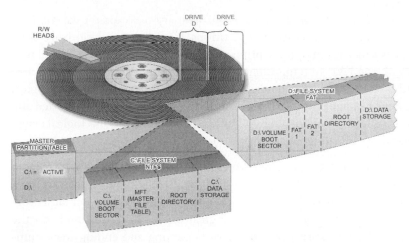

FIGURE 7.9 Partitions on an HDD.

All Windows 2000 and Windows XP versions are capable of using different file management system including File Allocation Table (FAT) and FAT32 file systems, as well as Master File Table (MFT)–based NTFS systems. The default file system for Windows 2000 and Windows XP is called *NTFS5*. These file systems are covered in detail in Chapter 13, "Major Operating System Structures."

EXAM ALERT

Remember the types of file management systems that Windows can work with.

FAT-based systems provide for two partitions on a physical hard disk drive. The first partition is referred to as the *primary partition* and must be created on the disk first. After the primary partition has been established and properly configured, an additional partition referred to as an *extended partition* can be created on any unused disk space that remains. In addition, the extended partition may be subdivided into 23 logical drives (the letters of the alphabet minus a, b, and c). These drives are dependent on the extended partition, so it cannot be deleted if logical drives have been defined within it.

NOTE

When a drive is partitioned in the Microsoft operating system environment, each logical drive is assigned a different drive letter (such as C, D, E, and so on) to identify it to the system.

NTFS systems can accommodate up to four primary partitions. Like the FAT system, NTFS also supports extended partitions. If extended partitions are used, the system has a maximum of three primary partitions and a single extended partition. As with the FAT system, extended partitions cannot be marked as active in the NTFS system. NTFS extended partitions can also be divided into logical drives. However, only primary partitions and logical drives can be formatted and assigned a drive letter. The total number of primary partitions plus logical drives cannot exceed 23 for a single hard drive.

When the primary partition is created on a hard disk, a special table is created in its master boot sector called the *partition table*. This table is used to store information about the partitions and logical drives on the disk. It includes information about where each partition and logical drive begins and ends on the physical drive. This is expressed in terms of beginning and ending track numbers. Each time a logical drive is added to the system, a complete disk structure, including a boot sector and preliminary directory management structure, is created. Its beginning and ending locations are also recorded in the partition table when the new drive is created.

The table also includes a setting that identifies the partition or logical drive that is active. The *active partition* is the logical drive that the system will boot to. On a partitioned drive, only one logical drive can be active at a time. When the system checks the drive's master boot sector looking for a Master Boot Record (MBR) during bootup, it encounters the partition table and checks it to determine which portion of the disk has been marked as active. With this information, the system jumps to the first track of the active partition and checks its boot sector for a partition boot record (an MBR for that partition). If an operating system has been installed in this partition, the boot sector will contain an MBR for it and the system will use it to boot up. This arrangement enables a single physical disk to hold different operating systems that the system can boot to.

Most PCs can have multiple physical hard-disk drive units installed in them. In a system using a Microsoft operating system, the primary partition is on the first disk drive designated as drive C:. The system files must be located in this partition, and the partition must be set to active for the system to boot up from the drive.

In local and wide area networks, the concept of logical drives is carried a step further. A particular hard-disk drive may be a logical drive in a large system of drives along a peer-to-peer network. On the other hand, a very large centralized drive may be used to create several logical drives for a server/client type of network.

In Windows 2000 and Windows XP, the disk partitioning function is performed using the Disk Management utility. This utility can be used to partition drives, and will show you the basic layout of the system's disks, including the following:

▶ The size of each disk

▶ The size and file system type used in each logical drive

▶ The size and location of any unformatted (free) space on the drive

However, these advanced disk utilities can also provide many advanced functions associated with enterprise (large-scale business-oriented) computing systems. The Disk Management utility can be used to create both traditional primary and extended partitions for Windows 2000 and Windows XP systems. They can also be used to create *volumes* (partitions that involve space on multiple physical drives) like those shown in Figure 7.10.

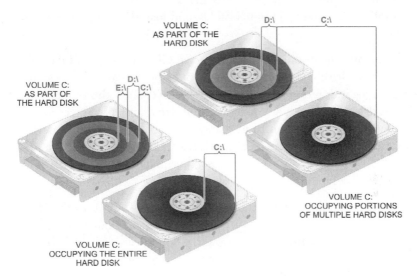

FIGURE 7.10 Volume types.

The high-level format procedure is performed by the operating system and fills in or re-creates the preliminary logical structures on the logical drive during the partitioning process. These structures tell the system what files are in the logical disk and where they can be found. Windows 2000 and Windows XP both support multiple types of file systems and partitions. In either of these systems, you may use the format process to create FAT and root directory structures for the partition. These structures are compatible with older operating systems. However, their native file system structure relies on a more flexible MFT structure used in the NTFS file management system.

> **NOTE**
>
> Hard disk drives also require a low-level format that marks off the disk into cylinders and sectors and defines their placement on the disk. System-level interface devices, such as IDE and SCSI drives, come with automatic low-level formatting routines already performed. Therefore, no low-level formatting needs to be performed on these drives before they can be partitioned and high-level formatted. Low-level formatting will not produce physical damage, but it may cause the loss of prerecorded bad track and sector information, as well as loss of information used to control the read/write heads for proper alignment over the tracks. If this occurs, it will normally be necessary to send the drive to the manufacturer to restore this information to the disk.

Installing CD-ROM/DVD Drives

Before installing an internal CD-ROM or DVD drive, confirm its master/slave or SCSI ID configuration setting. Afterward, install the drive unit in one of the drive bays, connect the power and signal cables, and load the drive's driver software if needed.

Figure 7.11 illustrates the installation of an internal CD-ROM drive. Of course, the interface for the drive and the system board must be the same. If the system board interface type is different from that of the HDD (that is, the system board supports PATA drives and the new drive is a SCSI drive), it will be necessary to install a compatible host adapter card in one of the expansion slots to interface the drive to the system. However, there are IDE-to-USB conversion kits that enable you to treat IDE drives as a USB plug-in peripheral. Finally, refer to the drive's documentation regarding any necessary jumper or switch settings.

To connect the drive to the system, hook up the CD-ROM drive to the HDD signal cable, observing proper orientation. Connect the audio cable to the drive and to the sound card's CD Input connection (if a sound card is installed).

Configuring CD-ROM Drives

As previously indicated, the CD-ROM drive must be properly configured for the system it is being installed in. In a PATA system, the master/slave setting must be confirmed. In a SCSI system, the ID setting must be correct. In a SCSI system, the only requirement is that a valid ID setting be configured. In a PATA system, however, some thought may be required as to how to configure the drive.

In a single-HDD system, the CD-ROM drive can be set up as the slave drive on the primary interface. However, the operation of the drives is much cleaner if the CD-ROM is set up as the master drive on the secondary PATA interface. In this manner, each drive has access to a full IDE channel instead of sharing one. Likewise, in a two-HDD system, the CD-ROM drive would most likely be configured as the master or single drive on the secondary interface. If the system also contains a sound card that has a built-in IDE interface, it should be disabled to prevent it from interfering with the primary or secondary interfaces.

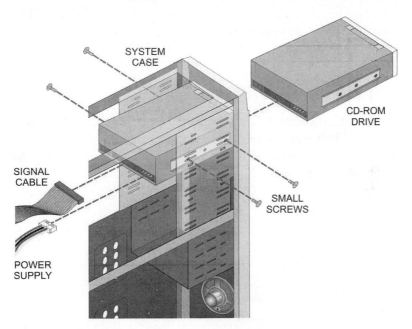

FIGURE 7.11   Installing an internal CD-ROM drive.

After the hardware has been installed, it will be necessary to install its software drivers. Consult the drive's documentation for instructions on software installation. Typically, all that is required is to insert the OEM driver disk into the floppy drive and follow the manufacturer's directions for installing the drivers. If the drive fails to operate at this point, reboot the system using single-step verification and check the information on the various boot screens for error messages associated with the CD-ROM drive.

Installing CD-RW and DVD-RW Drives

The hardware installation process involved with rewriteable CD-ROM and DVD drives is identical to that used with standard CD-ROM and DVD drives. However, prior to the Windows XP operating system, rewriteable CD-RW and DVD-RW drives required third-party application packages to perform write and rewrite functions. These applications had to be installed from the OEM CD that was packaged with the drive, or a CD had to be obtained from an independent supplier.

In the Windows XP environment, rewriteable drives are supported directly from the operating system and don't require any third-party applications. When you insert a blank disc into one of these drives, the operating system detects it and pops up a dialog box that asks you what you want to do with the disc. Most users still prefer to install a third-party program to manage all of the functions of these drives.

Installing a Floppy Disk Drive

The FDD installation procedure follows the sample procedure described earlier. Simply slide the FDD into one of the system unit's open drive bays, install two screws on each side to secure the drive to the system unit, and connect the signal and power cables to the drive. Figure 7.12 illustrates the steps required to install a floppy drive.

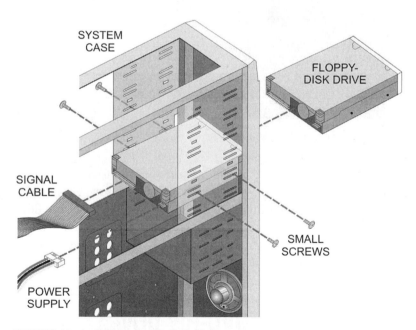

FIGURE 7.12   Installing a floppy disk drive.

The PC-compatible FDD unit uses a 34-pin signal cable that connects to BERG connectors at all points. Older FDD signal cables were designed to accommodate two FDD units, as illustrated in Figure 7.13. If the drive was the only floppy in the system, or was intended to operate as the A: drive, it was connected to the connector at the end of the cable. If it was being installed as a B: drive, the drive was attached to the connector toward the center of the cable. In new PCs, if a floppy drive is present at all, the signal cable is designed to accommodate only one drive.

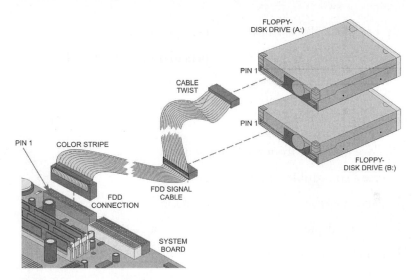

FLOPPY-
DISK DRIVE (A:)

PIN 1

CABLE
TWIST

PIN 1

PIN 1

COLOR STRIPE

FLOPPY-
DISK DRIVE (B:)

FDD
CONNECTION

FDD SIGNAL
CABLE

SYSTEM
BOARD

FIGURE 7.13   Connecting floppy drives.

On some Pentium system boards and on all-in-one system boards, check the system board's documentation for an FDD-enabling jumper and make certain that it is set correctly for the FDD installed. In newer systems, the FDD enabling function should be set in the Advanced CMOS Setup screen.

Reinstall the system unit's power cord and boot up the computer. As the system boots, move into the CMOS Setup utility and configure the CMOS for the type of FDD being installed.

Installing External Storage Devices

External storage devices normally connect to adapter cards installed in the system board's expansion slots. They also tend to employ separate, external power supply units. Several newer storage technologies, such as removable hard drive media, have been designed to take advantage of the enhanced parallel port specifications of modern systems. These devices can be connected directly to the system's parallel port or can be connected to the system through another device that is connected to the port. The device's installation software is used to configure it for use in the system.

The general procedure for installing external storage devices is the following:

1. Configure the device for operation

    a. Refer to the device's user's manual regarding any IRQ and COM jumper or switch settings

    b. Record the card's default IRQ and COM settings

    c. Set the device's configuration jumpers to operate at the default setting

2. Install the device's adapter card (if necessary)

    a. Turn the system off

    b. Remove the cover from the system unit

    c. Locate a compatible empty expansion slot

    d. Remove the expansion slot cover from the rear of the system unit

    e. Install the adapter card in the expansion slot

    f. Reinstall the screw to secure the card to the back panel of the system unit

3. Make the device's external connections

    a. Connect the device's signal cable to the appropriate connector at the rear of the system.

    b. Connect the opposite end of the cable to the device

    c. Verify that the power switch or power supply is turned off

    d. Connect the power supply to the external storage unit

4. Configure the device's software

    a. Turn the system on

    b. Check the CMOS setup to ensure that the port setting is correct

    c. Run the device's installation routine

Upgrading and Optimizing Disk Drives

As with other modules in the PC, the hard disk and CD-ROM/DVD drives can be upgraded as new or better components become available, or as the system's application changes. PC technicians must be capable of upgrading the various components of the system—including its disk drives. The technician should also be able to optimize the operation of the drive to obtain the best performance possible for a given system configuration.

HDD Upgrading

One of the key components in keeping the system up to date is the hard disk drive. Software manufacturers continue to produce larger and larger programs. In addition, the types of programs found on the typical PC are expanding. Many newer programs place high demands on the hard drive to feed information, such as large graphics files or digitized voice and video, to the system for processing.

Invariably, the system will begin to produce error messages stating that the hard drive is full. The first line of action is to use software disk utilities, such as CHKDSK and DEFRAG, to optimize the organization of the drive. The second step is to remove unnecessary programs and files from the hard drive. Programs and information that are rarely or never used should be moved to an archival media, such as removable disks or tape.

There may come a time when it is necessary to determine whether the hard drive needs to be replaced to optimize the performance of the system. One guideline suggests that the drive should be replaced if the percentage of unused disk space drops below 20%.

Another reason to consider upgrading the HDD involves its capability to deliver information to the system. If the system is constantly waiting for information from the hard drive, replacing it should be considered as an option. Not all system slowdowns are connected to the HDD, but many are. Remember that the HDD is the mechanical part of the memory system, whereas everything else is electronic.

As with the storage space issue, HDD speed can be optimized through software configurations, such as a more efficient disk cache. However, after it has been optimized in this manner, any further speed increases must be accomplished by upgrading the hardware.

When considering an HDD upgrade, determine what the real needs are for the hard drive. Multimedia-intensive applications can place heavy performance demands on the hard-disk drive. Moving large image, audio, and video files into RAM on demand requires high performance from the drive. Critical HDD specifications associated with disk drive performance include the following:

▶ Access time—The average time, expressed in milliseconds, required to position the drive's read/write heads over a specified track/cylinder and to reach a specified sector on the track.

▶ Track-seek time—The amount of time required for the drive's read/write heads to move between cylinders and settle over a particular track following the seek command being issued by the system.

▶ Data transfer rate—The speed, expressed in megabytes per second (MBps), at which data is transferred between the system and the drive.

These factors should be checked thoroughly when upgrading an HDD unit for speed-critical applications. In contemporary systems, the choice of hard drives for high-performance applications is between SATA drives and SCSI drives. The SATA drives are competitive and relatively easy to install, whereas the high-end SCSI specifications offer additional performance, but require additional setup effort and an additional host adapter card.

Disk Drive Subsystem Enhancements

When upgrading a PATA hard drive, make sure that the system board supports the type of PATA drive you are installing. If your system board will support only ATA-100 drives, there is little reason to purchase an ATA-133 drive, unless you plan to upgrade the system board in the near future.

Also verify that the correct cabling is being used to connect the new drive to the system. You should know that installing a new ATA-100 or ATA-133 drive in a system using the old 40-wire IDE cable will cause the drive's operation to be diminished to the level of the old drive. Without new cables, communication with the drives will be limited to the lesser standard determined by the 40-conductor signal cable. Check the master/slave jumper settings to see that they are correct for the new system before the drive is actually mounted in the system.

EXAM ALERT

Be aware of the effects of using newer PATA devices with older IDE signal cables.

When upgrading SCSI systems, prepare a scheme for SCSI identification and termination ahead of time and ensure that you have the necessary cabling and terminators. Take care to ensure that the new drive is correctly configured and terminated for its position in the system. Verify that the SCSI host adapter will support the new drive type. For example, a standard SCSI-I host adapter will not support a Fast-Wide SCSI drive. The physical cable and the communication speed differences between the two specifications will not match.

Likewise, when you upgrade a SCSI component, you should be aware that the SCSI host controller and the SCSI devices have the capability to adapt to lower functionality. If you upgrade one or more SCSI devices in a system, but do not upgrade the SCSI host adapter, the devices will probably operate, but they will operate only at the maximum performance level of the adapter.

On the other hand, if you update the SCSI adapter and one or more SCSI devices, but you still have some older SCSI devices installed, devices that can operate at higher performance levels will attempt to do so. However, slower devices will work at their designated speed. The fact that the controller must slow down to work with the slower devices will effectively slow the operation of the entire SCSI system.

EXAM ALERT

Be aware of how conducting partial upgrades on IDE and SCSI systems affects the performance of the devices involved and the drive system.

Before upgrading the HDD unit, make certain that the existing drive is providing all the performance that it can. Also, determine how much performance increase can be gained through other upgrading efforts before changing out the hard drive.

If the drive is being upgraded substantially, such as from a 10GB IDE/PATA drive to a 500GB IDE/PATA drive, check the capabilities of the system's ROM BIOS. If the current BIOS does not support the drive type or size you intend to install, you must upgrade it to support the new hard drive installation. The best place to find out the type and size of hard drives your current BIOS supports is the system board's documentation. The best place to find out whether a new BIOS version is available to support the new hard drive is the system board manufacturer's Internet support site. This website typically makes provisions for downloading the new BIOS material and loader utility.

EXAM ALERT

Be aware that the BIOS might be a size-limiting factor in disk drive partition sizes.

After the drive upgrade has been performed, you should verify the system's operation. When you start up the system, its power-on self test (POST) routines will examine the drive's configuration and notify you if it has been detected. This is the most basic verification. An additional level of verification occurs at boot-up. After the operating system starts up, you can open a file manager to see if the drive exists and how much space it presents to the system. You can also see the file system structure on the drive.

Finally, you should determine how much longer the unit in question is likely to be used before being replaced. If the decision to upgrade the HDD stands, ultimately, the best advice is to get the biggest, fastest hard drive possible. Don't forget that a different I/O bus architecture might add to the performance increase.

Challenge #3

Your PATA hard drive is continually producing "Out of Hard Drive Space" error messages. These messages continue to be a problem even after you have optimized the drive through the defrag utility and removed as much old information as possible. You are thinking of upgrading to a new high-speed, high-capacity 500GB ATA-133 drive. What system considerations do you need to resolve before buying this drive?

Installing Video/Monitor Systems

The video display system is one of the easiest systems to add to the computer. The components associated with the typical video display subsystem are depicted in Figure 7.14. The video adapter card typically plugs into one of the system's expansion slots. In some installations, you may need to connect an additional power connector to the video adapter card to supply power for the fan unit. Next, the monitor's signal cable plugs into the video adapter card. The monitor's power cable can be plugged into a commercial wall outlet.

While this configuration is true for most PC systems, many new system boards provide onboard VGA video as part of their chipsets and architecture. To upgrade the video capabilities of these systems, you must disable the onboard video capabilities before using an adapter card-based video display system. To do so, you must access the CMOS Setup utility and disable the onboard video function there.

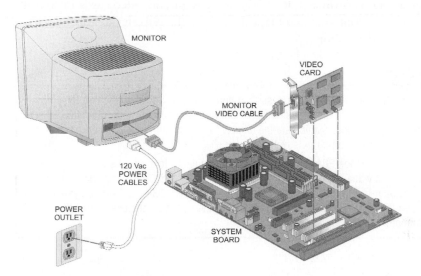

FIGURE 7.14   Video system components.

There are three common expansion slots types used with video cards. The oldest is the original PCI bus. However, the AGP slot found on a great number of ATX system boards was designed specifically for video adapter cards. Most new PCs use the 16X PCIe slot for video controllers. In some high-end gaming systems, dual PCIe slots are used for the video adapter subsystem.

After the video card has been installed and the monitor has been connected to the video card and plugged into the power outlet, the drivers for the video card must be loaded or installed. A Windows operating system should automatically detect the video card, start the system with basic VGA video drivers, tell you that it has found the new card, and then automatically load the correct video drivers. The only time that you should need to be directly involved with the system's video drivers is when the PnP process fails or the video card is not recognized by the operating system. The new device recognition function of the PnP process will ask you to select the driver for the new video card. At this point you can select the Windows Autodetect option or you can manually install a driver from the adapter's utility disk. The default values for VGA/PCI-compatible adapters include a standard 640 × 480 pixel screen resolution at 16 colors, with a refresh rate of 60Hz.

The video adapter's color, resolution, and refresh settings can be manually optimized through the Display icon in the Windows Control Panel. Some users prefer higher color values (32-bit instead of 16- or 24-bit operation), whereas others prefer higher screen resolutions (1024 × 768 or higher). Generally, the fastest refresh rate possible is desirable. Some high-end video cards include an auto-optimize function that automatically adjusts the refresh rate for the selected resolution and monitor type.

NOTE

LCD displays cannot be adjusted as described here. These panels come with a fixed number of pixels to work with (called its *native resolution*). To cope with other resolutions settings, these displays must manipulate the display image by removing pixel information to make it fit the physical constraints of the display.

However, most notebook PCs provide a VGA port connector that permits a CRT, a better LCD display, or a video projector to be used instead of the built-in display unit. Windows XP provides built-in support for dual displays. To add a CRT VGA display to a system, simply open the Display icon on the Control Panel and configure the system for dual display operation.

EXAM ALERT

Be aware that dual displays can be configured to work on Windows XP systems.

Installing Standard PC Input Devices

In a Windows-based system, the steps for installing a keyboard or a mouse are simple: plug the device's cable into the appropriate connector at the back of the unit. Then, turn the system on and let the operating system detect and automatically configure them.

Although the traditional method of connecting keyboards and pointing devices to the system has involved plugging the device's PS/2 connector into the proper socket on the back of the system unit, other options have appeared. Newer keyboards, mice, and pointing devices often use a USB port instead of the more traditional PS/2 port. This connection may also involve wireless links, such as infrared (IR) or radio frequency (RF) between the device and a small receiver that plugs into the USB port.

The only additional steps that may be required to get a different type of pointing device operational are to ensure that its port hardware is properly selected and enabled and that its driver software has been loaded into the operating system.

If the driver for the device is proprietary and cannot be identified by the system during the PnP phase of the startup process, you will need to select a device driver program for the device, or use one obtained from the device manufacturer. These drivers might be located on a CD (or a floppy if it's really old) that comes with the device, on the manufacturer's website, or on one of the third-party driver websites on the Internet. If you cannot find the driver in any of these locations, you will need to contact the device manufacturer through other means to obtain it.

Installing Scanners

Although some older scanners employed proprietary adapter cards, most scanners connect to one of the system's standard I/O ports, such as the system's EPP or ECP-enabled parallel port, as illustrated in Figure 7.15. When using one of these ports to support a scanner, it is important to use an approved IEEE-1284-compliant cabling. Older parallel printer cables were designed for unidirectional low-speed communications and may prevent a bidirectional high-speed device like a scanner from working correctly.

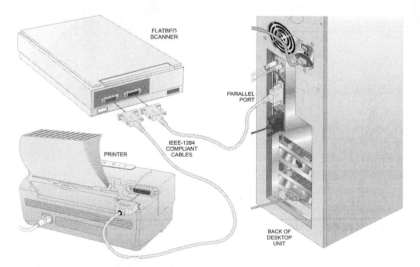

FIGURE 7.15   Connecting an IEEE-1284-compliant scanner.

Newer scanners may employ a SCSI bus extension or a USB port connection. These scanners must be installed in accordance with the appropriate SCSI or USB installation procedures. They will usually require that a supporting software application be installed in the system to take advantage of their feature sets.

Installing Bar Code Scanners

Bar code scanners are typically connected to the computer system using a PS/2 or USB cable. However, there are also versions that employ wireless Bluetooth connections to the computer. Some models are connected into the keyboard input using a Y-cable arrangement. In this scenario, the keyboard remains a usable input device. The hard-wired devices receive power through their interface cables, whereas the wireless scanners are battery operated. These connections are depicted in Figure 7.16.

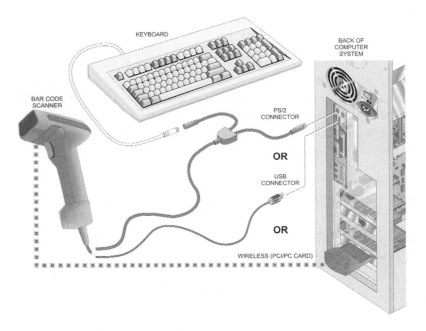

FIGURE 7.16 Connecting a bar code scanner.

Installing Sound Cards

Installing a sound card is similar to installing any other adapter card. Install the card in one of the system's vacant expansion slots and secure it to the back panel of the system unit. Plug the microphone and speakers cables into the proper 1/4 inch RCA minijacks (or 1/8 inch or 3/32 inch submini RCA jacks) on the card's backplate. After the card has been installed, the operating system should detect the card and load the proper software drivers for it. If not, you will have to manually install the sound card drivers in the same manner as previously described for other adapter card-based peripherals. Figure 7.17 depicts the connectors located on the back of a typical sound card.

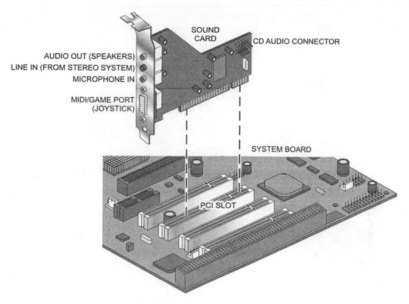

FIGURE 7.17 Sound card connections.

Installing Digital Cameras

Digital cameras are mobile devices that are mostly plugged into the computer simply to download pictures. The most widely used interface for connecting digital cameras and camcorders to PCs is USB. Some cameras can also communicate through IEEE-1394 FireWire ports. USB and FireWire ports feature hot-swap capabilities that permit the camera to be plugged into the system and removed while power is still applied. Figure 7.18 shows a typical digital camera connection scheme.

Software applications for downloading the pictures from the camera must be loaded on the PC before any transfers can be conducted. Likewise, the software supplied with the camera can be used to display the images and typically offers a limited number of graphic manipulation features (for example, rotate, color balance, crop, and resize). Most digital cameras deliver the images to the PC in a JPEG format. This format is compact, but it can be manipulated with virtually any commercial graphic design software.

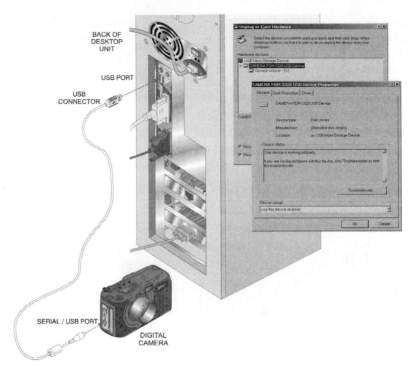

FIGURE 7.18 Digital camera connection.

Installing Adapter Card–Based Peripherals

In addition to installing hard drives and peripheral devices that connect to standard I/O ports, technicians must be able to successfully install and configure peripheral devices (or systems) that connect to the system in other ways—such as through the system's expansion slots. The steps for installing these types of peripherals and systems are generally very similar from device to device:

1. Remove the system unit's cover and take out an expansion slot cover.

2. Check the adapter card's user's manual for any manual configuration information and set up the card as required.

3. Insert the card into the empty expansion slot.

4. Connect any necessary internal and external cabling to the adapter card (such as power for a fan unit and/or signal cables for the peripheral device).

5. Connect any external power supply connections to the peripheral device.

6. Start the machine. The Windows operating system should detect the new device if it is PnP-compatible and install the correct drivers for it. If Windows does not detect the device, or it does not install the drivers, you will need to load drivers for the device from its installation media (disk or CD) or from an external source.

7. Shut down the system, turn it off, and reinstall the system unit's outer cover.

This process can be used to install diverse I/O devices such as modems and LAN adapters, as well as scanners and other devices that use adapter cards in expansion slots. However, for many devices, the advent of newer hot-swap I/O buses, such as USB and FireWire, has reduced this process to more or less just connecting the device to the bus.

Whenever you are installing adapter cards in PCs, you must be aware of all the dimensions of the cards you're installing. Even though a system board may contain four or five expansion slots, you may not be able to physically install more than a few adapters due to the spacing of the connectors. In some cases, such as high-end video adapter cards, the fan units may take up the space above an adjacent slot making it difficult or impossible to install another card in it.

Upgrading Adapters

Normally, updating adapters in a PC involves installing NICs, modems, or other proprietary adapter cards. You should always use the following guidelines for upgrading adapter card–based peripherals in a system:

1. Verify compatibility—When you are installing adapter cards, you should verify their compatibility with the system board, its adapter slot, and the other cards installed in the system. For example, if you are upgrading a PCI card, you should make sure that the voltage is compatible with the available PCI slot. If your PCI slots support only 3.3V adapters, the card you are upgrading to also needs to be 3.3V. PCI cards that operate on 3.3V and those that use 5V are configured differently. Therefore, a 3.3V card will fit only in a 3.3V slot, where as 5V cards will only fit in a 5V slot. On the other hand, some PCI cards support both 5V and 3.3V operation. There is less to worry about with such dual-voltage cards.

2. Perform BIOS upgrade—A system BIOS upgrade is not required when upgrading adapter cards, but some adapter cards contain their own specific BIOS. The BIOS may need to be upgraded to permit the adapter to work with the other components in the system. If in doubt, refer to the installation documentation and the manufacturer's website for specific information pertaining to the adapters you are using.

3. Obtain the latest drivers—In most cases, the drivers that came with an adapter card include the necessary drivers for the operating system you are using. However, the latest driver on the CD-ROM or floppy disk supplied with the component is often not the latest driver available for the noted operating system. Check the manufacturer's website for newer versions.

4. Implement ESD best practices—To prevent the adapter from being damaged, make sure that it is enclosed in an antishock bag when not in use. Make sure that you wear an antistatic device when handling the adapter. Most adapters include static sensitive components that can be damaged by very small electromagnetic shocks, so take extra care when handling or installing your adapter cards.

5. Verify upgrade—There are specific attributes that are common when verifying proper installation of a variety of adapter cards. For instance, all adapters use resources, such as IRQ, I/O memory, and/or base memory address. You must make sure that none of these settings conflict with those of other hardware devices in the system. You can check this in Windows by checking the system properties in the Control Panel and looking at the Hardware tab for hardware errors. Some adapter cards require jumper settings to be preset for these attributes, whereas others do not require jumpers or include jumperless BIOS.

Installing Devices Using USB, IEEE-1394, PCMCIA, and IrDA

Most new I/O ports and buses (such as USB, IEEE-1394, PCMCIA, and IrDA) feature hot insertion and removal capabilities for their devices. These are in addition to the traditional PnP operation. The devices that connect to these ports and buses are designed so that they can be plugged in and removed as needed. Installing these devices is practically a hands-off operation.

> **NOTE**
>
> Installation of PCMCIA devices is covered in more detail in Chapter 10, "Portable Computer Fundamentals."

Installing USB and IEEE-1394 (FireWire) Devices

Installing a USB or FireWire device usually involves the following steps:

1. Enable the USB resources in the CMOS setup screen, as illustrated in Figure 7.19. In some cases, this involves enabling the port and reserving an IRQ resource for the device.

2. Plug the device into an open USB connector.

3. Wait for the operating system to recognize the device and configure it through the PnP process.

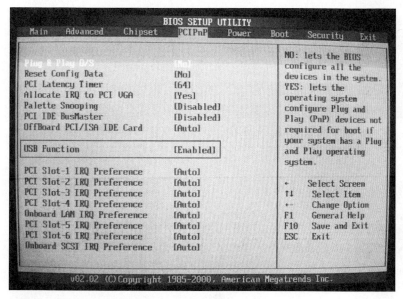

FIGURE 7.19 Enabling the USB resources.

Microsoft's Windows 2000 and Windows XP operating systems will detect the presence of the USB or FireWire device and start the Found New Hardware Wizard program, depicted in Figure 7.20, to guide the installation process. Follow the instructions provided by the wizard to set up the new device—there is no need to shut down or turn off the computer.

Installing IrDA Devices

Installing an IrDA device in an infrared-enabled system is a fairly simple process. When an IrDA device is installed in the system, a Wireless Link icon appears in the Windows Control Panel as depicted in Figure 7.21. (Remember, infrared port operations must first be enabled through the CMOS Setup utility.) When another IrDA device comes within range of the host port, the Infrared icon will appear on the Windows desktop and in the taskbar. In the case of an IrDA printer, a printer icon will appear in the Printer folder.

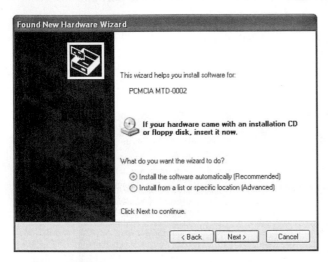

FIGURE 7.20 The Windows Found New Hardware Wizard.

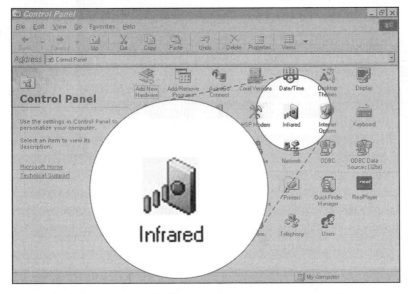

FIGURE 7.21 The Windows Wireless Link icon.

EXAM ALERT

Be aware that IrDA operations must be enabled in CMOS before any infrared activities can occur.

Right-click the Infrared icon on the taskbar to turn on the infrared communication function. Make sure that the Enable Infrared Communication check box is checked. To turn off infrared communications, make sure that this item is not checked. When infrared communication has been turned off, the Search for Devices Within Range and Enable Plug and Play functions are also turned off. To engage support for infrared plug-and-play devices, right-click the Infrared icon on the taskbar.

Make sure that the Enable Plug and Play option is checked. Conversely, to turn off support for plug-and-play device installation, make sure that this item is not checked. It will be available only if the infrared and searching functions are enabled. Click the Related Topics option if the taskbar icon is not visible.

EXAM ALERT

Be aware of how to know that an IrDA-capable device is within range of a host system.

Right-click the Infrared icon on the taskbar to install software for an infrared device. Make sure that the Enable Plug and Play check box is checked and verify that the new device is within range. If you are not sure whether the device you are installing is plug-and-play capable, check its user's guide. If it is not a plug-and-play device, install its drivers by accessing the Add New Hardware icon in the Control Panel.

Windows provides an Infrared Monitor utility that can be used to track the computer's activity. When this utility is running, it will alert you when infrared devices are within range of your computer by placing the Infrared icon on the taskbar. The Infrared Monitor not only notifies you when the computer is communicating with an infrared device, but it also indicates how well it is communicating. Other functions that can be performed through the Infrared Monitor include controlling how the system reports the status of the infrared activity it detects and what types of infrared activity it can conduct.

Upgrading Peripheral Devices

Devices that come under this category include printers, external modems, external CD devices, and input devices, such as the keyboard and mouse. The steps involved in this process are similar to those listed for upgrading adapter cards presented earlier in this chapter. You should use the general procedure that follows when you are upgrading a system's peripheral devices.

1. Verify compatibility—Because peripheral devices can vary greatly in their configuration and use, you should always refer to the device's documentation to ensure that it will work properly with your system. Because external devices must connect to the computer through its interface ports (serial and parallel ports, USB, FireWire, and in some cases, external SCSI connectors), you must ensure that the proper port is available for the device to be installed.

2. Perform firmware upgrade—Prior to installing a peripheral, consult the manufacturer's website for any updates that may exist for its firmware or any updated device drivers that may be available. To apply firmware updates, you must first obtain the firmware update tool from the manufacturer.

3. Obtain the latest drivers—In most cases, the installation software that came with the peripheral will have the necessary drivers for the operating system you are using. The latest driver on the installation CD or floppy disk is usually only the latest driver available at the time the peripheral shipped.

4. Implement ESD best practices—Peripherals tend to be less sensitive to electrostatic damage than PC board devices and are often directly grounded through their power cords. However, because peripheral devices tend to be expensive, you may still want to properly ground yourself before working with them. It is always better to be safe than sorry.

5. Verify the upgrade—Because peripheral devices can vary greatly in their configuration and use, there are a variety of ways that you can test your upgrade. For instance, with a printer you can print a test page, print a page from a client, or print multiple print jobs to test the queue. For a Zip disk, this may include moving data onto the disk and then trying to examine the data on another computer later.

6. Check system resources—Normally, peripherals use the resources associated with the port they are attached to. If the peripheral tests okay, you will not usually have to verify system resources.

Exam Prep Questions

1. What distinctive feature enables you to quickly identify an Ultra ATA 66 interface cable?

   ○ **A.** The connectors are blue.

   ○ **B.** The cable is blue.

   ○ **C.** The cable has 40 wires.

   ○ **D.** The cable has 80 wires.

2. Which of these standard SCSI devices has the highest priority?

   ○ **A.** SCSI-0

   ○ **B.** SCSI-1

   ○ **C.** SCSI-6

   ○ **D.** SCSI-7

3. Which SCSI ID is typically used for the system's internal hard-disk drive?

   ○ **A.** SCSI-0

   ○ **B.** SCSI-1

   ○ **C.** SCSI-7

   ○ **D.** SCSI-8

4. Which SCSI ID is typically used for the system's SCSI adapter?

   ○ **A.** SCSI-0

   ○ **B.** SCSI-6

   ○ **C.** SCSI-7

   ○ **D.** SCSI-8

5. After installing a scanner at the end of a SCSI daisy chain, you discover that both the scanner and your SCSI CD-ROM drive have stopped working. What is likely to be the problem?

   ○ **A.** The ribbon cable is bad.

   ○ **B.** The scanner is using an incompatible protocol.

   ○ **C.** Both devices are set to slave.

   ○ **D.** Both devices are using the same ID number.

6. When you install SCSI devices in a system, which device or devices should be terminated?

   ○ **A.** All SCSI devices.

   ○ **B.** The first and the last SCSI devices.

   ○ **C.** Only the last SCSI device.

   ○ **D.** SCSI devices do not require termination.

7. How are SCSI devices identified and differentiated from each other?

   ○ **A.** By the order in which they are connected on the cable.

   ○ **B.** The jumpers determine master/slave/single status.

   ○ **C.** An ID number that is assigned to the device.

   ○ **D.** A drive letter that is assigned to the device.

8. What is the highest drive letter that can be assigned to a logical drive in a FAT-based
   system?

   ○ **A.** S

   ○ **B.** W

   ○ **C.** Z

   ○ **D.** H

9. How many additional logical drives can be created in a computer using a FAT-based
   operating system?

   ○ **A.** 1

   ○ **B.** 8

   ○ **C.** 23

   ○ **D.** 26

10. If you connect four two-partition IDE drives to a system board, what will the drive des-
    ignation be for the primary partition on the master drive of the secondary IDE con-
    troller?

    ○ **A.** C:

    ○ **B.** D:

    ○ **C.** E:

    ○ **D.** F:

11. What describes the typical configuration setting options associated with an IDE drive?

- ○ **A.** Primary or secondary
- ○ **B.** Master or slave
- ○ **C.** Master secondary or alternate primary
- ○ **D.** Primary master or secondary master

12. You are preparing to install new adapter cards in a desktop PC. Which of the following actions should you take first?

- ○ **A.** Put on an antistatic wrist strap
- ○ **B.** Unplug the computer from the AC power source
- ○ **C.** Unplug the power supply from the system board
- ○ **D.** Roll back any existing drivers for the card

13. How do you install dual monitors on a Windows XP laptop PC?

- ○ **A.** Right-click on the desktop display, select the Dual monitors option from the menu, and extend the desktop
- ○ **B.** Click on the Display icon in the Control Panel and configure the settings for multiple monitors on the Settings tab
- ○ **C.** Click on the Add Hardware icon in the Control Panel, select the Dual Monitor option, and configure the dual monitor settings
- ○ **D.** Navigate to the Device Manager, expand the Display node and configure the options under the Dual Monitor tab

14. What is the default file system installed for Windows 2000?

- ○ **A.** NTFS4
- ○ **B.** FAT32
- ○ **C.** FAT16
- ○ **D.** NTFS5

Answers and Explanations

1. D. Ultra DMA (UDMA) interfaces (ATA-4/Ultra ATA 66 and Ultra ATA 100) extend the high data throughput capabilities of the ATA-3 bus by doubling the number of conductors in the IDE signal cable to 80. Although the number of wires has doubled, the IDE connector has remained compatible with the 40-pin IDE connection, but each pin has been provided with its own ground conductor in the cable.

2. D. The priority levels assigned to SCSI devices are determined by their ID numbers, with the highest numbered device receiving the highest priority.

3. A. Historically, manufacturers have classified the first internal hard drive as SCSI-0.

4. C. Traditionally, SCSI host adapter cards are set to SCSI-7 by default from their manufacturers.

5. D. Each SCSI device in a chain must have a unique ID number assigned to it. Even though there are a total of eight possible SCSI ID numbers for each controller, only six are available for use with external devices. If two SCSI devices are set to the same ID number, one or both will be invisible to the system.

6. B. The SCSI daisy chain must be terminated with a resistor at both ends.

7. C. The priority levels assigned to SCSI devices are determined by their ID numbers, with the highest numbered device receiving the highest priority. Each SCSI device in a chain must have a unique ID number assigned to it.

8. C. The extended partition may be subdivided into 23 logical drives (all the letters in the alphabet minus a, b, and c).

9. C. The partition may be subdivided into 23 additional logical drives (all the letters of the alphabet minus a, b, and c).

10. C. The hierarchy of assigning logical drive designations in the IDE interface calls for primary partitions to be assigned sequentially from ID1 master, ID1 slave, ID2 master, to ID2 slave. This is followed by assigning drive letters to the extended partitions for each drive in the same order.

11. B. You should confirm that the IDE drive is configured as a master or slave drive before installing the unit in the drive bay.

12. B. You should always remove power from the system before adding or removing devices from inside the system unit. You should also use an antistatic wrist strap or other ESD prevention devices to protect the system from damage due to the discharge of potentially harmful electrostatic buildup from your clothes or body. The system should be disconnected from the AC power source before touching the system with a wrist strap on. It is not enough to just turn the system off because some portions of ATX and BTX systems remain energized even when the system is turned off.

13. B. Most notebook PCs provide a VGA port connector that permits a CRT, a better LCD display, or a video projector to be used instead of the built-in display unit. Windows XP provides built-in support for dual displays. To add a CRT VGA display to a system, simply click the Display icon on the Control Panel and configure the system for dual display operation.

14. D. When partitions are created on a disk they have all the record-keeping structures required for them to work with the file management systems of particular operating systems. All Windows 2000 and Windows XP versions are capable of using different file management system including File Allocation Table-based FAT and FAT32 file systems, as well as Master File Table–based NTFS systems. The default file system for Windows 2000 and Windows XP is called NTFS5.

Challenge Solutions

1. The extended partition of the hard drive should show up as the E: drive. The primary partition will naturally be C:, and the master drive on IDE2 will be designated as drive D:. This will leave the F: designation for the slave drive on IDE2.

2. The terminator packs should be installed on the printer and the CD-ROM drive. The host adapter does not represent either end of the chain; it is in the middle of the chain.

3. If the drive is being upgraded substantially, such as from a 500MB IDE drive to a 10GB EIDE drive, check the capabilities of the system's ROM BIOS. If the system's BIOS doesn't support large LBA or ECHS enhancements, the drive capacity of even the largest hard drive will be limited to 528MB. All newer BIOS support large LBA and ECHS enhanced drives.

CHAPTER EIGHT

Basic Troubleshooting and Preventive Maintenance Techniques

Terms you'll need to understand:

✓ Preventive maintenance

✓ Software diagnostics

✓ POST cards

✓ POST

✓ Self-test routines

✓ Error messages

✓ Software diagnostic utilities

✓ Hardware failure

✓ Configuration error

✓ Beep codes

✓ Antistatic strap

✓ Multimeter

Techniques to master:

Essentials 1.3—Identify tools, diagnostic procedures, and troubleshooting techniques for personal computer components.

- ✓ Recognize the basic aspects of troubleshooting theory, for example:

    - ✓ Perform backups before making changes.

    - ✓ Assess a problem systematically and divide large problems into smaller components to be analyzed individually.

    - ✓ Verify even the obvious, determine whether the problem is something simple, and make no assumptions.

- ✓ Research ideas and establish priorities.

- ✓ Document findings, actions, and outcomes.

✓ Identify and apply basic diagnostic procedures and troubleshooting techniques, for example:

- ✓ Identify the problem, including questioning user and identifying user changes to computer.

- ✓ Analyze the problem, including potential causes, and make an initial determination of software and/or hardware problems.

✓ Test related components, including inspection, connections, hardware/software configurations, Device Manager, and consult vendor documentation.

✓ Evaluate results and take additional steps if needed, such as consultation, use of alternative resources, and manuals.

✓ Document activities and outcomes.

✓ Recognize the names, purposes, characteristics, and appropriate application of tools, for example: BIOS, self-test, hard drive self-test, and software diagnostics test.

Essentials 1.4—Perform preventative maintenance on personal computer components.

✓ Identify and apply basic aspects of preventative maintenance theory, for example:

✓ Visual/audio inspection

✓ Driver/firmware updates

✓ Scheduling preventative maintenance

✓ Use of appropriate repair tools and cleaning materials

✓ Ensuring proper environment

✓ Identify and apply common preventative maintenance techniques for devices, such as input devices and batteries.

Depot Technician 1.2, IT Technician 1.2—Identify tools, diagnostic procedures, and troubleshooting techniques for personal computer components.

✓ Recognize names, purposes, characteristics, and appropriate application of tools, for example:

✓ Multimeter

✓ Antistatic pad and wrist strap

✓ Specialty hardware/tools

✓ Loop back plugs

✓ Cleaning products (vacuum, cleaning pads)

Basic PC Troubleshooting

This chapter covers a portion of the Diagnostic Procedures and Troubleshooting techniques areas of the CompTIA A+ Certification—Essentials examination under Objective 1.3, as well as the Basic Preventive Maintenance areas under Essentials exam Objective 1.4. Finally, the Tools portions of Objectives 1.2 for both the Depot Technician and IT Technician exams are covered here.

Troubleshooting and repairing PC systems and peripherals requires a more complete knowledge base and a different skill set from what the average end user possesses. This chapter addresses basic troubleshooting practices associated with hardware-related problems. Later chapters deal with troubleshooting and repairing operating-system-related problems.

To be an effective PC troubleshooter, you must combine good equipment knowledge with proper tools, good diagnostic techniques, and deductive reasoning skills. These skills are based on careful observation and an organized approach to solving problems. They can be applied to diagnose and repair most defective equipment. The general process for diagnosing and troubleshooting equipment can be summarized as follows:

1. Gather information to identify the nature of the problem. This can involve the questioning the user and identifying any changes that have been made to the system. After the problem has been identified, you should assess the problem systematically and divide complex problems into smaller components to be analyzed individually. Next, you should analyze the potential causes of the individual problems and make an initial assessment of whether they are hardware or software related. During this analysis, you should verify even obvious potential causes—the classic is the unplugged power cord.

2. Inspect components related to the possible cause, including their connections and configuration settings. Test the system after each component is checked or modified to see what symptoms it will produce as the system is changed. Evaluate the results of all changes and establish priorities for additional steps. Do not assume anything—verify the impact of each step.

3. Research manufacturer websites and documentation for information related to the problem. Also consider whether you need to consult with others to gain insight into the possible cause of the problem you are working on. You may need to involve others in the process as a normal

matter of practice. Some problems may require consultation with management or other professionals such as the network administrator.

4. Finally, document your activities, actions, and outcomes. Good notes become a technician's personal knowledge base and can be used over and over. They also provide documentation when questions arise concerning how a problem was handled.

Diagnostic and Repair Tools

Anyone who wants to work on any type of equipment must have the proper tools for the task. The following sections discuss the tools and equipment associated with the testing and repair of digital systems.

The well-prepared technician's tool kit should contain a wide range of both flat-blade and Phillips-head screwdriver sizes. At a minimum, it should have a small jeweler's and a medium-size flat-blade screwdriver, along with a medium-size Phillips screwdriver. In addition, you may want to include a small set of miniature nut drivers, a set of Torx drivers, and a special nonconductive screwdriver-like device called an *alignment tool*.

You also need a couple of pairs of needle-nose pliers. These pliers are available in a number of sizes. You need at least one pair with a sturdy, blunt nose and one with a longer, more tapered nose. You also might want to get a pair that has a cutting edge built in to its jaws. You may perform this same function with a different type of pliers called *diagonals*, or *crosscuts*. Many technicians carry a pair of surgical forceps in addition to their other pliers.

You may want to include other hand tools in your tool kit:

- ▸ A telescopic magnet for retrieving screws and nuts that get dropped into the system unit or printer. This tool can save a lot of disassembly/reassembly time when metal objects get loose in the system.

- ▸ A small flashlight for examining the insides of enclosed system units and peripherals.

- ▸ Wire crimpers for fastening connectors to telephone and network cables. There are many times when you may need to make a test cable or replace a damaged connector in the end of an existing network or telephone cable.

- ▸ A multimeter for making common electrical tests on computers, peripherals, and cabling.

▶ A network cable tester for testing continuity and correct connections.

▶ Antistatic devices to prevent the buildup and discharge of potentially destructive static charges. These devices include antistatic wrist and ankle straps, antistatic mats, and antistatic storage and shipping containers.

> **NOTE**
>
> You should always be sure to use the correct tools for the job. This lessens the chances of breaking components or ruining screws because tools slipped or did not fit.

In addition to these hardware tools, the technician should have a collection of software tools at his disposal. Typical software tools used by computer technicians include the following:

▶ Emergency boot/start disks to get failing systems started

▶ Hardware diagnostic utility packages

▶ Embedded operating system software tools and utilities

▶ Antivirus and malware utilities

Gathering Information

One of the most important aspects of troubleshooting anything is the gathering of information about the problem at hand and its symptoms. One of the best sources for this type of information is the computer user. The next most important source of information is actually observing the system to see what it is doing. The PC technician should be able to effectively acquire information from the customer (user) and the system concerning the nature of a problem and then be able to practice basic troubleshooting methods to isolate and repair the problem.

Assessing the Situation

The most important aspect of checking a malfunctioning device is to be observant. Begin by talking to the PC user or the person who reported the problem. You can obtain many clues from this person. Gather information from the user regarding the environment the system is being used in, any symptoms or error codes produced by the system, and the situations that existed when the failure occurred. Ask the user to demonstrate the procedures that led to the malfunction in a step-by-step manner. This communication can help you narrow down a problem to a particular section of the computer.

Part of the technician's job is to determine whether the user could be the source of the problem—either trying to do things with the system that it cannot do or not understanding how some part of it is supposed to work. Carefully listening to the user is a good way to eliminate the user as a possible cause of the problems. Attempt to gain a full understanding of the process the user is trying to perform.

If you do suspect that the user is part of the problem, remove the user from the situation and operate the equipment yourself. This will enable you to personally observe the system's symptoms as they occur. Attempt to limit the problem to the hardware involved, the software package being used, and then to the operator.

EXAM ALERT

Be well aware that the user is one of the most common sources of PC problems. In most situations, your first troubleshooting step should be to talk to the user.

Challenge #1

You have been called to a business to repair a printing problem. When you arrive, you are told that the user is having trouble printing spreadsheets from his Microsoft Excel program. You are not an Excel or spreadsheet guru, so how do you go about servicing this problem?

Assessing the Environment

Take note of the environment that the equipment is being used in and how heavy its usage is. If the system is located in a particularly dirty area, or an area given to other environmental extremes, it may need to be cleaned and serviced more frequently than if it were in a clean office environment. The same is true for systems subjected to heavy or continuous use. In an industrial environment, check with the management to see whether any office or industry maintenance standards for servicing apply.

Finally, use simple observation of the wear and tear on the equipment to gauge the need for additional or spot maintenance steps. Look for signs of extended use (such as frayed cords, missing slot covers, keyboards with letters worn off, and so on) to spot potential problems resulting from age or usage.

Initial Troubleshooting Steps

Always try to use the system to see what symptoms you produce. Next, try to isolate the problem to either software- or hardware-related problems. Finally, isolate the problem to a section of the hardware or software. You may need to check the BIOS's advanced CMOS configuration screens for any incorrect enabling settings.

Perform an Initial Inspection

Successful troubleshooting is the result of careful observation, deductive reasoning, and an organized approach to solving problems. These techniques are common to repairing any type of defective equipment. Although we are demonstrating these techniques as they apply to repairing computer systems, it is quite possible to adapt them to other systems as well.

Some extreme problems may present themselves as soon as you approach the system. In cases where you observe smoke or flames coming from a PC, immediately remove power from the system and take steps to get any dangerous conditions under control—use a proper Class C fire extinguisher on any flames (after totally removing power from the system).

EXAM ALERT

Know how to handle extreme PC problems.

Observe the symptoms produced by the system to associate the malfunction with a section of the system responsible for that operation. If there is no prior knowledge of the type of malfunction, you should proceed by performing a careful visual inspection of the system. Check the outside of the system first. Look for loose or disconnected cables. Consult all the external front-panel lights. If no lights are displayed, check the power outlet, the plugs and power cords, as well as any power switches that may affect the operation of the system. You may also want to check the commercial power-distribution system's fuses or circuit breakers to ensure that they are functional.

Don't forget to listen to the system. Listen for the sounds of the power supply and processor fans, the hard drive spindle motor turning, and the sounds coming from the system speaker. If a user or customer reports a symptom that includes a particular sound and you cannot hear it, do not assume that it has fixed itself. This often indicates that a mechanical component, such as a cooling fan, was making noise but has now completely failed. Check all fans and drives to make sure they are turning when they should be.

EXAM ALERT

Remember to follow up on noise reports even if they do not show up in your presence.

If part of the system is active, try to localize the problem by systematically removing peripheral devices from the system. Try to revive the system, or its defective portion, by restarting it several times. You should try to restart the system after each correctional step is performed.

Consult any additional user's or operations manuals liberally. Indeed, many of the computer's peripheral systems, such as hard drives and printers, have some level of self-diagnostics built in to them. Generally, these diagnostics programs produce coded error messages. The key to recognizing and using these error messages is usually found in the device's user's guide. In addition, the user's guide may contain probable cause and suggested remedy information and/or specialized tests to isolate specific problems.

Document the Process

Take the time to document the problem, including all the tests you perform and their outcomes. Your memory is never as good as you think it is, especially in stressful situations such as with a down computer. This recorded information can prevent you from making repetitive steps that waste time and may cause confusion. This information will also be very helpful when you move on to more detailed tests or measurements.

Observe the Bootup Procedure

Unless the system is on fire, the first real diagnostic step is normally to turn the system on and carefully observe the steps of the bootup process. This procedure can reveal a great deal about the nature of any problems in a system. Faulty areas can be included or excluded as possible causes of errors during the bootup process. The observable actions of a working system's cold-boot procedure are listed as follows, in their order of occurrence:

1. When power is applied, the power supply and system fans activate.

2. The system's power light and CD-ROM/DVD power lights come on.

3. The hard disk drive activity light flashes and it can be heard spinning up to speed (although some newer models are so quiet that you may have to listen very closely).

4. The BIOS message displays on the monitor (this may occur later on some monitors that take longer to come alive), followed by processor type and memory count information.

5. The video display and keyboard lights flash as the rest of the system components are being reset.

6. The system produces a single beep, indicating that it has completed its power-on self tests (POST) of the system's basic hardware components and initialization process. After this point, the operation of the machine has shifted to looking for and loading an operating system.

7. The floppy disk drive access light comes on briefly (if enabled in the CMOS boot sequence) before switching to the hard drive activity light. If the computer does not have a floppy disk drive, like many newer systems these days, skip to the next item.

8. HDD and CD-ROM/DVD interface configuration information is displayed onscreen.

9. At this point in the process, the BIOS is looking for additional instructions (boot information)—first from the floppy drive and then from the hard drive (assuming that the CMOS setup is configured for this sequence).

10. When the system finds the boot files, the drive light will come on, indicating that the system is loading the operating system and configuration files.

11. On Windows machines, the Starting Windows message appears onscreen (unless it has been disabled to provide faster starting).

12. Windows loads its GUI desktop components and takes over control of the system.

EXAM ALERT

Be familiar with the order of the series of observable events that occur during the normal PC boot/start process.

The exact order of events in the startup process of a given computer may differ slightly from the description provided here. The order is affected by CMOS setup configurations and the speed of the display when it starts up. The point is that if a section of the computer is defective, you should observe only some (or possibly none) of these events. By knowing which sections of the computer are involved in each step, you can suspect a particular section of causing the problem when the system does not advance past that step.

Challenge #2

A friend is having trouble starting her computer and has asked you for help. When you turn the system on, the video display comes on and you can hear the disk drive spinning. Several different screens display and then you hear a single beep from the computer. From your knowledge of system bootups, what can you tell your friend about her system?

Symptoms/Error Codes

Most PCs have reasonably good built-in self-tests that run each time the computer is powered up. These tests can prove very beneficial in detecting hardware-oriented problems within the system. Whenever a self-test failure or setup mismatch is encountered, the BIOS may indicate the error through a blank screen, a visual error message on the video display, or an audio response (*beep codes*) produced by the system's speaker.

> **NOTE**
>
> If the system speaker is faulty or disconnected the system will not be able to produce the beep codes to help the troubleshooting process. This possibility should always be checked as part of the troubleshooting process if no sounds are being produced.

Some PCs issue numerically coded error messages on the display. Conversely, other PCs display a written description of the error. Table 8.1 defines the beep codes produced by a particular BIOS version from American Megatrends (AMI). The exact error messages and codes will vary from different BIOS manufacturers and from version to version.

TABLE 8.1   Beep Code and Error Message Examples

BEEP CODE	MESSAGES
1 beep	RAM refresh failure
2 beeps	Parity circuit failure
3 beeps	Base 64KB RAM failure
4 beeps	System timer failure

TABLE 8.1 *Continued*

BEEP CODE	MESSAGES
5 beeps	Processor failure
6 beeps	Keyboard controller/gate A20 failure
7 beeps	Virtual mode exception error
8 beeps	Display memory read/write failure
9 beeps	ROM BIOS checksum failure
10 beeps	CMOS shutdown register read/write error
1 long, 2 short beeps	Video controller failure
1 long, 3 short beeps	Conventional and extended test failure
1 long, 8 short beeps	Display test failure

VISUAL DISPLAY ERROR MESSAGES

SYSTEM HALTED ERRORS

CMOS INOPERATIONAL	Failure of CMOS shutdown register test
8042 GATE A20 ERROR	Error getting into Protected mode
INVALID SWITCH MEMORY FAILURE	Real/Protected mode change over error
DMA ERROR	DMA controller failed page register test
DMA #1 ERROR	DMA device # 1 failure
DMA #2 ERROR	DMA device # 2 failure

NONFATAL ERRORS—WITH SETUP OPTION

CMOS BATTERY LOW	Failure of CMOS battery or CMOS checksum test
CMOS SYSTEM OPTION NOT SET	Failure of CMOS battery or CMOS checksum test
CMOS CHECKSUM FAILURE	CMOS battery low or CMOS checksum test failure
CMOS DISPLAY MISMATCH	Failure of display type verification
CMOS MEMORY SIZE MISMATCH	System Configuration and Setup failure
CMOS TIMER AND DATE NOT SET	System Configuration and Setup failure in timer circuitry

NONFATAL ERRORS—WITHOUT SETUP OPTION

CH-X TIMER ERROR	Channel X (2, 1, or 0) timer failure
KEYBOARD ERROR	Keyboard test failure
KB/INTERFACE ERROR	Keyboard test failure
DISPLAY SWITCH SETTING NOT PROPER	Failure to verify display type

(continues)

TABLE 8.1 *Continued*

BEEP CODE	MESSAGES
KEYBOARD IS LOCKED	Unlock it
FDD CONTROLLER ERROR	Failure to verify floppy disk setup by system configuration file
HDD CONTROLLER FAILURE	Failure to verify hard disk setup by system configuration file
C: DRIVE ERROR	Hard disk setup failure
D: DRIVE ERROR	Hard disk setup failure

If you receive a beep code of 1 beep, 2 beeps, or 3 beeps, reseat the DRAM modules in their slots. If the error continues after restarting the system, replace the memory with known good chips. If the beep code consists of 4, 5, 7, or 10 beeps, troubleshoot the system board. Unless your repair area can support IC-level rework, you may have to replace the system board.

For six beeps, check parts of the system relating to the keyboard. For example, swap the keyboard for a known good one and check to see if the system board has a keyboard fuse. Eight beeps indicate a video adapter memory error. Replace the video card (or the memory devices on the video adapter if possible). If the system produces nine beeps, indicating a faulty BIOS device, you must replace or flash the BIOS with an updated version.

▶ Hard disk install failure—Cannot find or initialize the hard drive controller or the drive. Make sure the controller is installed correctly. If no hard drives are installed, be sure the Hard Drive selection in Setup is set to NONE.

▶ Hard disk(s) diagnosis fail—The system may run specific disk diagnostic routines. This message appears if one or more hard disks return an error when the diagnostics run.

▶ Primary master hard disk fail—POST detects an error in the primary master IDE hard drive.

▶ Primary slave hard disk fail—POST detects an error in the secondary master IDE hard drive.

▶ Resuming from Disk, Press Tab to Show POST Screen—Phoenix Technologies offers a save-to-disk feature for notebook computers. This message may appear when the operator restarts the system after a save-to-disk shutdown.

▶ Secondary master hard disk fail—POST detects an error in the primary slave IDE hard drive.

▶ Secondary slave hard disk fail—POST detects an error in the secondary slave IDE hard drive.

EXAM ALERT

Be aware of which devices are checked during the POST process and what types of failures and error codes/messages they produce.

Determining Hardware/Software/Configuration Problems

One of the earliest steps in troubleshooting a computer problem (or any other programmable system problem) is to determine whether the problem is due to a hardware failure or to faulty software. In most PCs, you can use a significant event that that occurs during the bootup process as a key to separating hardware problems from software problems: the single beep that most PCs produce between the end of the POST and the beginning of the bootup process.

Errors that occur, or are displayed, before this beep indicate that a hardware problem of some type exists. Up to this point in the operation of the system, only the BIOS and the basic system hardware have been active. Problems with the system's microprocessor, RAM, and ROM are the primary items checked during the POST process. Problems that occur with these devices should produce a failure during the POST and may or may not produce a beep-coded message as indicated in the previous section. Failures with other devices examined during the POST generally produce error messages and beep codes.

EXAM ALERT

Be aware of device problems that would stop the system during the POST process.

The operating system does not come into play until after the beep occurs. You can group errors that occur before the beep into two distinct categories:

▶ Hardware failures

▶ Configuration errors

Hardware Failures

Hardware failures associated with the system's basic components are typically the easiest items to troubleshoot. They tend to produce very distinct symptoms (such as no video, no lights, or no disk drive activities). Depending on how much of the system is working, the POST will normally detect these types of problems and generate a beep-coded message or an error code.

> **NOTE**
>
> If the system produces an error message (such as The System Has Detected Unstable RAM at Location x) or a beep code message before the single beep, the system has found a problem with the system's hardware. In this case, a bad memory device is indicated.

Configuration Problems

Configuration problems tend to occur whenever a new hardware option is added to the system or when the system is used for the very first time. These problems result from mismatches between the system's programmed configuration, held in CMOS memory, and the actual equipment installed in the system. The POST typically detects configuration errors and produces error code messages onscreen to identify them.

If the startup process reaches the point where the system's CMOS configuration information is displayed onscreen, you can safely assume that no hardware configuration conflicts exist in the system's basic components. After this point in the bootup process, the system begins loading drivers for optional devices and additional memory. If the error occurs after the CMOS screen displays and before the bootup tone, you must clean-boot the system and single step through the remainder of the bootup sequence.

The BIOS and operating system use plug-and-play techniques to detect new hardware that has been installed in the system. These components work together with the device to allocate system resources for the device. In some situations, the PnP logic will not be able to resolve all the system's resource needs, and a configuration error will occur. In these cases, the user must manually resolve the configuration problem.

There are several port and device enabling functions controlled through the BIOS CMOS Setup utility. If these settings are not enabled, the device will not be able to interact with the system when its hardware is installed. You may need to access and configure settings in the system's CMOS Setup utility the first time you start a newly constructed system, when you add a new device that is enabled through the CMOS utility, or when it becomes necessary to replace the system board's CMOS backup battery.

If you encounter configuration errors, refer to the installation instructions found in the new component's user manual. Table 8.2 lists typical configuration error codes and messages produced when various types of configuration mismatches occur.

TABLE 8.2   Common Configuration Error Messages

CONFIGURATION ERROR MESSAGE	MEANING
CMOS System Option Not Set	Failure of CMOS battery or CMOS checksum test
CMOS Display Mismatch	Failure of display type verification
CMOS Memory Size Mismatch	System configuration and setup failure
Press F1 to Continue	Invalid configuration information
CMOS Time and Date Not Set	Failure of CMOS battery

It is important to observe the system's symptoms to determine in which part of the system's operation the fault occurs. The configuration error messages described in the table occur and are reported before the single beep tone is produced at the end of the POST routines. If you cannot confirm a configuration error, the problem most likely is a defective component. The most widely used repair method with PC systems involves substituting known good components for suspected bad components.

Another option to examine when a configuration error occurs is to reset the contents of the CMOS to one of its default levels. As described in Chapter 2, "PC System Boards," the CMOS Setup utility typically offers two default auto-configuration options: Auto Configure with Power-On Defaults and Auto Configure with BIOS Defaults. The Power-On Defaults option provides the most conservative system options from the CMOS, and the most effective method of detecting CMOS-related system problems. It replaces any user-entered configuration information in the CMOS. The BIOS default option places the system at its most basic configuration and provides more flexibility than the power-on option. This selection also replaces the entered configuration settings with a new set of parameters from the BIOS, and likely gets you back into the CMOS Setup screen. If these default values fail to boot the system, it indicates possible hardware problems such as a bad component.

The contents of the CMOS can also be cleared and reset manually using the hardware reset process described in Chapter 2 for recovering from lost BIOS passwords. Unplug the system from the AC power source and remove the

CMOS battery from the system board. You may also be able to place a shorting block on the battery's reset pins to return the CMOS setup to its most basic settings.

After the POST

After the beep tone is produced, the system shifts over to the process of booting up and begins looking for and loading the operating system. Errors that occur between the beep and the presentation of the operating system's user interface (command prompt or desktop GUI) generally can be divided into three distinct types for troubleshooting purposes. These error types also correspond to three possible sources, which are summarized in the following list that includes the typical error messages types associated with each source:

- ▶ Hard Drive Failure or Configuration Problems—Physical or configuration problem with the boot drive

  - ▶ `General Failure Error Reading Drive X` (where "X" represents the letter of the drive, such as C:)

- ▶ Boot Failure—Corrupted or missing boot files

  - ▶ `Bad or Missing MBR`

  - ▶ `Non-System Disk or Disk Error`

  - ▶ `Bad File Allocation/Master File Table`

- ▶ OS Startup Failure—Corrupted or missing operating system files

  - ▶ `Bad or Missing NTOSKRNL File`

Conversely, bootup and OS startup problems are typically associated with the hard disk drive and the operating system. In these cases, checking the drive hardware is generally the last step of the troubleshooting process. Unless some specific symptom indicates otherwise, you should check for missing or corrupted boot and operating system files first.

Challenge #3

A remote customer calls and complains that he is receiving a `Bad or Missing MBR` error message and the system stops operating. The customer thinks he should replace his hard drive and wants you to order it for him. What should you tell him?

Using a Multimeter

A number of test instruments can help you isolate computer hardware problems. One of the most basic pieces of electronic troubleshooting equipment is the multimeter. *Multimeters* are available in both analog and digital readout form and can be used to directly measure electrical values of voltage (V), current in milliamperes (mA), or amperes (A), and resistance in ohms. Therefore, these devices are referred to as VOMs (volt-ohm-milliammeters) for analog types, or DMMs (digital multimeters) for digital types.

Figure 8.1 depicts a digital multimeter. With a little practice, you can use this device to check diodes, transistors, capacitors, motor windings, relays, and coils. This particular DMM contains facilities built into the meter to test transistors and diodes. These facilities are in addition to its standard functions of current, voltage, and resistance measurement; however, in computer repair work only the voltage and resistance functions are used extensively.

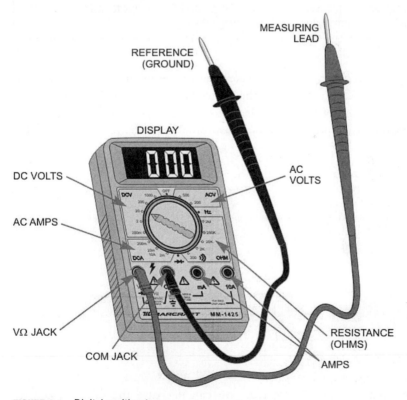

FIGURE 8.1   Digital multimeter.

The first step in using the multimeter to perform tests is to select the proper function. For the most part, you never need to use the current function of the multimeter when working with computer systems; however, the voltage and resistance functions can be very valuable tools.

In computer troubleshooting, most of the tests are DC voltage readings. These measurements usually involve checking the DC side of the power-supply unit. You can make these readings between ground and one of the expansion-slot pins, or at the system board power-supply connector. It is also common to check the voltage level across a system board capacitor to verify that the system is receiving power. The voltage across most of the capacitors on the system board is 5V (DC). The DC voltages that can typically be expected in a PC-compatible system are +12V, +5V, –5V, and –12V. The actual values for these readings may vary by 5% in either direction.

CAUTION

It is normal practice to first set the meter to its highest voltage range to make certain that the voltage level being measured does not damage the meter.

The DC voltage function is used to take measurements in live DC circuits. It should be connected in parallel with the device being checked. This could mean connecting the reference lead (black lead) to a ground point and the measuring lead (red lead) to a test point to take a measurement, as illustrated in Figure 8.2.

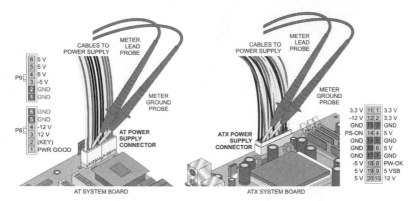

FIGURE 8.2 DC voltage check.

As an approximate value is detected, you can decrease the range setting to achieve a more accurate reading. Most meters allow for overvoltage protection;

however, it is still a good safety practice to decrease the range of the meter after you have achieved an initial value.

The second most popular test is the resistance, or continuity, test.

> **CAUTION**
>
> Unlike voltage checks, resistance checks are always made with power removed from the system.

Failure to turn off the power when making resistance checks can cause serious damage to the meter and can pose a potential risk to the technician. Resistance checks require that you electrically isolate the component being tested from the system. For most circuit components, this means desoldering at least one end from the board.

The resistance check is very useful in isolating some types of problems in the system. One of the main uses of the resistance function is to test fuses. You must disconnect at least one end of the fuse from the system. You should set the meter on the 1 kilohm resistance setting. If the fuse is good, the meter should read near 0 ohms. If the fuse is bad, the meter reads infinite. The resistance function also is useful in checking for cables and connectors. By removing the cable from the system and connecting a meter lead to each end, you can check the cable's continuity conductor by conductor to verify its integrity.

You also use the resistance function to test the system's speaker. To check the speaker, disconnect the speaker from the system and connect a meter lead to each end. If the speaker is good, the meter should read near 8 ohms (although a smaller speaker may be 4 ohms). If the speaker is defective, the resistance reading should be 0 for shorts or infinite for opens.

Only a couple of situations involve using the AC voltage function for checking microcomputer systems. The primary use of this function is to check the commercial power being applied to the power-supply unit. As with any measurement, it is important to select the correct measurement range; however, the lethal voltage levels associated with the power supply call for additional caution when making such measurements. The second application for the AC voltage function is to measure ripple voltage from the DC output side of the power-supply unit. This particular operation is very rarely performed in field-service situations.

EXAM ALERT

Know what readings to expect from a multimeter when testing fuses, speakers, and typical power-supply voltages in a PC.

Challenge #4

One of your new technicians has asked you about a problem she is having with a customer's computer. The customer's computer seems to be operating correctly but is not producing and sound from the speaker during startup or normal operations. She has checked all the system's software settings and found nothing apparently wrong. She has asked you to explain how to check the speaker hardware. What should you tell her?

Using Software Diagnostic Packages

Many companies produce disk-based diagnostic routines that check the system by running predetermined tests on different areas of its hardware. The diagnostic package evaluates the response from each test and attempts to produce a status report for all of the system's major components. Like the PC's built-in self-tests, these packages produce visual and beep-coded error messages. Figure 8.3 depicts the Main menu of a typical self-booting software diagnostic package.

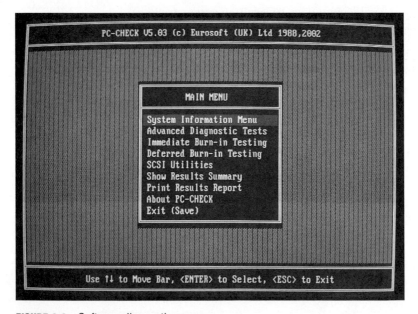

FIGURE 8.3 Software diagnostic menu.

This menu is the gateway to information about the system's makeup and config-uration, as well as the entryway to the program's Advanced Diagnostic Test functions. You can find utilities for performing low-level formats on older hard drive types and for managing SCSI interface devices through this menu. Additionally, options to print or show test results are available here, as is the exit point from the program.

The most common software-troubleshooting packages test the system's memo-ry, microprocessor, keyboard, display monitor, and the disk drive's speed. If at least the system's CPU, disk drive, and clock circuits are working, you may be able to use one of these special software-troubleshooting packages to help local-ize system failures. They can prove especially helpful when you're trying to track down non-heat-related intermittent problems.

If a diagnostic program indicates that multiple items should be replaced, replace the units one at a time until the unit starts up. Then replace any units removed prior to the one that caused the system to start. This process ensures that there were not multiple bad parts. If you have replaced all the parts and the unit still does not function properly, the diagnostic software is suspect.

For enterprises that repair computers, or build computers from parts, diagnos-tic programs that perform continuous burn-in tests are valuable tools. After the system has been built or repaired, these programs are used to run continuous tests on the system for an extended burn-in period, without any intervention from a technician or operator.

The tests performed in a burn-in situation are similar to standard software util-ity tests. However, they are usually used for reliability testing instead of general troubleshooting. Different parts of the system can be selected for the burn-in tests. Because the burn-in tests are designed for use in an unattended manner, you must be careful to select only tests that apply to hardware that actually exists in the system. The diagnostic keeps track of how many times each test has been run and how often it failed during the designated burn-in period, as depicted in Figure 8.4.

If a diagnostic tool indicates that multiple components have failed, use the one-at-time exchange method, starting with the first component indicated, to isolate the original source of the problem. Test the system between each component exchange and work backward through the exchanged components after the sys-tem has started to function again.

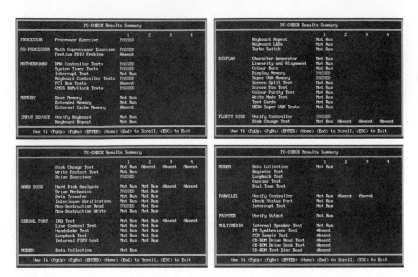

FIGURE 8.4 The burn-in test report.

Using POST Cards

Most BIOS program chips do not have an extensive set of onboard diagnostics built in to them. Therefore, several companies produce POST cards and diagnostic software to aid in hardware troubleshooting. A *POST card* is a diagnostic device that plugs into the system's expansion slot and tests the operation of the system as it boots up. These cards can be as simple as interrupt and DMA channel monitors or as complex as full-fledged ROM BIOS diagnostic packages that carry out extensive tests on the system.

POST cards are normally used when the system appears to be dead, or when the system cannot read from a floppy or hard drive. The firmware tests on the card replace the normal BIOS functions and send the system into a set of tests. The value of the card lies in the fact that the tests can be carried out without the system resorting to software diagnostics located on the hard disk or in a floppy drive.

The POST routines located in most BIOS chips will report two types of errors: fatal and nonfatal. If the POST encounters a fatal error, it stops the system. The error code posted on the indicator corresponds to the defective operation. If the POST card encounters a nonfatal error, however, it notes the error and continues through the initialization routine to activate as many additional system resources as possible. When these types of errors are encountered, the POST card must be observed carefully because the error code on its indicator must be coordinated with the timing of the error message or beep code produced by the BIOS routines.

Simple POST cards come with a set of light-emitting diodes (LEDs) on them that produce coded error signals when a problem is encountered. Other cards produce beep codes and seven-segment LED readouts of the error code. Figure 8.5 depicts a typical POST card.

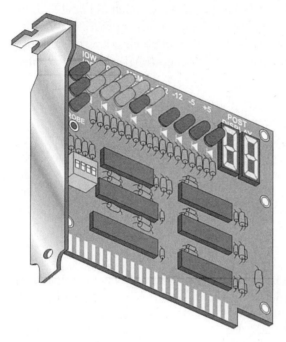

FIGURE 8.5   A typical POST card.

Field-Replaceable Unit Troubleshooting

Field-replaceable units (FRUs) are the portions of the system that you can conveniently replace in the field. Exchanging FRUs is the level of troubleshooting most often performed on PCs. FRU troubleshooting involves isolating a problem within one section of the system. A section consists of one device such as a keyboard, video display, video adapter card, I/O adapter card, system board, disk drive, printer, and so on. These are typically components that can be exchanged for a replacement on site and that require no actual repair work.

After a hardware error has been indicated, start troubleshooting the problem by exchanging FRU components (cards, drives, and so on) with known good ones. Because there may be metal oxide semiconductor (MOS) devices on the board, you should ground yourself before performing this test. You can do so by touching an exposed portion of the unit's chassis, such as the top of the power supply. Turn off the power and exchange suspected or indicated devices from the system one at a time. Make sure that you restore the power to test and evaluate the system after each exchange.

Check cabling connections after plugging them in. Check for missed connections and bent pins. Also, check the routing of cables. Try to establish connections that do not place unnecessary strain on cables. As much as possible, route them away from major IC devices. Some ICs, such as microprocessors, can run hot enough to eventually damage cables. Also avoid cooling fans because they produce high levels of electromagnetic interference (EMI) that can be introduced into the signal cables.

After you have isolated the problem, and the computer boots up and runs correctly, work backward through the troubleshooting steps and reinstall any original adapters and other components removed during the troubleshooting process. Working backward, one component at a time, through components that have been removed from the system enables you to make certain that only one failure occurred in the machine. If the system fails after installing a new card, check the card's default configuration settings against those of the devices already installed in the system.

Alternative Resources

You should make use of all the resources at your disposal. These include consulting with other technicians and managers about difficult or unfamiliar problems. Also refer to all available user and installation/configuration guides.

Basic Preventive Maintenance

It has long been known that one of the best ways to fix problems with complex systems is to prevent them before they happen. This is the concept behind preventive maintenance procedures. Breakdowns never occur at convenient times. By planning for a few minutes of nonproductive activities, hours of repair and recovery work can be avoided.

Cleaning

Cleaning is a major part of keeping a computer system healthy. Therefore, the technician's tool kit should contain a collection of cleaning supplies. Along with hand tools, you will need a lint-free soft cloth (chamois) for cleaning the plastic outer surfaces of the system.

Outer-surface cleaning can be accomplished with a simple soap-and-water solution, followed by a clear water rinse. Care should be taken to make sure that none of the liquid splashes or drips into the inner parts of the system. A damp soft cloth is easily the best general-purpose cleaning tool for use with computer equipment.

The cleaning should be followed by the application of an antistatic spray or antistatic solution to prevent the buildup of static charges on the components of the system. A solution composed of 10 parts water and one part common household fabric softener makes an effective and economical antistatic solution.

Another common problem is corrosion, or oxidation buildup, at electrical contact points. These buildups occur on electrical connectors and can reduce the flow of electricity through the connection. Some simple steps can be used to keep corrosion from becoming a problem. The easiest step in preventing corrosion is observing the correct handling procedures for printed circuit boards and cables. Never touch the electrical contact points with your skin because the moisture on your body can start corrosive action.

Even with proper handling, corrosion may occur over time. This oxidation can be removed in a number of ways. The oxide buildup can be gently rubbed off with an emery cloth, a common pencil eraser, or a special solvent wipe. It can also be dissolved with an electrical-contact cleaner spray.

Socket-mounted devices should be *reseated* (removed and reinstalled to establish a new electrical connection) as part of an anticorrosion effort. This also overcomes the chip-creep effect that thermal cycling has on socket-mounted devices. Remember that these devices should be handled according to the metal oxide semiconductor handling guidelines to make certain that no electrostatic discharge damage occurs.

EXAM ALERT

Be aware of the cause of chip creep in sockets.

If you use an emery cloth or rubber eraser to gently clean your contacts, always rub toward the outer edge of the board or connector to prevent damage to the contacts. Rubbing the edge may lift the foil from the PC board. Printed circuit-board connectors are typically very thin. Therefore, rub only hard enough to remove the oxide layer and take time to clean up any dust or rubber contamination generated by the cleaning effort.

Cleaning other internal components, such as disk-drive read/write heads, can be performed using lint-free foam swabs and isopropyl alcohol or methanol. It's most important that the cleaning solution be one that dries without leaving a residue.

Preventive Maintenance Procedures

The environment around a computer system, and the manner in which the computer is used, determines greatly how many problems it will have. Occasionally dedicating a few moments of care to the computer can extend its mean time between failures (MTBF) period considerably. This activity, involving maintenance not usually associated with a breakdown, is called *preventive maintenance (PM)*.

Computer equipment is susceptible to failures caused by dust buildup, rough handling, and extremes in temperature.

EXAM ALERT

Know what environmental conditions or activities are most likely to lead to equipment failures.

Dust

Over time, dust builds up on everything it can gain access to. Many computer components generate static electrical charges that attract dust particles. In the case of electronic equipment, dust forms an insulating blanket that traps heat next to active devices and can cause them to overheat. Excessive heat can cause premature aging and failure. The best dust protection is a dust-tight enclosure; however, computer components tend to have less than dust-tight seals. In addition, power supply and microprocessor fans pull air from outside through the system unit.

Another access point for dust is uncovered expansion-slot openings. Missing expansion-slot covers adversely affect the system in two ways. First, the missing covers permit dust to accumulate in the system, forming the insulating blanket previously described, which causes component overheating. Second, the heat problem is complicated further by the fact that missing slot covers disrupt the designed airflow patterns inside the case, causing components to overheat because of missing or inadequate airflow.

> **EXAM ALERT**
>
> Be aware of the effect that missing expansion slot covers have on the operation of the system unit.

Smoke is a more dangerous cousin of dust. Like dust particles, smoke collects on all exposed surfaces. The residue of smoke particles is sticky and clings to surfaces. In addition to contributing to the heat buildup problem, smoke residue is particularly destructive to moving parts, such as floppy disks, fan motors, and so forth.

Dust buildup inside system components can be taken care of with a soft brush. A static-free vacuum or compressed air can also be used to remove dust from inside cases and keyboards. Be sure to use a static-free vacuum because normal vacuums are by their nature static generators. The static-free vacuum has special grounding to remove the static buildup it generates. Dust covers are also helpful in holding down dust problems. These covers are placed over the equipment when the equipment is not in use and are removed when the device is needed.

> **EXAM ALERT**
>
> Know that computer vacuums have special grounding to dissipate static buildup that can damage computer devices.

Rough Handling

Rough handling is either a matter of neglect or a lack of knowledge about how equipment should be handled. Therefore, overcoming rough-handling problems requires that technicians be aware of proper handling techniques for sensitive devices such as hard disk drives and monitors, and that they adjust their component-handling practices to compensate.

Heat Buildup Problems

Excessive heat can cause premature aging and failure of electronic components. Identifying and controlling heat buildup problems requires some effort and planning. Microcomputers are designed to run at normal room temperatures. If the ambient temperature rises above 85 degrees Fahrenheit, *heat buildup* can become a problem. High humidity can also lead to heat-related problems and failures.

> **EXAM ALERT**
>
> Be aware of the effects that high humidity has on computer equipment.

To combat heat problems, make sure that the area around the system is uncluttered so that free airflow around the system can be maintained. Make sure the power supply's fan is operational. If it is not, replace the power-supply unit. Likewise, be sure that the microprocessor fan is plugged in and operational. It is very easy for a high-speed microprocessor to fry if its fan fails. A good general rule is to install a fan on any large IC device running above 33MHz.

You should check the computer's ventilation frequently to make sure that papers and other desk clutter are not cutting off airflow to the unit. Check for other sources of heat buildup around the computer and its peripherals. These sources include the following:

- ▶ Direct sunlight from an outside window
- ▶ Locations of portable heaters in the winter
- ▶ Papers/books piled up around the equipment

> **EXAM ALERT**
>
> Be aware that direct sunlight is a source of heat buildup in computer equipment.

Challenge #5

When you arrive at a customer's office to repair one of their key computers, you trace the problem down to a defective microprocessor. The system has apparently been upgraded several times over its lifetime—there are several open expansion slots and loose cables inside the system unit. There is also a layer of dust on all the internal components. What should you tell the manager when she asks you about what you have found?

If heat buildup still exists, check the outer cover to make sure that it is secured firmly to the machine and that all the expansion-slot covers are in place. Otherwise, the designed airflow characteristics of the case can be disrupted. Also, make certain that the air vents in the case are not blocked and are free from dust. Finally, add an additional case fan to draw more air through the system unit.

EXAM ALERT

Be aware of steps that can be taken to minimize the chances of system overheating.

With notebooks and other portables, make sure they are setting on a hard, flat surface. Placing portables on soft or uneven surfaces can block airflow that is designed to exit underneath the unit.

EXAM ALERT

Know how portable PCs handle airflow for cooling.

Protecting Display Systems

The PM associated with monitors consists of periodic cleaning, dusting, and good common-sense practices around the monitor. Aerosol sprays, solvents, and commercial cleaners should be avoided because they can damage the screen and cabinet. A simple cleaning solution, described earlier, is fine for cleaning the monitor. Make sure that the monitor's power cord is disconnected from any power source before washing. The monitor's screen should be dried with a soft cloth after rinsing.

EXAM ALERT

Always remember to remove power from a system or component before washing it.

The monitor should not be left on for extended periods with the same image displayed on the screen. Over a period of time, the image will become permanently "burned" into the screen. Most monitors have built-in screen-blanking circuitry to shut off the display if no activity is detected over a given period of time. Likewise, modern operating systems offer power management and screen protection options through the operating system.

If it is necessary to display the same information on the screen for a long period of time, turn the intensity level of the monitor down, or install a screen saver program to alter the screen image periodically. LCD monitors and televisions, as well as plasma televisions, are very susceptible to screen burning, and can be affected in as little as a few hours.

Very dangerous voltage levels (in excess of 25,000 volts; more than enough to kill or badly injure someone) exist inside the CRT monitor's housing. Therefore, you should remove the monitor's outer cabinet only if you are fully qualified to work on CRT-based equipment. Figure 8.6 shows the areas of the monitor that should be avoided if you must work inside its housing.

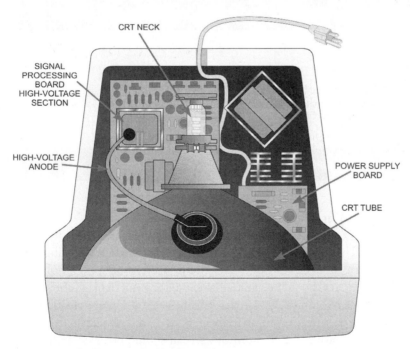

FIGURE 8.6 Caution areas inside the monitor.

Caring for LCD Displays

The life and usefulness of the LCD panels used in displays for portables and desktops can be extended through proper care and handling. The screen should be cleaned periodically with a glass cleaner and a soft, lint-free cloth. Spray the cleaner on the cloth and then wipe the screen. Never spray the cleaner directly on the screen. Also, avoid scratching the surface of the screen. It is relatively easy to damage the front polarizer of the display. Take care to remove any liquid droplets from the screen because they can cause permanent staining. After cleaning, allow 30 minutes for complete drying.

> **EXAM ALERT**
>
> Know how to safely clean LCD displays.

The screen should be shielded from bright sun light and heat sources. Moving the computer from a cooler location to a hot location can cause damaging moisture to condense inside the housing (including the display). It should also be kept away from ultraviolet light sources and extremely cold temperatures. The liquid crystals can freeze in extremely cold weather. A freeze/thaw cycle may damage the display and cause it to be unusable.

Protecting Hard Disk Drives

The primary preventive maintenance tasks associated with modern hard disk drives revolve around protecting them from shock hazards and overheating. Rough handling is responsible for more physical hard drive problems than anything else. While hard drives are not any more susceptible to heat than other PC components, it is a good practice to ensure that there is ample room for airflow around the drive to cool it.

> **EXAM ALERT**
>
> Be aware that hard drives can overheat if there is not enough airflow space around their housings.

The second most important task in protecting hard disk drives is to protect their logical structures and data from corruption. This involves installing and maintaining antivirus and spy ware products, as well as performing regular disk optimization activities such as defragmentation. You should also perform periodic backup and restore operations.

If a hard disk drive is to be transported or shipped, make sure to pack it properly. The forces exerted on the drive during shipment may be great enough to cause the read/write heads to slap against the disk surfaces, causing damage to both. Pack the drive unit in an oversized box with antistatic foam all around the drive. You can also pack the drive in a box-within-a-box configuration, again using foam as a cushion.

If the drive malfunctions, the electronic circuitry and connections can be tested; but when it comes to repairs within the disk chamber, factory service or a professional service facility with a proper clean room is a must!

To recover quickly from hardware failures, operator mistakes, and acts of nature, some form of software backup is essential with a hard disk system. Copies of the system backup should be stored in a convenient, but secure, place. In the case of secure system backups, such as client/server networks, the backup copies should be stored where the network administrators can have access to them, but not the general public (a locked file cabinet). Left unsecured, these copies could be used by someone without authority to gain access to the system, or to its data.

Even emergency repair disks associated with the Windows operating system should be stored in a secure location. These disks can also be used by people other than administrators to gain access to information in client/server networks. Many companies maintain a copy of their backup away from the main site. This is done for protection in case of disasters such as fire.

> **EXAM ALERT**
>
> Be aware of the precautions that should be employed with storing system backups.

A number of hard-disk drive software utilities are designed to optimize and maintain the operation of the hard-disk drive. They should be used as part of a regular preventive maintenance program. The primary HDD utilities are the CHKDSK, Defrag, and Backup utilities that have been available with different Microsoft operating systems since early the early days of MS-DOS. These utilities should be used regularly to keep the disk drive subsystem running to the best of its potential.

Protecting Removable Media Drives

Unlike hard disk drives, tape drives, floppy drives, and CD-ROM/DVD drives are at least partially open to the atmosphere, and their media may be handled on a regular basis. This opens these drive units up to a number of maintenance concerns not found in hard disk drives. Also, the removable cartridges, disks, or discs can be adversely affected by extremes in temperature, exposure to magnetic and electromagnetic fields, bending, and airborne particles that can lead to information loss.

Protecting Removable Media

Because magnetic tapes and floppy disks store information in the form of magnetized spots on their surfaces, it is only natural that external magnetic fields have an adverse effect on their stored data. Never bring tape cartridges or floppies near magnetic field[nd]producing devices, such as CRT monitors, television sets, or power supplies. They should also never be placed on or near appliances such as refrigerators, freezers, vacuum cleaners, and other equipment containing motors. All these items produce electromagnetic fields that can alter information stored on removable media.

Proper positioning of the drive and proper connection of peripheral interface cables help to minimize noise and radio frequency interference (RFI). RFI can cause the drive to operate improperly. Magnetic fields generated by power supplies and monitors can interfere with the magnetic recording on disks and tapes. The drive and signal cables should be positioned away from these magnetic field sources as well. Magnets should never be brought near any type of computer-related drive unit.

Additional measures to protect tape cassettes, disks, and discs include storing them in a cool, dry, clean environment, out of direct sunlight. Excessive temperatures will cause the disk and its jacket, or the tape and cartridge, to warp. Also, you should never physically touch the surface of a magnetic tape, floppy disk, or CD/DVD disc. In all cases, the natural oils from your skin can cause physical damage to the floppy's coating and partially block the laser in a CD-ROM or DVD drive, causing it to be unreadable. Floppies and tape cartridges have protective retractable guards to prevent accidental contact with the disk or tape surface. Do not manually retract these guards. Take care when inserting the disk into the drive so as not to damage the disk, its jacket, or the drive's internal mechanisms.

Maintaining Removable Media Drives

So far, each preventive action has involved the disk or disc. However, periodic manual cleaning of the read/write heads of tapes and floppies or of the laser-reading mechanism in CD-ROMs and DVDs can prevent failures and bigger maintenance problems. Cleaning the read/write heads in tape and floppy drives removes residue and oxide buildup from the face of the head to ensure accurate transfer of data from the head to the disk. Likewise, cleaning CD-ROM and DVD drives removes contaminants and buildup from the laser lens in the drive.

Cleaning kits are available for floppy drives and CD/DVD drives, as well as for different types of tape drives. In the case of floppies and tape drives, cleaning should be done by manually cleaning the heads. Automatic cleaning kits often include abrasive disks that scrub the faces of the read/write heads to remove buildup. These kits can eventually wear away the read/write head and damage it. On the other hand, CD-ROM/DVD-drive cleaning kits offer cleaning discs that brush the laser lens to remove dust and other contaminates. It is also common practice to keep discs free from smudges and dust by wiping them gently with a soft cloth.

Manual cleaning operations involve removing the cover of the drive, gaining access to the read/write heads, and cleaning them manually with a swab that has been dipped in alcohol. Together, these steps provide an excellent preventive maintenance program that should ensure effective, long-term operation of the drive.

The cleaning solution for manual cleanings can be isopropyl alcohol, methanol, or some other solvent that does not leave a residue when it dries. Common cotton swabs are not recommended for use in manual cleaning because they tend to shed fibers. These fibers can contaminate the drive and, in certain circumstances, damage the read/write mechanisms. Instead, cellular foam swabs, or lint-free cloths, are recommended for manual head cleaning.

Protecting Input Devices

Input peripherals generally require very little preventive maintenance. An occasional dusting and cleaning should be all that's required. The keyboard's electronic circuitry is open to the atmosphere and should be vacuumed when you are cleaning around your computer area. Dust buildup on the keyboard circuitry can cause its ICs to fail because of overheating. The keyboard is the peripheral most vulnerable to damage caused by dust. To remove dirt and dust particles from inside the keyboard, disassemble the keyboard and carefully brush particles away from the board with a soft brush. A lint-free swab can be used to clean between the keys.

EXAM ALERT

Remember that dust can settle into the keyboard through the cracks between the keys.

When using a trackball mouse, keep its workspace clear, dry, and free from dust. Periodically remove and clean the trackball. Use a lint-free swab to clean the X and Y trackball rollers, as shown in Figure 8.7. Using a sharp instrument, such as an X-acto knife, can place cuts and divots in the roller and permanently damage the mouse.

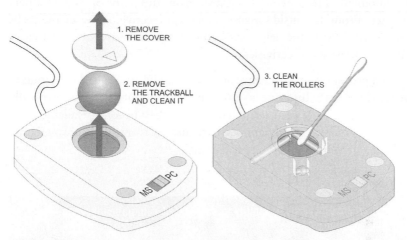

FIGURE 8.7   Cleaning the rollers in a trackball mouse.

EXAM ALERT

Know how to properly clean a trackball mouse.

The life and usefulness of a touch pad can be extended through proper care and handling. Clean the pad periodically with mild soap and water and a soft, lint-free cloth. Rinse the residue from the pad by wiping it with a cloth dampened in clear water. Never pour or spray liquids directly on the computer or the touch pad. Allow 30 minutes for complete drying. Touch pads should be shielded from bright sunlight and heat sources, as well as extremely cold temperatures. Never use sharp or pointed objects to tap the pad because these items can damage the surface of the pad.

Preventive Maintenance Scheduling

Most PC components have recommended maintenance programs and schedules designed by their manufacturers. These schedules are typically available in the device's documentation. You may also be able to obtain the manufacturer's maintenance schedule from their website.

EXAM ALERT

Know where to obtain a maintenance schedule for typical PC components.

For those devices where you cannot find an official maintenance schedule, the following is a reasonable schedule that can be used to effectively maintain most computer equipment. The schedule is written from the point of view of a personal computer. From an outside maintenance perspective, some of the steps will need to be shared with the daily users. In fact, for the most part, users carry out the daily and weekly PM activities.

Software-based preventive maintenance activities can be automated in Windows environments. PCs with Internet access can be configured to automatically obtain product updates and security patches when they become available from Microsoft. The Windows Automatic Update utility is available through the Windows 2000 and Windows XP Control Panel.

EXAM ALERT

Remember that Windows has the capability to be updated automatically when new features become available.

In addition, the Windows Scheduled Task utility can be used to schedule periodic software maintenance operations, such as backing up data and system state information and running antivirus scanning programs.

Daily Activities

Back up important data from the unit. This can be done to CD-R/RW discs, backup tape, another network drive, or some other backup media. Check computer ventilation to make sure that papers and other desk clutter are not cutting off airflow to the unit. Check for other sources of heat buildup around the computer and its peripherals. These sources include the following:

▶ Direct sunlight from an outside window

▶ Locations of portable heaters in the winter

▶ Papers/books piled up around the equipment

Weekly Activities

Clean the outside of the computer and its peripheral equipment. Wipe the outsides of the equipment with a damp cloth. The cloth can be slightly soapy. Wipe dry with an antistatic cloth. Clean the display screen using a damp cloth with the antistatic solution described earlier in this chapter. An antistatic spray can also be used for static build-up prevention.

Run CHKDSK/f on all hard drives to locate and remove any lost clusters from the drives. The CHKDSK command must be run from the command prompt in all versions. Run a current virus-check program to check for hard drive infection. Back up any revised data files on the hard drive. Inspect the peripherals (mice, keyboard, and so on), and clean them if needed.

Monthly Activities

Clean the inside of the system. Use a long-nozzle vacuum cleaner attachment to remove dust from the inside of the unit. Wipe the nozzle with antistatic solution before vacuuming. A soft brush can also be used to remove dust from the system unit.

Clean the inside of the printer using the same equipment and techniques as those used with the system unit. Check system connections for corrosion, pitting, or discoloration. Wipe the surface of any peripheral card's edge connectors with a lubricating oil to protect it from atmospheric contamination. Vacuum out the keyboard. Clean the X and Y rollers in the trackball mouse using a lint-free swab and a noncoating cleaning solution.

Defragment the system's hard drive using the Defrag utility. Remove unnecessary temporary (TMP) files from the hard drive. Check software and hardware manufacturers for product updates that can remove problems and improve system operation. Back up the entire hard disk drive.

Six-Month Activities

Every six months, perform an extensive PM check. Apply an antistatic wash to the entire computer/peripheral work area. Wipe down books, the desktop, and other work area surfaces with antistatic solution. Disconnect power and signal cables from the system's devices, and reseat them. Clean the inside of the printer. Run the printer's self-tests.

Use a software diagnostic package to check each section of the system. Run all system tests available, looking for any hint of pending problems.

Annual Activities

Reformat the hard drive by backing up its contents and performing a high-level format. Reinstall all the application software from original media and reinstall all user files from the backup system. Check all floppy disks in the work area with a current antivirus program.

Clean the read/write heads in the floppy drive, using a lint-free swab. Cotton swabs have fibers that can hang up in the ceramic insert of the head and damage it. Perform the steps outlined in the monthly and semiannual sections.

Although this is a good model PM schedule, it is not the definitive schedule. Before establishing a firm schedule there are several other points you should take into consideration. These points include any manufacturer's guidelines for maintaining the equipment. Read the user's guides of the various system components and work their suggested maintenance steps into the model.

Over time, adjust the steps and frequency of the plan to effectively cope with any environmental or usage variations. After all, the objective isn't to complete the schedule on time, it's to keep the equipment running and profitable.

Exam Prep Questions

1. What multimeter reading would you expect to receive from measuring a good 2-amp fuse?

   - ○ **A.** 0 ohms
   - ○ **B.** 2 ohms
   - ○ **C.** 15 ohms
   - ○ **D.** 30 ohms

2. Which multimeter reading should you expect from measuring a good speaker?

   - ○ **A.** Infinite
   - ○ **B.** 0 ohms
   - ○ **C.** 4 ohms
   - ○ **D.** 8 ohms

3. What meter reading would you expect from an open speaker?

   - ○ **A.** 0 ohms
   - ○ **B.** 4 ohms
   - ○ **C.** 8 ohms
   - ○ **D.** Infinity (or a blank display)

4. What are the voltages that should be expected when testing a PC?

   - ○ **A.** −1.2VDC, +1.2VDC, −0.5VDC, +0.5VDC
   - ○ **B.** −1.2Vac, +1.2Vac, −0.5Vac, +0.5Vac
   - ○ **C.** −3.3VDC, +3.3VDC, −1.5VDC, +1.5VDC
   - ○ **D.** −12VDC, +12VDC, −5VDC, +5VDC

5. What is the most important factor to consider when assessing the situation at a new troubleshooting call?

   - ○ **A.** The power supply
   - ○ **B.** The operating system
   - ○ **C.** The user
   - ○ **D.** The system configuration

6. What type of problem causes a `Press F1 to Continue` error message to be displayed?

   ○ **A.** A floppy disk drive is defective.

   ○ **B.** The operating system is missing from the hard drive.

   ○ **C.** The system needs to be reconfigured.

   ○ **D.** The video display is defective.

7. Which type of computer component can you usually replace in the field?

   ○ **A.** ERU

   ○ **B.** FSU

   ○ **C.** FRU

   ○ **D.** FRC

8. What event marks the transition from basic hardware problems to bootup problems?

   ○ **A.** The operating system bootup screen appears.

   ○ **B.** A single beep sound.

   ○ **C.** The power light comes on.

   ○ **D.** The operating system bootup is completed.

9. What questions should you ask the user when you are first examining a defective unit? (Select all that apply.)

   ○ **A.** How much experience do you have with this type of computer?

   ○ **B.** What were you doing when the problem occurred?

   ○ **C.** Was there an error message? What did it say?

   ○ **D.** Is the unit new? Did it ever work?

10. Which of the following items would not be considered to be an FRU that can be replaced in the field?

   ○ **A.** Chassis

   ○ **B.** Hard disk drive

   ○ **C.** CPU

   ○ **D.** Video card

11. What is the most commonly used repair technique for PC systems?

- ○ **A.** Replace all possible FRUs

- ○ **B.** Test each component on a test rig

- ○ **C.** Use a multimeter to test the signals from each component

- ○ **D.** Substitute known-good parts for suspected bad components

12. What is the most common type of malfunction observed after the installation of a new hardware or software component?

- ○ **A.** Hardware problems

- ○ **B.** Operating system problems

- ○ **C.** Configuration problems

- ○ **D.** Corrupted or missing files

13. After the system successfully POSTs, you see the error message `Bad or Missing Command Interpreter`. What type of problem is this?

- ○ **A.** Hardware

- ○ **B.** Configuration

- ○ **C.** Bootup

- ○ **D.** Operating system

14. Which of the following is not a software tool commonly used by a repair technician?

- ○ **A.** Emergency boot disk

- ○ **B.** Software diagnostics utility

- ○ **C.** Hardware diagnostic utility

- ○ **D.** Antivirus utility

15. Where should cleaning agents be applied to an LCD display on a notebook PC?

- ○ **A.** Directly to the plastic screen guard.

- ○ **B.** To a cloth or cleaning rag.

- ○ **C.** To a sponge.

- ○ **D.** Cleaning agents should not be used on an LCD display.

16. What action can you perform to reduce the number of redundant steps and efforts required to troubleshoot a problem?

○ **A.** Document each troubleshooting step and its outcome

○ **B.** Identify the source of the problem before beginning the troubleshooting process

○ **C.** Start at the beginning of the troubleshooting process and do not skip troubleshooting steps

○ **D.** Interrogate the user to determine how to conduct your troubleshooting process efficiently

17. Which of the following actions must you perform first when troubleshooting a customer's equipment?

○ **A.** Gather information from the user and assess the problem systemically

○ **B.** Inspect each component related to the possible cause

○ **C.** Test each component involved and evaluate the results of each test

○ **D.** Document the possible causes of the problem the system is displaying

Answers and Explanations

1. A. One of the main uses of the resistance function is to test fuses. You must disconnect at least one end of the fuse from the system. You should set the meter on the 1 kilohm resistance setting. If the fuse is good, the meter should read near 0 ohms. If it is bad, the meter reads infinity.

2. D. Disconnect the speaker from the system and connect a meter lead to each end. If the speaker is good, the meter should read near 8 ohms (although some smaller speakers may be 4 ohms).

3. D. If the speaker is defective, the resistance reading should be 0 for shorts or infinite for opens.

4. D. The DC voltages that can normally be expected in a PC-compatible system are +12V, +5V, –5V, and –12V. The actual values for these readings may vary by 5% in either direction.

5. C. The most important thing to do when checking a malfunctioning device is to be observant. Begin by talking to the person who reported the problem. You can obtain many clues from this person. Careful listening also is a good way to eliminate the user as a possible cause of the

problems. Part of the technician's job is to determine whether the user could be the source of the problem—either trying to do things with the system that it cannot do or not understanding how some part of it is supposed to work.

6. C. The system has encountered invalid configuration information during the bootup process. Either the configuration has been set up incorrectly, or the hardware was unable to confirm the configuration settings.

7. C. *Field-Replaceable Units (FRUs)* are portions of the system that you can conveniently replace in the field. These are typically components that can be exchanged for a replacement onsite and require no actual repair work.

8. B. One of the first steps in troubleshooting a computer problem (or any other programmable system problem) is to determine whether the problem is due to a hardware failure or to faulty software. In most PCs, you can use a significant event that occurs during the bootup process as a key to separating hardware problems from software problems: the single beep that most PCs produce between the end of the POST and the beginning of the bootup process.

9. B, C, D. When first examining a defective unit, gather information from the user regarding the environment the system is being used in, any symptoms or error codes produced by the system, and the situations that existed when the failure occurred.

10. A. FRU troubleshooting involves isolating a problem within one section of the system. A section consists of one device such as a keyboard, video display, video adapter card, I/O adapter card, system board, disk drive, printer, and so on.

11. D. The most widely used repair method involves substituting known-good components for suspected bad components.

12. C. When you are installing new hardware or software options, be aware of the possibility of a configuration error. If you encounter configuration (or setup) errors, refer to the installation instructions found in the new component's user's manual.

13. C. After the single beep tone has been produced in the startup sequence, the system shifts over to the process of booting up to the operating system. The `Bad or Missing Command Interpreter` error message is associated with bootup problems.

14. B. Typical software tools used by computer technicians include emergency boot/start disks to get broken systems started, antivirus utilities, and hardware diagnostic software packages.

15. B. Aerosol sprays, solvents, and commercial cleaners should be avoided when cleaning LCD displays because they can damage the screen and cabinet.

16. A. Take the time to document the problem, including all the tests you perform and their outcomes. This recorded information can prevent you from making repetitive steps that waste time and may cause confusion. This information will also be very helpful when you move on to more detailed tests or measurements.

17. A. First, you must gather information to identify the nature of the problem. This can involve questioning the user and identifying any changes that have been made to the system. After the problem has been identified, you should assess the problem systematically and divide complex problems into smaller components to be analyzed individually.

Challenge Solutions

1. Begin by having the user (who is supposed to be familiar with Excel) demonstrate the problem to you in a step-by-step manner. Have the user describe the process he or she is trying to complete. Then, remove the operator from the situation and begin the troubleshooting process to limit the problem to the hardware involved, the software package being used, and then the operator.

2. Because the system reaches the single beep, you can tell that the basic hardware in her system is working okay. Between the time the system is turned on and the single beep is presented, the system is performing POST tests and initializing basic system hardware components. After the beep, the system searches for a boot record and tries to load an operating system. The problem must be related to one of these activities.

3. You should tell your customer that the error could be caused by a bad hard drive, but that it is more likely a missing or corrupted bootup file that can be restored without replacing the hard drive. At the very least, more extensive troubleshooting should be conducted before buying a new drive.

4. Your friend needs to check the speaker using an ohmmeter. She must remove the speaker from the system, gain access to the speaker itself, and measure across its two leads (caution her that all electrical power and signal sources must be removed from the speaker). The resistance reading on the meter should be about 8 ohms (although 4 ohms is a common value as well). If the reading is infinity (blank display), the speaker wire has opened (broken). If it is zero, the coil of wires has shorted (meaning that the signal cannot go through the coil to be applied to the physical speaker).

5. You should tell her that the microprocessor has failed and you believe that it is related to heat buildup in the computer. Explain the importance of making sure that all the back panel slot covers are in place and the need for periodic cleaning—both of which you have taken care of for now. Also, describe other environmental issues the manager can be aware of that can cause such failures to occur.

CHAPTER NINE

Advanced PC Troubleshooting

Terms you'll need to understand:

✓ Indicator lights

✓ Beep codes

✓ Documentation

✓ Soft memory errors

✓ Hard errors

✓ Degaussing

✓ Autodetect function

✓ Microsoft download service

✓ Emergency repair disk

✓ Disk boot failure

✓ Invalid drive

✓ Invalid drive specification

✓ Buffer underrun errors

✓ Loopback test plug

✓ Drive mismatch error

✓ Invalid media type

Techniques you'll need to master:

Essentials 1.3—Identify tools, diagnostic procedures, and troubleshooting techniques for personal computer components.

✓ Recognize and isolate issues with display, power, basic input devices, storage, memory, thermal, and POST errors (for example, BIOS and hardware).

✓ Apply basic troubleshooting techniques to check for problems (such as thermal issues, error codes, power, connections including cables and/or pins, compatibility, functionality, software, and drivers) with components. For example:

    ✓ Motherboards

✓ Power supply

✓ Processor/CPUs

✓ Memory

✓ Display devices

✓ Input devices

✓ Adapter cards

Depot Technician 1.2—Identify tools, diagnostic procedures, and troubleshooting techniques for personal computer components.

✓ Identify the steps used to troubleshoot components (for example, check proper seating, installation, appropriate component, settings, and current driver). For example:

> ✓ Power supply
>
> ✓ Processor/CPUs and motherboards
>
> ✓ Memory
>
> ✓ Adapter cards

Technical Support Technician 1.2—Identify tools, diagnostic procedures, and troubleshooting techniques for personal computer components.

✓ Recognize and isolate issues with display, peripheral, multimedia, specialty input devices, and storage.

✓ Apply steps in troubleshooting techniques to identify problems (for example, physical environment, functionality, and software/driver settings) with components including display, input devices, and adapter cards.

IT Technician 1.2—Identify tools, diagnostic procedures, and troubleshooting techniques for personal computer components.

✓ Recognize and isolate issues with display, peripheral, multimedia, specialty input devices, internal and external storage, and CPUs.

✓ Identify the steps used to troubleshoot components (for example, check proper seating, installation, appropriate component, settings, and current driver). For example:

> ✓ Power supply
>
> ✓ Processor/CPUs and motherboards
>
> ✓ Memory
>
> ✓ Adapter cards
>
> ✓ Display and input devices

Advanced Diagnostics

This chapter covers a portion of the Diagnostic Procedures and Troubleshooting Techniques areas of the CompTIA A+ Certification—Essentials examination under Objective 1.3. Similar and related topics are presented in the Depot Technician, Tech Services Technician, and IT Technician exam objectives.

One of the primary responsibilities of every PC technician is to diagnose and troubleshoot computer problems. The technician should be able to identify common symptoms associated with computer components and use those symptoms to effectively troubleshoot and repair problems. Numerous sources of problems and symptoms are discussed here, beginning with those that relate to the power supply.

Tech Services Technician Objective 1.2 specifies that PC technicians working in job titles associated with the Tech Services exam should be able to apply basic troubleshooting techniques to displays, peripherals, multimedia and specialty input devices, and storage systems for physical environment, functionality, and software/driver settings—in contrast to thermal issues, error codes, power, and connections, which are covered in Essentials 1.3.

Likewise, Depot Technician Objective 1.2 and IT Technician Objective 1.2 specify that those technicians should be able to troubleshoot power supplies, processors, motherboards, memory, and adapter cards for proper seating, installation, correct component settings, and drivers—in contrast to thermal issues, error codes, power, and connections, which are covered in Essentials 1.3. The IT Technician Objective 1.2 also includes troubleshooting display and input devices under this definition.

> **NOTE**
>
> The topics specified in these different exam and objective areas are so closely related that it makes sense to present them as a contiguous discussion. You will need to study this material in this chapter for any of the four exams you intend to challenge.

Isolating Power Supply Problems

Typical symptoms associated with power supply failures include the following:

▶ No indicator lights visible, with no disk drive action and no display on the screen. Nothing works, and the system is dead.

▶ The On/Off indicator lights are visible, but there is no disk drive action and no display on the monitor screen. The system fan may or may not run.

▶ The system produces a continuous beep tone.

The power supply unit is connected to virtually every other component in the system. Therefore, it has the capability to affect all the other components if it fails. Figure 9.1 illustrates the interconnections of the power supply unit with the other components in the system.

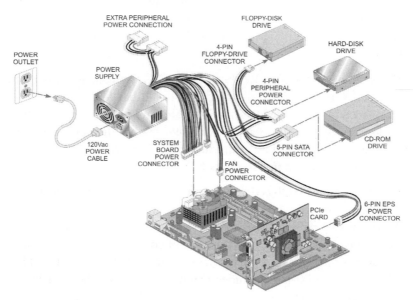

EXTRA PERIPHERAL
POWER CONNECTION

FLOPPY-DISK
DRIVE

HARD-DISK
DRIVE

POWER
OUTLET

4-PIN
FLOPPY-DRIVE
CONNECTOR

POWER
SUPPLY

4-PIN
PERIPHERAL
POWER
CONNECTOR

120Vac
POWER
CABLE

SYSTEM
BOARD
POWER
CONNECTOR

FAN
POWER
CONNECTOR

5-PIN SATA
CONNECTOR

CD-ROM
DRIVE

PCIe
CARD

6-PIN EPS
POWER
CONNECTOR

FIGURE 9.1 Power supply interconnections.

Checking a Dead System

When a system is inoperable, there are no symptoms to give clues as to where to begin the isolation process. In addition, it is impossible to use troubleshooting software or other system aids to help isolate the problem. The first step in troubleshooting any dead system is to visually inspect the system. Check for unseated cards, loose cables, or foreign objects within the system unit.

When the system exhibits no signs of life—including the absence of lights—the best place to start looking for the problem is at the power supply. The operation of this unit affects virtually every part of the system. Also, the absence of any lights working usually indicates that no power is being supplied to the system by the power supply.

1. Start with the external connections of the power supply. This is the first step in checking any electrical equipment that shows no signs of life.

2. Confirm that the power supply cord is plugged into a functioning outlet.

3. Check the position of the On/Off switch.

4. Examine the power cord for good connection at the rear of the unit.

5. Check the setting of the 110/220 switch setting on the outside of the power supply. The normal setting for equipment used in the United States is 110.

6. Check the power at the commercial receptacle using a voltmeter or by plugging in a lamp (or other 110-volt device) into the outlet.

> **EXAM ALERT**
>
> Remember the first step of checking out electrical equipment that appears dead.

If power is reaching the power supply and nothing is happening, the most likely cause of a totally dead system is the power supply unit. However, be aware that in ATX/BTX and NLX systems, if the cable that connects the system board to the power switch has become loose, the power supply will appear dead. Use a voltmeter to check for the proper voltages at one of the system's option's power connectors. (All system voltages should be present at these connectors.) If any voltage is missing, check the power supply by substitution.

> **CAUTION**
>
> Before changing any board or connection, always turn the system off first. In ATX/BTX/NLX-style systems, you should disconnect the power cable from the power supply. This is necessary because even with the power switch in the off position in these units, there are still some levels of voltage applied to the system board.

Other Power Supply Problems

If the front panel indictor lights are on and the power supply fan is running, but no other system action is occurring, you should consider the power supply as one of the most likely sources of a problem. The presence of the lights and the fan operation indicate that power is reaching the system and that at least some portion of the power supply is functional. This type of symptom results from the following two likely possibilities:

► A portion of the power supply has failed or is being overloaded. One or more of the basic voltages supplied by the power supply is missing while the others are still present.

► A key component on the system board has failed, preventing it from processing, even though the system has power. A defective capacitor across the power input of the system board can prevent it from operating.

Adding and Removing Power Supplies

Figure 9.2 illustrates the steps involved in removing the power supply from a PC. To exchange the power supply, all of its connections to the system must be removed.

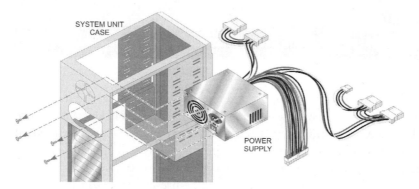

FIGURE 9.2   Removing a power supply.

Typical steps for removing a power supply:

1. Disconnect the exterior power connections from the system unit.

   A. Unplug the power cable from the commercial receptacle.

2. Disconnect the interior power connections.

   A. Disconnect the power supply connections from the system board.

   B. Disconnect the power supply connector from the floppy disk drive (if installed).

   C. Disconnect the power supply connector from the hard disk drive.

   D. Disconnect the power supply connector from the CD-ROM/DVD drive.

3. Remove the power supply unit from the system.

    A. Remove the four retaining screws that secure the power supply unit to the rear of the system unit.

    B. Store the screws properly.

    C. Remove the power supply from the system unit by lifting it out.

Reverse these steps for installing a power supply.

Troubleshooting the System Board

Troubleshooting problems related to the system board can be difficult because of the system board's relative complexity. Because so many system functions at least partially rely on the system board, certain symptoms can be masked by other symptoms. If you suspect a system board problem, you should do the following:

▶ Observe the steps that led to the failure and determine under what conditions the system failed. Were any unusual operations in progress?

▶ Note any error messages or beep codes produced.

▶ Refer to the documentation for the system board and peripheral units to check for symptoms and technical notes related to the symptoms observed.

▶ Examine the advanced CMOS setup parameters to make certain that all the appropriate system board–enabling settings have been made.

The microprocessor, RAM modules, ROM BIOS, and CMOS battery are typically replaceable or upgradeable units on the system board. If enough of the system is operational to perform tests on these units, you can replace them. If symptoms suggest that one or more of these devices may be defective, you can exchange them with a known-good unit of the same type.

System Board Symptoms

Because so much of the system's operation is based on the system board and its components, a problem with it can produce a variety of symptoms. Typical symptoms associated with system board hardware failures include the following:

▶ The On/Off indicator lights are visible and the display is visible on the monitor screen, but there is no disk drive action and no bootup.

▶ The On/Off indicator lights are visible, the hard drive spins up, but the system appears dead and there is no bootup.

▶ The system locks up during normal operation.

▶ The system produces a beep code with one, two, three, five, seven, or nine beeps.

▶ The system produces a beep code of one long and three short beeps.

▶ The system will not hold the date and time.

▶ An `8042 Gate A20 Error` message displays—`Error getting into Protected mode`.

▶ An `Invalid Switch Memory Failure` message displays.

▶ A `DMA Error` message displays—`DMA Controller failed page register test`.

▶ A `CMOS Battery Low` message displays, indicating failure of the CMOS battery or a CMOS checksum test.

▶ A `CMOS System Option Not Set` message displays, indicating failure of the CMOS battery or a CMOS checksum test.

▶ A `CMOS Checksum Failure` message displays, indicating the CMOS battery is low or a CMOS checksum test failure.

▶ An IBM `201` error code displays, indicating a RAM failure.

▶ A parity check error message displays, indicating a RAM error.

Typical symptoms associated with the system board's CMOS setup failures include the following:

▶ A `CMOS Inoperational` message displays, indicating failure of the CMOS shutdown register.

▶ A `CMOS Display Mismatch` message displays—`Failure of display type verification`.

▶ A `CMOS Memory Size Mismatch` message displays—`System Configuration and Setup failure`.

▶ A `CMOS Time & Date Not Set` message displays—`System Configuration and Setup failure`.

Typical symptoms associated with failures of the system board's I/O include the following:

- ▶ `Error initializing hard drive controller.` The system has detected a failure related to the IDE hard disk interface built in to the system board. The problem is most likely in the system board's IDE controller circuitry, but could be connected to the disk drive unit as well.

- ▶ The speaker doesn't work. The rest of the system works, but no sounds are produced through the speaker.

- ▶ `Keyboard Interface Error.` Although the message says the problem is with the keyboard controller on the system board, it is more often related to an unplugged or failed keyboard.

- ▶ The keyboard does not function after being replaced with a known-good unit.

Most of the hardware problems that occur with PCs involve the system board. Because the system board is the center of virtually all the computer's operations, it is only natural that you must check it at some point in most troubleshooting efforts. The system board is normally the last step of various troubleshooting schemes used for different system components. It occupies this position for two reasons. First, the system board supports most of the other system components, either directly or indirectly. Second, it is the system component that requires the most effort to replace and test.

Configuration Checks

Manipulating CMOS configuration settings requires you to have a good deal of knowledge about the particular function being configured. When users attempt to tweak these settings, they often create configurations that the system cannot work with (for example, data transfer timing errors and speed mismatches). When this happens, the system can crash and refuse to run. In cases where there are serious configuration circumstances, don't forget that you have the option to select default configuration options through the CMOS Setup utility.

Incorrectly configured enabling parameters cause the corresponding hardware to fail. Therefore, check for the presence of port and device enabling functions in the BIOS Features and Chipset Features screens as a part of every hardware configuration troubleshooting procedure. Advanced CMOS configuration and enabling settings in these screens usually include the disk drives, keyboard, and video options, as well as onboard ports and buses.

If the CMOS backup battery fails or has been changed, the contents of the CMOS setup will be lost. After replacing the battery, it is always necessary to run the CMOS Setup utility to reconfigure the system. The values stored in CMOS must accurately reflect the configuration of the system; otherwise, an error occurs. Accessing these values to change them normally requires pressing a predetermined key combination during the bootup process.

Hardware Checks

If the system's CMOS configuration appears to be correct and a system board hardware problem is suspected, you may need to exchange the system board for a working unit. Because most of the system must be dismantled to exchange it, a few items are worth checking before doing so.

Check the system board for signs of physical problems, such as loose cables and devices. If nothing is apparently wrong, check the power supply voltage levels on the system board. Check for +3.3VDC, +5VDC, and +12VDC on the system board, as illustrated in Figure 9.3. If these voltages are missing, turn off the system, disconnect power to all disk drives, and swap the power supply unit with a known-good one.

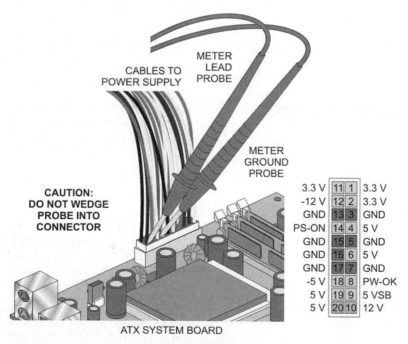

FIGURE 9.3 The system board voltage check location.

RAM

The system board's memory is a very serviceable part of the system. RAM failures basically fall into two major categories and create two types of failures:

- ▶ Soft-memory errors—Errors caused by infrequent and random glitches in the operation of applications and the system. You can clear these events just by restarting the system.

- ▶ Hard-memory errors—These errors are caused by permanent physical failures that generate Non-Maskable Interrupt (NMI) errors in the system and require that the memory units be checked by substitution.

Check the RAM count to ensure that it matches the amount of physical RAM actually installed in the system. If not, swap RAM devices around to see whether the count changes. Use logical rotation of the RAM devices to locate the defective part. The burn-in tests in most diagnostic packages can prove helpful in locating borderline RAM modules. Swap the RAM modules out, one at a time, to isolate defective modules. These modules are also swapped out when a system upgrade is being performed. Take care when swapping RAM into a system for troubleshooting purposes to make sure that the new RAM is the correct type of RAM for the system and that it meets the system's bus speed rating. Make sure that the replacement RAM is consistent with the installed RAM. Mixing RAM types and speeds can cause the system to lock up and produce hard-memory errors.

> **EXAM ALERT**
>
> Know what type of failures hard- and soft-memory errors are and how they affect the system.

Microprocessor

In the case of the microprocessor, the system may issue a slow, single beep, with no display or other I/O operation as a symptom. This indicates that an internal error has disabled a portion of the processor's internal circuitry (usually the internal cache). Internal problems also may allow the microprocessor to begin processing, but then cause it to fail as it attempts operations. This may cause the system to continuously count RAM during the bootup process. It also may lock up while counting RAM. In either case, the only way to remedy the problem is to replace the microprocessor.

If a new or upgraded processor fails immediately when the system is started, you should check the processor's pins or contacts to make sure that they are not bent or damaged. Bent pins will keep the processor from physically seating correctly in the socket and broken/missing pins will prevent it from working when the system is turned on.

> **EXAM ALERT**
>
> Know what things to look for when a new or upgraded processor fails immediately on startup.

If the system consistently locks up after being on for a few minutes, this is a good indication that the microprocessor's fan is not running or that some other heat buildup problem is occurring. The key indicator here is that the failure is linked to the time required to heat up and cool down. You also should check the microprocessor if its fan has not been running, but the power is on. This situation may indicate that the microprocessor has been without adequate ventilation and has overheated. When this happens, you must replace the fan unit and possibly the microprocessor. Check to make certain that the new fan works correctly; otherwise, a second microprocessor will be damaged.

> **EXAM ALERT**
>
> Know the effects on the system of heat buildup and microprocessor fan failures.

Socket- or slot-mounted processors should be removed and reseated when you encounter these types of problems. Sockets and slots are convenient for repair and upgrade purposes, but they can also attract corrosion between the pins of the device and those of the socket. Over time, the corrosion may become so bad that the electrical connection becomes too poor for the device to operate properly.

BIOS

As with the microprocessor, a bad or damaged ROM BIOS will typically stop the system completely. However, a damaged BIOS may also cause the bootup sequence to automatically move into the CMOS Setup utility, but never return to the bootup sequence. In some systems, you can physically replace the defective BIOS device with a version that matches the chipset used by the system. If the BIOS IC device is not removable, the system board will have to be replaced.

When new devices (microprocessors, RAM devices, hard drives) are added to the system, there is always a chance that the existing BIOS version will not support them. In these situations, the system may or may not function, depending on which device has been installed and how its presence affects the system. To compensate for these possible problems, always check the websites of the device and the system board manufacturers to obtain the latest BIOS upgrade and support information.

Problems with key system board components produce symptoms similar to those described for a bad power supply. Both the microprocessor and the ROM BIOS can be sources of such problems. You should check both by substitution when dead system symptoms are encountered but the power supply is good.

Cooling Systems

Microprocessor-based equipment is designed to provide certain performance levels under specified environmental conditions. One of the key design elements for microprocessor performance is operating temperature. With Pentium class microprocessors, PC systems are designed to maintain the operating temperature for the device in the range of 30–40 degrees C.

To accomplish this, Pentium class chipsets provide a microprocessor temperature control system that includes a temperature-sensing thermocouple device embedded in the system board under the microprocessor socket (or in the microprocessor cartridge). The thermocouple senses the current temperature of the microprocessor and produces an analog voltage signal that is proportional to the temperature. A special health controller monitors this signal and supplies the microprocessor with a digital representation of the temperature measurement.

The microprocessor compares this reading to an ideal setting established in the CMOS configuration and sends a digital code to the health controller, which in turn generates an analog speed control signal that is applied to the microprocessor's cooling fan. This signal slows the fan down if the measured temperature is too low, and speeds it up if it's too hot.

The ideal operating temperature setting varies among microprocessor types and manufacturers. In addition, the location of the CMOS configuration setting varies among BIOS versions. Some CMOS Setup utilities provide a separate Health screen whereas others integrate it into their Power Management screen. Many systems include an additional fan control circuit for use with an optional chassis (case) fan. In these cases, the system board features additional BERG connectors for the chassis temperature sensor and fan control cable.

If temperature-related problems like those described in the previous section occur, you should access the CMOS Hardware Health configuration screen, and check the fan speed and processor temperature readings. If they are outside the designated range, you may enter a different value for the temperature set point. If no fan speed measurement is shown, check to see whether the fan is actually turning. If not, you should turn the system off as soon as possible, check the operation of the fan, and replace it before the microprocessor is damaged.

Other alternatives when dealing with thermal problems in a PC include installing an additional chassis fan to help move cooler air through the system unit, changing the microprocessor fan for one that runs faster over a given range of temperatures, and flashing the BIOS to provide different fan control parameters. Also, check for missing slot covers that can disrupt air flow in the case, and route internal signal cables so that they do not block the flow of air through the case.

CMOS Batteries

The second condition that causes a configuration problem involves the system board's CMOS backup battery. If a system refuses to maintain the time and date information, the CMOS backup battery, or its recharging circuitry, is usually faulty. After the backup battery has been replaced, check the contacts of the battery holder for corrosion.

> **EXAM ALERT**
>
> Be aware that a defective battery can cause the system to continually lose track of time.

If the battery fails or if it has been changed, the content of the CMOS configuration will be lost. After replacing the battery, it is always necessary to run the CMOS Setup utility to reconfigure the system.

> **Challenge #1**
>
> You receive a call from a customer who complains that his Windows XP system continually loses its time and date information. What advice can you give this customer about his system?

Troubleshooting Keyboard Problems

Most of the circuitry associated with the keyboard is contained in the keyboard itself. However, some keyboard interface circuitry is located on the system board. Therefore, the steps required to isolate keyboard problems are usually confined to the keyboard, its connecting cable, and the system board. To isolate keyboard problems, check the keyboard and the system board.

Keyboard Symptoms

Typical symptoms associated with keyboard failures include the following:

▶ No characters appear onscreen when entered from the keyboard.

▶ Some keys work, whereas others do not.

▶ A Keyboard Is Locked—Unlock It error displays.

▶ A Keyboard Error—Keyboard Test Failure error displays.

▶ A KB/Interface Error—Keyboard Test Failure error displays.

▶ An error code of six short beeps is produced during bootup.

▶ Wrong characters are displayed.

▶ An IBM-compatible 301 error code displays.

Keyboard Configuration Checks

You should be aware that several keyboard configuration settings stored in CMOS can affect the operation of the keyboard. These include keyboard enabling, NumLock key condition at startup, typematic rate, and typematic delay. The *typematic* information applies to the keyboard's capability to repeat characters when the key is held down. The typematic rate determines how quickly characters are repeated, and the delay time defines the amount of time the key can be held before typematic action occurs. A typical typematic rate setting is six characters per second; the delay is normally set at 250 milliseconds.

Basic Keyboard Checks

Watch the keyboard's NumLock and Scroll Lock lights during the bootup process. These lights should flash when the system attempts to initialize the keyboard. The system's POST routines may also return keyboard-related error messages and codes.

The key switches of the keyboard can wear out, resulting in keys that don't make good contact (no character is produced when the key is pushed) or ones that remain in contact (stick) even when pressure is removed. A stuck key will produce an error message when the system detects it. However, the system has no way of detecting an open key. If you detect a stuck key, you can clean it to try to return it to acceptable service (desoldering and replacing individual key switches with a good key from a manufacturer or a similar keyboard would quickly drive the cost of the repair beyond the cost of a new unit).

EXAM ALERT

Know the most common conditions that will produce a keyboard error message.

If the keyboard produces odd characters on the display, check the Windows keyboard settings in the Control Panel's Device Manager. If the keyboard is not installed, or is incorrect, install the correct keyboard type. Also, make certain that you have the correct language setting specified under the Control Panel's Keyboard icon.

The condition of the NumLock key can cause portable PCs to produce incorrect characters. Notebook PCs do not have a separate 10-key numeric keypads. If the NumLock key function is engaged, the system will remap different keys to the locked numbers. In most cases, the only indicator that the NumLock key function is engaged is a small light near a small icon representing a numeric keypad. Unless you look closely, you probably won't realize that there is a numeric keypad associated with the keyboard (small numbers are embossed on the alpha keys). The NumLock-On setting can be disabled using the Fn key along with a designated function key (also denoted by a small numeric keypad icon). If the NumLock light remains lit after you've tried to turn it off, you should inspect the Fn key to make sure that it is not stuck.

EXAM ALERT

Know why a portable PC's keyboard might produce the wrong characters.

Keyboard Hardware Checks

If you suspect a keyboard hardware problem, you must first isolate the keyboard as the definite source of the problem (a fairly easy task). Because the keyboard is external to the system unit, detachable, and inexpensive, begin by exchanging the keyboard with a known-good keyboard.

If the new keyboard works correctly, return the system to full service and repair the defective keyboard appropriately. Remove the back cover from the keyboard and check for the presence of a fuse in the +5VDC supply and check it for continuity. Disconnecting or plugging in a keyboard with this type of fuse while power is on can cause it to fail. If the fuse is present, replace it with a fuse of the same type and rating.

EXAM ALERT

Be aware that standard PS/2 six-pin mini-DIN keyboards cannot be hot swapped and that doing so can cause damage to the keyboard and system board.

If replacing the keyboard does not correct the problem, and no configuration or software reason is apparent, the next step is to troubleshoot the keyboard receiver section of the system board. Normally, this ultimately involves replacing the system board.

Troubleshooting Wireless Keyboards

When a wireless keyboard stops working, there are generally two primary checks to make: Check the batteries in the keyboard and click the Reset button on its host port receiver. Low batteries can also cause the system to produce incorrect characters on the display. You can check the keyboard's battery status under the Control Panel's Keyboard icon.

As video display screens get larger, many users are tempted to work farther from the PC. You may need to move the keyboard closer to the receiver if you cannot enter information from the keyboard, or if characters get dropped or scrambled. Also, make sure that both devices are sufficiently removed from other wireless devices (such as cordless phones or wireless access points) that can scramble their communications.

There are basically two technologies used for wireless keyboards and mice: 27MHz radio frequency technology and Bluetooth networking technology. The 27MHz RF technology is most susceptible to interference from other RF-based consumer electronics devices typically found in the home or office. Bluetooth technology hops from frequency to frequency in a designed fashion, so it is not as susceptible to interference as the other technology. However, these devices operate in the 2.4GHz frequency range. This places them in potential conflict with 802.11 B/G wireless networking devices, as well as microwave ovens and some cordless phones. Large metal objects nearby, such as metal desks, can also create scrambled signals.

Many wireless keyboard models provide a channel selection switch to enable users to switch to other channels to escape interference problems. If the channel-switching option is not present or does not help, you will need to remove the cause of the interference, switch to a different technology, or adopt a wired keyboard solution.

Having the wrong driver installed for the wireless keyboard can also cause wrong characters to appear. This is not typically a problem for wired keyboards.

Check the keyboard driver by accessing the Hardware tab of the Control Panel's Keyboard icon. On this tab, you can select a different driver to use with the wireless keyboard.

If the wireless keyboard receiver employs a USB connection to the PC, use the Safely Remove Hardware icon to stop the keyboard's USB service, unplug the receiver, and reattach it to the system. The system should detect the USB keyboard as new and reload its drivers.

Troubleshooting Mouse Problems

Most of the problems with mice are related to a few items:

- ▶ Its port connection
- ▶ The mouse driver
- ▶ The trackball in a trackball mouse or a trackball unit
- ▶ The operation of the mouse buttons

In newer systems, the mouse is typically connected to a USB port or to the dedicated PS/2 mouse port on the back of the unit. ATX, BTX, and NLX systems use the same six-pin mini-DIN connector for the keyboard and mouse, and they do not work interchangeably. Although plugging the mouse into the keyboard connector should not cause any physical damage, it will cause problems with the operation of the system. These connections tend to be color coded, so check to make sure that the mouse is connected to the green connector.

The second reason for mouse failures is using the wrong driver for the mouse or its port. For USB and PS/2 mice, installation and configuration is a fairly routine process. Connect the mouse to the USB or PS/2 mouse port and let the system autodetect it and install the basic Windows mouse drivers. However, specialty mice—including some wireless and infrared mice—along with other pointing devices require special drivers that must be supplied by the manufacturer and loaded from the disk or disc that accompanies the device.

For wireless mice, check the batteries to make sure that they are supplying sufficient power for the mouse circuitry to operate.

Mouse Hardware Checks

Isolate the mouse from its connection port. Replace the mouse to test its electronics. If the replacement mouse works, the original mouse is probably defective. If its electronics are not working properly, few options are available for actually servicing the mouse. The low cost of a typical mouse generally makes it a throwaway item if simple cleaning does not fix it.

If the replacement mouse does not work, chances are very good that the mouse's electronics are working properly. In this case, the mouse driver or the port hardware must be the cause of the problem. If the driver is correct for the mouse, the port hardware and CMOS configuration must be checked.

The system board typically contains all the port hardware electronics and support, so it must be replaced to restore the port/mouse operation at that port. However, if the system board mouse port is defective, another option is to install a mouse that uses a different type of port (for example, use a USB mouse to replace a PS/2 mouse).

When a trackball mouse is moved across the table, it picks up dirt or lint, which can hinder the movement of the trackball. This can cause the cursor to periodically freeze and jump onscreen. You can remove the trackball from the mouse by a latching mechanism on its bottom. Twisting the latch counterclockwise enables you to remove the trackball. Then you can clean dirt out of the mouse.

EXAM ALERT

Be aware of the condition that causes the cursor to jump and freeze on the display.

The other mechanical part of the mouse is its buttons. These can wear out under normal use. When they do, the mouse should be replaced. However, before doing so, make sure to check the properties of the mouse in the operating system to ensure that the button functions have not been altered (for example, set up for left-hand use).

Mouse Configuration Checks

When a mouse does not work in a Windows system, restart the system and move into Safe Mode to start the operating system with the most basic mouse driver available. If the mouse does not operate in this mode, you must check the mouse hardware and the port it is connected to.

If the mouse works in Safe Mode, the problem exists with its driver configuration. The installed driver may be corrupt, or it could be having a conflict with some other driver. To check the driver, consult the Device Manager entry. If the Device Manager shows a conflict with the mouse, remove the driver and allow the system's PnP process to reinstall it.

If the correct driver for the installed mouse is not available, you will need to install one from the manufacturer. This typically involves placing the manufacturer's driver disk or disc in the appropriate drive and load the driver using the Update Driver (Requires Disk from OEM) option on the Device Manager Mouse Properties page. If the OEM driver fails to operate the mouse in Windows, you should contact the mouse manufacturer for an updated Windows driver.

Troubleshooting Optical and Wireless Mice

If you have an optical mouse that is operating erratically, you may have a dirty LED or sensor on the bottom of the mouse. Dust, or even a hair, may block the optical detector. It may also pick up moisture or lotion from contact with human skin through a mouse pad. Some optical mice are sensitive to bright light and may operate erratically if subjected to a strong light source (such as use on a glass-top desk or table). You may also experience poor tracking with an optical mouse when you use it on a mouse pad. Avoid glossy, or very dark, mouse pads because they may alter the reflected light's characteristics and provide erroneous operation. Test the optical mouse on a normal white sheet of paper. Likewise, using an optical mouse on an uneven surface can cause it to lose track and respond erratically.

Like wireless keyboards, there are generally two primary checks to make if your wireless mouse stops working: Check the batteries in the mouse and click the Reset button on the host port receiver. Move the receiver closer to the mouse and make sure that both are sufficiently removed from other wireless devices that can scramble their communications. If the receiver employs a USB connection to the PC, use the Safely Remove Hardware icon to stop the mouse service, unplug the mouse, and then reattach it to the system. The system should detect the mouse as new and reload its drivers.

For optical mice, blow away any debris buildup at the lens area and clean this area with a cotton swab. Move the mouse receiver closer to the mouse work area if possible.

Restart the PC in Safe Mode and attempt to use the mouse in this mode. If the mouse will not work in this setting, remove all the mouse drivers listed in the Device Manager and restart the system. You should also download and install the latest drivers for the optical and wireless mouse. You can typically find the latest driver information at the mouse manufacturer's website. You may want to use a diagnostic program on the system to check the mouse port's operation. Finally, check for viruses; as there are some viruses that can produce mouse and keyboard error symptoms.

Challenge #2

After you upgrade from a two-button PS/2 mouse to a new wheel mouse, you cannot get it to work with the system. You return it to the distributor and exchange it for another one. It also will not work. When you try one from your co-worker's machine, it works fine. What should you conclude about the wheel mouse?

Troubleshooting Video Systems

Figure 9.4 depicts the components associated with the video display. It may be most practical to think of the video information as starting out on the system board. In reality, the keyboard, one of the disk drives, or some other I/O device may be the actual originating point for the information. In any case, information intended for the video display monitor moves from the system board to the video adapter (usually through a video card installed in one of the system board's expansion slots). On the adapter, the screen information is converted into the configured screen image format and stored in the video screen memory. Finally, the information is applied to the monitor through the video signal cable.

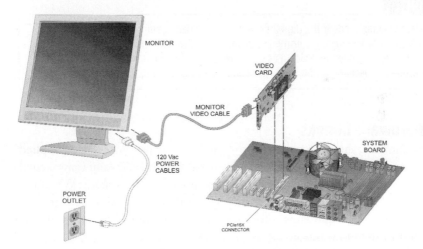

FIGURE 9.4 Video-related components.

Basically, two levels of troubleshooting apply to video problems: configuration and hardware problems. In the case of hardware problems, the components involved include the video adapter card, the monitor, and, to a lesser degree, the system board. Common symptoms associated with display problems include the following:

▶ No display.

▶ Wrong characters display onscreen.

▶ Diagonal lines display onscreen (no horizontal control).

▶ Display scrolls (no vertical control).

▶ An error code of one long and six short beeps is produced by the system.

▶ A `Display Switch Setting Not Proper—Failure to Verify Display Type` error displays.

▶ A `CMOS Display Mismatch—Failure to Verify Display Type` error displays.

▶ An error code of one long and two short beeps is produced by the system (indicates a display adapter problem).

▶ LCD display is blank (backlight failure).

▶ Limited color output—The system will supply only basic colors through the video display.

> **CAUTION**
>
> The following sections cover the digital portion of the video system. Troubleshooting an actual CRT monitor is discussed immediately following the video adapter troubleshooting sections. Only experienced technicians should participate in troubleshooting internal CRT monitor problems because of the very high voltages present there.

Video Hardware Checks

The video monitor should come on fairly quickly after power has been applied to it. With newer monitors, the monitor is normally only asleep and is awakened through the video adapter card when power is applied to the system. When the system is shut down, the monitor's circuitry senses that no signal is present from the video adapter card and slips into a monitoring mode as long as its power switch is left in the On position.

If the monitor does not wake up early in the system's startup process and present a display, you should assume that some type of hardware problem exists—the bootup action and operating system have not been introduced to the system before the single beep tone is produced. If you can see BIOS information displayed during this time, you do not have a hardware failure problem. Likewise, video problems that occur after the single beep are more likely to be related to operating system configuration settings.

If you suspect a video display hardware problem, the first task is to check the display's On/Off switch to see that it is in the On position. Also check the monitor's power cord to see that it is plugged in to either the power supply's monitor outlet or an active 120VAC commercial outlet. Check the monitor's intensity and contrast controls to make certain that they are not turned down.

Check to see that there is no hardware configuration problem existing between an adapter card–based video display and an onboard video adapter. Consult the system board's documentation to determine whether it has an onboard video adapter. If so, swap the monitor between the two displays' ports to determine whether the other port is active.

Check the components associated with the video display monitor. Start by disconnecting the monitor's signal cable from the video adapter card at the rear of the system unit and disconnecting its power cord from the power supply connector or the 120VAC outlet. Then exchange the monitor for a known-good one of the same type (that is, VGA for VGA). In the case of system boards with built-in video, move the monitor to the other video display port to see whether it is active.

If a video problem still exists, exchange the video controller card with a known-good one of the same type. Remove the system unit's outer cover. Disconnect the monitor's signal cable from the video controller card. Swap the video controller card with a known-good one of the same type. Reconnect the monitor's signal cable to the new video adapter and reboot the system.

Other symptoms that point to video adapter card problems include a shaky video display and a high-pitched squeal from the monitor or system unit. In these cases where you can see something on the display, but it is not usable, you should attempt to uninstall the old video drivers and let the system detect the video adapter during the system startup. If this action does not clear up the symptoms, replace the video adapter card with a known-good one. If the system still does not perform properly after swapping the video adapter card, the source of the problem may be in the system board.

Windows Video Checks

If you can read the contents of the display through the startup process, but then cannot see it after the system boots, you have an operating-system-related video problem. Because Windows operating systems are graphically based programs, navigation can be nearly impossible if video problems are severe enough to prevent you from seeing the display.

If the Windows video problem prevents you from being able to use the display, restart the system, press the F8 function key when the `Starting Windows` message appears, and select the Safe Mode option. This should load Windows with the standard 640×480×16-color VGA driver (the most fundamental driver available for VGA monitors), and should furnish a starting point for installing the correct driver for the monitor being used.

After you have gained access to a usable display, the next step involves checking the installed video drivers. You can access the Windows video information through the Control Panel's System icon. Inside the System Properties page, access the Device Manager through the Hardware tab and select the Display Adapters entry from the list. Click the node to the left of the Monitor icon and double-click the desired driver under the Display Adapters entry. The adapter's Properties page should pop up onscreen. The Device Status box normally presents the message The device is working properly if the system hasn't detected a problem. However, if a conflict or error has been detected, the system will note it in this box. You can click the Troubleshooters button to gain access to the Windows troubleshooting guidelines for the display.

If you have updated the display adapter with a new video driver and cannot use the display, you can also select the Driver tab and click the Roll Back Driver button to return to the driver that was in use before the update occurred.

EXAM ALERT

Know how to cope with video problems where you do not have access to a usable display.

Clicking the Driver tab reveals the driver file in use with the display adapter. From this page you have the option to uninstall the current driver (this will remove the driver from the system, so Windows will not load this driver the next time the system starts), update the Driver, or roll back the Driver, as illustrated in Figure 9.5.

NOTE

It is a good idea to uninstall old drivers before installing or updating to newer versions.

Selecting the Resources tab displays the video adapter's register address ranges and the video memory address ranges. It also provides a Conflicting Devices dialog box that provides information about other devices that may be interfering with the operation of the video adapter.

FIGURE 9.5 Device Manager driver options.

You can also gain access to the Windows video information by double-clicking the Control Panel's Display icon. At the top of the Display page is a series of file folder tabs. Of particular interest is the Settings tab. Under this tab, the Advanced button provides access to the Adapter, Monitor, and Troubleshooting tabs for the video display system.

Under the Adapter tab, information about the adapter's manufacturer, version number, and current driver files is given. Clicking the Properties button displays the adapter's General, Driver, and Resource tabs. The General tab provides general information about the adapter and features a troubleshooter button that can be used to start a diagnostic routine for the adapter. It also shows the device's current operational status. When things go wrong, the Driver tab provides options for updating, removing, and rolling back the driver to a previous version. Through these options, you can have Windows search various sources, including the Internet, for updated drivers and provide a list of available drivers to select from.

Having the wrong driver installed for a given video adapter card can cause the Limited Colors symptom presented earlier in the chapter. If the Color Quality setting cannot be adjusted through the Settings tab of the Control Panel's Display icon, use the Advanced button to continue on to the adapter's properties. You can access this page by clicking the Properties button on the Adapter tab. Select the Driver tab to uninstall, roll back or update the display adapter's driver. If you uninstall the current driver, you can simply restart Windows and allow it to detect the display adapter and attempt to install the correct driver.

The Windows XP Roll Back Driver feature will return the system to the driver that was being used before the current video display driver. The Update Driver option will ask you to select a driver to use from several options.

EXAM ALERT

Be aware of why a PC might not be able to display a full array of color output on the video display.

The Monitor tab provides general information about the monitor and features a troubleshooter button that can be used to start a diagnostic routine for the monitor. Like the Adapter tab, the Monitor tab shows the device's current operational status.

If the video problem disappears when lower settings are selected, but reappears when a higher resolution setting is used, refer to the Color Palette box under the Control Panel's Display option, Settings tab, and try the minimum color settings. If the problem goes away, contact the Microsoft Download Service (MSDL) or the adapter card maker for a compatible video driver. If the video problem persists, reinstall Windows. If the video is distorted or rolling, try an alternative video driver from the list.

Challenge #3

One of your customers has called you to his facility to repair a desktop computer that doesn't show anything on the display. When you start it up, you hear the system fans come on and the hard drive spin up. You also hear the system beeps when they are supposed to occur. The monitor power light is on. What piece of equipment should you retrieve from your repair kit for these symptoms?

Diagnosing Display Problems

Examine the power cord to see that it is plugged in and check to see that the monitor's power switch is in the On position. Verify the external settings to see that the brightness and contrast settings are not turned off. If the problem produces a blank display, disconnect the monitor's signal cable from its video adapter card. If a raster appears, a video card problem is indicated. The final step in isolating the video display as the source of the problem is to exchange it for a known-good one. If the replacement works, the problem must be located in the monitor.

Some display problems can be caused by incorrectly set front panel display settings. The monitor's front panel controls (either analog or digital) establish parameters for brightness, contrast, screen size and position, and focus. Typical problems associated with these controls include the following:

- ▶ Fuzzy characters
- ▶ Poor or missing colors
- ▶ Incomplete displays

There can be several causes of fuzzy characters on the display. The first step in troubleshooting this problem is to reset the display resolution to standard VGA values. If the fuzzy characters remain, check the intensity and contrast controls to see whether they are out of adjustment. With a CRT display, you may need to remove built-up electromagnetic fields from the screen through a process called *degaussing*. This can be done using a commercial degaussing coil. However, newer monitors have built-in degaussing circuits that can be engaged through their front panel controls. These monitors normally perform a degauss operation each time they are turned on. However, sometimes the user might need to perform this operation.

The monitor's front panel controls can also be used to adjust the red/green/blue color mixture for the display. If the monitor is showing poor colors, or only one color, examine the color settings using the front panel controls. If these settings are responsive to change, the problem exists in either the video adapter or the signal cable (broken or bad pin or conductor), or the monitor's color circuitry is deteriorating.

LCD displays can be calibrated to display correct colors as determined by a color calibration program or by using a set of transparent strips of color film. The transparent strips are standard colors that the screen can be calibrated to. The individual strips are placed on the screen and the colors are adjusted to match.

Incomplete displays are often the result of improperly set horizontal and vertical placement and size settings. These settings are also adjusted through the display's front panel controls.

Troubleshooting HDDs

Typical symptoms associated with hard disk drive failures include the following:

- ▶ The computer does not boot up when turned on.

- ▶ The computer boots up to a distribution CD in the CD-ROM drive (or the Windows 2000 Emergency Start disk in the FDD drive), but not to the hard drive, indicating that the system files on the HDD are missing or have become corrupt.

- ▶ No motor sounds are produced by the HDD while the computer is running. (In desktop units, the HDD should always run when power is applied to the system—this also applies to portables because of their advanced power-saving features.)

- ▶ An IBM-compatible 17xx error code is produced on the monitor screen.

- ▶ An HDD Controller Failure message displays, indicating a failure to verify hard disk setup by system configuration file error.

- ▶ A C: or D: Fixed Disk Drive Error message displays, indicating a hard disk CMOS setup failure.

- ▶ An Invalid Media Type message displays, indicating that the controller cannot find a recognizable track/sector pattern on the drive.

- ▶ A No Boot Record Found, a Non-System Disk or Disk Error, or an Invalid System Disk message displays, indicating that the system boot files are not located in the root directory of the drive.

- ▶ The video display is active, but the HDD's activity light remains on and no bootup occurs, indicating that the HDD's CMOS configuration information is incorrect.

- ▶ An Out of Disk Space message displays, indicating that the amount of space on the disk is insufficient to carry out the desired operation.

- ▶ A Missing Operating System, a Hard Drive Boot Failure, or an Invalid Drive or Drive Specification message displays, indicating that the disk's master boot record is missing or has become corrupt.

- ▶ A Current Drive No Longer Valid message displays, indicating that the HDD's CMOS configuration information is incorrect or has become corrupt.

Figure 9.6 depicts the relationship between the hard disk drive and the rest of the system. It also illustrates the control and signal paths through the system.

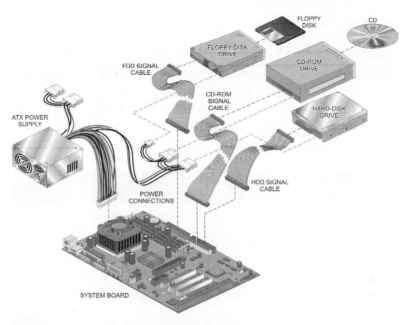

FIGURE 9.6 Hard disk drive–related components.

EXAM ALERT

Be able to describe the conditions indicated by `Invalid Drive` or `Drive Specification`, `Missing Operating System`, and the `Hard Drive Boot Failure` error messages.

The PC's hard drive subsystems typically consist of a controller, one or more signal cables, a power cable, and the drive units. The controller may be an integral part of the system board's chipset (as it is in PATA/SATA systems), or it may be mounted on an adapter card (as is the case with most SCSI and RAID systems). If the controller is integrated into the system board, the system board becomes a logical extension of the components that make up the HDD subsystem. Modern PCs rely on the PnP process and their operating systems to configure the drive and handle its operation.

The troubleshooting procedure typically moves from basic observation to setup and configuration, to formatting, and, finally, into the hardware component isolation process.

Basic HDD Checks

Start the system and listen for sounds of the hard drive spinning up (a low whine or clicking noise). If you do not hear any drive noises, there is a chance that the drive is not working mechanically. However, newer hard drives are very quiet and you may not be able to hear them run from outside the case. Verify that its power connector and interface cable are securely attached to the drive. Also check the HDD's activity light during the startup sequence. If the light does not come on at any time during the process, the system may not recognize that the drive is installed. If there is a loud, clicking noise coming from the drive, the drive has lost its alignment and is looking for its starting track.

EXAM ALERT

Know what a loud, clicking hard disk drive indicates.

If you think the hard drive is spinning, or if you see the access light come on, the next step is to get the system to boot up to some alternative, such as a simple boot disk, an emergency start disk, or a setup/distribution CD. This will enable you to examine the system to determine how extensive the problem is.

After you get the system started and can look around inside, the next objective is to determine whether the hard disk drive problem is a simple file system (boot) problem, or something more serious. The quickest way to determine this is to attempt to access the primary partition of the drive. This can be accomplished by executing a directory (DIR) command from the command prompt to attempt to access the C: drive.

If the system can see the contents of the drive, the boot files have been lost or corrupted, but the architecture of the disk is intact. If any one of these files is missing, you will typically receive some type of Disk Boot Failure message onscreen. The No (or Missing) ROM BASIC Interpreter message presented in the symptoms list may also be produced by this condition.

You may be able to correct a missing boot or system file problem by reinstalling the specified files from the operating system's emergency repair disk or its distribution CD. These operations are performed from the command prompt, so you will need to be familiar with command-line functions and the different files involved in the operating system's boot process.

In either Windows 2000 or Windows XP, you should boot to the distribution CD and run the Recovery Console. Start the system with the distribution CD in the drive. When you start the Recovery Console, you are prompted to choose the folder that contains the Windows 2000 or Windows XP installation that you are trying to repair, and then to log on as Administrator. Choose the option to Repair (Press the R Key) the Installation. This will produce the Recovery Console command-line environment.

Most of the typical command-line navigation and operational functions are available through this utility. You can obtain a listing of these commands by typing **Help** at the command prompt. You can also obtain information on a specific command by typing **help** *commandname* at the command prompt. However, for the symptoms described here, you will be using the FIXBOOT and FIXMBR commands. The FIXBOOT command will write a new boot sector into the drive specified in the command statement (that is, FIXBOOT D: will replace the boot record in drive D). You should use the FIXMBR command to repair the master boot record of a drive. The default drive for this command is the boot drive (the drive where the primary partition is located).

NOTE

You will need to enter the Administrator's password to access the Recovery Console. The password protection for the Recovery Console only permits two incorrect attempts by default. On the third incorrect attempt, the system will stop accepting further entries for a predetermined amount of time (referred to as *lockout time*).

After running the FIXBOOT and FIXMBR commands, you should remove the CD from the drive and reboot. If the problem has not been resolved, restart the system and select the Install option. The system may ask whether you want to repair the installation that is already in place. If you select Y, you will be offered the repair option again. Selecting the N option will create a clean install of the operating system.

NOTE

If the drive can be accessed but it will not boot, you should back up any important information on the drive to a different media before attempting any type of repair. This can involve copying the data to another hard drive that you temporarily install for this purpose, or to a USB thumb drive, a tape drive, or other backup device. You should do this while you still have access to the data—it may not survive some steps you employ to return the drive to service.

If the system cannot see the drive after booting to an alternative source, an Invalid Drive message or an Invalid Drive Specification message should be returned in response to any attempt to access the drive. Under these conditions, the drive or its disks have a serious problem and you will need to examine the HDD subsystem's configuration and hardware components as directed in the following sections.

HDD Configuration Checks

While you're booting up the system, observe the BIOS's HDD type information displayed on the monitor. If the drive has a hardware problem, the system may not be able to recognize or configure it.

Possible error messages associated with HDD configuration problems include the `Drive Mismatch Error` message and the `Invalid Media Type` message. If the system produces an error message like these, open the CMOS Setup utility and verify that the drive is enabled there. If not, select the Autodetect option, enable it, and attempt to boot the system.

On PATA drives, verify the master/slave jumper settings, illustrated in Figure 9.7, to make sure that they are set correctly for the drive's logical position in the system. Determine whether the system might be using the Cable Select option also depicted in the figure. This setting requires a special CSEL signal cable designed to determine the master/slave arrangements for multiple PATA drives. Likewise, check the ID configuration settings and terminator installations for SCSI drives. Exchange the HDD power connector with another one from the power supply to make certain that it is not a source of problems.

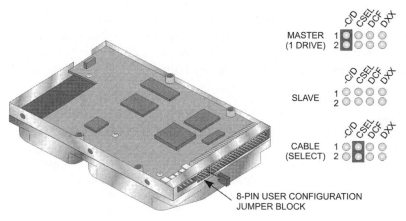

FIGURE 9.7 PATA master/slave settings.

With SATA drives, there is no master/slave setting to deal with. However, you may need to access the CMOS Setup utility to disable PATA drives and enable SATA drives. You can also experience problems loading drivers for these drive types. If the operating system does not recognize the SATA drive, use the Windows Device Manager utility to confirm that the latest drivers for the host adapter have been installed. If the drive is connected to the system board, the drivers should be those provided by the manufacturer. If the drive is connected to the system through a PCI card, the drivers should be those distributed by the manufacturer of the PCI card. The drive must also be partitioned and formatted through the operating system. This is done through Windows 2000 or Windows XP during the operating system installation process.

> **EXAM ALERT**
>
> Know that there can be only one master drive selection on each PATA channel.

If the drive is a SCSI drive, check to see that its ID is set correctly and that the SCSI chain has been terminated correctly. Make sure that every SCSI device has a unique ID address. Any of these errors will result in the system not being able to see the drive. Also, check the CMOS Setup utility to make sure that SCSI support has been enabled along with large SCSI drive support.

> **EXAM ALERT**
>
> Know that in newer systems, SCSI drive support and large drive support are both enabled in the BIOS.

Challenge #4

You are updating a working computer for your boss. The upgrade consists of adding a new microprocessor to the system, along with additional RAM and a second PATA hard drive. When you restart the system, the system will not boot to the original hard drive. As a matter of fact, neither drive will work. What should you check first?

HDD Hardware Checks

If you cannot access the hard disk drive when you boot from another location or media, and the drive's configuration settings appear correct, you must troubleshoot the hardware components associated with the hard disk drive. These components include the drive, its signal cable, and the IDE channel controller circuitry on the system board.

Check the HDD signal cable for proper connection at both ends. Exchange the signal cable for a known-good one. With PATA drives, make certain that the correct type of signal cable is being used. Do not get the newer 80-conductor/40-pin version confused with the older and much slower 40-conductor/40-pin version.

SATA cables have also been known to be a source of disk drive problems. Because the SATA specification does not use a shielded cable, SATA cables are susceptible to induced noise from other system components. Therefore, you should not place SATA devices or cables near each other or near PATA cables. Also, do not tie-wrap SATA cables together or put sharp bends in them; doing so modifies their insulation and decreases their noise resistance.

Check SCSI drives to make sure that the disk drive system is properly terminated.

If you have more than one device attached to a single interface cable, make sure that they are of the same type (that is, all are PATA devices or all are ATA100 devices). Mixing device types will create a situation where the system cannot provide the different types of control information each device needs. The drives are incompatible and you may not be able to access either device.

> **EXAM ALERT**
>
> Be aware that mixing drive types on a single signal cable can disable both devices.

The next logical step may seem to be to replace the hard drive unit. However, it is quite possible that the hard drive may not have any real damage. It may just have lost track of where it was and now it cannot find its starting point. In this case, the most attractive option is to reformat the hard disk. This action gives the hard drive a new starting point to work from. Unfortunately, it also destroys anything that you had stored on the disk.

If the reformatting procedure is not successful, or the system still won't boot from the hard drive, you must replace the hard disk drive unit with a working one.

Troubleshooting CD-ROM and DVD Drives

The troubleshooting steps for a CD-ROM and DVD drives are nearly identical to those of an HDD system. The connections and data paths are very similar. Basically, three levels of troubleshooting apply to CD-ROM problems. These are the configuration level, the operating system level, and the hardware level. Figure 9.8 shows the parts and drivers associated with CD-ROMs.

Basic Checks

In most systems, the CD-ROM and DVD drives share a controller or host adapter with the hard disk drive. If the system is using PATA drives, you should verify their master/slave jumper settings to make sure that they are set correctly. Normally, the CD-ROM or DVD drive should be set up as the master on the secondary PATA channel. In this manner, each drive has its own communications channel and does not need to share. If three or four PATA devices are installed in the system, you must determine which devices can share the channels most effectively.

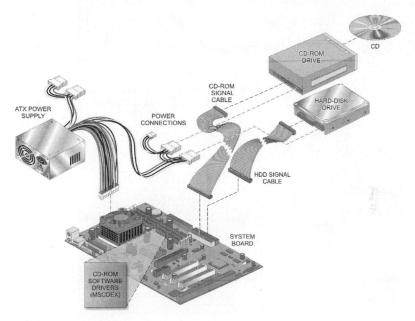

FIGURE 9.8   Components and drivers associated with CD-ROMs.

Windows Checks

In the Windows operating systems, you can access the contents of the CD-ROM or DVD through the CD Drive icon in the desktop's My Computer window. The CD-ROM drive's properties information is contained in the Device Manager utility. The properties of the installed CD-ROM drive can be viewed by expanding the node beside the DVD/CD-ROM Drives icon and double-clicking the driver listed there. Figure 9.9 shows a typical set of CD-ROM specifications.

CD-ROM/DVD Hardware Checks

If the configuration and software checks do not remedy the CD-ROM or DVD problem, you must troubleshoot the drive's related hardware. Basically, the hardware consists of the drive unit, the signal cable, the power cord, the media, and the controller or host adapter. The controller may be mounted on a host adapter card or, in a Pentium system, on the system board. For external drives, you must also check the plug-in power adapter.

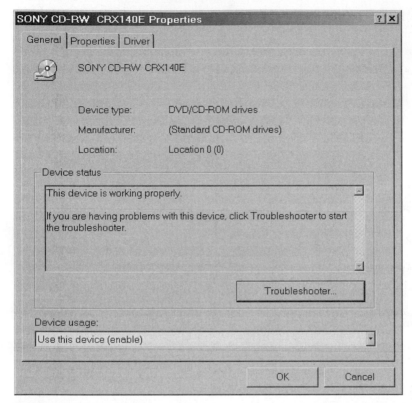

FIGURE 9.9   The CD-ROM drive properties.

In most systems, the CD-ROM and DVD drives share a controller or host adapter with the hard disk drive. Therefore, if the hard drive is working and the CD-ROM drive is not, the likelihood that the problem is in the CD-ROM or DVD drive unit is very high.

Before entering the system unit, check for simple user problems:

- ► Is there a CD or DVD in the drive?
- ► Is the label side of the disk facing upward?
- ► Is the disk a CD-ROM or some other type of CD?

If the drive is inoperable and there is a CD or DVD locked inside, you should insert a straightened paper clip into the tray-release access hole that's usually located beside the ejection button. This will release the spring-loaded tray and pop out the disc.

NOTE

Not all CD/DVD drives have this feature.

EXAM ALERT

Know how to retrieve a CD from a disabled CD-ROM drive.

If no simple reasons for the problem are apparent, exchange the CD-ROM drive with a known-good one of the same type. For external units, simply disconnect the drive from the power and signal cables, and then substitute the new drive for it. With internal units, you must remove the system unit's outer cover and disconnect the signal and power cables from the drive. Remove the screws that secure the drive unit in the drive bay. Install the replacement unit, start the system, and attempt to access it.

If the new drive does not work, check the drive's signal cable for proper connection at both ends. Exchange the signal cable for a known-good one.

If the controller is built in to the system board and becomes defective, it is still possible to install an IDE or SATA host adapter card in an expansion slot and use it without replacing the system board. This action can also be taken to upgrade PATA systems to SATA systems so that they can use additional IDE devices. The onboard IDE controller may need to be disabled before the system will address the new host adapter version.

EXAM ALERT

Remember that card-mounted IDE host adapters can be used to repair system boards with defective onboard IDE controllers and to upgrade older PATA systems.

Writable Drive Problems

An additional set of problems comes into play with writeable and rewriteable CD-ROM or DVD drives. These problems are concentrated in three basic areas:

▶ The quality of the drive's controller circuitry

▶ The makeup and version of the drive's read/write application interface software

▶ Compatibility with the operating system's multimedia support systems

The quality of the drive is based on the controller IC that oversees the operation of the drive. In less expensive drives, the BIOS extension on the drive may not support all the read/write functions to coordinate with the application package or the operating system's drivers. Although all newer CD-ROM and DVD drives are ATAPI compatible, they may not have an effective method of controlling *buffer underrun errors*. These errors occur when the system transfers data to the drive faster than the drive can buffer and write it to the disc. The ATAPI compatibility of the chipset ensures that the CD-ROM and DVD read functions work fine, but the nonstandard writing part of the drive may not produce satisfactory results.

You can use a few techniques to minimize buffer underruns. These include placing the CD-ROM or DVD writer on an IDE channel of its own, which keeps the drive from competing with other drives for the channel's available bandwidth. Also, conducting the write operation on the same drive as the read operation and using reduced write speed options in the read/write application software can minimize data flow problems.

In addition, the read/write application software for the drive may not be compatible with the operating system version in use or with the controller chip on the drive. Likewise, the operating system's multimedia enhancement drivers (DirectX in Windows operating systems) may not be compatible with the controller or the read/write application. It is best to consult the operating system's hardware and software compatibility lists before buying and installing a CD-RW or DVD-RW drive in a system. This typically means using a more expensive drive, but for now you do seem to get what you pay for when it comes to rewritable drives.

If the drive has already been purchased and installed, check the drive's documentation for suggestions and check the drive manufacturer's website for newer read/write applications and driver versions. You may also be able to locate a flash program for the drive's BIOS to upgrade it so that it provides better support for the write function.

Some CD-ROM and DVD R/W applications are incompatible with different drive BIOS versions or DirectX versions. Check the parties involved to find a collection of components that are all compatible with each other.

Troubleshooting FDDs

Typical symptoms associated with floppy disk drive (FDD) failures during boot up include the following:

- ▶ FDD errors are encountered during bootup.

- ▶ The front-panel indicator lights are visible, and the display is present on the monitor screen, but there is no disk drive action and no bootup.

- ▶ An IBM-compatible 6xx (that is, 601) error code displays.

- ▶ An FDD Controller Error message displays, indicating a failure to verify the FDD setup by the system configuration file.

- ▶ The FDD activity light stays on constantly, indicating that the FDD signal cable is reversed.

> **EXAM ALERT**
>
> Recognize the symptom produced by installing a floppy drive cable backwards.

Additional FDD error messages commonly encountered during normal system operation include the following:

- ▶ Disk Drive Read Error messages.

- ▶ Disk Drive Write Error messages.

- ▶ Disk Drive Seek Error messages.

- ▶ No Boot Record Found message, indicating that the system files in the disk's boot sector are missing or have become corrupt.

- ▶ The system stops working while reading a disk, indicating that the contents of the disk have become contaminated.

- ▶ The drive displays the same directory listing for every disk inserted in the drive, indicating that the FDD's disk-change detector or signal line is not functional.

A number of things can cause improper floppy disk drive operation or failure. These items include the use of unformatted disks, incorrectly inserted disks, damaged disks, erased disks, loose cables, drive failure, adapter failure, system board failure, or a bad or loose power connector. Basically, three levels of troubleshooting apply to FDD problems: the configuration, the software, and the hardware. No Windows-level troubleshooting applies to floppy disk drives. Figure 9.10 depicts the components associated with the operation of the floppy disk drive.

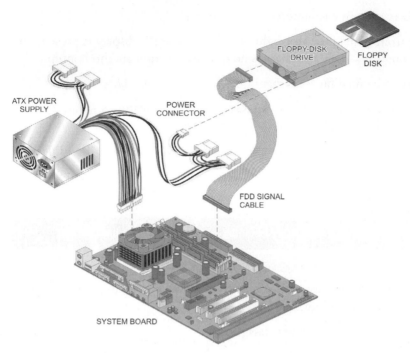

FIGURE 9.10 FDD-related components.

Basic FDD Checks

If there is a problem reading or writing to a particular floppy disk, try the disk in a different computer to determine whether it works in that machine. If not, there is most likely a problem with the format of the disk or the files on the disk. In the case of writing to the disk, you could be dealing with a write-protected disk, but the system will normally inform you of this when you attempt to write to it. However, if the other computer can read and write to the disk, you must troubleshoot the floppy drive hardware.

Hardware troubleshooting for floppy disk drives primarily involves exchanging the FDD unit for another one that is working. If necessary, exchange the signal cable with a known-good one. If neither of these actions repairs the problem, the only other option with most PC-compatible systems is to exchange the system board with a known-good one.

If there is a problem booting the system to the hard drive, you can insert the bootable disk in the floppy drive and turn on the system. If the system does not boot up to the floppy, examine the advanced CMOS setup to check the system's boot order. It may be set so that the FDD is never examined during the boot-up sequence.

If the system still will not boot up with the CMOS setting established to check the FDD first in the boot seek order, check the disk drive cables for proper connection at both ends. In many systems, the pin-1 designation is difficult to see. Reversing the signal cable causes the FDD activity light to stay on continuously. The reversed signal cable will also erase the master boot record from the disk, making it nonbootable. Because this is a real possibility, you should always use an expendable backup copy of the boot disk for troubleshooting FDD problems.

Troubleshooting Tape Drives

Because the fundamentals of recording on tape are so similar to those used with magnetic disks, the troubleshooting process is also very similar. The basic components associated with the tape drive are the tape drive, the signal cable, the power connection, the controller, and the tape drive's operating software. The tape itself can be a source of several problems. Common points to check with the tape include the following:

- ▶ Is the tape formatted correctly for use with the drive in question?
- ▶ Is the tape inserted securely in the drive?
- ▶ Is the tape write-protected?
- ▶ Is the tape broken or off the reel in the cartridge?

As cartridge tapes are pulled back and forth, their mylar base can become stretched over time. This action can cause the tape's format to fail before the tape actually wears out. To remedy this, you should retension the tape periodically using the software's retension utility. Cartridge tapes are typically good for about 150 hours of operation. If the number of tape errors begins to increase dramatically before this time, try reformatting the tape to restore its integrity. After the 150-hour point, just replace the tape.

If the tape is physically okay and properly formatted, the next item to check is the tape software. Check the software setup and configuration settings to make sure that they are correct for any hardware settings. Refer to the tape drive's documentation for a list of system requirements, and check the system to make sure that they are being met.

If any configuration jumpers or switches are present on the controller, verify that they are set correctly for the installation. Also run a diagnostic program to check for resource conflicts that may be preventing the drive from operating (such as IRQ and base memory addressing).

The software provided with most tape drives includes some error-messaging capabilities. Observe the system and note any tape-related error messages it produces. Consult the drive's documentation for error-message definitions and corrective suggestions. Check for error logs that the software may keep. You can view these logs to determine what errors have been occurring in the system.

Because many tape drives are used in networked and multiuser environments, another problem occurs when you are not properly logged in or enabled to work with files being backed up or restored. In these situations, the operating system may not allow the tape drive to access secured files, or any files, because the correct clearances have not been met. Consult the network administrator for proper password and security clearances.

If you have read/write problems with the drive, begin by cleaning its read/write heads. Consult the user's guide for cleaning instructions for floppy and tape drive read/write heads. The heads should be cleaned after about 20 backups or restores.

You can also try to use a different tape to see whether it works. Make certain that it is properly formatted for operation. It should also be a clean tape, if possible, to avoid exposing any critical information to potential corruption. If cleaning does not restore the drive to proper operation, continue by checking the drive's power and signal cables for good connection and proper orientation.

Troubleshooting Other Removable Storage Systems

Troubleshooting nontypical removable storage systems is very similar to troubleshooting an external hard drive or tape drive. The systems often consist of an external unit with a plug-in power adapter (anything with a motor in it usually requires an additional power source). It typically connects to the system through one of the standard I/O port connections. This requires a signal cable to be run between the system and the device. Depending on the exact type of storage device being used, there may be a removable media cartridge or container.

Inside the computer, there must be a device driver installed for the device. This is typically a function of the system's PnP process. The system should detect the external storage and load the driver for it automatically. If the system cannot locate the proper driver, it will present a prompt asking you to supply the location where the driver can be found. For the most part, external storage systems do not need a support application to be installed. However, you should refer to the device's documentation and follow its installation procedures to determine whether the device can be installed with just a driver.

Check the power supply at the external unit to make sure that power is being applied. Most external media devices have power lights to indicate that power is present. Next, check the removable media, if present, by exchanging it with another cartridge or tape. Next, you should open the Device Manager utility under the Windows Control Panel's System icon to make sure that the device has been recognized there and to check for conflicting device driver information.

If the Device Manager cannot see the device after the proper driver has been loaded, and the storage device has power, the final step in checking the system is to check the signal cable by substitution. The only other step usually available is to test the entire storage system on another machine (in most cases, there isn't a second storage system available to use as a source of known-good parts).

Troubleshooting Port Problems

The PC-compatible computer features a wide array of peripheral connection ports. Figure 9.11 illustrates the components involved in the operation of the legacy serial, parallel, and game ports. Failures in these ports tend to end with poor or no operation of the peripheral. Generally, there are only four possible causes for a problem with a device connected to an I/O port:

- ▶ The port is defective.
- ▶ The software is not configured properly for the port.
- ▶ The connecting signal cable is bad.
- ▶ The attached device is not functional.

Basic Port Checks

Check the CMOS Setup utility to determine whether the port in question has been enabled, and, if so, whether it has been configured correctly. The system's USB and infrared ports must be enabled in the Peripherals page of the CMOS Setup utility.

A modern parallel port must be enabled and configured with the proper protocol to interface with advanced peripherals. For typical printer operations, the setting can normally be set to SPP mode. However, devices that use the port in a bidirectional manner need to be set to EPP or ECP mode for proper operation. In both cases, the protocol must be set properly for both the port and the device to carry out communications.

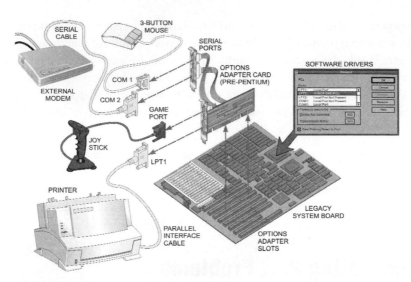

FIGURE 9.11 Components associated with I/O ports.

If serial or parallel port problems are occurring, the CMOS configuration window is the first place to look. Read the port assignments in the boot-up window. If the system has not detected the presence of the port hardware at this stage, none of the more advanced PnP levels will find it either. If values for any of the physical ports installed in the system do not appear in this window, check for improper port configuration.

Because the system has not loaded an operating system at the time the configuration window appears, the operating system cannot be a source of port problems at this time. If all configuration settings for the ports appear correct, assume that a hardware problem exists.

USB Port Checks

Because nearly any type of peripheral device can be added to the PC through the USB port, the range of symptoms associated with the USB device can include all the symptoms listed for peripheral devices in this chapter. Therefore, problems associated with USB ports can be addressed in three general areas:

▶ The USB hardware device

▶ The USB controller

▶ The USB drivers

The first step in troubleshooting USB problems is to check the CMOS setup screens to make sure that the USB function is enabled there. If the USB function is enabled in BIOS, check in the Windows Control Panel, System, Device Manager to make certain that the USB controller appears there. In Windows 2000, the USB controller should be listed under the Universal Serial Bus Controllers entry, or in the Human Interface Devices entry (using the default Devices by Type setting). In Windows XP, the USB controller's configuration is located under the Control Panel, Administrative Tools, Computer Management, Device Manager.

EXAM ALERT

Know what the first step should be if you encounter a system that will not support a USB device.

If the controller does not appear in Device Manager, or a yellow warning icon appears next to the controller, the system's BIOS may be outdated. Contact the BIOS manufacturer for an updated copy of the BIOS.

If the controller is present in the Device Manager, right-click the USB controller entry and click the Properties tab. If there are any problems, a message appears in the Device Status window, depicted in Figure 9.12, describing any problems and suggesting what action to take.

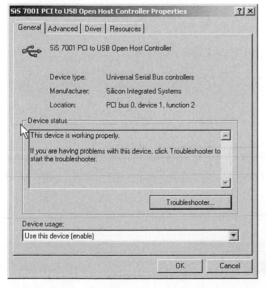

FIGURE 9.12 The USB Controller Properties page.

If the BIOS and controller settings appear to be correct, the next items to check are the USB port drivers. These ports have a separate entry in the Device Manager that you can access by clicking the Universal Serial Bus Controllers option, right-clicking the USB Root Hub entry, and then clicking the Properties tab.

If a USB device does not install itself automatically, you may have conflicting drivers loaded for that device, and you may need to remove them.

To use the Windows 2000/XP Professional Device Manager utility to troubleshoot USB problems in an administered network environment, you must be logged on as an administrator or as a member of the Administrators group.

To remove potentially conflicting USB drivers, follow these steps:

1. Disconnect any USB devices connected to the system and start the system in Safe Mode.

2. Under Windows 2000, you are asked about which operating system to use. Use the up-arrow and down-arrow keys to highlight Windows 2000 Professional or Windows 2000 Server, and then press Enter. If alert messages appear, read each alert and then click OK to close it.

3. Open the Device Manager, click the USB device, and then click the Remove option. Your particular USB device may be listed under the Universal Serial Bus Controller, Other Devices, Unknown Devices, or a particular device category (such as the Modem entry if the device is a USB modem).

4. Click the Start menu, select the Shut Down option followed by the Restart entry, and then click OK.

5. Connect the USB device directly to the USB port on your computer. If the system does not autodetect the device, you must install the drivers manually. You may need to obtain drivers from the device manufacturer to perform this installation.

You may encounter situations where mismatched USB ports and devices refuse to work together. In some older PCs that have USB 1.1, ports may not be able to work with some newer USB 2.0 devices. In these cases, the system may recognize the device but won't work with it.

EXAM ALERT

Be aware of the consequences of mixing USB 2.0 devices and USB 1.1 ports.

IEEE-1394 Adapters and Ports

Because Pentium-based PCs have largely adopted USB as the default high-speed bus, FireWire buses are implemented by installing an adapter card in the system to furnish the physical connection points. Many sound cards also provide IEEE-1394 connectors to handle transfer of high speed streaming audio between the card and other peripherals. Also, there is no direct BIOS support for IEEE-1394 buses in the typical PC. However, IEEE-1394 adapter cards are Plug and Play–compliant and can converse with the Windows operating systems.

The FireWire devices that attach to the bus connection do not communicate directly with the system; they work with the controller on the adapter card. Therefore, after the adapter card has been installed, you must troubleshoot it as you would any other adapter-card-based peripheral. The system should detect the new card when it is installed and load the driver for it automatically. If the system cannot locate the proper driver, it will present a prompt asking you to supply the location where the driver can be found.

Next, access the Device Manager to make sure that the device has been recognized there and to check for conflicting device driver information (for example, an exclamation point in a yellow circle). If the Device Manager cannot see the device after the proper driver has been loaded, and the attached device has power, the next step is to check the IEEE-1394 cabling and connectors for continuity and good connections. Also, verify that the correct FireWire cables are being used (a four-pin device cannot draw power through the FireWire bus). If the device employs its own power supply, make sure that power is being applied to it.

If the FireWire bus runs particularly slowly, and you have multiple devices attached to the system, you may have a situation where the slower device in the middle of the chain is slowing everything down. Move the slower device (such as a camcorder) to the end of the signal chain.

Legacy Port Problem Symptoms

Typical symptoms associated with legacy serial, parallel, or game port failures include the following:

- A 199, 432, or 90x IBM-compatible error code displays on the monitor (printer port).
- The online light is on, but no characters are printed by the printer.
- An 110x IBM-compatible error code displays on the monitor (serial port).

▶ A `Device Not Found` error message displays, or you have an unreliable connection.

▶ The input device does not work on the game port.

As you can see from the symptoms list, I/O ports do not tend to generate many error messages onscreen.

Basic Legacy Ports Check

Run a software diagnostic package to narrow the possible problem causes. Running a disk- or disc-based diagnostic program is not normally a problem in this situation because port failures do not generally affect the main components of the system. Software diagnostic packages usually require you to place a loopback test plug in the parallel or serial port connector to run tests on the port. The loopback plugs simulate a printer device by redirecting output signals from the port into port input pins.

Figure 9.13 describes the signal-rerouting scheme used in a parallel port loopback plug. The serial loopback plug is wired differently from a parallel loopback plug so that it can simulate the operation of a serial device.

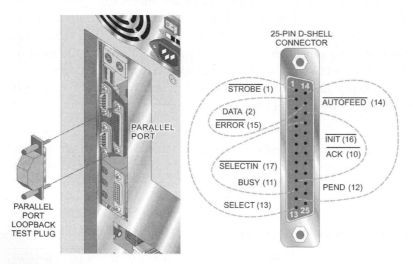

FIGURE 9.13 Parallel port loopback connections.

You can use a live printer with the port for testing purposes. However, this action elevates the possibility that the printer might inject a problem into the troubleshooting process. If there is a printer switch box between the computer and the printer, remove the print-sharing equipment, connect the computer directly to the printer, and try to print directly to the device. You can also use a live serial device with the port for testing purposes but, as with the printer, this elevates the possibility that nonport problems can be injected into the troubleshooting process.

EXAM ALERT

Be aware that print-sharing equipment (such as switch boxes) can be responsible for parallel port/printer problems and should be removed as part of port testing.

Troubleshooting Sound Cards

Some very basic components are involved in the audio output of most computer systems: a sound card, some speakers, the audio-related software, and the host computer system. Several software diagnostic packages enable you to test sound card operation. Most sound cards perform two separate functions. The first is to play sound files; the second is to record them. You may need to troubleshoot problems for either function.

Sound Card Configuration Checks

If sound problems are occurring in the multimedia system, two of the first things to check are the hardware and audio software configuration settings. Refer to the sound card manufacturer's documentation for proper installation and operating procedures.

Checking the system for resource conflicts in Windows is relatively easy. Access the System icon in the Control Panel and select the Hardware tab. From this point, click the Device Manager button and select the Sound, Video, and Game Controller option. If the system detects any conflicts, it places an exclamation point within a circle on the selected option. From the Device Manager, verify that the correct audio driver is installed and that its settings match those called for by the sound card manufacturer. If the driver is missing, or wrong, add the correct driver to the system through the Control Panel's Add/Remove Hardware Wizard (called Add Hardware in Windows XP). The main page of the sound card's Properties window displays all the resources the driver is using for the card. The Conflicting Devices List window provides information about any conflicting resource that the system has detected in conjunction with the sound card.

If the Windows PnP function is operating properly, you should be able to remove the driver from the system, reboot the computer, and allow the operating system to redetect the sound card and assign new resources to it. If the driver is not installed, or is incorrect, add the correct driver from the available drivers list. If the correct driver is not available, reinstall it from the card's OEM disk or obtain it from the card's manufacturer.

You should also check the volume and mute settings in the Windows environment to make sure that there is enough output to be heard. These settings are located under the Control Panel's Sounds and Audio Devices icon in Windows XP. There is a Windows audio device Troubleshooter button under the Hardware tab that will conduct a guided series of tests on the audio subsystem.

Sound Card Hardware Checks

Figure 9.14 depicts the system's sound-card–related components. Provided that the sound card's configuration is properly set, and the software configuration matches it, the sound card and speakers will need to be checked out if problems exist. Most of these checks are very simple. They include ensuring that the speakers are plugged in to the Speaker port. It is not uncommon for the speakers to be mistakenly plugged in to the card's MIC (microphone) port.

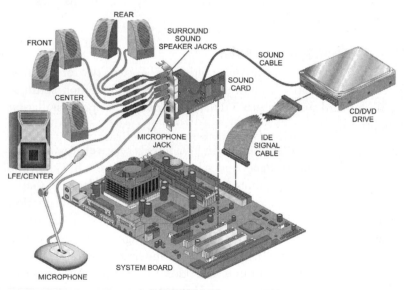

FIGURE 9.14 Sound-card-related components.

One common problem when dealing with audio output from a CD/DVD player is the sound cable that comes from the back of the drive and connects to the sound card or system board (for built-in audio adapters). If no sound is being produced from the CD/DVD drive, check this cable and connection.

Likewise, if the sound card will not record sound, make certain that the microphone is installed in the proper jack (not the speaker jack), and that it is turned on. Some microphones use batteries; check to see if this is so and that it is active. Check the amount of disk space available on the drive to ensure that there is enough to hold the file being produced.

In the case of stereo speaker systems, it is possible to place the speakers on the wrong sides. This will produce a problem when you try to adjust the balance between them. Increasing the volume on the right speaker will instead increase the output of the left speaker. The obvious cure for this problem is to physically switch the positions of the speakers.

EXAM ALERT

Know how to correct a balance problem that occurs with add-on stereo speakers.

If the system will not produce sound, troubleshoot the audio output portion of the system. Do the speakers require an external power supply? If so, is it connected, and are the speakers turned on? If the speakers use batteries for their power source, check them to see that they are installed and good. Check the speakers' volume setting to make certain they are not turned down.

Troubleshooting Front Panel Connections

Many system boards include additional embedded I/O port connectors that allow PC system manufacturers to create front panel–mounted versions of the systems' most popular ports. This approach provides customers with easier access to USB and IEEE-1394 ports, as well as removable media readers.

Other connections commonly mounted on the system's front panel include additional audio and video connections. This makes it easier for users to connect and disconnect peripherals such as speakers, microphones, and other A/V equipment to and from the system.

These connections are implemented on the system boards as BERG-pin connections, as illustrated in Figure 9.15. They connect to the front panel ports through extension cables supplied by the system board manufacturer. The ports can be enabled or disabled through the system's CMOS Setup utility.

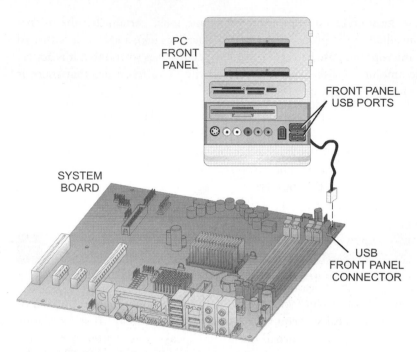

FIGURE 9.15 Front panel port connections.

If the front-mounted ports do not work, check the CMOS Setup to make sure that they are enabled there. Also check the connection to the system board. Finally, check the system board's documentation to determine that the correct cabling is being used because these port connection implementations may be proprietary to the system board manufacturer.

Exam Prep Questions

1. What is the first step in checking out electrical equipment that appears dead?

   ○ **A.** Check the power supply connection to the motherboard

   ○ **B.** Check the motherboard battery

   ○ **C.** Check to see that the power cord is plugged in

   ○ **D.** Check to see that the power light is on

2. What type of failures are hard-memory errors?

   ○ **A.** Infrequent errors in the OS and applications

   ○ **B.** RAM failures that generate NMI errors

   ○ **C.** Errors in the storage and retrieval of data to the hard drive

   ○ **D.** Errors caused by a physical jolt to the system

3. How can you correct soft-memory errors?

   ○ **A.** Replace the microprocessor.

   ○ **B.** Remove all RAM modules.

   ○ **C.** Replace all RAM modules.

   ○ **D.** Restart the computer.

4. What are the consequences of mixing RAM types and speeds within a system?

   ○ **A.** No effect.

   ○ **B.** The system will run slower.

   ○ **C.** Only part of the RAM will be recognized by the system.

   ○ **D.** A system crash.

5. What are the effects of heat buildup and microprocessor fan failure on the system?

   ○ **A.** The system locks up.

   ○ **B.** The system shuts down.

   ○ **C.** The system restarts.

   ○ **D.** The system slows down.

6. A defective _____ can cause the system to continually lose track of time.

  ○ **A.** RAM module

  ○ **B.** Microprocessor

  ○ **C.** Battery

  ○ **D.** BIOS ROM

7. What is a common condition that will produce a keyboard error message?

  ○ **A.** The operating system keyboard settings are incorrect.

  ○ **B.** A key is stuck down.

  ○ **C.** A key is stuck open.

  ○ **D.** The keyboard is plugged in wrong.

8. Which of the following connectors are used for devices that can be hot swapped?

  ○ **A.** Five-pin DIN

  ○ **B.** Six-pin PS/2 mini-DIN

  ○ **C.** RS-232C serial port

  ○ **D.** USB port

9. When you move the cursor across the screen, it randomly jumps and freezes. What should you do to correct this?

  ○ **A.** Replace the mouse.

  ○ **B.** Unplug the mouse and then plug it back in.

  ○ **C.** Reinstall the mouse driver.

  ○ **D.** Clean the dirt from inside the mouse.

10. What are the consequences of installing the FDD cable in reverse?

  ○ **A.** The FDD light stays on and erases the boot record on the disk.

  ○ **B.** The FDD doesn't spin.

  ○ **C.** The FDD light flashes, and the drive reads the disk but cannot write to it.

  ○ **D.** The FDD will still work normally.

11. What condition is indicated by the `Missing Operating System` error message?

   ○ **A.** The drive is not formatted.

   ○ **B.** The MBR is missing or corrupt.

   ○ **C.** Operating system files are missing or corrupt.

   ○ **D.** The HDD cable is not attached.

12. What condition is indicated by the `Hard Drive Boot Failure` error message?

   ○ **A.** The drive is not formatted.

   ○ **B.** The MBR is missing or corrupt.

   ○ **C.** Operating system files are missing or corrupt.

   ○ **D.** The HDD cable is not attached.

13. How many master drive selections are there for each IDE channel?

   ○ **A.** 1

   ○ **B.** 2

   ○ **C.** 3

   ○ **D.** 4

14. What does mixing IDE drive types on a single signal cable do?

   ○ **A.** It disables the master device.

   ○ **B.** It disables the slave device.

   ○ **C.** It disables both devices.

   ○ **D.** The system will work normally.

15. What action can be taken when you encounter an `Invalid Drive or Drive Specification` error message?

   ○ **A.** Reinstall the operating system.

   ○ **B.** Reformat the drive.

   ○ **C.** Repartition the drive.

   ○ **D.** Repartition and reformat the drive.

16. How can a CD be retrieved from a disabled CD-ROM drive?

    ○ **A.** Use a thin knife to gently pry the door open.

    ○ **B.** Press the Open/Close button.

    ○ **C.** Eject the disk using the operating system.

    ○ **D.** Insert a paper clip into the tray-release access hole in the front panel.

17. What must you do first if you want to troubleshoot a USB problem on a Windows 2000 system?

    ○ **A.** Open Device Manager.

    ○ **B.** Log on as a member of the Administrators group.

    ○ **C.** Select the USB driver and click the Properties button.

    ○ **D.** Restart the system.

18. How can a balance problem that occurs with add-on stereo speakers be corrected?

    ○ **A.** Replace the speakers.

    ○ **B.** Replace the sound card.

    ○ **C.** Adjust the sound balance in the operating system.

    ○ **D.** Swap the speaker positions.

19. You have been sent to a job location where the customer's new printer does not print from the host computer. When you arrive you find that the computer is running on the Windows 98 operating system and that a print-sharing switch box is inline between the computer and two different printers. The new printer is a laser printer and the old printer is an ink jet printer. The ink jet printer works fine. What action should you take?

    ○ **A.** Remove the printer-switching device.

    ○ **B.** Check for proper laser printer drivers.

    ○ **C.** Check to make sure that the parallel port is enabled in CMOS.

    ○ **D.** Set the printer port for basic SPP mode operation.

20. What action should be taken to clear up fuzzy characters on a CRT display?

    ○ **A.** Replace the video card.

    ○ **B.** Degauss the CRT.

    ○ **C.** Reinstall the video driver.

    ○ **D.** Reinstall the operating system.

21. What condition is indicated by the `Invalid Media Type` error message?

    ◯ **A.** The drive is not formatted.

    ◯ **B.** The MBR is missing or corrupt.

    ◯ **C.** Operating system files are missing or corrupt.

    ◯ **D.** The HDD cable is not attached.

22. When the system boots, you can hear the fans start, and the keyboard and drive lights flicker, but no display appears. What should you do first to troubleshoot this problem?

    ◯ **A.** Replace video card with a known-good one of the same type.

    ◯ **B.** Unplug the monitor from the video card and then plug it back in.

    ◯ **C.** Exchange the monitor with a known-good one of the same type.

    ◯ **D.** Replace the power supply with a known-good one of the same type.

23. Booting to Windows results in a distorted image that prevents you from manipulating the operating system. What can you do to correct this problem?

    ◯ **A.** Reboot the system to the command line.

    ◯ **B.** Boot to Safe Mode and reinstall/configure the driver.

    ◯ **C.** Replace the video card.

    ◯ **D.** Replace the monitor.

24. An Energy Star–compliant monitor _____.

    ◯ **A.** Uses more energy than non-Energy Star–compliant monitors

    ◯ **B.** Shuts off automatically

    ◯ **C.** Adjusts for room lighting automatically

    ◯ **D.** Switches to low-power mode when no signal change occurs for a given period of time

25. In newer systems, where are SCSI drive support and large drive support enabled?

    ◯ **A.** In the Device Manager

    ◯ **B.** In the CMOS Setup utility

    ◯ **C.** In the CONFIG.SYS file

    ◯ **D.** In the Registry

Answers and Explanations

1. C. Begin by checking the external connections of the power supply. This is the first step in checking any electrical equipment that shows no signs of life. For example, confirm that the power supply cord is plugged into a functioning outlet, and check the position of the On/Off switch.

2. B. Soft-memory errors are errors caused by infrequent and random glitches in the operation of applications and the system. You can clear these events just by restarting the system. Hard-memory errors are permanent physical failures that generate NMI errors in the system and require that the memory units be checked by substitution.

3. D. You can clear soft-memory errors just by restarting the system.

4. D. Make sure that the replacement RAM is consistent with the installed RAM. Mixing RAM types and speeds can cause the system to lock up and produce hard-memory errors.

5. A. If the system consistently locks up after being on for a few minutes, this is a good indication that the microprocessor's fan is not running or that some other heat buildup problem is occurring.

6. C. A defective motherboard battery can cause the system to continually lose track of time.

7. B. A stuck keyboard key will produce an error message when the system detects it.

8. D. Only the USB port has hot-swap capabilities. The standard sixpin PS/2 mini-DIN keyboards cannot be hot swapped. Neither can the standard RS-232C serial port. Doing so can cause damage to the keyboard, the port, and the system board.

9. D. Most of the problems associated with mice involve the trackball. As the mouse is moved across the table, the trackball picks up dirt or lint, which can hinder the movement of the trackball, typically evident by the cursor periodically freezing and jumping onscreen. On most mice, you can remove the trackball from the mouse by using a latching mechanism on its bottom. Twisting the latch counterclockwise enables you to remove the trackball. Then you can clean dirt out of the mouse.

10. A. When the FDD signal cable is reversed, the FDD activity light stays on constantly and the boot record on the disk will be erased.

11. B. A `Missing Operating System` message indicates that the disk's master boot record is missing or has become corrupt.

12. B. A `Hard Drive Boot Failure` message indicates that the disk's master boot record is missing or has become corrupt.

13. A. There can be only one master drive selection on each IDE channel.

14. C. Mixing IDE device types will create a situation in which the system cannot provide the different types of control information each device needs. The drives are incompatible, and you may not be able to access either device.

15. D. If the system cannot see the drive after booting to the disk, an `Invalid Drive` message or an `Invalid Drive Specification` message may be displayed in response to any attempt to access the drive. First, partition the drive and then install an operating system to make the drive usable.

16. D. If the CD-ROM drive is inoperable and there is a CD locked inside, you should insert a straightened paper clip into the tray-release access hole that's usually located beside the ejection button. This will release the spring-loaded tray and pop out the disc.

17. B. To use the Windows 2000/XP Device Manager utility to troubleshoot USB problems, you must be logged on as an administrator, or as a member of the Administrators group.

18. D. In the case of stereo speaker systems, it is possible to place the speakers on the wrong sides. This will produce a problem when you try to adjust the balance between them. Increasing the volume on the right speaker will increase the output of the left speaker, and vice versa. The obvious cure for this problem is to physically switch the positions of the speakers.

19. A. You should remove the printer-switching mechanism and try to print directly from the computer. The fact that two different types of printers are attached to the port through the switch should indicate that the drivers being used are not correct for the laser printer. However, you should still check the printer directly from the port.

20. B. There can be several causes of fuzzy characters on the display. The first step in checking out this problem is to reset the display resolution to standard VGA values. If the fuzzy characters remain, check the intensity and contrast controls to see if they are out of adjustment. Finally, you may need to remove built-up electromagnetic fields from the screen through a process called *degaussing*. This can be done using a commercial degaussing coil; however, newer monitors have built-in degaussing circuits that can be engaged through their front panel controls. These

monitors usually perform a degauss operation each time they are turned on; however, sometimes the user may need to perform this operation.

21. A. An `Invalid Media Type` message indicates that the controller cannot find a recognizable track/sector pattern on the drive.

22. B. If the video problem produces a blank display, disconnect the monitor's signal cable from its video adapter card. If a raster appears, a video card problem is indicated.

23. B. If the Windows video problem prevents you from seeing the desktop, restart the system, press the F8 function key when the Starting Windows message appears, and select Safe Mode. This should load Windows with the standard 640×480×16-color VGA driver (the most fundamental driver available for VGA monitors) and should furnish a starting point for installing the correct driver for the monitor being used.

24. D. If the monitor is an EPA-certified, Energy Star–compliant, power-saving monitor, it can revert to a low-power mode when it does not receive a signal change for a given period of time.

25. B. Check the CMOS Setup utility to make sure that SCSI support has been enabled, along with large SCSI drive support.

Challenge Solutions

1. You should tell the customer that you think that his system board battery is defective, or that its charging circuitry is bad. If a system refuses to maintain time and date information, check the backup battery and check the contacts of the battery holder for corrosion. Tell the customer to remove the system board battery if possible and clean its contacts with a contact cleaner or by gently using a pencil eraser. If cleaning the battery terminals does not cause the clock to keep proper time, replace the battery with a new one and allow it to completely charge.

2. If you install a new mouse in a working system and it does not work when you restart the system, chances are very good that the driver software or a port configuration setting must be the cause of the failure.

3. Because the system's light comes on and the hard drive spins, you can at least initially conclude that the system has power and that the power supply is working (although you might want to rethink these assumptions in some rare cases). The single beep indicates that the system has made it

through the POST test and that most of the basic hardware (including the video controller) is working; however, the POST tests cannot check the monitor's internal operation (only its video adapter). Therefore, you should bring a replacement monitor to swap out the existing one. The presence of the light on the monitor indicates only that it is plugged in and turned on—not that it is working. If swapping the monitor does not clear up the problem, check the video driver to make sure that it is correct, and replace the video adapter card last.

4. Check the drive to make sure that the master/slave jumper setting is set properly for the drive's logical position in the system. There can be only one master drive selection on each IDE channel. If you have more than one device attached to a single interface cable, make sure that all the devices are of the same type (for example, all are EIDE devices or all are ATA100 devices). Mixing IDE device types can create a situation where the system cannot provide the different types of control information each device needs. The drives are incompatible and you may not be able to access either device.

CHAPTER TEN

Portable Computer Fundamentals

Terms you'll need to understand:

- ✓ AC adapter
- ✓ DC adapter
- ✓ Battery
- ✓ Docking station
- ✓ Port replicator
- ✓ LCD panel
- ✓ PCMCIA
- ✓ Mini PCI
- ✓ Function (Fn) key
- ✓ Bluetooth
- ✓ Infrared

- ✓ Cellular
- ✓ Stylus/digitizer
- ✓ ACPI
- ✓ Touch pad
- ✓ Pointing stick/track point
- ✓ Backlight
- ✓ Notebook computer
- ✓ PC Card
- ✓ Native resolution
- ✓ Active matrix
- ✓ Passive matrix

Techniques you'll need to master:

Essentials 2.1—Identify the fundamental principles of using laptops and portable devices.

- ✓ Identify names, purposes and characteristics of laptop-specific
  - ✓ Form factors, such as memory and hard drives
  - ✓ Peripherals (such as docking station, port replicator, and media/accessory bay)
  - ✓ Expansion slots (PCMCIA I, II, and III, card, and express bus)

- ✓ Ports (for instance, mini PCI slot)
- ✓ Communication connections (such as Bluetooth, infrared, cellular WAN, ethernet)
- ✓ Power and electrical input devices (such as auto-switching and fixed-input power supplies, batteries)

✓ LCD technologies (active and passive matrix; resolution such as XGA, SXGA+, UXGA, WUXGA; contrast radio; native resolution)

✓ Input devices (such as stylus/digitizer, function [Fn] keys, and pointing devices such as touch pad, point stick, and track point)

✓ Identify and distinguish between mobile and desktop motherboards and processors, including throttling, power management, and Wi-Fi.

Essentials 2.2—Install, configure, optimize, and upgrade laptops and portable devices.

✓ Configure power management.

✓ Identify the features of BIOS-ACPI.

✓ Identify the difference between suspend, hibernate, and standby.

✓ Demonstrate safe removal of laptop-specific hardware such as peripherals, hot-swappable devices, and non-hot-swappable devices.

Depot Tech 2.1/IT Tech 2.1—Identify the fundamental principles of using laptops and portable devices.

✓ Identify appropriate applications for laptop-specific communication connections, for example:

  ✓ Bluetooth

  ✓ Infrared devices

  ✓ Cellular WAN

  ✓ Ethernet

✓ Identify appropriate laptop-specific power and electrical input devices and determine how amperage and voltage can affect performance.

✓ Identify the major components of the LCD including inverter, screen, and video card.

Depot Tech 2.2/ IT Tech 2.2—Install, configure, optimize, and upgrade laptops and portable devices.

✓ Demonstrate the safe removal of laptop-specific hardware including peripherals, hot-swappable, and non-hot-swappable devices.

✓ Identify/describe the effect of video sharing on memory upgrades.

Inside Portables

This chapter covers the names, purposes, and characteristics of portable PC systems area of the CompTIA A+ Certification—Essentials examination under Objective 2.1. It also covers the Install, configure, optimize and upgrade laptops and portable devices areas of the CompTIA A+ Certification—Essentials examination under Objective 2.2.

Portable computers represent a large and growing portion of the personal computer market. Therefore, the computer technician must be aware of how they vary from traditional desktop units. Every technician should be aware of typical portable computer components that can be exchanged in the field. A technician should be able to install, connect, and configure these components to upgrade or repair an existing system.

Portable computers typically contain all the devices that users need to perform work away from the office; however, there are additional items that users have become accustomed to using with their computers. For this reason, portables offer a wide range of I/O and expansion options to accommodate external Field Replacement Unit (FRU) devices.

NOTE

A major portion of Depot Tech Objective 2.2 and IT Tech Objective 2.2 is identical to the material in Essentials Objective 2.2. Also, the DT 2.2 and IT 2.2 objectives use the same wording about removal of portable peripherals (hot-swap and non-hot-swap devices) and the impact of video sharing memory in portables.

Depot Tech Objective 2.1 and IT Tech Objective 2.1 use different formats to say the same things about communications connections, power and electrical input devices, and major LCD display components.

The topics specified in these different exam/objective areas are so closely stated that it makes sense that they are presented as the same discussion. You will need to study this material in this chapter for any of the four exams you intend to challenge.

Portable computers have two ideal characteristics: They are compact and lightweight. Portable PC designers work constantly to decrease the size and power consumption of all the computer's components. Special low-power chipsets and disk drives have been developed to extend battery life.

EXAM ALERT

Be aware that portable PCs are different from desktop PCs in that their major concerns center on power consumption and thermal handling capabilities.

Portable cases have been designed to be as small as they can be while providing as many standard features as possible. Figure 10.1 shows the inside of a typical portable computer. Notice how the components are interconnected by the design. The system board is designed so that it wraps around other components whose form factors cannot be altered—such as the disk drive units. The components also tend to be layered in portable designs. Disk drives cover portions of the system board, whereas the keyboard unit covers nearly everything. The internal battery may slide into a cutout area of the system board, or more likely, it may be located beneath the system board.

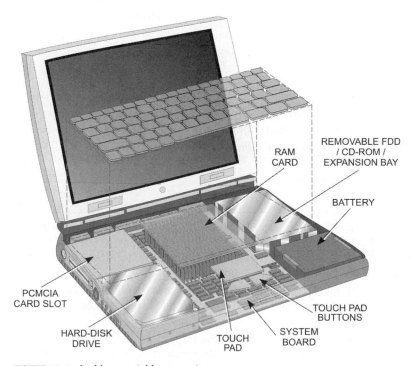

RAM CARD

REMOVABLE FDD / CD-ROM / EXPANSION BAY

BATTERY

PCMCIA CARD SLOT

TOUCH PAD BUTTONS

HARD-DISK DRIVE

TOUCH PAD

SYSTEM BOARD

FIGURE 10.1 Inside a portable computer.

Portable System Boards

System boards for portable computers are not designed to fit a standardized form factor, as illustrated in Figure 10.2. Instead they are designed to fit around all the components that must be installed in the system. Therefore, system boards used in portable computers tend to be proprietary to the model they are designed for. Mounting hole positions are determined by where they will best suit the placement of the other system components.

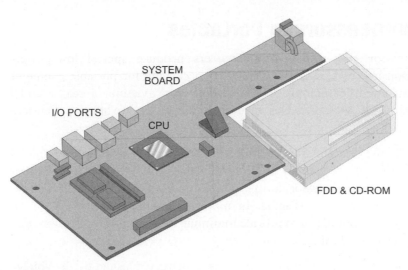

SYSTEM
BOARD

I/O PORTS

CPU

FDD & CD-ROM

FIGURE 10.2   Typical notebook system board.

The second item to notice is that none of the "standard" expansion slots or adapter cards is present on the portable's system board. These system board designs typically include the standard I/O and video circuitry as an integral part of the board. They also provide the physical connections for the unit's parallel and serial I/O ports, as well as onboard connectors for the disk drives, display unit, and keyboard units.

The computer's external I/O connections, such as serial and parallel port connectors, are arranged on the system board so that they align with the corresponding openings in the portable case. It would be highly unlikely that a system board from another portable would match these openings. On the maintenance side, a blown parallel-port circuit would require that the entire system board be replaced to correct the problem. In a desktop unit, a simple I/O card could be installed in an expansion slot to overcome such a situation.

The most widely used I/O connections in most notebook computers include of two or more USB ports, an external VGA monitor connector, a built-in LAN connection, a built-in modem port, the external microphone and speaker jack sound card connections, and a pair of PC Card slots. Older notebooks included legacy parallel printer ports, PS/2 external mouse/keyboard connectors, and proprietary docking port expansion buses. With most portable systems, the different port connectors are located on the back and sides of the unit. Other models may place most of their port connectors on the back of the unit. Some connectors may be hidden behind hinged doors for protection. These doors usually snap closed.

Microprocessors in Portables

Microprocessor and chipset manufacturers produce special low-power-consumption microprocessors and chipsets specifically for portable computer systems. Standard Pentium processors produce large amounts of heat, even by desktop standards. Most portables currently in the market are based on Pentium devices.

To minimize the heat buildup condition, Intel has produced a complete line of mobile Pentium processors for use in portable systems. Mobile devices differ from standard microprocessor devices in terms of both their internal construction and their external packaging. In mobile microprocessors, both design aspects have been optimized to provide minimum size and power consumption, as well as maximum heat reduction.

The mobile Pentium MMX processor was constructed using Intel's Voltage Reduction Technology, which enables the processor to run at lower core voltages (1.8–2.0 Vdc) and thereby consume less energy and generate less heat. The package style created for the mobile Pentium is referred to as a *Tape Carrier Package (TCP)*. The microprocessor chip is embedded in a polyimide film (tape) that is laminated with a copper foil. The leads of the IC are etched into the foil and attached to the processor.

The tape package arrangement makes the mobile package much smaller and lighter than the pin grid array (PGA) and staggered pin grid array (SPGA) packages used with the standard Pentium devices. It also mounts directly to the PC board instead of plugging into a bulky heavy socket. A special insertion machine cuts the strip of microprocessors into individual 24mm units as it is soldered to the system board. The system board furnishes a heat sink area beneath the processor that helps to dissipate heat. A layer of thermal conductive paste is applied to this connection prior to the soldering process to increase the heat transfer away from the processor. This design enables the full-featured Pentium processor to run at competitive speeds without additional heat sinks and fan modules. The cross-section of the complete mobile Pentium attachment is depicted in Figure 10.3.

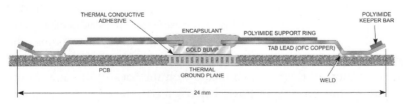

FIGURE 10.3 The mobile Pentium installation.

The attachment of the mobile microprocessor to a system board makes the arrangement permanent for all practical purposes. To allow for microprocessor upgrading, portable system boards often employ mobile processors mounted on plug-in daughter boards, or modules. Intel produced two Pentium plug-in variations. One is a mobile Pentium mounted on a 4 inch by 2.5 inch by 0.3 inch mobile module, referred to as an *MMO*. This module is attached to the system board via screws and plugs through a 280-pin connector. The other Intel module is a minicartridge for the Pentium II.

Pentium IIIM and 4M Processors

With the Pentium IIIM and Pentium 4M processors, Intel began to design mobile processors with a real concentration on the needs of portable computers. Intel's previous mobile processor designs were all based on processors designed specifically for desktop computers. Even with Intel's efforts to design more mobile-friendly processors, the core architecture of these processors was still based on desktop processor cores. This continued to limit the amount of power savings that Intel could engineer into the finished products.

The Pentium IIIM design included the following:

- ▶ 1.2GHz core
- ▶ 133MHz FSB
- ▶ 512KB L2 cache
- ▶ Socket 478
- ▶ 830 chipset

Likewise, the Pentium 4M design included the following:

- ▶ 2.6GHz core
- ▶ 400MHz FSB
- ▶ 512KB L2 cache
- ▶ Socket 478
- ▶ i845MP chipset

Both processors were built on 0.13 micron technology and provide a number of power-saving features not found in the desktop versions of these processors. These features include the enhanced SpeedStep technology that enables the system to be throttled back based on software performance requirements, and a Deeper Sleep Alert State that enables the processor to run on very little power and still be capable of waking up very rapidly.

Pentium M Processors

The Pentium M processor was the first line of Intel mobile processors designed specifically to address the limitations of earlier mobile processors. The *Wall Street Journal* carried a very interesting column about the difficulties Intel had in changing the mindset of its design engineers in producing new notebook systems for the market. The engineers had been so conditioned to produce the next fast processor that when the company identified that notebook users really wanted extended battery life and integrated networking, Intel had to become very stern with the engineers to get them to think in terms of slower processors and different chipset features to achieve the desired results.

The Pentium M brought together a Pentium III core with a Pentium 4 bus interface (instead of using a modified desktop Pentium 4). The processor core has been optimized for greater power saving to provide extended battery life. The voltage level for standard Pentium M processors is a low 1.5V. Low and ultra-low version cores run on 1.18V and 1.1V, respectively. The Pentium M processor's power dissipation varies from 5 watts when idle to 27 watts when fully loaded.

The Pentium M processors also employ a more flexible SpeedStep technology that provides better control of the system's clock frequency and Mobile Voltage Positioning (MVP IV) technology, which dynamically lowers voltage based on processor activity to reduce power usage based on the tasks it is performing. For example, a 1.6GHz Pentium M can throttle its clock speeds to 600MHz, 800MHz, 1000MHz, 1200MHz, 1400MHz, and 1600MHz. Older mobile processors such as the Pentium 4M had fewer possible steps to work with.

The Pentium M processors are combined with improved, power-efficient Intel 915 Express and 855 chipsets to provide notebook computers that can operate for five or more hours on a single battery. Pentium M versions come in a variety of core clock speeds ranging from 1GHz to 2.26GHz that feature 400 and 533 FSB speeds. They also employ 478-pin Micro FCPGA, 479-pin Micro FCBGA packaging, and ZIF socket technology that is designed to provide a range of thinner processors. Execute-disable bit technology has been included to prevent certain classes of malicious buffer overflow attacks when combined with a supporting operating system. Intel also modified the 1MB and 2MB L2 cache structures so that they avoid turning on sections of the cache that are not being used. This technique significantly decreases power usage associated with the cache.

The first Pentium M processors (Banias) were built using .13 micron technology and either carried no identifying number scheme or a 705 number. Advanced versions (Dothan) began to show up using a 7XX numbering series that does not relate directly with the processor's clock speed. The Dothan versions are built on 90nm technology that provides decreased power consumption.

Centrino

In its battle to change the perception of performance associated with portable PCs, Intel introduced a product badging system, called *Centrino*, that identified the product as supporting those qualities that Intel had determined were essential for portable computers. A massive Centrino advertising campaign was designed to focus customer attention away from sheer clock speed as the major factor in defining performance. Intel also decided to stop using clock speed as part of the processor's specification.

The major emphasis of the Centrino specification is that the chipsets and the Pentium M processors deliver outstanding performance while providing lower power usage. Users can use these systems to work for up to five hours without having to swap the battery or plug into an external power source. This relates to being able to work on a cross-country flight without having to give up halfway across the country. The second emphasis point in the Centrino specification is seamless, built-in wireless networking.

Pentium M Celerons

Intel produced its original Banias 512 Celeron M processor by removing half of the L2 cache from a Pentium M processor. It followed up with a Dothan 1024 Celeron M version that had half the cache of the 90nm Pentium M versions. All the Pentium M Celeron processors are designed to fit the Socket 479 specification and feature a 400MHz FSB rating. Core speeds for the different Celeron M versions range from 900MHz to 1.7GHz.

Intel produced a more advanced Yonah 1024 Pentium M based on its advanced Core Solo processor designed for desktop units. This processor boosted the front side bus speed to 533MHz and brought XD-bit protection to the Celeron M series. However, it still has only half the L2 cache of the Pentium M processors. The Yonah version of the Celeron M processor employs the FCPGA6 (478-pin) package and socket.

The other Celeron M version in production is the Northwood 256 processor. The L2 cache in this version of the Celeron M is only 256KB. This Celeron version employs a Socket 478 design and 400MHz FSB. Different Northwood versions have been produced with Core frequencies between 1.4GHz and 2.5GHz.

None of these units supports the variable clock speed SpeedStep functionality, and their battery life characteristics are much shorter than the standard Pentium M–powered systems. By definition, any portable computers based on one of the Celeron M processors cannot be branded with the Centrino label.

Core Duo Processors

Intel has unveiled a series of special low-power-consumption dual-core processors for mobile computing environments. Intel branded these products under the Intel Core Duo product name. They are mainly found in Intel's high-end Centrino mobile products and in some new Viiv applications.

As with the Pentium D and Pentium EE products used in desktop PCs, the Core Duo processors are optimized for multithreaded applications and multitasking operations. They can simultaneously execute multiple applications such as graphics-intensive games or serious computing applications while downloading large audio/video files from the Internet or running antivirus security programs in the background. In addition, special energy-efficient power-management technologies built in to the Core Duo architecture transfer power only to those areas of the processor that need it, thereby enabling laptops to save power.

Structurally, the Core Duo processor consists of two Pentium cores, a 2MB L2 cache that is shared by the two cores, and a bus arbiter that coordinates the activities of the L2 cache and FSB accesses. These processors communicate with the system board's chipset over a 166MHz quad-pumped (667MHz) front side bus. Figure 10.4 depicts a Core Duo processor.

FIGURE 10.4   The Core Duo processor.

At the same time the Core Duo was rolled out, Intel also introduced the Core Solo processor, which is a single-core version of the Core Duo product. Like the Core Duo, the Core Solo processor communicates with the chipset using a 667MHz FSB. Future versions of the Core Duo processor are scheduled to have a BIOS-configurable option that will permit one of the Cores to be turned off to reduce power consumption.

Intel has implemented a naming scheme for its Core processors that uses a T to mark a performance processor and an L to mark a low-power processor. The letters are followed by a four-digit code that, like the Pentium M, is not directly related to clock speed as performance.

Both Core processors employ the 478-pin FCPGA6 package and socket. However, the pinout of these processors and new chipset functions make the Core processors incompatible with previous Pentium M system boards. The Core Duo is matched up with the 945GTExpress chipset that delivers a 533/667 FSB and supports up to 4GB of dual channel DDR 667 memory. The chipset also provides PCIe x16 expansion slots and 3GBps SATA interfaces for PCs. In addition, the Core Duo became the first Intel processor to be used in Apple Macintosh production systems.

AMD Mobile Processors

Not to be outdone, AMD has continued to press ahead with its own line of mobile processors. These inlcude the AMD mobile Athlon, Athlon 64, Sempron, and Turion 64 and 64 X2 mobile processors.

AMD produced a wide array of Socket-A–compatible mobile processors. These include several mobile Athlon 4, and Athlon XP, Athlon XP-M processors. These processors featured 128KB, 256KB, or 512KB L2 cache options and 200MHz or 266MHz FSB ratings. One variation, the Athlon XP-M Dublin, featured 126/256KB L2 cache and the 800MHz HyperTransport technology discussed in Chapter 3, "Processors." Clock speeds for these processors range from 850MHz to 2.2GHz.

The mobile Athlon 64 processors increased the performance of AMD's mobile processor line by offering 512KB/1024KB L2 caches along with 800MHz HyperTransport technology. All of these processors are Socket-754–based and run at clock speeds between 1.6GHz and 2.6GHz.

The mobile Sempron processors are available in several Socket 754-compatible versions and a low-power Socket S1 version. The Sempron processors feature either 128KB, 256KB, or 512KB L2 caches and 800MHz HyperTransport interfacing. They are also available in 1.6GHz, 1.8GHz, 2.0GHz, and 2.2GHz frequencies.

Turion is the product name AMD has assigned to its newest line of 64-bit mobile processors. These processors compete with the Intel Pentium M and dual core processors. The Turion 64 is Socket-754–compatible and feature full speed 512KB or 1024KB L2 cache. These processors also make use of the 800MHz HyperTransport technology.

The Turion 64 X2 is a dual core mobile processor designed to compete with the dual core Intel processors. These processors are designed for Socket S1 and to work with DDR2 800 memory modules. The Turion 64 X2 processors employ a full-speed 256KB or 512KB L2 cache per core, and an 800MHz HyperTransport interface that provides a bandwidth of 10.7GBps.

Portable Memory

A special form factor DIMM, called the *Small Outline DIMM (SODIMM)*, has been developed for use in notebook computers. SODIMMs are significantly smaller than the standard DIMM so that they take up less space in notebook computers. Figure 10.5 depicts a 72-pin, a 144-pin, and a 200-pin SODIMM. The 72-pin SODIMM has a 32-bit data bus, whereas the 144-pin version is 64 bits wide.

> **EXAM ALERT**
>
> Know what types of memory devices are commonly used in portable PCs.

A new small form factor memory module referred to as *MicroDIMM* has been introduced for the micro devices market (subnotebook PCs) where size and performance are crucial. These units are nearly square 144-pin 32Mb×64 plug-in modules that are available with either SDRAM or DDR RAM components on board. Figure 10.6 shows a MicroDIMM module. MicroDIMMs are approximately 1.54 inches (38.0 mm) by approximately 1 inch (25.4 mm) high and unlike SODIMMs do not have any notches along their edge connector contacts. The height of MicroDIMM modules varies among different manufacturers.

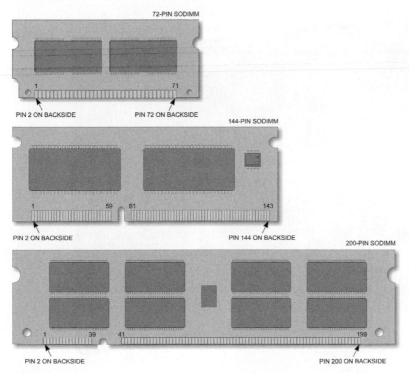

FIGURE 10.5   SODIMM packages.

A microDIMM module slides into a specialized spring-loaded socket where two plastic clips snap into place to hold it securely. To release the module from the socket, simply spread the clips apart and the spring will shove the module out of the socket.

Challenge #1

Your friend has brought you his notebook computer and wants you to upgrade the memory in it. He has also brought several 184-pin 512MB RIMM modules that he had in his office. What can you tell your friend about his upgrade?

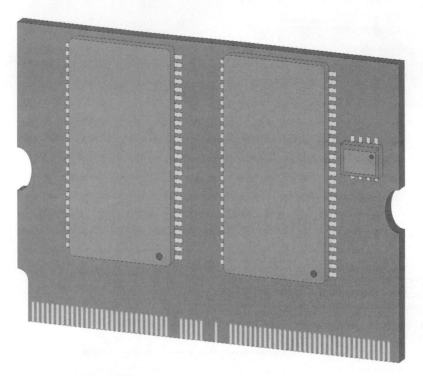

FIGURE 10.6 MicroDIMM.

Upgrading Portable Memory

The key to upgrading or replacing internal RAM in a portable computer can be found in its documentation. Only memory modules recommended by the portable manufacturer should be installed, and only in the configurations suggested.

The voltage level support for the memory devices in portable computers is very critical. Using RAM devices that electrically overload this supply will cause memory errors to occur.

If the type of RAM device being installed is not one of the recommended types, the notebook might not be able to recognize the new memory. If the new RAM is being added to expand the existing banks of memory, the system might not recognize this additional RAM. The problem will show up in the form of a short memory count during the POST routines. However, if only the new RAM type is installed, the system could present a number of different symptoms, including the following:

▶ Not working at all

▶ Giving beep-coded error messages

▶ Producing soft memory errors

▶ Producing short memory counts in the POST

▶ Locking up while booting the operating system

EXAM ALERT

Know why notebook computers show short memory counts during the bootup process.

As with disk drives, changing memory in a portable PC may involve disassembling the computer case. Figure 10.7 shows the replacement of a SODIMM module in a particular notebook computer. The location of and process of accessing the memory in the unit vary from manufacturer to manufacturer and from model to model. You should always disconnect the AC power adapter from the portable and remove its battery before removing and replacing its memory modules.

EXAM ALERT

Be aware that it is good practice to remove all power sources from the portable PC before upgrading its memory.

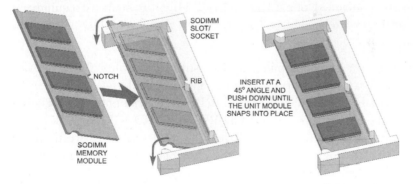

FIGURE 10.7 Replacing a SODIMM module.

In notebook computers, it is also possible to increase memory by installing PC Card–based memory cards, described later in this chapter. These memory units can increase the portable computer's memory capabilities without the need to take it apart. In addition, they can be removed when additional memory space is not in high demand. A newer memory add-on technology that has found some favor in the notebook computer arena is the USB plug-in memory module.

Portable PCs typically use a technique called *shared video memory*. Under shared memory, the system uses a portion of its main memory to hold screen information for the display. In desktop PCs this memory is distributed to the video adapter card. The disadvantage of shared memory is that it takes up RAM that applications would normally use. In addition, DRAM devices used for system memory are typically not as fast as specialized video memory used on standalone display adapter cards. System performance also suffers because of bus contention issues created by the processor and video controller requiring access to the same memory devices. If you are upgrading memory in the portable system, you must take into account that the amount of RAM available for use by the system will not be the same as the installed RAM.

> **EXAM ALERT**
>
> Be aware that in portable PCs that employ shared video memory, the amount of installed RAM and the amount of reported RAM will be different.

Portable Drives

Smaller 2 1/2-inch form-factor hard disk drives (HDD), low-profile 3 1/2-inch floppy disk drives (FDD), and combination FDD/CD-ROM drives have been developed to address the portable computer market's need for compact devices. Older portables included one FDD and one HDD as standard equipment. Newer models tend to include a CD-ROM drive and an HDD as standard internal units.

More expensive notebook computers may substitute a DVD or CD-RW drive for the standard CD-ROM drive. Although internal DVD-RW drives can be installed in portable computers, they tend to be installed in only very high-end versions. On the other hand, external CD-RW and DVD-RW units are widely used with portable computers. These drive units are described in greater detail later in this chapter. Figure 10.8 shows the placement of drives in a notebook unit that includes one of each drive type.

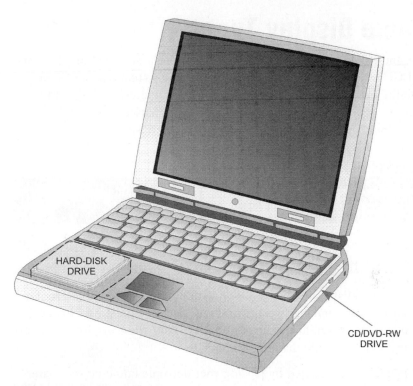

FIGURE 10.8 Portable disk drives.

Upgrading/Replacing Portable Drives

Some portable PC models include swappable drive bays that enable the combination of internal drives in the unit to be changed as dictated by the work being performed. In some units, a disk drive that is not needed for a particular task may be removed and replaced by an extra battery. Three basic considerations should be observed when replacing disk drives in a portable computer:

- ▸ Their physical size and layout
- ▸ Their power consumption
- ▸ Whether the BIOS supports the new drive

Replacing an internal disk drive in a portable computer typically involves taking the computer case apart to gain access to the drive. Some older portables did feature hot-swappable internal drives, but these units have largely disappeared from the portable market.

Portable Display Types

Notebook and laptop computers use non-CRT displays, such as Liquid Crystal Display (LCD) and gas-plasma panels. These display systems are well suited to the portability needs of portable computers. They are much lighter and more compact than CRT monitors and require much less electrical energy to operate. Both types of display units can be operated from batteries.

EXAM ALERT

Know that notebook display panels are powered by a low-voltage DC power source such as a battery or converter.

Liquid Crystal Displays

The most common flat-panel displays used with portable PCs are LCDs. They are relatively thin, flat, and lightweight, and require very little power to operate. In addition to reduced weight and improved portability, these displays offer better reliability and longer life than CRT units.

The LCD panel is constructed by placing thermotropic liquid crystal material between two sheets of glass. A set of electrodes is attached to each sheet of glass. Horizontal (row) electrodes are attached to one glass plate; vertical (column) electrodes are fitted to the other plate. These electrodes are transparent and let light pass through. A picture element or pixel is created in the liquid crystal material at each spot where a row and a column electrode intersect. Special plates called *polarizers* are added to the front and back of the display.

The complete LCD panel is mounted in a frame that also contains the control circuitry for the panel's electrode matrix. In a notebook computer, the frame is mounted between the two halves of its flip-up display housing. The display is physically attached to the body of the notebook by a pair of built-in hinges. The display is free to rotate around a pair of rods in the main body. Electrically, a single cable is generally used to connect the entire panel assembly to the system board using a plug-and-socket arrangement.

When an LCD panel fails, the most common repair is to replace the entire display panel/housing assembly. To replace the LCD panel, you must use an identical panel to ensure that it fits the plastic display housing. The upper half of the notebook body must be removed to provide access for plugging the display's signal cable into the system board.

LCD Operation

When a pixel is off, the molecules of the liquid crystal twist from one edge of the material to the other, as depicted in Figure 10.9. The spiral effect created by the twist polarizes light and prevents it from passing through the display. When an electric field is created between a row and a column electrode, the molecules move, lining up perpendicular to the front of the display. This permits light to pass through the display, producing a single dot onscreen.

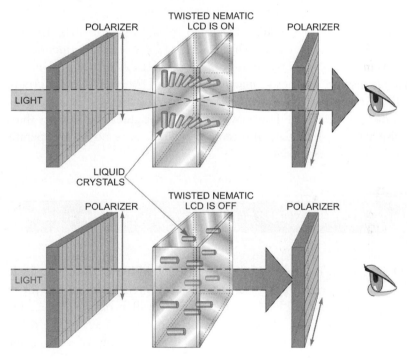

FIGURE 10.9 LCD operation.

Depending on the orientation of the polarizers, the energized pixels can be made to look like a dark spot on a light screen or a light dot on a dark screen. In most notebook computers, the display is lit from behind the panel. This is referred to as *backlighting*. The level of backlighting is controlled through a small adjustable wheel built in to the LCD panel's housing.

Because no current passes through the display to light the pixels, the power consumption of LCD displays is very low. The screen is scanned by sequentially activating the panel's row and column electrodes. The pixels appear to be continuously lit because the scanning rate is very high. The electrodes can be controlled (turned on and off) using very low DC voltage levels. LCDs constructed in this manner are referred to as *dual-scan*, or *passive-matrix*, displays. Advanced passive-matrix technologies are referred to as *Color Super-Twist Nematic (CSTN)* and *Double-layer Super-Twist Nematic (DSTN)* displays.

EXAM ALERT

Know what type of electrical power is used by an LCD panel.

An improved type of LCD is similar in design to the passive-matrix designs, except that it places a transistor at each of the matrix row-column junctions to improve switching times. This technology produces an LCD display type called an *active-matrix* display. The active matrix is produced by using thin-film transistor (TFT) arrays to create between one and four transistors for each pixel on a flexible, transparent film. TFT displays tend to be brighter and sharper than dual-scan displays; however, they also tend to require more power to operate and are therefore more expensive.

EXAM ALERT

Be aware of the technologies available for LCD displays and which is more desirable.

Color LCD displays are created by adding a three-color filter to the panel. Each pixel in the display corresponds to a red, blue, or green dot on the filter. Activating a pixel behind a blue dot on the filter will produce a blue dot onscreen. Like color CRT displays, the dot color on the screen of the color LCD panel is established by controlling the relative intensities of a three-dot (RGB) pixel cluster.

The images produced by color LCD panels are heavily influenced by the backlight that shines through the panel and provides its brightness. The backlight also alters the actual color of the pixels produced on the screen and tends to wash them out. The measure of how distinguishable colors are on a video display is its *contrast ratio*. The higher this value, the better the colors should appear on the screen. However, with LCD and other flat panel displays, this specification can be misleading. The quality of the image is affected by the angle at which it is viewed.

The construction of LCD displays prevents them from providing multiple resolution options like an adapter-driven CRT display can. The resolution of the LCD display is dictated by the construction of the LCD panel, and this value is known as its *native resolution*. To display image signals specified in higher or lower resolutions (DVD, HDTV, and so on) requires the video display system to convert the image to the native resolution to be displayed correctly.

If the display image has more pixels than the display's native resolution, it will lose some of its picture information and sharpness when displayed. On the other hand, if the image has fewer pixels than the display, you will see all the pixels displayed, but there will be no increased quality because of the additional resolution capabilities of the display. The additional picture elements added to fill in the image may make the image look worse.

The life and usefulness of the portable's LCD panel can be extended through proper care and handling. The screen should be cleaned periodically with a glass cleaner and a soft, lint-free cloth. Spray the cleaner on the cloth and then wipe the screen. Never spray the cleaner directly on the screen. Also, avoid scratching the surface of the screen. It is relatively easy to damage the front polarizer of the display. Take care to remove any liquid droplets from the screen because they can cause permanent staining. After cleaning, allow 30 minutes for complete drying.

The screen should be shielded from bright sunlight and heat sources. Moving the computer from a warmer location to a cold location can cause damaging moisture to condense inside the housing (including the display). It should also be kept away from ultraviolet light sources and extremely cold temperatures. The liquid crystals can freeze in extremely cold weather. A freeze/thaw cycle may damage the display and cause it to be unusable.

Portable Keyboards

The most widely used notebook keyboard is the 84-key version. The keys are slightly smaller and shorter than those found in full-size keyboards. A number of keys or key functions may be combined or deleted from a notebook keyboard. A typical notebook keyboard is illustrated in Figure 10.10.

Because portable keyboards tend to be more compact than the detachable models used with desktop units, many of the keys are typically given dual or triple functions. The portable keyboard normally contains an Fn function key. This key activates special functions in the portable, such as display brightness and contrast. Other common Fn functions include Suspend mode activation and LCD/external-CRT device selection.

FIGURE 10.10 An 84-key notebook keyboard.

Newer keyboard models may also include left and right Windows keys (WIN keys) and an application key. The WIN keys are located next to the Alt keys and provide specialized Windows functions, as described in Table 10.1. Similarly, the application key is located near the right WIN key or the Ctrl key, and provides context-sensitive help for most applications.

TABLE 10.1   WIN Key Definitions

KEYSTROKE	ACTION
WIN/E	Start Windows Explorer
WIN/F	Start Find Files or Folders
WIN/L	Lock Windows XP computer
Ctrl/WIN/F	Find the computer
WIN/M	Minimize All
Shift/WIN/M	Undo Minimize All
WIN/R	Display Run dialog box
WIN/F1	Start Help
WIN/Tab	Move through taskbar objects
WIN/Break	Show System Properties dialog box

EXAM ALERT

Know the basic WIN key shortcut functions.

Trackballs

In some applications, such as notebook computers, it is desirable to have a pointing device that does not require a surface to be moved across. The *trackball* can be thought of as an inverted mouse that allows the user to directly manipulate it. Trackballs may be separate units that sit on a desk or clip to the side of the computer and connect to one of the system's serial ports. In many laptop and notebook computers, trackballs are frequently built directly into the system housing and connected directly to its I/O circuitry. Like mice, trackballs may come with one to three buttons.

Touch Pads

Hewlett-Packard introduced the first touch screen monitor in 1983. These screens divide the display into rows and columns that correspond to X and Y coordinates on the screen. This technology has been adapted to notebook computers in the form of touch pad pointing devices, such as the one illustrated in Figure 10.11.

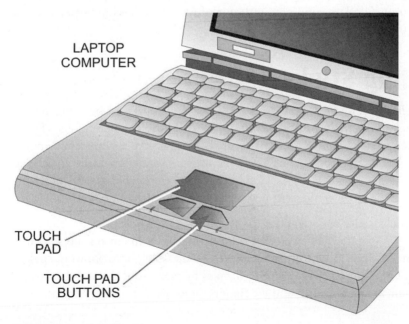

LAPTOP
COMPUTER

TOUCH
PAD

TOUCH PAD
BUTTONS

FIGURE 10.11 A touch pad.

This pointing device normally takes the place of the mouse as the pointing device in the system. The user controls the screen cursor by moving a finger across the pad surface. Small buttons are included near the pad to duplicate the action of the mouse buttons. With some touch pads, single and double button clicking can be simulated by tapping a finger on the pad.

The touch pad contains a gridwork of electrical conductors that organize the pad into a row and column format. When the user presses the touch pad, the protective layer over the grid flexes and causes the capacitance between the two grids within the pad to change. This produces a signal change that is detected by the touch pad controller at one X-grid line and one Y-grid line. The controller converts the signal generated between the two strips into an approximate X,Y position on the video display.

The human fingertip is broad and does not provide a fine enough pointing device to select precise points on the screen. Therefore, accurately locating a small item on the screen may be difficult. The touch pad software designers have created drivers that take this into account and compensate for it.

Touch pads are available as built-in units in some portables, whereas others are designed as add-ons to existing units. These units clip onto the body of the computer, or sit on a desktop, and plug into one of the system's serial ports, just as a mouse or trackball does.

Pointing Sticks

Some notebook computers feature a small fingertip operated pointing device called the *pointing stick*, or *TrackPoint* in IBM ThinkPad notebooks. These devices, depicted in Figure 10.12, are small joystick-like devices that enable users to position screen cursors by applying pressure to the top of the stick. The stick is positioned between the G, H, and B keys on the keyboard, and additional mouse click buttons are located just below the spacebar.

Pointing sticks sense force applied to the top of the stick through changing resistance of a material. The velocity of the cursor movement on the screen is proportional to the amount of force applied to the stick. The pointing stick is preferred over other types of pointing devices by many touch typists because it doesn't require users to relocate their fingers away from the home row of keys.

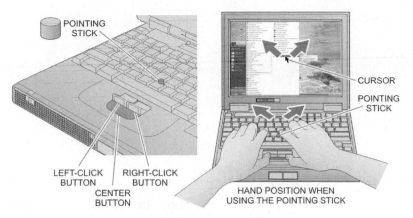

POINTING STICK

CURSOR

POINTING STICK

LEFT-CLICK BUTTON

RIGHT-CLICK BUTTON

CENTER BUTTON

HAND POSITION WHEN USING THE POINTING STICK

FIGURE 10.12 The pointing stick.

External Portable I/O

Personal computer users are creatures of habit as much as anyone else. Therefore, as they moved toward portable computers, they wanted the types of features they had come to expect from their larger desktops and towers. These features typically include an alphanumeric keyboard, a video display, and a pointing device.

Most portables offer standard connectors to enable full-size keyboards and VGA monitors to be plugged in. The VGA connector is usually the standard 15-pin D-shell type; the external keyboard connector is generally a USB port. When an external keyboard is plugged in, the built-in keyboard is disabled. The portable's BIOS software permits the user to enable either or both displays while the external monitor is connected.

Figure 10.13 shows the port connections associated with most portable systems. This example places the connectors on the back of the unit, just as they would be in a typical desktop. Other units may have some of these connectors along the sides instead. High-end portables may include an array of other connectors, such as external microphone and speaker jacks. Some connectors may be hidden behind hinged doors for protection. These doors usually snap closed.

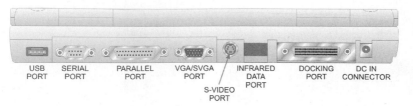

FIGURE 10.13 Notebook back-panel connections.

Peripheral Storage Devices

External storage devices normally connect to option adapter cards installed in the system board's expansion slots. They also tend to employ separate, external power-supply units. Several newer storage technologies, such as removable hard drive media, have been designed to take advantage of the enhanced parallel port specifications of modern systems. These devices can be connected directly into the system's parallel port or to the system through another device that is connected to the port. The device's installation software is used to configure it for use in the system.

External FDDs

Typically, the first item to be left out of a new notebook design is the internal floppy drive. So much of the latest software is distributed on CD-ROM that those drives now have preference in newer designs. However, so many applications still use floppies that an external FDD is almost always an add-on option for a new notebook. Because software is available on floppies and because so many users have cherished data stored on floppies, an additional unit usually makes sense.

The external floppy drives comes as a complete unit with an external housing and a signal cable. As with other external devices, it requires an independent power source, such as an AC adapter pack. The few remaining external floppy drive models available typically employ a USB interface for their signal cables.

External CD-ROM Drives

Prior to the CD-ROM drive becoming an accepted part of the notebook PC, some manufacturers produced external CD-ROM drives for use with these machines, and they are still available as add-ons to all types of PCs. External CD-ROM drives typically connect to a SCSI host adapter or to an enhanced parallel port. The latter connection requires a fully functional, bidirectional parallel port and a special software device driver.

Figure 10.14 illustrates the installation of an external SCSI CD-ROM drive. Because the drive is external, connecting the CD-ROM unit to the system usually involves connecting a couple of cables together. First, connect the CD-ROM's power supply to the external drive unit. Before making this connection, verify that the power switch, or power supply, is turned off. Connect the signal cable to the computer. Finally, connect the opposite end of the cable to the external CD-ROM unit. Complete the installation by installing the CD-ROM driver software on the system's hard disk drive.

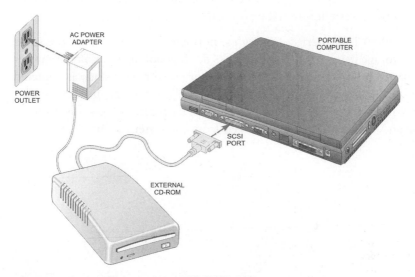

FIGURE 10.14 Installing an external CD-ROM drive.

External CD-RW and DVD-RW Drives

The process for external read/write CD-ROM and DVD drives is similar to installing external CD-ROM and DVD drives. These units connect to the system through a USB port, a FireWire port, an external SCSI connector, or a cardbus adapter. Using these ports and buses, the operating system's PnP operation can detect any new hardware attached to the system when it is installed. However, most of the devices are nonstandard in nature and require that the OEM applications package be installed from the OEM CD that was packaged with the drives to control them.

In the Windows XP environment, read/write CD-ROM and DVD drives are supported directly from the operating system and don't require any third-party applications. When you insert a blank disc into one of these drives, the operating system detects it and pops up a dialog box that asks what you want to do with the disc. Most users still prefer to install a third-party program to manage all the functions of these drives.

Removable Storage

For most portable PCs, the main removable storage system is the CD-RW/DVD drive. As long as you have a writable CD-R disks you have additional storage. Portables are also likely to feature internal PC Card slots that can hold hot-swappable memory cards. These cards can be added to the system or removed while the system is in full operation.

Through modern I/O interface strategies, portable PCs can employ the same removable storage devices that desktop units do. It is not uncommon for a notebook computer to feature different flash memory card reader slots, as depicted in Figure 10.15. These slots are designed to handle CF cards, memory sticks, SD cards, and others. Like the PC Card devices, flash card devices are also hot-swappable and can be inserted or removed from the system at any time.

FIGURE 10.15 Portable PC memory card slots.

Virtually all new notebook computers employ USB ports as their main I/O interface. Some models provide additional USB ports to extend the number of USB devices that can be plugged into the system. These devices include USB flash drives that can increase the system's storage capacity significantly. USB devices, including memory devices using USB interfaces, can be connected to the system and removed at any time. USB memory drives automatically load USB drivers and function as another drive in the system (for example, drive D:).

All the devices are hot-swappable. They give portable systems a great deal of flexibility in meeting storage needs. However, you must remember to eject them through the operating system software before you physically remove them from the system.

Installing External Storage Devices

Following is the general procedure for installing external storage devices:

1. Configure the device for operation.

    A. Refer to the device's user's manual regarding any configuration jumper or switch settings.

    B. Record the card's default configuration settings.

    C. Set the device's configuration jumpers to operate at the default setting.

2. Install the device's PCMCIA adapter card (if necessary).

    Install the PC Card in the PCMCIA slot. The system should detect the presence of the new card in the slot and automatically configure it for operation.

3. Make the device's external connections.

    A. Connect the device's signal cable to the appropriate connector at the rear of the system.

    B. Connect the opposite end of the cable to the device.

    C. Verify that the power switch or power supply is turned off.

    D. Connect the power supply to the external storage unit.

4. Configure the device's software.

    A. Turn the system on.

    B. Check the CMOS setup to ensure that the port setting is correct.

    C. Run the device's installation routine.

PC Cards

In 1989, the Personal Computer Memory Card International Association (PCMCIA) developed the PCMCIA bus standard that was primarily intended to accommodate the needs of the space-conscious notebook and subnotebook computer markets. A small form-factor expansion-card format, referred to as the *PC Card* standard, was also adopted for use. This format was derived from earlier proprietary laptop/notebook memory-card designs. Over time, the entire standard has come to be referred to as the PC Card standard. This is somewhat easier to say than PCMCIA. The interface is designed so that cards can be inserted into the unit while it is turned on (hot insertion).

The PC Card standard defines a methodology for software programmers to write standard drivers for PC Card devices. This methodology is referred to as *socket services* and provides for a software head to identify the type of card being used, its capabilities, and its requirements. Although the card's software driver can be executed directly on the card (instead of moving it into RAM for execution), the system's PC Card enablers must be loaded before the card can be activated.

> **EXAM ALERT**
>
> Be aware that the PC Card enablers must be loaded in the operating system before the system can interact with a PC Card in one of its slots.

With the PC Card enablers loaded, a PC Card can be installed in the system by inserting the card into one of the system's PCMCIA slots, as illustrated in Figure 10.16. If the computer is running, the card services will detect that the card has been installed and the operating system will perform a PnP configuration process for it. If the card is present when the system is started up, it will be configured as part of the normal PnP boot process. Likewise, if the card is removed from the slot, the PC Card services will also detect this event and deactivate the device in the operating system.

Cardbus

The latest variation of the PCMCIA standard is *Cardbus*. Cardbus is a redefined and enhanced 32-bit version of the PC Card standard. The main purpose of this new specification is to extend the PCMCIA bus to higher speeds with more powerful devices and to provide support of 32-bit I/O and memory data paths.

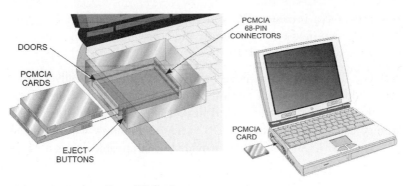

FIGURE 10.16 Inserting a PC Card.

The Cardbus slot has intelligent software that interrogates the card when it is inserted into the slot. If the slot finds that the card is a PC Card, it configures itself to function like a conventional PCMCIA slot. However, if an advanced Cardbus card has been inserted, the slot reconfigures itself to use the 32-bit bus width, increases speed, and uses the low-voltage capabilities of the Cardbus specification.

Whereas the Cardbus slot is designed to work with older PCMCIA and PC Card devices, the same is not true concerning using Cardbus cards in older slot types. The Cardbus card is keyed with a physical sheath around its pins so that it will not plug into the traditional PC Card socket. On the software side, for a Cardbus device to work in a given system, its operating system must support 32-bit data paths.

You can use the following procedure to determine whether a particular system is a Cardbus-enabled system:

1. Insert the Cardbus card into your system's PC Card slot. If it doesn't insert completely, the slot is not a Cardbus slot.

2. Check the system's BIOS setup and verify that the PC Card option is set to the Cardbus option. If no option exists for Cardbus, the system does not support Cardbus devices.

Adding PC Card Memory

Different types of PC Cards have been developed to increase the memory capabilities of notebook computers without tearing the system apart. The original PCMCIA card was developed as an add-on memory device. Additional memory is still a function of the PC Card industry. ATA flash cards provide semiconductor memory that operates like disk-based mass storage. These cards include

intelligent controllers that provide a PC Card version of the ATA (IDE) interface, as well as a sophisticated error detection and correction system. This system is similar to the systems used in IDE disk drives.

Similarly, the Type III PC Card specification was developed specifically to provide an effective add-on disk-drive function through the PCMCIA line. These
mini drives can be as small as 1.8 inches and fit in Type II PC Card slots. Their
formatted storage capacities can exceed 5GB. They also comply with both the
PCMCIA PC Card and ATA standards to provide hot-swappable drives for laptop PCs.

Advanced PC Card I/O

Several companies have developed high-speed serial interfaces based on the PC
Card/Cardbus format. In particular, many PC Card–based USB interfaces have
been developed. These interfaces permit up to 127 USB devices to be added to
the system in a PnP/hot-swap manner.

Likewise, PC Card–based FireWire ports enable portable computers to connect
to a variety of FireWire-based A/V equipment, such as CD and DVD burners,
digital cameras and camcorders, digital VCRs, high-resolution printers, scanners, cable set-top boxes, and game controllers.

Even SCSI interfaces have been produced on PC Cards to permit notebook
computers to interface with SCSI-based peripherals in the PC environment.
These cards offer quick and easy connections to Ultra SCSI and SCSI II (Fast
SCSI) devices. These cards typically provide a high-density (HD) 50-pin cable
and a HD 50F-to-Centronics 50M adapter that can be used to attach it to standard Ultra or Fast SCSI peripherals.

Installing PC Cards

Portable computers do not include standard desktop expansion slots for adding
peripheral devices to the system, but they do typically include a couple of PC
Card slots. Most notebooks provide two PCMCIA slots that can accept a wide
variety of I/O device types. PC Cards are relatively easy to install in a PnP system that has the PCMCIA card services function running. Slide the card into an
open PC Card slot and turn the machine on. The PnP function should detect
the card in the slot and configure it with the proper driver for the type of device
it is.

The operating system must support the PCMCIA slots at two levels: at the socket level (universal support for all PCMCIA devices) and at the card level (specific drivers to handle the function of the particular cards installed). Because

PCMCIA cards are hot-swappable, the operating system's socket service must update the system when a new card is installed or an existing card is removed. If it does not, the system will lose track of its actual resources. The card services portion delivers the correct device driver for the installed PC Card (for example, when a PC Card modem is removed and replaced with a LAN card, the operating system must automatically update its capability to control and use the new card).

In many cases, the PC Card must furnish a standard I/O connector for connection to the full-sized world. Often these connections are made through nonstandard connectors at the PC Card end, but terminate in standard connectors at the I/O device end. For example, a PC Card LAN card, such as the one depicted in Figure 10.17, is not physically thick enough to accommodate the standard RJ-45 plug used with ethernet networks. To overcome this, a thin connector is attached to the card and a standard connector is used at the other end of the cable. Depending on their specific function, some PC Cards require an external power supply to acquire enough power to operate efficiently.

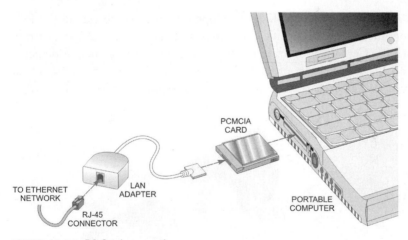

FIGURE 10.17 PC Card connections.

Installing PC Card Support

There are three possibilities for the card services utility to deliver the proper driver to the card:

▶ The Windows operating systems will immediately recognize the card and install the driver without restarting.

- ▶ The operating system recognizes the card and has its driver, but needs to reboot the operating system for the driver to be loaded.

- ▶ The operating system does not recognize the card that has been installed and requires an external driver to be loaded.

At different times, you may want to stop a PC Card driver from being loaded. To turn off support for a PC Card, access the Device Manager tab and expand the PC Card slot node. Then double-click the PC Card controller and in the Device Usage area, check the Disable in This Hardware Profile check box option.

The proper procedure for removing a PC Card from the computer begins with clicking the PC Card status indicator on the taskbar. Then select the command to stop the operation of the PC Card you want to remove. When the operating system prompts you, physically remove the PC Card from the system.

Mini PCI Express Cards

The Mini PCI specification has been developed in an effort to extend the PCI bus into portable PCs. This specification extends the PCI version 2.2 standard to operate on a PC Card–like socket and slide-in card. This arrangement is depicted in Figure 10.18. This version of the PCI bus only implements the 3.3V, 32-bit PCI specification. Therefore, no special keying is required for Mini PCI cards.

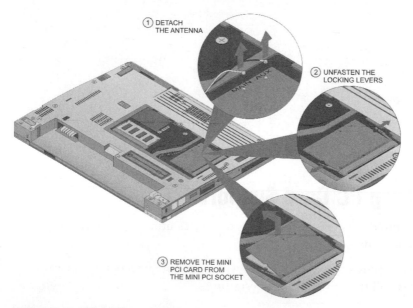

FIGURE 10.18 Mini PCI components.

There are three Mini PCI slot and card form factors: Type I, Type II, and Type III. Type I and II cards use a 100-pin connector as the PC Card slots do. However, the Type III cards employ a 124-pin edge connector interface similar to a traditional adapter card used in desktop PCs. For cards that provide an external interface, Type I and III cards provide support for a remote RJ-45 connector. The Type II cards include mounted RJ-11 and RJ-45 connectors. Typical applications associated with the Mini PCI card designs include PATA and SATA conroller cards, wireless network cards, modems, and sound cards.

The Mini PCI form factor also defines eight card sizes as described in Table 10.2.

TABLE 10.2—Mini PCI Card Specifications

MINI PCI CARD CONNECTOR	BOARD TYPE	DIMENSIONS
100-Pin Stacking	Type IA	7.5×70×45mm
100-Pin Stacking	Type IB	5.5×70×45mm
100-Pin Stacking	Type IIA	7.5×70×45mm
100-Pin Stacking	Type IIB	17.44×78×45mm
124-Pin Card Edge	Type IIIA	5.5×78×45mm
124-Pin Card Edge	Type IIIB	5×64.7×55.8mm
124-Pin Card Edge	Type IIIA	2.4×59.6×50.95mm
124-Pin Card Edge	Type IIIB	2.4×59.6×44.6mm

Challenge #2

You are traveling away from your office and want to get as much work done on the airplane as possible. You notice that the notebook takes several minutes to perform the PnP configuration portion of the boot process. Your notebook has a PC Card modem and network card, and you want to disable these devices while you are traveling so that their drivers do not need to be loaded. How can you do this without permanently removing the devices (because you want to use them when you get back to the office)?

Networking Portables

When the portable computer returns to the office, there is usually a gap between what is on the portable and what is on the desktop machine. One alternative is to use a docking station to allow the notebook to function as both a portable and a desktop system. This concept is explored later in this chapter. The other alternative is to make the portable computer network-ready so that it can plug into the network in the office.

There are PC Card network adapters that can be used with a network socket device to enable the portable to be connected to the office network. The socket device has internal circuitry that prevents the open net connection from adversely affecting the network when the portable is removed. Some network adapters use the system's parallel port and a pocket LAN adapter to connect portables to the network. The LAN adapter works between the network, the computer, and its printer, as shown in Figure 10.19.

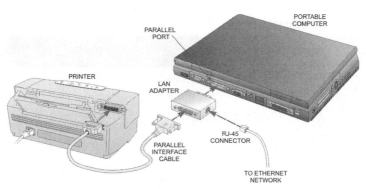

FIGURE 10.19 Networking portables.

Notebook computers can also be used in dial-up networking environments. Therefore, several newer portable models include built-in modems as standard equipment. Other portables can be configured for dial-up operations by simply installing a PC Card modem. These modems slide into Type II PCMCIA slots and connect to the telephone jack through a special phone cable. The cable plugs into a small slot on the card and into the phone jack using a standard RJ-11 connector. Other PC Card modems possess a pop-out RJ-11 port that can be used with standard telephone cables instead of a proprietary cable like the one just described.

Wireless Networking with Portables

Notebook computers are natural selections for use as wireless networking clients. Because they are portable, they can be used anywhere within any wireless access point's hot spot. Many enterprises are creating hot spots to enable traveling computer users to access their access point, for a fee. Notebook computers typically use PC Card–based wireless network adapters like the one depicted in Figure 10.20.

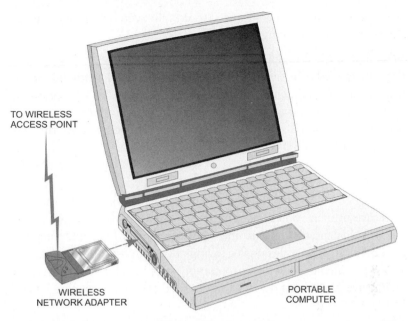

FIGURE 10.20   Wireless networking a notebook computer.

The wireless PC Card adapter slides into one of the notebook's PCMCIA slots and should be autodetected by the system. The card communicates with a remote access point through the embedded antenna that sticks out of the computer's PC Card slot. The device should be capable of functioning on the wireless LAN, provided that the card's driver and the operating system's networking components have been set up properly for communications.

Installing Wireless Networking in Portables

Notebook computers typically employ a wireless PCMCIA adapter to communicate with the network's access point. For the most part, the installation process involves inserting the wireless card in the PCMCIA slot and supplying the OEM driver from the manufacturer's CD. Part of configuring the driver involves identifying the name of the access point that the card should use. Afterward, you need to configure networking support in the operating system.

Because wireless units can and do move, there are certain wireless connectivity issues that you must be aware of. Type 802.11b cards have a limited range of operation (about 500 feet). This estimation relies on a clear line-of-sight pathway existing between the card and the access point. The signals used under this wireless specification do not travel well through objects. In addition, if the card is used in a multiple access point environment, it will always try to communicate with the access point it has been configured to use. To switch to another access point, this setting must be reconfigured.

Many wireless configuration applications include a built-in power meter program that shows the relative signal strength being received from the access point. When you're positioning a computer that has a wireless network card, you should use this tool to maximize the location of the computer. Likewise, if you are operating in a multiple access point environment, you can use this tool to identify the best access point to use in a given location.

Built-in Wi-Fi

As mentioned earlier in this chapter, embedded WLAN adapters have become a common feature of many notebook computer designs. Notebook computers with built-in WAN adapters often include a physical On/Off button to activate this feature. This button provides power savings by permitting the user to disable the circuitry while not online and to comply with regulations that require the transmit/receive portions of devices to be turned off while traveling by air.

EXAM ALERT

Be aware that portable PCs with built-in Wi-Fi typically have an activate/deactivate button that is used to conserve energy by turning the wireless circuitry off when not needed.

There is one important consideration when purchasing or recommending wireless networking for portable computers. By definition, the wireless networking modules in Centrino-branded notebooks were originally limited to 802.11b wireless connectivity. However, Intel eventually saw the advantage of upgrading the Centrino brand and has produced 802.11 b/g and 802.11 a/b/g wireless networking modules. On the other hand, Pentium M portables have always been free to include the latest standards and features in wireless networking. In particular, these units include multimode WLAN adapters that support 802.11a/b/g WLAN capabilities. In general, non-Centrino notebooks offer longer battery life and greater networking performance than the Centrino models do.

802.11b products, like those in Centrino laptops, use the same 2.4GHz frequency band used by cordless phones, microwave ovens, security cameras, and Bluetooth devices. These devices can interfere with the WLAN signal, slowing or disabling the connection. In addition, you should recall that the maximum data transmission rate for these devices is 11Mbps under ideal conditions.

On the other hand, the 802.11a wireless products run up to 54Mbps in the 5GHz spectrum. This frequency band is much more restrictive and offers less interference than the 802.11b channel. The 5GHz band also offers more usable channels (13) to avoid conflicts with other WLAN access points. 802.11g devices also communicate at a 54MHz rate, but do so in the 2.4GHz spectrum. This makes these devices subject to the same interference problems as the 802.11b products. However, it is still a good idea to have backward compatibility with 802.11b systems because of the large installed base of these products still in use.

Portable Power Sources

Notebooks use detachable, rechargeable batteries and external power supplies, as illustrated in Figure 10.21. (Battery sizes vary from manufacturer to manufacturer.) They also employ power-saving circuits and ICs designed to lengthen the battery's useful time. The battery unit contains a recharging circuit that enables the battery to recharge while it is being used with the external power supply. As with other hardware aspects of notebook computers, no standards exist for their power-supply units.

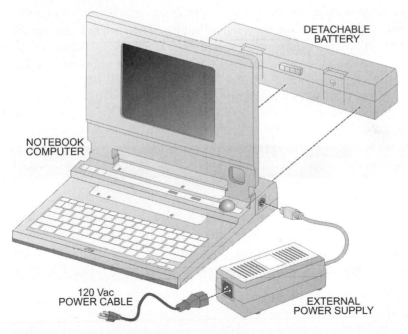

FIGURE 10.21 Laptop/notebook power supplies.

In a fashion similar to other computer power supply types, portable power supplies, also referred to as *AC adapters*, convert commercial AC voltage into a single DC voltage that the computer can use to power its components and recharge its batteries. Similar DC-to-DC controllers are available that permit notebook computers to draw power from a DC source such as cigarette lighter sockets in automobiles. From manufacturer to manufacturer, however, these AC and DC power converters often employ different connector types and possess different DC voltage and current-delivery capabilities. Therefore, a power supply from one notebook computer will not necessarily work with another portable model.

> ### EXAM ALERT
>
> Be aware that the external power supply used with portable systems converts AC voltage into a DC voltage that the system can use to power its internal components and recharge its batteries.

When obtaining a replacement or accessory adapter or controller, the best choice is to get the suggested model from the notebook manufacturer. But if you must get the device from a third party, be sure to match the output voltage level of the original. Also make certain that the replacement unit is capable of delivering at least as much current as the original supply. The specifications for the portable PC's DC power requirements should be located on the bottom of the unit, as well as on the AC power converter. Other sources of information related to obtaining a replacement AC adapter include the portable PC manufacturer's website and its users' documentation.

> ### EXAM ALERT
>
> Know how to locate information about a replacement AC power adapter for portable PCs.

Because the premise of portable computers is mobility, it is assumed that it can run without being plugged into an AC outlet. The question for most portables is how long it will run without being plugged in. This is the point where portable designs lead the industry. They continuously push forward in three design areas:

- ► Better battery design
- ► Better power-consumption devices
- ► Better power management

Power Consumption

As mentioned earlier, power consumption consideration has been built in to most devices intended for use with portable computers. Most PC chipsets provide a Standby mode that turns off selected components, such as the hard drive and display, until a system event, such as a keyboard entry or a mouse movement, occurs. An additional power-saving condition, called *Suspend mode*, places the system in a shutdown condition except for its memory units.

The *Hibernate mode* writes the contents of RAM memory to a hard drive file and completely shuts the system down. When the system is restarted, the feature reads the hibernate file back into memory and normal operation is restarted at the place it left off.

> **EXAM ALERT**
>
> Be aware of the different power-saving modes available to extend the operating time of portable PCs.

Power Management

Each sector of the portable computer market has worked to reduce power consumption levels, including software suppliers. Advanced operating systems include power management features that monitor the system's operation and turn off some high-power-consumption items when they are not in use (Standby mode), and will switch the system into a low-power-consumption sleep mode (Suspend mode) if inactivity continues.

These modes are defined by a Microsoft/IBM standard called the *Advanced Power Management (APM)* standard. The hardware producers refer to this condition as *green mode*. The standard is implemented through the cooperation of the system's chipset devices and the operating system. Control of the APM system is provided through the BIOS CMOS Setup utility.

Most new portable computers possess a number of automatic power-saving features to maximize battery life. Some can be controlled through the Power menu of the Advanced CMOS Setup utility. If the Hard Disk Timeout value is set to 3 minutes, the Standby Timeout to 5 minutes, and the Auto Suspend value to 10 minutes, the following activities will occur:

1. The hard disk will spin down after three minutes of inactivity (Standby).

2. After two additional minutes of inactivity, the system will enter the Suspend mode.

3. After 10 additional inactive minutes, the system will store the hibernation file on the hard drive and shut down.

The Suspend mode can also be entered by pressing a key combination for those times when the user must step away from the computer for a few minutes, but does not want to shut down.

When the system suspends operation, the following events take place:

1. The video screen is turned off.

2. The CPU, DMA, clocks, and math coprocessor are powered down.

3. All controllable peripheral devices are shut down.

The amount of time the unit can remain in Suspend mode is determined by the remaining amount of battery power. For this reason, data should be saved to the hard drive before voluntarily going to Suspend mode. Pressing the computer's power button will return the system to its previous operational point.

ACPI

The Advanced Configuration and Power Interface (ACPI) is a power management specification supported in all modern versions of the Microsoft Windows operating systems. It was designed to improve APM activities previously described by enabling the operating system to control the amount of power provided to each device or peripheral in the system. In addition, the specification permits power management functions to evolve independently in hardware devices, such as the BIOS and the operating systems.

ACPI is particularly important in the portable computer market because it provides a greatly improved power management function, which extends the battery life of those systems. It also enables the system to be reactivated by input from an exernal device, such as a mouse movement or a key closure.

Just as PnP requires a compatible BIOS for proper operation, ACPI must also be supported at the BIOS level to work. If these two items are not compatible, you can receive a BIOS ACPI error telling you that they are not working together. This error has appeared with Windows XP installations and upgrades. In these cases it is necessary to upgrade the BIOS so that it supports ACPI operation.

In Windows 2000 and Windows XP, the power management functions are located in the Control Panel under the Power Options icon. These functions include options for configuring hard drive and display shutdown times, standby mode timing, and the hibernate functions. Standby settings are confgured under the Power Schemes tab, whereas the hibernation function is enabled under the Hibernate tab (Enable Hibernate Support in Windows 2000 and Enable Hibernation in Windows XP.

Docking Stations

A *docking station*, or docking port, is a specialized structure that permits the note-book unit to be inserted into it. When the notebook is inside, the docking port extends its expansion bus so that the notebook can be used with a collection of desktop devices, such as an AC power source, a full-sized keyboard and CRT monitor, as well as modems, mice, and standard PC port connectors. Figure 10.22 depicts a typical docking station.

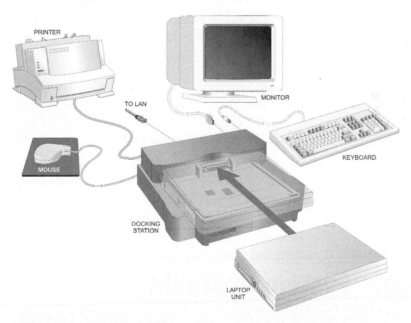

FIGURE 10.22 A docking station.

The notebook and the docking station communicate with each other through a special docking-port connector in the rear of the notebook. When the notebook is inserted into the docking station, an extension bus plugs into the expansion connector in the notebook. Most docking stations provide standard full-size expansion slots so that non-notebook peripheral devices, such as network adapters and sound cards, can be used with the system. Docking stations may also provide additional PCMCIA slots for the notebook computer. When the notebook is in the docking station, its normal I/O devices (keyboard, display, and pointing device) are usually disabled, and the docking station's peripherals take over.

Docking stations are proprietary to the portable computer they were designed to work with. The docking-port connection in the docking station must correctly align with the connector in the notebook. The notebook unit must also fit correctly within the docking station opening. Because no standards exist for these systems, the chances of two different manufacturers locating the connectors in the same place and/or designing the same case outline are very small.

Port Replicators

Many notebook computer manufacturers offer devices, called *port replicators*, that are similar to docking stations. These devices plug into the notebook computer and contain common PC ports such as serial and parallel ports. The purpose of these devices is to enable users to attach portable computers to standard, nonportable devices such as printers and monitors, full-size keyboards, and mice and speakers. With a port replicator, a portable user can have the portable computing experience while on the road, but a more traditional desktop computing experience when seated at a computer desk. Port replicators are commonly given to professional users who travel with their laptops, but want to work with a full-size keyboard, mouse, monitor, and other standard desktop computer amenities when at the office.

Notebook manufacturers typically offer port replicators as additional proprietary options for their computers. Although port replicators are similar to docking stations, they do not provide the additional expansion slots for adding adapter cards and disk drives found in docking stations.

Portable System Upgrading

As more and more desktop users began to use laptop and notebook computers, they demanded that additional peripheral systems be included. With the limited space inside portable units, it became clear that a new method for installing options would have to be developed.

Upgrading Batteries

The desktop world doesn't pay much attention to power-conservation issues. Conversely, portable computer designers must deal with the fact that they are tied to a battery. Older portable designs included the battery as an external, detachable device. These units normally contained rows of nickel cadmium (Ni-Cad) batteries wired together to provide the specified voltage and current capabilities for the portable. The housing was constructed both to hold the Ni-Cads and to attach to the portable case.

Newer portable designs have switched to nickel metal-hydride (NiMH), lithium-ion (Li-ion), or lithium-ion polymer batteries. These batteries are often housed in a plastic case that can be installed inside the portable's case. Other designs use plastic cases that attach to the outside of the portable case. These batteries typically provide up to two or three hours of operation. It is best to run the battery until the system produces a `Battery Low` warning message, indicator, or chime.

It should take about two to three hours to fully recharge the typical NiMH battery pack and about four to five hours for a Li-ion pack. Battery packs should always be fully recharged before using them. When the AC adapter is used, a trickle charge is applied to the battery pack to keep it in a fully charged condition. The AC adapter should be used whenever possible to conserve the battery.

> **EXAM ALERT**
>
> Be aware of which portable battery type provides the longest service between recharging.

Fuel Cells

A relatively new power source for portable computers and handheld devices is the fuel cell. *Fuel cells* are power-generating technologies that use electrochemical reactions between hydrogen and oxygen to produce electrical power. One fuel cell technology does this using hydrogen extracted from methanol, whereas the other major fuel cell technology employs pure hydrogen. In both cases, the reaction between the hydrogen and oxygen produces water vapor and heat.

Fuel cells small enough to be used with mobile computing systems are still primarily in the development stage, although some companies have produced prototypes already. Mobile computer manufacturers plan to routinely include fuel cells in their mobile products, including notebook PCs, digital still cameras,

PDAs, and cell phones. These units act as small wireless rechargers for the high-density lithium batteries already being used in notebook computers and PDAs. Current fuel cell designs in this category have about 10 times the energy capacity of a similar-size typical portable computer battery.

Upgrading PC Cards

Three types of PCMCIA card currently exist. All three PC Card types adhere to the same credit card size form factor of 2.12 inches by 3.37 inches; however, they are created in three thicknesses:

▶ Type I—PCMCIA Type I cards, introduced in 1990, are 3.3mm thick and work as memory-expansion units.

▶ Type II—In 1991, PCMCIA Type II cards were introduced. They are 5mm thick and support virtually any traditional expansion function (typically a modem or LAN card), except removable hard-drive units. Type II slots are backward compatible, so Type I cards will work in them.

▶ Type III—Currently, PCMCIA Type III cards are being produced. These cards are 10.5mm thick and are intended primarily for use with removable hard drives. Both Type I and Type II cards can be used in a Type III slot.

All three PC Card types employ a 68-pin, slide-in pin and socket arrangement. They can all be used with 8-bit or 16-bit data bus machines and operate on +5V or +3.3V supplies. The design of the cards enables them to be installed in the computer while it is turned on and running. Figure 10.23 shows the three types of PCMCIA cards.

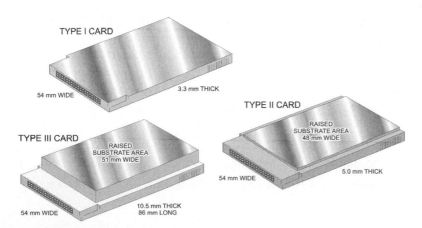

FIGURE 10.23 PCMCIA card types.

Most portable designs include only two Type II–size PC Card slots. These slots can physically accommodate two Type I or Type II cards or a single Type III card. Type III cards use only one of the two 68-pin JEIDA connectors, but take up the entire opening. The PCMCIA interface is designed so that cards can be inserted into the unit while it is turned on (hot-swappable).

EXAM ALERT

Memorize the physical sizes of the three card standards. Also, know what applications each type of card is capable of performing.

EXAM ALERT

Be aware that a single Type III PCMCIA card will usually take up both physical slots on a notebook computer.

Even PC Card hard drives (with disks the size of a quarter) can be found in the notebook market. Other common PC Card adapters include fax/modems, SCSI adapters, network adapters, and IDE host adapters. The PCMCIA standard provides for up to 255 adapters, each capable of working with up to 16 cards. If a system implemented the standard to its extreme, it could, theoretically, work with more than 4,000 PC Cards installed.

Exam Prep Questions

1. What functions are performed by the external power supply of a portable computer system?

   ○ **A.** Converting commercial AC voltage into DC voltage for system usage and battery charging

   ○ **B.** Converting commercial DC voltage into AC voltage for system usage and battery charging

   ○ **C.** Storing commercial power to recharge the battery

   ○ **D.** Increasing the voltage of commercial power for the computer

2. _____ is a redefined and enhanced 32-bit version of the PC Card standard whose main purpose is to extend the PCMCIA bus to higher speeds with more powerful devices and to provide support of 32-bit I/O and memory data paths.

   ○ **A.** Cardbus

   ○ **B.** Rambus

   ○ **C.** PCbus

   ○ **D.** IEEE bus

3. In a portable computer system, the operating system must support the PCMCIA slots at two levels. What are they?

   ○ **A.** At the socket level (universal support for all PCMCIA devices)

   ○ **B.** At the card level (specific drivers to handle the function of the particular card installed)

   ○ **C.** At the Device Manager level (a Device Manager version with support for PC Cards)

   ○ **D.** At the BIOS level (built-in BIOS support for PC Cards)

4. In a portable PC that has PCMCIA slots, the _____ portion of the operating system's socket services delivers the correct device driver for an installed PC Card when it is hot swapped into the system.

   ○ **A.** Card services

   ○ **B.** Autodetect

   ○ **C.** Driver Bank

   ○ **D.** Universal PnP

5. Which of the following options is not a legitimate way in which the Card Services utility in a Windows 2000–based portable PC delivers the proper drivers to the PCMCIA card hot-swapped into the system?

   ○ **A.** The Windows 2000 PC Card Wizard starts up to guide the user through the driver installation process.

   ○ **B.** The operating system recognizes the card and has its driver, but needs to reboot the operating system for the driver to be loaded.

   ○ **C.** The operating system does not recognize the card and requires that an external driver be loaded.

   ○ **D.** The operating system immediately recognizes the card and installs the driver without restarting.

6. At different times when you are traveling, you need to prevent the PC Card driver from being loaded. To turn off support for a PC Card in Windows, you must _____.

   ○ **A.** Access the Device Manager and expand the PC Card slot node. Then double-click the PC Card controller and in the Device usage area, check the Disable in This Hardware Profile check box option.

   ○ **B.** Access the Add/Remove Hardware wizard through the Control Panel, double-click the PC Card controller option, and check the Disable in This Hardware Profile check box option.

   ○ **C.** Access the Add/Remove Programs wizard through the Control Panel, select the PC Card controller option, and check the Disable in This Hardware Profile check box option.

   ○ **D.** Access the System node in the MMC, select the PC Card controller option, and click the Disable in This Hardware Profile entry.

7. What is the maximum distance that an 802.11b-rated wireless network card should be located away from its designated access point?

   ○ **A.** Less than 500 feet

   ○ **B.** Less than 110 feet

   ○ **C.** 1 mile

   ○ **D.** Up to 5 miles

8. What type of electrical power is required by the LCD panel of a notebook computer?

   ○ **A.** 100Hz AC

   ○ **B.** Low-voltage DC

   ○ **C.** Low-voltage AC

   ○ **D.** 100Hz DC

9. What type of RAM do you typically find in a notebook PC?

   ○ **A.** RIMM modules

   ○ **B.** SoDIMM modules

   ○ **C.** PCMCIA modules

   ○ **D.** SD modules

10. Which power-saving mode provides the best power saving and still permits the computing session to be activated later?

    ○ **A.** Hibernate mode

    ○ **B.** Suspend mode

    ○ **C.** Standby mode

    ○ **D.** Shutdown mode

11. A sales person from your company has contacted you asking how she can configure her new notebook PC to go into Hibernate mode to conserve her battery life on long trips. How can she get to the Hibernate configuration page from the Windows XP desktop?

    ○ **A.** Start, All Programs, System Tools, Power Options, Hibernate

    ○ **B.** Start, Control Panel, Power Options, Hibernate tab, Enable Hibernate

    ○ **C.** Start, Control Panel, Power Options, Advanced tab, Enable Hibernate

    ○ **D.** Start, Settings, Power Options, Hibernate, Enable

12. Which PCMCIA slot type can handle all the various PC Card device formats?

    ○ **A.** Type I

    ○ **B.** Type II

    ○ **C.** Type III

    ○ **D.** Mini PCI

13. You have installed 1GB of SDRAM in a notebook used by the sales staff. After some time, one of the sales people tells you that the notebook is showing only 700MB available. What should you tell the salesperson?

   ○ **A.** Someone must have removed a memory module and you will need to check the machine before it goes back into the field.

   ○ **B.** One of the machine's modules must have gone bad and it will need to be replaced before it goes back into the field.

   ○ **C.** The machine has BIOS shadowing configured in the CMOS, so the missing RAM capacity is being used to hold a copy of the BIOS so that the system can access it faster.

   ○ **D.** Notebooks often use shared video memory, which uses a portion of the system's installed memory capacity for video display support.

14. What happens on a Windows XP machine when you press the Windows Logo key along with the L key?

   ○ **A.** It bypasses the Windows logo when the system starts up.

   ○ **B.** It brings the Windows Logon dialog box to the display.

   ○ **C.** It brings the network Logon dialog box to the screen.

   ○ **D.** It locks the keyboard so that other users cannot access the system.

15. What are the main differences between desktop and notebook PC designs? (Select all that apply.)

   ○ **A.** Thermal handling capabilities

   ○ **B.** Power consumption levels

   ○ **C.** Processor speeds

   ○ **D.** Memory size

Answers and Explanations

1. A. Portable power supplies, also referred to as *AC adapters*, convert commercial AC voltage into a single DC voltage that the computer can use to power its components and recharge its batteries.

2. A. Cardbus is a redefined and enhanced 32-bit version of the PC Card standard. The main purpose of this new specification is to extend the PCMCIA bus to higher speeds with more powerful devices and to provide support of 32-bit I/O and memory data paths.

3. **A, B.** The operating system must support the PCMCIA slots at two levels: at the socket level (universal support for all PCMCIA devices) and at the card level (specific drivers to handle the function of the particular card installed).

4. **A.** Because PCMCIA cards are hot-swappable, the operating system's socket service must update the system when a new card is installed or an existing card is removed. If it does not, the system will lose track of its actual resources. The Card Services portion delivers the correct device driver for the installed PC Card (that is, when a PC Card modem is removed and replaced with a LAN card, the operating system must automatically update its capability of controlling and using the new card).

5. **A.** Windows 2000 does not supply a PC Card Installation Wizard.

6. **A.** To stop a PC Card driver from being loaded, turn off support for a PC Card. Access the Device Manager tab and expand the PC Card slot node. Then double-click the PC Card controller and in the Device usage area, check the Disable in This Hardware Profile check box option.

7. **A.** Type 802.11b cards have a limited range of operation (about 500 feet.). This estimation relies on a clear line-of-sight pathway existing between the card and the access point. The signals used under this wireless specification do not travel well through objects.

8. **B.** LCD panels operate with low-voltage DC power.

9. **B.** Notebook and other portable computer manufacturers do not use traditional DIMM modules in their designs. Special form factor DIMMs, called *small outline DIMM* (*SODIMMs*), wrtr developed specifically for use in notebook computers.

10. **A.** Hibernate mode saves the computing session that is stored in RAM to the hard disk then shuts the system down. When the system is reactivated, the computing session is fully restored back into memory and restarted at the place it left off.

11. **B.** The Windows XP Power Options icon provides access to power management functions. These functions include options for configuring standby and hibernate functions. Standby settings are confgured under the Power Schemes tab, while the hibernation function is enabled under the Hibernate tab (Start, Control Panel, Power Options, Hibernate tab, Enable Hibernate).

12. C. PCMCIA Type III cards are 10.5mm thick and are intended primarily for use with removable hard drives. Both Type I and Type II cards can be used in a Type III slot.

13. D. Under shared memory, the system uses a portion of its main memory to hold screen information for the display. In desktop PCs, this memory is distributed to the video adapter card. The disadvantage of shared memory is that it takes up RAM that applications would normally use. If you are upgrading memory in the portable system, you must take into account that the amount of RAM available for use by the system will not be the same as the installed RAM.

14. When the Windows logo key is pressed along with the L key, the system locks and the user must press the Ctrl, Alt, Del key combination to log back into the machine.

15. A, B. Notebook PC need to be small and lightweight to be practical. This limits the amount of free airspace inside the units. In addition, there are no large fans, such as those used in the power supply unit and on the microprocessors in portable units. In addition, portables are designed to operate on batteries when the user is traveling. The amount of power consumed by the PC directly affects how long the PC will be functional when running on the battery alone. Therefore, portable manufacturers strive to make their products as power-friendly as possible to conserve energy and lengthen the useful time between recharges.

Challenge Solutions

1. You will probably need to tell your friend that you need the user's manual for his notebook and that you doubt that the large RIMM modules he has supplied will work in the notebook computer. Notebook computers typically employ Small Outline DIMM devices (SODIMMs) that use different pin configurations (72-/144-pin versions) and operate from different voltage levels than normal DIMM devices.

2. The unused PC Card adapters could be temporarily disabled by making sure that the Enable Infrared Communication check box is checked. To turn off infrared communications, make sure this item is not checked. When infrared communication has been turned off, the Search for Devices Within Range and Enable Plug and Play options are also turned off. To engage support for infrared Plug-and-Play devices, right-click the Infrared icon on the taskbar.

CHAPTER ELEVEN

Maintaining and Repairing Portable Computers

Terms you'll need to understand:

✓ External monitor

✓ Fn keys

✓ Pixilation

✓ Antenna wires

✓ LCD cutoff switch

✓ Backlight

✓ Stylus/digitizer

Techniques to master:

Essentials 2.3/Depot Tech 2.3/ IT Tech 2.3—Identify/identify/use tools, basic diagnostic procedures, and troubleshooting techniques for laptops and portable devices.

✓ Use procedures and techniques to diagnose power conditions, video, keyboard, pointer and wireless card issues, for example:

   ✓ Verify AC power (for example, LEDs, swap AC adapter)

   ✓ Verify DC power

   ✓ Remove unneeded peripherals

   ✓ Plug in external monitor

   ✓ Toggle Fn keys

   ✓ Check LCD cutoff switch

✓ Verify backlight functionality and pixilation

✓ Stylus issues (for example, digitizer problems)

✓ Unique laptop keypad issues

✓ Antenna wires

Essentials 2.4—Perform preventative maintenance on laptops and portable devices.

✓ Identify and apply common preventative maintenance techniques for laptops and portable devices; for example, cooling devices, hardware and video cleaning materials, operating environments including temperature and air quality, storage, transportation, and shipping.

Troubleshooting Portable Systems

This chapter covers the Troubleshooting and Maintaining Portable PC Systems area of the CompTIA A+ Certification—Essentials examination under Objective 2.3. It also covers the preventive maintenance for portable PCs area of the Essentials examination under Objective 2.4.

For the most part, troubleshooting procedures and techniques are the same for portable PCs as they are for desktop PCs. However, the unique structures and components associated with portable PCs require some special troubleshooting knowledge. Therefore, PC technicians must be aware of how their service requirements are different.

> **NOTE**
>
> Depot Tech Objective 2.3 and IT Tech Objective 2.3 use wording that is nearly identical to the wording of the Essential 2.3 Objective dealing with troubleshooting portable issues.
>
> The topics specified in these different exam/objective areas are so closely stated that it makes sense that they are presented as the same discussion. You will need to study this material in this chapter for any of the four exams you intend to challenge.

From a service point of view, the greatest drawback of portable computers is that conventions and compatibility disappear. The continued minimization of the system comes at a cost. Most notably, the number of I/O ports, memory, and disk drive expansion capabilities are limited. In addition, there is no chance to use common, full-size options adapter cards that are inexpensive and easy to find.

One of the biggest problems for portable computers is heat buildup inside the case. Because conventional power supplies (and their fans) are not included in portable units, separate fans must be designed into portables to carry the heat out of the unit. The closeness of the portable's components and the small amount of free air space inside their cases also adds to heat-related design problems.

The internal PC boards of the portable computer are designed to fit around the nuances of the portable case and its components, rather than to match a standard design with standard spacing and connections. Therefore, interchangeability of parts with other machines or makers goes by the wayside. The only source of most portable computer parts, with the exception of PC cards and disk drive units, is the original manufacturer. Even the battery case may be proprietary. If the battery dies, you must hope that the original maker has a supply of that particular model.

Access to the notebook's internal components is usually challenging. Each case design has different methods for assembly and disassembly of the unit. Even the simplest upgrade task can be difficult with a notebook computer. Although adding RAM and options to desktop and tower units is a relatively easy and straightforward process, the same tasks in notebook computers can be difficult.

In some notebooks, it is necessary to disassemble the two halves of the case and remove the keyboard to add RAM modules to the system. In other portables, the hinged display unit must be removed to disassemble the unit. Inside the notebook, you may find that several of the components are hidden behind other units. Figure 11.1 demonstrates a relatively simple disassembly process for a notebook unit.

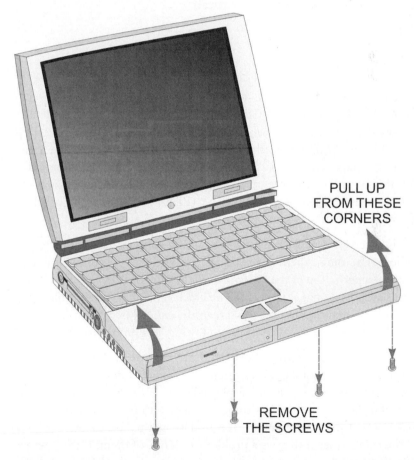

PULL UP
FROM THESE
CORNERS

REMOVE
THE SCREWS

FIGURE 11.1 Disassembling a notebook computer.

In this example, a panel in front of the keyboard can be removed to gain access to the notebook's internal user-serviceable components. Four screws along the front edge of the unit's lower body must be removed. Afterward, the LCD panel is opened and the front panel of the notebook's chassis is pulled up and away to expose a portion of the unit's interior.

Common LCD Display Problems

The most common problems associated with LCD displays are the following:

- A cracked screen
- A screen with lines (horizontal or vertical)
- A dim display
- No display

There are relatively few components to worry about in the LCD display of a portable computer. These are the LCD panel, the inverter, the video cable, the case-closed switch, the exterior bezel, an internal metal frame, and hinges. Of these items, only the LCD panel, the inverter, the video cable, and the case-closed switch are active components. The other item to consider is the video adapter, but this component is integrated into the notebook's system board and cannot be treated as an Field Replacable Unit (FRU) component. Figure 11.2 shows the components of a notebook computer LCD display.

A cracked LCD screen usually occurs because the computer has been dropped or mishandled. The outer shells on many notebook PCs are getting thinner. Placing heavy objects on top of the notebook can flex the back cover of the notebook and cause the LCD panel to crack. The crack can appear as a visible crack or it can look like liquid floating on the screen. In either case, you will need to replace the LCD panel as described in the following section of this chapter.

If lines appear in the screen (either horizontal or vertical), you should plug an external display into the notebook's external VGA port to determine whether the problem is with the display or the display adapter. If the lines do not appear on the external display, there is either some problem with the LCD panel or the video signal ribbon cable that connects the LCD panel to the adapter. Inspect the pins of the cable to see if there is a problem with one of them. If the pins are okay and the external display is good, the problem is with the LCD panel and you will need to replace it.

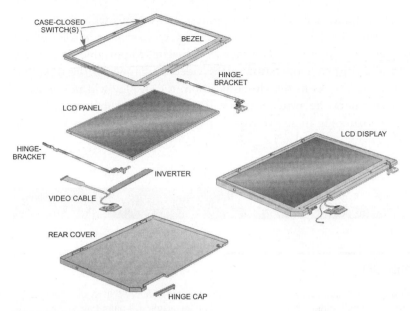

FIGURE 11.2   LCD display components.

If you have a dim screen on a portable system, there are two likely candidates: the LCD panel and the inverter card. The inverter provides power for the LCD panel's backlight. In most cases of a dim screen, the inverter is the source of the problem. This unit is normally a separate unit and is much less expensive to replace than an LCD panel. You can install a generic inverter to get the display running, but you must install the correct inverter for the display to receive optimal brightness and uniformity from the display. Refer to the following section for information related to replacing the inverter. If replacing the inverter does not restore the brightness to the display, you are looking at replacing the LCD panel.

EXAM ALERT

Know what components are typically related to dim LCD displays.

If there is no display on the portable's display, there are a couple of portable PC-specific items to check before using the same troubleshooting procedures you would for a desktop PC. The Fn key of portable computers can be used to redirect the video output to the external VGA port. If you suspect this to be the case, you will need to check the user's guide for directions in redirecting the video back to the main display. Conversely, if you are having problems with the built-in LCD display, it is a common practice to plug an external monitor into the external VGA port and redirect the video output there. This will allow you to determine whether the video problem is in the LCD display or in the built-in video display adapter circuitry. The other item specific to portables is the case closed switch that suspends operation of the video display when the display is down. If this switch sticks in the closed position, the display will not activate. You must troubleshoot the switch action and may need to adjust or replace it. Once again, you can plug in an external monitor to verify the operation of the internal video adapter circuitry.

EXAM ALERT

Know what the Fn key of a portable PC can be used for.

Challenge #1

A customer drops off a portable PC at your service desk complaining that system will not boot up. The unit is still under warranty and the customer wants it repaired at no cost. When you inspect the system you determine that the power light and hard drive light comes on when you turn the system on. You also notice that the LCD display has drops of liquid in it. What action should you take?

Replacing the LCD Panel

When an LCD panel fails, the most common repair is to replace the entire display panel/housing assembly. You must use an identical panel to ensure that it fits the plastic display housing.

To replace the LCD display on a portable PC, you must begin by locating all the screws that hold the panel between the front and back halves of the plastic bezel. Most displays are held together by between four and six small machine screws. These screws are typically hidden under small pieces of rubber and may be located on the front of the display or on its sides. Use a sharp tool such as an Exacto knife to remove the covers from the screws. Finally, use a screwdriver to remove the all the screws from the bezel and place them in a container.

Next, pull the two halves of the bezel shell apart. Separate the two halves at the seam that divides them. The front bezel typically snaps off fairly easily. If not, check for any missed screws in the frame. Work around the frame until the two halves are separated. You may need to work with the button that controls the latch because it may need to be in a certain position to separate the two halves.

With the front of the bezel removed, you should see the LCD panel and its metal frame as depicted in Figure 11.3.

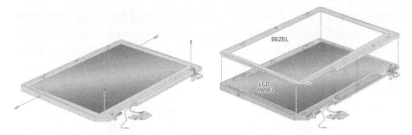

FIGURE 11.3   An open LCD display panel.

After removing the front half of the bezel from the display, cover the keyboard with a protective cloth. Pull the LCD panel and its metal bracket forward, away from the rear half of the bezel to gain access to the screws that hold the LCD panel to the metal bracket. Remove the screws and store them securely.

After releasing the LCD panel from its frame, gently tilt the LCD panel forward onto the protective covering on the keyboard. Remove the video cable from the rear of the LCD panel. Remove any pieces of tape or clips that secure the video cable to the rear of the LCD panel. Take care to avoid damaging the video signal cable or its pins. Portable PCs that feature wireless networking may place the antenna behind the LCD panel. If present, this item must also be gently removed form the LCD panel before replacing it.

Unplug the LCD panel's inverter cable from the inverter module. In some units, you may need to release the inverter module from the system by removing its retaining screws to gain access to the connector. At this point, the LCD panel is completely free from the system. Remove the LCD panel from the frame and check for its manufacturer's part number. Use this number to order the replacement LCD panel. Reinstalling the replacement LCD panel is a matter of reversing the preceding steps. Remember that the LCD panel is delicate and must be handled properly to avoid damage.

Challenge #2

One of your company's outside sales persons has called you to ask about increasing the brightness of his notebook's LCD display. His display has been dim since there was a power surge at the hotel he was staying in. He was wondering if there was some adjustment you could suggest to increase the brightness of his display. What can you tell your co-worker about his display?

Troubleshooting Portable Keyboards

If you have problems with the keyboard in a portable system, it is not as easy (or as cheap) to replace as desktop keyboards. Therefore, if you have a problem that affects only selected keys, such as sticky or inoperable keys, you should clean the keyboard out first. The keys may have built up dust or particles that keep the switches from making contact; use static-free compressed air to blow dust, dirt, or liquids out of the keyboard.

Check for spyware on the system because these types of malware monitor the keystrokes you make and can affect the operation of the keyboard. Check the portable's user's manual for an explanation of its function keys. In some units, a function key (such as F11 or F13) can be used to disable the keyboard. Check the keyboard to system board connector because a single bad connection in this connector can produce errors that appear in groups of keys.

If the keyboard problem is associated with all its keys, you may have a loose connection. Moving can jar connectors loose; check the keyboard connection to the system board to make sure that it is securely plugged in.

In either case, you can run a diagnostic program (either the one supplied by the portable manufacturer or a third-party diagnostic) to check for failures before you begin to disassemble the portable. You might also consider using a desktop keyboard with the portable if it has a PS/2 or USB port.

Troubleshooting Touch Pads

When troubleshooting touch pad problems, there are really only three components to consider: the touch-sensitive pad, the internal or I/O port the pad is attached to, and its driver software. Review the user's manual for the pad to check its software setup for possible configuration problems. Examine the I/O port connection (or internal connector) and configuration to make sure it is properly set up to support the pad. As with other internal portable connections, internal touch pad connections may be loosened whenever the system is taken apart for repair purposes.

EXAM ALERT

Be aware that the connections for different portable components can be loosened during disassembly and assembly processes.

If the pad is an add-on unit, check the port specification to make sure that it is compatible with the touch pad unit. Reinstall the touch pad driver software, carefully reviewing each step. Check for the presence of diagnostic routines in the touch pad's software. Check the I/O port settings.

Smaller transparent touch pads or touch screens, such as those on PDAs, work with a special pen called a *stylus*. The stylus is required to interact with the touch pad because the screen icons and menus are too small to be manipulated by human fingers. The coordinates of the touch pad are calibrated with the screen elements displayed underneath. When the alignment between the screen elements and the touch pad coordinates gets out of calibration, the system will not correctly interpret the input taps from the touch pad stylus.

The alignment can get out of calibration because of temperature and humidity changes, differences in users' perception, or a hard system reset. To correct this problem you must access the touch screen's recalibration utility and establish the starting point and length and width points. The touch screen can become so out of calibration that it is impossible to initiate the recalibration process. In this case you should check the Internet to download a third-party calibration utility. You should also check the device manufacturer's website to download an updated version of the device's driver—particularly if you are experiencing frequent recalibration problems.

Troubleshooting Portable Unique Storage

Other than CD-ROM/DVD drives and floppy drives, all the removable storage devices associated with portable computers are purely electronic devices—they have no movable parts. Therefore, causes for failures in these devices are limited to just a few possibilities: the part failed, the part has been physically damaged, the system does not recognize the device, or the system is not configured correctly to use the device. If the device has failed or has been damaged to the point where it will not work, it is likely that you will need to replace it. On the other hand, if the system does not recognize the device, or it can see the device but cannot work with it, typically you need to straighten out its driver arrangements.

The general procedure for troubleshooting USB devices is covered in detail in Chapter 9, "Advanced PC Troubleshooting." When you plug a USB memory device into the USB port, the system should recognize it and automatically load its drivers. At that point, you should be able to see the device listed as a drive in the My Computer window of any Windows operating system.

If the USB device does not appear, you should use the Device Manager utility to check for conflicting device drivers. You may also need to check the CMOS configuration pages to make certain that the USB ports are enabled there. If Windows will not work with the device you are trying to install, you need to obtain a Windows-compatible device driver for the device.

Although the Windows PnP process will automatically detect USB devices when they are inserted into the USB port, removing USB devices is not so automatic. Before you remove a USB device from a Windows system you should click on the Safely Remove Hardware (hot plugging) icon in the notification area of the taskbar. Unplugging or removing a device without using this icon to stop its operation may cause the system to generate an `Unsafe Removal of Device` error message and/or crash. In Windows 2000, you may occasionally receive this error message even after using the Safely Remove Hardware utility. This is usually the product of connecting USB 1.1 hub devices to the main USB hub of the system.

EXAM ALERT

Be aware of the Safely Remove Hardware icon for dealing with removable storage devices.

All the different flash memory card readers used with portable computers should automatically recognize the presence of the device when it is inserted. If not, you should use the Device Manager utility to check the status of the device and to determine whether there are any conflicts with its driver.

These types of devices can also generate error messages and failures when they are removed or turned off during an operation that involves them. For example, if you remove an SD card and then reinsert it into the system, the system may not use it. In the Device Manager utility you will find a yellow triangle with an exclamation point beside the device. The operating system has not released the system resources dedicated to the device and believes that a new device has been installed. It cannot issue another set of resources to the device. This problem has been corrected in newer Windows Service Pack updates. These updates can be downloaded and installed from the Microsoft website.

You may also encounter problems with removable media devices when you reformat them under Windows. If you run the Windows Format utility to reformat a removable media device from the Windows Explorer, other devices, such as digital cameras, may not be able to recognize the device. This indicates that the PC and the camera are not using the same file system. You must make sure that the devices are set to the same file system type when using the formatting utility. This typically involves setting the operating system's formatting utility to use File Allocation Table (FAT) or FAT16 formatting.

In Windows XP versions, this primarily occurs with older digital cameras that had memory devices that had to be formatted as FAT16. The default file system setting for the Windows XP Format utility is FAT32 (not FAT for removable devices that have previously been formatted as FAT, or contain less than 2GB of storage). If the camera, or other removable media device, does not support FAT32, it will not be able to recognize its own memory device. To correct this problem, change the file system setting in the Format menu to FAT. This problem is not so much of an issue with newer digital cameras and later service pack versions of Windows XP. Another alternative is to simply use the software that comes with the removable device to reformat its memory media.

You may also have access and usage problems with removable media devices that have been formatted as NTFS. These problems generally appear when users who have not logged in with administrative rights try to manipulate these removable media devices without having sufficient rights to perform the operation.

Troubleshooting Infrared Ports

The IrDA protocols for infrared communications specify communication ranges up to 2 meters (6 feet), but most specifications usually state 1 meter as the maximum range. All IrDA transfers must have a clear line of sight between the transmitter and receiver. The receiver must be situated within 15 degrees of center with the line of transmission. Therefore, you should test a failing infrared connection by placing the infrared transceivers as close together as possible and straight in line with each other.

Many Windows operating systems support infrared devices. The properties of installed IrDA devices can be viewed through their Device Managers. Make sure that the Enable Infrared Communication check box is checked. To engage support for infrared plug-and-play devices, right-click the Infrared icon on the taskbar. Make sure that the Enable Plug and Play option is checked. It will be available only if the infrared and searching functions are enabled. If the taskbar icon is not visible, click the Related Topics option.

Right-click the Infrared icon on the taskbar to install software for an infrared device. Make sure that the Enable Plug and Play check box is checked and verify that the new device is within range.

Windows also provides an Infrared Monitor utility that can be used to track the computer's activity. When this utility is running, it will alert you when infrared devices are within range of your computer by placing the Infrared icon on the taskbar. The Infrared Monitor not only notifies you when the computer is communicating with an infrared device, but also indicates how well it is communicating.

Troubleshooting PCMCIA

The process for troubleshooting PC Cards is nearly identical to troubleshooting other I/O adapter cards. PCMCIA cards can be plugged into the system at any time and the system should recognize them. In most cases, the Windows operating system will have a copy of the necessary driver software for the PCMCIA adapter being installed and will install it automatically when it detects the adapter. Most Windows operating system versions will display messages telling you that Windows is installing the drivers required. In most cases, the operating system will recognize the PC card device and automatically load the correct device driver for it. However, if the system does not recognize the device, it will prompt you for the manufacturer's drivers that should be located on the CD (or floppy for older devices) that came with the device.

In cases where the operating system does not have the necessary driver software, when it detects the adapter, it will display a prompt asking the user for a path to the location where the driver can be loaded. PCMCIA manufacturers typically supply drivers for various operating systems on a floppy disk or a CD that comes with the adapter.

To verify that the PC Card device is working, access Device Manager under the Windows Control Panel's System applet. If there is a problem with the PC Card device, it will be appear in Device Manager. If the adapter's icon shows an exclamation mark on a yellow background, the card is not functioning properly. Turn the system off and reinsert the device it in a different PCMCIA slot. If the same problem appears, there are three possible sources of problems: the card may be faulty, the PC card controller in the PC may be faulty, or the operating system may not support the device in question.

If Windows Device Manager displays the PCMCIA socket but no name for the card, the card insertion has been recognized but the socket could not read the device's configuration information from the card. This indicates that a problem exists with the PCMCIA socket installation. To correct this problem, remove the PCMCIA socket listing from the device manager, reboot the computer, and allow the Windows PnP process to detect the socket and install the appropriate driver for it. If the names of the PCMCIA cards do not appear after the restart, the reinstallation process was not successful. Therefore, the PCMCIA socket you are using is not supported by the operating system version.

If the names of other PCMCIA cards do appear in Device Manager, but the card in question does not, it is likely that the card has been damaged. To test the PC Card device, insert a different PC Card device of any type in the slot. If the other card works, it is very likely that the card in question has been damaged.

As with other PCMCIA devices, PC Card hard drives are self-contained. Plug them into the PCMCIA slot and the system should detect them (they are hot swappable). If the system does not detect the card/hard drive, use the troubleshooting steps described for other PCMCIA devices.

Like USB devices, PC Card devices must be logically ejected from the system before physically removing them. Click on the Safely Remove Hardware icon in the taskbar before you remove the device from the system. If not, you could lose data.

Troubleshooting Portable Power Issues

If you turn your portable computer on and nothing happens, the first things to check out include the AC power adapter and the battery. If the power adapter is plugged in, the computer should start up when the on/off switch is engaged. Check for the presence of a power light on the AC adapter and verify that it is on. If not, either power is not reaching the adapter or it is defective. However, if the computer is running on battery power and the system will not start, the battery could be bad or might need to be charged. Remove all unnecessary peripherals from the system to reduce the load on the portable's battery and/or power adapter.

Verify that the battery doesn't need a recharge by trying to start the system with the AC power adapter plugged in. Check the power indicator in the system display panel. If it is on, power is being supplied to the portable. If the indicator is not on, make sure that the power cord is securely connected to a live power source. Check all the power connections to make sure that the AC adapter jack is securely connected to the AC adapter port. If the portable still won't start up, you must troubleshoot the system board. If the system runs from the AC adapter, the battery needs to be recharged or replaced.

EXAM ALERT

Be aware that you can test the battery of a portable PC by plugging in or unplugging the AC power adapter.

Although a dead system is a classic battery/power supply problem, you may encounter several other battery-related problems with portable computers. These include problems that present the following types of symptoms:

▶ Receiving warning messages about the battery not charging.

▶ Intermittent system shutdowns when operating only on the battery.

▶ The computer does not recognize its network connection when operating with only the battery.

▶ The computer and input devices are slow when operating with only the battery.

▶ The computer loses the time and date information when operating on battery power.

A loose or improperly installed battery can cause these problems. They can also appear when the battery is toward the end of its charge/recharge cycle. Check the installation and attempt to recharge the battery using the portable computer's AC adapter.

The actual life of a laptop computer battery varies from just under one hour to over six hours in each sitting. If you are experiencing battery life cycles that are significantly shorter than this (for example, 10 to 15 minutes), you may have a problem referred to as *battery memory*. Battery memory is a condition that occurs with some types of batteries in which the battery becomes internally conditioned to run for less time than its designed capacity (for example, if you routinely operate the computer using the battery for an hour and then plug it back in to an AC source, the battery can become conditioned to run only for that amount of time).

To correct battery memory problems, you must fully discharge the battery and then recharge it. To accomplish this, turn the portable's Power Management feature off by accessing the Power Management icon in the Windows Control Panel. Then restart the computer and access the CMOS Setup utility during bootup. Disable the power management functions in the CMOS settings. Finally, start the portable computer using only the battery and allow it to run until it completely discharges the battery and quits. Then recharge the battery for at least 12 hours. Repeat this process several times watching for consistently increasing operating times.

> **CAUTION**
>
> This procedure is a generic description of restoring some of the usefulness of a rechargeable battery. Exact procedures for particular battery types vary, as do procedures from manufacturer to manufacturer. For safety reasons, you should always use the manufacturer's recommended procedure for recharging batteries.

The reality is that portable computer batteries will eventually need to be replaced. The capability of all rechargeable batteries to hold a full charge lessens as they age. Nickel metal-hydride (NiMH) batteries have a useful life of about 600 charges, whereas lithium ion batteries, the newest batteries, eliminate that, and they also last for about 1,200 charges. Nothing can be done to extend the lives of these batteries much beyond these values—they will need to be replaced.

Adding peripheral devices to portable systems does not typically present the same load on their power supplies as it does on a desktop system—most portable peripherals come with their own power sources. However, you should still be aware that adding peripherals that do not have their own separate power source to the portable would draw current from the system. This can be exceptionally problematic if the system is running on its battery. That's why the first step in troubleshooting general portable computer problems involves removing any unnecessary peripherals from the system and checking the AC adapter/battery system.

Troubleshooting Docking Stations/Port Replicators

Docking stations offer an internal power supply designed to operate the portable and its peripheral attachments. They typically include an external parallel port for printers, a serial port for serial devices (mice and modems), USB ports, external VGA/DVI video and full-size keyboard/mouse connections, and audio connections for external speakers. In addition, the docking station can host several types of external storage devices including, full-sized FDD/HDD/CD-ROM/DVD drives.

Docking stations may also include one or two PCI slots that allow full-size desktop adapter cards (SCSI or specialized video or LAN card) to be added to the system when it is docked. They may also provide multiple PCMCIA slots that add to the existing PC Card capabilities of the portable it is supporting.

For the most part, these connections are physical extensions of the ports provided by the portable. Therefore, if the port works on the portable and doesn't when connection is made through the docking station, generally something is wrong with the docking station/port replicator. However, many portable computers employ special keystroke combinations (Fn function key + some other key) to activate external devices such as video display monitors or full-size keyboards.

For example, some portables will detect that the external video display has been attached. Others will use an Fn key combination to switch the display to the external monitor only, and then use another Fn key combination to send the display to both the LCD panel and the external display (that is, internal, external, or both). If a peripheral device is not working, one of the first steps to take is to refer to the portable's documentation to ensure that the external device has been activated.

For audio problems, make sure the speakers are connected to the correct RCA minijacks (not the Line-in or Microphone jack). Check the documentation to make sure that the sound output has not been muted using an Fn key combination or by an external switch.

Under Windows operating systems, the hardware profile information for the portable computer can be configured differently for docked and undocked situations. When the computer is docked and turned on, its configuration is reset and the Eject PC option will appear on the Start menu. However, when the computer is not docked, the Eject PC option is automatically removed from the Start menu.

The Windows operating system uses hardware profiles to determine which drivers to load when the system hardware changes (docked or undocked). It uses the Docked Profile to load drivers when the portable computer is docked and the Undocked Profile when the computer starts up without the docking station. These hardware profiles are created by the operating system when the computer is docked and undocked if the system is PnP-compliant. If a portable is not PnP-compliant, you must manually configure the profile by enabling and disabling various devices present when docked and undocked.

The first check to make when you encounter docking station/port replicator problems is the same as with any other electronic device: check the power cord and docking power supply. Also, use the presence or activity levels of any indicator lights to determine whether they are correct.

Next, verify that the portable has been properly inserted in the docking station or port replicator. If a single connection does not work, bypass the docking station/replicator and try to operate the peripheral directly with the portable unit. Check the power supply for both the docking station and the peripheral device and make sure that both are turned on. Reboot the portable while it is attached to the docking station. Then check any signal cables between the docking station and the peripheral.

If the PS/2 mouse connection does not work, verify that it has not been installed in the PS/2 keyboard connector by mistake. Make sure the mouse port is enabled in the CMOS Setup utility. Likewise, if you are using a serial mouse, make sure that the port is enabled in CMOS and that it is connected to the correct port. Check the serial port's configuration settings to verify that a proper device driver has been installed for the serial mouse. If the portable's touch pad works but the external mouse does not, check the documentation for an Fn key combination requirement for the mouse.

Portable Preventative Maintenance

Preventative maintenance procedures for portable PCs are mostly identical to those used with desktop PCs. However, the mobile nature of portable PCs makes them susceptible to some issues not normally associated with desktop PCs.

Rough Handling

Portable computers are designed to endure the minor jolts and jars associated with travel and mobility. However, this doesn't include being dropped on the floor of the Orlando airport, or even a short drop onto a tabletop. Such occurrences typically damage portable PCs and can often destroy them. Therefore, the best preventative maintenance activity you can engage in is not dropping the PC.

The list of bad things that happen when a portable PC is dropped include the following:

- ▶ Hard drive head damage or misalignment—The HDD read\write heads are probably the most fragile mechanisms in the PC. When HDDs are dropped even a short distance, the heads can slap the drive's platters, damaging both the heads and the platters (where the data is stored).

- ▶ Video display damage—The physical integrity of the display can be compromised when the PC is dropped or jolted. The display screen can crack, the components of the screen can become misaligned, or its inter-connections can come loose.

▶ System board components popping off—The forces involved in a portable PC hitting the floor can dislodge components from the system board.

▶ Physical damage to the case—Portable PC cases are constructed mostly of plastic and can withstand only a given amount of force. Dropping the computer can break the plastic structure in the case and allow internal components to break loose.

▶ Internal connections coming loose—Internal connections between the keyboard, disk drives, video display, built-in pointing devices, and the system board can come loose.

Dropping the portable is not the only type of rough handling that can damage portable PCs. You should be careful when placing notebook computers in overhead bins or under the seat in front of you on airplanes. LCD displays are particularly susceptible to compression and can't handle being compressed for long periods of time. Resting your feet on the PC, or placing items on top of it, can pop the screen loose. The same thing happens when you leave objects inside the portable and try to close it. Pencils, pens, and notepads are often left inside the unit and pop the LCD screen loose when closed.

Preventing such damage from occurring requires users to be aware of the potential problems and take care to avoid situations and activities that can cause them. A good padded carrying case is the best precaution for minimizing minor shock-induced damage.

Likewise, special protection should be provided when shipping portable PCs. Portables should be shipped in its original shipping carton if possible. The manufacturer's foam and protective devices are designed to provide the best protection for the PC. If the original packaging is not available, the box-within-a-box shipping method should be used to provide protection.

Performing regular data backups is the best way to protect from data loss caused by impact-induced damage.

EXAM ALERT

Be aware that internal connections of portable PCs can come loose and create problems with specific portable subsystems.

Thermal Issues

Many portable PC case designs place fan and air vents on the bottom of the case. To properly dissipate heat, the system forces the hot air out through the space created under the computer. Therefore, the portable should be placed on a hard flat surface when it is running. Placing the unit on your lap or a soft surface can reduce the airflow leaving the case and cause overheating. If the system shows signs of overheating even when being used on a hard flat surface, it may require elevating the unit from the table.

EXAM ALERT

Be aware of operating environmental factors that can cause overheating in portable PCs.

Likewise, the screen should be shielded from bright sunlight and heat sources. Moving the computer from a cooler location to a hot location can cause damaging moisture to condense inside the housing (including the display). Portables should also be kept away from ultraviolet light sources and extremely cold temperatures. The liquid crystals can freeze in extremely cold weather. A freeze/thaw cycle may damage the display and cause it to be unusable.

Cleaning

Clean the portable PC in the same manner as a desktop PC. The screen should be cleaned periodically with a glass cleaner and a soft, lint-free cloth. You can also use clean water and a mild soap to clean the display. Stronger cleaning agents such as citrus-based and ammonia-based cleansers can damage the viewing screen and should not be used. Never spray the cleaner directly on the screen.

EXAM ALERT

Know which techniques and tools should be used to clean portable PCs.

Exam Prep Questions

1. What is the most common repair for a failed LCD monitor?

   ○ **A.** Demagnetizing the LCD screen

   ○ **B.** Replacing the signal cable

   ○ **C.** Replacing the LCD panel

   ○ **D.** Replacing the computer

2. What is the suggested cleaning solution for portable displays?

   ○ **A.** Water and mild soap

   ○ **B.** Water and citrus-based cleaning solutions

   ○ **C.** Water and ammonia

   ○ **D.** Water and antistatic spray

3. Which components are typically linked to dim LCD displays?

   ○ **A.** The backlight bulb

   ○ **B.** The inverter

   ○ **C.** The LCD panel

   ○ **D.** The screen dimmer module

4. You have just installed a new processor in a laptop PC. When you restart the system you discover that the keyboard works properly but the touch pad does not. What should you do to overcome this problem?

   ○ **A.** Use the keyboard to start the operating system installation. When the process moves into the GUI phase, the touch pad will become active.

   ○ **B.** You have installed an incompatible processor type that must be replaced.

   ○ **C.** The touch pad connector may have been loosened during the installation—reconnect it.

   ○ **D.** The portion of the system board responsible for the touch pad has been shorted out. You need to install a USB touch pad or mouse.

5. Which of the following is the best way to detect a bad battery in a Windows XP–based laptop PC?

   ○ **A.** Check the voltage with a multimeter

   ○ **B.** Check the battery indicator in the Systray portion of the taskbar

   ○ **C.** Disconnect the AC adapter and measure the time it takes for the system to fail

   ○ **D.** Check the battery level in the Control Panel's ACPI applet

6. A customer can't configure the correct resolution for the LCD display on a notebook PC. What steps can you take to fix the problem?

   ○ **A.** Use the Device Manager to verify that the installed video driver is correct for the installed video card

   ○ **B.** Connect a video projector to the external display port

   ○ **C.** Install a video adapter card that is compatible with the monitor

   ○ **D.** Install an external monitor to determine whether the problem is in the display panel

Answers and Explanations

1. C. When an LCD panel fails, the most common repair is to replace the entire display panel/housing assembly.

2. A. The screen should be cleaned periodically with a glass cleaner and a soft, lint-free cloth. You can also use clean water and a mild soap to clean the display. Stronger cleaning agents such as citrus-based and ammonia-based cleansers can damage the viewing screen and should not be used. Never spray the cleaner directly on the screen.

3. B. If you have a dim screen on a portable system, there are two likely candidates: the LCD panel and the inverter card. The inverter provides power for the LCD panel's backlight. In most cases of a dim screen, the inverter is the source of the problem. This unit is normally a separate unit and is much less expensive to replace than an LCD panel.

4. C. Installing a new processor should not affect the operation of the keyboard or the touch pad. However, the close physical proximity of the components inside a notebook PC make it likely that a connector could become disconnected when the system is taken apart and put back together.

5. C. Whenever the system shuts down earlier than normal will indicate that the battery either is bad or that it is having a battery memory problem where it becomes internally conditioned to run for less time than the designed capacity.

6. D. If the resolution of the LCD display cannot be found, you should plug an external display into the notebook's external VGA port to determine whether the problem is with the display or the display adapter. If the lines do not appear on the external display, there is either some problem with the LCD panel or the video signal ribbon cable that connects the LCD panel to the adapter.

Challenge Solutions

1. A cracked LCD screen usually occurs because the computer has been dropped or mishandled. The crack can appear as a visible crack or it can look like liquid floating on the screen. In either case you will need to replace the LCD panel. In most cases, the warranty does not cover damage from the portable being dropped, so you will probably have to tell the customer that his notebook is not covered.

2. If you have a dim screen on a portable system, there are two likely candidates: the LCD panel and the inverter card. The inverter provides power for the LCD panel's backlight. In most cases of a dim screen, the inverter is the source of the problem. This unit is normally a separate unit and is much less expensive to replace than an LCD panel.

CHAPTER TWELVE

Windows Operating Systems

Terms you'll need to understand:

✓ Windows Explorer

✓ My Computer

✓ Control Panel

✓ Command prompt

✓ My Network Places

✓ Taskbar

✓ Systray

✓ Start menu

✓ GUI

✓ Icons

Techniques to master:

Essentials 3.1—Identify the fundamentals of using operating systems.

✓ Identify differences between operating systems (Mac, Windows, Linux) and describe operating system revision levels including GUI, system requirements, application, and hardware compatibility.

✓ Describe features of operating system interfaces, for example:

    ✓ Windows Explorer

    ✓ My Computer

    ✓ Control Panel

    ✓ Command Prompt

    ✓ My Network Places

    ✓ Taskbar/systray

    ✓ Start menu

Operating Systems

This chapter covers the Operating System Types and Interfaces areas of the CompTIA A+ Certification—Essentials examination under Objective 3.1. The computer technician must be familiar with the functions and structures of different operating systems that may be encountered in the field. Although a PC technician might encounter several operating systems, most operating systems associated with personal computers fall into the Microsoft product line of Windows 2000 Professional, Windows XP Professional, Windows XP Home Edition, and Windows XP Media Center Edition. However, technicians are also likely to run into other systems running Apple Mac OS, UNIX, Novell, and Linux operating systems.

> **NOTE**
>
> Unless otherwise noted, operating systems referred to within this chapter include Microsoft Windows 2000, XP Professional, XP Home, and Media Center.

Every portion of the system must be controlled and coordinated so that the millions of operations that occur every second are carried out correctly and on time. *Operating systems* are programs designed to control and coordinate the operation of the computer system. As a group, they are easily some of the most complex programs devised.

A *disk operating system* (*DOS*) is a collection of programs used to control overall computer operation in a disk-based system. These programs work in the background to allow the user of the computer to input characters from the keyboard, to define a file structure for storing records, or to output data to a monitor or printer. The DOS is responsible for finding and organizing your data and applications on the disk.

The DOS can be divided into three distinct sections:

- ▶ Boot files—Take over control of the system from the ROM BIOS during startup

- ▶ File management files—Enable the system to manage information within itself

- ▶ Utility files—Permit the user to manage system resources, troubleshoot the system, and configure the system

PC operating systems act as a bridge between application programs and the computer hardware. These application programs allow users to create files of data pertaining to certain applications such as word processing, remote data communications, business processing, and user programming languages.

Network operating systems (NOSs) are designed to extend the control of disk operating systems to provide for communications and data exchanges between computers connected by a communication media. Notable network operating systems include Windows NT Server, Windows 2000 Server, Windows Server 2003, Linux, UNIX, and Novell NetWare.

Graphical User Interfaces

Another form of operating environment, referred to as a *graphical user interface (GUI)*, has gained widespread popularity in recent years. GUIs, like the Microsoft Windows desktop depicted in Figure 12.1, employ a graphics display to represent procedures and programs that can be executed by the computer. These programs routinely use small pictures, called *icons*, to represent different programs. The advantage of using a GUI is that the user doesn't have to remember complicated commands to execute a program.

FIGURE 12.1 A graphical user interface screen.

Major Operating System GUIs

The most widely used disk operating systems with personal computers are the Windows line of operating systems from Microsoft. Windows is a GUI-based operating system that enables users to navigate through the system using a series of pop-up windows and menus.

Many personal computer users run versions of a freely distributed, open-source operating system called *Linux*. Linux is a very powerful, command-line operating system that can be used on a variety of hardware platforms, including PC and Apple Macintosh systems.

A community of programmers works with the Linux oversight committee to continually upgrade and enhance the basic Linux structure to keep it current and competitive. In addition, several companies have developed proprietary additions to the basic Linux structure to produce their own *distributions* (Linux-speak for versions) of the operating system. Major Linux distributions include: Red Hat, SUSE, Slackware, Mandrake, Fedora, FreeBSD, Debian, and others. Although Linux is primarily thought of as a command-line-based operating system, multiple GUI-based desktop overlays have been developed to enable users to control the system in a manner similar to the Windows and Apple operating systems.

The other major line of the personal computers comes from Apple Computer. These personal computers are not compatible with the IBM line of PCs. They have distinctly different hardware designs and do not directly run software packages developed for the PC environment. All Apple computers originally ran proprietary versions of the Apple operating system. However, newer Apple Macintosh computers run on a proprietary version of Linux named Mac OS X. Although the structure of Mac OS X is Linux based, the user-interaction portions of the system employ Apple's trademark GUI-based desktop. This gives the Mac a very powerful and stable engine with very user-friendly interfaces to work with.

> **EXAM ALERT**
>
> Know which type of operating system kernel is used with Apple Mac systems.

For many years the vast majority of business PCs ran on a network operating system called Novell NetWare. However, Microsoft has taken over a large share of this market with Enterprise versions of its Windows operating systems. Originally, Novell developed and upgraded the complete structure of the NetWare operating system, including the proprietary network management system, file management system, user and group control management, and directory services.

Novell still maintains a reasonable share of networked business users. Therefore, the computer technician must be aware of NetWare and how to work with it in a network environment. In an attempt to regain some of the desktop market, Novell has embraced its own version of the Linux operating system.

The Windows NT Product Line

All current Windows operating system versions have been derived from Microsoft's Windows NT (New Technology) line of operating systems. The Windows NT product was originally developed in two parts: the NT Workstation and the NT Server operating systems.

The server software has retained the Server nomenclature through several iterations: Windows 2000 Server and Server 2003. However, with the advent of Windows 2000 and then Windows XP, Microsoft changed the name of the workstation software to Windows 2000 Professional and Windows XP Professional.

It also introduced market-specific variations of the Windows XP operating system: Windows XP Home Edition and Windows XP Media Center Edition. In this chapter we will examine the most current Windows NT workstation operating system versions: Windows 2000 Professional and all the varieties of Windows XP.

The Windows 2000 and Windows XP Professional operating systems belong to Microsoft's line of enterprise products designed specifically to perform in a client/server network environment. They are designed primarily for the business computing market. Windows XP Home and XP Media Center Edition are derivative operating systems designed for the home or small office/home office market. These versions include peer-to-peer networking functions for stand-alone and workgroup environments.

A client/server network is one in which standalone computers, called *clients*, are connected to and administered by master computers called *servers*. Collectively, the members of the group make up a network structure called a *domain*. Figure 12.2 depicts a typical domain-based network arrangement. The members of the domain share a common directory database and are organized in levels. Every domain is identified by a unique name and is administered as a single unit having common rules and procedures.

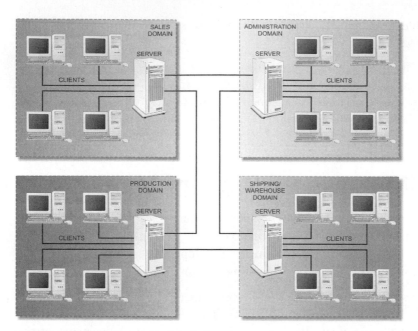

FIGURE 12.2 A client/server or domain-based network.

In peer-to-peer workgroup settings, all the nodes may act as servers for some processes and as clients for others. In a domain-based network, the network is controlled from a centralized server (domain controller). In Windows networks, this concept is embodied by the location where the administration and security databases are kept. In the workgroup, each machine maintains its own security and administration databases. In a domain environment, the server is responsible for keeping the centralized user account and security databases.

Enterprise networks are designed to facilitate business-to-business or business-to-customer operations. Because monetary transactions and customers' personal information travel across the network in these environments, enterprise networks feature facilities for additional, highly protective, security functions. These networks consist of multiple domains (called *trusted domains*) that are linked together, but managed independently.

Most enterprise networks are actually intranets. An *intranet* is a network built on the TCP/IP protocol that belongs to a single organization. It is in essence a private Internet. Like the Internet, intranets are designed to share information and services, but are accessible only to the organization's members, with authorization. Figure 12.3 depicts an intranet structure where a local web server provides Internet applications, such as email, FTP, and web browsing for the network without using the public telephone system.

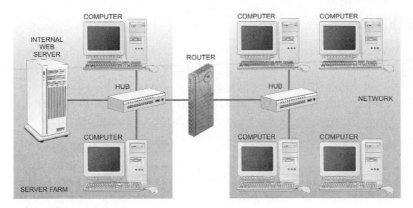

FIGURE 12.3 An intranet.

A relatively new term, *extranet*, is being used to describe intranets that grant limited access to authorized outside users such as corporate business partners, as illustrated in Figure 12.4. This makes the extranet a partially private, partially public network arrangement. In the figure, a customer web server is placed between the company's intranet and the Internet. Part of this server's job is to authenticate users from the outside by asking them for a valid password before they can access the contents of the server. Some type of firewall device or software typically blocks unauthorized outside users from accessing the intranet site.

> **NOTE**
>
> Business-to-business (B2B) relationships are the main reason for establishing an extranet.

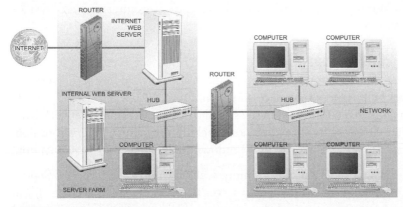

FIGURE 12.4 An extranet.

Windows 2000

Windows 2000 is the successor of the Windows NT 4.0 operating system. Windows 2000 introduced built-in support for many new technologies including DVD drives, USB devices, accelerated graphics ports (AGPs), multifunction adapter cards, and a full line of PC Cards. Finally, Windows 2000 provided a new distributed directory service for managing resources across an enterprise, FAT32 support, and the Internet Explorer 5 web browser.

Windows 2000 comes in two basic variations: the corporate workstation version, titled Windows 2000 Professional, and the network server version, called Windows 2000 Server. The server product is also available in two extended enterprise versions: Windows 2000 Advanced Server and Windows 2000 Datacenter Server.

Windows 2000 Professional

The workstation side of Windows 2000 is named Windows 2000 Professional. This operating system is designed to be the reliable, powerful desktop for the corporate computing world. It has been designed to be easier to set up and configure than its predecessors. Windows 2000 Professional employs several wizards, such as the New Hardware Wizard and the Network Connection Wizard, to make installation and configuration processes easier for users.

Windows 2000 Professional extended and improved the Windows 95/98 user interface and brought Plug-and-Play to the NT workstation line. The hardware supported by Windows 2000 Professional was upgraded significantly from previous workstation versions. Although it offered many improvements over previous Windows NT versions, Windows 2000 Professional proved to be too complex for most general consumer usage. For this reason, Microsoft continued to upgrade its Windows 9x product for the general consumer market with its release of Windows Me.

Windows 2000 Server

On the server side, Windows 2000 offers a more scalable and flexible server platform than its Windows NT predecessors. Windows 2000 Server actually comes in three versions that correspond to the size and complexity of the network environment they are used in. These versions include the standard Server edition, the Advanced Server edition, and the Windows 2000 Datacenter Server edition.

The standard Server edition offers a more scalable and flexible file server platform. It also functions as an application server that handles large data sets. It can be used to implement a standards-based, secured Internet/intranet server.

NOTE

Recall that an intranet is simply a private, web-based network, typically established by an organization for the purpose of running an exclusive website not open to the public (that is, company websites for internal company use only). Intranets can be based on local or wide area networks, or constructed as combinations of the two.

The standard Windows 2000 Server package can manage up to 4GB of RAM and is capable of distributing work between two microprocessors at a time. This type of operation is referred to as *Symmetrical Multiprocessing (SMP)*. If Windows 2000 Server has been installed as an upgrade to an existing Windows NT 4.0 Server, it can support up to four different microprocessors simultaneously.

The Advanced Server edition can support up to eight symmetrical processors and up to 8GB of memory. These features enable it to function well in medium-size networks running between 100 and 500 concurrent users. In other respects, the Advanced Server product is the same as the standard Server version. However, some enterprise versions of applications will run only on the Enterprise version of the operating system.

The Windows 2000 Datacenter Server edition can handle up to 64GB of RAM and 32 processors. This will enable it to support up to 1,000 simultaneous users with heavy processing demands.

Both the Advanced and Datacenter Server editions employ a pair of high-availability features that allow them to effectively handle the traffic levels found on medium and large websites. These features are Network Load Balancing (NLB) and Microsoft Cluster Server (MSCS). The load-balancing feature enables the operating system to distribute IP requests to the most available web server in a cluster of up to 32 web servers.

Windows XP

Windows XP is the current version of Microsoft's desktop operating system. Windows XP represents another level of meshing the stable kernel of the Windows NT operating system line with the consumer-oriented ease of use associated with its Windows 9x line of products. The Windows XP operating system is available in four versions:

- ▶ Windows XP Home Edition—The Windows XP Home Edition is designed to replace the Windows 95/98/Me operating systems. It is primarily intended for consumer and entertainment markets and provides many enhancements, such as more powerful and streamlined Internet access than any of its predecessors. The networking element has been downgraded in the Home Edition. It has been restricted to peer-to-peer networking and cannot be joined to a client/server domain network.

▶ Windows XP Professional—Windows XP Professional is designed and positioned to compete with Windows NT Workstation and Windows 2000 Professional operating systems. It contains features that make it more suitable as a client in enterprise network. These features include such items as simpler remote access and domain membership, enhanced security and reliability features, multiple processor support, and multiple language availability. The A+ certification focuses primarily on this Windows XP version.

▶ Windows XP 64-bit Edition—The Windows XP 64-Bit Edition is a high-end version of the operating system designed to run on Intel Itanium processors. These processors are employed in high-data-volume environments. This Windows XP version supports up to 16GB of physical memory and 16TB of virtual memory. Unlike its NT predecessors, Windows XP does not feature matching workstation and server operating system versions.

NOTE

There are actually two versions of Windows XP 64–Bit Edition: an original Windows XP 64-Bit Edition and a Windows XP Professional x64 Edition. The original version was designed to work with Itanium-based workstations. The latter was designed to work with AMD Opteron and Athlon 64 microprocessors as well as Intel Xeon and Pentium 4 processors that include EMT64T extensions. These two operating system versions are specific to certain hardware platforms and cannot be substituted for each other.

▶ Windows XP Media Center Extension—Windows XP Media Center Edition (XP MCE) is a special version of Windows XP Professional that includes a special multimedia-centered application, called the Media Center, which provides a TV remote control interface for viewing and recording television, a DVD player, and an audio/video record/playback system. Like the Home Edition, MCE's networking capabilities have been limited to the peer-to-peer environment.

Windows 2003 Server

While Microsoft decided to call its next workstation operating system Windows XP, the next version of the Server product line is called Windows Server 2003. As with the Windows 2000 series of server operating systems, the 2003 series includes standard, Enterprise (advanced), and Datacenter editions. The capabilities and qualities of these editions are similar to those stated for their Windows 2000 predecessors.

In addition to those editions already mentioned, Microsoft is producing a Windows Server 2003—Web edition that is designed for web services and hosting support. It contains only features required specifically to support development and deployment of web services and applications.

> **NOTE**
>
> Remember that information about specific server operating systems is not part of the A+ certification objective map. These systems are mentioned here for your information and knowledge base.

Windows Vista Operating Systems

Windows Vista is a radically different collection of operating system versions from Microsoft designed specifically to significantly improve security in the Windows operating systems line. Vista features a significantly upgraded GUI called Windows Aero, which provides a vastly different navigation system and organizational structure. Microsoft has chosen to roll Vista out as an upgradeable line of products that add features at each level. These versions are Windows Vista Starter, Windows Vista Home Basic, Windows Vista Home Premium, Windows Vista Business, Windows Vista Enterprise, and Windows Vista Ultimate.

> **NOTE**
>
> CompTIA did not include Windows Vista operating systems in the 2007 A+ exam structure.

Navigating Windows 2000/XP

When Windows 2000 or Windows XP is started, it produces the basic desktop screen depicted in Figure 12.5. The desktop is the primary graphical user interface for all Windows versions. As with previous Windows products, the desktop uses icons to quickly locate and run applications.

FIGURE 12.5 The Windows 2000 desktop.

Windows is a *task-switching* environment. Under this type of environment, several applications can run at the same time. In some cases, a particular application might be running on the desktop while others are running out of view. When you have multiple applications open in Windows, the window currently being accessed is called the *active* window and appears in the foreground (on top of the other windows). The activity of the other open windows is suspended, as denoted by their gray color, and their applications run in the background.

Select key combinations can be used to navigate through the Windows environment using the keyboard. The most common keys include the Alt, Esc, Tab, and Enter keys. These keys are used to move between the different Windows structures and make selections (that is, the Tab key is used to move forward through different options, whereas the Shift+Tab combination is used to move backward through available options).

Special key combinations enable the user to move between tasks easily. By pressing the Alt and Tab keys together, you can quickly select one of the open applications. Similarly, the Alt+Esc key combination enables the user to cycle through open application windows. Pressing the Ctrl+Esc keys will pop up the Start menu.

Windows 2000/XP Desktops

The desktop interface provides an easy method for starting tasks and making resource connections. Small graphic symbols called icons are used to represent programs and utilities that can be accessed by double-clicking the icon. Double-clicking the icon starts the application or brings up its window. The standard icons generated when Windows is installed are located along the left border of the screen. Notice that the standard desktop icons for Windows 2000 include My Computer, My Network Places, and the Recycle Bin. However, if the operating system is installed on a standalone unit that does not have a network card installed, the My Network Places icon will not be present on the desktop.

A separate screen area called the *taskbar* runs across the bottom of the screen, and the Start menu pops up from the Start button on the taskbar. The desktop icons are referred to as *shortcuts* because the primary method of accessing applications is through the Start menu. Figure 12.6 depicts the Windows 2000 desktop with the Start menu expanded.

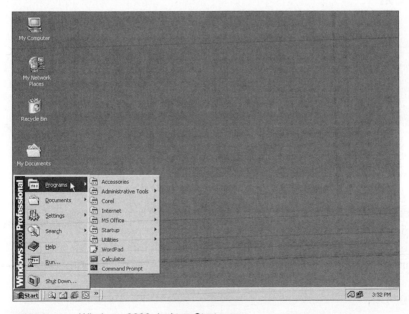

FIGURE 12.6 Windows 2000 desktop Start menu.

In addition to the normal Windows left-click and double-click functions, Windows 2000 and all versions of Windows XP employ the right mouse button for some activities. This is referred to as *right-clicking*, or as *alternate clicking* for right-handed users, and is used to pop up a menu of functions on the screen. The right-click menus in Windows are context-sensitive because the information they contain applies to the item that is being clicked.

Right-clicking techniques are employed to access context-sensitive options on the screen. Right-clicking a folder or file produces a pop-up menu. These menus enable the user to open, cut, or copy a folder (an icon that represents a directory), create a shortcut, delete or rename a folder, or examine properties of the folder. In the case of clicking one of the system's hardware devices, the menu will permit you to perform such functions as sharing the device, or checking its properties. These menus may have additional items inserted in their lists by applications that they serve.

Right-clicking in an open area of the desktop produces a pop-up menu similar to the one displayed in the right side of the figure. This menu enables the user to arrange icons on the desktop, create new folders and shortcuts, and see the properties of the system's video display.

Locating, Accessing, and Retrieving Information in Windows 2000 and XP

The major Windows 2000/XP user interfaces are the following:

- ▶ My Computer
- ▶ Start menu/taskbar
- ▶ Windows Explorer
- ▶ Internet Explorer
- ▶ My Network Places
- ▶ Windows 2000/XP dialog boxes (windows)

These interfaces provide user access to all the major areas of the system. In the following discussions, we will treat them as the same except where we specifically point out differences between operating system versions. Most of the time, these occurrences will involve the Windows XP version.

My Computer

The My Computer icon is the major user interface for Windows 2000 and XP. It enables the user to see the local system's contents and manage its files.

Double-clicking the My Computer icon will produce the Windows 2000 My Computer window, shown in Figure 12.7. This window displays all the system's disk drives as icons and represents the Control Panel as a folder. Double-clicking one of the drive icons produces a display of its contents onscreen.

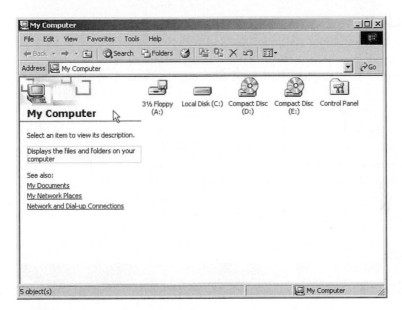

FIGURE 12.7   The My Computer window.

Right-clicking the My Computer icon produces a menu listing that provides options for opening the My Computer window, exploring the system drives and files through the Windows Explorer, working with network drives, creating shortcuts, renaming the selected folders and files, and accessing the properties of the system's installed devices.

EXAM ALERT

Know how to navigate to various parts of Windows through the My Computer icon.

Because Windows 2000 and Windows XP are designed to permit multiple users on a single machine, they both include a My Documents folder that acts a central repository for users' files. In reality, each user who has a profile on a given computer has an individual, dedicated My Documents folder for his or her files. The My Documents folder in Windows 2000 and Windows XP includes a My Pictures subfolder that acts as the default location to hold graphics files.

Windows XP also adds My Music and My Videos folders to the My Documents folder family. Windows XP Media Center Edition has gone even further and provided My TV, My Photos, My Video, and My Radio folders to provide each user with personal storage areas for these types of files.

The Recycle Bin

The Recycle Bin is a storage area for deleted files that enables you to retrieve files if they are deleted by mistake. When you delete a folder or file from the Windows system, its complete path and filename are stored in a hidden file called Info in the Recycled folder. Files are renamed in a manner that makes them become invisible to the system. However, the system records their presence in the Recycle Bin. The system is free to reuse the space on the drive because it does not know that anything is there. As long as it hasn't been overwritten with new data, or it hasn't been removed from the Recycle Bin, a file can be restored from the information in the Recycle Bin. If a file has been thrown out of the bin but has not been overwritten, it can be recovered using a third-party software utility for recovering deleted files.

> **EXAM ALERT**
>
> Know what happens to files moved into the Recycle Bin.

The Recycle Bin icon should always be present on the desktop. It can be removed only through the Registry. If its icon is missing, there are two alternatives for restoring it: establish a shortcut to the Recycle Bin using a new icon, or reinstall Windows. This action will always place the Recycle Bin on the desktop.

If the Empty the Recycle Bin command is unavailable or the Recycle Bin appears full but you cannot view its contents, the Recycled folder that holds the contents of the Recycle Bin may have become damaged. With some versions of Windows, you can restore the operation of the Recycle Bin, by using the `attrib` command from the Command Prompt to remove the system and hidden attributes and then using the `del` command to delete the folder. When you reboot the system Windows will re-create the folder and its operation.

In the case of removable media, such as floppy disks and removable hard drives, the Recycle Bin does not retain the files deleted from these media. When a file or folder is removed from one of these devices, the information is deleted directly from the system.

My Network Places

The My Network Places applet enables the user to create shortcut icons to network shares on the desktop. A *network share* is an existing shared resource (that is, a printer, drive, modem, or folder) located on a remote system. The new icon acts as an alias to link the system to the share point on the remote unit.

The Network and Dial-Up Connections option enables you to see all the network connections that exist for the local computer. The My Network Places folder includes a convenient Computers Near Me view that identifies local area network devices. The Add Network Place options enable you to more easily establish connections to other servers on the network. The user can establish shortcuts to virtually every server on the network.

In the Windows XP operating system, the My Network Places icon opens to a display of the local network, as shown in Figure 12.8. As the figure illustrates, the Network Tasks pane offers options to Add a Network Place and View Network Connections. In larger network environments, you may also have a Search Active Directory option.

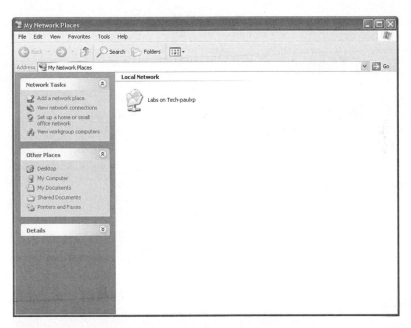

FIGURE 12.8   The Windows XP Local Network window.

The Add a Network Place option can be used to create shortcuts to network locations and websites. It can also be used to sign up for personal web storage space. As its name indicates, the Search Active Directory option enables the user to search the Active Directory structure for network shares, computers, and users.

EXAM ALERT

Be aware that information deleted from removable media is not moved into the Recycle Bin. Therefore, no recovery is possible for this information.

Challenge #1

A customer has called your help desk to complain that she has mistakenly removed a project that she have been working on for several months from her hard drive. She wants to know if your company can extract erased data from disk drives. With good questioning techniques, you determine that she is using a Pentium 4 machine with lots of RAM and a huge hard-disk drive. In addition, she has a R/W CD-ROM drive and she is running Windows 2000 Professional. She does not have a tape drive for backup, and because the system is very new, she has never performed a backup on it. What, if anything, can you do to help this customer?

Drop-Down Menus

Most Windows 2000 and XP dialog boxes include menu bars that provide pop-up menus when you click their titles. You can also press the Alt key and the underlined character (for example, the Alt+F combination will pop up the File menu). Typical menu bar options on most windows include File, Edit, View, and Help. Options that apply to the current window are displayed as dark text. Options that are not applicable to the window are grayed out.

EXAM ALERT

Know what is indicated when menu options are grayed.

File Menus

The Windows drop-down File menu performs basic file management–related functions for files and folders, including Open, Close, and Save operations that users constantly perform on files. In addition, the menu provides options that enable the user to rename the file or folder, create a shortcut for it, or establish properties for it.

Windows 2000 and XP offer extended common dialog boxes for File/Open, File/Print, and File/Save options. These dialog boxes provide easy organization and navigation of the system's hard drives, as well as providing navigation columns that grant quick access to frequently used folders, such as the My Documents and My Pictures folders. The File menu also includes an entry at the top of the menu titled New. Clicking this option produces the New options submenu used to create new folders, shortcuts, and files.

The File option on the My Computer and Windows Explorer menu bars can be used to perform many disk maintenance procedures. When a disk drive icon is selected, clicking the File option will produce a menu that includes provisions for opening, exploring, formatting the drive, sharing the drive with the network community, searching the contents of the drive, or displaying its properties.

The File menu's Properties option displays general information about the drive, such as file system type, capacity, free space, and used space. This option also has tabs that provide you with access to the system's drive maintenance tools and utilities through the Tools tab.

View Menu

The View menu option, shown in Figure 12.9, is one of the most used features of the menu bar. It can be used to alter the manner in which the contents of the window are displayed. Drives and folders can be displayed as small icons, changed to large icons, displayed as a list, or displayed with name, type, size, and free space details. Windows 2000 and XP dialog boxes also include an image preview function that enables users to locate graphics files efficiently. This is made possible through the use of thumbnail views. The dialog boxes can be resized to accommodate as many thumbnail images as desired.

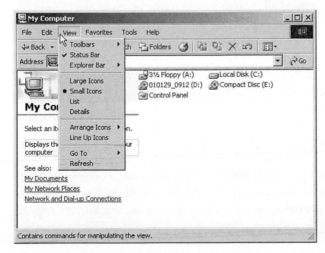

FIGURE 12.9 The Windows View menu.

Other options in the menu can be used to organize the icons within the window. A check mark located next to the menu option indicates that the item is currently in use. A large dot next to the item indicates that it is the currently selected option.

EXAM ALERT

Be aware of what the check mark and the dot in a pop-up menu indicate about the option.

Tools Menu

This information can also be displayed in several formats using the View option. Selecting the Folder Options entry in the Tools menu produces the Folder Options window. This window consists of four tabs (screens): General, View, File Types, and Offline Files.

NOTE

Windows XP Home Edition does not support offline files and folders.

The General tab supplies information about how the desktop will display windows as the user browses through multiple windows. The View tab is used to define how the folders and files in the selected window will be displayed onscreen. This screen also determines which types of files will be displayed. To see hidden and system files, select the View tab and click the Show Hidden Files and Folders option button. Files with selected extensions will be hidden. The File Types tab lists the types of files that the system can recognize. New file types can be registered in this window.

EXAM ALERT

Know how to show hidden files in Windows 2000/XP systems.

The Taskbar

Across the bottom of the display is an area called the taskbar. This area employs icons to display all the applications currently running in the system. Each time a program is started, or a window is opened, a corresponding button appears on the taskbar. To switch between applications, just click the desired program button to make it the active window. The button will disappear from the taskbar if the program is closed. Right-clicking the taskbar at the bottom of the screen produces a menu that can be used to control its appearance and open windows onscreen.

A small window at the extreme right side of the taskbar shows programs and events that occur in the background (mouse drivers, antivirus programs, volume control). This area is referred to as the *notification area*, or more commonly as the *systray*. On most systems, at the least the time of day clock is displayed here. The icons in this area provide quick links to programs and services, such as the volume control icon, that are running in the background.

> **NOTE**
>
> The terms *systray* and *system tray* are commonly used to describe the notification area of the taskbar. However, these are not technically correct in describing this area.

In Windows 2000 and XP, the taskbar is located at the bottom of the display by default. However, it can be moved around the display by clicking and dragging it to the left, right, or top of the screen. When moved to the top of the screen, the Start menu will drop down from above instead of pop up from the bottom. It can also be hidden just offscreen by clicking its edge and then dragging it toward the edge of the display.

If the taskbar is hidden, pressing the Ctrl+Esc key combination will retrieve it. This will pop up the Start menu along with the taskbar. Enter the Start, Settings, Taskbar, and Start Menu option to change the taskbar settings so that it will not be hidden. You can also locate an absent taskbar by moving the mouse around the edges of the screen until the shape of the cursor changes. Likewise, pressing the Tab key will cycle control between the Start menu, the Quick Launch icons, the taskbar, and the desktop icons. The Tab key can be helpful in navigating the system if the mouse fails.

> **EXAM ALERT**
>
> Know how to move around the desktop, Start menu, and taskbar using the keyboard.

Start Menu

Windows 2000 and Windows XP operations typically begin from the Start menu that pops up when the Start button is clicked. The Start menu provides the user with access to the system regardless of what else is occurring in the system. In doing so, it provides access to the system's installed applications, a search engine for finding data in the system, and the operating system's Help file structure.

The Windows 2000 Start menu contains entries for Programs, Documents, Settings, Find, Help, Run, and Shut Down options. Placing the cursor over designated menu items will cause any submenus associated with that option to pop up onscreen. An arrow to the right of the option indicates that a submenu is available. To open the selected item, left-click it and its window will appear on the desktop.

Windows 2000 and Windows XP feature intelligent, personalized Programs menus. These operating systems monitor the user's program usage, and after the first six accesses, arrange the menu options according to those most frequently used. The menu options displayed change based on their usage. Less frequently used programs are not displayed in the list, but can be accessed by clicking the double arrow at the bottom of the list. The hidden portion of the list will appear after a short delay. When this occurs, the six most frequently used applications are highlighted. This reduces screen clutter and makes it easier for users to access their most used items.

The operating system keeps track of personalized settings for each user who has a user profile established on the system. When a user logs on to the system, a profile folder is created in the Documents and Settings folder. This folder is labeled with the user's identification and contains personalized settings for the user's Desktop, My Documents folder, and Start Menu, as well as customized Internet options.

There may also be two general profile folders under the Documents and Settings folder: Administrator and All Users. The Administrative folder contains personalized settings for the Administrators account in a domain-based networking environment. The All Users folder contains information that will apply to all users who log on to the system.

EXAM ALERT

Know how to install programs and options that will apply to all users who access a given PC.

The Programs submenu has several options that include Accessories, Startup, and Windows Explorer. The Programs, Accessories entry is of particular interest to technicians because it provides access to some of the most frequently used

Windows operating system tool groups and utilities. These groups include Communications, Accessibility, Entertainment, and System Tools.

The System Tools group contains many utilities that are used to maintain and optimize the system, as illustrated in Figure 12.10. Access to many of these tools has been grouped into an Administrative Tools Console under the Windows 2000 and XP Control Panel. However some system tools are available only through this menu Path. For example, you can only get to the Character Map utility through the /Accessories/System Tools path. This utility is used to move and insert special characters, such as symbols and mathematical characters into documents, as well as for using, displaying, or printing foreign characters from another language.

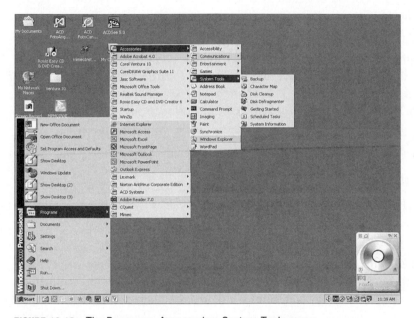

FIGURE 12.10   The Programs, Accessories, System Tools menu.

EXAM ALERT

Know how to access the Windows Character Map and what it is used for.

Windows supports the Unicode character set. *Unicode* is a character set standard established to represent nearly all the written languages of the world. This character set enables Windows to be a global tool that can be used around the world.

EXAM ALERT

Know what Unicode is and what it is used for.

The Start menu's Documents entry displays a list of documents previously opened and provides direct access to the user's My Document folder.

The Settings option displays values for the system's configurable components. It combines previous Windows functions, such as copies of the Control Panel, Network and Dial-Up Connection and Printers (Print Manager) folders, as well as access to the taskbar. The contents of the Windows 2000 and Windows XP Control Panels can be cascaded as a submenu of the Start button for quick access. The My Documents menu can also be cascaded off the Start menu for fast access to documents.

The Windows 2000 and XP Search utility includes powerful search capabilities for searching the local hard drive and the web to locate folders, files, mail messages, and shared computers. The HTML-like Search function in Windows 2000 and XP replaces the Start menu's Find option from previous Windows desktops. The Search feature provides three distinct search options:

▶ For Files and Folders

▶ On the Internet

▶ For People

The For Files and Folders option opens a powerful search function with advanced search options, such as case-sensitive searches. These options are available through the Advanced button. Selecting the On the Internet option brings up a search bar that establishes a link to a predetermined Internet search engine such as Yahoo!or Google. The Search for People option opens a Lightweight Directory Access Protocol (LDAP) dialog window.

Enabling the Microsoft Index Server function produces particularly fast searches. The Indexing Service runs in the background to provide content indexing on the local hard drive. Windows 2000 and XP Professional versions include a local version of the indexing service that operates with the local hard drive. In a network environment that uses Windows 2000 Server, the server can perform the content indexing service. The Index Service Management tools are located in the Start, Programs, Administrative Tools path. Searching with the context index feature enabled allows the user to write Boolean logic expressions (such as AND, OR, and NOT) for finding specific content quickly.

The Help file system provides extensive information about many Windows functions and operations. It also supplies an exhaustive list of guided troubleshooting routines for typical system components and peripherals.

The Run option is used to start programs or open folders from a command-line dialog box. To start an executable file, type its filename into the dialog box and click the OK button. The Browse button can be used to locate the desired file by looking through the system's file structure.

The Start button is also used to correctly shut down Windows. The Shut Down option shuts down the system, restarts the computer, or logs the user off. It must be used to avoid damaging files and to ensure that your work is properly saved. When it is clicked, the Shut Down Windows dialog box appears. After you select an option from the dialog box, the operating system will tell you to wait, and then it will give you a screen message telling you that it is okay to turn off the system.

Windows 2000 and XP enable individuals in multiuser systems to log on to and operate in personalized Windows environments specifically configured to their work needs. The Log Off User option is used to return the system to its natural setup. The Log Off entry may not appear in some installations, such as standalone machines that are not connected to a network environment.

Start menu items can easily be renamed in Windows 2000. You can accomplish this by right-clicking the menu item and choosing the Rename option from the context-sensitive pop-up menu. Then type the new name into the text entry box. This is all accomplished without opening the Start menu.

Additional items can be added to the Start menu so that they can be used directly from the menu. By doing so, the normal method of clicking Start, pointing to the Programs option, and moving through submenus can be avoided. To move a frequently used item to the top of the Start menu, drag its icon to the Start button on the taskbar. It is also possible to move all of your frequently used programs to the Programs submenu. Frequently used items can be moved to the taskbar, the Quick Launch toolbar, or user-created toolbars for easy access.

Windows 2000 Control Panel

The Windows Control Panel, shown in Figure 12.11, is the primary user interface for configuring and managing the Windows system. It contains a collection of Windows-specific applications and utilities (referred to as *applets*) that control different components of the operating system. The Control Panel can be accessed through the Start\Settings path.

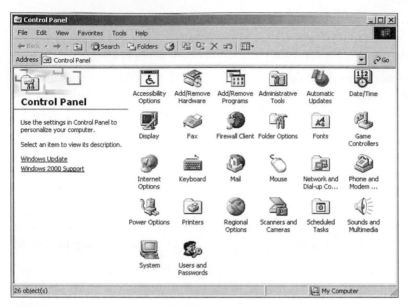

FIGURE 12.11   Windows 2000 Control Panel icons.

The Control Panel icon provides access to the configuration information for each of the system's installed devices specific to its type. Double-clicking any of the device icons will produce a Properties dialog box for that device. Each dialog box is different in that it contains information specific to the selected device. The dialog box will also have a number of folder tabs along its top. These tabs are labeled with the type of information it holds and can be used to review and change settings and drivers for the device. Clicking a tab will display additional information and options for the designated topic.

The Control Panel also provides support for infrared device control, an Internet configuration tool, a Power Management utility, support for scanners/digital cameras, and additional modem and communication control functions in the form of a Phone and Modem utility. The final addition to the Control Panel is the Users and Passwords icon that provides tools to establish and manage profiles for multiple users on the system.

The Windows Task Scheduler utility is located under the Control Panel's Scheduled Tasks icon. This utility is used to schedule operating system and application operations so that they start and run automatically. This enables users and technicians to schedule routine tasks such as backups and defragmentation operations to occur without a user or technician being involved. Also, these tasks can be scheduled to run at the most convenient times, such as the middle of the night when no one is using the machine. Tasks can be scheduled to run daily, weekly, monthly, or at prescribed times and dates.

However, the most important uses of the Control Panel tools for the technician are the following:

▸ Adding or removing new hardware or software components to the system

▸ Modifying system device settings

▸ Modifying desktop items

These functions are performed through two configuration wizards: Add/Remove Hardware (Add Hardware in Windows XP) and Add/Remove Programs (Add/Remove Programs and Windows Components in Windows XP). Windows 2000 and XP bring the most widely used administrative tools together in the Administrative Tools applet. The other control panel widely used by technicians is the System applet.

Installation Wizards

The Add/Remove Hardware (Add Hardware) icon brings the Add/Remove Hardware Wizard into action. It initially asks whether you want to Add/Troubleshoot a Device or Uninstall/Unplug a Device. Next, the wizard runs a new PnP enumeration on the system to see if it can detect any new hardware. If the system does not detect any new hardware, it asks you to Choose a Hardware Device to Troubleshoot.

The Devices list also offers a Add a New Device option. If you select this option, you are given the choice of having Windows conduct another search for the new hardware through a PnP-style detection process, or you can select the hardware from a list of Windows-supported hardware products.

If the device must be installed manually because Windows could not detect it, Windows will produce a Choose a Hardware Device component list similar to the one shown in Figure 12.12. The Add New Hardware Wizard will guide the manual installation process from this point and prompt the user for any necessary configuration information. If the device is not present in the list, click the Have Disk button to manually load drivers supplied by the device's manufacturer.

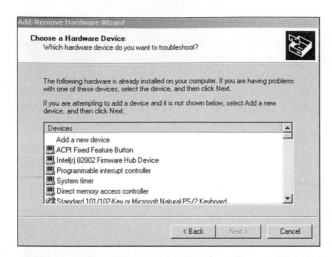

FIGURE 12.12 The Hardware Wizard's device selection page.

The Add/Remove Programs icon leads to the Change or Remove Programs screen. You can use this page to install new programs by clicking the Add New Programs button and specifying where to look for the program files. Conversely, programs listed in the Programs window can be removed from the system by highlighting their title and clicking the Change or Remove Programs button.

The Add/Remove Windows Component button is used to add or remove selected Windows components, such as communications packages or additional system tools. For example, when Service Pack 2 (SP2) was introduced for Windows XP, many users found that their existing system did not do well with the new upgrade. The Add or Remove Programs and Windows Components utility was used to remove the new service pack update in these machines.

Challenge #2

A friend gave you a copy of several quaint old MS-DOS-based games on CD. When you put the CD into the drive, there is no auto-run action. You want to install the games on your PC, but you're not sure how to go about it. Where should you look first to install the games under Windows 2000?

Administrative Tools

The Windows 2000 and Windows XP operating system versions have taken a different approach to system administration and preventive maintenance by concentrating many of the system's administration tools in a single location, under the Control Panel's Administrative Tools icon. The tools are combined in the Windows 2000/XP Computer Management Console, shown in Figure 12.13. You can access the Management Console by right-clicking the My Computer icon and selecting the Manage option from the pop-up menu. As the figure illustrates, the console includes three primary Microsoft Management Consoles (MMCs):

▶ System Tools

▶ Storage

▶ Services and Applications

The contents of the different consoles vary depending on which snap-in tools administrators decide to add to them.

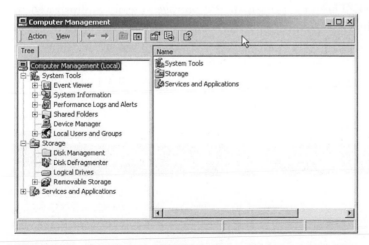

FIGURE 12.13   The Windows 2000/XP Computer Management console.

The System Tools console, shown in Figure 12.14, provides a collection of tools that can be used to view and manage system objects. They can also be used to track and configure all the system's hardware and software, and to configure network options and view system events.

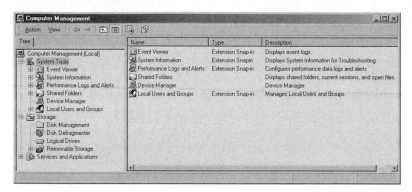

FIGURE 12.14   The System Tools options.

Likewise, the Storage console provides a standard set of tools for maintaining the system's disk drives. These tools include the Disk Management tool, the Disk Defragmenter utility, and a Logical Drives utility.

The Removable Storage node is used to establish unified sharing and managing of removal storage devices, such as disk drives, tape drives, and optical drives that have removable media. This utility works with data management applications and utilities, such as Backup, so that they can share these devices.

The Disk Management tool enables the user to create and manage disk partitions and volumes. The organization of the Storage console is illustrated in Figure 12.15. The Disk Defragmenter is used to optimize file operations on disks by rearranging their data into the most effective storage pattern for reading and writing. Finally, the Logical Drives tool shows a listing of all the logical drives in the system, including remote drives that have been mapped to the local system.

EXAM ALERT

Be aware of where the Disk Management tools are located in Windows 2000.

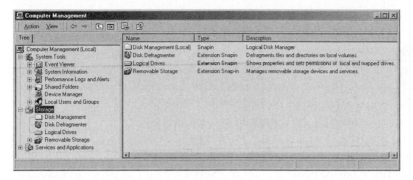

FIGURE 12.15 The Storage console options.

The Services and Applications entry includes an advanced set of system management tools. These tools include the Windows Management Instrumentation (WMI) tools, a listing of all the system's available services, and access to the Windows 2000 Indexing functions, as shown in Figure 12.16. The WMI tools are used to establish administrative controls with another computer, provide logging services, view user security settings, and enable the Windows 2000/XP advanced scripting services.

EXAM ALERT

Be aware of the capabilities associated with the Services and Applications node of the MMC.

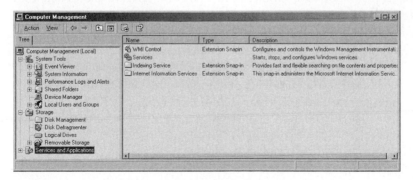

FIGURE 12.16 The Services and Applications options.

Some of the Windows 2000/XP management consoles are not loaded when the operating system is installed. However, they are available for installation from the Windows 2000/XP CDs. These consoles are referred to as *snap-ins*. In addition to the Control Panel path, all the installed MMCs can be accessed under the Start/Programs/Administrative_Tools path. Extended discussions of these tools are presented throughout the remainder of the text as they apply to managing and troubleshooting the operating system.

The System Icon

One of the main Control Panel icons is the System icon. Clicking this icon produces the System Properties window. This window features tabs for General information, Network Identification, Hardware, User Profiles, and Advanced in Windows 2000 and General, Computer Name, Hardware, Advanced, System Restore, Automatic Updates, and Remote in Windows XP.

▶ The General tab supplies information about the system's operating system version, microprocessor type, and RAM capacity, as well as its ownership and registration.

▶ The Network Identification (Computer Name) tab provides information about the system's full computer name and network relationship. It also provides access to the Network Identification Wizard, which is used to join the computer to a workgroup or domain network structure.

▶ The Hardware tab provides three important utilities used to manage the system's hardware components: the Hardware Wizard, the Device Manager, and Hardware Profiles. The Hardware Wizard is the same tool described earlier in this chapter in connection with the Add/Remove Hardware Wizard in the Control Panel. The Device Manager is a major hardware device configuration and troubleshooting tool. The Hardware Profiles button provides a window that can be used to establish different hardware configuration profiles to be implemented at startup. Normally, only multiple user systems require additional profiles.

▶ The User Profiles tab identifies the profiles that have been configured for all the different users defined in the system. These profiles contain tailored desktop settings and other information specific to each user.

▶ The Advanced tab provides access to the system's Performance Options, Environmental Variables, and Startup/Recovery configurations. The Performance Options button is used to configure how applications use memory, which ultimately affects the speed of the system. Environmental variables direct the system to certain types of information it needs to operate. The Startup and Recovery options direct the computer's operation on startup and define a course of action for when errors cause the computer to stop processing.

▶ The System Restore tab tracks changes made to the system and enables users to undo changes that produce undesired consequences.

▶ The Automatic Updates tab provides settings that can be configured to periodically check for Windows updates and install them as specified by the user.

▶ The Remote tab can be used to configure Windows XP for Remote Assistance and Remote Desktop options. Remote Assistance is a helpful utility that can be used to permit others to access and control a system from a remote location. The Remote Desktop option enables users to log in to their computer and desktop from a remote computer and use it as if they were setting at their computer.

EXAM ALERT

Memorize the types of information provided by the General tab of the System Properties page.

The Display Icon

The final major Control Panel function is to enable users to customize the Windows desktop. This customization is performed through the Display icon and includes such things as setting screen colors, changing the Windows wallpaper, and selecting screen savers. *Wallpaper* is the pattern that shows behind the various application windows. *Screen savers* are screen displays that remain in motion while the system is setting idle. This utility prevents a single display from remaining on the screen for a prolonged time. With older CRT displays this would cause the image to be "burned into" the screen. When this occurred, the image became a permanent ghost on the screen and the monitor was ruined. Advances in CRT and LCD displays have removed the need for screen savers and they are now more widely used to personalize the display.

Windows Explorer

File management functions in Windows are performed through the Windows Explorer interface. The Windows 2000/XP Windows Explorer graphically displays the entire computer system in a hierarchical tree structure on the left side of the screen. This enables the user to manipulate all the system's drives and software. The inclusion of the My Network Places icon links Windows Explorer directly to the My Network Places dialog window and extends the Windows Explorer structure to include network and domain structures. Likewise, the Internet Explorer icon supplies the system with a tightly linked web connection.

This manager is located under the Start/Programs/Accessories path in Windows 2000 and XP. By clicking the Windows Explorer entry, the system's directory structure will appear, as shown in Figure 12.17. You can access the Windows Explorer by right-clicking the Start button or by clicking the My Computer icon and selecting the Explore option.

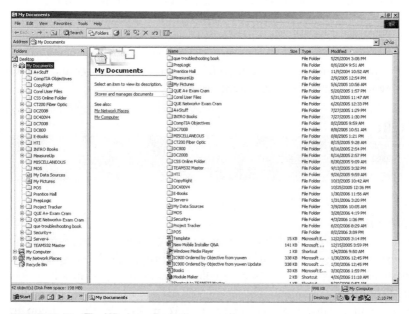

FIGURE 12.17   The Windows Explorer screen.

The Windows Explorer enables the user to copy, move, and erase files on any of the system's drives. Its screen is divided into two parts. The left side displays the system's directory tree, showing all the directories and subdirectories of its available drives.

In the Windows environment, directories and subdirectories are referred to, and depicted as, folders (and subfolders). Any drive or directory can be selected by clicking its icon or folder. You can expand the content of a folder by clicking the (+) sign beside it. Conversely, you can contract the same folder by clicking on the minus (–) sign in the same box.

The Windows Explorer is not limited to showing the directories, subdirectories, and files on local drives. It will also display drives and folders from throughout the network environment. The contents of the local drives are displayed at the top of the directory tree. If the system is connected to a network, the additional resources available through the network are displayed below those of the local system as a continuation of its tree structure.

The right side of the Windows Explorer screen displays the files of the selected directory. Applications can be started from this window by double-clicking their executable file. Double-clicking a file produced by an associated application will cause Windows to open the application and load the selected file.

The Windows Explorer toolbar comes with a collection of about 20 add-on buttons that can be used to customize its available options. You can modify the toolbar by right-clicking the toolbar and then selecting the Customize option from the pop-up menu. Additional buttons include Move To, Copy To, Search, Map Drive, Favorites, and Full Screen. The Full Screen option and can be used to toggle between maximized and normal window sizes.

The status bar at the bottom of the screen provides information about the number and size of the files in the selected directory. The View menu on the Windows Explorer menu bar can be used to set the display for large or small icons, as well as for simple or detailed lists. The Explorer's View functions are the same as those described for the My Computer menu bar.

The Windows Explorer is also used to perform functions such as formatting and copying disks. Right-clicking a folder icon will produce a menu that includes a Send To option. Moving the mouse to this entry will produce a submenu that can be used to send a selected folder or file to a floppy drive or to the desktop. Several files or folders can be selected for copying using the Shift key.

The contents of the right-click menu in Windows Explorer change depending on the item that is selected. Because the right-click function is context-sensitive, the menu produced for a folder will be different from the one displayed for a document file. Each menu will have options that apply to the selected item. Right-clicking a document file will produce options that enable the user to copy, cut, rename, open, or print the document from the Windows Explorer. This menu also provides options to create a shortcut for the document or to change its attributes.

By default, Windows Explorer does not show SYS, INI, or DAT files. To change file attributes from the Explorer, right-click the desired file, select the Properties option from the pop-up list, move to the General page, and click the desired attribute boxes. To see hidden and system files in Windows Explorer, click the Tools menu option, select the Folder Options entry, click the View tab, and check the Show All Files box. If you experience difficulty with this operation from the Windows environment, you can always access the file from the command prompt and change its attributes with the ATTRIB command.

EXAM ALERT

Be familiar with efficient methods of changing file attributes from the Windows Explorer.

EXAM ALERT

Know which file types are normally not shown in Windows Explorer.

If Windows cannot identify the application associated with the selected file, the operator will need to start the application and then manually open the file. However, the user can also register the file's extension type under the Tools/Folder Options/File Types path from the menu bar. This will produce the Registered File Types dialog box.

EXAM ALERT

Know how to navigate to various parts of the Windows operating system using the Windows Explorer.

To create a new folder in Windows Explorer, select a parent directory by highlighting it in the left window. Then click the File menu button, move the cursor to the New entry, slide across to the Folder option, and click it. A new unnamed folder icon will appear in the right Explorer window.

EXAM ALERT

Be aware of the different locations in Windows where new folders can be created, and remember the primary method of creating a new folder.

The same process is used to create new files. A file icon can be produced for any of the file types registered. Right-clicking the new icon will produce the menu with options for renaming the icon, creating a shortcut for it, and establishing its properties (including its attributes).

A small arrow in the lower-left corner of an icon identifies it as a shortcut. When a shortcut is created, Windows does not place a copy of the file or application in every location that references it. Instead, it creates an icon in each location and defines it with a link to the actual location of the program in the system. This reduces the amount of disk space required to reference the file from multiple locations.

Windows XP Interface Variations

The Windows XP Media Center Edition (MCE) is a special extension to the Windows XP Professional operating system that is designed to turn the Media Center PC into a device that users can use to watch and record TV programming, store videos, and create electronic picture albums as well as download, manipulate, and listen to music.

MCE is a Microsoft-exclusive, preinstalled application that provides a large-font user interface to accommodate television viewing from across a room. The 72-point font used in the MCE menus is referred to as the "10-foot" font. Microsoft has developed its own infrared remote control, receiver, and IR blaster, along with a new wireless keyboard to work with the MCE interface. In addition to watching televison, users can remotely accessible the interface for video recording and playback, DVD playback, photo viewing, and music playback. The MCE portion of the operating system converts the system's hard drive and video products into a personal video recorder (PVR).

In most other respects, Media Center Edition is a Windows XP Professional system. However, the networking options for MCE are limited to workgroup connections. Computers running Media Center Edition cannot be connected to a domain-based network.

EXAM ALERT

Be aware of the networking limitations of Windows XP Home and MCE versions.

Microsoft has limited distribution of XP Media Center Edition to OEM system builders and Microsoft Developer Network (MSDN) subsribers, but not to retail distributers. This has been done primarily to ensure that MCE is associated with high-quality products and produces high levels of consumer happiness with Microsoft's efforts in the consumer entertainment market.

Although the Windows XP desktop and Start menu can be configured to look like the old Windows 2000 Start menu (referred to as the *Classic theme*), they have been redesigned to offer a more compartmentalized arrangement, as illustrated in Figure 12.18.

FIGURE 12.18   The Windows XP Start menu.

To be more appealing to consumers, the "My…" collection has been expanded to include Documents (and Recent Documents), Pictures, Music, Favorites, Computer, and Network Places. These represent the personalized settings for the logged-in user. They also make up one of the biggest sections of the revised Start menu.

Most of the other Start menu items are similar to those that users are familiar with from previous versions of Windows. This includes quick-access applications along the left side of the menu, the Control Panel Printers and Faxes options, and the Help and Support Search and Run options at the bottom right of the menu. The Log Off and Shut Down buttons have been set off by themselves at the bottom of the menu. The one item that looks significantly different is the All Programs entry. This button is the new version of the Programs option from the Windows 2000 menu.

Resting the cursor over the green arrow icon will pop up the All Programs menu. As the figure shows, the Windows XP All Programs menu contains the usual entries from previous Programs menus. Technicians should be most familiar with the contents of the Accessories and Administrative Tools options. These two locations provide the most direct access to most of the diagnostic and maintenance tools provided by the Windows XP operating system.

One additional technician-related entry to note in the All Programs menu is the Remote Assistance icon. This utility can be used to let remote computer users, such as remote technicians or administrators, take over the local computer and operate it from their desktop. This feature must be activated locally and usually involves turning control over to a trusted individual for assistance purposes.

Figure 12.19 shows the Accessories menu listings. The most interesting entries in the Accessories menu include Communications, Entertainment, and System Tools.

▶ The Communications entry provides tools and wizards that assist in setting up local area and dial-up networking functions. The Remote Desktop Connection Wizard in this menu enables you to access desktops on remote computers and use them as if you were sitting in front of those machines.

▶ The Entertainment option primarily involves audio and video functions associated with the PC.

▶ The System Tools submenu is a very important area for technicians. This entry can be used to access the disk and system management tools used to perform preventive maintenance on the system and to optimize its performance.

One other entry that you may need to be aware of in the Accessories menu is the Accessibility option. This entry provides system customization features that can be implemented to accommodate users who have physical barriers to using the computer system.

The Administrative Tools menu, whose contents are displayed in Figure 12.20, is another key location for technicians. This applet provides access to the system's major administration and management tools. Important entries in this submenu include the Computer Management applet that has tools for managing the system's disk systems as well as both local and remote computers, the Local Security Policy option that is used to configure local security policies, and the Event Viewer and Performance tools that are used to monitor system events and performance so that problems can be spotted and corrected before major failures occur.

FIGURE 12.19 Key XP All Programs menu extensions.

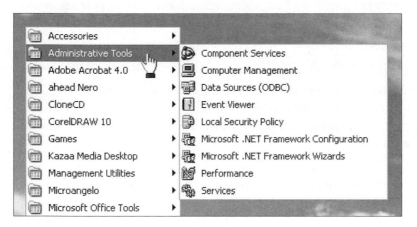

FIGURE 12.20 Windows XP Administrative Tools.

Windows XP Control Panel

The Windows XP Control Panel, depicted in Figure 12.21, also offers some additional features and functionality not found in previous versions. In Windows XP, the Control Panel option is included directly on the Start menu instead of in a submenu. Under the native Windows XP version of the Control Panel, the applets are organized into nine related categories.

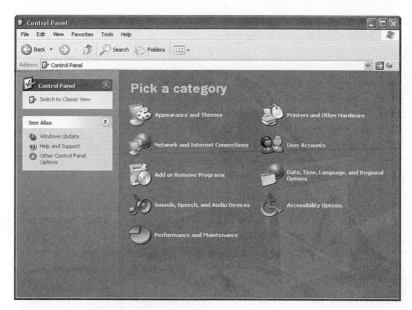

FIGURE 12.21   Windows XP Control Panel.

When you access some of these options, two corresponding dialog windows pop up in the left window: See Also and Troubleshooters. The See Also window lists other related topics that might be important to the activity you are attempting to perform. The Troubleshooters window provides direct access to related Windows Help Troubleshooters to solve context-specific problems. The Add or Remove Programs and User Accounts options do not have either of these two options when they are accessed. Similarly, the Date, Time, and Accessibility Options provide only a See Also window.

If you select the Switch to Classic View option in the upper-left dialog box, you should see all the normal Windows 2000–type Control Panel options for adding and removing hardware and software components, as well as a collection of individual control panels for different devices and Windows services. The Windows XP Control Panel also features an Administrative Tools applet that performs the same function as the entry from the Start, Programs menu of the same name.

In addition, the Classic View Control Panel includes advanced applets for Wireless Networking and Speech functions not found in other versions. There are also taskbar and Start menu options that can be used to customize these structures and control what items are displayed through them, such as the capability to lock the taskbar so that it cannot be moved or changed.

For the technician, one of the most important options in the Windows XP Control Panel is the Performance and Maintenance group depicted in Figure 12.22. This group contains the Administrative Tools and System icons. However, the System icon is the link to information about the computer system and to the device manager that is used to change the properties of the system's hardware devices.

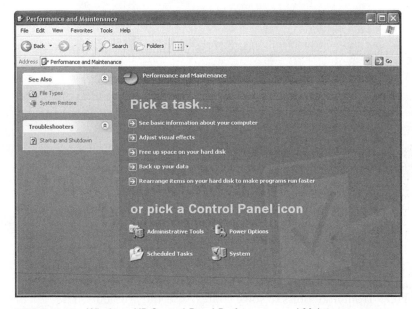

FIGURE 12.22   Windows XP Control Panel Performance and Maintenance group.

Windows XP Media Center Interfaces

The major features of the Windows XP Media Center Edition are appropriately connected to using the computer to handle multimedia functions such as viewing and recording television and other video sources, recording and listening to music, and storing, manipulating, and viewing pictures and graphics. Microsoft has accomplished this by adding a new Media Center option to the Start menu.

The Media Center Start page, depicted in Figure 12.23, provides a listing of content areas sorted by type. The options appear in a large font used to make the menu easier to read from a distance (made possible by the use of an infrared TV remote control). As you move the cursor across the menu options, most will pop up icons that represent recently used content for that content area. These pop-up icons enable users to move directly to desired content more quickly (that is, users do not have to click the main menu item to access the desired content area).

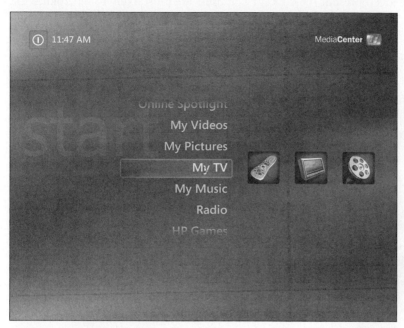

FIGURE 12.23 Media Center Start page options.

On earlier versions of Media Center Edition (MCE), Microsoft used the standard Minimize, Maximize, and Close buttons in the upper-right of the Start page. However, the 2005 version of MCE changed to a single Shut Down button located just to the left of the onscreen clock. When you move the cursor over this button, it turns red and pops up a Shut Down message. Click the button to open the Close Media Center options box. From this options box, you can close Media Center, log off, shut down the system, restart the computer, or enter standby mode, in order from left to right.

When you right-click an object in MCE, a context-sensitive menu pops up on the display. This pop up also occurs when you press the Details/More Info button on the remote control. The menu provides access to the object's details, as well as activity options for what actions can be performed on the object.

My TV

When you select the My TV option from the Start menu, the My TV main screen, depicted in Figure 12.24 appears. This screen provides a menu of TV options that includes Live TV, Recorded TV, Guide, Search, and Movies. It also displays listings of recently recorded shows and upcoming scheduled recordings. These lists provide direct access to these categories of content. The idea is that these two areas represent the content that users are most likely to be looking for.

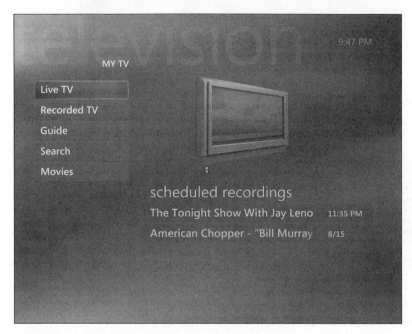

FIGURE 12.24 My TV.

The Live TV option brings up the current programming on the selected television channel. It also features a small control overlay that is used to pause a live show, navigate through it, or view the remaining time in a show.

The Recorded TV option brings up the Recorded TV page. This screen provides a small menu that includes Sort by Date and Sort by Title options. The Sort by Date option lists your recorded TV programs alphabetically and combines each episode of a recorded TV series into a single title.

The Scheduled option produces the Scheduled screen. Like the Recorded TV page, the Scheduled page presents a Sort By, Series, History menu. It also displays information about the shows you have scheduled to record in the future. The History option provides access to the complete list of recorded TV on the machine.

My TV also features a conflict resolution interface. If the user attempts to schedule two programs to be recorded at the same time, this interface reminds you with Only one show can be recorded at one time and asks you to select the program you prefer to record. However, MCE will attempt to find another instance of the same episode at a different time in the program guide. If so, it will automatically reschedule the recording for that time. This problem can be overcome in MCE systems by using TV capture cards that feature multiple TV tuner capabilities. Windows XP MCE is capable of handling up to three logical TV tuners simultaneously.

The My TV program guide, depicted in Figure 12.25, allows users to search through the channels they receive for TV programming that they want to watch or record. It also features a user interface for editing TV channel information. This feature permits users to navigate through their TV channel listing while they are viewing the channels and remove any channels that they do not receive through their service. You can also access viewing filter settings that enable users to limit the types of programming that can be viewed through the system. Unlike competing TV services, the Media Center Edition program guide does not charge a monthly fee for usage.

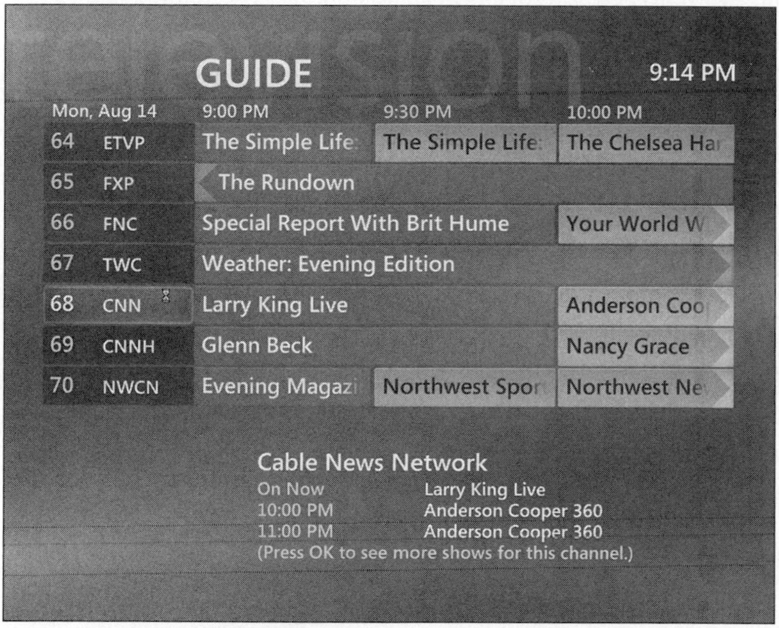

FIGURE 12.25   My TV program guide.

My Music

When you select the My Music option from the MCE Start menu, the My Music main page is displayed. It includes a selection menu and a graphical album list. The menu enables users to change the view to display all their music by artist, playlist, song, or genre. The menu also lets the user search for music. As with the other Start menu options, the My Music Start option presents the user's recent music. If you access the My Music page, the entire album list will be displayed along with the albums' cover art.

Under MCE, users can add music to a playlist while it is being played. To add more music to a list, you navigate to where the new music to be added is located and click the Add to Queue button. This will attach the new music to the end of the playlist. The same operation can be performed from the remote control. Press the More Info button on the remote and then select the Add to Queue option. Users can also use the menu to edit the playlist queue to move songs up or down the queue or remove them from the list.

You can save the updated playlist as a Media Player–compatible playlist using the Save as Playlist button. This button brings up the Queue screen illustrated in Figure 12.26. This enables users to access the playlist from both the Media Center and the Windows Media Player (WMP) utility. Availability in the WMP enables users to copy that music to portable devices for mobile listening purposes.

FIGURE 12.26 My Music Queue screen.

The playlist can also be burned to a CD or DVD using the Create CD/DVD option. This will bring up the Create CD/DVD page. At this point you must specify whether you are burning an audio CD or a data CD if you've placed a blank CD in the drive, or a data DVD, video DVD, or DVD slide show if you've loaded a blank recordable DVD disc in the drive.

You can also use MCE to load music and save it to the hard drive. To accomplish this, place an audio CD in the drive with MCE open. The title appears at the top of the My Music main screen, where you can choose to copy the music to the drive.

My Pictures

The MCE My Pictures option allows users to view and edit graphics through the MCE interface. Users can choose to play all pictures, or particular folders of pictures, in a slideshow fashion. They can also view and import graphics from CompactFlash cards, digital camera interfaces, or other portable storage formats.

Right-clicking an image brings up a menu of actions you can perform on the image. If you select the Picture Details option from the menu, the image will be displayed in the Picture Details page with a menu of editing options.

The Create CD/DVD option in My Pictures can be used to store pictures, folders, and slideshows on optical discs. The slideshow storage option is available only if the DVD option is chosen.

Other Features

The My Videos option is used to play digitized video stored on the system. Windows XP Media Center Edition includes version 2.1 of the Windows Movie Maker application. Likewise, the Play DVD option plays DVDs. Windows XP MCE includes FM and Internet Radio playback support with the capability to timeshare FM radio. For example, you can pause, rewind, and fast-forward through FM radio transmissions. However, MCE does not allow you to save FM recordings. A third-party Internet radio service is required to access Internet radio through the Radio option.

Command Prompt Procedures

Although "DOS is dead" for consumers, the technician must often resort to the command-line interface to isolate and correct problems within the Windows operating system. All Windows operating systems provide command-line interfaces that work separately from their GUIs for just this purpose.

To access the MS-DOS emulator in Windows 2000 or Windows XP, select the Run option from the Start menu and enter **CMD** (or **COMMAND**) in the Run dialog box. This will produce the command-line prompt.

EXAM ALERT

Know how to access the command prompt interface in Windows 2000/XP.

Challenge #3

A co-worker has just upgraded her old Windows Me computer to Windows 2000 Professional. The computer is connected to the company network and serves as a client to the company's file server. She wants to access the command prompt to run an older MS-DOS application, but she cannot find the MS-DOS icon in the Control Panel, so she asks you how to get to the command line in Windows 2000. What can you tell her?

To perform in the technical support area of the personal computer environment, you must be able to use the command-line functions and utilities available with the Windows operating systems.

Working from the Command Line

The command line is the space immediately following the drive letter prompt on the screen. All command-line functions and actions are typed in the space immediately to the right of the prompt. These commands are executed by pressing the Enter key on the keyboard. The command prompt for using the C: hard disk drive as the active directory is displayed in Figure 12.27.

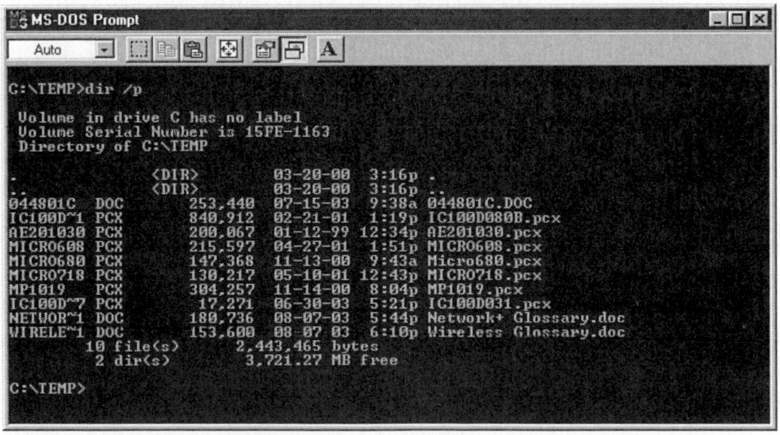

FIGURE 12.27   The command prompt.

From the command prompt, all command-line functions can be entered and executed. Application programs can also be started from this prompt. These files can be discerned by their filename extensions. Files with COM, EXE, or BAT extensions can be started directly from the prompt. The COM and EXE file extensions are reserved by Microsoft operating systems and can be generated only by programs that can correctly configure them. BAT files are simply ASCII text files that have been generated using command-line functions. Because BAT files contain operating system commands mixed with COM and EXE files, Microsoft operating systems can execute them from the command line.

EXAM ALERT

Know which file types can be executed directly from the command-line prompt.

Programs with other types of extensions must be associated with one of these three file types in order to be executed. The user can operate application software packages such as graphical user interfaces, word processors, business packages, data communications packages, and user programming languages (for example, Visual Basic and C++). For example, the core component of a word processor could be a file called WORDPRO.EXE. Document files produced by word processors are normally given filename extensions of DOC (for document) or TXT (for text file).

To view one of the documents electronically, you would first need to run the executable file and then use its features to load, format, and display the document. For example, Adobe Acrobat files normally have an extension of PDF. To execute a file with this extension, it is necessary to run the Adobe Acrobat application and then use the application to load and display different PDF files for use.

The user can also enter operating-system batch commands on the command line to perform different functions. These commands can be grouped into drive-level commands, directory-level commands, and file-level commands. The format for using command-line statements in a Microsoft command-line environment is

COMMAND (space) *SOURCE location* (space) *DESTINATION location*

COMMAND (space) *location*

COMMAND

The first example illustrates how command-line operations that involve a source and a final destination, such as moving a file from one place to another, are entered. The second example illustrates how single-location operations, such as formatting a disk in a particular disk drive, are specified. The final example applies to commands that occur in a default location, such as obtaining a listing of the files on the current disk drive.

You can modify the performance of various commands by placing one or more software switches at the end of the basic command. A switch is added to the command by adding a space, a foreslash (/), and a single letter:

COMMAND (space) *option/switch*

Drive-Level Command-Line Operations

The following command-line function pertains to drive-level operations. While there were several drive level commands available in the MS-DOS environment, there are only a few such command of interest in the Windows 2000/XP environment. The command must be typed at the command prompt.

▶ CONVERT: This command is used to in Windows 2000 and Windows XP to convert disks (volumes) from FAT-based disks into NTFS disks that typically provide more efficient disk management. The format for using this command is

```
C:\>CONVERT C: /FS:NTFS:
```

This will convert a FAT-based drive C: into an NTFS-based disk drive C: by installing the NTFS file system on the disk.

EXAM ALERT

Remember the function of the CONVERT command.

▶ FORMAT: This command is used to prepare a new disk, or a removable storage device, for use with an operating system. Actual data locations are marked off on the disk for the tracks and sectors, and bad sectors are marked. In addition, the directory is established on the disk. New disks must be formatted before they can be used.

```
C:\>FORMAT X
```
creates the tracks, sectors, and file system structure on the specified disk (in this case the X: drive).

```
C:\>FORMAT X:/S
```
causes three system files (boot files IO.SYS, MSDOS.SYS, and COMMAND.COM) to be copied into the root directory of the disk after it has been formatted. The new disk will now boot up without a DOS disk.

`C:\>FORMAT D:/Q` causes the system to perform a quick format operation on the D: disk or device. This amounts to removing the FAT and root directory from the disk.

▶ DISKCOPY: This command is used to make duplicate copies of floppy disks.

`C:\>DISKCOPY A:`

The `DISKCOPY` command can only be used with floppy disks and must be used on disks of the same capacity.

▶ DISKCOMP: This command is used to compare the contents of two disks. It compares the data on the disks not only to see that they are alike, but also to verify that the data is in the same place on both disks. This command is normally used to verify the contents of backup disks and is typically performed after a `DISKCOPY` operation has been performed.

`C:\>DISKCOMP A: B:`

EXAM ALERT

Know how to use disk-level commands.

Directory-Level Command Line Operations

In hard drive–based systems it is common to organize related programs and data into areas called *directories*. This makes them easier to find and work with because modern hard drives are capable of holding large amounts of information.

The following list of commands is used for directory-based operations in Microsoft systems. The format for using them is identical to that for the disk-related commands discussed earlier.

▶ DIR: The `Directory` command gives a listing of the files on the disk that is in the drive indicated by the drive specifier.

`C:\>DIR` or `DIR C:` (If DIR is used without any drive specifier, the content of the drive indicated by the prompt will be displayed.) The command may also be used with modifiers to alter the way in which the directory is displayed.

`C:\>DIR/W` displays the entire directory at one time across the width of the display.

`C:\>DIR/P` displays the content of the directory one page at a time. You must press a key to advance to the next display page.

▶ MKDIR (MD): Will create a new directory in an indicated spot in the directory tree structure.

C:\>MD C:\DOS\XXX will create a new subdirectory named XXX in the path that includes the root directory (C:\) and the DOS directory.

▶ CHDIR (CD): Will change the location of the active directory to a position specified by the command.

C:\>CD C:\DOS will change the working directory from the C: root directory to the C:\DOS directory.

▶ RMDIR (RD): Remove Directory will erase the directory specified in the command. You cannot remove a directory until it is empty or if it is currently active.

C:\>RD C:\DOS\forms would remove the DOS subdirectory "forms," provided it is empty.

Files and Filenames

Disk-based systems store and handle related pieces of information in groups called *files*. The system recognizes and keeps track of the different files in the system by their filenames. Therefore, each file in the system is required to have a filename that is different from that of any other file in its directory.

If two files having the same name were present within the same directory of the system, the computer would become confused and fail to operate properly. This is because it could not tell which version of the file it should work on. Each time a new file of information is created, it is necessary to give it a unique filename by which the operating system can identify and store it.

The following commands are used to carry out file-level operations. The format for using them is identical to that for the disk- and directory-related commands discussed earlier. However, the command must include the filename and its extension at the end of the directory path. Depending on the operation, the complete path may be required, or a default to the currently active drive will be assumed.

▶ COPY: The file copy command copies a specified file from one place (disk or directory) to another.

C:\>COPY C:filename.ext E:filename.ext

C:\>COPY C:\directory\filename.ext C:\directory\ is used if the file is to have the same name in its new location; the second filename specifier can be omitted.

▶ XCOPY: This command copies all the files in a directory, along with any
subdirectories and their files. This command is particularly useful in
copying files and directories between disks with different formats (for
example, from a 1.2MB disk to a 1.44MB disk) :

```
C:\>XCOPY C:\Temp A: /s
```

This command would copy all the files and directories from the \Temp
directory on drive C: (except hidden and system files) to the disk in drive
A:. The /s switch instructs the XCOPY command to copy directories and
subdirectories.

▶ DEL or ERASE: This command allows the user to remove unwanted files
from the disk when typed in at the command prompt:

```
C:\>DEL filename.ext
C:\>ERASE B:filename.ext
```

A great deal of care should be taken when using this command. If a file is
erased accidentally, it may not be retrievable.

▶ REN: Enables the user to change the name or extension of a filename:

```
C:\>REN A:filename.ext newname.ext
C:\>COPY A:filename.ext B:newname.ext
```

Using this command does not change the contents of the file, only its
name. The original filename (but not the file) is deleted. If you want to
retain the original file and filename, a copy command, using different
filenames, can be used.

▶ FC: This file-compare command compares two files to see if they are the
same. This operation is normally performed after a file copy has been
performed to ensure that the file was duplicated and located correctly:

```
C:\>FC C:\directory\filenameA.ext C:\directory\:filenameB.ext
```

If the filename was changed during the copy operation, the command
would have to be typed as

```
C:\>FC  C:\directory\filename.ext C:\directory\newname.ext
```

▶ ATTRIB: Changes file attributes such as Read-only (+R or –R), Archive
(+A or –A), System (+S or –S), and Hidden (+H or –H). The + and –
signs are to add or subtract the attribute from the file.

```
C:\>ATTRIB +R C:\DocumentsandSettings\My Documents\memos.doc
```

This command sets the file MEMOS.DOC as a read-only file. Read-only attributes protect the file from accidentally being overwritten. Similarly, one of the main reasons for giving a file a Hidden attribute is to prevent it from accidentally being erased. The System attribute is reserved for use by the operating system and marks the file as a system file.

A common error message encountered when working with command-line operations is the "bad command or file name" error message. This type of error message generally occurs when the path specified to the location of a file is incorrect, or when the filename is missing or misspelled.

Command-Line Shortcuts

Microsoft operating systems provide some command-line shortcuts through the keyboard's function keys. Some of the most notable are the F1 and F3 function keys. The F1 key will bring the previous command back from the command-line buffer, one character at a time. Likewise, the F3 key will bring back the entire previous command through a single keystroke.

When using filenames in command-line operations, the filename appears at the end of the directory path in the source and destination locations.

The * notation is called a wild card and allows operations to be performed with only partial source or destination information. Using the notation as *.* tells the software to perform the designated command on any file found on the disk using any filename and extension.

A question mark (?) can be used as a wild card to represent a single character in a filename or extension. Multiple question marks can be used to represent multiple characters in a filename or extension.

Data from a command can be modified to fit a prescribed output format through the use of filter commands. The main filter commands are More, Find, and Sort. The filter command is preceded by a pipe symbol (|) on the command line, when output from another command is to be modified. For example, to view the contents of a batch file that is longer than the screen display can present at one time, type Type C:\xxx.bat¦more. If the information to be modified is derived from another file, the less than (<) symbol is used.

Exam Prep Questions

1. You are running a DOS program under Windows and its display has taken up the entire screen. What can you do If you want to switch to another application while this one is running?

   ○ **A.** Ctrl+Esc

   ○ **B.** Ctrl+Tab

   ○ **C.** Alt+Tab

   ○ **D.** Alt+Esc

2. What desktop's shortcut key combination enables the user to cycle through open application windows?

   ○ **A.** Alt+Tab

   ○ **B.** Ctrl+Esc

   ○ **C.** Shift+Tab

   ○ **D.** Alt+Esc

3. How can you move around the desktop, Start menu, and taskbar by just using the keyboard?

   ○ **A.** Esc

   ○ **B.** Tab

   ○ **C.** Arrow keys

   ○ **D.** Ctrl

4. Which method is used to change file attributes from the Windows Explorer?

   ○ **A.** Right-click the file and select Properties

   ○ **B.** Edit the appropriate Registry entry with Regedt32

   ○ **C.** Highlight the file and choose the Select Options entry in the System Tools menu

   ○ **D.** Highlight the file and choose the Select Options entry in the View menu

5. How do you rename a file in Windows?

    ○ **A.** Double-click the file and enter the new name

    ○ **B.** Right-click the file and then select Rename from the pop-up menu

    ○ **C.** Click the file and enter the new name

    ○ **D.** Click the file and then select Rename from the pop-up menu

6. How can hidden and system files be shown in the Windows 2000 system?

    ○ **A.** Double-click My Computer, click File, select Properties from the menu, click the View tab, and then click the Show Hidden Files button

    ○ **B.** Double-click My Computer, click Tools, select Folder Options from the menu, click the View tab, and then click the Show Hidden Files and Folders button

    ○ **C.** Double-click My Computer, click View, select Options from the menu, click the View tab, and then click the Show Hidden Files button

    ○ **D.** Double-click My Computer, click Edit, select Folder Options from the menu, click the View tab, and then click the Show Hidden Files button

7. What is indicated when menu options are grayed out?

    ○ **A.** Options applicable to the selected item

    ○ **B.** Options not applicable to the selected item

    ○ **C.** Options currently in use

    ○ **D.** Options that are not installed

8. What does a check mark in a pop-up menu indicate about an option?

    ○ **A.** The option was previously deleted.

    ○ **B.** The option is currently selected.

    ○ **C.** The item needs to be installed.

    ○ **D.** The item is currently in use.

9. What does a dot in a pop-up menu indicate about an option?

    ○ **A.** The item is currently in use.

    ○ **B.** The item needs to be installed.

    ○ **C.** The option is currently selected.

    ○ **D.** The option is not available.

10. What happens to a file moved into the Recycle Bin?

   ○ **A.** The filename is changed to make it invisible to the system.

   ○ **B.** The file is deleted.

   ○ **C.** The file is archived and held for later deletion.

   ○ **D.** The file is overwritten.

11. What happens to information that is deleted from a removable media?

   ○ **A.** It is deleted from the file system.

   ○ **B.** It is moved into the Recycle Bin.

   ○ **C.** It is relocated to the System Backup directory.

   ○ **D.** The file is archived and held for later deletion.

12. How do you navigate to various parts of Windows through the Windows Explorer?

   ○ **A.** Expand a folder listing by clicking the minus sign (–) and repeat until you locate the target file/folder

   ○ **B.** Expand a folder listing by clicking the plus sign (+) and repeat until you locate the target file/folder

   ○ **C.** Expand a folder listing by clicking the star sign (*) and repeat until you locate the target file/folder

   ○ **D.** Expand a folder listing by clicking the backslash sign (\) and repeat until you locate the target file/folder

13. What action is required to install hardware devices not directly supported by Windows systems?

   ○ **A.** The system must be rebooted.

   ○ **B.** You must install a driver for a similar device from the same manufacturer.

   ○ **C.** The item cannot be installed.

   ○ **D.** It must be installed manually.

14. What type of information is provided by the General tab of the System Properties page? (Select all that apply.)

○ **A.** Microprocessor type and RAM capacity

○ **B.** Operating system version

○ **C.** Date of OS installation

○ **D.** Registered owner

15. Which method is used to change file attributes from the Windows Explorer?

○ **A.** Right-click the file and select Properties

○ **B.** Edit the appropriate Registry entry with Regedt32

○ **C.** Highlight the file and choose the Select Options entry in the System Tools menu

○ **D.** Highlight the file and choose the Select Options entry in the View menu

16. Which file types are usually not shown in Windows Explorer? (Select two answers.)

○ **A.** PCX

○ **B.** DAT

○ **C.** BMP

○ **D.** INI

17. How do you create a new folder using Windows Explorer?

○ **A.** Select a parent directory, click the File menu, and then select New Folder

○ **B.** Select a parent directory, click the Edit menu, and then select New Folder

○ **C.** Select a parent directory, click the Edit menu, select New, and then Folder

○ **D.** Select a parent directory, click the File menu, select New, and then Folder

18. Where are the disk drive tools located in Windows 2000?

○ **A.** System Information

○ **B.** System Tools

○ **C.** Device Manager

○ **D.** Computer Management

19. How is the MS-DOS emulator accessed in Windows 2000 and Windows XP?

   ○ **A.** PROMPT

   ○ **B.** CMD

   ○ **C.** RUN

   ○ **D.** DOS

20. How do you install a hardware device in a Windows system if the operating system does not have the device on its hardware compatibility list and does not have any existing drivers that are compatible with the device?

   ○ **A.** Install the device and allow the PnP process to configure the card

   ○ **B.** Install the device and click the Have Disk button when prompted

   ○ **C.** Install the device and manually configure it through the Device Manager

   ○ **D.** Install the device and access the Add/Remove Hardware Wizard to install it automatically

21. Which Windows utility can be used to automate many maintenance and administrative functions?

   ○ **A.** The Task Manager utility

   ○ **B.** The Device Manager

   ○ **C.** The Scheduled Tasks utility

   ○ **D.** The MSCONFIG utility

22. What type of kernel structure does the Apple OS X operating system employ?

   ○ **A.** Linux

   ○ **B.** UNIX

   ○ **C.** Windows NT

   ○ **D.** Windows Longhorn

23. What key combination opens the Start menu in Windows XP?

   ○ **A.** Ctrl+Esc

   ○ **B.** Alt+Esc

   ○ **C.** Ctrl+Alt+Esc

   ○ **D.** Shift+Esc

Answers and Explanations

1. C. If a DOS application takes up the entire screen in Windows, it will be necessary to press the Alt+Enter key combination to switch the application into a window. The Alt+Tab key combination switches the screen to another application.

2. D. Special key combinations enable the user to move between tasks easily. The Alt+Esc key combination enables the user to cycle through open application windows.

3. B. Pressing the Tab key will cycle control between the Start menu, the Quick Launch icons, the taskbar, and the desktop icons. This key can also be helpful in navigating the system if the mouse fails.

4. A. Changing file attributes from the Windows Explorer involves right-clicking the desired file, selecting the Properties option from the pop-up list, moving to the General page, and clicking the desired attribute boxes.

5. B. A file icon can be produced for any of the registered file types. Right-clicking the icon will produce a pop-up menu with options to rename the icon, create a shortcut for it, and establish its properties (including its attributes).

6. B. The View window is used to define how the folders and files in the selected window will be displayed onscreen. It also determines which types of files will be displayed. To see hidden and system files, double-click My Computer, click Tools, select Folder Options from the menu, click the View tab, and then click the Show Hidden Files and Folders button.

7. B. Options that are not applicable to the selected item will be grayed out.

8. D. A check mark located next to a menu option indicates that the item is currently in use.

9. C. The large dot next to an item indicates that it is the currently selected option.

10. A. The Recycle Bin is a storage area for deleted files, and it enables you to retrieve such files if they are deleted by mistake. When you delete a folder or file from the Windows system, its complete path and filename are stored in a hidden file called Info in the Recycled folder. Files are renamed in a manner that they become invisible to the system; however, the system records its presence in the Recycle Bin. The system is free to reuse the space on the drive because it does not know that anything is

there. As long as it hasn't been overwritten with new data, or it hasn't been removed from the Recycle Bin, the file can be restored from the information in the Recycle Bin. If it has been thrown out of the bin but has not been overwritten, it can be recovered using a third-party software utility for recovering deleted files.

11. A. In the case of removable media, such as floppy disks and removable hard drives, the Recycle Bin does not retain the files deleted from these media. When a file or folder is removed from one of these devices, the file information is deleted directly from the file system.

12. B. In the Windows environment, directories and subdirectories are referred to, and depicted as, folders (and subfolders). Any drive or directory can be selected by clicking its icon or folder. You can expand the content of the folder by clicking on the node (+ sign) beside the folder. Conversely, the content of the same folder can be contracted by clicking on the minus (–) sign node in the same box.

13. D. If the device must be installed manually because Windows could not detect it, selecting the No option and clicking Next will produce a hardware component list. The Add New Hardware Wizard guides the manual installation process from this point and prompts the user for any necessary configuration information. If Windows does not support the device, you must click the Have Disk button and load a driver supplied by the device's manufacturer.

14. A, B, D. The General tab supplies information about the system's operating system version, registered owner, microprocessor type, and RAM capacity, as well as its ownership and registration.

15. A. Changing file attributes from the Windows Explorer involves right-clicking the desired file, selecting the Properties option from the pop-up list, moving to the General page, and clicking the desired attribute boxes.

16. B, D. By default, Windows Explorer does not show SYS, INI, or DAT files.

17. D. To create a new folder in Windows Explorer, select a parent directory by highlighting it in the left window. Then click the File menu, move the cursor to the New entry, slide across to the Folder option, and click it. A new unnamed folder icon will appear in the right Explorer window.

18. D. The Windows 2000 Computer Management console can be accessed by Alt+clicking the My Computer icon and selecting the Manage option from the pop-up menu. The console includes the System Tools, Storage, and Services and Applications consoles. The Storage console provides a

standard set of tools for maintaining the system's disk drives. These tools include the Disk Management tool, the Disk Defragmenter utility, and a Logical Drives utility.

19. B. To access the MS-DOS emulator in Windows 2000 or XP, select the Run option from the Start menu and type CMD into the Run dialog box.

20. B. If the device is not on the operating system's hardware compatibility list, drivers for it must be supplied by the device manufacturer. These usually accompany the device in the form of an installation CD or floppy. When the system's PnP function finds the device but cannot configure it, it will ask for a disk or disc. If it does not, you will have to click the Have Disk button and supply a path to the driver file.

21. C. The System File Checker is one of many Windows utilities that can be run manually, or can be configured to run automatically when the system starts up. The Scheduled Tasks utility can be used to configure SFC to run at specified intervals.

22. A. All Apple computers originally ran proprietary versions of the Apple operating system. However, newer Apple Macintosh computers run on a proprietary version of Linux named Apple OS X. While the structure of OS X is Linux based, the user interaction portions of the system employ Apple's trademark GUI-based desktop.

23. A. Pressing the Ctrl+Esc key combination will pop up the Start menu along with the taskbar in Windows 2000/XP.

Challenge Solutions

1. You should have the customer check the Recycle Bin and restore the data herself. Because the drive is large and she has made no indication that she cleaned out the bin after the data was erased, there is no reason to think that the data is not in the Recycle Bin.

You should tell the caller to press the Alt and F keys at the same time to pop up the application's File menu. Next, the caller should press the S or A key to save the work to disk. The user may also need to press the Enter key to activate the command.

After the work has been saved, the user should press the Ctrl+Esc key combination to bring up the Start menu, and from there, use the up/down arrow keys to move to the Shut Down option. Pressing the Enter key will start the shutdown process.

2. Your best bet is to try the Add/Remove Software applet in the Control Panel. This utility is responsible for installing all software in the Windows environment.

3. She must access the command prompt through the Windows 2000 Start/Run menu option. In the Run dialog box that pops up, she must type **CMD** and click the OK button to access the command prompt.

13

Major Windows Structures

Terms you'll need to understand:

- ✓ BOOT.INI
- ✓ NTLDR
- ✓ Registry
- ✓ Active partition
- ✓ Primary partition
- ✓ Extended partition
- ✓ File allocation tables
- ✓ Master file tables
- ✓ Root directory
- ✓ NTFS
- ✓ Files
- ✓ Directories
- ✓ Permissions
- ✓ Logical partitions
- ✓ POST
- ✓ Bootup
- ✓ CDFS

Techniques you'll need to master:

Essentials 3.1: Identify the fundamentals of using operating systems.

- ✓ Identify names, purposes, and characteristics of the primary operating system components, including Registry, virtual memory, and file systems.

- ✓ Identify the names, locations, purposes, and characteristics of operating system files, for example:
    - ✓ BOOT.INI
    - ✓ NTLDR
    - ✓ NTDETECT.COM
    - ✓ NTBOOTDD.SYS
    - ✓ Registry data files

Essentials 3.1/Technical Support 2.1/IT Technician 3.1: Identify concepts and procedures for creating, viewing, managing disks, directories, and files in operating systems, for example:

- ✓ Disks (for example, active, primary, extended, and logical partitions)

- ✓ File systems (for example, FAT 32, NTFS)

- ✓ Directory structures (for example, create folders, navigate directory structures)

- ✓ Files (for example, creation, extensions, attributes, permissions)

Introduction

This chapter covers three major portions of the Windows Operating System areas of the CompTIA A+ Certification—Essentials examination under Objective 3.1. The three areas covered in this chapter are identifying the names, purposes, and characteristics of the primary operating system components, including the Registry, virtual memory, and file system; identifying the names, locations, purposes, and characteristics of key operating system files; and identifying concepts and procedures for creating, viewing, and managing disks, directories, and files in operating systems.

> **NOTE**
>
> Unless otherwise noted, operating systems referred to in this chapter are Microsoft Windows 2000, XP Professional, XP Home, and Media Center Edition.

PC technicians must be familiar with the functions and structure of operating systems that they may encounter in the field. Currently, the major operating system lines associated with personal computers are Windows 2000 Professional, Windows XP Professional, Home Edition, and Media Center Edition.

> **NOTE**
>
> A major portion of Tech Support Technician Objective 2.1 and IT Technician Objective 3.1 is identical to the material in Essentials Objective 3.1. Essentials 3.1—creating, viewing, and managing disks directories and files—and 2.1/3.1—creating, viewing, and managing disks, directories, and files—are the same.
>
> The topics specified in these different exam/objective areas are so closely stated that it makes sense that they are presented as the same discussion. You will need to study this material in this chapter for any of the four exams you intend to challenge.

The PC Hardware Startup Process

The system startup sequence is basically a hardware-oriented operation until the bootstrap process begins. At this point, the hardware begins looking for an operating system to take over control of the hardware to increase its functionality. This process represents the starting point of everything related to operating systems. With the exception of some hardware configuration information collected during the initialization phase of the startup process and eventually passed to the operating system, modern operating systems do not care what goes on prior to the bootup process. In fact, until the bootstrap process occurs, the system runs the same—no matter which operating system is eventually started to take over control of the system.

The key components and events of the PC-compatible hardware startup are the following:

▶ System Startup or Reset—When the system is started up or reset, the microprocessor is reset so that it begins taking instructions from a specified location in the ROM BIOS address range to test and initialize the system for operation.

▶ POST—The POST is actually a series of tests that are performed each time the system is turned on. The different tests check the operation of the microprocessor, the keyboard, the video display, the floppy and hard disk drive units, as well as both the RAM and ROM memory units.

▶ Initial POST checks—The first instruction that the microprocessor executes causes it to jump to the POST test, where it performs standard tests such as the ROM BIOS checksum test (that verifies that the BIOS program is accurate), the system's various DRAM tests (that verify the bits of the memory), as well as a test of the system's CMOS RAM (to make certain that its contents have not changed because of a battery failure). During the memory tests, the POST displays a running memory count to show that it is testing and verifying the individual memory locations. During these tests, the BIOS determines whether the system is being started from an off condition or being reset from some other state. When the system is started from an off condition, a *cold boot* is performed. However, simultaneously pressing the Ctrl, Alt, and Delete keys while the system is in operation (or selecting the Restart option from the Windows Shutdown menu) will generate a reset signal in the system and cause it to perform a shortened bootup routine. This operation is referred to as a *warm boot*, and it allows the system to be shut down and restarted without turning it off. This function also allows the computer's operation to be switched to another operating system.

▶ System initialization—During this part of the program, startup values stored in the ROM BIOS IC are moved into the system's programmable devices to make them functional. These include the IRQ and DMA channel configurations along with the standard I/O addresses that make the system PC-compatible.

▶ Plug-and-Play configuration—During the initialization process, the Plug-and-Play (PnP) BIOS checks the devices installed in the expansion slots to see what types they are, how they are configured, and which slots they are in. It then assigns each adapter a *software handle* (name) and stores its name and configuration information in a RAM table. Next, the BIOS performs an enumeration process to verify the adapter information against the system's basic configuration for resource conflicts. If no conflicts are detected, all the devices required for bootup will be activated.

▶ CMOS setup checks—During the initialization process, the BIOS checks the battery-powered CMOS RAM configuration storage area to determine what types of options are installed in the system. In PnP systems, these settings are established by the PnP process's autodetect functions. However, the boot sequence places a prompt on the screen that permits the user to enter the CMOS Setup utility to manually configure settings during this period. This prompt usually calls for pressing the Del or Esc key and is available for only a short period of time. Some newer BIOS versions use the F6 or F8 function key to enter the CMOS Setup utility.

▶ Additional POST checks—After the final memory test and basic system configuration steps have been performed, the remaining I/O devices and adapters are tested.

▶ BIOS extensions—After the POST and initialization processes have been completed, the BIOS checks the area of memory between C0000 and DFFFF for BIOS extension programs. IBM system designers created this memory area so that new or nonstandard BIOS routines could be added to the basic BIOS structure. These extended firmware routines match software commands from the system to the hardware they support. Therefore, the software running on the system does not have to be directly compatible with the hardware. The BIOS extension code on a network card may contain an initial program load (IPL) routine that will cause the local computer to load up and operate with an operating system from a remote computer. This is the principle behind diskless workstations that boot up to remote computers and have no local disk drives.

At the successful completion of these tests, most systems produce a single beep tone through the system speaker to announce the end of the hardware portion (POST/initialization) phase of the startup process and the beginning of the software portion (bootup) of the startup sequence.

The Windows 2000/XP Boot Process

All Windows NT (New Technology) operating system versions, which include Windows 2000 and all Windows XP variations, can work with two very different disk-management structures. These Windows NT versions can work with the file allocation table (FAT)–based file management system used with older, consumer-oriented Microsoft operating systems (MS-DOS, Windows 3.x, and Windows 9x/Me). However, they also offer their own proprietary Windows NT File System (NTFS). The NTFS structure is designed to provide better data security and operate more efficiently with larger hard drives than FAT systems do.

The Windows PC starts by running its POST, performing an initialization of its intelligent system devices, and performing a system boot process. When the BIOS accesses the Master Boot Record (MBR) on the hard drive, the MBR examines the disk's partition table to locate the active partition. The boot process then moves to the boot sector of that partition (referred to as the *partition boot sector*) located in the first sector of the active partition. Here the MBR finds the code to begin loading the secondary bootstrap loader from the root directory of the boot drive.

In the case of a Windows NTFS partition, the operating system loader is the NT loader file named NTLDR. This file is responsible for loading the complete operating system into memory. Afterward, NTLDR passes control of the system over to the kernel and support files that make up the Windows operating system. The major events in the startup are the following:

1. NTLDR checks system RAM memory, and the OS loader V5.0 message appears on the screen.

2. NTLDR switches the processor to 32-bit flat memory mode.

3. NTLDR starts the minifile system (FAT or NTFS) to read disk files. With the minifile system in place, the NTLDR can locate and read a special hidden boot loader menu file named BOOT.INI. If more than one operating system option is defined in the BOOT.INI file, NTLDR uses this text file to generate the Advanced Boot Options menu that is displayed on the screen. If no selection has been made after a given time delay, the default value is selected.

4. NTLDR reads the BOOT.INI file and displays the Advanced Boot Options menu onscreen. If Windows 2000 or Windows XP is designated as the operating system to be used, the NTLDR program executes a hardware detection file called NTDETECT.COM. This file is responsible for collecting information about the system's installed hardware devices and passing it to the NTLDR program. This information is later used to upgrade the Windows Registry files that keep track of all the system's users, hardware devices, and settings. If a different operating system is to be loaded, as directed by the Advanced Boot Options menu

entry, the NTLDR program loads a file called BOOTSECT.DOS and passes control to it. From this point, the BOOTSECT file is responsible for loading the desired operating system.

5. NTLDR runs NTDETECT.COM to gather system hardware information. Ntdetect checks for key hardware items.

6. NTLDR loads the NTOSKRNL and HAL files into memory and passes the hardware information to it.

7. NTLDR reads the SYSTEM Registry key, places it in memory, and implements the hardware profile (configuration and control set) from the proper Registry.

8. NTLDR loads startup device drivers into memory. At this point, Windows 2000 will place a progress bar on the screen along with the `Starting Windows 2000` message. No such message is displayed in Windows XP versions. Prior to this point, the user had the option to access the Advanced Options menu by pressing the F8 function key. This action is normally taken to enter a diagnostic startup mode because something has gone wrong on a previous startup attempt. Figure 13.1 shows a typical Advanced Options menu.

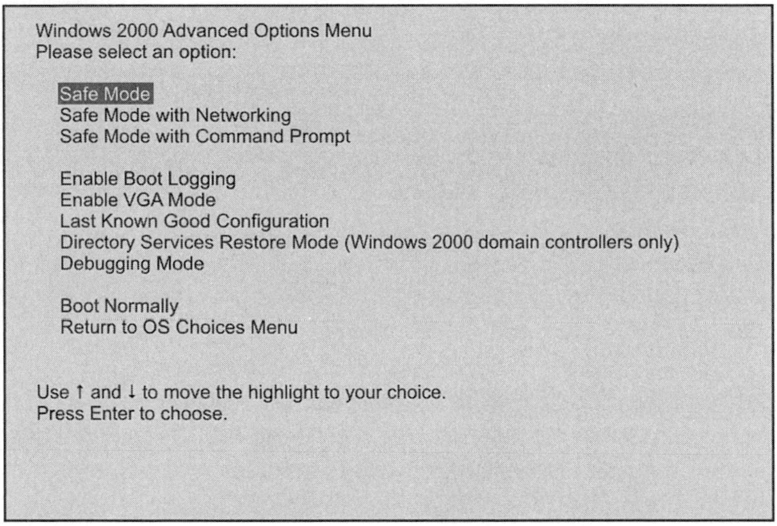

```
Windows 2000 Advanced Options Menu
Please select an option:

Safe Mode
Safe Mode with Networking
Safe Mode with Command Prompt

Enable Boot Logging
Enable VGA Mode
Last Known Good Configuration
Directory Services Restore Mode (Windows 2000 domain controllers only)
Debugging Mode

Boot Normally
Return to OS Choices Menu


Use ↑ and ↓ to move the highlight to your choice.
Press Enter to choose.
```

FIGURE 13.1 Windows 2000 Advanced Options boot menu.

9. NTLDR passes control to the NTOSKRNL file. When NTOSKRNL gains control of the system, it initializes the HAL.DLL file along with the BOOTVID.DLL file and shifts the video display to graphics mode.

It then initializes the drivers prepared by NTLDR and uses the NTDE-TECT information to create a temporary hardware hive in memory.

10. NTOSKRNL creates the Registry's Hardware key from the information gathered earlier by NTDETECT and executes additional device drivers.

11. NTOSKRNL starts the SMSS.EXE session file to carry out prestart functions such as running a boot-time version of CHKDSK, called AUTOCHK, and utilities to verify the readiness of the system. It also establishes parameters concerning the Windows 2000/XP virtual memory paging file (PAGEFILE.SYS) to hold RAM memory swap pages.

12. The Win32 subsection runs the WINLOGON.EXE and LSASS.EXE programs; the Ctrl+Alt+Delete window is presented on the display, and the logon screen is displayed.

13. The SCREG.EXE service controller program starts and loads all remaining services specified in the Registry, including the Windows 2000/XP shell and desktop.

EXAM ALERT

Memorize the files involved in the Windows 2000/XP startup process and know the order of their execution.

NOTE

If the Windows 2000 or XP system employs a SCSI disk drive and the system does not have a BIOS with SCSI support, a driver file named NTBOOTDD.SYS must be present in the root directory of the system partition. This condition must also be noted in the BOOT.INI file by placing a mark in its SCSI(x) or Multi(x) locations.

EXAM ALERT

Be aware of what the NTBOOTDD.SYS file does in a Windows 2000/XP system.

Windows 2000/XP Structures

When fully loaded into the system, the Windows 2000/XP logical structure exists as depicted in Figure 13.2. It is a modular operating system that allows for advances in computing technology to be integrated into the system. The operating system exists in two basic layers, referred to as *modes*. These two levels are the Kernel mode and the User mode.

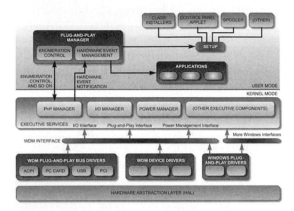

FIGURE 13.2 Windows 2000/XP organizational structure.

Basically, the operating system runs in the Kernel mode, whereas applications run in the User mode. The Kernel mode is the operating mode in which the program has unlimited access to all memory, including those of system hardware, User mode applications, and other processes (such as I/O operations). The User mode is a more restrictive operating mode in which no direct access of hardware is permitted.

Application programming interfaces (APIs) are routines, protocols, and tools built in to the operating system that provide application designers with consistent building blocks to design their applications with. For the user, these building blocks lead to consistent interfaces being designed for all applications.

The Windows 2000/XP Hardware Abstraction Layer (HAL) is a library of hardware drivers that operate between the actual hardware and the rest of the system. These software routines act to make the architecture of every device look the same to the operating system. The microkernel works closely with the HAL to keep the system's microprocessor as busy as possible. It does this by scheduling threads for introduction to the microprocessor on a priority basis. Microkernel architecture is used in operating systems such as Windows 2000 and Windows XP to permit additional services to be added to the operating system without rewriting the kernel. This tends to provide a more stable operating system structure.

The PnP manager employs the enumeration process to discover PnP devices installed in the system. Afterward, it loads appropriate drivers and creates Registry entries for those devices. These drivers and entries are based on information (INF) scripts developed by Microsoft and the hardware vendors for the device being configured. The PnP manager then allocates the system's resources (IRQ settings, DMA channels, and I/O addresses) to the devices that require them.

The power manager interacts with key system components to conserve energy (especially useful for portable computers) and reduce wear on system devices. Both managers depend on PnP-compliant system components as well as the APM and ACPI power management standards described in Chapter 10, "Portable Computer Fundamentals."

System Memory Management

Most modern operating systems, including Windows 2000, Windows XP, UNIX, and Linux, do not employ the address segmentation features of the Intel microprocessors to divide up the computer's memory allocations. Because segments can overlap, memory usage errors can occur when an application attempts to write data into a space being used by the operating system or by another application.

Using the *flat memory model*, the memory manager sections map each application's memory space into contiguous pages of physical memory. Using this method, each application is mapped into a truly unique address space that cannot overlap any other address space. The lack of segment overlap reduces the chances of applications interfering with each other and helps to ensure data integrity by providing the operating system and other processes with their own memory spaces.

In Windows 2000 and 32-bit versions of Windows XP, the memory management scheme employs a full 32-bit architecture with a flat memory model that provides direct access to up to 4GB of memory. In this model, the Virtual Memory Manager (VMM) assigns unique memory spaces to every active 32-bit and 16-bit application. Under Windows XP Professional x64 Edition, this structure is expanded to provide a 64-bit memory model that provides the capability to access up to 128GB of RAM.

Virtual Memory

The term *virtual memory* is used to describe memory that isn't what it appears to be. Virtual memory is actually disk drive space that is manipulated to seem like RAM. Software creates virtual memory by swapping files between RAM and the disk drive, as illustrated in Figure 13.3. This memory management technique effectively creates more total memory for the system's applications to use. However, because there is a major transfer of information that involves the hard disk drive, an overall reduction in speed is encountered with virtual memory operations.

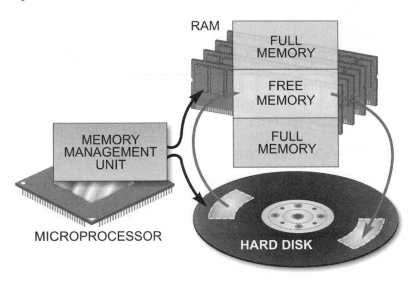

RAM

FULL MEMORY

FREE MEMORY

FULL MEMORY

MEMORY MANAGEMENT UNIT

MICROPROCESSOR

HARD DISK

FIGURE 13.3 Virtual memory operations.

Windows 2000/XP establishes virtual memory by creating a PAGEFILE.SYS file on the disk when the operating system is installed. Its default size is typically set at 1.5 times the amount of RAM installed in the system. It is possible to optimize the system's performance by distributing the swap file space between multiple drives. It can also be helpful to relocate the swap file away from slower or heavily used drives to faster or less used drives. The swap file should not be placed on mirrored or striped volumes. Also, don't create multiple swap files on logical disks that exist on the same physical drive.

EXAM ALERT

Memorize the filename of the Windows 2000/XP virtual memory swap file.

EXAM ALERT

Be aware that you can use the swap file to optimize the operation of Windows 2000 and Windows XP systems.

When the Windows 2000/XP VMM has exhausted the physical RAM locations available, it maps memory pages into virtual memory addresses, as described in

Figure 13.4. The VMM shifts data between RAM memory and the disk in 4KB pages. This theoretically provides the operating system with a total memory space that equals the sum of the system's physical RAM and the capacity of the hard disk drive.

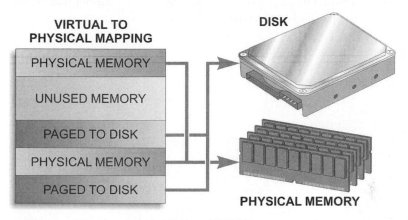

FIGURE 13.4   Virtual memory in Windows 2000/XP.

To take advantage of high RAM capacity, Windows automatically tunes itself to take advantage of any available RAM. The VMM dynamically balances RAM between paged memory and the virtual memory disk cache.

In Windows 2000, the VMM functions are located under the Control Panel's System icon. Click its Advanced tab followed by the Performance Options button to view the dialog window depicted in Figure 13.5. In Windows XP, the pathway to the Virtual Memory dialog window runs through the System icon's Advanced tab. Click the Settings button in the Performance section to obtain the Performance Options page. Select the Advanced tab and click the Change button in the Virtual Memory area of the page.

FIGURE 13.5   The system Performance Options window.

Clicking the Change button in the dialog window will produce the Virtual Memory dialog window shown in Figure 13.6. Through this dialog window, you can establish and configure an individual swap file for each drive in the system. By highlighting a drive, you can check its virtual memory capabilities and settings. Entering new values in the dialog windows and clicking the Set button will change the values for the highlighted drive.

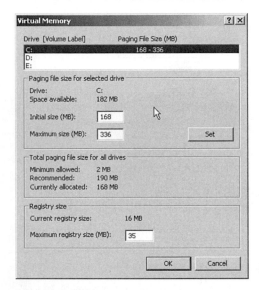

FIGURE 13.6   The Virtual Memory dialog window.

Windows 2000/XP Registries

Windows 2000 and Windows XP use a multipart database, called the *Registry*, to hold system and user configuration information. The Registry is primarily used to hold information about system hardware that has been identified by the enumeration or detection processes of the Plug-and-Play system. When a device is installed in the system, the operating system detects it, either directly or through the system's bus managers, and then searches the Registry and installed media sources for an appropriate driver. When the driver is found, it is recorded in the Registry along with its selected settings.

Some devices, such as PCMCIA devices, can be inserted and removed under hot conditions (while power is on). The system will detect the removal or insertion of the device, and automatically adjust its Registry configuration.

The Registry also holds information that enables the system to serve and track multiple users. It does this by retaining user-specific and configuration-specific information that can be used to customize the system to different users, or to different configuration situations.

The Windows 2000/XP Registries use English-language descriptions and a hierarchical organization strategy as depicted in Figure 13.7. The hierarchy is divided into Headkeys, Keys, Subkeys, and Values. If you examine the My Computer heading using the RegEdit option from the Start menu's Run option, you will find five categories listed. The head keys all start with an HKEY notation. Under My Computer the categories are

▸ HKEY_CLASSES_ROOT

▸ HKEY_CURRENT_USER

▸ HKEY_USERS

▸ HKEY_LOCAL_MACHINE

▸ HKEY_CURRENT_CONFIG

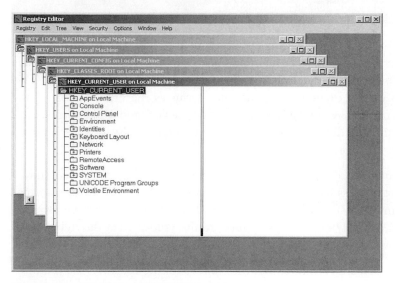

FIGURE 13.7 The Windows 2000/XP Registry.

Most of the HKEY titles should appear very descriptive of their contents. The Classes_Root key divides the system's files into two groups by file extension type and by association. This key also holds data about icons associated with the file.

The Current_User key holds data about the user-specific configuration settings of the system, including color, keyboard, desktop, and start settings. The values in the Current_User key reflect those established by the user that is currently logged in to the system. If a different user logs in, the content of the Users key is moved into the Current_User key.

The Users key contains the information about the various users that have been defined to log in to the system. The information from the Current_User key is copied into this section whenever a user logs off the system, or when the system is shut down.

The Local_Machine key contains information about the system's hardware. All of the hardware drivers and configuration information are contained in this key. The system will not be able to use peripheral devices that are not properly documented in the Local_Machine key.

The Current_Config key works with the Local_Machine key branch containing current information about hardware devices.

EXAM ALERT

Memorize the basic function of each Registry key.

Keys are descriptive section headers that appear at the left side of the Registry Editor window. *Values* are definitions of topics organized under the keys. This organization can be thought of in the same terms as the organization of any book; the head keys are similar to chapter titles, the keys and subkeys are equivalent to the major and minor headings of the chapters, and values are equal to the sentences that convey information.

Values can contain a wide variety of information types. They can contain interrupt and port address information for a peripheral system, or simply information about an installed application program. The information can be encoded into binary, DWORDS, or strings. Values are always located at the right side of the RegEdit window.

In Windows 2000 and Windows XP, the contents of the registries are physically stored in five files referred to as *hives*. Hives represent the major divisions of all the Registry's keys, subkeys, subtrees, and values. The hives of the Windows 2000/XP Registry are the following:

▶ The SAM hive

▶ The SECURITY hive

▶ The SOFTWARE hive

▶ The SYSTEM hive

▶ The DEFAULT hive

These files are stored in the \Winnt\System32\Config directory along with a backup copy and log file for each hive.

Configuration information about every user who has logged in to the system is maintained in a named subfolder of the \Winnt\Profiles directory. The user settings portion of the Registry is stored in the NTUSER.DAT file located in the \Documents_and_Settings\userxxx folder. The System portions of the Registry are stored in the SOFTWARE, SYSTEM, SECURITY, and SAM hives. These files are stored in the \Winnt\System32\Config folder. The major Windows hives and their files are described in Table 13.1.

TABLE 13.1   Major Windows Hives and Their Files

SUBTREE/KEY	FILE	LOG FILE
HKEY_LOCAL_MACHINE\SOFTWARE	SOFTWARE	SOFTWARE.LOG
HKEY_LOCAL_MACHINE\SECURITY	SECURITY	SECURITY.LOG
HKEY_LOCAL_MACHINE\SYSTEM	SYSTEM/SYSTEM.ALT	SYSTEM.LOG
HKEY_LOCAL_MACHINE\SAM	SAM	SAM.LOG
HKEY_CURRENT_USER	NTUSER.DAT	NTUSER.DAT.LOG
HKEY_USERS\DEFAULT	DEFAULT	DEFAULT.LOG
HKEY_CURRENT_CONFIG	SYSTEM/SYSTEM.ALT	SOFTWARE.LOG

The HKEY_LOCAL_MACHINE subtree is the Registry's major branch. It contains five major keys. The SAM and SECURITY keys hold information such as user rights, user and group information for domain or workgroup organization, and password information. The HARDWARE key is a database built by device drivers and applications during bootup. The database is updated each time the system is rebooted. The SYSTEM key contains basic information about startup, including the device drivers loaded and which services are in use. The Last Known Good Configuration settings are stored here. Finally, the SOFTWARE key holds information about locally loaded software, including file associations, OLE information, and configuration data.

The second most important subtree is HKEY_USERS. It contains a subkey for each local user who accesses the system. These subkeys hold desktop settings and user profiles.

The contents of the Registry can be edited directly using the Windows 2000/XP RegEdit utility: Regedt32.exe. The editor used to manage the Windows 2000/XP Registry is Regedt32. However, in some instances, such as Registry searches, the older RegEdit utility offers superior operation, even in Windows 2000 and XP. This file is located in the \Winnt\System32 folder.

Most changes to the Registry should be performed through the wizards in the Windows 2000/XP Control Panels. These wizards are designed to safely and correctly make changes to the Registry in a manner that the operating system can understand. Editing the Registry directly opens the possibility of changing an entry in a manner that the operating system cannot accept, and thereby, of crashing the system. In either event, it is a good practice to back up the contents of the Registry before installing new hardware or software or directly modifying the Registry.

> **EXAM ALERT**
>
> Be aware of the utility used to directly edit Registry entries of the various operating systems.

Windows 2000/XP File Systems

All Windows NT operating system versions can employ two different disk management structures: FAT systems and NTFS structures. The Windows 2000/XP component responsible for implementing and managing these file systems (along with the CDFS file system used with CR-ROM drives and the UDF file system used with DVDs and other digital media devices) is the Installable File System (IFS) Manager section of the I/O Manager. The following sections will cover the structures and operations associated with both major Windows file systems.

Managing Partitions

Physical hard-disk drives can be divided into multiple logical drives. This operation is referred to as *partitioning* the drive. When a physical drive is partitioned, it is divided into multiple logical drives that are handled by the file management system as separate, independent drives. This is because each logical drive has been given logical structures required to let it operate as an independent drive unit.

Under MS-DOS, partitioning became necessary because the capacity of hard drives exceeded the capability of the existing FAT structure to track all the possible sectors. Dividing the physical disk space into multiple logical drives where each new drive contains another complete file-tracking structure solved this dilemma. The operating system sees each logical drive on the hard drive as a completely new disk that it assigns a new, unique drive letter to.

Figure 13.8 illustrates the concept of creating multiple logical drives on a single hard drive. This is usually done for purposes of organization and increased access speeds. The operating system's partitioning utility creates the disk's boot sector and establishes partition parameters (partition table) for the system's use.

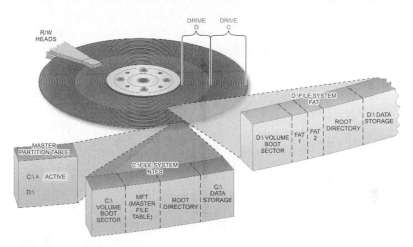

FIGURE 13.8   HDD partitions.

FAT systems provide for two partitions on an HDD unit. The first, or the *primary partition*, must exist as drive C. After the primary partition has been established and properly configured, an additional partition, referred to as an *extended partition*, is also permitted. However, the extended partition may be subdivided into 23 logical drives. The extended partition cannot be deleted if logical drives have been defined within it.

The *active partition* is the logical drive that the system will boot to. The system files must be located in this partition, and the partition must be set to Active for the system to boot from the drive.

An NTFS system can accommodate up to four primary partitions. It also supports extended partitions. If extended partitions are used, the system has a maximum of three primary partitions and a single extended partition. As with the FAT system, extended partitions cannot be marked as active in the NTFS system. NTFS extended partitions can also be divided into logical drives. However, only primary partitions and logical drives can be formatted and assigned a drive letter. The total number of primary partitions plus logical drives cannot exceed 32 for a single hard drive.

You may also hear or see partitions referred to as *volumes* when dealing with Windows 2000 and Windows XP. In instances involving a single physical drive, these terms will work interchangeably. However, *volume* takes on a different meaning when applied to contiguous memory spaces that span multiple physical drives—such as RAID volumes.

In local and wide area networks (LANs and WANs), the concept of logical drives is carried a step further. A particular hard disk drive may be a logical drive in a large system of drives along a peer-to-peer network. On the other hand, a very large, centralized drive may be used to create several logical drives for a client/server type of network. This is accomplished by creating a logical mapping between the operating system and the desired drive, so that the local system handles the mapped drive as one of its own drives.

In some applications, partitioning is used to permit multiple operating systems to exist on the same physical drive. Because each partition on the drive contains its own boot sector, FAT, and root directory, each partition can be set up to hold and boot up to a different operating system.

On a partitioned drive, a special table, called the *partition table*, is created in the boot sector at the very beginning of the disk. This table holds information about the location and starting point of each logical drive on the disk, along with information about which partition has been marked as active and a master boot record. The partition table is located at the beginning of the disk because this is the point where the system looks for bootup information. When the system checks the MBR of the physical disk during the boot process, it also checks to see which partition on the disk has been marked as active. It then jumps to that location, reads the information in that partition boot record, and boots to the operating system in that logical drive.

Challenge #1

You have a customer who has a new computer with Windows 2000 Professional installed on it. However, she has several Linux-based applications that she routinely uses and wants to move those applications to the new computer. How can you help her do this?

High-Level Formatting

The high-level format procedure is used to load the operating system into a partition on the disk. In the case of disks with multiple partitions, it is possible to load different operating systems in each partition. Most operating systems are capable of operating with different file systems.

For example, Windows 2000 and Windows XP can work with either FAT partitions or NTFS partitions. This is referred to as creating a *dual boot* system. However, under some configurations, the system will not be able to use space in both partitions at the same time. Some thought must go into setting up and operating disks that contain multiple partition formats. Likewise, other operating systems, such as Linux and NetWare, can be loaded into partitions on disks that also contain Windows versions.

FAT Disk Organization

In a FAT-based system, the formatting operation re-creates the two file allocation tables (FATs) along with a root directory on the disk. Figure 13.9 describes the organization of a FAT disk and illustrates the position of the boot sector, the file allocation tables, and the root directory. The remainder of the disk is dedicated to data storage. As mentioned previously, the first area on each logical disk or partition is the boot sector. Although all formatted partitions have this sector, they do not all have the optional master boot record located in the sector. Only disks created to be bootable disks have this record.

File Allocation Tables

The second logical section of a FAT disk is occupied by the file allocation tables. This area consists of information about how the disk is organized. Basically, the system logs two copies of disk space usage and availability in these tables.

In older versions of MS-DOS, the amount of space dedicated to tracking the sectors on the disk was 16 bits. Therefore, only 65,536 sectors could be accounted for. This parameter limited the size of an MS-DOS partition to 32MB (33,554,432 bytes). To more effectively manage the space on larger disks, modern disk operating systems versions divide the disk into groups of logically related sectors, called *allocation units* or *clusters*. In a FAT-based system, the cluster is the smallest piece of manageable information.

EXAM ALERT

Know what the smallest unit of storage in a disk-based system is.

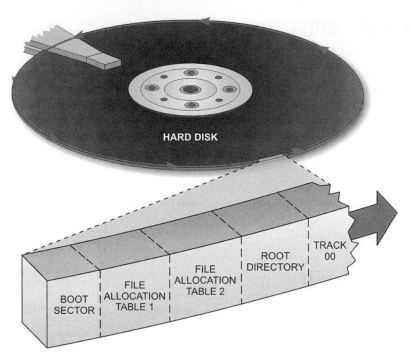

FIGURE 13.9 FAT disk organization.

The sectors on a FAT disk hold 512 bytes each. Files, on the other hand, can be any length. Therefore, a single file may occupy several sectors on the disk. The operating system's disk handling routine breaks a file into sector-sized chunks and stores it in a cluster of sectors. In this manner, DOS uses the cluster to track files instead of sectors. Because the file allocation table has to handle information only for a cluster, instead of for each sector, the number of files that can be tracked in a given length table is greatly increased.

EXAM ALERT

Know the size of sectors in an IBM/PC-compatible disk.

If the FAT becomes corrupted, chained files can become cross-linked with each other, making them useless. For this reason, two complete copies of the FAT are stored consecutively on the disk under the FAT-based disk structure. The first copy is the normal working copy, and the second FAT is used as a backup measure in case the contents of the first FAT become corrupted.

The Root Directory

The next section following the FAT tables is the disk's root directory. This is a special directory that is present on every FAT-based disk. It is the main directory of every logical disk and serves as the starting point for organizing information on the disk. The location of every directory, subdirectory, and file on the disk is recorded in this table.

Each directory and subdirectory (including the root directory) can hold up to 512 32-byte entries that describe each of the files in them.

EXAM ALERT

Remember the number of entries that directories in a FAT-based system can hold.

Because each root directory entry is 32 bytes long, each disk sector can hold 16 entries. Consequently, the number of files or directories that can be listed in the root directory is dependent on how many disk sectors are allocated to it. On a hard disk drive, 32 sectors are usually set aside for the root directory. Therefore, the root directory for such a disk can accommodate up to 512 entries.

Directory Structures

Technically, every directory on a disk is a subdirectory of the root directory. All additional directories branch out from the root directory in a treelike fashion. Therefore, a graphical representation of the disk drive's directory organization is called a *directory tree*. Figure 13.10 depicts the directory organization of a typical hard drive.

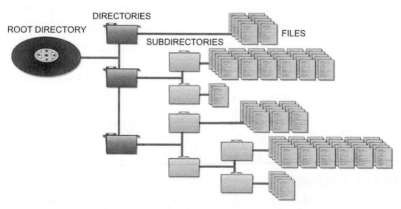

FIGURE 13.10 The Microsoft directory tree structure.

The organizational structure of a computer's logical disks or partitions is typically described as being like a common office file cabinet. Think of the drives in a computer as the filing cabinet structure. Our example has three drawers that can be opened. Think of these drawers as disk drives labeled A, B, and C/D. Inside each drawer are hanging folders that can hold different types of items. Think of these as directories (although Microsoft refers to them as folders in its Windows products).

The hanging folders may contain different types of items or other individual folders. Think of these individual folders as subdirectories. For organizational purposes, each hanging folder and each individual folder must have a unique label on it.

Inside each hanging folder, or individual folder, are the items being stored. In a real filing cabinet, these items are usually documents of different types. However, pictures and tapes and other items related to the folders can also be stored in them.

Think of the items inside the folders as files. Disk-based systems manage data blocks by giving them filenames. Recall that a file is simply a block of logically related data that is given a single name and treated as a single unit. Like the contents of the folders, files can be programs, documents, drawings or other illustrations, sound files, and so on.

To find an item in the cabinet, you need to know which drawer, hanging folder, and folder that it is located in. This concept can be translated directly to the computer system. To locate a particular file, you need to know which drive, directory, and subdirectory it is located in. From the command line, the path to any file in the system can be written as a direction to the computer so that it will know where the file is that it is being directed to. This format for specifying a path is as follows:

C:*directory name**subdirectory_name**filename*

where the C: specifies the C disk drive. The directory name, subdirectory_name, and filename would naturally be replaced by real names. The backslash (\\) after each item indicates the presence of a directory or subdirectory. The first slash represents the root directory, which is present on all logical disks.

The FAT32 File System

The OSR2 version of Windows 95 introduced an enhanced FAT32 file management system as an upgrade for the existing FAT16 file system. FAT32 was designed to optimize storage space and is based on the fact that the size of the registers in the operating system's FAT determines the size of the clusters for a given size disk partition.

Smaller cluster sizes are better because even a single byte stored in a cluster will remove the entire cluster from the available storage space on the drive. This can add up to a lot of wasted storage space on larger drives. The default cluster size set by Microsoft for FAT32 is 4KB. Table 13.2 describes the relationships between clusters and maximum partition sizes for various FAT entry sizes.

TABLE 13.2   FAT Relationships

FAT TYPE	PARTITION SIZE	CLUSTER SIZE (IN BYTES)
FAT12	16MB	4096
FAT16	32MB	2048
FAT16	128MB	2048
FAT16	256MB	4096
FAT16	512MB	8192
FAT16	1GB	16384
FAT16	2GB	32768
FAT32	<260MB	512
FAT32	8GB	4096
FAT32	16GB	8192
FAT32	32GB	16384
FAT32	>32GB	32768

The structure of the FAT32 system makes it incompatible with other versions of Windows file systems, including FAT16 and NTFS. Therefore, it is also not compatible with disk utilities and troubleshooting packages designed for those file systems.

NTFS Disk Organization

The Windows NTFS structure uses 64-bit entries to keep track of storage on the disk (in contrast to the 16- and 32-bit entries used in FAT and FAT32 systems). When a partition is formatted in an NTFS system, several system files and the MFT are created on the disk. These files contain the information required to implement the file system structure on the disk. The system files produced during the NTFS formatting process include the following:

► A pair of MFT files (the real one and a shorter backup version)

► A Log file to maintain transaction steps for recovery purposes

- ▶ A Volume file that includes the volume name, NTFS version, and other key volume information

- ▶ An Attribute definition table file

- ▶ A Root Filename file that serves as the drive's root folder

- ▶ A Cluster Bitmap that represents the volume and shows which clusters are in use

- ▶ The partition boot sector file

- ▶ A Bad Cluster file containing the locations of all bad sectors identified on the disk

- ▶ A Quota Table for tracking allowable storage space on the disk for each user

- ▶ An Upper Case Table for converting lowercase characters to Unicode uppercase characters

Unicode is a 16-bit character code standard, similar to 8-bit ASCII, used to represent characters as integer numbers. The 16-bit format allows it to represent over 65,000 different characters. This is particularly useful for languages that have very large character sets.

EXAM ALERT

Know what Unicode is and what it is used for.

Figure 13.11 illustrates the organization of an NTFS disk volume. The first information in the NTFS volume is the 16-sector Partition Boot Sector. The sector starts at physical sector 0 and is made up of two segments: the BIOS Parameter Block and the Code section. The BIOS Parameter Block holds information about the structures of the volume and disk file system. The Code section describes the method to be used to locate and load the startup files for the specified operating system. This code loads the Windows 2000/XP bootstrap loader file NTLDR in Intel-based computers running Windows 2000 or XP.

Master File Tables

The core component of the NTFS system is the Master File Table (MFT). This table replaces the file allocation tables in FAT-based systems and contains information about each file stored on the disk. The MFT contains information about each folder and file on the volume. The NTFS system relates to folders and files as a collection of attributes. All the folder's, or file's, elements (that is, filename, security information, and data) are considered to be attributes. The system allocates space in the MFT for each file or folder based on the cluster size being used on the disk.

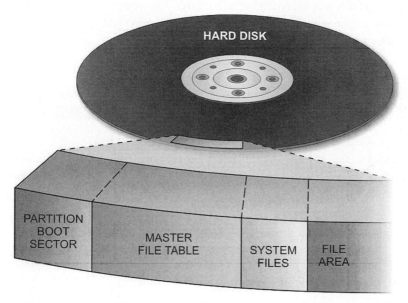

FIGURE 13.11 The organization of an NTFS disk volume.

For large files that cannot be identified by a single MFT record, multiple MFT records are employed. The first record contains a pointer to the additional MFT records. The original MFT record contains the file's or folder's standard information, followed by index links to other MFT records that, in turn, have index links to the actual data runs. In these cases, the data is stored outside the table and can theoretically range up to 16EB (an exabyte equals 2^{60}).

Like FAT systems, NTFS systems use the cluster as the basic unit of disk storage. In Windows 2000 and XP, NTFS clusters could range between 512 bytes and 64KB, depending on the size of the drive and how the disk was prepared. The smaller cluster size of the NTFS format makes it more efficient than FAT formats for storing smaller files. It also supports larger drives (more than 1GB) much more efficiently than FAT16 or FAT32 structures. The NTFS system is more complex than the FAT systems and, therefore, is not as efficient for smaller drives.

NTFS Advantages

The Windows 2000 operating system supports several file management system formats, including FAT, FAT16, FAT32, CDFS (the Compact Disk File System is used on CD-ROM disks), and NTFS4, along with its own NTFS5 format. The latter version enables administrators to establish disk quotas limiting the amount of hard drive space users can have access to. The new NTFS system also offers enhanced system security. NTFS5 provides an encrypted file system and secure network protocol and authentication standards.

> **EXAM ALERT**
>
> Be aware of the different file system types supported by Windows 2000 and Windows XP.

In most situations, the NTFS system offers better performance and features than a FAT16 or FAT32 system. The exceptions to this occur when smaller drives are being used, when other file systems are being used on the same drive, or when the operating system crashes.

In most other situations, the NTFS system offers the following:

- ▶ More efficient drive management because of its smaller cluster size capabilities

- ▶ Support for very large drives made possible by its 64-bit clustering arrangement

- ▶ Increased folder and file security capabilities

- ▶ Disk quotas governing how much disk space individual users can take up

- ▶ Disk compression that enables the system to create more available disk space by compressing folders and files

- ▶ File encryption that encodes data that is stored on the hard drive, making it much more difficult for data to be stolen

- ▶ Recoverable file system capabilities

- ▶ Built-in RAID support

> **EXAM ALERT**
>
> Memorize the advantages associated with using the NTFS file system.

In Windows 2000 and Windows XP, the administrator has the tools to limit what the user can do to any given file or directory. This is accomplished through two types of security permissions: share permissions and NTFS permissions.

The NTFS structure provides recoverable file system capabilities, including a hot-fix function and a full recovery system to quickly restore file integrity. The NTFS system maintains a copy of the critical file system information. If the file system fails, the NTFS system will automatically recover the system from the backup information as soon as the disk is accessed again. In addition, NTFS maintains a transaction log to ensure the integrity of the disk structure even if the system fails unexpectedly.

Security is a very big issue in large business networks. The NTFS file system provides security for each file in the system, as well as complete file access auditing information to the system administrator. NTFS files and folders can have permissions assigned to them whether or not they are shared. Data security is also improved by the capability Windows has to support mirrored drives. *Mirroring* is a technique of storing separate copies of data on two different drives. This protects the data from loss because of hard drive failures. This is a very important consideration when dealing with server applications. Additional fault tolerance capabilities such as disk mirroring, drive duplexing, striping, and support for uninterruptible power supplies (UPS) are provided with the Windows 2000 and Windows XP operating systems.

Challenge #2

You have a physical disk in your computer that has two partitions, both of which are formatted with FAT16. In one partition you are running Windows 95, and in the other you are running Windows NT 4.0. Because Windows 95 is becoming outdated and you do not want to keep it up, you upgrade the Windows 95 partition to Windows 2000 and use the NTFS5 file system. When you start the system up using the Windows 2000 partition, there is no problem. However, when you boot into the Windows NT 4.0 partition, the new partition is not available. What should you do to correct this problem?

Managing Windows 2000/XP NTFS

Windows 2000 and Windows XP are based on NTFS version 5.0. This version of NTFS enables the user to establish disk space quotas for users and locate files by owner. The NTFS system provides administrators with tools to manage user access and usage rights to individual files and directories. A special administrative list called the Access Control List (ACL) is used to view which files a user can have access to. This feature was new to the NT environment, but had been available in the Novell NetWare products for some time.

The Disk Management utility is a graphical tool that handles two distinctive types of disks: basic disks and dynamic disks. This tool enables the administrator to handle dynamic volumes, created on dynamic disks. A *basic disk* is a physical disk that contains partitions, drives, or volumes created with Windows NT 4.0 or earlier operating systems. *Dynamic disks* are physical disks created through the Windows 2000 Disk Management utility. These disks can hold only dynamic volumes (not partitions, volumes, or logical drives). However, with dynamic disks, the four-volume limit inherent with other Microsoft operating system versions has been removed.

There are five types of dynamic volumes:

▶ Simple volume—Contains disk space from a single disk and can be easily extended, if necessary, as depicted in Figure 13.12.

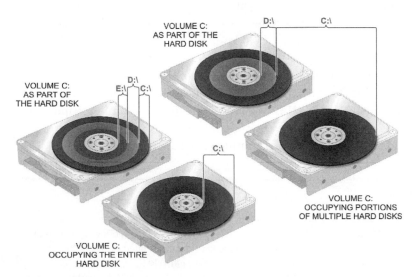

FIGURE 13.12 Simple volumes.

▶ Spanned volume—Contains disk space from two or more disks (up to a maximum of 32), as illustrated in Figure 13.13. The amount of disk space derived from each disk can vary.

▶ Mirrored volumes—Two volumes on different disks that are the same size and contain the same data, as shown in Figure 13.14. In the event that one of the disks fails, the other will continue functioning, providing disk fault tolerance (RAID 1).

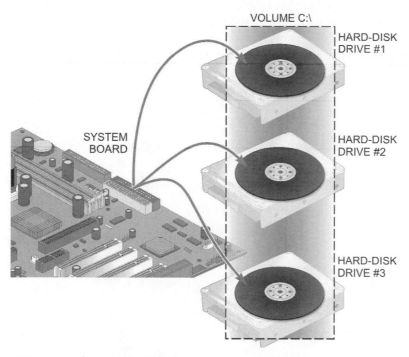

FIGURE 13.13 Spanned volumes.

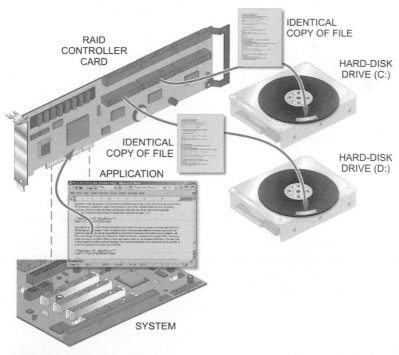

FIGURE 13.14 Mirrored volumes.

▶ Striped volume—Contains disk space from two or more disks (up to a maximum of 32), as illustrated in Figure 13.15. The amount of disk space derived from each disk must be the same.

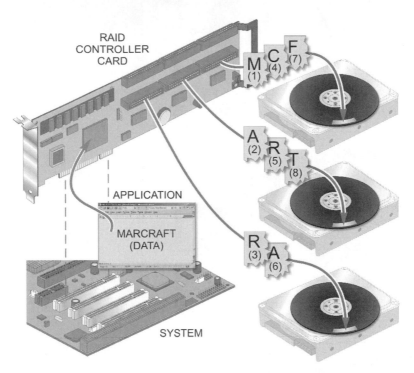

FIGURE 13.15   Striped volumes.

▶ RAID 5 volume—Also known as *striped volume with tolerance*, provides disk fault tolerance. The data is divided into 64KB chunks and is written to all drives in a fixed order. A five-disk RAID 5 configuration is shown in Figure 13.16.

NOTE

Although the figures for striping, mirroring, and RAID 5 all show a RAID controller card being used (this is the preferred method), Windows 2000 Server and Windows Server 2003 can perform these functions strictly using software. In fact, software RAID functionality can be obtained only through server operating systems—not Windows 2000 or XP Professional. However, you can create striped volumes in Windows 2000/XP Professional without installing a RAID controller.

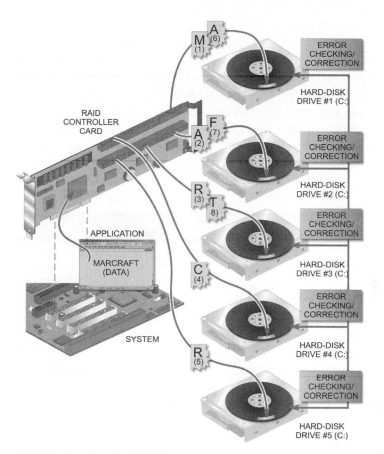

FIGURE 13.16 Five-disk RAID 5 system.

Only systems running Windows 2000 or Windows XP Professional can access dynamic volumes. Therefore, basic volumes should be established on drives that Windows 9x or Windows NT 4.0 systems need to access. If a dynamic volume is present on a drive, the file management systems associated with the other operating systems will not be able to see or access the dynamic drives or volumes.

NOTE

Windows XP Home Edition does not support spanned volumes.

To install Windows 2000 or Windows XP on a dynamic volume, it must be either a simple or a mirrored volume, and it must be a volume that has been upgraded from a basic volume. Installing Windows 2000 on the volume requires that it have a partition table, which dynamic volumes do not have unless they have been upgraded from a basic volume. Basic volumes are upgraded by upgrading a basic disk to a dynamic disk. Under Windows 2000, basic volumes are converted to dynamic volumes using the Disk Management tool (follow the path Start/Run, enter **DISKMGMT.MSC** into the text box, and then click the OK button). Windows 2000 and XP will not support dynamic volumes on portable computers. Likewise, mirrored and RAID 5 volumes are supported only on Windows 2000 Servers.

> **EXAM ALERT**
>
> Know what the requirements are for creating a dynamic volume in Windows 2000.

Dynamic volumes are managed through the Windows 2000/XP Disk Management snap-in tool, depicted in Figure 13.17, located under the Computer Management console. To access the Disk Manager, follow the Start/Settings/Control Panel/Administrative Tools path. Double-click the Computer Management icon and click the Disk Management entry. Because working with dynamic volumes is a major administrative task, you must be logged in as an administrator or as a member of Windows 2000's Administrators group to carry out the procedure. Also, system and boot volumes cannot be formatted as dynamic volumes.

> **EXAM ALERT**
>
> Know what is required to install Windows 2000/XP in a dynamic volume.

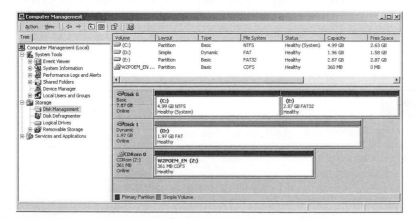

FIGURE 13.17 Windows 2000 Disk Management snap-in.

Formatting Volumes in Windows 2000/XP

Formatting a partition or volume prepares the logical structure to accept data by creating the file system in it. If a partition or volume has not been formatted, it does not contain a file system and cannot be accessed through the operating system or any applications. In the Windows 2000/XP environment, many actions can be performed to initiate formatting. These include the following:

▶ Use the Volume Creation Wizard in the Disk Management utility when the volume is created.

▶ In the Disk Management utility, right-click a volume that has already been created and select the Format option from the Action menu.

▶ In Windows Explorer, right-click the desired drive letter and select the Format option from the pop up menu.

▶ At a command prompt, type the command **Format** along with the appropriate switches.

CAUTION

If you format an existing partition or volume, any data residing in the structure will be lost. The Windows XP Professional operating system protects its system files by preventing the system and boot partitions from being formatted.

Typical options that will be presented during the formatting process are the following:

▶ Volume label—An 11-character name for the volume that will be displayed in Disk Management, Windows Explorer, and other utilities to identify it. You should make the label descriptive of the type of information that is stored on the volume.

▶ File system—This option permits you to choose FAT (for FAT16), FAT32, or NTFS for the file system type that will be installed in the partition or volume.

▶ Allocation unit size—This setting enables you to manipulate the default cluster size for any of the file systems. This setting should be left at the default value unless you are highly skilled at manipulating disk parameters.

▶ Perform a quick format—This option is used when you want to remove the files and folders on the volume without checking for bad sectors. This should be selected only if you have previously performed a full format and verified that the disk does not have damaged areas.

▶ Enable file and folder compression—The compression option is available only for partitions or volumes that are formatted with NTFS. It specifies that all files placed on the disk will be compressed by default. The compression option is always available on NTFS volumes and can be enabled at any time.

Files and Filenames

Disk-based systems store and handle related pieces of information in groups called *files*. The system recognizes and keeps track of the different files in the system by their filenames. Therefore, each time a new file is created, it is given a unique filename that the operating system can use to identify and store it.

Actually, computers can have different files with the same names, but the files must be located in different directories; and so each file in a given directory must have a different filename from that of any other file in the directory. If two files with the same filename were present in the same directory, the computer would have no mechanism to differentiate between them, so it would become confused and fail to operate properly.

File Types

Files are created by application programs or through programming packages. In the file cabinet representation of disk-based systems, it was mentioned that the items being stored could be programs, documents of different types, pictures, tapes, and other items related to the folders. Each application creates files in a format that it can interpret (that is, PPT files for PowerPoint slide shows and XLS files for Excel spreadsheets). File extensions are linked to these applications by association. However, if you arbitrarily saved a text file with a .ppt extension, the application can recognize that the information in the file is not arranged in an order that it recognizes and will return an error message (it will not load or open the file).

Inside the file, information can exist in two basic formats: binary and text-based (ASCII). Computers understand binary information—humans don't. Programs and data not intended for human consumption exist in the form of binary files that cannot be read. However, text files or communication files that may contain readable characters are normally stored and transmitted in some form of encoded text file (ASCII is the most widely accepted text-based character format).

Binary information is convenient and efficient for the computer to use. ASCII is convenient and much more efficient when humans are involved. However, for the computer, ASCII has a lot of overhead that reduces its efficiency. ASCII files can also be corrupted more easily than binary files.

Windows 2000/XP Files

Filenames in Windows 2000 can be up to 215 characters long, including spaces. Windows XP filenames can be up to 255 characters long. Windows 2000 and XP employ a proprietary method for reducing long filenames to MS-DOS–compatible 8.3 filenames. Instead of simply truncating the filename, inserting a tilde, and then assigning a number to the end of the filename, the Windows 2000 and XP systems perform a mathematical operation on the long name to generate a truly unique MS-DOS–compatible filename.

Windows 2000/XP filenames cannot contain the following characters:

/\:*?"<>|.

> **EXAM ALERT**
>
> Know which characters can not be used in a Windows 2000 filename.

Windows 2000 and XP create properties sheets for each file and folder in the system. These sheets contain information about the file (or folder), such as its size, location, and creation date. When you view the file's properties, you can also see its attributes, file type, the program that is designed to open it, and when the file was last opened or modified.

> **Challenge #3**
>
> A customer has an important business file on his Windows 2000 machine that has boot problems. He can gain access to the drive using a start disk. However, when he views the disk from the command line, he cannot find the FutureBusinessPlansandMarketing.doc file. He has asked you to help him locate the file because he must give a presentation based on it in one hour. When you view the drive, there are literally several hundreds of files on the drive. What can you do for him?

File Encryption and Compression

The NTFS file system employed in Windows 2000 and Windows XP Professional provides two new file types that technicians must deal with. These are *encrypted files* and *compressed files*. The Windows 2000 NTFS system provides an Encrypted File System (EFS) utility that is the basis of storing encrypted files on NTFS volumes. After a file or folder has been encrypted, only the user who encrypted it can access it. The original user can work with the file or folder just as with a regular file. However, other users cannot open or share the file (although they can delete it).

> **NOTE**
>
> Windows XP Home does not provide the capability to encrypt files, as does Windows XP Professional.

For other users to be able to access the file or folder, it must first be decrypted. The encryption protection disappears when the file or folder is moved to a non-NTFS partition. Only files on NTFS volumes can be encrypted. Conversely, system files and compressed files cannot be encrypted.

Files and folders can be encrypted from the command line using the cipher command. Information about the cipher command and its many switches can be obtained by typing **cipher** /**?** at the command prompt. Files can also be encrypted through the Windows Explorer. Encryption is treated as a file attribute in Windows 2000 and Windows XP. Therefore, to encrypt a file, you need to access its properties page by right-clicking it and selecting the Properties option from the pop-up menu. Move to the Advanced screen under the General tab and click the Encrypt Contents to Secure Data check box, as illustrated in Figure 13.18. Decrypting a file is a simple matter of clearing the check box.

FIGURE 13.18 Encrypting a file.

File and Folder Compression

The Windows Explorer can also be used to compress files and folders on NTFS volumes. Like encryption, Windows 2000 and Windows XP treat NTFS compression as a file attribute. To compress a particular file or folder, right-click it in the Windows Explorer; then select the Properties option, followed by the Advanced button to access its advanced properties screen. Click in the Compress Contents to Save Disk Space check box to compress the file or folder. Likewise, an entire drive can be compressed through the My Computer icon. From the File menu, select the Properties option, and then click in the Compress Drive to Save Disk Space check box.

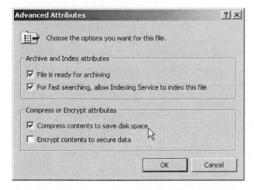

FIGURE 13.19   Compressing a file.

As with the encryption function, Windows 2000 and XP files and folders can be compressed only on NTFS volumes. If you move a file into a compressed folder, the file will be compressed automatically. These files cannot be encrypted while they are compressed. Compressed files can be marked so that they are displayed in a second color for easy identification. This is accomplished through the Folder Options setting in the Control Panel. From this page, select the View tab and click in the Display Compressed Files and Folder with Alternate Color check box. The only other indication that you will have concerning a compressed or encrypted file or folder is an attribute listing when the view setting is configured to display in web style.

NTFS Permissions

The NTFS5 system includes security features that enable permission levels to be assigned to files and folders on the disk. NTFS permissions set parameters for operations that users can perform on the designated file or folder. They can be assigned directly by an administrator, or they can be inherited through group settings, such as the default Everyone group.

NTFS permissions can be configured as Allow or Deny options. If a user has only Read permissions to a particular folder or file, but is assigned to a group that has wider permissions for that folder or file, the individual would gain those additional rights through the group. On the other hand, if the user is assigned the Deny option for a given permission level, they would be denied that permission level even if it were granted by another group that they were a part of. In a server environment, the default permission setting for files is No Access.

Standard NTFS folder permissions include the following:

▸ Read—This permission enables the user or group to view the file, folder, or subfolder of a parent folder along with its attributes and permissions.

▸ Write—This permission enables the user or group to add new files or subfolders, change file and folder attributes, add data to an existing file, and change display attributes within a parent folder.

▸ Read & Execute—The Read & Execute permission enables users or groups to make changes to subfolders, display attributes and permissions, and run executable file types.

▸ Modify—The Modify permission enables users to delete the folder and makes it possible for users to perform all the activities associated with the Write and Read & Execute permissions.

▸ List Folder Contents—This permission enables users or groups to view files and subfolders within the folder.

▸ Full Control—The Full Control permission enables the user or group to take ownership of the folder and to change its permissions, as well as perform all the other activities possible with all the other permissions.

Standard NTFS file permissions include the following:

▸ Read—This permission enables the user or group to view the file along with its attributes and permissions.

▸ Write—This permission enables the user or group to overwrite the file, change its attributes, and view its ownership and attributes.

▶ Read & Execute—The Read & Execute permission enables users or groups to run and execute an application, along with all the options available through the Read permission.

▶ Modify—The Modify permission enables users to modify and delete the file and to perform all the activities associated with the Read, Write, and Read & Execute permissions.

▶ Full Control—The Full Control permission enables the user or group to take ownership of the file and to change its permissions, as well as perform all the other activities possible with all the other permissions.

Whereas the NTFS system provides permission-level security for files and folders, other file systems running under Windows do not. For example, when a file is moved from an NTFS partition to a FAT partition, the NTFS-specific attributes are discarded. However, NTFS permissions do apply over a network connection.

EXAM ALERT

Know what happens to permissions when you move a file from an NTFS partition to a partition using another file system.

NOTE

NTFS is the preferred file system for Windows XP Home. However, several features are not available in the Home edition. For typical home users this is not an issue; however, many corporate environments require the more advanced NTFS features available only in Windows XP Professional. Windows XP Home does not offer any type of file- or folder-level security. Share permissions are available in the same fashion as Windows XP Professional.

Challenge #4

Your training group is bringing in a group of subject matter experts (SMEs) to design a training manual for a new software application your company has developed. You do not want the SMEs to be able to make changes to the application files but they do need to be able to run them for evaluation. During their work the members of the team will need to share their document copies with each other for review and correlation, so you establish a common folder Review1 for this purpose. In addition, each worker will need their own folder to keep original copies of their work that only they and management can access. How would you go about using NTFS permissions to accomplish these objectives?

Exam Prep Questions

1. What action does the operating system take when it runs out of available RAM?

   ○ **A.** It writes data to memory addresses that are not used frequently.

   ○ **B.** It writes data to the hard disk drive.

   ○ **C.** It writes data to virtual memory.

   ○ **D.** It writes data to cache.

2. What is the basic function of the HKEY_CURRENT_USER Registry key?

   ○ **A.** User-specific configuration

   ○ **B.** User logon data

   ○ **C.** PnP status data

   ○ **D.** Current information about devices

3. What is the basic function of the HKEY_USERS Registry key?

   ○ **A.** User-specific configuration

   ○ **B.** User logon data

   ○ **C.** PnP status data

   ○ **D.** Current information about devices

4. Which Windows utility can be used to make changes to the Registry in Windows 2000?

   ○ **A.** REGEDIT32

   ○ **B.** SYSEDIT

   ○ **C.** REGEDIT

   ○ **D.** POLEDIT

5. What is the swap file in Windows 2000 and Windows XP called?

   ○ **A.** SWAP.SYS

   ○ **B.** PAGEFILE.SYS

   ○ **C.** WIN386.SWP

   ○ **D.** WINSWAP.SWP

6. What are the names of the files involved in the Windows 2000/XP boot process, and in what order are they executed?

   ○ **A.** BOOT.INI, NTLDR, NTOSKRNL.EXE, NTDETECT.COM

   ○ **B.** NTLDR, BOOT.INI, NTOSKRNL.EXE, NTDETECT.COM

   ○ **C.** BOOT.INI, NTLDR, NTDETECT.COM, NTOSKRNL.EXE

   ○ **D.** NTLDR, BOOT.INI, NTDETECT.COM, NTOSKRNL.EXE, HAL.DLL

7. In a Windows 2000 or XP system, the NTBOOTDD.SYS file is used to _____.

   ○ **A.** Boot the system

   ○ **B.** Enable SCSI disk drives

   ○ **C.** Detect boot errors

   ○ **D.** Enable double-density booting

8. What are the primary characteristics of an extended partition? (Select all that apply.)

   ○ **A.** It is the first partition on the drive.

   ○ **B.** It can be divided into 23 logical drives.

   ○ **C.** It cannot be deleted if logical drives have been defined within it.

   ○ **D.** It is the logical drive that the system will boot to.

9. What is the smallest unit of storage on a disk that can be manipulated by the operating system?

   ○ **A.** Pixel

   ○ **B.** Bit

   ○ **C.** Cluster

   ○ **D.** Byte

10. What is the size of a sector in a PC-compatible disk?

   ○ **A.** 512 bytes

   ○ **B.** 8 bytes

   ○ **C.** 16 bytes

   ○ **D.** 1024 bytes

11. How many items can be placed in a directory in a FAT-based system?

   ○ **A.** 128

   ○ **B.** 256

   ○ **C.** 512

   ○ **D.** 1024

12. What is the maximum number of items that can exist in the root directory of a FAT-based disk?

   ○ **A.** 255

   ○ **B.** 256

   ○ **C.** 512

   ○ **D.** 1024

13. Which file system is the most efficient for storage of small files?

   ○ **A.** FAT

   ○ **B.** VFAT

   ○ **C.** FAT32

   ○ **D.** NTFS

14. Which of the following are advantages associated with using the NTFS file system? (Select all that apply.)

   ○ **A.** Data security.

   ○ **B.** Larger drives.

   ○ **C.** It handles small drives efficiently.

   ○ **D.** It uses 64-bit entries to keep track of items.

15. What is the maximum number of characters that can be used for Windows 2000 file-names?

   ○ **A.** 64

   ○ **B.** 215

   ○ **C.** 255

   ○ **D.** 256

16. Which of the following characters cannot be used in a Windows 2000 filename? (Select two answers.)

   ○ **A.** :

   ○ **B.** *

   ○ **C.** &

   ○ **D.** #

17. What command is used to encrypt files and folders from the Windows 2000 command line?

   ○ **A.** Protect

   ○ **B.** Unicode

   ○ **C.** Encrypt

   ○ **D.** Cipher

18. How do you identify a compressed file in Windows 2000? (Select two answers.)

   ○ **A.** The file or folder is listed in a second color.

   ○ **B.** The file or folder is listed in italic.

   ○ **C.** The file or folder shows a compressed/archive attribute listing.

   ○ **D.** The file or folder is given a vice-clamp icon.

19. Which of the following file systems is not supported under Windows XP Professional?

   ○ **A.** HPFS

   ○ **B.** NTFS5

   ○ **C.** FAT

   ○ **D.** FAT32

Answers and Explanations

1. C. Virtual memory is disk drive space that is manipulated to seem like RAM. Software creates virtual memory by swapping files between RAM and the disk drive. This memory management technique effectively creates more total memory for the system's applications to use. When the system runs out of available RAM, it shifts data to the virtual memory

swap file on the disk drive; however, because this involves a major transfer of information on the hard disk drive, an overall reduction in speed is encountered with virtual memory operations.

2. A. The Current_User key holds data about the user-specific configuration settings of the system, including color, keyboard, desktop, and start settings. The values in the Current_User key reflect those established by the user who is currently logged on to the system. If a different user logs on, the contents of the Users key is moved into the Current_User key.

3. B. The Users key contains the information about the various users who have been defined to log on to the system. The information from the Current_User key is copied into this section whenever a user logs off the system or when the system is shut down.

4. C. Windows 2000 includes two Registry editors: RegEdit and RegEdt32. Both utilities enable you to add, edit, and remove Registry entries and to perform other basic functions; however, specific functions can be performed in only one editor or the other. RegEdt32 is the Registry editor that is used with Windows 2000 and XP.

5. B. The Windows 2000/XPT paging file (PAGEFILE.SYS) is used to hold RAM memory swap pages.

6. D. The Windows 2000/XP boot sequence includes NTLDR, BOOT.INI, NTDETECT.COM, NTOSKRNL.EXE, and HAL.DLL.

7. B. If the Windows 2000 or XP system employs a SCSI disk drive, a driver file named NTBOOTDD.SYS must be present in the root directory of the system partition. This condition must also be noted in the BOOT.INI file by placing a mark in its SCSI(x) or Multi(x) locations. The NTLDR program can also load driver files that have been renamed as NTBOOTDD.SYS to enable Windows NT 4.0 and Windows 2000 to use drives greater than 8GB in size (even EIDE drives).

8. B, C. After the primary partition of a FAT-based system has been established and properly configured, an additional partition, referred to as an *extended* partition, is also permitted; however, the extended partition can be subdivided into 23 logical drives. The extended partition cannot be deleted if logical drives have been defined within it.

9. C. To more effectively manage space on the disk, newer operating system versions divide the disk into groups of logically related sectors called *allocation units* or *clusters*. In a FAT-based system, the cluster is the smallest manageable piece of information.

10. A. The sectors on a FAT-based disk hold 512 bytes each, and files can be of any length.

11. C. Each directory and subdirectory (including the root directory) can hold up to 512 32-byte entries that describe each of the files in them.

12. C. Because each root directory entry is 32 bytes long, each disk sector can hold 16 entries. On a hard disk drive, 32 sectors are set aside for the root directory. Therefore, the root directory for such a disk can accommodate up to 512 entries.

13. D. The smaller cluster size of the NTFS file system makes it more efficient than FAT formats for storing smaller files.

14. A, B, D. The NT File System (NTFS) structure is designed to provide better data security and to operate more efficiently with larger hard drives than FAT systems do. The NTFS structure uses 64-bit entries to keep track of storage on the disk (in contrast to the 16- and 32-bit entries used in FAT and FAT32 systems). The smaller cluster size of the NTFS format makes it more efficient than FAT formats for storing smaller files. NTFS also supports larger drives (more than 1GB) much more efficiently than FAT16 or FAT32 structures.

15. C. Filenames in Windows 2000 can be up to 215 characters long, including spaces.

16. A, B. Windows 2000 filenames cannot contain the following characters: / \ : * ? " and |.

17. D. Files and folders can be encrypted from the command line by using the cipher command. Information about the cipher command and its many switches can be obtained by typing **CIPHER /?** at the command prompt.

18. A, C. Compressed files can be marked so that they are displayed in a second color for easy identification through the Folder Options setting in the Control Panel. From this page, select the View tab and click the Display Compressed Files and Folders with Alternate Color check box. The only other indication that you will have concerning a compressed or encrypted file or folder is an attribute listing when the view setting is configured to display in web style.

19. A. Windows 2000 and Windows XP support NTFS (NTFS5 is native to both OS versions). They also support the FAT, FAT16, and FAT32 file systems, along with CDFS.

Challenge Solutions

1. You must create two partitions on the disk and format one with a Windows 2000 file management system (that is, FAT32 or NTFS) and the other with a Linux file management system. Although this sounds simple, this is not always the case. You can take some steps, however, to make the process simpler. If the disk does not already have two partitions available, you must repartition the drive to create them. Afterward, you can install one operating system in each of the partitions. There are third-party utilities that can be used to repartition a disk without losing existing data, but this function is not directly available in Windows 2000.

2. Although the NTFS file system can be used with NTFS, FAT16, FAT32, and CDFS, the FAT16 file management system has no tools for working with the other file management formats. Therefore, it is not even aware of the NTFS partition. You should change the second partition to use NTFS so that it will be able to access the first partition.

3. Because it is a Windows 2000 drive, the filenames are truncated when they are viewed from the command line. The customer should be looking for a file named XXXXXX1.DOC.

4. Establish Read & Execute permissions on the folder containing the application's executable and support files. Set Full Control permissions for Everyone on the REVIEW1 folder. Finally, set Full Control permissions on the individual SME folders.

14

Installing and Upgrading Operating Systems

Terms you'll need to understand:

- ✓ Setup
- ✓ Hardware Compatibility List
- ✓ Attended local install
- ✓ Unattended remote install
- ✓ Upgrade
- ✓ Permissions
- ✓ File systems
- ✓ Disk cloning

- ✓ Drivers
- ✓ Unsigned drivers
- ✓ Patches
- ✓ Updates
- ✓ Stop error
- ✓ Sysprep
- ✓ Remote Installation Service

Techniques you'll need to master:

Essentials 3.2—Install, configure, optimize, and upgrade operating systems—references to upgrading from Windows 95 and NT may be made.

- ✓ Identify procedures for installing operating systems, including the following:
  - ✓ Verification of hardware compatibility and minimum requirements
  - ✓ Installation methods (boot media such as CD, floppy, or USB, network installation, drive imaging)

- ✓ Operating system installation options (for example, attended or unattended, file system type, network configuration)
- ✓ Disk preparation order (start installation, partition and format drive)
- ✓ Device driver configuration (install and upload device drivers)
- ✓ Verification of installation

✓ Identify procedures for upgrading operating systems, including the following:

    ✓ Upgrade considerations (hardware, application, and/or network compatibility)

    ✓ Implementation (back up data, install additional Windows components)

✓ Install/add a device including loading and adding device drivers and required software, including the following:

    ✓ Determine whether permissions are adequate for performing the task

    ✓ Device driver installation (automated and/or manual search and installation of device drivers)

    ✓ Using unsigned drivers (driver signing)

    ✓ Verify installation of the driver (Device Manager and functionality)

Introduction

This chapter covers the Installing and Upgrading Windows Operating Systems areas of the CompTIA A+ Certification—Essentials examination under Objective 3.2. Operating systems must be installed on new computers to make them work. In addition, operating system versions change at a rapid pace, and most computers will have their operating system upgraded at least once in their lifetime. Therefore, technicians must be able to install operating systems on new machines and repair operating system problems.

Technicians must also be able to upgrade older operating systems (for example, Windows 9x and Windows NT 4.0 systems to new versions such as Windows 2000 or Windows XP systems). This chapter deals with installing and upgrading Windows 2000/XP operating systems and getting them to a functional level.

Installing Windows 2000/XP

The first issue to deal with is hardware compatibility. Windows 2000/XP makes no claim to maintaining compatibility with a variety of hardware devices. You can find comprehensive listings of Windows 2000 and Windows XP–compatible products on the Microsoft website under the Windows Marketplace Tested Products page at http://testedproducts.windowsmarketplace.com/. This collection is a complete reference for products that have been tested for Windows compatibility. You can use this site to easily browse, search, and validate the testing status of products your organization has or is considering for purchase.

Previously, the Microsoft Hardware Compatibility List (HCL) found on the operating system's distribution CD and the Microsoft website were the definitive list of Windows-compatible hardware products. However, HCLs are no longer maintained as a comprehensive reference. If your hardware does not appear in the Windows Marketplace Tested Products list, you are on your own for technical support.

You can also find Windows-compatible products in the Windows Catalogs at http://www.windowsmarketplace.com/. You can also reach these catalogs from the Windows Start menu and the Windows XP Help and Support menu.

The second factor involves which file management system to use. Windows 2000/XP can be configured to use either a typical FAT-based file system or its own proprietary NTFS file system.

Installation Methods

Windows 2000/XP operating systems can be installed using two primary methods:

▶ Attended installations from the Windows distribution CD or a USB flash drive

▶ Unattended installations across a network connection using a copy of the installation files obtained from a network server

In both cases, the installer must have access to the operating system's installation files. This means the equivalent of the \i386 folder on the distribution CD. If the local unit has a bootable CD-ROM drive, you can insert the CD into the drive and boot directly to it. When the system starts, the CD will load and the installation can take place locally, straight from the CD. If the system does not support a bootable CD, you will need to start the system using a boot floppy, load the CD-ROM driver, and run the setup utility from the CD. This will require running the Winnt.exe or Winnt32.exe file from the \i386 folder on the Windows CD.

> **NOTE**
>
> Windows XP setup boot floppies are available for download from Microsoft. These disks are available for users who want to run setup but do not have a bootable CD-ROM drive. The boot floppies come as a six-disk set and you must have the files and drivers from all the disks to access the CD-ROM drive and start the setup process.

The requirements for installing an operating system from a USB flash drive are similar to those associated with installing from a CD-ROM. The major difference is that a BIOS capable of booting from a USB device is required. Otherwise, the process is the same. Typically, the operating system must be loaded into the flash drive using a third-party program that condenses the Windows setup files into a smaller operating system that will fit on the flash drive. In some cases it is also possible to add additional utilities to the drive, such as antivirus and other antimalware products.

In a network environment, it is possible to perform installations from a network server across the network connection. This is particularly efficient when you need to perform multiple installations of the operating system around the network (such as when a new operating system version is rolled out across a business or office environment). In these settings, the operating system files are placed on a distribution server and executed from the destination (receiving) computer.

To do this, you boot the destination computer to a start disk (floppy, CD, USB, or HDD) that has the MS-DOS Client for Microsoft Networks utility on it, connect to the shared folder on the server that holds the setup files, and execute the Winnt.exe or Winnt32.exe file. The disk drive of the destination drive must be partitioned and formatted before engaging the installation routine.

EXAM ALERT

Be aware that you must have a formatted local partition before you can perform a network installation.

Unattended Installations and Disk Images

In a large corporate network, it could literally take weeks to perform a network operating system upgrade for all the systems on the network. For these environments, network operating system manufacturers have provided options for automating the installation process using the network and one or more distribution servers. Two automation methods are offered for Windows 2000 and XP networks:

▶ Unattended automated installations using answer files

▶ Disk cloning using disk images

Using Answer Files

In an unattended installation using answer files, administrators run scripted answer files that have been created to provide automatic answers to all the questions normally asked by the setup/installation routine. An administrator can run multiple installations across the network at one time.

If circumstances require different answers for different computers on the network, a Uniqueness Database File (UDF) must also be created to supply the unique settings required for those computers.

The Windows 2000/XP Setup Manager Wizards can be used to create answer files for unattended Windows installations and for Sysprep disk image cloning. In addition, this wizard can be used to create answer files for use with the Windows Remote Installation Services (RIS) server. This service is available to conduct RIS image-based installations across the network. It can be used to deploy only Windows 2000 Professional and Windows XP Professional operating systems.

This system involves establishing an RIS server in the network and then booting up systems as RIS clients that can download the image from the server. These images can be CD-based images or Remote Installation Preparation (RIPrep) images created with the Windows RIPrep Wizard. The Windows 2000 and XP Setup Manager Wizards are not installed by default and can be found on the CD in the Support\Tools\deploy.cab folder.

NOTE

Be aware that RIS can be used to deploy only Windows XP Professional and Windows 2000 Professional. It cannot be used to deploy Windows 2000 Server or any down-level operating systems—including Windows XP Home Edition and Windows XP Media Center Edition.

Disk Cloning

The second high-volume automated installation method employs clone copies of a given installation and simply re-creates that exact installation on multiple computers across the network. *Disk cloning* requires that a disk image be created of a reference computer. The main components of this computer (motherboard, BIOS, disk drive controllers, and VGA video controller) must be an exact copy of the hardware and software that you want to clone. Peripheral components not supported directly at the kernel level of the operating system (such as mice, NICs, sound cards, and modems) do not have to be the same among machines for disk cloning to take place.

Remote Installation Services Images

You must establish an RIS server in the network and then boot up systems as RIS clients that can download the image from the server.

The general procedure for creating RIPrep images is as follows:

1. Install and configure the RIS service on a Windows server using the Windows Components option under the Control Panel's Add/Remove Programs icon.

2. Execute the command **Risetup.exe** from the Run option of the Start menu on the RIS server. The RIS Wizard will install the RIS software, create an initial CD-based image of the system, create RIS answer files in the form of setup information (.sif) files, and configure the Client Installation menu required for remote installation operations.

3. Authorize the RIS server. This is performed through the Server's Administrative Tools and requires that the DHCP administrative utility be configured to authorize the server.

4. Create a reference computer as a template for the clone image. Configure this system with "most common denominator" user and system settings. Also, install and configure any application programs that will be part of the disk image.

5. Copy the Administrator profile into the Default User profile to ensure that everyone will be able to use the settings applied in the previous step.

6. From the command prompt, run RIPrep to prepare the system for duplication and create a disk clone image. This will create an exact snapshot of the reference system that can be stored on the RIS server and copied to as many computers as desired.

7. On the RIS client end, you must boot the system to an RIS boot disk containing the PXE protocol and network adapter card. The RIS boot disk is created using the Remote Boot Floppy Generator (Rbfg.exe) utility under the \Remoteinstall\Admin folder of the RIS server. The network adapter card will automatically request an IP address from the network's DHCP server and attempt to locate the RIS server in the network.

8. When the client machine locates the RIS server and connects to it, it will automatically download the image—provided the administrator has signified that the computer should receive that image.

Creating Disk Images

The Sysprep tool is used to prepare the reference computer for cloning. Third-party cloning software is required to create and distribute the disk image file that is used to clone the installation process on the remote computers.

> **EXAM ALERT**
>
> Be aware of the tools used to create disk clone images in Windows.

The basic steps for creating a disk image are the following:

1. Install the Windows 2000 or Windows XP operating system on the reference computer and log on as Administrator.

> **EXAM ALERT**
>
> Remember that in a domain environment you must be logged in with Administrative rights to perform OS cloning and upgrade operations.

2. Install and configure any application packages that are to be part of the disk image.

3. Configure a default set of user settings and Windows components that can be applied to everyone who will use the computers being cloned (that is, Start menu, desktop, and so on).

4. Under the Control Panel's System icon, copy the Administrator profile to the Default User profile to ensure that everyone who logs on to one of the clone computers will receive the proper settings.

5. Copy the Sysprep.exe, Setupcl.exe, and Sysprpe.inf files into the Sysprep directory of the reference computer (or on a floppy disk).

6. From the command prompt, run the Sysprep utility to prepare the system for cloning.

7. Run a disk-cloning utility (such as Norton Ghost from Symantec or Casper XP from Future Systems Solutions) to create an exact snapshot of the system. This snapshot can be stored on a distribution server and then be copied to as many computers as desired. Because the snapshot contains an exact picture of the reference system, including its Registry and configuration files, the copies must be installed on systems that either have the same or very similar hardware configurations. It is particularly important that the Hardware Abstraction Layers (HALs) and disk controller types match. Differences in plug-and-play devices will automatically be detected and corrected during the first startup.

8. When the clone system is started for the first time, the system will request information about several user- and computer-specific settings, such as licensing, user and company names, computer name and administrator password, product key, regional options, and time zone settings.

The general steps for using a third-party disk-cloning program to make disk images are as follows:

1. Install the disk-cloning software on a computer system.

2. As part of the installation process, the disk-imaging software provides for making a boot floppy that can be used to run the software on the reference and target computers.

3. Prepare a reference computer with the exact installation that you want to clone.

4. Boot the reference computer using the disk-imaging boot disk.

5. Follow the instructions presented by the imaging software to create the bit-by-bit clone image of the system. This is typically a menu selection to create an image for the system. You must inform the cloning software where to store the image after it is completed (for example, a CD-ROM or remote network drive).

6. Allow the image to be copied to the destination (CD or network drive). This may take a few minutes.

7. Boot the target computer using the boot disk and create a new partition on the drive.

8. Tell the disk-cloning client where to get the image and where to write the image on the target. This is normally a menu function as well.

9. Configure the target computer after the cloning process has concluded.

Hard Disk Drive Preparation

When a disk is manufactured, its surface is electronically blank. Several levels of preparation must take place to prepare the disk for use by the system. Installing the operating system on a new hard drive has evolved into the four basic steps that follow:

1. Partition the drive for use with the operating system.

2. Format the drive with the basic operating system files.

3. Run the appropriate setup utility to install the complete operating system.

4. Load all the drivers necessary to enable the operating system to work with the system's installed hardware devices.

Therefore, before you can install Windows 2000 or XP on a drive, it must contain as least one partition to hold the system and boot files. Several disk partition options are available when performing a setup from the Windows XP distribution CD. Partitioning can also be performed with a partitioning utility prior to the installation of Windows 2000 or XP Professional. Some partitioning utilities, such as the FDISK utility, are limited in the size and number of partitions that they can create. Third-party disk-partitioning utilities tend to be much more flexible.

When you are partitioning the disk during the setup process, you will be given the following options:

▶ Create a new partition if the hard disk does not have any partitions, or if it has existing partitions but also has free (unpartitioned) space.

▶ Delete partitions if the hard disk has existing partitions that you do not want to preserve. Then you can create a new partition to install the operating system in. However, when you delete a partition, all the existing information in it is lost.

▶ Bypass the partitioning process if the hard disk has existing partitions that you want to install Windows XP into. Any other existing partitions will remain intact.

> **NOTE**
>
> During the setup procedure, you should create only the partition that will hold the operating system. In Windows 2000 or XP, it is more efficient to create any additional partitions using the Disk Management utility after the installation has been completed.

Managing Patches and Service Packs

In the Windows environment, you must address three parts of the operating system when installing a new version or upgrade:

▶ Operating system release version

▶ Operating system patches and service packs

▶ Third-party device drivers

The operating system release is the version of the installation media produced and distributed as a complete unit. However, because of the nature of product development and the pressures on software producers to bring new products to the market, new releases never seem to be complete or perfect. Therefore, manufacturers continue to develop and upgrade their operating systems after they have been released. Rather than providing customers with new versions of the operating system when new features are added or major problems are corrected, software manufacturers provide OEM patches for their products. Microsoft typically releases its patches in the form of updates, or in collections that include additional functionality or new device drivers, which it refers to as *service packs*. Patches and service packs are not typically required to run an operating system release. The fact that an operating system exists as a release means that it is a complete operating system.

> **NOTE**
>
> For security and stability reasons, you should always patch operating systems on PCs that are connected to the Internet. However, this is not the case with all PCs. Stable PC systems that are not connected to the Internet should not be patched unless doing so resolves some problem the current system has.

When you install a fresh copy of an operating system that has been on the market for some time, or when you upgrade an existing operating system to a new version, there is a definite order for installing the new components:

- ▶ Install the operating system release
- ▶ Install the OEM patches or the latest service pack
- ▶ Install the best device driver choices

When the new operating system version or upgrade is installed, it should automatically install its own drivers for the devices it detects. In most cases, these drivers will be adequate to start up the installed devices because they have been tested to work with the operating system and should provide a functioning system. OEM drivers may be more up to date than those provided with the original operating system and offer better operation than the Windows versions.

If a device is not listed in the operating system's Marketplace Tested Products page, the device manufacturer's driver offers the only choice for operating the device. The other condition that calls for using the equipment manufacturer's driver occurs when the device does not operate correctly with the Windows-supplied drivers. New drivers delivered in service packs may offer a better choice than using the original operating system drivers. However, if they do not produce the operation desired, the OEM drivers must be reinstalled.

After installing an operating system and its device drivers, you must check for additional patches and service packs. Microsoft supplies its service packs with ascending numerical values—SP1, SP2, and so on. Subsequent service packs contain all the fixes included in earlier service packs, so you do not have to install an earlier version of a service pack before you install the latest version.

> **EXAM ALERT**
>
> Be aware of the requirements for installing service packs.

Microsoft provides the latest updates for its operating systems, hardware, and application products through its Windows Updates website. The www.windowsupdate.com page offers updates and service packs for its operating systems. The site inspects your PC to see what updates have already been installed and offers only those updates that you do not have. The selection page enables you to select just those items you want to download.

EXAM ALERT

Be aware of the Windows Update site.

The Automatic Windows Updates service can be scheduled to run automatically on the PC so that the user or administrator does not need to remember to periodically look for updates. Selecting one of the update options under the Control Panel's Automatic Updates icon turns on the Automatic Updates feature. If you select the Automatic (Recommended) option, you will need to designate a day and time for this to occur. In many cases, the Download Updates for Me, but Let Me Choose When to Install Them option is more desirable because the download can take up network bandwidth and slow the operation of the PC down for some period of time.

EXAM ALERT

Know how to set up Windows Automatic Updates.

Troubleshooting General Setup Problems

One of the three major categories of operating system problems is setup problems (those that occur during installation or upgrading). This category of problems typically involves failure to complete an OS installation or upgrade operation. In some cases, this can leave the system stranded between an older OS version and a newer OS version, making the system unusable.

The other two categories of general operating system problems are startup problems and operational problems. These categories happen at different stages in the operation of the system and produce distinct types of errors.

Setup problems are errors that occur during the installation of the operating system on the hard disk drive. One of the most common OS setup problems occurs when the system's hardware does not support the operating system that is being installed. These problems can include the following:

- Microprocessor requirements
- Memory speed mismatches
- Insufficient memory
- Incompatible device drivers

The memory speed mismatch or mixed RAM problem may produce a Windows Protection Error message during the installation process. This error indicates that the operating system is having timing problems that originate from the RAM memory used in the system. Correcting this problem involves swapping the system's RAM for devices that meet the system's timing requirements.

EXAM ALERT

Be aware that RAM speed mismatches can cause OS installation failures.

It is not uncommon for mouse or video drivers to fail during the installation of an operating system. If the video driver fails, you must usually turn off the system and attempt to reinstall the operating system from scratch. Conversely, if the mouse driver fails during the installation, it is possible to continue the process using the keyboard. This problem usually corrects itself after the system reboots.

The best way to avoid hardware-compatibility problems is to consult Microsoft's website to ensure that the hardware you are using is compatible with the operating system version you are installing.

Installing Windows 2000 Professional

The minimum hardware requirements for installing Windows 2000 Professional on a PC-compatible system are somewhat higher:

- Microprocessor—133MHz Pentium (P5 equivalent or better)
- RAM—64MB (4GB maximum)
- HDD space—650MB or more free on a 2GB drive
- Display device—VGA monitor

For installation from a CD-ROM, a 12x drive is required. If the CD-ROM drive is not bootable, a high-density 3.5-inch floppy-disk drive is also required.

> **EXAM ALERT**
>
> **Memorize the minimum system requirements for installing Windows 2000 Professional.**

Before installing Windows 2000 Professional from the CD, it is recommended that the checkupgradeonly file be run. This file is located on the installation CD under \i386\winnt32 and checks the system for possible hardware compatibility problems. The program generates a text file report named upgrade.txt that can be found under the \Windows folder. It contains Windows 2000 compatibility information about the system, along with a list of potential complications.

If your system has hardware devices that are not on the Windows 2000 Marketplace Tested Products page, you should contact the manufacturers of the devices to determine whether they have new, updated Windows 2000 drivers. Many peripheral makers have become very proactive in supplying updated drivers for their devices—often posting their latest drivers and product compatibility information on their Internet websites, where customers can download them. Another option is to get a device that is listed on the Windows 2000 Catalog.

> **EXAM ALERT**
>
> **Know what to do if you encounter hardware devices not listed on the Windows 2000 Marketplace Tested Products page.**

To conduct a new Windows 2000 Professional installation, you will need the Windows 2000 Professional distribution CD. If the installation is being performed on a system that cannot boot to the CD-ROM drive, you will also need Windows 2000 Professional setup disks. The Windows 2000 installation process, also called Setup, occurs in two distinct phases: a text only phase and a graphical wizard-driven phase. The installation process begins with a text-based sequence of screens known as the *Text Mode* portion of Setup. This mode of operation continues until enough of the operating system structure is in place to switch to the GUI-based conclusion of the setup process. After the basic Windows files have been copied into the system, the setup process switches into GUI format and presents the Windows Setup Wizard to guide the completion of the setup process.

The first step in the setup process is to choose whether the installation is a clean install or an upgrade. If a new installation is being performed, the Setup program will install the Windows 2000 files in the \WINNT folder.

For a CD-ROM installation, boot the system to the existing operating system and then insert the Windows 2000 Professional distribution CD into the CD-ROM drive. If the system detects the CD in the drive, click the Install Windows 2000 option. If it does not, start Setup through the Run command prompt dialog box. In Windows 9x and NT 4.0, click the Start button and then select the Run option from the menu. At the prompt, enter the location of the Windows 2000 start file (Winnt.exe or Winnt32.exe) on the distribution CD (D:\i386\Winnt32.exe). In the case of 16-bit operating systems, such as MS-DOS or Windows 3.x, the Winnt.exe option should be used. Winnt32.exe is used with 32-bit operating systems.

To install Windows 2000 Professional across a network, it will be necessary to establish a shared connection between the local unit and the system containing the Windows 2000 Professional Setup files. You will also need a Windows 2000 Professional–compatible NIC. At the command prompt, enter the path to the remote Winnt32.exe file (or Winnt.exe file). The Windows 2000 Setup Wizard collects information about the system and the user during the installation process. The most important information that must be provided includes the type of file management system that will be used (FAT or NTFS), computer name and administrator password, network settings, and workgroup or domain operations. After the installation process is complete, restart the system and verify the operation of the operating system and its various components.

Challenge #1

You have been tasked with changing over an office computer that had been running Windows 95 to Windows 2000 Professional. Your company has purchased a new high-capacity hard drive for the machine. As you move through the preinstallation preparation, you notice that the machine contains a modem and a LAN card that you cannot find on the Microsoft HCL for Windows 2000 Professional. What should you do to get the system back in service?

After the Windows 2000 install is complete, you will need to apply Windows updates and service packs. Windows 2000 eventually generated a list of four service packs before Microsoft stopped mainstream support for this operating system. Windows 2000 SP4 contains all the updates delivered in the previous service packs.

In additions to security fixes and application compatibility improvements, Windows 2000 SP4 delivered USB 2.0 and 802.1x wireless networking support to the Windows 2000 platform. The Windows Automatic Updates service was delivered in SP3 and 128-bit encryption was delivered in SP2.

Windows 2000/XP Setup Problems

When an attempt to install Windows 2000 or Windows XP fails, a stop error will normally result. Stop errors occur when Windows 2000 or XP detects a condition from which it cannot recover. The system stops responding, and a screen of information with a blue or black background displays. Stop errors are also known as *Blue Screen errors*, or as the *Blue Screen of Death (BSOD)*.

Other problems can occur during the Windows 2000 installation process. These problems include items such as the following:

▶ Noncompliant hardware failures.

▶ Insufficient resources.

▶ File system–type choices.

▶ WINNT32.EXE fails to run from the command prompt.

EXAM ALERT

Be aware that you should check hardware manufacturers' websites for updated device drivers before installing Windows 2000 or Windows XP.

Ways to correct these particular installation-related problems include the following:

▶ Verify hardware compatibility—The hardware-compatibility requirements of Windows 2000 and Windows XP are stringent. When either of these operating systems encounters hardware that is not compatible during the setup phase, it will fail the install process. Make certain to check the appropriate HCL to ensure that your hardware is compatible with Windows 2000 or Windows XP. Because of Windows 2000/XP's relative intolerance for unapproved devices, you should verify that all the system's hardware components are listed on the Marketplace Tested Products page. If any component is not on the list, remove it, restart the installation process, and see whether the process advances past the error. Check the hardware manufacturers' websites for updated device drivers before installing the operating system.

▶ Verify minimum system resource requirements—Make certain that your hardware meets the minimum hardware requirements, including the memory, free disk space, and video requirements. When the Windows NT, Windows 2000, or Windows XP setup routine detects insufficient resources (for example, processor, memory, or disk space), it either informs you that an error has occurred and halts, or it hangs up and refuses to continue the installation.

▶ Establish the file system type—Determine the file system you are going to use. If you will dual boot to Windows 98 and have a drive that is larger than 2GB, you must choose FAT32. Choosing NTFS for a dual-boot system renders the NTFS partition unavailable when you boot into Windows 98. FAT16 does not support drives larger than 2GB. You can upgrade from FAT16 to FAT32, or from FAT32 to NTFS; however, you can never revert to the older file system after you have converted it, without potentially losing data. You should also be aware that Windows NT does not support FAT32 partitions. Consider using the lowest common file system during installation and upgrading later.

NOTE

Windows 2000 and Windows XP versions can format native FAT32 volumes up to 32GB in size. However, they can work with larger volumes created by third-party partitioning software. For volumes larger than 32GB, Microsoft advises using the NTFS file system to format the volume for more efficient use of the drive space.

▶ WINNT32 does not run from the command prompt—The Winnt32.exe program is designed to run under a 32-bit operating system and does not run from the command line. It is used to initiate upgrades from Windows 9x or Windows NT to Windows 2000 or Windows XP. From a 16-bit operating system, such as an MS-DOS or a Windows 9x machine that has been started to a command prompt, you must run the Winnt.exe program from the command line to initiate the installation of Windows 2000 or XP.

In most cases, a failure during the Windows 2000/XP setup process produces an unusable system. When this situation occurs, you should usually reformat the disk and reinstall the system files from the Windows 2000 or XP setup (boot) disks.

Installing Windows XP Professional

The installation process for Windows XP is considerably different from previous Windows installation processes in that Windows XP requires you to activate your copy of the operating system within 30 days after installing it. This process is electronic and is meant to ensure that the copy of XP being used is legitimate and is being used on only one computer. If you attempt to install it on a second computer and activate it, an error message will be generated, notifying you that the registration is already active.

For technicians this does not become a problem until an extensive system upgrade is performed or a hard drive must be replaced. When these events occur, it will be necessary to deal with Microsoft's licensing department to reactivate the license. The licensing agreement that comes with Windows XP enables a single copy to be legally installed on one desktop and one portable computer.

The minimum hardware requirements for installing Windows XP Professional on a PC-compatible system are the following:

▶ Microprocessor—Pentium II 233MHz or higher or compatible processor required. Pentium II 300MHz or compatible processor recommended. Dual processor configurations are also supported with Windows XP.

▶ RAM—64MB required. 128MB recommended. The more memory installed the better. Maximum supported RAM is 4GB.

▶ HDD space—2GB with 650MB of free space required. 2GB of free hard disk space recommended. A 1.5GB partition size is required, with 2GB recommended. Additional disk space is required for installing over a network. The maximum hard disk space supported for a partition is 2TB.

▶ Display device—A VGA-compatible or higher display adapter with a monitor capable of 800×600 resolution required. SVGA-compatible display adapter recommended.

▶ Input devices—Keyboard and mouse (or other pointing device) required.

▶ CD-ROM—A 12x or faster CD-ROM drive is recommended (this item is required to perform the setup operation from the CD-ROM). If the CD-ROM drive is not bootable, a high-density 3.5-inch floppy drive is also required.

EXAM ALERT

Memorize the minimum system requirements for installing Windows XP Professional.

Other installation hardware requirements associated with network installations include a high-density 3.5-inch drive for performing setup across the network using a network client or boot disk, along with an appropriate network adapter card.

All hardware devices included in a Windows XP Professional system must be listed on Microsoft's Windows XP Marketplace Tested Products page. Devices listed on the Windows XP page have been tested and are supported by Microsoft. Copies of the Windows XP Marketplace Tested Products page can be obtained at http://testedproducts.windowsmarketplace.com/. The products on this Microsoft website typically represent the most up-to-date listing.

Before installing Windows XP Professional from the CD, you should run the Windows XP version of the checkupgradeonly utility. This file is located on the installation CD under \i386\Winnt32 and checks the system for possible hardware compatibility conflicts. It generates a text file report named upgrade.txt that contains Windows XP compatibility information, along with potential complications for the system. This report can be accessed in the \Windows folder.

If the system has hardware devices that are not on the Windows XP Marketplace Tested Products page, Microsoft has not tested or approved it and, therefore, will not support it. You should contact the device manufacturer to determine whether new or updated Windows XP drivers are available for the device. Most peripheral makers are aware of the importance of supplying updated drivers for their devices, so they typically post their latest drivers and product compatibility information on their corporate Internet sites.

The Windows XP attended installation process is nearly identical to the Windows 2000 process. The installation occurs in two phases: Text mode and GUI mode. The installer needs to answer only a few questions asked by installation wizard during the procedure.

After the installation process has completed, you will need to update the operating system by installing updates and service packs. Windows XP has generated two service packs, with SP2 being the current version. Service Pack 1 (SP1a) basically delivered fixes and security updates for the original Windows XP platform. Service Pack 2 includes all the updates and fixes delivered by SP1. It also introduced several security features such as the Windows Firewall, the Windows Security Center, and Pop-up Blocker for Internet Explorer. These enhancements were included to provide better protection from viruses, worms, and hackers.

> **EXAM ALERT**
>
> Be aware of features added to Windows XP by SP2.

Windows XP MCE Hardware Requirements

Media Center Edition has more stringent hardware requirements than other versions of Windows XP:

▶ Microprocessor—Pentium 4, 1.6GHz or higher.

▶ Display device—DirectX 9 hardware-accelerated Graphical Procssing Unit (GPU). The term *GPU* is used to describe a dedicated graphics-rendering device that is optimized to manipulate and display screen images.

▶ RAM—256MB required (at least 512MB preferred).

▶ HDD—40GB (high speed ATA or better).

▶ Input devices—Remote control and wireless keyboard preferred. Media Center remote controls are generally standardized in terms of button labels, functionality, and layout.

▶ TV tuner card—Required to receive and process television and other A/V signals. MCE 2005 supports up to four tuners: two analog tuners and two HDTV tuners. Recording is limited to only two programs at a time. Media Center tuners must have a standardized driver interface, hardware MPEG-2 encoders, and closed caption support. The 2005 version of MCE is capable of encoding incoming TV signals at a maximum rate of 9Mbps.

▶ Video output device—High-end video card (with S-video, component video, or DVI TV video output). The 2005 version of MCE directly supports DTV displays and can display 720p and 1080i video on large screen displays.

▶ Sound card/speakers—Sound card with stereo speakers or headset minimum—a 5.1 or 7.1 channel surround system is preferred.

> **NOTE**
>
> Additional functionality, such as Media Center Extender support, use of multiple tuners, or HDTV playback/recording capabilities, presents higher system requirements.

Windows XP Setup Problems

As with the other Windows versions, many things can cause Windows XP installations to fail. If a setup attempt fails during the installation process, you will be left with a system that has no workable operating system in place. If this occurs, you must first determine whether any hardware/software application conflict problems exist that could keep the system from starting. If there are none, you should start up the system from some type of bootable media and attempt to determine what might be keeping Windows XP from installing. Finally, if nothing appears as a likely cause of the problem, attempt to reinstall the Windows XP operating system from scratch.

If the Windows Setup Wizard does not detect sufficient hard disk space on the drive, a stop error will be created. If this occurs, try to remove files and programs to free up the needed disk space. You can also create an additional partition to hold Windows XP, or delete the existing partition and create a larger partition.

You should also verify that the system's hard drive and CD-ROM drives are on the Windows XP Marketplace Tested Products page. If the drives are not acceptable to the system, it will be difficult to conduct the installation, and you will receive errors during the text-based portion of the Windows XP setup routine. If the drives are not on the page, you can attempt to load OEM drivers for the devices from an OEM CD-ROM or floppy by pressing the F6 key when prompted and accessing the drivers on the disk.

> **EXAM ALERT**
>
> Remember which function key is used to load OEM drivers during the Windows XP installation process.

BIOS-based antivirus utilities can prevent operating systems from being installed or upgraded. When the setup utility attempts to make the hard disk Windows XP bootable, a BIOS-based virus scanner will interpret this action as an attempt by a virus to infect the system. In these cases, the system will produce an error message indicating that a virus is attempting to infect the boot sector. To prevent this from happening, disable the virus protection through the CMOS Setup utility and then enable it again after the operating system has been installed.

Most other failures during the installation process involve hardware detection problems or component installation errors. If the Windows XP installation process fails during the hardware detection phase of the process, check the system for devices that are not listed on the Windows XP Marketplace Tested Products page. Because of Windows 2000/XP's relative intolerance for unapproved devices, you should verify that all the system's hardware components are listed on the page. If any component is not on the list, remove it, restart the installation process, and see whether the process advances past the error.

Windows XP MCE Setup Limitations

The 2005 version of Windows XP MCE does not support joining a domain-based network environment. Although it is based on Windows XP Professional, the Media Center Edition was designed for residential installations, and there fore not designed for domain environments. Although the XP Professional structure allows MCE users to access network resources on a domain, it will not allow you to join the domain. Some hackers offer procedures for altering Registry keys in Windows XP MCE 2005 so that it can join a domain in the same manner as a windows XP Professional system that is running SP2.

However, XP MCE 2005 systems that have been upgraded from XP Media Center Editions 2004, which did permit network domain membership, can continue to be joined to domains. The original version status of Windows XP MCE can be determined by checking the System Properties in Control Panel. The revision status information can be obtained from the About option of the MCE application.

Operating System Upgrading

As mentioned earlier, it is not uncommon for a computer to have its operating system upgraded several times during its lifespan. The first key to a successful operating system upgrade is to make sure that the new system will be compatible with the existing hardware, software applications, and network environment. Check the Microsoft website for hardware compatibility lists. Check the application manufacturer's website and documentation for Windows OS compatibility statements.

Before you perform an OS upgrade, you should always back up the contents of the existing drive. Although you may not need to back up the current operating system files, you should always make sure to back up the users' personal files and settings. The new operating system, or a restored OS after a failure, will get the system running; however, files such as personal documents, pictures, illustrations, and system settings and preferences cannot be recovered unless they have been backed up in some manner.

> **EXAM ALERT**
>
> Remember what types of files are most valuable in the eyes of users when doing backups.

You may also need to install additional Windows components for the new operating system after an upgrade. These components are accessed through Control Panel's Add/Remove Programs (Add or Remove Programs or Windows Components in Windows XP) applet. The auxiliary Windows components available through this applet include Accessibility Options for physically, visually, or aurally challenged users, communications packages, and additional system tools.

The following sections of this chapter cover upgrading from Windows 9x environments to the Windows Me, Windows 2000, and Windows XP operating systems.

Upgrading to Windows 2000

Systems can be upgraded directly to Windows 2000 Professional from Windows 9x operating systems, as well as from Windows NT 3.51 and 4.0 workstations. This includes older NTFS, FAT16, and FAT32 installations. When you install Windows 2000, it can recognize all three of these file system types. If the computer is running an older Microsoft operating system, that OS version must be upgraded to one of these versions before it can be upgraded to Windows 2000. Otherwise, a clean installation must be performed from a full version of the operating system. Table 14.1 lists the acceptable Windows 2000 upgrade routes.

TABLE 14.1   Windows Upgrade Routes

CURRENT OPERATING SYSTEM	UPGRADE PATH
Windows 95 and Windows 98	Windows 2000 Professional only
Windows NT 3.51 and 4.0 Workstation	Windows 2000 Professional only
Windows NT 3.51 and 4.0 Server	Any Windows 2000 product
Windows NT 3.1 and 3.5	Must be upgraded to NT 3.51 or 4.0 first, and then to Windows 2000
Windows 3.x	Must be upgraded to Windows 95 or 98 first, and then to Windows 2000 Professional

The easiest upgrade path to Windows 2000 is from the Windows NT 4.0 operating system. Upgrading from Windows 9x is potentially more difficult because the Windows 9x Registry structure requires significant changes to become the Windows 2000 Registry structure.

EXAM ALERT

Memorize the acceptable paths for upgrading from older Windows operating systems to Windows 2000.

Windows 2000 does not attempt to remain compatible with older hardware and software. Therefore, some applications may not be compatible with Windows 2000 and may run poorly or fail completely after an upgrade.

Challenge #2

One of your customers has an office network made up of a Windows 4.0 server with three Windows NT 3.5 workstations, two Windows 98 workstations, one Windows NT 4.0 workstation, and one Windows 3.51 workstation. The customer wants to test out Windows 2000 Professional on one computer to see how it works and to begin getting the users accustomed to Windows 2000. The customers wants want to do this with as little hassle as possible. What would you suggest that the company do to accomplish these goals?

Upgrading to Windows 2000 is suggested for users who have an existing Windows operating system that is compatible with Windows 2000 and who want to maintain the existing data and preference settings. Follow these steps:

1. To upgrade a system to Windows 2000 from a previous operating system using a CD-ROM installation disc, boot the system to the existing operating system and then insert the Windows 2000 Professional distribution CD into the CD-ROM drive.

2. If the system detects the CD in the drive, click the Install Windows 2000 option. If it does not, start Setup through the Run command. In Windows 9x and NT 4.0, click Start and select the Run option from the menu. In Windows 3.x and NT 3.51, click File and then select the Run option from that menu.

3. At the prompt, enter the location of the Windows 2000 start file (Winnt.exe or Winnt32.exe) on the distribution CD (for example, d:\i386\Winnt32.exe). In the case of Windows 3.x, the Winnt.exe option should be used.

4. Choose the Upgrade to Windows 2000 (Recommended) option.

5. Follow the instructions the Installation Wizard places on the screen, entering any information required.

6. Verify the operation of the operating system and its components.

> **EXAM ALERT**
>
> Be aware that in a current Windows 2000 system, you should be able to reinstall Windows 2000 by starting the system with the Windows 2000 distribution CD in the drive so that it can be autodetected.

To upgrade Windows 2000 Professional from a previous operating system across a network, it is necessary to establish a shared connection between the local unit and the system containing the Windows 2000 Professional setup files. Follow these steps:

1. Boot the local unit to the existing operating system and establish a connection with the remote unit.

2. At the command prompt, enter the path to the remote Winnt32.exe file (use the Winnt.exe file if an older 16-bit operating system is being used on the local unit). The Winnt file is used with 16-bit operating systems such as MS-DOS or Windows 3.x. The Winnt32 version is used with

32-bit operating systems, including Windows 95, 98, NT 3.5, and NT 4.0.

3. Choose the Upgrade Your Computer to Windows 2000 option.

4. Follow the instructions the Setup Wizard places on the screen, entering any information required.

5. Verify the operation of the operating system and its components.

Challenge #3

You place the Windows 2000 Professional distribution CD in the drive of a Windows 98 machine and nothing happens. You want to upgrade the system to Windows 2000, but there is no autodetection or self-starting feature for the CD-ROM. What do you need to do to install the Windows 2000 operating system?

Upgrading to Windows XP

Existing Windows installations can be migrated to the new operating system by either upgrading them or by performing a clean installation of Windows XP Professional. Upgrading is preferable in many situations because it provides for the preservation of existing users and groups, user settings, data, and installed applications.

Systems can be upgraded to Windows XP Professional from Windows 98 and Windows Me as well as Windows NT 4.0 (with Service Pack 5) workstations and Windows 2000. This includes FAT16, FAT32, and NTFS systems. As was the case with Windows 2000, the Windows XP operating system can recognize all three file system types.

If a computer is currently running Windows 98, Windows Me, Windows NT Workstation 4.0 (with Service Pack 5 installed), or Windows 2000 Professional, it can be upgraded directly to Windows XP. However, systems running Windows 95 or Windows NT Workstation 3.51 operating systems cannot upgrade directly to XP. Instead, they must have intermediate upgrades to bring them up to a Windows version that does support direct upgrading to Windows XP.

NOTE

Although older Windows operating systems can be upgraded using interim upgrades, the computer hardware that they are running on probably does not satisfy the minimum hardware requirements for Windows XP Professional.

As with new Windows operating system installations, generating a system compatibility report prior to running the upgrade process is a good idea. This way, you can detect and analyze potential problems and implement solutions. You can generate the report by using the WINNT32 checkupgradeonly command (D:\winnt32 /checkupgradeonly—where the D: is your CD-ROM drive) or by selecting the Check System Compatibility option on the Setup menu. Either action launches Setup for the purpose of generating the compatibility report only; the computer is not modified in any way.

Some steps involved in upgrading from Windows 98 to Windows XP Professional can be difficult. Although most operating system and user configuration settings upgrade easily, other items such as applications and device drivers may create problems. The majority of these issues will show up when the compatibility report is generated.

If any hardware or software incompatibilities are detected, the proper updates should be obtained and applied before proceeding with the upgrade. Any incompatible software detected should be uninstalled from the system until new compatible replacements can be loaded. Before you install Windows XP, you should take the time to check the system BIOS version to verify that it is the latest revision available. There may have been enhancements or updates made to the BIOS since its release from the vendor that Windows XP can make use of.

> **NOTE**
>
> As with Windows 2000 upgrades, remember to verify that BIOS-based virus protection is disabled before performing the Windows XP upgrade. This BIOS feature causes the Setup process to fail because it will interpret Setup's attempts to modify the boot sector as a virus activity.

To avoid losing them, you should always back up any important files and data before performing an upgrade. You should consult with the system's users before conducting a backup to make sure that you properly handle information that is important to them. Typically, this involves their documents, pictures, emails and other personal files. You should also scan for viruses and remove them from the system before conducting an upgrade. Finally, make sure to uncompress any drive compressed with anything other than NTFS compression before performing the upgrade. The only compression type supported by Windows XP Professional is NTFS compression. Third-party compression formats are not supported.

Performing Local Upgrades

To initiate a local upgrade from a bootable CD-ROM drive, insert the Windows XP Professional distribution CD into the drive and select the Install Windows XP option from the Setup menu, as illustrated in Figure 14.1. If the menu is not displayed automatically, run the Setup utility from the Windows XP CD. If you are upgrading from a distribution server, run the WINNT32 utility command.

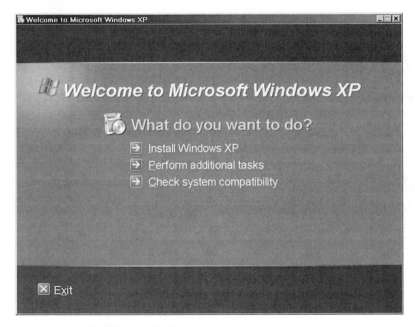

FIGURE 14.1 The Windows XP Setup menu.

The opening Windows Setup page, shown in Figure 14.2, asks whether an upgrade of the existing operating system is being conducted or a new version of Windows XP is being installed. If the New Installation option is specified, the existing operating system settings will be overwritten along with any existing applications. These applications must be reinstalled to retain their use.

FIGURE 14.2 The Windows XP Setup Wizard.

There are two types of upgrades: express and custom. An express upgrade automatically upgrades the existing Windows installation and maintains all current settings. A custom upgrade enables you to change the following:

▶ Installation partition

▶ Installation folder

▶ Language options

▶ File system type (NTFS conversions allowed)

Upgrading to Windows XP requires a minimum of administrative intervention and can be fully automated using answer files, as previously discussed in this chapter. The information required to perform a standard upgrade is very similar to that involved with the standard setup process.

Windows XP has special tools, called the *User State Migration Tools* (*USMT*) which administrators can use to transfer user configuration settings and files from systems running Windows 9x and NT systems to a clean Windows XP installation. This enables user information to be preserved without going through the upgrade process. In a USMT operation, user state information is backed up from the old operating system to a network server and then restored to the new Windows XP system. The following list describes the default settings transferred from the older system to the new Windows XP system by the USMT utility:

▶ The contents of the My Documents, My Pictures, Desktop, and Favorites folders

▶ Most user interface settings, including display properties, fonts, mapped network drives, network printers, browser settings, folder options, taskbar options, and files and settings associated with the Microsoft Office applications

▶ Files with industry standard extensions such as .doc, .ppt, .txt, and .xls

EXAM ALERT

Know which utility is used to transfer users' files and settings in an upgrade procedure.

Upgrade Problems

You will encounter many of the same problems performing an operating system upgrade that you do when performing a clean installation. These problems are usually related to the following:

▶ Insufficient hard drive or partition sizes

▶ Memory speed mismatches

▶ Insufficient memory problems

▶ Incompatible device drivers

While performing upgrade operations, you can also encounter problems created by version incompatibilities. New versions of operating systems are typically produced in two styles: full versions and upgrade versions. Generally, you cannot use a full version of the operating system to upgrade an existing operating system. Doing so will produce an `Incompatible Version` error message telling you that you cannot use this version to upgrade. You must either obtain an upgrade version of the operating system or partition the drive and perform a new installation (losing your existing data).

To determine the current version and service pack level of a Windows operating system running on a computer, right-click the My Computer icon, select the Properties option from the pop-up menu, and view the General tab of the System Properties window. Another way to get the version of Windows is to open Windows Explorer, click the Help menu, and select About Windows.

EXAM ALERT

Know how to display the current version of Windows information for a system.

Dual Booting

In a dual-boot system, a startup menu is established that can be used to boot the system into different operating systems on the disk. Depending on which operating system option the user selects from the menu, the system retrieves the correct set of files and then uses them to boot the system. Figure 14.3 shows the dual-boot menu containing information that varies depending on the exact operating systems involved.

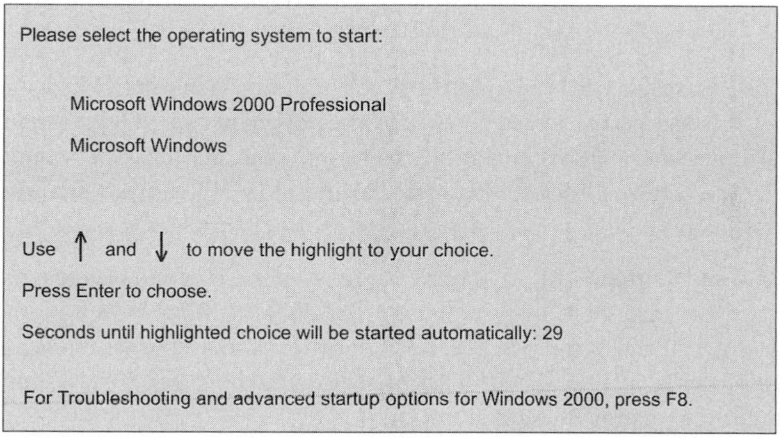

Please select the operating system to start:

    Microsoft Windows 2000 Professional

    Microsoft Windows

Use ↑ and ↓ to move the highlight to your choice.

Press Enter to choose.

Seconds until highlighted choice will be started automatically: 29

For Troubleshooting and advanced startup options for Windows 2000, press F8.

FIGURE 14.3 A dual-boot menu screen.

Dual Booting with Windows 2000/XP Operating Systems

Windows 2000 can be set up to dual boot with older MS-DOS or Windows 9x operating systems. This option provides a method for the system to boot into a Windows NT environment or into an MS-DOS/Windows 9x environment. In such cases, a startup menu appears on the display that asks which operating system should be used. Establishing either of these dual-boot conditions with Windows NT requires that the MS-DOS or Windows 9x operating systems be installed first. Make certain to install the Windows 2000 or Windows XP version in a new folder so that it does not overwrite the original operating system.

Although it is possible for Windows 2000 or Windows XP to share a partition with Windows 9x or Windows NT 4.0, this produces some potentially undesirable situations. Windows NT 4.0 supports both FAT 16 and NTFS, and either can be used on a dual boot system. Microsoft recommends using NTFS. However, Windows NT 4.0 cannot access an NTFS5 partition without SP4 or higher being installed. Windows NT 4.0 does not support FAT32 and can't be located on a FAT32 partition. As a general rule, you should install Windows 2000 or XP and the other operating system in separate partitions.

The major drawback of dual booting with Windows NT or Windows 2000 is that the other operating systems are not capable of using applications installed in the other operating system's partition. Therefore, software that is to be used by both operating systems must be installed in the system twice, once for each operating system partition. Even when you permit Windows 2000 or Windows XP to share the same partition with a Windows 9x or Windows NT operating system, you will need to reinstall the system's applications so that their installation routines can modify the Windows 2000/XP Registry.

Care must also be taken when formatting partitions in a Windows NT dual-boot system. The native file management formats of Windows 2000/XP and other operating systems are not compatible. If the disk is formatted with NTFS, the MS-DOS or Windows 9x operating system will not be able to read the files in the NTFS partition. These operating systems are not NTFS aware.

Windows 2000 and Windows XP can both operate with the FAT file systems. As a matter of fact, they can both be installed on FAT16, FAT32, or NTFS partitions. Windows 2000 and Windows XP also support the CDFS file system used with CD-ROM drives in PCs. The NTFS file system is the desired file system for use with these operating systems.

> **EXAM ALERT**
>
> Know which operating system versions are aware of other partition types in a dual-boot situation.

One reason to configure a dual-boot arrangement occurs when some of your key applications are not Windows XP compatible. In these situations, you can boot the computer into an older operating system to use those applications, and then run all the other applications under Windows XP. However, Windows XP does offer a Compatibility mode to make older applications run smoothly in an XP environment. To configure Compatibility mode for a given application, navigate to the program's .EXE file in Windows Explorer and right-click on its filename. Click on the Compatibility tab and select the best Compatibility mode for that application.

There are a few items to consider when dual booting. You should be aware that the system's active partition must be formatted with a file system that all the operating systems in the system can use. Windows 98 does not support NTFS and cannot boot from an NTFS partition.

NOTE

If you want to set up a dual-boot configuration with your current operating system, you will need to select the new installation option to preserve the existing operating system.

In dual-boot configurations, the boot process is controlled by a boot manager utility. This utility intercedes in the boot process and provides an option for selecting which operating system should be used to boot the system. If drive C: is formatted as NTFS, you will be unable to dual boot with any other operating system without employing a third-party boot manager utility. Therefore, Windows XP Professional should be the last operating system installed. The Windows XP boot manager is backward compatible with previous Microsoft operating systems; however, their boot managers are not compatible with Windows XP. For example, if you were to install Windows NT 4.0 as a second operating system in a dual-boot scenario after Windows XP Professional had been installed, the Windows NT 4.0 boot manager would overwrite the Windows XP boot manager, making it unbootable.

You should make sure that each operating system is installed into a different folder. If possible, they should even be placed in different volumes (drive letters). For example, if you install Windows XP in a folder where another operating system exists, the XP files will overwrite the previous operating system so that it will not boot. However, if you install Windows XP in a different folder on the same volume as an existing operating system, all the operating systems will function.

Although it is possible to dual boot FAT and NTFS volumes, from a security point of view it is recommended that FAT partitions be converted to NTFS partitions. The Windows Setup utility provides you with the option to convert the partition to the new version of NTFS, even though it was previously formatted as FAT or FAT32. This conversion process protects existing files—unlike formatting the partition. The conversion process can also be accomplished from the command line using the CONVERT command.

EXAM ALERT

Be aware of the command-line utility used to convert FAT or FAT32 partitions to NTFS partitions.

Loading and Adding Device Drivers

One of the reasons for the success of the PC-compatible system is its versatility. This versatility is the result of an open architecture that permits all types of devices to be added to it. This is accomplished through the use of software device drivers that interface diverse equipment to the basic system. Although the process for installing equipment and their drivers in a PC has become increasingly easy, the technician must still be able to install whatever drivers are necessary.

After installing or upgrading a device driver, you should verify that it works properly with the hardware it supports. The most straightforward method of verifying the functionality of the driver is to use the device to make sure that it does everything it is supposed to. You can also verify the installation of the driver through the Device Manager utility.

2000/XP Device Drivers

Windows 2000 and Windows XP offer support for a fairly wide range of disk drive types, VGA video cards, network interface cards, tape drives, and printers. To determine what devices the operating system supports, consult the Windows Catelogs for the version of Windows 2000/XP being used.

> **NOTE**
>
> Hardware compatibility information for the version of Windows 2000/XP being used can be obtained from the Microsoft website (http://testedproducts.windowsmarketplace.com/).

If drivers for the device being installed are not listed at this location, there is a good chance the device will not operate, or will not operate well in the Windows 2000/XP environment. If this is the case, the only recourse is to contact the device's manufacturer for Windows 2000 or Windows XP drivers. It is a good idea to check the manufacturer's website for updated drivers that can be downloaded.

> **EXAM ALERT**
>
> Know where to begin looking for Windows device drivers not supplied directly by Microsoft.

NOTE

Be aware that in an administrated client/server network, you need to have proper administrative permissions to add drivers to a system. If you are working in someone else's network, you usually need to contact the network administrator for a user account with permission levels and rights that will permit you to carry out the driver install/update.

Challenge #4

You are working in a music production facility that uses high-end MIDI devices (high-end professional sound cards and devices) to generate and manipulate musical instruments and sounds. You want to upgrade your production computers with these devices, but you worry that these specialized sound cards will not be compatible with the Windows 2000 Professional operating system. The cards and devices are working under Windows 98, and they tend to be somewhat expensive compared to other computer devices. How can you determine whether this upgrade solution is a good thing to do?

SATA Drivers

Drivers for SATA interfaces and devices are not native to Windows 2000 or Windows XP. If you are installing a SATA drive in an existing system that already has a boot drive, the drivers can be installed at any time. However, if the SATA drive is being installed as the boot drive, the SATA drivers will be loaded into the operating system during the Windows installation process.

In either case, you will need to check the CMOS configuration setup to make sure that the SATA communication channel and controller have been enabled. There should be no problem mixing SATA and PATA drives in a system that has the physical interfaces to do so. The operating system will prompt you for the SATA drivers during the installation process. At this point, you need to insert the disk or disc that has in the driver on it in an accessible drive and press the F6 function key. You will only have a limited amount of time to press the key and insert the media holding the driver.

To confirm the presence of the new SATA drivers for drives being added to an existing system, access the Device Manager utility and look for SCSI and RAID controller device entries (if the drive being installed is the boot drive, you will not be able to check the Device Manger). Click the + sign next to the SCSI device icon to reveal the presence of the serial ATA controller. With the drivers installed, you can move into the Computer Management console and select the Disk Management utility to partition the drive for use.

Finding Drivers

Device manufacturers often continue to develop improved device drivers for their products after they have been released into the market. These drivers offer more features and better performance for these devices than older drivers that were supplied on Windows distribution CDs. Therefore, you may want to locate new drivers for existing equipment to upgrade its performance under Windows 2000 or Windows XP.

To find a new or updated driver for a specific device, you should check the Microsoft Windows Catalogs at http://www.windowsmarketplace.com/ for the latest tested and approved drivers. You can also access the product vendor's website and search for your specific network operating system. Typically, you will need to know the specific make and model of your device. In most cases, the desired device driver can be downloaded directly from the vendor's website. There are also several third-party websites on the Internet where device drivers can be obtained for various pieces of hardware. These sites tend to be particularly useful for finding device drivers for older pieces of hardware, where original copies of drivers have been lost.

Driver Signing

Windows 2000 and Windows XP support a relatively wide array of newer hardware devices. These devices include DVD, USB, and IEEE-1394 devices. Microsoft works with hardware vendors to certify their drivers. These drivers are digitally signed so that they can be loaded automatically by the system.

Because poorly written device drivers had traditionally been a third-party problem for Microsoft, it created a Windows Hardware Quality Labs (WHQL) approval system for hardware manufacturers. Manufacturers that want to assure their customers that their products will work with Windows 2000 and XP operating systems can submit their equipment and drivers to Microsoft for certification. Microsoft grants tested drivers a digital signature that is embedded in the driver to show that it has been approved. When Windows 2000 or Windows XP loads the driver, the OS checks it for the signature.

Prior to the Windows Driver Signing system, manufacturers often provided poorly written drivers with their equipment that would crash systems or cause conflicts with other peripheral devices. Some manufacturers continue to provide unsigned drivers to reduce the cost of their product. The results of using unsigned drivers ranges from no effect to system lockups and crashes.

EXAM ALERT

Be aware of the consequences of using unsigned drivers in a Windows 2000 or XP system.

Driver signing is controlled through the Windows 2000/XP Control Panel's System icon. In the System applet, select the Hardware tab and click the Driver Signing button. The Driver Signing Options page will appear. On this page, you can establish how the system should react when it detects an unsigned driver. The options are as follows:

▶ Warn—This setting will cause Windows to notify the user when an unsigned driver has been detected. It will also produce an option to load or not load the driver.

▶ Block—As its title implies, this option will not permit any unsigned drivers to be loaded into the system.

▶ Disable (Ignore in Windows XP)—This option disables the digital signature check and automatically loads any driver without providing a warning to the user.

If you check the Apply Setting as System Default (Make This Action the System Default in Windows XP) check box, the signature verification setting will be applied to anyone who logs on to the system. Otherwise, only the currently logged-on user will be affected.

Because Windows 2000 and Windows XP are designed with centralized network security in mind, some administrative control issues may be encountered when loading device drivers into one of these systems. If the system detects a valid digital signature or the Designed for Windows Logo when it checks the driver, it will usually accept the driver without any problems. However, if no digital signature or logo exists, administrative privileges are required to load the driver into the system.

NOTE

You must be a member of the Administrators group to install drivers using the Add Hardware Wizard, or when a network policy setting has been established to restrict who can install devices.

Exam Prep Questions

1. What are the minimum hardware requirements for installing Windows 2000 Professional?

   ○ **A.** 80486DX/66 CPU, 32MB RAM, 650MB HDD space

   ○ **B.** Pentium 75 CPU, 32MB RAM, 650MB HDD space

   ○ **C.** Pentium 100 CPU, 64MB RAM, 650MB HDD space

   ○ **D.** Pentium 133 CPU, 64MB RAM, 650MB HDD space

2. What should you do if you encounter hardware devices not listed on the Windows 2000 Marketplace Tested Products page?

   ○ **A.** Download appropriate drivers from the device manufacturer's website.

   ○ **B.** Use a driver from a similar model from the same manufacturer in the Add New Hardware Wizard's list of supported devices.

   ○ **C.** Install the device without drivers.

   ○ **D.** Devices not directly supported in the Windows 2000 Marketplace Tested Products page cannot be installed.

3. Which command is used to start a Windows 2000 installation from a 16-bit operating system?

   ○ **A.** WIN2K

   ○ **B.** WINNT

   ○ **C.** WINNT16

   ○ **D.** WINNT32

4. Which command is used to start a Windows 2000 installation from a 32-bit operating system?

   ○ **A.** WIN2K

   ○ **B.** WINNT

   ○ **C.** WINNT16

   ○ **D.** WINNT32

5. _____ speed mismatches can cause OS installation failures.

    ○ **A.** Bus

    ○ **B.** RAM

    ○ **C.** Microprocessor

    ○ **D.** Disk drive

6. What should be checked before installing Windows 2000?

    ○ **A.** The hardware manufacturers' websites for updated device drivers

    ○ **B.** The expiration date for the operating system

    ○ **C.** The speed of the hard-disk drive

    ○ **D.** Your Internet connection

7. What utilities can prevent operating system upgrades from occurring?

    ○ **A.** Multiple-OS loader

    ○ **B.** Encryption

    ○ **C.** Compression/archive

    ○ **D.** Antivirus

8. How can the current version of Windows be displayed? (Select all that apply.)

    ○ **A.** Open Windows Explorer, click the Help menu, and select About Windows.

    ○ **B.** Open Windows Explorer, click the File menu, and select Properties.

    ○ **C.** Right-click My Computer and select Properties from the contextual menu.

    ○ **D.** Right-click the desktop and select Properties from the contextual menu.

9. What type of file system should you put on a partition if you intend to dual boot Windows 9x and Windows NT from that partition?

    ○ **A.** FAT

    ○ **B.** FAT32

    ○ **C.** NTFS

    ○ **D.** HPFS

10. It is not uncommon for the Windows 2000 operating system to occasionally need a therapeutic reinstallation. What must you do to accomplish this activity?

   ○ **A.** Start the system with the Windows 2000 distribution CD in the drive.

   ○ **B.** Start the system in Safe Mode and run Setup from the distribution CD.

   ○ **C.** Start the Windows system from the command prompt using the WIN command and the :D switch.

   ○ **D.** Start the system using the ERD and run the Emergency Repair Process.

11. Which of the following media can be used to perform attended Windows XP installs? (Select all that apply.)

   ○ **A.** A CD-ROM

   ○ **B.** An IrDA connection

   ○ **C.** A local area network

   ○ **D.** A USB drive

12. Patch management is defined as _____.

   ○ **A.** Installing new operating system releases to keep systems up to date

   ○ **B.** Downloading antivirus definition updates to keep systems safe from virus attacks

   ○ **C.** Removing software patches that are installed automatically when new applications are downloaded and installed on the system to recover wasted drive and memory capacity

   ○ **D.** Keeping the operating system up to date and secure

13. You have been asked to hook up an old dot matrix printer to a new Windows XP system. What is the best place to check to determine whether the printer will work with the new system?

   ○ **A.** Check the Microsoft HCL on the Microsoft website.

   ○ **B.** Check the printer manufacturer's documentation.

   ○ **C.** Check the Microsoft HCL on the Windows XP distribution disc.

   ○ **D.** Check on the Microsoft website under the Windows Marketplace Tested Products page.

14. Windows XP Professional can support up to _____ RAM.

   ○ **A.** 4GB

   ○ **B.** 16GB

   ○ **C.** 32GB

   ○ **D.** 64GB

15. Which of the following is a correct upgrade path? (Select all that apply.)

   ○ **A.** Windows Me to Windows XP

   ○ **B.** Windows 98 to Windows 2000

   ○ **C.** Windows 95 to Windows XP

   ○ **D.** Windows NT 3.5 to Windows XP

16. What is the minimum amount of memory required to install Windows 2000 Professional?

   ○ **A.** 8MB

   ○ **B.** 16MB

   ○ **C.** 32MB

   ○ **D.** 64MB

Answers and Explanations

1. D. The minimum hardware requirements for installing Windows 2000 Professional on a PC-compatible system are the following: Pentium 133 (P5 equivalent or better), 64MB RAM, 650MB or more of free space on a 2GB HDD, and a VGA monitor. For installation from a CD-ROM, a 12x drive is required. If the CD-ROM drive is not bootable, a high-density 3.5-inch floppy drive is also required.

2. A. If your system has hardware devices that are not on the Windows 2000 Marketplace Tested Products page, you should contact the manufacturers of the devices to determine whether they have new, updated Windows 2000 drivers. Many peripheral makers have become very proactive in supplying updated drivers for their devices—often posting their latest drivers and product compatibility information on their

Internet websites, where they can be downloaded by customers. Another option is to get a device that is listed on the Windows 2000 Marketplace Tested Products page.

3. B. The WINNT command is used with 16-bit operating systems such as DOS or Windows 3.x. The WINNT32 version is used with 32-bit operating systems, including Windows 95, 98, NT 3.5, and NT 4.0.

4. D. The WINNT32 version is used with 32-bit operating systems including Windows 95, 98, NT 3.5, and NT 4.0. The WINNT command is used with 16-bit operating systems such as DOS or Windows 3.x.

5. B. A memory speed mismatch or mixed RAM problem may produce a Windows Protection Error message during the installation process. This error indicates that the operating system is having timing problems that originate from the RAM memory used in the system. Correcting this problem involves swapping the system's RAM for devices that meet the system's timing requirements.

6. A. Contact the hardware vendors for all your components to determine whether they support Windows 2000 before starting the installation. At the same time, you can download the latest updates to the device drivers.

7. D. Active antivirus software might prevent Windows 98 from being installed on a system. These utilities see changes to the operating system's core files as a virus activity and will work to prevent them from occurring. Any antivirus programs should be disabled prior to running Windows 98 Setup. The antivirus program can be re-enabled after the setup process has been completed.

8. A, C. The simplest method to determine the current version of a Windows operating system running on a computer is to right-click the My Computer icon, select the Properties option from the pop-up menu, and select the General tab of the System Properties page.

9. A. The native file management formats of Windows 2000/XP and the other operating systems are not compatible. If the disk is formatted with NTFS, the Windows 9X operating system will not be able to read the files in the NTFS partition. The Windows 9X operating system is not NTFS aware. Windows NT and Windows 2000, however, can both operate with the FAT file systems used by Windows 9x. Therefore, it is recommended that logical drives in a dual-boot system be formatted with the FAT system.

10. A. Reinstalling Windows 2000 on an existing system typically requires only that the system be restarted with the Windows 2000 distribution CD in the drive.

11. A, D. Attended installations can be conducted from the Windows distribution CD or from a USB flash drive.

12. D. Rather than provide customers with a new version of the operating system when new features are added or major problems are corrected, software manufacturers provide OEM patches for their products. Microsoft typically releases patches in the form of updates, or in collections that include additional functionality or new device drivers that they refer to as service packs.

13. D. On the Microsoft website under the Windows Marketplace Tested Products page at http://testedproducts.windowsmarketplace.com/. This collection is a complete reference for products that have been tested for Windows compatibility.

14. A. Under Windows XP the maximum supported RAM is 4GB. The required RAM is 64MB and 128MB is recommended. The more memory installed the better.

15. A, B. If running Windows 98, Windows Me, Windows NT Workstation 4.0 (with Service Pack 5 installed), or Windows 2000 Professional, it can be upgraded directly to Windows XP. However, systems running Windows 95 or Windows NT Workstation 3.51 operating systems cannot upgrade directly to XP. Instead, they must have intermediate upgrades to bring them up to a Windows version that does support direct upgrading to Windows XP.

16. D. The minimum hardware requirements for installing Windows 2000 Professional on a PC-compatible system are a microprocessor running at 133MHz Pentium (P5 equivalent or better), RAM is minimum 64MB (4GB maximum), and HDD space is 650MB or more free on a 2GB drive.

Challenge Solutions

1. The best solution is to purchase a modem and LAN card that are listed on the Marketplace Tested Product page. This is your best guarantee of compatibility. The second best option is to determine the device manufacturer, attempt to locate the manufacturer's website, and download

Windows 2000–compatible drivers for the devices. Because the devices are not in the page, there is a very good chance that you will not be able to use them.

2. The best way for this company to test Windows 2000 Professional in its system is to upgrade the Windows NT 4.0 workstation. This is the most effective and easiest upgrade path to Windows 2000. The next best option would be upgrading the Windows NT 3.51 computer to Windows 2000 Professional. The other upgrade paths are more involved and may require more effort to ensure compatibility to successfully install the new operating system.

3. You will need to manually start the Windows 2000 Setup routine. To accomplish this, you must boot the system to the existing operating system with the Windows 2000 Professional distribution CD in the CD-ROM drive. Then start the Windows 2000 Setup Wizard from the command prompt (the Run dialog box in Windows). At the command prompt, enter the location of the Windows 2000 Winnt32.exe start file on the distribution CD (D:\i386\Winnt32.exe) and follow the instructions the Setup Wizard places on the screen.

4. Begin by checking for the MIDI devices and cards on the Windows 2000 Marketplace Tested Products page. This can be accomplished on the Windows 2000 distribution CD or at the Microsoft website. If the devices are not listed there, there is a good chance the devices will not operate or will not operate well with Windows 2000. Your only remaining recourse is to contact the device manufacturers for Windows 2000–compatible drivers. Begin by checking the manufacturer's websites for updated drivers that can be downloaded. Unless there is some other compelling reason to upgrade the operating system, the best choice is to stick with a system that is working and producing money.

CHAPTER FIFTEEN

Optimizing Operating Systems

Terms you'll need to understand:

✓ Services

✓ SERVICES.MSC

✓ MSCONFIG

✓ Disk Cleanup

✓ Patches

✓ Updates

✓ Bottlenecks

✓ System Monitor

✓ Task Manager

✓ Cleanmgr

✓ Disk Defragmenter

Techniques you'll need to master:

Essentials 3.2—Install, configure, optimize, and upgrade operating systems—references to upgrading from Windows 95 and NT may be made.

✓ Identify procedures and utilities used to optimize operating systems—for example, virtual memory, hard drives, temporary files, service, startup, and applications.

Tech Support Technician 2.2/IT Technician 3.2—Install, configure, optimize, and upgrade operating systems—references to upgrading from Windows 95 and NT may be made.

✓ Identify procedures and utilities used to optimize operating systems, for example:

    ✓ Virtual memory

✓ Hard drives (for example, disk defragmentation)

✓ Temporary files

✓ Services

✓ Startup

✓ Application

Essentials 3.4/Tech Support Tech2.4/IT Tech 3.4—Perform preventive maintenance on operating systems.

▶ Describe common utilities for performing preventive maintenance on operating systems—for example, software and Windows updates (service packs), scheduled backups/restore, restore points.

Introduction

This chapter covers the Optimizing Windows Operating Systems areas of the CompTIA A+ Certification—Essentials examination under Objective 3.2. It also covers the Basic Preventive Maintenance of Operating Systems areas that are generally testable under Objective 3.4 of the CompTIA A+ Certification— Essentials examination.

Windows operating systems have evolved to the point where they adapt well to most system settings and changes. Most of these adaptations are automatic in nature. However, some areas of the Windows system can be optimized to provide improved and extended performance. The PC technician must be aware of these areas and be able to implement them effectively for different computing environments.

> **NOTE**
>
> The Remote Support Technician Objective 2.2 and IT Tech Objective 3.2 use a different format to express the same subobjective described in the Essentials Objective 3.2 dealing with "Identifying procedures and utilities used to optimize operating systems."
>
> Similarly, the wording for Essentials Objective 3.4 and Remote Support Technician/IT Technician Objectives 2.4/3.4 is identical concerning "Perform preventive maintenance on operating systems."
>
> The topics specified in these different exam/objective areas are so closely stated that it makes sense that they are presented as the same discussion. You will need to study the material in this chapter for any of the four exams you intend to challenge.

Optimizing Windows 2000/XP Performance

The following activities should be performed periodically to tune up the performance of Windows-based PC systems:

- ▶ Optimize virtual memory management
- ▶ Perform disk defragmentation
- ▶ Establish and optimize various memory caches
- ▶ Perform effective temporary file management
- ▶ Manage system services

▶ Optimize the startup process

▶ Manage applications

Optimizing Virtual Memory

It is possible to optimize the system's performance by distributing its swap file (PAGEFILE.SYS) space among multiple drives. It can also be helpful to relocate the swap file away from slower or heavily used drives. The swap file should not be placed on mirrored or striped volumes. Also, don't create multiple swap files in logical disks that exist on the same physical drive.

> **EXAM ALERT**
>
> Remember that moving the Windows 2000/XP swap file to a faster or less-used drive partition will improve the performance of the system.

To take advantage of high RAM capacity, Windows automatically tunes itself to take advantage of any available RAM. The VMM dynamically balances RAM between paged memory and the virtual memory disk cache. However, you can manually optimize the system's memory usage so that it uses more or less memory for programs. If you devote more memory to programs, the programs will work faster.

In Windows 2000, the virtual memory management functions are located under Control Panel's System icon. Click its Advanced tab and then the Performance Options button to view the dialog window depicted in Figure 15.1.

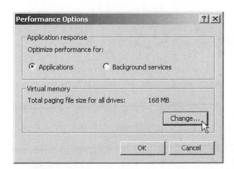

FIGURE 15.1 The system Performance Options window.

The path to the virtual memory management functions in Windows XP is a little different. To access the virtual memory settings in Windows XP, you must navigate to the Settings button in the Performance area of Control Panel's System properties. Clicking this button will produce the Performance Options dialog page. To manually configure the virtual memory settings, access the Advanced tab and click the Change button in the Virtual Memory area.

Clicking the Change button in the dialog window of either operating system will produce the Virtual Memory dialog window similar to the one shown in Figure 15.2. Through this dialog window, you can establish and configure an individual swap file for each drive in the system. By highlighting a drive, you can check its virtual memory capabilities and settings. Entering new values in the dialog windows and clicking the Set button will change the values for the highlighted drive.

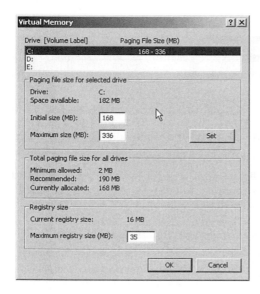

FIGURE 15.2 The Virtual Memory dialog window.

Optimizing the Disk Drive System

The performance of any operating system will deteriorate over time. Most of this deterioration is because of unnecessary file clutter and segmentation on the hard disk drive.

▶ Check for and remove lost file chains and clusters using the CHKDSK and CHKDSK /f commands. Cross-linked files can accumulate and cause the system to slow down. Use the CHKDSK utility to find and remove or repair cross-linked files that may be using up disk space.

▶ Use the DEFRAG utility to realign files on the drive that may have become fragmented after being moved back and forth between the drive and the system. DEFRAG is available through the Administrative Tools/Computer Management console and is used to reposition related files and sectors on a disk drive so that they are located in the most advantageous pattern for being found and read by the system. Performing a defrag operation can improve the disk drive's access and delivery times dramatically.

▶ Use the Windows Disk Cleanup utility to identify optional applications and certain types of temporary files that are not required for operation of the system. The temporary files that you can normally afford to remove from the system to gain needed disk space include Windows, Internet, and multimedia temp files.

Defragmenting Disk Drives

In the normal use of the hard disk drive, files become fragmented on the drive. This file fragmentation creates conditions that cause the drive to operate more slowly. *Fragmentation* occurs when files are stored in noncontinuous locations on the drive. This happens when files are stored, retrieved, modified, and rewritten because of differences in the sizes of the before and after files.

Because the fragmented files do not permit efficient reading by the drive, it takes longer to complete multisector read operations. The *defragmentation* process optimizes the operation of the disk drive by reorganizing its data into logically contiguous blocks. When data is arranged in this manner, the system does not need to reposition the drive's read/write heads as many times to read a given piece of data.

Some portions of files may become lost on the drive when a program is unexpectedly interrupted (such as when software crashes, for example, or during a power failure). These lost allocation units (chains) will also cause the drive to operate slowly. Therefore, it is customary to use the command-line CHKDSK command to find these chains and remove them before performing a defrag operation.

It may also be necessary to remove some data from the drive to defragment it. If the system is producing Out of Disk Space error messages, the defragmentation utility will not have enough room on the drive to realign clusters. When this happens, some of the contents of the drive will need to be transferred to a backup media (or discarded) to free up some disk space so that the realignment process can occur.

Using Disk Cleanup

Another disk management tool available in Windows operating systems is the Disk Cleanup utility. This utility can be used to remove certain types of disposable files and optional components from the system to clear additional disk space. The Disk Cleanup Wizard can clear space on the hard disk by removing temporary Internet files, removing any downloaded program files (such as ActiveX controls and Java applets downloaded from the Internet), emptying the Recycle Bin, and removing Windows temp files, as well as removing little-used Windows components and installed programs no longer in use.

> **NOTE**
>
> You should always carefully consider which files you are removing with the Disk Cleanup utility. You should not remove files when you do not know what they do, or when you do not know what the consequences of removing them will be.

The Disk Cleanup utility is accessed through the System Tools entry on the Start/Programs/Accessories path. It can also be initiated by typing `cleanmgr` in the Start, Run dialog box. When it is activated, the Disk Cleanup utility will calculate the amount of space that can be regained by emptying the Recycle Bin. It also examines the space saved by removing downloaded files, temporary files, and temporary Internet files. The View Files button can be used to view the individual files involved before discarding them.

The More Options tab enables the user to select optional components that were installed while there was plenty of space on the disk. Now that space has become a problem on the disk, the user has the option to remove them. They can always be restored if more space is cleared (or if a larger drive is installed) later.

> **EXAM ALERT**
>
> Know that you can improve the performance of the system by using the Disk Cleanup utility to free up additional hard disk drive space.

Managing Temporary Files

Temporary (TMP) files and backup (BAK) files are special types of files that the operating system creates when it needs to store an original copy of the file along with an updated copy. Over time, these types of files can accumulate and take up space on the hard drive. You should periodically remove unwanted or unused

.TMP and .BAK files from the system and maintain the operating system's various caches. There are two major cache locations for temporary files in the Windows environment: the Windows Temporary folder and the Temporary Internet Files folder.

Managing the Windows Temporary Folder

Windows operating systems are designed to collect information about their users so that they can serve them quicker and better. When users download information from the Internet or open archive files, the operating system places copies of these items in the system's Temporary folder. These copies may remain in the folder and create a security risk—particularly if they contain passwords, account information, or personal information. Other people who gain access to the PC—either correctly or by malicious activities—can access this information. In addition, the copies take up as much space as their originals. You can clear the contents of the folder through the Disk Cleanup utility, or you can manually delete the files in the folder at *user*\Local Settings\Temp—where user is the name of the person currently logged into the machine.

Managing the Temporary Internet Files Folder

Internet Explorer caches Internet files in the Temporary Internet Files folder for quick viewing. Each time you load a web page, Internet Explorer saves a copy of it in the Temporary Internet Files folder so that it will load faster the next time you try to access it. This technique allows Internet Explorer browser to download only content that has changed since the web page was last viewed, instead of downloading the entire page every time it is displayed. This feature improves the speed of web browsing and allows for offline browsing of the files. However, it also takes up hard disk drive space. It also compromises user security because these files can be viewed by anyone who gains access to the system.

NOTE

Temporary Internet files pose a security risk because their presence enables others to see what pages the user has been viewing since the last time the Temporary Internet files cache was cleared.

In Windows 2000 and XP, the Temporary Internet Files are stored in \\Documents and Settings*<username>*\Local Settings\Temporary Internet Files by default. However, prior to Windows XP SP2, if the system had only one user account, the *<username>* portion of the path was replaced with Administrator. With a clean install of Windows XP SP2, the single account will contain a username instead of Administrator.

The amount of disk space used to store temporary files can escalate rapidly with heavy web users. Therefore, you should periodically clear the Temporary Internet Files cache to improve system performance. There are two paths you can use to clear Temporary Internet files: through Internet Explorer and through the Control Panel.

To delete temporary Internet files through Internet Explorer, follow these steps:

1. In Internet Explorer, click the Tools menu and select the Internet Options entry from the drop-down menu to access the Internet Options window.

2. Access the General tab and click the Delete Files button in the Temporary Internet Files section to access the Delete Files dialog box.

3. Click the Delete All Offline Content check box to delete all the content stored offline. Then click the OK button to delete the files.

To delete temporary Internet files through Control Panel, access the Internet Options applet, select the General tab, and click the Delete Files button in the Temporary Internet Files section. In the Delete Files dialog box, click to select the Delete All Offline Content check box, and then click the OK button.

Deleting offline content may take several minutes if it has been some time since the cache was last cleared. Users should be aware that a special file named Index.dat still retains a history of the pages that have been accessed through the browser. This can constitute a security threat in some environments. In addition, cookie files can still remain in the Temporary Internet Files folder after the deletion process. These files are aliases for real cookie files stored in the Cookies folder. To delete these files and the cookie files, click the Delete Cookies button in the Temporary Internet Files section.

Cookies are small message files sent to browsers by web servers to identify the browser on subsequent visits. Cookies enable web service providers to produce custom web pages for users based on their browsing habits. Although cookies provide useful services to many web users, they can also provide a security threat in that information provided by users is almost always stored as a cookie. This information includes personal information, as well as credit card and other financial information disclosed on the Web. Web browsers provide options for rejecting cookies. In Internet Explorer, this option is located in the Tools menu under the Privacy tab of the Internet Options entry.

Optimizing System Services

Unused system services should be stopped or disabled to optimize system responsiveness and performance. In Windows XP, you can launch the Services control applet either through the Control Panel/Administrative Tools/Services path or by running the SERVICES.MSC command-line utility. This utility will produce a listing of all the user-controllable services running in the system. From this list you can stop or switch services to manual startup configuration—you should not disable any service unless you are absolutely sure that you will not need it and that no other vital service needs it.

> **EXAM ALERT**
>
> Remember to turn off unused services to increase system performance and responsiveness.

You can double-click any service to open its Properties page, as illustrated in Figure 15.3. The Properties page contains a General tab, a Log On tab, a Recovery tab, and a Dependencies tab. On the General tab, you can start, stop, pause, or resume a service as part of the optimization or troubleshooting process. On the Recovery tab, you can specify what action to take if the service fails. You can check the Dependencies tab to see what other services this service relies on for proper operation to make sure that you don't turn off services that it needs.

FIGURE 15.3 Service properties.

Modifying the Startup Process

The Windows startup process can be optimized by tuning the BIOS, modifying the timeout setting in the BOOT.INI file, and limiting the number of applications and programs that launch automatically when Windows starts up.

Applications designated to run at startup are located in the Startup folders for both user profiles (UserProfile\Start Menu\Programs\Startup) and for the All Users profile (All Users\Start Menu\Programs\Startup) under C:\Documents and Settings. You should delete any program shortcuts that are no longer needed.

You can also use the MSCONFIG.EXE command-line utility to fine-tune the applications that run at startup.

> **NOTE**
>
> In many cases, you may not be able to recognize the applications running in the startup process, and removing programs that the system needs to work may render the system unusable. There is an excellent website at http://www.sysinfo.org/startuplist.php that you can use to find information about the function and importance of startup applications you may encounter.

Altering BOOT.INI

The BOOT.INI file in Windows 2000/XP systems is a special, hidden read-only boot text file that is used to generate the OS Choices Boot Options menu during the 2000/XP startup process. The system reads the settings in the BOOT.INI file during the bootup process and places the menu on the screen to permit the user to select an operating system to boot to.

The menu can support starting different Windows 2000/XP versions and can provide for starting one non-Windows 2000/XP operating system as well. There is also an option on the menu that enables users to enter an Advanced Boot Options menu by pressing the F8 function key. If no selection is made within a specified timeframe, the bootup process continues on in default mode.

The BOOT.INI file contains two sections of text that can be read and modified. The default values of the BOOT.INI file are generated automatically by the system when the Windows 2000/XP operating system is installed. The following is an example of a BOOT.INI file where Windows 2000 Professional has been installed on the first partition and Windows XP Professional has been installed on the second partition. The OS Choices Boot Options menu is configured to display for 30 seconds during the startup process. The default setting indicates that the operating system defined for the first partition will be used to boot the system.

```
[boot loader]
timeout=30
default=multi(0)disk(0)rdisk(0)partition(1)\WINNT
[operating systems]
multi(0)disk(0)rdisk(0)partition(1)\WINNT="Windows 2000 Professional"
/fastdetect
multi(0)disk(1)rdisk(0)partition(2)\WINNT="Windows XP Professional"
/fastdetect
```

NOTE

You should always make a copy of the existing BOOT.INI file before making any edits to its structure.

In Windows 2000, you can access the BOOT.INI file using a text editor. Before doing so, you must change its attributes so that it becomes visible and so that you can open it. This can be done through My Computer, Windows Explorer or by using the `Attrib` command.

In Windows XP Professional, you can modify the BOOT.INI file through the Startup and Recovery dialog page. From this page, you can select the default operating system, change the OS Choices Boot Options menu timeout value, or manually edit the file. You can also use the BOOTCFG command-line utility to modify the BOOT.INI file.

NOTE

Be aware that the BOOTCFG command-line utility is available only in Windows XP Professional—not Windows XP Home or MCE versions.

Optimizing the Startup Menu

The Windows Start menu includes a folder named Startup that can be used to start programs each time Windows starts up. To automatically start the program, you simply drag and drop its shortcut icon into the Startup folder. Some applications automatically install their own shortcuts in the Startup folder when they are installed in the system. These programs can automatically run in the background using up system resources and slowing the operation of the system—even though the user is not aware of or using the application.

Although it is convenient to have some applications in the Startup folder, it is not a good practice to have many applications there. Therefore, you should periodically clean out the Startup folder. Because these items are shortcuts and not actual programs, deleting them will not affect the user's ability to access them, only the speed with which the user can bring them up.

Before deleting applications from the Startup folder, make sure that you know what they are supposed to do. Some protective programs such as antivirus and spyware programs should run each time the system is started up. Other fast start application shortcuts are not necessary and should be removed from the folder.

Using MSCONFIG to Optimize Startup

Start MSCONFIG from the command prompt and move to the Startup tab. Remove the checks from any applications that you do not want to run at startup. This action should be performed with some forethought—generally you do not want to disable anything in the \Windows folder. Using the MSCONFIG utility allows you to disable applications, try the system, and then restore them if you need to—as opposed to deleting them from the Startup folder.

As mentioned earlier in this section, removing necessary files from the startup process can render the system unusable. It is a good policy to remove only programs for which you know what they do and for which you know what the outcome of removing them will be. There are websites on the Internet that provide lists of startup-related applications that can help you make decisions as to whether you can safely remove them or not.

Monitoring System Performance

There are two Windows utilities that can be useful in monitoring the system's performance. These utilities are the Task Manager and the System Monitor. The three areas of the system that are most commonly monitored are Memory, Processor, and Disk Usage.

The amount of memory in the system has the most impact on its overall performance. Insufficient memory negatively impacts the operation of applications and services and can affect the performance of other hardware resources in the system. Next to memory usage, processor activity is the next most important component to monitor. If the processor becomes overloaded, requests for processor time begin to back up and the overall system performance is degraded. Finally, the performance of the hard disk system can also greatly affect the overall performance of the system.

Monitoring Performance with Task Manager

The Task Manager Performance tab, displayed in Figure 15.4, provides a quick summary of CPU and memory usage. Its history charts enable you to view recent trends in both statistics. The Totals, Physical Memory, Commit Charge, and Kernel Memory sections display summary processor and memory information.

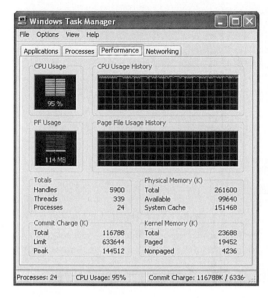

FIGURE 15.4 The Task Manager Performance tab.

Although the Performance tab can provide a quick view of the system's overall processor and memory usage, the Processes tab of Task Manager or the System Monitor utility can be used to obtain a better view of the system changes over time.

The Task Manager's Processes tab, depicted in Figure 15.5, displays the processor activity and memory usage of individual system processes and application programs. If you notice that a process or application appears to be taking up a disproportionate amount of processor time, you should identify the process or application's role and determine how to handle it—remove it or treat it as normal.

NOTE

It is not uncommon for the System Idle Process to show a high percentage of CPU usage. This indicates that the processor is lightly loaded and does not represent a problem—to the contrary. A very low Processor Idle Time reading indicates that the processor may be overloaded. If the report continually remains low, corrective action should be taken.

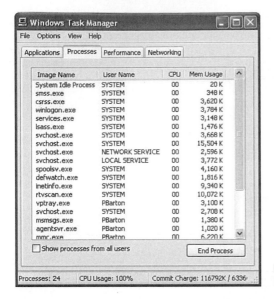

FIGURE 15.5   The Task Manager Processes tab.

Monitoring Application Performance with System Monitor

Most applications do not create significant performance problems as long as the system has sufficient processing power, hard disk space, and memory. If an application is running abnormally slow, and there are no virus problems, you probably have a system configuration problem, but you may also need to analyze application performance with the System Monitor. You may find that the system has a bottleneck that is the result of any particular application, or a group of applications, that is running on the system.

The System Monitor utility is designed to collect performance information. It provides more detailed information than the Task Manager display can generate. In addition, it enables you to monitor other systems remotely, to log information for future analysis, and to configure alerts to notify you of potential error conditions.

The System Monitor classifies information in three categories—as objects, instances, and counters:

▶ Objects—Objects are major hardware or software components of the system or the operating system. Typical objects include microprocessors, memory allocations, and OS services.

▶ Instances—Each occurrence of an object is considered an instance. For example, dual-processor systems would show two instances of processors.

▶ Counters—A counter is a particular aspect of an object that can be measured.

Using the System Monitor to track and analyze system performance involves creating and monitoring counters for different system objects. In Windows 2000 and XP, there are literally hundreds of counters to choose from. You can select counters to use through the Performance option under Control Panel's Administrative Tools icon. Figure 15.6 illustrates adding counters to the System Monitor display. Which objects you choose to monitor depends on whether you are trying to collect general baseline information, troubleshoot a performance problem, diagnose an issue with an application, and so forth.

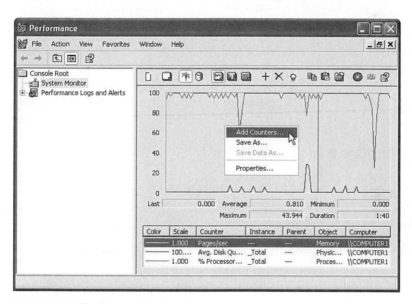

FIGURE 15.6 The System Monitor.

The Process object in System Monitor, depicted in Figure 15.7, is used to monitor selected performance counters on a per-application basis. Performance counters can be established for quantities such as % Processor Time, IO Data Bytes/Sec, Page Faults/Sec, Page File Bytes, and Thread Count. These counters can help to identify the resource usage of each application.

FIGURE 15.7 Monitoring application performance with System Monitor.

The System Monitor utility has no repair or problem-solving capabilities. However, carefully analyzing process counters will give you a better idea of how resources are being used. If the system doesn't have enough memory, processor, or hard disk resources, you will have to address these issues to correct the problem (that is, either upgrade the device causing the bottleneck or move applications to another location).

Using Performance Logs and Alerts

You can configure the Performance Logs and Alerts utility to log System Monitor counter information in a file and to generate alerts based on event levels that you configure. The Performance logs can be viewed and analyzed through System Monitor. This utility contains three components:

▶ Counter logs—These logs compile activity information for selected System Monitor counters taken at regular intervals.

▶ Trace logs—These logs monitor and record activity for selected System Monitor counters when a configured event occurs.

▶ Alerts—These logs monitor and record activity and notify administrators when a particular counter exceeds a configured threshold.

To enable performance logging, follow these steps:

1. Access Performance from the Control Panel's Administrative Tools icon.

2. Expand the Performance Logs and Alerts node, right-click the Counter Logs option, and select the New Log Settings option.

3. In the New Log Settings dialog window, enter a name for the log and click the OK button.

4. On the General tab, depicted in Figure 15.8, add the counters that you want to log and modify the sampling interval if necessary.

FIGURE 15.8 Configuring General log properties.

5. You can modify the name and location of the log file as well as the type of file on the Log Files tab, if necessary.

6. Configure the start and stop times for logging on the Schedule tab.

7. Click the OK button to save the log configuration and exit.

To view a performance log, follow these steps:

1. Open the Performance utility and select System Monitor.

2. Right-click the data display and select the Properties option from the menu.

3. On the Source tab, select the Log Files option and enter the name of the log file to be viewed, as illustrated in Figure 15.9, and click the OK button to continue.

4. Right-click the data display and select the Add Counters option.

5. Add the counters to be viewed and click the OK button. The available counters will be limited to those that are present in the log.

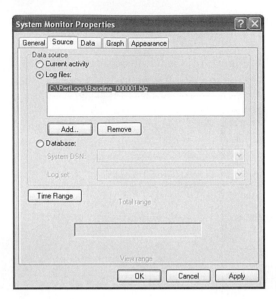

FIGURE 15.9 Configuring the data source.

Correcting Memory Performance Issues

One good indicator of low system memory is a high number of virtual memory accesses. This indicates that there is not enough memory and the system is having to transfer data back and forth between RAM and the disk drive. This condition also negatively affects the performance of the drive system. Insufficient system RAM also puts an unnecessary load on the microprocessor and can severely degrade its performance.

The most straightforward way to handle memory problems is to add more memory. However, if the system's RAM capacity is maxed out, or adding RAM is not cost effective, you can take several steps to improve memory-related performance:

- ▶ Remove unused or unnecessary operating system components.

- ▶ Remove unused or unnecessary network services.

- ▶ Minimize the number of applications that are opened simultaneously.

- ▶ Minimize the number of programs in the Startup group.

- ▶ Increase the initial size of the paging file to equal its maximum size setting.

- ▶ Increase the paging file size if usage approaches 100%.

- ▶ Ensure that there is sufficient hard disk space to support the growth of the paging file.

▶ Move the paging file to a volume other than the system and boot volumes.

▶ Offload resources to another system to reduce memory usage.

Correcting Processor Performance Issues

You can monitor several key counters to detect processor bottlenecks. These counters include measurements of the percentage of processor time counter, the interrupts per second counter, and the queue length. If these counters indicate that a processor usage problem exists, you can take several steps to correct the problem:

▶ Verify that the system has enough memory.

▶ If the rate of system interrupts is high, determine which device is causing the issue.

▶ Upgrade to a faster processor or add another processor if an additional socket is available. In some cases, you may be able to replace an existing single core processor with a dual core upgrade.

▶ Offload processes that are overloading the system to another computer.

To some degree, working with these counters requires that you be aware of what types of applications the system is running. For example, if single-threaded applications are using large amounts of processing time, upgrading to a faster processor will increase performance more than adding another processor because a single-threaded application can make use of only one processor at a time. On the other hand, if multithreaded applications are using a large amount of processing time, installing an additional processor will increase performance more than a faster processor. Multithreaded applications can take advantage of multiple processors simultaneously.

Correcting Disk System Performance Issues

You can detect disk bottlenecks by monitoring and evaluating physical and logical disk counters. Physical disk counters provide information about activity for the entire disk. Logical disk counters monitor performance of the individual volumes on the disks. If these counters indicate that a disk issue exists, you can take several steps to correct them:

▶ If the page file usage is high, add more RAM.

▶ Analyze and defragment the drive.

- ▶ Add an additional drive to the system and create a spanned volume to increase contiguous disk space.

- ▶ Add disk compression to increase space if processor performance is not an issue.

- ▶ Install faster drives.

- ▶ Configure stripe sets to increase performance.

- ▶ If one drive is used significantly more than others, distribute the workload evenly across all the disks in the system.

- ▶ Install additional HDD controllers if you have multiple disks attached to a single controller.

Challenge #1

You have been called to a customer's advertising agency to work on a PC. The system has two PATA hard drives in a system and one SATA drive. The system is used to create and manipulate large multimedia files. It keeps getting slower and slower. The customer would like to know why the machine is getting slower and how to get the performance out of the machine that it provided previously. When you examine the performance logs and alerts, you see that the system has a high number of virtual memory accesses. Having this information, what steps can you take to improve the system's performance?

Software Maintenance

Make sure to keep the system software updated with the latest service packs and patches. Microsoft offers an automated online update service that scans your system, downloads updates and security patches, and then installs them without your intervention. This same service can be run manually at any time. Simply access the Microsoft.com website and select the Microsoft Updates option. Many software application providers offer similar web-based update services for their products.

You should either set up protective utilities to automatically run periodically or set a schedule to run these utilities yourself. These utilities include antivirus programs and backup operations. In addition, antivirus programs require periodic updating to stay current with new viruses and worms releases. Most commercial antivirus solutions provide automatic web-based update functions to keep their products up to date. Finally, take time to educate the user about preventing malicious software attacks because a well-informed user is the most effective antivirus solution available.

In a Windows XP environment, you should periodically establish Restore Points while the system is running correctly. You should also make it a practice to set a new Restore Point just before you make a change to the system, and just after you have verified that the update is performing correctly.

Windows Update Services

The Windows Update service is offered through the Internet and enables the system to periodically check the Microsoft Updates site for enhancements. When the system connects with the site, the service compares the current status of the local Windows installation to the latest information on the site. It then provides a list of available updates for the computer. Users can select which updates are applicable to their use. Users can also access the Windows Update service at any time through the Start menu or through the Internet Explorer Tools menu.

The Windows Update service is also used to obtain service packs. These additions are important because they address major issues that have been detected in the operating system version since it was launched (or since the last service pack was issued). For larger network environments, administrators typically work through the Microsoft subscription service to automatically receive service packs when they are released.

EXAM ALERT

Be aware that Microsoft offers an online Windows Update service to deliver patches, Service Packs, and security updates to its users.

Automatic Updates

You can configure Windows to automatically check the Windows Update service. Enabling the Automatic Updates feature will cause Windows to routinely check for updates. These updates include security updates, critical updates, and Service Packs.

To turn on Automatic Updates in Windows XP, access the System icon in the Control Panel and click the Automatic Updates tab. In Windows 2000, you can double-click the Automatic Updates icon in Control Panel. In either operating system, Automatic Updates can be configured to download and install updates on a specified schedule or to notify the user when high-priority updates become available. You can click the Automatic (Recommended) option button and then enter day and time settings for Windows to install the updates under the Automatically Download Recommended Updates for My Computer and Install Them option.

NOTE

You must be logged on as an administrator or a member of the Administrators group to complete this procedure.

EXAM ALERT

Know how to obtain automatic updates for a Windows PC.

Exam Prep Questions

1. Which utilities can be used to view real-time system performance in Windows 2000/XP? (Select all that apply.)

   ○ **A.** System Information

   ○ **B.** System Monitor

   ○ **C.** Computer Management

   ○ **D.** Task Manager

2. How can you optimize a Windows system to improve drive access times and virtual memory performance?

   ○ **A.** Run the CHKDISK utility.

   ○ **B.** Run the Clean Up utility to improve free disk space.

   ○ **C.** Defrag the drive.

   ○ **D.** Convert the file system to FAT16.

3. A computer system installed several months ago is showing signs of increasingly slow operation. What steps can be preformed to improve system performance? (Select all that apply.)

   ○ **A.** Delete temporary files.

   ○ **B.** Defrag the system disk.

   ○ **C.** Run the FDISK utility revitalize the operating system.

   ○ **D.** Run the CHKDSK utility to clear unused files from the system.

4. Where in Windows 2000 and Windows XP can you go to optimize virtual memory management?

   ○ **A.** Help and Support Center

   ○ **B.** Programs/Accessories/System Tools

   ○ **C.** System Tools/Control Panel/Advanced tab

   ○ **D.** Control Panel/System

5. How do you configure the Automatic Updates feature for Windows 2000?

   ○ **A.** Use the Add Components utility to add the Automatic Updates feature to the system.

   ○ **B.** Double-click Automatic Updates in Control Panel and then click Automatic.

   ○ **C.** Use the Add/Remove Programs utility to install the Windows Automatic Updates utility.

   ○ **D.** Access the Microsoft Windows Update web page and click the Automatic Updates option.

6. What is the best way to update/patch a Windows XP Professional computer system?

   ○ **A.** Use the online Windows Update service.

   ○ **B.** Use a computer that is completely updated and burn all the patches onto an update CD.

   ○ **C.** Download Windows XP SP2 from Microsoft because all other XP patches are unnecessary.

   ○ **D.** Use the Task Scheduler utility to look for patches and updates on a regular schedule.

Answers and Explanations

1. B, D. System Monitor can be used to track the performance of key system resources for both evaluation and troubleshooting purposes. If system performance is suspect but there is no clear indication of what might be slowing it down, System Monitor can be used to determine which resource is operating at capacity and thereby limiting the performance of the system. Task Manager also has the facilities to provide real-time display of different system resources.

2. C. You should run the Defrag utility to optimize the storage patterns on the drive and thus improve read/write times and virtual memory performance.

3. A, B. The Windows 2000/XP Windows Cleanup utility can be used to identify certain types of temporary files that are not required for operation of the system. The temporary files that you can normally afford to remove from the system to gain needed disk space include Windows, Internet, and multimedia temp files. Use the DEFRAG utility to realign files on the drive that may have become fragmented after being moved back and forth between the drive and the system.

4. D. You can increase the performance of Windows 2000/XP by manipulating the size and placement of the virtual memory swap file. Page file
manipulation in Windows 2000/XP can be done in Control Panel's
System icon.

5. B. To turn on Automatic Updates in Windows XP, access the System
icon in Control Panel and click the Automatic Updates tab. In Windows
2000, you can double-click the Automatic Updates icon in the Control
Panel. In either operating system, Automatic Updates can be configured
to download and install updates on a specified schedule or to notify the
user when high-priority updates become available. You can click the
Automatic (Recommended) option button and then enter day and time
settings for Windows to install the updates under the Automatically
Download Recommended Updates for My Computer and Install Them
option.

6. A. The Windows Update service is offered through the Internet and
enables the system to periodically check the Microsoft Updates site for
enhancements. When the system connects with the site, the service compares the current status of the local Windows installation to the latest
information on the site. It then provides a list of available updates for the
computer. Users can select which updates are applicable to their use.
Users can also access the Windows Update service at any time through
the Start menu or through the Internet Explorer Tools menu.

Challenge Solutions

1. You could tell the customer that the large files it uses are causing the
system to transfer files back and forth between RAM and the virtual
memory page file. This generates additional disk accesses, which slows
the system down. To correct this, you can add more RAM to the system.
However, a less costly option is to increase the initial size of the paging
file to equal its maximum size setting, increase the paging file size if
usage approaches 100%, ensure that there is sufficient hard disk space to
support the growth of the paging file, and move the paging file to a volume other than the system and boot volumes.

16

CHAPTER SIXTEEN

Operating System Utilities

Terms you'll need to understand:

- ✓ DEFRAG
- ✓ NTBACKUP
- ✓ CHKDSK
- ✓ Format
- ✓ Device Manager
- ✓ Task Manager

- ✓ MSCONFIG.EXE
- ✓ Restore points
- ✓ Event Viewer
- ✓ REGEDIT.EXE
- ✓ REGEDT32.EXE

Techniques to master:

Essentials 3.3—Identify tools, diagnostic procedures, and troubleshooting techniques for operating systems.

- ✓ Identify the names, locations, purposes, and characteristics of operating system utilities; for example:
    - ✓ Disk management tools (DEFRAG, NTBACKUP, CHKDSK, Format)
    - ✓ System management tools (Device and Task Manager, MSCONFIG.EXE)
    - ✓ File management tools (Windows Explorer, ATTRIB.EXE)

Technical Support 2.1/ IT Technician 3.1—Locate and use operating system utilities and available switches; for example:

- ✓ Disk management tools (DEFRAG, NTBACKUP, CHKDSK, Format)

- ✓ System management tools
    - ✓ Device and Task Manager
    - ✓ MSCONFIG.EXE
    - ✓ REGEDIT.EXE
    - ✓ REGEDT32.EXE
    - ✓ CMD
    - ✓ Event Viewer
    - ✓ System Restore
    - ✓ Remote Desktop
- ✓ File management tools (Windows Explorer, ATTRIB.EXE)

Essentials 3.4/Tech Support Tech2.4/ IT Tech 3.4—Perform preventative maintenance on operating systems.

- ✓ Describe common utilities for performing preventative maintenance on operating systems; for example, software and Windows updates (service packs), scheduled backups/restore, and restore points.

Windows Disk Management Tools

This chapter covers a portion of the diagnostic procedures and troubleshooting techniques for operating systems areas of the CompTIA A+ Certification—Essentials examination under Objective 3.3. It also covers the Basic Preventive Maintenance of Operating Systems areas that are generally testable under Objective 3.4 of the CompTIA A+ Certification—Essentials examination.

Successful troubleshooting of operating systems requires tools. The Windows operating system includes a variety of different tools designed to help users and administrators optimize and repair problems related to the operating system, its peripherals, and applications. The major Windows diagnostic and management tools can be divided into three general categories:

▸ Disk management tools

▸ System management tools

▸ File management tools

> **NOTE**
>
> A major portion of Tech Support Technician Objective 2.1 and IT Technician Objective 3.1 are identical to the material in Essentials Objective 3.3. Essentials 3.3—Identify the names, locations, purposes, and characteristics of operating system utilities and Tech Support/IT Tech 2.1/3.1—Locate and use operating system utilities and available switches cover the same material. However, the advanced objectives include additional utilities not mentioned in Essential (REGEDIT.EXE, REGEDT32.EXE, CMD, Event Viewer, System Restore, and Remote Desktop).
>
> Likewise, the wording for Essentials 3.4 and Tech Support/IT Tech 2.4/3.4 is identical.
>
> The topics specified in these different exam/objective areas are so closely stated that it makes sense that they are presented as the same discussion. You will need to study this material in this chapter for any of the four exams you intend to challenge.

The operation of hard drives can slow down with general use. Files stored on the drive can be erased and moved, causing parts of them to be scattered around the drive. This causes the drive to reposition the read/write heads more often during read and write operations, thereby requiring more time to complete the process.

Four important Windows utilities can be used to optimize and maintain the operation of the hard disk drive: the Disk Cleanup, CHKDSK, defrag, and backup utilities. All these utilities have been available since early MS-DOS versions.

In Windows 2000 and Windows XP, these disk-drive tools are located in the Computer Management console under the Control Panel's Administrative Tools icon. The Storage node in the Computer Management console offers direct access to the Disk Management and Defragmentation utilities. The Backup and Defrag utilities are available through the Start/Programs/Accessories/System Tools menu path. The executable file for the Defrag program is under C:\Windows. The actual Windows 2000/XP NTBackup utility is located in the C:\WINNT\SYSTEM32 folder.

Another way to access the hard disk drive (HDD) tools in Windows 2000/XP is to open My Computer and right-click the icon for the hard disk drive you want to use. Next, select the Properties option from the context-sensitive pop-up menu. Then, click the Tools tab to gain access to the most useful Windows HDD utilities.

TIP

Remember where the main HDD utility programs are located in the Windows 2000/XP environments.

NOTE

Microsoft does not supply a built-in antivirus utility with its operating systems, so a third-party add on must be used.

You should use these HDD utilities periodically to tune up the performance of the system. To do so, perform these steps:

1. Periodically remove unnecessary TMP and BAK files from the system.

2. Check for and remove lost file chains and clusters using the CHKDSK utility.

3. Use the Defrag utility to realign files on the drive that may have become fragmented after being moved back and forth between the drive and the system.

Disk Cleanup

The Disk Cleanup utility enables you to remove temporary files, temporary Internet files, installed Windows components, and unused programs from the system to free up additional hard drive space. This utility scans the system's drives for these types of files and presents a display that it believes you can safely remove form the system. You can select items to be removed from the presented listing. You can also empty the content of the system's Recycle Bin through this utility.

The main reason for using the Disk Cleanup utility is to free up hard disk space because the system is running out of space. Because you may not always know which files in the Windows environment are useful, the Disk Cleanup utility provides a safe method of removing hard drive clutter.

In Windows 2000 and Windows XP, the Disk Cleanup utility is available through the Start/Programs (All Programs)/Accessories/System Tools path. You can also run the CLEANUPMGR version of the utility from the command prompt.

EXAM ALERT

Know what functions the Disk Cleanup utility can perform.

CHKDSK

The CHKDSK (Check Disk) command is a command-line utility that has remained in use with Windows 3.x, 9x, NT, 2000, and XP and is used to recover lost allocation units from the hard drive. Lost allocation units occur when an application terminates unexpectedly and causes the file management system to lose track of where some parts of the file are stored. The total file becomes segmented into undefined pieces that can still be read by the utility but cannot be associated with a particular filename in the file allocation table (FAT) or Master File Table (MFT).

Files can also become cross-linked when the file management system loses track of some portion of the file. In these cases, part of a second file might be written into a sector that actually belonged to another file and they become linked to each other at that spot. Figure 16.1 depicts a typical CHKDSK display. CHKDSK locates lost clusters and, when used with an /F switch, converts them into files that can be viewed with a text editor.

Over a period of time, lost units can pile up and occupy large amounts of disk space. To remove these lost units from the drive, an /F modifier is added to the command so that the lost units will be converted into files that can be investigated and then removed, if necessary. In some cases, the converted file is a usable data file that can be rebuilt for use with an application.

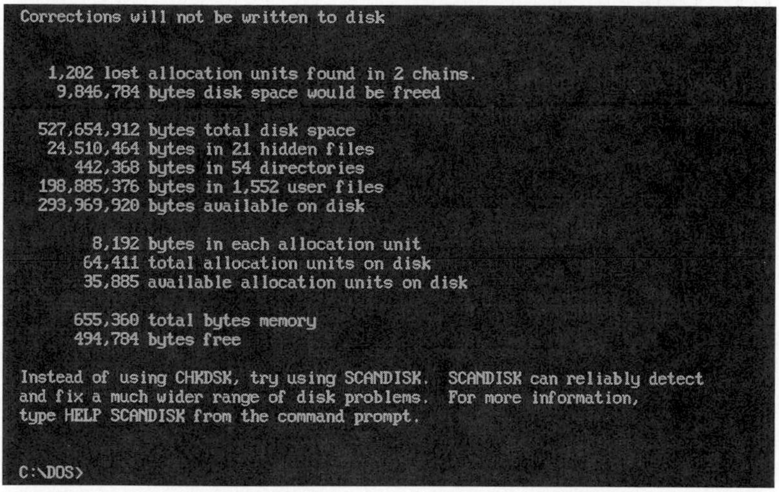

```
Corrections will not be written to disk

   1,202 lost allocation units found in 2 chains.
   9,846,784 bytes disk space would be freed

 527,654,912 bytes total disk space
  24,510,464 bytes in 21 hidden files
     442,368 bytes in 54 directories
 198,885,376 bytes in 1,552 user files
 293,969,920 bytes available on disk

       8,192 bytes in each allocation unit
      64,411 total allocation units on disk
      35,885 available allocation units on disk

     655,360 total bytes memory
     494,784 bytes free

Instead of using CHKDSK, try using SCANDISK.  SCANDISK can reliably detect
and fix a much wider range of disk problems.  For more information,
type HELP SCANDISK from the command prompt.

C:\DOS>
```

FIGURE 16.1   A Check Disk display.

The CHKDSK command can be run from the command prompt at any time. However, in Windows 2000 and Windows XP, the CHKDSK command is available only when working from the command line in the Recovery Console. The Windows 2000/XP version provides the /P switch for performing an exhaustive check of the drive and /R for finding bad sectors and recovering readable information from them, if possible.

A boot version of CHKDSK, called Autochk,exe, is run each time Windows restarts to scan all volumes for the presence of a "dirty bit" indicating that Windows detected a system error on the disk. If the dirty bit is present, autochk performs a CHKDSK /F operation on the disk in an effort to repair the problem. In some cases, this operation may take several hours to perform. To postpone the chkdsk operation to a more convenient time, administrator can use the CHKNTFS command from the command prompt to exclude volumes from the automatic CHKDSK operation.

EXAM ALERT

Be aware of the CHKDSK switches and what they do.

HDD Defragmentation

In the normal use of the hard disk drive, files become fragmented on the drive. This file fragmentation creates conditions that cause the drive to operate more slowly. Fragmentation occurs when files are stored in noncontiguous locations on the drive. This happens when files are stored, retrieved, modified, and rewritten because of differences in the sizes of the before and after files.

Because the fragmented files do not permit efficient reading by the drive, it takes longer to complete multisector read operations. The *defragmentation* process optimizes the operation of the disk drive by reorganizing its data into logically contiguous blocks. When data is arranged in this manner, the system does not need to reposition the drive's read/write heads as many times to read a given piece of data.

Some portions of files may become lost on the drive when a program is unexpectedly interrupted (such as when software crashes, for example, or during a power failure). These lost allocation units (*chains*) will also cause the drive to operate slowly. Therefore, it is customary to use the command-line CHKDSK command to find these chains and remove them before performing a defrag operation.

It may also be necessary to remove some data from the drive to defragment it. The defrag operation requires that at least 15% of the space on the volume being defragmented be free to operate. If the system is producing Out of Disk Space error messages, the defragmentation utility will not have enough room on the drive to realign clusters. When this happens, some of the contents of the drive will need to be transferred to a backup media (or discarded) to free up some disk space for the realignment process to occur.

> **EXAM ALERT**
>
> Be aware of the free space requirements for performing defrag operations.

Defragmentation operations can be conducted from the command line all Windows versions by entering **DEFRAG** at the command prompt. In Windows 2000, the Defragmenter utility is located under the Start/Programs/Accessories/ System Tools path. In Windows XP, the correct path is Start/All Programs/ Accessories/System Tools. In Windows 2000 and Windows XP, the Disk Defragmenter can also be accessed through the Control Panel/Administrative Tools/Computer Management path. To use the Defrag tool from this point, follow these steps:

1. Click the Disk Defragmenter option.

2. Click the desired drive to highlight it.

3. Click the Defragment button to begin the operation.

The DEFRAG main screen should appear, similar to that shown in Figure 16.2.

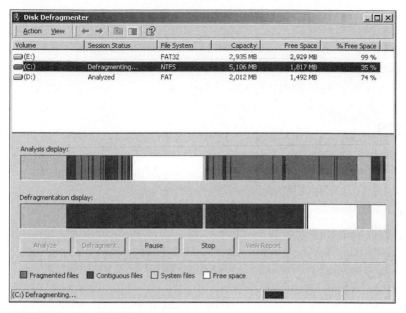

FIGURE 16.2 The DEFRAG main screen.

The Defragmenter contains a disk analysis tool that reports the current status of the volume's key parameters. Figure 16.3 shows a sample analysis report.

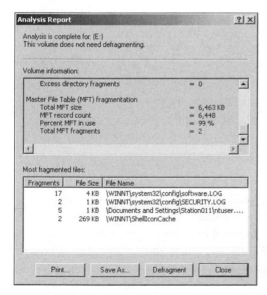

FIGURE 16.3 The Defrag Analysis Report.

Viewing the defragmentation operation is possible through the My Computer window. Right-click the drive icon and select the Properties option. From this point, click the Tools option and select Defrag. However, viewing the operation of the defragmentation process makes the operation longer. It is better to run this utility in a minimized condition.

Backups

Backup utilities enable the user to quickly create extended copies of files, groups of files, or an entire disk drive. This operation is usually performed to create backup copies of important information for use if the system's hard drive crashes or when its contents become corrupt.

Backup and Restore utilities (either those provided with Windows or by a third-party software vendor) can be used to back up and retrieve one or more files to another location, such as an external hard drive, a DVD, or a tape drive. Because a backup of related files is typically much larger than a single floppy disk, serious backup programs allow information to be backed up to a series of disks; they also provide file compression techniques to reduce the size of the files stored on the disk. However, it is impossible to read or use the compressed backup files in this format. To be usable, the files must be decompressed (expanded) and restored to their original format.

Backup Types

Most backup utilities provide different options for conducting backups. Typically, backups fall into four categories:

- ▶ Full or total
- ▶ Incremental
- ▶ Selective
- ▶ Differential (or modified only)

In a full or total backup process, depicted in Figure 16.4, the entire contents of the designated disk are backed up. This includes directory and subdirectory listings and their contents. This backup method requires the most time each day to back up, but also requires the least time to restore the system after a failure. Only the most recent backup copy is required to restore the system.

FIGURE 16.4 Full backup.

Partial backups are often used instead of full backups to conserve space on the backup media and consume less time for the administrator. Three partial backup techniques are used to store data, but conserve space on the storage media: incremental backups, selective backups, and differential backups.

▶ Incremental backup—In an incremental backup operation, shown in Figure 16.5, the system backs up those files that have been created or changed since the last backup. Restoring the system from an incremental backup requires the use of the last full backup and each incremental backup taken since then. This method requires the least amount of time to back up the system but the most amount of time to restore it.

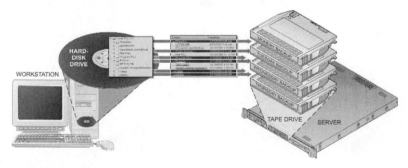

FIGURE 16.5 Incremental backup.

▶ Selective or copy backup—To conduct a selective backup, the operator moves through the tree structure of the disk marking, or tagging, directories and files to be backed up. After all the desired directories/files have been marked, they are backed up in a single operation. This form of backup is labor intensive and may inadvertently miss important data. A selective backup is illustrated in Figure 16.6.

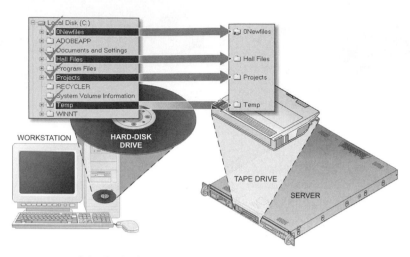

FIGURE 16.6 Selective backup.

▶ Differential or modified only backup—Specifying a differential backup causes the backup utility to examine each file to determine whether it has changed since the last full backup was performed. If not, it is bypassed. If the file has been altered, however, it will be backed up. This option is a valuable time-saving feature in a periodic backup strategy. To restore the system, you need a copy of the last full backup and the last differential backup. A differential or modified only backup operation is depicted in Figure 16.7.

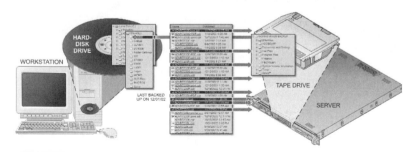

FIGURE 16.7 Differential backup.

EXAM ALERT

Know which backup type requires the least amount of time to perform and the least amount of effort to restore the system.

Windows Data Backup

You must be a member of the Administrator or Backup Operators groups, or have appropriate permissions to the information they are attempting to back up, to use the Windows 2000 or XP Backup utility. Members of these groups can back up and restore all data on a Windows computer, regardless of their permissions level. These groups are automatically assigned the Back Up Files and Directories and Restore Files and Directories user rights.

Any user can back up files they have at least the Read permission for. Likewise, they can restore anything they have at least the Write permission for. Users generally have these permissions to their own files so that they can perform backups and restores of their data as necessary.

To perform a backup of all data on a Windows 2000 or XP computer, follow these steps:

1. Log on as a user with appropriate permissions to back up the system.

2. Use the CHKDSK/F command to clean up lost file clusters. Instruct the program to convert any lost chains into files that can be checked later.

3. From the Start menu, select Programs (All Programs in Windows XP), Accessories, System Tools, and Backup.

4. From the Welcome window, launch the Backup Wizard in Windows 2000. In Windows XP, click the Advanced Mode link to switch into Advanced mode. You could perform the Backup using Wizard mode, but Advanced mode will provide more backup options to choose from.

5. From the Welcome tab, launch Backup Wizard or Backup Wizard (Advanced).

6. At the Welcome window, click the Next button.

7. At the What to Back Up window, select the Back Up Everything on My Computer option, and then click the Next button.

8. At the Where to Store the Backup (Backup Type, Destination, and Name in Windows XP) window, configure the type, location, and name for the backup, and then click the Next button.

9. At the Completing the Backup Wizard window, click the Advanced button to modify the Advanced settings, if necessary, and then click the Finish button to start the backup process.

NOTE

You can also access the Windows Backup utility through the command prompt. Type **Ntbackup** in the Start, Run dialog box window. The Ntbackup.exe utility can also be used to write scripts to automate the backup and restore process. For additional information about this option, type **Ntbackup /?** at the command prompt.

Advanced Backup Settings

Choosing the Advanced backup option will lead you through the following configuration pages:

▶ Type of Backup—Includes normal, differential, incremental, copy, and daily backup options.

▶ How to Back Up—Includes options for verifying the backup and enabling compression (if it's supported by your backup device). *Verifying the backup* means to compare the data that is on the tape with the data that was backed up, to make certain that all information was copied properly during the backup.

▶ Media Options (Backup Options in Windows XP)—This configuration option enables you to specify whether to replace the existing data on the backup media or append the new data to the end of the media.

▶ Backup Label—This setting enables you to assign a name to the backup. You should usually label backups with the date and time that the backup was performed and the contents of the backup.

▶ When to Back Up—You can launch the backup operation immediately or specify a later time and date for the backup.

You can schedule backups to occur repetitively at a designated time through the Schedule Jobs tab. Double-clicking any date in the calendar will launch the Backup Wizard, with the option to specify the time that the backup operation will start. You will also be prompted to set up a repetitive schedule during the process.

NOTE

Remember that it is possible for others to access the data from a stolen backup and restore it on another Windows system where they have Administrator privileges. Make sure that backup copies are stored securely.

Restoring Data

To restore data from a backup, start the Backup/Restore utility from the System Tools submenu and follow these steps:

1. From the Welcome window, select the Restore Wizard option. (Switch to Advanced mode in Windows XP and from the Welcome tab, launch the Restore Wizard [Advanced].)

2. At the Welcome window, click the Next button.

3. In the What to Restore window, select the appropriate backup file and the files and folders to be restored, as illustrated in Figure 16.8. Click the Next button to continue.

4. In the Completion window, click the Advanced button to specify additional options, if necessary.

5. Click the Finish button to start the restore process.

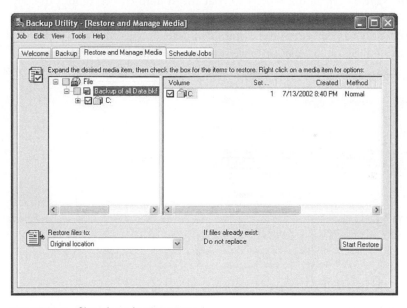

FIGURE 16.8 Choosing what to restore.

Advanced Restore Settings

If you choose to configure advanced restore settings, you will be presented with the following series of configuration pages:

▶ Where to Restore—This option enables you to restore to the original location, an alternative location, or a single folder. If you choose to restore to an alternative location, the wizard will ask you to supply a path to restore the files. The folder structure of the backup will be maintained. Selecting the restore to a single folder option will also require a path to use for the restore. However, this option will not preserve the existing folder structure.

▶ How to Restore—This option enables you to determine how the restore will handle files that already exist on the disk. The options include not replacing files on the disk (this is the default option), replacing the files on the disk only if they are older than the backup copy, and always replacing the files on the disk.

System State Data Backups

In addition to backing up data files and applications, it is often convenient to back up the key system configuration and information as well. This type of data is called the *System State* and is stored so that the system can be rebuilt quickly in case of a failure. Windows 2000 and Windows XP Backup utilities provide an option specifically to perform System State data backup, as illustrated in Figure 16.9. The System State data can be backed up by itself or as part of the regularly scheduled system backup operation.

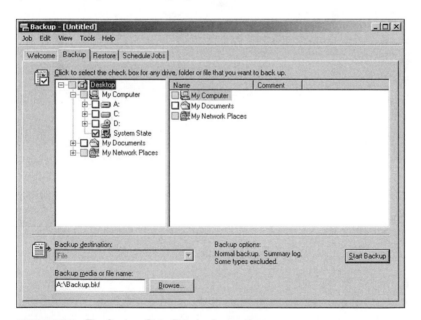

FIGURE 16.9 The System State Data backup option.

Backing up the System State data includes the following:

- The contents of the Registry

- The system startup files

- Files under Windows File Protection in Windows XP

- The COM+ class registration database (a database of information about Component Services applications)

When the System State data check box is checked, its individual components are listed in the details pane of the display. The components are dependent on one another and can be backed up and restored only as a set (there is no way to back up the components individually).

When the System State data is restored to a machine, any existing System State information will be overwritten and destroyed. This can be a problem if an older version of the System State data is copied back into the system (any newer configuration information would be lost).

Backup Scheduling

In business environments, backup operations are a very important part of most company preventive-maintenance programs. In these environments, the backup process is scripted into a schedule and a method for performing the backup function. To develop an acceptable backup schedule, you must consider a variety of issues, including when and what type of backup is required to ensure acceptable recovery in case of system failure. As a minimum, you must ask yourself the following questions when considering what type of backup method to use:

- How critical is your data?

- Can the business tolerate losing financial records for the past 24 hours?

- What systems must be reinstated first?

- How far back should your retain system settings?

- How far back might you be asked to go to recover a file?

Time is also a critical element in deciding your backup schedule. Although a full system backup would give you the best assurance of a quick system recovery, it also takes a fair amount of server downtime to perform. Can you afford to have productivity stop just to perform backups? This may not be an issue when backing up a small server system that is measured in megabytes, but when your

overall system's data is large—measured in multiple gigabytes or terabytes—
your server downtime for full backups could adversely affect overall company
productivity.

When determining your backup methodology, you must consider when to do
your backups and the form of media rotation you will use. The following provides you with a brief discussion on these issues:

▶ Daily Backup—Daily full-system backup provides the best assurance of
  at least being able to quickly recover all but the last 24 hours of your
  data. This is feasible only for small systems or portions of a system. For
  larger systems, a daily regiment of incremental or differential backups
  would at least assure recovery of your system, again excluding up to the
  last 24 hours. If your organization determines that specific data is too
  critical to potentially lose 24 hours worth of information, you may need
  to back up that specific data on a more rigorous schedule.

▶ Weekly Backup—Normally you can schedule weekly full-system backups
  during weekends, as long as your company requirements for uptime
  allow. The overall time required for your weekly backups will depend on
  the size of your system, and the frequency you apply. Very large companies may require maximum uptime, even during weekend timeframes. In
  these incidences, more aggressive data distribution, backup methods, and
  more controlled backup scheduling needs to be applied.

▶ Unscheduled Backups—Unscheduled backups occur whenever there is a
  need that is either unanticipated or does not fit into your regular schedule of backups. A good example is when your server is exhibiting symptoms of potential failure, or you are upgrading portions of the system. At
  these times, or anytime you are concerned that the normal backup
  schedule may not cover a potential loss of data, you should perform an
  unscheduled backup.

NOTE

Backup operations are typically scheduled to run at nonworking hours to lessen their
impact on the operation of the network. By scheduling backups to run in the middle of the
night or on a weekend, the large volume of data involved in a backup operation flows
across the network without affecting anyone's productivity.

Backup Media Rotation

After you ensure that your backup plan has the necessary attributes to ensure
initial system recovery, you must determine the need of your company to

retrieve historical copies of its data. The *backup media rotation* method you employ will determine the historical timeframe for which you will be able to retrieve data. There are numerous media rotation methods that can be employed, each having its own timeframe of recovery. The Grandfather-Father-Son method, shown in Figure 16.10, is the most common methodology employed today.

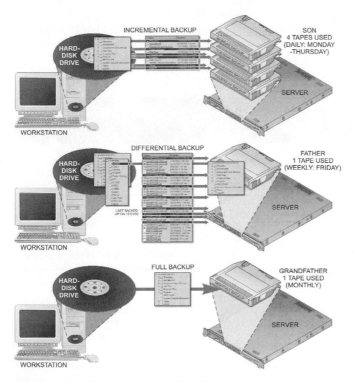

FIGURE 16.10 The Grandfather-Father-Son method.

The Grandfather-Father-Son method uses three different groupings of backup tapes: the *Grandfather* for monthly backups, the *Father* for weekly backups, and the *Son* for daily backups.

The Son uses four tapes—one for every weekday normally covering Monday through Thursday—typically applying the incremental backup method. The Father's weekly backup, normally performed on Friday, uses one tape applying the differential method of backup. After this, you reuse the corresponding Son tapes for the following daily backups. At month's end, you use one tape to run the Grandfather backup. This backup would be a full backup of the system. Depending on your company's needs, you may store these tapes to support an ongoing historical backup library, or reuse the tape for future backups.

NOTE

Storage media can become a security issue if they are not stored and accounted for properly. Some companies store multiple copies of their backups in different locations. Storage strategies are typically structured to counteract potential threats, such as fires and floods. One copy is typically stored on site, say in a locked cabinet located in an administrator's locked office, whereas another copy may be stored in a local fireproof safe, with an additional copy stored securely away from the building, such as in a bank's safety deposit box. In some cases, companies hire remote data storage companies to keep copies of their backups far away from the site (such as in a different city or state).

EXAM ALERT

Know how many tapes are required to restore using a Grandfather-Father-Son backup implementation.

NOTE

It is a good idea to periodically perform restore operations from backups to diverse locations. This will enable you to validate the backups. You do not want to wait until the system fails to find out that the backups you've been making on a regular basis don't work. Also, the worst time to learn how to restore data is when you are in the middle of a crisis.

TIP

Know how to ensure that backup operations are working correctly and will return the system to normal if needed.

Removable Storage Utility

The Windows 2000 and XP include a Removable Storage utility that provides a variety of services to system administrators. It enables them to set up, share, and manage the removable media devices attached to the computer. Both the Windows 2000 and third-party backup applications use the Removable Storage utility to keep track of the identity of all backup media they use. The utility facilitates the actual mounting of the media when requested by the application, and the application itself keeps track of the actual data written or retrieved from the media.

The Windows Removable Storage Management system does not recognize CD-R, CD-RW, or DVD-R devices as backup media, even though there are options to add these devices through the utility.

Windows 2000/XP System Management Tools

The Windows operating systems also include a number of tools and utilities designed to manage and troubleshoot the Windows environment. These tools typically include utilities for managing system configuration settings, device drivers, and system resources. In Windows 2000 and XP, a number of administrative, diagnostic, and troubleshooting tools are clustered under the Control Panel's Microsoft Management Console (MMC).

The System Tools console consolidates a number of utilities that can be used to configure and track all of the system's hardware and software components, in addition to configuring network options and viewing system events. The major tools gathered in this console by default include the following:

▶ Event Viewer

▶ System Information

▶ Performance Logs and Alerts

▶ Device Manager

▶ Local Users and Groups

Event Viewer

In Windows 2000 and Windows XP, significant events (such as system events, application events, and security events) are routinely monitored and stored. These events can be viewed through the Event Viewer utility depicted in Figure 16.11. As described earlier, this tool is located under the Control Panel/Administrative Tools/Computer Management path.

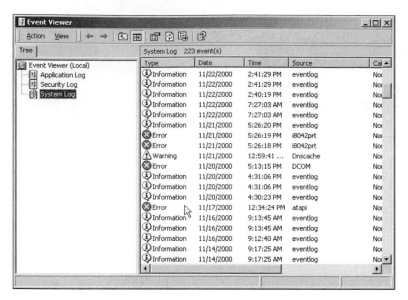

FIGURE 16.11 The Windows 2000 Event Viewer.

System events include items such as successful and failed Windows component startups, as well as successful loading of device drivers. Likewise, application events include information about how the system's applications are performing. Not all Windows applications generate events that the Event Viewer will log. Finally, security events are produced by user actions such as logons and logoffs, file and folder accesses, and creation of new Active Directory accounts.

Three default event logs track and record the events just mentioned. The system log records events generated by the operating system and its components. The application log tracks events generated by high-end applications. Likewise, the security log contains information generated by audit policies that have been enacted in the operating system. If no audit policies are configured, the security log will remain empty.

EXAM ALERT

Remember the types of information stored in the Windows security logs and where they can be viewed.

In addition to the default logs, some special systems such as domain controllers and DNS systems will have specialized logs to track events specifically related to the function of the system.

The Event Viewer produces three categories of system and application events:

▶ Information events—Events that indicate an application, a service, or a driver has loaded successfully. These events require no intervention.

▶ Warning events—Events that have no immediate impact, but that could have future significance. These events should be investigated.

▶ Error events—Events that indicate an application, a service, or a driver has failed to load successfully. These events require immediate intervention.

Notice in the figure that the Information events are denoted by a small "i" in a cloud, whereas exclamation marks (!) and Xs are used to identify Warning and Error events, respectively. You can double-click on these icons to obtain a detailed explanation of the event or error that occurred. These explanations often contain links to additional information about the condition or error.

EXAM ALERT

Be aware that detailed information about system errors can be obtained through the Event Viewer.

Under Windows XP, you can configure the system to write events to the system log when the system stops unexpectedly. These logs contain memory dump files that contain the contents of specified amounts of memory when the system failed. Administrators can configure this feature under the Advanced tab of the Control Panel's System icon. From the Startup and Recovery area of this tab, you can click on the Settings button and configure the options available for system failure, along with how much debugging information to store and where.

EXAM ALERT

Know what a memory dump is and how it can be used.

The memory dump file can be examined with the DUMPCHK.EXE utility located on the Windows XP distribution CD. DUMPCHK will display basic information about the memory dump and verify all the virtual and physical addresses in the file. If it detects any errors in the memory dump file, it will display them in the report. This feature is typically used by programmers to debug their applications.

> ## Challenge #1
>
> The president of the Acmeco Inc. has hired you as an IT consultant for his company. Acme has had some malicious activities occurring within the company network and he wants you to establish a method of tracking who logs in to each machine and when. All the workstation PCs are Windows XP Professional systems and the network server is a Windows 2000 Server. What do you need to do to accomplish this objective?

Windows 2000/XP System Information

The Windows 2000 System Information utility provides five subfolders of information about the system. These folders include a system summary, a list of hardware resources being used, a list of I/O components in the system, a description of the system's current software environment, and a description of the Windows Internet Explorer.

The System Information tool can be used to enable remote service providers to inspect the system's information across a LAN environment. To save system information to a file, right-click the System Information entry and select the Save As option from the resulting menu. Saving this information enables you to document events and conditions when errors occur. You can use the results of different system information files to compare situations and perhaps determine what changes may have occurred to cause the problem.

In Windows XP systems, the System Information tool can be accessed through the Start, Run menu by typing `msinfo32.exe` into the Run dialog box. You can also access the Windows XP System Information tool by navigating the Start/All Programs/Accessories/System Tools path and selecting the System Information option. Both methods will produce the Windows XP System Information console depicted in Figure 16.12.

The contents of the System Information utility can be saved or exported to a file so that it can be saved for troubleshooting or optimization purposes. Both of these functions can be performed through the utility's File menu. Using the Save option stores the data in a .NFO format that can be read again by the System Information utility. The export function saves the information to a text file that can be read with any standard text editor (for example, Notepad).

One of the biggest reasons to save the system information is for troubleshooting when system errors occur. By saving system information when the system is functioning properly, you can compare it to information obtained when a failure occurs. The other reason to save system information is to establish performance baselines that can be used to measure the effectiveness of changes that are made to the system. If an upgrade is performed and the System Information report shows diminished performance characteristics, you can reverse the upgrade effort.

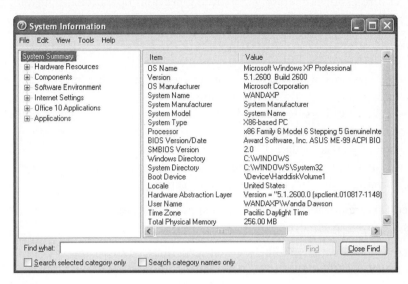

FIGURE 16.12   Windows XP System Information.

The Windows XP System Information Tools menu, depicted in Figure 16.13, provides additional access to many of the system's troubleshooting and administrative tools.

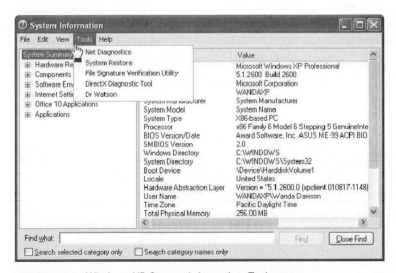

FIGURE 16.13   Windows XP System Information, Tools menu.

Windows XP System Restore

The Windows XP System Restore utility enables administrators to roll back the Windows XP Professional operating system to a previous operational state and configuration—without affecting any user's personal data. This feature extends the Last Known Good Configuration mode by allowing the system to be rolled back to predetermined restore points.

Restore points are records of information that are created at specific intervals and when certain events occur. Some restore points are created automatically on a 24-hour/daily basis. Others are created when significant events occur, such as when you upgrade the system hardware or software, perform a recovery operation, or when a new driver is loaded. However, restore points can also be created manually as a method of preserving the current state of the operating system prior to performing management activities. Such activities include the following:

▶ When you are updating a driver and it appears to cause problems with the system that rolling back the driver does not resolve

▶ When you are installing a new software program and it creates problems with the system that uninstalling the software does not resolve

▶ Anytime you need to get back to a point where you know the system was functioning correctly.

You should actually create a restore point anytime that you are making changes to the system that might make it unstable or that might disable it.

Task Manager

In Windows 2000 and Windows XP, Task Manager is a utility that can be used to determine which applications in the system are running or stopped, as well as which resources are being used. You can also determine general microprocessor and memory usage levels.

When an application hangs up in these operating systems, you can access the Task Manager window depicted in Figure 16.14 and remove it from the list of tasks. The Windows 2000 and Windows XP Task Managers can be accessed by pressing Ctrl+Alt+Delete or by pressing Ctrl+Shift+Esc.

You can also access Task Manager by right-clicking Task Manager and selecting Task Manager from the pop-up contextual menu. The Ctrl+Shift+Esc key sequence moves directly into Task Manager, whereas the Ctrl+Alt+Del selection opens the Windows Security menu screen, which offers Task Manager as an option.

FIGURE 16.14 Task Manager.

To use Task Manager, select the application from the list on the Applications tab and click the End Task button. If prompted, click the End Task button again to confirm the selection. The Performance tab provides a graphical summary of the system's CPU and memory usage. The Process tab provides information that can be helpful in tracking down problems associated with slow system operation.

Tasks that have stopped can also be restarted from Task Manager. Clicking the New Task button, or clicking the New Task(Run) option on the File menu, will bring up a the Run dialog box that provides access to a command prompt. Any stopped application, or file with a .EXE extension, can be restarted by entering its filename at the command prompt. For example, you can attempt to restart a stalled print spooler by entering **spoolsv.exe** at the command prompt and pressing the Enter button.

Challenge #2

You are using a commercial customer-tracking database application on a Windows 2000 Professional system when the system hangs up and will not do anything. What is the best method to safely gain control of the system and remove the offending application?

Device Manager

Hardware and configuration conflicts also can be isolated manually using the Windows 2000/XP Device Manager from the Control Panel's System icon. This utility is basically an easy-to-use interface for the Windows 2000/XP Registries. You can use Device Manager, depicted in Figure 16.15, to identify installed ports, update device drivers, and change I/O settings. From this window, the problem device can be examined to see where the conflict is occurring.

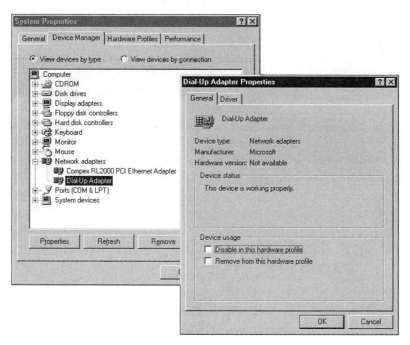

FIGURE 16.15 The Device Manager's display.

Under Windows 2000, two option buttons on the Device Manager page can be used to alter the way it displays the devices installed in the system. Clicking the left button (the page's default setting) displays the system's devices alphabetically by device type. The rightmost option button shows the devices by their connection to the system. In Windows XP, these display options are located in the View drop-down menu and includes options for displaying both devices and resources by type and connection. As with the Registry and Policy Editors, the presence of plus (+) and minus (–) signs in the nodes of the devices indicates expandable and collapsible information branches at those nodes.

The Device Manager will display an exclamation point (!) inside a yellow circle whenever a device is experiencing a direct hardware conflict with another device. The nature of the problem is described in the device's Properties dialog box. Similarly, when a red X appears at the device's icon, the device has been disabled because of a user-selection conflict.

> **EXAM ALERT**
>
> **Memorize symbols used by the Windows Device Manager.**

This situation can occur when a user wants to disable a selected device without removing it. For example, a user who travels and uses a notebook computer may want to temporarily disable device drivers for options that aren't used in travel. This can be accomplished through Device Manager's Disable in This Hardware Profile option. This will keep the driver from loading up until it is reactivated. Clicking the Properties button at the bottom of the Device Manager screen produces the selected device's Properties sheet. The three tabs at the top of the page provide access to the device's general information, driver specifications, and system resource assignments.

> **EXAM ALERT**
>
> **Be aware of how to temporarily disable device drivers that are not needed in certain situations, yet retain them in the system for future use.**

When a device conflict is suspected, click the offending device in the listing, make sure that the selected device is the current device, and then click the Resources tab to examine the conflicting device's list.

To change the resources allocated to a device, click the resource to be changed, remove the check mark from the Use Automatic Settings box, click the Change Setting button, and scroll through the resource options. Take care when changing resource settings. The Resource Settings window displays all the available resources in the system, even those that are already spoken for by another device. You must know which resources are acceptable for a given type of device and which ones are already in use.

To determine what resources the system already has in use, click the Computer icon at the top of the Device Manager display. The Computer Properties page provides ways to view and reserve system resources.

Through this page, you can click option buttons to display the system's use of four key resources: IRQ channels, DMA channels, I/O addresses, and memory addresses. The Reserve Resources page is used to set aside key resources to avoid conflicts with the PnP configuration operations. If a resource is reserved and Windows detects it as already in use, a warning dialog box displays onscreen and asks for a confirmation.

Normal causes for conflict include devices sharing IRQ settings, I/O address settings, DMA channels, or base memory settings. The most common conflicts are those dealing with the IRQ channels. Nonessential peripherals, such as sound and network adapters, are most likely to produce this type of conflict.

When a device conflict is reported through the Resource tab's Conflicting Device list, record the current settings for each device, refer to the documentation for each device to determine what other settings might be used, and change the settings for the most flexible device. If either device continues to exhibit problems, reset the configurations to their original positions and change the settings for the other device.

Make sure that the device has not been installed twice. When this occurs, it is usually impossible to determine which driver is correct. Therefore, it will be necessary to remove both drivers and allow the PnP process to redetect the device. If multiple drivers are present for a given device, remove the drivers that are not specific to the particular device installed in the system.

Windows XP Driver Rollback Feature

In Windows XP, Device Manager includes a new Driver Rollback option that can be used to replace an upgraded driver whenever it causes problems with the system. To roll back the driver, right-click the device in the Device Manager listing and select the Properties option. Click the Driver tab and then the Roll Back Driver button, depicted in Figure 16.16.

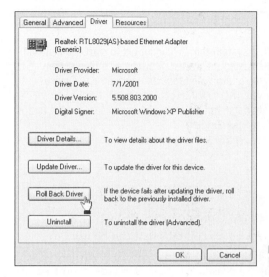

FIGURE 16.16 The Device Manager Roll Back Driver option.

The Driver Rollback feature enables you to quickly recover when you install a new driver for a device and the system does not function well with it. This can often result in a blue screen Stop error or a complete crash when you try to boot the system. However, most new driver problems do not result in bootup problems. Instead, they tend to create unstable system operation.

In cases where you cannot boot to the operating system you can boot into the Last Known Good Configuration start mode and the system should revert to the old driver. However, when a new driver installation creates an unstable system, you should access the Device Manager's Driver Rollback option for the offending device and revert to the previous driver.

The Driver Rollback feature tracks only one previous driver level. If you attempt to repair a driver problem by loading a new replacement before conducting the driver rollback operation, the utility will not be able to get back to the original driver. Therefore, you should always attempt to roll back the driver before you attempt to update it.

EXAM ALERT

Be aware of the limitations of the Driver Rollback feature.

Challenge #3

A co-worker has asked for your help with a system that he cannot get to start. He installed a new video display adapter and when he started the system it produced a blue screen and locked up. He successfully booted the system into Safe Mode and navigated to Device Manager where he tried to update the driver. This failed to get the system running, so he reentered Device Manager and tried the Uninstall option. Now he has no idea of what to do next to get the system running. What could you suggest?

MSCONFIG.EXE

The Windows XP command-line System Configuration Utility (MSCONFIG. EXE), depicted in Figure 16.17, provides several tabs that can be used to selectively omit startup sequences and actions that may be preventing the system from starting up normally. It can also be used to create a restore point before you begin troubleshooting the operating system.

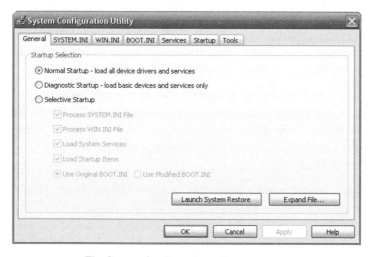

FIGURE 16.17 The System Configuration utility.

EXAM ALERT

Know what types of problems the **MSCONFIG.EXE** utility is used for.

Remote Desktop and Remote Assistance Features

Windows XP Professional offers two utilities that provide remote access to other computers. The first is the Remote Desktop utility that enables users to connect to their own Windows XP computer from a remote location. The second is Remote Assistance that enables technicians and mentors to remotely control another user's computer.

Using Remote Desktop, users can gain access to their remote Windows XP Professional desktop, applications, data, and network resources from another computer on the network. In addition, users who have been granted permission can also remotely connect to the system.

Remote Desktop enables users who work from various locations, such as PC Repair book authors, to access their main Windows XP Professional system running at the home office. This provides access to all the resources needed to write this book—source materials and research materials. Packing all this material in a suitcase and dragging it around the world can produce tennis elbow and numerous back pain problems. As I'm sure you are probably aware at this point in this book, books can be quite heavy.

For technicians and help desk personnel, the Remote Assistance feature is the more interesting utility. Instead of sometimes awkwardly trying to give less technically savvy users directions over a phone (or worse yet, in person), the Remote Assistance feature provides the user with the ability to electronically permit you to take control of his system from your remote location. Both systems must be configured for Remote Assistance before a connection can be made. After the Remote Assistance connection has been established, the communication provides interactive cooperation between the user and the helper.

If you've never tried to give troubleshooting information to someone over the phone, you probably can't imagine how many ways the conversation can head off in a wrong direction. Most technicians would rather be right there looking at what's going on. This is much less tiresome than trying to remember what you've already asked the other person to do and trying to understand and guide the feedback they are giving you.

Remote Assistance enables you to get online with the user and do just that—see what happens on the other end without having to run everything through another less technically savvy person. After you're connected to the user's desktop, you can view and take shared control of the desktop, chat, and send and receive files.

File Management Tools

The primary file management tool in all Windows versions is the Windows Explorer. Its File and Edit menus enable you to create, delete, rename, and reposition files and folders in the Windows system. It also provides access to the attributes associated with each file and folder in the system. This is a feature primarily intended for technicians.

During many repair processes, technicians need to access system files that are typically hidden from view. To show the hidden files in Windows 2000 and XP Explorer, select the drop-down Tools menu, click the Folder Options, click the View tab, and select the Show Hidden Files and Folders option. The command line also provides very powerful file management capabilities. You can always access a file from the command prompt and change its attributes with the ATTRIB command.

> **EXAM ALERT**
>
> Be aware of options available for viewing and altering attribute associated with hidden, system, and read-only files in the Windows environment.

System Editors

The Windows 2000 and XP operating systems contain several important editors:

- ▶ Two text editors—Edit and System Configuration Editor (SysEdit)
- ▶ Two Registry Editors—RegEdit and RegEdt32
- ▶ The Group Policy Editor (GPE)

The two command-line-based text editor programs—EDIT.COM and the System Configuration Editor (SYSEDIT.EXE) program—enable users to easily modify text files such as the BOOT.INI and other initialization files as needed. You can start the Edit version of the text editor by typing the **EDIT** command and the filename at the command prompt. To start the SysEdit function, select the Run option from the Start menu. Type **SYSEDIT** into the Run dialog box and click the OK button. The SysEdit commands are similar to those of other Windows-based text editing programs, such as Notepad or Write.

The Windows Registry is a very complex structure that can accumulate invalid entries and become corrupt. These are typically caused by incorrect removal of applications, missing or corrupt device drivers, or nonexistent startup programs.

Still other Registry problems are caused by viruses and spyware programs that track system activity. Over time, this corruption can cause the system to crash and not run, can provide unpredictable operation, or cause it to issue an error message indicating that a particular type of problem has occurred. Common Registry corruption errors include the following:

- ▶ Different Stop errors

- ▶ .DLL errors

- ▶ Runtime errors

- ▶ Missing file or program errors

When these symptoms or error messages appear, you will need to repair the Registry to get back to normal operations. This can be accomplished by performing a restore point operation, restoring the Registry from a backup, editing the Registry, or by reinstalling Windows.

Windows 2000 and Windows XP include two Registry editors: RegEdit and RegEdt32. RegEdit is an older Registry editor that was used with previous Windows versions but retains some features not available in the newer RegEdt32 version. Both utilities enable you to add, edit, and remove Registry entries and to perform other basic functions. However, specific functions can be performed in only one editor or the other. RegEdt32 presents each subtree as an individual entity in a separate window. The subtrees are presented as being part of the same entity in a single window, as illustrated in Figure 16.18.

EXAM ALERT

Be aware of which Windows utilities can be used to make changes to the Registry in Windows 2000 and Windows XP.

The Registry has a permissions system that is similar to NTFS permissions, which enables you to control access to the keys and assigned values. RegEdt32 enables you to view and set permissions through the Security menu. RegEdit does not allow you to access the permissions system.

The Find capabilities of RegEdt32 are accessed from the View menu and are very limited. You can search only for keys, not assigned values or their corresponding data. This is the equivalent of being able to search for folders in the file system, but not for files. Also, you can initiate a search in only one subtree at a time. The Find capabilities of RegEdit are accessed through the Edit menu and are very strong. You have the option to search for keys and assigned values, and you can search all subtrees at once. RegEdit also enables you to save frequently accessed Registry locations as favorites to enable quicker access.

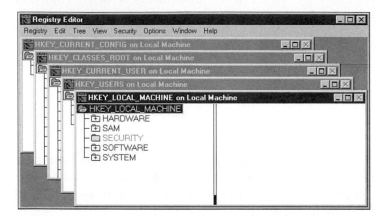

FIGURE 16.18   The RegEdt32 Registry Editor.

CAUTION

Editing the Registry with RegEdit or RegEdt32 should be done only when you have no other alternative. These editors bypass all the safeguards provided by the standard utilities and allow you to enter values that are invalid or that conflict with other settings. Incorrect editing of the Registry can cause Windows 2000 to stop functioning correctly, prompting a significant amount of troubleshooting or a reinstallation of the operating system.

Dr. Watson

The main tool for isolating and correcting application errors is the Dr. Watson utility provided in all Windows versions. These errors are commonly referred to as general protection faults (GPFs) and are caused by incorrect memory access attempts, either into another applications memory space, or into reserved operating system memory spaces. Dr. Watson is used to trace problems that appear under certain conditions, such as starting or using a certain application. When one of these conditions causes a GPF to occur, Windows XP will produce an error message saying *Program name* `has encountered a problem and needs to close` if possible. In Windows Vista, the message has changed to *Program Name* `has stopped working`. In other cases, these errors produce blue screen Stop errors.

When Dr. Watson is started, it runs in the background with only an icon appearing on the taskbar to signify that it is present. For problems that cannot be directly attributed to the Windows operating system, an application program might be the source of the problem and the Dr. Watson utility should be set up to run in the background as the system operates.

As the system operates, the Dr. Watson utility monitors the code moving through the system and logs its key events in the DRWTSN32.LOG file. When a system error occurs, the Dr. Watson log contains a listing of the events that were going on up to the time of the failure. This log provides programmers with a detailed listing of the events that led up to the failure. The information is automatically stored in the log file that can be provided to software developers, or to Microsoft, so that it can debug its software and produce patches for it. In many cases, the program will describe the nature of the error and possibly suggest a fix.

> **EXAM ALERT**
>
> Know which Windows utility can be used to monitor the operation of application packages and log errors so that they can be reported to software developers for repairing their programs.

The Dr. Watson utility is not located in any of the Windows 2000/XP menus. To use it, you must execute the program from the Start menu's Run option by typing the name **drwtsn32** into the dialog box and clicking OK to start the log file.

> **EXAM ALERT**
>
> Be aware of where the Dr. Watson utility is located and what it is used for.

Command-Line Utilities

Because technicians must frequently work form the command line, many of the tools you use must also be available from the command prompt. Many of the repair operations used to get the system and its logical subsystems back up and running involve using the command line. In all Windows versions, the command-prompt environment can be reached through the Start, Run dialog box. In Windows 2000/XP you can type **CMD** or **COMMAND**. Remember that in many cases, you will need to employ the **ATTRIB** command to change a file's attributes (hidden or read only) so that you can see and work with them.

The following list describes most of the major tools associated with maintaining and repairing the system's hard-disk drives.

▶ CHKDSK.EXE—This hard-disk–checking utility inspects the data on a specified disk for errors and corruption. It is used to find and possibly repair cluster chains that make up files that have become disconnected from each other.

▶ DEFRAG.EXE—This disk-drive utility organizes disjointed information on hard-disk drives into more efficient patterns to speed up the access and read times associated with finding and reading data from the drive.

▶ DISKPART.EXE—This Windows XP disk-partitioning utility is used to establish logical structures on a hard-disk drive.

Other available *operating system tools* enable administrators and technicians to manage files and memory usage in the PC system. These tools include the following:

▶ EXTRACT.EXE—The EXTRACT utility is used to pull needed files from the Windows distribution media so that they can be used to replace corrupted or missing files that are preventing the system from working.

▶ SFC.EXE—The System File Checker utility is a Windows 2000/XP command-line utility that checks the system's protected files for changed, deleted, or possibly corrupt files. If it finds such files, it attempts to extract the original correct versions of the files.

▶ MSCONFIG.EXE—The System Configuration Utility can be used to selectively omit startup sequences and actions that may be preventing the system from starting up normally. It can also be used to create a restore point before you begin troubleshooting the operating system.

▶ EDIT—This command opens the operating system's default text editor package. This editor can be used to alter and repair text-based files.

▶ MEM—This command is used to display the amount of used and free memory in a system.

Other command-line utilities are available for network troubleshooting purposes. As a matter of fact, the various Windows operating system versions contain a suite of TCP/IP troubleshooting utilities that are executed from the command prompt. The most widely used TCP/IP commands are

▶ IPCONFIG — This command-line utility enables you to determine the current TCP/IP configuration (MAC address, IP address, and subnet mask) of the local computer. It also may be used to request a new TCP/IP address from a DHCP server. IPCONFIG is available in both Windows 2000 and Windows XP.

▶ PING—This TCP/IP networking utility is used to verify network connections between computers.

▶ TRACRT—The Tracert utility is another very important network troubleshooting tool that is used from the command prompt. It provides route information for packets of information being sent across a network.

Be aware that these are only three of several TCP/IP utilities covered in detail in Chapter 23, "Networking Troubleshooing."

> **NOTE**
>
> As pointed out earlier in this chapter, any program/file in the Windows system that has an .EXE extension can be run from the command line. This includes executables such as the spoolsv.exe file, which handles the printing process for Windows.

Challenge #4

One of your customers thinks that there may be some corrupt files on the hard drive preventing it from booting up. She has called you back to see if there is some troubleshooting tool that she can use to check out the disk drive and possibly repair any corruption problems present. She thinks that there is, but is not sure as to what it is or how to use it. What advice should you give her?

Windows Troubleshooting Help Files

Windows 2000 and Windows XP come with built-in troubleshooting Help file systems. The Windows Troubleshooters are a special type of context-specific help that is available in Windows 2000 and XP. These interactive files enable you to pinpoint problems and identify solutions to problems by asking a series of questions and then providing you with detailed troubleshooting information based on your responses to those questions. This feature includes troubleshooting assistance for a number of Windows problems.

In both systems, the Troubleshooter utilities can be accessed from the Start menu, from the Help menu entry on the toolbar, or through Device Manager.

Selecting the Help entry from the Start or toolbar menus produces the Windows 2000 Help Topics window.

The Windows 2000 local Help screens are manipulated by making a selection from the various tabs (Contents, Index, and Search). Double-clicking the Troubleshooting and Maintenance entry on the Contents tab menu will expose the Windows 2000 Troubleshooters option. Selecting this option will produce the list of Troubleshooter routines depicted in the right pane of Figure 16.19.

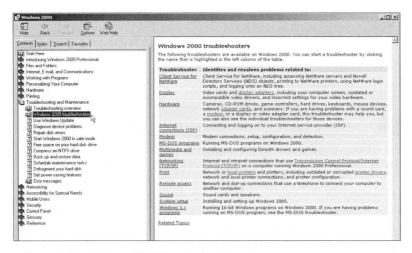

FIGURE 16.19   Windows 2000 Troubleshooter options.

This window contains a list of several entries with information about common Windows problems and situations. Clicking one of the listed topics will produce an interactive troubleshooting process in the right pane of the window that is associated with that particular problem (for instance, modem problems). The interactive text contains a step-by-step procedure for isolating the problem listed. Simply follow the questions and suggestion schemes provided.

The Index tab provides an index of topics that can be searched using key words (for example, Hardware/Conflict Troubleshooting). Several troubleshooting procedures can be accessed through this tab. Type the word **troubleshooting** into the keyword dialog box and select the appropriate topic from the list.

The Search tab can be used to conduct a search of all the Windows help and support materials for key topics, such as troubleshooting. Enter the word and click the List Topics button to conduct the search.

In Windows XP, clicking the Help and Support option from the Start menu produces the Help and Support window. This window looks considerably different from the Windows 2000 version. It also brings several new tools to the Help function.

One of the most significant improvements to the Help system in Windows XP is the search option that checks its local help files and produces a suggestion list of material as well as providing access to its full local text file. In addition, the search function will search the Microsoft Knowledge Base for extended information about the topic you enter.

Internet Help

You can activate the Windows 2000 or Windows XP online help functions by selecting a topic from the menu and then clicking the menu bar's Web Help button. Afterward, you must click the Support Online option at the lower right of the Help window. This action brings up the Internet Sign-In dialog box, if the system is not already logged on to the Internet. After signing in, the Microsoft technical support page appears.

Microsoft's online Product Support Services can provide a wealth of information about Microsoft products, including their operating systems. The URL for Product Support Services is www.Microsoft.com/support. Features of Microsoft Product Support include the following:

▶ Microsoft Knowledge Base—A searchable database of information and self-help tools. The Knowledge Base is used by Microsoft Technical Support to support their customers and is made available to you free of charge.

▶ Download Center—Enables you to search all available downloads for any Microsoft product, including service packs, patches, and updates.

▶ Facts by Product—Enables you to browse for information by product and includes a list of most frequently asked questions about each product.

▶ A listing of support phone numbers that can be used to access live assistance. A charge applies for phone support.

▶ Online Support Requests—Permits you to submit questions to Microsoft support personnel. A charge applies for online support.

Exam Prep Questions

1. What command can be used to repair segmented files in Windows?

   ○ **A.** DISKSCAN /F

   ○ **B.** CHECKDSK /F

   ○ **C.** SCANDISK /F

   ○ **D.** CHKDSK /F

2. Which backup methodology requires the least amount of time to perform and the most amount of time to restore the system?

   ○ **A.** Full

   ○ **B.** Differential

   ○ **C.** Incremental

   ○ **D.** Daily

3. The _____ process will provide more efficient and faster operation of your system.

   ○ **A.** Event logging

   ○ **B.** Defragmentation

   ○ **C.** Disk cleaning

   ○ **D.** Backup

4. Which method will *not* access the Windows 2000 defragmentation utility?

   ○ **A.** Click Start, Programs, Accessories, System Tools, and then select Disk Defragmenter

   ○ **B.** Click Start, Settings, Control Panel, Administrative Tools, and then double-click Computer Management

   ○ **C.** Click Start, Programs, Accessories, and then select Disk Defragmenter

   ○ **D.** Open My Computer, right-click the drive icon, select Properties from the contextual menu, click the Tools tab, and then click the Defragment Now button

5. Where are the disk drive tools located in Windows 2000?

   ○ **A.** System Information

   ○ **B.** System Tools

   ○ **C.** Device Manager

   ○ **D.** Computer Management

6. Where would you locate information about conflicts found in Device Manager?

   ○ **A.** Open Device Manager, double-click the device driver's name, and then click the Resources tab

   ○ **B.** Click Start, Programs, Accessories, System Tools, select System Information, and then click the Resources tab

   ○ **C.** Click Start, Settings, Control Panel, double-click System, and then click the Resources tab

   ○ **D.** Open Device Manager and then click the Resources tab

7. What does the exclamation point (!) inside a yellow circle mean when used by the Windows Device Manager?

   ○ **A.** The device has been disabled because of a user-selection conflict.

   ○ **B.** It indicates expandable and collapsible information branches.

   ○ **C.** The device is experiencing a direct hardware conflict with another device.

   ○ **D.** The device is not installed properly.

8. In Windows, how are device drivers temporarily disabled when they are not needed in certain situations, yet retained in the system for future use?

   ○ **A.** By opening Device Manager and selecting Disable in the device's Properties window

   ○ **B.** By opening Device Manager, right-clicking the device, and selecting Disable from the pop-up menu

   ○ **C.** By opening System Information, clicking Hardware Resources, and then right-clicking the device and selecting Disable

   ○ **D.** Click Start, Settings, Control Panel, open System, click Hardware Resources, and then right-click the device and select Disable

9. Where are the Backup and Restore functions located in Windows 2000?

   ○ **A.** Click Start, Programs, Accessories, System Tools, and then select Backup

   ○ **B.** Click Start, Settings, Control Panel, System, and then click the Backup tab

   ○ **C.** Click Start, Settings, Control Panel, and then double-click the Backup tool

   ○ **D.** Click Start, Programs, Accessories, and then select Backup

10. How can you remove a stalled application in a Windows 2000 system? (Select all that apply.)

   ○ **A.** Right-click the system tray, select Task Manager from the contextual menu, click the Applications tab, highlight the application, and click End Task

   ○ **B.** Press Ctrl+Alt+Esc, click Task Manager, click the Applications tab, highlight the application, and click End Task

   ○ **C.** Press Ctrl+Shift+Esc, click the Applications tab, highlight the application, and click End Task

   ○ **D.** Press Ctrl+Alt+Delete, click Task Manager, click the Applications tab, highlight the application, and click End Task

11. What is the function of the Dr. Watson utility?

   ○ **A.** It analyzes system failures.

   ○ **B.** It analyzes virus activity.

   ○ **C.** It detects and logs an application failure.

   ○ **D.** It detects and logs unauthorized user access.

12. Where is the Dr. Watson utility located?

   ○ **A.** From the Start menu's Run option, type the name **drwtsn32** into the dialog box, and click OK

   ○ **B.** Double-click the file named drwatson in Windows Explorer

   ○ **C.** Enter the name **drwatson** in the Search dialog box

   ○ **D.** From the desktop, click the Dr. Watson icon

13. In Windows 2000 or XP, which utility is used to control programs that run at startup?

   ○ **A.** STARTREG

   ○ **B.** MSCONFIG

   ○ **C.** REGEDIT

   ○ **D.** REGEDT32

14. What utility is used to directly edit Registry entries in Windows 2000 or XP?

   ○ **A.** EDIT

   ○ **B.** SYSEDIT

   ○ **C.** REGEDIT

   ○ **D.** REGEDT32

15. A user wants to back up his system information to a CD, but he doesn't have any CD burner software to work with. How does he do this in Windows XP Home Edition?

   ○ **A.** Use the Windows Backup utility to save to a CD

   ○ **B.** Windows XP Home will not back up to a recordable CD

   ○ **C.** Use the System State Backup utility

   ○ **D.** Use the Grandfather/Father/Son technique to back up the data

16. You have just installed a new high speed tape drive in a customer's server and backed up the entire system. How can you be sure that the new drive has done this successfully?

   ○ **A.** Check the size of the backup file to make sure that it is large enough to represent the stored data

   ○ **B.** Check the backup log to make sure that everything indicated was backed up to the tape

   ○ **C.** Place the backup tape in another drive and see if it can be read from a secondary storage device in case the first drive fails

   ○ **D.** Verify the backup by performing a restore operation from the tape

17. Which Windows command-line utility is used to move driver.cab files from an installation or recovery disk to a corrupted disk drive to repair it?

   ○ **A.** Expand

   ○ **B.** Extract

   ○ **C.** Move

   ○ **D.** Extend

18. Performing a System State backup will back up _____.

○ **A.** The entire operating system along with user configuration settings

○ **B.** Key operating system configuration settings and data so that the system can be rebuilt quickly in the event of a failure

○ **C.** Data that has changed since the last major backup

○ **D.** Tagged files and folders

19. What backup method requires the most time to perform?

○ **A.** Full

○ **B.** Differential

○ **C.** Incremental

○ **D.** Selective

20. How much free drive space is required to run the defrag utility on a volume in Windows XP?

○ **A.** 10%

○ **B.** 15%

○ **C.** 20%

○ **D.** 25%

21. Which Windows XP utilities work to keep the system's HDD running at its optimum capabilities? (Select all that apply.)

○ **A.** The CHKDSK utility

○ **B.** The DEFRAG utility

○ **C.** The Disk Management utility

○ **D.** The Device Manager

22. What utility can gather files that are distributed across different sections of a drive and place them into the same sections of the drive and place them into the same sections of the drive for optimization purposes?

○ **A.** Scandisk

○ **B.** Chkdsk

○ **C.** Dr. Watson

○ **D.** Defrag

Answers and Explanations

1. **D.** CHKDSK a command-line utility that is used to recover lost allocation units from the hard drive. These lost units occur when an application terminates unexpectedly and causes the file-management system to lose track of where some parts of the file are stored. The total file becomes segmented into undefined pieces that can still be read by the utility but cannot be associated with a particular filename in the FAT. Over a period of time, lost units can pile up and occupy large amounts of disk space. To remove lost units from the drive, you can add an /F switch to the command so that the lost units will be converted to files that can be investigated and removed if necessary. In some cases, the converted file is a usable data file that can be rebuilt for use with an application. The CHKDSK /F command is often used before running a drive-defragmentation program.

2. **C.** In an incremental backup operation, the system backs up files that have been created or changed since the last backup. Restoring the system from an incremental backup requires the use of the last full backup and each incremental backup taken since then. Therefore, this method requires the least amount of time to back up the system, but the most amount of time to restore it.

3. **B.** Because fragmented files do not provide for efficient reading, the drive takes longer to complete multisector read operations. The defragmentation program realigns the positioning of related file clusters to speed up the operation of drive access operations.

4. **C.** In Windows 2000, the Disk Defragmenter utility is located under the Start/Programs/Accessories/System Tools path. The Defragmenter can also be accessed through the Start/Settings/Control Panel/Administrative Tools/Computer Management path.

5. **D.** The Windows 2000 Computer Management console can be accessed by Alt+clicking the My Computer icon and selecting the Manage option from the pop-up menu. The console includes the System Tools, Storage, and Services and Applications consoles. The Storage console provides a standard set of tools for maintaining the system's disk drives. These tools include the Disk Management tool, the Disk Defragmenter utility, and a Logical Drives utility.

6. **A.** When a device conflict is suspected, click the offending device in the listing, right-click the item, select Properties from the pop-up menu, and

then click the Resources tab to examine the Conflicting Devices list. You can also access the Properties window by double-clicking the device driver name.

7. C. Device Manager will display an exclamation point (!) inside a yellow circle whenever a device is experiencing a direct hardware conflict with another device. The nature of the problem is described in the device's Properties dialog box.

8. A. This arrangement can be established through Device Manager's Disable in This Hardware Profile option. This setting, located in the Properties window for that particular device, keeps the driver from loading up until it is reactivated.

9. A. The Backup utility is located in the C:\Windows\Start Menu\Programs\Accessories\System Tools directory.

10. A, C, D. There are several methods for accessing Task Manager in Windows 2000: press Ctrl+Alt+Del and then click the Task Manager button; press Ctrl+Shift+Esc; right-click the system tray; select Task Manager from the pop-up contextual menu.

11. C. The Dr. Watson utility is very useful in detecting application faults. When activated, Dr. Watson intercepts the software actions, detects the failure, identifies the application, and provides a detailed description of the failure.

12. A. The Dr. Watson utility is not located in any of the Windows 2000/XP menus. To use it, you must execute the program from the Start menu's Run option by typing the name **drwtsn32** into the dialog box and clicking OK to start the log file.

13. B. The System Configuration Utility (MSCONFIG.EXE) enables you to examine the system's configuration through a check box system. By turning different configuration settings on and off, problem settings can be isolated, and corrected by a process of elimination. You can access this utility through the System Information screen. From the Tools menu, select the System Configuration Utility. This tool is especially useful in controlling which programs will load at startup.

14. C. Although there is a copy of the REGEDIT.EXE tool in Windows 2000 and XP, this version was designed to work with earlier Windows versions. REGEDT32 is the primary registry editor tool in both Windows 2000 and XP.

15. B. The Windows Removable Storage Management system does not recognize CD-R, CD-RW, or DVD-R devices as backup media, even though there are options to add these devices through the utility.

16. D. It is a good idea to periodically perform restore operations from backup copies to diverse locations. This will enable you to validate the backups. You do not want to wait until the system fails to find out that the backups you've been making on a regular basis don't work. Also, the worst time to learn how to restore data is when you are in the middle of a crisis.

17. B. Technicians should be aware of the EXTRACT command. This utility is used to pull needed files from the Windows distribution media so they can be used to replace corrupted or missing files that are preventing the system from working.

18. B. In addition to backing up data files and applications, it is often convenient to back up the key system configuration settings and data information as well. This type of data is called *System State data* and is stored so that the system can be rebuilt quickly in case of a failure.

19. A. The full backup process backs up the entire contents of the disk. This includes directory and subdirectory listings and their contents. This backup method requires the most time each day to backup, but requires the least time to restore the system after a failure.

20. B. The Defrag utility requires that at least 15% of a volume being defragmented be available as free space.

21. A, B. The CHKDSK and Defrag utilities are designed primarily to optimize the performance of the system's disk drives

22. B. The command-line version of the defragmenter (defrag.exe) moves scattered, randomized file segments into a logical pattern that provides optimum read and processing times for the drive's circuitry.

Challenge Solutions

1. First you will need to establish a security audit policy to create logs of security events that occur at each station. The security log contains information generated by audit policies that have been enacted in the operating system. If no audit policies are configured, the security log will remain empty. The Event Viewer can be used to examine the Security logs for each workstation PC and the network server.

2. In Windows 2000, pressing the Ctrl+Shift+Esc key combination directly accesses the Task Manager window so that you can remove nonfunctioning applications from the list of tasks.

3. Under these conditions, your best move is to use the Last Known Good Configuration startup option to get the system back up and running. The attempt to update the new driver removed the option to use the Device Rollback option (it can remember only one previous layer of drivers).

4. The CHKDSK utility can be used to check the disk for corruption and cross-linked files or bad allocation units. The /F switch can be used to cause the utility to repair the files if found. This utility should be on the boot disk. If so they can run it to check the C:\ drive by typing **CHKDSK C: /F** from the boot prompt.

CHAPTER SEVENTEEN

Basic Operating System Troubleshooting and Maintenance

Terms you'll need to understand:

✓ Device Manager

✓ Task Manager

✓ MSCONFIG.EXE

✓ Blue screen

✓ Restore points

✓ Emergency Repair Disk

✓ Automated System Recovery

✓ Safe Mode

✓ Recovery console

✓ Event Viewer

✓ Advanced Options menu

Techniques you'll need to master:

Essentials 3.3—Identify tools, diagnostic procedures, and troubleshooting techniques for operating systems.

✓ Identify basic boot sequences, methods, and utilities for recovering operating systems.

  ✓ Boot methods (Safe Mode, recovery console, boot to restore point)

  ✓ Automated System Recovery (ASR) (for example, Emergency Repair Disk [ERD])

✓ Identify and apply diagnostic procedures and troubleshooting techniques, for example:

  ✓ Identify problem by questioning user and identifying user changes to the computer.

  ✓ Analyze problem including potential causes and initial determination of software and/or hardware problem.

  ✓ Test related components, including connections, hardware and software configurations, Device Manager, and consult vendor documentation.

    ✓ Evaluate results and take additional steps if needed, such as consultation, alternative resources, and manuals.

    ✓ Document activities and outcomes.

✓ Recognize and resolve common operational issues, such as blue screen; system lockup; input/output device; application install, start or load, and Windows-specific printing problems (for example, print spool stalled, incorrect or incompatible driver for print).

✓ Explain common error messages and codes, for example:

    ✓ Boot (invalid boot disk, inaccessible boot drive, missing NTLDR)

    ✓ Startup (device/service failed to start, device/program in Registry not found)

    ✓ Event Viewer

    ✓ Registry

    ✓ Windows reporting

Technical Support 2.3/IT Technician 3.3—Identify tools, diagnostic procedures, and troubleshooting techniques for operating systems.

✓ Recognize and resolve common operational problems, for example:

    ✓ Windows-specific printing problems (for example, print spool stalled, incorrect/incompatible driver form print)

    ✓ Auto-restart errors

    ✓ Blue screen error

    ✓ System lockup

    ✓ Device driver failure (input/output devices)

    ✓ Application install, start, or load failure

✓ Recognize and resolve common error messages and codes, for example:

    ✓ Boot (invalid boot disk, inaccessible boot device, missing NTLDR)

    ✓ Startup (device/service has failed to start, device/program references in Registry not found)

    ✓ Event Viewer

    ✓ Registry

    ✓ Windows (reporting)

✓ Use diagnostic utilities and tools to resolve operational problems, for example:

    ✓ Bootable media

    ✓ Startup modes (for example, Safe Mode, Safe Mode with Command Prompt or Networking, step-by-step/single-step mode)

    ✓ Documentation resources (for example, user/installation manuals, Internet/web-based, training materials)

    ✓ Task and Device Manager

    ✓ Event Viewer

✓ MSCONFIG

✓ Recovery CD/Recovery partition

✓ Remote Desktop Connection and Assistance

✓ System File Checker (SFC)

IT Technician 3.3—Identify tools, diagnostic procedures, and troubleshooting techniques for operating systems.

✓ Demonstrate ability to recover operating systems (for example, boot methods, recovery console, ASR, ERD).

Introduction

This chapter covers a major portion of the Diagnostic Procedures and troubleshooting Techniques for Operating Systems areas of the CompTIA A+ Certification—Essentials examination under Objective 3.3. The second half of the PC system is software, and the main piece of software that technicians have to deal with is the operating system.

Unless you are installing a new operating system or upgrading a system to a new operating system, there are really only two categories of operating system problems that you must deal with: startup problems (those that occur when the system is booting up) and operational problems (those that occur during the normal course of operations). By isolating a particular software problem to one of these areas, the troubleshooting process becomes less complex.

▶ Startup problems usually produce conditions that prevent the system hardware and software from starting and running correctly. These problems fall into two major groups: hardware configuration problems and operating system bootup problems.

▶ Operational problems are problems that occur after the system has booted and has started running. These problems fall into three main categories: when performing normal application and file operations, when printing, and when performing network functions.

The PC technician must be able to identify and correct both startup and operational problems associated with the operating system, including printing problems related to the Windows environment.

NOTE

Major portions of Tech Support Technician Objective 2.3 and IT Technician Objective 3.3 are identical to the material in Essentials Objective 3.3.

The "Identify and apply diagnostic procedures and troubleshooting techniques" section of Essentials 3.3 is unique to that section and is not mentioned in the Tech Support Technician or IT Technician objectives.

Essentials 3.3 requires only "Explaining error messages and codes," whereas Tech Support Technician 2.3 and IT Technician 3.3 go further to require that you "Recognize and resolve" those messages and codes.

Tech Support Technician 2.3 and IT Technician 3.3 add "Auto-restart errors" to the list of problems under the "Recognize and resolve common error messages and codes" section of Essentials 3.3.

The "Use diagnostic utilities and tools to resolve operational problems" section is unique to Tech Support Technician 2.3 and IT Technician 3.3.

The "recovering operating systems" portions of Essentials 3.3 and IT Technician 3.3 are identical.

The topics specified in these different exam/objective areas are so closely stated that it makes sense that they are presented as the same discussion. You will need to study the material in this chapter for any of the four exams you intend to challenge.

General OS Troubleshooting Process

Troubleshooting operating system problems involves the same steps as any other logical troubleshooting procedure. The steps are just adapted to fit the structure of the operating system. Analyze the symptoms displayed, isolate the error conditions, correct the problem, and test the repair.

As with suspected hardware-related problems, begin troubleshooting startup and other operating system problems by talking to the person who reported the problem. Remember that one of your first tasks is to eliminate the user as a possible cause of the problem. In particular, you should determine whether the user has changed something such as hardware components or operating system configurations since the last time the system successfully booted.

Ask the user to demonstrate in a step-by-step manner the procedure that led to the malfunction. This communication can help you narrow a problem down to a particular section of the computer. Gain an understanding of the process the user is trying to complete. Next, remove the operator from the situation and observe the symptoms of the malfunction to verify the problem for yourself. Attempt to limit the problem to the hardware involved, the software package being used, and then the operator.

Perform tests and make changes to the operating system one at a time, taking time to evaluate the effects of the change before making additional changes. Don't forget to check related components such as configuration settings.

Take time to document the steps you take along with the outcome of each. This can prevent wasting time performing repetitive steps and can be helpful in repeat service efforts. In addition, properly documenting your troubleshooting efforts can save technicians who follow you time and effort because they will not need to perform the steps you did.

Finally, refer to any available information and troubleshooting resources to assist in the troubleshooting and repair process. These resources include user manuals, online tutorials, and vendor documentation. You may occasionally need to consult with others, such as manufacturer's reps or technicians, or other professionals.

Troubleshooting Startup Problems

Fortunately, only a few problems can occur during the startup process of a disk-based computer. These problems include the following:

- ▶ Hardware problems

- ▶ Configuration problems

- ▶ Bootup (or OS startup) problems

- ▶ Loading failure of the operating system desktop GUI

All four of the previously listed problem types can result in startup failures. Some prevent any activity from appearing in the system, others produce symptoms that can be tracked to a cause, and yet others produce error messages that can be tracked to a source.

NOTE

A key troubleshooting point occurs at the single beep in the bootup process of most computers. If the system produces an error message or a beep-coded error signal before the single beep, the problem is hardware related. On the other hand, if the error message or beep code is produced after the single beep occurs, the problem is likely to be associated with starting up the operating system. At this point, the problem becomes primarily a software problem (specifically, an operating system startup problem). You'll often hear these beeps referred to as *beep codes*. Beep codes vary from BIOS to BIOS. Check with the BIOS manufacturer's website to learn how to interpret the beep codes you hear on a malfunctioning computer.

General Bootup/Startup Problems

Under Windows operating systems, startup problems can be divided into two subgroups: *bootup problems* and *startup problems*. Generally, bootup problems involve the activities that occur between the single beep and the time the `Starting Windows` message appears on the screen. Startup problems occur between the appearance of the message and the appearance of the Windows desktop on the display. How you troubleshoot these problems depends somewhat on when these problems occur.

When you are dealing with starting up a disk operating system, the following four things can prove very useful to help you isolate the cause of startup problems:

- ▶ Error messages
- ▶ Clean boot disks (Emergency Start disks)
- ▶ Operating system startup tools
- ▶ System log files

If the system will not boot up correctly, there are two possible actions you can take:

- ▶ Boot the system into an alternative boot mode (Safe Mode, for instance).
- ▶ Boot the system to a different device, such as a floppy disk drive or a CD-ROM drive.

If the system fails to start up properly, the Windows operating systems offer a variety of alternative startup tools to work with. These tools can be used to start the system in minimized configurations or to look around the system after an alternative boot mode has been successful. They typically boot the system to some minimized configuration level that bypasses selected unnecessary configuration and GUI-related settings to establish a point to begin troubleshooting the problem.

If the system boots up from one of the minimized conditions, the problem exists in the bypassed files. You must replace these files to get the system up and running normally. Different Windows tools can be used to manually copy files back to the disk, or you may wind up reinstalling the operating system to restore the corrupt or missing files.

If none of the alternative boot methods get the system to a level where you can work with it, you must try to boot the system to an alternative device. To boot to an alternative drive, you must ensure that the system is configured to search for that drive in the CMOS Setup utility and have a bootable disk in that drive when you turn it on. This normally involves using some type of clean boot disk or the Setup disk to start the system. A *boot disk* (or disc) is one that has an operating system that can be used to start the system.

If the system boots to another device and you can see the drive, you may be able to save the data on the disk by repairing its boot files. If you cannot access the drive structure after booting to an alternative device, you have two possible alternatives: you can try to repartition and reformat the drive, or you can physically replace the drive. If the drive has a physical hardware failure, you will not be able to restructure the drive. In either case, you will not be able to save the data from the drive; you can only hope there is a current backup on a different media.

Windows 2000/XP Startup Tools

Both Windows 2000 and Windows XP provide a wealth of tools for recovering from a startup problem, including the following:

- ▶ Windows 2000/XP Safe Mode options
- ▶ Windows 2000/XP MSCONFIG.EXE utility
- ▶ Windows 2000/XP Recovery Console
- ▶ Windows 2000/XP Emergency Repair Disk
- ▶ Windows XP System Restore Function
- ▶ Windows XP Automated System Recovery
- ▶ Windows XP Driver Rollback option

Using Startup Modes

If the system does not startup normally, you must first try to start the system in a minimum configuration to establish a point from which to begin troubleshooting the problem. This should also be attempted if the system makes it past the Starting Windows message before it hangs up. Using minimal startup methods enables you to bypass any unnecessary configuration and typically involves using a clean boot disk or the Emergency Start disk to start the system.

If the system starts up from the minimal condition, the problem exists in the bypassed files. Restart the system and select a startup mode that single-steps through the configuration and startup file sequence.

The single-step startup procedure enables you to isolate the problem command. If the system crashes while trying to execute a particular command, restart the bootup process and skip the offending command. Repeat the process until the system reaches bootup. Track all offending commands so that you can correct them individually. Check the syntax (spelling, punctuation, and usage) of any offending lines.

The Windows 2000 and Windows XP operating systems incorporate a number of startup options that can be engaged to get the system up and running in a given state to provide a starting point for troubleshooting operations. The Advanced Options menu, depicted in Figure 17.1, contains several options that can be of assistance when you're troubleshooting Windows startup failures. To access this menu, hold down the F8 function key when the `Starting Windows` message is displaying onscreen.

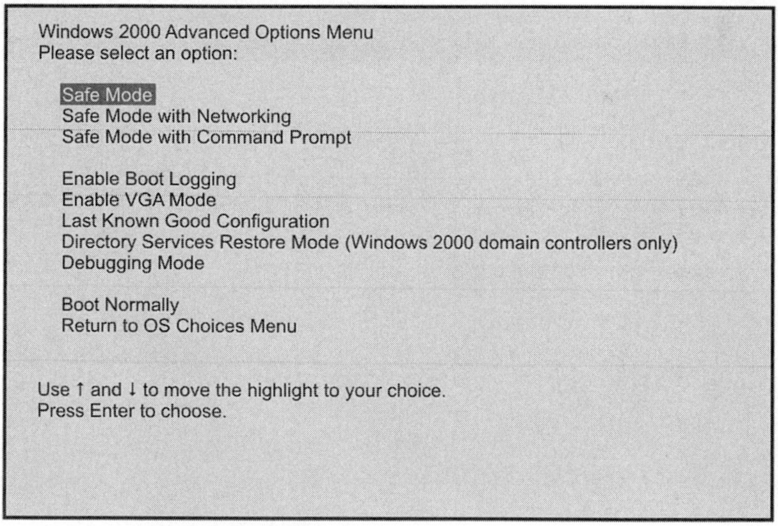

```
Windows 2000 Advanced Options Menu
Please select an option:

Safe Mode
Safe Mode with Networking
Safe Mode with Command Prompt

Enable Boot Logging
Enable VGA Mode
Last Known Good Configuration
Directory Services Restore Mode (Windows 2000 domain controllers only)
Debugging Mode

Boot Normally
Return to OS Choices Menu


Use ↑ and ↓ to move the highlight to your choice.
Press Enter to choose.
```

FIGURE 17.1 The Advanced Options menu.

Safe Mode

The Advance Options menu provides several variations of Safe Mode options that can be used to start the system using a minimized subset of the complete system. Windows 2000/XP has a Boot Normally start option and three Safe Mode startup options:

- ▶ Boot Normally
- ▶ Safe Mode

▶ Safe Mode with Networking

▶ Safe Mode with Command Prompt

Each option is customized for specific situations and disables selected portions of the system to prevent them from interfering with the startup process.

If Windows determines that a problem preventing the system from starting has occurred, or if it senses that the Registry is corrupt, it automatically attempts to restart the system in Safe Mode. This mode bypasses several startup files to provide access to the system's configuration settings. In Safe Mode, the minimal device drivers (keyboard, mouse, and standard-mode VGA drivers) are active to start the system. However, the CD-ROM drive will not be active in Safe Mode.

EXAM ALERT

Know what files are loaded into the system when it is started in Safe Mode.

Unless modified, the Safe Mode screen appears as depicted in Figure 17.2. Active functions appear onscreen along with the Safe Mode notice in each corner. However, there is no taskbar in Safe Mode.

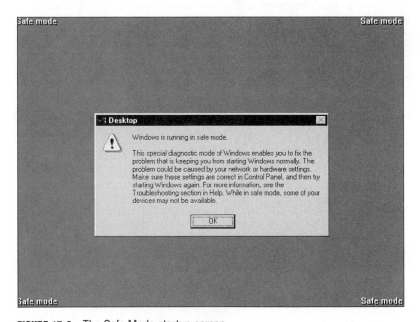

FIGURE 17.2   The Safe Mode startup screen.

The standard Safe Mode startup option is used when the system

- ▶ Will not start after the `Starting Windows` message appears onscreen

- ▶ Stalls repeatedly or for long periods of time

- ▶ Cannot print to a local printer after a complete troubleshooting sequence

- ▶ Has video display problems

- ▶ Slows down noticeably or does not work correctly

The only device drivers loaded in Safe Mode are the mouse driver, the standard keyboard driver, and the standard VGA driver. This should enable enough of the Windows structure to operate so that the offending portions can be isolated and repaired using step-by-step checking procedures.

The Safe Mode with Networking option loads the normal Safe Mode files and includes the basic network driver files. This mode is used in networked environments when the system

- ▶ Stops responding when a remote network is accessed

- ▶ Cannot print to a remote printer

- ▶ Stalls during startup and cannot be started using a normal Safe Mode startup

If the Safe Mode option will not start the system, reboot the computer and select the Safe Mode with Command Prompt option from the menu. Selecting this mode causes the system to boot to the command line, using the startup files and the Registry. The system will start in Safe Mode with minimal drivers (while not executing any of the startup files) and will produce the command-line prompt. It does load the command interpreter CMD.EXE. You can also use this mode to

- ▶ Employ command-line switches, such as `WIN d/x`

- ▶ Employ command-line instructions and text editors

Other Windows Startup Options

In addition to the different Safe Mode options, the menu also provides a number of other startup options carried over from previous Windows NT versions:

- ▶ Enable Boot Logging—This creates a log file called NTBTLOG.TXT in the root folder. This log is very similar to the BOOTLOG.TXT file described earlier in that it contains a listing of all the drivers and services that the system attempts to load during startup and can be useful when trying to determine what service or driver is causing the system to fail.

▶ Enable VGA Mode—When selected, this option boots the system normally, but uses only the standard VGA driver. If you have configured the display incorrectly and are unable to see the desktop, booting into VGA mode will enable you to reconfigure those settings.

▶ Last Known Good Configuration—This option will start Windows 2000 or XP using the settings that existed the last time a successful user logon occurred. All system setting changes made since the last successful startup are lost. This is a particularly useful option if you have added or reconfigured a device driver that is causing the system to fail.

▶ Debugging Mode—This starts Windows 2000 or XP in a kernel debug mode that will enable special debugger utilities to access the kernel for troubleshooting and analysis.

These startup modes play an important role in getting a Windows 2000 or Windows XP operating system up and running when it fails to start. You must press the spacebar while they are displayed on the screen to select one of the optional startup modes. If no selection is made, the system will continue with a normal startup sequence as previously outlined, using the existing hardware configuration information.

Challenge #1

You are working on a customer's Windows 2000 system and you notice that the display resolution is running well below what you expect from the video card. When you attempt to change the video driver to get better display performance from it, you see only horizontal streaks across the screen after you reboot the machine. Which Windows 2000 startup mode provides the best choice for quickly accessing the display setup so that you can correct it?

Using MSCONFIG.EXE

If a startup problem disappears when the system is started using any of the safe modes, use the command-line system configuration utility (MSCONFIG.EXE) to isolate the conflicting items.

Select the Diagnostic Startup option to start the system using only the basic device drivers and services. This option is equivalent to the standard Safe Mode startup. If the system starts using this option, advance to the Selective Startup option and restart the system. The Selective Startup option interactively loads device drivers and software options according to the check boxes enabled on the General tab.

Start the troubleshooting process with only one box checked. If the system starts up with that box checked, add another box to the list and restart. When the system fails to start, move into the tab that corresponds to the last option you enabled and step through the check boxes for that file, one at a time until the system fails again. You can use the Edit button to manually edit the lines of the file. This step-by-step process is used to systematically enable or disable items until all the problem items are identified.

The Expand File button is used to extract individual Windows files directly from the cabinet files on the distribution/installation media, under the I386 folder. The Launch System Restore button can be used to restore the system if changes made to the configuration increase the level of the problem. You should use this button to create a restore point before you begin troubleshooting.

EXAM ALERT

Know which Windows utility can be used to selectively turn startup options on and off for diagnostic purposes.

Windows XP Drive Rollback

If the system starts in Safe Mode, one of the possible causes of the failure is a wrong or corrupt device driver. In a Windows XP system, this condition can be corrected through the Device Manager's Driver Rollback function. To roll back the driver, you will need to access the Device Manager utility. From the Device Manager's main page, right-click the device in the listing and select the Properties option. Click the Driver tab and then the Roll Back Driver button.

EXAM ALERT

Know how to access the Windows XP Driver Rollback function.

Windows 2000/XP Recovery Console

The Recovery Console available in Windows 2000 and Windows XP is a command-line interface that provides you with access to the hard disks and many command-line utilities when the operating system will not boot (that is, after the Last Known Good Configuration and Safe Mode options have been tried). The Recovery Console can access all volumes on the drive, regardless of their file system type. However, if you have not added the Recovery Console option prior to a failure, you will not be able to employ it and you will need to use the Windows 2000 Setup disks or the Windows 2000/XP distribution CD instead. You can use the Recovery Console to perform tasks such as the following:

▶ Copy files from a floppy disk, CD, or another hard disk to the hard disk used for booting, enabling you to replace or remove files that may be affecting the boot process. Because of the security features in Windows 2000 and Windows XP, you are granted only limited access to certain files on the hard drive. You cannot copy files from the hard drive to a floppy or other storage device under these conditions.

▶ Control the startup state of services, enabling you to disable a service that could potentially be causing the operating system to crash.

▶ Add, remove, and format volumes on the hard disk.

▶ Repair the master book record (MBR) or boot sector of a hard disk or volume.

▶ Restore the Registry.

The Recovery Console can be permanently installed on a system so that it is accessible from the Advanced Options menu. It can be started at any time by booting from the Windows 2000 Setup disks or the Windows 2000/XP distribution CDs, choosing to repair an installation, and selecting Recovery Console from the repair options.

You can run the Recovery Console from the distribution CD for both Windows 2000 and Windows XP. To do so, start the system with the distribution CD in the drive and choose the Repair (Press the R Key) the Installation option. Enter the administrator's password to access the Recovery Console. The password protection for the Recovery Console permits only two incorrect attempts by default. On the third incorrect attempt, the system will stop accepting further entries for a predetermined amount of time (referred to as *lockout time*).

EXAM ALERT

Be aware of how to employ the Recovery Console utility when a system will not start.

When you start the Recovery Console, you are prompted to choose the folder that contains the Windows 2000 or Windows XP installation that you are trying to repair, and then to log on as Administrator. The commands that can be used with the Recovery Console include most of the MS-DOS-based commands. After you have logged on to the system, you can type **HELP** at the command line to obtain a list of available commands.

Table 17.1 displays the list of Recovery Console commands along with a brief description of each.

TABLE 17.1   Recovery Console Commands

Command	Description
ATTRIB	Changes attributes on one file or directory (wildcards are not supported)
BATCH	Executes commands specified in a text file
BOOTCFG	Scans hard disks to locate Windows installations and modifies or re-creates Boot.ini accordingly
CD	Displays the name of the current directory or switches to a new directory
CHDIR	Same as the CD command
CHKDSK	Checks a disk and displays a status report
CLS	Clears the screen
COPY	Copies a single file to another location (wildcards are not supported)
DEL	Deletes one file (wildcards are not supported)
DELETE	Same as the DEL command
DIR	Displays a list of files and subdirectories in a directory
DISABLE	Disables a Windows system service or driver
DISKPART	Manages partitions on a hard disk, including adding and deleting partitions
ENABLE	Enables a Windows system service or driver
EXIT	Quits the Recovery Console and restarts the computer
EXPAND	Expands a compressed file
FIXBOOT	Writes a new boot sector to the system volume
FIXMBR	Repairs the MBR of the system volume
FORMAT	Formats a disk for use with Windows XP
HELP	Displays a list of available commands
LISTSVC	Lists all available services and drivers on the computer
LOGON	Lists the detected installations of Windows XP and prompts for Administrator logon
MAP	Displays drive letter to physical device mappings
MAP ARC	Displays the ARC path instead of the Windows XP device path for physical device mappings

(continues)

TABLE 17.1 *Continued*

Command	Description
MD	Creates a directory
MKDIR	Same as the MD command
MORE	Displays a text file to the screen
RD	Removes a directory
REN	Renames a single file (wildcards are not supported)
RENAME	Same as the REN command
RMDIR	Same as the RD command
SET	Used to set Recovery Console environment variables
SYSTEM_ROOT	Sets the current directory to system_root
TYPE	Displays a test file to the screen (same as the MORE command)

One of the major Windows 2000/XP Recovery Console commands is the BOOTCFG command. This command can be used to change the configuration of the BOOT.INI file or to recover from bootup problems. The BOOTCFG command is available for use only in the Recovery Console.

> **EXAM ALERT**
>
> Be aware of the different commands available through the Recovery Console and how to use them.

Restoring the Registry

You can use the Recovery Console to restore the Windows 2000 or Windows XP Registries. Every time you back up the System State data with Windows 2000 Backup, a copy of the Registry is placed in the \Repair\RegBack folder. If you copy the entire contents of this folder or only particular files to \System32\Config (which is the folder where the working copy of the Registry is stored), you can restore the Registry to the condition it was in the last time you performed a System State data backup.

You can also accomplish this task through the Windows 2000 Backup/Restore function. You access it by navigating the Start/Programs/System Tools/Backup path. In Windows XP, the path is Start/All Programs/System Tools/Backup. It is recommended that you create a copy of the files located in \System32\Config prior to restoring the other files from backup. This way, you can restore the Registry to its original condition if necessary.

The Recovery Console can be started from the Repair option on the Windows 2000 Setup disks or distribution CD. You can also use the XP CD for XP systems. After installing the Recovery Console, you can access it through the Advanced Options menu at startup.

NOTE

If you have not added the Recovery Console option prior to a failure, you cannot employ it; you need to use the Windows 2000 Setup disks instead. You can also access the Recovery Console from the Windows XP Setup CD.

EXAM ALERT

Know which Windows 2000 utility can be used to restore backup copies of the Registry to the system.

Windows 2000 Startup and Emergency Repair Disks

In the Windows 2000 arena, the technician should have two different types of troubleshooting-related disks on hand: Setup disks and the Emergency Repair Disk (ERD).

Windows 2000 creates a four-disk set of Setup disks. These disks do not bring the system to a command prompt. Instead, they initiate the Windows Setup process. Under Windows 2000, you must place the distribution CD in the drive and launch the MakeBootDisk utility to create the four disk images for its Windows 2000 Setup disks. You can also create a setup disk from the command prompt using the MAKEBT32.EXE file for Windows 2000. These disks can also be made from the Start/Run/Browse/CD-ROM path. From the CD, select the BOOTDISK option followed by the MAKEBT32.EXE command.

Windows 2000 provides for an ERD to be produced. The ERD is different from the setup disks in that it is intended for use with an operational system when it crashes. It is not a bootable disk and must be used with the Setup disks or the distribution CD. Whereas the Setup disks are uniform for a given version of Windows 2000, the ERD is specific to the machine it is created from. It contains a copy of the Registry in Windows 2000. When dealing with the Windows 2000 ERD, it is necessary to manually copy the Registry files to the disk.

The Windows 2000 Setup routine prompts you to create an ERD during the installation process. The ERD can also be created using the Windows 2000 Backup utility located under the Programs/Accessories/System Tools path. Choosing this option will activate the Windows 2000 ERD Creation Wizard, depicted in Figure 17.3. The Windows 2000 ERD disk contains configuration information that is specific to the computer and that will be required during the emergency repair process.

EXAM ALERT

Know where ERDs are created in Windows 2000.

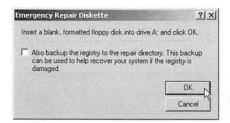

FIGURE 17.3 The ERD creation screen.

In many PC systems, you will need to make sure that the system is configured to check the floppy disk as part of the boot search sequence to use the Windows 2000 Setup and ERDs. This setting is configured in the CMOS Setup utility.

EXAM ALERT

Remember that the floppy disk drive must be enabled in the CMOS Setup utility to use Windows 2000 Setup and ERDs.

Performing an Emergency Repair in Windows 2000

The Windows 2000 ERD provides another repair option in the event that Safe Mode and the Windows 2000 Recovery Console do not enable you to repair the system. If you have already created an ERD, you can start the system with the Windows 2000 Setup CD or the Setup floppy disks, and then use the ERD to restore core system files. The Emergency Repair Process can perform the following functions:

- ▶ Repair the boot sector
- ▶ Repair the startup files
- ▶ Replace the system files

EXAM ALERT

Be aware that the Windows 2000 Emergency Repair Process is designed to repair the operating system only and cannot repair application or data problems.

To perform an emergency repair, follow these steps:

1. Boot the system from the Windows 2000 CD. If the system cannot boot from the CD, you will need to boot with the Setup Boot Disk, which is the first of four setup floppies that will be required. The setup floppies can be created with MAKEBOOT.EXE, which is in the \BOOTDISK folder off the root of the Windows 2000 CD.

2. When the text-mode portion of Setup begins, follow the initial prompts. When you reach the Welcome to Setup screen, press R to repair the Windows 2000 installation.

3. When prompted, choose the Emergency Repair Process by pressing R.

4. When prompted, press F for fast repair.

5. Follow the instructions and insert the Emergency Repair Disk into the floppy drive when prompted.

Windows XP Boot Disk

Although not Microsoft's recommended way of starting a failing Windows XP system, it is possible to make a Windows XP boot disk that can be used to bypass corrupted boot files at the root of the system volume and start the PC.

To create a Windows XP boot disk, follow these steps:

1. Start Windows XP and move into the My Computer windows.

2. Place a blank floppy disk in the disk drive.

3. Right-click the floppy drive icon in My Computer and select the Format option from the menu.

4. Verify the floppy parameters in the Format 3 1/2 Floppy (A:) page and click the Start button.

5. When the format operation is complete, copy the system's Ntldr, Ntdetect.com, and Boot.ini files to the floppy disk.

6. If Bootsect.dos and/or Ntbootdd.sys exist in the system, copy them to the floppy disk as well.

Ntldr and Ntdetect.com are generic files and can be used with any Windows XP installation. However, Boot.ini and Ntbootdd.sys are specific to the system that created them. Therefore, Windows XP boot disks may not work on different systems. Bootsect.dos cannot be used on any system other than the one that created it.

System File Checker

The System File Checker utility (SFC.EXE) is a Windows 2000/XP command-line utility that checks the system's protected files for changed, deleted, or possibly corrupt files. If it finds such files, it attempts to extract the original correct versions of the files from Windows files in the \system32\dllcache folder. SFC can be used to verify that the protected system files are the appropriate versions and to verify and replace files in the dllcache folder. The latter ensures that files used to replace invalid operating system files are actually valid.

System File Checker can be run manually or can be configured to run automatically when the system starts up. You can also use the Scheduled Tasks utility to configure SFC to run at specified intervals. You must have administrative privileges to run System File Checker. Table 17.2 lists the switches that can be used to modify the SFC operation. The actual run process is very quick on modern PCs and flashes on the screen for only an instant.

TABLE 17.2 SFC Switches

Switch	Action Performed
/scannow	This switch immediately scans all protected system files when it is activated. This operation is carried out only one time and requires access to the Windows 2000 or XP installation source files.
/scanonce	Scans all protected system files once at the next boot. Requires access to the Windows XP installation source files.
/scanboot	Scans all protected system files every time the system is booted. Requires access to the Windows XP installation source files.
/revert	This switch returns the scan to the default setting.
/purgecache	This switch purges the dllcache folder and immediately scans all protected file system files.
/cachesize=x	Sets the maximum size of the dllcache folder.

EXAM ALERT

Know which Windows utility can be used to establish the integrity of the Windows files.

Using Windows XP System Restore

To activate the Windows XP System Restore utility, navigate the Start/All Programs/Accessories/System Tools path, and then select the System Restore option from the menu.

> **NOTE**
>
> You must be a member of the Administrators group to use the System Restore feature.

To manually create restore points, select the Create a Restore Point option from the Welcome to System Restore screen (the Create a Restore Point option can also be accessed through the Start menu's Help and Support Center option). Click the Next button and enter the name for the restore point in the Restore Point Description dialog box, as illustrated in Figure 17.4. The System Restore utility will automatically add this name, along with the time and date, to the restore point list. Click Create to finish the process.

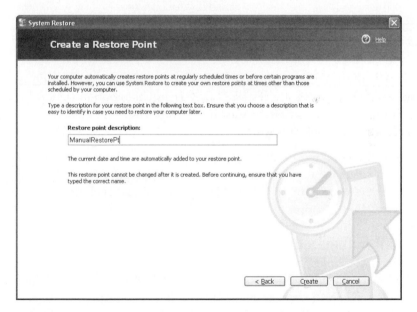

FIGURE 17.4 Creating a restore point.

Selecting the Restore My Computer to an Earlier Time option from the Welcome screen will enable you to select a restore point from a calendar and a list, as illustrated in Figure 17.5. Unless you need a restore point from earlier in the day, select the date on the calendar that you want to roll the system back to and, if there are multiple restore points for that day, choose the restore point you want to use.

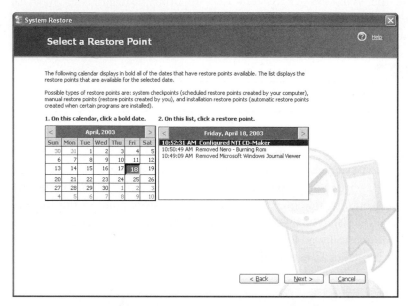

FIGURE 17.5 The Select a Restore Point screen.

After you have confirmed the restore point, the system will conduct the rollback and the system will automatically restart. There is an Undo option (Undo My Last Restoration) available that can be used if the restore operation did not solve the problem, or if the problem is worse.

To access the System Restore feature through the Start menu's Help and Support option, select the Performance and Maintenance option from its menu, click the Using System Restore to Undo Changes entry, and click the Run the System Restore Wizard option.

Windows XP Automated System Recovery

In the Windows XP Professional operating system, the Emergency Repair Disk has been replaced with an emergency startup tool called the Automated System Recovery (ASR). The ASR tool can be used to back up and restore the System State information, along with all the files stored on the system volume. As with the Windows 2000 Emergency Repair Disk, the ASR feature is considered to be the last resort that is used when you have been unable to recover the system using other methods, including Safe Mode, Last Known Good Configuration mode, and the Recovery Console.

> **NOTE**
>
> ASR is available only in Windows XP Professional—ASR is not available in Windows XP Home Edition. You can use the ASR Wizard if you install the Ntbackup program from the \Valueadd folder on the Windows XP Home Edition CD-ROM.

> **EXAM ALERT**
>
> Be aware that the ASR function replaces the Emergency Repair Process that was used in Windows 2000.

The ASR utility is a function of the NTBackup.exe backup utility. As with other backup options, ASR is a two-part system: backup and restore operations. ASR backups should be performed periodically to keep them up to date. On the other hand, an ASR restore operation is usually performed only in the case of a system failure. The contents of an ASR backup operation include the following:

- ▶ The System State data
- ▶ The system services
- ▶ The system components for all disks

In addition, an ASR floppy disk is created during the backup operation that contains additional information required for the ASR restore process. This disk contains two files:

- ▶ Asr.sif, which contains hard disk, partition, and volume configuration information along with general system information
- ▶ Asrpnp.sif, which contains PnP device configuration data

> **NOTE**
>
> Be aware that the ASR function can be used only to back up and restore system information. Therefore, you must make sure that you perform regular applications and data backup as well.

Conducting ASR Backups

ASR backup operations are performed through the Windows XP Backup utility as follows:

1. Access the Windows XP Backup utility and click the Next button on the Backup and Restore Wizard Welcome window.

2. From the Welcome window, switch to Advanced mode.

3. Click the Automated System Recovery Wizard button, as shown in Figure 17.6.

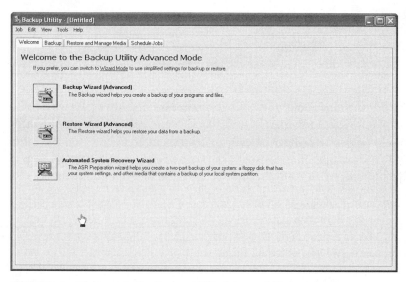

FIGURE 17.6 Welcome to the Backup Utility Advanced Mode screen.

4. Select a backup media type, specify the backup name, and click the Finish button to complete the ASR backup operation.

You should not place the ASR backup on the system or boot volume when specifying a location for the backup. The system volume is reformatted during an ASR restore, and depending on the condition of the system, the boot volume may be reformatted as well. You should also be aware that performing a restore operation from network shares is not an option with ASR. You must use local devices such as another hard disk, a CD-ROM, or a tape drive to hold the ASR backup.

NOTE

If the ASR backups are being used as a method of system restore, make sure that they are performed on a regular schedule.

ASR Restore Operations

The ASR restore process is launched from Windows XP Professional Setup as a part of the operating system install process (that is, the operating system is reinstalled and then the ASR backup information is used to complete the restoration of the system).

Three items are required to conduct the ASR restore operation. These items are

▶ The Windows XP distribution CD

▶ The ASR floppy disk

▶ The ASR backup

You should make sure that you have access to these items prior to launching an ASR restore operation.

To perform an ASR restore, boot the system using the Windows XP Professional CD and press the F2 function key when the Welcome to Setup screen is displayed. The ASR process should automatically start at this point. Then, when prompted, insert the ASR floppy disk and follow the onscreen prompts.

In the event that the ASR floppy disk is lost or damaged, the Asr.sif and Asrpnp.sif files can be recovered from the ASR backup. The Asf.inf and Asrpnp.inf files must reside at the root of the ASR floppy disk for them to be found during the ASR restore process.

Windows 2000/XP Startup Problems

If Windows 2000 or Windows XP fails to boot, the first troubleshooting step is to determine whether the computer is failing before or after the operating system takes control. If the startup process makes it to the beep that indicates the end of the POST, but you do not see the operating system's boot selection menu, the problem is probably one of the following:

▶ System partition

▶ Master Boot Record

▶ Partition boot sector

These types of problems are usually the result of hard disk media failures or a virus and must be repaired before the operating system will function. Typical symptoms associated with hard disk media failures include the following:

▸ A blue screen or Stop message appears.

▸ Bootup stops after the POST.

▸ The boot selection menu is never reached.

▸ An error message is produced.

▸ Unexpected reboot errors occur.

Windows 2000/XP may display a number of error messages related to these problems, such as the following:

▸ `Missing Operating System`

▸ `Disk Read Error`

▸ `Invalid Partition Table`

▸ `Insert System Disk`

▸ `Error Loading Operating System`

▸ `Inaccessible Boot Device`

▸ `Hard Disk Error` (or `Absent/Failed`)

▸ `At Least One Service or Driver Failed During Startup`

The `Error Loading Operating System` message from the preceding list indicates that the system partition was located but could not start the operating system. The system partition on that drive could be missing or misidentified.

The BOOT.INI or NTLDR files also could be missing or have become corrupted. If you receive a message stating `Kernel File Is Missing` or `NTLDR Could Not Be Found`, the partition boot sector is okay, but the NTLDR file is probably corrupt. An error stating that the NTLDR file cannot be found can also be caused by a missing BOOT.INI file.

To correct these problems, use the ATTRIB command-line utility to change the attributes. Copy the file over from the Startup disk to the root folder. All the startup files, including NTLDR, BOOT.INI, NTDETECT, and NTOSKRNL, can be restored from the ERD.

EXAM ALERT

Know which files must be present to boot Windows 2000/XP and how to correct problems associated with the Windows boot sequence.

The `Missing Operating System` and `Invalid Partition Table` errors indicate a problem with the Master Boot Record. In Windows 2000 and XP, you can use the Recovery Console's `FIXMBR` command to replace the Master Boot Record if the console has been installed beforehand. In Windows 2000, the Emergency Repair Process can be used to repair the boot sector.

You can also use the FDISK.EXE to restore an MBR in Windows 2000 or XP. Although this approach works well on a standalone drive, it does not work with disks that contain partitions or logical drives that are part of striped or volume sets. You also should not perform this procedure on drives that use third-party translation, partitioning, or dual-boot programs.

The `Inaccessible Boot Device` blue screen error occurs when applications, such as those furnished with CD-ROM recording packages, are removed from a Windows 2000 Professional system and the system cannot find boot information that has been referenced through the Registry. (That is, the application has written information directly into the Registry that the system is supposed to use for booting from CD-ROMs, but it is no longer there.)

You can use the Recovery Console to replace the System hive with an old copy that does not have the wrong value in it. Other options include disabling the CD-ROM service and copying the System hive from a similar (parallel) system. All these operations involve altering the system's Registry and, therefore, can seriously affect the system.

With some errors that occur during this time, the system will place a `Service or Driver Failed During Startup` message on the screen. This indicates that some information about a device or service that the system was looking for during the startup process was missing from the Registry or was corrupt. There are several tools you can use to investigate this problem: the Event Viewer utility, the Advanced Options menu's Boot Logging option, and the Recovery Console's `LISTSVC` command.

EXAM ALERT

Be aware of the Windows tools that can be used to troubleshoot services that fail to start during the startup process.

Start the system in Safe Mode and access the Event Viewer through the Start/Control Panel/Administrative Tools path. In the Event Viewer, open the system log and locate the offending service. Double-click the service to view a description of the error and obtain a link to the Microsoft Help and Support

Center, where an extended explanation is presented, along with possible corrective actions to be taken.

Challenge #2

A remote customer calls and complains that she is receiving a `Missing \System32\ system file` error message and the system stops operating. She thinks she should replace her hard drive and wants you to order it for her. What should you tell her?

Network Startup Problems

For network clients, such as Windows 2000 and Windows XP systems, there is one additional startup phase that could produce errors. This is the network logon phase (which is automatic in client/server network environments). During this period, the desktop should appear on the screen. However, several communication services are still being loaded into the system behind the scenes. Failure to load one of these services (or the device that supports it) will result in a `Device or Service Has Failed to Start` error message being displayed on the screen.

In most of these cases, you should still have a desktop display to work from. However, the system is working in a standalone fashion. In Windows 2000 or Windows XP systems, access the Event Viewer utility and expand the System node to view the event log of system events—such as loading the networking services. Even if no desktop is available, you can restart the system in Safe Mode and access the Event Viewer to use this log to isolate the cause of the error.

Authentication Problems

One last problem that can occur during startup (even though it is not actually a startup problem) is a logon problem. Basically, users cannot log on to systems when they don't have the proper authorization to do so. These problems tend to be very common in secure environments such as those that use Windows 2000 or Windows XP.

The most common logon problem is a forgotten or invalid username and password. Invalid usernames and passwords typically result from poor typing or from having the Caps Lock function turned on. Users also can be prevented from logging on because of station or time restrictions imposed. Check with the network administrator to see whether the user's rights to the system have been restricted.

When Windows 2000 or Windows XP is first installed, the only usable account is the Administrator account; the Guest account is disabled by default. If a user cannot log on, check the user's password. The password is case sensitive, so verify that the Caps Lock key is not an issue.

If you have forgotten the Administrator password and you have not created any other accounts with Administrator privileges, you must reinstall Windows 2000 or XP. Some third-party utilities may be able to help you recover the Administrator password, but you will usually find it easier to just reinstall the operating system at this point.

Common OS Operational Problems

After the system has reached a stable desktop display and the user has logged in, problems occurring in the system move into a category of problems called *operational* problems. These problems tend to manifest themselves in the following areas:

▶ Optional devices not checked by the system POST

▶ Applications

▶ Installing and Starting

▶ Printing operations

▶ Networking operations

Optional Devices Do Not Operate

The system's basic devices are configured as part of the system's PnP startup process in Windows 2000/XP systems; however, this doesn't mean that all the system's devices are in working order or that they will remain in working order while the system is on. Optional devices such as modems, sound cards, and advanced I/O devices may configure properly as part of the PnP process and then fail to operate after the system starts.

For example, many video cards are capable of displaying very high resolution screens at high refresh rates. However, some monitors do not have the same capabilities. When you configure the video card with settings that the monitor cannot display, symptoms may range from a simple blank screen to several ghost images being displayed onscreen. After the initial installation, the video drivers are always changed while Windows is operating.

To correct this problem, start the system in Safe Mode. This action causes Windows to load a basic VGA video driver, enabling you to then change the display properties of the video card. In a Windows 2000/XP system, you should select the VGA Mode option to gain access to the video configuration by loading a standard VGA driver.

Similarly, adding an input device such as a new mouse or joystick can create problems when the new device does not work under the Windows environment. In the Windows operating system, several tools help identify and isolate hardware-related problems. These tools include the Device Manager located under the Control Panel's System icon, the Hardware Troubleshooter procedures located under the Help entry of the Start menu, and the various hardware-related icons in the Control Panel.

Windows XP offers Device Driver Rollback, System Restore, and Disable the Device options that can be used to replace an updated driver (other than a printer driver) that may be causing problems. This option reinstalls the driver that was being used previous to the current driver and restores any driver settings that were updated when the driver was installed.

The System Restore feature can be used to restore the system and its applications to a previous operating configuration that was known to be working correctly at that point. You would resort to this method of changing the device driver in Windows XP after the Device Driver Rollback option did not repair the system.

The Disable the Device option should be used when you believe that a specific device is causing a system problem. This option disables the device and its drivers so that you can verify that it is the cause of whatever problem the system is experiencing.

Challenge #3

You believe your video display can produce a higher-resolution display than it is currently providing, so you change the video driver in your Windows XP Professional system. When you apply the new setting, you cannot see anything on the display. What should you do to regain control of your display?

Troubleshooting Stop Errors

Stop errors typically occur when new hardware or their device drivers have been installed, or when the system is running low on disk space. Stop errors also can occur on a system that has been running without a problem for months, but for whatever reason experiences a hardware error of some sort that causes the system to crash. You need to be aware that stop errors can happen for a variety of other reasons and can be very difficult to troubleshoot.

In Windows XP, stop errors may produce a condition where the system reboots seemingly for no reason. This is caused by a combination of a blue screen error and an Automatic Restart setting in Windows XP. The setting is designed to automatically reboot Windows when it detects a critical error in the system. Because the setting automatically kicks in when the system stops, you do not get to see the blue screen error message.

If the system is displaying this symptom, you must either check the error logs in the Event Viewer or disable the Automatic Restart feature to get to the error message so that you can begin to correct the problem causing the error. To disable the setting, right-click the My Computer icon and select Properties. In the Startup and Recovery section of the Advanced tab, click Settings and then remove the check from the Automatic Restart option in the System Failure section. You can also access the setting through the Advanced tab of the Control Panel's System icon. This will allow the blue screen error message to be displayed onscreen when it occurs.

There is no standard procedure for resolving stop errors, but you can do many things to potentially eliminate the error or to gain additional information about what caused it.

Use the following steps to troubleshoot blue screen/stop errors:

1. Restart the system to see whether the error will repeat itself. In many cases, a particular series of operations can cause the error. In these cases, restarting will correct the condition. However, if the stop error appears again, you will need to take additional action.

2. If you have recently installed new hardware in the system, verify that it has been installed correctly and that you are using the most current version of its device drivers.

3. Check the Microsoft's Windows Marketplace Tested Product page to verify that any newly installed hardware and device drivers are compatible with Windows 2000 or Windows XP.

4. Remove any newly installed hardware to see whether doing so relieves the stop error. If Windows starts, immediately use the Event Viewer to view any additional error messages that were generated before the stop error occurred. These messages will provide further information as to why the hardware caused the system to crash.

5. Try to start the operating system in Safe Mode. If you can start the system in Safe Mode, you can remove any newly installed software that could be causing the stop error. You can also remove or update device drivers that could be causing the stop error.

6. Attempt to start the system using the Last Known Good Configuration. This resets the system configuration to whatever the hardware configuration was the last time you were able to successfully boot the system, and it gives you the opportunity to try to install or configure a new hardware device again.

7. Verify that the latest operating system Service Pack has been installed.

8. Use TechNet or visit the Microsoft Support Center website and search for the particular stop error number to see whether you can get any additional information. The stop error number is noted in the upper-left corner of the stop screen.

9. Disable memory caching or shadowing options in the system CMOS Setup utility.

10. If possible, run diagnostic software on the system to check for memory errors.

11. Use a virus utility to check for viruses and eliminate any viruses if found.

12. Verify that the system's BIOS is the latest revision. If not, contact the manufacturer of your system to determine how to update the BIOS.

Windows 2000/XP Application Problems

Windows application problems tend to fall into two categories: the application will not install or the application will not start. A trio of Windows utilities are very useful for troubleshooting application problems:

▶ Event Viewer

▶ Task Manager

▶ System Monitor

Applications Will Not Install

Under Windows, most applications will autorun when their distribution CD is placed in the drive. The Autorun feature presents a user interface on the display that will guide the user through the installation process. If the Autorun feature in Windows 2000/XP is disabled in the drive's Properties page, the automatic interface will not start and the installation will not be performed.

You should check the distribution CD for the presence of the Autorun.inf file. If it is present and no autorun action occurs, you should examine the CD-ROM drive's Properties page to ensure that the Autorun function is enabled.

Some applications do not include the Autorun function as part of their installation scheme and are typically installed through the Control Panel's Add/Remove Programs applet. If an application is not on the Windows 2000 Application Compatibility Toolkit (ACT, the software equivalent of the HCL listing), the application may not install on the system or operate properly. This toolkit can be downloaded from the Microsoft MDSN Library web page at http://msdn2.microsoft.com/en-us/library/aa286552.aspx. The ACT utility will run on Windows 2003 Server, Windows XP, and 2000 Professional as well as on Windows 2000 Server with Service Pack 3 (SP3) installed.

Application Will Not Start

If an application will not start in Windows, you have several possibilities to consider:

▶ The application is missing or its path is incorrect.

▶ Part or all of the application is corrupted.

▶ The application's executable file is incorrectly identified.

▶ The application's attributes are locked.

▶ Incorrect application properties (filename, path, and syntax).

▶ Missing or corrupt Registry entries.

▶ Conflicting DLL files.

> **EXAM ALERT**
>
> Know what items to look for when applications will not start.

As with other GUI-based environments, Windows applications hide behind icons. The properties of each icon must correctly identify the filename and path of the application's executable file; otherwise, Windows will not be able to start it. Likewise, when a folder or file accessed by the icon or by the shortcut from the Windows Start menu is moved, renamed, or removed, Windows will not be able to find it when asked to start the application. Check the application's properties to verify that the filename, path, and syntax are correct. Applications' properties can be accessed by right-clicking their desktop icon, as well as by right-clicking their entry in the Start menu, My Computer page, or Windows Explorer screen.

EXAM ALERT

Be aware of the different methods of accessing an application's properties.

Most applications require Registry entries in order to run. If these entries are missing or corrupt, the application will not start. Corrupted or conflicting DLL files prevent applications from starting. To recover from these errors, you must reinstall the application.

Starting Applications from the Command Prompt

Another major operational problem that affects operating systems involves the application programs running in the system. Recall that in the Microsoft world, if the application is a BAT, EXE, or COM file, it should start when its name is properly entered on the command line. If such an application does not start in a command-line environment, you have a few basic possibilities to consider: It has been improperly identified, it is not located where it is supposed to be, or the application program is corrupted.

Check the spelling of the filename and reenter it at the command prompt. Also, verify that the path to the program has been presented correctly and thoroughly. If the path and filename are correct, the application may be corrupted. Reinstall it and try to start it again. Other possible reasons for programs not starting in a command-line environment include low conventional memory or disk space and file attributes that will not let the program start. In client/server networks, permission settings may not permit a user to access a particular file or folder.

Challenge #4

You have just installed a new Windows 2000 Professional operating system upgrade on a co-worker's machine. In the process of testing it, you discover that her word processor application will not start from the desktop icon. How should you go about troubleshooting this problem?

Locating Hidden Files

By default, Windows 2000 and Windows XP hide known filename extensions. If you cannot see filename extensions, open the Windows Explorer, click Tools, click Folder Options, click the View tab, and deselect the Hide File Extensions for Known Files option. Likewise, Windows 2000/XP by default does not display hidden or system files in Explorer. To see hidden or system files, open the Windows Explorer, click Tools, click Folder Options, click the View tab, and select the Show Hidden Files and Folders option.

> **EXAM ALERT**
>
> Be aware that Windows 2000 and Windows XP do not show hidden and system files by default. Also, know how to display these file types from the Windows environment.

Applying Task Manager to Application Problems

In Windows 2000 and XP, the Task Manager can be used to monitor the condition and operation of application programs and key Windows operating system services and components. In these operating systems, the Task Manager is available at any time and can be accessed by pressing the Ctrl+Alt+Delete key combination.

When the Task Manager appears, the Applications tab shows by default. This tab displays the applications that are currently running in the system along with a description of their status (that is, Running or Not Responding). When an application is present in this window and shows a Not Responding status, it has stalled and you should remove it. You can use this tab to remove these applications from the active system by highlighting the task and clicking the End Task button.

You should consult the Task Manager's Processes tab if the system is running slowly to determine whether an application is using more of the system's resources than it should. If the memory usage number for a given application consistently grows, the application may have a programming problem known as a *memory leak*. Over time, memory leaks can absorb all the system's free memory and crash the system.

Applying Event Viewer to Application Problems

Although blue screen stop errors are primarily associated with setup and configuration problems involving new hardware or software products, they can happen at any time. When a stop error occurs during the normal operation of a Windows 2000/XP system, you should restart the system and see if it reoccurs.

When the system restarts, use the Event Viewer utility to look for the source of the problem.

The Windows 2000 and Windows XP application logs can be used to examine the operation of the higher-end applications and some operating system services. The contents of this log can be examined through the Event Viewer utility to determine what conditions the system logged leading up to a failure, such as an application failing to start or stalling. The Event Viewer will show whether the application or service ran correctly. It may also indicate that conditions are present that you should take note of before they become failures.

Another indicator of application-related problems is the appearance of an Event Log Is Full error message. The event logs have a specified maximum file size that they can reach before they are considered full. By default, the event logs are set to overwrite any log data that is more than seven days old if they become full. Therefore, if events are occurring so quickly that the logs fill up before the default time, this indicates that an excessive number of system errors (events) are occurring. In addition, the Event Viewer will stop logging events until the seven days has passed. You should examine the full event log to determine what activity is accounting for so many loggable events. To clear the event logs so that the system will continue operating, access the Event Viewer and select the Clear All Events option from the Action menu list.

EXAM ALERT

Know how to clear an Event Log Full message in Windows XP.

In the case of failure events, the system usually generates a user alert through a pop-up dialog box on the screen. The information in the box will indicate the nature of the problem and refer you to the Event Viewer for details. The Event Viewer is available through the Start/Programs (All Programs in XP)/Administrative Tools/Event Viewer path.

EXAM ALERT

Know what items to look for when applications will not start.

Other Operational Problems

Because Windows 2000 and XP are typically used in client/server networks, some typical administrative problems associated with files, folders, and printers can pop up during their normal operations. These problems include the following symptoms:

- ▶ Users cannot gain access to folders.

- ▶ Users send a print job to the printer but cannot locate the documents.

- ▶ Users have Read permissions to a folder, but they can still make changes to files inside the folder.

- ▶ Users complain that they can see files in a folder but cannot access any of the files.

- ▶ Users complain that they cannot set any NTFS permissions.

- ▶ You cannot recover an item that was deleted by another user.

- ▶ You cannot recover any deleted items.

- ▶ You cannot find key files using Windows utilities.

A user's inability to gain access to folders can come from many places. In the Windows 2000/XP environment, the user might not have permissions that enable access to different files and folders. This is an administrative decision and can be overcome only by an administrator establishing permission levels that will permit access.

If the print job is not still in the local spooler or the print server, but Print Pooling is enabled, check all the printers in the pool. You cannot dictate which printer receives the print job. If the print job is visible in the spooler but does not print, this can be caused by the printer availability hours being set for times other than when the user submitted the print job.

If users have Read permission for a folder, but can still make changes to files inside the folder, their file permissions must be set to Full Control, Write, or Modify. These permissions are set directly on the file and override the folder permissions of Read. You can correct this by changing the permissions on the individual files or at the folder level and allowing the permissions to propagate to files within the folder.

When users complain that they can see files in a folder but cannot access any of the files, those users have most likely been assigned the List permission at the folder level. The List permission enables users to view the contents of the folder only and denies them all other permissions, including Read and Execute.

If you cannot set any NTFS permissions, the first item to check is that the file or folder is on an NTFS partition. FAT16 and FAT32 have no security options that can be assigned. If the partition is NTFS, the user must have Full Control permission to set any security permissions to a file or folder.

If the system can see files in a folder but cannot access any of them, the user might have been assigned the List permission at the folder level. The List permission enables users to view the contents of the folder only, denying them all other permissions, including Read and Execute.

In Windows, you cannot recover an item that was deleted by another user because the Recycle Bin is maintained on a user-by-user basis. If one user deletes something, only that user can recover it. You must log on as the user who deleted the items. Files and folders deleted from a floppy disk or network drive are permanently deleted and cannot be recovered. When the Recycle Bin fills to capacity, any newly deleted file or folder added causes older deleted items to be automatically deleted from the Recycle Bin.

> **EXAM ALERT**
>
> Be aware that files deleted from remote and removable storage devices do not appear in the Recycle Bin.

Windows-Related Printing Problems

In a Windows-based system, the Windows environment controls the printing function through its drivers. Check the printer driver using the Control Panel's Print applet to make certain that the correct driver is installed. Substitute the standard VGA driver and try to print a document.

Determine whether the Print option from the application's File menu is unavailable (gray). If it is, check the Windows Control Panel, Printers window for correct parallel port settings. Make certain that the correct printer driver is selected for the printer being used. If no printer type or the wrong printer type is selected, set the desired printer as the default printer. Check to see whether a printer switch box exists between the computer and the printer. If so, remove the print-sharing equipment and connect the computer directly to the printer.

Troubleshooting Windows Printing Problems

If a printer is not producing anything in a Windows environment even though print jobs have been sent to it, check the print spooler to see whether any particular type of error has occurred. To view documents waiting to be printed, double-click the desired printer's icon. While viewing the print spooler queue, check to make certain that the printer has not been set to the Pause Printing setting.

Return to the Printer folder, right-click the Printer icon, click Properties, and then select Details. From this point, select Spool Settings and select the Print Directly to the Printer option. If the print job goes through, a spooler problem exists. If not, the hardware and printer driver are suspect.

To check spooler problems, examine the system for adequate hard disk space and memory. If the Enhanced Metafile (EMF) Spooling option is selected, disable it, clear the spooler, and try to print. To check the printer driver, right-click the Printer icon, select the Properties option, and click the Details option. Reload or upgrade the driver if necessary.

> **EXAM ALERT**
>
> Remember how to test the operation of the Windows print spooler when the printer will not print.

If the printer operation stalls during the printing operation, some critical condition must have been reached to stop the printing process (that is, the system was running but stopped). Restart the system and try to print again. If the system still does not print, delete backed-up spool files (SPL and TMP) in the System/Spool/Printers directory.

> **Challenge #5**
>
> When you arrive at the customer's machine, the customer tells you that users have been sending files to the local printer but nothing comes out. When you check the local print queue, you see the files sitting there and determine that they are not moving. What steps should you take to get the printer back into operation?

Troubleshooting Windows-Related Network Printing Problems

The complexity of conducting printer operations over a network is much greater because the addition of the network drivers and protocols. Many of the problems encountered when printing over the network involve components of the operating system. Therefore, its networking and printing functions must both be checked.

When printing cannot be carried out across the network, verify that the local computer and the network printer are set up for remote printing. In the Windows operating systems, this involves sharing the printer with the network users. The local computer that the printer is connected to, referred to as the *print server*, should appear in the My Network Places window of the remote computer. If the local computer cannot see files and printers at the print server station, the File and Print Sharing function may not be enabled there.

EXAM ALERT

Be aware that not having File and Print Sharing enabled will cause computers to not "see" the other computers across the network.

In Windows, printer sharing can be accomplished at the print server in a number of ways. First, double-click the printer's icon in the Printer (or Printers and Faxes) dialog box, navigate the Printer/Properties/Sharing path, and then choose the desired configuration. The second method uses a right-click on the printer's icon, followed by selecting the Share entry in the pop-up context menu and choosing the desired configuration. The final method is similar except that you right-click the printer's icon, click Properties, click the Sharing tab, and then choose the configuration.

Run the printer's self-test to verify that its hardware is working correctly. If it will not print a test page, a problem exists with the printer hardware. Next, troubleshoot the printer hardware. When the operation of the hardware is working, attempt to print across the network again.

Next, determine whether the print server can print directly to the printer. Open a document on the print server and attempt to print it. If the file will not print directly to the local printer, a problem exists in the local hardware. Troubleshoot the problem as a local standalone printer problem.

If the local print server operation is working, verify the operation of the network by attempting to perform other network functions, such as transferring a file from the remote unit to the print server. In Windows 9x, open the Control Panel's Printer folder and select the Properties entry in the drop-down File menu. Check the information under the Details and Sharing tabs.

If other network functions are operational, verify the printer operation of the local computer. If possible, connect a printer directly to the local unit and set its print driver up to print to the local printer port. If the file prints to the local printer, a network/printer driver problem still exists. Reload the printer driver and check the network print path, as depicted in Figure 17.7. The correct format for the UNC network path is \\computer_name\shared_device_name.

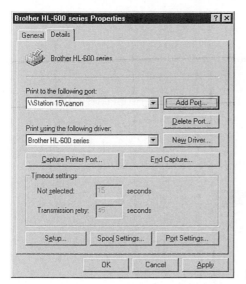

FIGURE 17.7 Checking the printer path.

If the printer operation stalls or crashes during the printing process, a different type of problem is indicated. In this case, the remote printer was functioning, the print server was operational, and the network was transferring data. Some critical condition must have been reached to stop the printing process. Check the print spooler in the print server to see whether an error has occurred. Also, check the hard disk space and memory usage in the print server.

> **EXAM ALERT**
>
> Know how to create a UNC path from a local computer to a remote printer or a directory located on a remote computer.

Using Remote Desktop/Assistance

When the remote user is accessing the remote computer, its desktop is locked down and local access by other users is not possible, except by an administrator. Users with administrative privileges can log on locally during the remote session. However, the remote session will be terminated.

Configuring the Remote Desktop Function

You must configure the Remote Desktop function in two parts: First, configure the remote target computer to accept Remote Desktop connections. Second, configure the local computer with Remote Desktop Connections or Terminal Services client software.

To configure the remote target computer to allow Remote Desktop connections, follow these steps:

1. Right-click the My Computer icon and select the Properties option from the pop-up menu.

2. In the Remote Desktop window of the Remote tab, select Allow Users to Connect Remotely to This Computer, as shown in Figure 17.8.

FIGURE 17.8 Enabling Remote Desktop.

3. Click the Select Remote Users button and add the appropriate user accounts (local administrators are automatically on the list and can access remote sessions without being invited). Verify that the accounts entered have passwords; these are required for Remote Desktop activities.

4. Click the OK button to return to the Remote tab. Click the OK button again to exit the Properties window.

Conducting Remote Desktop Sessions

To establish a Remote Desktop session from a Windows XP Professional computer, follow these steps:

1. Navigate the Start/All Programs/ Accessories/Communications path on the local computer to launch the Remote Desktop Connections client.

2. When the Remote Desktop Connection dialog box appears, as depicted in Figure 17.9, enter the name of the remote computer to access and click the Connect button. Clicking the Options button will display several tabs of configurable options, as shown in Figure 17.10. These options include

   ▶ General—On this tab, you can specify the username, password, and domain names that will be used for authentication. The tab also provides for saving and opening connection settings.

   ▶ Display—This tab includes options for configuring the parameters for the remote connection display. One of the key settings is how much of the local screen will be taken up by the remote desktop display. You want to be able to see the details of the remote screen but still have some access to the local desktop.

   ▶ Local Resources—This tab enables sound and keyboard configurations as well as which local devices to connect to when logged on to the remote computer.

   ▶ Programs—This tab provides the capability to automatically launch a program when a remote connection is established.

   ▶ Experience—This performance tab enables you to optimize the connection speed and control the display of the desktop background, themes, menu and window animation, and other items that can affect performance.

FIGURE 17.9 Establishing a Remote Desktop session.

> **NOTE**
>
> To use Remote Desktop connections, TCP port 3389 must be enabled if ICS, ICF, or another type of firewall is in use. The Windows Firewall link on the bottom of the System Properties/Remote page will automatically configure the Windows ICF for Remote Desktop operation.

FIGURE 17.10 Remote Desktop Connection properties.

3. Enter a username and password and click the OK button to log on to the remote computer.

4. If another user is also logged on to the remote system, a Logon Message dialog box will be displayed. To continue, you must click the Yes button. However, the other user will be logged off and any unsaved data the user has will be lost.

5. A Remote Desktop session like the one depicted in Figure 17.11 is established. In this case, the remote window is a fraction of the total display. It is possible to make the remote desktop cover the entire display. This setting is configured under the Options button described earlier.

FIGURE 17.11 A Remote Desktop session.

NOTE

After a connection has been established, the local desktop is locked for security reasons, preventing anyone from viewing the tasks that are being performed remotely.

6. Perform all the tasks you normally would if you were seated in front of the other computer.

7. When you're finished, end the remote session.

There are two acceptable methods of ending a remote session: Log off the remote computer normally, which will close all programs, log the user off, and then close the Remote Desktop connection; or disconnect by closing the Remote Desktop window or selecting Disconnect from the Start menu. This will leave the user logged on at the remote computer, and all programs will continue processing—the user will be reconnected to the same session the next time that user connects.

NOTE

One technique that does not work the same in a remote desktop as it does in the local setting is the Ctrl+Alt+Delete key combination. To access the Windows Security dialog box or the Task Manager utility on the remote unit, you must select the Windows Security option from the remote Start menu. Pressing Ctrl+Alt+Delete still brings up the local Security/Task Manager window.

Using Remote Assistance

Conducting a Remote Assistance session requires that both the user and the helper actively participate in establishing the connection. A Remote Assistance session is established in three phases:

1. The user requiring support sends a Remote Assistance invitation to the helper.

2. The helper responds to the invitation.

3. The user accepts the helper's assistance.

Establishing Remote Assistance Sessions

To send a Remote Assistance invitation, the user must perform the following steps:

1. Access the Help and Support screen from the Start menu.

2. Under the Ask for Assistance option, select Invite a Friend to Connect to Your Computer with Remote Assistance, followed by the Invite Someone to Help You option.

3. Select the utility you want to create the invitation with, as shown in Figure 17.12. As the figure illustrates, invitations can be sent directly to the helper using a Windows Messenger account or as an email attachment using Outlook. You can also create the invitation as a file and save it to a folder that the helper has access to, or send it as an email attachment. The email attachment or saved file will be given an .msrcindicent extension.

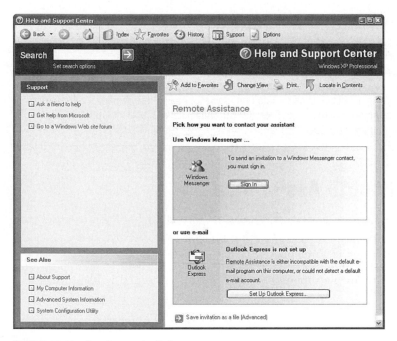

FIGURE 17.12 Creating an invitation.

4. When prompted, enter the requested information, including your name, a message, when the invitation should expire, and a password that the helper can use to establish the connection in a more secure fashion.

5. Click the Send Invitation option.

When the helper receives the invitation, the helper must respond in kind to continue the process. If the invitation was sent through Windows Messenger, the helper must accept the invitation using the Messenger pop-up window. Conversely, if the invitation was sent via email or as a file, the attached invitation must be accessed and opened to notify the user that the request has been accepted. When the user receives the confirmation, the user must click the Yes button in the Remote Assistance dialog box to establish the connection.

The Remote Assistance Consoles

After the Remote Assistance connection has been established, the user will receive the user's console displayed in Figure 17.13. The console provides a Chat History and Message Entry window for online chatting. The Connection Status window displays the connected helper information, along with the capabilities of the connection: View Only or In Control.

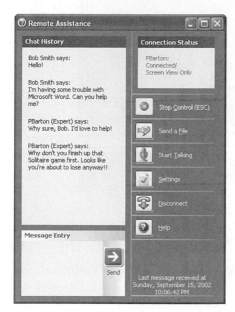

FIGURE 17.13 The Remote Assistance user's console.

Several other functions are available to the user through the buttons on the right side of the screen:

- ▶ Stop Control (ESC)—This button enables the user to regain control of the system after the helper has taken control.

- ▶ Send a File—You can use this option to send a file to the helper's computer.

- ▶ Start Talking—This feature is used to enable voice communications between computers with voice capabilities.

- ▶ Settings—The Settings button enables the user to adjust sound quality.

- ▶ Disconnect—This button is used to terminate the Remote Assistance connection.

- ▶ Help—Provides access to Remote Assistance help features.

On the helper end of the connection, the helper's console depicted in Figure 17.14 is displayed. This end of the connection has a corresponding Chat History and Message Entry window for online chatting. The other user's desktop is displayed in the Status window at the right side of the display.

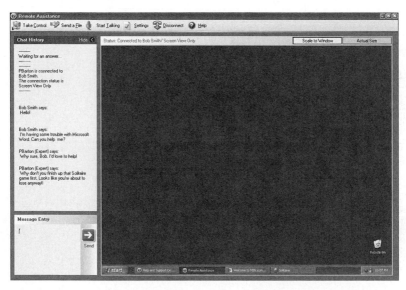

FIGURE 17.14   The Remote Assistance helper's console.

For the most part, the helper's console has a corresponding set of button options for those provided in the user's console. However, the notable exception is the Take Control/Release Control button. This button sends a request to the user to take shared control of the desktop. The user must accept the request to grant the helper access to the system. The user can cancel the connection at any time by clicking the Disconnect button or by pressing the Esc key.

When the helper establishes shared control of the user's system, the helper can fully manipulate the remote system as if he or she were physically sitting at it. This includes manipulating drivers, launching applications, and viewing event logs. However, the helper cannot move files from the user's computer to the helper's computer. The user's data is secure during the Remote Assistance connection.

Exam Prep Questions

1. What type of problem is the MSCONFIG.EXE utility used for?

   ○ **A.** Desktop configuration

   ○ **B.** Registry configuration

   ○ **C.** Network configuration

   ○ **D.** System configuration

2. In Windows 2000, which utility can be used to access hard drives and command-line utilities when the system does not boot?

   ○ **A.** Recovery Console

   ○ **B.** Computer Management console

   ○ **C.** Device Manager

   ○ **D.** REGEDT32.EXE

3. Which utility can be used to restore the Registry from a backup if you cannot boot to a GUI?

   ○ **A.** Backup

   ○ **B.** Regback

   ○ **C.** Recovery Console

   ○ **D.** Scanreg

4. Which of the following is not a function of the Emergency Repair Process in Windows 2000? (Select all that apply.)

   ○ **A.** Repairing the disk drive's boot sector

   ○ **B.** Repairing the system's startup files

   ○ **C.** Repairing corrupted data files

   ○ **D.** Repairing failed applications

5. Which drivers are loaded into the system when it is started in Safe Mode?

   ○ **A.** Standard mouse, keyboard, VGA drivers

   ○ **B.** Standard mouse, keyboard, VGA, CD-ROM drivers

   ○ **C.** Standard mouse, keyboard, VGA, network drivers

   ○ **D.** Standard mouse, keyboard, VGA, CD-ROM, network drivers

6. Which function key is used to access Safe Mode in Windows?

○ **A.** F1

○ **B.** F5

○ **C.** F8

○ **D.** F11

7. The Emergency Repair Process is designed to _____ and cannot be of assistance in repairing application or data problems.

○ **A.** Repair the file system

○ **B.** Repair the operating system

○ **C.** Repair the network configuration

○ **D.** Repair the desktop configuration

8. The _____ process will provide more efficient and faster operation of your system.

○ **A.** ScanDisk

○ **B.** Defragmentation

○ **C.** CHKDSK

○ **D.** Backup

9. What happens to information that has been deleted from removable media?

○ **A.** It is deleted from the file system.

○ **B.** It is moved into the Recycle Bin.

○ **C.** It is relocated to the System Backup directory.

○ **D.** The file is archived and held for later deletion.

10. What are the various methods of launching an application in the Windows XP environment? (Select all that apply.)

○ **A.** Start/All Programs, select the application's entry, and then select the shortcut to the executable file.

○ **B.** Start/Run, enter the full path and filename to the executable file, and then click the OK button.

○ **C.** Browse to the application's folder in Windows Explorer and then double-click the application's executable file.

○ **D.** Browse to the application's folder in Windows Explorer, click the executable file to highlight it, and then click the Edit menu and select the Open option.

11. The _____ in Windows 2000 and Windows XP can be used to remove nonfunctioning applications from the system.

   ○ **A.** Close Program tool

   ○ **B.** Task Manager tool

   ○ **C.** Close Application tool

   ○ **D.** Computer Management tool

12. How are hidden and system files displayed from the Windows 2000 environment?

   ○ **A.** Start/Settings/Control Panel/System/Folder Options/View tab; then select the Show Hidden Files and Folders option.

   ○ **B.** Open Windows Explorer/Tools/Folder Options; then select the Show Hidden Files and Folders option.

   ○ **C.** Start/Programs/Accessories/System Tools/Folder Options/View tab; then select the Show Hidden Files and Folders option.

   ○ **D.** Open Windows Explorer/Tools/Folder Options/View tab; then select the Show Hidden Files and Folders option.

13. What is a common reason for not seeing a remote printer in the Windows Network Places?

   ○ **A.** Inadequate access rights

   ○ **B.** File and printer sharing not enabled on the remote computer

   ○ **C.** Improper printer name

   ○ **D.** No driver loaded

14. How is a UNC path created from a local computer to a remote printer or to a directory located on a remote computer?

   ○ **A.** //Shared_resource_name

   ○ **B.** //Computer_name/shared_resource_name

   ○ **C.** \\Shared_resource_name

   ○ **D.** \\computer_name\shared_resource_name

15. Which types of deleted files do not appear in the Recycle Bin? (Select two answers.)

   ○ **A.** System files

   ○ **B.** Files from remote devices

   ○ **C.** Files from removable storage devices

   ○ **D.** Hidden files

16. When applications do not start in Windows, what items should be looked for? (Select all that apply.)

   ○ **A.** Conflicting DLL files

   ○ **B.** Incorrect application properties

   ○ **C.** Missing or corrupt Registry entries

   ○ **D.** Incompatibility with the installed operating system

17. During the boot process, your computer stalls and produces a blue screen with the words NTLDR missing displayed. Which of the following will best fix this problem?

   ○ **A.** Boot to the Advanced Options menu and start the system in Last Known Good Configuration.

   ○ **B.** Boot to Safe mode and run the Rollback feature from the Device Manager.

   ○ **C.** Boot to Safe mode and run the SFC utility.

   ○ **D.** Boot to Safe mode and run the MSCONFIG utility.

18. Which of the following is a valid bootup option when using Windows 2000 and Windows XP Professional distribution CDs to start the system?

   ○ **A.** The Last Known Good Configuration option.

   ○ **B.** Running the Automatic System Recovery option.

   ○ **C.** Opening the Recovery Console.

   ○ **D.** Running the MSCONFIG utility.

19. Which Windows utility can be used to selectively turn items off during the startup process for diagnostic purposes?

   ○ **A.** Safe Mode

   ○ **B.** MSCONFIG

   ○ **C.** SFC

   ○ **D.** Device Manager

20. Which of the following actions will write a new boot sector into the system volume of the boot drive?

   ○ **A.** Running the ASR Restore operation.

   ○ **B.** Running the Diagnostic Startup option from the Startup tab of the MSCONFIG utility.

   ○ **C.** Running the FIXBOOT command from the Recovery Console's command line.

   ○ **D.** By running the SYS C: command from the Windows command interpreter.

21. After upgrading a video adapter card's driver in Windows XP, the video display is scrambled. What action should you take to revert to the old driver version?

   ○ **A.** Boot into Safe Mode with command prompt only and remove the driver.

   ○ **B.** Boot into Safe Mode and run the Driver Rollback feature from the Device Manager.

   ○ **C.** Use the SFC utility to startup the system and roll back the driver.

   ○ **D.** Use the Recovery Console to reboot the system and then roll back the driver.

22. You need to reinstall Windows 2000 in an existing system that has failed. The system has a set of Emergency Start disks. Which of the following must occur so that the disks can be used to start the system, enabling you to carry out the repair function?

   ○ **A.** Change the HDD driver settings to the default value.

   ○ **B.** Change the boot sequence in the CMOS to include the FDD in the startup process.

   ○ **C.** Change the boot order in the BOOT.INI file.

   ○ **D.** The device driver for the FDD must be enabled.

Answers and Explanations

1. **D.** If a startup problem disappears when the system is started using any of the Windows safe modes, use the system configuration utility (MSCONFIG.EXE) to isolate the conflicting items. Of course, you may need to enter this command from the command line.

2. A. The Recovery Console is a command-line interface that provides you with access to the hard disks and many command-line utilities when the operating system does not boot. The Recovery Console can access all volumes on the drive, regardless of the file system type. However, if you have not added the Recovery Console option prior to a failure, you will not be able to employ it and will need to use the Windows 2000 Setup disks instead.

3. C. Every time you back up the System State data with Windows 2000 Backup, a copy of the Registry is placed in the \Repair\RegBack folder. If you must use the command line provided by the Recovery Console to restore the Registry, copy the entire contents of this folder or only particular files to \System32\Config (which is the folder where the working copy of the Registry is stored). You can restore the Registry to the same condition it was in the last time you performed a System State data backup. It is recommended that you create a copy of the files located in \System32\Config prior to restoring the other files from backup. This will enable you to restore the Registry to its original condition if necessary.

4. C, D. In Windows 2000, the Emergency Repair Process can be used to repair the boot sector, repair the startup files, and replace the system files. However, you should be aware that the Windows 2000 Emergency Repair Process is designed to repair the operating system only and cannot be of assistance in repairing application or data problems.

5. A. In Safe Mode, the minimal device drivers (keyboard, mouse, and standard-mode VGA drivers) are active to start the system. However, the CD-ROM drive will not be active in Safe Mode.

6. C. Safe Mode can be accessed at bootup by pressing the F8 key.

7. B. The Emergency Repair Process can perform the following functions: repair the boot sector; repair the startup files; and replace the system files. The Windows 2000 Emergency Repair Process is designed to repair the operating system only and cannot be of assistance in repairing application or data problems.

8. B. Because fragmented files do not provide for efficient reading by the drive, it takes longer to complete multisector read operations. The defragmentation program realigns the positioning of related file clusters to speed up the operation of drive access operations.

9. A. In the case of removable media, such as floppy disks and removable hard drives, the Recycle Bin does not retain the files deleted from these

media. When a file or folder is removed from one of these devices, the file information is deleted directly from the file system.

10. A, B, C. There are several acceptable methods of launching an application in the Windows environment: From the Start menu, select the Applications entry, click the folder where the desired application is, and double-click its filename; from the Start menu, select the Run entry, and then enter the full path and filename for the desired executable file; double-click the application's filename in Windows Explorer or in My Computer; click the File menu option from the menu bar in My Computer or Windows Explorer, and select the Open option; you can also Alt+click the application and choose Open.

11. B. In Windows NT, Windows 2000, and Windows XP, the Close Program dialog has been replaced by the Task Manager. This utility can be used to determine which applications in the system are running or stopped, as well as which resources are being used. You can also determine what the general microprocessor and memory-usage levels are. A nonfunctioning application can be removed using Task Manager in Windows 2000 and XP.

12. D. To see hidden or system files, open the Windows Explorer, click Tools, click Folder Options, click the View tab, and select the Show Hidden Files and Folders option. These files are not shown by default.

13. B. When printing cannot be carried out across the network, verify that the local computer and the network printer are set up for remote printing. In Windows, this involves sharing the printer with the network users. The local computer that the printer is connected to (referred to as the *print server*) should appear in the Windows 9x Network Neighborhood window of the remote computer. If the local computer cannot see files and printers at the print server station, file and print sharing may not be enabled there.

14. D. The correct format for the UNC network path to a shared network device is \\computer_name\shared_resource_name.

15. B, C. Files and folders deleted from a floppy disk or network drive are permanently deleted and cannot be recovered.

16. A, B, C. Windows 2000 and XP can all suffer from application problems such as incorrect application properties (filename, path, and syntax); missing or corrupt Registry entries; conflicting DLL files.

17. C. A Missing Operating System error, such as the Missing NTLDR error message, indicates a problem with the master boot record. In

Windows 2000 and XP, you can use the Recovery Console's `FIXMBR` command to replace the master boot record.

18. C. You can run the Recovery Console from the distribution CD for both Windows 2000 and Windows XP. To do so, start the system with the distribution CD in the drive and choose the option to Repair (Press the R Key) the installation. Enter the administrator's password to access the Recovery Console.

19. B. The Selective Startup option located under the MSCONFIG Diagnostic Startup selection interactively loads device drivers and software options according to the check boxes enabled on the General tab. Start the troubleshooting process with only one box checked. If the system starts up with that box checked, add another box to the list and restart. When the system fails to start, move into the tab that corresponds to the last option you enabled and step through the check boxes for that file, one at a time, until the system fails again.

20. C. The Recovery Console's `FIXBOOT` command writes a new boot sector to the system volume of the boot drive. You can run the Recovery Console from the Windows distribution CD.

21. B. Windows XP includes an option that can be used to revert to an older device driver when a driver upgrade causes problems with a device. This feature is called Driver Rollback and can be implemented through the Windows XP Device Manager.

22. B. To use the Windows 2000 Setup and ERDs, you must make sure that the system is configured to read the floppy disk drive through the CMOS Setup utility.

Challenge Solutions

1. In this situation, using Windows 2000 Professional, the most efficient mode that you can use to reset the video driver is VGA mode. In Windows 2000, you can change the video driver through this mode with a single reboot operation (although you would not need to reboot at all to change the resolution of the existing driver). Using Safe Mode to change the video driver in Windows 2000 would require that you reboot the system twice to complete the operation.

2. You should tell your customer that the error could be caused by a bad hard drive, but that it is more likely a missing or corrupted boot file that

can be restored without replacing the hard drive. At the very least, more extensive troubleshooting should be conducted before buying a new drive.

3. To correct this problem, start the system in Safe Mode. This action causes Windows to load a basic VGA video driver, enabling you to then change the display properties of the video card. In a Windows 2000/XP system, you should select the VGA Mode option to gain access to the video configuration by loading a standard VGA driver. In Windows XP, you can open the Device Manager located under the Control Panel's System icon to access its Device Driver Rollback, System Restore, and Disable the Device options. These options can be used to replace an updated driver (other than a printer driver) that may be causing problems. This option reinstalls the driver that was being used previous to the current driver and restores any driver settings that were updated when the driver was installed.

4. In Windows, the properties of each icon must correctly identify the filename and path of the application's executable file. If not, Windows will not be able to start the application. If the folder or file containing the executable was moved, renamed, or removed in the upgrade, Windows will not be able to find it when asked to start the application. Check the application's properties to verify that its filename, path, and syntax are correct. An application's properties can be accessed by right-clicking its desktop icon, as well as by right-clicking its entry in the Start menu, My Computer page, or Windows Explorer screen. One of the application's core files, such as a DLL, could have been erased or become corrupted in the upgrade. In this case, you would need to reinstall the application.

5. Begin by making sure that the printer is not in an offline condition and that the physical connection is correct. Next, change the settings in the printer's Properties page so that it prints directly to the port instead of to the spooler. If the information begins moving to the printer, reinstall the printer driver. This should reset the spooler in the process. Other options for repairing the spooler include extracting the spooler files from the Windows distribution CD or reinstalling the operating system.

CHAPTER EIGHTEEN

Printers and Scanners

Terms you'll need to understand:

✓ Scanner

✓ Printer

✓ Printer driver

✓ Inkjet printer

✓ Laser printer

✓ Dot matrix printer

✓ Dye sublimation printer

✓ Thermal printer

✓ Print server

✓ Bluetooth printer

✓ Test page

Techniques you'll need to master:

Essentials 4.1—Identify the fundamental principles of using printers and scanners.

✓ Identify the differences among types of printer and scanner technologies (laser, inkjet, thermal, solid ink, impact).

✓ Identify the names, purposes, and characteristics of printer and scanner components (memory, driver, firmware) and consumables (toner, ink cartridge, paper).

✓ Identify the names, purposes, and characteristics of interfaces used by printers and scanners, including port and cable types, for example:

   ✓ Parallel

   ✓ Network (NIC, print servers)

   ✓ USB

✓ Serial

✓ IEEE 1394/FireWire

✓ Wireless (Bluetooth, 802.11, infrared)

✓ SCSI

Essentials 4.2—Identify the basic concepts of installing, configuring, optimizing, and upgrading printers and scanners.

✓ Install and configure printers and scanners.

   ✓ Power and connect the device using local or network port.

   ✓ Install and update the device driver and calibrate the device.

   ✓ Configure the options and default settings.

   ✓ Print a test page.

✓ Optimize printer performance; for example, printer settings such as tray switching, print spool settings, device calibration, media types, and paper orientation.

Depot Technician 3.1/Remote Support Technician 3.1/IT Technician 4.1—Identify the fundamental principles of using printers and scanners.

✓ Describe the processes used by printers and scanners including laser, ink dispersion, thermal, solid ink, and impact printers and scanners.

Depot Technician 3.2/Remote Support Technician 3.2/IT Technician 4.2—Install, configure, optimize, and upgrade printers and scanners.

✓ Install and configure printers and scanners.

　　✓ Power and connect the device using local or network port.

　　✓ Install and update the device driver and calibrate the device.

　　✓ Configure options and default settings.

　　✓ Calibrate the device (604).

　　✓ Install and configure the print drivers (PCL, PostScript, GDI) (602/603).

　　✓ Validate compatibility with operating system and applications (602/603).

　　✓ Educate the user about basic functionality (602/603).

　　✓ Print a test page (604).

✓ Install and configure printer upgrades, including memory and firmware (602/604).

✓ Optimize scanner performance including resolution, file format, and default settings (All).

Introduction

This chapter covers the basic Printers and Scanners areas of the CompTIA A+ Certification—Essentials examination under Objectives 4.1. It also covers the Installation, Configuration, Optimization, and Upgrading of Printers and Scanners areas that are generally testable under Objective 4.2 of the Essentials examination.

Printers are the second most common output peripheral used with PCs. Computer technicians must understand how the different types of printers operate, what their typical components are, and what printer components can be serviced in the field.

Printers used with personal computers are available in many types and use various connection schemes. The computer technician must be able to connect any model of printer to any computer and configure them for operation.

> **NOTE**
>
> The Depot Technician 3.1/Remote Support Technician 3.1/IT Technician 4.1 objectives are identical to the "Identify the fundamental principles of using printers and scanners—Describe processes used by printers and scanners including laser, ink dispersion, thermal, solid ink and impact printers and scanners" objective portion of Essentials Objective 4.1.
>
> Likewise, the Depot Technician 3.1/Remote Support Technician 3.1/IT Technician 4.1 Objectives are nearly identical to the Essentials 4.2 objective. The Depot Technician version includes "Calibrate the device" and "Print a test page" entries in its list, and both the Depot Technician and IT Technician versions include an "Install and configure printer upgrades" entry.
>
> The entries for the "PCL/Post Script/GDI drivers," "Validate compatibility with operating system and applications," and "Educate the user about basic functionality" entries are shared by the Remote Support Technician and IT Technician exams.
>
> The topics specified in these different exam/objective areas are so closely stated that it makes sense that they are presented as the same discussion. You will need to study this material in this chapter for any of the four exams you intend to challenge.

Printer Types

In many instances, a permanent copy of a computer's output is desired. The leading hard-copy output device is the *character printer* (that is, letters, numbers, and graphical images). Character printers are the second most common output peripheral used with PCs (after the video display). As computer systems and their applications have diversified, a variety of printer systems have developed to fill the particular printing needs created by the marketplace.

There are two common classifications of printers based on how they produce characters on a page: impact and nonimpact printers. *Impact printers* place characters on the page by causing a hammer device to strike an inked ribbon. The ribbon, in turn, strikes the printing surface (paper). *Nonimpact printers* create characters without making physical contact with the paper.

Most impact printers have disappeared from the marketplace as improvements in nonimpact technologies and pricing have made them more desirable. The one situation where impact printers remain the logical choice is in office applications that print multipart forms and continuous forms. Several nonimpact methods of printing are used in computer printers. Older nonimpact printers relied on special heat-sensitive or chemically reactive paper to form characters on the page. Newer methods of nonimpact printing use ink droplets, squirted from a jet-nozzle device (inkjet printers), or a combination of laser/xerographic print technologies (laser printers) to place characters on a page. Currently, the most popular nonimpact printers use inkjet or laser technologies to deliver ink to the page.

Basically, there are two methods of creating characters on a page. One method places a character on the page that is fully shaped and fully filled in. This type of character is called a *fully formed character*. The other method involves placing dots on the page in strategic patterns to fool the eye into seeing a character. This type of character is referred to as a *dot-matrix character*.

Fonts

The term *font* refers to variations in the size and style of characters. With true fully formed characters, typically only one font is available without changing the physical printing element. With all other printing methods, however, it is possible to include a variety of font types and sizes.

The three common character fonts are *bitmapped* (or raster-scanned), *vector-based*, and *TrueType outline fonts*. Bitmapped fonts store dot patterns for all the possible size and style variations of the characters in the set. *Font styles* refer to the characteristics of the font, such as normal, bold, and italic styles. *Font size* refers to the physical measurement of the character. Type is measured in increments of 1/72 of an inch. Each increment is called a *point*. Common text sizes are 10-point and 12-point type.

Vector-based fonts store the outlines of the character styles and sizes as sets of mathematical formulas. Each character is composed of a set of reference points and connecting lines between them. These types of fonts can be scaled up and down to achieve various sizes. The vector-based approach requires much less storage space to store a character set and all its variations than would be necessary for an equivalent bitmapped character set. In addition, vector-based fonts can be scaled and rotated; bitmapped fonts typically cannot be scaled and rotated. Conversely, bitmapped characters can be printed out directly and quickly, but vector-based characters must be generated when called for.

EXAM ALERT

Be aware of the benefits and drawbacks of bitmapped characters.

EXAM ALERT

Know which font types are generated by establishing starting points and then calculating mathematical formulas.

TrueType fonts are a type of outline font commonly used with Microsoft Windows. These fonts are stored as a set of points and outlines used to generate a set of bitmaps. Special algorithms adjust the bitmaps so that they look best at the specified resolution. After the bitmaps have been created, Windows stores them in a RAM cache that it creates. In this manner, the font is generated only once when it is first selected. Afterward, the fonts are called out of memory, thus speeding up the process of delivering them to the printer. Each TrueType character set requires an FOT and a TTF file to create all its sizes and resolutions.

You can use the Windows Character Map to view all the characters that are available in a selected font. The Character Map can display Windows and Unicode character sets. The Character Map can also be used to place special characters and math symbols in documents.

EXAM ALERT

Be aware of the functions the Windows Character Map provides in printing operations.

Basic Printer Components

Although printers vary considerably from type to type and from model to model, some elements are common to all printers. These elements are depicted in Figure 18.1.

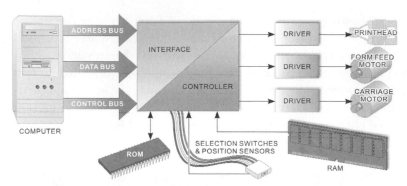

FIGURE 18.1 Common printer components.

Printer Interface

Like most other peripherals, the heart of a character printer is its interface/controller circuitry. The interface circuitry accepts data and instructions from the computer's I/O port. This includes decoding the computer's instructions to the printer, converting signal logic levels, and passing data to the printer's controller.

The most widely used connection interface for new printers is the USB port. This is followed by the direct network connection using CAT5 cables with RJ-45 connectors. Wi-Fi, Bluetooth, and infrared link printer interfaces common. However, there are still so many older printers using parallel printer ports and serial interfaces that you must be able to identify them and work with them. Some printers include an IEEE-1394 FireWire connection to support printing from digital cameras and Apple Macs.

Historically, parallel-port connections were the primary choice when the printer was located in close proximity to the computer. If the printer had to be located remotely, the RS-232 serial interface became more appropriate. Many manufacturers offered both connections as standard equipment. Other models offered the serial connection as an option. More is said about these two interfaces later in this section.

A third, less-common method of connecting printers to computers uses the SCSI interface as the connection port. As with other SCSI devices, the printer must be set up as a unique SCSI device, and proper connection and termination procedures should be observed.

EXAM ALERT

Be aware of the different types of interface connections commonly used with printers.

Printer Controllers

The controller section receives the data and control signals from the interface section and produces all the signals necessary to select, or generate, the proper character to be printed. It also advances the print mechanism to the next print position and feeds the paper at the proper times. In addition, the controller generates status and control signals that tell the computer what is happening in the printer.

Because of the complexity of most character printers, a dedicated *microcontroller* (processor) is typically employed to oversee the complete operation of the printer. The presence of the dedicated microprocessor provides greater flexibility, and additional options, for the printer. Along with the dedicated processor, the printer normally contains IC memory in the form of RAM, ROM, or both. A speed mismatch exists between the computer and the printer because the computer is usually capable of generating characters at a much higher rate than the printer can print them. To minimize this speed differential, printers typically carry onboard RAM memory buffers to hold characters coming from the computer. In this way, the transfer of data between the computer and the printer occurs at a rate that is compatible with the computer's operating speed. The printer obtains its character information from the onboard buffer.

In addition to character print information, the host computer can also store printer instructions in the buffer for use by the dedicated processor. The printer may also contain onboard ROM in the form of character generators, or printer initialization programs for startup. Some printers contain EPROM, instead of ROM, to provide a greater variety of options for the printer, such as downloadable type fonts and variable print modes.

Basically, the controller must produce signals to drive the print mechanism, the paper feed motor, the carriage motor, and possibly optional devices, such as single-sheet feeders and add-on tractors. Most of these functions are performed by precision stepper motors. There are hardware driver circuits between the motors and the controller to provide current levels high enough to activate the motors.

The controller also gathers information from the printer through a variety of sensing devices. These include position-sensing switches and user-operated, front-panel-mounted, mode-control switches. Some of the more common sensing switches include the home-position sensor, the end-of-paper sensor, and the carriage position sensor. The controller also responds to manual input command switches, such as On/Off Line, Form Feed (FF), and Line Feed (LF).

The sensors and switches can be treated as Field Replaceable Units (FRUs) in many printers. This is particularly true with more expensive laser printers. In most printers, the entire *operator control panel* can be exchanged for another unit. This effectively changes all the user-operated input switches at one time.

Dot-Matrix Printers

Dot-matrix characters are not fully formed characters. Instead, dot-matrix characters are printed in the form of dot patterns that represent the characters. The reader's eye fills in the gaps between the dots.

The printhead in a dot-matrix printer is a vertical column of print wires controlled by electromagnets. Dots are created on the paper by energizing selected electromagnets, which extend the desired print wires from the printhead. In the printhead, the permanent magnet keeps the wires pulled in until electromagnets are energized, causing them to move forward. The print wires impact an ink ribbon, which impacts the paper. Remember that the entire character is not printed in a single instant of time—it is printed in steps.

The components of a typical dot-matrix printer are depicted in Figure 18.2. They consist of a power supply board, a main control board, a printhead assembly, a ribbon cartridge, a paper-feed motor (along with its mechanical drive gears), and a printhead-positioning motor and mechanism.

EXAM ALERT

Remember what a main board in a printer is called.

Dot-Matrix Printer Mechanics

By the very nature of their operation, printers tend to be extremely mechanical peripherals. During the printing operation, the print mechanism must be properly positioned over each character cell in sequence. In most printers used with PCs, the character-positioning action involves holding the paper stationary and stepping the printhead carriage across the page. The printhead carriage rides on rods that extend across the front of the page.

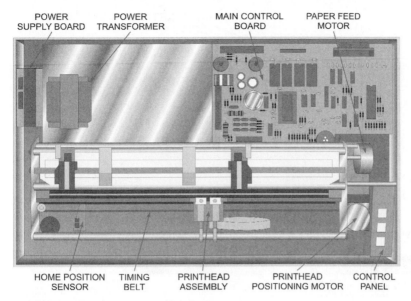

FIGURE 18.2 Parts of a dot-matrix printer.

In addition to positioning the print mechanism for printing, all printer types must feed paper through the print area. The type of paper-handling mechanism in a printer is somewhat dependent on the type of forms that will be used with the printer and its speed. There are two common methods of moving paper through the printer:

▶ Friction-feed uses friction to hold the paper against the printer's platen. The paper advances through the printer as the platen turns.

▶ Pin-feed pulls the paper through the printer by a set of pins that fit into the holes along the edge of the form, as shown in Figure 18.3. The pins may be an integral part of the platen or mounted on a separate motor-driven tractor.

Friction feed is normally associated with single-sheet printers. Platen pin-feed and pin tractors are usually employed with continuous and multilayer forms. These mechanisms can control paper slippage and misalignment created by the extra weight imposed by continuous forms. Platen pin-feed units can handle only one width of paper; tractors can be adjusted to handle various paper widths. Tractor feeds are used with very heavy forms, such as multiple-part, continuous forms, and are most commonly found on dot-matrix printers. Most inkjet and laser printers use single-sheet feeder systems.

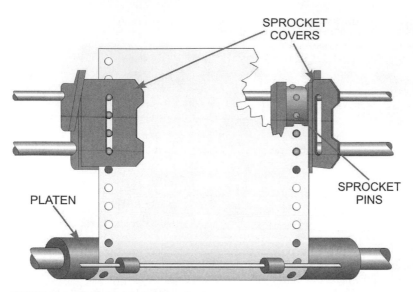

FIGURE 18.3 A tractor/pin-feed mechanism.

EXAM ALERT

Know the major purpose of a tractor-feed mechanism and where it is most commonly used.

Printhead Mechanisms

The printhead-positioning motor is responsible for moving the printhead mechanism across the page and stopping it in just the right places to print. The printhead rides back and forth across the printer on a pair of carriage rods. A timing belt runs between the printhead assembly and the printhead-positioning motor and converts the rotation of the motor into linear stepped movement of the printhead assembly across the page.

The paper-feed motor and gear train move the paper through the printer. This can be accomplished by driving the platen assembly. The platen can be used in two different ways to move the paper through the printer. After the paper has been wrapped halfway around the platen, a set of rollers is used to pin the paper to the platen as it turns. This is friction-feed paper handling. The platen may have small pins that can drag the paper through the printer as the platen turns. In either case, the paper-feed motor drives the platen to move the paper.

Thermal Printers

As mentioned earlier in this section, thermal printing techniques were at one time widely used with PC printing. These printers use heated elements to burn or melt dot pattern characters on special paper. There are two types of thermal printers: direct thermal printers and thermal wax transfer printers.

A direct transfer thermal printer works in much the same manner as the dot-matrix printer described in the preceding section. The major difference between the two technologies is that the print wires in the thermal printer are heated so that they can burn dot patterns into special thermal paper. Early facsimile (fax) machine technology was based on this type of thermal printing. Even now, thermal printers are widely used for bar code printing, battery-powered handheld printing devices, and credit card receipt printers.

The other difference between the two dot-matrix printers is that in the thermal printer, the printhead does not move across the page. Instead, different pins in a row of heating elements are extended as the paper passes over the print bar. This makes thermal printing quiet and efficient. There is also no ink ribbon to change or run out of.

The drawback to direct thermal printing is the special thermal paper required for operation (using regular paper would present a fire hazard). In addition, the paper does not age well. Over time, the entire page will darken and become difficult to read.

EXAM ALERT

Be aware of the drawbacks associated with thermal printers.

The other variation of thermal printer is the thermal wax transfer printer. In these units, a thermal printhead melts dots of wax-based ink from the transfer ribbon onto the paper. When the wax cools, it is permanently attached to the page. Unlike the direct thermal printer, thermal wax transfer printers do not require special paper to print on.

These printers are available in monochrome (one color) and multicolor versions. The multicolor versions can be three-color printers (cyan, magenta, and yellow—CMY color) or four-color printers (CMY + black = CMYK color). These thermal printers use a high volume of wax to print each page. Each page requires a complete page of wax to print, regardless of how many characters are placed on the page.

In Figure 18.4, the thermal printer feeds a sheet of paper into the thermal printing mechanism. In the print mechanism, the paper is brought together with a roll of color film that is coated with successive sheets of inked wax. Each sheet on the roll contains one of the basic colors (CMY and K) and is equal to the length and width of the sheet of paper.

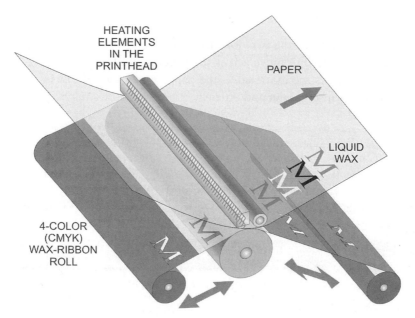

FIGURE 18.4 A color thermal printing.

As the paper moves through the print engine the first time, it is matched with one of the color sheets as it passes through a compression roller and a strip of thermal print heating elements (pins). The heating elements are turned on and off to melt selected dots of colored wax onto the paper. After completing the first pass, the paper and the film are separated from each other, the paper is repositioned for another run using the second color sheet, and the process is repeated to place the second set of color dots on the page. This cycle is repeated until all the colors have been applied to the page.

This type of printer is used in professional color printing because it provides vivid reproductions of picture and artwork. However, thermal printers can't actually produce images that approach real photographic quality because they use color dots to create the image of the picture, and photographs are made up of continuous tones.

Inkjet Printers

Inkjet printers produce characters by squirting a precisely controlled stream of ink drops onto the paper. The drops must be controlled very precisely in terms of their aerodynamics, size, and shape, or the drop placement on the page becomes inexact, and the print quality falters.

The drops are formed by one of two methods:

▶ Thermal shock heats the ink in a capillary tube, just behind the nozzle. This increases the pressure of the ink in the tube and causes it to explode through the opening.

▶ Mechanical vibration uses vibrations from a piezoelectric crystal to force ink through a nozzle.

The inkjet nozzle is designed to provide the proper shape and trajectory for the ink drops so that they can be directed precisely toward the page. The nozzle is also designed so that the surface tension of the ink keeps it from running out uncontrollably.

> **EXAM ALERT**
>
> Be able to identify the printer type that produces print by squirting ink at the page. Remember the techniques used to form the ink drops.

Some inkjet printers incorporate multiple jets to permit color printing. Four basic colors can be mixed to create a palette of colors by firing the inkjets in different combinations.

A special variety of inkjet printer referred to as a *solid inkjet printer* (also called *wax jet printer*) combines thermal printer technology with inkjet operations to produce brilliantly colored pictures and images. Instead of working with inks, these printers melt dyed waxes and then spray them on the page using inkjetlike dispersal methods. The wax base used for the printing process produces exceptionally bright colors on all types of paper. However, because these printers are slow and relatively expensive, they are typically found only in professional reproduction and advertising settings.

Inkjet Printer Components

Aside from the printing mechanism, the components of a typical inkjet printer are very similar to those of a dot-matrix printer. Figure 18.5 illustrates these components.

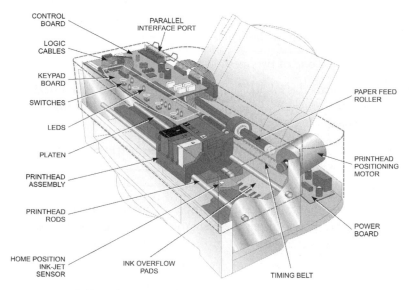

FIGURE 18.5   Inkjet printer components.

The ink cartridge snaps into the printhead assembly, which rides in front of the platen on a rail or rod. The printhead assembly is positioned through a timing belt that runs between it and the positioning motor. A flexible cable carries inkjet-firing information between the control board and the printhead. This cable folds out of the way as the printhead assembly moves across the printer.

The paper-feed motor turns a gear train that ultimately drives the platen. The paper is friction-fed through the printer, between the platen and the pressure rollers. Almost all inkjet printers used with microcomputer systems are single-sheet, friction-feed systems.

Laser Printers

A laser printer modulates a highly focused laser beam to produce CRT-like raster-scan images on a rotating drum, as depicted in Figure 18.6. This process was developed by Xerox and is referred to as *electrophotographic reproduction.*

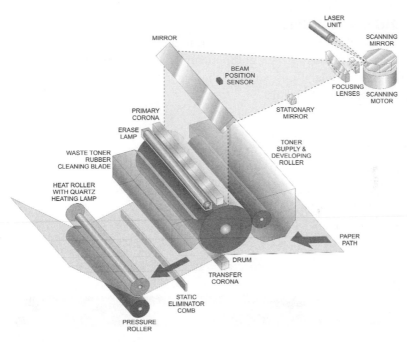

FIGURE 18.6   A typical laser printer.

The drum is coated with a photosensitive plastic, which is given a negative electrical charge over its surface. The modulated laser beam creates spots on the rotating drum. The spots written by the laser take on a positive electrical charge. A negatively charged toner material is attracted to the positively charged, written areas of the drum. The paper is fed past the rotating drum and the toner is transferred to the paper. A pair of compression rollers and a high-temperature lamp work together to fuse the toner to the paper. Thus, the image written on the drum by the laser is transferred to the paper.

The laser beam scans the drum so rapidly that it is not practical to do the scanning mechanically. Instead, the beam is bounced off a rotating polygonal (many-sided) mirror. The faces of the mirror cause the reflected beam to scan across the face of the drum as the mirror revolves. Using the highest dot densities available, these printers produce characters that rival typeset text.

Laser Printing Operations

From manufacturer to manufacturer and from model to model, the exact arrangement and combination of components in laser printers may vary. However, the order of operations is always the same. The six stages of operation in a laser printer are the following:

1. Cleaning

2. Conditioning

3. Writing

4. Developing

5. Transferring

6. Fusing

EXAM ALERT

Memorize the operational stages of a typical laser printer.

When character data is received from the host computer, it is converted into a serial bit stream, which is applied to the scanning laser. The photosensitive drum rotates as the pulse-encoded laser beam is scanned across it. The laser creates a copy of the image on the photosensitive drum in the form of a relatively positive-charged drawing. This operation is referred to as *registration*.

Before the laser writes on the drum, a set of erase lamps shines on the drum to remove any residual traces of the preceding image. This leaves the drum with a neutral electrical charge. A high voltage, applied to the primary corona wire, creates a highly charged negative field that conditions the drum to be written on by applying a uniform negative charge (–600V) to it.

As the laser writes on the drum, the drum turns through the toner powder, which is attracted to the charged image on the drum. Toner is a very fine powder, bonded to iron particles that are attracted to the charges written on the drum. The developer roller, in the toner cartridge, turns as the drum turns and expels a measured amount of toner past a restricting blade. A regulating AC voltage assists the toner in leaving the cartridge, but also pulls back some excess toner from the drum. Excess toner is recycled within the toner cartridge so that it can be used again.

Great care should be taken when installing a new drum unit in a laser printer. Exposing the drum to light for more than a few minutes may damage it. The drum should never be touched; this too, can ruin its surface. Keep the unit away from dust and dirt, as well as away from humidity and high-temperature areas.

EXAM ALERT

Know that you should never expose the drum of a laser printer to sunlight or any other strong light source.

The transfer corona wire (transfer roller) is responsible for transferring the toner from the drum to the paper. The toner is transferred to the paper because of the highly positive charge the transfer corona wire applies to the paper. The positive charge attracts the negative toner particles away from the drum and onto the page. A special static-eliminator comb acts to prevent the positively charged paper from sticking to the negatively charged drum.

EXAM ALERT

Know the functions of the two corona wires in a laser printer.

After the image has been transferred to the paper, a pair of compression rollers in the fusing unit (fuser) act to press the toner particles into the paper while they melt them to it. The top roller, known as the *fusing roller*, is heated by a quartz lamp. This roller melts the toner to the paper as it exits the unit; the lower roller, known as the *compression roller*, applies pressure to the paper. A cleaning pad removes excess particles and applies a silicon lubricant to prevent toner from sticking to the Teflon-coated fusing roller.

A thermal sensor in the fusing unit monitors the temperature of the unit. This information is applied to the control circuitry so that it can control the fuser temperature between 140°C and 230°C. If the temperature of the fuser is not controlled correctly, it may cause severe damage to the printer and may also present a potential fire hazard.

EXAM ALERT

Remember the purpose of the thermal fuse in laser printers.

A typical laser printer has sensors to determine what paper trays are installed, what size paper is in them, and whether the tray is empty. It also uses sensors to track the movement of the paper through each stage of the printer. This enables the controller to know where the page is at all times and properly sequence the activities of the solenoids and clutches.

Electrophotographic Cartridges

In Hewlett-Packard printers, the main portion of the printing system is contained in the electrophotographic cartridge. This cartridge contains the toner supply, the corona wire, the drum assembly, and the developing roller. Figure 18.7 depicts the HP configuration.

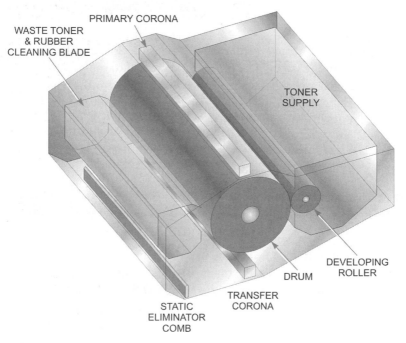

FIGURE 18.7 The HP cartridge configuration.

Color laser printers operate on the same principles as the monochrome version we have described as an example. However, color lasers use four color toners. From earlier discussions of other color printers, you might be able to guess that the four toners are combined in different ratios on the page to form the different colors in the spectrum.

Likewise, from the description of how images are written on the drum of a laser printer and transferred to the paper, you can probably imagine that the voltages used to control the attraction properties of the toner to the drum and paper are much more complex than they would be for a single-color laser printer. However, for the technician, color laser printers still work like their single-color relatives.

Dye Sublimation Printers

Earlier in this chapter we discussed thermal wax printers that could produce vivid high-quality graphics. However, the images they produce never approach photographic quality because of their dot composition. A variation of that printer type, called *dye sublimation printers*, has been produced to provide photographic quality, continuous tone images.

Figure 18.8 illustrates the dye sublimation process. Although the printing mechanism appears similar to that of the thermal wax printer described earlier, there are some distinct differences. In a dye sublimation printer, sheets of special paper or transparencies are fastened securely to a print drum. Clamping the page to the drum ensures good registration between the different colors that will be printed on the paper in successive color passes.

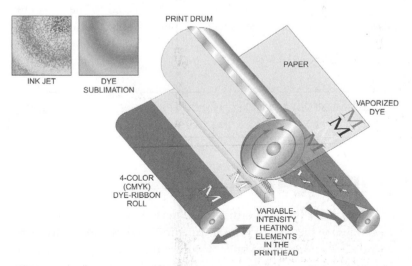

FIGURE 18.8 Dye sublimation printing.

The drum with the paper is rotated in conjunction with a continuous roll of plastic film containing successive CMYK color sheets that have the same dimensions as the page. At the point where the paper and film come together, a heating element strip is used to heat the color substance on the film so that it vaporizes (sublimates) and is absorbed into the paper. The heating element contains thousands of small heat points that can create extremely fine patterns of color dots. In addition, each element can be used to supply hundreds of different temperatures, which leads to hundreds of different amounts of ink transferred to the page, resulting in hundreds of shades that can be produced.

After the length of the page has been printed with one color, the drum cycles again and the process is repeated until all the colors have been transferred to the page.

These printers tend to be very slow and expensive. However, because of their capability to produce continuous-tone images, these printers are widely used by professional graphics businesses to produce posters and large-scale reproductions.

With the popularity of digital cameras continuing to increase, users have many more options about how they handle, view, and display their photographs. Because digital photographs can be viewed without sending them to a print house, many users store their images on an electronic storage medium such as a disk drive, flash drive, SD card, or CD. However, people often want to create hard copies of some of their photographs. For these occasions, small consumer versions of the dye sublimation printer have been introduced to the consumer market to enable users to reproduce electronic photographs without using a print service.

> **NOTE**
>
> Manufacturers have adapted several print technologies to produce personal photo-printing units.

Printer Installation

Generally speaking, one of the least difficult I/O devices to add to a PC system is a printer. Regardless of the type of printer being installed, the steps for adding a printer to a system are basically the same: Connect the printer's power cord to an AC power source. Connect the printer to the correct I/O port at the computer system. Make sure that the port is enabled. Set up the appropriate printer drivers. Configure the port's communication parameters, if a serial printer is being installed. Install the paper. Run the printer's self-test, and then print a document. These steps are summarized in Figure 18.9.

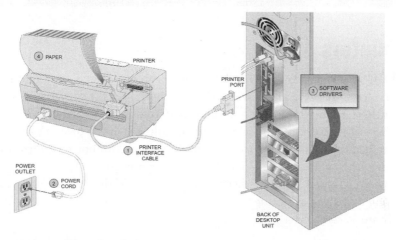

FIGURE 18.9   Printer installation steps.

NOTE

You may also need to check the peripheral port enabling settings in the CMOS Setup utility. Serial, parallel, IrDA, USB, and IEEE-1394 ports may need to be enabled through the CMOS utility. Likewise, the parallel and serial port modes are configured through this utility.

Traditional parallel and serial ports that have been used with printers for decades are quickly fading from prominence as newer, faster, more powerful interfaces are gaining acceptance. Therefore, it is not uncommon for printers to feature a variety of connection options.

After you have finished installing and configuring a printer, the final step is to educate the user about its operation. Use the printer's documentation to highlight key information the user will need access to after you are gone. Use pictures and illustrations to highlight your instructions as you go through the different processes with the user. Also, use the actual printer to demonstrate the operation of the system because you may invalidate the customer's warranty when you perform some steps. As with other training efforts, avoid using slang and jargon to instruct the user about the operation of the printer.

EXAM ALERT

Be aware that the printer install or upgrade is not complete until the user has been properly instructed in its operation.

USB Printers

To install a USB printer, connect the USB signal cable to the computer and to the printer, plug in the printer's power cord, and then allow the system to detect the printer through the PnP process when it is started up. When the operating system detects the new printer, it may automatically install the printer's drivers without any additional efforts. If the operating system does not recognize the printer, a Found New Hardware Wizard will appear, and you will need to select the proper driver from a Windows list or supply an OEM driver from a disc. If the operating system does not detect the printer, you must install it using the Add Hardware Wizard.

Networked Printers

If a printer is installed in a computer system that is part of a network, any other computer on the network can send work to the printer. Historically, the local computer is attached to the printer through one of the normal printing interfaces (parallel, serial, or USB ports) and is also connected to the other remote computers through its network connection. In addition to the signal cable, the local computer's operating system must be configured to permit the remote stations on the network to print through it to its printer. This relationship is known as *print sharing*.

Newer printers, called *network-ready printers*, come with built-in network interfacing that enables them to be connected directly into the local area network. Most network printers contain an integrated network controller and ethernet LAN adapter that enable printers to work on the LAN without a supporting host computer.

As with other devices that access the network, printers operate on the network at the maximum speed of its network adapter. For hard-wired network printers, this translates to 10/100/1000Mbps (1Gbps) operation compatible with wired ethernet operation. Printers equipped with 802.11x wireless network adapters will operate at 11 or 54Mbps. Bluetooth printers communicate with the rest of the network at 723kbps or 2.1Mbps.

> **EXAM ALERT**
>
> Be aware that the type of built-in network adapter that a network printer is equipped with determines its operating speed on the network.

Other printers may be connected directly to the local area network through a device called a *print server port*. This device resembles a network hub in appearance and can be used to connect up to three printers directly into the network.

Although some older network printers used coaxial cable connections, newer network printers feature RJ-45 jacks for connection to twisted-pair ethernet networks. It is relatively easy to determine whether a printer is networked by the presence of a coaxial or a twisted-pair network cable connected directly to the printer. The presence of the RJ-45 jacks on the back of the printer also indicates that the printer is network capable, even if it is not being used in that manner.

> **EXAM ALERT**
>
> Know how to identify the presence of a network-ready printer.

Wireless Printer Interfaces

Just as it is common to find printers with built-in network adapters, it is almost as common to find printer models that feature wireless 802.11 and Bluetooth connectivity. These interfaces provide relatively easy, no-wire methods of attaching printers to existing networks. These units typically offer an embedded wireless network adapter as one of multiple interface options. In some cases, the printer may need to be physically connected to the network or a host computer to be configured. Afterward it can be used as a wireless device.

Small, inexpensive 802.11b/g wireless print server hub devices (or *Wi-Fi adapters*) have been developed to eliminate the need for a dedicated PC to handle print functions. These hubs typically connect to the USB port of network-capable, wired printers (or multifunction printer/scanner/copier/fax devices) and transform them into wireless printers. Some models also provide web server functionality to enable remote configuration, printer management, and troubleshooting through a web browser.

The Bluetooth option enables users to print directly from notebooks, PDAs, or cell phones. Bluetooth can be added to an existing USB or parallel port printer through a small Bluetooth receiver that plugs into the port. It also makes printer placement a simple and dynamic activity. You need only to position the printer within the specified range (for example, 20 meters) of the Bluetooth device to achieve connectivity. Also, you can pick up the printer and relocate it to another room or office.

Bluetooth adapters feature flash RAM memory that can be flashed with the latest software updates to provide additional functionality. They also include traditional RAM memory to buffer pages of print data being sent to it across the network.

Infrared Printer Ports

Many portable computer designs include an IrDA-compliant port to provide wireless communication with devices such as character printers. Figure 18.10 illustrates an IrDA-connected printer. The IrDA specification calls for communication ranges up to 2 meters (6 feet), but most implementations state 1 meter as the recommended maximum range. All IrDA transfers are carried out in half-duplex mode and must have a clear line of sight between the transmitter and receiver. The receiver must be situated within 15 degrees of center with the line of transmission.

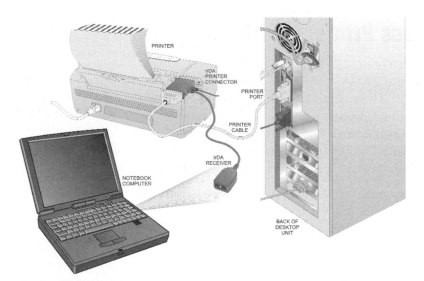

FIGURE 18.10   An IrDA printer connection.

The figure shows the infrared receiver mounted on a cable that connects to a standard port. This permits the receiver to be positioned in the best possible manner to maximize the IrDA line-of-sight and distance requirements.

Legacy Printer Interfaces

From the beginning of the PC era, a printer has been one of the most standard pieces of equipment to add to the system. This standardization has led to fairly direct installation procedures for most printers: Obtain an IBM Centronics printer cable, plug it into the appropriate LPT port on the back of the computer, connect the Centronic-compatible end to the printer, plug the power cord into the printer, load a device driver to configure the software for the correct printer, and print.

At the printer end of a Centronics parallel port, a 36-pin connector is used. Of course, the computer end of the cable must have a DB-25M connector to plug into the system's DB-25F LPT port.

The major limiting factor for parallel printer connections is length. although cables purchased from reputable suppliers are typically correct in length and contain all the shielding and connections required, cheaper cables and home-made cables often are lacking in some of these areas. The recommended signal cable lengths associated with standard parallel printers is 0–10 feet (3 meters), although some equipment manufacturers specify 6 feet (1.8 meters) maximum for their cables. You should believe these recommendations when you see them.

One note of caution concerning parallel printer cables: The IEEE has established specifications for bidirectional parallel printer cables (IEEE-1284). These cables affect the operation of Enhanced Parallel Port (EPP) and Extended Capabilities Port (ECP) parallel devices. Using an older, noncompliant unidirectional cable with a bidirectional parallel device will prevent the device from communicating properly with the system and may prevent it from operating.

Serial Printer Interface

In some applications, it is impossible to locate the printer close enough to the host computer to use the parallel connection. In these cases, serially interfaced printers come into play. Printers using an RS-232 serial interface connection add an extra level of complexity to the system. Unlike the parallel printer interface that basically plugs and plays on most systems, serial interface connections require additional hardware and software configuration steps. Serial printers are slightly more difficult to set up because serial printers are not PnP compliant, and the communication definition must be manually configured between the computer and the printer. The serial port must be configured for speed, parity type, character frame, and protocol.

In the PC world, RS-232 serial cables can take on several configurations. First, they may use either 9-pin or 25-pin D-shell connectors at either end of the cable. The cable for a particular serial connection must have the correct type of connector at each end. A typical printer serial cable has a female 9-pin D-shell connector (DB-9F) that connects to the PC's serial (COM) port and a male 25-pin D-shell connector (DB-25M) that plugs into the printer.

Likewise, the connection scheme inside the cable can vary from printer to printer. Normally, the Transmit Data line (TXD-pin 2) from the computer is connected to the Receive Data line (RXD-pin 3) of the printer. Also, the Data Set Ready (DSR-pin 6) is typically connected to the printer's Data Terminal Ready (DTR-pin 20) pin. These connections are used as one method to control the flow of information between the system and the printer. If the printer's character buffer becomes full, the printer will signal the computer to hold up sending characters by deactivating its DSR pin.

> **EXAM ALERT**
>
> Remember the types of connectors used at both the computer and the printer ends of an RS-232 serial printer cable.

The recommended signal cable lengths associated with serial printers is 10–50 feet (15.25 meters). Some references, however, use 100 feet as the acceptable length of an RS-232C serial cable. Serial connections are tricky enough without problems generated by the cable being too long. Make the cable as short as possible.

> **EXAM ALERT**
>
> Know the recommended maximum length of a standard parallel printer cable and an RS-232 cable.

Challenge #1

Your warehouse manager has come to you asking for a 20-foot printer cable so that he can move his wide carrlage dot-matrix printer out of his office and into the warehouse where the noise level caused by the dot-matrix printer will not be a problem. He must use the dot-matrix printer because he has to print multipart invoice forms. What can you suggest to the warehouse manager that would solve his problem?

Serial Printer Configuration

After the correct connector and cabling scheme has been implemented, the printer configuration must be established at both the computer and the printer. The information in both locations must match for communications to occur. On the system side of the serial-port connection, the software printer driver must be set up to match the settings of the printer's receiving section.

First, the driver must be directed toward the correct serial port. In a newer Windows-based system, this is typically COM1. If the system has an analog modem installed or built in, you should check the COM port setting of that device to make sure that there are no conflicts. Second, the selected serial port must be configured for the proper character framing. The number of start, stop, data, and parity bits must be set to match what the printer expects to receive. These values are often established through hardware configuration switches located on the printer.

The printer driver must also be set up to correctly handle the flow of data between the system and the printer. Incorrect flow control settings can result in slow response, lost characters, or continuous errors and retries. Flow control can be established through software or hardware handshaking.

Challenge #2

Your office manager has come to you complaining about the noise level in the accounting office caused by the dot-matrix printers they have to use. The wide carriage dot-matrix printers are required because everyone in the department must print multipart invoices. After they have been printed, the invoices are separated from each other and taken to the warehouse for processing. The warehouse is well beyond the 5 meter range of the USB printers you are using now. What option can you present to the office manager to lower the noise level in the accounting office?

Printer Drivers

All peripheral devices require device driver programs to coordinate their operation with the system. These programs are installed on the host computer and create a software interface between the operating system's printing subsystem, the port, and the printer's intelligent devices. For the most part, modern operating systems supply a variety of device drivers (including printer drivers) as an integral part of their packages.

When a new printer is installed, it should be detected by the system's PnP process the next time the system is started. In many cases, the operating system will be able to determine which type of printer is attached and automatically load a standard driver for it. In other cases, the PnP process will request that the user insert an OEM driver disk so that it can load a driver for the new drive.

When the new printer is not detected, the user must manually install the printer and its driver program through a configuration program (wizard) in the operating system. Figure 18.11 illustrates the functional position of a printer driver in the system.

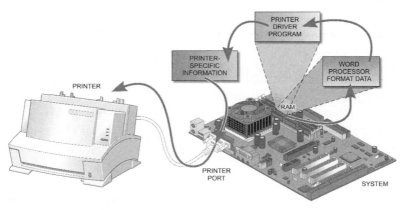

FIGURE 18.11   Printer driver position.

Printer drivers can also be a source of many printing problems and are generally one of the first things checked when a new printer installation does not function. These programs can also become corrupted in some operating systems when new devices are installed that write over .dll portions of their code. Therefore, it may be necessary to reload printer drivers in these situations.

Faulty or incorrect printer drivers will typically produce garbled print (because the driver is not giving the printer information that it can recognize) or no print at all. If you suspect that a printer driver problem is occurring, you must reinstall or replace the driver. In a PnP system, you can remove the existing driver through the installation wizard and restart the system so that it can detect the printer and install a new copy of the driver. In non-PnP systems, you must manually reinstall the driver.

If you are going to reinstall the driver, you should check the printer manufacturer's website for new updated drivers for the printer you are working with. Printer manufacturers typically supply proprietary driver programs that may be newer than the version in your operating system. Theoretically, these newer drivers should work better or offer improved features over the older version.

Special Print Drivers

There are applications, such as desktop publishing, where you will need to install specialty drivers to extend the font capabilities of the printer. The two most widely used drivers for this function are PostScript and PCL. PostScript and PCL are actually *Page Description Languages* (*PDLs*) that describe the arrangement of text and graphics on a printed page. In Windows, the default page descriptions for graphics output devices is supplied by its Graphics Device Interface (GDI) library. To implement PostScript and PCL functions on the PC, it is necessary to install the driver software for that PDL.

- ▶ PostScript, developed by Adobe, is the de facto PDL standard for printing in commercial typesetting and print houses. The driver enables the system to scale characters to size using an interpreter, thereby removing the necessity of storing a variety of font types and sizes in disk or in memory. It is recommended for use with color documents, documents that have complex page layout formatting, or documents that contain several graphical images. In addition, the PostScript driver offers more options and handles graphical processing more efficiently that other print drivers.

- ▶ *Printer Control Language* (*PCL*) is a page description command language developed by Hewlett-Packard for its LaserJet printers to support scalable fonts. Its use has been so widely accepted that PCL has become the de facto standard in many printer models. It is best suited for use with text documents that are monochrome and that have relatively simple formatting. With these types of pages, the PCL driver will offer quicker printing than a PostScript driver.

The printer has three options for accessing these types of fonts: internal fonts, soft fonts, and cartridge fonts. *Internal fonts* are those fonts are stored in the printer's onboard ROM and are always available. *Soft fonts* are downloadable fonts that reside on a disk somewhere and can be transferred to the printer's memory when needed. *Cartridge fonts* are provided in plug-in modules that are inserted directly into slots in the printer housing. The printer retrieves the fonts from the cartridge when called for.

When a page references one of these PDLs, the printer will check for the indicated font internally. If it does not find the font there, it will check with the host computer and download it into memory, if available. If the font is not available in the printer or the computer, the printer will attempt to convert a bitmapped font into a simulated PostScript font. This often produces pages with mangled text and graphic positioning and characters of much lower quality than expected.

PostScript and PCl soft font drivers for different printers can be downloaded to the host computer and must then be installed. These fonts are installed in Windows through the printer's Properties dialog box. In the dialog box, select the Device Settings tab, click External Fonts, and then select Properties. Next, you must tell the installation wizard where the fonts are located by entering the path to the folder or drive where the fonts reside. You must have Manage Printers permissions in a network environment to add these fonts to the system.

Printer Control Panel Configuration

Most printer models have an *operator control panel* of some sort that can be used to configure printer options. Some control panels are a collection of a few buttons whereas others have buttons and visual displays (usually small LCD screens). Some high-end printers feature touch screens that both display information about the printer and enable the user to configure printer settings through touch screen menus.

In any case, the use of the operator control panel to configure printer settings is often less than straightforward. Likewise, information that the printer supplies to the user through the control panel may also be cryptic in nature. Therefore, you should always refer to the printer's user's manual to determine what options are available and how to go about changing default settings when an application calls for something different. For example, in the case of PCL and PostScript printers described in the previous section, you may need to configure internal font usage through the control panel on the front of the printer. For some configuration items, it is possible to establish their settings through the printer driver (using the Properties page) or through the operator's control panel.

The operator's control panel is also the main source of information about the printer's operation and errors that occur. Like the computer, the printer or scanner may try to issue coded messages to you through beeps or flashing light sequences. The meaning of these coded messages and the recommended steps to correct them are located in the user's manual.

Printer Calibration

There are two common methods of adjusting printer output. The first is to adjust the output through the printer's driver settings. The other method involves using color management functions to match International Color Consortium (ICC) profiles. The key to using either method involves first correctly calibrating the display that you can match a test image printout to. This will enable you to effectively evaluate the quality of the image being produced.

There are several sources of good test images available on the Internet. These images are specially constructed to show the full capabilities of the printer (for example, crispness, color, grayscale, brightness, contrast). One of the easiest methods of obtaining printer test pages is to use an Internet search engine to search for "printer test page". These pages can be downloaded to your system and displayed on a calibrated monitor as the standard to adjust the printer output to.

Printer driver adjustments begin in the printer's properties window, as illustrated by the sample printer properties window. To achieve maximum control of the printing process, you must select a Custom Mode option and click the Advanced button to access the color management functions.

This page will enable you to adjust brightness, contrast, saturation, and CMYK color. You must adjust these settings and print test pages until you achieve the print output you want. It is best to make the first print using the default settings and then adjust one setting at a time until the desired qualities are achieved. You can change more than one adjustment at a time for expediency but you should always record the previous settings so that you can come back to them if needed.

You should also be aware that the actual appearance of printed material can changed based on the media type you are printing on. Many printer properties pages allow you to select a media type to compensate for changes caused by the media.

Color management is a set of tools used to establish and maintain consistent image appearance between different devices, such as cameras, displays, scanners, and printers. Each of these devices has different color responses when displayed. Also, no direct correlation exists between RGB color in monitors and CYMK colors in printers and scanners. However, color management acts to coordinate the appearance of these color types between the devices.

Color management is based on Image Color Management (ICM) standards established by the ICC. ICC profiles are files that map color settings between devices. Depending on the type of profile, the color match may be linked between printers and monitors, printers and scanners, or monitors and scanners. These profiles are identified by a common filename extension of *.icm*. ICC profiles can be downloaded from Internet sources and should be placed in the Windows ICC profile folder. In Windows 2000 this is WinNT\System32\ Spool\Drivers\Color, and in Windows XP is WINDOWS\system32\spool\ drivers\color.

After the profile has been installed, application programs that are ICM-aware, such as Photoshop, can use them. If the printer can use ICC profiles, they can be applied through the Printing Preferences dialog box. With the correct printer profile installed and a properly calibrated monitor, the match between the monitor and the printer output should be very good.

> **EXAM ALERT**
>
> Know how to correct color coordination problems in printers.

Printer Options and Upgrades

Printer FRU modules—in some printers, the microcontroller, RAM modules, and ROM/EPROM devices may be treated as FRU components. Many laser printers come with something less than their maximum amount of RAM installed. However, they also provide optional hardware to permit the memory to be upgraded if desired. Many high-speed laser printers require additional RAM to be installed to handle printing of complex documents, such as desktop-published documents containing large Encapsulated PostScript (EPS) graphics files.

ROM and EPROM devices that contain BIOS or character sets may be placed in sockets so that they can be replaced or upgraded easily. However, newer printers have shifted to using ROM devices that can be flashed. How replaceable these units are depends on the ability to source them from a supplier. In most cases, the question is not whether the device can be exchanged, but whether it makes economical sense to do so. For a given printer type and model, the manufacturer's service center can provide information about the availability of replacement parts.

In many cases, printers in business environments are becoming their own node of the company network. Increasingly, these printers are being equipped with their own built-in network adapters and computerlike peripherals so that they can function in a standalone manner. Figure 18.12 depicts a high-end laser printer intended for multiple-user or network printer applications.

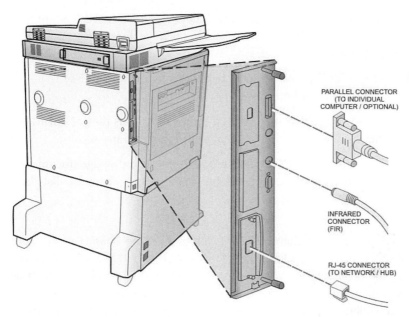

FIGURE 18.12 Standalone multiple-use printer.

Initially, these units were equipped only with an ethernet network adapter and enough electronics to let them function as a network node and provide printing services for other network nodes. However, to make them more efficient, it has become common to integrate other computer peripherals such as hard drives into the printer unit. For example, the hard disk drive (HDD) unit is used in a high-volume printer to store information coming to it from across the network. The HDD unit makes it possible for the printer to spool large amounts of data that it receives so that the network does not get congested waiting for the printer to print the user's documents.

In all but the most basic printer installation, several time- and labor-saving peripherals and devices can be attached to printers. The technician must be aware of these devices and their functions because they can fail in printer installations. It is not unusual for commercial office printers to offer several types of add-on components for their machines, such as the following:

- ▶ An automatic sheet feeder—A device that mounts on the printer to enable special paper types to be fed directly into the printer. This unit can be combined with a scanner unit so that hard copy documents can be scanned directly into the printer for printing.

- ▶ Multiple paper trays—Storage bins that can be used to supply different sizes and types of papers to the printer without having to manually load them or change paper in a single tray. They can also be used to store large volumes of standard paper so that the printer does not need human attention as often.

▶ A duplexer—A device that reroutes paper through the printer so that copies can be made on both sides.

▶ A collator—A device that sorts multipage documents as they are printed so that they are in a prescribed order (page 1, page 2, and so on).

▶ A stapler/stacker—An add-on that is used to staple multipage documents after they have been sorted and collated; it then stacks them for distribution.

As mentioned earlier in this chapter, laser printers share their basic technologies with other office machines, such as copiers, scanners, and plain paper faxes. Because of this, combination products have been developed to bring all these functions together in a single unit, like the one depicted in Figure 18.13. These units offer considerable savings over buying separate machines for each function.

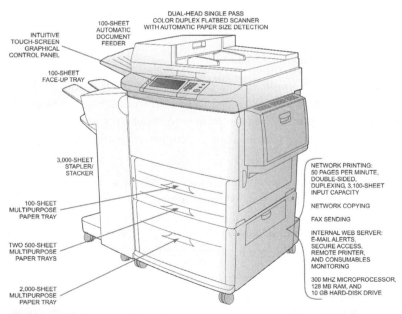

FIGURE 18.13 Office automation unit.

In combination units, the ELP drum provides the central function for each operation. In a scanner operation, the image is scanned from an inserted document and digitized. The digitized image can then be stored as an electronic file. Because the document is in a digital form, it can also be converted to a proper format for faxing to another fax machine. In addition, the unit can act as a laser printer that accepts information from a host computer, scans it on the drum, and prints it out.

Printing in Windows

Windows 2000 and Windows XP employ a print spooler–processing architecture that provides smooth printing in a background mode and quick return-to-application time. The key to this operation is in how the print spooler sends data to the printer. Data is moved to the printer only when it is ready to receive more. Therefore, the system never waits for the printer to digest data that has been sent to it.

The Windows print spooler, depicted in Figure 18.14, is actually a series of 32-bit virtual device drivers and DLLs. The spooler consists of the logical blocks between the client computer and the print device. These blocks process threads in the background and pass them to the printer when it is ready. In essence, the application prints to the Windows printer driver, the driver controls the operation of the spooler, and the driver prints to the printer from the spooler.

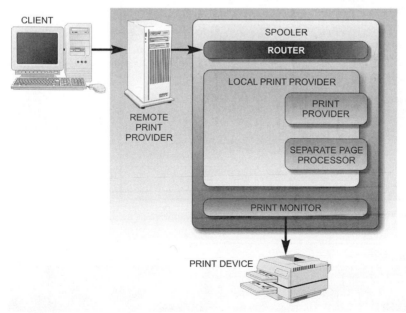

FIGURE 18.14 The Windows print spooler.

In a network printing operation, the print spooler must run on both the local server and the remote client systems. You can start and stop the local spooler process in Windows through the Control Panel's Administrative Tools/Services icon. Clicking this icon produces the Services listing that contains the Print Spooler entry. Simply select this entry from the list to access the Print Spooler Properties dialog box illustrated in Figure 18.15. After you stop the spooler service, it will be necessary to restart it before printing can occur again, unless the printer driver has been configured to bypass the spooler. Also, the local user is not capable of controlling the print operation to a server. The server print function is managed independently.

FIGURE 18.15 Windows XP Print Spooler Properties dialog box.

EXAM ALERT

Know which structure controls remote printing across a network and how to configure its operation.

To print an open file in Windows 2000 or Windows XP, simply move to the application's File menu and click the Print option. If the file is not open, it is still possible to print files in Windows 2000 and Windows XP. Under the My Computer icon, access the desired file, right-click it, and select the Print option from the pop-up menu. Files can be printed from the Windows Explorer screen by employing the same right-click menu method. The document can also be dragged-and-dropped onto a printer icon in the Printers folder, in the My Network Places listing, or on the desktop. Obviously, this option can be performed with both local and remote networked printers.

In Windows 2000, the settings for any printer can be changed through the My Computer icon on the desktop or through the Printers option under the Start menu's Settings entry. The process is the same for both routes: Simply double-click the Printer folder, right-click the desired printer, and select its Properties entry from the menu. In Windows XP, you can access these settings through the Printers and Faxes option in the Start menu. The rest of the process is the same as that used in Windows 2000.

To view documents waiting to be printed from the print spooler, double-click the desired printer's icon in the Printer folder. This will produce the existing print queue display, as illustrated in Figure 18.16. The print queue structure allows multiple files to be loaded onto a printer for printing. Closing the print window does not interrupt the print queue in Windows 2000 or Windows XP. The fact that the print spooler runs in its own virtual environment means that printer hang-ups will not lock up the system. The print jobs in the queue will be completed unless they are deleted from the list.

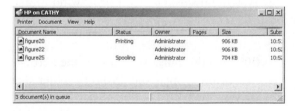

FIGURE 18.16 Windows print queue.

> **EXAM ALERT**
>
> Be aware of which Windows structure allows multiple files to be loaded onto a printer for printing.

The print queue window's menu options permit local printing operations to be paused and resumed. The Printer/Set as Default option permits you to designate the printer as the default printer to be used for print jobs. The menu can also be used to delete print jobs from the queue. This becomes necessary when print jobs sent to the spooler stop processing and need to be removed from the spooler to continue printing operations.

Right-clicking printer icon will produce a pop-up menu that can also be used to control printing operations that are performed by that printer. Both options offer a Properties option that can be used to access the printer's configuration and connection information.

> **EXAM ALERT**
>
> Know how to set a printer as the default printer in a network environment.

The Windows 2000 and Windows XP Printers dialog boxes enable users to sort between different printers based on their attributes. Windows 2000 Professional possesses the capability of printing across the Internet using the new standards-based Internet Printing Protocol (IPP). Using this protocol, Windows 2000 Professional and Windows XP can print to a URL, view the print queue status using an Internet browser, and install print drivers across the Internet.

Establishing Printers in Windows

Windows 2000 and Windows XP will automatically adopt any printers that have been established prior to their installation in the system. If no printers have been installed, the Setup routine will run the Add Printer Wizard to enable a printer to be installed. Each printer in the system possesses its own print window and icon to work from. The wizard can be accessed at any time through the Start menu.

To use the Start menu in Windows 2000 for this purpose, move to the Settings entry, and click Printers. To install a printer, open the Printers folder and double-click the Add Printer icon. In Windows XP, click the Start button and then click the Printers and Faxes icon. To access the Add Printer Wizard in Windows XP, select the Add a Printer option from the Printer Tasks window. From this point, the Add Printer Wizard guides the installation process. Because Windows 2000 and Windows XP have built-in networking support, the printer can be a local unit (connected to the computer) or a remote unit, located somewhere on the network.

To install local printers, choose the Local Printer (Local Printer Attached to This Computer in Windows XP) option and click the Next button. In the Windows XP dialog window, you should also have the Automatically Detect and

Install My Plug and Play Printer option checked. Normally, the LPT1 options should be selected from the list of printer port options. Next, the Add Printer Wizard will produce a list of manufacturers and models to choose from. This list will be similar to the one shown in Figure 18.17. Simply select the correct manufacturer and then the desired model from the list and inform the wizard about the location of the \I386 directory to fetch the driver from. If the \I386 directory has been copied to the hard drive, it will be faster to access the driver there. If not, the Windows 2000 or Windows XP distribution CD will be required.

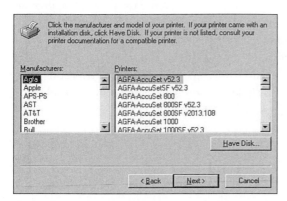

FIGURE 18.17 A list of printer manufacturers and models.

If the printer is not recognized as a model supported by the Windows 2000 or Windows XP driver lists, OEM drivers can be installed from a disk containing the OEMSETUP.INF file. Select the Have Disk option from the Add Printer Wizard screen. In Windows XP, you can also select the Windows Update option to search for updated drivers. After loading the driver, the wizard will request a name for the printer to identify it to the network system. Enter a unique name or use the default name supplied by Windows and continue.

EXAM ALERT

Know how to install device drivers in Windows if the particular printer is not listed in the standard Windows driver listings.

Finally, the Add Printer Wizard will ask whether the printer is to be shared with other units on the network. If so, the printer must have a unique name to identify it to others on the network and must be set as shared. The shared printer must also be set up for the different types of operating systems that may want to use it. The wizard will display a list of operating system types on the network. Any of or all the operating system types may be selected. The installation process is completed when the Finish button is clicked.

In Windows 2000, the Add Printer Wizard can also be accessed through the My Computer icon, the Control Panel, or by double-clicking the Printers folder or icon. However, in Windows XP, the My Computer path does not exist.

Printer Properties

Printer properties are all the defining features about a selected printer and include information that ranges from which port the printer uses, to what security features have been implemented with it. To examine or change the properties of a printer in Windows 2000, select the Printers option from the Start/Settings menu. In Windows XP, the path is Start/Printers and Faxes. Inside the Printer dialog page, click the desired printer to select it. From the File menu option, select the Properties entry to display the printer's Properties page, as depicted in Figure 18.18. Right-clicking the printer icon and then selecting the Properties option from the menu will also access this location.

FIGURE 18.18 Printer Properties page.

The General tab provides general information about the printer. This includes such information as its description, physical location, and installed driver name. The Ports tab lists the system's physical ports and the Scheduling tab displays the printer's availability, priority level, and spooling options. In Windows XP, the Scheduling tab has been replaced with a tab named Advanced. The Sharing tab shows the printer's share status and share name.

The Security tab provides access to three major components. These are the Permissions button, the Auditing button, and the Ownership button. The Permissions button enables the system administrator to establish the level of access for different users in the system. The Auditing button provides user and event-tracking capabilities for the administrator. Finally, the Ownership button displays the name of the printer's owner.

> **NOTE**
>
> Access to files and folders on NTFS volumes can be audited, allowing the tracking and discovery of potential security violations. However, this feature is not available on Windows XP Home Edition.

The Device Settings tab provides an array of information about the printer, including such items as paper tray sizes and font substitution tables. This feature is used to import downloadable font sets, install font cartridges, and increase the printer's virtual memory settings. The Device Settings tab is one of the most important tabs in a printer's Properties page.

Network Printing with Windows

Windows 2000 and Windows XP provide installation wizards to guide the network printer installation. If the physical printer is connected to a remote computer, referred to as a *print server*, the remote unit must supply the printer drivers and settings to control the printer. Likewise, the print server must be set up to share the printer with the other users on the network.

To install the network printer, access the My Network Places icon on the desktop, navigate the network to locate and open the remote computer's network name, right-click the remote unit's printer name, select the Connect option from the pop-up menu, and follow the directions provided by the Windows Add Printer Wizard. When the wizard produces a dialog box asking whether to install the selected printer, click the OK button. This should produce the Add Printer Wizard driver selection dialog box, shown in Figure 18.19. After the remote printer has been installed, the local computer can access it through the My Network Places icon.

Windows 2000 and Windows XP include a point-and print feature called Autopublish that enables you to install a printer driver on a client PC from any application. Active Directory also enables the user to browse the network for a specific printer type or location.

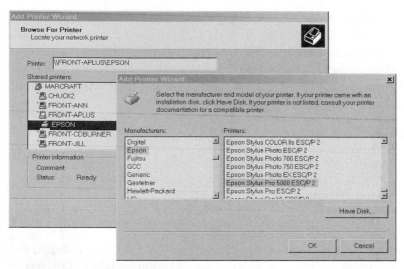

FIGURE 18.19   Installing a network printer in Windows.

The File/Print window includes a Find Printer button that you can use to search for printers locally, connected to the LAN, or connected across the Internet. After a printer has been located, Windows 2000 or XP will automatically install the driver for that printer on the client PC.

Scanners

Scanners convert pictures, line art, photographs, and text into electronic signals that can be processed by software packages such as desktop publishers and graphics design programs. These programs, in turn, can display the image on the video display or can print it out on a graphics printer.

Scanners are typically classified by the types of images they can reproduce. Some scanners can differentiate only between different levels of light and dark. These scanners are called *grayscale scanners*. *Color scanners*, on the other hand, include additional hardware that helps them distinguish among different colors. The software included with most scanners provides the user with at least a limited capability to manipulate the image after it has been scanned.

In a typical flatbed scanner, the scanner body remains stationary as the scan head moves past the paper. Figure 18.20 describes this process. The paper is placed face down on the scanner's glass window. The light source from the scanning mechanism is projected up through the glass and onto the paper. The lighter areas of the page reflect more light than the darker areas do.

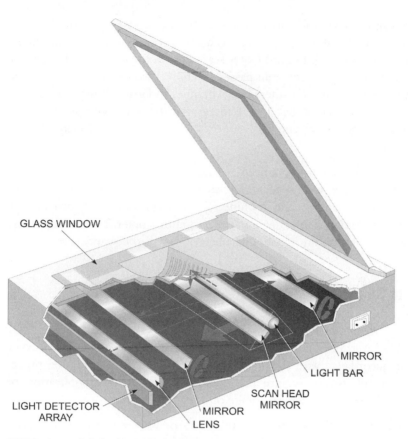

GLASS WINDOW

MIRROR

LIGHT BAR

SCAN HEAD
MIRROR

LIGHT DETECTOR
ARRAY

MIRROR

LENS

FIGURE 18.20   A flatbed scanner.

A precision positioning motor moves the scan head below the paper. As the head moves, light reflected from the paper is captured and channeled through a series of mirrors. The mirrors pivot to continually focus the reflected light on a light-sensitive diode. The diode converts the reflected light intensity into a corresponding digital value.

A normal flatbed scanner can achieve resolutions up to 4,800 or 9,600 dots per inch (dpi) or pixels. At these resolutions, each dot corresponds to about 1/90,000 of an inch. The higher the selected scanning resolution, the slower the computer and printer operate because of the increased amount of data that must be processed.

The digitized information is routed to the scanner adapter card in one of the PC's expansion slots. In main memory, the graphics information is stored in a format that can be manipulated by graphic design software.

Grayscale scanners can differentiate between varying levels of gray on the page. This capability is stated in shades. A good-quality grayscale scanner can differentiate between 256 levels of gray. Color scanners, on the other hand, use three passes to scan an image. Each scan passes the light through a colored filter to separate the colors from each other. The red, blue, and green filters create three different electronic images that can be integrated to form a complete picture. For intermediate colors, varying levels of the three colors are blended to create the desired shade.

Most scanners are currently produced as part of a multifunction office printer. These units combine several technologies to offer multiple standard office machine functions from a single machine. The functions normally provided by these units include the scanner, printer, fax, and photocopier. The heart of these machines is the photodrum technology shared among the scanner, the copier, and the printer.

Installing Scanners

Although some older scanners employed proprietary adapter cards, most scanners connect to one of the system's standard I/O ports. Newer scanners may employ a USB port or SCSI bus extension connection. These scanners must be installed in accordance with the appropriate SCSI or USB installation procedures. They will usually require that a supporting software application be installed in the system to take advantage of their feature sets.

Older scanners typically used the system's EPP- or ECP-enabled parallel port, as illustrated in Figure 18.21. When using one of the advanced parallel port options to support a scanner, it is important to use an approved IEEE-1284–compliant cabling. Older parallel printer cables were designed for unidirectional low-speed SPP communications and may prevent a bidirectional high-speed device such as a scanner from working correctly.

As with installing printers and other peripheral devices, there is more to installing a scanner than simply hooking it up to the computer and turning it on. First you should verify that the scanner is compatible with the system's I/O port options and its current operating system and applications. Make sure that there are device drivers available to support the scanner in question.

You should also take time to educate yourself or the user in the operation of the scanner being installed. Scanners can be configured to provide various levels of copy quality from basic draft level to near-perfect picture level. The trade-off for quality scanning is always file size and memory usage.

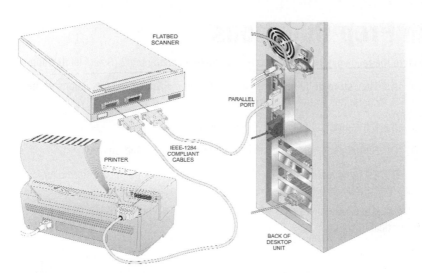

FIGURE 18.21   Connecting an IEEE-1284–compliant scanner.

The challenge is to balance these trade-offs to achieve the desired output results (for example, draft quality wedding photos will probably not make the customer happy, even though the files are smaller and they do not take up valuable storage space). These variables can be manipulated by configuring the scan for appropriate size/resolution and file format (some formats are more compact than others). Run test pages and experiment with how changing these variables affects the output.

Exam Prep Questions

1. Which of the following are true concerning bitmapped characters? (Select all that apply.)

   ○ **A.** They store dot patterns for all the possible size and style variations of the characters in the set.

   ○ **B.** Bitmapped fonts typically cannot be scaled and rotated.

   ○ **C.** Bitmapped characters can be printed out directly and quickly.

   ○ **D.** Each character is composed of a set of reference points and formulas.

2. Which font types are generated by establishing starting points and then calculating mathematical formulas?

   ○ **A.** Bitmapped fonts

   ○ **B.** Raster-scanned fonts

   ○ **C.** Vector-based fonts

   ○ **D.** TrueType outline fonts

3. What is the major purpose of a tractor-feed mechanism, and where is it most commonly used?

   ○ **A.** It is used on dot-matrix printers that print continuous forms.

   ○ **B.** It is used on inkjet printers that print continuous forms.

   ○ **C.** It is used on laser printers that print continuous forms.

   ○ **D.** It is used on color printers that print continuous forms.

4. How many print wires are in a high quality dot-matrix printhead?

   ○ **A.** 6, 10, or 1

   ○ **B.** 6, 12, or 14

   ○ **C.** 9, 12, or 18

   ○ **D.** 9, 18, or 24

5. What is the main circuit board in a printer called?

   ○ **A.** Printhead board

   ○ **B.** Main control board

   ○ **C.** Control panel

   ○ **D.** Sensor board

6. Which of the following is not a type of interface connection commonly used with printers?

   ◯ **A.** IrDA

   ◯ **B.** SCSI

   ◯ **C.** IDE

   ◯ **D.** USB

7. What types of connectors are used at the computer and the printer ends, respectively, of a parallel-printer cable?

   ◯ **A.** 36-pin Centronics and DB-25F

   ◯ **B.** DB-25M and 36-pin Centronics

   ◯ **C.** DB-25M and DB-9F

   ◯ **D.** DB-9M and DB-25M

8. What printer type produces print by squirting ink at the page?

   ◯ **A.** Thermal

   ◯ **B.** Inkjet

   ◯ **C.** Laser

   ◯ **D.** Dot-matrix

9. What techniques are used to form the ink drops in an inkjet printer? (Select two answers.)

   ◯ **A.** Electromagnetic acceleration

   ◯ **B.** Mechanical vibration

   ◯ **C.** Air pressure

   ◯ **D.** Thermal shock

10. What are the operational stages of a typical laser printer?

   ◯ **A.** Cleaning, conditioning, writing, transferring, developing, fusing

   ◯ **B.** Conditioning, writing, transferring, developing, fusing, cleaning

   ◯ **C.** Cleaning, conditioning, writing, developing, transferring, fusing

   ◯ **D.** Conditioning, writing, developing, transferring, fusing, cleaning

11. You should never expose the drum of a laser printer to _____.

◯ **A.** Cold temperatures

◯ **B.** A strong light source

◯ **C.** Air flow

◯ **D.** Toner dust

12. What are the functions of the two corona wires in a laser printer? (Select two answers.)

◯ **A.** They clean the drum.

◯ **B.** They fuse the toner to the paper.

◯ **C.** They transfer toner from the drum to the paper.

◯ **D.** They condition the drum to be written on.

13. What is the purpose of the thermal fuse in laser printers?

◯ **A.** It protects the paper from burning.

◯ **B.** It protects the fuser assembly from overheating.

◯ **C.** It fuses the toner image to the paper.

◯ **D.** It heats the fusing unit.

14. What is the HP laser printer cartridge called?

◯ **A.** Cartridge assembly

◯ **B.** HP cartridge

◯ **C.** Electrophotographic cartridge

◯ **D.** Cartridge unit

15. What problems can be created by using a noncompliant parallel cable with an IEEE-1284 bidirectional parallel device?

◯ **A.** The printer doesn't work.

◯ **B.** The printer output is jumbled.

◯ **C.** All characters print on the same line.

◯ **D.** Characters print but not graphics.

16. What type of connectors are used at the computer and the printer ends of an RS-232 serial printer cable, respectively?

- ○ **A.** 36-pin Centronics and DB-25F
- ○ **B.** DB-25M and 36-pin Centronics
- ○ **C.** DB-25F and DB-25M
- ○ **D.** DB-9F and DB-25M

17. What is the recommended maximum length of an RS-232 cable?

- ○ **A.** 10 feet (3 meters)
- ○ **B.** 30 feet (9 meters)
- ○ **C.** 50 feet (15 meters)
- ○ **D.** 100 feet (30 meters)

18. What are the recommended and maximum distances specified for IrDA printer connections?

- ○ **A.** 1 meter, 2 meters
- ○ **B.** 2 meters, 4 meters
- ○ **C.** 3 meters, 6 meters
- ○ **D.** 4 meters, 8 meters

19. How do you identify the presence of a network-ready printer? (Select two answers.)

- ○ **A.** RJ-11 jacks on the back of the printer.
- ○ **B.** RJ-45 jacks on the back of the printer.
- ○ **C.** RS-232 port on the back of the printer.
- ○ **D.** The network cable is connected to the printer.

20. How does a dot-matrix printer place characters on a page?

- ○ **A.** It squirts precisely controlled drops of ink onto the paper.
- ○ **B.** Magnetically charged ink particles are attracted to an ionized form on the paper.
- ○ **C.** Magnetically controlled pins place dots on the paper.
- ○ **D.** Fully formed metal characters force ink from a ribbon onto the paper.

21. What are the components found in a typical electrophotographic cartridge? (Select all that apply.)

    ○ **A.** Developing roller

    ○ **B.** Drum assembly

    ○ **C.** Compression roller

    ○ **D.** Corona wire

22. What is the function of the fuser unit in a laser printer?

    ○ **A.** It squirts the ink onto the paper.

    ○ **B.** It cleans the excess toner off the drum assembly.

    ○ **C.** It transfers toner to the paper.

    ○ **D.** It melts the toner onto the paper.

23. You are tasked with the installation of a new USB printer in a Windows XP Home system. Which of the following is the best procedure to use?

    ○ **A.** Place the manufacturer's installation disc in the drive and let the installation process install the correct drivers and tell you when to connect the printer.

    ○ **B.** Connect the printer to the computer, start up the computer system, and allow the Windows PNP process discover and install the proper driver for the printer.

    ○ **C.** Use the Add Printer Wizard and select a generic printer driver until the correct driver can be obtained from the Internet.

    ○ **D.** Insert the manufacturer's driver disc in the CD drive and let it configure the printer when Windows starts up.

24. The process that laser printers use to convert electronic images to printed documents is called _____.

    ○ **A.** Thermal image transfer

    ○ **B.** Dye sublimation

    ○ **C.** Toner fusing

    ○ **D.** Electrophotographic reproduction

25. What is the recommended maximum length of a standard parallel-printer cable?

   ○ **A.** 3 feet (1 meter)

   ○ **B.** 10 feet (3 meters)

   ○ **C.** 30 feet (9 meters)

   ○ **D.** 50 feet (15 meters)

26. Which of the following is a typical speed for data transfers between hard-wired, network printers and the network?

   ○ **A.** 54Mbps

   ○ **B.** 100Mbps

   ○ **C.** 2.4Gbps

   ○ **D.** 480MBps

Answers and Explanations

1. A, B, C. Bitmapped fonts store dot patterns for all the possible size and style variations of the characters in the set. Bitmapped fonts typically cannot be scaled and rotated. Bitmapped characters can be printed out directly and quickly.

2. C. Vector-based fonts store the outlines of the character styles and sizes as sets of mathematical formulas. Each character is composed of a set of reference points and connecting lines between them. These fonts can be scaled and rotated.

3. A. Pin tractors are usually employed with continuous and multilayer forms. These mechanisms can control paper slippage and misalignment created by the extra weight imposed by continuous forms. Tractors can be adjusted to handle various paper widths. Tractor feeds are used with very heavy forms, such as multiple-part, continuous forms, and are most commonly found on dot-matrix printers.

4. D. A typical printhead may contain 9, 18, or 24 print wires. The number of print wires used in the printhead is the major determining factor associated with a printer's character quality.

5. B. The main circuit board of a printer is referred to as the *main control board*.

6. C. The printer's interface may contain circuitry to handle serial data, parallel data, or a combination of the different interface types— Centronics parallel, RS-232 serial, SCSI, USB, or IrDA.

7. B. At the printer end of a parallel printer cable is a Centronics 36-pin connector. The computer end of the cable should have a DB-25M connector to plug into the system's DB-25F LPT port.

8. B. Inkjet printers produce characters by squirting a precisely controlled stream of ink drops onto the paper.

9. B, D. The drops are formed by one of two methods: thermal shock or mechanical vibration. Thermal shock heats the ink in a capillary tube, just behind the nozzle. This increases the pressure of the ink in the tube and causes it to explode through the opening. Mechanical vibration uses the vibrations from a piezoelectric crystal to force ink through a nozzle.

10. C. The six stages of operation in a laser printer are cleaning, conditioning, writing, developing, transferring, and fusing.

11. B. Exposing a laser printer's drum to light for more than a few minutes may damage it. The drum should never be touched; this too, can ruin its surface. Keep the unit away from dust and dirt, as well as from humidity and high-temperature areas.

12. C, D. A high voltage, applied to the primary corona wire, creates a highly charged negative field that conditions the drum to be written on by applying a uniform negative charge (–600V) to it. The transfer corona wire is responsible for transferring the toner from the drum to the paper.

13. B. A thermal fuse protects the fuser assembly from overheating and damaging the printer.

14. C. In Hewlett-Packard laser printers, the main portion of the printing system is contained in the electrophotographic cartridge.

15. A. The IEEE has established specifications for bidirectional parallel-printer cables (IEEE-1284). These cables affect the operation of EPP and ECP parallel devices. Using an older noncompliant unidirectional cable with a bidirectional parallel device will prevent the device from communicating properly with the system and may prevent it from operating. Some failures produce error messages, such as `Printer Not Ready`; others leave the data in the computer's print spooler. The symptom normally associated with this condition is that the parallel device refuses to operate.

16. D. A typical serial printer cable has either a female 9-pin D-shell connector (DB-9) or a female 25-pin D-shell connector that connects to the PC's serial (COM) port and a male 25-pin D-shell (DB-25M) that plugs into the printer.

17. C. RS-232 serial printers have a recommended maximum cable length of 50 feet (15 meters).

18. A. The IrDA specification calls for communication ranges up to 2 meters, but most implementations state 1 meter as the recommended range.

19. B, D. It is relatively easy to determine whether a printer is networked by the presence of a coaxial or a twisted-pair network cable connected directly to the printer. The presence of the RJ-45 jacks on the back of the printer also indicates that the printer is network capable, even if it is not being used in that manner.

20. C. Dot-matrix characters are printed in the form of dot patterns that represent the characters. The printhead in a dot-matrix printer is a vertical column of print wires controlled by electromagnets. Dots are created on the paper by energizing selected electromagnets, which extend the desired print wires from the printhead.

21. A, B, D. The electrophotographic cartridge contains the toner supply, the corona wire, the drum assembly, and the developing roller.

22. D. After the image has been transferred to the paper, a pair of compression rollers in the fusing unit press the toner particles into the paper while they melt the particles to it. The top compression roller, known as the *fusing roller*, is heated by a quartz lamp. This roller melts the toner to the paper as it exits the unit; the lower roller, known as the *compression roller*, applies pressure to the paper. A cleaning pad removes excess particles and applies a silicon lubricant to prevent toner from sticking to the Teflon-coated fusing roller.

23. B. To install a USB printer, connect the USB signal cable to the computer and to the printer, plug in the printer's power cord, and then allow the system to detect the printer through the PnP process when it is started up.

24. D. A laser printer creates an image on paper by writing the image on a special photographic drum, attracting a toner material to the image on the drum, transferring the toner to a page, and finally fusing it to the page. This process was pioneered by Xerox and is called *electrophotographic reproduction*.

25. B. Standard parallel printers have a recommended maximum cable length of 10 feet (3 meters).

26. B. A hardwired network printer is connected to the network through a built-in ethernet LAN adapter and will operate at UTP compatible speeds: 10Mbps, 100Mbps, or 1000 Mbps (1Gbps).

Challenge Solutions

1. You could install a serial printer in the warehouse. The range provided by the serial interface would enable you to move the printer to the warehouse without moving the computer out of the office.

2. In this situation, you could place the dot-matrix printer in the warehouse and connect it to the network. This would most likely involve setting up a print server computer in the warehouse to handle the networking part of the strategy. The accounting staff would then have to print across the network to the warehouse. The fact that several people must print to this printer makes using a serial printer interface (if available) impractical.

CHAPTER NINETEEN

Printer and Scanner Servicing

Terms you'll need to understand:

✓ Missing print

✓ Knowledge base

✓ Missing Beam errors

✓ Faint print

✓ Black pages

✓ White lines

✓ Smudged print

✓ Printer Not Ready

✓ Remanufactured toner cartridges

✓ Paper trays

✓ Paper jam error

✓ Ribbon cartridge

✓ Print spooler

✓ Windows Troubleshooters

✓ TWAIN drivers

Techniques you'll need to master:

Essentials 4.3—Identify tools, basic diagnostic procedures, and troubleshooting techniques for printers and scanners.

✓ Gather information about printer/scanner problems.

  ✓ Identify symptom.

  ✓ Review device error codes, computer error messages, and history (for example, event log, user reports).

  ✓ Print or scan test page.

  ✓ Use appropriate generic or vendor-specific diagnostic tools, including web-based utilities.

✓ Review and analyze collected data.

  ✓ Establish probable causes.

  ✓ Review service documentation.

  ✓ Review knowledge base and define and isolate the problem (for example, software versus hardware, driver, connectivity, printer).

✓ Identify solutions to identified printer/scanner problems.

  ✓ Define specific cause and apply fix.

✓ Replace consumables as needed.

✓ Verify functionality and get user acceptance of problem fix.

Remote Support Technician 3.3—Identify tools, diagnostic procedures, and troubleshooting techniques for printers and scanners.

✓ Gather information required to troubleshoot printer/scanner problems.

✓ Troubleshoot print failure (for example, lack of paper, clear queue, restart print spooler, recycle power on printer, inspect for jams, check for visual indicators).

Depot Technician 3.3/IT Technician 4.3—Identify tools and diagnostic procedures for troubleshooting printers and scanners.

✓ Gather information about printer/scanner problems.

✓ Review and analyze collected data about printer/scanner problems.

✓ Isolate and resolve identified printer/scanner problem, including defining cause, applying fix, and verifying functionality.

✓ Identify appropriate tools used for troubleshooting and repairing printer/scanner problems.

   ✓ Multimeter

   ✓ Screwdrivers

   ✓ Cleaning solutions

   ✓ Extension magnet

   ✓ Test patterns

Depot Technician 3.4/IT Technician 4.4—Perform preventative maintenance of printers and scanners.

✓ Perform scheduled maintenance according to vendor guidelines (for example, install maintenance kits, reset page counts).

✓ Ensure suitable environment.

✓ Use recommended supplies.

Introduction

This chapter covers the Printers and Scanners Troubleshooting areas of the CompTIA A+ Certification—Essentials examination under Objectives 4.3. It also covers the Preventive Maintenance of Printers and Scanners area that is generally testable under Objective 3.4 of the Depot Technician exam and Objective 4.4 of the IT Technician exam.

Printers are routinely connected to personal computers and they break down. Therefore, the computer technician should be familiar with common printer problems and be able to demonstrate effective service techniques.

> **NOTE**
>
> Objective 4.3 of the Essential exam covers essentially the same subobjectives as Depot Technician Objective 2.3 and IT Tech Objective 4.3. The latter two objectives list specific "tools" that you should be able to "identify," and the Essentials objective states that you should be able to "Use appropriate generic or vendor-specific tools...". Remote Support Technician Objective 3.3 uses broader statements to cover these topics: "Gather information..." and "Troubleshoot" specific print failures. Likewise, the Depot Technician Objective 3.4 states this as "Implement solutions to solve identified printer/scanner problems."
>
> The Depot Technician 3.4 and IT Technician 4.4 objectives use the same wording to cover Preventive Maintenance of Printers and Scanners. This includes "Use scheduled maintenance and vendor guidelines, suitable environment, and use recommended supplies."
>
> The topics specified in these different exam/objective areas are so closely stated that it makes sense that they are presented as the same discussion. You will need to study this material in this chapter for any of the four exams you intend to challenge.

Servicing Printers

The preliminary steps for troubleshooting printer problems are similar to those used with other electronic devices: Begin with the simple and obvious possibilities. This includes talking to the user or operator to gather information about the problem. Then check for simple causes, such as the printer not being plugged into the power source or not being connected to the host computer. It is a good practice to cycle the power on the printer off and back on to see whether problems clear up by resetting the printer system.

You should note any visual error indicators, codes, or messages presented by the printer. These messages are often coded and will require that you refer to the user's manual for explanation. It makes much more sense to look up the meaning of a code than to go directly to troubleshooting activities. The device is trying to make your life easier—listen to it. You may need to add paper, clear a jammed page from the printer, clear the printer queue, or restart the print spooler. Often, common problems such as low toner or a paper jam will be indicated through front panel LEDs or onscreen messages, making your job much simpler.

> **EXAM ALERT**
>
> Be aware of simple checks to make in response to error codes and messages presented by the printer.

However, if these simple things are not the cause of a problem you are trying to isolate, some organizations suggest that you divide the troubleshooting process into two activities: Review and analyze the data you've collected and then identify solutions for the problem. Use any printer diagnostic tools available. These include diagnostic utilities provided by the manufacturer as well as third-party tools. The Internet is a good source of general (and sometimes specific) printer troubleshooting information, as well as a source of troubleshooting utilities.

Begin the review process by establishing probable causes (hardware, software, drivers, or connectivity) for the symptoms you are observing. Then review the printer's (or multifunction device's) service documentation for information related to the problem. Also review any available knowledge bases for references to the problem being observed. In many cases, these knowledge bases have built-in search functions that let you go directly to information related to keywords used to describe the problem.

The next step is to identify solutions for the problem you're observing. The following sections of this chapter deal with typical problems encountered with dot-matrix, inkjet, and laser printers. They also include troubleshooting methods associated with each type of printer. Use this information to define a specific cause and apply a fix to the problem. When you're finished, always verify the printer's functionality and get the owner/user to sign off on the repair.

General Printer Troubleshooting

The classic first step in determining the cause of any printer problem is to determine which part of the printer-related system is at fault: the host computer, the signal cable, or the printer.

Most printers have built-in power supplies. Troubleshooting procedures for these power supplies are identical to those presented for computer power supplies. Check for the presence of indicator lights and motor noise when power is applied to the printer. Printers run their own POSTs when started, and they produce error messages when problems exist. For example, if the printer remains in a constant state of startup, this is equivalent to the computer not passing the POST portion of the bootup process. The meanings of these messages are either obvious or can be found in the printer's user manual.

> **CAUTION**
>
> Printer power supplies are typically open circuit boards and present possibly lethal voltages if the printer case is open.

Nearly every printer is equipped with a built-in self-test. The easiest way to determine whether the printer is at fault is to run its self-test routine. If the self-test runs and prints clean pages, most of the printer has been eliminated as a possible source of problems. The problem could be in the computer, the cabling, or the interface portion of the printer. If the printer fails the self-test, it will be necessary to troubleshoot the printer's problem.

> **EXAM ALERT**
>
> Know what it means if the printer produces a satisfactory self-test printout but does not print from the computer.

If the printer's self test runs successfully, it will be necessary to troubleshoot its interface, the signal cable (or other communication media), and the printer configuration on the host computer.

Main Control Board Problems

Even though the printer may run a self-test correctly, there is still an area of the printer that could be defective: its interface circuitry. Functions associated with this part of the printer are primarily confined to its main control board. Figure 19.1 illustrates the interface/controller position in a typical printer system.

The main board contains most of the printer's circuitry. Unlike PC system boards, printer main boards typically don't contain many Field Replacable Units (FRU) components. The exception is that the firmware on the printer's main board can be upgraded by replacing the IC or through the flash process. When main board problems occur with low-end dot-matrix and inkjet printers, the cost involved in replacing a main board often exceeds the value of the used product. Therefore, most printers in these categories are replaced when a hardware problem occurs.

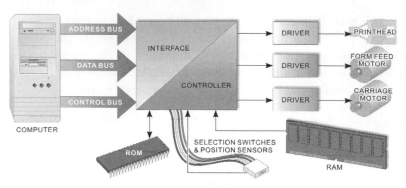

FIGURE 19.1   Printer interface/controller functions.

With more expensive laser printers, replacing a main board is still an acceptable practice. These printers also provide for additional RAM to be installed to increase the printer's buffer memory capacity. The print buffer holds data and instructions from the computer and provides speed matching between the slower printer and the faster computer interface.

If the printer has too little RAM, or defective RAM, the operation of the printer can be negatively affected or prevented. In these printers, the RAM is mounted on DIMM cards that can be replaced and tested by substitution. This option also allows for the printer's memory capabilities to be upgraded to provide more efficient (and error-free) operation when dealing with large files and complex document/image types.

The motors, sensors, and switches can be treated as FRUs in many printers. This is particularly true with more expensive laser printers. In most printers, the entire main control panel can be exchanged for another unit. This effectively changes all the user-operated input switches at one time.

Be sure, however, before you discard a low-end dot-matrix or inkjet printer (or replace the main board in a laser printer), that you check the printer's documentation and the manufacturer's website for possible explanations, configuration settings, and solutions for that printer.

Checking the Computer

At the host computer's end of the printing process, there are only three items to consider: the port circuitry is not enabled or has failed, the printer driver is incorrect or corrupted, or the printing application or subsystem is having problems.

The first place to check for host computer-related printing problems is the Advanced CMOS Setup screens to make certain that the port the printer is using has been enabled for operation. If the port is enabled and activated, use Device

Manager to check its resource allocations, its operational condition, and its driver information. If Device Manager indicates that the hardware portion of the port is functioning correctly, check for new or updated drivers for the printer being used. If it shows that the port is malfunctioning, use the built-in Windows Troubleshooters to isolate the cause of the problem.

If the connection between the printer and the computer is based on one of the newer interfaces, such as USB or IEEE-1394 ports, try removing power from the printer, disconnecting the interface cable from the computer, and removing its device driver from the system using Device Manager. Then restart the computer, reconnect the cable to the port, reapply power to the printer, and allow the system to recognize the "new" device and reconfigure it.

If no hardware or port problems are indicated, it will be necessary to troubleshoot the software side of the host system. Fortunately, Windows controls most of the printing for the software portion of the system through its drivers. Refer to the "Troubleshooting Windows Printing Problems" section of Chapter 17, "Basic Operating System Troubleshooting and Maintenance," to troubleshoot this portion of the system.

Checking Printer Cables

If the printer and the host computer show no signs of being the source of printing problems, the only component left to check is the communication link between the printer and the computer—that is, the cable or wireless link.

Printer signal cables can be tested for continuity using the resistance function of a digital meter or by substitution with a known-good cable. In the case of direct-connect, network-ready printers, you must check the LAN cable with a cable tester.

Determine whether the printer is connected to the system through a print-sharing device. If so, connect the printer directly to the system and test it. It is not a good practice to use laser printers with these types of devices. A better arrangement is to install—or just use a different port or port type to attach—an additional printer to the system. If access to several printers is required, it might be better to network the printers to the system.

EXAM ALERT

Be aware that laser printers are not good candidates for use with print-sharing devices.

The IEEE has established specifications for bidirectional parallel-printer cables (IEEE-1284). These cables affect the operation of Enhanced Parallel Port (EPP) and Extended Capabilities Port (ECP) parallel devices. Using an older, noncompliant unidirectional cable with a bidirectional parallel device will prevent the device from communicating properly with the system and may prevent it from operating. Some failures produce error messages, such as `Printer Not Ready`; others leave the data in the computer's print spooler. The symptom normally associated with this condition is that the parallel device refuses to operate.

EXAM ALERT

Be aware of the problems that can be created by using a noncompliant parallel cable with an IEEE-1284 bidirectional parallel device.

Challenge #1

You are called out to a customer's site to check his laser printer. The printer sits on the desk next to the host computer and is attached to the back of the system. When you start the printer, it shows no startup errors and prints a page from a self-test. Then you check the system's CMOS settings to verify that the printer port is enabled and that it is set for ECP operation. Still, you cannot get the system to print a page from the printer. What should you check next?

Troubleshooting Dot-Matrix Printers

Begin the troubleshooting process by running the dot-matrix printer's built-in self-test. As indicated earlier, if the self-test runs and prints clean pages, most of the printer has been eliminated as a possible source of problems. Check the host computer (if present), the cabling, or the interface portion of the printer. If the printer fails the self-test, however, you must troubleshoot the printer's problem based on the symptoms it produces.

Like other peripheral devices, printers can be configured to operate in different modes. In the case of dot-matrix printers, the configuration settings are normally entered into the printer through the buttons of its control panel. Typical dot-matrix configuration settings include printer mode, perforation skip (for continuous forms), automatic line feed at the bottom of the page, paper-handling type, ASCII character codes (7-bit or 8-bit), and basic character sets. Other quantities that can be configured on a dot-matrix printer can include print font, character pitch, and form length.

Dot-Matrix Printer Power Supply Problems

If the printer does not function and displays no lights, makes no sounds, and performs no actions, the power supply is generally involved. Check the online light. If the printer is offline, no print action will occur. A missing or improperly installed ribbon cartridge will also prevent the unit from printing. Plug a lamp or other device into the outlet to verify that it is operative. Check to see that the power cord is plugged securely into the printer and the socket. Make sure that the power switch is turned on.

Check the power supply's fuse to make sure that it is good. If the fuse is blown, replace it with a fuse of the same type and rating. Fuses do not usually blow unless another component fails. Another possible cause of excessive current occurs when a motor (or its gear train) binds and cannot move. Check the drive mechanisms and motors for signs of binding. If none of the printer sections work when everything is connected and power is applied, you should exchange the power-supply board for a new unit.

Dot-Matrix Consumables

One consideration that must be taken into account when buying a printer is the cost associated with the ongoing operation of the unit. There are generally two consumable items associated with dot-matrix printers that represent the ongoing cost of using the printer: ribbon cartridges and paper.

The single item in a dot-matrix printer that requires the most attention is the ribbon cartridge. It is considered a consumable part of the printer and must be changed often. The ink ribbon is stored in a controlled wad inside the cartridge and moves across the face of the platen, as depicted in Figure 19.2. A take-up wheel draws new ribbon out of the wad as it is used.

> **EXAM ALERT**
>
> Remember that the ribbon cartridge is the item in a dot-matrix printer that requires the most attention.

As the ribbon wears out, the printing will become faint and uneven. When the print becomes noticeably faint, the cartridge should be replaced. Most dot-matrix printers use a snap-in ribbon cartridge. To replace a typical ribbon cartridge, move the printhead carriage assembly to the center of the printer. Remove the old cartridge by freeing it from its clips or holders, and then lift it out of the printer. Tighten the ribbon tension by advancing the tension knob on the cartridge in a counterclockwise direction until the ribbon is taut. Snap the cartridge into place, making certain that the ribbon slides between the printhead and the ribbon mask. Slide the printhead assembly back and forth on the rod to check for proper ribbon movement.

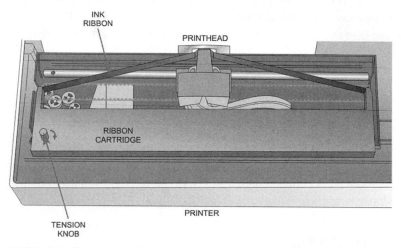

FIGURE 19.2 The printer ribbon cartridge.

The other consumable item associated with dot-matrix printers is paper. Unlike the other printer types, dot-matrix printers are capable of using a wide range of different paper types. Less-expensive dot-matrix printers typically work with paper of a single page width that can be inserted as single sheets through a single-sheet feeder mechanism. These sheets are usually 8.5×11 inch bond paper sheets in the United States. A similar A4 paper size defined by the International Standards Organization (ISO) is more prevalent outside the United States.

Paper Specifications

One of the biggest problems associated with any printer occurs when the wrong paper type or paper type setting is used. The most fundamental specification for paper is weight. Paper is specified in terms of its weight per 500 sheets at 17 inches × 22 inches (for example, 500 sheets of 17-inch × 22-inch, 21-pound bond paper will weigh 21 pounds).

Printhead Not Printing

If none of the printhead's print wires are being energized, the first step should be to exchange the control board for a known-good one of the same type. If the new control board does not correct the problem, replace the printhead. A power-supply problem could also cause the printhead not to print.

A related problem occurs when one or more of the print wires do not fire. If this is the case, check the printhead for physical damage. Also, check the flexible signal cable for a broken conductor. If the control board delivers any of the other print-wire signals, the problem is most likely the printhead mechanism. Replace the printhead as a first step. If the problem continues after replacing the printhead, however, exchange the control board for a new one.

If the tops of characters are missing, the printhead is misaligned with the platen. It may need to be reseated in the printhead carriage, or the carriage assembly may need to be adjusted to the proper height and angle.

If the output of the printer gets lighter as it moves from left to right across the page, it may be necessary to adjust the spacing between the platen and the printhead carriage rod to obtain proper printing.

To exchange a dot-matrix printhead assembly, make sure that it is cool enough to be handled. These units can get hot enough to cause a serious burn.

EXAM ALERT

Remember that the printhead of dot-matrix printers generates a great deal of heat and can be a burn hazard when you're working on these units.

Printhead Not Moving

If the printhead is printing but not moving across the page, a single block of print will be generated on the page. When this type of problem occurs, the related components include the printhead positioning motor, the timing belt, the home-position and timing sensors, the control board, and possibly the power-supply board.

With the power off, manually move the printhead to the center of the printer. Turn the printer on to see whether the printhead seeks the home position at the far-left side of the printer. If it moves to the left side of the printer and does not shut off, or does not return to the center of the printer, the home-position sensor is malfunctioning and should be replaced.

If the printhead moves on startup but does not move during normal printing, the control board should be replaced. In the event that the printhead assembly does not move at any time, the printhead-positioning motor should be replaced. If the print is skewed from left to right as it moves down the page, the printer's bidirectional mode settings may be faulty, or the home-position/end-of-line sensors may be defective.

Paper Not Advancing

When the paper does not advance, the output will usually be one line of dark blocks across the page. Examine the printer's paper-feed selector lever to make sure that it is set properly for the type of paper feed selected (friction feed, pin feed, or tractor feed). If the paper feed is set correctly, the printer is online, and the paper does not move, it will be necessary to troubleshoot the paper-feed motor and gear train. Check the motor and gear train by setting the printer to the offline mode and holding down the Form Feed (FF) button.

EXAM ALERT

Know the type of output that will be generated by a dot-matrix printer when the paper advance does not work.

Challenge #2

You get a call from your warehouse manager complaining about the serial printer you installed in his warehouse. It seems that soon after you installed the new dot-matrix printer, the text on the multipart forms became uneven from side to side and printed on an uphill slant. When you check out the printer, you determine that the paper is slipping from the weight of the multipart continuous forms. What can you do to fix this printing problem on the new printer?

If the feed motor and gear train work from this point, the problem must exist in the control board, the interface cable, the printer's configuration, or the computer system. If the motor and/or the gear train do not respond, unplug the paper-feed motor cable and check the resistance of the motor windings. If the windings are open, replace the paper-feed motor.

Troubleshooting Inkjet Printers

As with the dot-matrix printer, the first step in determining the cause of an inkjet printer problem is to determine which part of the printer system is at fault: the host computer, the signal cable, or the printer.

Inkjet Printer Configuration Checks

A color inkjet printer uses four ink colors to produce color images. These are cyan, magenta, yellow, and black (referred to as *CMYK color*). To create other colors, the printer prints a predetermined percentage of the basic colors in close proximity to each other. You can also configure the basic appearance of color and grayscale images produced by the inkjet printer.

Inkjet Consumables

Like dot-matrix printers, there are two consumable items typically related to inkjet printers: ink cartridges and paper. The single item in an inkjet printer that requires the most attention is the ink cartridge (or cartridges).

The density of the printout from an inkjet printer can be adjusted through its printing software. However, when the print becomes noticeably faint or the resolution becomes unacceptable, the ink cartridge needs to be replaced. Most inkjet printers use a self-contained, snap-in ink cartridge. Some models have combined ink cartridges that replace all three colors and the black ink at the same time. Other models use individual cartridges for each color.

EXAM ALERT

Be aware that print density can be adjusted through software in an inkjet printer.

EXAM ALERT

Know what the symptoms are of an inkjet printer cartridge going dry.

You can pop an ink cartridge out of the printhead assembly and thereby inspect the inkjets. If any of or all the jets are clogged, it is usually possible to clear them by running the printer's built in nozzle-cleaning function. In a Windows environment, this operation can be performed through the printer's Properties page. If this fails to clear the clogged jets, gently wipe the face of the cartridge with a nonfibrous swab. Small fibers left behind by typical cotton swabs can partially clog the jets and produce irregularly shaped ink drops that will not travel in the correct path to the paper. A gentle squeeze of the ink reservoir can also help to unblock a clogged jet. The surface tension of the ink keeps it from running out of the nozzle when it is not energized. Using solvents to clear blockages in the jets can dilute the ink, reduce its surface tension characteristics, and allow it to flow uncontrollably through the jet.

EXAM ALERT

Be aware of the consequences of using a solvent to unclog an inkjet nozzle.

To replace a typical ink cartridge, refer to its documentation and position the cartridge assembly as instructed in the manual (you will usually be asked to move the printhead carriage assembly to the center of the printer or completely to one end or the other). Remove the old cartridge by freeing it from its clips or holders and lifting it out of the printer. After replacing the ink cartridge, you should cycle the printer on so that it will go through its normal warm-up procedures. During these procedures the printer performs a thorough cleaning of the inkjet nozzles and gets the ink flowing correctly from the nozzles.

Printhead Not Printing

If the printhead is moving but not printing, begin by checking the ink supply in the print cartridge. The reservoir does not have to be completely empty to fail. Next, attempt to print from the self-test. If the printer does not print from the self-test, the components involved include the printhead, the flexible signal cable (between the control board and the printhead), the main control board, and possibly the power supply board.

If none of the inkjets is firing, you should exchange the ink cartridges for new ones. If a single inkjet is not firing, the output will appear as white lines on the page; replace the cartridge that is not working. If one of the jets is activated all the time, black or colored lines will be produced on the page. To isolate the cause of these problems, perform the following actions one at a time: replace the print cartridge, check the flexible cabling for continuity and for short-circuits between adjacent conductors, exchange the control board for a known-good one, and, finally, check the power supply.

Printhead Not Moving

If the printhead is printing but not moving across the page, a single block of print will usually be generated on the page. When this type of problem occurs, the related components include the printhead-positioning motor, the timing belt, the home-position sensor, the control board, and possibly the power supply.

With the power off, manually move the printhead to the center of the printer. Turn the printer on to see whether the printhead seeks the home position at the far end of the printer. If the printhead moves to the end of the printer and does not shut off, or if it does not return to the center of the printer, the home-position sensor is malfunctioning and should be replaced. If the printhead moves on startup, but does not move during normal printing, the control board should be replaced. In the event that the printhead assembly does not move at any time, check to see whether the printer is in maintenance mode. In this mode, the printer typically keeps the printhead assembly locked in the home position. If no mode configuration problems are present, the printhead-positioning motor should be replaced.

> **EXAM ALERT**
>
> Be aware of the maintenance mode setting in inkjet printers and know that this setting can adversely affect troubleshooting procedures.

Paper Not Advancing

When the paper does not advance in an inkjet printer, the output will usually be a thick, dark line across the page. Check the Control Panel to see that the printer is online. If the printer is online and the paper does not move, you must troubleshoot the paper-handling motor and gear train. Check the motor and gear train by setting the printer to the offline mode and holding down the Form Feed button.

If the printer's paper thickness selector is set improperly, or the rollers in its paper feed system become worn, the paper can slip as it moves through the printer and cause disfigured graphics to be produced. Check the printer's paper-thickness settings. If they are correct and the print output is disfigured, you need to replace the paper feed rollers.

> **EXAM ALERT**
>
> Know what types of problems can cause disfigured print in an inkjet printer.

Troubleshooting Laser Printers

Many of the problems encountered in laser printers are similar to those found in other printer types. For example, notice that most of the symptoms listed in the following section relate to the printer not printing, not printing correctly, and not moving paper through the printer.

Due to the extreme complexity of the laser printer's paper-handling system, paper jams are a common problem. This problem tends to increase in frequency as the printer's components wear from use. Basically, paper jams occur in all three main sections of the printer. These sections are

- ▶ The pickup area
- ▶ The registration area
- ▶ The fusing area

If the rubber separation pad in the pickup area is worn excessively, more than one sheet of paper may be drawn into the printer, causing it to jam. Additional, optional paper-handling features—such as duplexers (for double-sided copying) and collators (for sorting)—can contribute to the possibility of jams as they wear. Paper problems can also cause jams to occur. Using paper that is too heavy or too thick can result in jams, as can overloading paper trays. Similarly, using the wrong type of paper can defeat the separation pad and allow multiple pages to be drawn into the printer at one time. In this case, multiple sheets can move through the printer together, or they might result in a jam. Using coated paper stock can be hazardous because the coating may melt or catch fire.

CAUTION

Laser printers tend to have several high-voltage and high-temperature hazards inside. To get the laser printer into a position where you can observe its operation, it will be necessary to defeat some interlock sensors. This action will place you in potential contact with the high-voltage, high-temperature areas previously mentioned. Take great care when working inside a laser printer.

Laser Printer Consumables

In laser printers, the normal consumable items include toner and paper. As mentioned earlier, the toner cartridge in many laser printer models also contains the drum and the corona wires. Therefore, when you change the toner cartridge you also replace these components with new ones.

In most laser printers, the toner cartridges are designed so that they can be refilled. At present, the third-party refill cartridges (also known as *remanufactured toner cartridges*, or *RTCs*) typically are not as good as those from the manufacturer; however, they tend to be much cheaper than original equipment cartridges. If the output from the printer does not have to be very high quality, using refilled toner cartridges might be an option. To date, no regulations govern the disposal of laser-printer cartridges.

Although laser printers are capable of working with normal bond paper (and are most commonly used with this paper), a special grade of paper exists, referred to as *laser printer paper*. This paper is similar to the special inkjet papers described earlier in this chapter. However, laser printer paper is designed to work with the toner fusion and compression operations that occur in the laser printer. It is also designed to withstand the relatively high temperatures associated with these operations.

Printer Is Dead or Partially Disabled

If the printer does not start up, check all the normal, power-supply-related components (power cord, power outlet, internal fuses, and so on). If the printer's fans and lights are working, check other components that are associated with a defective power supply, including the main motor and gear train, the high-voltage corona wires, the drum assembly, and the fusing rollers.

If the high-voltage portion of the power supply that serves the corona wires and drum sections is defective, the image delivered to the page will be affected. If the high-voltage section of the power supply fails, the transfers of toner to the drum and then to the paper cannot occur. In addition, the contrast control will not be operational.

EXAM ALERT

Know what conditions will cause the contrast control on a laser printer not to work.

In cases of partial failure, the image produced will have a washed-out appearance. Replace the high-voltage section of the power supply and/or the drum unit. If a separate corona wire is used, let the printer cool sufficiently and replace the wire. Never reach into the high-voltage, high-temperature corona area while power is applied to the printer. Also, avoid placing conductive instruments in this area.

If the DC portion of the power supply fails, the laser beam will not be produced, creating a `Missing Beam` error message. The components involved in this error are the laser/scanning module, the control board, and the DC portion of the power supply.

Print on Page Is Missing or Bad

Many of the problems encountered in laser printers are associated with missing or defective print on the page. Normal print delivery problems fall into the following eight categories:

- ▶ Black pages
- ▶ White (blank) pages
- ▶ Faint print
- ▶ Smudged print
- ▶ Random specks on the page
- ▶ White lines along the page
- ▶ Faulty print at regular intervals on the page
- ▶ Print missing from some portion of the page

A black page indicates that toner has been attracted to the entire page. This condition could be caused by a failure of the primary corona, the laser-scanning module, or the main control board. If the laser is in a continuous on condition, the entire drum will attract toner. Likewise, if the primary corona is defective, the uniform negative charge will not be developed on the drum to repel toner. Replace the primary corona and/or drum assembly. If the problem continues, replace the laser-scanning module and the main control board.

On the other end of the spectrum, a white (or blank) page indicates that no information is being written on the drum. This condition usually involves the laser-scanning module, the control board, and the power supply. Another white-page fault occurs when the corona wire becomes broken, contaminated, or corroded, so that the attracting charge between the drum and the paper is severely reduced.

EXAM ALERT

Know what types of problems produce blank pages from a laser printer.

Specks and stains on the page may be caused by a worn cleaning pad or by a defective corona wire. If the cleaning pad is worn, it will not remove excess toner from the page during the fusing process. If the corona wire's grid does not regulate the charge level on the drum, dark spots will appear in the print. To correct these situations, replace the corona assembly by exchanging the toner cartridge or drum unit. Also, replace the cleaning pad in the fusing unit. If the page still contains specks after changing the cartridge, run several pages through the printer to clear excess toner that may have collected in the printer.

White lines that run along the length of the page are usually a sign of poorly distributed toner. Try removing the toner cartridge and gently shaking it to redistribute the toner. Another cause of white lines is damaged or weakened corona wires. Check and clean the corona wires, if they are accessible, or replace the module containing the corona wires.

Faint print in a laser printer can be caused by a number of things. If the contrast control is set too low, or the toner level in the cartridge is low, empty, or poorly distributed, the print quality can appear washed out. Correcting these symptoms is fairly easy; adjust the contrast control, remove the toner cartridge, inspect it, shake it gently (if it is a sealed unit), and retry it.

If the print does not improve, replace the toner cartridge. Other causes of faint print include a weakened corona wire or a weakened high-voltage power supply that drives it. Replace the unit that contains the corona wire. Replace the high-voltage power supply. Make sure that latent voltages have been drained off the high-voltage power supply before working with it.

Faults in the print output that occur at regular intervals along the page are usually caused by mechanical problems. When roller and transport mechanisms begin to wear in the printer, bad registration and bad print appear in cyclic form. This can be attributed to the dimensions of cyclic components such as the drum, the developing roller in the toner cartridge, or the fusing roller. When you have cyclic problems, examine the various mechanical components for wear or defects.

Missing print is usually attributed to a bad or misaligned laser-scanning module. If this module is not correctly installed, it cannot deliver lines of print to the correct areas of the page. Likewise, if the scanning mirror has a defect or is dirty, portions of the print will not be scanned on the drum. Another cause of missing print involves the toner cartridge and low or poorly distributed toner. If the toner does not come out of the cartridge uniformly, areas of missing print can be created. A damaged or worn drum can also be a cause of repeated missing print. If areas of the drum do not hold the charge properly, toner will not transfer to the drum or to the page correctly.

Smudged print is normally a sign of a failure in the fusing section. If the fusing roller's temperature or pressure is not sufficient to bond the toner to the page, the print will smudge when touched. When the heating element or lamp in the fusing area does not receive adequate AC power from the power supply, the toner will not adhere to the page as it should. This condition will result in smudged output. Examine the fuser unit, the power supply, and the fusing roller's heating unit. The printer may also produce `Fuser Error` messages on its display panel when fuser problems occur.

> **EXAM ALERT**
>
> Be aware of symptoms and error messages produced by fuser problems.

> **Challenge #3**
>
> One of your customers calls you, complaining that the pages coming out of the laser printer have spots where print does not show up. The customer has changed the toner cartridge, but nothing improved. Now the customer wants your advice on what to do next. What should you say?

Paper Does Not Feed or Is Jammed

If the paper does not feed at all, the place to begin checking is the paper-tray area. The paper trays have a complex set of sensors and pickup mechanisms that must all be functioning properly to begin the paper handling. Because of the complexity of the paper-pickup operation, jams are most likely to occur in this area.

Check the paper tray to make sure that there is paper in it and that it has the correct size of paper in it. Each tray in a laser printer has a set of tabs that contact sensor switches to tell the control circuitry that the tray is installed and what size paper is in it. A mechanical arm and photodetector are used to sense the presence of paper in the tray. If these switches are set incorrectly, the printer could print a page that is sized incorrectly for the actual paper size.

EXAM ALERT

Be aware of the consequences of incorrectly setting the paper tray switches in a laser printer.

If the printer's display panel indicates a `Paper Out` or `Paper Feed` error message, locate and actuate the paper detector by hand (lift it up). While holding the paper sensor, check the sensor switches by pressing each one individually. If the `Paper Out` message does not go out when any of the individual switches is pressed, replace that switch. If none of the switches show good, replace the paper sensor and arm. Also, check the spring-loaded plate in the bottom of the tray to make sure that it is forcing paper up to the pickup roller when the tray is installed in the printer.

The paper pickup roller must pull the top sheet of paper off the paper stack in the tray. The controller actuates a solenoid that engages the pickup roller's gear train. The pickup roller moves the paper into position against the registration rollers. If the printer's display panel shows a jam in the pickup area, check to make sure that the paper tray is functional, and then begin troubleshooting the pickup roller and main gear train. If the gear train is not moving, the main motor and controller board need to be checked. The power supply board may also be a cause of the problem.

EXAM ALERT

Remember which laser printer components are associated with `Paper Out` or `Paper Feed` errors.

If the paper feeds into the printer but jams after the process has begun, troubleshoot the particular section of the printer where the jam is occurring—pickup, registration, fusing area, and output devices (collators and duplexers). This information is generally presented to the user through the laser printer's display panel.

Another cause of laser printer jams is the presence of some obstruction in the paper path. Check for pieces of paper that have torn loose and lodged in the printer's paper path. In most laser printers, mechanical components are part of a replaceable module (the drum unit, the developing unit, or the fusing unit). If the motor and all the exposed gears are working, replace these units one at a time.

Many times, a paper jam error indication remains even after the paper has been removed from the laser printer. This is typically caused by a safety interlock error. Simply opening the printer's main access door should clear the error.

> **EXAM ALERT**
>
> Be aware that you may need to open the printer's access door to clear a paper jam after the jammed paper has been removed.

Troubleshooting Scanners

The scanning system is composed of three elements: the scanner, the interface cable, and the host computer. The scanning process is usually initiated by an application running on the host computer.

When the scanner receives the signal to perform the scan, the scanning mechanism will move the light source across the scanning area and then return it to its resting position. The light source should be on as long as power is supplied. If the light source is not shining, verify that the scanner is plugged into a working power source and that its On/Off switch (if present) is in the On position. The expected service life of a flatbed scanner lamp is 10,000 hours. To prolong the life of the bulb, you should turn the scanner off when not in use (if possible).

Some scanners have locking mechanisms that prevent the light source from moving inside the housing during transportation. If the light source is on but will not move when the system applies a scan request, refer to the scanner's documentation to determine whether your scanner has a locking mechanism. If so, check to make sure that the scanner is unlocked.

> **EXAM ALERT**
>
> Remember that some scanners have locking mechanisms that protect the light source from being damaged during transportation.

If possible, install the scanner on a different PC or another port. If the scanner fails to work on multiple systems, the problem is likely the signal cable or the scanner. Use a different cable or interface type if possible to limit the problem to the scanner.

Image Quality Problems

Use the following advice to troubleshoot image quality problems when scanning:

▶ If the system is scanning, but the quality of the scanned image is a problem, there are a few avenues to consider: the scanning surface, source image, conflicts with the system's display settings, and proper scanning size.

▶ If the scanning surface is dirty or smudged, this will be transferred to the scanned image. Use a damp, soft cloth to clean the glass, making sure to remove all dirt, dust, and other smudges.

▶ If you receive blurred images, the image may not be laying completely flat on the scanning area. Also, check to make sure that the scanner is setting on a relatively flat surface so that it does not rock or vibrate when the scanning module is in motion.

▶ If you receive scanned images that appear to have speckled areas, you may have scanner/monitor configuration mismatch problems. The image displayed on the monitor will only be as good as the quality that the monitor can produce. The good news is that the scanned image is actually better than it looks on the monitor. To improve the appearance of the image, improve the settings of the monitor.

▶ If you receive `Out of Memory` errors, or the system crashes when you are trying to scan an image, you may need to reconsider the dots per inch (DPI) setting for the scan. Consider the size of the file created by multiplying the number of bits used to represent a color pixel by the dots per inch resolution, times the area of the image; scanning larger images at high resolutions and color settings can quickly add up to gigabytes of storage. Consider scaling back one or more of these values to the most appropriate level for its intended use. Also consider saving the image in a compressed file format such as JPEG or TIFF, and/or using a compression utility to minimize the size of the file.

▶ Finally, the scanned image cannot get better than the original image. If you are trying to scan images that have dot patterns and they are different than that of the scanner, you will receive stripes in the image, moiré patterns, or blotches. To correct this problem, scan the image at a high resolution and then downsize the file with graphics application software later.

Checking the Host System

As with printers, there are only three items to consider at the host computer's end of the scanning process: the port circuitry is not enabled or has failed, the scanner driver is incorrect or corrupted, or the scanning application is having problems.

First, check the Advanced CMOS Setup screens to make certain that the port the scanner is using has been enabled for operation. If the port is enabled and activated, use Device Manager to check its resource allocations, its operational condition, and its driver information. If Device Manager indicates that the hardware portion of the port is functioning correctly, check for new or updated drivers for the scanner model being used. If it shows that the port is malfunctioning, use the built-in Windows Troubleshooters to isolate the cause of the problem.

If the connection between the scanner and the computer is based on one of the high speed serial interfaces such as USB or IEEE-1394 ports, try removing power from the scanner, disconnecting the interface cable from the computer, and removing its device driver from the system using Device Manager.

One of the most common types of drivers associated with scanners is the TWAIN driver. The TWAIN interface specification was designed to enable different types of image acquisition devices to communicate with TWAIN-compatible applications. If a TWAIN file is missing or damaged, the TWAIN application will generate an error message when you try to perform a scan operation. The scanner application software installs the TWAIN drivers when it is installed. You should uninstall and reinstall the scanner's TWAIN software.

> **EXAM ALERT**
>
> Know what types of devices are associated with TWAIN drivers.

Restart the computer, reconnect the cable to the port, reapply power to the scanner, and allow the system to recognize the "new" device and reconfigure it. If there are no hardware or port problems indicated, it will be necessary to troubleshoot the software side of the host system.

The order in which the scanner components are installed and activated can be important. For example, if you connect the hardware to the system before loading the supporting software, the Windows system may not be able to recognize the scanner to load the proper drivers for it. Remove any existing scanner drivers from the system using Device Manager and then reinstall the scanner and software in the recommended order.

Finally, check the software side of the system by trying to scan using the application that came with the scanner, if you are not already doing so. If this application will not scan the image, the chances of third-party software working are much less.

Interface Cables

If the scanner employs a parallel printer interface, it should have two available connections on the back. Verify that the cable from the host computer is connecting to the correct IN connection. If the scanner is connect to the PC along with a printer using this interface and cabling, you may receive IRQ conflict errors if both devices are activated at the same time. In addition, these EPP/ECP daisy-chained connections typically require bidirectional, IEEE-1284 cables. If older, non-IEEE-1284–compliant cables are used, the image acquisition device will probably fail to work. Finally, make sure that the EPP or ECP port mode settings are enabled correctly in the system's CMOS Setup utility.

As with more traditional printer connections, if a USB or IEEE-1394 interface is being used to connect a scanner to a computer, remove power from the scanner, disconnect the interface cable from the computer, and remove its device driver from the system using Device Manager. Then restart the computer, reconnect the cable to the port, reapply power to the scanner, and allow the system to recognize the "new" device and reconfigure it.

If the scanner is using a SCSI interface, check its ID configuration setting and termination requirements to determine whether it should have a terminating block installed.

Preventive Maintenance and Safety Issues

Because printers tend to be much more mechanical than other types of computer peripherals, they require more effort to maintain. Printers generate pollutants, such as paper dust and ink droplets, in everyday operation. These pollutants can build up on mechanical parts and cause them to wear. As the parts wear, the performance of the printer diminishes. Therefore, printers require periodic cleaning and adjustments to maintain good performance.

The best preventive maintenance practice for printers involves performing scheduled maintenance according to the manufacturer's guidelines. These activities include cleaning and lubricating the system and installing update kits to renew print mechanisms and supplies (such as ink or toner cartridges). You may be able to save you or your customer some money by using third-party supplies. However, you should never have a problem using manufacturer-recommended kits and supplies.

The conditions and environment around the printer or scanner will also affect its usefulness and life cycle. The environmental requirements for printers are identical to those of a computer or any other electronic device. Provide ample free air space around the printer, run its power and signal cables in such a manner that they are not a trip or catch hazard, and keep them out of direct sunlight and away from heat sources.

Dot-Matrix/Inkjet Printers

Clean the printer's roller surfaces. Use a damp, soft cloth to clean the surface of the platen. Rotate the platen through several revolutions. Do not use detergents or solvents on the rollers.

Use a nonfibrous swab dipped in alcohol to clean the face of the dot-matrix printhead. This should loosen up paper fibers and ink that may cause the print wires to stick. Apply a small amount of oil to the face of the printhead.

> **CAUTION**
>
> Cleaning the printer and its mechanisms periodically adds to its productivity by removing contaminants that cause wear. Vacuum the inside of the unit after applying antistatic solution to the vacuum's hose tip. Wipe the outside with a damp cloth, also using antistatic solution. Using a soft-bristled brush, remove any contaminant buildup from the printer's mechanical components. Never lubricate the platen assembly of the printer.

Most inkjet printers require cleaning and adjustments similar to those described for dot-matrix printers.

Laser Printers

Use a special laser toner vacuum cleaner and toner cloth to remove dust buildup and excess toner from the interior of the laser printer. Care should be taken to remove all excess toner from the unit. Vacuum or replace the printer's ozone filter as part of its preventive maintenance schedule. Because water can mix with the toner particles in the printer, using wet sponges or towels to clean up toner inside the laser printer can create a bigger mess than the original one you were cleaning up. Remove the toner cartridge before vacuuming.

Clean the laser printer's rollers using a damp cloth or denatured alcohol. Also, clean the paper-handling motor's gear train. Use a swab to remove buildup from the teeth of the gear train. If the gear train has been lubricated before, apply a light coating of oil to the gears using a swab. Make sure that the oil gets distributed throughout the gear train.

Clean the writing mechanism thoroughly. Use compressed air to blow out dust and paper particles that may have collected on the lenses and shutters. If possible, wipe the laser lens with lint-free wipes to remove stains and fingerprints.

If accessible, use a swab, dipped in alcohol, to clean the corona wires. Rub the swab across the entire length of the wires. Take extra care to not break the strands that wrap around the corona. If these wires are broken, the printer will be rendered useless until new monofilament wires can be reinstalled.

As with other printer types, you should maintain laser printers in accordance with the manufacturer's guidelines. This includes installing the manufacturer's maintenance kit designed for that printer. Don't forget to reset the page counter on those copiers and laser printers that have them.

EXAM ALERT

Remember acceptable methods for cleaning laser printers.

Laser Safety Issues

Laser printers contain many hazardous areas. The laser light used to write on the ELP drum can be very damaging to the human eye. In addition, there are several high-voltage areas in the typical laser printer as well as a high-temperature fuser area that should be avoided.

Exam Prep Questions

1. What does it mean if the printer produces a satisfactory self-test printout, but does not print from the computer?

   ○ **A.** The printer is the problem.

   ○ **B.** The printer is not the problem.

   ○ **C.** The cabling is the problem.

   ○ **D.** The computer is the problem.

2. What item in a dot-matrix printer requires the most attention?

   ○ **A.** Printhead

   ○ **B.** Ribbon cartridge

   ○ **C.** Tension knob

   ○ **D.** Control panel

3. What is the most likely cause of uneven or faded print in a dot-matrix printer?

   ○ **A.** Misaligned printhead

   ○ **B.** Misaligned platen

   ○ **C.** Worn-out ribbon

   ○ **D.** Worn-out printhead

4. How do you correct the problem of uneven or faded print in a dot-matrix printer?

   ○ **A.** Adjust the ink ribbon.

   ○ **B.** Replace the ink ribbon cartridge.

   ○ **C.** Replace the printhead.

   ○ **D.** Adjust the platen.

5. What causes the tops of characters to be missing in a dot-matrix printer?

   ○ **A.** The printhead is misaligned.

   ○ **B.** The printhead is too far away from the paper.

   ○ **C.** The ribbon is worn out.

   ○ **D.** The printhead is worn out.

6. How do you correct the problem in which the tops of characters are missing in a dot-matrix printer? (Select two answers.)

    ○ **A.** Reseat the printhead in the printhead carriage.

    ○ **B.** Reseat the platen.

    ○ **C.** Adjust carriage assembly to the proper height and angle.

    ○ **D.** Replace the ribbon.

7. What is the most likely cause of print that fades from one side of the page to the other in a dot-matrix printer?

    ○ **A.** The ribbon needs replacing.

    ○ **B.** The printhead/platen gap needs adjusting.

    ○ **C.** The platen's tension lever needs to be adjusted.

    ○ **D.** The printhead assembly must be replaced.

8. The _____ of dot-matrix printers generates a great deal of heat and can be a burn hazard when working on these units.

    ○ **A.** Ribbon

    ○ **B.** Platen

    ○ **C.** Printhead

    ○ **D.** Paper tray

9. What type of output will be generated by a dot-matrix printer when the paper advance does not work?

    ○ **A.** One or more dark lines running down the page.

    ○ **B.** One dark line across the page.

    ○ **C.** The whole page is black.

    ○ **D.** The whole page is white.

10. Where is print density adjusted in an inkjet printer?

    ○ **A.** Software

    ○ **B.** Control panel

    ○ **C.** Platen knob

    ○ **D.** System tray

11. What are the symptoms of an inkjet printer cartridge going dry? (Select two answers.)

   ○ **A.** Black streaks running down the page.

   ○ **B.** The resolution becomes unacceptable.

   ○ **C.** One dark line across the page.

   ○ **D.** The print becomes noticeably faint.

12. What are the consequences of using a solvent to unclog an inkjet nozzle? (Select all that apply.)

   ○ **A.** It dilutes the ink.

   ○ **B.** It reduces the ink's surface-tension characteristics.

   ○ **C.** It changes the color of the ink.

   ○ **D.** It allows ink to flow uncontrollably out of the jet.

13. Which inkjet printer setting can adversely affect troubleshooting procedures?

   ○ **A.** Tray Selector

   ○ **B.** Page Feed

   ○ **C.** Self-Test

   ○ **D.** Maintenance Mode

14. What types of problems can cause smudged or disfigured print in an inkjet printer? (Select all that apply.)

   ○ **A.** The platen is misaligned.

   ○ **B.** The paper thickness selector is improperly set.

   ○ **C.** The paper feed rollers are worn.

   ○ **D.** The ribbon is worn out.

15. Where are paper jams likely to occur in a laser printer? (Select all that apply.)

   ○ **A.** Fusing area

   ○ **B.** Registration area

   ○ **C.** Control area

   ○ **D.** Pickup area

16. Paper jams in a laser printer can be caused by _____. (Select all that apply.)

    ○ **A.** Using paper that is too thick

    ○ **B.** Incorrect paper settings

    ○ **C.** Using coated paper

    ○ **D.** Using colored paper

17. Which type of printer can be a source of electrocution, eye damage, and burns?

    ○ **A.** Laser

    ○ **B.** Dot-matrix

    ○ **C.** Inkjet

    ○ **D.** Dye sublimation

18. What type of problem will produce blank pages from a laser printer? (Select all that apply.)

    ○ **A.** The contrast is set too low.

    ○ **B.** Failure in the fusing section.

    ○ **C.** Bad or misaligned laser-scanning module.

    ○ **D.** A corona wire is broken, contaminated, or corroded.

19. What are the consequences of incorrectly setting the paper tray switches in a laser printer? (Select two answers.)

    ○ **A.** The pages are smudged.

    ○ **B.** The paper will not feed.

    ○ **C.** The page is sized incorrectly for the actual paper size.

    ○ **D.** The pages are all white.

20. After the jammed paper has been removed, what may need to be done to clear the paper jam?

    ○ **A.** Set the printer to the Online mode.

    ○ **B.** Disconnect the interface cable.

    ○ **C.** Open the printer's access door.

    ○ **D.** Use the Form Feed button.

21. What is an acceptable method for cleaning laser printers?

    ◯ **A.** Using wet sponges to mop up the excess toner inside the printer.

    ◯ **B.** Using a toner vacuum to clean dust and excess toner from the printer housing.

    ◯ **C.** Using an air hose to blow dust and excess toner out of the printer housing.

    ◯ **D.** Using a normal fabric softener sheet to remove the static charge from the toner so that it can be vacuumed or blown out of the printer housing.

22. You are troubleshooting a laser printer that is producing a `Fuser Error` message. Which of the following should you do first?

    ◯ **A.** Replace the fuser assembly.

    ◯ **B.** Turn the printer off and on repeatedly until the error message clears.

    ◯ **C.** Replace the paper in the printer.

    ◯ **D.** Replace the transfer corona wire.

23. After handling a printed document from a laser printer, you notice the letters smudge and the toner rubs off. What is the most likely cause for this problem?

    ◯ **A.** The contrast is set too low.

    ◯ **B.** The fusing section fails.

    ◯ **C.** The laser-scanning module is bad or misaligned.

    ◯ **D.** A corona wire is broken, contaminated, or corroded.

24. If an inkjet printer is printing text correctly but leaves a line through each character, what is the most likely cause of this problem?

    ◯ **A.** A printhead nozzle is partially clogged and must be cleaned out.

    ◯ **B.** The ink cartridge needs to be cleaned.

    ◯ **C.** The printer driver has been corrupted and must be replaced.

    ◯ **D.** The paper handling mechanism is malfunctioning.

25. You have been called to an advertising firm that has a flatbed scanner that will not scan. When you test it, the scanning light is on but it does not move across the page. Which of the following is the most likely cause of the problem?

   ○ **A.** The resolution setting of the scanning software is not compatible with the size of the picture being scanned.

   ○ **B.** The picture being scanned is too large for the resolution setting and memory available in the host system.

   ○ **C.** The scanner's light-positioning mechanism is locked.

   ○ **D.** The scanner's signal cable is faulty.

26. You purchase a 24-pound standard weight of 24-pound bond paper. How many sheets are involved, and what size are they?

   ○ **A.** 500 sheets, 8.5 inches × 11 inches

   ○ **B.** 500 sheets, 17 inches × 22 inches

   ○ **C.** 1000 sheets, 8.5 inches × 11 inches

   ○ **D.** 1000 sheets, 17 inches × 22 inches

Answers and Explanations

1. B. The easiest way to determine whether the printer is at fault is to run its self-test routine. If the self-test runs and prints clean pages, most of the printer has been eliminated as a possible source of problems. The problem could be in the computer, the cabling, or the interface portion of the printer. If the printer fails the self-test, however, it will be necessary to troubleshoot the printer's problem.

2. B. The single item in a dot-matrix printer that requires the most attention is the ribbon cartridge. It is considered a consumable part of the printer and must be changed often.

3. C. As the ribbon wears out, the printing will become faint and uneven.

4. B. When the print becomes noticeably faint, the cartridge should be replaced. Most dot-matrix printers use a snap-in ribbon cartridge. To replace a typical ribbon cartridge, move the printhead carriage assembly to the center of the printer. Remove the old cartridge by freeing it from its clips or holders, and then lift it out of the printer. Tighten the ribbon tension by advancing the tension knob on the cartridge in a counter-clockwise direction until the ribbon is taut. Snap the cartridge into place,

making certain that the ribbon slides between the printhead and the ribbon mask. Slide the printhead assembly back and forth on the rod to check for proper ribbon movement.

5. A. When the tops of characters are missing, the printhead is misaligned with the platen.

6. A, C. The printhead may need to be reseated in the printhead carriage, or the carriage assembly may need to be adjusted to the proper height and angle.

7. B. If the output of the printer gets lighter as it moves from left to right across the page, it may be necessary to adjust the printhead mechanism to obtain proper printing.

8. C. To exchange the printhead assembly, make sure that it is cool enough to be handled. These units can get hot enough to cause a serious burn.

9. B. When the paper does not advance, the output will normally be one line of dark blocks across the page.

10. A. The density of the printout from an inkjet printer can be adjusted through its printing software; however, when the print becomes noticeably faint or the resolution becomes unacceptable, the cartridge needs to be replaced.

11. B, D. When the print becomes noticeably faint or the resolution becomes unacceptable, the cartridge needs to be replaced.

12. A, B, D. The surface tension of the ink keeps it from running out of the nozzle when it is not energized. Using solvents to clear blockages in the jets can dilute the ink, reduce its surface tension characteristics, and allow it to flow uncontrollably through the jets.

13. D. In the event that the printhead assembly does not move at any time, check to see whether the printer is in maintenance mode. In the maintenance mode, the printer typically keeps the printhead assembly locked in the home position.

14. B, C. If the printer's paper thickness selector is set improperly or the rollers in its paper-feed system become worn, the paper can slip as it moves through the printer and cause disfigured graphics to be produced.

15. A, B, D. Because of the extreme complexity of the laser printer's paper-handling system, paper jams are a common problem. This problem tends to increase in frequency as the printer's components wear from use. Paper jams occur in all three main sections of the printer: the pickup area, the registration area, and the fusing area.

16. A, B, C. Using paper that is too heavy or too thick can result in jams, as can overloading paper trays. Similarly, using the wrong type of paper can defeat the separation pad and allow multiple pages to be drawn into the printer at one time. In this case, multiple sheets may move through the printer together, or they may result in a jam. Using coated paper stock can be hazardous because the coating may melt or catch fire.

17. A. Laser printers can be a source of electrocution, eye damage (from the laser), and burns (from the fuser assembly). The laser printer tends to have several high-voltage and high-temperature hazards inside it. To get the laser printer into a position where you can observe its operation, it will be necessary to defeat some interlock sensors. This action will place you in potential contact with the high-voltage, high-temperature areas in the printer. Take great care when working inside a laser printer.

18. C, D. A white (or blank) page indicates that no information is being written on the drum. This condition basically involves the laser-scanning module, the control board, and the power supply. Another white-page fault occurs when a corona wire becomes broken, contaminated, or corroded, so that the attracting charge between the drum and the paper is severely reduced.

19. B, C. The paper trays have a complex set of sensors and pickup mechanisms that must all be functioning properly. Each tray in a laser printer has a set of tabs that contact sensor switches to tell the control circuitry that the tray is installed and what size paper is in it. A mechanical arm and photodetector are used to sense the presence of paper in the tray.

20. C. A paper jam error indication may remain even after the paper has been removed from the laser printer. This is typically caused by a safety interlock error. Simply opening the printer's main access door should clear the error.

21. B. Use a special laser toner vacuum cleaner and toner cloth to remove dust buildup and excess toner from the interior of the laser printer. Clean the laser printer's rollers using a damp cloth or denatured alcohol.

22. A. When the printer produces a Fuser Error messages on its display panel, this is normally a sign of a failure in the fusing section. If the fusing roller's temperature or pressure is not sufficient to bond the toner to the page, the print will smudge when touched. When the heating element or lamp in the fusing area does not receive adequate AC power from the power supply, the toner will not adhere to the page as it should. This condition will also result in smudged output. Examine the fuser unit, the power supply, and the fusing roller's heating unit.

23. B. Smudged print in a laser printer is usually a sign of a failure in the fusing section. If the fusing roller's temperature, or pressure, is not sufficient to bond the toner to the page, the print will smudge when touched. Examine the fuser unit, the power supply, and the fusing roller's heating unit.

24. A. If a single inkjet is not firing, the output will appear as white lines on the page; replace the cartridge that is not working. If one of the jets is activated all the time, black or colored lines will be produced on the page. To isolate the cause of these problems, perform the following actions one at a time: replace the print cartridge, check the flexible cabling for continuity and for short-circuits between adjacent conductors, exchange the control board for a known-good one, and, finally, check the power supply.

25. C. Some scanners have locking mechanisms that prevent the light source from moving inside the housing during transportation. If the light source is on but will not move when the system applies a scan request, refer to the scanner's documentation to determine whether your scanner has a locking mechanism. If so, check to make sure that the scanner is unlocked.

26. B. Paper is specified in terms of its weight per 500 sheets at 17 inches × 22 inches (for example, 500 sheets of 17 inch × 22 inch, 21-pound bond paper will weigh 21 pounds).

Challenge Solutions

1. You have checked the host computer and the printer. The only item left unchecked in the printing subsystem is the signal cable.

2. You should contact the printer manufacturer to obtain a tractor feed mechanism for the printer. The tractor feed will move the heavy forms through the printer in a straight line. Tractor feeds must be obtained from the original printer manufacturer because they are proprietary to the printer they are mounted on.

3. Missing print is usually attributed to a bad or misaligned laser-scanning module. If this module is not correctly installed, it cannot deliver lines of print to the correct areas of the page. Likewise, if the scanning mirror has a defect or is dirty, portions of the print will not be scanned on the drum. Another cause of missing print involves the toner cartridge and low or poorly distributed toner. If the toner does not come out of the

cartridge uniformly, areas of missing print can be created. A damaged or worn drum can also be a cause of repeated missing print. If areas of the drum do not hold the charge properly, toner will not transfer to the drum or to the page correctly. Because your customer has already changed the toner cartridge, you should tell the customer to wait for a qualified printer technician. The problems indicate that they are beyond what users can be expected to repair.

CHAPTER TWENTY

Basic Networking Concepts

Terms you'll need to understand:

- ✓ TCP/IP
- ✓ Protocols
- ✓ UTP
- ✓ Bandwidth
- ✓ Full duplex
- ✓ Plenum
- ✓ Subnet
- ✓ IPX/SPX
- ✓ NWLINK
- ✓ NETBEUI
- ✓ NETBIOS
- ✓ Twisted pair
- ✓ Coaxial cable
- ✓ Peer-to-peer
- ✓ Client/server
- ✓ Network cards
- ✓ Bluetooth

Techniques you'll need to master:

Essentials 5.1—Identify the fundamental principles of networks.

- ✓ Describe basic networking concepts.
    - ✓ Addressing
    - ✓ Bandwidth
    - ✓ Status indicators
    - ✓ Protocols (for example, TCP/IP including IP, classful subnet, IPX/SPX including NWLINK, NETBEUI/NETBIOS)
    - ✓ Full duplex, half duplex
    - ✓ Cabling (twisted pair, coaxial cable, fiber optic, RS-232)
- ✓ Networking models including peer-to-peer and client/server
- ✓ Identify names, purposes, and characteristics of the common network cables.
    - ✓ Plenum/PVC
    - ✓ UTP (CAT3, CAT5/5e, CAT6)
    - ✓ STP
    - ✓ Fiber (single mode and multimode)
- ✓ Identify names, purposes and characteristics of network cables (RJ-45 and RJ-11, ST/SC/LC, USB, IEEE-1394/FireWire).

Local Area Networks

This chapter covers a portion of the Networking Fundamentals area of the CompTIA A+ Certification—Essentials examination under Objectives 5.1. Networks are often defined by their geographical size. For example, a network designed to connect computers together over a relatively small area is called a *local area network* or *LAN*. A larger network arrangement made up of interconnected LANs is referred to as a *campus area network* or *CAN*. These networks are typically thought of as connecting networks between buildings such as those found on a college campus. Even larger networks that may include wireless and fiber optic connections to span larger geographical distances such as several blocks of a residential area, or a complete city, are referred to as *municipal area networks* or *MANs*. Finally, networks designed to operate over large geographical areas are referred to as *wide area networks*, or *WANs*. The most famous wide area network is the Internet which connects networks of all kinds together to form a worldwide communications network.

The use of local area networks has grown immensely. These networks have become the backbone of small and medium-size businesses because they enable people to share and control business resources and information in a highly efficient manner. LANs also play a major role in large businesses, tying users together with each other and with other networks within the organization. Because LANs have become such an integral part of commercial computer systems, the PC technician must understand how they function.

> **EXAM ALERT**
>
> Know which type of networking applies to most businesses.

Local area networks are systems designed to connect computers together in relatively close proximity. These connections enable users attached to the network to share resources such as printers and modems. LAN connections also enable users to communicate with each other and share data among their computers.

When discussing LANs, we need to consider two basic topics: the LAN's topology (hardware connection method) and its protocol (communication control method). Let's first address CompTIA's definition of a network. CompTIA defines a network as a minimum of two computers connected together so that they can share resources. However, if only two units are connected, point-to-point communications software and a simple null modem could be employed.

> **EXAM ALERT**
>
> Be aware that under CompTIA's definition, a LAN can exist with only two computers.

The null modem could be constructed using the RS-232 serial cable, or it could be made up of a copper networking cable, using RJ-45 connectors. In this case, the cable would be known as a *crossover cable* instead of a null modem.

> **EXAM ALERT**
>
> Know that two computers can be connected together and communicate without the benefit of a network.

LAN Topologies

Network topologies are physical connection/configuration strategies. LAN topologies fall into four types of configurations: bus, ring, star, and mesh. You may also encounter hybrid networks composed of combinations of different network topologies.

Figure 20.1 illustrates all four topologies. The basics of the four topologies are

> ▶ Bus topology—In the bus topology, the nodes, or stations, of the network connect to a central communication link. This was easy to see in older bus topology LANs that employed coaxial cable. In these networks, each node connected into a single linear cable that provided the bus line. This concept may not be as apparent in newer bus networks that use hubs and twisted wire cables. In either case, each node along the bus has a unique address that differentiates it from the other users on the network. Information can be placed on the bus by any node. The information must contain the network address of the node, or nodes, that the information is intended for. Other nodes along the bus will ignore the information.

> **EXAM ALERT**
>
> Be able to recognize network topologies from this type of drawing.

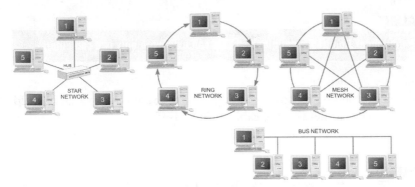

FIGURE 20.1   Star, bus, ring, and mesh configurations.

▶ Ring topology—In a ring network configuration, the communication bus is formed into a closed loop. Each node inspects the information on the LAN as it passes by. A repeater, built into each ring LAN card, regenerates every message not directed to it and sends it to the next appointed node. The originating node eventually receives the message back and removes it from the ring. Ring topologies tend to offer very high data-transfer rates but require additional management overhead. The additional management is required for dependability. If a node in a ring network fails, the entire network fails. To overcome this, ring designers have developed rings with primary and secondary data paths. If a break occurs in a primary link, the network controller can reroute the data onto the secondary link to avoid the break.

▶ Star topology—In a star topology, the logical layout of the network resembles the branches of a tree. All the nodes are connected in branches that eventually lead back to a central unit. Nodes communicate with each other through the central unit. The central station coordinates the network's activity by polling the nodes, one by one, to determine whether they have any information to transfer. If so, the central station gives that node a predetermined slice of time to transmit. If the message is longer than the time allotted, the transmissions are chopped into small packets of information that are transmitted over several polling cycles.

▶ Mesh topology—The mesh design offers the most basic network connection scheme. In this design, each node has a direct physical connection to all the other nodes in the network. Although the overhead for connecting a mesh network topology in a LAN environment is prohibitive, this topology is employed in two very large network environments: the public telephone system and the Internet.

Logical Topologies

It would be easy to visualize the connections of the physical topologies just described if the nodes simply connected to each other. However, this is typically not the case in newer LAN arrangements because most LAN installations employ connection devices, such as hubs and routers, which alter the appearance of the actual connection scheme. Therefore, the logical topology will not match the appearance of the physical topology. The particulars of the connection scheme are hidden inside the connecting device. As an illustration, Figure 20.2 shows a typical network connection scheme using a router. The physical topology appears as a star.

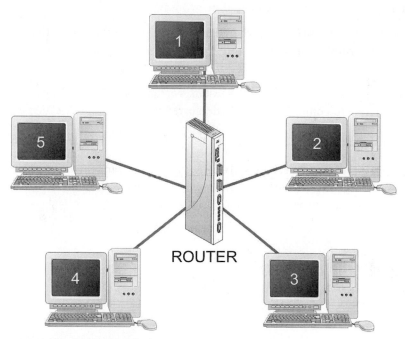

FIGURE 20.2   Logical topologies.

However, the internal wiring of the connecting router provides a logical bus topology. It is not uncommon for a logical ring or mesh topology to be implemented in a physical star topology.

NOTE

The most popular network topology in the world is the bus topology used with ethernet-based local area networks. Although all the other network topologies exist and may be in used somewhere, the majority of networks that PC technicians will encounter are ethernet-based bus technologies running on logical star configurations, constructed around hubs, switches, and routers.

Network Control Strategies

When you begin to connect computers to other computers and devices so that they can share resources and data, the issue of how and who will control the network comes up very quickly. In some applications, such as developing a book like this one, it is good for the author, artists, and pagination people to be able to share access to text and graphics files, as well as to devices such as printers. However, in a business network, companies must have control over who has access to sensitive information and company resources, as well as when and how much.

Control of a network can be implemented in two ways:

▶ As a *peer-to-peer network* (*P2P*) where each computer is attached to the network in a ring or bus fashion and is equal to the other units on the network.

▶ As a *client/server network* where dependent workstations, referred to as *clients*, operate in conjunction with a dedicated master computer called a *server*.

Figure 20.3 illustrates a typical peer-to-peer network arrangement. In this arrangement, the users connected to the network can share access to different network resources, such as hard drives and printers.

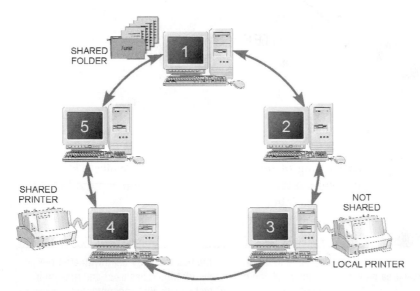

FIGURE 20.3 A peer-to-peer network.

EXAM ALERT

Be aware that resource sharing in a peer-to-peer network is determined at the local node.

In a peer-to-peer network, control of the local unit is fairly autonomous. The nodes in this type of network configuration usually contain local hard drives and printers that the local computer has control of. These resources can be shared at the discretion of the individual user. A common definition of a peer-to-peer network is one in which all the nodes can act as both clients and servers of the other nodes under different conditions.

EXAM ALERT

Be aware that the nodes in peer-to-peer networks can serve as both clients and servers for different functions.

Figure 20.4 depicts a typical client/server LAN configuration. In this type of LAN, control tends to be very centralized. The server typically holds the programs and data for its client computers. It also provides security and network policy enforcement. The major advantages of the client/server networking arrangement are

▶ Centralized administration

▶ Data and resource security

▶ Network services

In some cases, the client units do not even include a local hard drive or floppy drive unit. The boot process is performed through an extension of the onboard BIOS, and no data is stored at the client machine. This type of client is referred to as a *diskless workstation*.

EXAM ALERT

Know the characteristic differences between peer-to-peer and client/server networks.

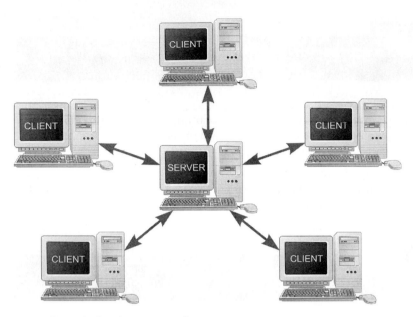

FIGURE 20.4 A client/server network.

Although peer-to-peer networks enable users to share resources and have a limited amount of local control over resources, they do not typically provide services for the different computers and devices attached to the network. In a client/server-based network, special computers running server operating systems can be tasked with automatically providing services to the network members, such as automatically assigning TCP/IP settings (DHCP and APIPA), domain naming services (DNS), and network address translation services (NATS).

EXAM ALERT

Be aware of service types provided in client/server networks verses those used in peer-to-peer environments.

Challenge #1

You are setting up a new production room for creating textbooks and multimedia presentations. You will employ writers, artists, document layout, and paste-up professionals, multimedia animators, and multimedia presentation designers. Your board of directors has asked you for input about how to set up the system. They are anticipating tying everyone into the company's existing client/server network, but someone has suggested looking into peer-to-peer networks. What will you recommend to them and why?

Network Connectivity Devices

Although each computer or device attached to the network must have a network interface adapter capable of physically connecting the computer to the network transmission media, other connectivity devices may be in the network to connect different portions of the network together and perform different network management functions. As described in the preceding section, these connectivity devices are usually hubs, switches, or routers. In large or complex networks, you may also find devices called *bridges* used to interconnect sections of the network. Although each device provides physical connectivity, each also has specific methods of operation that make it suitable for use in a specific network application. In some cases, a device with more features may be used to perform the functions of a lower-featured device.

A *hub* is a relatively simple connectivity device used to connect multiple network devices together so that they work like a single segment. When it receives a packet of network information at one of its ports, it sends that information out to all its other ports—making it a repeater. Hubs are also referred to as *concentrators* because their main function is to concentrate the network segment connections together in one place. However, hubs do possess some built-in intelligence that enables them to monitor their ports and detect excessive collisions (bad behavior) at a particular port and disconnect it from the other ports. This prevents a port from disabling the entire network segment. Hubs also provide port status lights that can be used to troubleshoot network connectivity problems. Hubs require a separate (usually DC) power supply to operate.

A *switch* connects network devices together to form a local area network. Instead of repeating a received messages at all its other ports, the switch can direct the information to its intended receiver if the address of the receiver is known. The switch keeps track of devices attached to it through a Media Access Control (MAC) address table. All network devices have a MAC address assigned to them when they are manufactured. Because the information is sent only to the port where it is intended, the performance of the entire network is improved greatly. For this reason, switches have largely replaced hubs as the most basic connectivity device in local area networks. If the address is not known, the switch will broadcast the information to all its ports in the same manner that a hub does. Like hubs, switches provide status lights for troubleshooting and require external power supplies to operate. Figure 20.5 shows a typical network switch connection scheme.

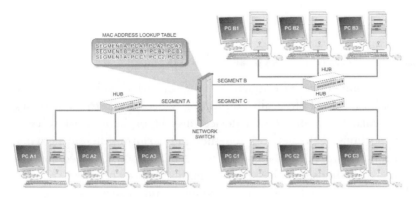

FIGURE 20.5 A network switch connection.

Routers are network connectivity devices that forward network information in a manner similar to switches. However, unlike switches, routers can forward information across different network segments. This gives routers the capability to join different networks through a process known as *routing*. For example, a router is commonly used to connect small residential networks to the biggest network in the world—the Internet.

Likewise, routers are used in commercial and governmental environments to break large networks into more manageable subnetworks. This enables different sections of organizations to have their own network space while still being able to share information with other parts of the organization when needed. Such an internetworked arrangement increases the efficiency of all segments of the network by confining information moving across the network to only those things that need to be shared. Otherwise, local network traffic is confined within the local network by the presence of the router. Figure 20.6 illustrates using routers to break networks into individual segments.

In large networks, routers communicate with other routers using a routing protocol to build and maintain routing tables. These tables are used to record the best route between different network locations. Unlike the MAC table used in switches, routing tables store address and hop information about the path between devices.

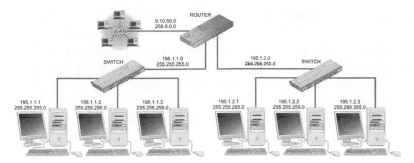

FIGURE 20.6 Segmenting a network.

Often, confusion exists about connectivity devices because of the way they are marketed. For example, switch and router functions are sometimes built into the same piece of equipment and marketed as a multiport router. Routers can be labeled by the function they perform (for example, a router connecting a network to the Internet may be referred to as an *edge router*, whereas a pair of routers connecting two network segments together is called a *core router*).

When routers are used to connect networks to always-on, broadband Internet connections, they are referred to as *Internet gateways*. In addition to performing the routing functions, Internet gateway routers typically supply a number of other Internet-related services, such as automatic address assignments and firewall services. These services are described in detail later in this chapter. You may also encounter routing switches (called *LAN switches*) that have routing capabilities built in to them.

A *network bridge*, sometimes referred to as a *network switch*, bridges network segments together and forwards traffic from one network to another. Like the switch, a bridge uses MAC addresses to guide information to the correct port; however, it also passes broadcast information to all of its ports. Therefore, the bridge gathers network connections into a single common segment, whereas a router separates them into different segments. Figure 20.7 illustrates the operation of a network bridge.

In a communication environment, there are three basic modes for transmitting data between two parties:

▶ Simplex mode—Data is transmitted in only one direction.

▶ Half-duplex mode—Data can be transmitted in both directions, but in only one direction at a time. A walkie-talkie is the typical example used to describe this type of communication; users can transmit information only when they have access to the communication media.

▶ Full-duplex mode—Data can be transmitted in both directions at the same time. This effectively doubles the operating speed of a connection using this mode. The telephone system is the typical example of a full-duplex communication system—users can talk and hear anytime a connection is present. Full-duplex communications require either dual physical communication links or a multiplexer/demultiplexer system to separate transmitted and received data from each other on the same communication media.

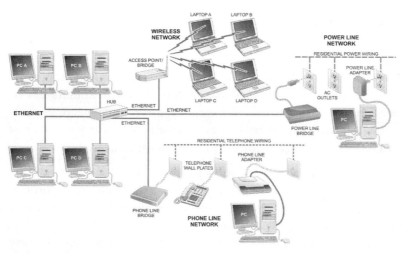

FIGURE 20.7   A network bridge arrangement.

In a computer network environment, communications between devices can occur in half-duplex or full-duplex modes depending on the type of equipment in use. Hubs and basic switches operate in half-duplex mode. There are also switches and routers that can operate in both half-duplex and full-duplex modes to provide much faster data handling when communicating with other full-duplex devices. These devices auto-negotiate with the network devices connected to their ports so that they can establish the highest possible transmission rates possible for both devices.

Network Transmission Media

Basically, four media are used to transmit data between computers:

▶ Copper cabling

▶ Fiber-optic cabling

> ▶ Infrared light
>
> ▶ Wireless radio frequency (RF) signals

Each media type offers advantages that make it useful for networking in certain conditions. The main media-related considerations include cost to implement, ease of installation, maximum data transmission rates, and noise immunity characteristics.

In the implementation phase of a network, the cost to install the medium is a primary concern. This cost exists in two facets: the actual relative cost of the media and its adapter/connections and the cost associated with installing and configuring the network.

Likewise, each media type has some limitations on its capability to transfer information. This factor also consists of two considerations: bandwidth and attenuation. *Bandwidth* is the media's total capability to carry data at a given instance. *Attenuation* is a measure of how much signal loss occurs as the information moves across the medium. As you will see in the following sections, some media types can literally carry a signal for miles and still deliver it as recognizable information.

The final media-related consideration is noise immunity capabilities. Stray electrical energy (referred to as *noise*) moves through the atmosphere as a natural course. Electrical machines and devices also generate electronic noise. These stray signals can interfere with organized data signals and make them unrecognizable. Therefore, cabling used to transmit data is expected to have some resistance to these stray signals.

Copper Cabling

Under the heading of copper cabling, there are basically two categories to consider: twisted-pair cabling and coaxial cabling. Twisted-pair cabling consists of two or more pairs of wires twisted together to provide noise reduction. The twist in the wires causes induced noise signals to cancel each other out. In this type of cabling, the number of twists in each foot of wire indicates its relative noise immunity level.

Twisted-Pair Cabling

When discussing twisted-pair cabling with data networks, there are two basic types to consider: Unshielded Twisted Pair (UTP) and Shielded Twisted Pair (STP). UTP networking cable contains four pairs of individually insulated wires, as illustrated in Figure 20.8. STP cable is similar with the exception that it contains an additional foil shield that surrounds the four-pair wire bundle. The shield provides extended protection from induced electrical noise and cross-talk by supplying a grounded path to carry the induced electrical signals away from the conductors in the cable.

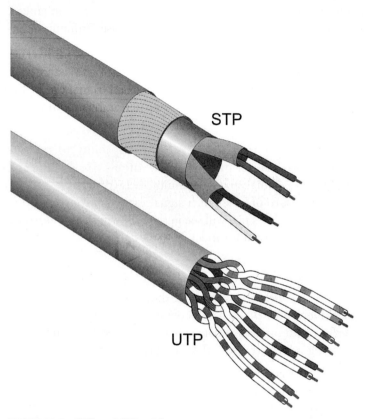

FIGURE 20.8 UTP and STP cabling.

One of the specifications associated with the physical layer of the OSI model is the EIA/TIA-568 specification for network wiring. Two groups have established this specification jointly—the Electronic Industry Association (EIA) and the Telecommunications Industry Association (TIA)—to standardize the use of UTP cable for different networking applications. These organizations have categorized different grades of cable along with connector, distance, and installation specifications to produce the EIA/TIA UTP wiring category (CAT) ratings for the industry (that is, CAT 5, CAT 5e, and CAT 6 cabling).

CAT 5 cabling is still currently the most widely used specification for data communication wiring. However, an enhanced CAT 5e version adds far-end cross-talk prevention to provide higher performance capabilities. It is often used for

1000Base-T networks. These cables are used in networks that operate at speeds of 10Mbps, 100Mbps, and 1Gbps.

The Category 6 (CAT6) specification provides even stricter regulation that gives it performance levels up to 250MHz. CAT6 is backward compatible with CAT3 and CAT5/5e specification. If can be used in 10Base-T, 100Base-TX, and 1000Base-T (Gigabit Ethernet) networks. Like CAT5, CAT6 has four-wire pairs of 23 AWG copper wire (slightly larger than 24 AWG wire used in CAT5).

CAT 5/5e and CAT 6 cables have a maximum length of 100 meters. This measurement includes a 90-meter horizontal cable designation and 10 meters of drop (connection) cables on either end. Table 20.1 lists the industry's various CAT cable ratings that apply to UTP data communication cabling.

TABLE 20.1   UTP Cable Category Ratings

CATEGORY	MAXIMUM BANDWIDTH	WIRING TYPES	APPLICATIONS
3	16MHz	100 Ω UTP; Rated Category 3	10Mbps ethernet; 4Mbps token ring
4	20MHz	100 Ω UTP; Rated Category 4	10Mbps ethernet; 16Mbps token ring
5	100MHz	100 Ω UTP; Rated Category 5	100Mbps TPDDI; 155Mbps ATM
5e	160MHz	100 Ω UTP; Rated Category 5E	1.2Gbps 1000Base-T High-Speed ATM
6	250MHz	100 Ω UTP; Rated Category 6	1.2Gbps 1000Base-T High-Speed ATM and beyond
7 Proposed	600– 862MHz	100 Ω UTP; Rated Category 7	1.2Gbps 1000Base-T High-Speed ATM and beyond

EXAM ALERT

Know what type of cabling is involved in the CAT 5 cable rating.

The connector and color-coded connection schemes specified for four-pair, EIA/TIA 568-A and 568-B CAT 5 and CAT 6 UTP network cabling configurations are illustrated in Figure 20.9. In both cases, the UTP cabling is terminated in an eight-pin RJ-45 plug. The color codes for attaching the connector to the cable are also provided in the figure.

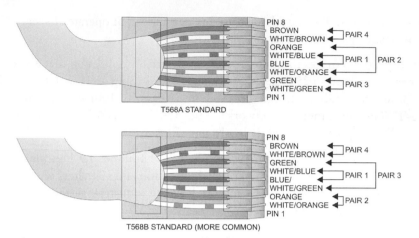

FIGURE 20.9 UTP cable connection specifications.

NOTE

Although the A+ exams and most of the networking industry refer to the connectors used with UTP networking cable as **RJ-45 connectors**, these are actually eight position, eight conductor (8P8C) connectors. True RJ-45 connectors used in telecommunication applications look similar to 8P8C connectors, but they are keyed and not compatible with 8P8C connectors.

UTP LAN connections are made through modular RJ-45 registered jacks and plugs. RJ-45 connectors are very similar in appearance to the RJ-11 connectors used with telephones and modems. However, the RJ-45 connectors are considerably larger than the RJ-11 connectors. Some ethernet adapters include 15-pin sockets that enable special systems, such as fiber-optic cabling, to be interfaced to them. Other cards provide specialized ST connectors for fiber-optic connections.

Coaxial Cable

Coaxial cable (often referred to simply as *coax*) is familiar to most people as the conductor that carries cable TV into their homes. Coaxial cable is constructed with an insulated solid or stranded wire core surrounded by a dielectric insulating layer and a solid or braided metallic shield. Both the wire and shield are wrapped in an outer protective insulating jacket, as illustrated in Figure 20.10.

In the past, coaxial cable was widely used for ethernet LAN media. However, because the thickness and rigidity of coaxial cable makes it difficult and time-consuming to install, the networking industry and network standards development groups have abandoned coaxial cable in favor of unshielded twisted-pair cabling.

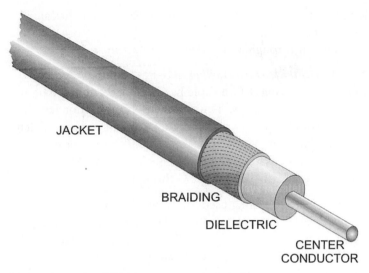

JACKET

BRAIDING

DIELECTRIC

CENTER
CONDUCTOR

FIGURE 20.10 Coaxial cable.

Coax cable continues to be used for some applications, such as Internet service delivered to residential settings through the commercial cable television (CATV) system. In addition, several varieties of coaxial cable are available for transporting video and high-data-rate digital information. These types of coax are used with computers, audio/video equipment, and intelligent home products in residential networks.

Coaxial Cable Specifications

Typically, coax cable is specified by an RG rating that is appropriate for a given application (such as RG-58 cable for use in ethernet data network applications or RG-59 for CATV). The RG designation stands for *radio grade*, a term used in military specifications. Some grades of coaxial cable have similar outer appearances (for example, RG-58 and RG-59). However, it is not advisable to mix different cable and terminator specifications as we once did when we switched from an older ArcNet LAN to an ethernet LAN. Make sure that you have the correct grade of cable and the corresponding correct terminator for the intended coaxial application.

Coaxial cables are typically categorized according to their size (diameter), shielding, and core construction, type of dielectric, impedance, velocity factor, fire rating, and attenuation rating.

▶ RG-6—RG-6 coaxial cable is the preferred type of coaxial cable for residential structured wiring. It is widely used for video distribution and also for connecting satellite receiving antenna systems to standard, digital, and high-definition television (HDTV) receivers. RG-6 cable has an impedance of 75 ohms and uses 18-gauge wire. This type of coaxial cable connects to equipment through a threaded F-connector.

▶ RG-8—Referred to as *thicknet coax cabling*, RG-8 was widely used in 10Base5 ethernet networking. RG-8 cable has an impedance of 50 ohms and uses 19/10-gauge wire centers. The thicknet cable does not actually connect to the network adapter in the computer. Instead, a device called a Medium Attachment Unit (MAU) is inserted inline with the cable. An interface cable referred to as an Attachment Unit Interface (AUI) connects the MAU to the network adapter card through a 15-pin AUI cable.

▶ RG-58—Thinnet ethernet cabling used for 10Base2 networks. RG-58 cable has an impedance of 50 ohms and uses 24-gauge wire centers. These cables attach to equipment through British Naval Connectors (BNCs). In 10Base2 LANs, the node's LAN adapter card is usually connected directly to the LAN cabling, using a T-connector for peer-to-peer networks or a BNC connector in client/server LANs.

▶ RG-59—RG-59 cable is widely used for CATV and video services. It is very similar in appearance to RG-58 cabling.

Fiber-Optic Cable

Fiber-optic cable is plastic or glass cable designed to carry voice or digital data in the form of light pulses. The signals are introduced into the cable by a laser diode and bounce along its interior until they reach the end of the cable, as illustrated in Figure 20.11. At the end, a light-detecting circuit receives the light signals and converts them back into usable information. This type of cabling offers potential signaling rates in excess of 200000Mbps. However, current access protocols still limit fiber-optic LAN speeds to 100Mbps and 1000Mbps (using the 802.3z Gigabit Ethernet standard).

Because light moving through a fiber-optic cable does not attenuate (lose energy) as quickly as electrical signals moving along a copper conductor, segment lengths between transmitters and receivers can be much longer with fiber-optic cabling. In some fiber-optic applications, the maximum cable length can range up to 2 kilometers.

Fiber-optic cable also provides a much more secure data transmission medium than copper cable because it cannot be tapped without physically breaking the conductor. Light introduced into the cable at one end does not leave the cable except through the other end. In addition, fiber-optic cable electrically isolates the transmitter and receiver so that usually no signal-level matching needs to be performed between the two ends.

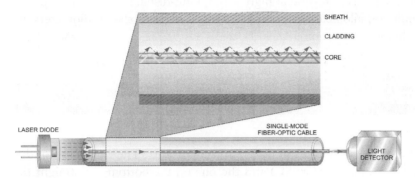

FIGURE 20.11   Transmitting over fiber-optic cable.

Getting the light out of the cable without significant attenuation is the key to making fiber-optic connections. The end of the cable must be perfectly aligned with the receiver and be free from scratches, film, or dust that would distort or filter the light.

Fiber-optic cabling offers the prospect of very high-performance links for LAN implementation. It can handle much higher data-transfer rates than copper conductors do and can use longer distances between stations before signal deterioration becomes a problem. In addition, fiber-optic cable offers a high degree of security for data communications. Because it does not radiate EMI signal information that can be detected outside the conductor, it does not tap easily, and it shows a decided signal loss when it is tapped into. Two basic types of fiber-optic cabling are used in networking applications:

▶ Multimode fiber-optic cable—Multimode fiber-optic cable is designed so that light travels in many paths from the transmitter to the receiver. Light rays that enter the cable reflect off the cladding at different angles as they move along the length of the cable. These rays disperse in the cladding and are useless as signals. Only those light rays introduced to the core of the cable within a range of critical angles will travel down the cable. Even with the excessive signal attenuation created by this method, multimode is still the most commonly used cable type because it is cheaper and will transmit light over sufficient distances for use in local area networks (less than 3,000 feet).

▶ Single-mode fiber-optic cable—In a single-mode fiber-optic cable, the diameter of the core is reduced so that just one wavelength of the light source travels down the wire. The light source for this type of cable is a laser. Laser diodes (LDs) produce the in-phase, single-frequency, unidirectional light rays required to travel down such a cable. These cables are normally reserved for use in high-speed, long-distance cable runs (up to 24 miles/40 kilometers in point-to-point configurations—5 kilometers in an ethernet installation).

Figure 20.12 depicts two types of fiber-optic connectors. The connector on the top is a subscriber connector (SC) and the one on the bottom is a straight tip (ST) connector. The SC connector is the dominant connector for fiber-optic ethernet networks. In both cases, the connectors are designed so that they correctly align the end of the cable with the receiver.

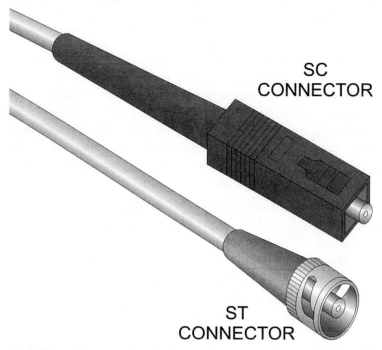

SC
CONNECTOR

ST
CONNECTOR

FIGURE 20.12   Fiber-optic cable.

Fiber-optic cable manufacturers have adopted a pseudo-standard method of color-coding the different types of fiber-optic cabling. Single-mode cable is typically provided with a yellow cable jacket, whereas multimode cable comes in an orange jacket. The core/cladding size (for example, 8.3m/125m) is stamped on the multimode cable jacket. However, some versions of multimode cable, such as plenum-rated cables, are available in blue, green, or red jackets. Single-mode and multimode cables are not interchangeable, so equipment requirements must always be checked before installing fiber-optic cable.

> **EXAM ALERT**
>
> Remember the methods commonly used to identify different types of fiber-optic cables.

Two newer connectors you may find when dealing with fiber optic network connectivity include the LC connector and the MT-RJ connector. The *LC connector* is a small form-factor (half size) SC connector developed by Lucent Technologies for use in telephone environments. Likewise, the MT-RJ *connector* is a small form-factor fiber optic connector that resembles an RJ-45 connector. It was designed by AMP to provide an inexpensive, easy-to-implement fiber connection method. These smaller fiber connectors provide higher connection densities than the ST and SC connectors and are as easy to connect and disconnect as RJ-11 and RJ-45 connectors. In addition, they fit in conventional RJ-45 faceplates and patch panel openings. Figure 20.13 depicts the LC and MT-RJ connectors.

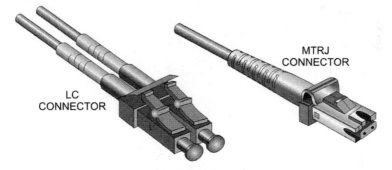

FIGURE 20.13   Small form-factor fiber connectors.

Plenum Cable

Another important rating for all cable types comes into play when you must install a cable in a space that is primarily involved in moving air throughout a facility. According to the National Electrical Code (NEC), a *plenum* is "a compartment or chamber to which one or more air ducts are connected and that forms part of the air distribution system." Likewise, the Building Industry Consulting Services International (BICSI) standards organization defines plenum as "a designated closed or open area that is used for transport of environmental air."

According to the NEC, when you are installing cables in plenums you must use special plenum-rated cables that are listed as Type CMP (Communications Plenum) cable. In certain cases, Type MPP (Multipurpose Plenum) cables offer an acceptable substitute for Type CMP cables. Plenum-rated cables are suitable for use in ducts, plenums, and other spaces used for environmental air because they have adequate fire-resistance and low smoke-producing characteristics. The reason for this requirement is that when the protective insulation placed around cabling burns, it gives off toxic gases. If these cables are located in a plenum area, the dangerous gases will be spread throughout the facility as part of the air circulation system.

Wireless Infrared Links

The Infrared Data Association (IrDA) infrared transmission specification makes provisions for multiple IrDA devices to be attached to a computer so that it can have multiple, simultaneous links to multiple IrDA devices. Figure 20.14 shows how IrDA links can be used to share computers and devices through a normal ethernet hub. In these scenarios, the IrDA link provides the high-speed transmission media between the ethernet devices.

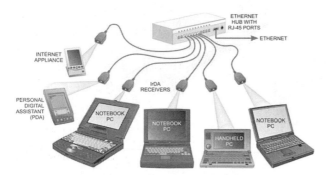

FIGURE 20.14   IrDA networking.

One drawback of infrared transmissions in general is that they provide line-of-sight communications over only short distances and can be interfered with easily. In addition, they have very narrow lines of sight (15 degrees from straight forward). IrDA devices cannot offer dependable communication paths if an object, such as a person, interrupts the path of the light from the transmitter to the receiver. They also cannot penetrate walls or other solid objects and they cannot communicate around corners.

Wireless RF Links

Recently, various Wireless Local Area Networking or Local Area Wireless Network (WLAN or LAWN) specifications have been introduced into the market. These networks connect computer nodes together using high-frequency radio waves. The IEEE organization has presented a group of wireless networking specifications under the IEEE-802.11x banner to describe its wireless networking standard. The IEEE 802.11x (also known as *Wireless Fidelity* or *Wi-Fi*) wireless standards have gained wide acceptance as the preferred wireless networking technology for both business and home network applications.

A typical wireless LAN, depicted in Figure 20.15, consists of a device known as an *access point* and any number of wireless network–capable devices. The wireless access point acts as a bridging device that connects the wireless network computers with the wired network. The access point uses antennas and a radio receiver/transmitter to communicate with the other devices through radio frequency signals. Conversely, it communicates with the host computer through a physical interface known as an *ethernet hub* or *router*, which provides connectivity between the access point and the wired ethernet LAN.

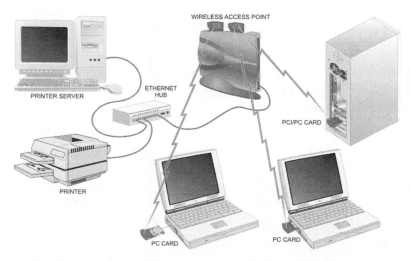

FIGURE 20.15   A wireless LAN.

Wireless network client computers also require a network interface consisting of a radio transmitter, receiver, and antenna. Wireless LAN (WLAN) adapters for PCs are typically available in the form of plug-in PCI and PCMCIA cards, or as attachable USB devices.

Each client computer that has a wireless network interface can communicate with other wireless equipped computers or with the access point. Wireless network computers are also able to communicate with wired network computers on an ethernet LAN using the access point as the connection between the two networks.

EXAM ALERT

Know what type of device is the main connection device used with 802.11x wireless networks.

Bluetooth

Although Wi-Fi networks dominate the desktop and portable computer networking environment, a separate networking specification for personal area networks (PANs) has gained widespread acceptance. This specification is called Bluetooth (or IEEE-802.15.1) and was developed by a consortium made up of Ericsson, IBM, Intel, Nokia, and Toshiba as an avenue to connect and exchange information between personal devices such as PDAs, cell phones, and digital cameras, as well as PCs, notebooks, and printers. The meshing together of personal computers, cell phones, web devices, LAN devices, and other intelligent devices in a common forum is referred to as *convergence*. The Bluetooth specification is intended to promote convergence of these systems.

Bluetooth devices use low power consumption, short-range radio frequency signals to provide a low cost, secure communication link. The specification provides three power level/range options that include 100mW/100meters, 2.5mW/10meters, and 1mW/1meter.

Bluetooth employs Adaptive Frequency Hopping Spread Spectrum (AFHSS) in the license-free 2.4GHz range to provide security and avoid crowded frequency ranges. The Bluetooth protocol divides the 2.4GHz frequency range into 79 1MHz communication channels. The frequency-hopping mechanism changes channels up to 1,600 times per second. Data transfer rates for Bluetooth 1.1 and 1.2 devices is 723.1Kbps and 2.1Mbps for Bluetooth 2.0 devices.

The most widely used application of Bluetooth is to provide point-to-point wireless communications between cell phones and hands-free headsets. It is also used to provide point-to-point communications between MP3 players, PDAs, and digital cameras and host computer systems. These devices can be connected to only one device at a time, and connecting to them will prevent them from connecting to other devices and showing up in inquiries until they disconnect from the other device. However, the standard also provides for constructing multipoint wireless networks using Bluetooth technologies.

Under the Bluetooth specification, up to eight devices can be grouped together to form a piconet. Any device can become the master device and assume control of the network by issuing a request broadcast. The other seven devices become slave devices until the master device releases its position. The master device uses time division multiplexing to rapidly switch from one slave device to another around the network. In this manner, the Bluetooth network operates like a wireless USB network. Any device in the network can assume the master device role when it is available.

In the PC networking environment, the Bluetooth specification allows several Bluetooth peripheral devices to communicate with a PC simultaneously. In particular, Bluetooth is used with desktop PCs, notebooks, Tablet PCs, and PDAs to communicate with wireless input and output devices such as mice, keyboards, and printers.

EXAM ALERT
Be aware of typical Bluetooth applications associated with PCs and networking.

Network Architectures

Networks are complex, multifaceted structures that require a tremendous amount of interaction between computer designers, network equipment designers, operating system manufacturers, and networking application providers. Several initiatives have been put forward to provide models to serve as blueprints for these groups to follow in designing their products. Although you should be aware that different hierarchical networking models exist, the most widely discussed initiative is the Open Systems Interconnection (OSI) model put forward by the International Standards Organization.

The layers of this model are shown in Figure 20.16. In the figure, each layer on the left is matched with a group of protocols that operate within it on the right. As you can see, many protocols are at work in network architectures. Local area networking environments are primarily concerned with the first four layers of the model, whereas layers four through seven are more widely dealt with in wide area network environments. Basically, the de facto network architecture used with local area networks since 2003 is ethernet.

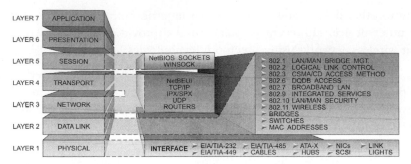

FIGURE 20.16 The OSI networking model.

Ethernet

Xerox developed ethernet in 1976. The standard specification for ethernet has been published by the Institute of Electrical and Electronics Engineers (IEEE) as the IEEE-802.3 ethernet protocol (refer to the Data Link level of the OSI model). Local area networks are designed so that the entire network runs synchronously at one frequency. Therefore, only one set of electronic signals may be placed on the network at one time. However, data can move in both directions between network locations. By definition, this makes local area network operations half duplex in nature (that is, information can travel in both directions, but not at the same time).

For this reason, LANs require that some method be used to determine which node can use the network's communications paths, and for how long. The network's access protocol handles these functions, and it is necessary to prevent more than one user from accessing the bus at any given time. If two sets of data are placed on the network at the same time, a data collision occurs and data is lost.

The ethernet methodology for access control is referred to as carrier sense *multiple-access with collision detection* (*CSMA/CD*). Using this protocol, a node that wants to transfer data over the network first listens to the LAN to determine whether it is in use. If the LAN is not in use, the node begins transmitting its data. If the network is busy, the node waits for the LAN to clear for a predetermined time, and then it takes control of the LAN.

If two nodes are waiting to use the LAN, they will periodically attempt to access the LAN at the same time. When this happens, a data collision occurs, and the data from both nodes is rendered useless. The receiver portion of the ethernet controller monitors the transmission to detect collisions.

When the transmitting node senses that the data bits are overlapping, it halts the transmission, as does the other node. The transmitting controller generates an abort pattern code that is transmitted to all the nodes on the LAN, telling them that a collision has occurred. This alerts any nodes that might be waiting to access the LAN that there is a problem.

The receiving node (or nodes) dump any data that it might have received before the collision occurred. Other nodes waiting to send data generate a random timing number and go into a holding pattern. The timing number is the waiting time that the node sits out before it tries to transmit. Because the number is randomly generated, the odds against two of the nodes trying to transmit again at the same time are very low.

The first node to timeout listens to the LAN to determine whether any activity is still occurring. Because it almost always finds a clear LAN, it begins transmitting. If two of the nodes do timeout at the same time, another collision happens and the abort pattern/number generation/timeout sequence begins again. Eventually, one of the nodes will gain clear access to the network and successfully transmit its data.

The ethernet strategy provides for up to 1,024 users to share the LAN. From the description of its collision-recovery technique, however, it should be apparent that with more users on an ethernet LAN, more collisions are likely to occur, and the average time to complete an actual data transfer will be longer.

Ethernet Specifications

Ethernet is classified as a bus topology that has been implemented across several network media, including

- ▶ Coaxial cable
- ▶ Twisted-pair copper cable
- ▶ Fiber-optic cable
- ▶ Wireless RF

Coaxial Ethernet Specifications

The original ethernet scheme was classified as a 10Mbps transmission protocol. The maximum length specified for ethernet is 1.55 miles (2.5km), with a maximum segment length between nodes of 500 meters. This type of LAN is referred to as a *10Base5 LAN* by the IEEE organization.

The *XXBaseYY* IEEE nomenclature designates that the maximum data rate across the LAN is 10Mbps, that it is a baseband LAN (versus broadband), and that its maximum segment length is 500 meters. One exception to this method is the 10Base2 implementation. The maximum segment length for this specification is 185 meters (almost 200).

> ### EXAM ALERT
>
> Be aware that the XXBaseYY system roughly uses the XX value to represent the distance (in meters) that a network segment can be located (the notable exception is the 185 meter Base2 value—it's almost 200 meters).

Coaxial ethernet connections can be made through 50-ohm RG-8 thicknet coaxial cable (10Base5) or thinnet coaxial cable (10Base2). The original 10Base5 connection scheme required that special transceiver units be clamped to the cable. A pin in the transceiver pierced the cable to establish electrical contact with its conductor. An additional length of cable, called the *drop cable*, was then connected between the LAN adapter card and the transceiver. The 10Base2 ethernet LAN uses thinner, industry-standard RG-58 coaxial cable, and has a maximum segment length of 185 meters. Both coaxial connection methods require that a terminating resistor be installed at each end of the transmission line. Ethernet systems use 52-ohm terminators.

> ### Challenge #3
>
> Your office is just getting networked, and you are in charge of the physical connections made to all the machines. In the CFO's office, you encounter a machine that has been running on a small accounting network for several years, but it doesn't have an RJ-45 jack for the network cable. How can this be, and what should you do about it?

Twisted-Pair Ethernet Specifications

The Unshielded Twisted Pair (UTP) specifications are based on telephone cable and are normally used to connect a small number of PCs together. The twisted pairing of the cables uses magnetic-field principles to minimize induced noise in the lines. The original UTP LAN specification (10Base-T) had a transmission rate that was stated as 1Mbps. Using UTP cable, a LAN containing up to 64 nodes can be constructed with the maximum distance between nodes set at 100 meters. Newer ethernet implementations are producing LAN speeds of up to 1Gbps (1000Mbps) using UTP copper cabling.

For these networks, the IEEE adopted 10Base-T, 100Base-T, and 100Base-TX designations, indicating that they operate on twisted-pair cabling and depend on its specifications for the maximum segment length. The 100Base designation is referred to as *Fast Ethernet*. The TX version of the Fast Ethernet specification employs two pairs of twisted cable to conduct high-speed, full-duplex transmissions. The cables used with the TX version can be CAT 5 UTP or STP. There is also a 100Base-FX Fast Ethernet designation that indicates the network in using fiber-optic cabling. This specification is described later in this chapter.

Network cards capable of supporting both transmission rates are classified as 10/100 ethernet cards. The recommended maximum length of a 10/100Base-T segment is 100 meters (actually, the maximum segment length of any ethernet connection designated with a T is 100 meters).

EXAM ALERT

Know what type of cable 10Base-T and 100Base-T networks use.

The latest ethernet designations for copper cabling are the 1000Base-T Gigabit Ethernet specification that delivers 1 gigabit (1000Mbps) data transfers over Category 5 UTP cable and the 1000Base-CX specification that provides for gigabit transfers over two pairs of STP cable.

UTP systems normally employ connection concentrators built into routers, switches, or hubs for connection purposes, as shown in Figure 20.17.

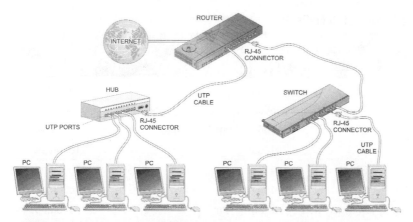

FIGURE 20.17 UTP network connectivity device.

Fiber Ethernet Standards

The IEEE organization has created several fiber-optic variations of the ethernet protocol. It classifies these variations under the IEEE-803 standard. These standards are referenced as the *10/100Base-F* specification. Variations of this standard include the following:

▶ 10Base-FP—This specification is used for passive star networks running at 10Mbps. It employs a special hub that uses mirrors to channel the light signals to the desired node.

▶ 10Base-FL—This specification is used between devices on the network. It operates in full-duplex mode and runs at 10Mbps. Cable lengths under this specification can range up to 2 kilometers.

▶ 100Base-FX—This protocol is identical to the 10Base-FL specification with the exception that it runs at 100Mbps. This particular version of the specification is referred to as *Fast Ethernet* because it can easily run at the 100Mbps rate.

▶ 1000Base–LX—Gigabit ethernet delivered over two multimode or single-mode optical fiber cables using longwave laser techniques.

▶ 1000Base-SX–Gigabit ethernet delivered over two multimode or single-mode optical fiber cables using shortwave laser techniques.

Table 20.2 summarizes the different Ethernet specifications. Other CSMA/CD-based protocols exist in the market. Some are actually Ethernet compatible. However, these systems may or may not achieve the performance levels of a true Ethernet system. Some may actually perform better.

TABLE 20.2   Ethernet Specifications

CLASSIFICATION	CONDUCTOR	MAX. SEGMENT LENGTH	NODES	MAX. LENGTH	TRANS. RATE
10Base2	RG-58	185m	30/1,024	250m	10Mbps
10Base5	RG-8	500m	100/1,024	2.5km	10Mbps
10Base-T	UTP/STP	100m/200m	2/1,024	2.5km	10Mbps
100Base-T	UTP	100m	2/1,024	2.5km	100Mbps
100Base-FX	FO	412m	1,024	5km	100Mbps
1000Base-T	UTP	100m	1,024	-	1000Mbps
1000Base-SX	FO (multimode)	275m–550m	1,024	-	1000Mbps
1000Base-LX	FO (single mode)	500m–550m–5km	1,024	-	1000Mbps

EXAM ALERT

Know the types of connectors and physical cable types used with each network media type.

Wireless Ethernet Standards

Wireless networking standards fall under the designation of 802.11x or Wi-Fi. Current standard versions include 802.11a, b, and g. These are sometimes referred to as *wireless ethernet standards*; however, true ethernet protocols are classified under IEEE-802.3 standards.

The current 802.11 wireless specifications include the following:

▶ 802.11—The original wireless LAN specification that furnishes 1 or 2Mbps data rates using advanced FHSS or DSSS spread spectrum signaling techniques in the 2.4GHz frequency range.

▶ 802.11a—An upgraded 802.11 specification that provides up to 54Mbps data rates in the 5.2GHz frequency range. The practical range for 802.11a signals is less than the 802.11b specification (225 feet, with direct line of sight).

▶ 802.11b—802.11 High Rate (802.11hr). This standard was the first 802.11 version to reach commercial acceptance and gained wide acceptance as the preferred wireless networking technology for both business and home network applications. It operates at transfer rates in the range of 11Mbps, with fallback operations at 5.5Mbps, 2Mbps, and 1Mbps. This version of the 802.11 specification provides ethernetlike functionality. Typically, the effective range of the 802.11b signal is from 100 to 300 meters, assuming a direct line of sight, and can be affected by intervening objects, such as walls and trees. The practical range for 802.11b is 150 feet.

▶ 802.11g—A newer WI-Fi wireless specification that delivers data transfer rates in excess of up to 54Mbps in the 2.4GHz band. The practical distance for 802.11g signals is the same as the 802.11b specification.

▶ 802.11n—A proposed 802.11x wireless specification based on multiple input, multiple output antennas that delivers data transfer rates in excess of up to 540Mbps in the 2.4GHz or 5.0GHz bands. The practical distance for 802.11n signals is expected to be about 50 meters.

There is also a group of 802.11 WLAN update standards that have been developed to support the general 802.11 specification. These include Quality of

Service (802.11e), Access Point Interoperability (802.11f), Interference (802.11h), and Security (802.11i also known as *WPA2*) .

Networking Protocols

When more than two computers are involved in the communications pathway, a network is formed and additional controls must be put into place to make certain that information is sent to the correct member of the network. This is in addition to controlling the flow of information on the network connection. A *network protocol* is a set of rules that governs how communications are conducted across a network. These protocols operate at the Network and Transport layers of the OSI model (as shown in Figure 20.16). For devices to communicate with each other on the network, they must all use the same network protocol.

Although many types of network protocols are in use throughout the world, four are widely accepted and must typically be dealt with in normal network environments:

- ▶ NetBEUI—NetBIOS Enhanced User Interface (NetBEUI) is a fast, efficient protocol, suitable for use on smaller Microsoft networks. It doesn't require any configuration to implement and is very simple to administer. NetBEUI is the fastest networking protocol because it has very low non-data overhead. However, NetBEUI is not a routable protocol and therefore cannot be used in complex, multisegment networks that use routers. Therefore, the NetBEUI protocol is not used much anymore because the TCP/IP protocol has become the protocol of choice for most networks.

- ▶ NWLink—NWLink is Microsoft's version of the Internetwork Packet Exchange/Sequenced Packet Exchange (IPX/SPX) network protocol used in Novell NetWare environments. Although NetWare has used IPX/SPX for the majority of its networking functions, with the release of Netware 5.0, Novell changed NetWare's primary protocol from IPX/SPX to TCP/IP. Even so, the majority of the installed NetWare networks continue to run IPX/SPX for at least some networking functions. IPX/SPX is a routable protocol and therefore is suitable for use in larger multisegment network environments. NWLink is relatively easy to install and manage and is also a routable protocol. Although IPX/SPX nearly became the most widely used network protocol, it has taken second place behind TCP/IP because of the Internet. The IPX/SPX protocol is slower than NetBEUI but it is faster than TCP/IP.

▶ AppleTalk—AppleTalk is used to communicate with Apple Macintosh computers. Historically, Apple has used AppleTalk for the majority of the functions in its networking environment. However, Apple now supports TCP/IP as well. AppleTalk is a routable protocol. In a PC environment, the AppleTalk protocol is usually implemented only to communicate with Macintosh computers on your network.

▶ TCP/IP—Transport Control Protocol/Internet Protocol (TCP/IP) is the most popular network protocol currently in use, largely because the Internet is based on it. However, TCP/IP has rapidly become the proto-col of choice for corporate networks because most operating systems support this protocol. This fact becomes very useful when you are trying to network different types of systems (Windows, Apple Macs, Linux machines) to one another. Also, TCP/IP is a routable protocol, so its packets can be transferred across many types of networks before they reach their final destination. Although TCP/IP is much slower than either IPX/SPX or NetBEUI, because it is a very reliable protocol it has the capability to ensure that data will be delivered to the receiver cor-rectly. These network protocols will be visited again later as we apply them to the Internet and when we set up LAN and WAN connections for different operating systems.

Exam Prep Questions

1. Under CompTIA's definition, a LAN can exist with as few as _____ computers.

  ○ **A.** Two

  ○ **B.** Tree

  ○ **C.** Four

  ○ **D.** Five

2. What are the major advantages of client/server over peer-to-peer networks? (Select all that apply.)

  ○ **A.** Less cable to maintain

  ○ **B.** Centralized administration

  ○ **C.** Data and resource security

  ○ **D.** Low cost

3. From the network topologies shown in the figure, identify the bus topology.

  ○ **A.** A

  ○ **B.** B

  ○ **C.** C

  ○ **D.** D

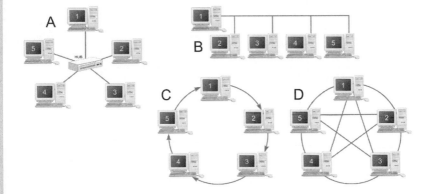

4. From the network topologies shown in question 4, identify the ring topology.

○ **A.** A

○ **B.** B

○ **C.** C

○ **D.** D

5. From the network topologies shown in question 4, identify the star topology.

○ **A.** A

○ **B.** B

○ **C.** C

○ **D.** D

6. From the network topologies shown in question 4, identify the mesh topology.

○ **A.** A

○ **B.** B

○ **C.** C

○ **D.** D

7. How is resource sharing organized in a peer-to-peer network?

○ **A.** By the user of the local machine

○ **B.** By the network administrator

○ **C.** By the server configuration

○ **D.** By the network manager

8. Nodes in _____ networks can serve as both clients and servers for different functions.

○ **A.** Client/server

○ **B.** Peer-to-peer

○ **C.** Token ring

○ **D.** Nondifferentiated

9. The main connection device for an 802.11x wireless network is _____.

   ○ **A.** A wireless hub

   ○ **B.** A wireless router

   ○ **C.** A wireless access point

   ○ **D.** A wireless modem

10. Which of the following network protocols is not routable?

    ○ **A.** TCP/IP

    ○ **B.** NetBEUI

    ○ **C.** IPX/SPX

    ○ **D.** AppleTalk

11. What is the maximum segment length associated with the 10Base2 networking standard?

    ○ **A.** 100m

    ○ **B.** 185m

    ○ **C.** 200km

    ○ **D.** 500m

12. What type of cable do 10Base-T and 100Base-T use?

    ○ **A.** UTP

    ○ **B.** STP

    ○ **C.** Fiber-optic

    ○ **D.** RG-58

13. An RJ-45 connector is most commonly used with _____.

    ○ **A.** Disk drive units

    ○ **B.** Fiber-optic cabling

    ○ **C.** Coaxial cabling

    ○ **D.** Unshielded twisted pair cabling

14. Which connector is not used with network cables?

   ○ **A.** BNC

   ○ **B.** RJ-45

   ○ **C.** SCSI

   ○ **D.** ST

15. What type of cabling is involved in the CAT5 cable rating?

   ○ **A.** Thin coaxial

   ○ **B.** UTP

   ○ **C.** STP

   ○ **D.** Thick coaxial

16. Which type of network employs SC connectors?

   ○ **A.** Token ring fiber-optic

   ○ **B.** Peer-to-peer UTP

   ○ **C.** Client/server UTP

   ○ **D.** Ethernet fiber-optic

17. Which type of cabling is used to support the 100Base-FX IEEE standard?

   ○ **A.** Fiber-optic

   ○ **B.** UTP

   ○ **C.** STP

   ○ **D.** Thick coaxial

18. Which fiber-optic cable type is the most widely used?

   ○ **A.** Single-mode cable

   ○ **B.** Multimode cable

   ○ **C.** FDDI cable

   ○ **D.** Plenum cable

19. What type of cabling would be best for cable runs that need to be run through air conditioning ducts that run through the facility?

- ○ **A.** Plenum cable
- ○ **B.** CAT 5e cable
- ○ **C.** Single-mode fiber-optic cable
- ○ **D.** Coaxial cable

20. When two devices can send signals to each other at the same time over the same wire, this is called _____ communication.

- ○ **A.** Simplex
- ○ **B.** Half duplex
- ○ **C.** Full duplex
- ○ **D.** Multi-quadraplex

21. Which of the following network types is best for sharing information and resources in a small business environment?

- ○ **A.** CAN
- ○ **B.** LAN
- ○ **C.** MAN
- ○ **D.** WAN

22. Which network components are compatible with 802.11g systems?

- ○ **A.** 802.11a
- ○ **B.** 802.11b
- ○ **C.** Bluetooth
- ○ **D.** 802.3

23. What networking technology supports several peripheral devices communicating with a PC simultaneously?

- ○ **A.** Wi-Fi
- ○ **B.** Bluetooth
- ○ **C.** Ethernet
- ○ **D.** IrDA

24. Which of the following network types does not have to interact with a centralized server?

   ○ **A.** A peer-to-peer LAN

   ○ **B.** A domain-based LAN

   ○ **C.** An Intranet

   ○ **D.** An Internet

25. What advantages do 802.11g networks have over 802.11b networks? (Select all that apply.)

   ○ **A.** Better data transfer rate

   ○ **B.** Greater useful transmission distance

   ○ **C.** Better frequency range

   ○ **D.** More simultaneous users

26. What is the maximum communicating speed of an 802.11g-rated wireless access point?

   ○ **A.** 2Mbps

   ○ **B.** 54Mbps

   ○ **C.** 5.5Mbps

   ○ **D.** 11Mbps

27. A customer wants to install a 1Gbps local area network in a facility. Which of the following cabling types will meet the user's expectations?

   ○ **A.** CAT3 cabling

   ○ **B.** CAT5 cabling

   ○ **C.** CAT6 cabling

   ○ **D.** Coaxial cabling

28. The 802.11x standard is used to identify which type of network?

   ○ **A.** Ethernet

   ○ **B.** Wi-Fi wireless

   ○ **C.** Fiber optic

   ○ **D.** Bluetooth wireless

29. Which wireless networking options offer the fastest communications? (Select all that apply.)

    ○ **A.** 802.11a

    ○ **B.** 802.11b

    ○ **C.** 802.11g

    ○ **D.** 802.15.1

Answers and Explanations

1. A. Under CompTIA's definition, a LAN can exist with as few as two computers.

2. B, C. The major advantages of the client/server networking arrangement include centralized administration and data and resource security.

3. B. In the bus topology, the stations, or nodes, of the network connect to a central communication link. Each node has a unique address along the bus that differentiates it from the other users on the network. Information can be placed on the bus by any node. The information must contain the network address of the node or nodes that the information is intended for. Other nodes along the bus will ignore the information.

4. C. In a ring network configuration, the communication bus is formed into a closed loop. Each node inspects the information on the LAN as it passes by. A repeater, built into each ring LAN card, regenerates every message not directed to it and sends it to the next appointed node. The originating node eventually receives the message back and removes it from the ring.

5. A. In a star topology, the logical layout of the network resembles the branches of a tree. All the nodes are connected in branches that eventually lead back to a central unit. Nodes communicate with each other through the central unit. The central station coordinates the network's activity by polling the nodes, one by one, to determine whether they have any information to transfer. If so, the central station gives that node a predetermined slice of time to transmit. If the message is longer than the time allotted, the transmissions are chopped into small packets of information that are transmitted over several polling cycles.

6. D. The mesh design offers the most basic network connection scheme. In this design, each node has a direct physical connection to all the other nodes in the network. Although the overhead for connecting a mesh network topology together in a LAN environment is prohibitive, this topology is employed in two very large network environments: the public telephone system and the Internet.

7. B. The local resources of PCs in a peer-to-peer network configuration can be shared at the discretion of the individual user at the local machine.

8. B. In a peer-to-peer network, local resources are shared with other network users by the operator at the local machine (as opposed to the network administrator in a client/server network).

9. C. A typical wireless LAN is centered on a wireless access point that acts as a bridging device that connects the wireless network computers with the wired network.

10. B. The NetBEUI protocol is an older protocol used with Microsoft networks. It is not routable, which puts it at a disadvantage in larger and mixed computer type networks where TCP/IP and IPX/SPX are widely used.

11. B. The 10Base2 LAN has a maximum segment length of 185m.

12. A. Newer ethernet implementations produce LAN speeds of up to 100Mbps using Unshielded Twisted Pair (UTP) copper cabling. For these networks, the IEEE adopted 10Base-T, 100Base-T, and 100Base-TX designations, indicating that they operate on twisted-pair cabling and depend on its specifications for the maximum segment length.

13. D. Unshielded Twisted Pair (UTP) cabling is terminated with an 8-pin RJ-45 plug.

14. C. A SCSI cable is used to connect SCSI devices to the computer.

15. B. EIA/TIA have categorized different grades of cable along with connector, distance, and installation specifications to produce the EIA/TIA UTP wiring category (CAT) ratings for the industry (for example, CAT3 and CAT5 cabling). CAT5 cabling is currently the most widely used specification for data communication wiring. For more information, see the section "Twisted-Pair Cabling."

16. D. The SC connector is the dominant connector for fiber optic ethernet networks. For more information, see the section "Fiber-Optic Cable."

17. **A.** The 100Base-FX Fast Ethernet designation indicates that the network is using fiber-optic cabling. For more information, see the section "Fiber Ethernet Standards."

18. **B.** Multimode fiber is the most widely used type of fiber-optic cabling. It is relatively cheap and transmits data over sufficient distances to make it useful for fiber-optic LAN environments.

19. **A.** Plenum cabling is a cable that has been rated as acceptable for use in locations that involve the movement of environmental air in a facility.

20. **C.** When a modem is used to send signals in only one direction, it is operating in simplex mode. Modems capable of both transmitting and receiving data are divided into two groups, based on their mode of operation. In half-duplex mode, modems exchange data, but only in one direction at a time. Multiplexing or full-duplex modems send and receive signal frequencies that allow both modems to send and receive data simultaneously.

21. **B.** The use of local area networks has grown immensely. These networks have become the backbone of small and large businesses because they enable people to share and control business resources and information in a highly efficient manner.

22. **B.** The 802.11g delivers data transfer rates up to 54 Mbps in the 2.4GHz band. The practical distance for 802.11g signals is the same as the 802.11b specification. Therefore network components are compatible with both standards.

23. **B.** Bluetooth can use up to eight devices that can be grouped together to form a piconet. Any device can become the master device and assume control of the network by issuing a request broadcast. The other seven devices become slave devices until the master device releases its position. The master device uses time division multiplexing to rapidly switch from one slave device to another around the network.

24. **A.** Peer-to-peer networks do not use dedicated server computers to provide services to other computers and devices on the network. Although peer-to-peer networks enable users to share resources and have a limited amount of local control over resources, they do not typically provide services for the different computers and devices attached to the network. In a client/server-based network, special computers running server operating systems can be tasked with automatically providing services to the network members such as automatically assigning TCP/IP settings (DHCP and APIPA), domain naming services (DNS), and network address translation services (NATS).

25. A. The 802.11b specification only provides data transfer rates up to 11Mbps, with fallback operations at 5.5Mbps, 2Mbps, and 1Mbps. Typically, the effective range of the 802.11b signal is from 100 to 300 meters, assuming a direct line of sight (practical range is 150 feet). The 802.11g specification delivers data transfer rates up to 54Mbps in the 2.4GHz band. The practical distance for 802.11g signals is the same as the 802.11b specification.

26. B. The 802.11g wireless networking specification delivers data transfer rates in excess of up to 54Mbps in the 2.4GHz band.

27. C. CAT6 cabling is a 250MHz, 100-ohm UTP rated Category 6. It is capable of 1.2Gbps over 1000Base-T wiring.

28. B. Wi-Fi wireless networking standards fall under the designation of 802.11x. Current standard versions include 802.11a, b, and g. These are sometimes referred to as *wireless Ethernet standards*; however, true Ethernet protocols are classified under IEEE-802.3 specifications.

29. A, C. The 802.11a specification provides up to 54Mbps data rates in the 5.2GHz frequency range. The 802.11g wireless networking specification delivers data transfer rates in excess of up to 54Mbps in the 2.4GHz band.

Challenge Solutions

1. A peer-to-peer network is very well suited to this type of environment. The different workers in this scenario need to be able to exchange different types of information among their different work areas. The administrative overhead is minimal in a peer-to-peer network. Also, the information these workers generate can be very intense when it passes across the network. Graphics and multimedia files tend to be quite large and can tie up a network. By creating a peer-to-peer network for the development staff, the main company network will not be required to handle these files.

2. In the case of the company's other network requirements, a client/server environment is much better suited for the accounting and warehouse/shipping functions. In most companies, the accounting and payroll information is considered confidential and protected. This typically includes inventory and shipping information. The advanced security functions associated with client/server systems are very important in these situations.

3. The computers in the accounting network use an older coaxial cabling for connectivity. You can either replace it with a UTP network so that you can hook it into your network, or add an ethernet network adapter card to the CFO's computer to make it a gateway between the two networks.

21

Installing Local Area Networks

Terms you'll need to understand:

✓ Network client

✓ Protocol

✓ Permissions

✓ Workgroup

✓ Server

✓ Connectivity

✓ Services

✓ Network shares

✓ Share permissions

✓ NTFS permissions

✓ Service Set Identifier (SSID)

Techniques you'll need to master:

Essentials 5.2—Install, configure, optimize, and upgrade networks.

✓ Install and configure network cards (physical address)

✓ Install, identify, and obtain wired and wireless connection

Remote Support Technician 4.2/IT Technician 5.2—Install, configure, optimize, and upgrade networks.

✓ Establish network connectivity:

   ✓ Install and configure network cards

   ✓ Obtain a connection

✓ Configure client options (such as Microsoft, Novell) and network options (such as domain, workgroup, tree)

✓ Configure network options

✓ Demonstrate the ability to share network resources:

   ✓ Models

   ✓ Configure permissions

   ✓ Capacities/limitations for sharing for each operating system

Installing and Configuring LAN Components

This chapter covers the Installing and Configuring Networks areas of the CompTIA A+ Certification—Essentials examination under Objectives 5.2. It also covers the Install, Configure, Optimize, and Upgrade networks information that is generally testable under Objective 4.2 of the Remote Support Technician exam and Objective 5.2 of the IT Technician exam.

Because PC technicians are typically responsible for maintaining the portion of the network that attaches to the computer, they must be able to install, configure, and service the network adapter card and cable.

> **NOTE**
>
> The Remote Support Technician 4.2 and IT Technician 5.2 objectives use the same wording to cover installing, configuring, optimizing, and upgrading networks. These listings cover the "Install and configure network cards (physical address)" and "Install, identify, and obtain wired and wireless connection" subobjectives from Essentials 5.2 and go on to complete the network installation and configuration process.
>
> The topics specified in these different exam/objective areas are so closely stated that it makes sense that they are presented as the same discussion. You will need to study this material in this chapter for any of the four exams you intend to challenge.

Installing and configuring LANs, as it applies to most PC technician positions, refers to the process of installing a network adapter (typically a card), connecting a transmission media to the card using a standard network connector of some type, configuring the PC's networking properties, and verifying the connection of the PC to the network.

Although some positions require that the PC technician go further than these simple steps, in most others, the network administrator takes over the more complex network configuration and administration duties. In most cases where there is a network administrator, the PC technician must work for or in conjunction with the administrator.

LAN Adapter Cards

In a LAN, each computer on the network requires a *network interface adapter*. This adapter may exist as a *Network Interface Card* (or *NIC*), or it may be built into the system board circuitry. In addition, every unit has to be connected to the network by some type of cabling or other communication media. Network cables are typically either twisted-pair wires, thick or thin coaxial cable, or fiber-optic cable. Other network communication media includes radio frequency or infrared light signals.

LAN adapter cards must have connectors that are compatible with the type of LAN cabling being used. Ethernet LAN cards come equipped with an RJ-45 connector. Figure 21.1 depicts a typical LAN card.

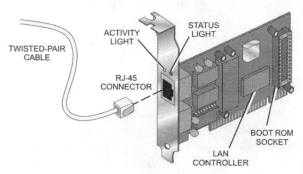

FIGURE 21.1 A typical LAN card (also known as NIC).

Another item that can be found on many LAN cards is a vacant ROM socket. This socket is included so that it can be used to install a boot ROM that will enable the unit to be used as a diskless workstation. One or more activity lights may also be included on the card's backplate. These lights can play a very important part in diagnosing problems with the LAN connection. Check the card's user manual for definitions of its activity lights.

Each adapter must have an adapter driver program loaded in its host computer to handle communications between the system and the adapter. These are the ethernet and token ring drivers loaded to control specific types of LAN adapter cards.

In addition to the adapter drivers, the network computer must have a network protocol driver loaded. This program may be referred to as the *transport protocol*, or just as the *protocol*. It operates between the adapter and the initial layer of network software to package and unpackage data for the LAN. In many cases, the computer may have several protocol drivers loaded so that the unit can communicate with computers that use other types of protocols.

Typical protocol drivers include the Internetwork Packet Exchange/Sequenced Packet Exchange (IPX/SPX) model produced by Novell, and the standard Transmission Control Protocol/Internet Protocol (TCP/IP) developed by the U.S. military for its ARPA network. Figure 21.2 illustrates the various LAN drivers necessary to transmit or receive data on a network.

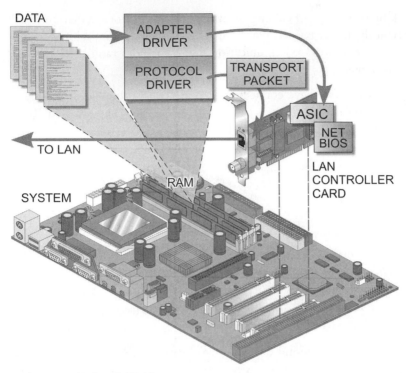

DATA

ADAPTER DRIVER

PROTOCOL DRIVER

TRANSPORT PACKET

ASIC

NET BIOS

TO LAN

LAN CONTROLLER CARD

RAM

SYSTEM

FIGURE 21.2   Various LAN drivers.

Installing LAN Cards

The process for installing a LAN card in a PC follows the basic steps for installing most peripheral cards in a PnP system. Consult the NIC's installation guide for any special settings that the card may require. If no special installation instructions exist for the card, place the adapter card in a vacant expansion slot, secure it to the system unit's backplate, and turn the system on.

As with other adapter cards, the system's PnP function should detect the presence of the network adapter and the operating system should load the correct device drivers for it. If Windows doesn't detect the network card, you will need to use the Add New Hardware Wizard to install the device. If the system does not install drivers for the adapter, you will be prompted to select a driver from a list provided by the operating system, or you will have to provide a driver supplied by the adapter's manufacturer or a third-party source.

Connect the LAN card to the network media and check the activity lights on the back of the NIC card to ensure that a connection to the network has been obtained. Figure 21.3 illustrates connecting the computer to the LAN using

UTP cable. As the figure illustrates, the line drop to the computer comes from a network connectivity device. In some office environments, the connection comes from a wall plate that has network cabling that runs back to the connectivity equipment.

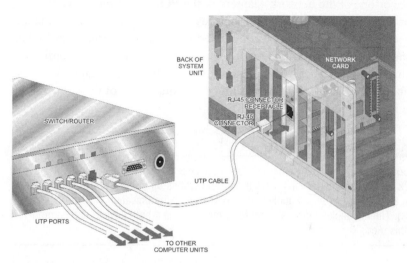

FIGURE 21.3   Connecting the computer to the LAN.

After the card has been installed and physically connected to the network transmission media, you must install and configure the client options and network protocols. These items are operating system–specific, so they will be dealt with later in this chapter.

The final step involved with installing the NIC card is to turn the computer on and check the activity light on the back of the card. If the light is blinking, the network has recognized the presence of the card, and the connection to the network is good. If not, you must troubleshoot the network cabling and the NIC.

Optimizing Network Adapters

In a networked system, by design, all the nodes in the network run at the same speed. That means that the performance of the network is limited by its slowest component. If the system is using mostly adapter cards and devices rated for 1GHz operation, but one or more of the cards or connectivity devices is rated for only 100MHz operation, the network will be limited to 100MHz operation. Therefore, all the adapters in the system should be updated to use the fastest speed the network architecture can accommodate.

In Windows 2000 and Windows XP, there may also be a problem with the speed and duplex settings for the adapter or the connectivity devices. Most network hubs and switches have the ability to auto-negotiate the network speed and communication duplexing with the PCs connected to them. However, if the connectivity device or one of the network adapters in the PCs, is configured incorrectly, the network segment will be force to run at less than its optimum performance. The connectivity devices should be configured for optimum performance when they are installed. Likewise, the network adapters can be manually configured through the Advanced tab of the network adapter's Properties page. Set these values to match the values of the actual speed and duplexing of the connectivity device the PC is connected to.

> **NOTE**
>
> Network adapters and connectivity devices typically have the capability to communicate in half duplex mode (communications move in both directions but in only one direction at a time—like a walkie-talkie) or full duplex mode (two-way communication occurring at the same time). The full duplex mode is faster for a given speed if both devices can communicate in this mode.

Installing Wireless LANs

Wireless LANs provide the maximum amount of flexibility for connecting home and office networking components. Because no wires are required to connect devices to the wireless network, users have considerable mobility. The wireless network is becoming a popular option for connecting devices in residential and small office environments. It is also becoming an economical choice for locations where installing cable is not practical or is prohibited by historic building codes or other restrictions.

The process for setting up a wireless network involves four steps:

1. Install the access point
2. Configure the access point
3. Install the client adapters.
4. Configure security.

Installing the Access Point

The access point (AP) is the mainstay of the wireless network; it serves as the central connection point for all the network devices within its range. It also provides the physical connection with wired networks, as illustrated in Figure 21.4.

The access point can be connected to a host computer that is a node on an existing hard-wired network, or it can be connected directly into a connectivity device such as a network hub, switch, or router. In many cases, the AP function is built directly into the router or gateway device. Installing the access point is normally a matter of connecting it to the network host, installing its power adapter, and loading its network drivers and protocols on the host computer.

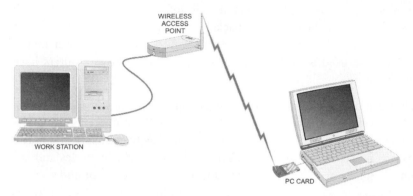

FIGURE 21.4 Wireless network components.

The antennas on the access point establish a range of transmission around the access point called a *hot spot*. Other wireless computing devices (*clients*) may access the network throughout the hot spot as long as they are within range of other wireless terminals or the access point. Wireless clients can be any type of computer or peripheral designed to use the same wireless protocol that the access point is using. These devices include desktop computers with wireless PCI cards, laptop computers using PCMCIA cards, and wireless peripheral equipment using built-in wireless interfaces.

Although the physical installation and configuration of wireless networks is typically simple when computers are close to each other and there are no physical barriers to their line-of-sight transmissions, installations can become more difficult when you have clients located at distances from the access point or when there are physical barriers of any type (walls, for instance). The radio frequency (RF) signal strength at wireless LAN clients can be negatively affected by signals bouncing off walls and objects in an indoor environment. The radio waves may arrive from multiple directions and in some cases can cancel or severely reduce the signal strength between portable users. This effect is called *multipath* and is eliminated by analyzing the signals with test instruments or moving the nodes to a different location. Radio emissions from other devices using the unlicensed 2.4GHz radio spectrum are also a source of electromagnetic interference for 802.11b wireless interfaces (802.11a/g devices operate in the 5GHz range and are not adversely affected by these devices). The WLAN adapter cards and the access point should be installed in such a way that they provide the maximum exposure for the antenna to maximize signal strength.

The first step in overcoming these types of obstacles is to perform a site survey to analyze the network signal strength in each section of the network. Site checks can be performed using specialized test equipment or with software built into wireless devices. Most access points include software-based signal strength analysis tools as part of their support package. Likewise, the wireless support built in to the Windows operating system provides a signal strength meter. These tools can be used to test for signal strength when the computers have been brought online.

The simplest site survey method involves setting up the AP in some initial position and then walking around the site with a portable computer, noting the power level at each section of the site. After the site has been mapped, you can locate network nodes to maximize connectivity between all the nodes and the access point. You may also find that you need to relocate the AP or add another AP to the network to gain better coverage. Generally, the best place to locate the AP is in the center of the area you need to cover. All the WLAN adapter cards and the access point should be installed in such a way that they provide the maximum exposure for the antenna to maximize signal strength. You should keep the AP's antenna as close to vertical as possible.

You may want to hang the AP on a wall or from the ceiling to get the best clear path for its wireless signals. Generally, the higher in the room the better because this avoids typical obstacles found in most rooms. However, you should be aware that the weakest signal points for the AP are typically directly above and below the unit. Also be aware that hanging the AP on an exterior wall will limit its useful range (unless you want to work outside, in which case you should put the access point near a window).

Typical obstacles to the wireless network signals include large metal or water-filled objects, such as filing cabinets and fish tanks. Other items that tend to affect wireless network communications include other 2.4GHz devices such as cordless telephones.

Configuring the Access Point

After the best location for the AP has been established and it has been connected to the network host, you will need to configure it for operation. Most APs provide their own browser-based wizard for this purpose. Other APs come with CD-based configuration programs. In either event, you will need to start a browser on one of the network's computers and access the AP.

Using the browser method to access the AP's configuration wizard involves entering its IP address in the browser's navigation window. The factory default IP address for many APs is in the private address range of 192.168.x.x. When the wizard starts, you will be guided through the configuration process. Information you will need to enter includes password, Service Set Identifier (SSID) name, and AP channel. The SSID is a 32-character identifier that is attached to the front end of packets sent across wireless networks. You can select 11 different channels for the AP's operation. The factory default channel setting for most APs is 6. If problems occur with this channel setting, try channel 1 or 11. If you are adding an AP to a network that already has an AP set to channel 6, set the second AP to channel 1 operation—never set two APs in the same network to the same channel.

Next, you will be asked to enable encryption and security features. This option should be bypassed until the wireless client computers have been set up. To complete the AP configuration, you must apply the settings to the AP. The AP will reset itself, momentarily dropping connectivity with the network. You will need to come back to the wizard to configure security settings after configuring the client computers.

Installing Wireless Clients

For most client computers, all that is necessary to start sharing data and resources wirelessly is to install the proper wireless adapter and configure the network software. The adapter card can be a PCI-based wireless adapter in a desktop unit, or a PC Card–based adapter in a notebook computer. Computers built to meet Intel's Centrino mobile technology standard have built-in wireless networking capabilities. No additional wireless adapter is needed. Simply configure the internal wireless adapter and push the button to activate the circuitry.

For most computers, simply install the wireless USB, PCI, or PC Card adapter card in the computer and turn it on. In Windows systems, the operating system will display a Found New Hardware Wizard page. Normally, you should select the Install the Software Automatically option. This will cause Windows to search for the appropriate driver. If the drivers are already installed, Windows will automatically use those drivers and attempt to establish a wireless network connection. If the drivers are not present, the operating system will produce a prompt asking for the location of the driver software. If there is more than one possible driver for the adapter, Windows will prompt the user to select the proper driver.

Many wireless network adapters come with additional software with their products to give them an advantage over their competitors. This software typically replaces Windows built-in wireless configuration software. However, other wireless adapters come with driver software that must be installed before you install the hardware. If you install the adapter first, the computer will not have the proper drivers installed and the adapter will not work.

Installing Network Connectivity Devices

For the most part, installing a hub or switch in a network involves attaching the network media connections to the device, connecting the power unit to the device, and turning on the power switch. In cases where a single router is being used, such as in a residential, home office, or small office environment, the physical installation process for routers is similar to that of a switch or hub. However, in the case of the router, it will need to be configured properly for its position (IP address) and role in the network (that is, providing DHCP and firewall services, as well as access point functions in a wireless network).

In the case of routers in larger, or multisegmented networks, you may be required to install connecting cables that link the router to another router. In situations where you are connecting multiple routers together in the network, you must give some thought to which device in the network is going to be responsible for handling the DHCP function. This function must be disabled on all other routers and server PCs to avoid confusion.

The CAT5 wiring scenarios presented in the previous section are normally wired in a *straight-through cable* arrangement (that is, Pin 1 at both ends of the cable wired together, as are all the other connections). However, you must be aware that not all CAT5 cables are wired this way.

A CAT5 crossover cable is a good tool to have for troubleshooting NICs and hubs. These cables can also be used to connect two computers together without a hub or other network connectivity device. They might also be required to connect two hubs together.

Figure 21.5 depicts the wiring specification for such a crossover cable. Notice that the wire pairs remain constant with the earlier straight-through CAT5 wiring examples. The only difference with the crossover cable is that the Transmit pair of one end (TX+ and TX–) is crossed over to match the Receive pair (RX+ and RX–) at the other end.

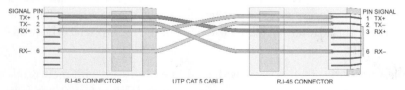

FIGURE 21.5 Crossover cabling.

Cabling from a NIC to a hub or router is usually performed with a straight-through cable. Crossover cables are typically used for connecting two hubs together. Hubs usually have markings on their ports to indicate whether a straight-through or crossover cable is required. The markings that are used to identify straight-through and crossover cables are

▸ MDI (Media Dependent Interface)—This connection requires an external crossover (either the cable or the other hub must perform the crossover function).

▸ MIDX (Media Independent Interface Crossover)—This type of connection can be switched so that the port performs the crossover function. This allows a straight-through cable to be used to make the connection when engaged.

If there is no marking on the port, it is generally assumed that the hub performs the crossover. However, you should always check the hub documentation to verify this arrangement.

> **NOTE**
>
> Crossover connections are made only from port to port and not between a regular port and the uplink port. An *uplink port* is a special MDI port on the hub or switch that is designed for linking two like devices together with a standard (straight-through) patch cable.

After the router has been connected, you must configure it for operation. Routers typically employ a browser-based wizard for this purpose. To begin the configuration process, start one of the computers in the network and open its browser. Next, enter the router's IP address in the browser's navigation window. The normal default value for most routers is the private network address 192.168.0.1. This should produce a configuration wizard screen similar to the one depicted in Figure 21.6.

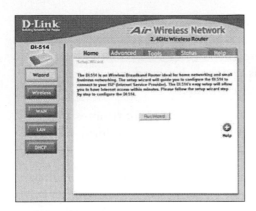

FIGURE 21.6 A router configuration screen.

The first thing you will be asked to do is enter a username and password to get into the wizard. Default usernames and passwords are normally available in the router's installation guide as well. If the device has previously been configured, you must either obtain the login information from the network administrator, or physically reset the router and use the default values to access the wizard. After the configuration wizard has been accessed, a number of items may need to be configured. The following paragraphs cover the generic features found on most routers.

▶ Administrative Password—It is a good idea to change the password from the default value. This setting should be a strong setting because the router protects the entire network. If the password is forgotten, you can always physically reset the router and reestablish the password setting. It's not a good idea to allow your browser to remember your username and password for this function if you are in an open environment where others can access the network through your computer.

▶ Router IP Address—Some routers allow you to change their IP addresses from the factory default. Changing the address can add an additional level of security to the network.

▶ DHCP Server—Where you set this configuration depends on how your network is set up. To communicate in a network, every client must have a unique IP address that identifies its location to the rest of the network. Network clients can be configured with constant IP addresses, called *static IPs,* or they can be assigned one from a list of available IP addresses. There are two possible sources for IP addresses in a local area network: a computer providing the Dynamic Host Configuration Protocol (DHCP) function or a router performing this function. If both DHCP devices are active in the network, confusion will occur as devices attempting to log on to the network receive conflicting information from the two sources.

If you are setting up a relatively small network, such as a residential or small office network, consider using static IP addressing and assigning each computer a unique address. In this case you would choose to disable the DHCP server function on the router (as you would if you have a DHCP server computer operating in the network). If you need to run the DHCP function on the router, you might want to consider limiting the number of IP addresses the router can issue to just a couple more than the number of computers you currently have connected to the network (for expansion purposes). DHCP is covered in detail later in this chapter.

▶ Access to Virtual Servers or Port Forwarding—*Virtual servers* are the computers in the local network that interface directly with the Internet. Unless you are running a web business where you have need to have servers connected to the Internet, disable this option.

▶ Exclusive Applications—This setting allows applications to access and receive information directly from the Internet without controls from the router. This is a potential point of attack and should be enabled only if the system must use software that requires this feature.

▶ Enable Access to Known MACs—Also known as *MAC filtering*, this option enables you to configure the router to permit devices with known MAC addresses to access it. If you enable this feature, you should allow only MAC addresses you recognize from your network to have access.

▶ Wireless AP—Many wireless access points also possess the capability to perform the routing functions. In network environments that have no wireless network devices, this function should be disabled.

▶ Remote Management—This feature permits you to access your network from a remote location to perform management functions. Unless you have specific need to do this, you should disable this setting. It can always be reset to Enable if you find that you need to perform remote management functions later.

▶ Discard Ping from WAN Side—This is a troubleshooting setting that enables you to hide your network from unknown Internet users who may be trying to verify your location for malicious purposes. Enabling this setting prevents them from getting responses back from ping operations and makes it look like your network is not present. If you are setting up the router as an internal connection, there is no need to enable this setting.

▶ UPnP—This setting (Universal Plug and Play) applies to allowing operating systems to manage standalone network devices such as the router. This option makes the router and the network more vulnerable to attacks; therefore, this setting should be disabled.

Challenge #1

You have been contracted to set up a network for a small business. The client has purchased a wireless access point/router device to provide Internet access to three computers he has in his small office complex. He has two desktop PCs that have built-in ethernet network adapters and a notebook PC with a wireless network adapter. What do you need to do to connect all the PCs to the router and get them to communicate with each other?

Installing Network Components in Windows 2000/XP Control Panels

After the network adapter card has been installed, the next step in setting up the computer on the network is to load and configure its drivers, protocols, and services. In most Windows 2000/XP installations, rebooting the computer and permitting Windows to detect the network adapter will accomplish the majority of these items.

In Windows 2000, the Networking Control Panel is located under the Network and Dial-Up Connections icon. It provides access to the Network and Dial-Up Connections window shown in Figure 21.7. This window provides several key functions associated with local and wide area networking. It is used to install new network adapter cards and change their settings, change network component settings, and to install TCP/IP.

In Windows XP, the Networking icon has been changed to the Network Connections icon. It does not offer the dial-up networking function included in the Windows 2000 applet, but it is used to configure and manage LAN and high-speed Internet access connection (DSL and cable modem connections). Clicking the icon produces the LAN or High-Speed Internet window shown in Figure 21.8.

The Network Tasks pane of the Network Connections window provides options for creating, viewing, repairing, renaming, and reconfiguring the displayed connection, as well as for disabling a network device.

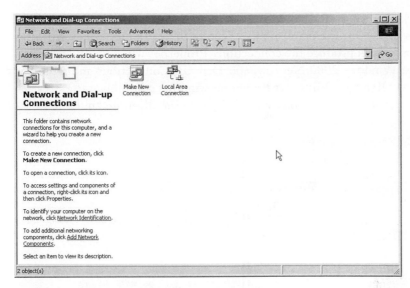

FIGURE 21.7 The Network and Dial-Up Connections window.

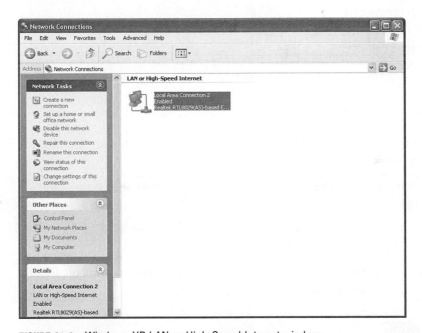

FIGURE 21.8 Windows XP LAN or High-Speed Internet window.

EXAM ALERT

Know how to view the status of a local area network connection.

Right-clicking the connection will produce a pop-up menu that contains the Properties option for the connection. Selecting this option in either operating system version will produce the connection's Properties window. The organization of the Windows 2000 Network and Dial-Up Connections and Windows XP LAN or High Speed Internet Properties windows consolidates the services, protocols, and adapters functions under a single tab, as illustrated in Figure 21.9.

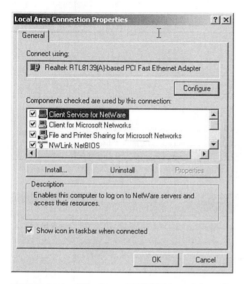

FIGURE 21.9 Windows 2000/XP Local Area Connection Properties.

The functions associated with the Windows 2000 Local Area Connection Properties include the following:

▶ Clients—Enables the system to use files and printers shared on other computers

▶ Services—Used to add, remove, or configure network services such as DNS, WINS, and DHCP functions

▶ Protocols—Used to add, remove, or configure network protocols for specific types of network environments

EXAM ALERT

A *protocol* is a set of rules governing how an operation will be performed. In local area networking, there are several layers of protocols involved.

To configure any of these functions for a given component, access the Local Area Connection Properties dialog box, highlight the desired component, and click the Install button. Each entry contains a list of primary and alternative drivers, protocols, and services that can be viewed by clicking the title in the window. These alternatives are included because many non-Microsoft networks are in use, and Windows attempts to support the most common ones. If a particular network component type is not supported in the standard listings, each Select Network page features a Have Disk button that permits the system to upload Windows-compatible drivers and protocols.

Other functions affecting the networking and dial-up connections in Windows 2000 and Windows XP include the following:

▶ Network Identification—Specifies the computer name and the workgroup or domain name to which the computer belongs. Under TCP/IP, computer names can be up to 63 characters, but should be limited to 15 characters or fewer. They can use the numbers 0–9, letters A–Z (and a–z), as well as hyphens. Using other characters may prevent other nodes from finding your computer or the network. This option is located under the System icon in the Control Panel.

▶ Bindings—Establishes a potential pathway between a given network service, a network protocol, and a given network adapter. The order of the bindings can affect the efficiency of the system's networking operations. To establish bindings, access the Network and Dial-Up Connections (Network Connections in XP) page and click the Advanced entry on its drop-down menu bar. Then select the Advanced Settings option from the menu.

EXAM ALERT

Memorize which network items can be set through the Windows 2000 Network and Dial-Up Connections applet's Local Area Connection Properties window.

The Windows XP Local Area Connections Properties window offers two tabs not available in the Windows 2000 version: the Advanced tab and the Authentication tab. The Advanced tab is used to enable the Windows XP Internet Connection Firewall (changed to Windows Firewall with Service Pack 2 installed). This feature is embedded in Windows XP so that it can act as an Internet firewall for itself or for a local area network attached to it. This feature is described in more detail in Chapter 24, "Security."

The Authentication tab is used to configure authentication protocols for conducting local area and wide area communications across a network. Recall that *authentication* is the process of identifying an individual as who they claim to be. This page, shown in Figure 21.10, is used to select standard protocols associated with particular network types, including ethernet and 802.1x wireless protocols.

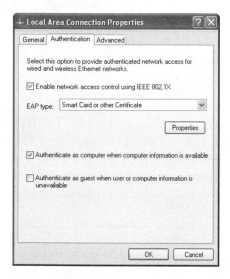

FIGURE 21.10 Windows XP Authentication tab.

Configuring Clients in Windows 2000/XP

Any network computer that uses the resources of another computer in the network is acting as its client. To use these resources, the local computer must have client software installed that will enable it to work with the other computer. In some networks, this may mean working with computers that have other types of operating systems running on them.

To add a new client to the computer, highlight the Client option in the Select Network Component Type dialog box, select the desired client from the list, and click the Add button. The new client will appear in the Installed Network Components window of the Network page.

Configuring Protocols in Windows 2000/XP

Because the boot-detection process loads the adapter driver, two types of clients to choose from, and a set of sharing parameters, most installation procedures require only that the appropriate protocols be loaded for the network type. In

Windows-based client/server LANs, TCP/IP has become the leading choice of networking protocols. Therefore, the TCP/IP protocol must be activated and configured properly for the computer to function on the LAN.

However, you may need to add the NetBEUI, AppleTalk, and IPX/SPX (also known as *NWLink*) protocols computer if the LAN contains computers with older Windows operating systems, Apple/Mac computers, or computers running Novell operating systems. You should also be aware that Microsoft offers separate TCP/IP protocols for local area and wide area networking. The additional TCP/IP protocol is used for dial-up Internet support. The procedure for adding protocols is the same as that described for adding clients.

Configuring TCP/IP in Windows 2000/XP LANs

When the TCP/IP protocol is installed, it can require several pieces of configuration information to fully implement. In a simple local area network, such as a peer-to-peer network, only an IP address and a subnet mask setting are required. However, in multisegmented client/server LANs, you may also be required to provide a default gateway (router) address, as well as an IP address for a DNS or WINS server.

TCP/IP is automatically installed in Windows 2000 and XP and configured to automatically obtain an IP address. There are three possible sources for IP addresses: Dynamic Host Configuration Protocol (DHCP), Automatic Private IP Addressing (APIPA), and manually assigned TCP/IP properties.

Manual TCP/IP Configuration

To manually configure TCP/IP values, select the TCP/IP protocol for the LAN from the listing in the Network and Dial-Up Connections (or Network Connections in Windows XP) window and click the Properties button. This will produce the General tab of the TCP/IP Properties page, as illustrated in Figure 21.11.

Through this page you can configure the computer to obtain an IP address using an automatic service, such as DHCP, or you can manually configure a static address for the computer. To manually configure TCP/IP, the Use the Following Address option must be enabled, and you must know the IP address and subnet mask settings you want to use. Remember that every computer on a network must have a unique IP address that identifies who it is. It must also have a subnet mask entry to limit the mobility of the transmission to those nodes within the subnet. (Without subnets, every TCP/IP communication could range across every connected network link in the world—the traffic would be unbelievable.)

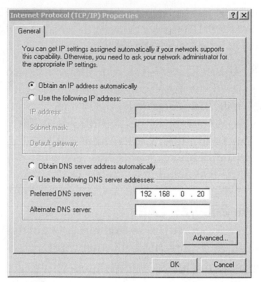

FIGURE 21.11   The TCP/IP Properties page.

If the Obtain an IP Address Automatically option is selected, the computer will attempt to locate a DHCP server when it boots onto the network. The DHCP server has the capability to provide it with all the TCP/IP configuration information it needs. If no DHCP server is found, Windows computers will default to a random IP address in the range of 169.254.XX.XX and a subnet mask of 255.255.0.0. The Automatic Private IP Address (APIPA) feature is very useful in smaller single-segment networks because it effectively autoconfigures such a network.

The Preferred and Alternate DNS Server boxes can be configured to provide a secondary source for DNS information in the event that the primary DNS server is unavailable. Click the Advanced button to access the Advanced TCP/IP Settings dialog window where you can configure additional TCP/IP settings.

Under the IP Settings tab, depicted in Figure 21.11, you can configure the following settings:

▶ IP Addresses—This dialog window is used to enter, remove, and edit IP addresses. It can contain multiple IP addresses that may be required for special situations. You can add as many IP addresses to the list as you want.

▶ Default Gateways—This dialog window is used to specify the IP address of the router (or other gateway device) that separates your network segment from other segments. The computer uses this address to communicate with IP addresses outside the local segment.

Three additional tabs can be used to configure TCP/IP functions for given implementations:

- ▶ DNS—This tab enables you to specify the IP addresses of Domain Name System servers that are responsible for reconciling DNS computer names to actual IP addresses. In a LAN, this is typically the domain server for your network. In a wide area network environment, such as the Internet, this is typically the IP address of the ISP. Various DNS suffixes can be attached to enable the DNS system to attempt to resolve incomplete domain names. This listing will attach specified domain suffixes (for example, mic-inc.net, mic-inc.com) to names it receives. These suffixes will be attached to the received name and tried in the order they are entered in the list.

- ▶ WINS—This tab is used to specify the IP addresses of a Windows Name System server that is used to resolve the NetBIOS/NetBEUI names associated with older Windows operating systems to IP addresses.

- ▶ Options—This tab is used to configure TCP, UDP, and IP address filtering. These settings are use to control the type of TCP/IP traffic that can reach the computer.

EXAM ALERT

Know where TCP/IP properties are established in Windows 2000 and XP.

Networking with Novell NetWare

In a Novell NetWare system, the root directory of the workstation should contain the files NETBIOS and IPX.COM. The NETBIOS file is an emulation of IBM's Network Basic Input/Output System (NetBIOS) and represents the basic interface between the operating system and the LAN hardware. This function is implemented through ROM ICs, located on the network card. The Internetworking Packet Exchange (IPX) file passes commands across the network to the file server.

The NETBIOS and IPX protocols must be bound together to navigate the Novell network from a computer using a Windows operating system. This is accomplished by enabling the NETBIOS bindings in the IPX protocol Properties in the Network Properties window.

The Open Datalink Interface (ODI) file is the Novell network shell that communicates between the adapter and the system's applications. Older versions of NetWare used a shell program called NETx.

EXAM ALERT

Be aware of the elements that are required to navigate through a Novell network from a computer running a Microsoft operating system.

Challenge #2

You are working on a Windows 2000 Professional client computer that has IPX loaded. You are working in a Novell LAN, however, and you find that you cannot browse the network. What should you check to gain access to the LAN?

Installing NetWare Clients and Protocols

For Windows computers to be able to communicate with Novell servers in a network, they must have the client service for NetWare installed and configured. As indicated earlier in this chapter, clients are installed through the Select Network Component Type dialog window. This window is located under the connection's Properties.

Similarly, in Windows 2000 and Windows XP systems, you must install the Client Service for NetWare (CSNW) option to provide the Windows client with the capability to communicate with NetWare servers. CSNW requires that the IPX/SPX protocol be installed on the client. It can be installed manually beforehand, or it will be installed automatically when the CSNW client is installed.

There are actually two pieces to the IPX/SPX implementation in Windows: the NWLink NetBIOS and NWLink IPX/SPX/NetBIOS Compatible Transport Protocol options. Both are required for interaction with Novell systems. To configure the IPX/SPX protocol, select the NWLink IPX/SPX/NetBIOS Compatible Transport Protocol option from the list in the dialog window and click the Properties button.

In certain instances, you may have to enter an internal network number and a frame type setting on the General tab of the IPX/SPX Properties page. The network number is used when certain NetWare-specific applications are installed. This number is generally obtained from the NetWare administrator. The frame type setting is used in ethernet networks to identify the type of ethernet packets that are being used. The Auto Frame Type Detection option permits the IPX function to determine what type of frame is actually being used on the network.

Installing Other Network Protocols

There are two other protocols of interest that you can install in a Windows system: Appletalk and NetBEUI. As mentioned earlier, Appletalk is required for Windows computers to communicate with Apple Macs running Apple operating systems in the network, and NetBEUI is required when the network contains computers running older Windows operating systems. Both protocols are available through the Select Network Component Type dialog window. They can be installed by clicking the Install button, selecting the Protocol option, clicking the Add button, selecting the desired protocol from the list, and clicking the OK button.

Sharing Network Resources

During the Windows 2000 or Windows XP setup processes, the system must be configured to function as a workgroup node or as part of a domain. A *workgroup* is a collection of networked computers assigned the same workgroup name. Any user can become a member of a workgroup by specifying the particular workgroup's name during the setup process. Conversely, a *domain* is a collection of networked computers established and controlled by a network administrator. As mentioned earlier in this chapter, domains are established for security and administration purposes.

The Setup routine requires that a computer account be established before a computer can be included in the domain. This account is not the same as the user accounts that the system uses to identify individual users. If the system has been upgraded from an older Windows NT version, Windows 2000 or XP will adopt the current computer account information. If the installation is new, the Setup utility will request that a new computer account be established. The network administrator normally assigns this account prior to running Setup. Joining the domain during setup requires a username and password.

In Windows 2000 or Windows XP systems using the TCP/IP protocol, computer names can range up to 63 characters in length and should be made up of the letters A through Z, numbers 0 through 9, and hyphens.

EXAM ALERT

Know the specifications for setting up computer names in a given operating system.

Network Shares

In a network environment, only *network shares* (shared directories and resources) can be accessed across the network. The sharing function is implemented at the computer that hosts the folder or resource (*resources* are devices capable of holding or manipulating data). In Windows operating systems, you can establish sharing for a folder by right-clicking it and selecting the Sharing (Sharing and Security in Windows XP) option from the menu. This will produce the Sharing tab of the file or folder's Properties page, as illustrated in Figure 21.12.

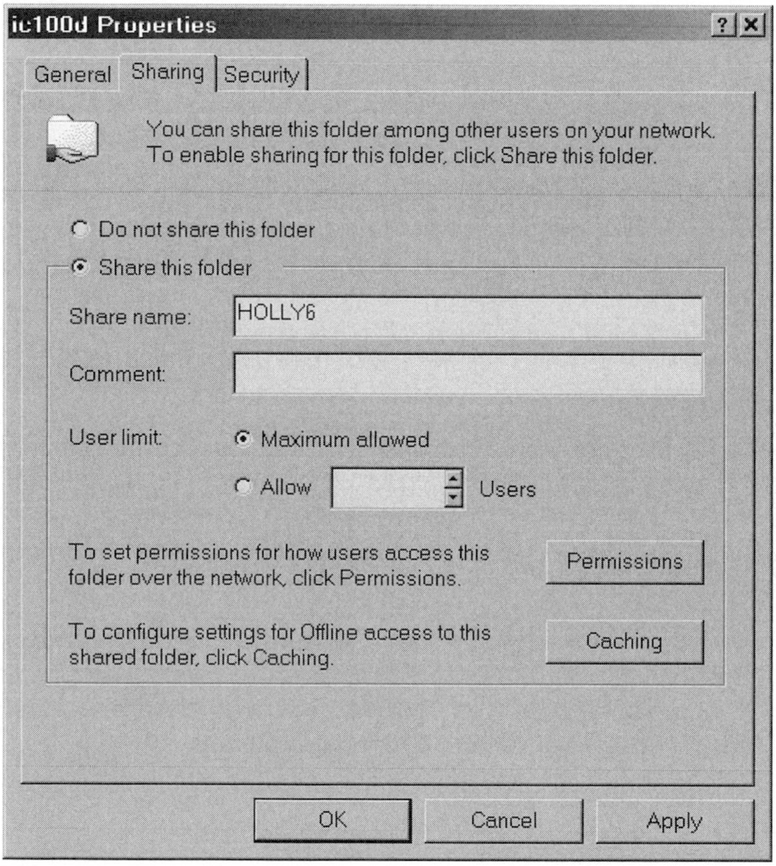

FIGURE 21.12 The file and folder Sharing tab.

Similarly, for resources such as disk drives and printers, you can institute sharing by right-clicking the device's icon and selecting the Sharing option from the menu. This will produce the Sharing tab from the device's Properties page. In both cases, the presence of a hand symbol under the folder or device's icon indicates that it has been shared. To configure a shared folder's Properties page, click the Share This Folder option button and fill in the Share Name dialog box. Then click the Permissions button to open the folder's Permissions dialog box to produce the Share Permissions dialog window shown in Figure 21.13.

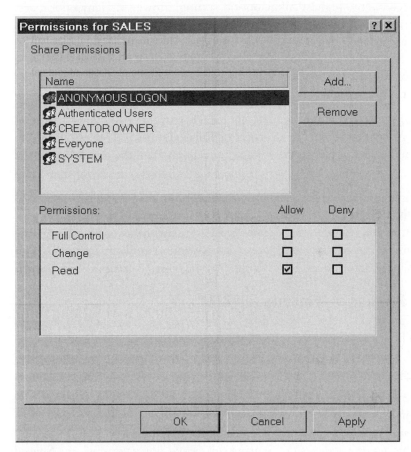

FIGURE 21.13 Share Permissions dialog window.

Standard share permission options in Windows 2000 and XP are the following:

▶ Read—This setting enables the user to view filenames and folder names, run applications, read files, view file and folder attributes, and navigate through the directory tree at levels beneath this folder.

▶ Change—This setting provides complete Read permissions, as well as the capability to create and delete files and folders, to edit files, and to change file and folder attributes.

▶ Full Control—This option enables the user to perform all the functions available with the Change permission and provides the capability to modify permissions and to take ownership of the folder.

It is possible for users to receive these permissions from different sources (that is, as members of different groups that have been assigned different permissions to the folder or resource). When this occurs, the different settings combine and the user receives the highest Allow option setting. However, Deny option settings override any Allow setting. For example, if a user has Full Control permissions for a certain folder from one group and only Read permissions from another group, the result will be Full Control. However, if a Deny permission is assigned for Full Control from another group, the user will receive only Read permissions for the folder.

To access the shared remote resource, the local operating system must first connect to it. After the connection has been established, the local operating system creates a new logical drive on the system to accommodate the new folder in the system.

Share permissions can be assigned only to the folder level. Windows 2000 and Windows XP NTFS permissions are much more robust than share permissions. NTFS permissions can be set at the file level in NTFS systems. However, share permissions are the only network access control option available for non-NTFS partitions.

Sharing Printers in Windows 2000/XP

Shared printers, also referred to as *networked printers*, receive data from computers throughout the network. As in other networks, these printers must be configured as shared printers in the Windows 2000/XP environment to allow remote computers to access them.

To share a printer under Windows 2000, select the Printers option from the Start/Settings path. In Windows XP, select the Printers and Faxes option from the Start menu. Right-click the printer to be shared and select the Sharing option. This action produces the Sharing tab. From this page, click the Shared As option, enter a share name for the printer, and click the OK button to complete the sharing process. Unlike in Windows 9x systems, you must have administrative rights to make these changes in Windows 2000 networks.

To connect to a printer on the network in Windows 2000, select the Printers option from the Start/Settings path and double-click the Add Printer icon. In Windows XP, you must select the Printers and Faxes option from the Start menu and click the Add a Printer option. The Welcome to the Add Printer Wizard page will be displayed. Click the Next button to move forward in the connection process. In the Local or Network Printer page, select the Network Printer (or A Network Printer or Printer Attached to Another Computer) option, and click the Next button to access the Specify a Printer dialog box.

In Windows 2000, you can enter the network printer name in this window. You should also use the UNC format to specify the path to the printer being connected to (that is, \\computer_name\share_name). If the printer's name is not known, click the Type the Printer Name option or click the Next button to access the Browse for Printer page.

In Windows XP, you have additional options to enter the UNC path and printer name or connect to a printer on the Internet (or a Small Office/Home Office [SOHO] network). There is also an option button that enables you to find a printer using Active Directory.

Connecting to a printer over the Internet (or the company intranet) is as simple as selecting the Connect to Printer on the Internet or your intranet option and entering the URL address of the printer. The URL must be expressed in standard HTTP addressing format (that is, http://servername/printer/). The connection wizard will guide the connection process from this point.

> **EXAM ALERT**
>
> Know how to correctly write a UNC path to a shared directory located on a remote computer.

NTFS Permissions

The NTFS5 system includes security features that enable permission levels to be assigned to files and folders on the disk. These permissions set parameters for operations that users can perform on the designated file or folder. As with the share permissions described earlier in this chapter, NTFS permissions can be configured as Allow or Deny options. Standard NTFS folder permissions include the following:

▶ Read—This permission enables the user or group to view the file, folder, or subfolder of a parent folder along with its attributes and permissions.

▶ Write—This permission enables the user or group to add new files or subfolders, change file and folder attributes, add data to an existing file, and change display attributes within a parent folder.

▶ Read & Execute—The Read & Execute permission enables users or groups to make changes to subfolders, display attributes and permissions, and run executable file types.

▶ Modify—The Modify permission enables users to delete the folder and makes it possible for users to perform all the activities associated with the Write and Read & Execute permissions.

- ▶ List Folder Contents—This permission enables users or groups to view files and subfolders within the folder.

- ▶ Full Control—The Full Control permission enables the user or group to take ownership of the folder and to change its permissions, as well as perform all the other activities possible with all the other permissions.

Standard NTFS file permissions include the following:

- ▶ Read—This permission enables the user or group to view the file along with its attributes and permissions.

- ▶ Write—This permission enables the user or group to overwrite the file, change its attributes, and view its ownership and attributes.

- ▶ Read & Execute—The Read & Execute permission enables users or groups to run and execute an application, along with all the options available through the Read permission.

- ▶ Modify—The Modify permission enables users to modify and delete the file and to perform all the activities associated with the Read, Write, and Read & Execute permissions.

- ▶ Full Control—The Full Control permission enables the user or group to take ownership of the file and to change its permissions, as well as perform all the other activities possible with all the other permissions.

Whereas the NTFS system provides permission-level security for files and folders, other file systems running under Windows do not. For example, when a file is moved from an NTFS partition to a FAT partition, the NTFS-specific attributes are discarded. However, NTFS permissions do apply over a network connection.

> **EXAM ALERT**
>
> Know what happens to permissions when you move a file from an NTFS partition to a partition using another file system.

Permissions can be assigned directly by the administrator, or they can be inherited through group settings, such as the default Everyone group. If a user has only Read permissions to a particular file, but is assigned to a group that has wider permissions, that individual would gain those additional rights through the group. In a server environment, the default permission setting for files is No Access.

> **NOTE**
>
> NTFS is the preferred file system for Windows XP Home. However, several features are not available in the Home edition. For typical home users this is not an issue; however, many corporate environments require the more advanced NTFS features available only in Windows XP Professional. Windows XP Home does not offer any type of file- or folder-level security. Share permissions are available in the same fashion as Windows XP Professional.

Challenge #3

Your training group is bringing in a group of subject matter experts (SMEs) to design a training manual for a new software application your company has developed. You do not want the SMEs to be able to make changes to the application files but they do need to be able to run them for evaluation. During their work the members of the team will need to share their document copies with each other for review and correlation so you establish a common folder, Review1, for this purpose. In addition, each worker will need their own folder to keep original copies of their work that only they and management can access. How would you go about using NTFS permissions to accomplish these objectives?

Mapping a Drive

A drive map is a very important tool in a network environment. It allows a single computer to act as though it possesses all the hard drives that reside in the network. The Network File Service (NFS) portion of the operating system coordinates the systems so that drives located on other physical machines show up as logical drives on the local machine. This shows up in the Windows Explorer and My Computer screens, as illustrated in Figure 21.14. It also makes the additional drives available through the command-line prompt.

The primary reason to map a drive in a network environment is because some applications cannot recognize volume names. They can see only drive letters. In Windows, the number of recognizable drive letters is 26 (A–Z). Some network operating systems can recognize an extended number of drive letters (that is, A–Z and AA–ZZ). However, by using unique volume names to identify drives, the system is capable of recognizing a large number of network drives.

For a local system to access a remote resource, the resource must be shared, and the local user must have a valid network user ID and password. The user's assigned rights and permissions are tied to his or her password throughout the network, either through individual settings or through group settings.

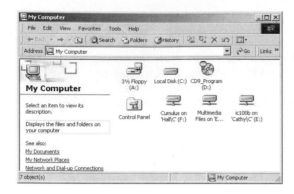

FIGURE 21.14 A mapped drive display.

To map (assign) a drive letter to a remote network computer or folder, open the Windows Explorer. From the Tools menu, select the Map Network Drive option to display the Map Network Drive dialog box. Windows will attempt to assign the next available drive letter to the computer or folder indicated in the Path text box. Establishing the map to the resource is a simple matter of entering the required path and share name in the text box, using the UNC format:

```
\\host_name(server name)\drive_path\shared_resource_name
```

The format always begins with double backslashes (\\).

EXAM ALERT

Be aware of how to apply the UNC format to shared resources.

The Reconnect at Logon check box must be selected in the Map Network Drive dialog box for the drive mapping to become a permanent part of the system. If the option is not selected when the user logs off, the mapped drive information disappears and needs to be remapped for any further use. If a red X appears on the icon of a properly mapped drive, this indicates that the drive is no longer available or that the connection to it has been lost. Its host computer may be turned off, the drive may have been removed, or it may no longer be on the same path. If the drive was mapped to a particular folder and the folder name has been changed, the red X also appears. In some cases, you can re-establish the network connection to the drive by double-clicking its icon.

EXAM ALERT

Know what causes a mapped drive to disappear from a system when it is shut down and restarted.

Exam Prep Questions

1. What does the activity of the light on the network adapter's backplate mean?

   ○ **A.** The connection is alive.

   ○ **B.** Data is being uploaded.

   ○ **C.** Data is being downloaded.

   ○ **D.** Data is being encrypted.

2. To view the status of a local area network connection you should check under _____.

   ○ **A.** My Network Places/Network Monitor

   ○ **B.** Network Neighborhood/Network Monitor

   ○ **C.** My Computer/Network Connections

   ○ **D.** Control Panel/Network Connections

3. What Windows tool can be used to configure most modern routers?

   ○ **A.** The Windows Explorer interface

   ○ **B.** The Device Manager utility

   ○ **C.** The MSCONFIG utility

   ○ **D.** An Internet Explorer web browser

4. You have been asked to make recommendation to improve the performance of a client's network. When you examine the network architecture, you find that it is based on hubs. What should you suggest to improve the LAN's performance?

   ○ **A.** Install higher-speed hubs to minimize system upgrade costs and maintain compatibility with the existing network structure.

   ○ **B.** Install high speed switches to replace the old hubs. This will provide more intelligent routing of the information around the network.

   ○ **C.** Install routers to replace the hubs. Router performance is so much better than hubs that the performance increase will be very noticeable.

   ○ **D.** Install a router to better control information movement in the network and replace the hubs with switches to improve network traffic.

5. In Windows 2000 and Windows XP, which networking component provides the rules that the computer will use to govern the exchange of information across the network?

   ○ **A.** Client

   ○ **B.** Adapter

   ○ **C.** Protocol

   ○ **D.** Service

6. For Windows XP, the Local Connections Properties window offers two tabs not available in the Windows 2000 version. What are the two tabs called?

   ○ **A.** General and Advanced

   ○ **B.** Authentication and Encryption

   ○ **C.** Advanced and Encryption

   ○ **D.** Advanced and Authentication

7. How is the UNC format applied to shared resources?

   ○ **A.** //shared_resource_name

   ○ **B.** //host_name/shared_resource_name

   ○ **C.** \\shared_resource_name

   ○ **D.** \\host_name\drive_path\shared_resource_name

8. Which of the following causes a mapped drive to disappear from a system when it is shut down and restarted?

   ○ **A.** The name of the mapped folder has been changed.

   ○ **B.** The Reconnect at Logon option is not selected.

   ○ **C.** The path to the mapped folder has changed.

   ○ **D.** The host computer for the mapped folder is turned off.

9. Where can the TCP/IP protocol be manually configured in Windows XP?

   ○ **A.** In the Properties page of the Network Connections window

   ○ **B.** In the Network Component Type screen through the Dial-up Connections page

   ○ **C.** In the Protocol Installation screen through the Local Area Connection page

   ○ **D.** In the Protocol screen of the Network Configuration page

10. Which network items can be set through the Windows 2000 Networking and Dial-Up Connection icon's Local Area Connections Properties page? (Select all that apply.)

   ○ **A.** Enabling the TCP/IP troubleshooting tools

   ○ **B.** Adding the DNS service

   ○ **C.** Configuring network protocols

   ○ **D.** Configuring network adapter cards

11. What is required to navigate through a Novell network from a computer running a Microsoft operating system?

   ○ **A.** Installing the NetBEUI protocol

   ○ **B.** Installing the IPX protocol

   ○ **C.** Binding the ODI and IPX protocols

   ○ **D.** Installing the Client Service for NetWare (CSNW) protocol

Answers and Explanations

1. A. The activity light on the backplate of the LAN card (if available) is used to determine whether the network is recognizing the network adapter card. If the light is active, the connection is alive.

2. D. In Windows 2000, the Control Panel's Network and Dial-Up Connections icon is used. In Windows XP, the Networking icon has been changed to the Network Connections icon.

3. D. After the router has been connected, you must configure it for operation. Routers typically employ a browser-based wizard for this purpose. To begin the configuration process, start one of the computers in the network and open its browser. Next, enter the router's IP address in the browser's navigation window. The normal default value for most routers is the private network address 192.168.0.1.

4. B. Instead of repeating received messages to all its other ports, the switch can direct the information to its intended receiver if the address of the receiver is known. Because the information is sent only to the port for which it is intended, the performance of the entire network is improved greatly. For this reason, switches have largely replaced hubs as the most basic connectivity device in local area networks. If the address is not known, the switch will broadcast the information to all of its ports in the same manner as a hub does.

5. C. The Protocol option is used to add, remove, and configure network protocols (rules) for specific types of network environments.

6. D. The Windows XP Local Area Connections Properties window offers two tabs not available in the Windows 2000 version: the Advanced tab and the Authentication tab. The Advanced tab is used to enable the Windows XP Internet Connection Firewall. The Authentication tab is used to configure authentication protocols for conducting local area and wide area communications across a network.

7. D. Establishing the map to the resource is a simple matter of entering the required path and share name in the dialog box, using the UNC format (*host_name**drive_path**shared_resource_name*).

8. B. The Reconnect at Logon option must be selected in the Map Network Drive page for the drive mapping to become a permanent part of the system. If the option is not selected when the user logs off, the mapped drive information disappears and needs to be remapped for any further use. If a red X appears on the icon of a properly mapped drive, this indicates that the drive is no longer available. Its host computer may be turned off, the drive may have been removed, or it may no longer be on the same path. If the drive was mapped to a particular folder, and the folder name has been changed, the red X also appears.

9. A. To manually configure TCP/IP values, select the TCP/IP protocol for the LAN from the listing in the Network Connections page and click the Properties button. This will produce the General tab of the TCP/IP Properties page. Through this page you can configure the computer to obtain an IP address using an automatic service, such as DHCP, or you can manually configure a static address for the computer. To manually configure TCP/IP, the Use the Following Address option must be enabled, and you must know the IP address and subnet mask settings you want to use.

10. B, C, D. The functions associated with the Windows 2000 Local Area Connection Properties page include adding, removing, or configuring network services (such as DNS, WINS, and DHCP), network protocols, and network adapter cards.

11. D. In Windows 2000 and Windows XP systems, you must install the Client Service for NetWare (CSNW) option to provide the Windows client with the capability to communicate with NetWare servers. CSNW requires that the IPX/SPX protocol be installed on the client. It can be installed manually beforehand, or it will be installed automatically when the CSNW client is installed.

Challenge Solutions

1. Set up the router and plug it into the power source. You must run CAT5 cables from the network adapters in each of the desktop PC to the router and plug them in. Configure the network adapter card in one of the PCs for TCP/IP operation. Next, read the router's installation documentation and locate the default IP address, username, and password for the router. Enter the IP address in the Address box of the PC's web browser. When the router's configuration utility appears, enter the default username and password to access the utility. Configure the DHCP settings for the network along with the wireless SSID setting and channel number for the router, but leave the other options disabled until you have all the systems in the network working. Configure the TCP/IP clients in the remaining desktop and notebook computer to automatically obtain the configuration information it needs. After the network is working correctly, set up encryption on the AP and wireless network adapters.

2. The NETBIOS and IPX protocols must be bound together to navigate the Novell network from a computer using a Windows operating system. You do so by enabling the NETBIOS bindings in the IPX Protocol Properties in the Network Properties window.

3. Establish Read & Execute permissions on the folder containing the application's executable and support files. Set Full Control permissions for Everyone on the REVIEW1 folder. Finally, set Full Control permissions on the individual SME folders.

CHAPTER TWENTY-TWO

Wide Area Networking

Terms you'll need to understand:

- ✓ TCP/IP
- ✓ Protocols
- ✓ SMTP
- ✓ IMAP
- ✓ HTML
- ✓ HTTP
- ✓ HTTPS
- ✓ SSL
- ✓ Telnet
- ✓ FTP
- ✓ DNS
- ✓ DSL

- ✓ Cable
- ✓ Satellite
- ✓ Dial-up
- ✓ Wireless (all 802.11x)
- ✓ Infrared
- ✓ Broadband
- ✓ Bluetooth
- ✓ VoIP
- ✓ Script support
- ✓ Proxy
- ✓ Security settings

Techniques you'll need to master:

Essentials 5.1/Remote Technician 4.1/IT Technician 5.1—Identify the fundamental principles of networks.

- ✓ Identify names, purposes, and characteristics (for example, definition, speed, and connections) of technologies for establishing connectivity, for example:

    - ✓ LAN/WAN
    - ✓ ISDN
    - ✓ Broadband (for example, DSL, cable, satellite)
    - ✓ Dial-up

- ✓ Wireless (all 802.11)
- ✓ Infrared
- ✓ Bluetooth
- ✓ Cellular
- ✓ VoIP

Remote Technician 4.1/IT Technician 5.1—Identify the fundamental principles or networks.

- ✓ Identify names, purposes, and characteristics of basic network protocols and terminologies, for example:

    - ✓ ISP

- ✓ TCP/IP (gateway, subnet mask, DNS, WINS, static and automatic address assignment)
- ✓ IPX/SPX (NWLink)
- ✓ NETBEUI/NETBIOS
- ✓ SMTP
- ✓ IMAP
- ✓ HTML
- ✓ HTTP
- ✓ HTTPS
- ✓ SSL
- ✓ Telnet
- ✓ FTP
- ✓ DNS

IT Technician 5.2—Install, configure, optimize, and upgrade networks.

- ✓ Install and configure browsers.
  - ✓ Enable/disable script support.
  - ✓ Configure proxy and security settings.

Introduction

This chapter covers the Connectivity areas of the CompTIA A+ Certification—Essentials examination under Objectives 5.1. In addition, it covers the basic network protocols and terminologies that are generally testable under Objective 4.1 of the Remote Support Technician exam and Objective 5.1 of the IT Technician exam. The chapter also covers a small section of the "Install, configure, optimize, and upgrade networks" objective under IT Technician 5.2. This section pertains to wide area networking situations.

With so many people going online, the technician must understand how the Internet is organized. The tremendous popularity of the Internet, with its heavy concentration on PC platforms, requires that the PC technician understand how the Internet is organized and how the PC relates to it. The successful technician also must be able to establish and maintain Internet connections using the major operating systems and dial-up networking software.

> **NOTE**
>
> The "establishing connectivity" portion under Objective 5.1 of the Essentials exam covers essentially the same subobjectives as Remote Support Technician Objective 4.1 and IT Technician Objective 5.1. The only difference is that the Remote Technician omits infrared, Bluetooth, cellular, and VoIP from its listing. Remote Technician 4.1 and IT Technician 5.1 go further in depth to list basic network protocols and terminologies associated with wide area networking.
>
> The topics specified in these different exam/objective areas are so closely related that it makes sense that they are presented as the same discussion. You will need to study the material in this chapter for any of the four exams you intend to challenge.

Internet Connectivity

The most famous wide area network (WAN) is the Internet. The Internet is actually a network of networks working together. The main communication path for the Internet is a series of networks, established by the U.S. government, to link supercomputers together at key research sites.

This pathway is referred to as the *backbone* and is affiliated with the National Science Foundation (NSF). Since the original backbone was established, the Internet has expanded around the world and offers access to computer users in every part of the globe.

The TCP/IP protocol divides the transmission into packets of information suitable for retransmission across the Internet. Along the way, the information passes through different networks that are organized at different levels. Depending on the routing scheme, the packets may move through the Internet using different routes to get to the intended address. At the destination, however, the packets are reassembled into the original transmission. This concept is illustrated in Figure 22.1.

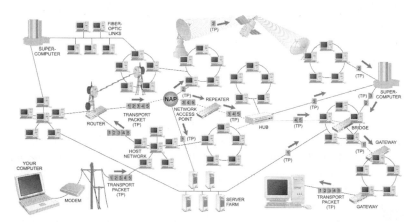

FIGURE 22.1 Packets moving through the Internet.

As a message moves from the originating address to its destination, it may pass through LANs, midlevel networks, routers, repeaters, hubs, bridges, and gateways. A *midlevel network* is simply another network that does not require an Internet connection to carry out communications.

A *repeater* receives, amplifies, and retransmits messages to keep them from deteriorating as they travel. *Hubs* are used to link networks together so that nodes within them can communicate with each other. *Bridges* connect networks so that data can pass through them as it moves from one network to the next. A special type of bridge called a *gateway* translates messages as they pass through so that they can be used on different types of networks (for example, Apple networks and PC networks).

Internet Service Providers

Connecting all the users and individual networks are Internet service providers (ISPs). *ISPs* are companies that provide the technical gateway to the Internet. These companies own blocks of access addresses that they assign to their customers to give them an identity on the network. Figure 22.2 illustrates the service provider's position in the Internet scheme and shows the various connection methods used to access the Internet.

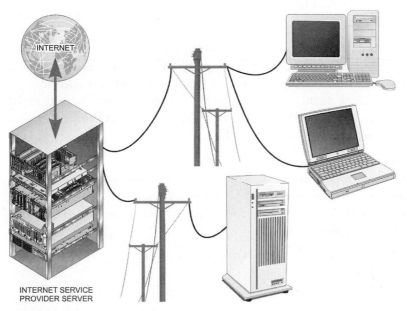

INTERNET

INTERNET SERVICE
PROVIDER SERVER

FIGURE 22.2 The service provider's position.

When you connect to a service provider, you are connecting to its computer system, which, in turn, is connected to the Internet through devices called routers. A *router* is a device that intercepts network transmissions and determines for which part of the Internet they are intended. It then determines what the best routing scheme is for delivering the message to its intended address. The routing schedule is devised based on the known available links through the Internet and the amount of traffic detected on various segments. The router then transfers the message to a network access point (NAP).

Services that most ISPs deliver to their customers include the following:

▶ Internet identity through IP addresses

▶ Email services through POP3 and SMTP servers

▶ Internet news service through Usenet archive servers

▶ Internet routing through DNS servers

EXAM ALERT

Be aware of common services that ISPs provide their Internet customers.

IP Addresses

The blocks of Internet access addresses that ISPs provide to their customers are called *Internet Protocol addresses*, or *IP addresses*. The IP address makes each site a valid member of the Internet. This is how individual users are identified to receive file transfers, email, and file requests. There are two versions of IP addressing currently in use: IPv4 and IPv6. IPv4 is the Internet Protocol version typically referenced due to its widespread use.

IPv4 addresses exist in the numeric format of XXX.YYY.ZZZ.AAA. Each address consists of four 8-bit (32bits total) fields separated by dots (.). This format of specifying addresses is referred to as *dotted decimal notation*. The decimal numbers are derived from the binary address that the hardware understands. For example, a binary network address of

10000111.10001011.01001001.00110110 (binary)

corresponds to

135.139.073.054 (decimal)

Each IP address consists of two parts: the network address and the host address. The network address identifies the entire network; the host address identifies an intelligent member within the network (a router, a server, or a workstation).

> **EXAM ALERT**
>
> Know what dotted decimal notation is and what IPv4 addresses represent.

Three classes of standard IP addresses are supported for LANs: Class A, Class B, and Class C. These addresses occur in four-octet fields like the preceding example.

► Class A addresses are reserved for large networks and use the last 24 bits (the last three octets or fields) of the address for the host address. The first octet always begins with a 0, followed by a 7-bit number. Therefore, valid Class A addresses range between 001.x.x.x and 126.x.x.x. This allows a Class A network to support 126 different networks with nearly 17 million hosts (nodes) per network.

> **NOTE**
>
> The 127.x.x.x address range is a special block of addresses reserved for testing network systems. The U.S. government owns some of these addresses for testing the Internet backbone. The 127.0.0.1 address is reserved for testing the bus on the local system.

▶ Class B addresses are assigned to medium-sized networks. The first two octets can range between 128.x.x.x and 191.254.0.0. The last two octets contain the host addresses. This enables Class B networks to include up to 16,384 different networks with approximately 65,534 hosts per network.

▶ Class C addresses are normally used with smaller LANs. In a Class C address, only the last octet is used for host addresses. The first three octets can range between 192.x.x.x and 223.254.254.0. Therefore, the Class C address can support approximately two million networks with 254 hosts each.

IPv6 is a newer IP addressing protocol developed to cope with the anticipated shortage of available IPv4 addresses in the future. Under IPv6, the IP address has been extended to 128 bits to accommodate a tremendous number of IP addresses. IPv6 also provides for authenticating the sender of a packet, as well as encrypting the content of a packet. Both Windows Vista and many Linux distributions include support for IPv6, but to date, it has not gained wide spread usage. The industry expects the new IP version to support mobile phones, automobile PCs, and a wide array of other IP-based personal devices.

IPv6 addresses are typically written in the form of eight groups of four hexadecimal digits, separated by colons—2001: 0db8:00a7:0051:4dc1:635b:0000.2ffe. Groups composed of four zeros can be expressed as double colons (::). However, it is illegal to have more than one double colon in an address. Leading zeros can also be omitted to make the number more manageable. When used in a URL, an IPv6 address must be enclosed in brackets—http://[2001: 0db8:00a7:0051:4dc1:635b:0000.2ffe].

Subnets

Sections of a network can be grouped together into subnets that share a range of IP addresses. These groups are referred to as *intranets*. An intranet requires that each segment have a protective gateway to act as an entry and exit point for the segment. In most cases, the gateway is a device called a router. A *router* is an intelligent device that receives data and directs it toward a designated IP address.

Some networks employ a firewall as a gateway to the outside. A *firewall* is a combination of hardware and software components that provides a protective barrier between networks with different security levels. Administrators configure the firewall so that it will pass data only to and from designated IP addresses and TCP/IP ports. A detailed discussion of firewalls is presented in Chapter 24, "Security."

Subnets are created by masking off (hiding) the network address portion of the IP address on the units within the subnet. This, in effect, limits the mobility of the data to those nodes within the subnet because they can reconcile addresses only from within their masked range. There are three common reasons to create a subnet:

▶ To isolate one segment of the network from all the others—Suppose, for example, that a large organization has 1,000 computers, all of which are connected to the network. Without segmentation, data from all 1,000 units would run through every other network node. The effect of this would be that everyone in the network would have access to all the data on the network, and the operation of the network would be slowed considerably by the uncontrolled traffic.

▶ To efficiently use IP addresses—Because the IP addressing scheme is defined as a 32-bit code, only a certain number of addresses are possible. Although 126 networks with 17 million customers might seem like a lot, in the scheme of a worldwide network system, that's not a lot of addresses to go around.

▶ To utilize a single IP address across physically divided locations—For example, subnetting a Class C address between remotely located areas of a campus would permit half of the 253 possible addresses to be allocated to one campus location and the other half to be allocated to hosts at the second location. In this manner, both locations can operate using a single Class C address.

A subnet is established by entering numbers to block any of or all the addresses associated with each octet of the IP address. For example, a subnet mask value of 255 blocks the entire octet, whereas a value of 254 blocks all but one of the addresses in the octet.

The default subnet mask for a Class A IP address is 255.0.0.0, whereas a Class B IP address typically uses a subnet mask of 255.255.0.0. For a Class C address, which is typically used in small organizations and residential networks, a subnet mask of 255.255.255.0 is commonly used. This blocks the first three octets (the network portion of the address) and leaves the addresses from the lower octet open for use with hosts. When you enter an IP address in Windows 2000 or Windows XP, the default subnet mask value for that class of IP address is automatically filled in.

EXAM ALERT

Know the standard subnet mask assignments for different IP address classes.

Private IP Classes

Because the Internet is basically a huge TCP/IP network in which no two computers connected to it can have the same address, networks connected to the Internet must follow a specific IP addressing scheme assigned by an ISP. However, any IP addressing scheme can be used as long as your network is not connected to the Internet. This is referred to as a *private network*.

When configuring a private network, you must design an IP addressing scheme to use across the network. Although technically you could use any IP addressing scheme you want in a private network without consulting an ISP, special ranges of network addresses in each IP class have been reserved for use with private networks. These are reserved addresses that are not registered to anyone on the Internet.

If you are configuring a private network, you should use one of these address options rather than creating a random addressing scheme. The total number of clients on the network typically dictates which IP addressing class you should use. The following list of private network IP addresses can be used:

▶ An IP address of 10.0.0.0, with the subnet mask of 255.0.0.0

▶ An IP address of 169.254.0.0, with the subnet mask of 255.255.255.0 (the Microsoft AIPA default)

▶ An IP address of 172.(16–32).0.0, with the subnet mask of 255.240.0.0

▶ An IP address of 192.168.0.0, with the subnet mask of 255.255.0.0

In addition, remember that all hosts must have the same network ID and subnet mask and that no two computers on your network can have the same IP address when you are establishing a private IP addressing scheme.

Internet Domains

The IP addresses of all the computers attached to the Internet are tracked using a listing system called the *domain name system* (*DNS*). This system evolved as a way to organize the members of the Internet into a hierarchical management structure.

The DNS structure consists of various levels of computer groups called *domains*. Each computer on the Internet is assigned a *domain name*, such as mic-inc.com. The "mic-inc" is the user-friendly domain name assigned to the Marcraft site.

In the example, the .com notation at the end of the address is a top-level domain that defines the type of organization or country of origin associated with the address. In this case, the .com designation identifies the user as a commercial site. The following list identifies the Internet's top-level domain codes:

.com = Commercial businesses

.edu = Educational institutions

.gov = Government agencies

.int = International organizations

.mil = Military establishments

.net = Networking organizations

.org = Nonprofit organizations

.au = Australia

.ca = Canada

.fr = France

.it = Italy

.es = Spain

.tw = Taiwan

.uk = United Kingdom

On the Internet, domain names are specified in terms of their fully qualified domain names (FQDN). An *FQDN* is a human-readable address that describes the location of the site on the Internet. It contains the hostname, the domain name, and the top-level domain name. For example, the name www.oneworld.owt.com is an FQDN.

The letters *www* represent the hostname. The hostname specifies the name of the computer that provides services and handles requests for specific Internet addresses. In this case, the host is the World Wide Web.

The .owt extension indicates that the organization is a domain listed under the top-level domain heading. Likewise, the .oneworld entry is a subdomain of the .owt domain. It is very likely one of multiple networks supported by the .owt domain.

At each domain level, the members of the domain are responsible for tracking the addresses of the domains on the next-lower level. The lower domain is then responsible for tracking the addresses of domains, or end users, on the next level below it.

DNS Name Resolution

Each domain must have a DNS name server that is responsible for registering its clients with the next higher level of the network. Any computer that provides domain name services is technically referred to as a *DNS* server. All DNS servers maintain a DNS database listing of name to IP address mappings that they are responsible for.

When a DNS client submits a name resolution request to a local DNS server, the server will search through its DNS database, and if necessary through the hierarchical DNS system, until it locates the hostname or FQDN that was submitted to it. At this point it resolves the IP address of the requested hostname and returns it back to the client.

Internet Access Methods

Most users connect to the Internet and other wide area networks via standard telephone lines, using analog dial-up modems. Dial-up connections are generally the slowest way to connect to a network, but they are inexpensive to establish and use. Other users who require quicker data transfers contract with the telephone company to use special, high-speed Digital Subscriber Line (DSL) or Integrated Services Digital Network (ISDN) lines. Still other users contract with a cable television provider for fast Internet access connections. All these connectivity types require a digital modem to conduct data transfers. Because the modems used with these technologies are digital, no analog conversion is required. These technologies are covered in detail later in this chapter.

Users who require very high data-transfer rates lease dedicated T1 and T3 lines from the telephone company. These applications generally serve businesses that put several of their computers or networks online. After information is transmitted, it may be carried over many types of communication links on its way to its destination. These interconnecting links can include fiber-optic cables, satellite uplinks and downlinks, UHF, and microwave transmission systems. Figure 22.3 illustrates different ways to access WANs.

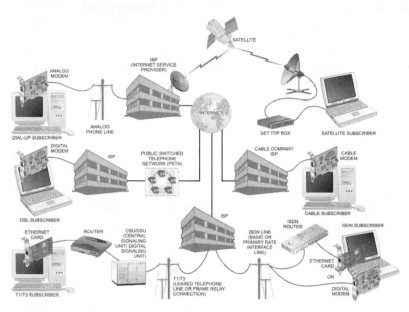

FIGURE 22.3 Methods of accessing wide area networks.

LAN Access to the Internet

As the figure illustrates, you can use several methods to contact an ISP to gain access to the Internet. You can dial it up directly using an analog modem and the plain old telephone system (POTS), or you can make arrangements with service providers for special always-on services such as DSL, ISDN, cable, or satellite services. These services can be obtained through direct links to the phone company or an ISP that provides such services. Most residential users access the Internet using one of these methods.

However, in commerce and industrial settings it is more common for users to work in a local area network (LAN) environment. In these environments, Internet access is generally provided through the existing LAN structure. One or more of the LAN's network devices are used to provide some type of gateway to the Internet, as illustrated in Figure 22.4. This arrangement may involve a third-party ISP, or in large organizations, the company may act as its own ISP.

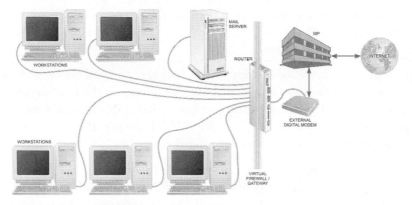

FIGURE 22.4 Internet gateways.

The network device that offers the gateway service may be a standalone router, or it could be one of the LAN's servers acting as a router for the LAN. The common use of a router as a gateway to the outside world has led to the terms *router* and *gateway* being used interchangeably. When the router is used as the gateway, the outside world sees only the router—not the individual computers attached to the LAN.

When a server is used as the gateway, it may be configured to perform several connection functions. Of course, the server's first function is to perform all the routing services for the LAN. This includes properly routing incoming messages to the proper node on the LAN and forwarding outgoing messages to the Internet. To accomplish this, the server must possess an Internet connection sharing service, such as Windows Internet Connection Sharing (ICS) or Network Address Translation Service (NATS) that will enable it to represent the other computers on the LAN.

The server may also act as a proxy server for the LAN. A *proxy server* is a computer used to perform services locally and forward requests for services that it cannot fulfill to an appropriate server. In this case, the proxy server function of the gateway computer could be used to cache (store) web pages that have recently been accessed from the Internet, so that if they are needed again, they can be accessed locally instead of over the Internet. This improves network performance by reducing the load placed on the bandwidth capabilities of the link between the company and the Internet. If the requested page is not in the proxy cache, the server forwards the request to the Internet for resolution.

The gateway computer may also act as a firewall. A *firewall* is a combination of hardware and software components that provides a protective barrier between networks with different security levels (that is, the LAN and the Internet). Rules for transmitting and receiving information between the networks can be established for the firewall so that specific types of items or addresses will not be allowed to pass between the networks.

In some versions of this LAN connection scheme, a router is placed between the gateway computer and the Internet. In this case, the router is the only device seen by the outside world, but its function is single-ended in that the LAN server still represents the other computers on the LAN. However, the router can still be used to provide the firewall services referred to earlier.

The physical connection between the LAN and the Internet can be a dial-up connection using the telephone network, or it may involve one of the newer, faster always-on access methods—ISDN, DSL, cable, or satellite. Corporate customers and large organizations may lease special multichannel T1 or T3 telephone lines for direct access to the Internet or ISP. The following sections of this chapter deal with these various Internet connectivity technologies.

Network Address Translation

The *NAT*, or *network address translation*, service is a protocol that enables a private IP address to be converted to a public IP address. One purpose for doing this is to conserve IP address assignments by encouraging the use of private IP addresses on a local area network, while still providing the computers on the network with Internet access. To access the Internet, the private IP addresses used by the network computers must be replaced with a public IP address for the Internet. NAT is the protocol used to make the switch in IP addresses.

The second reason for doing this is because it effectively hides the internal structure of the network from the Internet—making it harder for outsiders to gain access to a specific PC or network device. Outsiders see the network as a single entity represented by one public IP address.

Some connectivity devices integrate the modem, router, and switch functions into a single unit that can perform the NAT process. Under NAT, when the modem or router receives a response from the Internet, it translates the public address to the corresponding private address of the correct computer.

EXAM ALERT

Know what functions the NAT service can provide for a network.

Dial-up Access

As distances between computer terminals increase, it soon becomes impractical to use dedicated cabling to carry data. Fortunately, there is already a very extensive communications network in existence: the public telephone network. Unfortunately, the phone lines were designed to carry analog voice signals instead of digital data. The design of the public phone system limits the frequency at which data may be transmitted over these lines.

The world's largest communications network is the public telephone system. When computers use this network to communicate with each other, it is referred to as *dial-up networking* (DUN). Computers using this connectivity method connect to the phone system through analog modems and communicate with each other using audio tone signals. To use the telephone system, a modem must duplicate the dialing characteristics of a telephone and be able to communicate within the frequencies that occur within the audible hearing range of human beings (after all, this is the range that telephone lines are set up to accommodate). A modem allows a computer to communicate with other computers through the telephone lines.

Installing Analog Modems

Modems can be either internal or external devices, as illustrated in Figure 22.5. An *internal modem* is installed in one of the computer's expansion slots, and has its own interfacing circuitry. An *external modem* is usually a box that resides outside the system unit and is connected to one of the computer's USB or RS-232 serial ports. The latter units depend on the interfacing circuitry of the computer's serial ports. External modems also require a separate power source.

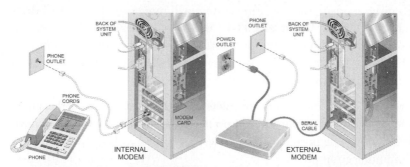

FIGURE 22.5   Internal and external modems.

In both cases, the modem typically connects to the telephone line through a standard 4-pin RJ-11 telephone jack. The RJ designation stands for *registered jack*. A second RJ-11 jack in the modem allows an additional telephone to be connected to the line for voice usage. A still smaller 4-pin RJ-12 connector is used to connect the telephone handset to the telephone base. Be aware that an RJ-14 jack looks exactly like the RJ-11, but that it defines two lines to accommodate advanced telephone features such as Caller ID and Call Waiting.

The procedures for installing a modem vary somewhat, depending on whether it is an internal or external device. To install an internal modem, you must remove the cover from system unit, locate a compatible empty expansion slot, remove the expansion slot cover from the rear of the system unit, and install the modem card in the system. Connect the phone line to the appropriate connector on the modem. Then connect the other end of the phone line to the commercial phone jack. Finally, replace the system unit cover. All modern modems should automatically be configured through the plug-and-play procedure.

It is somewhat simpler to install an external modem. There is no need to remove the system unit cover to install an external modem. Simply connect the serial signal cable to the USB or serial COM port connector on the rear of the system, and connect the opposite end of the cable to the USB or RS-232 connector of the external modem unit. Next, connect the phone line to the appropriate connector on the modem and the other end to the phone system jack. You can also connect a telephone to the appropriate connector on the modem. Finally, verify that the power switch or power supply is turned off, connect the power supply to the external modem unit, and verify this connection arrangement.

Modem Configuration

With PCI-based internal modems, the configuration process is simple because these cards possess PnP capabilities that enable the system to automatically configure them with the resources they need to operate. If the PnP process does not recognize a given modem, the operating system will request that the OEM driver disk be inserted in the floppy or CD-ROM drive so that the OS can obtain the drivers required to support the modem. In some cases, these drivers may need to be loaded through the Windows Add/Remove Hardware (Add Hardware in XP) applet in the Control Panel.

With external modems, the system interacts with the host port and the port's UART interacts with the system. Even if no device connected is to a COM port, the computer knows the port is there. Software supplied with the modem controls the communication process.

After the modem hardware has been installed, you will need applications to make use of the modem. These applications can be third-party calling programs—usually supplied with the modem—or programs built in to the operating system, such as browsers (Internet Explorer or Firefox) and email programs

(Outlook or Outlook Express). These programs must be configured to work with the modem hardware.

Establishing the Windows 2000/XP Dial-up Configuration

Under Windows 2000 and Windows XP, the operating system should detect (or offer to detect) the modem through its plug-and-play facilities. It may also enable you to select the modem drivers manually from a list in the Control Panel's Phone and Modem Options applet. After the modem has been detected, or selected, it appears in the Windows 2000 or Windows XP Modems tab. The settings for the modem can be examined or reconfigured by selecting it from the list and clicking its Properties tab. In most cases, the device's default configuration settings should be used.

Both operating systems provide all the software tools required to establish an Internet connection. These include the TCP/IP network protocol and the Dial-up Networking component. The Dial-up Networking component is used to establish a link with the ISP over the public telephone system. This link also can be established over an ISDN line. All Windows 2000 and Windows XP versions feature the built-in Microsoft Internet Explorer web browser and a personal web server.

The Windows 2000 operating systems feature a New Network Connections folder, located in the My Computer window. To create a dial-up connection in Windows 2000, click the Make New Connection icon in the My Computer/Network Connections folder. Similarly, to create a new connection in Windows XP, you must navigate the Start/My Network Places/View network connections path and click the Create a New Connection option in the Network Tasks pane, as illustrated in Figure 22.6.

FIGURE 22.6 Creating a new network connection.

These actions will open the Windows 2000/XP Network Connection Wizard (New Connection Wizard in XP) that guides the connection process. The wizard requires information about the type of connection, the modem type, and the phone number to be dialed. The connection types offered by the wizard include private networks, virtual private networks, and other computers. The Network Connection Wizard enables users to employ the same device to access multiple networks that may be configured differently. This is accomplished by enabling users to create connection types based on who they are connecting to rather than on how they are making the connection.

Establishing Dialing Rules

For Windows 2000 or XP to connect to a network or dial-up connection, it must know what rules to follow to establish the communication link. These rules are known as the *dialing rules*. In Windows 2000 and XP, the dialing rules are configured through the Phone and Modem Options icon in the Control Panel. If the connection is new, a Location Information dialog window displays, enabling you to supply the area code and telephone system information.

To create a new location, click the New button on the Dialing Rules tab and move through the General, Area Code Rules, and Calling Card tabs to add information as required. The default rules for dialing local, long distance, and international calls are established under the General tab. These rules are based on the country or region identified on this page. Ways to reach an outside line (such as dialing 8 or 9 to get an outside line in a hotel or office building) are established here. Similarly, the Area Code Rules information modifies the default information located under the General tab. As its name implies, the information under the Calling Cards tab pertains to numbers dialed using a specific calling card or long-distance company.

Establishing Dial-up Internet Connections

The Windows 2000 Internet Connection Wizard provides an efficient way to establish Internet connectivity. In Windows XP, the Internet connection is established through the New Connection Wizard. You can use the Internet or New Connection Wizard to set up the web browser, the Internet email account, and the newsgroup reader. To create the Internet connection for an existing account with an ISP, you need to know the following:

► The ISP's name

► The username and password

► The ISP's dial-in access number

The Internet Connection Wizard collects this information and then creates the Internet connection.

To connect to the Internet in Windows 2000, select the Internet Connection Wizard option from the Start/Programs/Accessories/Communications path. Likewise, to connect to the Internet in Windows XP, you must select the New Connection option from the Accessories, Communications menu. If the connection is new, the Location Information dialog boxes, along with the dialing rules defined in the preceding section of this chapter, will appear. You also need to click the I Want to Sign Up for a New Internet Account option, click the Next button, and follow the wizard's instructions.

In a Windows XP system, the New Connection Wizard produces the Network Connection Type screen shown in Figure 22.7. In this screen you can choose to Connect to the Internet, Connect to a Network at My Workplace, or Set Up an Advanced Connection.

FIGURE 22.7 Windows XP Network Connection Type page.

Establishing Internet Connection Sharing

Sharing an Internet connection enables several computers to be connected to the Internet through a single dial-up connection. These connections can be made individually, or simultaneously, with the users maintaining the ability to use the same services they did when they were connected directly to the Internet.

To establish Internet Connection Sharing (ICS), you must log on to the computer using an account that has Administrator rights. In a Windows 2000 system, click Start, Settings and select the Network and Dial-up Connections option. Right-click the connection to be shared and then select the Properties option from the pop-up menu. The Internet connection's Sharing screen displays.

Under the Internet Connection Sharing tab, select the Enable Internet Connection Sharing for This Connection check box. If the connecting computer is supposed to dial in to the Internet automatically, click the Enable On-Demand Dialing check box. Clicking the OK button causes protocols, services, interfaces, and routes to be configured automatically.

In Windows XP, access the Network Connections, select the connection you want to share, and then select the Change settings of this connection option from the Network Tasks pane. On the Advanced tab, enable the Allow Other Network Users to Connect Through This Computer's Internet Connection setting. On this tab you can also enable settings that will automatically dial out when another computer on the network tries to access the Internet and permit other network users to control the shared Internet connection.

ISDN Connections

Integrated Services Digital Network (ISDN) service offers high-speed access to the public telephone system. However, ISDN service requires digital *imodems* (also referred to as *Terminal Adapters*, or TAs). Not only does the end user require a digital modem, but the telephone company's switch gear equipment must be updated to handle digital switching. This fact has slowed implementation of ISDN services until recently.

Three levels of ISDN service are available: Basic Rate Interface (BRI) services, Primary Rate Interface (PRI) services, and Broadband ISDN (BISDN) services. BRI services are designed to provide residential users with basic digital service through the existing telephone system. The cost of this service is relatively low, although it is more expensive than regular analog service. BRI service is not available in all areas of the country, but it is expanding rapidly.

Typical residential telephone wiring consists of a four-wire cable. Up to seven devices can be connected to these wires. Under the BRI specification, the telephone company delivers three information channels to the residence over a two-wire cable. The two-wire system is expanded into the four-wire system at the residence through a network terminator. The ISDN organizational structure is depicted in Figure 22.8.

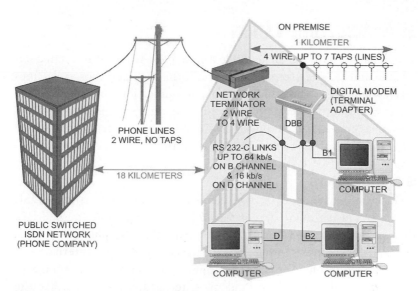

FIGURE 22.8 The ISDN organizational structure.

The BRI information channels exist as a pair of 64 Kbps channels and a 16Kbps control channel. The two 64 Kbps channels, called *bearer* or *B* channels, can be used to transmit and receive voice and data information. The 16 Kbps D channel is used to implement advanced control features such as call waiting, call forwarding, caller ID, and others. The D channel also can be used to conduct packet-transfer operations.

PRI services are more elaborate ISDN services that support the very high data rates needed for live video transmissions. This is accomplished using the telephone company's existing wiring and advanced ISDN devices. The operating cost of PRI service is considerably more expensive than that of BRI services. The higher costs of PRI tend to limit its usage to larger businesses.

The fastest, most expensive ISDN service is broadband ISDN. This level of service provides extremely high data-transfer rates (up to 622Mbps) over coaxial or fiber-optic cabling. Advanced transmission protocols are also used to implement broadband ISDN.

ISDN modems are available in both internal and external formats. In the case of external devices, the analog link between the computer and the modem requires D-to-A and A-to-D conversion processes at the computer's serial port and then again at the modem. Of course, with an internal digital modem, these conversion processes are not required.

Digital Subscriber Lines

Telephone companies have begun to offer a new high-bandwidth connection service to home and business customers in the form of digital subscriber lines (DSL). This technology provides high-speed communication links by using the existing telephone lines to generate bandwidths ranging up to 24Mbps or more. However, distance limitations and line quality conditions may reduce the actual throughput that can be achieved with these connections.

Modems and Splitters

As with ISDN connections, DSL communication requires a special DSL modem (also known as an *ADSL Terminal Unit* [ATU]) to provide the interface between the computer (or the computer network) and the DSL phone line. DSL modems are available in both internal and external configurations. Internal DSL modems are installed in one of the host computer's expansion slots, similar to the installation of an analog dial-up modem. External DSL modems, like the one depicted in Figure 22.9, connect to the computer through a USB port or a network adapter card. They also require separate power supplies. In many cases, an ethernet router is installed between the DSL modem and the LAN to provide equal access to the Internet connection. Usually, CAT 5 UTP cable is used to connect the DSL modem to a port on the router.

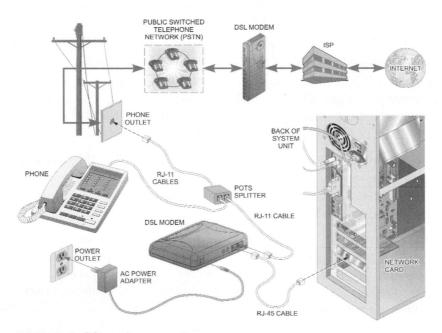

FIGURE 22.9 DSL modem connections.

Challenge #1

A client complains that after replacing his DSL modem, his home DSL connection isn't working. When you inspect his computer, you note that none of the lights on the DSL modem are on. You notice that the only two cables that plug into the DSL modem connect via the RJ-11 and RJ-45 connectors. You are able to ping port 127.0.0.1. What is the most likely problem with the DSL connection?

Installing a device called a *POTS splitter* in the DSL connection separates the telephone voice band (0–4KHz) and the DSL band used to transmit digital information. This enables the DSL phone line connection to be used for both telephone/voice and data communications. Depending on the DSL service provider, the splitter may be manually installed at the subscriber location (splitter-based DSL), or the signal splitting may be provided remotely from the telephone exchange carrier local office (splitterless DSL). A splitter variation referred to as d*istributed splitter* DSL service lowers the complexity at the subscriber location, but is more complex to implement at the local office.

With most new DSL installations, line splitters are not required. Instead, telephone line filters are used to separate voice information from communications data. This is achieved by placing line filters on all the lines used by telephones. These filters are placed inline with the phones so that users do not hear the sound of the digital communications going on. Note that no line filter should be placed inline with the network and computer equipment because it will prevent the digital data from reaching it.

EXAM ALERT

Be aware of the consequences of placing a line filter inline with the computer and network equipment in a DSL installation.

Challenge #2

Your company moves to a new location. Because the company is small, you use a DSL connection to connect all users to the Internet. When setting up the network, you connect the DSL modem using an RJ-11 connector to the phone outlet, connect the DSL modem to a router using a CAT 5 cable, and plug the DSL modem into a power source.

(continues)

(continued)

> You connect all the workstations to the router using CAT 5 cable, and you put line filters on all phone lines, including the phone line used for the DSL modem. When testing the system, however, no users can connect to the Internet. When you unplug the DSL modem and remove all the line filters, the phone line is still operational. What is the most likely solution to this situation?

There are several advantages to using DSL connection rather than standard dial-up connections. Some of these advantages include the following:

▶ The speed of DSL connections (1.5Mbps) is much higher than that of dial-up connections using regular modems (56Kbps).

▶ The Internet connection can remain open while the phone line is used for voice calls.

▶ DSL service employs existing telephone wires between the home and the telephone-switching center (referred to as the *local office*).

▶ The local exchange carrier that offers DSL usually provides the DSL modem as part of the installation.

However, there are disadvantages associated with using DSL technologies:

▶ A DSL connection works better when you are closer to the provider's central office.

▶ The ADSL connection is faster for receiving data than it is for sending data over the Internet.

▶ DSL service is not available in all locations.

DSL Versions

The term *xDSL* is used to refer to all types of DSL collectively. There are two main categories of DSL: asymmetric DSL (ADSL) and symmetric DSL (SDSL). Two other types of xDSL technologies that have some promise are high-data-rate DSL (HDSL) and symmetric DSL (SDSL).

SDSL is referred to as symmetric because it supports the same data rates for upstream and downstream traffic. Conversely, ADSL (also known as *rate-adaptive DSL*) supports different data transfer rates when receiving data (referred to as the *downstream rate*) and transmitting data (known as the *upstream rate*). SDSL supports data-transfer rates up to 3Mbps in both directions, whereas ADSL has data-transfer rates of from 1.5 to 9Mbps downstream and from 16 to 640Kbps upstream. Both forms of DSL require special modems that employ sophisticated modulation schemes to pack data onto telephone wires. However, you should be aware that access speeds vary from provider to provider, even if they use the same central office (CO) to provide service.

> **EXAM ALERT**
>
> Be aware that ADSL provides different upload and download speeds.

xDSL is similar to the ISDN arrangements just discussed in that both operate over existing copper POTS telephone lines. Also, they both require shorter geographical cable runs (less than 20,000 feet) to the nearest CO than traditional telephone lines. However, as just stated, xDSL services offer much higher transfer speeds. In doing so, the xDSL technologies use a much greater range of frequencies on the telephone lines than the traditional voice services do. In addition, DSL technologies use telephone lines as a constant (always-on) connection, so users can have access to the Internet and email on a 24/7 basis. There is no need to connect with an ISP each time you want to go online.

In the telephone system, users are connected to the local exchange, or central office, by their local loop connection. DSL takes advantage of the local loop by operating in unused bandwidth of the connection. The DSL portion of the local loop requires a DSL modem at the subscriber's end of the loop and a device called a *DSLAM* (*Digital Subscriber Line Access Multiplexer*) located at the CO that multiplexes and demultiplexes voice and data signals for the DSL line. The DSLAM passes traditional voice signals on to the line, but adds a higher-frequency DSL band to the line to carry the DSL information to the subscriber's location. This higher-frequency requirement is what limits the geographical distance of a DSL line.

> **EXAM ALERT**
>
> Know that the maximum distance that is specified between the subscriber location and the local office for ADSL is less than 20,000 feet.

Asymmetric DSL Versions

Asymmetric DSL (ADSL) works by splitting the phone line into two frequency ranges. The frequencies below 4KHz are reserved for voice, and the range above that is used for data. This makes it possible to use the line for phone calls and data network access at the same time. This type of DSL is called *asymmetric* because more bandwidth is reserved for receiving data than for sending data. Asymmetrical variations include ADSL, G.lite ADSL, RADSL, and VDSL. The collection of ADSL standards facilitates interoperability among all standard forms of ADSL.

▶ Asymmetric DSL (ADSL)—Full-rate ADSL offers differing upload and download speeds and can be configured to deliver up to six megabits of data per second (6000K) from the network to the customer; that is up to 120 times faster than dial-up service and 100 times faster than ISDN. ADSL enables voice and high-speed data to be sent simultaneously over the existing telephone line.

▶ G.lite ADSL—The G.lite standard was specifically developed to meet the plug-and-play requirements of the consumer market. It is a medium bandwidth version of ADSL that provides Internet access at up to 1.5 megabits downstream and up to 500 kilobits upstream.

▶ Rate-Adaptive DSL (RADSL)—RADSL is a nonstandard version of ADSL, although standard ADSL also permits an ADSL modem to adapt speeds of data transfer.

▶ Very High Bit Rate DSL (VDSL)—VDSL offers transfer rates of up to 52Mbps over distances up to 50 meters on short loops, such as from fiber to the curb. VDSL lines are usually served from neighborhood cabinets that link to a central office through fiber-optic cabling. This type of DSL is particularly useful for campus-type environments.

▶ Very High Bit Rate DSL 2 (VDSL2)—An improved VDSL version that offers transfer rates of up to 250Mbps over distances up to 500 meters. Unlike VDSL loops, VDSL2 loops are not limited to short distances.

EXAM ALERT

Be aware that ADSL has the slowest upstream rate and VDSL has the fastest upstream rate.

Table 22.1 illustrates the downstream performance of ADSL as a function of the distance from the subscriber to the local office.

TABLE 22.1   ADSL Performance Versus Local Loop Length

CABLE LENGTH (FEET)	BANDWIDTH AVAILABILITY (Kbps)
18,000	1,544
16,000	2,048
12,000	6,312
9,000	8,448

One disadvantage of ADSL service is that when the ADSL local loop length increases, the available bandwidth decreases for both upstream (not shown) and downstream traffic. These numbers assume 24-gauge wire; performance decreases significantly if 26-gauge wire exists on the local loop.

Symmetric DSL Versions

As with ADSL, there are several varieties of symmetric DSL. These versions include SHDSL, HDSL, HDSL-2, and IDSL. The equal upstream and downstream speeds make symmetric DSL versions useful for LAN access, video conferencing, and for locations that host their own websites.

- ▶ Symmetric DSL (SDSL)—SDSL is a proprietary version of symmetric DSL that may include bit rates to and from the customer ranging from 128Kbps to 2.32Mbps. SDSL is an umbrella term for a number of supplier-specific implementations over a single copper pair providing variable rates of symmetric service.

- ▶ Symmetric HDSL (SHDSL)—Also known as *G.shdsl*, SHDSL is the newest industry standard symmetric DSL version. This service can operate at bit rates ranging from 192Kbps up to 2.3Mbps, depending on the type of customer and installation parameters. Overall, it achieves 20% better useful distance than previous versions of symmetric DSL (for example, 1.2Mbps transmissions at distances over 20,000 feet using 26 AWG wire).

- ▶ SHDSL is designed for data-only applications that require high upstream bit rates. Although SHDSL does not carry voice like ADSL does, new voice-over-DSL techniques permit these services to be used for transmitting digitized voice and data.

- ▶ High Data Rate DSL (HDSL)—This DSL variety delivers symmetric service at speeds up to 2.3Mbps in both directions. Available at 1.5 or 2.3Mbps, this symmetric fixed-rate application does not provide standard telephone service over the same line.

> **EXAM ALERT**
>
> Be aware that HDSL does not use phones and data on the same lines.

▶ High Data Rate DSL–second generation (HDSL2)—This HDSL delivers 1.5Mbps service each way, supporting voice, data, and video using either ATM (asynchronous transfer mode), private-line service, or frame relay over a single copper pair. This standard for this symmetric service gives a fixed 1.5Mbps rate both upstream and downstream. HDSL2 does not provide standard voice telephone service on the same wire pair. The HDSL2 standard employs one pair of wires to transmit data at 1.5Mbps, whereas HDSL requires two pairs.

▶ Integrated Services Digital Network DSL (IDSL)—This DSL type supports symmetric data rates of up to 144Kbps using existing phone lines. It is unique in that it has the capability to deliver services through a remote device, called a *digital loop carrier* (*DLC*), which is positioned in planned neighborhoods to simplify the distribution of cable and wiring from the phone company.

Cable Modems

Another competitor in the high-speed Internet connection market involves the local cable television service companies. These companies act as ISPs and provide Internet access through their existing broadband cable television networks. To accomplish this, the cable companies offer special cable modems that attach the computer to an existing cable TV (CATV) network connection in the home.

A *cable modem* typically features two main connections: one to the host computer's USB port or 10/100 ethernet network adapter and the other to the CATV coaxial cable outlet on the wall. A CAT 5 UTP cable usually provides the communication path between the cable modem and the NIC card for the ethernet-type connection. The cable modem employs an F-Type connector (similar to a BNC connector) to attach the coaxial cable from the cable distribution system to the cable modem. Figure 22.10 illustrates this connection scheme.

> **NOTE**
>
> Not all cable modems provide a coaxial connection for the television as illustrated in the figure. In these cases a signal splitter must be used to channel the signal to the television.

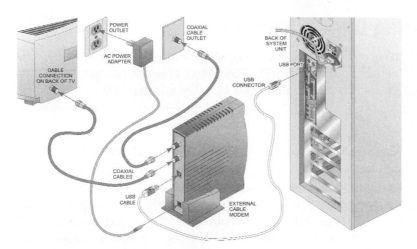

FIGURE 22.10   A cable modem configuration.

When a cable modem subscriber configures multiple computers in a LAN environment, the connection between the cable modem and the network can be made through a gateway/router. This places the router between the modem and the other computers on the network. As with the LAN/Internet connection scheme described earlier, the router provides each computer on the LAN with equal access to the Internet through the modem.

A cable modem is similar to an ASDL modem because it establishes two different transmission rates, which provide for the uploading of data (information leaving the subscriber PC to the server) to have a slightly slower speed than downloading information (the server sending information to the subscriber). The typical cable modem transfers data at speeds up to 38Mbps downstream and 10Mbps upstream. For comparison, this is about 1,000 times faster than the fastest analog modem connections using dial-up service. However, these rates vary depending on the number of users on the cable (because cable Internet access is a shared service).

In North America, the standard for cable modems is called Data Over Cable Service Interface Specification (DOCSIS). To deliver DOCSIS data services over a cable television network, one 6MHz radio frequency (RF) channel is typically allocated for downstream traffic to residential subscribers. Another frequency channel is used to carry upstream signals.

The DOCSIS standard specifies downstream data rates between 27 and 36Mbps using radio frequencies in the 50 to 750MHz range. The upstream rates are specified between 320 and 10Mbps using RF ranges between 5 and 42MHz.

Installing Digital Modems

Although dial-up modems continue to play a part in the WAN connectivity, they tend to be limited in their capability to move data. However, several high-speed broadband communications technologies have become available to most users. These technologies include ISDN, DSL, cable modems, and satellite communication links.

Each of these technologies is provided through a service provider that supplies the service for a fee. These technologies also all involve some type of specialized digital modem to make the connection. Figure 22.11 illustrates a typical digital modem connection scheme. Although each digital modem type employs different connection media, the structure of the physical installation is identical for all the technologies. The modem sits between the computer and the outside service media (such as telephone wires, CATV cable, or satellite dish).

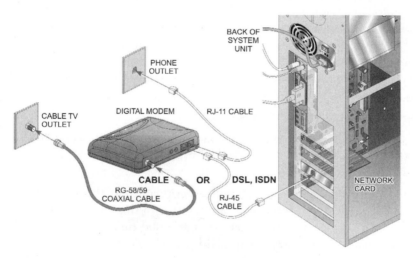

FIGURE 22.11   Installing digital modems.

The host system sees the digital modems in ISDN, DSL, and cable modem connections through a network adapter card, so the system must be configured for network operation. No OEM drivers need to be loaded for these devices to function. In the case of the satellite connection, the host computer's USB port is used. Because satellite modems are not typical connectivity devices, you might need to load OEM drivers supplied by the manufacturer for the system to work with the PC.

In residential installations, this connection scheme is usually direct. However, in business environments, one computer is typically used as a gateway between the internal LAN and the external network (that is, the Internet). Some LAN connection schemes include a router between the gateway computer and the outside network to represent the complete LAN as a single unit. This makes unauthorized access to the internal LAN harder for outsiders to accomplish.

Following are the basic steps for installing a broadband cable modem or DSL modem:

1. Obtain the digital modem and support documentation from the service company. This should come as part of the cable or DSL service agreement.

2. Install a network adapter card in the host computer.

3. For broadband DSL connections, place filters on all phone and fax connections throughout the residence, except for the one the DSL modem will use. Note: This must include telephone connections to satellite receivers, answering machines, and computer fax modems.

4. Connect the digital modem to the commercial connection (the broadband interface for the cable or the telephone line) and power up the modem. For cable modems, connect the CATV cable to the modem. Connect the DSL modem to the phone line.

5. Connect the digital modem to the network adapter or a router. In both cases, this involves connecting a CAT 5 cable between the digital modem and NIC (or router). If a router is used, the host computer must be connected through the router.

6. Start the host computer and configure the network connection for DHCP operation. Verify that all the status lights on the digital modem are active. Typically, these are Power, Activity, and Link lights. The Power and Link lights should be on and solid; the Activity lights may flicker depending on the activity level of the network.

7. Configure authentication for the connection. Depending on the service provider's requirement, you may need to run its installation disk. Typical required information includes account number, username, and password (assigned by the service provider when the kit is delivered). There are two processes you may encounter for configuring authentication for the connection: Point-to-Point Protocol over Ethernet (PPoE) and non-PPoE. If there is an installation CD, the authentication process will be performed automatically as part of the setup. However, if no installation CD is provided, you must manually configure the router to perform the authentication process.

Under the PPoE method, the authentication requires that a username and password (supplied by the service provider) be entered in the router's configuration table. Under the non-PPoE method, the MAC address of the NIC or router connected directly to the digital modem must be supplied to the service provider (usually over the telephone).

8. Verify that you have received an IP address from the router (`ipconfig /all`). The IP address of the machine should be in the range supplied by the router (typically 192.168.1.X). You should also see a gateway address that should match the address of the router (typically 192.168.1.1).

9. Ping the default gateway (router) to confirm connectivity.

10. Open a browser and attempt to access a website (for example, www.mic-inc.com).

If you cannot access the Internet, obtain a known IP address from the Web and attempt to ping it instead of the domain name. If this does not work, contact the technical support service of the service provider.

Satellite Internet Access

Two major companies (DirecTV and Dish Network) have successfully entered the market for television distribution using signals delivered to the customer via satellite. In these distribution systems, television signals are transmitted to a satellite in orbit around the earth (uplinked) and then retransmitted to satellite receiver dishes installed in residences and offices (downlinked). These companies have not been content to simply compete for television distribution markets. They have also taken on the cable distribution companies by providing Internet access via satellite link.

These services have been provided using two methods: two-way satellite link and separate uplink and downlink channels using satellite and dial-up telephone lines. In most satellite systems, the dish has no uplink capabilities, so it cannot send data to retrieve information from the Web. This function must be supplied through the telephone or wireless modem connection. Download speeds are very good (up to 1.5Mbps), but upload speeds are limited to the 56Kbps speed of the dial-up modem. In other systems, the dish is equipped with multiple transceivers that provide both uplinks and downlinks through the satellite link.

Instead of sending web page requests to a web server on the Internet, the uplink service routes the request to the satellite system's network operation center. The network operation center requests the desired page and returns it to the user through the satellite's downlink. The page request operation can only occur at the speed of the uplink connection and the additional steps to get the page to the user may result in a noticeable delay known as *latency*.

As with other Internet connection services, satellite Internet performance is affected by the number of concurrent users accessing the service. The satellite's bandwidth is divided among all the users accessing it. Likewise, natural interference from high winds or heavy rains can diminish the performance of the satellite dish.

EXAM ALERT

Be aware of factors that create noticeable delays in satellite Internet systems.

Figure 22.12 depicts a typical satellite/Internet communications configuration.

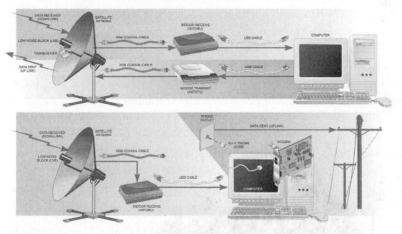

FIGURE 22.12 Satellite Internet access.

As the figure illustrates, the satellite dish is the transmitter and receiver for both the television and Internet signals. The dish holds a device known as a *Low Noise Block (LNB) converter* that receives the satellite signal, removes the noise from it, and converts it to a digital signal that is compatible with the satellite receiver. RG-6 coaxial cable is used to connect the LNBs and the satellite receiver. The receiver unit separates the received demodulated signal into the individual television and Internet channels. It typically furnishes multiple methods for connecting to the television sets in the facility, including through RG-59 coaxial cabling and S-video/optical audio cabling options.

Most receiver models employ a dial-up connection for the uplink portion of the Internet operation, but employ the satellite channel to provide very high-speed downloads and streaming media service. However, some more expensive models provide an always-on uplink through the satellite system as well. On the downlink side, the Internet access signal is considered to be just another channel coming from the satellite that gets filtered out and sent to the computer system, usually through a standard USB port. However, when the satellite uplink method is included, two USB satellite units are required. These units are the receiver (also called the *indoor receive unit*, or *IRU*) and an additional *indoor transmit unit* (*ITU*) . The ITU unit is connected to a digital-to-RF converter mounted on a dish that performs the uplink function. The IRU unit shares the USB connection to the computer with the ITU unit.

Wireless Internet Access

In a wireless network environment, the access point is the key components. As described earlier in this chapter, the access point can be connected to a hub or a computer in the LAN that will act as its host for the wired network. Several industries are beginning to employ this concept to provide Internet services to their customers who carry Internet-ready wireless computing devices. New service providers, such as restaurants, hotels, and airports, install access points that provide their customers with Internet access within the hot spot they establish. Customers with wireless-equipped portable computers can connect to the Internet while in a Wi-Fi–enabled hot spot such as an airport, hotel lobby, fast food restaurant, or coffee shop. Wi-Fi (Wireless Fidelity) is a trademark used by wireless LANs that operate on an unlicensed radio spectrum and are therefore restricted to limited transmitter power covering an area of 200–300 feet from the antenna (the practical range is about 150 feet). In most cases, this Internet connectivity is a for-pay service that the customer signs up for.

Broadband wireless Internet access has also begun to appear in some markets. This service employs a long-range wireless modem to transmit to and receive signals from cellular towers instead of using traditional dial-up phone line connections. The wireless broadband modem connects to the computer or network connectivity device. Then you install the software that comes with the modem, and it's up and working. You can connect the modem into a wireless router/AP and have both wired and wireless Internet access throughout the network. The modem is highly portable. It can be taken along with the computer to other areas where the broadband wireless hosting service is available and it will work there as well.

Cellular telephones, personal digital devices, and tablet PCs have become major technologies involved in the wireless Internet market. Cell phones are widely used to send and receive text messages, email, graphics transmissions, and

Internet downloads. Many PDA manufacturers have included wireless Internet access capabilities with their devices. *Tablet PCs* are small computer systems that offer a trade-off between PDAs and notebooks. They feature touch-screen operation like a PDA has, but tend to include items such as multiple-gigabyte hard drives and USB ports. They typically work with docking stations, just like a laptop, to provide removable drives and usually have built-in wireless networking. National ISPs or telephone providers typically supply the actual Internet access service.

Voice Over IP

Another technology that has advanced rapidly since the last version of this book came out is Voice over IP, or VoIP technology. Sending and receiving data over the Internet has become an efficient, robust, and inexpensive process for billions of people. It was only a matter of time before someone considered replacing the data payload in the IP packet with digitized voice information. Instead of communicating over a fixed-connection circuit switched network (the telephone system), VoIP employs the packet-switching technology used on the Internet to provide low-cost, worldwide voice communications.

The major advantage of VoIP communications for the user is cost savings. Most conventional telephone users pay a monthly flat fee for local telephone calls and a per-minute charge for long-distance calls. Because VoIP calls typically use the Internet, these calls are combined into the monthly flat fee structure of the Internet connection. In addition, VoIP users can drop their standard telephone service and use the Internet connection for both data and voice traffic.

The savings is also worldwide. International calls, which can be very costly through the telephone network, can be made with no additional cost through the Internet. Conversely, VoIP users can place and receive fee-less calls from anywhere in the world as long as they have Internet access. All VoIP calls perform like local telephone calls regardless of where they are made to or from.

IP telephony can be integrated into other Internet services, such as audio and video conferencing and instant messaging. Like other IP-based services, VoIP is susceptible to viruses, worms, and other malicious hacking. Although this is rare, it is possible, and the VoIP industry is developing encrypting tools to prevent these types of activities from occurring.

VoIP Operations

VoIP communications are sometimes referred to as *broadband phones* because they are most often used with DSL connections. Although VoIP does not require DSL connections to operate, the quality of service is certainly better with a broadband connection. VoIP can also be carried out over cable modem connections to the Internet.

There are three commonly used connectivity schemes for placing VoIP calls:

▶ Using an analog telephone adapter (ATA) to interface conventional telephones to the computer so that it can use VoIP drivers to take advantage of its Internet connection. Commercial VoIP companies bundle ATA devices with their proprietary hosting services and application and driver software packages. The installation process is straightforward: install the ATA, connect the phone to it, load and configure the VoIP drivers and software, and make IP telephony calls.

▶ Through special IP phones that connect directly to the network (router or hub) using an RJ-45 connector instead of the standard RJ-11 telephone connector. These phones contain all the circuitry and firmware to perform VoIP operations without a host computer.

▶ Computer-to-computer VoIP using the computer's sound card, microphone, and speakers, along with third-party VoIP application software and an Internet connection. This removes all costs from the VoIP operation except the ISP's hosting fee.

VoIP communications are not limited strictly to the Internet. IP telephony can be used on an IP-based network, such as a LAN. IP telephony calls can be placed to other VoIP devices as well as to normal telephones on the PSTN.

When you initiate a VoIP call by picking up the handset or activating the application package, a connection is established with the call processor running at the VoIP service provider's location. The local VoIP equipment (ATA, IP phone, or VoIP software) returns a dial tone to your handset or speakers, telling you that a connection to the Internet exists. When you dial a number, a special mapping database program running on the call processor, referred to as a *soft switch*, translates the number into an IP address and establishes a session with the remote number when the handset on the other end picks up.

The Internet handles the VoIP conversation just as it would email or web page accesses. Packets pass back and forth between the two computers and are converted into analog voice signals by the ATA, IP phone, or VoIP software, depending on the type of connection being used. These elements also keep the session open between the two end users while the call is in progress. When you end the call by hanging up, the handset sends a signal to the ATA (or its equivalent), which in turn sends a signal to the soft switch, terminating the session. Figure 22.13 illustrates the operation of a VoIP call.

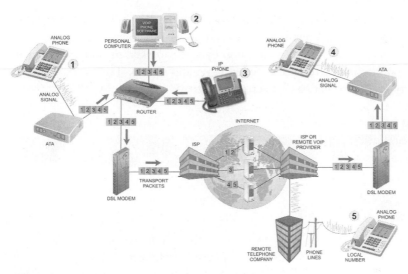

FIGURE 22.13   VoIP calls.

TCP/IP

The key to the Internet is the Transmission Control Protocol/Internet Protocol (TCP/IP). The U.S. Department of Defense originally developed the TCP/IP protocol as a hacker-resistant, secure protocol for transmitting data across a network. It is considered to be one of the most secure of the network protocols. Because the U.S. government developed TCP/IP, no one actually owns the TCP/IP protocol, and so it was adopted as the transmission standard for the Internet. Because of its capability to connect to many types of computers and servers, TCP/IP is used in the majority of all computer networks and is the preferred network protocol for all current Windows operating system versions.

However, the main reason that TCP/IP is the most widely used network protocol today is the Internet. No matter what type of computer platform or software is being used, information must move across the Internet in the form of TCP/IP packets. This protocol calls for data to be grouped together in bundles called *network packets*. The TCP/IP packet is designed primarily to allow for message fragmentation and reassembly.

EXAM ALERT

Know what TCP/IP is and what it does.

The TCP/IP protocol was so widely accepted by the Internet community that virtually every network operating system supports it, including Apple, MS-DOS/Windows, UNIX, Linux, OS/2, and even networked printers. It can also be used on any topology (ethernet, token ring, and so on). Therefore, all these computer types can exchange data across a network using the TCP/IP protocol.

EXAM ALERT

Know the advantages of using the TCP/IP protocol.

The TCP/IP Suite

The TCP/IP protocol includes many options that network technicians and administrators must understand to ensure proper configuration and operation of TCP/IP systems. First, the TCP/IP protocol is not a single protocol—it is actually a *suite of protocols* that was originally developed by the Department of Defense in 1969. TCP/IP consists of two main parts: *Transmission Control Protocol* (*TCP*) and *Internet Protocol* (*IP*). These protocols work together with a number of other protocols in a structure referred to as a protocol stack.

The most important function of the network protocol is to make sure that information gets to the network location it is intended for. Ultimately this is the real function of the TCP/IP protocol. It accomplishes this by routing packets of information to locations specified by IP addresses. A TCP/IP header contains two addresses: the source address that the message comes from and the destination address that it is being sent to.

Because humans don't relate to strings of numbers very well, computers are typically identified by name. For information to get to the address humans want it to go, there has to be some resolution between the numerical IP addresses understood by computers and the alphanumeric names we give them. To accomplish this, TCP/IP relies on a group of protocols and services that represent special advanced name and address resolution functions:

- ▶ DNS (Domain Name System)—A service that works with the hierarchical DNS naming system employed by the Internet.

- ▶ WINS (Windows Internet Name Service)—A service that works with the Microsoft naming system used with earlier Microsoft networks.

▶ DHCP (Dynamic Host Configuration Protocol)—A protocol that ISPs and other networks use to automatically assign user IP addresses from a rotating pool of available addresses.

▶ ARP (Address Resolution Protocol)—This protocol/utility is used to modify tables that translate IP-to-ethernet addresses.

In addition to these supporting protocols associated with IP/computer name resolution, the TCP/IP protocol suite includes support for

▶ Electronic mail transportation

▶ File and print services

▶ Web browsing

▶ Network troubleshooting

In addition to its domain name tracking function, the DNS system resolves (links) individual domain names of computers to their current IP address listings. Some IP addresses are permanently assigned to a particular domain name so that whenever the domain name is issued on the Internet it always accesses the same IP address. This is referred to as *static IP addressing*. However, most ISPs use a dynamic IP addressing scheme for allocating IP addresses.

If an ISP wanted to service 10,000 customers within its service area using static IP addressing, it would need to purchase and maintain 10,000 IP addresses. However, because most Internet customers are not online all the time, their IP addresses are not always in use. This allows the ISP to purchase a reasonable number of IP addresses that it can hold in a bank and dynamically assign to its users as they log on to their service. When a user logs out, the IP address returns to the bank for other users.

The Internet software communicates with the service provider by embedding the TCP/IP information in a Point-to-Point Protocol (PPP) shell for transmission through the modem in analog format. The communications equipment at the service provider's site converts the signal back to the digital TCP/IP format. Older units running the UNIX operating system used a connection protocol called *Serial Line Internet Protocol* (*SLIP*) for dial-up services.

Domain Name Service

To communicate with another computer in a TCP/IP network, your computer must have the IP address of the destination host. As users, we generally specify the name of a computer when establishing connections, such as Marcraft1, not the IP address. These names need to be converted into the IP address of the destination computer. The process of matching a computer name to an IP address is called *name resolution*. The Domain Name Service (DNS) can be used to perform name resolution for any TCP/IP client.

DNS runs on one or more servers in the network. These servers have databases that are used to perform the DNS-name-to-IP-address resolution function for the network. If your network employs DNS for name resolution, you must configure all the clients with the IP address of one or more DNS servers. Procedures for enabling and configuring DNS as part of the TCP/IP package are presented in later sections of this chapter. DNS is also the name resolution service used for the Internet.

Windows Internet Naming Service

Although the DNS naming service is used exclusively by the Internet, it is not the only name-resolution service available to PCs. In the case of older Windows LANs, the Windows Internet Naming Service (WINS) service can be installed on one or more servers in the network to perform name resolution on TCP/IP networks. The WINS service can be used to translate IP addresses to NetBIOS names within a Windows LAN environment. As with a DNS system, a Windows Name server must be running the WINS server software present in the network to maintain the WINS database used for resolving IP addresses/NetBIOS names for the LAN.

Pre–Windows 2000 clients can use WINS for name resolution of other Windows computers on the network. However, they will still employ DNS for the name resolution of hosts on the Internet. To use WINS for name resolution, you must configure the clients with the IP address of one or more WINS servers. Each client in a WINS network must contain the WINS client software and be WINS enabled.

> **EXAM ALERT**
>
> Know what DNS and WINS are, what they do, and how they are different.

Dynamic Host Configuration Protocol

The Dynamic Host Configuration Protocol (DHCP) is an Internet protocol that can be used to automatically assign IP addresses to devices on a network using TCP/IP. Using DHCP simplifies network administration because software, rather than an administrator, assigns and keeps track of IP addresses. For this reason, many ISPs use the dynamic IP addressing function of DHCP to provide access to their dial-up users. The protocol automatically delivers IP addresses, subnet mask and default router configuration parameters, and other configuration information to the devices on the network.

The dynamic addressing portion of the protocol also means that computers can be added to a network without manually assigning them unique IP addresses. In fact, the devices can be issued a different IP address each time they connect to the network. In some networks, the device's IP address can change even while it is still connected. DHCP also supports a mix of static and dynamic IP addresses.

EXAM ALERT
Be aware that IP address assignments change regularly in a DHCP system.

DHCP is an open standard, developed by the Internet Engineering Task Force (IETF). It is a client/server arrangement in which a DHCP client contacts a DHCP server to obtain its configuration parameters. The DHCP server dynamically configures the clients with parameters appropriate to the current network structure.

The most important configuration parameter carried by DHCP is the IP address. A computer must be initially assigned a specific IP address that is appropriate to the network to which the computer is attached and that is not assigned to any other computer on that network. If a computer moves to a new network, it must be assigned a new IP address for that new network. DHCP can be used to manage these assignments automatically.

DHCP is particularly convenient when traveling with portable PCs. Users can set up traveling accounts to automatically obtain DHCP information (IP address, subnet mask, gateway address, and DNS address) from network hosts such as hotels and airport kiosks that provide high speed Internet connections for their customers.

In the case of wireless Internet connections, you will also need to configure your wireless adapter to work with the host's access point. This involves configuring your adapter with the SSID of the AP. Many free hot spots are set up for open access—meaning that they require no encryption. In these cases you will not have to set up encryption types and keys to match the host AP. However, in some hot spots, you will be required to configure a matching encryption type and key.

EXAM ALERT
Be aware of how DHCP can be used to establish Internet connectivity when traveling.

Challenge #3

You work as a service representative for an Internet service provider. One day, you receive a call from a customer wondering why her IP address changes periodically. She doesn't have a problem with the operation of her computer, so what do you tell her?

Internet Resources

The Internet is constructed of resources, or services, offered to users. The range of services available includes file transfers, database access, email, and access to linked documents on the World Wide Web.

A uniform resource locator (URL) is used to access services on the Internet. A URL is composed of two parts. The first part specifies an Internet resource that's to be accessed. HTTP and FTP are examples of an Internet resource. Frequently, the resource is the name of a particular protocol. For example, both FTP and HTTP are well-established protocols used on the Internet. The second part of a URL lists the name of the server. The server name is followed by the directory path and filename of a particular document.

Consider the fictitious URL http:\\help.com/documents/security.txt. The URL consists of the following parts:

► http—The protocol, or service, that will be accessed.

► help.com—The server name (also called the *hostname* or *domain name*) that is accessed for files.

► /documents/—The directory path from which one or many specific files may be accessed.

► security.txt—The name of the file to be accessed.

EXAM ALERT

Be able to identify the individual parts of a URL.

Other common ways of referring to an Internet name is to call it a *web address*, *Internet address*, or *website*. This is a reference to the static IP addresses assigned to the server name.

The World Wide Web

The World Wide Web (WWW) is a menu system that ties together Internet resources from around the world. These resources are scattered across computer systems everywhere. Web servers inventory the Web's resources and store address pointers, called *links*, to them.

To access a website, the user must place the desired URL on the network. Each URL begins with http:// or https://. These letters stand for *Hypertext Transfer Protocol* and identify the address as a website. The rest of the address is the name of the site being accessed (for example, http://www.mic-inc.com is the home page of Marcraft, located on a server at One World Telecommunications). Each website begins with a home page. The home page is the menu to the available contents of the site.

There are numerous types of resources available on the Internet. Typical Internet resources include the following:

▶ The Hypertext Transfer Protocol (HTTP) is used to access linked documents on the World Wide Web. The documents are prepared with the Hypertext Markup Language (HTML).

▶ The Hypertext Transfer Protocol Secure (HTTPS) is used to access linked documents on the World Wide Web that are located on a secure server. A secure server typically requires that a password be entered before access is granted. In some applications, https:// means that documents are encrypted (using the Secure Sockets Layer protocol as described in detail later in this chapter) before sending them to a user that connects to the secure site.

▶ The File Transfer Protocol (FTP) is used to copy files to and from a remote server. When a URL has the ftp:// prefix, it means that the user is accessing a site from which files can be downloaded or uploaded.

▶ The mailto: prefix is used to access an email server. After the email server is accessed (usually after entering a username and password), the email application is started, and the user can read or write email.

▶ The news: prefix starts the newsgroup application on the Internet. A newsgroup is a bulletin board arranged by specific discussion group titles such as the Internet, networking, or computers. There are thousands of newsgroups on the Internet.

▶ The gopher:// prefix is used to access the database area of the Internet. Largely replaced by the World Wide Web, Gopher consists of a series of linked menu items.

- ▶ The telnet:// prefix is used to connect a user to a remote server. After the connection is established, the user has access to software or tools located on the server. When telnet is specified, a separate telnet application begins on the user's workstation. Like Gopher, telnet is being used less and less. Network operating systems such as Windows 2000/XP and Novell NetWare contain remote access services that have largely replaced telnet.

- ▶ The Simple Mail Transfer Protocol (SMTP) is used to send email across the Internet. Email uses conventions that are somewhat different from those used with other services.

- ▶ The file:// prefix is used to access a file on a local server that supports Internet applications. For example, assume that the URL http://inet.com/document/help.txt is accessed. After the help.txt file is open, it may include references to other documents on the inet.com server. The file:// prefix can be used to directly connect to one of the other documents.

File Transfer Protocol

A special application, called the File Transfer Protocol (FTP), is used to upload and download information to and from the Net. FTP is a client/server type of software application. The server version runs on the host computer, and the client version runs on the user's station.

To access an FTP site, the user must move into an FTP application and enter the address of the site to be accessed. After the physical connection has been made, the user must log on to the FTP site by supplying an account number and password. When the host receives a valid password, a communication path opens between the host and the user site, and an FTP session begins.

Around the world, thousands of FTP host sites contain millions of pages of information that can be downloaded free of charge. However, most FTP sites are used for file transfers of things such as driver updates and large file transfers that are too large for email operations.

EXAM ALERT

Memorize the different file types associated with Internet operations and know what their functions are.

FTP Authentication

FTP sites exist on the Internet in two basic formats: private and public. To access most private FTP sites, you must connect to the site and input a username and password designated by the FTP host. Most public FTP sites employ anonymous authentication for access to the site. Anonymous authentication is an interaction that occurs between the local browser and the FTP host without involving the remote user. (That is, no username or passwords are required to gain access.)

EXAM ALERT

Be aware that FTP sites employ anonymous authentication for access.

Email

One of the most widely used functions of WANs is the electronic mail (email) feature. This feature enables Internet users to send and receive electronic messages to each other. As with the regular postal service, email is sent to an address from an address. With email, however, you can send the same message to several addresses at the same time, using a mailing list.

On the Internet, the message is distributed in packets, as with any other TCP/IP file. At the receiving end, the email message is reassembled and stored in the recipient's mailbox. When recipients open their email program, the email service delivers the message and notifies the users that it has arrived. Standard email reader protocols include the POP3 and IMAP4 standards. POP3 is typically used in individual subscriber email accounts, whereas IMAP4 is often used in large network environments. Likewise, it includes a standard SMTP email utility for outgoing email. When setting up an email account, you must supply the following configuration information:

▶ Account name

▶ Password

▶ POP3 or IMAP4 server address

▶ SMTP server address

The default email program in Windows 2000 and Windows XP is Outlook Express. In this program, these configuration settings can be accessed through its Tools menu. From the Tools option, select the Accounts entry, highlight an account name, and click the Properties button. Then click the Servers tab to access the email account configuration, as depicted in Figure 22.14.

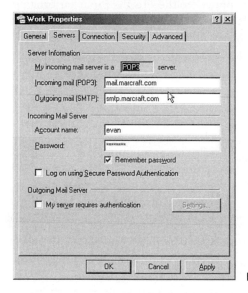

FIGURE 22.14   Email account configurations.

Secure Sockets Layer Protocol

The Secure Sockets Layer (SSL) protocol is used to authenticate users or e-commerce servers on the Internet and to encrypt/decrypt messages (particularly credit card purchases) by using a security process called *public-key encryption*. SSL encrypts data that moves between the browser and the server.

EXAM ALERT

Be aware that SSL is used to protect credit card information during online transactions.

The SSL protocol consists of a digital certificate that the e-commerce site must possess before a web browser can authenticate web servers at the e-commerce site. The digital certificate is issued by a certificate authority (CA). The role of the CA in the SSL session is to authenticate the holder of a certificate (such as an e-commerce server) and to provide a digital signature that will reveal whether the certificate has been compromised. CA certificates are preinstalled in all modern web browsers.

The reason sites need to be authenticated is that it's relatively easy to copy a complete website and then repost it using a domain name that's very similar to the real site. For example, it is easy to mistake the site micrsoft.com, for microsoft.com. A purchaser may be lured to the first site, make a purchase, and never receive the purchased item.

A connection to a certificate server that uses SSL will use a URL that begins with https://. For example, a site called https://buy.now.com is a secure site in which messages between the browser and server are encrypted. The browser indicates that the connection is secure by displaying a locked padlock, or key, near the bottom corner of the browser.

EXAM ALERT

Know that when a website URL starts with https:// it is using SSL.

Telnet

Telnet is a service that enables you to "telephone-net" into another computer so that you can utilize its resources in a command-line interface environment. Although most web browsers do not include a client for telnet access, most operating systems include a utility that will enable you to launch telnet. In Windows, you can enter telnet from the command line. In other operating systems, a terminal emulator utility may be required in addition to a telnet client. A *terminal emulator* is a software package that allows a computer to mimic a dumb terminal.

Telnet enables users at remote computers to connect to a remote server. The client computer doesn't have to be running the same operating system as the remote server. This is a good solution for situations where the PC environment is radically different from that of the other computer (such as a Linux or Novell system, or a mainframe computer).

EXAM ALERT

Know how to connect to servers running different operating systems.

Table 22.2 summarizes common Internet service protocols and includes the well-known port number for each resource. In networking terms, port numbers are used to represent services running on computers. Network security systems open and close ports to control access to systems and services.

TABLE 22.2   Common Internet Protocols and Well-Known Port Numbers

URL PREFIX	DESCRIPTION	PORT NUMBER
http://	Specifies an address on the World Wide Web	80
https://	Specifies a secure address on the World Wide Web that employs the SSL protocol	443
ftp://	Specifies file transfers	20/21
mailto:	Initiates email	24
news:	Initiates access to newsgroups	144
gopher://	Initiates access to database information	70
telnet://	Initiates direct access to a remote computer	23
SMTP:	Initiates email over the Internet	25
file://	Initiates access to a file on a local server	59

Web Browsers

As the Internet network has grown, service providers have continued to provide more user-friendly software for exploring the World Wide Web. These software packages are called *web browsers* and are based on hypertext links. Browsers use hypertext links to interconnect the various computing sites in a way that resembles a spider's web.

Browsers are to the Internet what Windows is to operating environments. Graphical browsers such as Netscape Navigator and Microsoft Internet Explorer enable users to move around the Internet and make selections from graphically designed pages and menus instead of operating from a command line. The original Internet operating environment was a command-line program called UNIX. Fortunately, the UNIX structure and many of its commands were the basis used to create MS-DOS. Therefore, users who are DOS literate do not require extensive training to begin using UNIX. With the advent of a variety of browsers, however, it is unlikely that most users will become involved with UNIX.

The first graphical browser was known as Mosaic. It allowed graphical pages to be created using a mixture of text, graphics, audio, and video files. It translated the HTML files used to create the Web and that ultimately link the various types of files.

EXAM ALERT

Be aware of the different file types used with the Internet.

The Netscape Navigator and the Microsoft Internet Explorer browsers quickly followed Mosaic. Both provide a graphical interface for viewing web pages. Links to search engines are useful for finding information on the Internet. Both have links to built-in email facilities and to their respective creator's home pages.

EXAM ALERT

Memorize the Internet-related abbreviations and acronyms.

Establishing Internet Browser Security Options

A variety of user-selectable options can be established for web browsers. Some of these options are personal preferences, such as colors, fonts, and toolbars. However, some security-related activities involve the browser and searching the Internet. These include configuring scripting, proxies, and security levels through the user's browser. In Microsoft IE, these functions are located on the Security tab under the Tools/Internet Options path, depicted in Figure 22.15.

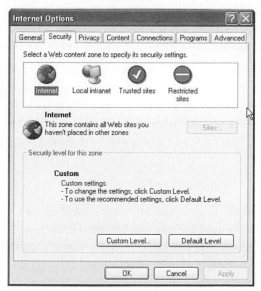

FIGURE 22.15 IE Security tab.

Highlighting the Intranet, Trusted Sites, or Restricted sites icon will enable the Sites button. This button can be used to add or remove sites to or from each of these different zone classifications. The security settings attached to these different zone types can be modified by clicking the Custom Level button. The Internet icon enables security settings to be established for all websites that have not been classified as one of the other zone types.

In each zone type, clicking the Custom Level button will produce a list of individual controls that can be enabled, disabled, or configured to present a user prompt when the browser encounters a related object. These objects represent web page components, such as animated scripts, file downloads, user identification logins, which may be encountered by accessing or viewing a given website.

The Reset Custom Settings dialog box features a drop-down window for establishing general levels of security settings for all the items in the selected zone type's list.

Configuring Script Support

Scripts are executable applications that provide interactive content on websites. They are also capable of retrieving information in response to user selections. However, the user may not have to do anything to run a script program—they are embedded in the website that they access. There are a couple of reasons why you would consider controlling scripts encountered on websites. Scripts are one of the main sources of virus infections. Hackers configure scripts to contain viruses that clients may download unwittingly. Scripts also facilitate automatic pop-up windows that appear without warning on the client's browser. These windows normally contain unrequested advertisements that tend to annoy users.

The capability to load and run scripts in a browser can be controlled through the browser's Tools/Internet Options/Security tab. The list of individual web page components that you can control includes different script types, such as ActiveX and JavaScript. As with the other security objects, you can configure the browser to enable, disable, or present a user prompt whenever it encounters one of these scripted items.

Configuring Proxy Settings

A *proxy server* is a barrier that prevents outsiders from entering a local area network. All addressing information sent to the Internet will use the IP address of the proxy server. Because the IP address of the workstation that's connecting to the Internet isn't used, an outside intruder has no way of accessing the workstation. Client access is configured from the web browser of the workstation. To configure a workstation using the Microsoft Internet Explorer browser for a proxy server, follow these steps:

1. Start Microsoft Internet Explorer. From the toolbar menu, choose Tools, Internet Options.

2. Select the Connection tab and click the LAN Setting button. This will produce the Local Area Network (LAN) Settings dialog box, similar to Figure 22.16.

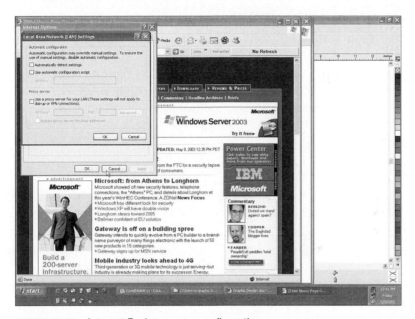

FIGURE 22.16 Internet Explorer proxy configuration.

3. Check the Use a Proxy Server for your LAN option and enter the name of the proxy server in the Address field. An IP address may be entered in the Address field instead of the server name.

4. Enter the port number of the server in the Port field. The port number is usually a well-known port number.

5. Click the Apply button, followed by the OK button.

When fully configured, the proxy server will supply the client with the addresses and port numbers for Internet services (HTTP, FTP, and so on) that are available to it.

Most commercial web browsers provide for proxy configuration in a manner that's similar to the preceding steps described. For example, follow these steps to configure the workstation proxy settings for Netscape Navigator:

1. From the Netscape Navigator toolbar menu, choose Options, and then select the Network Preferences entry from the menu. Click the Proxies tab in the Preferences dialog box.

2. Click the Manual Proxy Configuration option button, and then click the View button.

3. Enter the name or IP address of the proxy server for each service, along with the port number of the service.

4. Click the Apply button, followed by the OK button.

Navigator also permits you to use an automatic proxy configuration for workstations by entering the address where the proxy configuration file is located. Enter the address in the Automatic Proxy Configuration field of the Preferences dialog box.

Exam Prep Questions

1. What services do all ISPs provide to their Internet customers? (Select all that apply.)

   ○ **A.** Spam filtering

   ○ **B.** Internet identity through IP addresses

   ○ **C.** DNS routing

   ○ **D.** Email services

2. Which of the following are advantages of employing IPv6 addressing over IPv4 addressing? (Select all that apply.)

   ○ **A.** IPv6 provides dynamic IP addressing.

   ○ **B.** IPv6 makes more IP addresses available.

   ○ **C.** Piv6 provides authentication and encryption.

   ○ **D.** IPv6 provides invisible IP addresses.

3. Which protocol type is used specifically for authenticating users in a credit card–based e-commerce setting?

   ○ **A.** SMTP

   ○ **B.** SSL

   ○ **C.** HTTP

   ○ **D.** SLIP

4. In most satellite systems, the dish has _____ capabilities.

   ○ **A.** No downlink

   ○ **B.** Both uplink and downlink

   ○ **C.** No dial-up networking

   ○ **D.** No uplink

5. Download speeds in satellite Internet systems range up to _____.

   ○ **A.** 1.5Mbps

   ○ **B.** 622Mbps

   ○ **C.** 2.3Mbps

   ○ **D.** 9Mbps

6. A _____ is a computer used to perform services locally; it then forwards requests for services that it cannot fulfill to an appropriate server.

- ○ **A.** Proxy server
- ○ **B.** Firewall router
- ○ **C.** Router
- ○ **D.** Gateway

7. A client complains that she cannot get her DSL Internet connection working. On the phone, she mentions that the ethernet cable that plugs into the DSL modem will not plug properly into the computer's 56K modem. What should you tell the customer about her connection problem?

- ○ **A.** A DSL modem plugs into a workstation via a network interface card, not a 56K modem.
- ○ **B.** She needs to replace the ethernet cable with a phone line.
- ○ **C.** She needs to change the modem settings using the Control Panel wizards to enable DSL.
- ○ **D.** She needs to add a DSL line filter to the phone outlet that the DSL modem plugs into.

8. You are looking at wireless network cards because you travel frequently and want to have one to provide Internet access in airports and other hot spots. You see one that is labeled as Wi-Fi compatible and you wonder what type of range you can expect to have with it. What is the most likely range for this card?

- ○ **A.** 50 to 100 feet
- ○ **B.** 200 to 300 feet
- ○ **C.** 500 to 1000 feet
- ○ **D.** 2500 to 3000 feet

9. Modems used in dial-up networking applications produce _____ signals that are compatible with the telephone system.

- ○ **A.** Digital/parallel
- ○ **B.** Analog/parallel
- ○ **C.** Digital/serial
- ○ **D.** Analog/serial

10. A customer calls to ask your advice about getting DSL service for a computer. You know that a distance limit applies to DSL installations, and you find that the customer lives 4.1 miles from the nearest telephone office. What should you tell the customer about the service?

    ○ **A.** The customer needs to live within 2.8 miles (15,000 feet) of the telephone company office, so the customer should consider another form of Internet connectivity.

    ○ **B.** The customer needs to live within 3.7 miles (20,000 feet) of the telephone company office, so the customer should consider another form of Internet connectivity.

    ○ **C.** The customer needs to live within 5.7 miles (30,000 feet) of the telephone company office, and so should have no problem using DSL services for Internet connectivity.

    ○ **D.** The customer needs to live within 7.5 miles (40,000 feet) of the telephone company office, and so should have no problem using DSL services for Internet connectivity.

11. A residential customer who has just switched their Internet access over to a satellite system has called to find out why they sometimes experience delays in the satellite system delivering Internet connectivity to them. How do you explain this delay to the customer?

    ○ **A.** Modern satellite systems should not have any delay periods.

    ○ **B.** There is a downlink delay time associated with connecting to the satellite source.

    ○ **C.** The dish requires an azimuth correction period to switch to a different satellite.

    ○ **D.** This is due to connection latency caused by additional parties in the communications link.

12. You are setting up a small peer-to-peer network in your home office and have decided to use simple private IP addressing with static addresses. Which of the following IP addresses is reserved specifically for use as a private address?

    ○ **A.** 192.255.0.1

    ○ **B.** 170.124.0.1

    ○ **C.** 169.254.0.1

    ○ **D.** 135.254.0.1

13. You are traveling and you want to add yourself to the free wireless network in your hotel. Which of the following will you need to do to join the hotel's wireless network using your Windows XP laptop with built-in Wi-Fi? (Select all that apply)

○ **A.** Configure the SSID on your laptop to match the local access point.

○ **B.** Configure WEP, WPA, or WPA2 encryption settings on your laptop to match the local AP settings if required.

○ **C.** Configure the Proxy Server settings in Internet Explorer.

○ **D.** Configure your Wi-Fi channel setting to match the local AP.

14. A cable modem is attached to a router using _____ connector.

○ **A.** An F-Type

○ **B.** An RJ-11

○ **C.** An RJ-45

○ **D.** A BNC

15. How many bits make up an IPv4 address?

○ **A.** 32

○ **B.** 64

○ **C.** 128

○ **D.** 256

16. Which TCP/IP utility can be used to control a remote Linux PC from a local Windows 2000 Professional PC?

○ **A.** FTP

○ **B.** Telnet

○ **C.** SNMP

○ **D.** Remote Access

17. A sales person from your office reports that she can't connect to the Internet or send and receive email from her laptop while traveling outside the office. What can be done to fix her problem?

    ○ **A.** Order a wireless network card for her portable.

    ○ **B.** Establish a roaming profile for her that will automatically obtain network connectivity wherevershe is.

    ○ **C.** Set up a new connection for traveling and configure it to automatically obtain an IP address, subnet mask, gateway address, and DNS address from the host network using DHCP.

    ○ **D.** Set up automatic private IP addressing in the TCP/IP Properties page to provide connectivity wherever she is.

18. One of your coworkers is trying to solve an Internet connection problem for a customer. When he tries to access a website by using its name, the system cannot find the page. However, when he tries to connect to the numeric IP address he has on the customer's work order, it connects. He doesn't know where to look to solve this problem. What can you tell him about which TCP/IP service resolves IP addresses to domain names?

    ○ **A.** DNS

    ○ **B.** DHCP

    ○ **C.** FTP

    ○ **D.** TCP

19. You are setting up a small office network for a business client and using private IP addressing in the range of 192.168.X.X. When you begin to configure the first PC, you enter **192.168.0.1**. What is the standard subnet mask you would use for this IP address?

    ○ **A.** 255.0.05.0

    ○ **B.** 255.255.0.0

    ○ **C.** 255.255.255.0

    ○ **D.** 255.255.255.254

20. What is the purpose of the NAT service? (Select all that apply.)

   ◯ **A.** To represent the network as a single entity to the Internet environment.

   ◯ **B.** To prevent internal users from accessing outside Internet locations.

   ◯ **C.** To configure safe communications between two remote systems without using encryption services.

   ◯ **D.** To prevent outsiders from the Internet from making direct contact with internal network users.

21. What type of protocol is commonly associated with the World Wide Web?

   ◯ **A.** FTP

   ◯ **B.** TCP/IP

   ◯ **C.** HTTP

   ◯ **D.** PPP

22. Anonymous authentication is used for which type of Internet service?

   ◯ **A.** Web server

   ◯ **B.** Email server

   ◯ **C.** FTP server

   ◯ **D.** Secure server

23. How can you identify when an Internet website is using Secure Sockets Layer?

   ◯ **A.** Its address starts with FTP://.

   ◯ **B.** Its address starts with HTTPS://.

   ◯ **C.** Its address ends with .SSL.

   ◯ **D.** Its address starts with WWW.

24. Which of the following Windows services is responsible for performing dynamic IP addressing?

   ◯ **A.** NATS

   ◯ **B.** WINS

   ◯ **C.** DHCP

   ◯ **D.** DNS

Answers and Explanations

1. B, C, D. Services that most ISPs deliver to their customers include Internet identity through IP addresses, email services through POP3 and SMTP servers, Internet news service through Usenet archive servers, and Internet routing through DNS servers.

2. B, C. The address field for IPv6 is extended to 128 bits, which creates a tremendous number of possible IP addresses. IPv6 also provides for authenticating the sender of a packet as well as encrypting the content of a packet.

3. B. The Secure Sockets Layer (SSL) protocol is used to authenticate users or e-commerce servers on the Internet and to encrypt/decrypt messages using a security process called public-key encryption.

4. D. In most satellite systems, the dish has no uplink capabilities, so it cannot send data to retrieve information from the Web. This function must be supplied through a telephone or wireless modem connection.

5. A. Download speeds in satellite systems are very good (up to 1.5Mbps), but upload speeds are limited to the 56Kbps speed of the dial-up modem (unless an RF transmitter is installed in the dish).

6. A. A proxy server is a computer used to perform services locally; it then forwards requests for services that it cannot fulfill to an appropriate server.

7. A. A DSL modem plugs into a workstation via a network interface card, which uses an RJ-45 connector. A 56K modem connects directly into a phone line and does not interact with a DSL modem in any fashion.

8. B. Wi-Fi (Wireless Fidelity) is used by wireless LANs that operate on the unlicensed radio spectrum and are therefore restricted to limited transmitter power covering an area of 200–300 feet from the antenna (the practical range is about 150 feet). Realistic usage ranges must take into account environmental factors such as clear line of sight, AP signal strength, electrical congestion, and so on.

9. D. A modem is used to convert the parallel, digital signals of the computer into serial analog signals, which are better suited for transmission over wire.

10. B. DSL connectivity requires short geographical cable runs (less than 20,000 feet) to the telephone company's nearest CO.

11. D. Instead of sending web page requests to a web server on the Internet, the uplink service routes the request to the satellite system's network operation center. The network operation center then requests the desired page from the real web server and returns it to the user through the satellite's downlink. The page request operation can only occur at the speed of the uplink connection and the additional steps to get the page to the user may result in a noticeable delay known as *latency*.

12. C. The following IP addresses can be used for private IP addressing: an IP address of 10.X.X.X with the subnet mask of 255.0.0.0., an IP address of 169.254.0.X with the subnet mask of 255.255.255.0 (the Microsoft APIPA default), an IP address of 172.(16–32).0.X with the subnet mask of 255.240.0.0., or an IP address of 192.168.X.X with the subnet mask of 255.255.0.0.

13. A, B. Information you will need to configure your system with includes a service set identifier (SSID) name and possibly encryption information (none, WEP, WPA, or WPA2). This information must match that of the host AP you are connecting to.

14. C. A cable modem typically features two main connections one to the host computer's USB port or an ethernet network adapter and the other to the CATV coaxial cable outlet on the wall. A CAT5 UTP cable/RJ-45 normally provides the communication path between the cable modem and the PC's network adapter. A cable modem has an F-Type connector that is used to attach the coaxial cable from the cable system to the cable modem.

15. A. IPv4 addresses exist in the numeric format of XXX.YYY.ZZZ.AAA. Each address consists of four 8-bit (32-bits total) fields separated by dots (.). This format of specifying addresses is referred to as *dotted decimal notation*. The decimal numbers are derived from the binary address that the hardware understands.

16. B. Telnet is a service that enables you to "telephone-net" into another computer so that you can utilize its resources in a command-line interface environment. Although most web browsers do not include a client for telnet access, most operating systems include a utility that will enable you to launch telnet. Telnet enables users at remote computers to connect to a remote server. The client computer doesn't have to be running the same operating system as the remote server. This is a good solution for situations where the PC environment is radically different from that of the other computer (such as a Linux or Novell system, or a mainframe computer).

17. C. Set up a new connection for traveling and configure it to automatically obtain an IP address, subnet mask, gateway address, and DNS address from the host network using DHCP.

18. A. To communicate with another computer in a TCP/IP network, a computer must have the IP address of the destination host. Users generally specify the name of a computer when establishing connections, not the IP address. These names must be converted into the IP address of the destination computer. The process of matching a computer name to an IP address is called *name resolution*. The Domain Name Service (DNS) can be used to perform name resolution for any TCP/IP client.

19. C. A subnet mask value of 255 blocks the entire octet, whereas a value of 254 would block all but one of the addresses in the octet. For a Class C address such as 192.168.0.1, which is typically used in a residential network, a subnet mask of 255.255.255.0 is employed. This blocks the first three octets and leaves the addresses from the lower octet open for use.

20. A, D. The NAT, or network address translation, service is a protocol that enables private IP addresses to be converted to a public IP address. One purpose for doing this is because it effectively hides the internal structure of the network from the Internet—making it harder for outsiders to gain access to a specific PC or network device. Outsiders see the network as a single entity represented by one public IP address.

21. C. The World Wide Web (WWW) can be accessed using the Hypertext Transfer Protocol (HTTP).

22. C. Most public FTP sites employ anonymous authentication for access to the site. Anonymous authentication is an interaction that occurs between the local browser and the FTP host without involving the remote user (that is, no username or password is required to gain access).

23. B. When a website URL address starts with https://, the site employs the Secure Socket Layer protocol for secure e-commerce activities.

24. C. A Dynamic Host Configuration Protocol (DHCP) server, or a router with DHCP capabilities, will automatically assign a unique IP address to DNS clients on the network.

Challenge Solutions

1. DSL modems require an external power source to function and the user has failed to reconnect its power source. If you do not see the power converter plugged in to the modem (and you don't have any lights), this should be a major clue—the system does not have power applied to it.

2. If a filter is put on the DSL connection, the Internet connection may not work correctly. These filters are designed to separate DSL signals from the normal phone traffic. The DSL line needs a clear path to the DSL provider.

3. Many ISPs use the dynamic IP addressing function of DHCP to provide access to their dial-up users. The protocol automatically delivers IP addresses, subnet mask and default router configuration parameters, and other configuration information to the devices on the network. The dynamic addressing portion of the protocol also means that computers can be added to a network without manually assigning them unique IP addresses. In fact, devices can be issued a different IP address each time they connect to the network. In some networks, a device's IP address can even change while it is still connected.

23

Network Troubleshooting

Terms you'll need to understand:

✓ IPCONFIG.EXE

✓ PING.EXE

✓ TRACERT.EXE

✓ NSLOOKUP.EXE

✓ Firewall

✓ Cable tester

✓ Static IP addresses

✓ Automatic IP address assignment

✓ Status indicators

✓ Electrical interference

Techniques you'll need to master:

Essentials 5.3—Identify tools, diagnostic procedures, and troubleshooting techniques for networks.

✓ Explain status indicators; for example, speed, connection and activity lights, and wireless signal strength.

Remote Support Technician 4.3/IT Technician 5.3—Use tools and diagnostic procedures to troubleshoot network problems.

✓ Identify names, purposes, and characteristics of tools, for example:

    ✓ Command-line tools (for example, IPCONFIG.EXE, PING.EXE, TRACERT.EXE, NSLOOKUP.EXE)

    ✓ Cable testing device

✓ Diagnose and troubleshoot basic network issuess, for example:

    ✓ Driver/network interface

    ✓ Protocol configuration

    ✓ TCP/IP (for example, gateway, subnet mask, DNS, WINS, static and automatic address assignment)

    ✓ IPX/SPX (NWLink)

    ✓ Permissions

    ✓ Firewall configuration

    ✓ Electrical interference

IT Technician 5.4—Perform preventative maintenance of networks, including securing and protecting network cabling.

Basic Network Troubleshooting

This chapter covers the Network Troubleshooting areas of the CompTIA A+ Certification—Essentials examination under Objectives 5.3. The Remote Support Technician 4.3 and IT Technician 5.3 objectives advance this discussion by requiring that the technician "use" the tools and techniques from Essentials 5.3. It then lists those tools. The chapter also covers network-related preventive maintenance activities that are generally testable under Objective 5.4 of the IT Technician exam.

Networking and internetworking are such an integral part of the personal computer environment that the PC technician should be familiar with common networking problems and be able to demonstrate effective service techniques for diagnosing and troubleshooting network problems.

> **NOTE**
>
> The Remote Support Technician 4.3 and IT Technician 5.3 objectives build directly on the materials required for Essentials Objective 5.3. The major difference between these objectives is the use of *identify* in Essentials and *use* in Remote Support and IT Technician objectives.
>
> The topics specified in these different exam/objective areas are so closely stated that it makes sense that they are presented as the same discussion. You will need to study this material in this chapter for any of the four exams you intend to challenge.

First, gather information to identify the nature of the problem. Question the user and identify any changes that have been made to the system since it was running last. If the installation is new, the system should be inspected as a setup problem. Check to see whether any new hardware or new software has been added. Has any of the cabling been changed? Have any new protocols been installed? Has a network adapter been replaced or moved? If any of these events has occurred, begin by checking it specifically.

If the problem does not appear in, or is not related to, the standalone operation of the unit, it will be necessary to check the portions of the system that are specific to the network. These elements include the network adapter card, the network-specific portions of the operating system, and the network drop cabling. Figure 23.1 depicts the network-specific portions of a computer system.

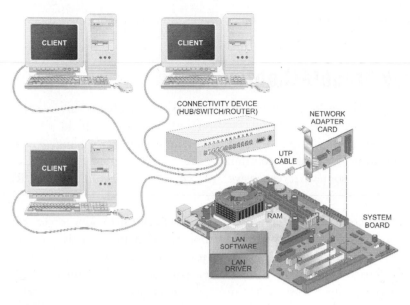

FIGURE 23.1 Network-related components.

In a network, no node is an island, and every unit has an impact on the operation of the network when it is online. Unlike working on a standalone unit, the steps performed on a network computer may affect the operation of all the other units on the network. Changes made in one part of a network can cause problems and data loss in other parts of the network. You should be aware that changing hardware and software configuration settings for the adapter might have adverse effects when the system is returned to the network. In addition, changing hard drives in a network node can have a negative impact on the network when the unit is brought back online.

Diagnostic efforts and tests run across the network can use a lot of the network's bandwidth. This reduced bandwidth causes the operation of all the units on the network to slow down. This occurs because of the added usage of the network.

EXAM ALERT

Be aware of the effects that running applications across the network can have on its performance.

Because performing work on the network can affect so many users, it is good practice (and required in most companies) to involve the network administrator in any such work being performed. This person can run interference for any work that must be performed that could disable the network or cause users to lose data.

Network Troubleshooting Tools

The most frequent hardware-related cause of network problems involve bad cabling and connectors. There are several specialized, handheld devices designed for testing the various types of data communication cabling. These devices range from inexpensive continuity testers, to moderately priced data cabling testers, to somewhat expensive time domain reflectometry (TDR) devices.

The inexpensive continuity testers can be used to check for broken cables and bad connections between cables and connectors. This function can also be performed by the simple DMM. Data cabling testers are designed to perform a number of different types of tests on twisted pair and coaxial cables. These wiring testers normally consist of two units: a master test unit and a separate load unit, as illustrated in Figure 23.2.

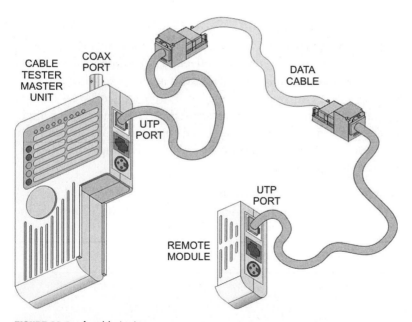

FIGURE 23.2   A cable tester.

The master unit is attached to one end of the cable and the load unit is attached at the other. The master unit sends patterns of test signals through the cable and reads them back from the load unit. Many of these testers feature both RJ-45 and BNC connectors for testing different types of cabling. When testing twisted-pair cabling, these devices can normally detect such problems as broken wires, crossed-over wiring, shorted connections, and improperly paired connections.

TDRs are sophisticated testers that can be used to pinpoint the distance to a break in a cable. These devices send signals along the cable and wait for them to be reflected. The time between sending the signal and receiving it back is converted into a distance measurement. The TDR function is normally packaged along with the other cable testing functions just described. TDRs used to test fiber optic cables are known as *optical time domain reflectometers* (*OTDRs*).

OS-Based Network Troubleshooting Tools

The main operating-system-related troubleshooting tools are the TCP/IP troubleshooting tools that are automatically installed along with the rest of the TCP suite. All TCP/IP utilities are controlled by commands entered and run from the command prompt. Because they are troubleshooting utilities that return information to the screen, they cannot simply be initiated from the Start/Run dialog box. These tools include the following:

EXAM ALERT

Know where TCP/IP utilities are initiated.

- ► Address Resolution Protocol (ARP)—This utility enables you to modify IP-to-ethernet address-translation tables.

- ► PING—This utility enables you to verify connections to remote hosts.

- ► NETSTAT—This utility enables you to display the current TCP/IP network connections and protocol statistics. A similar command, called NBTSTAT, performs the same function using NetBIOS over the TCP/IP connection.

- ► Trace Route (TRACERT)—This utility enables you to display the route, and a hop count, taken to a given destination. The route taken to a particular address can be set manually using the ROUTE command.

EXAM ALERT

Know which TCP/IP utility can be used to display the path of a transmission across a network.

▶ IPCONFIG—This command-line utility enables you to determine the current TCP/IP configuration (MAC address, IP address, and subnet mask) of the local computer. It also may be used to request a new TCP/IP address from a DHCP server. IPCONFIG is available in both Windows 2000 and Windows XP. The IPCONFIG utility can be started with two important option switches: /renew and /release. These switches are used to release and update IP settings received from a DHCP server. Another useful switch is the /all switch used to view the full TCP/IP configuration settings for all adapter cards in the local machine. This includes the IP address, subnet mask, and default gateway values, as well as the Windows Naming Service (WINS) and Domain Naming Service (DNS) settings.

EXAM ALERT

Know which TCP/IP utilities can be used to release and renew IP address information from a DHCP server.

▶ PATHPING—PATHPING is a TCP/IP utility that combines the features of the PING and TRACERT commands. It sends packets to each router on the way to a final destination over a period of time and computes results for each hop. It can be used to pinpoint which routers or links are causing network problems.

EXAM ALERT

Know which TCP/IP utilities show the host IP address.

▶ NSLOOKUP.EXE—This is a Windows 2000/XP TCP/IP utility that can be entered at the command prompt to query Internet (DNS) name servers interactively. It has two modes: interactive and noninteractive. In interactive mode, the user can query name servers for information about various hosts and domains. Noninteractive mode is used to print only the name and requested information for a host or domain. NSLOOKUP is available only when the TCP/IP protocol has been installed.

EXAM ALERT

Know where TCP/IP utilities are run from.

Although all these utilities are useful in isolating different TCP/IP problems, the most widely used are PING and TRACERT.

The PING utility sends Internet Control Message Protocol (ICMP) packets to a remote location and then waits for echoed response packets to be returned. The command waits for up to one second for each packet sent and then displays the number of transmitted and received packets. You can use the command to test both the name and IP address of the remote unit. For example, if you know the hostname of a computer on the network, you can use PING/*hostname* to determine its IP address. A number of switches can also be used to set parameters for the PING operation. Figure 23.3 depicts the information displayed by a typical PING operation.

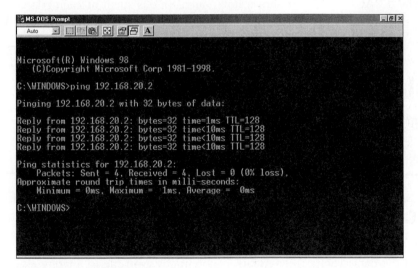

FIGURE 23.3 A PING operation.

Most Internet servers do not respond to ICMP requests created by pinging. However, you can use the PING utility to access *www.somewebsitename.com*. By doing so, you can get a reply that will verify that TCP/IP, DNS, and gateway are working. The TRACERT utility traces the route taken by ICMP packets sent across the Net, as described in Figure 23.4. Routers along the path return information to the inquiring system and the utility displays the hostname, IP address, and round-trip time for each hop in the path.

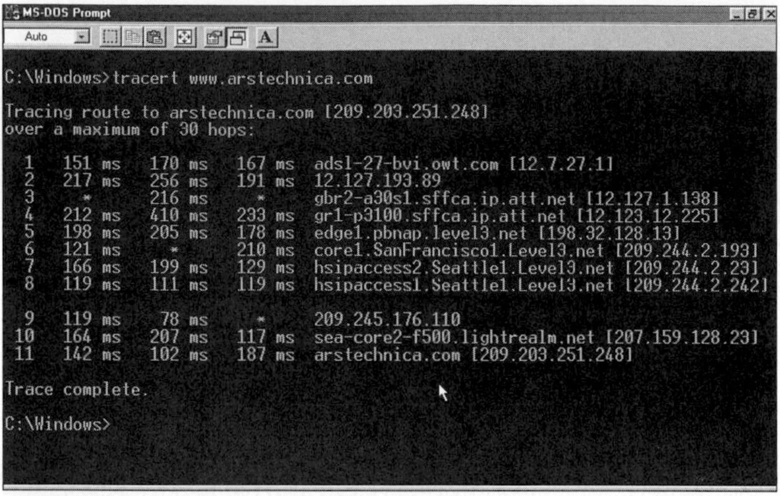

```
MS-DOS Prompt                                                    _ □ ×
Auto    ▼   🗊 🖺 🖺 🖾 🖆 🖥 A

C:\Windows>tracert www.arstechnica.com

Tracing route to arstechnica.com [209.203.251.248]
over a maximum of 30 hops:

  1   151 ms   170 ms   167 ms  adsl-27-bvi.owt.com [12.7.27.1]
  2   217 ms   256 ms   191 ms  12.127.193.89
  3     *      216 ms     *     gbr2-a30s1.sffca.ip.att.net [12.127.1.138]
  4   212 ms   410 ms   233 ms  gr1-p3100.sffca.ip.att.net [12.123.12.225]
  5   198 ms   205 ms   178 ms  edge1.pbnap.level3.net [198.32.128.13]
  6   121 ms     *      210 ms  core1.SanFrancisco1.Level3.net [209.244.2.193]
  7   166 ms   199 ms   129 ms  hsipaccess2.Seattle1.Level3.net [209.244.2.23]
  8   119 ms   111 ms   119 ms  hsipaccess1.Seattle1.Level3.net [209.244.2.242]

  9   119 ms    78 ms     *     209.245.176.110
 10   164 ms   207 ms   117 ms  sea-core2-f500.lightrealm.net [207.159.128.23]
 11   142 ms   102 ms   187 ms  arstechnica.com [209.203.251.248]

Trace complete.

C:\Windows>
```

FIGURE 23.4 A TRACERT operation.

Because the TRACERT report shows how much time is spent at each router along the path, it can be used to help determine where network slowdowns are occurring.

Troubleshooting LAN Problems

The components involved in the LAN subsystem include the network adapter, the connection media, the LAN connectivity devices, and the networking software configuration. Tools involved in LAN troubleshooting include activity/status lights, cable testers, and network troubleshooting utilities.

Service Access Problems

One of the major concerns in most network environments is data security. Because all the data around the network is potentially available to anyone else attached to the network, all network administration software employs different levels of security. Passwords are typically used at all software levels to lock people out of hardware systems, as well as out of programs and data files.

Logon problems are the most common type of problem associated with secure network environments such as LANs. Logon passwords and scripts are designed to keep unauthorized personnel from accessing the system or its contents. In LAN environments, administrators are typically responsible for setting up accounts and passwords for all users. Administrators normally enact password policies that dictate how users interact with the system passwords.

Access to network accounts is based on the user's account name and password, which are asked for each time the user logs on to the network. Forgetting or misspelling either item will result in the user being denied access to the network. Password entries are typically case sensitive, so forgetting to properly capitalize key characters, or having the CapsLock key engaged, will prevent the system from authenticating users and providing them access.

Additional passwords may be used to provide access to some parts of the system and not to others (for example, lower-level accounting personnel may be allowed access to the accounts receivable and payable sections of the business management software package, but not be allowed into the payroll section). A series of passwords may be used to deny access to this area.

Network administrators can control access and privilege levels to programs and data through the operating system's security system. These settings can be established to completely deny access to certain information or to allow limited access rights to it. An example of limited rights would be the ability to read data from a file, but not be able to manipulate it (write, delete, print, or move it) in any way.

Be aware that established security settings can prevent technicians from using any, or all, of the system's resources. In addition, using security settings to limit access to applications can give the applications the appearance of being defective. Because of this, the service technician must work with the network administrator when checking a networked machine. The administrator can provide the access and the security relief needed to repair the system. The administrator can also keep the technician away from data that might not be any of the technician's business.

Checking the NIC

A major cause of connectivity problems is the physical layer. The first step in troubleshooting local network connectivity is to try to obtain a connection with the network. Check to see that the computer is physically connected to the network and check the activity/status lights on the backplate of the LAN card to determine whether the network recognizes the adapter. If the lights are glowing, the NIC sees network traffic and the connection is alive. If not, check the adapter in another PC.

EXAM ALERT

Be aware of what activity of the light on the network adapter's backplate means.

Most network adapter cards come from the manufacturer with a disk or CD-ROM of drivers and diagnostic utilities for that particular card. You can run these diagnostic utilities to verify that the LAN hardware is functioning properly.

Malfunctioning network adapters can cause problems with other computers on the LAN. For example, if a network adapter starts transmitting bad data, all other computers on the same network segment may not be able to send or receive data. If the faulty adapter fails to transmit or receive any data at any time, the problem can be easily isolated because the remaining network adapters on the segment are operating correctly.

The most troubling type of NIC failure is when the problem device captures all the network data and continuously retransmits it erroneously. This condition will shut down all the computers on the affected segment, and thereby complicate the troubleshooting problem. Each computer may have to be tested individually.

To verify the operation of the network adapter, access the Device Manager and double-click on Network Adapters. Ensure that the appropriate network adapter model is listed without either a yellow ! or red X next to it. If a red X appears, the device is disabled in the hardware profile. To enable it, double-click the network adapter and clear the option Disable in This Hardware Profile.

Determine whether any entries are listed as Unsupported or Other Devices. If unsupported devices are listed, double-click the entry and examine the details. If there is no network adapter listed, you must install it according to the manufacturer's instructions. If the network adapter has an exclamation point beside it, the operating system does not recognize the device. You should double-click the entry and click the Troubleshooters button. Simply follow the instructions presented by the Help and Support center to isolate and correct the problem. After making changes through the Device Manager, restart the system so that the changes will take effect.

EXAM ALERT

Know which network utility can be used to identify the address of a known remote location.

Checking Cabling

Cabling is one of the biggest problems encountered in a network installation. Is it connected properly? Are all the connections good? Is the cable type correct? The network cable may be the wrong type of cable. For example, a crossover cable does not function correctly as a regular network cable. The most efficient way to test a network cable is to use a cable tester to check its functionality.

> **EXAM ALERT**
>
> Be aware that cabling faults represent the number one reason for LAN failures.

With UTP cabling, unplug the cable from the adapter card and plug it into the cable tester. The tester performs the tests required to analyze the cable and connection. The easiest way to resolve cabling issues is to replace the network cable with one that works.

> **EXAM ALERT**
>
> Know what type of device is commonly used to make checks on LAN cables.

Checking Connectivity Devices

If no activity shows in the lights on the back of the NIC, check the network's local connectivity devices, such as switches, routers, and bridges that may not be functioning properly. Check the power, status, and activity lights on these devices to determine their interaction with the node you are troubleshooting. These network connectivity devices often provide several indicator lights that can be used to troubleshoot hardware connectivity problems. Typical status and activity lights include the following:

- ▶ PWR—Shows that the device is receiving power and that its power supply is functioning.

- ▶ ACT—The activity light that blinks when the device is transmitting or receiving data to/from the network adapter.

- ▶ Speed indicator lights—If the device has speed indicator lights, they will be illuminated when the device is properly connected to a network adapter; the light corresponding to the operating speed of the link will be illuminated.

> **NOTE**
>
> Different types and models of connectivity devices may have different numbers of lights and definitions. Always consult the device's documentation for descriptions of its link and activity light meanings.

> **EXAM ALERT**
>
> **Know how to interpret the operation of the activity lights on the back of a network adapter.**

The link/active light on the connectivity device should be blinking for the port you're using. If not, the network cable may not be connected to the correct port on the network device. To resolve this issue, verify that the network cable is connected to the correct port on the network device. You should lose the network signal if you connect the cable to the uplink port on a hub, on a switch, or on a router instead of on a regular port. Plug the network cable into another open port on the connectivity device. If you are not sure where to connect the network cable, see the hardware documentation.

Some hubs, switches, and routers disable the port next to the uplink port when the uplink port is being used. To resolve this issue, verify that the port next to the uplink port is empty. If you cannot locate the uplink port, refer to the hardware's documentation. If the link light on the network adapter remains off, you may have a defective or disabled network adapter.

If the physical link between the local network card and the connectivity device is good, you will need to check the logical operation of the network. In Windows systems, this involves using the TCP/IP tools that come with the operating system.

Windows-Related LAN Problems

Some typical networking problems can occur during normal Windows 2000 or Windows XP operations, including such things as the following:

- ▶ The user cannot see any other computers on the local network.
- ▶ The user cannot see other computers on different networks.
- ▶ The clients cannot see the DHCP server, but do have an IP address.
- ▶ The clients cannot obtain an IP address from a DHCP server that is on the other side of a router.

If a client cannot see any other computers on the network, improper IP addressing may be occurring. This is one of the most common problems associated with TCP/IP in networks that use automatic TCP/IP configuration. Users must have a valid IP address and subnet mask to communicate with other computers. If the IP address is incorrect, invalid, or conflicting with another computer in the network, you will be able to see your local computer, but will not be able to see others on the network.

Incorrect IP addressing can occur for two reasons: incorrectly set manual TCP/IP configurations or missing automatic TCP/IP configurations. If the network client PCs and devices are configured to automatically obtain TCP/IP information when they start up, they will attempt to contact a DHCP device to obtain their settings. The DHCP device may be a router, or a server that has been configured to provide network clients with all the TCP/IP configuration information they need.

In large networks, each segment of the network would require its own DHCP server to assign IP addresses for that segment. If the DHCP device is missing or not functioning, none of the clients in that segment would be able to see the network.

DHCP settings are administered through the TCP/IP Properties window. In Windows 2000, this window is located under Start, Settings, Networking and Dial-Up Connections. From this point, open the desired Local Area or Dial-Up Connection and click the Properties option. To manually configure TCP/IP values in Windows XP, select the TCP/IP protocol for the local area network by right-clicking the Local Area Connections icon in the Network Connections page and then clicking the Properties option. These actions will produce the General tab of the TCP/IP Properties page in their respective operating systems.

Through the TCP/IP Properties page, you can configure the computer to obtain an IP address using an automatic service, such as DHCP, or you can manually configure a static address for the computer. To manually configure TCP/IP, the Use the Following Address option must be enabled and you must know the IP address and subnet mask settings you want to use. Remember that every computer on a network must have a unique IP address that identifies who it is. It must also have a subnet mask entry to limit the mobility of the transmission to those nodes within the subnet.

If a Windows client cannot locate a DHCP device when it starts up on the network, it will default to a random IP address in the range of 169.254.XX.XX and a subnet mask of 255.255.0.0. The APIPA feature is very useful in smaller single segment networks because it effectively auto-configures such a network. It also provides an important clue that DHCP problems are occurring in a DHCP environment.

Begin the troubleshooting process for this type of problem by checking the TCP/IP Properties under the Network icon. Next, check the current TCP/IP settings using the command-line IPCONFIG/ALL utility. They will display the current IP settings and offer a starting point for troubleshooting. Afterward, use the PING utility to send test packets to other local computers that you find. The results of this action indicate whether the network is working.

> **EXAM ALERT**
>
> Know the primary TCP/IP tools used to troubleshoot network problems.

Challenge #1

You installed a new Windows XP Professional client in your network and manually assigned it a valid IP address. However, when you try to browse the network, nothing shows up. What should you do to begin troubleshooting this problem?

If users can see other local computers in a TCP/IP network, but cannot see remote systems on other networks, the problem may be routing. Check to make certain that the address for the default gateway listed in the TCP/IP properties is valid. Use the NET VIEW command to see whether the remote computer is available. If the user is relying on the My Network Places feature to see other computers, a delay in updating the Browse list may cause remote systems to not be listed. The NET VIEW command directly communicates with the remote systems and displays available shares.

Challenge #2

You have been called to a customer site to repair a networking problem. The user cannot see any other computers on the network. You check the drivers for the NIC and the protocols that are installed in the operating system, and they appear to be okay. You also check the network adapter and see that the light on its back panel is not glowing. What items should you check next?

If the clients have an IP address of 169.254.xxx.xxx, it is because they cannot communicate with the DHCP server. Windows 2000 automatically assigns the computer an IP address in the 169.254 range if it cannot be assigned one from a DHCP server. Check the previously discussed procedures to determine what the problem may be.

Many routers do not pass the broadcast traffic generated by DHCP clients. If clients cannot obtain an IP address from a DHCP server that is on the other side of a router, the network administrator must enable the forwarding of DHCP packets or place a DHCP server on each side of a router.

Challenge #3

You work in a large corporation that has just converted all its Windows NT Workstation client computers in your network over to Windows 2000 Professional. The network uses a DHCP server to provide IP addresses for the clients. In the process of upgrading the system, you also moved one of the workstations to a new location in the network. However, when you bring the network back up, all the clients come up perfectly except the unit that was relocated—it cannot connect to the network. What should you look for as you try to get the unit back in operation?

Verifying TCP/IP Configurations

There are two TCP/IP utilities that are particularly important in confirming and troubleshooting a system's TCP/IP configuration. These are the IPCONFIG and PING utilities. To verify the configuration of a new TCP/IP installation, begin by running the IPCONFIG utility from the command prompt to verify that the connection has been properly initialized. Then use the PING utility to test the TCP/IP operations. This is accomplished by pinging different IP addresses in the following order:

1. PING address 127.0.0.1 to perform a loopback test that will verify that TCP/IP has successfully been loaded in the local computer.

2. PING the local adapter's IP address to ensure that it has been initialized.

3. PING the default gateway (router) address to verify that TCP/IP is working on both devices.

4. PING the address of another computer on the same network segment to make sure that the default gateway is functional.

If only one of the pinged devices does not return a reply, it has a problem. If neither device replies, the local computer may have a problem. Have someone else check your TCP/IP configuration settings to make sure that no values have been transposed as they were being entered.

EXAM ALERT

Know which Windows tools to use to check out network-related problems.

Challenge #4

You are supposed to demonstrate the operation of the company's network to some executives and you want to display the path that your TCP/IP packets are traveling to get to a remote network location. Which utilities can you use to accomplish this?

Troubleshooting Wireless Networks

Communicating across a wireless network link involves two distinct functions: associating and authenticating. *Associating* is the process of establishing a connection between the local wireless network adapter and the remote AP (or wireless adapter in a peer-to-peer setting). This means creating a wireless link between the adapter and the AP.

In a wireless network, or a wireless link in a mixed network, the link status indictor you should refer to for troubleshooting on the client end is the wireless signal strength indicator, depicted in Figure 23.5. If the signal strength level is too low, the client will not be able to communicate with the network.

Connectivity and transfer speeds in 802.11x networks are based on having a clear line of sight between the wireless clients and the AP. The presence of walls and other objects between these devices will diminish the communication speed, or block the signal between the devices. If the wireless connection seems slow, check for an auto-negotiate connection setting in the AP/router. These settings can be set to a low default value that keeps the device from performing up to its full rated capabilities.

EXAM ALERT

Remember that wireless networking is based on a clear line of sight between the wireless devices.

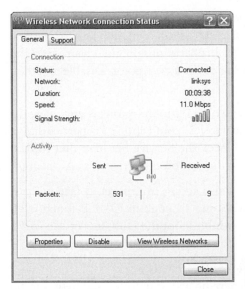

FIGURE 23.5 Wireless signal strength indictor.

Also check for devices such as 2.4GHz cordless phones that can interfere with or disable Wi-Fi communications. If you encounter interruptions in networking when the cordless phone is being used, try switching the AP and network adapters to a different communication channel.

Also note the number of packets that are sent and received. If packets are sent but not received, the logical configuration of the WLAN adapter or the wireless AP/router is incorrect.

Although the signal strength indicator may show that a connection exists, if no communications occur between the local unit and remote units, the network link is probably not configured properly. The status indicator shows only that the local adapter sees an AP or another wireless adapter, not that communications are going on.

When dealing with portable PCs that have built-in wireless networking, you should check that your wireless network adapter is switched on. Some laptops come with buttons that can be used to disable the wireless network function when not in use. This is a power-saving feature used to extend the battery cycle life.

EXAM ALERT

Be aware of the On/Off button and light in portable PCs that feature built-in wireless networking.

Use the Device Manager to ensure that the wireless adapter is enabled. In Device Manager, right-click the wireless network adapter and click Properties. On the Advanced tab, select the Channel Property option and ensure that the number corresponds to the channel setting of the access point. Disable and then re-enable the wireless connection.

The first key to establishing wireless network communications is *association*. In Windows XP, you should navigate to the wireless connection's Properties dialog window and select the Association tab. Check the Service Set Identifier (SSID) setting. This setting should match the configuration of the wireless AP/router.

Check the local IP settings. If your AP is also acting as a router, it may be configured to automatically provide IP addressing through its DHCP function. If the IP addressing is incorrect, you must troubleshoot the DHCP problem at the network router or server to re-establish connectivity.

Wireless network adapters can also be configured to work in a peer-to-peer mode (also referred to as *ad hoc mode*), where no access point is used between the PCs. In this environment, all the wireless clients should be using static IP addresses in the same range. In small networks, it is often convenient to use a simple default addressing scheme similar to the following:

- ▶ PC-A IP address—192.168.0.2

- ▶ PC-B IP address—192.168.0.3

- ▶ Router/gateway address—192.168.0.1 (this address is usually reserved for the gateway)

- ▶ Each PC should have the same subnet mask (that is, 255.255.255.0)

Make sure that the security settings are set to the same encryption type (WEP/WPA), level (64-bit, 128-bit, and so on) as the AP/router (or the other computers in a peer-to-peer setting) and that they are using identical encryption keys. If possible, you may want to disable encryption long enough to get the connection up and running; however, this will leave the network more vulnerable to outside access while it is disabled. Both WEP and WPA can make establishing a connection more difficult—fight one battle at a time.

Other wireless network items to check include making sure that the network adapter is in the right mode—ad-hoc mode for peer-to-peer operations, or infrastructure mode for use in wireless networks with APs or AP/routers. Make sure that the access point is enabled. If it is using the access control list (ACL) function, make sure that the list contains the correct MAC address for the local wireless adapter.

It is also a good idea to remove any unused network connections from the Preferred Networks list on the wireless network's tab. This will speed up connection time by eliminating the need to move through unavailable network connections (they are checked in the order they are listed).

EXAM ALERT

Remember to remove unused network connections from the Preferred Networks list to speed up connection times on wireless networks.

Troubleshooting Network Printing Problems

The complexity of conducting printer operations over a network is much greater because of the addition of the network drivers and protocols. Many of the problems encountered when printing over a network involve components of the operating system. Therefore, its networking and printing functions must both be checked.

When printing cannot be carried out across a network, verify that the local computer and the network printer are set up for remote printing. In the Windows operating systems, this involves sharing the printer with the network users. The local computer the printer is connected to, referred to as the *print server*, should appear in the My Network Places window of the remote computer. If the local computer cannot see files and printers at the print server station, the file and print sharing function may not be enabled there.

EXAM ALERT

Be aware that not having File and Print Sharing enabled will cause computers not to see the other computers across the network.

In Windows, printer sharing can be accomplished at the print server in a number of ways. First, double-click the printer's icon in the Printer (or Printers and Faxes) dialog box, navigate the Printer/Properties/Sharing path and then choose the desired configuration. The second method uses a right-click on the printer's icon, followed by selecting the Share entry in the pop-up context menu, and then choosing the desired configuration. The final method is similar, except that you right-click the printer's icon and click Properties, Sharing tab, and then choose the configuration.

Use the IPCONFIG, PING, and TRACERT utilities, just as you would with any other network devices, to verify and troubleshoot network connectivity between the local PC and the remote printer/print server.

Use the PING address 127.0.0.1 to perform a loopback test that will verify that TCP/IP has successfully been loaded in the local computer. Then PING the local adapter's IP address to ensure that it has been initialized. Next, PING the default gateway (router) address to verify that TCP/IP is working on both devices. Finally, PING the address of the remote computer or network ready printer to make sure that the default gateway is functional.

If only one of the pinged devices does not return a reply, it is the device that has the problem. If none of the devices reply, the local PC may have a problem.

> **EXAM ALERT**
>
> Be aware of causes for different PING responses associated with a remote printer.

If the networking between the local PC and the remote print server or network-ready printer is working, run the printer's self-test to verify that its hardware is working correctly. If it will not print a test page, there is obviously a problem with the printer hardware. Next, troubleshoot the printer hardware. When the operation of the hardware is working, attempt to print across the network again.

Next, determine whether the print server can print directly to the printer. Open a document on the print server and attempt to print it. If the file will not print directly to the local printer, a problem exists in the local hardware. Troubleshoot the problem as a local standalone printer problem. If the local print server operation is working, verify the operation of the network by attempting to perform other network functions, such as transferring a file from the remote unit to the print server.

If other network functions are operational, verify the printer operation of the local computer. If possible, connect a printer directly to the local unit and attempt to print to it through the local printer port. If the file prints to the local printer, a network/printer driver problem still exists. Reload the printer driver and check the network print path, as depicted in Figure 23.6. The correct format for the UNC network pathname is *computer_name**shared device_name*.

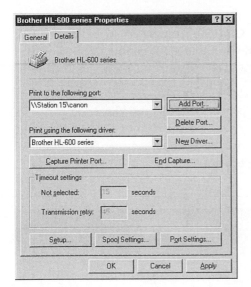

FIGURE 23.6 Checking the printer path.

If the remote printer operation stalls or crashes during the printing process, a different type of problem is indicated. In this case, the remote printer was functioning, the print server was operational, and the network was transferring data. Some critical condition must have been reached to stop the printing process. Check the print spooler in the print server to see whether an error has occurred. This will require that you physically access the print server computer. To do so you will need to log in with administrative privileges. If the print server is a Windows machine, open Printers and Faxes and double-click the printer where you want to view the documents waiting to print. The print queue displays information about a document such as print status, owner, and number of pages to be printed. From this location, you can cancel or pause printing for any document you send to the printer.

EXAM ALERT

Be aware that not all print servers are Windows-based PCs.

In Windows XP, changes made to the print server properties will affect all the printers attached to the print server. To access the server properties, open the Printers and Faxes icon, click the File menu, and select Server Properties. You must be logged on with administrative privileges to configure print server properties. Options available through the server properties include configuring ports, updating printer drivers, and setting spooler options.

Also, check the hard disk space and memory usage in the print server. To verify the available hard disk space, open My Computer and determine whether there is enough room left on the drive. If not, you will need to consider removing files to free up additional space on the drive, or moving the print spooler file to another drive.

Other steps to take include using the print server's Event Viewer to check its Event logs for printing errors. You may also want to stop and restart the print spooler service (spoolsv.exe) though the Services snap-in under Computer Management to create a fresh printing environment.

> **EXAM ALERT**
>
> Know how to create a UNC path from a local computer to a remote printer or to a directory located on a remote computer.

Troubleshooting WAN Problems

The structure and components involved in troubleshooting wide area networks are very similar to those listed for local area networks. Two additional components you will have to contend with in WANs are Internet-specific software, such as the browser, and third-party service providers.

Wide area networking employs modem devices not typically involved in local area networks. There are two types of modems that a technician may have to contend with: analog dial-up modems and digital broadband modems. From an installation and troubleshooting perspective, the differences between these modem types are configuration and connection media.

In the Internet environment, ISPs establish Internet access accounts for each user. As with local area network accounts, these accounts are based on the user's account name and password that are asked for each time the user logs on to the account. Forgetting or misspelling either item will result in the ISP rejecting access to the Internet. Most accounts are paid for on a monthly schedule. If the account isn't paid up, the ISP may cancel the account and deny access to the user. In either of these situations, if the users attempt to log on to the account, they will repeatedly be asked to enter their account name and password until a predetermined number of failed attempts has been reached.

Challenge #5

Your friend has called you on the telephone because he cannot get on the Internet and he doesn't know enough about his computer or the Internet to fix his problem. When you ask him to describe what is happening, he tells you that he gets to the login screen that asks for his username and password, but each time he puts them in, the same screen reappears. He wants to know if you think he has a virus. What two things can you tell him to check? Is one of those items running an antivirus program?

Troubleshooting Broadband Problems

A typical broadband Internet connection consists of a broadband connection and service, a digital modem, a gateway device such as a router, a network adapter card, and a PC.

Common broadband network symptoms include no connection, slow connections, and some Internet services failing to work. The tools used to troubleshoot broadband connection problems typically include ISP documentation, status lights, and TCP/IP utilities.

Checking Activity Lights

Begin by checking the status lights on all the equipment, including the digital modem, the router (or gateway), and the PC's NIC. Check the digital modem lights. External cable and DSL modems provide status lights called Power, DSL (Activity), and LINE SYNC (Link) for monitoring modem status as well as incoming and outgoing traffic. The conditions of these lights can tell you whether the modem is communicating with the PC and with the service provider. Typically, Power and Link should be on and solid; Activity may flicker depending on the activity level of the network. Refer to the modem's user manual for information about the status light conditions. Internal modems use their software packages to communicate this information through the PC display. If the Link light does not show activity, the connection to the service provider has been interrupted.

Checking Physical Connections

The next step is to check the modem's physical connections. Unplug and reconnect the various connections throughout the broadband system, including the telephone lines, cable connections, and CAT5/6 connections. Confirm that all the connections are plugged into the proper ports and that all the devices have power applied.

Verify that the type of network and telephone (or coax) cables are correct for connecting the PC, modem, and router together with the outside service. If the connecting cables are not the originals from the equipment manufacturers, make sure that a standard cable has not been substituted for a crossover cable or vice versa. In the case of cable modems, refer to the user manual to verify that the grade of cable is correct.

In the case of a DSL connection, use a telephone handset to test the phone line for a dial tone. If the dial tone is present, the phone line is working properly. If there is no dial tone, you have a telephony problem and must contact the service provider. Likewise, with cable modem connections, you should check the cable signal coming to a television set that is connected to the cable service. In both cases, receiving a signal on another device associated with the service connection suggests that the service and media are working to your location. It does not mean that the data service is available through the branch attached to the PC.

> **NOTE**
>
> Be aware that although the presence of a dial tone on the line is an indicator of connectivity, it does not mean that the line has DSL functionality or that it is performing at its maximum capabilities.

In the case of broadband systems that connect to the PC using a USB connection, disconnect any other USB devices from the system. Then disconnect and reconnect the USB cable at the PC. If there are any connectivity devices between the modem and the PC, route the connection directly to the host computer.

Checking the Filters

Any other telephony devices using the DSL broadband connection must have inline filters in place to avoid conflicts with the data signals. Missing or improperly installed filters may prevent the successful connection to the DSL service. You should check for filters inline with equipment such as the base units of cordless telephones, satellite boxes, fax machines, and residential alarm systems. These devices can produce electrical interference that will prevent the DSL connection from working properly.

Restarting the Equipment

Before digging into the more difficult aspects of troubleshooting the broadband system, you should remove power from all the broadband devices, including the computer, the cable or DSL modem, and any connectivity devices (routers, gateways, or switches). After a short wait, turn on the modem, the router, and the PC, in that order. Allow 30 seconds for the modem to initialize and synchronize with the broadband signal. If this fails to provide the WAN connection, reboot the PC and try connecting again.

Checking the Connectivity Equipment

Check the power, status, and activity lights on the router to determine whether there is interaction with the node you are troubleshooting. If the physical link between the local network card and the connectivity device is good, you will need to check the logical operation of the network.

Start the host computer and check the system for DHCP operation. From the command line, perform an `ipconfig /all` operation to verify that you have received an IP address from the router (or a DHCP server in the LAN). The IP address of the local PC should be in the range supplied by the router (typically 192.168.1.X). You should also see a gateway address that matches the address of the router (typically 192.168.1.1). If not, open a web browser window, access the router's admin page, and enable DHCP service from the router.

Checking the PC

First, PING address 127.0.0.1 from the command prompt to perform a loopback test on the local system. This will verify that TCP/IP has successfully loaded in the local PC. If the PING operation returns a `Request timed out` message, the local PC is not communicating with its own network adapter, and the TCP/IP configuration settings should be checked.

If the loopback test is successful, use IPCONFIG to obtain the IP address of the default gateway (router). Then PING the address to verify that TCP/IP is working on both devices and to confirm connectivity between them. If you receive a `Request timed out` message, a problem may exist with the default gateway. If possible, PING the address of another computer on the same network segment to make sure that the default gateway is functional.

Open a browser and attempt to access a website (www.mic-inc.com). If you cannot access the Internet using this name address, obtain a known IP address, such as your service provider's DNS server, and attempt to PING it. This will test whether a successful Internet connection exists. If it fails, check the gateway address settings to make sure that they are correct.

EXAM ALERT

Be aware that when you can access a local network address, but cannot access the Internet, you may have a gateway address problem.

If the IP address works, but the FQDN does not, there is a DNS server problem. Check the DNS server addresses in the TCP/IP properties to make sure that they are correct. You should also check any firewall settings to make sure that an incorrectly set port filter is not blocking the DNS service. If these checks do not reveal the source of the problem, contact technical support for the service provider.

> **NOTE**
>
> If some Internet functions work whereas others do not, it is a good idea to check router port blocking and firewall settings to see whether that function is being filtered. This requires familiarity with the well-known TCP/UTP port numbers associated with different services.

> **EXAM ALERT**
>
> Be aware of the symptoms associated with a missing DNS service.

Additional Checks

Check with your service provider's technical support services to determine whether it has some type of outage. If you're connected to the Internet, check your ISP's website for a status update. Also make sure that your account is active. One common reason for interruption of service is that the account has expired. Service can be shut off when users cancel or replace their credit cards and forget to update their billing information.

If all other steps have failed, turn off the modem, the router, and the PC. Then disconnect the units from each other and from the broadband connection. Next, uninstall and reinstall the modem's configuration and setup software. Also remove the modem drivers from the system. Then reconnect the broadband components and run the installation CD to set up the system again. The fresh installation should remove the problems that have prevented the connection from functioning properly.

Troubleshooting Dial-Up Problems

Most of the dial-up WAN troubleshooting steps from the local computer level involve the analog modem. Typical symptoms associated with modem failures include the following:

▸ No response from the modem.

▸ Modem does not dial out.

▸ Modem does not connect after number has been dialed.

▸ Modem does not transmit after making connection with remote unit.

▸ Cannot get modem installed properly for operation.

▸ Garbled messages are transmitted.

▸ Cannot terminate a communication session.

▸ Cannot transfer files.

Troubleshooting Modem Hardware

Some of the most common sources of analog modem problems involve the incoming phone line and the communications service. Inspect the telephone connection and any signal cabling connections to see that they are made correctly and functioning properly. Typical error messages related to the incoming phone line or service include the following:

▸ `No Dial Tone`—This error indicates a bad or improper phone-line connection, such as the phone line being plugged into the modem's line jack rather than the phone jack.

▸ `Port In Use`—This error indicates a busy signal or an improper configuration parameter.

▸ `Disconnected`—This message occurs for a number of reasons, including a noisy phone line or random transmission errors. You can usually overcome this type of error by retrying the connection.

A section on troubleshooting analog modems has to be subdivided into two segments:

▸ External modems

▸ Internal modems

Troubleshooting an internal modem involves the same basic process as any other I/O card. If you are troubleshooting an external modem, it must be treated as an external peripheral, with the USB or serial port being treated as a separate I/O port. Figure 23.7 shows the components associated with internal and external modems.

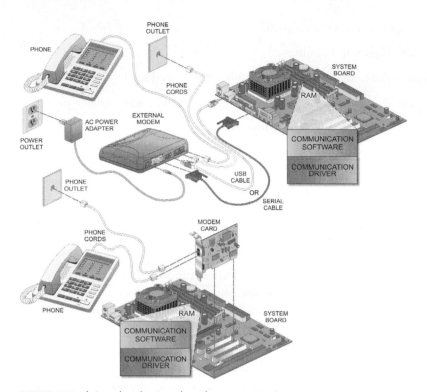

FIGURE 23.7 Internal and external modem components.

Loopback Tests

Most modems can perform self-tests on their circuitry. Modems have the capability to perform three kinds of self-diagnostic tests:

- ▶ The local digital loopback test

- ▶ The local analog loopback test

- ▶ The remote digital loopback test

In a *local digital loopback test*, data is looped through the registers of the port's UART. When testing an RS-232 port, a device called a *loopback plug* (or *wrap-plug*) channels the output data directly back into the received data input, and only the port is tested. Many modems can extend this test by looping the data through the local modem and back to the computer (the *local analog loopback test*). Some modems even possess the capability to loopback data to a remote computer through its modem (*remote digital loopback test*). In this manner, the entire transmit and receive path can be validated, including the communication line (the telephone line). One of the most overlooked causes of transmission problems is the telephone line itself. A noisy line can easily cause garbled data to be output from the modem. Figure 23.8 illustrates port, analog, and digital loopback tests.

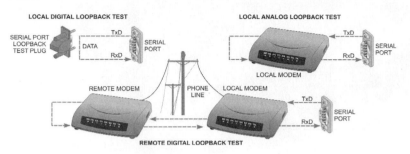

FIGURE 23.8   Loopback tests.

If transmission errors occur frequently, you should use the various loopback tests to locate the source of the problem. Begin by running the remote digital loopback test. If the test runs successfully, the problem is likely to be located in the remote computer.

If the test fails, run the Local Digital Loopback Test with Self Tests. If the test results are positive, the problem may be located in the local computer. On the other hand, you should run the local analog loopback test if the local digital test fails.

If the local analog test fails, the problem is located in the local modem. If the local analog test is successful, and problems are occurring, you should run the local analog test on the remote computer. The outcome of this test should pinpoint the problem to the remote computer or the remote modem.

If the modem is an internal unit, you can test its hardware by exchanging it with a known-good unit. If the telephone line operates correctly with a normal handset, only the modem, its configuration, or the communications software can be causes of problems. If the modem's software and configuration settings appear to be correct and problems are occurring, the modem hardware is experiencing a problem and it will be necessary to exchange the modem card for a known-good one.

Front Panel Lights

With an external modem, you can use the front panel lights as diagnostic tools to monitor its operation. You can monitor the progress of a call and its handling, along with any errors that may occur. Figure 23.9 depicts the front panel lights of a typical external modem.

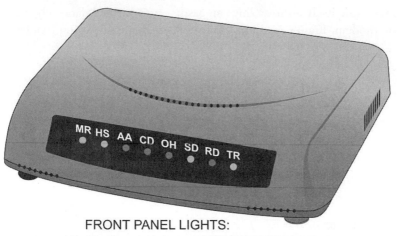

FRONT PANEL LIGHTS:

MR - MODEM READY   OH - OFF-HOOK
HS - HIGH SPEED   SD - SEND DATA
AA - AUTO ANSWERING   RD - RECEIVE DATA
CD - DATA CARRIER DETECT TR - TERMINAL READY

FIGURE 23.9 Typical modem front panel indicators.

The Modem Ready (MR), Terminal Ready (TR), and Auto Answer (AA) lights are preparatory lights that indicate that the modem is plugged in, powered on, ready to run, and prepared to answer an incoming call. The MR light becomes active when power is applied to the modem and the modem is ready to operate. The TR light becomes active when the host computer's communication software and the modem contact each other. The AA light just indicates that the Auto Answer function has been turned on.

The Off-Hook (OH), Ring Indicator (RI), and Carrier Detect (CD) lights indicate the modem's online condition. The OH light indicates that the modem has connected to the phone line. This action can occur when the modem is receiving a call, or when it is commanded to place a call. The RI light becomes active when the modem detects an incoming ring signal. The CD light activates when the modem detects a carrier signal from a remote modem. As long as this light is on, the modem can send and receive data from the remote unit. If the CD light will not activate with a known-good modem, a problem with the data communication equipment exists.

The final three lights indicate the status of a call in progress. The Send Data (SD) light flickers when the modem transmits data to the remote unit, whereas the Received Data light flickers when the modem receives data from the remote unit. The High Speed (HS) light becomes active when the modem is conducting transfers at its highest possible rate. If an external modem will not operate at its highest rated potential, check the specification for the UART on the adapter card to make certain that it is capable of operating at that speed.

Modem Configuration Checks

If the hardware is functional, the operating system's driver and resource configuration settings must be checked. Each user should have received a packet of information from the ISP when the service was purchased. These documents normally contain all the ISP-specific configuration information needed to set up the user's service. This information should be consulted when installing and configuring any Internet-related software. Improper software setup is the most common cause of modems not working when they are first installed.

Check the modem documentation for any manufacturer-specified hardware configuration settings for the modem. Check the modem manufacturer's website for updated drivers that will work with the operating system you have.

Windows Modem Checks

To check the Windows configuration for the modem, move into the Device Manager utility and check the modem for resource conflicts. If there is a conflict with the modem, an exclamation point (!) should appear alongside the modem listing. If a conflict is indicated, double-click the modem driver under the Modems node to move into the General tab of the modem's Properties page. Check the message in the Device Status window to see what type of conflict is indicated. The conflict must be resolved between the modem and whatever device is sharing its resources. Click the Troubleshooter button to access and run the Windows Modem Troubleshooter.

If no conflict is indicated, move into the Diagnostics tab. Click the Query Modem button to cause Windows to communicate with the modem hardware. If no problems are detected by this test, Windows displays a listing of the AT communications commands that it used to test the hardware, as illustrated in Figure 23.10. If an error is detected during the Windows testing, an error message displays onscreen. These messages are similar to those previously listed.

If the modem tests are okay, check the User Name and Password settings. This can be accomplished through the Start/Settings/Network and Dial-Up Connections path in Windows 2000. In Windows XP, the path is Start/Connect To/Show All Connections.

FIGURE 23.10 Modem properties query modem response.

In the Windows 2000 Network and Dial-Up Connections (or Show All Connections in Windows XP) window, right-click the desired connection icon and select the Properties option from the list. Check the phone number and modem type on the General tab. Next move into the Networking tab and confirm the Type of Dial-Up Server I Am Calling setting. For Windows Internet dial-up service, this is typically a PPP Windows Internet connection. Also, disable the NetBEUI and IPX/SPX components on the page, and make certain that the TCP/IP component is enabled.

Most ISPs use DHCP to assign IP, DNS, and gateway addresses to clients for dial-up accounts. Therefore, in a dial-up situation, the Server Assigns IP Address option and the Server Assigns Name Server Address option are normally enabled. Check the ISP-supplied information to make sure that these settings do not need to be configured manually. If so, set up the page to match the ISP-specified settings. In the case of intranets with in-house clients, the network administrator determines how the values are assigned—statically or via DHCP.

Troubleshooting Browser Problems

As with other access problems, correct spelling is a leading cause of browser problems. If you cannot access a website, check the spelling of the fully qualified domain name to make sure that it is spelled exactly as it should be. If the spelling is wrong, no communications will take place.

Many websites won't work properly if cookies are disabled. Disabling cookies prevents websites from storing in your browser small pieces of information that the site uses to remember who you are, as well as for personalized actions such as logging in or making purchases. The local user can control how remote websites interact with the local browser.

Likewise, many websites will not work properly if JavaScript is disabled. Websites use JavaScript to provide sophisticated applications and dynamic features to enhance the site's presentation. Although JavaScript is harmless on trusted sites, on other sites it can be a source of pop-up ads and other bothersome browser windows.

The browser security setting is another source of problems. If the security setting is too high, access will be restricted to specified sites only. A medium security setting generally provides sufficient protection for normal web browsing.

Slow connection speeds can cause web pages to load slowly or fail to load at all. A full page cache can cause the browser to perform slowly or not at all. The *cache* is a memory area where the browser saves copies of previously visited web pages. The cache enables the browser to load frequently visited pages more quickly. You should occasionally clear the cache to improve the browser's performance.

> **EXAM ALERT**
>
> Know that a full page cache will cause web browsers to run slowly.

Troubleshooting Internet Connection Sharing

Windows 2000 and Windows XP enable networked computers to share a single connection to the Internet. This feature is known as Internet Connection Sharing (ICS) and must be configured on the connection host and the client computers in the network. ICS is configured on the host computer through the Advanced tab of its Local Area Connection properties. On this tab, check the Allow Other Network Users to Connect Through This Computer's Internet Connection check box.

Each client computer must be configured to automatically obtain an IP address. The ICS service dynamically assigns the client computers an IP configuration using an IP address in the range of 192.168.0.x, with a subnet mask of 255.255.255.0. It also produces a default gateway address of 192.168.0.1 and a DNS server address of 192.168.0.1.

If the ICS function is not working, follow these steps:

1. Verify that the ICS host computer is configured to share its Internet connection. Also be certain that the ICS host is not enabled to automatically obtain an IP address.

2. Check the client's IP configuration settings to ensure that they are within the ranges listed in the previous paragraph. The x value in the IP address must be between 2 and 254.

3. If the clients' IP address is 169.254.0.0, the ICS function is not supplying the IP address. This address is the default for the APIPA function. From the command prompt, run the IPCONFIG /RENEW command to determine whether an appropriate address can be obtained. If not, you should examine the physical connections for the network and be certain that the ICS function is enabled properly.

4. Check the ICS host's connection to the Internet. If the clients are receiving the proper IP configurations but cannot connect to the Internet, the problem most likely involves the host-to-ISP connectivity.

5. Check the network for other DHCP services that might be conflicting with the ICS function (such as a wireless router configured to provide DHCP services).

Troubleshooting Software Firewall Issues

Some connection problems can be the result of misconfigured proxy or firewall settings. Whereas corporate and business environments rely on hardware firewalls and have skilled administrators to manage them, personal and residential networks typically rely on software firewalls, such as Zone Alarm or the Windows XP ICF (Windows Firewall with Service Pack 2 or later).

If you are having Internet connectivity problems getting WAN access or some services, such as incoming or outgoing mail, do not function, temporarily disable your security software and set the Internet Explorer security level to its default. This should minimize interference with the connection. If you are able to connect to the Internet or use the desired service under this condition, you must reconfigure the firewall settings. This will involve identifying services (or ports) that are being blocked and then configuring them to allow communications to take place or the identified service to function.

Exam Prep Questions

1. What effects will running diagnostic applications across the network have on the network's performance?

   ○ **A.** The unit running the application will not have access to other parts of the network.

   ○ **B.** The units on the network may slow down.

   ○ **C.** The units on the network will communicate faster.

   ○ **D.** The units on the network may crash.

2. What does the activity of the light on the network adapter's backplate mean?

   ○ **A.** The connection is alive.

   ○ **B.** Data is being uploaded.

   ○ **C.** Data is being downloaded.

   ○ **D.** Data is being encrypted.

3. You have been sent to troubleshoot an Internet connectivity problem. When you try to PING the site's fully qualified domain name, the site cannot be located; however, you can PING its IP address. What network function should be checked?

   ○ **A.** DNS

   ○ **B.** DHCP

   ○ **C.** WINS

   ○ **D.** FTP

4. When you enter **IPCONFIG** in the Run dialog box, you get a momentary black box on the display followed by a normal command prompt screen. What is occurring with this command?

   ○ **A.** The TCP/IP utility has not been configured on the local machine.

   ○ **B.** The network adapter is bad. Therefore, there is no information for the IPCONFIG utility to return.

   ○ **C.** The local host is not communicating with the client computer. Therefore, there is no information for the IPCONFIG utility to report.

   ○ **D.** This is a normal response for running a TCP/IP utility from the Run dialog box.

5. After running the IPCONFIG utility, you try to PING the local adapter's IP address but no reply is returned. What does this indicate?

　　○　**A.** TCP/IP has not been loaded into the system.

　　○　**B.** The local adapter's IP address has not been initialized.

　　○　**C.** TCP/IP is not working on the gateway device.

　　○　**D.** The default gateway is not functional.

6. A computer on your network is not able to see any other computers on the network. When you check the adapter's TCP/IP configuration, you find that the IP address is 169.254.0.0. What does this indicate?

　　○　**A.** The network adapter in the machine is bad or has not been initiated.

　　○　**B.** The cable connecting the PC to the local switch is bad.

　　○　**C.** The DNS function for the network is not working and Automatic Private IP Addressing has been performed by the local PC.

　　○　**D.** The DHCP function for the network is not working and Automatic Private IP Addressing has been performed by the local PC.

7. You have just finished configuring a notebook PC with built-in wireless networking. However, when you start the system, you find that you can't connect to any network. What should you check first?

　　○　**A.** Run IPCONFIG /ALL to check the local network configuration settings.

　　○　**B.** Check the notebook for an external button to enable its internal antenna.

　　○　**C.** Check the notebook's TCP/IP configuration.

　　○　**D.** Run Ping 127.0.0.1 to ensure that the local network adapter's IP address has been initialized.

8. What command would be used to establish network connectivity?

　　○　**A.** IPCONFIG /all

　　○　**B.** IPCONFIG /release

　　○　**C.** IPCONFIG /renew

　　○　**D.** IPCONFIG /registerdns

9. Which IP address will invoke the TCP/IP loopback function?

- ○ **A.** 127.0.0.1
- ○ **B.** 10.0.0.1
- ○ **C.** 169.192.0.1
- ○ **D.** 172.254.0.1

10. Generally, whenever a user tells you that a LAN connection is not working, what is the first thing to check?

- ○ **A.** Check the network adapter drivers to see that they are configured properly.
- ○ **B.** PING a known IP address to see whether the network cable and connectivity are good.
- ○ **C.** Check for the presence of link lights on the back of the network adapter.
- ○ **D.** Run IPGONFIG to see whetherthe local network hardware is functioning.

11. A user can access an associate's computer on the network but can't access the Internet through the network gateway. What is the most likely cause of this problem?

- ○ **A.** The subnet mask configuration is incorrect.
- ○ **B.** The DNS service is not working.
- ○ **C.** The DHCP service is not working.
- ○ **D.** The gateway address is configured incorrectly.

12. If you try to ping the loopback address and nothing happens, what is most likely the problem?

- ○ **A.** TCP/IP is not working on the local machine.
- ○ **B.** The network cable is bad.
- ○ **C.** The local connectivity device is turned off.
- ○ **D.** The network adapter in the local machine is defective.

Answers and Explanations

1. B. Performing diagnostic efforts and running tests across the network can consume a significant amount of the network's bandwidth. This reduced bandwidth causes the operation of all the units on the network to slow down. This slowdown is because of the added network traffic.

2. A. The activity light on the backplate of the LAN card (if available) is used to determine whether the network is recognizing the network adapter card. If the light is active, the connection is alive.

3. A. To PING the site's FQDN, your DNS must submit a name resolution request to a local DNS server. The server will search through its DNS database, and if necessary through the hierarchical DNS system, until it locates the host name or FQDN that was submitted to it. At this point, it resolves the IP address of the requested hostname and returns it to the client.

4. D. This is a normal response for running a TCP/IP utility from the Run dialog box. Because they are troubleshooting utilities that return information to the screen, they cannot simply be initiated from the Start/Run dialog box.

5. B. The PING utility can be used for testing the TCP/IP operations. Pinging the local adapter's IP address and receiving no reply is indicates that the adapter's IP address has not been initialized.

6. D. If network clients have an IP address of 169.254.xxx.xxx, it is because they cannot communicate with the DHCP server. Windows 2000/XP automatically assigns the computer an IP address in the 169.254 range if it cannot be assigned one from a DHCP server.

7. B. When dealing with portable PCs that have built-in wireless networking, you should check that your wireless network adapter is switched on. Some laptops come with buttons that can be used to disable the wireless network function when not in use. This is a power-saving feature used to extend the battery cycle life.

8. C. The IPCONFIG utility can be started with two important option switches: /renew and /release. These switches are used to release and obtain new IP settings received from a DHCP source. The /release switch dumps the old TCP/IP configuration and the /renew switch requests a new set of TCP/IP information to use.

9. A. PING address 127.0.0.1 will perform a loopback test that verifies TCP/IP has been successfully loaded in the local computer.

10. C. The first step in troubleshooting local network connectivity is to try to obtain a connection with the network. Check to see that the computer is physically connected to the network and check the activity/status lights on the backplate of the LAN card to determine whether the network recognizes the adapter. If the lights are glowing, the NIC sees network traffic and the connection is alive. If not, check the adapter in another PC.

11. D. If you can access a node on the local network but cannot access the Internet, check the gateway address setting to make sure that it is configured correctly.

12. A. Pinging address 127.0.0.1 will perform a loopback test that will verify that TCP/IP has successfully been loaded in the local computer.

Challenge Solutions

1. Use the IPCONFIG/ALL utility for Windows 2000/XP systems to display the current IP settings and offer a starting point for troubleshooting.

2. You should check the drop cable to the computer to make sure that it is plugged in and that it is wired correctly (check its color code). Also, check the device the cable is connected to (the hub, switch, or router).

3. Check to see if there is a router between the old and new segments that the computer is attached to. Many routers do not pass the broadcast traffic generated by DHCP clients. If clients cannot obtain an IP address from a DHCP server that is located on the other side of a router, the network administrator must enable the forwarding of DHCP packets or place a DHCP server on each side of the router.

4. TRACERT is the traditional TCP/IP tool used to show packet routes to a remote location.

5. Forgetting or misspelling either the username or password will result in the ISP refusing access to the Internet. Typically, passwords entries are case sensitive, so forgetting to properly capitalize key characters, or having the Caps Lock key engaged will prevent the system from authenticating users. Also, if the account isn't paid up, the ISP may have canceled the account and denied your friend access. In either case, when he attempts to log on to his account, he will repeatedly be asked to enter their account name and password until a predetermined number of failed attempts has been reached. Running an antivirus program has nothing to do with logging in.

24

Security

Terms you'll need to understand:

- ✓ Smart cards
- ✓ Biometrics
- ✓ Authentication
- ✓ Viruses
- ✓ Trojans
- ✓ Worms
- ✓ Spam
- ✓ Spyware
- ✓ Adware
- ✓ Grayware
- ✓ Software firewall
- ✓ SSID
- ✓ Encryption
- ✓ Data migration
- ✓ WPA.x
- ✓ MAC filtering
- ✓ Accounts
- ✓ User profiles
- ✓ Administrator account
- ✓ Guest account
- ✓ Group account
- ✓ Permissions
- ✓ Auditing
- ✓ Social engineering
- ✓ Dumpster divers
- ✓ Incidence reporting policy
- ✓ Polarizing films
- ✓ Data migration

Techniques you'll need to master:

Essentials 6.1—Identify the fundamental principles of security.

- ✓ Identify names, purposes, and characteristics of hardware and software security, for example:
  - ✓ Hardware deconstruction/recycling
  - ✓ Smart cards/biometrics (for example, key fobs, cards, chips, and scans)

- ✓ Authentication technologies (for example, username, password, biometrics, smart cards)

- ✓ Malicious software protection (for example, viruses, Trojans, worms, spam, spyware, adware, grayware)

- ✓ Software firewalls

- ✓ File system security (for example, FAT32 and NTFS)

- ✓ Identify names, purposes, and characteristics of wireless security, for example:
  - ✓ Wireless encryption (for example, WEP.x and WPA.x) and client configuration
  - ✓ Access points (for example, disable DHCP/use static IP, change SSID from default, disable SSID broadcast, MAC filtering, change default username and password, update firmware, firewall)
- ✓ Identify names, purposes, and characteristics of data and physical security.
  - ✓ Data access (basic local security policy)
  - ✓ Encryption technologies
  - ✓ Backups
  - ✓ Data migration
  - ✓ Data/remnant removal
  - ✓ Password management
  - ✓ Locking workstation (hardware, operating system)
- ✓ Describe importance and process of incidence reporting.

Depot Technician 4.1—Identify the names, purposes, and characteristics of physical security devices and processes.

- ✓ Control access to PCs, servers, laptops, and restricted spaces.
  - ✓ Hardware
  - ✓ Operating systems

Remote Support Technician 5.1/IT Technician 6.1—Identify the fundamental principles of security.

- ✓ Identify the names, purposes, and characteristics of access control and permissions.
  - ✓ Accounts including user, admin, and guest
  - ✓ Groups
  - ✓ Permission levels, types (for example, file systems and shared), and actions (such as read, write, change, and execute), components, restricted spaces

IT Technician 6.1—Identify the fundamentals and principles of security.

- ✓ Identify the purposes and characteristics of auditing and event logging.

Essentials 6.2—Install, configure, upgrade, and optimize security.

- ✓ Install, configure, upgrade, and optimize hardware, software, and data security, for example:
  - ✓ BIOS
  - ✓ Smart cards
  - ✓ Authentication technologies
  - ✓ Malicious software protection
  - ✓ Data access (basic local security policy)
  - ✓ Backup procedures and access to backups
  - ✓ Data migration
  - ✓ Data/remnant removal

Depot Technician 4.2/Remote Support Technician 5.2/IT Technician 6.2—Install, configure, optimize, and upgrade security.

- ✓ Install and configure hardware, software, wireless, and data security, for example:
    - ✓ Smart card readers
    - ✓ Key fobs
    - ✓ Biometric devices
    - ✓ Authentication technologies
    - ✓ Software firewalls
    - ✓ Auditing and event logging (enable/disable only)
    - ✓ Wireless client configuration
    - ✓ Unused wireless connections
    - ✓ Data access (permissions, security policies)
    - ✓ Encryption and encryption technologies
    - ✓ File systems (converting from FAT32 to NTFS only)

Essentials 6.3—Identify tools, diagnostic procedures, and troubleshooting techniques for security.

- ✓ Diagnose and troubleshoot hardware, software, and data security issues, for example:
    - ✓ BIOS
    - ✓ Smart cards, biometrics
    - ✓ Authentication technologies
    - ✓ Malicious software
    - ✓ File system (FAT32, NTFS)
    - ✓ Data access (basic local security policy)
    - ✓ Backup
    - ✓ Data migration

Remote Support Technician 5.3/IT Technician 6.3—Identify tools, diagnostic procedures, and troubleshooting techniques for security issues.

- ✓ Diagnose and troubleshoot software and data security issues, for example:
    - ✓ Software firewall issues
    - ✓ Wireless client configuration issues
    - ✓ Data access issues (permissions, security policies)
    - ✓ Encryption and encryption technology issues

Essentials 6.4—Perform preventative maintenance for computer security.

- ✓ Implement software security preventive maintenance techniques such as installing Service Packs and patches and training users about malicious software prevention technologies.

Essentials 6.1/Remote Support Technician 5.4/IT Technician 6.4:

- ✓ Perform preventive maintenance for security.
- ✓ Recognize social engineering and address social engineering situations.

Introduction

This chapter covers the Security areas of the CompTIA A+ Certification—
Essentials examination under Objectives 6.1, 6.2, 6.3, and 6.4. It also covers the
security information that is generally testable under Objectives 4.1 and 4.2 of
the Depot Technician exam, Objectives 5.1, 5.2, 5.3, and 5.4 of the Remote
Support Technician exam, and Objectives 6.1, 6.2, 6.3, and 6.4 of the IT
Technician exam.

Three levels of security are commonly associated with desktop and portable
PCs: hardware-oriented possession and access limitation, local and network
policies and permissions governing access to information on the PC, and protection from external sources seeking to steal, damage, or disrupt data on the
PC. The PC technician must be able to understand these threats, install software to prevent them from affecting PCs, and instruct users about how to avoid
them.

NOTE

Depot Technician Objectives 4.1 and 4.2 are completely covered by a portion of the
Essentials 6.1 subobjectives. A portion of the IT Technician Objective 6.1 is the same as
Remote Support Technician Objective 5.1. IT Technician 6.1 adds "Auditing" to the
Remote Support Technician listing. Remote Support Technician Objective 5.2 is the same
as IT Technician Objective 6.2 except that the Remote Support Technician subobjective
includes "Smart cards, key fobs, and biometric devices," as does Depot Technician
Objective 4.2. The Remote Support Technician 5.3 and IT Technician 6.3 objectives use
the same wording to cover "Software firewall issues, data access issues, encryption
issues." Likewise, Remote Support Technician Objective 5.4 and IT Technician Objective
6.4 employ the same language to cover "Recognize social engineering."

The topics specified in these different exam/objective areas are so closely stated that it
makes sense that they are presented as the same discussion. You will need to study the
material in this chapter for any of the four exams you intend to challenge.

Computer Security

Computer security is implemented on multiple levels that include physical
denial of use, limited access to system resources, and active protection against
individuals and software intent on corrupting or stealing data. When dealing
with server systems, it is common to strictly limit physical access to the server
hardware by placing it in protected rooms that have automatic locks on the door
and the computer chassis. These systems also include audible alarms and esca-
lating security notices if anyone attempts to get past these safeguards. However,

this is not practical with PC systems that may be used by different users and that, in many cases, are portable.

Access Control

In a domain-based networked computer environment, security is not only a matter of securing access to the information in the network, it also involves the security of the server hardware and the physical environment. This requires limiting physical access to the servers and placing alarms on their server computers, racks, and rooms. Then also install locks on the server room access doors, the individual server racks, and on each server chassis (system unit).

The first physical security feature that should be in place is a lockable server case or chassis. If individuals do not have a key to the server, they cannot get into it. A lockable server rack can be used to keep multiple servers safe from unauthorized entry. Good server racks include sensors that will cause the system to issue alerts to administrators when the cabinet is opened. The system can also use the input from these sensors to log when and for how long the cabinet was open. In addition, the server's security system can be configured so that these alerts are paged or send via email to network administrators or technicians. Likewise, each server chassis in the rack should be equipped with a locking front panel and an intrusion alarm so that it can also create an alert if the server chassis is opened. The locking front panel prevents unauthorized access to the server's drives and front panel controls.

Finally, the server room door should be lockable, preferably using a security keypad. It should be designed to lock automatically when it shuts. If you are designated to work in the server room, you should make sure that the door closes behind you when you enter or exit the room. Propping the door open may make it a little easier for you to come and go, but it also provides access for people who are not authorized to be in the room. If the door has windows for viewing purposes, they should be made of security glass that has wire screens embedded in the glass to prevent individuals from gaining access by breaking the glass.

The network administrator is generally responsible for determining which personnel can have access to the server room and may require a logbook entry for anyone working inside the server room. The presence of unauthorized individuals in the server room should be reported to the network administrator. Violations of any server room security measures should be reported to the network administrator for corrective action.

Backup Tape Access

A good security system limits access to network backup tapes. Backup tapes typically contain a company's valuable proprietary data. Anyone who gains access to those tapes could retrieve this information and misuse it. Backup tapes should be stored in rooms or cabinets that can be locked with a key. There should also be a sign-in/sign-out sheet for tracking access to the tapes. There should be two sets of backup tapes kept—one onsite and the other offsite. In both locations, fireproof safes are the most secure containers for backup tapes.

Passwords

The first line of protection for access to servers and server rooms, as well as information in individual PCs, is the password. Passwords are used to prevent access to a room, a computer, or the contents of the computer depending on where it is implemented. For passwords to be effective, they must possess a certain amount of complexity. Their length, width, and depth must be sufficient to thwart password-cracking techniques. The longer the password is, the more difficult it is to crack. Typically, passwords should consist of between six and nine characters.

Password width relates to the number of different types of characters incorporated. Combinations of numbers, special characters, and uppercase/lowercase letters make passwords stronger. Windows operating systems do not incorporate case sensitivity and do not differentiate between characters such as "W" and "w". Passwords can contain control characters, alternate characters, and even spaces in some operating systems. Ideally, all the following character sets should be drawn from when creating passwords:

- ▶ Uppercase letters such as A, B, C

- ▶ Lowercase letters such as a, b, c

- ▶ Numerals such as 1, 2, 3

- ▶ Special characters such as $, ?, &

- ▶ Alternate characters (special characters created in combination with the Alt key)

Password depth refers to how difficult it is to guess its meaning. Although a good password should be easy to remember, it should be difficult to guess. The meaning of a password should not be something that could be easily guessed or deduced through simple reasoning. Passwords must be changed regularly to continue being effective. Some environments require users to change passwords as often as once a month, whereas in other settings, passwords are changed every three or four months. Many administrators choose to prevent users from reusing their passwords through the use of a password history.

You should be aware that users quickly become frustrated if they can't remember their passwords—especially if it is due to complexity or change requirements. However, the act of writing down or storing passwords should be avoided whenever possible. Users should never talk about their passwords with anyone, other than known system administrators, no matter how harmless or legitimate such conversation might seem. This includes third-party service personnel who might find it convenient to temporarily use the operator's password to perform work on their PC. These technicians should be granted the proper level of access and their own temporary access information from the network administrator. Such discussions should be conducted in person, and never over the telephone or through email.

EXAM ALERT

Remember that true password security involves the users safeguarding their password from others. Be aware of situations where the users might realistically need to share their password.

You can use several items to educate users about effective and noneffective password strategies. Phrases can be used to create passwords that cannot be easily guessed but that do not need to be written down to be remembered. The first letters in each word of a memorable phrase can be used to create the password (for example, Ihnybtf—"I have not yet begun to fight!"). You can also convert some of the letters into alternative characters (for example, the number "4" can be substituted wherever the letter "f" is used).

On the other hand, users should avoid using conventional words with numbers added to their ends, or with numbers substituted for similar-looking letters. Using a zero for the letter O will not provide much password security. The same caution is recommended for using conventional words in reverse. How long can using "krowten" hold off a determined or sophisticated hacker?

PC Hardware Security

Although it is not practical to limit physical access to PCs in most situations, several methods are commonly used to limit possession of the computer and to limit what unauthorized people can do with the computer. These methods can be as simple as installing polarizing films over displays to prevent others from viewing information displayed on the screen, or as extreme as chaining computer equipment to furniture or other suitable structures to keep it from being removed.

Polarizing screens are placed in front of displays and permit the user sitting directly in front of the display to view the information onscreen. The polarizing feature prevents others from viewing the screen from an angle.

Some portable systems also have lockable docking stations that secure the notebook and docking station to a structure such as a desk. Other organizations encase the system units inside furniture to keep them from being removed. Access doors provide access to the drive openings and the on/off switch. This leaves only the keyboard, video display, and pointing devices vulnerable to removal.

When it's not feasible to physically lock up the hardware, hardware devices can be used to make the system unusable by people other than authorized users. These devices include such items as smart cards and biometric devices.

Smart Cards

Smart cards are authentication tools that contain information about its owners, such as their passwords, personal identification numbers (PINs), network keys, digital certificates, and so on. Physically, smart cards exist as smart, credit-card-like devices, ID badges, and plug-in devices that communicate with a smart card reader.

The smart card reader may communicate with the reader through magnetic stripes or wirelessly. The reader generally is installed in the PC, or it attaches to or plugs into one of the PC's serial, USB, or PCMCIA ports. Figure 24.1 depicts a typical smart card device used with PCs.

Internally, all smart card designs contain a microprocessor and memory devices that are embedded in the card structure. The memory section of the smart card holds user-specific identification information, as well as all the programming it needs to communicate with the host system—the Card Operating System (COS). The programmability of the smart card enables it to work with changing password strategies and to pass tokens and certificates back and forth with network hosts to provide secure network interactions.

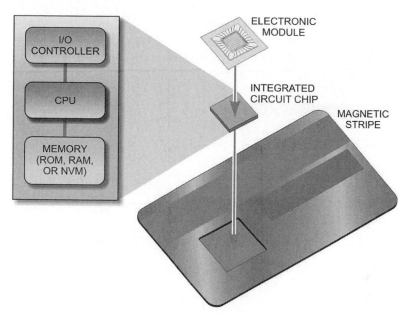

FIGURE 24.1 Smart cards.

Some organizations that use smart cards issue their employees smart cards that they can use get into their buildings, log on to their PCs, and access appropriate applications. The card system combines the users' secret PINs (something the users alone know) with tokens generated by the network's Certificate Authority authentication system to generate a unique pass code. The pass code validates the users and their access to different resources.

The IC devices in smart cards are embedded in a manner that makes them resistant to tampering. As a matter of fact, tampering with a smart card generally disables it. In addition, some care must be taken with smart cards because even bending one may render it unusable.

Windows 2000 and XP support Personal Computer/Smart Card (PC/SC) compliant smart card readers through the PnP process. Therefore, no external device drivers need be loaded for these smart-card readers. However, the Windows Smart Card Services must be enabled in the Computer Management console. Windows also provides smart card–secured login support when authenticating to Active Directory domains.

In Windows 2000, right-click the connection (Dial-up, VPN, or Incoming) that you want to use the smart card in the Network and Dial-up Connections window and choose Properties. In Windows XP, click the desired connection in Network Connections and select the Change Settings of This Connection option under Network Tasks. In either Windows 2000 or XP, click the Typical (Recommended Settings) option on the Security tab, depicted in Figure 24.2. Next, click the Use Smart Card option in the Validate My Identity as Follows dialog box.

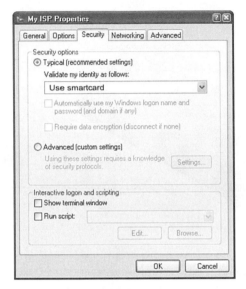

FIGURE 24.2   Selecting smart card validation.

Checking the Advanced (Custom Settings) check box and clicking the Settings button will bring up the Advanced Security Settings window. On this page, you can configure custom security settings for data encryption and logon security. Under the Logon Security entry, click the Use Extensible Authentication Protocol (EAP) option; then click Smartcard or Other Certificate (Encryption Enabled), click Properties, and choose the appropriate setting for the certificate you want to use: Use My Smartcard or Use a Certificate on This Computer.

NOTE

EAP is an extension of the PPP protocol and is the authentication protocol associated with smart cards, token cards, and secure VPNs. It offers better protection against brute force attacks (where all possible combinations of characters is attempted) and password-guessing attempts than other authentication protocols.

Biometric Authentication Devices

Biometric authentication involves using uniquely personal physiological characteristics to verify that people are who they say they are. Every person possesses unique physical characteristics that differentiate him or her from everyone else.

Even identical twins have separate and distinctive DNA, voice patterns, fingerprints, eye features, and other characteristics. The qualities most often involved in biometric authentication include voice patterns, fingerprints, palm prints, signatures, facial features, and retinal and iris scans, as shown in Figure 24.3.

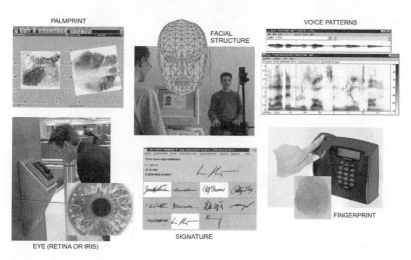

FIGURE 24.3 Typical biometric authentication methods.

In each case, a biometric scanning device is required to convert the physiological quantity into a digital representation. The results are stored in a database where they can be used in an authentication process. The underlying application will use the truly unique qualities of the data as a basis to compare to future access requests. If the data from a future authentication request matches the key points of the stored version, access will be granted.

Not all biometric scanning devices are equally accurate at authenticating users. The characteristics of the human eye—iris and retinal scans—tend to make it the most reliable source of authentication. Whereas fingerprint readings tend to be more accurate than voice scans, fingerprints can be stored on a clear surface and used later. On the other hand, illnesses and user stress levels can affect voiceprints.

In general, biometric scanners are getting significantly more sophisticated—including face-scanning devices, searchable databases, and supporting application programs. However, the biometric authentication device most widely used with PCs is the fingerprint scanner. Some manufacturers offer miniature touch pad versions that sit on the desk and connect to the system though a cable and USB connector. Other fingerprint scanners are built into key fobs that plug directly into the USB port. Some manufacturers even build these devices into the top of the mouse. Figure 24.4 shows different fingerprint scanner devices designed for use with PCs.

FIGURE 24.4 Fingerprint scanners.

Most fingerprint scanners come with password-management software that enables users to manage access to Internet accounts, encrypted documents, and other options secured with a password. For USB-based scanners, the scanner's application software is generally installed in the host machine first. Next, the scanner is physically attached to one of the system's USB ports. When the system is started up, the PnP process should detect the new hardware component and bring up its Installation Configuration Wizard to guide you through the setup process.

The setup process typically involves entering passwords and usernames for different accounts. Because the users will not be asked to input their passwords, passwords can be long and quite complex. This makes it much harder for the password to be cracked.

The password manager's Enrollment Wizard will prompt you to identify which finger, or fingers, you intend to use. Afterward, it will ask you to place that finger firmly and securely on the scanner pad and press selected keys to submit the scan into the system. The fingerprint scanner application uses the image to build the authentication database. The reason for scanning multiple fingerprints is to provide login options for occurrences such as injured/bandaged fingers. The other finger scans serve as a backup for these occasions. The user may also be asked to repeat the scanning process multiple times on each finger to ensure that a good print is taken and stored. Likewise, you can use multiple fingerprint reads to identify multiple users for a single computer.

NOTE

Some fingerprint scanners actually store the scanned images and the account access information on the device. This allows the identification file to travel with the user if the user works with different computers at different locations.

After the fingerprint scanner software has been installed and configured, the password manager will prompt you to scan in your fingerprint rather than type a password on future login attempts. Software supplied with some fingerprint scanner models can log users in to local Windows systems as well as into a domain environment with a quick, simple finger scan. This feature undermines keystroke-logging spyware that attempts to monitor and steal passwords and usernames.

The fingerprint scanner support software typically includes encryption functions that incorporate the fingerprint as the key. The supporting applications often include utilities for storing other information routinely used in authenticated transactions.

Microsoft provides a proprietary fingerprint scanner for standalone and home computers. However, this scanner does not work with domain logins. Therefore, it is not practical for use in domain-based business environments. In addition, it will not work with non-IE web browsers such as Firefox.

Information Disposal/Destruction Policies

People and businesses generate and collect piles of information each day in the normal course of living and working. Without proper forethought and planning, these piles can become a source of information for unauthorized and/or malicious people and businesses. Access to certain types of information can enable these people to commit crimes such as identity theft, intellectual property theft, and monetary theft. For this reason, it is a good idea to have an information disposal and destruction policy. This policy should address the handling of information in the following areas:

- Waste paper handling
- Electronic file storage
- Network information

Waste paper includes documents, notes, memos, files, and folders that are no longer useful in day-to-day activities. All these items should be shredded and removed or shredded and burned because they may contain information that others could use to do damage.

However, not all old files and folders should be destroyed. Some types of information are required to be stored for various periods of time after they are no longer current. Files such as tax records, bank records, personnel files, and audit files may need to be protected rather than destroyed.

Environmental Security Issues

People with sinister motives are not the only threats to computers and data—so are the environmental conditions around the server room and the computer/networking equipment. The presence of dust on the equipment or discolored ceiling tiles (indicating that there may be a water leak of some type) should gain your attention because these are environmental indicators of possible future problems. Dust can build up on electromechanical equipment and cause it to wear or overheat, and the leak could drip liquid into the equipment, causing it to fail.

> **EXAM ALERT**
>
> Be aware that the presence of water in a server room, or near networking/computing equipment, poses a security risk to equipment and data.

Software Security

Files and folders of electronic information can collect on hard drives, backup tapes, floppy disks, and CD-ROMs. As with waste paper products, old floppies, backup tapes, and CD-ROMs should be erased and destroyed when they are no longer useful. Methods used to destroy storage media such as outdated floppy disks and tape backups include incineration, shredding, using acid, or preferably by demagnetizing.

You can demagnetize floppy disks and backup tapes using strong magnets to electronically erase them. Simply erasing the files from the disk or tape does not actually remove the recorded data from them. Several commercially available software tools can restore erased data from a magnetic disk. Other stronger tools can be used to restore old data from magnetic disks even after they have been overwritten.

> **EXAM ALERT**
>
> *Degaussing* is a magnetic method used to remove data from floppy disks, tape back-ups, and even hard drives.

Waste paper and obsolete magnetic storage materials cannot simply be disposed of without being destroyed first. Unscrupulous individuals called *Dumpster divers* go through trash receptacles, trying to find items such as credit card information, account information, shipping receipts, phone numbers, and even scribbled passwords that they can use to undermine people's lives and businesses.

> **EXAM ALERT**
>
> Be aware that enforcing a policy that requires the destruction of waste paper and obsolete magnetic media that is no longer used is the best prevention against Dumpster diving.

Another major security threat that is often overlooked occurs when systems are updated with new hard disk drives. It is a simple matter to migrate any desired data over to the new drive and put the old drive away in case it can be used for something else later. However, that information still resides on the old drive and left alone, it can remain for many years. Because the drive is no longer in a machine where physical and electronic access to its data is controlled, it becomes a security risk.

Data migration operations can become a security problem when the data is not removed from the old machine and it is assigned to a new user. For example, if a manager receives a new notebook and transfers his data from the old machine to the new machine without removing the data when he is finished, and that machine is then reissued to an employee, the employee can gain access to the data. It's not difficult to see how this could be a problem because the employee has access to potentially sensitive information.

When information from an NTFS partition is moved to a FAT partition, the NTFS attributes and security features are lost. Even moving files between different NTFS partitions on different drives can change the security level of data. Migrating NTFS data to a partition that has lower permission levels than the original partition will cause the data to inherit the lesser permissions of the target folder.

It is a good security move to convert any FAT or FA32 partitions to NTFS so that the stronger NTFS and share permissions can be used to provide stronger control over access to data on the drive. This will also allow you to use the NTFS encrypting file system to protect files on the drive.

Disposal and Destruction Policies

Without a disposal and destruction policy, the same thing can happen when old computers are decommissioned and replaced. The drives still hold their information for a long time and, generally, no one is paying attention to where they are and who might be accessing them. At a minimum, the data on these drives should be erased. There are also commercially available software tools for cleaning information from drives. However, these tools generally do not conduct the low-level format procedure on the hard drive required to completely erase it. Many hard drive manufacturers provide downloadable low-level format tools that can be used to remove any remnant of data from their drives.

> **NOTE**
>
> If a hard drive is to be stored or reused in a different capacity, it should be low-level formatted before it is removed from the original system. This will provide some measure of security for the data it originally held.

If a hard disk drive is not going to be reused, it should be rendered physically unusable—not just logically unusable. This can involve opening the outer cover of the drive and physically scarring its disk surfaces. Scratching the surface with a sharp implement, hammering the disks, or pouring acid on the disk surfaces will render the drive and the information in it useless. You can also use a powerful magnet to magnetically erase data from the disks. However, this method must be applied thoroughly to the disks, as some data remnants may remain on the disk surfaces that professional data collectors can still detect.

Backup tapes and discs pose the same security risks as hard drives do. Old backup tapes contain information that, in the wrong hands, can be used in a mischievous or malicious manner. The network administrators or their designated subordinates are typically responsible for controlling access to backup tapes. Current tapes should be kept in a physically secure place (in a locked cabinet or in a locked room) away from general access. However, these copies should be handy to the administrators in case they need access to them to restore the system.

In many companies, multiple backup copies are created. At least one copy is kept offsite so that it will survive any catastrophic failures, such as fires or floods. In some cases, copies are performed over the Internet to remote third-party facilities to add additional physical security to the data. When the tapes become obsolete, they should be physically and logically destroyed in the same manner as hard disk drives.

Windows Network Security

One of the main features of the Windows 2000 and Windows XP Professional operating systems is their array of security options. As operating systems designed to work in business networks, data security is one of the most important functions of the Windows NT line of products. The Windows 2000 and XP Professional operating systems provide security in four forms:

- ▶ User security in the form of user logon and psswords is required to access the system.

- ▶ User security between users of the same computer controls access to local data.

- ▶ Identification of attempted security breaches through audit trails.

- ▶ Memory usage protection between applications running on the same hardware.

All users must have a user account on a particular computer to gain access to its operation. In a workgroup setting, this account must be set up on each computer. However, in a domain environment, the account can be established on the domain server.

When Windows 2000 or XP is first installed, a master administrator account is established. The administrator account has rights and permissions to all the system's hardware and software resources. The administrator uses this account to grant rights and permissions to other users as necessary. The administrator can deal with users on an individual basis or may gather users into groups that can be administered uniformly. In doing so, the administrator can assign permissions or restrictions on an individual or an entire group. The value of using groups lies in the time saved by being able to apply common rights to several users instead of applying them one by one.

Each user and group in the Windows environment has a *profile* that describes the resources and desktop configurations created for them. Settings in the profile can be used to limit the actions users can perform, such as installing, removing, configuring, adjusting, or copying resources. When users log in to the system, it checks their profile and adjusts the system according to their information. In Windows 2000 and Windows XP Professional, this file is located at \Documents and Settings\login_name\NTuser.dat.

> **NOTE**
>
> The location given for the ntuser.dat file assumes a clean install of Windows 2000 or XP or an upgrade from Windows 2000 or 98/Me. If the system was upgraded from Windows NT 4.0, the ntuser.dat file would be located at \WinNT\Profiles.

The Windows 2000 or 2003 Server operating system can be used to establish profiles for the entire network from a central location. Its administration package can also be used to establish roaming profiles that enable users to log in to any workstation on the network and work under their own profile settings. The administrator can also cause the content of each user's local My Documents folder to reside on the server instead of the local desktop. This option provides safe, centralized storage for user files by enlisting the server's security and backup functions to safeguard the data.

Portable computer users in the business world typically spend some time connected to a company network and other times traveling away from the network connection. The Windows Synchronization Manager enables the user to select network files and folders and to travel without an active connection to a server. When the client wants to take files, the files are moved from the server to the portable and the Synchronization Manager synchronizes the time and date version information concerning the files. While the portable client is offline, the user can continue to use the files under their network names. When the user returns to the network environment, the client resynchronizes the files with the server versions and the newer copy overwrites the older version.

Windows 2000/XP Professional portability features are not limited to mobile computers. Many organizations have mobile employees that work at different computers within a given location. To accommodate this type of mobility, Windows 2000 and Windows XP provide for roaming profiles that can be employed to store each user's desktop, Start menu setup, and My Document folder on the server and redirect them to the local client where the user logs in. Windows 2000 and XP can also automatically install applications the users require on the local client when they log on.

Administering Windows Networks

The sheriff on any network is the *network administrator*. These individuals create user and group accounts for network members that include specific access rights and permissions to the network and its resources. Network users are allowed or denied access to read, modify, and examine files and folders based on the access control policy that is established for them either as individuals or by their position in different network groups. In most organizations, the network administrators establish policy statements that control who has access to the network and its resources and what those users can do with them.

Windows 2000 and XP Professional are both designed for use in an administrated LAN environment. As such, they must provide network administrators with the tools necessary to control users and data within the network. To empower the network administrator, Windows 2000 and XP furnish five powerful administrative tools:

- ▶ System policies

- ▶ User profiles

- ▶ Groups and group policies

- ▶ Network share permissions

- ▶ NTFS rights

Each of these tools is designed to enable administrators to limit or grant users' access to files, folders, services, and administrator-level services.

Windows 2000/XP Policies

The overall operation of the Windows network environments is governed by system policies. Basically, policies give administrators control over users. Using system policies, the network administrator can give or limit users' access to local resources, such as drives and network connections. Administrators can establish policies that force certain users to log in during specified times and lock them out of the system at all other times. System Policies also enable the administrator to send updates and configure desktops for network clients. Fundamentally, any item found in the Control Panel can be regulated through system policies.

User Profiles

Windows 2000 and Windows XP employ profiles to provide customized operating environments for users. Users are assigned a profile directory under their username the first time they log in to a given Windows system. This profile contains system information and settings that become particular to the user and that are stored under the Documents and Settings directory.

Inside the directory, the system creates the ntuser.dat file, along with various other data files. As discussed previously, this file contains the user portion of the Windows Registry. This file contains the user-specific settings that have been established for this user. When the user logs on to the system, the User and

System hive portions of the Registry are used to construct the user-specific environment in the system.

The first time a user logs on to a system, the default User Profile directory is copied into the directory established under the user's name. When the user makes changes to the desktop, Start menu, My Documents, and so on, the data is stored in the appropriate files under the username. Windows 2000 and Windows XP provide methods of storing user profiles on the server in a networked environment. This prevents the user's profile directories from being re-created at each machine the user logs in to. Instead, these operating systems provide roaming profiles that are downloaded from the server to the client when the user logs in. Changes made during sessions are uploaded to the server when the user logs out.

Group Policies

Windows 2000 and Windows XP environments function on Group Policy Objects (GPOs). Group policies are the Windows 2000/XP tools for implementing changes for computers and users throughout an enterprise. The Windows 2000 and XP group policies can be applied to individual users, domains, organizational units, and sites. In addition, the Windows 2000/XP policies are highly secure.

In Windows 2000 and Windows XP Professional systems, policies are established through the Group Policy Editor (GPE) shown in Figure 24.5. Administrators use this editor to establish which applications different users have access to, as well as to control applications on the user's desktop.

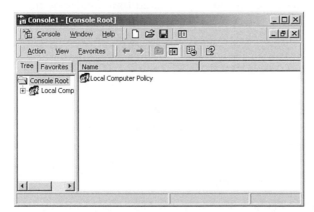

FIGURE 24.5 The Windows 2000 Group Policy Editor.

With group policies, administrators can institute a large number of detailed settings for users throughout an enterprise, without establishing each setting manually. GPOs can be used to apply a large number of changes to machines and users through the Active Directory. These changes appear in the GPE under three headings:

▶ Software Installation Settings

▶ Windows Settings

▶ Administrative Templates

Each heading appears in two places: the first version is listed under Computer Configuration and the second copy is found under User Configuration. Values will usually differ between the versions of the headings because the user and computer settings will be different.

▶ The Software Installation Settings heading can be used to install, update, repair, and remove applications.

▶ The Windows Settings portion of the GPO contains startup and shutdown scripts as well as security settings. The Security Setting portion of this heading covers such topics as account policies, password policies, and user rights assignments, to name a few.

▶ The Administrative Templates portion of the GPO stores changes to the Registry settings that pertain to the HKEY_LOCAL_MACHINE.

Administrative Security Settings

Administrative activities associated with implementing network security policies include the following:

▶ Establishing user and group accounts

▶ Implementing authentication options

▶ Enabling system auditing and event logging

▶ Establishing firewall settings

▶ Establishing and implementing malicious software protection policies

Establishing User and Group Accounts

These accounts are configured to allow or deny access to system and network resources. In a Windows environment, the administrator can use local and group policies, share permissions, and NTFS permissions to restrict access to resources to just those individuals or groups that need them. Even if a user is granted access to certain resources, the administrator can limit the scope of activities the user can conduct with different files and folders.

Local users and groups exist in the local Windows 2000 or XP accounts database. They are used to gain initial access to the computer, control access to its local resources, and to control access to network resources. These accounts are created and managed through the Local Users and Groups utility under Computer Management, as depicted in Figure 24.6.

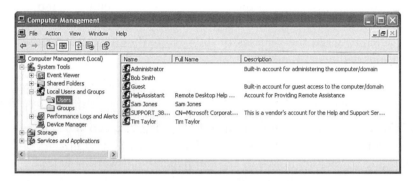

FIGURE 24.6   Managing local user and group accounts.

There are several default user accounts in Windows 2000 and XP. These accounts include the following:

- ▶ Administrator—The main administrative management account that has full access to the system and all its management tools.

- ▶ Guest account—A catchall account used to provide access to users who do not have a user account on the computer. This account should be disabled after user accounts have been established.

- ▶ HelpAssistant—A special Windows XP account used with its Remote Assistance utility to authenticate users connecting through it. This account is enabled whenever a remote assistance invitation is created, and it is automatically disabled when all invitations have expired.

- ▶ SUPPORT_XXXXX—A special Microsoft account used to provide remote support through the Help and Support Service utility.

The Windows default user accounts can be renamed but not deleted. The initial Windows Administrator account password is set up during the Windows installation process.

Administrators use group accounts to collectively deal with user accounts that have common needs. Groups save administrators time by allowing them to issue user rights and resource access permissions to everyone in the group at once. You cannot use a group account to log on to a computer. You can gain access to a system only by logging on with a legitimate user account.

The default group accounts in Windows 2000 and XP Professional include the following:

- ▶ Administrators—Members of this group have full access to the computer and its tools and can perform all management functions. This group automatically includes the Administrator user account as a member.

- ▶ Guests—This default group has minimized access to the system, and all members share the same user profile. The Guest user account is automatically a member of this group.

- ▶ Power Users—Power Users is a special group that has permissions to perform many management tasks on the system but does not have the full administrative privileges of the Administrator account. Power Users can create and manage users and groups that they create. However, they do not have access to files and folders on NTFS volumes unless they are granted permissions to them through other sources. There are no members in this group when it is created.

- ▶ Backup Operators—As the name implies, members of this group can back up and restore all files on the computer. Through the Backup utility, members of this group have access to the system's entire file system. There are no members in this group when it is created.

- ▶ Network Configuration Operators—Members of this group can manage different aspects of the system's network configuration. In particular, they can modify TCP/IP properties, enable, disable, and rename connections, and perform IPCONFIG operations. This group is empty when it is created.

- ▶ Users—This is a catchall group with limited default permissions. Except for the Guest account, all user accounts created on the system, including the Administrator account, are made members of this group by default.

- ▶ Remote Desktop Users—Members of this Windows XP group have user rights to log on to the system remotely to perform Remote Desktop activities. The group has no members by default.

EXAM ALERT

Remember the default capabilities of the standard groups in the Windows environment.

NOTE

Whenever possible, the default group accounts in Windows should be used to assign permissions. Creating additional groups generates additional system management requirements.

Domain User and Group Accounts

Windows 2000 and XP Professional systems also support domain user and Group accounts when used in a domain environment. Domain accounts are created on Windows domain controllers through the Active Directory Users and Computers utility and are stored in the Active Directory database. When a Windows 2000 or Windows XP computer is placed in a domain environment, some group memberships are automatically changed to reflect this:

▶ The Domain Admins group is added to the local Administrators group so that domain administrators will have administrative control over all the computers in their domain.

▶ A Domain Users group is added to the local Users group.

▶ A Domain Guests group is added to the local Guests group.

These groups are all are a function of the Windows domain controllers and exist only in Windows domain environments. The automatic addition of these groups in domain environments makes it easier for domain administrators to configure access to the local computer's resources. The groups are not permanent additions and can be removed at the administrator's discretion.

Implementing Authentication Options

Windows 2000 and Windows XP offer a much-improved security structure over previous Windows versions. The new security features apply to both LAN and wide area communications. The main security improvement is the adoption of the Kerberos authentication protocol. *Authentication* is a process that verifies that users on the network are who they say they are.

The Kerberos protocol enables users to authenticate without sending a password over the network. Instead, the user acquires a unique key from the network's central security authority at login. The domain controller referred to as the *Key Distribution Center* (*KDC*) provides the security authority.

When a client makes a request to access a network resource or program, it authenticates itself with the KDC as described in Figure 24.7. The KDC responds by returning a session ticket to the client that is used to establish a connection to the requested resource. The ticket can be used to authenticate the client's access to services and resources for only a limited amount of time. During that time, the client presents the ticket to the application server that verifies the user and provides access to the requested program.

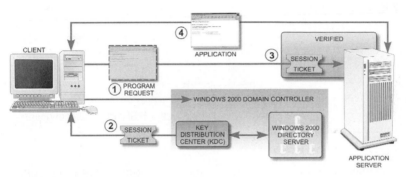

FIGURE 24.7   Kerberos protocol operations.

The key is cached on the local machine so that the user can reuse the key at a later time to access the resource. Keys are typically good for about eight hours, so there is no need for repeated interaction between the user and the KDC. This reduces the number of interactions that must be made across the network and thereby reduces the traffic load on the network in general. In addition, no passwords are circulated during the process, so there is no chance of compromising them.

Digital certificates are another major security feature in the Windows 2000 and Windows XP operating systems. Digital certificates are password-protected, encrypted data files that include data that identifies the transmitting system and can be used to authenticate external users to the network through virtual private networks (VPNs).

VPNs use message encryption and other security techniques to ensure that only authorized users can access the message as it passes through public transmission media. In particular, VPNs provide secure Internet communications by establishing encrypted data tunnels across the WAN that cannot be penetrated by others.

When the certificates are combined with security standards such as the IP Security (IPSec) protocol, secure, encrypted TCP/IP data can be passed across public networks such as the Internet. IPSec is a secure, encrypted version of the IP protocol. IPSec client software connects remote users to a VPN server by creating an encrypted tunnel across the Internet to the remote user, as illustrated in Figure 24.8.

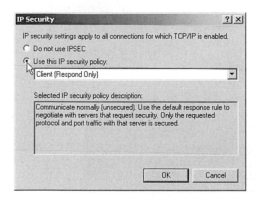

FIGURE 24.8 IP Security protocol operations.

In addition to IPSec, Windows 2000 and Windows XP continue to offer Point-to-Point Tunneling Protocol (PPTP) and Layer 2 Tunneling Protocol (L2TP) as alternative security technologies for VPNs. L2TP can be used in conjunction with IPSec to pass the IPSec packets through routers that perform network address translation.

Password Policies

The main user authentication tool is the username and password login. In Windows 2000 and XP Professional, there are two types of user related logons to contend with: the interactive Windows logon to the local machine and the Network logon. The first logon validates the user for local computer resources, whereas the latter confirms the user's credentials for accessing remote resources.

The administrator also sets the network password policy for how often users must change their passwords as well as setting length and complexity requirements. The options in the Password Policy folder, shown in Figure 24.9, enable administrators to make user accounts and passwords more secure. Password policies apply to all users who log on to the system and cannot be configured for individual users.

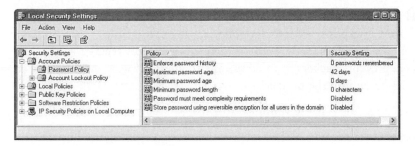

FIGURE 24.9 Password policies.

As the figure indicates, the Password Policy folder is accessed through the Local Security Settings utility. From this folder, administrators can configure the following settings:

▶ Enforce Password History—This option is used to specify the number of passwords that will be tracked for each user. When users attempt to change their password, they will not be permitted to reuse any of the passwords being tracked.

▶ Maximum Password Age/Minimum Password Age—These two settings enable administrators to set passwords so that they expire after the specified number of days, and also to prevent users from changing their password for some specific number of days. When apassword expires, the user is prompted to change it, ensuring that even if a password becomes public, it will be changed within a short period of time to close the security breach.

▶ Minimum Password Length—This option is used to specify the minimum number of characters that a password may contain. This allows the administrator to force users to employ passwords that are longer and harder to guess. A password of at least eight characters is recommended for secure systems.

▶ Passwords Must Meet Complexity Requirements—Administrators can use this option to force users to use more secure, complex passwords that include some combination of lowercase letters, numbers, symbols, and capitalized characters. The administrator sets the level of complexity by establishing password filters at the domain controller level.

▶ Store Password Using Reversible Encryption for All Users in the Domain—This is a special Active Directory domain option that permits passwords to be recovered in emergency cases.

Account Lockout Policy

Windows provides a password lockout policy setting that enables administrators to enact password policies that prevent users from repeatedly trying to access the system. This prevents hackers from being able to guess the account password so that they can break into the network.

In Windows 2000 and XP, the administrator has lockout policy settings for

▶ How long the account will be locked out after a preconfigured number of failed login attempts—*Account Lockout Duration*. Setting this value to 0 will prevent the account from unlocking until the administrator manually resets it.

▶ How many times account access can be attempted before the account is locked out—*Account Lockout Threshold*. The default value for this setting is 0, which disables the account lockout function.

▶ The amount of time that can pass before the account lockout value is returned to 0—*Reset Account Lockout Counter After*.

> **EXAM ALERT**
>
> Be aware of the default lockout setting for failed access attempts in Windows.

Enabling System Auditing and Event Logging

In a Windows network, auditing is established at the server level and event logging can be set up at the local level. The auditing functionality of Windows 2000 and Windows XP enables the user and operating system activities on a computer to be monitored and tracked. This information can then be used to detect intruders and other undesirable activity.

The auditing system consists of two major components: an *audit policy*, which defines the types of events that will be monitored and added to the system's security logs, and *audit entries*, which consist of the individual entries added to the security log when an audited event occurs. The system administrator implements audit policy. Audit entries are maintained in the security log, which can be viewed through the Event Viewer. For auditing to be an effective security tool, the security log should be reviewed and archived regularly.

Auditing is configured through the Audit Policy option located under the Administrative Tools menu, as shown in Figure 24.10.

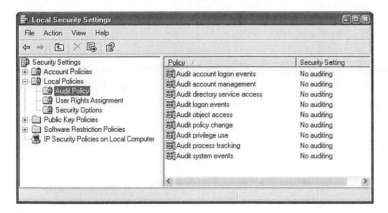

FIGURE 24.10   Configuring auditing.

In the right pane, open the policy to be configured (or right-click it and select Properties). This will produce the Local Security Setting window, depicted in Figure 24.11. Place check marks beside the option or options that should be tracked and audited—Success, Failure, or both—and click the OK button to save the setting and close the policy setting window.

FIGURE 24.11   Establishing a local security policy setting.

In domain-based environments, auditing can be automated through Active Directory group policies to save administrators the time that would be involved in setting up audit policies on all the computers in their network.

NOTE

You must be logged in as an administrator to configure audit policy.

Auditing must be configured both as a general system policy setting and on each object (file, folder, and printer) that requires auditing. With this in mind, when you are configuring an audit policy, you must consider what effect the policy will have on the system and its performance. If you were to set up auditing on every file, folder, and printer in a system, the auditing process would place so much extra work on the system that the system could literally slow to a halt.

To configure auditing on a file or folder on an NTFS disk, open Windows Explorer, right-click the file or folder to be audited, and select the Properties option. Move to the Security tab and click the Advanced button. From the Auditing tab, click the Add button to bring up the Select User or Group window. Add the users or groups whose access should be audited (if you want to audit all accesses, select the Everyone group) and click the OK button. This will bring up the Auditing Entry window depicted in Figure 24.12. Select the items to configure the type of accesses that you want to audit for the object and then click the OK button to exit.

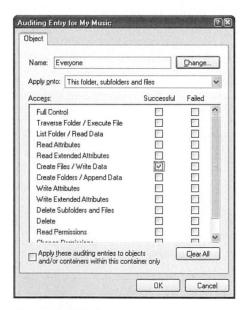

FIGURE 24.12   Configuring an auditing entry.

> **NOTE**
>
> To audit files and folders, they must exist on an NTFS disk.

The process for configuring auditing on a printer is very similar. The printer's properties are accessed through the Printer folder and the options for events to audit on printers include successful and failed attempts to

- ► Print

- ► Manage printers

- ► Manage documents

- ► Read permissions

- ► Change permissions

- ► Take ownership

Establishing Wireless Security

Although wireless networks are gaining popularity for their ease of installation, a number of security issues exist concerning using them to communicate personal or otherwise sensitive information. Transmissions from wireless network devices cannot be confined to the local environment of a residence or business. Although the range is typically limited to a few hundred feet, radio frequency signals can easily be intercepted even outside the vicinity of the stated security perimeter. Any unauthorized mobile terminal can accomplish this using an 802.11 receiver.

To minimize the risk of security compromise on a wireless LAN, the IEEE-802.11b standard provides a security feature called *Wired Equivalent Privacy* (*WEP*). WEP provides a 128-bit mathematical key encryption scheme for encrypting data transmissions and authenticating each computer on the network. Enabling the WEP function adds security for data being transmitted by the workstations. WEP is included on most access points (APs) and is relatively easy to install.

EXAM ALERT

Be aware of the security-related problems associated with wireless networking and know how to compensate for them.

All the computers in the network must be configured to use the same key to communicate. Therefore, if you enable WEP on the AP, you will need to enable the same WEP key on each computer in the network. WEP is enabled and configured by returning to the browser-based configuration wizard and accessing the WEP settings page (the same page as the SSID and channel settings). If the configuration wizard provides for multiple encryption levels, you should select the highest (strongest) level of encryption.

You will also need to enter the WEP key value (password), either in the form of a hexadecimal number string or as an ASCII character string. The ASCII option is easier for most people to work with. Record this string for use with the network's client computers. Each client computer will need to have the key installed the next time it attempts to connect to the network. When requested by the system, enter and confirm the WEP key.

Although WEP is a strong encryption method, serious hackers can crack it. This has led the wireless industry to create a stronger Wi-Fi Protected Access (WPA) standard. WPA adds improved data encryption using Temporary Key Integrity Protocol (TKIP) and IEEE 802.1X Extensible Authentication Protocol (EAP) user authentication protocol to provide increased security. This combination requires users to use usernames and passwords to access the network. After the user logs in, the AP generates a temporary key that is used to encrypt data transfers between the AP and the client computer.

A newer version of WPA, called WPA2, is supported in Windows XP. This WPA version fully implements the security mechanisms for wireless networks called for in the IEEE-802.11i standard. The original WPA standard implemented only a subset of this standard. WPA2 mandates both TKIP and AES encryption capabilities for secure data transmissions. WPA2 provides excellent wireless LAN security using a high level of encryption and choice of strong and stronger authentication protocols.

> **NOTE**
>
> Be aware that there are two organizations involved in this discussion: the Wi-Fi Alliance and the IEEE organization. Therefore, the definitions used by either side may not correspond to those used by the other. In particular, you may encounter two versions of WPA and WPA2: one that supports a single version of EAP and another that supports five different types of EAP developed by different vendors. This may make it difficult to match products that are certified as WPA or WPA2 compliant.

If possible, you should set up the router to use WPA-PSK along with a strong encryption key. The PSK option enables WPA to use pre-shared keys instead of a separate certificate authority (CA) computer to provide user authentication. The PSK option allows a password to be set on the router and shared with the rest of the users. If the router does not offer WPA as an option, check the router manufacturer's website for a firmware upgrade. While you are there, you should also check for driver upgrades to enable WPA-PSK to work on the wireless network cards.

If WPA is not an option, you should enable WEP with 128-bit encryption. In addition, after you've installed and authenticated all the wireless clients, you should set the SSID Broadcast option to Disable so that outsiders do not use SSID to acquire your address and data. Also change the SSID name from the default value if you have not already done so.

> **EXAM ALERT**
>
> Know which wireless security options should be used in given scenarios.

Establishing Firewall Settings

Firewalls are configured to pass only those services actually needed and used by the network's users. In a business network environment, the administrator controls firewall installations and configurations. This is done at the router/gateway and server levels of the network. In Windows XP, the local user can configure the built-in Internet Connection Firewall (ICF)—changed to simply *Windows Firewall* with SP2 installed.

The Windows Firewall feature is designed to provide protection from outside attacks by preventing unwanted connections from Internet devices. Computers connected directly to the Internet are vulnerable to attacks from the outside. Recall that a *firewall* is a device (or program) that is placed between an internal network, such as a corporate intranet, and an outside network (the Internet). The firewall is used to inspect all traffic going to and coming from the outside network and can be programmed to control traffic flow between the networks based on desirable properties.

The Windows Firewall service is designed to protect individual computers that are directly connected to the Internet through dial-up, LAN, or high-speed Internet connections. Proper installation and configuration of the Windows Firewall service can provide a strong protective barrier between Windows XP Professional and the outside network. When combined with the Windows ICS service, Windows Firewall can be configured to provide Internet access to multiple computers through a single connection. Windows Firewall should be enabled on the shared external connection to secure communication for all internal clients.

Firewalls work by examining the front end (header) of network packets as they are received. Depending on how the firewall is configured, it may look at the header information and permit it to pass through the firewall or block it from going through. By default, the Windows Firewall service will block all connection requests initiating from outside its network. It will permit only incoming traffic to come through that it recognizes as a response to a request from inside the network. The firewall knows which responses are acceptable because it maintains a table of outgoing connection information for itself and any computers on the local network that are sharing the Windows Firewall connection.

However, the Windows Firewall function can be configured with filters to enable specific traffic to enter the network. For example, if web or FTP services are running on the internal network and must be made available to external customers, you can configure a filter to open the firewall to let just that service pass through.

Normally, these filters are configured around services recognized by the TCP and UDP networking protocols. These protocols use port numbers to identify specific processes such as HTTP or FTP. These ports are 16-bit numbers that refer incoming messages to an application that will process them. Many of the port numbers are standardized and are referred to as *well-known ports*. Similarly, their associated applications are called well-known services.

Table 24.1 lists several well-known port numbers and their provided services. The Internet Assigned Numbers Authority (IANA) has assigned standard port numbers ranging from 0 to 1023 to specific services. Port numbers from 1024 through 65535 are called *ephemeral ports* and are not assigned by the organization. Instead, they are frequently employed in user-developed programs.

TABLE 24.1 Well-Known Ports

SERVICE	WELL-KNOWN PORT NUMBER
FTP	21, 20
Telnet	23
SMTP Mail	25
HTTP (WWW)	80
POP3 (Mail)	110
News	144
HTTP	443
PPTP	1723
IRC	6667

When the firewall examines the incoming packet, it can read the source and destination IP addresses of the packet and any TCP/UDP port numbers. It will use the IP address and port information in the packet headers to determine whether an incoming packet should be routed into the internal network. If you have configured the firewall with the IP address of an internal computer that provides

FTP services and opened ports 20 and 21, the firewall will recognize the IP address and port numbers in the incoming header as valid and route the packet to that computer. However, all other incoming requests will still be blocked.

To enable the ICF function in Windows XP prior to SP2, open the Network Connections applet, right-click the connection (dial-up, LAN, or high-speed Internet) that you want to protect, and select the Properties option from the menu. Then, in the Internet Connection Firewall section of the Advanced tab, check the Protect My Computer and Network by Limiting or Preventing Access to This Computer from the Internet check box and click the OK button. In a network that is using ICS, only the outgoing Internet connection should use the ICF feature. The other computers in the internal network should not have their ICF enabled.

With the addition of Windows XP SP2, the Windows operating system implemented the Windows Security Center. Under this update, the ICF became known simply as the Windows Firewall and was moved under the Security Center icon in the Control Panel. To enable the Windows Firewall function in Windows XP SP2, you can still open the Network Connections applet, right-click the connection (dial-up, LAN, or high-speed Internet) that you want to protect, and select the Properties option from the menu. However, the route through the Control Panel/Security Center icon is more convenient.

Inside the Security Center, click on the Windows Firewall icon and select the desired level of firewall filtering on the General tab. If you select the On (Recommended) option, you can configure the firewall to allow connections from different programs and services through the Exceptions tab. The firewall's Advanced tab is used to enable network connections for use. You can use the adjacent Settings button to configure services running on the network that Internet users can access.

The Settings button in the Security Logging area of the Advanced tab can be used to create networking logs for troubleshooting purposes. The default log file can be found at \Windows\pfirewall.log.

Using the Encrypting File System

Windows 2000 and Windows XP both provide effective local hard drive security through their Encrypting File System (EFS) feature. The EFS feature enables the user to encrypt files stored on the drive using keys only the designated user (or an authorized recovery agent) can decode. This prevents theft of data by those who do not have the password or a decoding tool.

> **NOTE**
>
> EFS prevents files from being accessed by unauthorized users, including those trying to bypass the operating system and gain access using third-party utilities. However, EFS is not available on Windows XP Home Edition.

Windows 2000 and XP Professional users can implement the EFS option to encrypt their files and folders on NTFS drives. To do so, they simply click the Encrypt Contents to Secure Data check box in the file or folder's Advanced Attributes windows. Users can open these files and folders just as they would any ordinary files or folders. However, if someone gains unauthorized access to the computer, that person will not be able to open the encrypted files or folders. EFS is simple to use because it is actually an attribute that can be established for files or folders.

The EFS feature further enhances the security of files on portable computers by enabling users to designate files and folders so that they can be accessed only by using the proper encryption key. Public key encryption techniques employ two keys to ensure the security of the encrypted data: a public key and a private key. The public key (known to everyone) is used to encrypt the data, and the private or secret key (known only to the specified recipient) is used to decrypt it. The public and private keys are related in such a way that the private key cannot be decoded simply by possessing the public key.

> **EXAM ALERT**
>
> Know how to enable file encryption in the Windows environment.

Locking the Computer

Users should never leave their computer unattended after they have logged on. Doing so opens the door for others to access and manipulate their computer, data, and network. All users should be trained to either log off or lock their computers when they are away from them, even if only for a few minutes. Locking the computer protects it from intruders and preserves the current system state. When the computer is unlocked, the applications and data that were active in the system are still open, making it much easier for users to pick up where they left off. Users should also be instructed to make sure they log off at the end of the day. This closes all applications and ensures that data files are saved.

In Windows 2000 and XP, the computer can be locked from the keyboard by pressing Ctrl+Alt+Delete to open the Windows Security dialog box, as shown in

Figure 24.13. Click the Lock Computer button. The Unlock Computer dialog box will appear and the user will need to enter the username and password in the Unlock Computer dialog box and click the OK button to unlock the computer. If the user who locked the computer is unavailable to unlock it, an administrator will have to do so. In this event, the current user will be logged off, all applications will be closed, and any unsaved data will be lost

FIGURE 24.13 The Windows Security dialog box.

Users can also click the Change Password button on the Windows Security dialog box to change their password at any time. Doing so will bring up the Change Password dialog box, as shown in Figure 24.14, with the user's User Name and Log On To information already present. The user simply needs to enter the old and new passwords as indicated and click the OK button. If all the information was entered correctly, a message will appear indicating that the password was successfully changed. If not, a different message will be displayed indicating that there is a problem and that the information needs to be entered again.

FIGURE 24.14 The Change Password dialog box.

Administrators can use this dialog box to change users' passwords, but in Windows-based networks they can use their much more powerful Local Users and Groups utility or the Active Directory Users and Computers utility to change user passwords without knowing the old one. In either utility, the administrator can change a user's password by right-clicking the user's account and selecting the Set Password entry in the context menu.

Malicious Program Security

Increased connectivity through networks and the Internet have made PCs vulnerable to an array of different types of malware and grayware. *Malware* is the term used to describe programs designed to be malicious in nature. The term *grayware* describes programs that have behavior that is undisclosed or that is undesirable. Common malware and grayware programs include the following:

▶ Viruses

▶ Trojan horses

▶ Worms

▶ Spyware

▶ Adware

▶ Hacking tools

The first three entries in the list belong to the malicious malware category and are generally associated with computer viruses. The last three entries fall into a category of mischievous and obnoxious grayware programs.

Viruses

Computer viruses are destructive programs designed to replicate and spread on their own. Viruses are created to sneak into personal computers. This most often occurs when users download programs from the Internet or open infected email attachments. Many "free" products obtained from the Internet have something attached to them—either a virus or spyware or some other form of malware. If a deal is free or seems too good to be true, it probably is. You should download only materials that you are reasonably sure you can trust. Also, open only email attachments from trusted sources. No one is hoping to do you a favor or give you money, trips, or gifts on the Internet.

Sometimes viruses take control of a machine to leave a humorous message, and sometimes they destroy data. After they infiltrate one machine, they can spread into other computers through infected disks that friends and co-workers pass around, or through local and wide area network connections. There are basically three types of viruses, based on how they infect a computer system:

▶ A boot sector virus—This type of virus copies itself onto the boot sector of floppy and hard disks. The virus replaces the disk's original boot sector code with its own code. This allows it to be loaded into memory before anything else is loaded. After it is in memory, the virus can spread to other disks.

▶ A file infector—*File infectors* are viruses that add their virus code to executable files. After the file with the virus is executed, it spreads to other executable files. A similar type of virus, called a *macro virus*, hides in the macro programs of word processing document files. These files can be designed to load when the document is opened or when a certain key combination is entered. In addition, these types of viruses can be designed to stay resident in memory after the host program has been exited (similar to a terminate-and-stay-resident [TSR] program), or they might just stop working when the infected file is terminated.

▶ Trojan horses—This type of virus appears to be a legitimate program that might be found on any system. Trojan horse viruses are more likely to do damage by destroying files, and they can cause physical damage to disks. In newer definitions, Trojan horses are not referred to as viruses because they do not replicate or attach themselves to other files. Instead they are made to appear to be applications so that users will be tricked into using them. Although they appear to work properly, they have a malicious code hidden inside that gathers information by monitoring network behavior. Some Trojan horses establish an additional user or administrator account, whereas others remain dormant in the background until a back door becomes available for an attack. Back door Trojan horses make use of specific service port numbers to invade systems. Therefore, a firewall or router must be used to limit access to these ports to reduce the threat of these types of attacks. For example, a Trojan horse might be designed to mimic the operation of the system's telnet service. If a user opens the telnet service, the user would be unaware that the malicious code was recording each activity that occurred.

▶ Computer worms—*Computer worms* are malicious programs that destroy the host by replicating until the disk space, memory, and other system resources have been consumed. They do not infect other programs as viruses do. Worms are typically introduced into the system when users view an email attachment that contains the worm.

EXAM ALERT

Be able to identify different types of virus and know how they are different from other malicious software programs.

A number of different viruses have been created from these three virus types. They have various names, but they all inflict basically the same damage. After the virus file has become active in the computer, it resides in memory when the system is running. From this point, it might perform a number of types of operations that can be as complex and damaging as the author designs them to be.

For example, a strain of boot sector virus, known as *CMOS virus*, infects the hard drive's master boot record and becomes memory-resident. When activated, the virus writes over the system's configuration information in the CMOS area. Part of what gets overwritten is the HDD and FDD information. Therefore, the system cannot boot up properly. The initial infection comes from booting from an infected floppy disk. The virus overwrites the CMOS once in every 60 bootups.

A similar boot sector virus, referred to as the *FAT virus*, becomes memory resident in the area of system memory where the OS kernel files are located. This allows it to spread to any non–write-protected disks inserted into the computer. In addition, the virus moves the system pointers for the disk's executable files to an unused cluster and rewrites the pointers in the FAT to point to the sector where the virus is located. The result is improper disk copies, inability to back up files, large numbers of lost clusters, and all executable files being cross-linked with each other.

In another example, a file infector virus strain called the *FAT table virus*, infects EXE files but does not become memory-resident. When the infected file is executed, the virus rewrites another EXE file.

EXAM ALERT

Know how the different types of viruses attack the system.

Likewise, TSR viruses create copies of themselves in system memory. Then they intercept system events such as a disk access and use this operation to infect files and sectors on the disk. In this manner, TSR viruses are active both when an infected program runs and after it terminates. Because the resident copy of these viruses remains viable in memory, even if all the infected files are deleted from the disk, it is very difficult to fully remove these viruses from the system.

Removing TSR viruses by restoring all the files from distribution disks or back-up copies does not work well because the resident copy of the virus remains active in RAM and infects the newly created files.

Virus Symptoms

Because viruses tend to operate in the background, it is sometimes difficult to realize that the computer has been infected. Typical virus symptoms include the following:

- ► Hard disk controller failures.

- ► Disks continue to be full even when files have been deleted.

- ► System cannot read write-protected disks.

- ► The hard disk stops booting, and files are corrupted.

- ► The system will boot to floppy disk but will not access the HDD.

- ► An `Invalid Drive Specification` message is displayed when you attempt to access the C: drive.

- ► CMOS settings continually revert to default values even though the system board battery is good.

- ► Files change size for no apparent reason.

- ► System operation slows down noticeably.

- ► Blank screen when booting (flashing cursor).

- ► Windows crashes.

- ► The hard drive is set to DOS compatibility, and 32-bit file access suddenly stops working.

- ► Network data transfers and print jobs slow down dramatically.

Common practices that increase the odds of a machine being infected by a virus include use of shareware software, software of unknown origin, or bulletin board software. One of the most effective ways to reduce these avenues of infection is to buy shrink-wrapped products from a reputable source.

EXAM ALERT

Know how viruses are spread.

Establishing and Implementing Malicious Software Protection

It is common to install a number of defensive products to protect PCs and their data from unauthorized access and malicious interference. The products most widely used for these purposes include the following:

▶ Antivirus programs

▶ Antispyware programs

▶ Spam blockers

▶ Pop-up blockers

Antivirus Software

Another means of virus protection involves installing a virus-scanning (antivirus) program that checks disks and files before using them in the computer. Several other companies offer third-party virus-protection software that can be configured to operate in various ways. If the computer is a standalone unit, it might be nonproductive to have the antivirus software run each time the system is booted up. It would be much more practical to have the program check floppy disks or writable CD-ROM disks because this is the only possible non-network entryway into the computer.

A networked or online computer has more opportunity to contract a virus than a standalone PC because viruses can enter the unit over the network or through the modem. Therefore, all computers with connections to the Internet should be protected by an antivirus solution before they are ever attached to the Internet. In these cases, setting the software to run at each bootup is more desirable. In addition, most antivirus software includes utilities to check email and files downloaded to the computer through network or Internet connections.

> **EXAM ALERT**
>
> Be aware that any computer connected to the Internet is a potential target for viruses and other malicious software types.

Most antivirus suppliers provide their products in multiple formats. They usually sell boxed commercial versions as well as Internet download versions. In addition, they typically provide automatic update services that periodically notify you of new threats and provide new virus definition databases (these programs work by comparing the characteristics of received files to profiles associated with known virus types). A subscription service is usually provided to continue the update service after the initial usage period has expired.

As indicated earlier, when an antivirus application is installed on the system, it can be configured to provide different levels of virus protection. You will need to configure when and under what circumstances you want the virus software to run.

Challenge #1

A customer calls you to his site complaining that the wide-carriage, dot-matrix printer in his Accounting department is running very slowly and that users cannot get all their invoices printed for today's shipping purposes. When you check their print queue, you see that the print jobs for the invoices are stacked up in the queue but that they aren't being processed. The Accounting manager tells you that they typically don't have any problems getting their invoices printed and that nothing out of the ordinary has been done to the computer to make it slow down. What items should you check to determine the cause of the slowdown?

Boot Sector Virus Protection provided through the system CMOS is not exactly a virus protection tool. What this feature does is provide a warning whenever the boot sector is accessed for writing. The warning screen allows you to disable the access or to continue. This feature can be extremely annoying if you use programs that need to write to the boot sector as part of their normal operation. Boot Sector Virus Protection is completely useless for SCSI drives because they use their own BIOS on the controller.

Removing Viruses

Even if users are meticulous about keeping their antivirus software updated and regularly run virus scans on their PCs, it is still possible to pick up a virus. New viruses appear at a fast pace and sometimes they will hit your PC before your antivirus program can be updated to protect the system.

If you can access your antivirus program, immediately run a scan on your PC using the current virus definitions. If this does not identify the virus and stop its operation, download the latest virus signatures from the manufacturer and re-scan your system. Microsoft also offers a Malicious Software removal Tool for Windows 2000 and Windows XP. This tool is available as a download from the Microsoft Update, Windows Update, or Microsoft Download Center.

If you can reach the Internet from the infected machine, there are several free removal tools and scanning utilities that can be downloaded and run to identify and possibly remove viruses from your infected machine. There are also virus definitions sites that you can find on the Internet. These sites list the virus, what it does, and where it gets installed in the system.

You can use the MSCONFIG utility to check for suspicious programs that get launched at startup. Also check the Task Manager for suspicious programs running on the system (typical applications running in Windows are well documented on the Internet). Perform a Google search on any suspect programs or services running in the system before you stop or remove it—it might just be a program or service you actually need.

If the virus has made it impossible for you to access updated virus signatures and utilities, you may need to obtain an antivirus tool on a CD. You can use this CD to boot the system and run a virus scan. This will probably require that you create the CD from an uninfected PC and download the newest security patches and definitions.

In cases of severe infections, your only option may be to partition your drive and reinstall the operating system and applications. Hopefully, you have a recent backup copy of your important files.

EXAM ALERT

Be aware of options available after a PC has been infected with a virus.

Grayware

Grayware is a general classification for applications that have behavior that is undisclosed or that may be annoying or undesirable. Grayware programs can perform a variety of undesired and threatening actions, such as irritating users with pop-up advertising, logging user keystrokes, and exposing computer vulnerabilities to attack. The different categories of grayware include the following:

▶ Spyware—Programs that hide and record Internet surfing habits, typically without the user's consent.

▶ Adware—Programs that display unintentional advertising on the system's screen.

▶ Dialers—Programs that invade and change Internet configuration settings. The infected system dials preconfigured telephone numbers through a modem. These numbers are typically long distance numbers, toll numbers, or international numbers that can leave the host with large telephone bills.

- ▶ Jokes—Programs that invade the system and alter the operation of the system in a nondestructive way.

- ▶ Password crackers—Programs designed to steal usernames, passwords, and account information.

- ▶ Spam—Undesirable junk email and unsolicited advertisements.

Although grayware programs do not harm the performance of infected computers, they do adversely affect their operation. In addition, they can introduce significant security, confidentiality, and legal risks to an organization.

Spyware

Spyware programs are generally introduced to the system through Internet downloads that appear to be useful programs (similar to Trojan horses). They can also be acquired through music-sharing downloads. Unlike viruses and Trojan horses, spyware programs typically don't self-replicate. After spyware is installed on the system, it monitors the system's operation and collects information such as usernames, passwords, credit card numbers, and other confidential information. The program then transmits the information to its author while the host system is online.

Although most spyware is used to gather marketing information, it can also be used in malicious activities such as identity theft and credit card fraud. Some spyware has been delivered to user computers in the form of rogue antispyware programs that actually contain spyware. Some spyware products are designed so that they can disable antivirus and firewall software. Others can alter browser security settings to open the system to other types of attacks.

One particularly troubling method of distributing spyware is where programmers create fake notices that tell users they have been infected and that they need to download their antispyware product. The downloaded product is actually a spyware product.

Some spyware programs include other programs designed to protect them. In these cases, the protective program watches for efforts, either by software or by the user, to uninstall or terminate it. When this occurs, the protective program reinstalls the spyware or regenerates the Registry key that starts it. One way to circumvent this type of spyware is to start the system in Safe Mode and run the antispyware program.

Spyware-infected computers can accumulate a number of spyware components after the initial infection. This leads to degraded system performance because of elevated microprocessor, disk, and network activity created by the spyware.

Users may also encounter problems connecting to the Internet because of spyware activity. Some spyware versions even disable a competitor's spyware programs when they find them in a system. If a system becomes infected with several pieces of spyware, there may be no alternative but to back up its important data and perform a full clean install of the operating system and applications.

Because of its popularity, Microsoft Windows presents the biggest target for both mischievous and malicious malware and grayware writers. Therefore, Windows receives an unrivaled percentage of all the attacks associated with viruses and spyware. This fact has led some Windows customers to adopt other operating system platforms, such as Linux or Mac OS X, which are much less of a malware target.

Spyware Prevention

Several companies have created antispyware products. These include companies that specialize in antispyware products, companies that already specialize in antivirus products, and most recently Microsoft. Microsoft has licensed an antivirus product it relabeled as Windows Defender that will ship free with its future operating system versions (it is currently available as a free download for Windows XP, Windows 2000, and Windows 2003).

Windows XP Service Pack 2 (SP2) introduced several security features to the Windows operating system, such as the Windows Firewall, the Windows Security Center, and Pop-up Blocker for Internet Explorer. These enhancements were included to provide better protection from viruses, worms and hackers.

EXAM ALERT

Be aware of the security features added to Windows XP by SP2.

There are basically two types of antispyware products available: those that find and remove spyware after it has been installed and those that block spyware when it is trying to install. Both of these methods stand a better chance of keeping computers free from spyware when they are combined with user information about how to avoid spyware.

The detect-and-remove method is by far the simpler type of antispyware product to write. Therefore, several commercially available products use this method. Like antivirus software packages, this type of antispyware product relies on databases of existing definitions to recognize spyware threats. These databases must be updated frequently to recognize new spyware versions that have been identified.

The real-time prevention type of antispyware product does not rely on histori-cal data to identify spyware. Instead, it monitors certain configuration parame-ters and notifies the user when suspicious installation activity occurs. The user then has the option to allow or block the installation effort. Some antispyware products incorporate both methods of dealing with spyware.

In addition to installing antispyware applications, users can fight spyware in a number of other ways:

▶ Install a web browser other than Internet Explorer (for example, Mozilla Firefox).

▶ Download a newer Internet Explorer version that offers better security features.

▶ Work with an ISP htat uses its firewalls and proxies to block sites that are known to distribute spyware.

▶ Download software only from reputable sites to prevent spyware down-loads that come attached to other programs.

Adware

Adware programs introduce unwanted, unsolicited advertising displays to web browser screens. They can also be designed to gather user selection information from the browser. This information is used to tailor future advertising to the user. Adware is typically introduced to the system through downloads such as free software. Users actually agree to install these programs by accepting the End User Licensing Agreement (EULA) included in most software packages. Other adware programs are packaged with spyware so that they can do double duty to collect user preference information and tailor ads to take advantage of the acquired knowledge.

One of the problems with adware is that those who create adware products believe they are doing nothing wrong by clogging up people's computers with unasked for pop-up advertising. They also don't think there is anything wrong with placing things on other people's property without the owner's knowledge.

Spam

The term *spam* is used to describe the distribution of unsolicited undesirable email and advertisements. Spam is easy to create and cheap to distribute, so spammers use SMTP relay servers to flood the Internet with multiple copies of the same spam message. Getting rid of spam is time-consuming for the receivers. Because spam is legal in many places, it is difficult to regulate or elim-inate.

Malicious spammers can use SMTP relay techniques to flood email servers and create DoS attacks. The attack directs so many email messages at the server that it cannot handle the level of traffic. This effectively prevents clients that use that server from sending or receiving real email.

On a local level, users can establish spam filters and spam blockers through their ISPs or email service providers. These filters examine key features of email received to determine whether each piece is likely to be real email or spam. Suspected emails are rerouted to a holding area and do not show up in the user's email program.

Social Engineering

There are some malicious computer activities for which the only prevention method is to educate customers about them. Social engineering is one of these activities. Social engineers exploit people's human nature to fool them into providing information about themselves, their business, or their computer/network. They accomplish this by using trickery, deceit, lies, gifts, or acts of kindness to first establish a level of trust. They then use this trust relationship to gain information.

Typical social engineering ploys include using free sales pitches or personal notes of affection to get users to click something that downloads malicious code to their system. Other social engineering efforts can go to great lengths to get users to surrender their login information. For instance, the programmer may design a login screen that exactly mimics a login screen that you expect to see from a trusted site or company. In the background, the login screen passes your information back to the programmer.

Social engineering activities aren't limited to just the computer and network. It can also be used on a personal basis. For example, humans as a group typically desire to be helpful and friendly, particularly when the other person is in a position of importance to them (employers, co-workers, potential clients, relatives, or friends). The social engineer uses this fact to establish apparent relationships with people to gain their confidence and trust. After trust is established, the target feels freer to divulge personal and potentially secret information to the social engineer.

To combat such activities in the workplace, employees must be educated to the fact that these attacks occur and given examples of strategies used to get information from them. Organizations should have social engineering awareness training programs to bring these activities to their employees' attention. They should also have an incident reporting policy that tells employees how to report suspicious efforts in obtaining information from them.

Phishing

Many social engineers have devised techniques to illegally acquire information about people and companies through fraudulent means called *phishing*. On the Internet, phishing sites spoof (pretend to be) reputable sites but their real intent is to acquire user information such as usernames, passwords, and credit card information. Phishing expeditions typically begin with an email or instant messenger communication that points the target toward the spoofed site. These sites are often look-alikes for sites where financial activities are conducted, such as banks, online auction sites, and online stores or payment systems. They also tend to feature URLs that are closely related to the spoofed site—such as a misspelled URL, or using a part of the real URL as a subdomain.

These communications often ask the target to verify account or billing information to update what appears to be a legitimate account. After the attackers have acquired the information, they can manipulate the user's account for whatever purposes they want—such as stealing money from a financial account to stealing the victim's identity.

Users should also be educated about how to handle suspicious requests properly. They should know to ignore the request, delete the email message, and report the incident to their supervisors. However, they should not forward the request as this also poses a security risk.

Pharming

Phishing expeditions can often be detected by closely examining the URL of the spoofed site. To compensate for this possibility, attackers have developed URL-hijacking techniques, referred to as pharming, to switch fake addresses with real ones. These techniques exploits the Internet's DNS service to hijack legitimate URLs associated with HTTP pages. Then the attacker substitutes the link to the fake site so that when users enter the real URL address in their browser they are automatically routed to the spoofed page.

Pharming can also be performed in the local area network environment. The LAN's router can be attacked and reprogrammed to provide incorrect DNS server specification to the entire network. Under this scenario, every Internet access performed could be rerouted to a bogus DNS server established by the attacker, without the users knowing.

Residential-grade wireless routers are particularly vulnerable to pharming because they tend to be less well administered. Many are configured to work with only their default parameters configured. If attackers locate this router and guess the default administrative password, they can alter the router's firmware and administration for their use. These changes will be virtually undetectable for the vast majority of users.

To check for pharming activities, you can use the TCP/IP NSLOOKUP command to check the domain names associated with questionable IP addresses.

Session Hijacking

Session hijacking is a method of gaining unauthorized access to someone's computer by stealing cookies from one of user's legitimate Internet sessions. Recall that cookies are used to authenticate computers to remote servers and are routinely stored on user computers to provide quick access to web pages.

Attackers steal can steal these cookies by using a packet sniffer to capture cookies as they are passed across the network. They can also steal the cookie information from the PC if they can access the system by tricking it into believing the code it is receiving is from a trusted location such as the server. Once the attackers have obtained the cookie information, they can gain access to other privileged information.

> **EXAM ALERT**
>
> Know what type of malicious activity is associated with session hijacking.

Identity Theft

Much of the malicious activity associated with the Internet centers around the practice of identity theft. Identity theft is the use of someone else's personal identifiers to impersonate them for illegal activities. After attackers have gained access to someone else's personal information, they can use that information to obtain goods and services at that person's expense, misdirect authorities in the commission of crimes, assume the other person's identity, or obtain credit in that person's name.

As described earlier, identity theft is not limited to online or computer-based activities. Many identity thieves will go Dumpster diving to get information necessary to steal another person's identity. However, phishing, pharming, and social engineering efforts continue to fool computer users into giving up their personal information. As a technician, one of the best ways to limit these activities is to understand how these efforts work and educate your customers about how to avoid getting taken.

Exam Prep Questions

1. You install a new wireless network for a client. However, your client has been reading about network security and asks you to increase the security of the network while maintaining the wireless nature of the network. What do you suggest to accomplish this?

   ○ **A.** Turn on Wired Equivalent Privacy.

   ○ **B.** Connect all workstations to the wireless access point using CAT 5.

   ○ **C.** Install more wireless access points throughout the network.

   ○ **D.** Change the encryption from 40-bit keys to 16-bit keys.

2. Do viruses normally attack the system's CMOS settings?

   ○ **A.** Yes, this is how a virus attacks most computers.

   ○ **B.** No, viruses do not normally attack CMOS settings.

   ○ **C.** Yes, this is how viruses attack all computers.

   ○ **D.** No, viruses never attack CMOS settings.

3. How are most computer viruses spread from computer to computer?

   ○ **A.** By downloading programs from the Internet.

   ○ **B.** By individuals sharing infected files through disks and CDs, as well as over local area network connections.

   ○ **C.** By not formatting disks before using them.

   ○ **D.** By transferring files over modems.

4. _____ are relationships that enable users to move between domains and perform certain types of operations.

   ○ **A.** Trusts

   ○ **B.** Permissions

   ○ **C.** Rights

   ○ **D.** Privileges

5. The members of a _____ share a common directory database and are organized in levels.

    ◯ **A.** Workgroup

    ◯ **B.** Tree

    ◯ **C.** Group

    ◯ **D.** Domain

6. Which of the following is the strongest wireless encryption protocol?

    ◯ **A.** WPA

    ◯ **B.** WEP

    ◯ **C.** WPA2

    ◯ **D.** CHAPS

7. Members of the Power Users group have been trying to access the files of a user who has left the company. However, they can't get into them. Why is this?

    ◯ **A.** Power Users don't have access rights to a user's files and folders unless they created the user or they have been granted permissions through some other source.

    ◯ **B.** Only a file's owner or an administrator can access secured files.

    ◯ **C.** Power Users members have access to only their own files and system hardware configuration functions.

    ◯ **D.** Power Users have access to only the files allowed by an administrator.

8. You have been asked to connect a single Windows XP system to a broadband modem for Internet access. Which of the following actions should you take first to protect the PC from the Internet?

    ◯ **A.** Turn on the Windows Firewall feature and enable the file sharing option.

    ◯ **B.** Turn on the Windows ICS feature and enable file and printer sharing.

    ◯ **C.** Install an antivirus software package before connecting to the Internet.

    ◯ **D.** Install spam blocker, adware, and firewall protection software before accessing the Internet.

9. There are technicians in the server room when you enter and you notice that the door has been braced open. What should you do?

 ○ **A.** Tell the technicians to close the door when they leave.

 ○ **B.** Report the security breach to the network supervisor.

 ○ **C.** Close the door and note the security breach in the server room log book.

 ○ **D.** Tell the technician they are creating a security breach and close the door yourself.

10. Which of the following is considered malicious software?

 ○ **A.** Adware

 ○ **B.** Pop-ups

 ○ **C.** Spam

 ○ **D.** Worms

11. Which of the following malicious software types is actually a virus?

 ○ **A.** Trojan horse

 ○ **B.** Spam

 ○ **C.** Worm

 ○ **D.** Spyware

12. Your company is donating several PCs to a local school, but your superiors are very concerned about other being able to retrieve proprietary information from the hard disk drives. Which of the following is a way to ensure sensitive data from an HDD is not retrievable?

 ○ **A.** Partition and completely reformat the drive.

 ○ **B.** Reinstall the operating system over the existing OS structure.

 ○ **C.** Delete all the files on the drive and perform a disk defrag operation.

 ○ **D.** Physically destroy the drive's platters with a hammer or a strong acid.

13. You are installing a wireless network in your apartment and will be performing work-related functions on days when you telecommute from home. Which of the following steps should you take to protect your wireless network from potential unauthorized user access in your apartment complex? (Select all that apply.)

    ○ **A.** Set up MAC address filtering on each card.

    ○ **B.** Configure the AP so that it doesn't broadcast the SSID.

    ○ **C.** Set up WEP on all network nodes.

    ○ **D.** Minimize the distance between network connections.

14. After a system becomes infected with a virus, what actions can be taken to remove it? (Select all that apply.)

    ○ **A.** Run an antivirus program to detect and remove the virus.

    ○ **B.** Reinstall the operating system over the infected OS structure.

    ○ **C.** Partition the drive and reinstall the operating system.

    ○ **D.** Install your original antivirus software CD and run it.

15. Which type of computer activity involves taking control of a legitimate user's web application session while it is in progress?

    ○ **A.** Social engineering

    ○ **B.** Spoofing

    ○ **C.** Session hijacking

    ○ **D.** Phishing

Answers and Explanations

  1. A. To minimize the risk of security compromise on a wireless LAN, the IEEE 802.11b standard provides a security feature called Wired Equivalent Privacy (WEP). WEP provides a method for encrypting data transmissions and authenticating each computer on the network.

  2. B. No, viruses do not normally attack CMOS settings. Most viruses attack files on disk drives and hang out in memory when the system is running. Only one type of infrequently encountered virus, known as CMOS virus, attacks the information stored in the CMOS area.

3. B. Although most infections come from downloading programs from the Internet or email attachments, after viruses infiltrate one machine, they typically spread into other computers through infected files that friends and co-workers share on disk or CD, or through local area network connections.

4. A. Trusts are relationships that enable users to move between domains and perform prescribed types of operations.

5. D. A client/server network is one in which standalone computers, called *clients*, are connected to and administered by a master computer called a *server*. Collectively, the members of the group make up a body called a *domain*. The members of the domain share a common directory database and are organized in levels. Every domain is identified by a unique name and is administered as a single unit having common rules and procedures.

6. C. WEP is a strong encryption method, but serious hackers can crack it. This has led the wireless industry to create a stronger Wi-Fi Protected Access (WPA) standard. A newer version of WPA, called WPA2, fully implements the security mechanisms for wireless networks called for in the IEEE-802.11i standard, making it the strongest encryption method typically used with wireless networks.

7. A. Power Users is a special group that has permissions to perform many management tasks on the system but does not have the full administrative privileges of the Administrator account. Power Users can create and manage users and groups they create.

8. C. Be aware that any computer connected to the Internet is a potential target for viruses and other malicious software types. Therefore, all computers with connections to the Internet should be protected by an antivirus solution before they are ever attached to the Internet.

9. B. The server room door should be lockable, preferably using a security keypad. It should be designed to lock automatically when it shuts. If you are designated to work in the server room, you should make sure that the door closes behind you when you enter or exit the room. Propping the door open may make it a little easier for you to come and go but it also provides access for people who are not authorized to be in the room. Violations of any server room security measures should be reported to the network administrator for corrective action.

10. D. Malware is the term used to describe programs designed to be malicious in nature. The common malware programs are viruses, Trojan horses, and worms.

11. A. Computer viruses, such as a Trojan horse virus, are destructive programs designed to replicate and spread on their own. After they infiltrate one machine, they can spread into other computers through infected disks that friends and coworkers pass around or through local and wide area network connections.

12. D. If a hard disk drive is not going to be reused, it should be damaged to the point where it is physically unusable—not just logically unusable. This can involve opening the outer cover of the drive and physically scarring its disk surfaces: scratching the surface with a sharp implement, hammering the disks, or pouring acid on the disk surfaces.

13. B, C. All the computers in the network must be configured to use the same key to communicate. Therefore, if you enable WEP on the AP, you will need to enable the same WEP key on each computer in the network. In addition, you should set the SSID Broadcast option to Disable so that outsiders do not use SSID to acquire your address and data.

14. A, C. If you can access your antivirus program, immediately run a scan on your PC using the current virus definitions. If this does not identify the virus and stop its operation, download the latest virus signatures from the manufacturer and rescan your system. If you can reach the Internet from the infected machine, there are several free removal tools and scanning utilities that can be downloaded and run to identify and possibly remove viruses from your infected machine. There are also virus definitions sites that you can find on the Internet. These sites list the virus, what it does, and where it gets installed in the system. In cases of severe infections, your only option may be to partition your drive and reinstall the operating system and applications. Hopefully, you have a recent backup copy of your important files.

15. C. *Session hijacking* is a method of gaining unauthorized access to someone's computer by stealing cookies from one of their legitimate Internet sessions.

Challenge Solution

1. This is a classic symptom of a virus infection in which the virus is using excessive amounts of memory, slowing down the computer's operation. The other possible cause of this symptom is a nearly full hard drive. The lack of disk drive space for the print spooler and other temporary files caused by either of these situations makes it difficult for the system to process information for the printer. Check the hard drive's Temporary folder for TMP files that have accumulated there.

CHAPTER TWENTY-FIVE

Safety and Environmental Issues

Terms you'll need to understand:

- ✓ Material Safety Data Sheets (MSDs)
- ✓ Disposal procedures
- ✓ Electrostatic discharge (ESD)
- ✓ Grounds
- ✓ Uninterruptible Power Supply (UPS)
- ✓ Surge suppressor
- ✓ Fire extinguisher
- ✓ Eye protection
- ✓ Brownouts
- ✓ Voltage sags
- ✓ Voltage spikes
- ✓ Transients
- ✓ Electrocution Shock (ESD) hazards
- ✓ Burn hazards
- ✓ Cardiopulmonary Resuscitation (CPR)

Techniques you'll need to master:

Essentials 7.1—Describe the aspects and importance of safety and environmental issues.

- ✓ Identify potential hazards and proper safety procedures.
- ✓ Use Material Safety Data Sheets (MSDSs) or equivalent documentation and appropriate equipment documentation.
- ✓ Use appropriate repair tools.
- ✓ Describe methods to handle environmental and human (electrical, chemical, physical) accidents, including incident reporting.

Essentials 7.2—Identify potential hazards and implement proper safety procedures, including ESD precautions and procedures, safe work environment, and equipment handling.

Essentials 7.3—Identify proper disposal procedures for batteries, display devices, and chemical solvents and cans.

Depot Technician Objectives 5.1/ IT Technician Objectives 7.1—Identify potential hazards and proper safety procedures, including power supply, display devices, and environment (trip, liquid, situational, atmospheric hazards, high-voltage, and moving equipment).

Work Area and Safety Issues

This chapter covers the Safety and Environmental Issues areas of the CompTIA A+ Certification—Essentials examination under Objectives 7.1, 7.2, and 7.3. It also covers the "Identify potential hazards and proper safety procedures" information that is specified in Objective 5.1 of the Depot Technician exam and Objective 7.1 of the IT Technician exam.

Safety is an issue in every profession. PC technicians must be aware of the potential hazards to personnel and equipment encountered when working with lasers, high-voltage equipment, and moving parts. They must also be aware of the potential causes and damaging effects of electrostatic discharge (ESD) so that they can prevent its occurrence. Many of the materials used in the construction of computer-related equipment can be ecologically harmful. Also, many of the products used to service computer equipment can have an adverse effect on the environment. Therefore, the technician should be aware of requirements associated with the disposal of this equipment and these materials.

> **NOTE**
>
> The Depot Technician 5.1 and IT Technician 7.1 objectives use the same wording to cover "Identify potential hazards and proper safety procedures." The information in these objectives expands the information specified in the "Identify potential hazards and proper safety procedures" and "Identify potential hazards and implement proper safety procedures including ESD precautions and procedures, safe work environment, and equipment handling" subobjectives from Essentials 7.1 and 7.2.
>
> The topics specified in these different exam/objective areas are so closely stated that it makes sense that they are presented as the same discussion. You will need to study this material in this chapter for any of the four exams you intend to challenge.

Being prepared is the most crucial element in a safe working environment. Simple steps that are often overlooked may prevent serious injuries to you or the people working around you. The tools and materials you work with have an important role in job safety. When dealing with safety considerations, knowing and understanding your working environment (and the potential hazards that may arise) is an important part of any safety program. For example:

▶ Always read any safety warnings that pertain to your equipment.

▶ Attend any safety training courses such as basic first aid and cardiopulmonary resuscitation (CPR), both offered by the American Red Cross.

The Work Area

The first order of business when you're working on any type of electronic equipment is to prepare a proper work area. You need a clear, stable, flat workspace to rest the PC system and its components on. Make sure that your workspace is large enough to accommodate the equipment. Confirm that you have an adequate number of power receptacles to handle all the equipment you may need. Try to locate your workspace in a low-traffic area.

The work area should include antistatic protection devices to protect static sensitive devices from electrostatic discharges (ESD). These discharges can build up on moving surfaces (including people) and damage the integrated circuit devices in the PC. The most common antistatic device is a grounding strap placed around the wrist or ankle while a technician is working on equipment. Antistatic mats for the floor and table are advised as well. These devices all work to channel static discharges away from sensitive devices.

Good lighting is a prerequisite for the work area because the technician must be able to see small details, such as part numbers, cracked circuit foils, and solder splashes. An adjustable lamp with a shade is preferable. Fluorescent lighting is particularly desirable. In addition, a magnifying glass helps to read small part numbers.

Cabling can become a trip or catch hazard if not managed properly. Cables should be run neatly and out of the walkway. If possible, signal and power cables should be just long enough to make the necessary connections without creating stress on the connector. Additional cable lengths should be coiled and secured neatly. If temporary cabling must be run in or across a walkway, it should be taped down to the floor or covered with a protective cover strip to prevent it from becoming a trip hazard.

EXAM ALERT

Know how to organize and run cables in a safe manner.

Power cables and signal cables should not be bundled together because electrical noise radiating from the power cable can disrupt digital signals moving across the signal cable. Power cables and signal cables should be run parallel to each other and be separated by at least 12 inches. If signal cables must cross power cables, they should do so at a 90-degree angle.

Liquids and electronic equipment do not play well together. Liquid refreshments such as water, coffee, and soft drinks should not be brought into the work area. The presence of water in the work area from other sources, such as leaking pipes or ceilings, should always be a cause for alarm and correction. Water leaks in the work area are generally the responsibility of the building maintenance supervisor. If the business does not have someone on staff that is responsible for building infrastructure, you should report the situation to whoever is responsible for the PCs and/or network so that they can properly shut the systems down.

EXAM ALERT

Be aware of how to handle potential environmental hazards in the work area.

Personal Safety

A good internal safety policy should be in place on every job site. For example, designate the location of the first aid kit, eyewash station, and chemical showers, as well as how to use each of them. A well thought out safety policy provides rules to which members of the organization can turn for guidance in the day-to-day execution of their work in an ever-changing environment.

When well prepared, a safety policy establishes the basic points of operational philosophy on which all employees can agree. These serve as the foundation for answering questions such as what to do? in the event of an emergency. Find and study the safety procedures for your organization.

Basic first aid and CPR certifications should be taken and renewed before their expiration. Safety training can also increase the level of commitment of employees to the organization and increase their perception that the organization is a good and safe place to work. Increased commitment can result in less turnover and absenteeism, thus increasing an organization's productivity.

Hand and Power Tool Safety

About 7% of industrial accidents involve the unsafe use of hand tools. These accidents result from using the wrong tool for the job, using the right tool incorrectly, or failing to follow approved safety guidelines. The following checklist provides some basic guidelines for the proper use of hand tools:

▶ Know the precise purpose for each tool in your toolbox, and use it only for the specific task it was designed to do.

▶ Never use any hand tool or power tool unless you are trained to do so.

- ▶ Inspect tools before each use; replace or repair tools if worn or damaged.

- ▶ Clean tools after every use and keep cutting edges sharp.

- ▶ Never test a cutting edge with your fingers; instead test it on scrap material.

- ▶ Select the right size tool for the job; don't use cheaters. A *cheater* is a tool that will do the job, but is the wrong tool for the job to be performed.

- ▶ Carry tools correctly; never place sharp or pointed tools in your pockets.

- ▶ When carrying tools by hand, point cutting edges away from you and toward the ground.

- ▶ Wear personal protective equipment, such as safety goggles, face shields, and gloves, as required.

When working with any tool, make sure to follow the manufacturer's recommended directions. Be sure to wear clothing that doesn't hang loosely or dangle. Safety guards for all tools should be in place and operable. Proper tool maintenance will also help to prevent disaster. If a tool is damaged or not operating properly, replace it immediately.

Avoiding High-Voltage Hazards

In most IBM compatibles, there are only two potentially dangerous areas: inside the CRT display and inside the power supply unit. Both of these areas contain electrical voltage levels that are lethal; however, they reside in self-contained units, and you will usually not be required to open either unit.

In fact, you should never enter the interior of a CRT cabinet unless you have been trained specifically to work with this type of equipment. The tube itself is dangerous if accidentally cracked. In addition, extremely high voltage levels (in excess of 25,000 volts) may be present inside the CRT housing, even up to a year after electrical power has been removed from the unit.

EXAM ALERT

Be aware of the voltage levels that are present inside a CRT cabinet.

In repair situations, the high-voltage charge associated with video displays must be discharged. This is accomplished by creating a path from the tube's high-voltage anode to the chassis. With the monitor unplugged from the commercial power outlet, clip one end of an insulated jumper wire to the chassis ground of the frame. Clip the other end to a long, flat-blade screwdriver that has a well-insulated handle. While touching only the insulated handle of the screwdriver, slide the blade of the screwdriver under the rubber cup of the anode and make contact with its metal connection. This should bleed off the high-voltage charge to ground. Continue the contact for several seconds to ensure that the voltage has been fully discharged.

> **EXAM ALERT**
>
> Be aware that a long, flat-blade screwdriver is the proper tool to use for discharging the high-voltage anode of a CRT tube.

Never open the power-supply unit. Some portions of the circuitry inside the power supply carry extremely high voltage levels and have very high current capabilities. Generally, no open shock hazards are present inside the system unit. However, you should not reach inside the computer while power is applied to the unit. Jewelry and other metallic objects pose an electrical threat, even with the relatively low voltage present in the system unit.

Do not defeat the safety feature of three-prong power plugs by using two-prong adapters. The equipment ground of a power cord should never be defeated or removed. This plug connects the computer chassis to an earth ground through the power system. This provides a reference point for all the system's devices to operate from, and supplies protection against electrical shock. In defeating the ground plug, a very important level of protection is removed from the equipment. You should remove all power cords associated with the computer and its peripherals from the power outlet during thunderstorms.

> **EXAM ALERT**
>
> Know the best way to protect computer equipment in an electrical storm.

Periodically examine the power cords of the computer and peripherals for cracked or damaged insulation. Replace worn or damaged power cords promptly. Never allow anything to rest on a power cord. Run power cords and connecting cables safely out of the way so that they don't become trip hazards or catch hazards.

Handling Shock and Electrocution

Basic first aid and CPR training should be taken and renewed annually. It is unlikely that the victim, when treated by a trained first-aid provider, will come to any additional harm, provided that the care and treatment is rendered in accordance with the provider's level of training. If there is the threat of death for the victim, first aid provided by an untrained person is better than the alternative. If first aid is administered quickly, but with due care, the victim may not suffer any additional harm.

To get expert medical assistance, call 911 as soon as possible. If you are attending to a casualty, get a bystander to telephone for help. If you are on your own, you will have to leave the victim momentarily to make a call. Use common sense, take your time, and act rationally. Before calling 911, remember to collect all valuable information, such as the following:

- ▶ The type of injury or illness the victim has

- ▶ The time the accident took place

- ▶ The address or location of the accident

- ▶ Information from the victim's medical alert bracelet or necklace, if any

- ▶ Any other important information that would help prepare the emergency response team before they arrive

EXAM ALERT

Remember that calling for qualified help is usually the first step in handling medical emergencies.

After medical assistance has been notified, you have more time to thoroughly examine the casualty by conducting a head-to-toe secondary examination. Your main goals are to attend to the victim's wounds and to keep the victim calm. Inform medical technicians of any and all relevant information when they arrive.

The human body is an electricity conductor. When a victim receives an electric shock, the electricity is conducted through the body. A casualty may receive significant burns, or the electric shock may interfere with the heart's electrical system. Electrical burns to the victim may be greater than they appear on the surface. When attending to a victim exposed to electricity, danger is the priority. Be alert for danger to yourself and to other rescuers, and approach the scene with caution. Electricity can be considered as two distinct types: residential voltage and high voltage.

It is critical that the casualty be disconnected from the electrical source, either by

▶ Turning off the power supply, disconnecting any plugs from the outlet, and isolating the electricity supply at the main power board if possible

▶ Removing the casualty from the electrical source by separation with non-conducting materials—for example, a wooden stick or board, a rope, or a blanket

CAUTION

Be careful not to touch the casualty's skin before the electrical source is disconnected. Also, be alert for the presence of water or conducting materials that may be in contact with you or the victim.

Avoiding Laser and Burn Hazards

Laser printers contain many hazardous areas. The laser light can be very damaging to the human eye. In addition, there are multiple high-voltage areas in the typical laser printer, and a high-temperature area to contend with as well.

It is sometimes necessary to bypass safety interlocks to isolate problems. When doing so, proper precautions must be observed, such as avoiding the laser light, being aware of the high temperatures in the fuser area, and taking proper precautions with the high-voltage areas of the unit. The laser light is a hazard to eyesight, the fuser area is a burn hazard, and the power supplies are shock hazards. Another potential burn hazard is the printhead mechanism of dot matrix, thermal wax, and dye sublimation printers. During normal operations, these elements become hot enough to be a burn hazard if touched.

EXAM ALERT

Know the areas of the computer system that are dangerous for personnel and how to prevent injury from these areas.

Because computers have the potential to produce these types of injuries, it is good practice to have a well-stocked first-aid kit in the work area. In addition, a Class-C fire extinguisher should be on hand. Class-C extinguishers are the type specified for use around electrical equipment. You can probably imagine the consequences of applying a water-based fire extinguisher to a fire with live electrical equipment around. The class, or classes, that the fire extinguisher is rated for are typically marked on its side.

Treating Burns and Scalds

Never clean burns or break blisters. Never remove any clothing that may stick to the burn. Also, never apply any type of grease, ointment, or medication on a severe burn. The three degrees of burns are

▶ First degree—Discoloration of skin surface (redness), mild swelling, and pain. Usually additional medical treatment is not necessary.

▶ Second degree—Deep burn with red or spotted appearance, blisters, considerable pain, swelling, and the surface of the skin appears wet. Burns may be potentially serious, requiring additional medical treatment depending on extent and location.

▶ Third degree—Severe tissue destruction with a charred appearance, but no pain. Seek professional medical help immediately.

For minor burns (first and second degree burns over less than 15% of an adult's body), cool the burn. Apply cool wet cloths or immerse in water. Apply a cold compress to the area to reduce swelling and conduct heat away from the skin. Do *not* use ice! Blot the burn gently and apply a dry sterile patch if necessary. The burn victim may want to take an over-the-counter pain reliever to lessen pain.

For major burns (that is, third degree burns and lesser burns over more than 15% of the body), call for emergency help right away. Make sure that the victim is no longer in contact with the heat source and is away from smoke if present. Do not remove burnt clothing or place the burned area in cold water. Make sure that the victim is breathing (if not, start CPR immediately). Cover the burn area with a cool, moist, sterile bandage.

Challenge #1

Your company is setting up a new sever room to house its main server systems. You are working with an electrician who is installing electrical outlets and running network cabling through the walls of the server and overhead in the ceiling to the places where you are setting up workstation PCs. You walk into the server room and find the electrician on the floor with a piece of cabling in his hand. The electrician is unconscious. The cabling disappears into the wall and you have no idea of where it runs to. Describe the steps you should take and the logical order they should be performed in given this situation. Also comment on any things that you should avoid while doing so.

System Protection

Computer technicians should be aware of potential environmental hazards and know how to prevent them from becoming problems. A good place to start checking for environmental hazards is with the incoming power source.

Power Line Protection

Digital systems tend to be sensitive to power variations and losses. Even a very short loss of electrical power can shut a digital computer down, resulting in loss of any information that has not been saved to a mass storage device. Typical power supply variations fall into two categories:

▶ *Transients*—Overvoltage conditions that can be classified as spikes (measured in nanoseconds) or as surges (measured in milliseconds).

▶ *Sags*—Undervoltage conditions that include voltage sags and brownouts. A voltage sag typically lasts only a few milliseconds, whereas a brownout can last for a protracted period of time.

The effects of power supply variations are often hard to identify as power issues. Brownouts and power failures are easy to spot because of their duration. However, faster-acting disturbances can cause symptoms not easily traced to the power source. Spikes can be quite damaging to electronic equipment, damaging devices such as hard drives and modems. Other occurrences may just cause data loss. Sags may cause the system to suddenly reboot because it thinks the power has been turned off. These disturbances are relatively easy to detect because they typically cause any lights in the room to flicker.

In general, if several components go bad in a short period of time, or if components go bad more often than usual at a given location, these are good indicators of power-related issues. Likewise, machines that crash randomly could be experiencing power issues. If "dirty" power problems are suspected, a voltage-monitoring device should be placed in the power circuit and left for an extended period of time. These devices observe the incoming power over time and will produce a problem indicator if significant variations occur.

> **EXAM ALERT**
>
> Be aware of how undervoltage and overvoltage situations are categorized (that is, their time lengths).

Surge Suppressors

Inexpensive power line filters, called *surge suppressors*, are good for cleaning up dirty commercial power. These units passively filter the incoming power signal to smooth out variations. There are two factors to consider when you choose a surge suppressor:

▶ Clamping speed

▶ Clamping voltage

EXAM ALERT

Know what type of devices will protect systems from minor power sags and power surges.

Surge suppressors protect the system from damage up to a specified point; however, large variations, such as surges created when power is restored after an outage, can still cause considerable data loss and damage. In the case of startup surges, making sure that the system is turned off, or even disconnected from the power source until after the power is restored, is one option.

Uninterruptible Power Supplies

In the case of a complete shutdown or a significant sag, the best protection against losing programs and data is an uninterruptible power supply (UPS).

EXAM ALERT

Know what type of device prevents power interruptions that can corrupt data.

Uninterruptible power supplies are battery-based systems that monitor the incoming power and kick in when unacceptable variations occur. The term *UPS* is frequently used to describe two different types of power backup systems. The first is a standby power system, and the second is a truly uninterruptible power system. The standby system monitors the power input line and waits for a significant variation to occur. The batteries in this type of unit are held out of the power loop and draw only enough current from the AC source to stay recharged.

Uninterruptible systems do not keep the batteries offline. Instead, the batteries and converters are always actively attached to the output of UPS. When an interruption in the supply occurs, no switching of the output is required. The battery/inverter section simply continues under its own power.

Standby systems generally don't provide a high level of protection from sags and spikes. They do, however, include additional circuitry to minimize such variations. Conversely, an uninterruptible system is an extremely good power-conditioning system. Because it always sits between the commercial power and the computer, it can supply a constant power supply to the system.

When dealing with either type of UPS system, the most important rating to be aware of is its volt-ampere (VA) rating. The VA rating indicates the capability of the UPS system to deliver both voltage (V) and current (A) to the computer, simultaneously. This rating differs from the device's wattage rating, and the two should not be used interchangeably. The wattage power rating is a factor of multiplying the voltage and current use, at any particular time, to arrive at a power consumption value.

Another significant specification for UPS systems is the length of time they can supply power. Because the UPS is a battery-powered device, it uses an ampere-hour rating. This is the same time notation system as that used for automobile batteries and other battery-powered systems. The rating is obtained by multiplying a given current drain from the battery by a given amount of time (for example, a battery capable of sustaining 1.5 amps of output current for one hour would be rated at 1.5 amp-hours).

The primary mission of the UPS is to keep the system running when a power failure occurs (usually long enough to conduct an orderly shutdown of the system). Because it's a battery-based system, it cannot keep the system running infinitely. For this reason, you should not connect nonessential, power-hungry peripheral devices such as laser printers to the UPS. If the power goes out, it is highly unlikely that you will have to print something before shutting the system down. If a UPS is used to keep a system in operation during a power outage, the high current drain of the laser printer would severely reduce the length of time that the UPS could keep the system running.

If the UPS is connected inline with the computer's power source, when a power line disruption occurs, the UPS will kick in and keep the computer running until the batteries are drained or the power is restored. However, UPS systems have the capability to communicate with a host computer so that an orderly shutdown of the system can be performed. The host computer can be a standalone desktop/tower unit that the UPS is guarding, or in a network environment, it can be a server that has network management capabilities for all the computers on the network. The host computer is typically connected to the UPS through a serial interface cable.

When a disruption occurs, the UPS notifies the power management system in the host computer's operating system of the failure. The power management utility for most operating systems can be configured to begin a prescribed shut-down schedule. This option is designed to give the system enough time to safely store any key information and prepare to be shut down. In the case of a server-managed network situation, the server can shut down different programs, com-puters, and support equipment at different times to conserve the battery life of the UPS, yet stay online as long as necessary.

The server can also be configured to notify system users that a shutdown will be occurring so that they can complete their tasks and shut down properly. At the same time, the host computer can issue a page or email alert to an administra-tor or service person to notify him or her that a problem has occurred and needs to be investigated.

The host computer sees the UPS device as another peripheral device. As a mat-ter of fact, when the UPS is first installed, the system's PnP process should detect the UPS as it would any other peripheral attached to one of its serial ports. Afterward, the system will see the UPS as another one of its installed devices.

Checking UPS Operation

A UPS system is a major component of any server system that must have a high level of availability. The UPS provides continued operation when power prob-lems arise and provides safety for data in process. However, a UPS is still an electronic device and is subject to failure. If the safety component of a system fails, the entire system becomes vulnerable.

Therefore, the UPS should be tested at regular intervals to ensure that it is func-tioning properly. The simplest UPS test is to unplug the UPS from the wall while the computer is running to make it supply power to the system through its batteries alone. You should measure the performance of the system against its configured shutdown schedule.

NOTE

Of course, you should be aware that any UPS testing should be performed while the com-puter is not in active use and when there is no chance of data loss occurring because of unexpected test results.

If the UPS does not supply the expected amount of backup time when it's test-ed, it may be overloaded, or its batteries may be wearing out. The first option is to unplug less-important equipment, such as laser printers, from the UPS. Afterward, attempt to recharge the batteries and retest the system. If this does not restore backup time to acceptable levels, consider replacing the batteries in the UPS.

Other common problems that can occur with UPS systems include the UPS not turning on, the UPS not turning off, the host computer running only on the UPS batteries, and the UPS not controlling the shutdown of the host computer. If the UPS system does not come on, verify the function of its on/off switch. If the switch functions properly, check the AC supply to the UPS by substituting a lamp or other handheld AC device in its outlet to verify that power is reaching the outlet. If power is available at the outlet, check the AC power cord at the outlet and the UPS. Next, check the input circuit breaker UPS, if present, to determine whether it is set or tripped. Finally, check the battery connector to make certain that it is fully engaged.

If the UPS operates on battery power even though AC power is available, the input circuit breaker may be tripped or the unit's input voltage sensitivity may be set too high. You should reduce the load on the UPS by unplugging any unnecessary items. After the auxiliary devices have been removed, reset the breaker. Some inexpensive power generators can distort the input voltage to the UPS. To combat this, you may need to move the UPS to a different outlet on a different power circuit, or adjust the UPS unit's voltage sensitivity setting.

Likewise, if the UPS does not turn off, an internal UPS fault has occurred and the unit should not be used. Instead, the UPS unit should be replaced and serviced immediately. UPS systems do not always use standard serial cables for communication. If the cable is incorrect, loose, or missing, the computer's power management functions will not be able to communicate with the UPS to control it.

EXAM ALERT

Be aware that the UPS system will not be able to control the operation of the computer without the serial communications cable installed.

Challenge #2

Your company has been hired to move Acme Co.'s data processing network into a larger facility where it is going to ramp up its staff. Your team is supposed to move their main servers and workstations to the new facility and connect them. The new location is in an older, highly industrialized portion of town and you are pretty sure that that section of town is susceptible to occasional brownouts and frequent power fluctuations. What should you suggest to your customer's management team to make sure the move and continued operations go well?

Electrostatic Discharge

The first step in avoiding electrostatic discharge (ESD) is being able to identify when and why it occurs. Electrostatic discharges are the most severe form of electromagnetic interference (EMI). The human body can build up static charges that range up to 25,000 volts. These buildups can discharge very rapidly into an electrically grounded body or device. Placing a 25,000-volt surge through any electronic device is potentially damaging to it.

At this point you may be wondering why the 25,000 volts associated with video monitors is deadly, whereas the 10,000 to 25,000 volts associated with ESD is not harmful to humans. The reason is the difference in current-delivering capabilities created by the voltage. Electronics instructors reiterate that it isn't the voltage that will kill you, it's the current (amperage). The capability of the voltage associated with a video monitor to push current through your body is significant (several amps), whereas the same capability associated with static is very low (micro-amps—thousandths of an amp). Therefore, it is possible for a lower voltage device with a higher current rating (such as a 110VAC power supply) to be much more dangerous than a higher voltage source that has a lower current-producing capability (such as static).

> **EXAM ALERT**
>
> Know that high voltage ratings do not make a particular contact point more dangerous than one with a lower voltage but a higher current potential.

Static can easily discharge through digital computer equipment. The electronic devices that are used to construct digital equipment are particularly susceptible to damage from ESD. As a matter of fact, ESD is the most damaging form of electrical interference associated with digital equipment.

The most common causes of ESD are the following:

- Moving people
- Improper grounding
- Unshielded cables
- Poor connections
- Moving machines
- Low humidity (hot and dry conditions)

EXAM ALERT

Memorize the conditions that make ESD more likely to occur.

When people move, their clothes rub together and can produce large amounts of electrostatic charge on their bodies. Walking across carpeting can create charges in excess of 1,000 volts. Motors in electrical devices, such as vacuum cleaners and refrigerators, also generate high levels of ESD. Some repair shops do not permit compressed air to be used for blowing dust out of keyboards and other computer equipment because it has been linked, erroneously, to creating ESD.

EXAM ALERT

Be aware that compressed air can be used to blow dust out of components and that it does not create ESD.

ESD is most likely to occur during periods of low humidity. If the relative humidity is less than 50%, static charges can accumulate easily. ESD generally does not occur when the humidity is greater than 50%. Air conditioning works by removing moisture from the atmosphere. Therefore, its presence can increase the potential for ESD by lowering the humidity even further. Anytime the static charge reaches around 10,000 volts, it is likely to discharge to grounded metal parts. In many high-ESD situations, it is useful to install a humidifier to raise the level of humidity in the work area.

Challenge #3

You have been asked to consult on the design of your company's new repair facility near Phoenix, Arizona. In particular, management wants to know how to equip the work areas of its new facility. You have not been to the site, but you know that it is in a hot desert environment. Also, the building will be air-conditioned. How should you advise management about precautions that should be taken with the work area?

Don't apply liquid or aerosol cleaners directly to computer equipment. Spray cleaners on a cloth and then apply the cloth to the equipment. Freon-propelled sprays should not be used on computer equipment because they can produce destructive electrostatic charges.

MOS Handling Techniques

The integrated circuit devices used to build PCs and other digital devices are built on different versions of metal oxide semiconductor (MOS) technology. MOS devices are sensitive to voltage spikes and static electricity discharges. The level of static electricity present on your body may be high enough to destroy the inputs of a MOS device if you touch its pins with your fingers (in practice this level of damage may require multiple electrostatic discharges). Professional service technicians employ a number of precautionary steps when they are working on systems that may contain MOS devices. These technicians normally use a grounding strap, like the one depicted in Figure 25.1. This antistatic device can be placed around the wrist or ankle to ground the technician to the system being worked on. These straps release any static present on the technician's body and pass it harmlessly to ground potential.

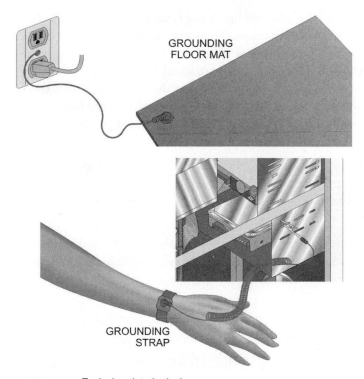

GROUNDING
FLOOR MAT

GROUNDING
STRAP

FIGURE 25.1 Typical antistatic devices.

Antistatic wrist or ankle straps should never be worn while working on higher voltage components, such as monitors and power supply units. Some technicians wrap a copper wire around their wrist or ankle and connect it to the grounded side of an outlet. This is not a safe practice because the resistive feature of a true wrist strap is missing. As an alternative, most technicians' work areas include antistatic mats made out of rubber or other antistatic materials that they stand on while working on the equipment. This is particularly helpful in carpeted work areas because carpeting can be a major source of ESD buildup. Some antistatic mats have ground connections that should be connected to the safety ground of an AC power outlet.

EXAM ALERT

Know when not to wear an antistatic wrist strap.

To avoid damaging static-sensitive devices, the following procedures will help to minimize the chances of destructive static discharges:

▶ Before touching any components inside the system, touch an exposed part of the chassis or the power supply housing with your finger. Grounding yourself in this manner ensures that any static charge present on your body is removed. This technique should be used before handling a circuit board or component. Of course, you should be aware that this technique works safely only when the power cord is attached to a grounded power outlet. The ground plug on a standard power cable is the best tool for overcoming ESD problems.

▶ Be aware that normal operating vibrations and temperature cycling can degrade the electrical connections between ICs and sockets over time. This gradual deterioration of electrical contact between chips and sockets is referred to as *chip creep*.

▶ Use antistatic sprays or solutions on floors, carpets, desks, and computer equipment. An antistatic spray or solution, applied with a soft cloth, is an effective deterrent to static.

▶ Install static-free carpeting in the work area. You can install an antistatic floor mat as well. Install a conductive tabletop to carry static away from the work area. Use antistatic mats on the work surface.

▶ Use a room humidifier to keep the humidity level above 50% in the work area.

EXAM ALERT

Be aware of the effects that temperature cycling can have on socket-mounted devices.

Understanding Grounds

The term *ground* is often a source of confusion for the novice because it actually encompasses a collection of terms. Generically, *ground* is simply any point from which electrical measurements are referenced. However, the original definition of ground actually referred to the ground. This ground is called *earth ground*.

The movement of electrical current along a conductor requires a path for the current to return to its source. In early telegraph systems and even modern power transmission systems, the earth provides a return path and, hypothetically, produces an electrical reference point of absolute zero. This type of ground is shown in Figure 25.2.

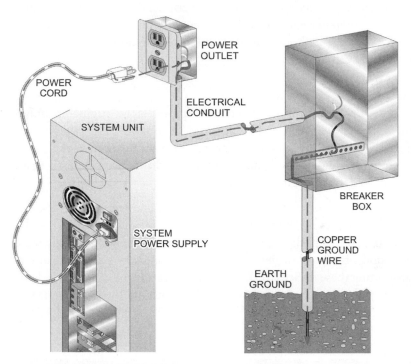

FIGURE 25.2 Power transmission system.

Grounding is an important aspect of limiting EMI in computer systems. Left unchecked, EMI can distort images on the video display, interfere with commercial communication equipment (such as radios and televisions), and corrupt data on floppy disks. In addition, EMI can cause signal deterioration and loss due to improper cable routing. If a signal cable is bundled with a power cord, for example, radiation from the power cord may induce current into the signal cable, affecting the signals that pass through it. Good grounding routes the induced EMI away from logic circuitry and toward ground potential, preventing it from disrupting normal operations. Unlike ESD, which is destructive, the effects of EMI can be corrected without damage.

EXAM ALERT

Remember that ESD is destructive and EMI is not.

Because a computer system is connected to an actual earth ground, it should always be turned off and disconnected from the wall outlet during electrical storms. This includes the computer and all its peripherals. The electrical pathway through the computer equipment can attract lightning on its way to earth ground. The extremely high electrical potential of a lightning strike is more than any computer can withstand.

Protection During Storage

The best storage option for most computer equipment is the original manufacturer's box. These boxes are designed specifically to store and transport the device safely. They include form-fitting protective foam to protect the device from shock hazards. The device is normally wrapped in a protective antistatic bag or wrapper to defeat the effects of ESD.

Monitors, printers, scanners, and other peripheral equipment should be stored in their original boxes, using their original packing foam and protective storage bag. The contours of the packing foam for these devices are not generally compatible from model to model or device to device. Foam is also the best packaging for transporting these devices. If the original boxes and packing materials are not available, make sure to use sturdy cartons and cushion the equipment well on all sides before shipping.

EXAM ALERT

Know that the best device for transporting computer equipment is the original manufacturer's packaging, including the antistatic foam and bags used to pack it.

Hardware Disposal Procedures

Most computer components contain some level of hazardous substances. Printed circuit boards consist of plastics, precious metals, fiberglass, arsenic, silicon, gallium, and lead. CRTs contain glass, metal, plastics, lead, barium, and rare earth metals. Batteries from portable systems can contain lead, cadmium, lithium, alkaline manganese, and mercury.

Although all these materials can be classified as hazardous materials, so far there are no widespread regulations when it comes to placing them in the landfill. Conversely, local regulations concerning acceptable disposal methods for computer-related components should always be checked before disposing of any electronic equipment.

Laser printer toner cartridges can be refilled and recycled. However, this should be done only for draft-mode operations where very good resolution is not required. Ink cartridges from ink-jet printers can also be refilled and reused. Like laser cartridges, they can be very messy to refill and often do not function as well as new cartridges do. In many cases, the manufacturer of the product has a policy of accepting spent cartridges.

EXAM ALERT

Remember that toner cartridges from a laser printer should be recycled.

For both batteries and cartridges, the desired method of disposal is recycling. It should not be too difficult to find a drop site that will handle the recycling of these products. On the other hand, even nonhazardous Subtitle-D dumpsites can handle the hardware components if need be. Subtitle-D dumpsites are non-hazardous, solid waste dumpsites that have been designed to meet EPA standards set for this classification. These sites are designed to hold hazardous materials safely.

EXAM ALERT

Remember that the proper disposal method for batteries is to recycle them.

All hazardous materials are required to have Material Safety Data Sheets (MSDS) that accompany them when they change hands. These sheets are also required to be on hand in areas where hazardous materials are stored and commonly used. The hazardous material supplier must provide these information sheets. Likewise, if you supply hazardous material to a third party, you must also supply the MSDS for the material. These sheets inform workers and management about hazards associated with the material and how to handle it safely. They also provide instructions about what to do if an accident occurs involving the material.

Exam Prep Questions

1. A _____ is an undervoltage condition that lasts for an extended period of time.

   ○ **A.** Sag

   ○ **B.** Brownout

   ○ **C.** Surge

   ○ **D.** Spike

2. A _____ is an undervoltage condition that lasts for a very short period of time.

   ○ **A.** Surge

   ○ **B.** Spike

   ○ **C.** Sag

   ○ **D.** Brownout

3. A _____ is used to protect computer equipment from power line variations or power outages.

   ○ **A.** Preliminary ESD

   ○ **B.** Surge protector

   ○ **C.** USPS

   ○ **D.** UPS

4. A _____ is used to protect computer equipment from very small overvoltage occurrences.

   ○ **A.** USPS

   ○ **B.** UPS

   ○ **C.** Surge suppressor

   ○ **D.** Preliminary ESD

5. Which device should not be connected to a UPS system?

   ○ **A.** Mail server

   ○ **B.** Laser printer

   ○ **C.** Web server

   ○ **D.** Workstation

6. In terms of maintenance issues, how are the effects of ESD and EMI different?

    ⭕ **A.** ESD is not destructive, whereas EMI can be very destructive.

    ⭕ **B.** EMI is not destructive, whereas ESD can be very destructive.

    ⭕ **C.** EMI improves system efficiency, whereas ESD can be very destructive.

    ⭕ **D.** ESD improves system efficiency, whereas EMI can be very destructive.

7. Which voltage level is more dangerous, 110VAC at 5 amps, or 25,000VDC at 5 microamperes?

    ⭕ **A.** Neither is particularly dangerous.

    ⭕ **B.** 5 amps is much more dangerous than 5 microamperes.

    ⭕ **C.** Both are extremely dangerous.

    ⭕ **D.** 25,000 volts is much more dangerous than 110 volts.

8. Damaging electrostatic discharge is most likely to occur when_____.

    ⭕ **A.** Working around rubber mats

    ⭕ **B.** Using test instruments on a system

    ⭕ **C.** The humidity is low

    ⭕ **D.** You accidentally get too close to the power supply unit while it is operating

9. You should not wear a wrist grounding strap when _____.

    ⭕ **A.** Replacing an adapter card

    ⭕ **B.** Repairing a motherboard

    ⭕ **C.** Repairing a CRT

    ⭕ **D.** Adding or replacing RAM

10. _____ is the gradual deterioration of the electrical connection between the pins of an IC and its socket.

    ⭕ **A.** Rust

    ⭕ **B.** Degradation

    ⭕ **C.** Chip creep

    ⭕ **D.** Tarnish

11. What is the best device for transporting computer equipment?

○ **A.** An antistatic bag

○ **B.** A server rack

○ **C.** A sturdy carton filled with styrofoam peanuts

○ **D.** The original packaging

12. What is the recommended method for handling an empty toner cartridge?

○ **A.** Recycle it

○ **B.** Throw it in the trash

○ **C.** Burn it in a certified incinerator

○ **D.** Turn it in to a licensed computer retailer

13. What is the recommended method for handling a dead battery?

○ **A.** Recycle it

○ **B.** Throw it in the trash

○ **C.** Burn it in a certified incinerator

○ **D.** Recharge it

14. What are the voltage levels commonly found in a CRT?

○ **A.** 25 volts

○ **B.** 250 volts

○ **C.** 25,000 volts

○ **D.** 250,000 volts

15. What is the best tool for releasing the charge on a CRT anode?

○ **A.** Your finger

○ **B.** Terrycloth towel

○ **C.** Wrist strap

○ **D.** Screwdriver

16. The local weather report indicates that an electrical storm with severe winds is likely to occur in your area overnight. What reasonable precautions should you take to protect your computers?

   ○ **A.** Monitor the computers until the storm passes

   ○ **B.** Plug the computers into a surge protector

   ○ **C.** Turn off the computers

   ○ **D.** Unplug the computers

17. What type of fire extinguisher should be used around computers?

   ○ **A.** Class A

   ○ **B.** Class B

   ○ **C.** Class C

   ○ **D.** Class D

18. The _____ of dot-matrix printers generates a great deal of heat and can be a burn hazard when working on these units.

   ○ **A.** Ribbon

   ○ **B.** Platen

   ○ **C.** Printhead

   ○ **D.** Paper tray

19. Which type of printer can be a source of electrocution, eye damage, and burns?

   ○ **A.** Laser

   ○ **B.** Dot matrix

   ○ **C.** Ink jet

   ○ **D.** Daisy wheel

20. What type of equipment should be used to minimize the chances of ESD during normal computer maintenance work?

   ○ **A.** Surge protector

   ○ **B.** Terrycloth towel

   ○ **C.** Wrist strap

   ○ **D.** Screwdriver

21. What is the purpose of the antistatic wrist strap?

   ○ **A.** To protect the equipment from electrostatic discharge

   ○ **B.** To protect the technician from injury

   ○ **C.** To render the technician electrically neutral

   ○ **D.** To protect technicians working on high voltage equipment such as power supplies and CRT monitors

22. If you enter a work area and find a technician unconscious on the floor and it appears they have come into contact with a power circuit nearby, what should you do first?

   ○ **A.** Call emergency services first

   ○ **B.** Start CPR immediately

   ○ **C.** Turn the power off first

   ○ **D.** Remove the victim from the danger area and then begin CPR

23. You are preparing to travel to a job to upgrade the RAM in customer's PC. Which of the following are correct statements concerning the handling of the RAM modules?

   ○ **A.** Lay the RAM devices on a sheet of foil while they are waiting to be installed

   ○ **B.** Store the RAM devices in antistatic bags to transport them

   ○ **C.** Unplug the power supply from the system board while installing the RAM modules

   ○ **D.** Use compressed air to blow any dust accumulation off the modules before installing them

24. When you enter a user's workspace you see water on the floor and stained ceiling tiles overhead. There are server systems in the work area along with several networked PCs. What should you do first in this situation?

   ○ **A.** Shut down the PCs and notify the network administrator immediately

   ○ **B.** Notify the building maintenance supervisor

   ○ **C.** Notify the network security administrator

   ○ **D.** Clean up the water immediately and look for the source of the leak

25. You are preparing to install new adapter cards in a desktop PC. Which of the following actions should you perform first?

    ○ **A.** Put on an antistatic wrist strap and connect yourself to the system

    ○ **B.** Unplug the computer from the AC power source

    ○ **C.** Unplug the power supply from the system board

    ○ **D.** Roll back any existing drivers for the card

26. While working in a customer's facility you observe several CAT5 cables on the floor in different areas of the workplace. What should you do about this situation?

    ○ **A.** Tape the cables down so that they are not a trip or catch hazard

    ○ **B.** Remove the cables from the walkways

    ○ **C.** Recommend that the customer replace these cables with cables that can be routed out of the way

    ○ **D.** Disconnect the cables and run new cables that can be run out of the walkway

Answers and Explanations

1. B. A *brownout* is an undervoltage condition that lasts for a sustained period of time.

2. C. A *voltage sag* is an undervoltage condition that lasts for a few milliseconds.

3. D. The uninterruptible power supply (UPS) is the best protection against losing data or damaged components when power interruptions or variations occur.

4. C. A surge suppressor can protect an electrical device from small power variations up to a point, but it cannot handle sustained power line problems. If the ratings of the suppressor are exceeded, the device it is guarding could be damaged.

5. B. The laser printer should not be attached to the UPS. It is not required in an emergency situation and it consumes a considerable amount of power.

6. B. Electrostatic discharge (ESD) can send severe overvoltages into electrical equipment that have the potential to cause permanent damage to

sensitive electronic components. EMI occurs when strong electromagnetic fields distort signals within the system, causing a partial or complete system crash. Unlike ESD, which is destructive, the effects of EMI can be corrected without damage.

7. B. "It isn't the voltage that will kill you, it's the current (amperage)." The capability of the voltage associated with a video monitor to push current through your body is significant (several amps), whereas the same capability associated with static is very low (micro-amps, thousandths of an amp). Therefore, it is possible for a lower voltage device with a higher current rating (such as a 110VAC power supply) to be much more dangerous than a higher voltage source that has a lower current capability (such as static).

8. C. ESD is most likely to occur during periods of low humidity. If the relative humidity is less than 50%, static charges can accumulate easily. ESD generally does not occur when the humidity is greater than 50%. In many high-ESD situations, it is useful to install a humidifier to raise the level of humidity in the work area.

9. C. A wrist strap is a conductor designed to carry electrical charges away from your body. In high-voltage environments such as those found inside a power supply unit or a monitor, however, this safety device becomes a potential path for electrocution.

10. C. *Chip creep* is the degradation of the contact between an IC and its socket, and it occurs because of the effects of temperature cycling on the IC pins and the socket contacts.

11. D. The best storage option for most computer equipment is the original manufacturer's box.

12. A. Laser printer toner cartridges can be refilled and recycled.

13. A. For both batteries and cartridges, the desired method of disposal is recycling.

14. C. Extremely high voltage levels (in excess of 25,000 volts) may be present inside the CRT housing, even up to a year after electrical power has been removed from the unit.

15. D. In repair situations, the high-voltage charge associated with video displays must be discharged. This is accomplished by creating a path from the tube's high-voltage anode to the chassis. With the monitor unplugged from the commercial power outlet, clip one end of an insulated jumper wire to the chassis ground of the frame. Clip the other end to a long flat-blade screwdriver that has a well-insulated handle. While

touching only the insulated handle of the screwdriver, slide the blade of the screwdriver under the rubber cup of the anode and make contact with its metal connection. This should bleed off the high-voltage charge to ground. Continue the contact for several seconds to ensure that the voltage has been fully discharged.

16. D. For complete protection from potential lightning strikes, you should completely disconnect the computers from the commercial power source (unplug them from the outlets) so that there is no path for the lightning to follow.

17. C. A Class-C (CO_2) fire extinguisher should always be on hand. Class-C extinguishers are the type specified for use around electrical equipment.

18. C. To exchange the printhead assembly, make sure that it is cool enough to be handled. These units can get hot enough to cause a serious burn.

19. A. Laser printers can be a source of electrocution, eye damage (from the laser), and burns (from the fuser assembly). The laser printer tends to have several high-voltage and high-temperature hazards inside it. To get the laser printer into a position where you can observe its operation, it will be necessary to defeat some interlock sensors. This action will place you in potential contact with the high-voltage, high-temperature areas in the printer. Take great care when working inside a laser printer.

20. C. Professional service technicians employ a number of precautionary steps when they are working on systems that may contain MOS devices. These technicians generally use a grounding strap. This antistatic device may be placed around the wrist or ankle to ground the technician to the system being worked on. These straps release any static present on the technician's body and pass it harmlessly to ground potential.

21. A. Technicians protect the equipment from electrostatic discharge by using grounding straps devices that are placed around the wrists or ankles to ground the technician to the system being worked on. These straps release any static present on the technician's body and pass it harmlessly to ground potential.

22. A. The victim in this case is in need of expert medical assistance, call 911 as soon as possible. If you are attending to a casualty, get a bystander to telephone for help. If you are on your own, you will have to leave the victim momentarily to make a call. Use common sense, take your time, and act rationally.

23. B. PC boards containing static-sensitive devices are normally shipped in special antistatic bags. These bags are good for storing ICs and other

computer components that may be damaged by ESD. They are also the best method of transporting PC boards with static-sensitive components.

24. B. Liquids such as water, coffee, and soft drinks should not be brought into the work area. The presence of water in the work area from other sources should always be a cause for alarm and correction. Water leaks in the work area are generally the responsibility of the building maintenance supervisor.

25. B. Most adapter card manufacturers advise you to unplug the power from the AC power source before installing new devices in the system. Always read the manufacturer's install instructions first.

26. A. If temporary cabling must be run in or across a walkway, it should be taped down to the floor or covered with a protective cover strip to prevent it from becoming a trip hazard.

Challenge Solutions

1. In the situation described in this challenge, you first step should be to get additional help if available. The electrician is unconscious and you do not know what has happened to him. Is the cable he is holding energized? Because you do not know this, you should not come into contact with him until you're sure. If no other help is nearby, try to find the power source (breaker box or subpanel) for the room and turn it off. If this cannot be accomplished, you should find some electrically insulated material to move the cable away from the electrician. After the electrocution safety issue has been handled, you must evaluate the electrician's condition and arrange for any medical help needed. Also begin first aid and CPR if necessary.

2. You should suggest that the company install a UPS system to protect at least its servers and at least install surge suppressors on the workstation PCs. The UPS will protect the servers and the key business information stored on them) during brownouts and other fluctuations. The surge protectors will provide some protection to the workstations against the power line fluctuations.

3. The facility should be equipped with a humidifier system to overcome the effects of the hot, dry climate and the air-conditioning. It should also have antistatic floor mats, antistatic desk mats, and antistatic wrist straps for the technicians.

CHAPTER TWENTY-SIX

Professionalism and Communication

Terms you'll need to understand:

✓ Jargon

✓ Acronyms

✓ Marketing

✓ Technical support

✓ Active listening

✓ Feedback

✓ Soft skills

✓ Customer service

✓ Body language

✓ Phone support

Techniques to master:

Essentials 8.1/Remote Support Technician 6.1/IT Technician 8.1

Use good communication skills, including listening, tact, and discretion, when communicating with customers and colleagues.

✓ Use clear, concise and direct statements

✓ Allow the customer to complete statements—avoid interrupting

✓ Clarify customer statements— ask pertinent questions

✓ Avoid using jargon, abbreviations, and acronyms

✓ Listen to customers

Essentials 8.2/Remote Support Technician 6.2/IT Technician 8.2

Use job-related professional behavior, including notation of privacy, confidentiality, and respect for the customer and customer's property.

✓ Behavior

   ✓ Maintain a positive attitude and tone of voice

   ✓ Avoid arguing with customers and/or becoming defensive

   ✓ Do not minimize customers' problems

   ✓ Avoid being judgmental and/or insulting or calling the customer names

   ✓ Avoid distractions and interruptions when talking with customers

✓ Property

✓ Telephone, laptop, desktop computer, printer, monitor, and so on

Customer Service Skills

This chapter covers the Professionalism and Communication areas of the CompTIA A+ Certification—Essentials examination under Objectives 8.1 and 8.2. It also covers those same subobjectives for the Remote Support Technician objectives 6.1 and 6.2 and IT Technician objectives 8.1 and 8.2 examinations.

One thing that is very apparent from these exam objectives is that employers want their people to have good interpersonal skills. Mostly, they want employees to be aware of those behaviors that contribute to satisfying customers. These behaviors include such things as the quality of technician-customer personal interaction, the way a technician conducts him or herself professionally within the customer's business setting, the credibility and confidence projected by the technician, which in turn engenders customer confidence, and the resilience, friendliness, and efficiency that can unexpectedly delight the customer above and beyond the solving of a technical problem.

> **NOTE**
>
> The Remote Support Technician Objectives 6.1 and 6.2 and IT Technician Objectives 8.1 and 8.2 use the same wording as the subobjectives from Essentials 8.1 and 8.2. The topics specified in these different exam/objective areas are stated the same, so it makes sense that they should be presented as the same discussion. You will need to study the material in this chapter for any of the four exams you intend to challenge.

The object of this section is to discuss customer service skills that employers find desirable in their employees. Many companies have formal customer service guidelines that they make all employees aware of. However, these guidelines are not universal throughout the industry. Therefore, we offer a set of generic guidelines for your consideration.

For the most part, a high level of technical proficiency alone is not enough to sustain a career in the world of computer service. For most of the service jobs available, good customer skills are just as important as good technical skills. In most cases, they are equal partners for a successful career. Good customer service skills are a must for those of us who work directly with the public.

Customer service is part of any company's sales and marketing effort and should be considered as such. As a part of the customer service team, you should think of yourself as part of the sales and marketing team as well. Marketing makes potential customers aware of the company's products and services. The salespeople follow up on the marketing efforts to ensure that the marketing materials are received and understood, and to convert the potential customer into an actual customer. After customers have chosen your company, the customer service effort comes into play to keep them as customers. In every type of business, it costs far less to hang on to an existing customer than to find and convince new ones.

Good customer service typically involves the following:

- Educating customers by providing useful and practical information, problem resolution, and support

- Informing customers of goods and services

- Relating to customers by learning their needs and concerns

- Delivering goods and services to customers in a timely manner and in a form desired by the customers

- Supporting customers to the degree that they feel supported but not overwhelmed

Customer service may take the form of *general support* or *technical support*. General support provides nontechnical care of the customer, whereas technical support deals with product installation, application, repair, and maintenance. In general, customer service supports the customer through education, personal service, and customer satisfaction monitoring.

Customer education refers to providing direction on the proper use of the product and advising customers of new services or product developments. *Personal service* involves answering questions and addressing specific concerns about products and services. This aspect also concerns assisting in the resolution of service or product problems. The customer service person solicits feedback from the customer concerning products and services.

The feedback aspect of customer service is one of the most important functions and one of the most underused. This phase is used to provide logs of customer problems and complaints, maintain positive feedback and suggestions, produce policy decisions to improve products and services, and promote goodwill in customers. Ideally, feedback should be solicited from the customer during every contact. You should routinely inquire about how the customer, and the product, is doing.

All of these customer service functions typically involve person-to-person activity. Therefore, the customer service personnel must be able to communicate effectively with users, and potential users, of technical equipment. As indicated earlier, they must be able to educate and support the user in the safe and proper use of such equipment.

Both field and bench technicians must possess good interpersonal skills to properly handle customers. Some service managers have said, "We don't fix computers, we fix customers." How service people are perceived is as important as how well they perform. In the end, it is *customer satisfaction* (with the product, the service, and the supplier) that creates a successful business—and continued employment.

Customer service skills are generally referred to as *soft skills* because they cannot be tested easily with a written, or hands-on, test. However, they are skills that can be learned and practiced. The following paragraphs contain key points to consider in the area of providing customer service.

Prepare

Review customer history before contacting them or going to their site to perform work. In particular, see whether the problem you are going to work on is a recurring problem or a new occurrence. Check the urgency of the call and the customer's priority level.

Research the type of equipment the call is concerning to determine whether you will need any special tools or parts for the repair. Make sure that your documentation is in order. It may be necessary to check the customer's status with your company. Make certain that you have all the manuals, replacement parts, and tools you will likely need. Do you have the ESD prevention equipment, meters, hand tools, and so on that you need? Make sure that the tools and parts are in good working order.

Prioritize commitments and set realistic schedules. Resist the urge to overbook appointments. If it takes 30 minutes to get across town, never schedule an appointment there for a half-hour after you should be finished at the first site. Maintain time allotments established for completion of different tasks.

The best-laid plans of men and concrete often go astray. There will be occasions where you just won't be able to keep an appointment. A previous service call runs long, the car breaks down, traffic on the freeway is stopped, and so on. When these occasions come up, make contact with the affected customers as soon as possible to let them know about your situation. Likewise, there may be occasions when the customer is not ready for you. They may have had things come up between the time they scheduled your appointment and the time you arrived that changed their need for the equipment. Always ask the customer if they are ready for you to work on their machines before you begin your work.

Always notify customers, as soon as possible, about any appointment changes, service delays, complications, or setbacks that may occur. Apologize for the inconvenience and ask how they would like to proceed. These things happen to everyone, and your best defenses against customer dissatisfaction are promptness and good communication.

Establish Rapport

A good practice is to learn your customers by name and greet them with it. Collect business cards and include copies in customer folders—have them in your pocket during the call. Always deal with them as individuals, not by stereotypes such as order entry person, receptionist, manager, and so forth.

Be as open, friendly, and approachable as your personality will allow. This is an area that most of us can always work on. Politeness is a valuable quality to possess. However, it should never be forced, contrived, or overdone. Your greatest weapon in this area is your expertise. Avoid politically or racially sensitive topics, as well as religious discussions and comments/discussions that might get you into a sexual harassment situation. These have no place in business settings.

Establish Your Presence

Make eye contact when you speak to customers. Maintain alert body posture and calm facial expressions. Keep a calm voice level when perplexing situations arise. Your presence can be used to set the excitement level of the customer. If you appear calm, collected, and confident, the customer probably won't get too excited either. Avoid moodiness in the workplace. This can undermine your credibility with the customer. You begin each new customer contact with a 100% rating. At the end, you will be left with whatever points you have not given away. Doing an efficient, professional, and complete job does more to ingratiate you to customers than almost anything else you can do.

If customers get to the point where they are sure that you will always be able to solve their problems, you have the best rapport that could be achieved in a business setting.

Be Proactive

Provide customers with appropriate preventive-maintenance plans and explain how they contribute to the continued productivity of their equipment. Take time to illustrate proper methods of handling consumables and items to be on the watch for. Show them how to properly install and change printer ribbons, ink cartridges, toner cartridges, and the like. Demonstrate the use of virus protection products, backup utilities, and advise the customer of potential environmental hazards, such as improper disposing of toner cartridges.

Challenge #1

A customer calls with a RAM problem that has been common in a particular model of computer. What should you tell the customer about the product?

A. "Oh yeah, we have that happening all over. We're getting everyone fixed up ASAP."

B. "We've had a whole batch of bad RAM in those machines."

C. Troubleshoot the problem as you would any other phone support problem.

D. Offer to send the customer replacement RAM.

Alert your customers to potential system problems or productivity-related issues concerning their systems. Identify noisy system components that may need care in the near future. Suggest system changes that could improve performance, and explain how this is possible. Keep customers aware of service bulletins and advisories concerning their equipment.

Research customer requests for recommendations, and advise about future directions and equipment. However, this option should normally be taken only if requested by the customer. Also be sensitive to the level of the person you are making recommendations to. There are workers that have never met a new piece of hardware or software they didn't like. However, their superiors may be quite happy without the production, downtime, and cost trade-offs that changing could bring. Don't incite the customer's employees with the latest and greatest product if their management hasn't signaled the way.

Listen and Communicate

One of the attributes that makes a good customer service or repair person is the ability to *actively listen* to the customer. Real listening means not just hearing what the customer has to say, but trying to pin down what the customer means. The technique for doing this is called *active listening*. Using active listening involves focusing on the customer's comments, repeating key information to let the customer know that you are following what they are saying, and avoiding distractions such as visual or audible activities that draw away your attention away from the customer.

EXAM ALERT

Be able to describe the components of active listening.

Mentally (and maybe physically) identify key points as the customer describes the nature of the problem. Don't interrupt customer descriptions before you have all the details. Even if you are sure that you know what is going on after the first sentence, have the patience to listen to the complete description. This is not only common courtesy, but also serves to uncover extra data about the problem.

Challenge #2

You are sent to set up a desktop publishing computer for a publisher, and you discover that the company is using a publishing program that you know does not have all the features of a competing program. You're sure that the company could be much more productive using the other program. How do you convey this to the customer?

A. You don't because the company is installing a new program and does not need to be told this isn't the best.

B. Get the supervisor alone and recommend the other program in private.

C. Mail an advertisement of the better product to the manager.

D. Tell the operators about the features of the other product in confidence so that they will know what to look for the next time.

Pay attention to the customer's body language and other nonverbal clues. Pay attention to body posture, hand gestures, facial cues, and voice inflection to gauge anger, franticness, and so on.

You should also be aware of your body language and what it is saying. Folding your arms while someone is speaking to you signals that you are not interested in what they are saying and that you are simply waiting for them to finish.

Failure to make eye contact when you are talking conveys lack of commitment and may be taken as a sign you are being less than truthful. Closing books, returning pens to your pocket, or gathering tools while the customer is talking to you also sends a sign that you are finished and not paying real attention. Make sure to always pay serious attention to the customer.

Listening is also a good way to eliminate the user as a possible cause of the problems occurring. Many cartoons have been created in service newsletters about the strangest user-related calls ever received. Part of your job is to determine whether the user could be the source of the problem—either trying to do things with the system that it cannot do, or not understanding how some part of it is supposed to work. If you find this to be the case, work with the user to clarify the realistic uses of the system. This is a point where it may be appropriate to suggest advanced training options. However, such suggestions should be made discreetly.

Challenge #3

You arrive on a service call, and the office supervisor turns on the malfunctioning machine. She begins to explain what she thinks the problem is, but you can tell from the operation of the machine that it is something else. What course of action should you pursue?

A. Listen to the explanation until she is finished, and then fix the machine.

B. Sit down and fix the machine while she is describing the rest of the problem to you.

C. Begin troubleshooting the problem she is describing until she leaves, and then fix the problem.

D. Stop the explanation, and tell her that you are pretty sure that you already know what the problem is.

The ability to communicate clearly is the other trait most looked for in service people. Allow customers to talk through their problems but try to guide and control the discussion to make certain that it stays focused. If you simply let the conversation go in any direction, you may waste a significant amount of the customer's and your time. Also, you're the one with the knowledge of what might cause problems. The customer may not have good diagnostic skills or system knowledge, so they will not know how to optimize the conversation.

EXAM ALERT

Be aware that you need to control the conversation with the customer to optimize your time usage.

Use probing questions for clarification purposes and to make sure they understand what the user is describing at each step. In doing so, they may come up with clues they haven't thought of before. Help them to think through the problem by asking organized questions. With equipment down, the customer may be under some stress and might not be thinking as rationally as usual. Choose words and questions that do not put the customer, or their employees, in a bad light. (For example, "What have you done now?" is not likely to set the proper tone with a customer who has more problems than he or she needs for the moment.) Adjust the pace and flow of your conversation to accommodate the customer.

Avoid quick analysis statements. Repeatedly changing your position kills customer confidence. Also, avoid or minimize surprises that pop up (such as unexpected charges or time requirements). Try to manage the customer's expectations by being as up front as possible about what you can accomplish and the scope of services you can provide. If the customer has a networking problem, and you are the computer repair person, the customer shouldn't be allowed to believe that you are going to get everything working before you leave (unless the network falls within the scope of your normal work).

If the person you are working with in a company is the MIS person, network administrator, or engineer, take his or her lead and follow instructions. Avoid situations of who knows more. Try to quickly recognize the technical abilities of the people you are working with. Adjust your conversation to accommodate them. For technically challenged customers, avoid jargon. It will be confusing to them and can be a cause of customer dissatisfaction with you, even if you do a great job.

Clarify your terminology with such people, and be careful to avoid talking down to them or patronizing them. On the other hand, if customers are technically literate, be careful not to insult their intelligence by overexplaining things to them. In this case, use technical terms as appropriate, and use them correctly. Watch for signs of misunderstanding, and explain things in greater detail as necessary.

Challenge #4

While working with a relatively inexperienced customer over the telephone, you become aware that the customer is having great difficulty following your directions. How can you help the customer even though he cannot see you?

A. Send the customer fax drawings of steps to perform.

B. Ask the customer if you can talk to someone else to get a fresh perspective on the problem.

C. Check your conversation, and try to communicate more clearly.

D. Ask the customer to fax you drawings of what he is experiencing.

There are some words and phrases that should automatically be avoided when talking to customers. Some key phrases that lose customers include the following:

▶ I don't know—Although this statement may be true, using it with a customer really means you don't care enough to go find out. Try to substitute "I will have to find out and get back to you about that" instead. Write down the question, do the research, and make certain to follow up with the customer when you do know.

▶ What was your name/problem?—These questions show that you have not paid close enough attention to what the customer has already said, possibly causing a doubt that you are paying attention to anything. People usually call because they need a problem solved. This phrase will not go far in convincing them that you have the answers they need. Keep a writing instrument by the telephone and write down names and related information as soon as it is given.

▶ I can't help you—Again, this may be a true statement; however, using this statement by itself indicates that you are not interested in helping, either. Add something such as "But, you might try…" in an attempt to be helpful to the customer.

▶ I'm/he's/she's busy—So is everyone else. Saying this indicates that the recipient is less important than something else. Therefore, it almost automatically wounds the customer's ego and creates a bad atmosphere. If you/he/she is involved in something that cannot be interrupted right away, try to phrase the rejection so that it is delivered with a promise to get back to the caller as soon as possible, and indicate that the customer's call is of value. Also ask whether the customer would like to leave a message for the other individual.

You may also run into situations where you do not speak the same language as the customer. When this occurs, you will need to find someone who can interpret for you to perform the customer-questioning segment of the troubleshooting process. You should contact your management to see whether there is someone in the organization who has the ability to interact with this customer. Finally, you may be able to communicate with the customer on a graphical level using drawings.

> **EXAM ALERT**
>
> Know how to communicate with customers that do not have the same language you do.

Follow Up

A key part of any technical work on equipment that involves a user is to educate the user about the equipment, its usage or the cause/effects of repair work you perform. After an installation, you should coach the user on the proper usage and care for the device (PC, printer, and so on). The job is not complete until you've educated the user.

> **EXAM ALERT**
>
> Be aware that the last step in an installation or repair process is to educate the user.

The best tool for training users is typically the actual equipment or software they will be expected to use. If you are coaching one or two users, it is best to pull up a chair and get to an equal level with them. This allows you to make the training more personable and less formal. Use the documentation that comes with the hardware or software as part of the training process. Point out and mark key topic areas in the documentation that you know the users will need after you're gone. However, do not read the manuals to them—this is an instant cure for insomnia and very ineffective training. Also be careful to use language that the user can relate to. Use proper terminology. Avoid jargon or industry slang when coaching users.

> **EXAM ALERT**
>
> Know how to coach users after you've installed new hardware or software.

Because you are typically working in close proximity with the user in coaching situations, be aware of your body position—particularly your hands. Although it may be totally innocent, resting your hand on someone's shoulder, or patting them on the back, can be misconstrued and cause problems.

Follow up on unresolved issues. For incomplete calls, such as those requiring additional parts, assess the customer's need and restore as much functionality to the system as possible, or needed. Clean up and organize parts removed from the system so that they will not be in the way or be removed before your return to the site. Keep the customer informed about progress of unresolved issues, such as when parts are expected. If problems are intermittent, set up a schedule and procedure to work with the customer to pin down circumstances that cause the problem to reoccur.

Be Responsive

Concentrate on the customer's problem or request. Give preeminence to the customer's sense of urgency. Relegate paperwork and administrative duties to a secondary level until the customer's problems have been fully aired. Don't undermine the customer's sense of urgency. Work with the customer's priorities. Schedule steps to fulfill any unresolved problems to show commitment to getting the problems solved. In this way, customers will be assured that they are not being left adrift.

Don't multitask while working directly with a customer. Focus on the task at hand, and keep it in the forefront. Avoid distractions in the customer's presence. Act on the customer's complaints.

Challenge #5

A customer who has picked up a repaired computer from your store brings it back within a few hours, complaining that it doesn't work. What should you say?

A. "What happened to it?"

B. "Sometimes I can't believe our technicians can find their way home at night. I'll get this thing fixed up for you."

C. "It was working when it left here. I don't know what could have happened to it. Let's take a look at it."

D. "Did it ever work when you got it home?"

Be Accountable

Document your promises and dates so that you can demonstrate accountability to your customers. Follow up on return dates for yourself and/or equipment. Take personal responsibility for being the single point for the service call—contacting specialists, dealing with parts vendors, and so on. It's your show—run it unless your organization has someone in the structure who is supposed to take over this responsibility.

You may also encounter situations where you should not assume accountability for different things. For example, working in a customer's residence when they are not there can be problematic. If they decide something is missing and you were there by yourself whose guess problem it will become. Even when they find the item later, the damage has been done. Likewise, never assume responsibility for anyone's children, or being alone with their children.

In residential settings, you may be subject to the presence of children who could be a distraction or a problem in getting your work completed in an efficient manner. If this is the case, you should explain this to the customer and ask them to remove the children from the work area. This is not your responsibility and could cause problems if you directly confront the child or children.

> **EXAM ALERT**
>
> Be aware of situations where you should not assume responsibility.

Challenge #6

An irate customer calls, complaining that a technician from your company has recently performed a software upgrade on the customer's system and now the modem will not connect with other modems. How should you handle the customer?

A. "I'm sure none of our technicians would have left a condition like that. Let's see what the problem is."

B. "Give me the technician's name, and I'll have him get back to you as soon as he returns to the office."

C. "Please describe the symptoms to me so that I can see what might be causing the problem."

D. "This is really easy. Take the top off of the computer, and check to see that the card is installed securely."

Be Flexible

Effective customer service means that you must be flexible and readily adaptable to meet the needs of customers. This does not mean that the customer is always right. But it does mean that you should be looking for the best way to help customers meet their needs. This may involve looking for new and innovative methods of servicing the customer.

If a problem runs beyond the scope of your position, or your capabilities, take the initiative to move it to the next level of authority. Never leave customers hanging without a path to get their problems addressed. Provide alternatives when possible: downtime scheduling, loaner equipment availability, and so on. This is also true for requests for work to be performed that are outside of your assignment or your company's agreement with the customer. Escalate the request so that management can take proper action in deciding how the particular customer should be handled.

> **EXAM ALERT**
>
> Know how to handle request that fall outside of your agreed upon or contracted scope of work.

In some cases you may have the opportunity to do something extra for a customer that will put you and your company in a good light. For example, if a customer asks you to install an application while you are upgrading their operating system, you can check to determine whether it is legal software, whether the company policy allows for this person to have this software, and then install it for the customer. You might want to make sure that this activity does not take up more time than you can afford to give away free.

Be Professional

You should always make certain that your attire is clean, neat, and appropriate. It should also be businesslike and is probably described by your company's policies. Avoid excessive jewelry, or jewelry that might be offensive to your range of customers. Also, hold down the cologne or perfume—be moderate. Practice good hygiene by keeping hair washed and groomed, fingernails trimmed and clean, and breath fresh (use mouthwash or breath mints as needed, but not chewing gum).

You should establish a good rapport with your customers, but you should always maintain a professional distance from them. You cannot afford to be their support, or confidant, in dealings with the company you work for. The apparent opportunity to gain the inside track with the customer, at your company's expense, cannot work out in your favor. Remember, the customer sees you as an extension of that company. So, you can only be as good as your company is to the customer. If your computer is broken, you don't need a friend, you need the best repair person you can find.

It is important for technicians to display a certain level of confidence in the workplace. This gives customers a feeling of confidence in you as well (at least until you do something to make them feel otherwise). However, over-confidence, or overly assertive communications can diminish your professional appearance with the customer. Recognize that there is a professional way to communicate with customers. There is a difference between saying "You broke this PC" and "Help me understand how the computer got to this point." The first statement is overly assertive and judgmental, whereas the second is inquiring and nonjudgmental. The assertive statement sets up a level of separation between the technician and the user, whereas the inquisitive statement brings the two together to investigate the problem.

The same is true when dealing with co-workers. Although there is often some competitiveness within highly trained groups, this can foster an unhealthy work environment if not properly restrained. Overly assertive conversations with co-workers can create the same adversarial conditions as it does with customers. If you have a personality that tends to use this approach with people, work on controlling and minimizing this trait.

> **EXAM ALERT**
>
> Be aware of assertive language and its impact on working relationships.

Establish Integrity

The news media periodically produces undercover exposés about service rip-offs in different industries. Integrity is the greatest asset a service person has. This is the factor that creates continuous customer relationships and repeat business. After it has been breached, it is nearly impossible to restore.

It is beneficial to establish your relationship with the customer based on your abilities and integrity. Have something good to say about the customer's facilities, if possible. If not, don't comment on them at all. The same goes for equipment that customers have chosen. They aren't paying you for consulting services, and disparaging comments about their choices won't win you any points.

From time to time, you may be exposed to customer information that is of a sensitive nature. Respect the confidentiality of this information. Never reveal financial information that you have obtained from a customer's system. This includes friends, and especially employees, of the customer.

Put simply, bad things happen sometimes. If you damage a customer's property in the process of your work, you should take responsibility for the damage. Hiding inflicted damage or passing it off on the customer can put you and your company in an embarrassing situation if it comes into question. When damage occurs, make sure that you document the extent of the damage and the circumstances surrounding how it occurred. Let your management know and then let the customer know. Your company probably has policies in place that spell out your responsibilities in this area.

> **EXAM ALERT**
>
> Know how to handle inflicted damage situations.

Along with reporting damage to customers when it occurs, you will occasionally have to give customers other types of bad news—such as "you can't repair their system or recover their data from a damaged drive. The best way of giving bad news is to simply give it to the customer as soon as you have determined the extent of the problem and be honest with them about the extent of the problem they have. Avoiding giving the customer the bad news, or delaying it, only wastes the customer's time and can cause them to doubt your abilities.

> **EXAM ALERT**
>
> Be aware of the best practice for giving customers bad news.

Challenge #7

The technician received a telephone call from a customer who buys thousands of dollars of computer equipment from his company each year. The purchaser cannot get the company's computer to work with a printer that was purchased through another supplier. She wants the technician to get the system running. How should the technician react?

A. "I'm really sorry, but we can't work on equipment purchased from another vendor."

B. "Sure, how can I help you?"

C. "Let me clear this with my supervisor."

D. "You'll have to tell my supervisor that you want me to do this. I'm sure that it will be all right because you do so much business with us."

Avoid distracting employees while you are working at a customer's site. Work as unobtrusively as possible. *Ask permission* to use the customer's facilities, such as the telephone, copier, or other equipment. For example, if paper is required to test a printer you are repairing, ask an appropriate person for it. Don't just get it for yourself. Also ask permission from a supervisor if you must borrow equipment, enter areas of a facility that you have not expressly been authorized to be in, or move equipment around. Remember to straighten up the work area before leaving it (for example, don't leave the paper from the print tests laying around).

Also consider the impact your work will have on the customer or user's work area. If you are going to have to dismantle the user's PC, you might want to consider the best location to do this. Should you perform this operation at the user's desk, at some convenient place within their facility, or should you take the machine to your work area? This decision may be dictated by time pressures (does the PC need to be returned to service as quickly as possible?) or by appearance (would the appearance of a disassembled computer on a user's desk be improper for the facility you are working in?). Also, the user may need to do other things at their desk while their computer is down.

EXAM ALERT

Be aware of the impact of where you perform different activities has on a given customer/location/situation.

Never break copyright regulations by illegally loading or giving away software. One of the leading causes of computer virus infection is pirated software. Not only do you run this risk in giving away copies, it's illegal and can get you introduced to various people you never really wanted to meet, such as lawyers and judges. On top of that, it could cost you your job. Tell customers that ask you to install suspect software that it is illegal to do so and you cannot do it for them.

Pornographic materials on computers fall into the same category as illegal copies of programs. Having such materials on your PC is reason for immediate termination in most companies. If you are exposed to illegal software or pornographic material on a customer's computer, you should report this to your supervisor. If you discover illegal software or pornographic material on one of your company's computers, report it to the proper authority in your organization (provided you are not authorized by your company's policies to handle this situation yourself).

> **EXAM ALERT**
>
> Be aware of how to handle the presence of illegal or pornographic materials on customer and in-house computers.

Handle Conflicts Appropriately

Successfully servicing customers often means providing a positive solution to their problems under negative circumstances. Inevitably, you will run into a customer who is having a bad day. No matter what you do, you will not be able to keep the customer from getting angry. What you can do is realize that this is the case and attempt to de-escalate the situation.

This usually involves letting customers get pent-up frustrations off their chest by simply listening to them. The best thing to do is let customers vent verbal frustrations without reply. It can be very frustrating to let customers vent without interrupting them, but that is an important part of successfully handling irate customers. Take notes during the emotional explosion and note the key issues. Taking notes and trying to figure out the real issues should keep you preoccupied so that the emotional part does not affect you as much.

When you do reply, remain calm, talk in a steady voice, and avoid making inflammatory comments. Also, try to avoid taking a defensive stance because this signals a conflict point. Realize that criticism given out by customers is generally not personal—so don't take it personally. Information delivered with an aggressive attitude will normally lead to an aggressive or retaliatory response from the customer.

After the customer has poured out the full story, try to redirect the conversation to creating solutions to the problems. Go over the important details, one at a time, and explain how you will handle each concern (or who you must turn to for a final answer). Here again, be exact. Give the customers a time when you will be getting back to them with answers. Be specific if possible—next Tuesday morning is a better answer than some time next week. Reassure the customer that you are fully capable of fixing their problem, and then follow up by fixing the problem and returning their system to working order.

If the customer is too angry to work through the details with you, conclude the encounter by trying to do or offer something to lessen the frustration level, and make certain to follow up as you've indicated. As soon as possible, withdraw from the confrontation and let the situation cool off. Inform your superiors of the situation as quickly as possible so that you have inside support and so that a plan of relief can be implemented.

Telephone Techniques

All the listening and communications skills are equally valuable when performing phone support work. Because you cannot see the customer, or interpret body language, it is even more important to quickly assess the state of the customer. It is also important to determine the technical abilities of the user as quickly as possible. Asking a receptionist to remove the cover of a computer is not normally an accepted practice.

When giving instructions over the phone, be precise. Provide detailed instructions for work to be done, and ask lots of questions about what is happening on the other end. Cellular or cordless phones are valuable tools for customers using phone support. At your end of the phone, take good notes of what the user has been instructed to do so that you can review them as needed.

Try to answer the phone on the second or third ring. First-ring answers can be startling for customers, catching them unprepared. Customers will often assume that you are not available soon after the third ring. Voice-mail answering systems are normally set up to assume the same thing, so your call may automatically get routed there after only a few rings. Many people do not care for being switched to a machine.

When you're placing a call, let it ring up to 6 times if you are calling a business and 10 times if calling a residence. Longer time may be required to get to the phone from some parts of a residence, such as the garage or basement.

Avoid rounds of phone tag by leaving a good time to call in your message. Don't forget to leave the telephone number where you can be reached at that time.

Also provide a reason for the call along with any other pertinent information. Doing so will enable the other party to have any relevant documents or notes for the conversation. Do not leave the time or date of your call as part of your message unless the greeting tells you to do so. Most automated answering systems do this automatically.

Always identify your company and provide your name when making or receiving telephone calls. Attempt to use the caller's name at least once, if not twice, in the conversation. This action personalizes the call and lets the customer know you are paying attention (it also reminds you to pay attention).

Avoid putting customers on hold if possible. If you must put them on hold, make certain to get their name and phone number in case anything happens. If you expect that a customer may be on hold for more than 30 seconds, ask whether you can call the customer back. Their time is as valuable as yours and, unless they are calling on a toll-free or local line, they are paying for the call.

Take notes during the conversation and recap the important points before hanging up. Reaffirm all commitments made and include times and dates of any appointments or services scheduled. Always include date, time, and reasons for calls, as well as the customer's name and company information. These items can be very beneficial when preserved in note form. Good notes prevent missed, lost, or forgotten communications from ruining a good customer relationship.

Telephone Etiquette

Telephones are great communications devices. Cell phones enable us to be reached, or to reach out from almost anywhere in the world—including in a customer's place of business. There are many people who cannot resist taking a call almost anywhere, under almost any circumstances. This tendency does not make for good customer service.

You should avoid taking personal calls when you are at work. If you see that a friend is calling you on your cell phone while you are at work, or in a customer's business, let the call go to voice mail. If you are in the middle of a serious conversation with a customer, you should not interrupt the conversation to answer your cell phone.

On the other hand, if you are working on a piece of equipment at the customer's facility, you could check to see who is calling. If the call is from someone you think you should speak with, or is a call you think it is important to take, answer the call, keep the conversation to a minimum, and call the other party back after you finish the customer's job. If you are in the customer's immediate presence when you see that a call could be important, tell the customer that you must take the call and excuse yourself from their presence to respond to the call.

If you decide to take a call at a customer's business (or residence) and it begins to looks as though it is going to take some time, you should tell the other party that you will have to reconnect with them at a different time. Customers will notice that you are on the phone and, if they are paying for your time, they will feel like they aren't getting good value from you.

EXAM ALERT

Know how to handle telephone calls when working at a customer or users location.

Handle Paperwork and Finish Up

There are a number of nontroubleshooting, nonrepair activities that must be handled to have an efficient organization. As a service person, you are not alone. As indicated at the beginning of this chapter, you are part of a team that must communicate effectively for the system to operate smoothly. Other members of the team won't be able to do their jobs effectively if you don't follow through on yours. When the last nut has been tightened and the last cord plugged in on a service call, process the paperwork as soon as possible so that it can be moving through your system.

Note any abnormalities, unusual situations, or memory-based activities in writing. For example, suppose that you loan a customer an extension cord and do not write a memo or work ticket entry about it. Would you reasonably expect to remember the place and situation after a couple of weeks, and dozens of service calls, have gone by? At some point, you, or one of your co-workers, will need that equipment, and there will be no record of where it is.

Follow up with people you have delegated tasks to so that you make sure that those tasks are being taken care of. Use an organizational aid to coordinate jobs, appointments, and activities with co-workers.

Maintain an Orderly Work Area

Handle jobs one at a time so that components from one job do not get mixed up with components from another job. Store equipment not being used so that there is ample room to work, and so that these items do not become a safety hazard.

Keep an inventory of parts and equipment in your area of responsibility. Promptly order parts needed for a job, and keep a log of when they should arrive. If the parts do not arrive as scheduled, you should have a reminder that they are still missing. This reminder will allow you to track repair parts so that when customers call to check on their equipment or problem, you will have the information at hand.

Tag parts brought into the work area so that they do not get lost or mishandled. Store them so that they will not be damaged by environmental factors, such as ESD. Include all pertinent information about the part, including the problem description, repair notes, and customer name and location.

If you are working in a customer's residence or business location, keep the work area as orderly as possible. Also protect the customer's equipment and environment from inflicted damages caused by your work.

Exam Prep Questions

1. Identify the customer satisfaction elements that create a successful business. (Select all that apply.)

   ○ **A.** Satisfaction with the organization (supplier)

   ○ **B.** Satisfaction with the product

   ○ **C.** Satisfaction with your personality

   ○ **D.** Satisfaction with the service received

2. Choose the items that negatively affect your perception as a professional. (Select all that apply.)

   ○ **A.** Use of breath mints

   ○ **B.** Wearing jeans

   ○ **C.** Chewing gum

   ○ **D.** Wearing polo shirts

3. You have just finished repairing a remote printer connection at a customer's office and need some paper to test it. The paper tray is empty and no one is nearby. What should you do?

   ○ **A.** Look for the supply closet

   ○ **B.** Find someone who works in the office and ask that person to get it for you

   ○ **C.** Find a manager from the office and ask permission to get and use their material

   ○ **D.** Leave a note for the operator to test the printer connection and get back to you if any problems occur

4. What are the definite downsides of illegally sharing copies of copyrighted software with customers or their employees? (Select all that apply.)

   ○ **A.** The customer may acquire a virus from your copy.

   ○ **B.** This action is illegal and could get you fired or your customer sued.

   ○ **C.** The customer will be disappointed in your ethics.

   ○ **D.** The customer will likely call the software supplier for support.

5. When dealing with an irate customer, what action on your part should be avoided to ensure that a conflict point isn't established?

    ◯ **A.** Contacting your boss to escalate the problem resolution to a higher level

    ◯ **B.** Aggressively defending your personal techniques and abilities

    ◯ **C.** Attempting to divert the conversation to a solutions-oriented discussion

    ◯ **D.** Going over details one at a time with the customer because this will appear as a waste of time to that customer

6. If you must put customers on hold, at what point should you consider asking them if you can call them back?

    ◯ **A.** 10 minutes

    ◯ **B.** 5 minutes

    ◯ **C.** 1 minute

    ◯ **D.** 30 seconds

7. You receive a call from an office where Jim, another member of your team, has just repaired a computer system for them. Jim has left their offices and they are telling you that the machine is down again. Which of the following is a proper customer service response?

    ◯ **A.** "The machine was working when Jim left your office. I can't imagine what could have happened to it. I'm busy right now and I know Jim is on another appointment already. I'll have someone get back to you as soon as possible."

    ◯ **B.** "I'm not familiar with what Jim was working on at your place, but I will try to help you or have Jim get back to you as soon as possible."

    ◯ **C.** "I can't help you but I will have Jim get back to you as soon as he can get free."

    ◯ **D.** "Give me your name and I will have Jim get back to you as soon as he can."

8. You are at a job site with one of your company's best customers when one of the managers asks you to repair a printer that you know your company does not sell or service. How should you handle this request?

    ◯ **A.** Simply perform the work as requested.

    ◯ **B.** Offer to perform the work on your own time.

    ◯ **C.** Refer the request to your management.

    ◯ **D.** Decline the work because it is not your responsibility.

9. When answering customer phone calls, what pieces of information should you always remember to include in your conversation? (Select all that apply.)

- ○ **A.** Your phone or extension number
- ○ **B.** Your name
- ○ **C.** The date and time
- ○ **D.** The company's name

10. When you are performing troubleshooting or other customer support functions over the telephone, which of the following are key parts of a successful customer satisfaction effort? (Select all that apply.)

- ○ **A.** Use precise directions and terminology.
- ○ **B.** Include plenty of anecdotes to keep the customer calm.
- ○ **C.** Ask questions before and after each instruction has been performed.
- ○ **D.** Make sure that the customers use a corded phone so that they can clearly hear your instructions.

11. You have been called into your service manager's office and told that your communications with your subordinates tends to be very assertive. The manager explains that some of your assertiveness is good and some is counter-productive. Which of the following is an example of good assertive communication?

- ○ **A.** Telling a co-worker, "You don't know what you're doing."
- ○ **B.** Telling an employee, "You are the reason were losing this account."
- ○ **C.** Saying "You don't understand what the goal is here" to a co-worker.
- ○ **D.** Saying "Tell me why you can't get this machine back to the customer today" to an employee.

12. A customer spends several minutes telling you the problems they are having with their PC. You are reasonably sure that you comprehend their problem, so how should you handle the customer at this point?

- ○ **A.** Repeat each portion of the problem back to the customer for verification.
- ○ **B.** Report the problem to your supervisor to let them know why your call is taking so long to complete.
- ○ **C.** Tell the customer the service is no longer available.
- ○ **D.** Tell the customer the you understand the problem and will fix the problem without any further delay.

13. When dealing with customers over the telephone, you should _____.

- ○ **A.** Control the call and gather important information about the problem
- ○ **B.** Allow the customer to guide the call because they are the one who has seen the problem
- ○ **C.** Let the customer explain everything and write it down
- ○ **D.** Take control of the conversation as soon as you have a good idea of what the problem is

14. You have been called to the service desk to deal with an angry customer who has returned a computer that has been brought in several times for the same problem, but it still does not work. What is the best way to handle this situation?

- ○ **A.** Tell the customer that you have not worked on this computer before but you're the best and that you are sure you will get it fixed for them.
- ○ **B.** Tell the customer that the machine qualifies as a lemon, under the "Lemon law" and replace it for them with a new unit.
- ○ **C.** Offer to send the machine off to a depot facility for a detailed troubleshooting process.
- ○ **D.** Try to calm the customer, review all the problems with them, perform a standard troubleshooting process based on the information and symptoms you receive, and correct the problem.

15. While working on a user's computer, their phone rings. Which of the following should you do?

- ○ **A.** Answer the phone and take a message for the person.
- ○ **B.** Don't touch the phone; let the message system get the call.
- ○ **C.** Answer the call and ask the caller to wait while you find the user.
- ○ **D.** Answer the call, and tell the caller to call back later.

Answers and Explanations

1. **A, B, D.** In many ways, how service people are perceived is as important as how well they perform. In the end, it is customer satisfaction (with the product, the service, and the supplier) that creates a successful business— and continued employment.

2. **B, C.** You should always make certain that your attire is clean, neat, and appropriate. It should also be businesslike. Avoid excessive jewelry, or

jewelry that might be offensive to your range of customers. Also, hold down the cologne or perfume—be moderate. Practice good hygiene by keeping hair washed and groomed, fingernails trimmed and clean, and breath fresh (use mouthwash or breath mints as needed, but not chewing gum). Refer to your company's policies for clarification.

3. C. Find a manager from the office and ask permission to get and use their material.

4. A, B. Never break copyright regulations by illegally loading or giving away software. One of the leading causes of computer virus infection is pirated software. Not only do you run this risk in giving away copies, it's illegal, and it can get you introduced to various people you never really wanted to meet, such as lawyers and judges. On top of that, it could cost you your job.

5. B. Avoid arguing with the customer. When you do reply, remain calm, talk in a steady voice, and avoid making inflammatory comments. Also, try to avoid taking a defensive stance, because this signals a conflict point. Realize that criticism given out by customers is generally not personal—so don't take it personally. Information delivered with an aggressive attitude will normally lead to an aggressive, or retaliatory response from the customer.

6. D. Avoid putting customers on hold if possible. If you must put them on hold, make certain to get their name and phone number in case anything happens. If you expect that the customer may be on hold for more than 30 seconds, ask if you can call the customer back. Their time is as valuable as yours, and, unless they are calling on a toll-free or local line, they are paying for the call.

7. B. Take responsibility for being the single point of contact for the customer. In this case, the only answer option that leads to customer satisfaction is for you to attempt to deal with the problem. You may reach a point where you need to turn the problem back over to Jim, but you should not put the customer off without trying to help first.

8. C. Take the initiative to move it to the next level of authority. Never leave customers hanging without a path to get their problems addressed.

9. B, D. Always identify your company and provide your name when making or receiving telephone calls. Attempt to use the caller's name at least once, if not twice, in the conversation. This action personalizes the call and lets the customer know you are paying attention. (It also reminds you to pay attention.)

10. A, C. When giving instructions over the phone, be precise. Provide detailed instructions for work to be done, and ask lots of questions about what is happening on the other end.

11. D. Recognize that there is a professional way to communicate with customers. There is a difference between saying "You broke this PC" and "Help me understand how the computer got to this point." The first statement is overly assertive and judgmental while the second is inquiring and non-judgmental. The assertive statement sets up a level of separation between the technician and the user, whereas the inquisitive statement brings the two together to investigate the problem. Overly assertive conversations with co-workers can create adversarial conditions. If you have a personality that tends to use this approach with people, work on controlling and minimizing this trait.

12. D. Mentally (and maybe physically) identify key points as the customer describes the nature of the problem. Don't interrupt customer descriptions before you have all the details. Even if you are sure that you know what is going on after the first sentence, have patience to listen to the complete description. Then fix the problem.

13. A. The ability to communicate clearly is the other trait most looked for in service people. Allow customers to talk through their problems but try to guide and control the discussion to make certain that it stays focused. If you simply let the conversation go in any direction, you may waste a significant amount of the customer's and your time. Also, you're the one with the knowledge of what might cause problems. The customer may not have good diagnostic skills or system knowledge, so they will not know how to optimize the conversation.

14. D. Avoid arguing with the customer. When you do reply, remain calm, talk in a steady voice, and avoid making inflammatory comments. After the customer has poured out the full story, try to redirect the conversation to creating solutions to the problems. Go over the important details one at a time and explain how you will handle each concern, or who you must turn to for a final answer.

15. B. Avoid distracting employees while you are working at a customer's site. Ask permission to use the customer's facilities, such as the telephone, copier, or other equipment. In this case, there is no reason for you to answer someone else's telephone unless they have specifically asked you to.

Challenge Solutions

1. C. You should handle each call using a professional troubleshooting approach without jumping to conclusions. In this case, there is no need to tell customers that this is a widespread problem or to discuss the scope of the problem at all. This does nothing to ingratiate customers to you or your company—it also does not fix their problem. Doing an efficient, professional, and complete job will do more to ingratiate you to the customer than distancing yourself from the product. Also, there is always a chance that the problem the customer is having is not the common malfunction that has been associated with that model; simply offering to send RAM without conducting a troubleshooting process will miss this possibility and will not make the customer happy. It will also cost the company the price of the misdiagnosed RAM.

2. A. Be sensitive to the level of the person you are making recommendations to. There are people who have never met a new piece of hardware or software they didn't like. However, their superiors may be quite happy without the production, downtime, and cost trade-offs that changing could bring. Don't incite the customer's employees with the latest and greatest product if their management hasn't signaled the way. In this case, the company has just made an investment, and you should assume that they have done some research and gotten comfortable with what they purchased. Diminishing the product at this point will not win you any points—where were you when the company was making its decision?

3. A. Mentally (and maybe physically) identify key points as the customer describes the nature of the problem. Don't interrupt customer descriptions before you have all the details. Even if you are sure that you know what is going on after the first sentence, have patience to listen to the complete description. This is not only common courtesy but also serves to uncover extra data about the problem.

4. C. Try to quickly recognize the technical abilities of the people you are working with. Adjust your conversation to accommodate them. For technically challenged customers, avoid jargon and acronyms. It will be confusing to them and can be a cause of customer dissatisfaction with you, even if you do a great job.

5. D. The only thing you can say to the customer without assuming a defensive position is to ask if it ever worked after it left the shop. All the other answer options establish a defensive or accusatory tone: "What happened to it," "It was working when it left here," or "I can't believe

the level of people I have to work with." None of these does anything positive for the customer. "Did it work" is an investigative question with no overtones.

6. C. Take personal responsibility for being the single point for the service call—contacting specialists, dealing with parts vendors, and so on. It's your show, run it (unless your organization has someone in the structure that is supposed to take over this responsibility). Don't try to establish or transfer blame. Quick, efficient help from you can calm customers and return them to some level of satisfaction with your company and products—and maybe even you.

7. C. If a problem runs beyond the scope of your position or your capabilities, take the initiative to move it to the next level of authority. Never leave a customer hanging without a path to follow to get the problems addressed.

CHAPTER TWENTY-SEVEN

Advanced PC Component Installations and Upgrades

Terms you'll need to understand:

✓ Pin 1

✓ ZIF socket

✓ Health configuration

✓ Advanced cooling systems

✓ Voltage regulator module

Techniques you'll need to master:

Depot Technician Objective 1.1—
Install, configure, optimize, and
upgrade personal computer components

✓ Add, remove, and configure
internal storage devices, motherboards, power supplies,
processor/CPUs, memory and
adapter cards, including the following:

  ✓ Drive preparation

  ✓ Jumper configuration

  ✓ Storage device power and
cabling

  ✓ Selection and installation
of appropriate motherboard

  ✓ BIOS setup and
configuration

✓ Selection and installation
of appropriate CPU

✓ Selection and installation
of appropriate memory

✓ Installation of adapter
cards, including hardware
and software/drivers

✓ Configuration and optimization of adapter cards,
including adjusting
hardware settings and
obtaining network card
connection

✓ Add, remove, and configure
systems

IT Technician Objective 1.1—Install, configure, optimize, and upgrade personal computer components

✓ Add, remove, and configure personal computer components, including selection and installation of appropriate components; for example:

- ✓ Storage devices
- ✓ Motherboards
- ✓ Power supplies
- ✓ Processors/CPUs
- ✓ Memory
- ✓ Display devices
- ✓ Input devices (for example, basic, specialty, and multimedia)
- ✓ Adapter cards
- ✓ Cooling systems

Introduction

This chapter covers the advanced Installation, Configuration, Optimizing and Upgrading of Personal Computer Components area of the CompTIA A+ Certification—Depot Technician examination under Objectives 1.1 and IT Technician examination under Objective 1.1.

Unlike most peripheral systems, which can be physically installed and then detected through PnP, other components in the PC require additional planning to install and optimize. For the most part, these components are related to the system board. The other major PC component that requires some consideration before installing or upgrading is the power supply unit. PC technicians should be able to install, connect, and configure these components to upgrade or repair an existing system.

> **NOTE**
>
> Depot Technician Objective 1.1 and IT Technician Objective 1.1 use different ways of saying the same thing. The Depot Technician objective list is more explicit about configuring and optimizing, whereas the IT Technician 1.1 Objective is more specific about selecting appropriate components. Many of the items listed as subobjectives were covered under the "Basic Installation and Configuration" section of the Essentials 1.1 objective. However, both the Depot Technician 1.1 and IT Technician 1.1 objectives include power supplies, system boards, processors, memory devices, and cooling systems not covered in other sections.
>
> The topics specified in these different exam/objective areas are so closely stated that it makes sense that they are presented as the same discussion. You will need to study this material in this chapter for any of the four exams you intend to challenge.

System Board Compatibility Issues

Component form factors come into play when assembling new systems, as well as in repair and upgrade situations where system boards are being replaced. Therefore, the first consideration when installing or replacing a system board is whether it will physically fit the environment and whether it will work with the other system components. In both cases, you must deal with the following basic compatibility issues:

- The system board's form factor
- The case's form factor
- The power supply connection types

▶ The disk drive connection types (PATA/SATA/FDD)

▶ Front panel connection types (USB/IEEE-1394/SD Card Readers)

▶ The system board's power requirements

System boards of different types have different mounting-hole patterns. The hole pattern of the replacement system board must match that of the case. If not, the replacement board cannot be installed or grounded properly. Some clone system boards do not observe standard sizes (only compatible standoff spacing). If the case has a power supply that mounts in the floor of the unit, there may not be enough open width in the case to accommodate an extra-wide system board. The same can be said for a full-height disk drive bay. If the disk drive bay reaches from the floor of the case to its top, there will be no room for a wide system board to fit under it.

In addition to the mounting hole alignment issue, the case openings for expansion slots and port connections must be compatible with those of the system board. Likewise, expansion slot placement is likely to vary between different form factors. The bad alignment created by this situation can make it difficult to install I/O cards in some systems. Similarly, I/O connectors mounted directly on the backs of system boards may not line up with openings in other form factor case styles. The types of adapter cards in the system are another point of consideration when installing or replacing a system board. Make sure that the new board has enough of the correct types of expansion slots to handle all the different adapter cards in the system.

System boards typically include a small panel called an *I/O shield* that can be installed in the back panel of the system unit to accommodate the system board's particular I/O port arrangements. These shields are designed to replace the I/O shield supplied by the case manufacturer. The I/O shield that comes with the system unit case may be held in place by tabs or screws. The replacement shields are typically designed to snap into place in a standardized opening in the back panel.

Power supply size, orientation, and connectors present another compatibility consideration. The ATX specification calls for this device to be placed toward the right rear of the board so that its fan can push air directly across the microprocessor. Under the BTX specification, the processor placement is moved toward the front center of the board so that a front-mounted thermal (cooling) unit can direct fresh air across it.

> ## Challenge #1
>
> You have been called in as a computer consultant for the world's third-largest banking organization. It wants to upgrade its existing computer systems to Pentium-class systems. When you arrive, you discover that old Windows 3.11 operating systems are still running on 80386 computers. These systems use baby AT system boards, 2/3-size multi-I/O cards, 9-pin serial mice, and 500MB IDE hard drives. What should you advise the customer to do to upgrade the machines with the least cost and the most advantage?

Replacing System Boards

Generally, system boards are removed for one of two possible reasons. Either the system board has failed and has to be replaced, or the user wants to install a new system board with better features. In either case, it will be necessary to remove the current system board and replace it. The removal procedure can be defined in five steps:

1. Remove all external I/O systems.

2. Remove the system unit's outer cover.

3. Remove the option adapter cards.

4. Remove the cables from the system board.

5. Remove the system board.

Removing the External I/O Systems

Unplug all power cords from the commercial power outlet. Remove all peripherals from the system unit. Disconnect the mouse, keyboard, and monitor signal cable from the unit. In the past, these connections would have all been made at the rear of the unit. However, new case and system designs provide additional USB, IEEE-1394, audio, and video connections as well as flash card readers on the front of the machine. These connections are tied to the system board through cabling (often called *header cables*) that must be removed before the system board can be exchanged. Figure 27.1 illustrates the system unit's back panel connections.

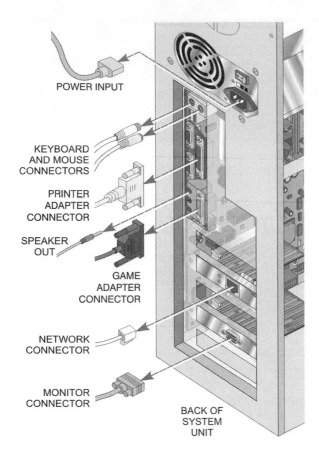

POWER INPUT

KEYBOARD
AND MOUSE
CONNECTORS

PRINTER
ADAPTER
CONNECTOR

SPEAKER
OUT

GAME
ADAPTER
CONNECTOR

NETWORK
CONNECTOR

MONITOR
CONNECTOR

BACK OF
SYSTEM
UNIT

FIGURE 27.1   System unit back panel connections.

Removing the System Unit's Cover

Unplug the AC power cord from the system unit. Determine which type of case you are working with. If the case is a desktop model, does the cover slide off the chassis in a forward direction, bringing the front panel with it, or does it raise off the chassis from the rear? If the back lip of the outer cover folds over the edge of the back panel, the lid raises up from the back after the retaining screws are removed. If the retaining screws go through the back panel without passing through the lip, the outer cover will slide forward after the retaining screws have been removed.

Remove the screws that hold the cover to the chassis. Store the screws properly. Next, remove the system unit's outer cover and set it aside. Slide the case forward. Tilt the case upward from the front and remove it from the unit. Or lift the back edge of the outer cover to approximately 45 degrees, and then slide it toward the rear of the chassis.

> **NOTE**
>
> Although these are common types of system unit case designs, you should be aware that there are a wide assortment of case designs you may encounter. Some will have swing out access doors and panels, whereas others have door handles and key locks. In each case you will need to exam the external appearance of the case to determine how it comes apart.

Removing the Adapter Cards

Remove any cables or connectors from the adapter card, noting where they originate. If the card is free of connections, remove the retaining screws that secure the adapter cards to the system unit's back panel. Finally, remove the adapter cards from the expansion slots. It is a good practice to place adapter cards back into the same slots they were removed from, if possible. Store the screws properly.

Removing the Cables from the System Board

The system board provides an operator interface through a set of front panel indicator lights and switches. These indicators and switches connect to the system board by BERG connectors, as depicted in Figure 27.2.

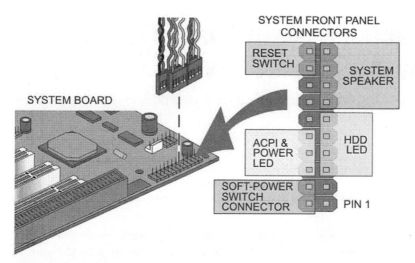

FIGURE 27.2 Front panel connections.

The front panel connectors must be removed to exchange the system board for a new one. Because it is quite easy to get these connections reversed, make sure that you mark them before removing them from their connection points. Record the color and function of each connection. Trace each wire back to its front panel connection to determine what its purpose is. This will ensure that all the wires are reinstalled correctly after the exchange is completed.

Remove the HDD and CD-ROM/DVD drive signal cables from the system board. Disconnect the power supply connections from the system board as well.

Removing the System Board

Verify the positions of all jumper and switch settings on the old system board. Record these settings and verify their meanings before removing the board from the system. This may require the use of the board's user manual, if available. Remove the grounding screws that secure the system board to the chassis. Store the screws properly.

In some cases you will be able to lift the system board straight out of the chassis, as illustrated in Figure 27.3. However, in other cases, you will need to guide some portion of the board around overhanging disk drive cages and power supply mounts. Normally, you simply need to tilt the board back and forth to clear these obstacles on the way out. Be careful not to snag any of the system board devices on these structures as you remove the board from the case. The same will be true when you install the replacement system board in the unit.

Replacing System Board Field Replaceable Unit Devices

The system board contains a few serviceable devices on the system board. These include

- ▶ The microprocessor
- ▶ The system RAM modules
- ▶ Specialized support ICs

As with the system board itself, there are really only two possible reasons for replacing any of these devices: to replace a failed unit or to upgrade the unit. In either case, technicians must be able to exchange the device and return the system to proper operation.

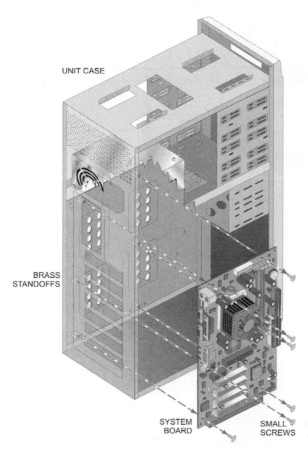

UNIT CASE

BRASS
STANDOFFS

SYSTEM
BOARD

SMALL
SCREWS

FIGURE 27.3 Removing the system board.

Installing Microprocessors

PC manufacturers mount microprocessors in sockets so that they can be replaced easily. This enables a failed microprocessor to simply be exchanged with a working unit. More often, though, the microprocessor is replaced with an improved version to upgrade the speed or performance of the system.

As the typical microprocessor's pin count increased, special Zero Insertion Force (ZIF) sockets were designed that permit the microprocessor to be placed in the socket without force and then clamped in place. An arm-activated clamping mechanism in the socket shifts to the side, locking the pins in place. A ZIF socket and microprocessor arrangement is depicted in Figure 27.4.

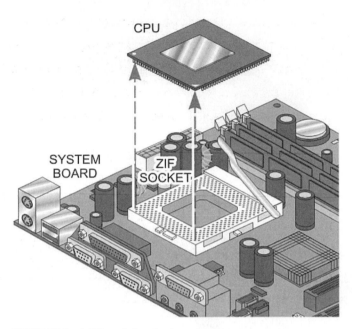

FIGURE 27.4 A ZIF socket and microprocessor.

After the microprocessor has been locked in place, the heat sink and fan unit must be installed. The fan unit is typically attached to the heat sink block using small machine screws. The combined heat sink/fan unit clamps into place on top of the microprocessor. Before you install the fan/heat sink unit, you must apply thermal compound to the heat sink (usually a small drop) and spread it across the heat sink/microprocessor contact surface.

To release the microprocessor from the socket, the lever arm beside the socket must be pressed down and away from the socket. When it comes free from the socket, the arm raises up to release the pressure on the microprocessor's pins.

A notch and dot in one corner of the CPU marks the position of the processor's pin 1. The dot and notch should be located at the free end of the socket's locking lever for proper installation. Both the CPU and the socket have one corner that does not have a pin (or pin hole) in it. This feature prevents the CPU from being inserted into the socket incorrectly.

If the processor does not appear to set completely flush in the socket, remove it before clamping it into place. Check for bent pins that may not be lining up properly with the socket. Also make certain that the processor's pin configuration lines up properly with the socket. If you force the processor into the socket, you may break the pin off and ruin the processor.

EXAM ALERT

Be aware of the potential to damage the processor if it does not seat properly in the socket.

Installing Slot Processors

From the Pentium II processor forward, Intel has offered microprocessors in Single Edge Cartridges (SEC). These processors mount vertically in an edge connector slot on the system board. The slot concept is very similar to the expansion slot connectors used with adapter cards. Because the cartridge mounts vertically on the system board, special mechanical supports must be installed on the system board to help hold it in place. These supports are normally preinstalled on the system board by its manufacturer.

The processor cartridge slides into the upright supports as illustrated in Figure 27.5. It should be pressed firmly into the slot to ensure good contact.

Configuring Processor Speeds

Pentium microprocessors are available in a number of speed ratings, and many use a dual-processor voltage arrangement. In addition, the processor may be a Pentium clone manufactured by a company other than Intel.

The microprocessor's internal core voltage supply is controlled through a voltage regulator module (VRM) located on the system board. Previous Pentium system board generations employed jumpers to establish the proper +3V and CPU core voltage settings for the particular type of microprocessor being installed. These boards also used jumpers to establish the external/internal clock ratio for the microprocessor, as well as its external front-side bus frequency. Newer systems autodetect the type of microprocessor installed through the PnP BIOS and configure these settings for their optimum values.

Fans, Heat Sinks, and Cooling Systems

Modern processors generate a considerable amount of heat. To prevent this heat from reaching a destructive level for the device, all Pentium processors require CPU cooling fans and heat sinks. As Figure 27.6 illustrates, these devices come in many forms, including simple heat sinks and fan-cooled, active heat sinks.

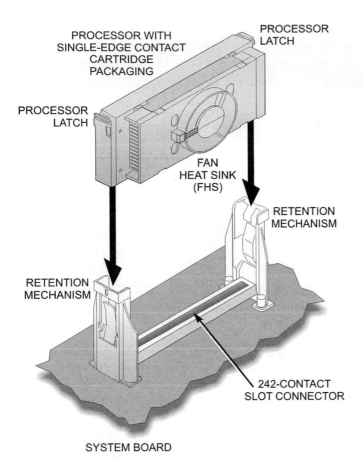

FIGURE 27.5 Installing a cartridge processor.

Heat sinks are finned metal slabs that can be clipped onto the top of the microprocessor (heat sinks for other major chipset devices—such as the North Bridge—may be permanently attached to the top of the device). The fins increase the surface area of the heat sink, enabling it to dissipate heat more rapidly. Active heat sinks add a fan unit to move air across the heat sink. The fan moves the heat away from the heat sink and the microprocessor more rapidly.

A special heat-conducting thermal compound is typically used with snap-on heat sinks to provide good thermal transfer between the microprocessor and the heat sink. Power for the fans is usually obtained from one of the system's power connectors or from a special jumper block on the system board. These items must be installed before operating the microprocessor.

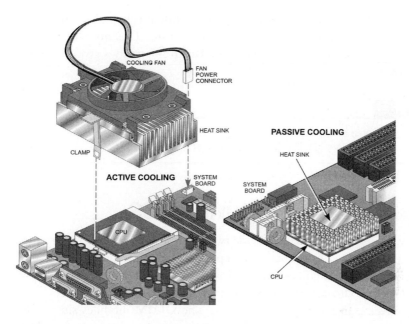

FIGURE 27.6   Typical microprocessor cooling systems.

Cartridge-mounted Pentium processors require heat sinks and cooling systems to dissipate the tremendous amount of heat they generate. Slot-based cartridge processors (Pentium II, III, and 4 processors) also require special heat sink and fan support structures that work with the cartridge package. These units mount vertically on the system board beside the processor cartridge and provide support for the heat sink as well as the fan unit. The support mechanism is designed so that it plugs into standard predrilled holes in the system board. The fan unit receives power and speed control information from the system board through a two- or three-wire cable and connector. The fan unit can be removed from the support mechanism and replaced for repair or upgrading purposes.

ATX-style systems employ power supplies that use a reverse-flow fan that brings in cool air from the back of the unit and blows it directly on the microprocessor. For this arrangement to work properly, the system board must adhere to the ATX form factor guidelines and have the microprocessor in the correct position. In theory, this design eliminates the need for special microprocessor-cooling fans. Because slot processors are typically used in ATX-style systems, the processor cartridge assembly is typically mounted directly beneath the power supply vent to achieve additional cooling benefits.

The BIOS in Pentium systems interrogates the processor during startup and configures it appropriately. This prevents the user from subjecting the processor to potentially destructive conditions, such as overclocking. In addition, these systems can monitor the health of the processor while it is in operation and take steps to compensate for problems such as overheating. This normally involves speeding up or slowing down the processor fan to maintain a given operating temperature.

NOTE

Even with automated temperature and speed control features, PC enthusiasts still over-clock Pentium processors to enhance the operation of their machines.

Installing Memory Modules

Modern system boards typically provide two or more dual inline memory module (DIMM) sockets. These sockets accept small piggyback memory modules that can contain various combinations of RAM devices. DIMMs use edge connectors that snap into a retainer on the system board. DIMM sockets accept 168-pin, 184-pin, or 240-pin DIMM units. The DIMM modules simply slide vertically into the socket and are locked in place by a tab at each end. These processes are illustrated in Figure 27.7. DIMM modules are keyed so that they cannot be plugged in backward.

Physically installing the RAM devices is all that is usually required. The system's PnP operation automatically detects the type of RAM installed and establishes proper settings for it during the boot process. Steps can be taken to optimize key RAM parameters through the CMOS Setup utility. However, only technicians who are aware of the implications of the changes they are making should change these parameters.

EXAM ALERT

Know that DIMM modules are keyed and that it is almost physically impossible to plug them in wrong.

On some Pentium system boards, the DIMM sockets are organized so that slots 1 and 2 make up bank-0, and slots 2 and 3 form bank-1. Each bank can be filled with single-sided (32-bit) DIMMs or double-sided (64-bit) DIMMs. The system can be operated with only bank-0 full. It will also operate with both banks full. However, it cannot be operated with a portion of any bank filled (a bank in use must be full).

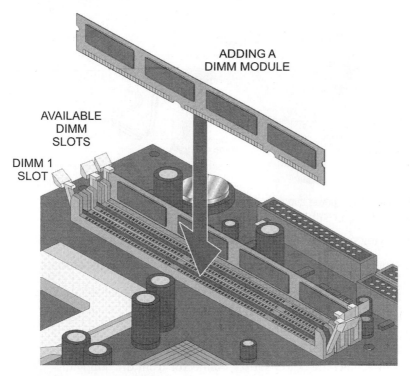

ADDING A
DIMM MODULE

AVAILABLE
DIMM
SLOTS

DIMM 1
SLOT

FIGURE 27.7   Installing a DIMM module.

Challenge #2

An employee in a remote office has called you for information about how to replace a system board in one of the desktop computers. She saw smoke coming from the microprocessor on the current system board and wants to replace it. Write a description of the process for replacing the system board that you can fax to her office. (The phone cord cannot reach the location of the failed computer.)

Replacing Power Supplies

The function of the power supply is to convert commercially available AC power into various levels of DC electrical power and deliver them to the system's components. To exchange the power supply, its connections to the power source and other devices must be removed. Figure 27.8 illustrates the typical power supply connections in a PC. The only other step involved in exchanging the power supply is to remove the screws that bind it to the system unit case.

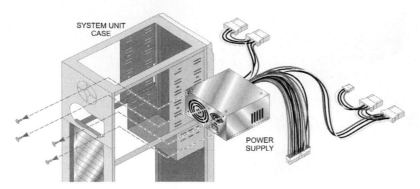

FIGURE 27.8 Removing a power supply.

Use the following procedure to remove a power supply unit from a system:

1. Disconnect the exterior power connections from the system unit.

   a. Unplug the power cord from the commercial receptacle.

2. Disconnect the interior power connections.

   a. Disconnect the power supply connections from the system board.

   b. Disconnect the power supply connector from the floppy disk drive (if present).

   c. Disconnect the power supply connectors from the hard disk drive(s).

   d. Disconnect the power supply connectors from the optical drive(s).

3. Remove the power supply unit from the system.

   a. Remove the four retaining screws that secure the power supply unit to the rear of the system unit.

   b. Store the screws properly.

   c. Remove the power supply from the system unit by lifting it out.

Installing Power Supplies

When ordering a replacement power supply, you must remember to take into account its form factor and its wattage rating requirements. The *wattage* rating is a measurement of the total power the supply can deliver to the system. More heavily equipped systems (that is, more disk drives and peripherals) require power supplies with higher wattage ratings.

Power Supply Upgrade Considerations

One consideration that may not be apparent when system components are being upgraded is the power supply. Each time a new drive or device is added to the system, more current is required. The power supply unit in a computer comes with a given power rating (in watts). The voltage level for a given location in the world is fixed (that is, 120 or 220VAC) and the power required can be calculated by multiplying the voltage level by the maximum current rating (in amperes) of all the devices in the system.

In the field, it is difficult to accumulate the current values for all the devices in the system. For example, upgrading the processor can easily increase the power consumption in the system by more than 20 watts. A typical Pentium processor may require 65 watts of power to operate. Advanced Pentium processors have increased their power consumption to more than 80 watts. Replacing RAM with faster or bigger RAM devices tends to increase power consumption as well. Simply increasing the installed memory from 128MB to 256MB by adding an additional DIMM will almost double the power consumption of the system's memory (that is, from 6 watts to 12).

Adding adapter cards to the system also significantly increases the amount of power the power supply must deliver to the system board. A typical adapter card may require 12 to 15 watts with good connections to the slot. A high-end video adapter used for games may consume up to 100 watts. However, disk drive devices tend to consume more power than most other system devices because they use motors to spin the disk or disc and to position the read/write mechanism. A typical hard disk drive can require up to 20 or 30 watts each.

As you can see from these paragraphs, it is relatively easy to consume hundreds of watts of power for a normal system. The typical power supply used with basic Pentium desktop systems is 300 watts. One third of this value must be reserved for startup of the computer. During this time, the system will require more power than it does when it is running. For systems using the high-end video card mentioned earlier, the power supply might need to be capable of delivering 500 watts or more of power.

In any event, there are two ways to determine that the system will need a power supply upgrade. The first is to approximate how much each device will require and double that value to provide for operating safety and the startup surge. The second method involves purchasing all the upgrade items and turning on the system to discover that it will not start.

System Upgrading and Optimizing

The modular design of the PC-compatible system enables portions of the system to be upgraded as new, or better, components become available, or as the system's application changes. PC technicians must be capable of upgrading the system's BIOS as part of a system upgrade. Technicians should also be able to optimize PC hardware to obtain the best performance possible for a given system configuration. The following sections cover upgradeable components found in common PC systems, including information about when and how to upgrade them.

System Board Upgrading

There are typically four serviceable components on the system board:

▶ The microprocessor

▶ The RAM modules

▶ The CMOS backup battery

▶ The ROM BIOS

Of the four items listed, three—the microprocessor, the RAM modules, and the cache memory—can be exchanged to increase the performance of the system. These devices are usually mounted in sockets to make replacing or upgrading them an easy task.

Great care should be taken when exchanging these parts to avoid damage to the ICs from electrostatic discharge. In addition, care should be taken during the extraction and replacement of the ICs to avoid misalignment and bent pins. Make sure to correctly align the IC's pin #1 with the socket's pin #1 position. In the case of microprocessors that plug into standard sockets, the force required to insert them may overstress the system board if it is not properly supported.

Microprocessor Upgrades

Microprocessor manufacturers generally offer their different microprocessor types in multiple speed ratings. This strategy enables the end user to realize speed and performance increases by upgrading their microprocessor and its support systems to use faster, or multi-core processors.

Upgrading the processor is a fairly easy operation after gaining access to the system board. In most cases, you can simply remove the heat sink and fan unit form the board, remove the microprocessor from its socket and replace it with the upgrade processor, apply new thermal grease to the heat sink, and then reattach the fan/heat sink unit to the processor. However, you should check the system board's documentation before selecting an upgrade microprocessor for it. You must make certain that the system board will support the new processor in terms of the following:

▶ Physical compatibility—Socket versus slot or socket type-A versus socket type-B compatibility. When you move a microprocessor to a new board, it must be socket compatible, voltage compatible, and speed compatible with the new board.

▶ Speed/clocking ratings—There is no need to purchase a 2GHz processor with a 200MHz front-side bus capability if the system supports only 1.2GHz operation using a 133MHz front-side bus speed. If you do so, the new processor will be limited to operating at all the system board's lower capabilities.

▶ Technology—A 0.13 micron processor will not work in a socket system designed to support processors built with 0.18 micron technology.

▶ Logical upgradability—Verify that the existing BIOS can be upgraded to support the new microprocessor specifications.

Table 27.1 shows the upgrade paths available to the major microprocessor types used in PCs.

TABLE 27.1 Microprocessor Upgrade Paths

SOCKET TYPE	MICROPROCESSOR
Slot A	AMD Athlon
Socket 462 (Socket A)	AMD Athlon, Duron, Athlon XP, Athlon XP-M, Athlon MP, Sepron
Socket 423	Pentium 4 (1.3GHz–2.0GHz)
Socket 478	Pentium 4 (1.4GHz–2.2GHz)
Socket 603	Pentium 4 Xeon (1.4GHz–2.2GHz)
Socket 418	Itanium/Intel (733MHz–800MHz)
FC-LGA775 (Socket T)	Pentium 4 Extreme Edition (3.2GHz–3.7GHz)
	Pentium D (2.667GHz–3.6GHz)
	Celeron D (2.133GHz–3.333GHz)

(continues)

TABLE 27.1 *Continued*

SOCKET TYPE	MICROPROCESSOR
Socket 563	Athlon XP-M (1.333GHz–2.333GHz)
Socket 754	Athlon 64 (2.133GHz–3.333GHz)
Socket 939	Athlon 64 (2.133GHz–3.333 GHz)
	Athlon 64 FX (2.2GHz–2.8GHz)
	Opteron (1.4GHz–2.4GHz)
Socket 940	Opteron (1.6GHz–3.0GHz)
	Athlon 64 FX (2.2GHz–2.8GHz)

There are three places in a Windows-based PC where you can go to determine the speed of a currently installed microprocessor. You can view the microprocessor's speed on the System Properties tab. To access this location, right-click My Computer and then select Properties from the menu. Click the General tab and view the microprocessor information displayed in the Computer area. You can also view the microprocessor's information through the System Information utility. To view the microprocessor's speed through this path, click the Start button and select the Run option. In the Run dialog box, type **Msinfo32**, click the OK button followed by the System Summary option. The processor speed will be displayed in the Processor line. Finally, you can use Device Manager to determine the current microprocessor's speed. click on the Start button and select the Run option. In the Run dialog box, type **Devmgmt.msc**, and then click OK. Expand the Processors node to view the microprocessor information.

> **EXAM ALERT**
>
> Know how to determine the operating speed of an installed processor in a Windows system.

After the new processor has been installed, you should verify the operation of the upgrade. The initial test will be to boot up the system and see whether you receive an error code and to verify that the system recognizes the newly installed processor.

Bus System Issues

Different portions of the system's buses run at different speeds. When an upgrade microprocessor is installed in a system, the coordination between it and the other devices requires that the timing relationships among all the buses be recalculated. This process begins with the microprocessor and its front-side bus. However, the other buses in the system must run at predetermined speeds to maintain compatibility with the types of devices they serve. The chipset devices must be reset so that they can act to synchronize the movement of information between the different buses.

Most current system boards feature autodetection functions as part of the PnP process that automatically detects the presence of the new processor on the board and synchronizes the different bus speed configurations. These systems exchange information with the system's PnP BIOS during the configuration portion of the boot procedure to obtain the optimum chipset settings.

However, some microprocessor-related settings on system boards may still be enabled and configured through onboard jumpers. Incorrectly setting processor-related jumpers causes a high number of failures for both new installations and upgrades. You should always refer to the system board's installation guide or user's manual for definitions of these settings. In particular, the Core Voltage, Bus Frequency, and Bus Ratio settings must be properly configured for the new processor. If these items are not set correctly, you may have the following types of problems:

▶ Overheating and destroying the new microprocessor

▶ Inability to start the system

▶ Encountering random errors during normal operations

▶ Failure to start the operating system

▶ Receiving incorrect processor type or incorrect processor speed messages during the POST

EXAM ALERT

Know why a computer would show an incorrect processor type or speed message after a processor upgrade has been conducted.

On many system boards it is possible to tweak the board to clock the microprocessor above its stated characteristics. In these systems, the microprocessor clock is set at a higher speed than the IC manufacturer suggests. This is referred to as *overclocking the processor*. This typically involves manually setting the processor configurations for higher microprocessor clock settings. Overclocking the processor normally includes updating the BIOS to support the upgraded processor and improving the processor's cooling system.

Installing Additional Processors

Some system boards provide multiple processor sockets or slots that permit additional processors to be added to distribute the processing load. You can use all, some, or just one of the available sockets by removing the terminator from the socket and installing the new processor. When possible, adding additional processors represents the most effective means to upgrade the performance of the computer. However, several steps should be taken before installing additional processors:

1. Verify processor compatibility—Ensure that the additional processor you are installing is compatible with the socket type on the board (preferably the same brand of processor that is already being used on the board). You should also check the production run number of the processor to ensure that it is within one production run of its companion processors. In the case of Intel processors, this is referred to as a *stepping level*. For optimum stability, you should install the same make, model, and clock speed for all processors. This would include using the same bus speed and multiplier settings and the same cache size to ensure that there is no speed difference between cache feeds. Refer to the multiprocessor system board's manual or online documentation for detailed information about processor compatibility issues.

2. Perform a BIOS upgrade—Multiple processor system boards include a BIOS version with multiple processor support. This BIOS should be sufficient when installing directly compatible additional processors. However, for major upgrades, such as installing newer and faster processors, the BIOS may have to be upgraded. In many cases, newer BIOS versions are developed by the system board's manufacturer to permit the installation of faster processors as they enter the market. Therefore, check the manufacturer's Internet support site to determine whether your system board can support the processor type and speed you intend to use.

3. Verify upgrade—Verifying a processor upgrade is fairly simple. Boot the system to see whether an error code is generated and to verify that the system recognizes the newly installed processor.

NOTE

You should not interpret an automatic entry into the CMOS Setup utility as an error when the system is initially booted after adding an additional processor. This is the process that systems often use to recognize new processors. You can use the system's CMOS Setup utility (or its administrative tools package) to ensure that the system board is recognizing all the installed processors and that they are working properly.

Managing Symmetric Multiprocessing

The task-scheduling capabilities of Windows enable it to control multiple microprocessors on a single system board. In the case of system boards with multiple microprocessors, the Windows microkernel provides synchronization between the different processors. The Symmetrical Multiprocessing (SMP) function enables threads of any process to be applied to any available processor in the system. The SMP function also enables microprocessors within a system to share memory space with and assign threads to the next available microprocessor.

Using SMP, the processing load is distributed evenly among all the installed processors, regardless of what type of task is being performed. However, in an Asymmetrical Multiprocessing (AMP) scheme, each processor is capable of processing only a particular type of task. Therefore, the processing load is distributed based on the tasks that each processor can perform. This technique permits conditions to occur in which one processor is very busy while others are idle.

Windows 2000 Professional and XP Professional both offer SMP support for dual (2x) processor operations. Similarly, Windows 2000 Server can support up to 4 (4x) simultaneous processors, whereas the Advanced and Datacenter versions of the Server package support 8x and 16x SMP, respectively (or 32 processors using a special OEM version of Windows 2000 Datacenter). With versions of the server running more than four processors, the hardware manufacturer must supply a special, proprietary version of the Windows 2000 HAL.DLL file for the machines.

If you upgrade a system to use additional processors, or if you upgrade the existing processors on a multiprocessor board, you will need to update the HAL file. This operation is performed through Device Manager. Access Device Manager and expand the Computer node. The currently installed HAL will be displayed, as illustrated in Figure 27.9. Then, to update the installed HAL, right-click the existing HAL and select the Update Driver option from the menu.

Firmware Upgrades

The physical microprocessor upgrade should also be accompanied by a logical upgrade. For major upgrades, such as installing newer and faster processors, the BIOS may need to be upgraded as well. Later BIOS versions are often developed by the system board's manufacturer to permit installation of faster processors as they come on the market.

When the microprocessor is upgraded, the BIOS should be flashed with the latest compatibility firmware. If the BIOS does not possess the flash option and does not support the new microprocessor, a new BIOS chip that does support it must be obtained. If not, the entire system board will typically need to be upgraded.

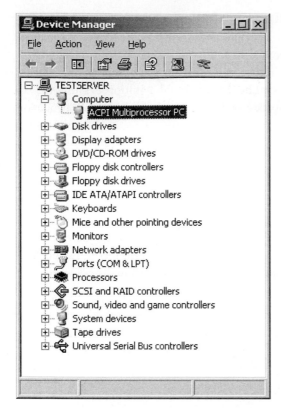

FIGURE 27.9 Updating the HAL in a multiple-processor system.

When you *flash* firmware, you direct the system board to send electrical charges into a ROM chip that will rewrite its programming. To flash the ROM device, you must have a program from its vendor that can be downloaded into the IC. This program will write the updated information into the chip so that the physical device now holds the latest version of information.

The same technique is used for flashing the system's ROM BIOS, as well as the various ROM BIOS extensions associated with video cards, network cards, modems, and RAID controllers. Each peripheral device will have its own utility program for flashing its ROM devices.

Although many types of devices exist whose BIOS you can flash, the general process to do so remains the same:

- ▶ Document the CMOS settings.
- ▶ Back up the original BIOS program. In case the process fails, you can use the original BIOS program to attempt to restore the settings back to its original form.

▶ Flash the BIOS with the new program according to the directions of the device manufacturer.

EXAM ALERT

Know what precautions to take before upgrading the system's BIOS.

A graphical representation of this process is shown in Figure 27.10.

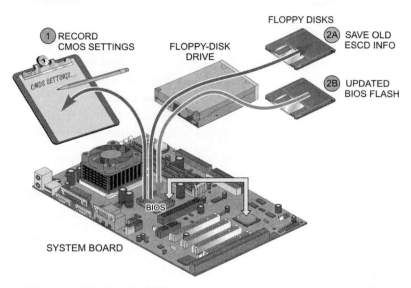

FLOPPY DISKS

① RECORD
   CMOS SETTINGS

FLOPPY-DISK
DRIVE

②A SAVE OLD
    ESCD INFO

②B UPDATED
    BIOS FLASH

CMOS SETTINGS....

BIOS

SYSTEM BOARD

FIGURE 27.10 Flashing the BIOS.

Cooling System Upgrades

In any modern PC, the cooling system will included a passive heat sink device and a processor-cooling fan. These items work alongside the power supply fan to cool the system and the processor. A special thermal compound (thermal grease) is placed between the heat sink and the processor to increase the rate of heat transfer to the heat sink. A small drop of this compound (generally the size of a BB) should be applied to the surface of the processor. A small amount is all that's needed to fill the imperfections in the metal and create a more efficient heat transfer between the processor and the heat sink. In some situations, additional case fans are installed to increase or redirect the airflow through the chassis.

NOTE

Be aware that applying too much thermal compound to the heat sink will result in it overflowing the surface when the heat sink is attached to the processor and could cause damage. A drop the size of a BB is sufficient.

EXAM ALERT

Know how thermal compound should be applied to the processor and heat sink.

When microprocessors are upgraded (or overclocked), the processor-cooling system may also have to be improved. In most cases, the new microprocessor comes with a properly sized heat sink and fan. These are referred to as *boxed processors* and provide longer warranties than standalone OEM (original equipment manufacturer) processors. However, OEM processors do not include a fan or heat sink, and you must research and locate a proper cooling system for them.

To accomplish this, you must find the microprocessor's operating temperature specification. For Pentium processors, the recommended operating temperature was 30° C. However, with the appearance of the Pentium III and Pentium 4 processors, Intel switched to 35° C. The AMD processors typically run much hotter than Intel versions (45–50° C). Then you must find a fan that is rated to work with that processor's temperature/speed specification.

The health configuration settings in the system's CMOS Setup utility can be set to automatically control the fan speed to provide optimum cooling. This setting can also be switched to permit manual configuration of the cooling system. These settings work in conjunction with fan speed control values obtained from the BIOS. If the cooling system fails to maintain the processor temperature, it can shut down the system and prevent it from starting back up. Optimizing the speed of the fan lowers the relative dust accumulation that can lead to thermal failure.

Some computer manufacturers include air baffles (guides) that channel air through the chassis in specific paths. Others include foam filters at chassis openings to filter the incoming air, removing dust particles that accumulate on electronic devices and cause overheating.

EXAM ALERT

Be aware of additional steps that can be taken to make PCs run cooler.

At present, high-end servers and gaming computers are available with liquid cooled and refrigerated processor cooling systems. Only serious hardware users employ these options with their PCs. However, future processor development plans are considering liquid versus refrigerated cooling systems as standard equipment.

Memory Upgrades

Upgrading system board memory is also a fairly simple process. Having more RAM on board allows the microprocessor to access more data directly from memory, without having to access the disk drive. This can speed up system operation considerably depending on the overall condition of the system. Normally, upgrading memory amounts to installing new memory modules in vacant DIMM slots. If the slots are already populated, it will be necessary to remove them to install faster or higher-capacity modules. However, if you do simply add more RAM to an existing memory configuration, you should make sure to obtain RAM devices that match the devices already installed in the system.

Although a 168-pin, 184-pin, or 240-pin DIMM from one system board can physically be transferred to another, it must still have a sufficient speed rating to work in the new system. Consult the system board's documentation to determine what speed the memory devices must be rated for. You should be aware that RAM and other memory devices are rated in access time instead of clock speed. Therefore, a 4-nanosecond (ns) RAM device is faster than an 4.5-nanosecond device.

You should never mix memory types when upgrading a system board. If the new memory modules are not technically compatible with the existing memory, the old memory should be removed. Remember that just because the memory modules are physically compatible, it does not mean that they will work together in a system. Mismatched memory speeds and memory styles (registered/unregistered, buffered/unbuffered, ECC, and so on) can cause significant problems in the operation of the system. These problems can range from preventing bootup to creating simple soft memory errors.

You must ensure that the memory type and size you want to install is supported by the system board and that it does not already have the maximum amount of memory installed. The system board's documentation will include information on the type, configuration, and size of memory it will accept. In addition, verify that the memory you want to install is compatible with the memory currently installed on the board. For example, if the memory currently installed in the machine is rated as PC2-6400, you would not want to install an additional PC2-3200-type memory module.

EXAM ALERT

Identify key considerations for upgrading memory in a PC system.

Normally you should use the same type, brand, and speed of memory devices for RAM upgrades. Because the information detailing the RAM module's type and speed is rarely annotated on the device, you may have to check the signal to clock rate (CAS) for comparison. For instance, if your current memory modules are described as CAS3 units, you should get CAS3 type memory for a compatible replacement or for adding additional memory.

There are two simple ways to determine the amount of RAM currently installed in a Windows-based PC. You can examine the installed RAM information through the System Information utility. To view the installed RAM information through this utility, click the Start button and navigate the Programs (All Programs in XP)/Accessories/System Tools path, and then select the System Information option. The total physical memory size is presented in the Details pane, along with information about the operating system name, version, manufacturer, and directory location. You can also access this information by typing `Msinfo32.exe` in the Start menu's Run dialog box.

The other path where system memory information is displayed is through the Computer Management console. To use this path, access Computer Management through Control Panel, right-click the Computer Management (Local) option in the console tree, and then click the Properties option.

EXAM ALERT

Be aware of how to obtain information about what types of RAM devices can be used to upgrade a PC system.

EXAM ALERT

Be aware of the consequences of mixing memory types in a PC.

To verify the memory upgrade, attempt to observe the memory test display during the POST process to ensure that the system sees the additional memory. Afterward, boot into the operating system and verify that it also recognizes the installed memory. In some cases, the system may detect the presence of the new RAM modules but not be able to correctly identify them. If the system's front side bus speed cannot be increased to the maximum capabilities of the RAM modules, the memory type displayed during the POST will not reflect the actual memory type installed. In these cases, you should access the CMOS Setup utility to check the system's front side bus configuration settings to determine whether they can be manually reconfigured.

EXAM ALERT

Know why the memory type displayed during the POST process may show an incorrect type and what possible options you have to correct this situation.

Challenge #3

A customer has brought in his Socket-370-based ATX computer and has told you that he wants to upgrade the system to get another year of good operation out of it. The system currently has a Celeron 600MHz processor, 64MB of DRAM, and a 2GB hard drive installed. What items can you suggest for upgrading this machine without replacing the system board? What additional system upgrades might be required to support these changes?

NOTE

Before upgrading the system board's FRU units, compare the cost of the proposed component upgrade against the cost of upgrading the system board itself. In many cases, the RAM from the original board can be used on a newer, faster model that should include a more advanced microprocessor. Before finalizing the choice to install a new system board, however, make sure that the current adapters, software, and peripherals will function properly with the updated board. If not, the cost of upgrading may be unexpectedly higher than simply replacing an FRU component.

Exam Prep Questions

1. Under what conditions would you normally expect to upgrade the system's BIOS?

   ○ **A.** When the power comes on but the screen stays blank.

   ○ **B.** When you upgrade the microprocessor.

   ○ **C.** When you forget the CMOS password.

   ○ **D.** When the battery goes dead.

2. Which pin is used to align a microprocessor for insertion in a socket?

   ○ **A.** Pin 0

   ○ **B.** Pin 1

   ○ **C.** Pin 10

   ○ **D.** Pin 8

3. When installing RAM memory modules, which of these potential problems is the most unlikely?

   ○ **A.** Installing two sticks of RAM with different memory sizes.

   ○ **B.** Installing one stick of RAM with tin contacts and a second stick with gold contacts.

   ○ **C.** Installing two sticks of RAM with different bus speeds.

   ○ **D.** Installing a DIMM in a SIMM slot.

4. What factors must be taken into account when ordering a new power supply?

   ○ **A.** Current capabilities and form factor

   ○ **B.** Total BTU and number of connectors

   ○ **C.** Form factor and wattage

   ○ **D.** Noise and total BTU

5. What system board feature is used to manage the installation and replacement of a socket-mounted microprocessor?

   ○ **A.** The ROM BIOS

   ○ **B.** An HSF

   ○ **C.** A ZIF socket

   ○ **D.** The operating system

6. You suspect that a PC in a graphic design studio is running slowly because of limited RAM capacity and typically large graphics files. Where can you go to determine what type of RAM devices could be used to upgrade the system?

   ○ **A.** The PC's installation and user documentation.

   ○ **B.** The system manufacturer's website.

   ○ **C.** The Device Manager utility.

   ○ **D.** The Event Viewer utility.

7. Friends have asked you to check out their PC. They have tried to upgrade its CPU and RAM using a *How To* book they purchased at the local bookstore. The system shows no signs of operating except that the power light comes on when you press the On/Off switch. When you open up the system unit, you notice that the fan and heat sink unit are simply setting on top of the processor and not locked down. Also the processor socket's locking arm is not clamped down. What should you do first in this situation?

   ○ **A.** Lock the processor securely in place by closing the socket's locking arm.

   ○ **B.** Check for thermal grease on the heat sink.

   ○ **C.** Check the processor for bent pins.

   ○ **D.** Snap the fan/heat sink unit into position and make sure that its power connection is properly attached.

8. Identify three sources of determining the speed of the currently installed microprocessor in a Windows XP Professional PC.

   ○ **A.** Through the System Information utility.

   ○ **B.** Through the Device Manager utility.

   ○ **C.** Through Control Panel's Processors icon.

   ○ **D.** Through the System Properties dialog box.

9. Identify two sources of determining the amount of RAM currently installed in a Windows XP Professional PC.

   ○ **A.** Through the System Information utility.

   ○ **B.** Through the Device Manager utility.

   ○ **C.** Through Control Panel's Memory icon.

   ○ **D.** Through the System Properties dialog box.

10. Which of the following properly describes the correct technique for installing thermal compound between a new microprocessor and its heat sink?

- ○ **A.** A thin layer.
- ○ **B.** An even layer.
- ○ **C.** Around the edges of the heat sink.
- ○ **D.** Around the edges of the microprocessor.

11. You have been tasked with upgrading the existing memory in one of the production room PCs with additional RAM. What are the most important considerations you must take into account before ordering the new RAM for this machine?

- ○ **A.** The PC's current RAM type and speed.
- ○ **B.** The speed of the PC's current microprocessor.
- ○ **C.** The PC's front side bus speed.
- ○ **D.** The PC's total RAM capacity.

12. Your company is sending you to install several PCs in a facility located in the desert southwest portion of the United States. The area is very hot and dry in the summer months and is prone to dust storms in the spring and fall of the year. Which of the following is the best scenario for installing the PCs under these circumstances?

- ○ **A.** Install the PCs in a dust-free area.
- ○ **B.** Install the PCs in an air-conditioned area.
- ○ **C.** Install foam dust filters in the air intake vents of the PCs.
- ○ **D.** Install a microprocessor air conditioning system.

13. After you upgrade a desktop PC by installing new PC133 DRAM modules, you start the system and see that it is still identifying the RAM as PC100. What action should you take to determine why this is occurring?

- ○ **A.** Use the CMOS Setup utility to check the system's front side bus settings to determine what they are and whether they can be reconfigured.
- ○ **B.** Return the memory modules to the supplier for the correct type.
- ○ **C.** Access the system's memory device drivers through the Device Manager utility and reconfigure the memory type setting.
- ○ **D.** Access the system's North Bridge device drivers through the Device Manager utility and reconfigure the memory bus speed settings.

Answers and Explanations

1. **B.** If you install a new microprocessor in a system that does not have an autodetect function for the microprocessor, you must make sure that the BIOS version will support the new processor. A BIOS upgrade is necessary when the existing BIOS cannot support the new microprocessor.

2. **B.** There are notches and dots on the various ICs that provide important keys when replacing a microprocessor. These notches and dots specify the location of pin 1. This pin must be lined up with the pin-1 notch of the socket.

3. **D.** DIMM slots are keyed, and it is almost physically impossible to plug them in wrong.

4. **C.** When ordering a replacement power supply, you must remember to take into account its form factor and its wattage rating requirements. The wattage rating is a measurement of the total power the supply can deliver to the system. More heavily equipped systems (that is, with more disk drives and peripherals) require power supplies with higher wattage ratings.

5. **C.** Zero Insertion Force (ZIF) sockets permit the microprocessor to be placed in the socket without force and then be clamped in place. An arm-activated clamping mechanism in the socket shifts to the side, locking the pins in place.

6. **A.** Consult the system board's documentation to determine what speed the memory devices must be rated for. You should be aware that RAM and other memory devices are rated in access time instead of clock speed.

7. **C.** If the processor does not appear to set completely flush in the socket, remove it before clamping it into place. Check for bent pins that may not be lining up properly with the socket. Also make certain the processor's pin configuration lines up properly with the socket. If you force the processor into the socket, you may break the pin off and ruin the processor.

8. **A, B, D.** There are three places in a Windows-based PC where you can go to determine the speed of a currently installed microprocessor. You can view the microprocessor's speed on the System Properties tab. You can also view the microprocessor's information through the System Information utility. Finally, you can use Device Manager to determine the current microprocessor's speed. Click the Start button and select the

Run option. In the Run dialog box, type **Devmgmt.msc**, and then click OK. Expand Processors to view the microprocessor information.

9. **A, D.** There are two simple ways to determine the amount of RAM currently installed in a Windows-based PC. You can examine the installed RAM information through the System Information utility. The other path where system memory information is displayed is through the Computer Management console.

10. **A.** A special thermal compound (thermal grease) is placed between the heat sink and the processor to increase the rate of heat transfer to the heat sink. A small drop of this compound (generally the size of a BB) should be applied to the surface of the processor. A small amount is all that's needed to create a thin layer to fill the imperfections in the metal and create a more efficient heat transfer between the processor and the heat sink.

11. **A.** You should never mix memory types when upgrading a system board. If the new memory modules are not technically compatible with the existing memory, the old memory should be removed. Remember that just because the memory modules are physically compatible, it does not mean that they will work together in a system. Mismatched memory speeds and memory styles (registered/unregistered, buffered/unbuffered, ECC, and so on) can cause significant problems in the operation of the system. These problems can range from preventing bootup to creating simple soft memory errors.

12. **C.** Some computer manufacturers include air baffles (guides) that channel air through the chassis in specific paths. Others include foam filters at chassis openings to filter the incoming air, removing dust particles that accumulate on electronic devices and cause overheating.

13. **A.** Access the CMOS Setup utility to determine whether you can manually reconfigure the system's FSB settings.

Challenge Solutions

1. You must advise the customer to completely upgrade the systems. The cases and power supplies are AT-style devices, and new system boards will not physically fit into these cases. Also, the newer ATX system will support 9-pin serial mice, but they are really set up for PS/2 mini-DIN

mice. Finally, even the keyboards are physically incompatible (5-pin DIN) with the ATX system boards that you would need to install to upgrade the systems.

2. Although the microprocessor is an FRU device, it would not be a good idea to replace it in a unit where the original smoked. You could quickly ruin a perfectly good (and expensive) microprocessor by doing so.

   a. Remove all the external I/O systems attached to the computer.

   b. Remove the system unit's outer cover.

   c. Remove all the option adapter cards installed in the system.

   d. Remove the power supply and front panel cables from the system board.

   e. Remove the system board. Remove the grounding screws that secure the system board to the chassis. Store the screws properly.

   f. Install the new system board and perform steps d through a in reverse order. If the system board does not already have the micro-processor and memory modules installed, you will have to add these at this point.

3. The Celeron processor can be upgraded directly to a Pentium III and the installed RAM can be expanded considerably. The hard drive capacity and speed can be increased as well. As a precaution, you should check the BIOS version to make certain that it will support these changes. If not, you must obtain a BIOS version that will support the new processor.

Index

NUMBERS

4:2:2 connections. *See* Digital Component Video connections

+5V power supplies, 14

+12V power supplies, 14

A

AC adapters, 15
portable computers, 473
troubleshooting, 501-503

AC voltage, checking via multimeter, 345

access control (security)
backup tapes, 1076
lockable server cases/chassis, 1075
passwords, 1076-1077

Accessories menu (Windows XP), 549

account lockout policies, Windows 2000/XP security, 1098

accountability (customer service techniques), 1171

ACPI (Advanced Configuration and Power Interface), power management, 476

active heat sinks, 148

active listening (customer service techniques), 1164

active partitions, Windows 2000/XP file systems, 591

active termination, SCSI adapter cards, 295

active-matrix displays, LCD displays, 454

activity lights, troubleshooting broadband connections, 1053

adapter cards

I/O cards

IEEE-1394 FireWire cards, 34

internal modem cards, 32

LAN (Local Area Network) cards, 32

SATA (Serial ATA) Disk Drive cards, 34

SCSI (Small Computer System Interface) cards, 33, 90

sound cards, 33

TV tuner cards, 33

USB (Univeral Serial Bus) cards, 34

wireless network cards, 34

LAN, 934-937

peripheral installations, 314-315

removing, system board installations, 1195

SCSI cards

address configuration, 293-294

installing, 292-293

termination, 295-296

system units, 8, 31

video adapter cards, VGA (Video Graphics Array) cards, 31

adapters

AC, 15

FireWire (IEEE-1394), troubleshooting, 419

upgrading, 315-316

Add a New Device option (Control Panel), 537

Add New Hardware wizard (Windows 2000), 537

Add Printer Wizard (Windows 2000/XP), 834-835

Add/Remove Hardware wizard (Windows 2000), 537

Add/Remove Programs icon (Windows 2000), 538

Add/Remove Windows Component utility (Windows 2000), 538

adding items to Start menu, 535

administrative passwords, routers, 944

Administrative Tools icon (Windows 2000), 539-542

Administrative Tools menu (Windows XP), 549

Administrator Accounts (Windows 2000/XP), 1087, 1092-1093

ADSL (Asymmetric DSL), 993-995

Advanced BIOS Features Setup screen (CMOS setup utility), 100-101

Advanced Chipset Features Setup screen (CMOS setup utility), 101

Advanced Pentium/PCIe chipsets, 68

Advanced tab

System Properties window, 542-543

Windows 2000/XP Local Area Connection Properties dialog, 949

adware, 1114, 1117

AGP (Accelerated Graphics Port)

expansion slots, 80-82

slot connectors, 29

All Programs menu (Windows XP), 549

AMD (Advanced Micro Devices) processors

Athlon 64 processors, 136

Athlon XP processors, 136

dual-core processors

Athlon processors, 137-139

Opteron processors, 141

Duron processors, 137

K6PLUS-3D processors, 135

K75 processors, 136

Mobile processors, portable computers, 445

Slot A Athlon processors, 135

AMR (Audio Modem Risers)

expansion slots, 82-83

slot connectors, 30

analog modems, installing, 983-984

annual preventive maintenance activities, 363-364

anonymous authentication (FTP), 1013

answer files, unattended Windows 2000/XP installations, 625

antispyware applications, 1116

antistatic devices, 331

antivirus software, 1112

AP (access points), wireless LAN installations, 938-940

API (application programming interfaces), Windows 2000/XP, 582

APM (Advanced Power Management), 475

AppleTalk, 921

applications

   installing, troubleshooting, 770

   not starting, troubleshooting, 771

   performance (Windows 2000/XP), monitoring via System Monitor, 678

      disk system performance, 683-684

      memory performance, 682

      Performance Logs and Alerts utility, 680-681

      processor performance, 683

   starting from Command Prompt, troubleshooting, 772

ARP (Address Resolution Protocol), 1007, 1035

ASIC (application-specific integrated circuits), 21

aspect ratio (digital resolution), 268

ASR utility (Automated System Recovery), 760

   backups, 761

   restore operations, 763

Asynchronous SRAM (Static RAM), 163

AT (Advanced Technology) buses. *See* ISA (Industry Standard Architecture) slot connectors

ATA (Analog Telephone Adapters), 1004

ATA (AT Attachment) disk drive interfaces, 200-202

Athlon 64 processors, 136

Athlon dual-core processors, 137-139

Athlon XP processors, 136

attended installations

   Windows 2000/XP, 624

   Windows XP Professional, 640

ATTRIB command (Windows OS file/file-name command line operations, 563

ATX (Advanced Technology Extended) form factor, 10, 60-61

audio

   connections, 239

   fidelity, 271

   portable computers, troubleshooting, 504

   resolution, 271

   sound cards, 270-273, 312

auditing, Windows 2000/XP security, 1098-1100

authentication

   biometric authentication, 1080-1083

   FTP, 1013

   troubleshooting, startup problems, 766

   Windows 2000/XP

      digital certificates, 1095

      IPSec, 1096

      KDC, 1095

      Kerberos protocol, 1094-1095

      VPN, 1095

Authentication tab (Windows 2000/XP Local Area Connection Properties dialog), 950

automatic sheet feeders (printers), 829

automatic updates, software maintenance, 685

Automatic Updates tab (System Properties window), 543

B

back panel connections (peripherals), 42-44

backlights (LCD displays), 453, 493

Backup Label configuration page (Backup utility), 702

Backup Operator Accounts (Windows 2000/XP), 1093

backup tapes

demagnetizing, 1084

disposal of, 1086

security, 1076

Backup utility (Windows 2000/XP), 701-702

backups

ASR utility (Windows XP), 761

Backup utility (Windows 2000/XP), 701-702

differential backups, 700

full backups, 698

Grandfather-Father-Son method, 707

incremental backups, 699

media rotation, 707-708

Restore utility (Windows 2000/XP), 703

scheduling, 705-706

selective backups, 699

system state, 704

barcode scanners, 257, 312

batteries

disposal procedures, 1149

portable computers

fuel cells, 479

troubleshooting, 501-503

upgrading, 479

beep codes, 338

examples of, 336

hardware failures, 340

troubleshooting system boards, 379

beverages, work area safety, 1132

Bindings function (Windows 2000/XP), 949

biometric authentication, 1080-1083

biometric input devices, 256

BIOS (Basic Input/Output Systems)

bootup, phases of, 24, 26

CMOS RAM, 27

CMOS setup utility, 28

Advanced BIOS Features Setup screen, 100-101

Integrated Peripherals setup screen, 103

extensions, PC hardware setup process, 578

firmware, 24

PCI local bus expansion slots, 75-76

PNP (Plug-and-Play), 27

POST (Power-On Self Tests), 24

troubleshooting, 384

BISDN (Broadband ISDN) services, 988-989

bitmapped fonts, 800-801

black page errors (laser printers), troubleshooting, 869

blank (white) page errors (laser printers), troubleshooting, 869

blue screen errors, 765, 769, 773

Bluetooth, 819, 912, 971

body language (customer service techniques), 1165-1166

Boot Disk (Windows XP), troubleshooting startup process, 757

boot failures, troubleshooting, 342

boot-sector viruses, 1109-1110

BOOT.INI files

modifying, 674-675

Windows 2000/XP boot process, 579

bootups, procedure observances (troubleshooting), 334-335

bottlenecks, monitoring Windows 2000/XP application performance, 678

BRI (Basic Rate Interface) services, 988-989

bridges, WAN Internet connectivity, 972

brightness (video displays), 47

broadband connections, troubleshooting
activity lights, 1053
connectivity equipment checks, 1055
filter checks, 1054
PC checks, 1055-1056
physical connections, 1053-1054
restarting equipment, 1054
brownouts, 1138
BSOD (Blue Screen of Death), 636
BTX (Balanced Technology Extended) form factor, 10, 62-63
BTX Thermal Module, 149
buffer overflow attacks, 134
buffer registers, 163
buffer underrun errors, 410
bulk data transfers, USB, 235
burn-in tests, 347
burn/laser hazards, 1136-1137
Burst-mode SRAM (Static RAM), 163
buses
configuring, 146
enumerating, 231
speeds, 72
system board upgrades, 1208-1209
topologies (LAN), 891

C

cable modems, 996-997
cables
coaxial cables, 904-906
copper cables
coaxial cables, 904-906
twisted-pair cables, 901-903
fiber-optic cables, 906-908
FireWire buses (IEEE-1394), 237
GND (Ground) wire, 232
interface cables, troubleshooting scanners, 876
LAN, troubleshooting, 1041
plenum cables, 909-910
printer cables, troubleshooting, 857-858
RS-232, 248
SCSI, 208-209
serial printer interfaces, 822
signal cables, system units, 8
system boards, removing from, 1195-1196
testers, 331, 1034
twisted-pair cables, 901-903
UTP, Ethernet specifications, 916-917
Vbus wire, 232
work area safety, 1131
cache memory, 16, 152, 166-167
calibrating printers, 827
cameras (digital), 313
CAN (Campus Area Networks), 890
Cardbus, portable computers, 464-465
cartridge fonts (printers), 825
case design (system units), 7
CAT 5 cabling
crossover cables, wireless LAN installations, 942
specifications, UTP cables, 902-903
CAT 6 cabling specifications, UTP cables, 903
CD, Create CD/DVD option (Windows XP MCE), 557
CD-R disks, 196-197
CD-ROM disks, 195
CD-ROM drives
CD-R disks, 196-197
CD-ROM disks, 195
CD-RW disks, 196-197
data storage, 36, 193-194
external CD-ROM drives, portable computers, 460
installing, 300-301
troubleshooting
basic checks, 406
hardware checks, 407-409

Windows checks, 407

writable drives, 409-410

CD-RW disks, 196-197

CD-RW drives

external CD-RW drives, portable computers, 461

installing, 301

Celeron processors, portable computers, 443

Centrino processors, portable computers, 443

Centronics standard, parallel printer ports, 246

CF (CompactFlash) cards, 216

Change or Remove Programs screen (Windows 2000), 538

Change permissions (network shares), 957

character printers, 799

CHDIR (CH) command (Windows OS directory-level command line operations), 562

chipsets, 17, 67

Advanced Pentium/PCIe chipsets, 68

ASIC (application-specific integrated circuits), 21

bus speeds, 72

CMOS setup utility, Advanced Chipset Features Setup screen, 101

Dual-Core Intel chipsets, 69-72

CHKDSK (Check Disc) command (Windows Disk Management tools), 668, 694

CHKDSK.EXE utility (Windows 2000/XP), 726

Class A addresses, 974

Class B addresses, 975

Class C addresses, 975

Classic View option (Control Panel), 551

cleaning (preventive maintenance), 350-352, 507

cleanmgr, 670

client/server networks, 515

diskless workstations, 895

LAN network control strategies, 894-895

Clients function (Windows 2000/XP Local Area Connection Properties dialog), 948

clock speeds (microprocessors), 144

clone processors, 18, 145

cloning (disk)

Sysprep tool, 627

Windows 2000/XP installations, 626-628

clusters, 593

CMOS (Complementary Metal Oxide Semiconductors)

backup batteries, troubleshooting, 386

configuration checks, troubleshooting system boards, 381-382

HDD installations, 286

PATA drive installations, 288

PC hardware setup process, 578

SATA drive configuration, 291

setup failures, troubleshooting system boards, 380

viruses, 1110

CMOS Display Mismatch error message, 341

CMOS Memory Size Mismatch error message, 341

CMOS RAM, 27

CMOS setup utility, 28, 96

Advanced BIOS Features Setup screen, 100-101

Advanced Chipset Features Setup screen, 101

disk drive support, 99-100

health configuration settings, 1214

IDE controller, 103

Integrated Peripherals setup screen, 103

PC Health menu screen, 106

PnP/PCI Configuration screen, 102

port implementation, 104-105

Power Management fields, 106

Security Configuration screen, 107-108

time/date, 98-99

CMOS System Option Not Set error message, 341

CMOS Time and Date Not Set error message, 341

CNR (Communication Networking Risers)

expansion slots, 82-83

slot connectors, 30

coaxial cables, 904-906

coaxial Ethernet specifications, 915-916

collators (printers), 830

color space conversion, video capture cards, 259

command line (Windows OS), 559

directory-level operations

CHDIR (CH) command, 562

DIR command, 561

MKDIR (MD) command, 562

RMDIR (RD) command, 562

drive-level operations

CONVERT command, 560

DISKCOMP command, 561

DISKCOPY command, 561

FORMAT command, 560

file/filename operations

ATTRIB command, 563

COPY command, 562

DEL command, 563

ERASE command, 563

FC command, 563

REN command, 563

XCOPY command, 563

Command Prompt, starting applications from, 772

command-line utilities (Windows 2000/XP)

CHKDSK.EXE utility, 726

DEFRAG.EXE utility, 726

DISKPART.EXE utility, 726

EDIT utility, 726

EXTRACT.EXE utility, 726

IPCONFIG utility, 726

MEM utility, 726

MSCONFIG.EXE utility, 726

PING utility, 727

SFC.EXE utility, 726

TRACRT utility, 727

communication (customer service techniques), 1166-1169, 1177-1179

Component Video connections, 241

Composite Video connections, 240

compound USB devices, 231

compressed files

Windows 2000/XP files, 610-611

Windows Explorer, 611

concentrators. *See* hubs

confidence (customer service techniques), 1173

configuration errors (hardware), troubleshooting, 340-341

configuring

analog modems, 984

I/O ports, 317

printers

operator control panels, 826

serial printer interfaces, 823

Windows 2000/XP, 836-837

Windows 2000/XP dial-up access, 985

conflict management (customer service), 1176-1177

connections

FireWire buses (IEEE-1394), 236-237

Line In/Line Out, sound cards, 272

multimedia, sound cards, 272

connectors

expansion slots

AGP, 29, 80-82

AMR, 30, 82-83

CNR, 30, 82-83

ISA, 30

PCI, 29, 73-76

PCI-X, 30, 76-77

PCIe, 30, 77-80

system boards, 17, 28

legacy, 244-245

MIDI, 242

    data transfers, 244

    MMC, 243

    patch cords, 243

multimedia

    audio, 239

    Component Video, 241

    Composite Video, 240

    Digital Component Video, 241

    DVI, 241

    HDMI, 242

    S-Video, 241

PS/2, 229

RS-232, 248

SCSI, 208-209

Series-A, 232

Series-B, 232

continuity testers, 1034

contrast (video displays), 47

contrast ratio (LCD displays), 454

Control Panel (Windows 2000), 535-536

    Add a New Device option, 537

    Add/Remove Programs icon, 538

    Administrative Tools icon, 539-542

    Display icon, 543

    installation wizards, 537

    System icon, 542-543

Control Panel (Windows XP), 550-552

control transfers, USB, 235

CONVERT command (Windows OS drive-level command line operations), 560

cooling systems

    installing, 1199-1201

    microprocessors

        BTX Thermal Module, 149

        fans, 148-149

        heat sinks, 148-149

        water-based systems, 150

    system board upgrades, 1213-1214

    thermal compound/paste, 148

    troubleshooting, 385

copper cables

    coaxial cables, 904-906

    twisted-pair cables, 901-903

copy backups. *See* selective backups

COPY command (Windows OS file/file-name command line operations), 562

Core Duo processors, portable computers, 444

core routers, 899

CPU (system boards), 16-17

    bus speeds, 72

    clone processors, 18

    Pentium package types, 18-20

crackers (passwords), 1115

Create CD/DVD option (Windows XP MCE), 557

crimpers (wire), 330

crossover cables, wireless LAN installations, 942

CRT (Cathode Ray Tube) video displays, 46, 260-261

Current_Config key (Windows 2000/XP Registry), 588

Current_User key (Windows 2000/XP Registry), 587

customer education, 1161

customer service, 1160

    accountability, 1171

    body language, 1165-1166

    communication, 1166-1169, 1177-1179

confidence, 1173

conflict management, 1176-1177

customer education, 1161

feedback, 1161

flexibility, 1172

follow ups, 1169

general support, 1161

integrity, 1173-1175

jargon, avoiding, 1167

legal issues, 1176

listening, 1164-1166

paperwork, handling, 1179

permission, asking, 1175

personal service, 1161

preparation, 1162

presence, 1163

proactive, being, 1164

professionalism, 1172-1173

rapports, 1163

responsiveness, 1170

work area management, 1179

customizing Windows 2000/XP startup process

BOOT.INI files, 674-675

MSCONFIG, 676

Startup menu optimization, 675

D

daily backups, 706

daily preventive maintenance activities, 362

data migration, security threats, 1085

data storage, 34

CD-ROM drives, 36

installing storage devices, 300-301

optical storage, 193-197

CD-RW drives, installing storage devices, 301

disk drive interfaces

ATA interfaces, 200-201

floppy interfaces, 203-204

IDE interfaces, 200-201

internal disk drive interfaces, 199

SATA interfaces, 202

DVD drives, 37

installing storage devices, 300

optical storage, 197-198

DVD-RW drives, installing storage devices, 301

external storage devices, 303

FDD (floppy disk drives), 38, 190-191, 302-303

floppy drives, 38

HDD (hard disk drives), 34

CMOS setups, 182

controllers, 181

installing storage devices, 283-286

sub-system components, 180

internal storage devices, 282

PVR, 182-183

RAID systems, 185-188

removable media devices

preventive maintenance procedures, 359-360

troubleshooting, 498

removable storage, 39, 213

flash memory, 214-217

portable computers, 462-463

Removable Storage utility (Windows 2000/XP), 708

system connections, 40-41

SCSI, 204

adapter cards, 292-296

cables/connectors, 208-209

Serial SCSI, 207-208

signaling, 210-213

specifications, 205-207

tape drives, 38, 191-192

USB devices, troubleshooting, 497-498

data transfers

MIDI connections, 244

USB, 235

date/time

CMOS setup utility, 98-99

CMOS Time and Date Not Set error message, 341

DC voltage, checking via multimeter, 344

DDR-DRAM sockets, 95

DDR-SDRAM (Double Data Rate-SDRAM), 162, 171

DDR2 (Double Data Rate-SDRAM 2), 162, 172

DDR2-DRAM sockets, 95

dead systems, troubleshooting, 376-377

Debugging Mode (Windows 2000/XP), troubleshooting startup process, 750

Default Gateways option (Windows 2000/XP IP Settings tab), 952

DEFRAG command (Windows Disk Management tools), 669, 695-698

DEFRAG.EXE utility (Windows 2000/XP), 726

defragmenting

Disk Defragmenter tool (System Tools console), 540

HDD, 669

degaussing, 399

DEL command (Windows OS file/filename command line operations, 563

demagnetizing

backup tapes, 1084

floppy disks, 1084

depth (passwords), 1077

device drivers

driver signing, 656-657

finding, 656

SATA, 655

Windows 2000/XP, 654

Device Manager utility (Windows 2000/XP), 716-719, 751, 768

Device Settings tab (Printer Properties page), printer property configuration, 837

DHCP (Dynamic Host Configuration Protocol), 1007-1009

DHCP servers, wireless LAN installations, 944

diagnostic/repair tools, 330

multimeters, 343-345

POST cards, 348-349

software diagnostic packages, 346-347

diagnostics. *See* troubleshooting

dial-up connections

analog modems

configuring, 984

installing, 983-984

establishing, 986-987

dialing rules, 986

DLS versus, 992

ICS, 987-988

troubleshooting, 1056

front panel lights, 1059-1060

loopback tests, 1058-1059

modem configuration checks, 1061

modem hardware, 1057

Windows 2000/XP access, configuring, 985

dialers (grayware), 1114

differential backups, 700

digital cameras, 313

digital certificates, Windows 2000/XP authentication, 1095

Digital Component Video connections, 241

digital modems, 998-999

digital resolution (monitors), 268

digital television display standards, 269-270

DIMM (Dual Inline Memory Modules), 22

MicroDIMM, portable computers, 446

modules, installing, 1202

packages, 168

sockets, 95

SODIMM, portable computers, 446

DIR command (Windows OS directory-level command line operations), 561

directory trees, FAT disks, 595-596

directory-level command line operations (Windows OS)

CHDIR (CH) command, 562

DIR command, 561

MKDIR (MD) command, 562

RMDIR (RD) command, 562

Disk Cleanup utility (Windows Disk Management tools), 669-670, 693-694

disk cloning

Sysprep tool, 627

Windows 2000/XP installations, 626-628

Disk Defragmenter tool (System Tools console), 540

disk drives (system units), 8

CD-ROM, portable computers, 460

CD-RW, portable computers, 461

CMOS support, 99-100

controllers, 181

DVD-RW, portable computers, 461

FDD, portable computers, 460

interfaces

ATA interfaces, 200-202

floppy drive interfaces, 203-204

IDE interfaces, 200-201

internal disk drive interfaces, 199

system board connections, 17

PATA connections

I/O ports, 86-88

IDE controller (CMOS setup utility), 104

SATA connections

I/O ports, 86-89

IDE controller (CMOS setup utility), 104

disk images, Windows 2000/XP installations, 625-628

Disk Management tools (Windows), 540, 692-693

backups

Backup utility, 701-702

differential backups, 700

full backups, 698

incremental backups, 699

media rotation, 707-708

Restore utility, 703

scheduling, 705-706

selective backups, 699

system state backups, 704

CHKDSK command, 694

DEFRAG command, 695-698

Disk Cleanup utility, 693-694

Removable Storage utility, 708

disk system performance, 683-684

DISKCOMP command (Windows OS drive-level command line operations), 561

DISKCOPY command (Windows OS drive-level command line operations), 561

diskless workstations, 895

DISKPART.EXE utility (Windows 2000/XP), 726

Display icon (Windows 2000), 543

displays (video)

brightness, 47

contrast, 47

CRT, 46, 260-261

dot pitch, 267

external monitors, portable computers, 493

horizontal/vertical positioning, 47

horizontal/vertical sizing, 47

installing, 308-309

LCD (liquid crystal display) monitors, 46

polarizing screens, 452, 1078

portable displays, 452-455

preventive maintenance procedures, 355-356

resolution, 265-268

screen memory, 263

skew, 47

touch screens, 254-256

troubleshooting, 393

   degaussing, 399

   diagnosing problems, 398-399

   hardware checks, 394-395

   LCD displays, 492-495

   video checks, 395-398

DMA (Direct Memory Access), I/O transfers, 227

DNS (Domain Name Servers), 1006-1007

name resolution, 979

structure of, 978

DNS tab (Windows 2000/XP), 953

docking stations, 477

port replicators, 478

troubleshooting, 503-504

DOCSIS (Data Over Cable Service Interface Specification), 997

documentation

customer service techniques, 1179

previewing in Windows 2000/XP, 833

troubleshooting, 334

Documents and Settings folder (Start menu), 532

Domain Accounts (Windows 2000/XP), 1094

domains

DNS

   name resolution, 979

   structure of, 978

WAN Internet connectivity, 978

DOS (disk operating systems), 512-513

dot pitch (monitors), 267

dot-matrix printers, 804

friction-feed, 805

pin-feed, 805

preventive maintenance, 877

printhead mechanisms, 806

troubleshooting, 858

   paper, 859-863

   paper feed issues, 862-863

   power supplies, 859

   printhead not moving, 862

   printhead not printing, 861

   ribbon cartridges, 859-860

dotted decimal notation, 974

Download Center (Microsoft Product Support Services), 729

Dr. Watson utility (Windows 2000/XP), 724-725, 736

DRAM (Dynamic RAM), 160

EDRAM, 161

packages, 169

refreshing, 164

SDRAM

   DDR-SDRAM, 162, 171

   DDR2, 162, 172

   ECC-SDRAM, 165-166

   EDDR-SDRAM, 162

   EDO-DRAM, 161

   ESDRAM, 162

   RDRAM, 162, 172

   SDS-DRAM, 162

   SGRAM, 162

   speed ratings, 170

   VCM-SDRAM, 162

sockets, 95

speed ratings, 170, 173

drive arrays

mirrored arrays, 184-186

RAID systems, 185-188

striped arrays, 184-185

Drive Mismatch Error messages, 404

drive-level command line operations (Windows OS)

CONVERT command, 560

DISKCOMP command, 561

DISKCOPY command, 561

FORMAT command, 560

Driver Rollback function (Windows XP), troubleshooting

operational problems, 768

startup process, 751

Driver Rollback option (Device Manager utility), 718-719

drivers

printers, 824

cartridge fonts, 825

internal fonts, 825

PCL, 825

PDL, 825-826

PostScript, 825

soft fonts, 825

signing, device drivers, 656-657

TWAIN drivers, scanners, 875

drop-down menus (Windows 2000/XP)

File menus, 528-529

Tools menu, 530

View menu, 529-530

DSHD (double-sded, high-density) floppy disks, 191

DSL (Digital Subscriber Lines), 979

ADSL, 993-995

dial-up access versus, 992

DSLAM, 993

HDSL, 995

HDSL2, 996

IDSL, 996

modems, 990

SDSL, 992, 995

SHDSL, 995

splitters, 991

xDSL, 992-993

DSLAM (Digital Subscriber Line Access Multiplexer), 993

DSSD (double-sded, single-density) floppy disks, 191

dual booting, 593, 651-653

dual channel memory, 173

Dual-Core Intel chipsets, 69-72

dual-core processors

AMD

Athlon processors, 137-139

Opteron processors, 141

Intel, 130-132

EIST, 134

EM64T, 134

hyperthreading, 134

SpeedStep technology, 134

XD-bit virus protection, 133

duplexers (printers), 830

Duron processors, 137

dust, preventive maintenance procedures, 353

DVD, Create CD/DVD option (Windows XP MCE), 557

DVD drives

data storage, 37, 197-198

installing, 300

troubleshooting

basic checks, 406

hardware checks, 407-409

Windows checks, 407

writable drives, 409-410

DVD-RW drives

external DVD-RW drives, portable computers, 461

installing, 301

DVI (Digital Video Interface)

connections, 241

video cards, 264

DVR (digital video recorders). *See* PVR (personal video recorders)

dye sublimation printers, 815-816

dynamic volumes

NTFS disk volumes

mirrored volumes, 602

RAID 5 volumes, 604

simple volumes, 602

spanned volumes, 602

striped volumes, 604

Windows 2000/XP volumes

formatting, 607-608

installations, 605

E

EAP, 1080

ECC-SDRAM (Error Correction Code-SDRAM), 165-166

echo operations, 252

ECP (Extended Capabilities Port), 105, 247

EDDR-SDRAM (Enhanced DDR-SDRAM), 162

edge routers, 899

EDIT utility (Windows 2000/XP), 726

EDO-RAM (Extended Data Out-DRAM), 161

EDRAM (Enhanced DRAM), 161

EDTV (Enhanced Definition TV), 270

EEPROM (Electrically-Erasable Programmable Read Only Memory), 23

EFS (Encrypting File System) feature (Windows 2000/XP), 1105-1106

EIDE (Enhanced IDE) disk drive interfaces, 201

EIST (Enhanced Intel SpeedStep Technology), Intel dual-core processors, 134

electrocution/shock, 1134-1135

electrophotographic cartridges (laser printers), 814

electrophotographic reproduction. *See* laser printers

ELP drums (printers), 830

EM64T, Intel dual-core processors, 134

email, 1013

employees

customer service, 1160

accountability, 1171

body language, 1165-1166

communication, 1166-1169, 1177-1179

confidence, 1173

conflict management, 1176-1177

customer education, 1161

feedback, 1161

flexibility, 1172

follow ups, 1169

general support, 1161

integrity, 1173-1175

jargon, avoiding, 1167

legal issues, 1176

listening, 1164-1166

paperwork, handling, 1179

permission, asking, 1175

personal service, 1161

preparation, 1162

presence, 1163

proactive, being, 1164

professionalism, 1172-1173

rapports, 1163

responsiveness, 1170

work area management, 1179

safety

hand tools, 1132-1133

high-voltage hazards, 1133-1134

laser/burn hazards, 1136-1137

shock/electrocution, 1134-1135

Enable Boot Logging (Windows 2000/XP), troubleshooting startup process, 749

Enable VGA Mode (Windows 2000/XP), troubleshooting startup process, 750

encryption, Windows 2000/XP files, 610

Enforce Password History option (Windows 2000/XP), 1097

enterprise networks, 516

environmental assessments (troubleshooting), 332

environmental security, 1084

EPP (Enhanced Parallel Ports), 105, 247

EPS (Entry-Level Power Supply) specification, 13-14

ERASE command (Windows OS file/filename command line operations, 563

ERD (Emergency Repair Disks), troubleshooting startup process, 755-756

error checking RAM

ECC-SDRAM, 165-166

parity checking, 164-165

error codes (beep codes), 338

examples of, 336

hardware failures, 340

Error events (Event Viewer utility), 711

error messages

CMOS Display Mismatch, 341

CMOS Memory Size Mismatch, 341

CMOS System Option Not Set, 341

CMOS Time and Date Not Set, 341

Drive Mismatch Error, 404

Event Log Is Full, 774

examples of, 336-338

hardware configuration, 341

hardware failures, 340

Invalid Drive, 400

Invalid Drive Specification, 400

Invalid Media Type, 400, 404

memory access violation errors, 136

Missing Beam (laser printers), 869

Out of Memory (scanners), 874

Parity Error messages, 166

Press F1 to Continue, 341

Printer Not Ready, 858

troubleshooting system boards, 380

ESD (electrostatic discharges)

causes of, 1143

grounds, 1147

minimizing, 1146

MOS, 1145-1146

storage, protection during, 1148

ESDRAM (Enhanced SDRAM), 162

Ethernet, 914

coaxial specifications, 915-916

fiber specifications, 918

twisted-pair specifications, 916-917

wireless specifications, 919-920

ettiquette (telephone), customer service techniques, 1178-1179

Event Log Is Full error messages, 774

event logging, Windows 2000/XP security, 1098-1100

Event Viewer utility (Windows 2000/XP), 709-711, 773-774

expansion slots

AGP, 29, 80-82

AMR, 30, 82-83

CNR, 30, 82-83

ISA, 30

PCI, 29, 73-76

PCI-X, 30, 76-77

PCIe, 30, 77-80

system boards, 17, 28

Explorer (Windows), 543-546, 611

extended partitions, 297, 591

external CD-ROM drives, portable computers, 460

external CD-RW drives, portable computers, 461

external data storage devices, installing, 303

external DVD-RW drives, portable computers, 461

external FDD (floppy disk drives), portable computers, 460

external modems, 983

external monitors, portable computers, 493

external storage, portable computers, 462-463

EXTRACT.EXE utility (Windows 2000/XP), 726

extranets, 517

F

Facts by Product (Microsoft Product Support Services), 729

faint print (laser printers), troubleshooting, 870

fans
installing, 1199-1201
microprocessor cooling systems, 148-149

FAT (file allocation tables)
disks
directory trees, 595-596
FAT clusters, 593
FAT32 file systems, 596-597
root directories, 595
NTFS partitions, moving to, 1085
viruses, 1110

FC command (Windows OS file/filename command line operations), 563

FC-PGA (Flip Chip Pin Grid Array) 370 sockets, 128

FDD (floppy disk drives), 38
DSHD disks, 191
DSSD disks, 191
external FDD, portable computers, 460
installing, 302-303
troubleshooting, 410
basic checks, 412
error messages, 411

feedback (customer service), 1161

fiber Ethernet specifications, 918

fiber-optic cables, 906-908

fidelity (audio), 271

File Management tools (Windows)
Dr. Watson utility, 724-725
RegEdit utility, 723
RegEdt32 utility, 723-724
SYSEDIT.EXE, 722

File menus (Windows 2000/XP), 528-529

files
compression, Windows Explorer, 611
infectors, 1109
NTFS permissions
Full Control, 960
List Folder Contents, 960
Modify, 959-960
Read, 959-960
Read & Execute, 959-960
Write, 959-960

file:// prefix, 1012

filters, troubleshooting broadband connections, 1054

finding
device drivers, 656
hidden files, troubleshooting, 773

fingerprint scanners, 257, 1082-1083

firewalls, 976, 981
troubleshooting, 1064
wireless security, 1103
enabling ICF function in Windows XP, 1105
well-known ports table, 1104

FireWire (IEEE-1394), 244
adapters, troubleshooting, 419
buses
cables, 237
connections, 236-237
infrared ports, 237-238
device installations, 317
ports, troubleshooting, 419-421

firmware, 24, 1211

flash memory, 214
CF (CompactFlash) cards, 216
memory sticks, 216-217
SD (Secure Digital) cards, 217
USB flash drives, 215

flashlights, 330

flat memory model, 583

flexibility (customer service techniques), 1172

flip chips, 92

floppy disk drives. *See* FDD (floppy disk drives)

floppy disks, demagnetizing, 1084

floppy drives, data storage, 38

Fn keys, troubleshooting portable computers, 505-505

follow ups (customer service techniques), 1169

fonts (printers)

bitmapped fonts, 800-801

cartridge fonts, 825

internal fonts, 825

print drivers, 825-826

soft fonts, 825

text sizes, 800

TrueType outline fonts, 800-801

vector-based fonts, 800

viewing characters, 801

For Files and Folders option (Start menu), 534

form factors, 10

ATX system boards, 60-61

BTX system boards, 62-63

defining, 9

LPX system boards, 66

NLX system boards, 66

FORMAT command (Windows OS drive-level command line operations), 560

formatting Windows 2000/XP

file systems, 593

volumes, 607-608

Found New Hardware Wizard, 317

FPT (Forced Perfect Termination), SCSI adapter cards, 295

friction-feed (dot-matrix printers), 805

front panel connections, troubleshooting, 423-424, 1059-1060

FRU (Field Replaceable Units)

replacing

cooling system installation, 1199-1201

fan installation, 1199-1201

heat sink installation, 1199-1201

microprocessor installation, 1197

microprocessor speed configuration, 1199

slot processor installation, 1199

troubleshooting, 349-350

FTP (File Transfer Protocols), 1010-1013

fuel cells, portable computers, 479

full backups, 698

Full Control permissions

network shares, 957

NTFS, 960

full-duplex mode (network bridges), 900

G

G.shdsl. *See* SHDSL

game ports, 249

gateways (internet), 899

LAN, 981

WAN Internet connectivity, 972

general support (customer service), 1161

General tab

Printer Properties page, printer property configuration, 836

System Properties window, 542

gimbals (joysticks), 45, 254

GND (Ground) wire, 232

gopher:// prefix, 1011

GPF (General Protection Faults), Dr. Watson utility, 725, 736

Grandfather-Father-Son backup method, 707

grayware, 1114

green mode, power management, 475

grounds (ESD), 1147

Group Accounts (Windows 2000/XP), 1091-1092

    Administrator Accounts, 1093

    Backup Operator Accounts, 1093

    Domain Accounts, 1094

    Guest Accounts, 1093

    Network Configuration Accounts, 1093

    Power User Accounts, 1093

group policies (Windows 2000/XP), 1090-1091

group profiles (Windows 2000/XP), 1087

Guest Accounts (Windows 2000/XP), 1092-1093

GUI (graphical user interfaces), 513-514

H

HAL (Hardware Abstraction Layer), Windows 2000/XP, 582

half-duplex mode (network bridges), 899

hand tools, safety checklist, 1132-1133

hard-memory errors, 383

hardware

    disposal procedures, 1148-1149

    security

        biometric authentication devices, 1080-1083

        information disposal/destruction policies, 1083-1084

        polarizing screens, 1078

        smart cards, 1078-1080

    troubleshooting

        after POST errors, 342

        configuration errors, 340-341

        failures, 340

Hardware tab (System Properties window), 542

HCL (Hardware Compatibility Lists), 623

HDD (hard disk drives)

    CMOS setups, 182

    controllers, 181

    data storage, 34

    defragmenting, 669, 695-698

    Disk Cleanup utility, 670

    disposal of, 1085-1086

    installing, 283-286, 289-291

    optimizing, 668

        defragmenting disk drives, 669

        Disk Cleanup utility, 670

    partitions, 296-299

    PATA drive configurations, 287-288

    portable drives, 450-451

    preventive maintenance procedures, 357-358

    SATA drives, installing, 289-291

    security, 1085

    sub-system components, 180

    troubleshooting, 400

        basic checks, 401-403

        boot failures, 342

        configuration checks, 404-405

        configuration failures, 342

        hardware checks, 405-406

        hard drive failures, 342

    upgrades, 305-307

    volumes, 299

    Windows 2000/XP installation, 629

HDMI (High Definition Media Interface)

    connections, 242

    video cards, 264

HDSL (High Data Rate DSL), 995

HDSL2 (High Data Rate DSL 2nd generation), 996

HDTV (High Definition TV), 270

health configuration settings (CMOS setup utility), 1214

heat buildup

    portable computers, 490

    preventive maintenance procedures, 354-355, 507

heat sinks, 148-149, 1199-1201

help

Help screen (Windows 2000/XP), 728

Internet, 729

troubleshooter utilities (Windows 2000/XP), 727-728

Help file system (Start menu), 535

Help screen (Windows 2000/XP), 728

HelpAssistant (Windows 2000/XP), 1092

helper's console (Remote Assistance), 786

Hibernate mode, portable computers, 475

hidden files, finding, 773

high-level formatting, Windows 2000/XP file systems, 593

high-voltage hazards, 1133-1134

hijacking (sessions), 1120

hives (Windows 2000/XP Registry), 588-589

horizontal/vertical positioning, video displays, 47

horizontal/vertical retraces, CRT monitors, 261

horizontal/vertical sizing, video displays, 47

host addresses (IP addresses), 974

hot swapping USB devices, 231

How to Back Up configuration page (Backup utility), 702

How to Restore configuration page (Restore utility), 704

HTTP (Hypertext Transfer Protocol), 1010-1011

HTTPS (Hypertext Transfer Protocol Secure), 1011

hubs, 897

root hubs, USB, 233

WAN Internet connectivity, 972

HVD (High-Voltage Differential), SCSI signaling, 211

hyperthreading, Intel dual-core processors, 134

I

I/O (Input/Output)

cards

IEEE-1394 FireWire cards, 34

internal modem cards, 32

LAN (Local Area Network) cards, 32

SATA (Serial ATA) Disk Drive cards, 34

SCSI (Small Computer System Interface) cards, 33, 90

sound cards, 33

TV tuner cards, 33

USB (Universal Serial Bus) cards, 34

wireless network cards, 34

FireWire buses (IEEE-1394), 236-238

legacy connectors, 244-245

MIDI connections, 242-244

multimedia connections

audio, 239

Component Video, 241

Composite Video, 240

Digital Component Video, 241

DVI, 241

HDMI, 242

S-Video, 241

ports

ATX back panel connections, 84

CMOS setup utility, 104-105

configuring, 317

connectors, 226

game ports, 249

infrared ports, 237-238

legacy ports, 244-245

parallel printer ports, 246-247

PATA disk drive connections, 86, 88

RS-232 serial ports, 248

SATA disk drive connections, 86-89

SCSI adapter cards, 90

standard types, 229

USB ports, 229, 233

programming, 226

PS/2 connectors, 229

system boards

connections, 17

troubleshooting, 381

system resource allocations, 227

transfers, initiating, 226-227

USB

architectures, 233-234

bus enumerating, 231

compound devices, 231

data transfers, 235

desktop connection schemes, 230

device speed ratings, 235-236

GND (Ground) wire, 232

hot swapping devices, 231

ports, 229, 233

root hubs, 233

Series-A connectors, 232

Series-B connectors, 232

Vbus wire, 232

ICF function (firewalls), enabling in Windows XP, 1105

ICS (Internet Connection Sharing), 987-988

IDE (Integrated Drive Electronics) disk drive interfaces, 200-201

IDE controller (CMOS setup utility), 103

IDSL (Integrated Services Digital Network DSL), 996

IEEE-1394 (FireWire), 207-208

adapters, troubleshooting, 419

buses

cables, 237

connections, 236-237

infrared ports, 237-238

device installations, 317

ports, troubleshooting, 419-421

image quality, troubleshooting (scanners), 874

imodems, 988

impact printers, 800

incremental backups, 699

indentity theft, 1120

Index Server function (Start menu), 534

Index tab (Help screen), 728

indicator lights, troubleshooting

power supplies, 377

system boards, 379

information disposal/destruction policies (security), 1083-1084

information events (Event Viewer utility), 711

Infrared, 971

infrared ports, 237-238, 499-500

ink cartridges

inkjet printers, 810, 863-864

laser printers, troubleshooting, 868-870

RTC, 868

inkjet printers, 809

components of, 810

ink cartridges, 810, 863-864

mechanical vibration printing method, 809

paper-feed motors, 810

preventive maintenance, 877

solid inkjet printers, 809

thermal shock printing method, 809

troubleshooting

configuration checks, 863

ink cartridges, 863-864

paper, 866

paper feed issues, 866

printhead not moving, 865

printhead not printing, 865

input devices

keyboards, troubleshooting, 496

preventive maintenance procedures, 360-361

touch pads, troubleshooting, 496-497

inspections (troubleshooting), 333

installation wizards, Windows 2000, 537

installing

adapter card-based peripherals, 314-315

analog modems, 983-984

AP, wireless LAN installations, 938-940

applications, troubleshooting, 770

cooling systems, system boards, 1199-1201

digital cameras, 313

digital modems, 998-999

DIMM modules, 1202

external storage devices, portable computers, 463

fans, system boards, 1199-1201

FireWire IEEE-1394 devices, 317

heat sinks, system boards, 1199-1201

IrDA devices, 317-319

LAN adapter cards, 936-937

microprocessors, system boards, 1197-1199

monitors, 308-309

Netware (Novell) clients/protocols, Windows 2000/XP networking, 954-955

PC cards, 466-467

power supplies, 378-379, 1204

printers, 816-817

Bluetooth, 819

IrDA printer ports, 820

legacy printer interfaces, 821

networked printers, 818-819

serial printer interfaces, 821-822

USB printers, 818

Wi-Fi adapters, 819

Windows 2000/XP, 834-835

RAM modules, 1202

routers, wireless LAN installations, 942

SATA drives, 289-291

scanners, 311-312, 840-841

slot processors, system boards, 1199

sound cards, 312

storage devices

CD-ROM drives, 300-301

CD-RW drives, 301

DVD drives, 300

DVD-RW drives, 301

external storage devices, 303

FDD, 302-303

HDD, 283-286

internal storage devices, 282

SCSI adapter cards, 292-296

system boards, removing

adapter cards, 1195

cables, 1195-1196

external I/O systems, 1193

previous system board, 1196

system unit covers, 1194

USB devices, 317

video systems, 308-309

Windows 2000 Professional, 633-638

Windows 2000/XP, 623

attended installations, 624

disk cloning, 626-628

disk image creation, 627-628

dynamic volumes, 605

HDD preparation, 629

patches, 630-632

RIS images, 626

service packs, 630-632

troubleshooting setup problems, 632-633

unattended installations, 624-625

Windows XP Professional, 638-639

attended installations, 640

MCE hardware requirements, 640-641

MCE setup limitations, 642

troubleshooting setup problems, 641-642

wireless LAN, 938

AP configuration, 940

AP installation, 938-940

CAT5 crossover cables, 942

DHCP servers, 944

Mac filtering, 945

Port Forwarding, 945

remote management, 945

router configuration, 943, 945

router installation, 942

UPnP, 946

Virtual Servers, 945

Wireless AP, 945

wireless client installation, 941

wireless networks, portable computers, 471

Integrated Peripherals setup screen (CMOS setup utility), 103

Integrated Video Controllers, VGA (Video Graphics Array) cards, 31

integrity (customer service techniques), 1173-1175

Intel processors

dual-core processors, 130-134

Pentium processors, 122-123

Itanium processors, 130

MMX processors, 124

Pentium II processors, 125-127

Pentium III processors, 127

Pentium 4 processors, 128-129

Pentium Pro processors, 124

Xeon processors, 128

interface cables, troubleshooting scanners, 876

interlaced displays (digital resolution), 268

interlaced scanning, CRT monitors, 261

internal data storage devices, installing, 282

internal disk drive interfaces, 199

internal fonts (printers), 825

internal modem cards, 32

internal modems, 983

Internet

access methods, 979

cable modems, 996-997

dial-up access, 983-988, 992

digital modems, 998-999

DSL, 979, 990-996

ISDN, 979, 988-989

LAN, 980-982

satellite access, 1000-1002

VoIP, 1003-1004

wireless access, 1002

connectivity

bridges, 972

domains, 978

gateways, 972

hubs, 972

IP addresses, 974-977

ISP, 972-973

midlevel networks, 972

packets, 971

repeaters, 972

routers, 973

gateways, 899

help, 729

Internet Connection Wizard (Windows 2000), 986

interrupt transfers, USB, 235

interrupt-driven I/O (I/O transfers), 226

intranets, 516, 975-976

Invalid Drive error messages, 400

Invalid Drive Specification error messages, 400

Invalid Media Type error messages, 400, 404

IP (Internet Protocol) addresses

classes of, 974

dotted decimal notation, 974

host addresses, 974

intranets, 975-976

network addresses, 974

private IP classes, 977

routers, 944

static IP addresses, 1007

subnets, 975-976

WAN Internet connectivity, 974-977

IP Addresses option (Windows 2000/XP IP Settings tab), 952

IP Settings tab (Windows 2000/XP), 952

IPCONFIG utility (Windows 2000/XP), 726, 1036, 1045, 1055

IPSec, Windows 2000/XP authentication, 1096

IPX/SPX (Internetwork Packet Exchange/Sequenced Packet Exchange), 920

IrDA (Infrared Data Association)

device installations, 317-319

links, 910

ports

implementation via CMOS setup utility, 105

printer ports, 820

troubleshooting infrared ports, 499-500

IrDA-FIR protocol, infrared ports, 238

IrDA-SIR protocol, infrared ports, 238

IrLPT protocol, infrared ports, 238

IrTran-P protocol, infrared ports, 238

IRU (Indoor Receive Units), 1002

ISA (Industry Standard Architecture) slot connectors, 30

iSCSI (Internet SCSI), 207-208

ISDN (Integrated Services Digital Network), 979, 988-989

isochronous transfers, USB, 235

ISP (Internet Service Providers), WAN Internet connectivity, 972-973

Itanium processors, 130

ITU (Indoor Transmit Units), 1002

J - K

jargon, avoiding (customer service techniques), 1167

jokes (grayware), 1115

joysticks, 45, 250, 254

K6PLUS-3D processors, 135

K75 processors, 136

KDC (Key Distribution Center), Windows 2000/XP authentication, 1095

Kerberos protocol, Windows 2000/XP authentication, 1094-1095

Kernel mode (Windows 2000/XP), 582

keyboards, 6, 44, 251

back panel connections, 42-44

echo operations, 252

encoders, 252

portable keyboards, 455-456

preventive maintenance procedures, 360

PS/2 connectors, 229

shortcuts (Windows 2000/XP), 522

troubleshooting, 386, 496

basic checks, 387

configuration checks, 387

hardware checks, 388

wireless keyboards, 389

Knowledge Base (Microsoft), 729

L

L1 cache memory, 152

L2 cache memory, 152

L3 cache memory, 152

LAN (Local Area Networks), 32, 947-948

adapter cards, 934-937

CAN, 890

client configuration, 950

gateways, 981

hubs, 897

Internet access, 980-982

MAN, 890

NAT, 982

network adapters, optimizing, 937

network bridges, 899-900

network control strategies

    client/server networks, 894-895

    P2P, 894-896

protocol configuration, 950-953

routers, 898-899, 981

switches, 897

topologies

    bus, 891

    logical, 893

    mesh, 892

    ring, 892

    star, 892

transport protocol, 935

troubleshooting

    cable checks, 1041

    connectivity device checks, 1041-1042

    NIC checks, 1039-1040

    printing problems, 1049-1051

    service access problems, 1038-1039

    windows related problems, 1042-1045

    wireless networks, 1046-1048

wireless LAN, installing, 938-946

laptops, 7, 437

dissassembling, 491-492

displays, 452-455

docking stations, 477-478

external CD-ROM drives, 460

external CD-RW drives, 461

external DVD-RW drives, 461

external FDD, 460

heat buildup, 490

Hibernate mode, 475

memory

    MicroDIMM, 446

    SODIMM, 446

    upgrades, 448-449

PC cards

    adding memory to, 465

    Cardbus, 464-465

    installing, 466-467

    Mini PCI Express cards, 468-469

    upgrading, 480

peripheral storage devices, 460

portable drives, 450-451

portable keyboards, 455-456

power supplies, 474

    AC adapters, 473

    DC adapters, 473

    fuel cells, 479

    power consumption, 475

    power management, 475-476

    upgrading batteries, 479

preventive maintenance

    cleaning, 507

    heat buildup, 507

    rough handling, 505-506

removable storage, 462-463

security, 1088

styluses, 458, 497

system boards, 438

    AMD Mobile processors, 445

    Centrino processors, 443

    Core Duo processors, 444

    microprocessors, 440-441

    Pentium IIIM processors, 441-442

    Pentium 4M processors, 441-442

    Pentium M processors, 442-443

touch pads, 457-458

trackballs, 457

troubleshooting, 490

    audio, 504

    docking stations, 503-504

    Fn keys, 504-505

infrared ports, 499-500

keyboards, 496

LCD displays, 492-495

PCMCIA cards, 500-501

port replicators, 503-504

power supplies, 501-503

removable media devices, 498

touch pads, 496-497

USB devices, 497-498

VGA connectors, 459

wireless networks, 470

built-in WiFi, 472

installing, 471

laser printers, 811-813

electrophotographic cartridges, 814

paper, 868

power supplies, 868

preventive maintenance, 877-878

safety issues, 878

troubleshooting, 866-867

black page errors, 869

faint print, 870

ink cartridges, 870

Missing Beam error messages, 869

missing print, 870

paper, 868

paper jams, 871-872

partial/total failures, 868

power supplies, 868

roller errors, 870

smudged print, 871

specks/stains, 870

toner cartridges, 868

white (blank) page errors, 869

white line errors, 870

xspecks/stains, 870

laser/burn hazards, 1136-1137

Last Known Good Configuration option (Windows 2000/XP), troubleshooting startup process, 750

latency, 1001

LCD (liquid crystal display) monitors, 46

portable displays, 452-455

preventive maintenance procedures, 357

troubleshooting, 492-495

LDTV (Low Definition TV), 269

legacy connectors, 244-245

legacy device resources, 228

legacy ports, 244-245

legacy printer interfaces, installing, 821

legal issues (customer service), 1176

lighting (work area safety), 1131

Line In/Line Out connections, sound cards, 272

Linux, 514

liquids (work area safety), 1132

List Folder Contents permissions (NTFS), 960

listening (customer service techniques), 1164-1166

Live TV option (Windows XP MCE), 554

LNB (Low Noise Block) converters, 1001

Local Area Connection Properties dialog (Windows 2000/XP)

Advanced tab, 949

Authentication tab, 950

Clients function, 948

Protocols function, 948

Services function, 948

Local Network window (Windows XP), 527

Local_Machine key (Windows 2000/XP Registry), 588-589

lockable server cases/chassis, 1075

locking computers (wireless security), 1106-1108

Log Off User option (Start menu), 535

logical drives, 296-299

Logical Drives tool (System Tools console), 540

logical topologies (LAN), 893

logs (event), Windows 2000/XP security, 1098-1100

loopback tests, 420, 1058-1059

low-profile desktops (system units), 7

LPX (Low-Profile Extended) form factor, system boards, 66

LVD (Low-Voltage Differential), SCSI signaling, 211-212

M

MAC (Media Access Control) address switches, 897

Mac filtering, wireless LAN installations, 945

magnetic tape drives, data storage, 191-192

mailto: prefix, 1011

maintenance (preventive). *See also* troubleshooting
cleaning, 350-352, 507
dot-matrix printers, 877
dust, 353
HDD (hard disk drives), 357-358
heat buildup, 354-355, 507
inkjet printers, 877
keyboards, 360
laser printers, 877-878
mice, 360
monitors, 355-356
removable media drives, 359-360
rough handling, 353, 505-506
scheduling, 361
annual activities, 363-364
daily activities, 362
monthly activities, 363
six-month activities, 363
weekly activities, 362
smoke, 353
touch pads, 361

MAN (Multiple Area Networks), 890

mapping network drives, 961-962

marketing, customer service, 1160

master boot sectors (primary partitions), 298

Maximum Password Age/Minimum Password Age option (Windows 2000/XP), 1097

MCE (Media Center Edition)
Windows XP, 547
Movie Maker application, 557
Start page, 552-557
Windows XP Professional
hardware requirements, 640-641
setup limitations, 642

MDI (Media Dependent Interface) connections, wireless LAN installations, 943

mechanical vibration printing method (inkjet printers), 809

Media Options configuration page (Backup utility), 702

media servers, 62

MEM utility (Windows 2000/XP), 726

memory
access violation errors, 136
cache memory, 16, 152, 166-167
CMOS Memory Size Mismatch error message, 341
CMOS RAM, 27
DIMM modules, installing, 1202
dual channel memory, 173
EEPROM (Electrically-Erasable Programmable Read Only Memory), 23
flash memory, 214
CF (CompactFlash) cards, 216
memory sticks, 216-217
SD (Secure Digital) cards, 217
USB flash drives, 215
flat memory model, 583
memory access violation errors, 136
PC cards, adding to, 465
performance, 682

portable computers

   MicroDIMM, 446

   SODIMM, 446

   upgrades, 448-449

primary memory (system boards), 16, 22-23

RAM (Random Access Memory), 16, 23

   cache memory, 166-167

   CMOS RAM, 27

   DIMM (Dual Inline Memory Modules), 22, 168

   DRAM, 160-161, 164, 169-170, 173

   dual channel memory, 173

   error checking, 164-165

   hard-memory errors, 383

   installing RAM modules, 1202

   RIMM, 169

   soft-memory errors, 383

   SRAM, 160, 163

   troubleshooting, 383, 856

   volatile memory, 22

ROM (Read-Only Memory), 16, 22-23

shared video memory, 450

system board upgrades, 1215-1216

virtual memory, 583-584, 667

volatile memory, 22

Windows 2000/XP

   flat memory model, 583

   virtual memory, 583-584, 667

memory sticks, 216-217

menus, grayed options, 528

mesh topologies (LAN), 892

MFT (Master File Table), NTFS disks, 598

mice (peripherals). *See* mouses (peripherals)

Micro BTX system boards, 63

microcontrollers, printers, 803

MicroDIMM, portable computers, 446

microdrive cards. *See* CF (CompactFlash) cards

microphones, sound cards, 272

microprocessors (system boards), 16-17

AMD processors

   Athlon 64 processors, 136

   Athlon XP processors, 136

   Duron processors, 137

   K6PLUS-3D processors, 135

   K75 processors, 136

   Slot A Athlon processors, 135

bus speeds, 72

cache memory, 152

characteristics summary table, 142-143

clock speeds, 144

clone processors, 18, 145

configuring, 146

cooling systems

   BTX Thermal Module, 149

   fans, 148-149

   heat sinks, 148-149

   water-based systems, 150

dual-core processors

   AMD, 137-141

   Intel, 130-134

flip chips, 92

installing, 1197

overclocking, 147, 1209

OverDrive processors, 91

Pentium processors, 18-20, 122-123

   Itanium processors, 130

   MMX processors, 124

   Pentium II processors, 125-127

   Pentium III processors, 127

   Pentium 4 processors, 128-129

   Pentium Pro processors, 124

   Xeon processors, 128

portable computers, 440-441

power supplies, 145

slotket processors, 92

socket specifications, 91-95

speed configuration, 1199

system board upgrades, 1210-1211

troubleshooting, 383-384

upgrades, 1206-1208

ZIF sockets, 1197

Microsoft Index Server function (Start menu), 534

Microsoft Knowledge Base (Microsoft Product Support Services), 729

MIDI (Musical Instrument Digital Interface) connections, 242

data transfers, 244

MMC, 243

patch cords, 243

midlevel networks, 972

MIDX (Media Independent Interface Crossover) connections, wireless LAN installations, 943

Mini PCI Express cards, 468-469

mini-DIN connectors. See PS/2 connectors

Minimum Password Length option (Windows 2000/XP), 1097

mirrored drive arrays, 184-186

mirrored volumes, NTFS disks, 602

Missing Beam error messages, laser printers, 869

missing print (laser printers), troubleshooting, 870

MKDIR (MD) command (Windows OS directory-level command line operations), 562

MMC (MIDI Machine Control), 243

MMX processors, 124

modems

analog modems, installing, 983-984

cable modems, 996-997

digital modems, 998-999

DSL, 990

external modems, 983

imodems, 988

internal modems, 983

ISDN, 989

null modem connections, 249

troubleshooting, 1057, 1061-1062

modified only backups. See differential backups

Modify permissions (NTFS), 959-960

monitors. See video, displays

monthly preventive maintenance activities, 363

MOS (metal oxide semiconductors), ESD, 1145-1146

motherboards. See system boards

mouses (peripherals), 6, 44

back panel connections, 42-44

PS/2 connectors, 229

trackball mouses, 45, 253

troubleshooting

configuration checks, 391

hardware checks, 390-391

optical mouses, 392

wireless mouses, 392

wheel mouses, 45

Movie Maker application (Windows XP MCE), 557

MSCONFIG.EXE (System Configuration utility), 676, 720, 726, 750

MSDS (Material Safety Data Sheets), 1149

multimedia connections

audio, 239

Component Video, 241

Composite Video, 240-242

Digital Component Video, 241

DVI, 241

S-Video, 241

sound cards, 272

multimeters, 330, 343-345

multiprocessors, VRM (Voltage Regulator Modules), 145

My Computer window (Windows 2000/XP), 524-525

My Documents folder (Windows 2000/XP), 525

My Music option (Windows XP MCE), 555

My Network Places window (Windows 2000/XP), 527

My Pictures option (Windows XP MCE), 557

My TV option (Windows XP MCE), 554-555

My Video option (Windows XP MCE), 557

N

naming Start menu items, 535

NanoBTX system boards, 63

NAT (network address translation), 982

native resolution, LCD displays, 455

NET VIEW command, troubleshooting LAN, 1044

NetBEUI (NetBIOS Enhanced User Interface), 920

NETBIOS, Windows 2000/XP networking, 953

NETSTAT utility, network troubleshooting, 1035

NetWare (Novell)

ODI, 953

Windows 2000/XP networking, 953-955

Network Administrator (Windows 2000/XP), 1088

Network Configuration Operator Accounts (Windows 2000/XP), 1093

Network Connection Wizard (Windows 2000), 985

Network Identification (Computer Name) tab (System Properties window), 542

Network Identification function (Windows 2000/XP), 949

networks

adapters, optimizing in LAN, 937

addresses (IP addresses), 974

AppleTalk, 921

bridges, 899-900

cable testers, 331

CAN, 890

client/server networks, 515

diskless workstations, 895

LAN network control strategies, 894-895

connectivity devices

hubs, 897

network bridges, 899-900

routers, 898-899

switches, 897

copper cables

coaxial cables, 904-906

twisted-pair cables, 901-903

enterprise networks, 516

Ethernet, 914

coaxial specifications, 915-916

fiber specifications, 918

twisted-pair specifications, 916-917

wireless specifications, 919-920

extranets, 517

fiber-optic cables, 906-908

intranets, 516

IrDA links, 910

LAN, 946-948

adapter cards, 934-937

bus topologies, 891

CAN, 890

client configuration, 950

hubs, 897

Internet access, 980-982

logical topologies, 893

MAN, 890

mesh topologies, 892

network bridges, 899-900

network control strategies, 894-896

optimizing network adapters, 937

protocol configuration, 950-953

ring topologies, 892

routers, 898-899

star topologies, 892

switches, 897

transport protocol, 935

troubleshooting, 1038-1051

Local Network window (Windows XP), 527

MAN, 890

mapping drives, 961-962

midlevel networks, 972

NetBEUI, 920

NWLink, 920

P2P, LAN network control strategies, 894-896

plenum cables, 909-910

printers

    installing, 818-819

    Wi-Fi adapters, 819

    Windows 2000/XP, 837

private networks, 977

shares, 527, 956

    Change permissions, 957

    Full Control permissions, 957

    NTFS permissions, 958

    Read permissions, 957

TCP/IP, 921

troubleshooting, 1032

    ARP, 1035

    cabling testers, 1034

    continuity testers, 1034

    IPCONFIG utility, 1036, 1045, 1055

    LAN, 1038-1051

    NETSTAT utility, 1035

    NSLOOKUP.EXE utility, 1036

    OTDR, 1035

    PATHPING utility, 1036

    PING utility, 1035-1037, 1045, 1055

    printing, 777-778

    startup problems, 766

    TDR devices, 1034-1035

    TRACERT utility, 1035-1038

WAN, 1052-1064

wiring testers, 1034

wireless networks

    IrDA links, 910

    portable computers, 470-472

    RF links, 911-912

    troubleshooting, 1046-1048

wireless RF links, 911-912

workgroups, 955

New Connection Wizard (Windows XP), 985, 987

news: prefix, 1011

NIC (Network Interface Cards), 934, 1039-1040

NLX (New Low-Profile Extended) form factor, 11, 66

NMI (Non-Maskable Interrupt) signals, parity checking, 165

non-impact printers, 800

NOS (network operating systems), 513

notebooks, 437

    displays, 452-455

    dissassembling, 491-492

    docking stations, 477-478

    external CD-ROM drives, 460

    external CD-RW drives, 461

    external DVD-RW drives, 461

    external FDD, 460

    heat buildup, 490

    Hibernate mode, 475

    memory

        MicroDIMM, 446

        SODIMM, 446

        upgrades, 448-449

    PC cards

        adding memory to, 465

        Cardbus, 464-465

        installing, 466-467

        Mini PCI Express cards, 468-469

        upgrading, 480

    peripheral storage devices, 460

    portable drives, 450-451

portable keyboards, 455-456

power supplies, 474

  AC adapters, 473

  DC adapters, 473

  fuel cells, 479

  power consumption, 475

  power management, 475-476

  upgrading batteries, 479

preventive maintenance

  cleaning, 507

  heat buildup, 507

  rough handling, 505-506

removable storage, 462-463

styluses, 458, 497

system boards, 438

  AMD Mobile processors, 445

  Centrino processors, 443

  Core Duo processors, 444

  microprocessors, 440-441

  Pentium IIIM processors,
    441-442

  Pentium 4M processors, 441-442

  Pentium M processors, 442-443

touch pads, 457-458

trackballs, 457

troubleshooting, 490

  audio, 504

  docking stations, 503-504

  Fn keys, 504-505

  infrared ports, 499-500

  keyboards, 496

  LCD displays, 492-495

  PCMCIA cards, 500-501

  port replicators, 503-504

  power supplies, 501-503

  removable media devices, 498

  touch pads, 496-497

  USB devices, 497-498

VGA connectors, 459

wireless networks, 470

  built-in WiFi, 472

  installing, 471

Novell NetWare

  ODI, 953

  Windows 2000/XP networking,
    953-955

NSLOOKUP.EXE utility, network troubleshooting, 1036

NTBOOTDD.SYS, Windows 2000/XP boot process, 581

NTFS (NT File Systems)

  FAT, moving to (security issues),
    1085

  file/folder permissions, 960

    Full Control, 960

    List Folder Contents, 960

    Modify, 959-960

    Read, 959-960

    Read & Execute, 959-960

    Write, 959-960

  NTFS disks, 597

    advantages of, 600-601

    MFT, 598

    mirrored volumes, 602

    RAID 5 volumes, 604

    simple volumes, 602

    spanned volumes, 602

    striped volumes, 604

    Unicode, 598

  permissions (network shares), 958

  Windows 2000/XP file permissions,
    612-613

NTLDR (NT Loader file), Windows 2000/XP boot process, 579-580

NTOSKRNL.EXE files, Windows 2000/XP boot process, 581

null modem connections, 249

NWLink, 920

O

ODI (Open Datalink Interface), Novell Network, 953

old computers, disposal of, 1085-1086

Online Support Requests (Microsoft Product Support Services), 729

operating systems

Windows 2000

installing, 623-633

upgrades, 643-645, 650-653

Windows 2000 Professional, installing, 633-638

Windows XP

installing, 623-633

upgrades, 643, 646-653

Windows XP Professional, installing, 638-642

operational problems, troubleshooting, 742, 775

applications

applying Event Viewer to, 773-774

applying Task Manager to, 773

installing, 770

not starting, 771

starting from Command Prompt, 772

hidden files, finding, 773

networks, 777-778

optional devices do not operate, 767-768

printers, 776-778

stop errors, 768-770

operator control boards (printers), 804, 826, 855-856

Opteron dual-core processors, 141

optical data storage

CD-ROM drives, 193-197

DVD drives, 197-198

optical mouses, troubleshooting, 392

optimizing

HDD, 305-306, 668

defragmenting disk drives, 669

Disk Cleanup utility, 670

SCSI systems, 307

Startup menu (Windows 2000/XP), 675

system services, 673

virtual memory, 667

Options tab (Windows 2000/XP), 953

OS (operating systems)

DOS (disk operating systems), 512-513

GUI (graphical user interfaces), 513-514

NOS (network operating systems), 513

startup failures, troubleshooting, 342

Windows 2000, 518

Advanced Server edition, 519

client/server networks, 515

command line, 559-564

Control Panel, 535-543

Datacenter Server edition, 519

desktops, 523

Explorer, 543-546

File menus, 528-529

keyboard shortcuts, 522

My Computer window, 524-525

My Documents folder, 525

My Network Places window, 527

Professional edition, 518

Recycle Bin, 526

right-clicking, 524

Standard Server edition, 518-519

Start menu, 531-535

System Tools console, 540

taskbar, 530

Tools menu, 530

user interfaces, 524

View menu, 529-530

Windows Server 2003, 521

Windows Vista, 521

Windows XP, 519

64-bit edition, 520

Accessories menu, 549

Administrative Tools menu, 549

All Programs menu, 549

client/server networks, 515

command line, 559-564

Control Panel, 550-552

desktops, 523

Explorer, 543-546

File menus, 528-529

Home edition, 519

keyboard shortcuts, 522

Local Network window, 527

MCE (Media Center Edition), 520, 547, 552-557

My Computer window, 524-525

My Documents folder, 525

My Network Places, 527

Professional edition, 520

Recycle Bin, 526

right-clicking, 524

Start menu, 531-535, 548

taskbar, 530

Tools menu, 530

user interfaces, 524

View menu, 529-530

OTDR (optical time domain reflectometers), 1035

Out of Memory error messages (scanners), 874

overclocking, 147, 1209

OverDrive processors, 91

P - Q

P2P (peer-to-peer networks), LAN network control strategies, 894-896

packets, Internet connectivity, 971

paper

dot-matrix printers

feed issues, 862-863

specifications, 860

troubleshooting, 859-863

inkjet printers, troubleshooting, 866

laser printers, troubleshooting, 868, 871-872

paper trays (printers), 829

paper-feed motors (inkjet printers), 810

paperwork, handling (customer service techniques), 1179

parallax errors, 256

parallel printer ports

Centronics standard, 246

ECP, 247

EPP, 247

implementation via CMOS setup utility, 104

parity checking, RAM, 164-165

Parity Error messages, 166

partition tables, 298, 592

partitions, 296, 299

extended partitions, 297

NTFS system support, 298

partition tables, 298

primary partitions, 297-298

Windows 2000/XP file systems, 590-592

passive heat sinks, 148

passive termination, SCSI adapter cards, 295

passive-matrix displays, LCD displays, 454

passwords

changing, 1077

crackers (grayware), 1115

depth, 1077

routers, 944

width, 1076

Windows 2000/XP security, 1096-1097

Passwords Must Meet Complexity Requirements option (Windows 2000/XP), 1097

PATA drives

configuring, 287-288

connections

I/O ports, 86-88

IDE controller (CMOS setup utility), 104

interface specifications, 212-213

troubleshooting, 404-405

patch cords, MIDI, 243

patches, Windows 2000/XP installation, 630-632

PATHPING utility, network troubleshooting, 1036

PC cards

adding memory, 465

advanced I/O, 466

Cardbus, 464-465

installing, 466-467

Mini PCI Express cards, 468-469

upgrades, 480

PC hardware setup process

BIOS extensions, 578

CMOS setup checks, 578

PnP configuration, 577-578

POST checks, 577-578

system initialization, 577

system startup/reset, 577

PC Health menu screen (CMOS setup utility), 106

PC/SC (Personal Computer/Smart Card), 1079

PCI (Peripheral Component Interconnect) expansion slots, 29, 73-76

PCI-to-PCIe bridges, 80

PCI-X (PCI-Extended) expansion slots, 30, 76-77

PCIe (PCI Express)

expansion slots, 30, 77-80

power connectors, 14

PCL (Printer Control Language), print drivers, 825

PCMCIA (Personal Computer Memory Card International Association) cards

adding memory, 465

advanced I/O, 466

Cardbus, 464-465

installing, 466-467

Mini PCI Express cards, 468-469

troubleshooting, 500-501

upgrades, 480

PDL (Page Description Language), print drivers, 825-826

peer-to-peer workgroups, client/server networks, 516

pen drives. *See* USB, flash drives

Pentium processors, 122-123

Itanium processors, 130

MMX processors, 124

Pentium II processors, 125-127

Pentium III processors, 127

Pentium IIIM processors, portable computers, 441-442

Pentium 4 processors, 128-129

Pentium 4M processors, portable computers, 441-442

Pentium M Celeron processors, portable computers, 443

Pentium M processors, portable computers, 442-443

Pentium Pro processors, 124

Xeon processors, 128

performance

application performance (Windows 2000/XP), monitoring

disk system performance, 683-684

memory performance, 682

processor performance, 683

System Monitor, 678-681

system performance (Windows 2000/XP), monitoring, 676-677

Windows 2000/XP, optimizing in

HDD, 668-670

monitoring application performance, 678-684

monitoring system performance, 676-677

software maintenance, 684-685

startup process, 674-676

system services, 673

temporary file management, 670-672

virtual memory, 667

Performance Logs and Alerts utility (System Monitor), 680-681

Performance Options dialog (Windows 2000/XP), 585

peripheral power connectors, 14

peripheral storage, portable computers, 460

peripherals, 41

  adapter card peripheral installations, 314-315

  back panel connections, 42-44

  Integrated Peripherals setup screen (CMOS setup utility), 103

  keyboards, 6, 44, 251

    echo operations, 252

    portable keyboards, 455-456

    preventive maintenance procedures, 360

    PS/2 connectors, 229

    troubleshooting, 386-389, 496

  mouses (peripherals), 6, 44

    back panel connections, 42-44

    pointing devices, 252-253

    PS/2 connectors, 229

    trackball mouses, 45, 253

    troubleshooting, 390-392

    wheel mouses, 45

  pointing devices, 6, 44

    joysticks, 45, 250, 254

    mouses, 45, 252-253

    portable computers, 458

    PS/2 connectors, 229

    touch pads, 45, 457-458

    trackballs, 45, 457

    troubleshooting, 390-392

  printers

    automatic sheet feeders, 829

    calibration, 827

    cartridge fonts, 825

    character printers, 799

    collators, 830

    configuring, serial printer interfaces, 823

    controllers, 803

    dot-matrix printers, 804-806, 858-863, 877

    drivers, 824-826

    duplexers, 830

    dye sublimation printers, 815-816

    ELP drums, 830

    fonts, 800-801

    impact printers, 800

    inkjet printers, 809-810, 863-866, 877

    installing, 816-822

    interfaces, 802

    internal fonts, 825

    laser printers, 811-814, 866-872, 877-878

    non-impact printers, 800

    operator control panels, 804, 826

    paper trays, 829

    preventive maintenance, 877-878

    processors, 803

    soft fonts, 825

    stapler/stackers, 830

    thermal printers, 807-808

    troubleshooting, 853-872

    upgrades, 828

    Windows 2000/XP, 831-837

  scanners, 838

    barcode, 257

    biometric, 256

    fingerprint, 257

    installing, 840-841

    troubleshooting, 873-876

  video displays, 6

    brightness, 47

    contrast, 47

    CRT, 46, 260-261

    dot pitch, 267

    external monitors, portable computers, 493

    horizontal/vertical positioning, 47

    horizontal/vertical sizing, 47

installing, 308-309

LCD (liquid crystal display) monitors, 46

portable displays, 452-455

preventive maintenance procedures, 355-356

resolution, 265-268

screen memory, 263

skew, 47

touch screens, 254-256

troubleshooting, 393-399

permission, asking (customer service techniques), 1175

personal safety

hand tools, 1132-1133

high-voltage hazards, 1133-1134

laser/burn hazards, 1136-1137

shock/electrocution, 1134-1135

personal service (customer service), 1161

pharming, 1119

phishing, 1119

physical drives

partitions, 296-299

volumes, 299

PicoBTX system boards, 63

pin-feed (dot-matrix printers), 805

PING utility (Windows 2000/XP), 727, 1035-1037, 1045, 1055

Pipeline SRAM (Static RAM), 163

plenum cables, 909-910

PnP (Plug-and-Play), 27

CMOS setup utility, PnP/PCI Configuration screen, 102

PC hardware setup process, 577-578

PCIe expansion slots, 80

UPnP, 946

PnP manager (Windows 2000/XP), 582

PnP/PCI Configuration screen (CMOS setup utility), 102

pointing devices, 6, 44

joysticks, 45, 250, 254

mouses, 6, 44

back panel connections, 42-44

PS/2 connectors, 229

trackballs, 45, 253, 457

troubleshooting, 390-392

wheel mouses, 45

portable computers, 458

PS/2 connectors, 229

touch pads, 45

portable computers, 457-458

preventive maintenance procedures, 361

troubleshooting, 496-497

trackballs, 45, 253, 457

polarizing screens, 452, 1078

polling (I/O transfers), 226

Port Forwarding, wireless LAN installations, 945

port replicators, 478, 503-504

portable computers, 7, 437

disassemblin, 491-492

displays, 452-455

docking stations, 477-478

external CD-ROM drives, 460

external CD-RW drives, 461

external DVD-RW drives, 461

external FDD, 460

heat buildup, 490

Hibernate mode, 475

memory

MicroDIMM, 446

SODIMM, 446

upgrades, 448-449

PC cards

adding memory to, 465

Cardbus, 464-465

installing, 466-467

Mini PCI Express cards, 468-469

upgrading, 480

peripheral storage devices, 460

pointing devices, 457-458, 497

portable drives, 450-451

portable keyboards, 455-456

power supplies, 474

   AC adapters, 473

   DC adapters, 473

   fuel cells, 479

   power consumption, 475

   power management, 475-476

   upgrading batteries, 479

preventive maintenance

   cleaning, 507

   heat buildup, 507

   rough handling, 505-506

removable storage, 462-463

security, 1088

styluses, 458, 497

system boards, 438

   AMD Mobile processors, 445

   Centrino processors, 443

   Core Duo processors, 444

   microprocessors, 440-441

   Pentium IIIM processors, 441-442

   Pentium 4M processors, 441-442

   Pentium M Celeron processors, 443

   Pentium M processors, 442-443

touch pads, 457-458

trackballs, 457

troubleshooting, 490

   audio, 504

   docking stations, 503-504

   Fn keys, 504-505

   infrared ports, 499-500

   keyboards, 496

   LCD displays, 492-495

   PCMCIA cards, 500-501

   port replicators, 503-504

   power supplies, 501-503

   removable media devices, 498

   touch pads, 496-497

   USB devices, 497-498

   VGA connectors, 459

   wireless networks, 470

   built-in WiFi, 472

   installing, 471

portable displays, 452-455

portable drives, 450-451

portable keyboards, 455-456

portable power, troubleshooting, 501-503

ports, 41

   back panel connections, 42-44

   ECP, 247

   EPP, 247

   FireWire (IEEE-1394), troubleshooting, 419-421

   game ports, 249

   I/O (Input/Output) ports

      ATX back panel connections, 84

      CMOS setup utility, 104-105

      connectors, 226

      PATA disk drive connections, 86-88

      SATA disk drive connections, 86-89

      SCSI adapter cards, 90

   infrared, 237-238, 499-500

   IrDA printer ports, 820

   legacy, 228, 244-245

   loopback test plugs, 420

   parallel printer ports, 246-247

   RS-232 serial ports, 248

   standard types, 229

   troubleshooting

      basic checks, 415

      FireWire (IEEE-1394) ports, 419-421

      front panel ports, 423-424

      USB ports, 416-418

   USB ports, 229, 233, 416-418

   well-known ports table, firewalls, 1104

POST (Power-On Self Tests), 24

cards, 348-349

checks (PC hardware setup process), 577-578

PC hardware setup process, 577

PostScript, print drivers, 825

POTS splitters, 991

Power Management fields (CMOS setup utility), 106

power manager (Windows 2000/XP), 583

power supplies, 1203

+5, 14

+12V, 14

AC adapters, 15

batteries, 479

EPS (Entry-Level Power Supply)

power connectors, 14

specifications, 13

installing, 378-379, 1204

microprocessors, 145

PCIe (PCI Express) power connectors, 14

peripheral power connectors, 14

portable computers, 473

AC adapters, 473

DC adapters, 473

power consumption, 475

power management, 475-476

troubleshooting in, 501-503

printers

dot-matrix printers, 859

laser printers, 868

troubleshooting, 854, 859, 868

protection

ESD, 1143-1148

sags, 1138

surge suppressors, 1139

transients, 1138

UPS, 1139-1142

VA ratings, 1140

removing, 378-379, 1203

soft switches, 13

system board power connectors, 12-13

system units, 8, 11

troubleshooting, 375

adding/removing power supplies, 378-379

dead system checks, 376-377

indicator light functionality, 377

system boards, 382

upgrades, 1205

power tools, safety checklist, 1132-1133

Power User Accounts (Windows 2000/XP), 1093

PPP protocol, EAP, 1080

preparation (customer service techniques), 1162

presence (customer service techniques), 1163

Press F1 to Continue error message, 341

preventive maintenance. *See also* troubleshooting

cleaning, 350-352, 507

dot-matrix printers, 877

dust, 353

HDD (hard disk drives), 357-358

heat buildup, 354-355, 507

inkjet printers, 877

keyboards, 360

laser printers, 877-878

monitors, 355-356

mouses, 360

removable media drives, 359-360

rough handling, 353, 505-506

scheduling, 361

annual activities, 363-364

daily activities, 362

monthly activities, 363

six-month activities, 363

weekly activities, 362

smoke, 353

touch pads, 361

previewing documents in Windows 2000/XP, 833

PRI (Primary Rate Interface) services, 988-989

primary memory (system boards)

cache memory, 16

RAM (Random Access Memory), 16, 22-23

ROM (Read-Only Memory), 16, 22-23

primary partitions, 297

master boot sectors, 298

partition tables, 298

Windows 2000/XP file systems, 591

Printer Not Ready error messages, 858

Printer Properties page (Windows 2000/XP)

Device Settings tab, 837

General tab, 836

Security tab, 837

printers, 6, 47

automatic sheet feeders, 829

cables, troubleshooting, 857-858

calibration, 827

character printers, 799

collators, 830

configuring, 823

controllers, 803

dot-matrix printers, 804

friction-feed, 805

paper, 859-863

pin-feed, 805

power supplies, 859

preventive maintenance, 877

printhead mechanisms, 806

ribbon cartridges, 859-860

troubleshooting, 858-863

drivers, 824

PCL, 825

PDL, 825-826

PostScript, 825

duplexers, 830

dye sublimation printers, 815-816

ELP drums, 830

fonts

bitmapped fonts, 800-801

cartridge fonts, 825

internal fonts, 825

soft fonts, 825

text sizes, 800

TrueType outline fonts, 800-801

vector-based fonts, 800

viewing characters, 801

impact printers, 800

inkjet printers, 809

components of, 810

ink cartridges, 810, 863-864

mechanical vibration printing method, 809

paper, 866

paper-feed motors, 810

preventive maintenance, 877

solid inkjet printers, 809

thermal shock printing method, 809

troubleshooting, 863-866

installing, 816-817

Bluetooth, 819

IrDA printer ports, 820

legacy printer interfaces, 821

networked printers, 818-819

serial printer interfaces, 821-822

USB printers, 818

Wi-Fi adapters, 819

interfaces, 802

laser printers, 811-813

black page errors, 869

electrophotographic cartridges, 814

faint print, 870

ink cartridges, 868-870

missing print, 870

paper, 868

paper jams, 871-872

partial/total failures, 868

power supplies, 868

preventive maintenance, 877-878

roller errors, 870

safety issues, 878

smudged print, 871

specks/stains, 870

troubleshooting, 866-872

white (blank) page errors, 869

white line errors, 870

non-impact printers, 800

operator control panels, 804, 826

paper trays, 829

parallel printer ports, 246-247

power supplies, troubleshooting, 859

preventive maintenance, 877-878

processors, 803

serial printer interfaces, 823

sharing, Windows 2000/XP, 958-959

stapler/stackers, 830

thermal printers, 807-808

toner cartridges, disposal procedures, 1149

troubleshooting, 776, 853

   cables, 857-858

   computer checks, 856-857

   dot-matrix printers, 858-863

   identifying solutions, 854

   inkjet printers, 863-866

   LAN, 1049-1051

   laser printers, 866-872

   networks, 777-778

   operator control boards, 855-856

   power supplies, 854

   Printer Not Ready error messages, 858

   probable causes, 854

   self-tests, 855

upgrades, 828

Windows 2000/XP

   designating in, 833

   installing in, 834-835

network printers, 837

previewing documents in, 833

property configuration, 836-837

sorting documents in, 834

spoolers, 831-832

printhead mechanisms (dot-matrix printers), 806

printhead not moving

   dot-matrix printer errors, 862

   inkjet printer errors, 865

printhead not printing

   dot-matrix printer errors, 861

   inkjet printer errors, 865

private IP classes, 977

private networks, 977

proactive, being (customer service techniques), 1164

processors

   overclocking, 1209

   performance, 683

   printers, 803

   slot processors, installing, 1199

   system board upgrades, 1210-1211

Product Support Services (Microsoft), 729

professionalism (customer service techniques), 1172-1173

program guides, My TV option (Windows XP MCE), 555

programming I/O (I/O transfers), 226

Programs submenu (Start menu), 532

progressive displays (digital resolution), 268

properties sheets (Windows 2000/XP), 609

Protocols function (Windows 2000/XP Local Area Connection Properties dialog), 948

proxy servers, 981, 1018-1020

PS/2 connectors, 229

PVR (personal video recorders), data storage, 182-183

R

RAID 5 volumes, NTFS disks, 604

RAID systems, data storage, 185-186, 188

RAM (Random Access Memory), 16

cache memory, 166-167

CMOS RAM, 27

DIMM (Dual Inline Memory Modules), 22-23

DIMM packages, 168

DRAM, 160

EDRAM, 161

packages, 169

refreshing, 164

SDRAM, 161, 170

speed ratings, 170, 173

dual channel memory, 173

error checking

ECC-SDRAM, 165-166

parity checking, 164-165

modules, installing, 1202

operator control boards (printers), 856

RIMM, 169

SRAM, 160, 163

troubleshooting, 383, 856

volatile memory, 22

rapports (customer service techniques), 1163

raster lines, CRT monitors, 261

RDRAM (Rambus DRAM), 162, 172

Read & Execute permissions (NTFS), 959-960

Read permissions

network shares, 957

NTFS, 959-960

Recorded TV option (Windows XP MCE), 554

Recovery Console (Windows 2000/XP), troubleshooting startup process, 751-754

Recycle Bin (Windows 2000/XP), 526

refreshing DRAM (Dynamic RAM), 164

RegEdit utility (Windows 2000/XP), 723

RegEdt32 utility (Windows 2000/XP), 723-724

Registry (Windows 2000/XP), 586, 722

Current_Config key, 588

Current_User key, 587

hives, 588-589

Local_Machine key, 588-589

RegEdit utility, 723

RegEdt32 utility, 723-724

restoring, Recovery Console (Windows 2000/XP), 754

Users key, 588-589

Remote Assistance (Windows 2000/XP), 721, 783

establishing sessions, 784

helper's console, 786

user's console, 785

Remote Desktop (Windows 2000/XP), 721, 779-783, 1093

remote management, wireless LAN installations, 945

Remote tab (System Properties window), 543

removable media devices, troubleshooting, 498

removable media drives, preventive maintenance procedures, 359-360

removable storage, 39-41, 213

flash memory, 214

CF (CompactFlash) cards, 216

memory sticks, 216-217

SD (Secure Digital) cards, 217

USB flash drives, 215

portable computers, 462-463

Removable Storage utility (Windows 2000/XP), 708

troubleshooting, 414

Removable Storage node (System Tools console), 540

removing

power supplies, 378-379, 1203

viruses, 1113

REN command (Windows OS file/filename command line operations, 563

renaming Start menu items, 535

repair/diagnostic tools, 330

multimeters, 343-345

POST cards, 348-349

software diagnostic packages, 346-347

repeaters, WAN Internet connectivity, 972

replacing

FRU, installing

cooling systems, 1199-1201

fans, 1199-1201

heat sinks, 1199-1201

microprocessors, 1197-1199

slot processors, 1199

portable drives, 451

system boards, removing

adapter cards, 1195

cables, 1195-1196

external I/O systems, 1193

system board, 1196

system unit covers, 1194

replicators (port), troubleshooting, 503-504

resistance checks, multimeters, 345

resolution

audio, 271

video displays, 265-266

digital resolution, 268

dot pitch, 267

LCD, native resolution, 455

responsiveness (customer service techniques), 1170

restore points, 714, 759

Restore utility (Windows 2000/XP), 703-704

restores

ASR restores (Windows XP), 763

Registries (Windows 2000/XP), 754

restore points, 714

System Restore utility (Windows 2000/XP), 714

RG-6 specification, coaxial cables, 905

RG-8 specification, coaxial cables, 906

RG-58 specification, coaxial cables, 906

RG-59 specification, coaxial cables, 906

ribbon cartridges, dot-matrix printers, 859-860

right-clicking, Windows 2000/XP, 524

RIMM, 169

ring topologies (LAN), 892

RIS (Remote Installation Services), Windows 2000/XP installations, 626

RMDIR (RD) command (Windows OS directory-level command line operations), 562

roaming profiles (Windows 2000/XP), 1088

roller errors (laser printers), troubleshooting, 870

ROM (Read-Only Memory), 16, 22-23

root directories, FAT disks, 595

root hubs, USB, 233

rough handling, preventive maintenance procedures, 353, 505-506

routers, 898, 973

administrative passwords, 944

internet gateways, 899

IP addresses, 944

LAN, 899, 981

wireless LAN installations, 942-945

RS-232 serial ports, 248

RTC (remanufactured toner cartridges), 868

Run option (Start menu), 535

S

S-Video connections, 241

Safe Mode (Windows 2000/XP), troubleshooting

  operational problems, 768

  startup process, 747-749

safety, 1130

  laser printers, 878

  personal safety

    hand tools, 1132-1133

    high-voltage hazards, 1133-1134

    laser/burn hazards, 1136-1137

    shock/electrocution, 1134-1135

  work area

    cables, 1131

    lighting, 1131

    liquids, 1132

sags (power supply protection), 1138

SAS (Serial Attached SCSI), 207

SATA (Serial Advanced Technology Attachment)

  device drivers, 655

  Disk Drive cards, 34

  disk drive

    connections, 86-89, 104

    installing, 289-291

    troubleshooting, 404-406

  interfaces, 202, 212-213

satellite Internet access, 1000

  IRU, 1002

  ITU, 1002

  latency, 1001

  LNB converters, 1001

scalds/burns, 1137

scanners, 838

  barcode, 257, 312

  biometric, 256, 1081-1082

  fingerprint, 257, 1082-1083

  installing, 311, 840-841

  troubleshooting, 873

    host system checks, 875

    image quality problems, 874

    interface cables, 876

    Out of Memory error messages, 874

    TWAIN drivers, 875

Scheduled option (Windows XP MCE), 554

scheduling

  backups, 705-706

  preventive maintenance, 361

    annual activities, 363-364

    daily activities, 362

    monthly activities, 363

    six-month activities, 363

    weekly activities, 362

SCREG.EXE, Windows 2000/XP boot process, 581

scripts, configuring for web browsers, 1018

SCSI (Small Computer System Interface), 33

  adapter cards

    address configuration, 293-294

    I/O ports, 90

    installing, 292-293

    termination, 295-296

  cables/connectors, 208-209

  data storage, 204

  drives, troubleshooting, 405-406

  HDD

    installations, 285

    upgrades, 307

  Serial SCSI, 207-208

  signaling, 210-213

  specifications, 205-207

SD (Secure Digital) cards, 217

SDRAM (Synchronous DRAM), 161

  DDR-SDRAM, 162, 171

  DDR2, 162, 172

ECC-SDRAM, 165-166

EDDR-SDRAM, 162

EDO-DRAM, 161

ESDRAM, 162

RDRAM, 162, 172

SDS-DRAM, 162

SGRAM, 162

sockets, 95

speed ratings, 170

VCM-SDRAM, 162

SDS-RAM (Single Data Rate-DRAM), 162

SDSL (Symmetric DSL), 992, 995

SDTV (Standard Definition TV), 270

Search tab (Help screen), 728

Search utility (Start menu), 534

SEC (Single-Edge Contact) cartridges, 125

security, 1074

    access control

        backup tapes, 1076

        lockable server cases/chassis, 1075

        passwords, 1076-1077

    adware, 1117

    backup tapes, disposal of, 1086

    buffer overflow attacks, 134

    data migration, 1085

    encryption, Windows 2000/XP files, 610

    environmental issues, 1084

    grayware, 1114

    hardware

        biometric authentication devices, 1080-1083

        information disposal/destruction policies, 1083-1084

        polarizing screens, 1078

        smart cards, 1078-1080

    HDD, disposal of, 1085-1086

    identity theft, 1120

    pharming, 1119

    phishing, 1119

    session hijacking, 1120

social engineering, 1118

software

    demagnetizing backup tapes/floppy disks, 1084

    HDD, 1085

    moving FAT partitions to NTFS partitions, 1085

spam, 1117

spyware, 1115-1116

viruses, 1108

    antivirus software, 1112

    boot-sector viruses, 1109-1110

    file infectors, 1109

    removing, 1113

    symptoms of, 1111

    Trojan horses, 1109

    worms, 1109

web browsers, 1017

Windows 2000/XP

    account lockout policies, 1098

    administrative security settings, 1091

    Administrator Accounts, 1087

    auditing, 1098-1100

    authentication, 1094-1096

    Domain Accounts, 1094

    event logging, 1098-1100

    Group Accounts, 1091-1093

    group policies, 1090-1091

    group profiles, 1087

    Network Administrator, 1088

    password policies, 1096-1097

    portable computers, 1088

    roaming profiles, 1088

    System Policies, 1089

    User Accounts, 1087, 1091-1092

    user profiles, 1087-1090

wireless networks

    EFS feature (Windows 2000/XP), 1105-1106

    firewalls, 1103-1105

    locking computers, 1106-1108

WEP, 1101-1102

WPA, 1102

XD-bit virus protection, 133

Security Configuration screen (CMOS setup utility), 107-108

Security tab (Printer Properties page), printer property configuration, 837

See Also window (Windows XP), 551

selective backups, 699

self-tests

POST (Power-On Self Tests), 24

cards, 348-349

checks (PC hardware setup process), 577-578

PC hardware setup process, 577

printers, 855

SEPP (Single-Edged Processor Package) cartridges, 127

serial ports, RS-232, 248

serial printer interfaces

configuring, 823

installing, 821-822

Serial SCSI (Small Computer System Interface), 207-208

Series-A connectors, 232

Series-B connectors, 232

servers, lockable server cases/chassis, 1075

service packs, Windows 2000/XP installation, 630-632

Services function (Windows 2000/XP Local Area Connection Properties dialog), 948

session hijacking, 1120

Settings option (Start menu), 534

SFC.EXE utility (System File Checker)

switches list, 758

troubleshooting startup process, 758

Windows 2000/XP, 726

SGRAM (Synchronous Graphics RAM), 162

shadow masks, CRT monitors, 262

shared video memory, 450

shares (network), 956

Change permissions, 957

Full Control permissions, 957

NTFS permissions, 958

Read permissions, 957

sharing

Internet connections. See ICS, 987

printers, Windows 2000/XP, 958-959

Sharing tab (Windows 2000/XP), 956

SHDSL (Asymmetric HDSL), 995

sheet feeders (printers), 829-830

shock/electrocution, 1134-1135

shortcuts

keyboard, Windows 2000/XP, 522

Windows OS command line, 564

Shut Down option (Start menu), 535

signal cables, system units, 8

simple volumes, NTFS disks, 602

simplex mode (network bridges), 899

situational assessments (troubleshooting), 331

six-month preventive maintenance activities, 363

sizing video displays, 47

skewing video displays, 47

Slot 1 socket specification, 92-93

Slot 2 socket specification, 92

Slot A Athlon processors, 135

Slot A specification, 93

slot connectors

AGP (Acclerated Graphics Port), 29

AMR (Audio Modem Riser), 30

CNR (Communications and Networking Riser), 30

ISA (Industry Standard Architecture), 30

PCI (Peripheral Component Interconnect), 29

PCI-X (PCI Extended), 30

PCIe (PCI Express), 30

system boards, 17, 28

slot processors, installing, 1199

slotket processors, 92

smart cards

connection configuration, 1079

EAP, 1080

IC devices, 1079

PC/SC, 1079

programming, 1078

smoke, preventive maintenance procedures, 353

SMTP (Simple Mail Transfer Protocol), 1012

smudged print (laser printers), troubleshooting, 871

social engineering, 1118

Socket 7 specification, 91

Socket 8 specification, 92

Socket 370 specification, 92

Socket 423 specification, 93

Socket 462 specification, 93

Socket 563 specification, 93

Socket 754 specification, 93

Socket 939 specification, 93

Socket 940 specification, 93

Socket AM2 specification, 93

Socket F specification, 94

Socket LGA775 specification, 93

Socket S1 specification, 94

sockets

DDR-DRAM, 95

DDR2-DRAM, 95

DIMM, 95

DRAM, 95

FC-PGA 370, 128

SDRAM, 95

services, PC cards, 464

specifications, 95

Slot 1, 92-93

Slot 2, 92

Slot A, 93

Socket 7, 91

Socket 8, 92

Socket 370, 92

Socket 423, 93

Socket 462, 93

Socket 563, 93

Socket 754, 93

Socket 939, 93

Socket 940, 93

Socket AM2, 93

Socket F, 94

Socket LGA775, 93

Socket S1, 94

SODIMM (Small Outline DIMM), portable computers, 446

soft fonts (printers), 825

soft skills. *See* customer service

soft switches, 13

soft-memory errors, 383

software

antivirus software, 1112

diagnostic packages, 346-347, 420

diagnostic/repair software, 331

firewalls, troubleshooting, 1064

grayware, 1114

maintenance, 684-685

security

demagnetizing backup tapes/floppy disks, 1084

HDD, 1085

moving FAT partitions to NTFS partitions, 1085

spyware, 1115-1116

solid inkjet printers, 809

sound cards, 33, 270-273

installing, 312

troubleshooting

configuration checks, 421-422

hardware checks, 422-423

spam, 1115-1117

spanned volumes, NTFS disks, 602

speakers, 6

specks/stains (laser printers), troubleshooting, 870

Speech function (Windows XP), 551

SpeedStep technology, Intel dual-core processors, 134

spikes (voltage), 1138

splitters, 991

spoolers (printers), 831-832

SPP (Standard Parallel Port), implementation via CMOS setup utility, 104

spyware, 1114-1116

SRAM (Static RAM), 160, 163

SSID (Service Set Identifiers), AP configuration, 941

SSLP (Secure Socket Layer Protocol), 1014

stackers/staplers (printers), 830

stains/specks (laser printers), troubleshooting, 870

standard I/O connections, system boards, 17

stapler/stackers (printers), 830

star topologies (LAN), 892

Start button (Start menu), 535

Start menu (Windows 2000/XP), 531, 548

adding items to, 535

Documents and Settings folder, 532

For Files and Folders option, 534

Help file system, 535

Index Server function, 534

Log Off User option, 535

Programs subment, 532

renaming items, 535

Run option, 535

Search utility, 534

Settings option, 534

Shut Down option, 535

Start button, 535

System Tools group, 533

Start page (Windows XP MCE), 552

My Music option, 555

My Pictures option, 557

My TV option, 554

My Video option, 557

starting applications from Command Prompt, troubleshooting, 772

startup failures (OS), troubleshooting, 342

Startup menu (Windows 2000/XP), optimizing, 675

Startup Mode (Windows 2000/XP), troubleshooting startup process, 746-747

startup problems, troubleshooting, 742-744, 763-765

authentication, 766

Boot Disk (Windows XP), 757

Debugging Mode (Windows 2000/XP), 750

Driver Rollback function (Windows XP), 751

Enable Boot Logging (Windows 2000/XP), 749

Enable VGA Mode (Windows 2000/XP), 750

ERD (Windows 2000), 755-756

general bootup/startup problems, 745

Last Known Good Configuration option (Windows 2000/XP), 750

MSCONFIG.EXE utility (Windows 2000/XP), 750

networks, 766

Recovery Console (Windows 2000/XP), 751-754

Safe Mode (Windows 2000/XP), 747-749

SFC.EXE utility (Windows 2000/XP), 758

Startup Mode (Windows 2000/XP), 746-747

System Restore (Windows XP), 759-763

startup process (Windows 2000/XP), modifying, 674

  BOOT.INI files, 674-675

  MSCONFIG, 676

  Startup menu optimization, 675

static

  antistatic devices, 331

  ESD

    causes of, 1143

    grounds, 1147

    minimizing, 1146

    MOS, 1145-1146

    protection during storage, 1148

static IP addresses, 1007, 1048

stop errors

  troubleshooting, 768-770

  Windows 2000 Professional installations, 636

  Windows XP Professional installations, 641

storage devices, peripheral storage, 460

Store Password Using Reversible Encryption for All Users in the Domain option (Windows 2000/XP), 1097

storing data, 34

  CD-ROM drives, 36

  disk drive interfaces

    ATA interfaces, 200-201

    floppy interfaces, 203-204

    IDE interfaces, 200-201

    internal disk drive interfaces, 199

    SATA interfaces, 202

  DVD drives, 37

  ESD protection, 1148

  FDD (floppy disk drives), 38, 190-191

  HDD (hard disk drives), 34

    CMOS setups, 182

    controllers, 181

    sub-system components, 180

  installing storage devices

    CD-ROM drives, 300-301

    CD-RW drives, 301

    DVD drives, 300

    DVD-RW drives, 301

    external storage devices, 303

    FDD, 302-303

    HDD, 283-286

    internal storage devices, 282

    SCSI adapter cards, 292-296

  optical storage

    CD-ROM drives, 193-197

    DVD drives, 197-198

  PVR, 182-183

  RAID systems, 185-188

  removable media devices, troubleshooting, 498

  removable media drives, preventive maintenance procedures, 359-360

  removable storage, 39, 213

    flash memory, 214-217

    portable computers, 462-463

    Removable Storage utility (Windows 2000/XP), 708

    system connections, 40-41

  SCSI, 204

    cables/connectors, 208-209

    Serial SCSI, 207-208

    signaling, 210-213

    specifications, 205-207

  tape drives, 38, 191-192

  USB devices, troubleshooting, 497-498

STP (Shielded Twisted Pair) cables, 901

striped drive arrays, 184-185

striped volumes, NTFS disks, 604

styluses (portable computers), 44-45, 458, 497

subnets, intranets, 975-976

support (Internet), 729

SUPPORT_XXXXX (Windows 2000/XP), 1092

suppressors (surge), 1139

surge suppressors, 1139

Suspend mode, portable computers, 476

switches, 897-899

Symmetic multiprocessing, system board upgrades, 1211

Synchronization Manager (Windows 2000/XP), 1088

Synchronous SRAM (Static RAM), 163

SYSEDIT.EXE (System Configuration Editor), 722

Sysprep tool, disk cloning, 627

system boards (system units), 8

ATX, 60-61

BTX, 62-63

chipsets, 17, 21, 67

Advanced Pentium/PCIe chipsets, 68

bus speeds, 72

Dual-Core Intel chipsets, 69-72

compatibility issues, 1191-1192

cooling systems, installing, 1199-1201

disk drive interface connections, 17

expansion slots

AGP (Accelerated Graphics Port), 29, 80-82

AMR (Audio Modem Riser), 30, 82-83

CNR (Communications and Networking Riser), 30, 82-83

ISA (Industry Standard Architecture), 30

PCI (Peripheral Component Interconnect), 29, 73-76

PCI-X (PCI Extended), 30, 76-77

PCIe (PCI Express), 30, 77-80

fans, installing, 1199-1201

heat sinks, installing, 1199-1201

LPX, 66

microprocessors, 16-17

bus speeds, 72

installing, 1197

Pentium package types, 18-20

speed configuration, 1199

NLX, 66

portable computers, 438

AMD Mobile processors, 445

Centrino processors, 443

Core Duo processors, 444

microprocessors, 440-441

Pentium IIIM processors, 441-442

Pentium 4M processors, 441-442

Pentium M processors, 442-443

power connectors, 12-13

primary memory

RAM (Random Access Memory), 22-23

ROM (Read-Only Memory), 22-23

replacing

removing adapter cards, 1195

removing cables, 1195-1196

removing external I/O systems, 1193

removing system board, 1196

removing system unit covers, 1194

slot processors, installing, 1199

standard I/O connections, 17

system configuration settings, 27-28

troubleshooting

beep codes, 379

BIOS, 384

CD-ROM drives, 406-410

CMOS batteries, 386

CMOS configuration checks, 381-382

CMOS setup failures, 380

cooling systems, 385

DVD drives, 406-410

error messages, 380

FDD, 410-412

FireWire (IEEE-1394) devices, 419-421

front panel connections, 423-424

HDD, 400-406

I/O failures, 381

indicator lights, 379

keyboards, 386-389

microprocessors, 383-384

monitors, 393-399

mouses, 390-392

ports, 415-418

power supplies, 382

RAM, 383

removable storage systems, 414

replaceable/upgradeable components, 379

sound cards, 421-423

tape drives, 413-414

upgrades

bus system issues, 1208-1209

cooling system upgrades, 1213-1214

firmware upgrades, 1211

memory upgrades, 1215-1216

microprocessor upgrades, 1206-1208

processor installation, 1210

Symmetric multiprocessing, 1211

system configuration settings, 27-28

System icon (Windows 2000), 542-543

System Information utility (Windows 2000/XP), 712-713

system initialization (PC hardware setup process), 577

System Management tools (Windows), 709

Device Manager utility, 716-719

Event Viewer utility, 709-711

MSCONFIG.EXE, 720

Remote Assistance feature, 721

Remote Desktop utility, 721

System Information utility, 712-713

System Restore utility, 714

Task Manager utility, 714

System Monitor, monitoring application performance, 678

disk system performance, 683-684

memory performance, 682

Performance Logs and Alerts utility, 680-681

processor performance, 683

system performance (Windows 2000/XP), monitoring, 676-677

System Policies (Windows 2000/XP), 1089

System Properties window (Windows 2000), 542-543

system protection, power supplies

ESD, 1143-1148

sags, 1138

surge suppressors, 1139

transients, 1138

UPS, 1139-1142

VA ratings, 1140

System Restore (Windows XP), 543, 714

ASR utility, 760-763

restore points, creating, 759

troubleshooting

operational problems, 768

startup process, 759-763

system services, optimizing, 673

system startup/reset (PC hardware setup process), 577

system state backups, 704

System Tools console (Windows 2000), 540

System Tools group (Start menu), 533

system units, 6

adapter cards, 8

IEEE-1394 FireWire cards, 34

internal modem cards, 32

LAN (Local Area Network) cards, 32

SATA (Serial ATA) Disk Drive cards, 34

SCSI (Small Computer System Interface) cards, 33

sound cards, 33

TV tuner cards, 33

USB (Universal Serial Bus) cards, 34

video adapter cards, 31

wireless network cards, 34

case design, 7

disk drives, 8

power supplies, 8, 11-13

signal cables, 8

system boards, 8

chipsets, 17, 21

disk drive interface connections, 17

expansion slot connectors, 17, 28-29

microprocessors, 16-20

power connectors, 12-13

primary memory, 16, 22-23

standard I/O connections, 17

system configuration settings, 27-28

systray (taskbar), 531

T

TA (Terminal Adapters). *See* imodems

tape drives

data storage, 38, 191-192

troubleshooting, 413-414

Task Manager (Windows 2000/XP), 714

application problems, applying to, 773

system performance, monitoring, 676-677

taskbar (Windows 2000/XP), 530

TCP/IP (Transmission Control Protocol/Internet Protocol), 921, 1005

ARP, 1007

DHCP, 1007-1009

DNS service, 1006-1007

LAN, configuring in, 951-953

static IP addressing, 1007

WINS, 1006, 1008

TDR (time domain reflectometry) devices, 1034-1035

technical support (customer service). *See* general support (customer service)

telephone skills (customer service techniques), 1177-1179

telescoping magnets, 330

telnet, 1015

telnet:// prefix, 1012

temporary files, managing, 670

Temporary Internet Files Folder, 671-672

Windows Temporary Folder, 671

Temporary Internet Files Folder, managing, 671-672

tests (self)

POST (Power-On Self Tests), 24

cards, 348-349

checks (PC hardware setup process), 577-578

PC hardware setup process, 577

printers, 855

text sizes (fonts), 800

thermal compound/paste (cooling systems), 148

thermal modules, BTX system boards, 62

thermal printers, 807-808

thermal shock printing method (inkjet printers), 809

thumb drives. *See* USB flash drives

time/date

CMOS setup utility, 98-99

CMOS Time and Date Not Set error message, 341

toner cartridges, disposal procedures, 1149

Tools menu (Windows 2000/XP), 530

topologies (LAN)

bus, 891

logical, 893

mesh, 892

ring, 892

star, 892

touch pads, 45

portable computers, 457-458

preventive maintenance procedures, 361

troubleshooting, 496-497

touch screens, 254, 256

towers (system units), 7

TRACERT (Trace Route) utility, network troubleshooting, 1035-1038

trackball mouses, 45, 253, 457

TrackPoint pointing device (IBM), 458

TRACRT utility (Windows 2000/XP), 727

transferring data, USB, 235

transients (power supply protection), 1138

transport protocols, LAN, 935

Trojan horses, 1109

troubleshooter utilities (Windows 2000/XP), 727-728

Troubleshooters window (Windows XP), 551

troubleshooting, 329, 375. *See also* preventive maintenance; Windows Disk Management tools

AC adapters, 501-503

batteries, 501-503

beep codes, 336-340

BIOS, 384

blue screen errors, 765, 769, 773

boot failures, 342

bootups, procedure observances, 334-335

broadband connections

activity lights, 1053

connectivity equipment checks, 1055

filter checks, 1054

PC checks, 1055-1056

physical connections, 1053-1054

restarting equipment, 1054

burn-in tests, 347

CD-ROM drives

basic checks, 406

hardware checks, 407-409

Windows checks, 407

writable drives, 409-410

CMOS batteries, 386

cooling systems, 385

diagnostic/repair tools, 330

multimeters, 343-345

POST cards, 348-349

software diagnostic packages, 346-347

dial-up connections, 1056

front panel lights, 1059-1060

loopback tests, 1058-1059

modem configuration checks, 1061

modem hardware, 1057

documentation, 334

DVD drives

basic checks, 406

hardware checks, 407-409

Windows checks, 407

writable drives, 409-410

environmental assessments, 332

error messages

examples of, 336-338

hardware configuration, 341

hardware failures, 340

FDD (floppy disk drives), 410

basic checks, 412

error messages, 411

firewalls, 1064

FireWire (IEEE-1394) devices

adapters, 419

ports, 419-421

front panel connections, 423-424

FRU (Field-Replaceable Units), 349-350

general OS process, 743-744

hardware

after POST errors, 342

configuration errors, 340-341

failures, 340

HDD (hard disk drives), 400-401

basic checks, 401-403

configuration checks, 404-405

failures, 342

hardware checks, 405-406

inspections, 333

keyboards, 386

basic checks, 387

configuration checks, 387

hardware checks, 388

wireless keyboards, 389

LAN

cable checks, 1041

connectivity device checks, 1041-1042

NIC checks, 1039-1040

printing problems, 1049-1051

service access problems, 1038-1039

windows related problems, 1042-1045

wireless networks, 1046-1048

memory, RAM, 383

microprocessors, 383-384

modems, 1057, 1061-1062

monitors, 393

degaussing, 399

diagnosing problems, 398-399

hardware checks, 394-395

LCD displays, 492-495

video checks, 395-398

mouses

configuration checks, 391

hardware checks, 390-391

optical mouses, 392

wireless mouses, 392

networks, 1032

ARP, 1035

cabling testers, 1034

continuity testers, 1034

IPCONFIG utility, 1036, 1045, 1055

LAN, 1038-1048

NETSTAT utility, 1035

NSLOOKUP.EXE utility, 1036

OTDR, 1035

PATHPING utility, 1036

PING utility, 1035-1037, 1045, 1055

TDR devices, 1034-1035

TRACERT utility, 1035-1038

wireless networks, 1046-1048

wiring testers, 1034

operational problems, 742, 775

application installations, 770

applications will not start, 771

applying Event Viewer to application problems, 773-774

applying Task Manager to application problems, 773

finding hidden files, 773

networks, 777-778

optional devices do not operate, 767-768

printers, 776-778

starting applications from Command Prompt, 772

stop errors, 768-770

OS startup failures, 342

PATA drives, 404-405

portable computers, 490

audio, 504

docking stations, 503-504

Fn keys, 504-505

infrared ports, 499-500

keyboards, 496

LCD displays, 492-495

PCMCIA cards, 500-501

port replicators, 503-504

power supplies, 501-503

removable media devices, 498

touch pads, 496-497

USB devices, 497-498

ports

basic checks, 415

FireWire (IEEE-1394) ports, 419-421

front panel ports, 423-424

USB ports, 416-418

power supplies, 375

adding/removing power supplies, 378-379

dead system checks, 376-377

indicator light functionality, 377

system boards, 382

printers, 853

cables, 857-858

computer checks, 856-857

dot-matrix printers, 858-863

identifying solutions, 854

inkjet printers, 863-866

LAN, 1049-1051

laser printers, 866-872

operator control boards, 855-856

power supplies, 854

Printer Not Ready error messages, 858

probable causes, 854

self-tests, 855

Remote Assistance (Windows 2000/XP), 783

establishing sessions, 784

helper's console, 786

user's console, 785

Remote Desktop (Windows 2000/XP), 779-783

removable storage systems, 414

SATA drives, 404-406

scanners, 873

host system checks, 875

image quality problems, 874

interface cables, 876

Out of Memory error messages, 874

TWAIN drivers, 875

SCSI drives, 405-406

situational assessments, 331

software, diagnostic packages, 420

sound cards

configuration checks, 421-422

hardware checks, 422-423

startup problems, 742-744, 764-765

authentication, 766

Boot Disk (Windows XP), 757

Debugging Mode (Windows 2000/XP), 750

Driver Rollback function (Windows XP), 751

Enable Boot Logging (Windows 2000/XP), 749

Enable VGA Mode (Windows 2000/XP), 750

ERD (Windows 2000), 755-756

general bootup/startup problems, 745

Last Known Good Configuration option (Windows 2000/XP), 750

MSCONFIG.EXE utility (Windows 2000/XP), 750

networks, 766

Recovery Console (Windows 2000/XP), 751-754

Safe Mode (Windows 2000/XP), 747-749

SFC.EXE utility (Windows 2000/XP), 758

Startup Mode (Windows 2000/XP), 746-747

System Restore (Windows XP), 759-763

system boards

beep codes, 379

BIOS, 384

CD-ROM drives, 406-410

CMOS batteries, 386

CMOS configuration checks, 381-382

CMOS setup failures, 380

cooling systems, 385

DVD drives, 406-410

error messages, 380

FDD, 410-412

FireWire (IEEE-1394) devices, 419-421

front panel connections, 423-424

HDD, 400-406

I/O failures, 381

indicator lights, 379

keyboards, 386-389

microprocessors, 383-384

monitors, 393-399

mouses, 390-392

ports, 415-418

power supplies, 382

RAM, 383

removable storage systems, 414

replaceable/upgradeable components, 379

sound cards, 421-423

tape drives, 413-414

tape drives, 413-414

video systems, 393

degaussing, 399

diagnosing problems, 398-399

hardware checks, 394-395

video checks, 395-398

voltage, multimeters, 343-345

WAN, 1052

broadband connections, 1053-1056

dial-up connections, 1056-1061

software firewalls, 1064

web browsers, 1063-1064

Windows modem checks, 1061-1062

web browsers, 1063-1064

Windows 2000

installing, 632-633

upgrades, 650-653

Windows 2000 Professional installations, 636-638

Windows XP

installing, 632-633

upgrades, 650-653

Windows XP Professional installations, 641-642

wireless networks, 1046-1048

TrueType outline fonts, 800-801

TSR (Terminate and Stay Resident) viruses, 1110

TV tuner cards, 33

TWAIN drivers, scanners, 875

twisted-pair cables

STP, 901

UTP, 901-903, 916-917

Type of Backup configuration page (Backup utility), 702

U

Ultra ATA (AT Attachment) disk drive interfaces), 202

unattended installations, Windows 2000/XP, 624-625

Unicode

NTFS disks, 598

Windows support, 533

unscheduled backups, 706

updates (automatic), software maintenance, 685

upgrades

adapters, 315-316

batteries, portable computers, 479

cooling systems, 1213-1214

firmware, 1211

HDD, 305-307

memory, 1215-1216

microprocessors, 1206-1208

operating systems, 643

PC cards, 480

peripherals, 320

portable computers

batteries, 479

memory, 448-449

portable drives, 451

power supplies, 1205

printers, 828

system boards, 1206

bus system issues, 1208-1209

cooling system upgrades,
1213-1214

firmware upgrades, 1211

memory upgrades, 1215-1216

microprocessor upgrades,
1206-1208

processor installation, 1210

Symmetric multiprocessing, 1211

Windows 2000, 643-645, 650-653

Windows XP, 646-647

local upgrades, 648-649

troubleshooting, 650-653

**UPnP (Universal Plug and Play), wireless
LAN installations, 946**

**UPS (uninterruptible power supplies),
1139-1142**

**URL (uniform resource locators),
1010-1011**

USB (Universal Serial Buses)

architectures, 233-234

bus enumerating, 231

cards, 34

cables

GND (Ground) wire, 232

Vbus wire, 232

compound devices, 231

connectors, 232

data transfers, 235

desktop connection schemes, 230

devices

installations, 317

speed ratings, 235-236

troubleshooting storage devices,
497-498

flash drives, 215

hot swapping devices, 231

ports, 229, 233, 416-418

printers, installing, 818

root hubs, 233

**User Accounts (Windows 2000/XP), 1087,
1091-1093**

Administrator accounts, 1092

Domain Accounts, 1094

Guest Accounts, 1092

HelpAssistant, 1092

SUPPORT_XXXXX, 1092

user interfaces, Windows 2000/XP, 524

User mode (Windows 2000/XP), 582

**user profiles (Windows 2000/XP),
1087-1090**

User Profiles tab (System Properties window), 542

user's console (Remote Assistance), 785

**Users key (Windows 2000/XP Registry),
588-589**

**UTP (Unshielded Twisted Pair) cables,
901-903, 916-917**

V

VA (volt-ampere) ratings, 1140

Vbus wire, 232

**VCM-SDRAM (Virtual Channel Memory-
SDRAM), 162**

vector-based fonts, 800

**vertical resolution (digital resolution),
268**

vertical/horizontal positioning, video displays, 47

vertical/horizontal retraces, CRT monitors, 261

vertical/horizontal sizing, video displays, 47

VGA (Video Graphics Array)

cards, 31

connectors, portable computers, 459

resolution (monitors), 266

video

adapters, 263

cards, 264-265

adapter cards, 31

capture cards, 258-259

editing cards, 260

connections

Component Video, 241

Composite Video, 240

Digital Component Video, 241

DVI, 241

HDMI, 242

S-Video, 241

displays, 6

brightness, 47

contrast, 47

CRT, 46, 260-261

dot pitch, 267

external monitors, portable computers, 493

horizontal/vertical positioning, 47

horizontal/vertical sizing, 47

installing, 308-309

LCD (liquid crystal display) monitors, 46

polarizing screens, 452, 1078

portable displays, 452-455

preventive maintenance procedures, 355-356

resolution, 265-268

screen memory, 263

skew, 47

touch screens, 254-256

troubleshooting, 393-399

PVR, data storage, 182-183

shared video memory, 450

system installations, 308-309

View menu (Windows 2000/XP), 529-530

virtual memory

optimizing, 667

Windows 2000/XP, 583-584

Virtual Memory dialog (Windows 2000/XP), 586

Virtual Servers, wireless LAN installations, 945

viruses, 1108

antivirus software, 1112

boot-sector viruses, 1109-1110

file infectors, 1109

removing, 1113

symptoms of, 1111

Trojan horses, 1109

worms, 1109

XD-bit virus protection, 133

Vista (Windows), 521

VoIP (Voice Over IP), 1003-1004

volatile memory, 22

voltage

checking, multimeters, 343-345

sags, 1138

spikes, 1138

volumes. *See* partitions

VPN (virtual private networks), Windows 2000/XP authentication, 1095

VRM (Voltage Regulator Modules), 145, 1199

W

WAN (wide area networks)

Internet access methods

cable modems, 996-997

dial-up access, 983-988

digital modems, 998-999

DSL, 979, 990-996

ISDN, 979, 988-989

LAN, 980-982

satellite access, 1000-1002

VoIP, 1003-1004

wireless access, 1002

Internet connectivity

bridges, 972

domains, 978

gateways, 972

hubs, 972

IP addresses, 974-977

ISP, 972-973

midlevel networks, 972

packets, 971

repeaters, 972

routers, 973

Internet resources

email, 1013

file:// prefix, 1012

FTP, 1010-1013

gopher:// prefix, 1011

HTTP, 1010-1011

HTTPS, 1011

mailto: prefix, 1011

news: prefix, 1011

SMTP, 1012

SSLP, 1014

telnet, 1015

telnet:// prefix, 1012

URL, 1010-1011

WWW, 1011

TCP/IP, 1005

ARP, 1007

DHCP, 1007-1009

DNS service, 1006-1007

static IP addressing, 1007

WINS, 1006-1008

troubleshooting, 1052

broadband connections, 1053-1056

dial-up connections, 1056-1061

software firewalls, 1064

web browsers, 1063-1064

Windows modem checks, 1061-1062

web browsers, 1016

configuring proxy servers, 1018-1020

configuring script support, 1018

establishing security options, 1017

warning events (Event Viewer utility), 711

waste paper, 1084

water-based microprocessor cooling systems, 150

web browsers, 1016

establishing security options, 1017

proxy servers, configuring, 1018-1020

script support, configuring, 1018

troubleshooting, 1063-1064

weekly backups, 706

weekly preventive maintenance activities, 362

WEP (Wired Equivalent Privacy), 1101-1102

wheel mouses, 45

When to Back Up configuration page (Backup utility), 702

Where to Restore configuration page (Restore utility), 703

white (blank) page errors (laser printers), troubleshooting, 869

white line errors (laser printers), troubleshooting, 870

Wi-Fi

adapters, printers, 819

portable computers, 472

width (passwords), 1076

Win32, Windows 2000/XP boot process, 581

Windows 2000, 518

Add Printer Wizard, 834-835

Add/Remove Windows Component utility, 538

Administrator Accounts, 1087, 1092-1093

Advanced Server edition, 519

API, 582

Backup Operator Accounts, 1093

Bindings function, 949

boot process
  BOOT.INI, 579
  NTBOOTDD.SYS, 581
  NTLDR, 579-580
  NTOSKRNL, 581
  SCREG.EXE, 581
  Win32, 581

Change or Remove Programs screen, 538

command line, 559
  directory-level operations, 561-562
  drive-level operations, 560-561
  file/filename operations, 562-563
  shortcuts, 564

command-line utilities
  CHKDSK.EXE utility, 726
  DEFRAG.EXE utility, 726
  DISKPART.EXE utility, 726
  EDIT utility, 726
  EXTRACT.EXE utility, 726
  IPCONFIG utility, 726
  MEM utility, 726
  MSCONFIG.EXE utility, 726
  PING utility, 727
  SFC.EXE utility, 726
  TRACRT utility, 727

Control Panel, 535-536
  Administrative Tools icon, 539-542
  Display icon, 543
  installation wizards, 537
  System icon, 542-543

Datacenter Server edition, 519

Debugging Mode, troubleshooting startup process, 750

desktops, 523

device drivers, 654

Device Settings tab, printer property configuration, 837

dial-up access, configuring, 985

Disk Management tools, 692
  backup media rotation, 707-708
  Backup utility, 701-702
  CHKDSK command, 694
  DEFRAG command, 695-698
  differential backups, 700
  Disk Cleanup utility, 693-694
  full backups, 698
  incremental backups, 699
  Removable Storage utility, 708
  Restore utility, 703
  scheduling backups, 705-706
  selective backups, 699
  system state backups, 704

DNS tab, 953

Domain Accounts, 1094

dynamic volume installations, 605

Enable Boot Logging, troubleshooting startup process, 749

Enable VGA Mode, troubleshooting startup process, 750

ERD, troubleshooting startup process, 755-756

Event Viewer, applying to application problems, 773-774

Explorer, 543-546

FAT disks
  directory trees, 595-596
  FAT, 593
  FAT32 file systems, 596-597
  root directories, 595

File Management tools
  Dr. Watson utility, 724-725
  RegEdit utility, 723
  RegEdt32 utility, 723-724
  SYSEDIT.EXE, 722

File menus, 528-529

files
    compressed files, 610-611
    encryption, 610
    filename limitations, 609
    NTFS permissions, 612-613
    properties sheets, 609
    types of, 608-609
formatting volumes, 607-608
Found New Hardware Wizard, 317
General tab, printer property config-
    uration, 836
Group Accounts, 1091-1093
group policies, 1090-1091
group profiles, 1087
Guest Accounts, 1092-1093
HAL, 582
Help screen, 728
HelpAssistant, 1092
high-level formatting, 593
installing, 623
    attended installations, 624
    disk cloning, 626-628
    disk image creation, 627-628
    HDD preparation, 629
    patches, 630-632
    RIS images, 626
    service packs, 630-632
    troubleshooting setup problems,
        632-633
    unattended installations, 624-625
Internet Connection Wizard, 986
IP Settings tab, 952
Kernel mode, 582
keyboard shortcuts, 522
LAN, 946-948
    client configuration, 950
    protocol configuration, 950-953
Last Known Good Configuration
    option, troubleshooting startup
    process, 750

Local Area Connection Properties
    dialog
    Advanced tab, 949
    Authentication tab, 950
    Clients function, 948
    Protocols function, 948
    Services function, 948
memory
    flat memory model, 583
    virtual memory, 583-584
MSCONFIG.EXE utility, trou-
    bleshooting startup process, 750
My Computer window, 524-525
My Documents folder, 525
My Network Places window, 527
Network Administrator, 1088
Network Configuration Accounts,
    1093
Network Connection Wizard, 985
Network Identification function, 949
networking via NetWare (Novell),
    953-955
NTFS disks, 597
    advantages of, 600-601
    MFT, 598
    mirrored volumes, 602
    RAID 5 volumes, 604
    simple volumes, 602
    spanned volumes, 602
    striped volumes, 604
    Unicode, 598
optimizing
    application performance, 678-683
    application system performance,
        683-684
    HDD, 668-670
    monitoring system performance,
        676-677
    software maintenance, 684-685
    startup process, 674-676
    system services, 673

temporary file management, 670-672

virtual memory, 667

Options tab, 953

partitions, 590-592

Performance Options dialog, 585

PnP manager, 582

power manager, 583

Power User Accounts, 1093

printers

    designating, 833

    installing, 834-835

    network printers, 837

    previewing documents, 833

    property configuration, 836-837

    sharing, 958-959

    sorting documents, 834

    spoolers, 831-832

Professional edition, 518

Recovery Console, troubleshooting startup process, 751-754

Recycle Bin, 526

Registry, 586, 722

    Current_Config key, 588

    Current_User key, 587

    hives, 588-589

    Local_Machine key, 588-589

    RegEdit utility, 723

    RegEdt32 utility, 723-724

    restoring, 754

    Users key, 588-589

Remote Assistance, 783

    establishing sessions, 784

    helper's console, 786

    user's console, 785

Remote Desktop, 779-783, 1093

right-clicking, 524

roaming profiles, 1088

Safe Mode, troubleshooting

    operational problems, 768

    startup process, 747-749

security

    account lockout policies, 1098

    administrative security settings, 1091

    Administrator Accounts, 1087

    auditing, 1098-1100

    authentication, 1094-1096

    Domain Accounts, 1094

    EFS feature, 1105-1106

    event logging, 1098-1100

    Group Accounts, 1091-1093

    group policies, 1090-1091

    group profiles, 1087

    Network Administrator, 1088

    password policies, 1096-1097

    portable computers, 1088

    roaming profiles, 1088

    System Policies, 1089

    User Accounts, 1087, 1091-1092

    user profiles, 1087-1090

Security tab, printer property configuration, 837

SFC.EXE utility, 758

Sharing tab, 956

Standard Server edition, 518-519

Start menu, 531-535

Startup Mode, troubleshooting startup process, 746-747

startup problems, troubleshooting, 763-766

SUPPORT_XXXXX, 1092

Synchronization Manager, 1088

System Management tools

    Device Manager utility, 716-719

    Event Viewer utility, 709-711

    Remote Assistance feature, 721

    Remote Desktop utility, 721

    System Information utility, 712-713

    System Restore utility, 714

    Task Manager utility, 714

System Policies, 1089

System Properties window
   Advanced tab, 542-543
   Automatic Updates tab, 543
   General tab, 542
   Hardware tab, 542
   Network Identification
     (Computer Name) tab, 542
   Remote tab, 543
   System Restore tab, 543
   User Profiles tab, 542
System Tools console, 540
Task Manager, applying to application problems, 773
taskbar, 530
Tools menu, 530
troubleshooter utilities, 727-728
upgrades, 643-645, 650-653
User Accounts, 1087, 1091-1093
user interfaces, 524
User mode, 582
user profiles, 1087-1090
View menu, 529-530
Virtual Memory dialog, 586
WINS tab, 953
WMI tools, 541

Windows 2000 Professional, installing, 633-638

Windows Disk Cleanup utility, HDD optimization, 669

Windows Disk Management tools, 692-693
   backups, 698
     Backup utlity, 701-702
     differential backups, 700
     full backups, 698
     incremental backups, 699
     media rotation, 707-708
     Restore utlity, 703
     scheduling, 705-706
     selective backups, 699
     system state backups, 704
   CHKDSK command, 694

   DEFRAG command, 695-698
   Disk Cleanup utility, 693-694
   Removable Storage utility, 708

Windows Explorer, 543-546

Windows File Management tools
   Dr. Watson utility, 724-725
   RegEdit utility, 723
   RegEdt32 utility, 723-724
   SYSEDIT.EXE, 722

Windows Movie Maker application (Windows XP MCE), 557

Windows OS (operating systems)
   client/server networks, 515
   command line, 559
     directory-level operations, 561-562
     drive-level operations, 560-561
     file/filename operations, 562-563
     shortcuts, 564
   Windows 2000, 518, 524
     Advanced Server edition, 519
     command line, 559-564
     Control Panel, 535-543
     Datacenter Server edition, 519
     desktops, 523
     Explorer, 543-546
     File menus, 528-529
     keyboard shortcuts, 522
     My Computer window, 524-525
     My Documents folder, 525
     My Network Places window, 527
     Professional edition, 518
     Recycle Bin, 526
     Standard Server edition, 518-519
     Start menu, 531-535
     System Tools console, 540
     taskbar, 530
     Tools menu, 530
     user interfaces, 524
     View menu, 529-530
   Windows Server 2003, 521

Windows Vista, 521

Windows XP

  64-bit edition, 520

  Accessories menu, 549

  Administrative Tools menu, 549

  All Programs menu, 549

  command line, 559-564

  Control Panel, 550-552

  desktops, 523

  Explorer, 543-546

  File menus, 528-529

  Home edition, 519

  keyboard shortcuts, 522

  Local Network window, 527

  MCE (Media Center Edition), 547

  MDE (Media Center Edition), 552-557

  Media Center edition, 520

  My Computer window, 524-525

  My Documents folder, 525

  My Network Places, 527

  Professional edition, 520

  Recycle Bin, 526

  right-clicking, 524

  Start menu, 531-535, 548

  taskbar, 530

  Tools menu, 530

  user interfaces, 524

  View menu, 529-530

Windows Server 2003, 521

Windows System Management tools, 709

  Device Manager utility, 716-719

  Event Viewer utility, 709-711

  MSCONFIG.EXE, 720

  Remote Assistance feature, 721

  Remote Desktop utility, 721

  System Information utility, 712-713

  System Restore utility, 714

  Task Manager utility, 714

Windows Temporary Folder, managing, 671

Windows Update Services, software maintenance, 685

Windows Vista, 521

Windows XP, 519

  64-bit edition, 520

  Accessories menu, 549

  Add Printer Wizard, 834-835

  Administrative Tools menu, 549

  Administrator Accounts, 1087, 1092-1093

  All Programs menu, 549

  API, 582

  ASR utility, 760-763

  Backup Operator Accounts, 1093

  Bindings function, 949

  Boot Disk, troubleshooting startup process, 757

  boot process, 579

    BOOT.INI, 579

    NTBOOTDD.SYS, 581

    NTLDR, 579-580

    NTOSKRNL, 581

    SCREG.EXE, 581

    Win32, 581

  command line, 559

    CHKDSK.EXE utility, 726

    DEFRAG.EXE utility, 726

    directory-level operations, 561-562

    DISKPART.EXE utility, 726

    drive-level operations, 560-561

    EDIT utility, 726

    EXTRACT.EXE utility, 726

    file/filename operations, 562-563

    IPCONFIG utility, 726

    MEM utility, 726

    MSCONFIG.EXE utility, 726

    PING utility, 727

    SFC.EXE utility, 726

    shortcuts, 564

    TRACRT utility, 727

  Control Panel, 550-552

Debugging Mode, troubleshooting startup process, 750

desktops, 523

device drivers, 654

Device Manager, Driver Rollback function, 751, 768

Device Settings tab, printer property configuration, 837

dial-up access, configuring, 985

Disk Management tools, 692-693

   backup media rotation, 707-708

   Backup utility, 701-702

   CHKDSK command, 694

   DEFRAG command, 695-698

   differential backups, 700

   Disk Cleanup utility, 693-694

   full backups, 698

   incremental backups, 699

   Removable Storage utility, 708

   Restore utility, 703

   scheduling backups, 705-706

   selective backups, 699

   system state backups, 704

DNS tab, 953

Domain Accounts, 1094

dynamic volume installations, 605

Enable Boot Logging, troubleshooting startup process, 749

Enable VGA Mode, troubleshooting startup process, 750

Event Viewer, applying to application problems, 773-774

Explorer, 543-546

FAT disks

   directory trees, 595-596

   FAT, 593

   FAT32 file systems, 596-597

   root directories, 595

File Management tools

   Dr. Watson utility, 724-725

   RegEdit utility, 723

   RegEdt32 utility, 723-724

   SYSEDIT.EXE, 722

File menus, 528-529

files

   compressed files, 610-611

   encryption, 610

   filename limitations, 609

   NTFS permissions, 612-613

   properties sheets, 609

   types of, 608-609

firewalls, enabling ICF function, 1105

formatting volumes, 607-608

General tab, printer property configuration, 836

Group Accounts, 1091-1093

group policies, 1090-1091

group profiles, 1087

Guest Accounts, 1092-1093

HAL, 582

Help screen, 728

HelpAssistant, 1092

high-level formatting, 593

Home edition, 519

installing, 623

   attended installations, 624

   disk cloning, 626-628

   disk image creation, 627-628

   HDD preparation, 629

   patches, 630-632

   RIS images, 626

   service packs, 630-632

   troubleshooting setup problems, 632-633

   unattended installations, 624-625

IP Settings tab, 952

Kernel mode, 582

keyboard shortcuts, 522

LAN, 946-948

   client configuration, 950

   protocol configuration, 950-953

Last Known Good Configuration option, troubleshooting startup process, 750

Local Area Connection Properties
dialog
Advanced tab, 949
Authentication tab, 950
Clients function, 948
Protocols function, 948
Services function, 948
Local Network window, 527
MCE (Media Center Edition), 520,
547
Movie Maker application, 557
My Music option, 555
My Pictures option, 557
My TV option, 554
My Video option, 557
Start page, 552
Media Center edition, 520
memory
flat memory model, 583
virtual memory, 583-584
MSCONFIG.EXE utility, trou-
bleshooting startup process, 750
My Computer window, 524-525
My Documents folder, 525
My Network Places, 527
Network Administator, 1088
Network Configuration Accounts,
1093
Network Identification function, 949
networking via NetWare (Novell),
953-955
New Connection Wizard, 985-987
NTFS disks, 597
advantages, 600-601
MFT, 598
mirrored volumes, 602
RAID 5 volumes, 604
simple volumes, 602
spanned volumes, 602
striped volumes, 604
Unicode, 598

optimizing
application performance, 678-683
application system performance,
683-684
HDD, 668-670
monitoring system performance,
676-677
software maintenance, 684-685
startup process, 674-676
system services, 673
temporary file management,
670-672
virtual memory, 667
Options tab, 953
partitions, 590-592
Performance Options dialog, 585
PnP manager, 582
power manager, 583
Power User Accounts, 1093
printers
designating, 833
installing, 834-835
network printers, 837
previewing documents, 833
property configuration, 836-837
sharing, 958-959
sorting documents, 834
spoolers, 831-832
Professional edition, 520
Recovery Console
commands list, 753-754
restoring Registries, 754
troubleshooting startup process,
751-754
Recycle Bin, 526
Registry, 586, 722
Current_Config key, 588
Current_User key, 587
hives, 588-589
Local_Machine key, 588-589
RegEdit utility, 723
RegEdt32 utility, 723-724

restoring, 754

Users key, 588-589

Remote Assistance, 783

establishing sessions, 784

helper's console, 786

user's console, 785

Remote Desktop, 779-783, 1093

right-clicking, 524

roaming profiles, 1088

Safe Mode, troubleshooting

operational problems, 768

startup process, 747-749

security

account lockout policies, 1098

administrative security settings, 1091

Administrator Accounts, 1087

auditing, 1098-1100

authentication, 1094-1096

Domain Accounts, 1094

EFS feature, 1105-1106

event logging, 1098-1100

Group Accounts, 1091-1093

group policies, 1090-1091

group profiles, 1087

Network Administrator, 1088

password policies, 1096-1097

portable computers, 1088

roaming profiles, 1088

System Policies, 1089

User Accounts, 1087, 1091-1092

user profiles, 1087-1090

Security tab, printer property configuration, 837

See Also window, 551

SFC.EXE utility, 758

Sharing tab, 956

Speech function, 551

Start menu, 531-535, 548

Startup Mode, troubleshooting startup process, 746-747

startup problems, troubleshooting, 763-766

SUPPORT_XXXXX, 1092

Synchronization Manager, 1088

System Management tools

Device Manager utility, 716-719

Event Viewer utility, 709-711

MSCONFIG.EXE, 720

Remote Assistance feature, 721

Remote Desktop utility, 721

System Information utility, 712-713

System Restore utility, 714

Task Manager utility, 714

System Policies, 1089

System Restore

ASR utility, 760-763

creating restore points, 759

troubleshooting operational problems, 768

troubleshooting startup process, 759-763

Task Manager, applying to application problems, 773

taskbar, 530

Tools menu, 530

troubleshooter utilities, 727-728

Troubleshooters window, 551

upgrades, 646-647

local upgrades, 648-649

troubleshooting, 650-653

User Accounts, 1087, 1091-1093

user interfaces, 524

User mode, 582

user profiles, 1087-1090

View menu, 529-530

Virtual Memory dialog, 586

WINS tab, 953

Wireless Networking function, 551

Windows XP Professional, installing, 638-639

attended installations, 640

MCE

hardware requirements, 640-641

setup limitations, 642

troubleshooting setup problems, 641-642

WINS (Windows Internet Name Service), 1006-1008

WINS tab (Windows 2000/XP), 953

wire crimpers, 330

Wireless AP, wireless LAN installations, 945

wireless clients, wireless LAN installations, 941

wireless keyboards, troubleshooting, 389

wireless mouses, troubleshooting, 392

Wireless Networking function (Windows XP), 551

wireless networks

cards, 34

Ethernet specifications, 919-920

Internet access, 1002

IrDA links, 910

LAN, installing

AP installation, 938-940

CAT5 crossover cables, 942

DHCP servers, 944

Mac filtering, 945

Port Forwarding, 945

remote management, 945

router configuration, 943-945

router installation, 942

UPnP, 946

Virtual Servers, 945

Wireless AP, 945

wireless client installation, 941

portable computers, 470

built-in WiFi, 472

installing on, 471

RF links, 911-912

security

EFS feature (Windows 2000/XP), 1105-1106

firewalls, 1103-1105

locking computers, 1106, 1108

WEP, 1101-1102

WPA, 1102

troubleshooting, 1046-1048

wireless RF links, 911-912

wiring testers, 1034

wizards

Add New Hardware wizard (Windows 2000), 537

Add Printer Wizard (Windows 2000/XP), 834-835

Add/Remove Hardware wizard (Windows 2000), 537

installation wizards, Windows 2000, 537

Internet Connection Wizard (Windows 2000), 986

Network Connection Wizard (Windows 2000), 985

New Connection Wizard (Windows XP), 985-987

WMI (Windows Management Instrumentation) tools, 541

work areas

managing (customer service techniques), 1179

safety

cables, 1131

lighting, 1131

liquids, 1132

workgroups, 955

workstations (diskless), 895

worms, 1109

WPA (Wi-Fi Protected Access) standard, wireless networks, 1102

writable CD-ROM/DVD drives, troubleshooting, 409-410

Write permissions (NTFS), 959-960

WWW (World Wide Web), 1011

X - Y - Z

XCOPY command (Windows OS file/file-name command line operations, 563

XD-bit (Execute Disable Bit) virus protection, Intel dual-core processors, 133

xDSL, 992-993

Xeon processors, 128

XGA (Extended Graphics Array) standard, screen resolution, 266

yearly preventive maintenance activities, 363-364

ZIF (Zero Insertion Force) sockets, 1197

THIS BOOK IS SAFARI ENABLED

INCLUDES FREE 45-DAY ACCESS TO THE ONLINE EDITION

The Safari® Enabled icon on the cover of your favorite technology book means the book is available through Safari Bookshelf. When you buy this book, you get free access to the online edition for 45 days.

Safari Bookshelf is an electronic reference library that lets you easily search thousands of technical books, find code samples, download chapters, and access technical information whenever and wherever you need it.

TO GAIN 45-DAY SAFARI ENABLED ACCESS TO THIS BOOK:

- Go to **www.examcram.com/safarienabled**
- Complete the brief registration form
- Enter the coupon code found in the front of this book on the "Copyright" page

If you have difficulty registering on Safari Bookshelf or accessing the online edition, please e-mail customer-service@safaribooksonline.com.

informIT